SOMATOFORM DISORDERS

Somatization Disorder
Conversion Disorder
Hypochondriasis
Body Dysmorphic Disorder
Pain Disorder

FACTITIOUS DISORDERS

Factitious Disorder

DISSOCIATIVE DISORDERS

Dissociative Amnesia
Dissociative Fugue
Dissociative Identity Disorder (Multiple Personality Disorder)
Depersonalization Disorder

SEXUAL AND GENDER IDENTITY DISORDERS

Sexual Dysfunctions
Sexual Desire Disorders: Hypoactive Sexual Desire Disorder;
Sexual Aversion Disorder / Sexual Arousal Disorders: Female Sexual
Arousal Disorder; Male Erectile Disorder / Orgasmic Disorders:
Female Orgasmic Disorder (Inhibited Female Orgasm); Male
Orgasmic Disorder (Inhibited Male Orgasm); Premature Ejaculation /
Sexual Pain Disorders: Dyspareunia; Vaginismus / Sexual Dysfunction
Due to a General Medical Condition / Substance-induced Sexual
Dysfunction
Paraphilias
Exhibitionism / Fetishism / Frotteurism / Pedophilia / Sexual
Masochism / Sexual Sadism / Voyeurism / Transvestic Fetishism
Gender Identity Disorders
Gender Identity Disorder: in Children; in Adolescents or Adults
(Transsexualism)

EATING DISORDERS

Anorexia Nervosa
Bulimia Nervosa

SLEEP DISORDERS

Primary Sleep Disorders
Dyssomnias: Primary Insomnia; Primary Hypersomnia; Narcolepsy;
Breathing-related Sleep Disorder; Circadian Rhythm Sleep Disorder
(Sleep-Wake Schedule Disorder) / Parasomnias; Nightmare Disorder
(Dream Anxiety Disorder); Sleep Terror Disorder; Sleepwalking
Disorder / Sleep Disorders Related to Another Mental Disorder
Sleep Disorder Due to a General Medical Condition
Substance-induced Sleep Disorder

IMPULSE CONTROL DISORDERS NOT ELSEWHERE CLASSIFIED

Intermittent Explosive Disorder
Kleptomania
Pyromania
Pathological Gambling
Trichotillomania

ADJUSTMENT DISORDERS

Adjustment Disorder
With Anxiety / with Depressed Mood / with Disturbance of Conduct /
with Mixed Disturbance of Emotions and Conduct / with Mixed
Anxiety and Depressed Mood

Axis II

Mental Retardation
Mild Mental Retardation / Moderate Mental Retardation / Severe
Mental Retardation / Profound Mental Retardation

PERSONALITY DISORDERS

Paranoid Personality Disorder
Schizoid Personality Disorder
Schizotypal Personality Disorder
Antisocial Personality Disorder
Borderline Personality Disorder
Histrionic Personality Disorder
Narcissistic Personality Disorder
Avoidant Personality Disorder
Dependent Personality Disorder
Obsessive-Compulsive Personality Disorder

OTHER CONDITIONS THAT MAY BE A FOCUS OF CLINICAL ATTENTION

Psychological Factors Affecting Medical Condition
Medication-induced Movement Disorders
Relational Problems
Relational Problem Related to a Mental Disorder or General Medical
Condition / Parent-Child Relational Problem / Partner Relational
Problem / Sibling Relational Problem
Problems Related to Abuse or Neglect
Physical Abuse of Child / Sexual Abuse of Child / Neglect of Child /
Physical Abuse of Adult / Sexual Abuse of Adult
Additional Conditions That May Be a Focus of Clinical Attention
Bereavement / Borderline Intellectual Functioning / Academic
Problem / Occupational Problem / Child or Adolescent Antisocial
Behavior / Adult Antisocial Behavior / Malingering / Phase of Life
Problem / Noncompliance with Treatment / Identity Problem /
Religious or Spiritual Problem / Acculturation Problem / Age-related
Cognitive Decline

TO THE INSTRUCTOR

WileyPLUS is built around the activities you perform

Prepare & Present

Create outstanding class presentations using a wealth of resources, such as PowerPoint™ slides, image galleries, interactive simulations, and more. Plus you can easily upload any materials you have created into your course, and combine them with the resources Wiley provides you with.

Create Assignments

Automate the assigning and grading of homework or quizzes by using the provided question banks, or by writing your own. Student results will be automatically graded and recorded in your gradebook. *WileyPLUS* also links homework problems to relevant sections of the online text, hints, or solutions— context-sensitive help where students need it most!

*Based on a spring 2005 survey of 972 student users of *WileyPLUS*

TO THE STUDENT

You have the potential to make a difference!

Will you be the first person to land on Mars? Will you invent a car that runs on water? But, first and foremost, will you get through this course?

WileyPLUS is a powerful online system packed with features to help you make the most of your potential, and get the best grade you can!

With Wiley**PLUS** you get:

A complete online version of your text and other study resources

Study more effectively and get instant feedback when you practice on your own. Resources like self-assessment quizzes, tutorials, and animations bring the subject matter to life, and help you master the material.

Problem-solving help, instant grading, and feedback on your homework and quizzes

You can keep all of your assigned work in one location, making it easy for you to stay on task. Plus, many homework problems contain direct links to the relevant portion of your text to help you deal with problem-solving obstacles at the moment they come up.

The ability to track your progress and grades throughout the term.

A personal gradebook allows you to monitor your results from past assignments at any time. You'll always know exactly where you stand.

If your instructor uses *WileyPLUS*, you will receive a URL for your class. If not, your instructor can get more information about *WileyPLUS* by visiting www.wiley.com/college/wileyplus

---

"It has been a great help, and I believe it has helped me to achieve a better grade."

Michael Morris, *Columbia Basin College*

69% of students surveyed said it helped them get a better grade. *

Abnormal Psychology
Tenth Edition

Ann M. Kring

University of California, Berkeley

Gerald C. Davison

University of Southern California

John M. Neale

State University of New York at Stony Brook

Sheri L. Johnson

University of Miami

WILEY

John Wiley & Sons, Inc.

PUBLISHER   Jay O'Callaghan
EXECUTIVE EDITOR   Christopher T. Johnson
ASSOCIATE EDITOR   Jessica Bartelt
DEVELOPMENTAL EDITORS   Joanne Tinsley, Len Neufeld
EXECUTIVE MARKETING MANAGER   Jeffrey Rucker
PRODUCTION MANAGER   Jeanine Furino
SENIOR PRODUCTION EDITOR   Sandra Dumas
DESIGN DIRECTOR   Harry Nolan
SENIOR ILLUSTRATION EDITOR   Anna Melhorn
PHOTO EDITOR   Hilary Newman
PHOTO RESEARCHER   Elyse Rieder
MEDIA EDITOR   Lynn Pearlman
PRODUCTION MANAGEMENT SERVICES   Suzanne Ingrao
COVER PHOTOS & CHAPTER OPENERS   ©Ted Kinsman/Photo Researchers

This book was set in 10.5/12 Berkeley Book by Techbooks and printed and bound by
Von Hoffmann Corporation. The cover was printed by Phoenix Color Corporation.

This book is printed on acid-free paper. ∞

To order books or for customer service, please call 1-800-CALL-WILEY (225-5945).

Library of Congress Cataloging in Publication Data:

Kring, Ann M., Gerald C. Davison, John M. Neale, Sheri L. Johnson.

ISBN-13 978-0-471-69238-6
ISBN-10 0-471-69238-7

Printed in the United States of America

10 9 8 7 6 5 4 3 2

To

Angela Hawk

Kathleen C. Chambers, Eve H. Davison, and Asher Davison

Gail and Sean Neale

Richard White

About the Authors

ANN M. KRING is Associate Professor of Psychology at the University of California at Berkeley where she has served as the Director of the Clinical Science Program and Psychology Clinic. She received a B.S. from Ball State University and her M.A. and Ph.D. from the State University of New York at Stony Brook. Her internship in clinical psychology was completed at Bellevue Hospital and Kirby Forensic Psychiatric Center, in New York. Before moving to Berkeley, she was on the psychology faculty at Vanderbilt University (1991–1998). At both Vanderbilt and UC Berkeley, she has taught a course in abnormal psychology every year. She is on the editorial board of the *Journal of Abnormal Psychology, Emotion, Applied and Preventive Psychology,* and *Journal of Personality Research*, and was formerly an Associate Editor for *Cognition and Emotion*. She is currently a member of the Executive Board for the Society for Research in Psychopathology.

In 1997 she was awarded a Young Investigator award from the National Alliance for Research on Schizophrenia and Depression, and in 2006 she was awarded the Joseph Zubin Memorial Fund Award in recognition of her research in schizophrenia. Her current research focus is on emotion and psychopathology, with a specific interest in the emotional features of schizophrenia, the linkage between attention and emotion in schizophrenia, and the social and emotional features of social anxiety and depression. A second major focus of Kring's research is on the origins and consequences of individual differences in emotional expressivity and how gender and social context shape the experience and expression of emotion.

GERALD C. DAVISON is Professor and Chair of the Department of Psychology at the University of Southern California, where he was also Director of Clinical Training from 1979 to 1984. He earned his B.A. from Harvard in 1961, was a Fulbright Scholar in Germany the following year, and obtained his Ph.D. from Stanford in 1962. From 1994 to 1996 he served as Interim Dean of the USC Annenberg School for Communication. Previously he was on the psychology faculty at the State University of New York at Stony Brook.

Dr. Davison is a Fellow of the American Psychological Association and has served on the Board of Scientific Affairs, on the Committee on Scientific Awards, on the Council of Representatives, and on the Continuing Professional Education Committee. He is also a Charter Fellow of the American Psychological Society, on the Advisory Board of the Society for the Exploration of Psychotherapy Integration, a past president of the Association for Advancement of Behavior Therapy, and a Distinguished Founding Fellow of the Academy of Cognitive Therapy. He served two terms on the National Academy of Sciences/National Research Council Committee on Techniques for the Enhancement of Human Performance. In 2006–2007 he is Chair of the Council of Graduate Departments of Psychology as well as President of the Society of Clinical Psychology (Division 12 of the American Psychological Association).

In 1988 Davison received an outstanding achievement award from APA's Board of Social and Ethical Responsibility; in 1989 was the recipient of the Albert S. Raubenheimer Distinguished Faculty Award from USC's College of Letters, Arts and Sciences; in 1993 won the Associates Award for Excellence in Teaching, a university-wide prize; in 1995 received the Distinguished Psychologist Award from the Los Angeles County Psychological Association; in 1997 was given the Outstanding Educator Award of the Association for Advancement of Behavior Therapy; in 2003 received the Lifetime Achievement Award from AABT; and in

2005 was the recipient of the USC Mellon Award for Excellence in Mentoring. At USC he was a Faculty Fellow in the Center for Excellence in Teaching from 2001 to 2003.

Among his more than 130 publications, his book *Clinical Behavior Therapy*, co-authored in 1976 with Marvin Goldfried and reissued in expanded form in 1994, is one of two publications that have been recognized as Citation Classics by the Social Sciences Citation Index; it appears in German and Spanish translation. Davison is also on the editorial board of several professional journals, including *Behavior Therapy, Cognitive Therapy and Research, Journal of Cognitive Psychotherapy, Journal of Psychotherapy Integration, Journal of Clinical Psychology*, and *Clinical Psychology: Science and Practice*. His publications emphasize experimental and philosophical analyses of psychopathology, assessment, and therapeutic change. His current research program focuses on the relationships between cognition and a variety of behavioral and emotional problems via his articulated thoughts in simulated situations paradigm.

JOHN M. NEALE is Professor Emeritus of Psychology at the State University of New York at Stony Brook, where he regularly taught the undergraduate course in abnormal psychology. He received his B.A. from the University of Toronto and his M.A. and Ph.D. from Vanderbilt University. His internship in clinical psychology was as a Fellow in Medical Psychology at the Langley Porter Neuropsychiatric Institute. In 1975 he was a Visiting Fellow at the Institute of Psychiatry, London, England. In 1974 he won the American Psychological Association's Early Career Award for his research on cognitive processes in schizophrenia. In 1991 he won a Distinguished Scientist Award from the American Psychological Association's Society for a Science of Clinical Psychology. He has been on the editorial boards of several journals and has been Associate Editor of the *Journal of Abnormal Psychology*. Besides his numerous articles in professional journals, he has published books on the effects of televised violence on children, research methodology, schizophrenia, case studies in abnormal psychology, and psychological influences on health. Schizophrenia was a major focus of his research, and he also conducted research on the influence of stress on health.

SHERI L. JOHNSON received her B.A. from Salem College in 1982 and her Ph.D. from the University of Pittsburgh in 1992. She completed an internship and postdoctoral fellowship at Brown University, and she was a clinical assistant professor at Brown from 1993–1995. Since that time, she has been teaching in the Department of Psychology at the University of Miami, where she is currently an Associate Professor of Psychology with a joint appointment in the Department of Psychiatry and Human Behavior. She regularly teaches courses on abnormal psychology at undergraduate and graduate levels.

In 1993, Johnson received the Young Investigator Award from the National Alliance for Research in Schizophrenia and Depression. In 2001 and 2005, she received the Award for Excellence in Graduate Teaching from the Department of Psychology at the University of Miami. Dr. Johnson's previous books include *Psychological Treatments of Bipolar Disorder*, which has been published in paperback, and *Stress, Coping and Depression*. She is currently co-editing a book on *Emotion and Psychopathology*. She has published more than 60 articles and chapters. She is an associate editor for *Applied and Preventive Psychology* and *Cognition and Emotion*, and she serves on the editorial board for *Psychology and Psychotherapy* and *Journal of Cognitive Psychotherapy: An International Quarterly*. She is a member of the Executive Board for the Emotion Research Group and for the Society for Research in Psychopathology. Her work has been supported by grants from the National Alliance of Research on Schizophrenia and Depression, the National Institute of Mental Health, and the National Cancer Institute. Her research is focused on understanding the psychological and socioenvironmental factors that shape the course of mania and major depression.

Preface

It has been more than thirty years since the first edition of this book was published. Emerging from conversations about teaching abnormal psychology between Davison and Neale, then young faculty at Stony Brook, came the first edition of a textbook that was different from the texts available at the time in its balance and blending of research and clinical application; in its use of paradigms as an organizing principle; and in its effort to involve the reader in the problem solving engaged in by clinicians and scientists. These qualities have continued to be the cornerstones of subsequent editions of the book, and we have been both surprised and delighted at the favorable reception the book has received, and perhaps more importantly, the impact it has had on the lives of so many students of abnormal psychology throughout the years.

With this the tenth edition of the book, we continue to emphasize the recent and comprehensive research coverage that has been the hallmark of the book, yet we have also greatly expanded the pedagogical features, by adding clinical cases, figures, tables, and clarifying writing to make this material accessible to a broad audience. We continue to emphasize an integrated approach, showing how psychopathology is best understood by considering multiple perspectives, and how these varying perspectives can provide us with the clearest accounting of the causes of these disorders as well as the best possible treatments.

We have chosen diamonds as the cover image and theme for this edition to reflect the fact that the book contains the most up-to-date, cutting edge, sharp, and clear presentations of the theories and research on the descriptions, causes, and treatments for psychopathology. In addition, the diamonds convey our view that psychopathology is best understood by adopting different angles or perspectives on any given clinical problem.

Ann Kring joined the book in the ninth edition, and she has expanded her contributions in this edition. We are delighted in this new edition to be joined by Sheri Johnson. She brings to our collaboration an interest and expertise in mood disorders, including bipolar disorder and major depression. In her research, she translates the findings from basic laboratory studies into the development of psychological interventions. For example, her work on mania incorporates research and theory from basic studies in emotion and cognition, and this has been translated into a psychosocial intervention that emphasizes goal setting for individuals with bipolar disorder. This translational approach to research reflects, we believe, one of the most promising approaches to the study of psychopathology, and we are excited to have this approach further represented in the book.

Goals of the Book

With each new edition, we update, make changes, and streamline features to enhance both the scholarly and pedagogical characteristics of the book. We also devote considerable effort to couching complex concepts in prose that is sharp, clear, and vivid. In the past thirty years, the domains of psychopathology and intervention have become increasingly multifaceted and technical. Therefore a good abnormal psychology textbook must engage the careful and focused attention of students so that they can acquire a deep and critical understanding of the issues and the material. Some of the most exciting breakthroughs in psychopathology research and treatment that we present in the book have come in areas that are complex, such as molecular genetics, neuroscience, and cognitive science. Rather than oversimplify these complex issues, we have instead added a number of new pedagogical features to enhance understanding of this vital material.

Our goals in writing this textbook are not only to present up-to-date theories and research in psychopathology and intervention but also to convey some of the intellectual excitement that is associated with the search for answers to some of the most puzzling questions facing humankind. A reviewer of an earlier edition once said that our book reads like a detective story, for we do more than just state the problem and then its solution. Rather, we try to involve the student in the search for clues, the follow-up of hunches, and the evaluation of evidence that are part and parcel of the science and art of the field. We try to encourage students to participate with us in a process of discovery as we sift through the evidence on the origins of psychopathology and the effectiveness of specific interventions.

In this edition, we also emphasize ways in which we can take away the stigma that is unfortunately still associated with different forms of mental illness. Psychopathology is something that affects all of us in one way or another. As many as half of us may experience symptoms of one disorder at some time or another, and most of us know someone who has suffered from one disorder or another. Despite the ubiquity of psychopathology, the stigma associated with it can keep some from seeking treatment, keep our legislatures from providing adequate funding for treatment and research, and keep some terms as accepted popular vernacular ("crazy", "nuts", "schizo"). Thus, another of our goals for the book is combat this stigma and present a positive and hopeful view on the causes and treatments of mental illness.

Paradigms as an Organizing Principle

A recurrent theme in the book is the importance of major points of view, perspectives, or, to use Kuhn's (1962) phrase, paradigms. Our experience in teaching undergraduates has made us very much aware of the importance of making explicit the unspoken assumptions underlying any quest for knowledge. In our handling of the paradigms, we have tried to make their premises clear. Long after specific facts are forgotten, we hope students will retain a grasp of the basic problems in the field of psychopathology and understand that the answers one arrives at are, in an important but often subtle way, constrained by the questions one poses and the methods employed to ask those questions.

Throughout the book we discuss four major paradigms: genetic, neuroscience, psychoanalytic, and cognitive behavioral. We also emphasize the importance of factors that are important to all paradigms, including emotion, gender, culture, ethnicity, and socioeconomic status. A related issue is the use of more than one paradigm in studying abnormal psychology. Rather than force an entire field into, for example, a cognitive behavioral paradigm, we argue from the available information that different problems in psychopathology are amenable to analyses within different frameworks. For instance, genetic factors are important in bipolar disorder and attention-deficit/hyperactivity disorder, but genes do their work via the environment. In disorders such as depression, cognitive factors are essential, but neurotransmitters also exert an influence. For still other disorders, for example, dissociative disorders, psychoanalytic theories can enhance our understanding, but cognitive factors involving consciousness are also important to consider. Furthermore, the importance of a diathesis–stress approach has become increasingly evident. Emerging data indicate that many, perhaps most, disorders arise from subtle interactions between genetic or psychological predispositions and stressful life events. Our coverage continues to reflect these hypotheses and findings, strengthening the basic position we took in our very first edition that a diathesis–stress paradigm is necessary for understanding most psychological disorders.

Organization of the Tenth Edition

In Chapters 1 through 4 we place the field in historical context, present the concept of paradigms in science, describe the major paradigms in psychopathology, review the text revision of the fourth edition of the Diagnostic and Statistical Manual of Mental Disorders (DSM-IV-TR), discuss critically its validity and reliability, provide an overview of major approaches and techniques in clinical assessment, and then describe the major research methods of the field. These chapters are the foundation upon which

the later chapters can be interpreted and understood. As in previous editions, specific disorders and their treatment are discussed in Chapters 5 through 14. We continue to provide up-to-date coverage of late life and psychological disorders in Chapter 15. In Chapter 16 we cover discuss process and outcome research on treatment and controversial issues surrounding the therapy enterprise. In Chapter 17 we have continued to update and strengthen our chapter on legal and ethical issues.

Throughout the book we have included considerable material on culture and ethnicity in the study of psychopathology and intervention as well as discussion of the different ways abnormal behavior is conceptualized in cultures other than our own. In Chapter 2, we present a separate section that emphasizes the importance of culture and ethnicity in all paradigms. We point to the important role of culture and ethnicity in the other chapters as well. For example, in the Diagnosis and Assessment chapter (3), we have extended our earlier discussions of cultural bias in assessment and ways to guard against this selectivity in perception. We have expanded and updated information on ethnicity with respect to how stress impacts health in Chapter 7, and we have updated coverage of culture and ethnicity in schizophrenia (Chapter 11). And in Chapter 16 we have expanded our discussion of cultural and ethnic factors in psychological interventions.

We have added an expanded and up-to-date discussion of genetics and psychopathology throughout the book. We repeatedly emphasize that psychopathology is best understood by considering how genes do their work via the environment. Thus, rather than asking whether genes or the environment are more important in a particular disorder, we emphasize that both of these factors are important. Exciting new discoveries have made it clear that genes (nature) and the environment (nurture) work together, not in opposition to one another. Without the genes, a behavior might not be possible. But without the environment, genes could not express themselves and thus contribute to the behavior. Genes are remarkably flexible at responding to different types of environments. In turn, human beings are quite flexible at adapting to different environments.

New to This Edition

The tenth edition has undergone a substantial revision. The chapters covering the disorders all have a consistent organization, presenting sections on clinical descriptions, etiology, and treatments of the various disorders. The book now has 17 chapters, and we have streamlined the writing across all the chapters to increase the clarity of presentation and to highlight the key issues in the field. We have placed particular emphasis on updating theories and research on the role of genetics, neuroscience, cognition, gender, sociocultural factors, and life events in psychopathology.

We have heard from students and professors alike about the need for additional pedagogy, and we have added a number of features to aid the reader in this edition. We have added forty new Clinical Case boxes to the book in order to illustrate what the different disorders look like in the context of real people's lives. "Quick Summaries" have been added at several points in each chapter in order to summarize some of the more complex material. In addition, "Check Your Knowledge Questions" have been added at several points in each chapter so that students may do a quick check to see if they are understanding and integrating the material. There are over 75 new photos to provide students with additional real-world examples and applications of abnormal psychology. In addition, we have added over 35 new colorful illustrations and over 40 new tables to provide additional visual clarification and explanation for more complex material. The glossary has been substantially revised and updated. The end of chapter summaries are consistent across the chapters, using a bulleted format and summarizing the descriptions, causes, and treatments of the disorders covered. Finally, the book's website has been substantially updated to provide additional resources for students.

One of the strengths of the book has always been its current and forward-looking coverage of research in the descriptions, causes, and treatments of psychopathology, and this tradition is strongly maintained in this edition with the addition of over 1000 new references.

New and Expanded Coverage

We are excited about the new features of this edition. Some of the major new material in this tenth edition includes:

Chapter 1: Introduction and Historical Overview
Three new clinical cases
New section on stigma and mental illness
Historical material on psychoanalysis, behaviorism, genetics placed here
Reorganized and refocused section describing definitions of abnormal

Chapter 2: Current Paradigms in Psychopathology
Paradigms reorganized to include: genetic, neuroscience, psychoanalytic, cognitive behavioral
New section on factors that cut across paradigms: gender and sociocultural factors
New section on gene-environment interactions, gene environment correlations
Updated and expanded information on behavior and molecular genetics and neuroscience

Chapter 3: Diagnosis and Assessment
New organization—diagnosis and assessment are now in one chapter
New material on brain imaging
New section on the assessment of stress and life events
Updated and expanded coverage of cultural factors in diagnosis and assessment
New section previewing the DSM-V

Chapter 4: Research Methods in the Study of Psychopathology
New section covering meta-analysis

Updated example of single-case experimental design
Material on epidemiological and behavioral genetics research integrated as examples of the use of correlational methods

Chapter 5: Anxiety Disorders
Substantially reorganized so that clinical descriptions for all disorders covered first
New section on factors common across the anxiety disorders
Several new clinical cases
New sections on gender and cultural issues in anxiety disorders
Updated research on neurobiology, personality, life events, and cognition
Updated coverage of comorbidity among anxiety disorders

Chapter 6: Somatoform Disorders and Dissociative Disorders
New section on cognitive-behavioral model of somatoform disorders
Updated coverage of body dysmorphic disorder
Updated research on controversy about DID and repressed memories
Updated research on the unconscious and cognitive psychology
New Focus on Discovery box on the treatment of pain disorder
New section explaining dissociation as a coping mechanism, more discussion of dissociation and memory

Chapter 7: Stress and Health
Chapter has been renamed to emphasize ways in which stress affects all aspects of health
Updated research on stress and the immune system
Section on theories of the stress-illness link revised and reorganized substantially
Updated research on gender and ethnicity
Updated research on asthma
Sections on cardiovascular disorders and treatment streamlined

Chapter 8: Mood Disorders
Increased coverage of life events and socioenvironmental facets of mood disorders
Increased coverage of new neurobiological models
Broader focus on affect and emotion in mood disorders
Increased coverage of the risk factors for mania
New discussion on public health issues in the treatment of depression
New research findings for cognitive therapy
New findings on neurobiology of suicide and prevention of suicide

Chapter 9: Eating Disorders
New research findings on binge eating disorder
New Focus on Discovery box on obesity
Expanded section on ethnicity and eating disorders
Updated research on dietary restraint

Chapter 10: Substance-Related Disorders
Updated statistics on prevalence rates for all disorders
Updated statistics for costs associated with substance dependence
New section on the unfortunate stigma of substance-related disorders
New research findings on secondhand smoke
New research findings on how the brain is affected by drugs
Treatment section streamlined; new information on biological treatments added

Chapter 11: Schizophrenia
New research on molecular genetics
New research on prefrontal cortex, hippocampus in schizophrenia
Updated and reorganized section on symptoms
Updated research on ethnicity
Updated and reorganized treatment section
New Focus on Discovery box on historical conceptions of schizophrenia

Chapter 12: Personality Disorders
Updated material on the inter-rater reliability and stability of personality disorders
Updated research on the overlap of cluster A with schizophrenia
Reorganized material on the etiology of borderline personality disorder, to emphasize the research data on abuse
Updated material on the course of borderline personality disorder
New research on the etiology of narcissistic personality disorder

Chapter 13: Sexual and Gender Identity Disorders
Re-organized and shortened material on the etiology of sexual dysfunctions, to reflect that the risk factors often increase risk for a range of sexual dysfunctions
New section on normative sexual behavior
Incorporated current debates regarding whether GID should be a diagnosis

Chapter 14: Disorders of Childhood
Updated information on culture and ADHD, neurobiological and genetic factors in ADHD
Updated research on neurobiological factors in dyslexia
Updated section on Head Start
Updated section on autism, including epidemiology, causes, and treatment
New Focus on Discovery box on controversies in developmental psychopathology, including suicide and antidepressant treatment
New sections covering mood and anxiety in children.

Chapter 15: Late Life and Psychological Disorders
New section on myths about aging
Reorganized material on psychological disorders, to cover issues that influence all disorders

Reduced material on therapy with adults; emphasis on new empirical research on treatment outcome in late life
Refocused material on nursing homes, alternative living settings, and community care

Chapter 16: Psychological Treatment
Increased emphasis on culture and ethnicity
Increased discussion of empirically supported treatments
Increased discussion of therapy process research and mechanisms of change
New section on motivational interviewing and third wave of cognitive behavioral therapy

Chapter 17: Legal and Ethical Issues
Greater clarity added to definition and discussion of insanity defense
Two new Clinical Case boxes
Updated material on *Tarasoff*
Updated material on insanity pleas in the states
Updated material on forced medication and competency
New information on informed consent among patients with schizophrenia, dementia

Special Features for the Student Reader

Several new features of this book are designed to make it easier for students to master and enjoy the material; all these elements are designed to make it user friendly.

Clinical Case Boxes. We have expanded and added a number of new clinical cases throughout the book to provide a clinical context for the theories and research that occupy most of our attention in the chapters and to help make vivid the real-life implications of the empirical work of psychopathologists and clinicians.

Focus on Discovery Boxes. There are many in-depth discussions of selected topics encased in Focus boxes throughout the book. This feature allows us to involve the reader in specialized topics in a way that does not detract from the flow of the regular text. Sometimes a Focus box expands on a point in the text; sometimes it deals with an entirely separate but relevant issue, often a controversial one. We have added a number of new boxes in this edition, replacing a number of the older boxes.

Quick Summaries. We have added short summaries throughout the chapters to allow students to pause and assimilate the material. These should help students to keep track of the multifaceted and complex issues that surround the study of psychopathology.

End of Chapter Summaries. Summaries at the end of each chapter have been completely rewritten in bulleted form. In Chapters 5-14, we organize these by clinical descriptions, etiology, and treatment—the major sections of every chapter covering the disorders. We believe this format will make it easier for readers to review and remember the material. In fact, we even suggest that the student read it before beginning the chapter itself in order to get a good sense of what lies ahead. Then re-reading the summary after completing the chapter itself will enhance the student's understanding and provide an immediate sense of what has been learned in just one reading of the chapter.

Check your Knowledge Questions. Throughout each chapter, we provide between three and six boxes that ask questions about the material covered in the chapter. These questions are intended to help students assess their understanding and retention of the material, as well as provide them with samples of the types of questions that often are found in course exams. The answers to the questions in these boxes are at the end of each chapter, just before the list of key terms. We hope that these will be useful aids for students as they make their way through the chapters.

Glossary. When an important term is introduced, it is boldfaced and defined or discussed immediately. Most such terms appear again later in the book, in which case they will not be highlighted in this way. All of these terms are listed again at the end of each chapter and definitions appear at the end of the book in a glossary. The glossary has been substantially revised and updated in this edition.

DSM-IV-TR Table. The endpapers of the book contain a summary of the current psychiatric nomenclature found in the text revision of the fourth edition of the Diagnostic and Statistical Manual of Mental Disorders, known as DSM-IV-TR. This provides a handy guide to where particular disorders appear in the "official" taxonomy or classification. We make considerable use of DSM-IV-TR, though in a selective and sometimes critical vein. Sometimes we find it more effective to discuss theory and research on a particular problem in a way that is different from DSM's conceptualization.

Supplements

Several supplements have been prepared, free to adopters of the text, to enhance and facilitate teaching from this textbook. These supplements include:

Wiley Plus. New to the tenth edition, this exciting online resource provides a number of valuable tools for instructors, including tools for preparing class presentations and assignments, tracking student progress, and administering the course. The content of the book is fully integrated with this invaluable online resource.

Abnormal Psychology Videotapes, updated and revised for the tenth edition, feature short video clips of actual patients, their problems, and the professional care they receive. These interviews cover several of the major disorders discussed in the text.

Instructor's Resource Manual, written by David Smith of the University of Notre Dame, includes chapter summaries, lecture launchers, perspectives on the causes and treatment of each disorder, key points students should know, key terms,

discussion stimulators, and guides to instructional films and websites.

Instructor's PowerPoint slides, written by Sandra Kerr of West Chester University, provide lecture-ready slides that include the figures and tables from the text, so that the instructor can create a custom classroom presentation.

Test Bank, written by Stephanie McMurrich of the University of Miami, contains nearly 2000 multiple choice questions. It is available in printed form as well as on CD. Computerized Test Bank (Diploma for Windows; Exam for Mac), an easy-to-use computerized test bank, contains the same questions as the printed version. Instructors can customize exams by adding new questions or editing existing ones.

Study Guide, written by Douglas Hindman of Eastern Kentucky University, includes a summary of each chapter, a list of key concepts, important study questions, and practice tests written in collaboration with the test bank author to ensure consistency and to encourage active reading and learning. Students find it to be a very helpful study guide.

Book Website (http://www.wiley.com/college/kring) includes an on-line Instructor Resource section and an on-line Student Resource section, as well as active learning links to several interesting sites related to the field of abnormal psychology. On-line Student Quizzes for which students can receive immediate feedback are also on the site.

Acknowledgments

It is a real pleasure to acknowledge the contributions of a number of colleagues to this tenth edition. Their thoughtful comments and expert feedback have helped us to refine and improve the book. A special thank you goes out to:

Ted Beauchaine, *University of Washington*
Allison Harvey, *University of California, Berkeley*
Jutta Joormann, *University of Miami*
Janice Kiecolt-Glaser, *Ohio State University*
Richard McNally, *Harvard University*
Jack Nitzcke, *University of Wisconsin*

In addition, we recognize the following reviewers of previous editions, for it was with their assistance that the tenth edition had the strong base on which to build:

David Arnold, *University of Massachusetts*; Jack J. Blanchard, *University of Maryland*; John Burns, *Chicago Medical School*; Laura Heatherington, *Williams College*; John Kassel, *University of Illinois at Chicago*; Joni Mihura, *University of Toledo*; Judith Moskowitz, *University of California, San Francisco*; Brady Phelps, *South Dakota State University*; Kathleen M. Pike, *Columbia University*; Judy Rauenzahn, *Kutztown University*; Melanie Domenech Rodriguez, *Utah State University*; Randall Salekin, *University of Alabama*; Carol Terry, *University of Oklahoma*; Mary Pat Kelly, *University of California-Irvine*; Judith LeMaster, *Scripps College*; David Greenway, *University of Southwestern Louisiana*; Drew Gouvier,

Louisiana State University-Baton Rouge; Michael R. Hufford, *University of Montana*; C. Chrisman Wilson, *Tulane University*; Kathy Hoff, *Utah State University*; Jose M. Lafosse, *University of Colorado-Denver*; Kent Hutchinson, *University of Colorado*; Tibor Palfai, *Boston University*; Daniel L. Segal, *University of Colorado-Colorado Springs*; Ann Rosen Spector, *Rutgers University*; William T. McReynolds, *University of Tampa*; Kristine Lynn Brady, *California School of Professional Psychology, San Diego*; Debra Hollister, *Valencia Community College*; Gay Melville, *Trident Technical College*; Joseph Lowman, *University of North Carolina at Chapel Hill*; Mitchell Earleywine, *University of Southern California*; Thomas Bradbury, *University of California, Los Angeles*; Frances K. Grossman, *Boston University*; Brad Schmidt, *Ohio State University*; Cooper Holmes, *Emporia State University*; Christopher Layne, *University of Toledo*; Robert D. Coursey, *University of Maryland*; Larry Jamner, *University of California-Irvine*; Kelly Champion, *Gustavus Adolphus College*; D. Growe, *Oakland Community College*; Robert Higgins, *Oakland University*; Mike Connor, *California State University-Long Beach*; James Linder, *California State University-Long Beach*; Paul Rokke, *North Dakota State University*; William G. Iacono, *University of Minnesota*; J. Tate, *Middle Tennessee State University*; Joanne Lindoerfer, *University of Texas*; John Hall, *LaSalle University*; Benjamin Blanding, *Rowan University*; John Suler, *Rider University*; Christine Gayda, *Stockton College*; Herbert Rappaport, *Temple University*; Davis Burdick, *Stockton College*; Michael Zinser, *University of Colorado, Denver*; Scott Hamilton, *Colorado State University*; Charles Gelso, *University of Maryland*; Donald Strassberg-Carson, *University of Utah*; James Alexander-Carson, *University of Utah*; Melissa Alderfer, *University of Utah*; Jennifer Skeem, *University of Utah*; Gretchen Gimpel, *Utah State University*; L. Dennis Madrid, *University of Southern Colorado*; James Cameron, *University of Southern Colorado*; Bob Coursey, *University of Southern Colorado*; Gordon D. Atlas, *Alfred University*.

We would also like to give a big thanks to Asher Davison for contributing to the substantial revision and updating of the glossary. We also thank Amy Hansford and Stephanie McMurrich who helped with research and library work. And, we are tremendously appreciative of the wisdom and guidance that Charles Carver provided throughout the process.

We have also benefited greatly over the years from the skills and dedication of the folks from Wiley. For this edition, we have many people to thank. Specifically, we thank our Executive Editors, Chris Johnson, who saw us through to the finish, and Ryan Flahive, who was there at the beginning; Executive Marketing Manager Jeffrey Rucker; Production Manager, Jeanine Furino; Photo Editor Hillary Newman; Illustration Editor Anna Melhorn; and the Outside Production Service, Suzanne Ingrao of Ingrao Associates. We also extend a special thanks for the generous help and timely support from Jessica Bartelt, the Associate Editor for Psychology. Her efficiency and enthusiasm kept our spirits up when time was short, and everything seemed to run more smoothly and positively whenever she was involved. Finally, we thank Anne Smith for her guidance and direction in launching this edition as well as her steadfast support of previous editions.

One aspect of our textbook that previous users have liked is its readability and its ability to engage the reader in a collaborative quest with the authors for answers to some of the most perplexing problems facing psychology. We have worked very hard on this edition to present complex material in an engaging and understandable manner. Our efforts would have failed were it not for the work of our two terrific developmental/line editors, Joanne Tinsley and Len Neufeld. We are extremely grateful for their careful attention and dedication to the project. We know the book is much stronger, clearer, more interesting, and tighter thanks to their efforts.

From time to time, students and faculty colleagues have written us their comments on the book; these communications are always welcome. Readers can e-mail us: akring@berkeley.edu, gdaviso@rcf.usc.edu, sjohnson@miami.edu.

Finally and most importantly, our heartfelt thanks go to the most important people in our lives for their continued support and encouragement along the way. A great big thanks to: Angela Hawk (AMK), Kathleen Chambers, Eve and Asher Davison (GCD), Gail and Sean Neale (JMN), and Richard White (SLJ), to whom this book is dedicated with love and gratitude.

DECEMBER 2005
Ann M. Kring, *Berkeley, CA*
Gerald C. Davison, *Los Angeles, CA*
John M. Neale, *Hilton Head, SC*
Sheri L. Johnson, *Miami, FL*

Brief Contents

Contents

4

Research Methods in the Study of Psychopathology   100

5

Anxiety Disorders   121

6

Somatoform Disorders and Dissociative Disorders   158

7

Stress and Health 188

8

Mood Disorders 229

9

Eating Disorders 270

10

Substance-Related Disorders 296

11

Schizophrenia   349

12

Personality Disorders   386

13

Sexual and Gender Identity Disorders 413

14

Disorders of Childhood   449

15

Late Life and Psychological Disorders 496

16

Psychological Treatment   529

17

Legal and Ethical Issues   563

1 Introduction and Historical Overview

Learning Goals

1. Be able to explain the meaning of stigma as it applies to people with mental illness.
2. Be able to describe and compare different definitions of abnormality.
3. Be able to explain how the causes and treatments of mental illness have changed over the course of history.
4. Be able to describe the historical forces that have helped to shape our current view of mental illness, including biological, psychoanalytic, and behavioral views.
5. Be able to describe the different mental health professions, including the training involved and the expertise developed.

Clinical Case: Jack

Jack dreaded family gatherings. His parents' house would be filled with his brothers and their families, and all the little kids would run around making a lot of noise. His parents would urge him to "be social" and spend time with the family, even though Jack preferred to be alone. He knew that the kids called him "crazy Uncle Jack." In fact, he had even heard his younger brother Kevin call him crazy Jack when he stopped by to see their mother the other day. Jack's mother admonished him, reminding Kevin that Jack had been doing very well on his new medication. "Schizophrenia is an illness," his mother had said.

Jack had not been hospitalized with an acute episode of his schizophrenia for over 2 years. Even though Jack still heard voices, he learned not to talk about them in front of his mother because she would then start hassling him about taking his medication or ask him all sorts of questions about whether he needed to go back to the hospital. He hoped he would soon be able to move out of his parents' house and into his own apartment. The landlord at the last apartment he tried to rent rejected his application once he learned that he had a mental illness. His mother and father needed to cosign the lease, and they had inadvertently said that Jack was doing very well with his illness. The landlord asked about the illness, and once his parents mentioned schizophrenia, the landlord became visibly uncomfortable. The landlord called later that night and said the apartment had already been rented. When Jack's father pressed him, the landlord admitted "he didn't want any trouble" and that he was worried that people like Jack were violent.

Clinical Case: Felicia

Felicia didn't like to think back to her early school years. Elementary school was not a very fun time. She couldn't sit still or follow directions very well. She often blurted out answers when it wasn't her turn to talk, and she never seemed to be able to finish her class papers without many mistakes. If that wasn't bad enough, the other girls often laughed at her and called her names. She still remembers the time she tried to join in with a group of girls during recess. They kept running away, whispering to each other, and giggling. When Felicia asked what was so funny, one of the girls laughed and said, "You are hyper, girl! You fidget so much in class, you must have ants in your pants!"

When Felicia started fourth grade, her parents took her to a psychologist. She took a number of tests and answered all sorts of questions. At the end of these testing sessions, the psychologist diagnosed Felicia with attention-deficit/hyperactivity disorder (ADHD). Felicia began seeing a different psychologist, and her pediatrician prescribed the medication Ritalin. She enjoyed seeing the psychologist because she helped her learn how to deal with the other kids' teasing and how to do a better job of paying attention. The medication helped too—she was able to concentrate better and didn't seem to blurt out things as much anymore.

Now in high school, Felicia is much happier. She has a good group of close friends, and her grades are better than they have ever been. Though it is still hard to focus sometimes, she has learned a number of ways to deal with her distractibility. She is looking forward to college, hoping she can get into the top state school. Her guidance counselor has encouraged her, thinking her grades and extracurricular activities will make for a strong application.

We all try to understand other people. Determining why another person does or feels something is not easy to do. In fact, we do not always understand our own feelings and behavior. Figuring out why people behave in normal, expected ways is difficult enough; understanding abnormal human behavior, such as the behavior of Jack, Felicia, and José (see p. 4), can be even more difficult.

This book is about the range of abnormality as it pertains to psychological disorders. We will consider the description, causes, and treatments of a number of different disorders. We will also demonstrate the numerous challenges professionals in this field face. For example, we often must have a tolerance for conflicting data and tentative conclusions. Then, we must have the endurance to work with such uncertain material. As you approach the study of **psychopathology**, the field concerned with the nature, development, and treatment of psychological disorders, keep in mind that the subject offers few hard and fast answers. Nevertheless, as we proceed you will see that these uncertainties do not detract from the field's interest and importance.

Another challenge we face in studying abnormal psychology is to remain objective. Our subject matter, human behavior, is personal and powerfully affecting, making objectivity difficult. The pervasiveness and potentially disturbing effects of abnormal behavior intrude on our own lives. Who has not experienced irrational thoughts, fantasies, and feelings? Most of us have known someone, a friend or a relative, whose behavior was upsetting and impossible to fathom, and we realize how frustrating and frightening it can be to try to understand and help a person suffering psychological difficulties. You can see that this personal impact of our subject matter requires us to make a conscious, determined effort to remain objective.

The other side of this coin is that our closeness to the subject matter adds to its intrinsic fascination; undergraduate courses in abnormal psychology are among the most popular in the entire college curriculum, not just in psychology departments. Our feeling of familiarity with the subject matter draws us to the study of abnormal psychology, but it also has a distinct disadvantage: we bring to our study our preconceived notions of what the subject matter is. Each of us has developed certain ways of thinking and talking about abnormal behavior, certain words and concepts that somehow seem to fit. As you read this book and try to understand the mental disorders it discusses, we may be asking you to adopt different ways of thinking and talking from those to which you are accustomed; indeed, they may be different from those we ourselves use when we are not wearing our professional hats.

Perhaps the most challenging of all, we must not only recognize our own preconceived notions of mental disorder and abnormality, but we must also confront and work to change the stigma we often associate with these conditions. **Stigma** refers to the pernicious beliefs and attitudes held by a society that are ascribed to groups considered deviant in some manner, such as the mentally ill. More specifically, stigma has four characteristics (see Figure 1.1):

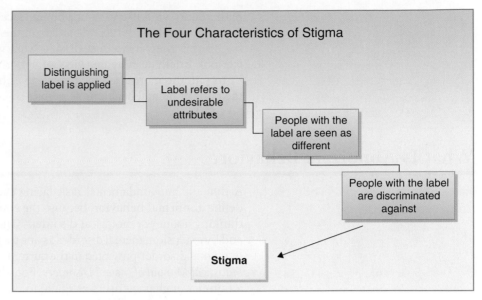

Figure 1.1   The four characteristics of stigma.

1. A label is applied to a group of people that distinguishes them from others (e.g., "crazy").
2. The label is linked to deviant or undesirable attributes by society (e.g., crazy people are dangerous).
3. People with the label are seen as essentially different from those without the label, contributing to an "us" versus "them" mentality (e.g., we are not like those crazy people).
4. People with the label are discriminated against unfairly (e.g., a clinic for crazy people can't be built in our neighborhood).

The case of Jack illustrates how stigma can lead to discrimination. Jack was denied an apartment due to his mental illness. The landlord believed Jack's mental illness meant he would be violent. This belief is based more in fiction than reality, however. A person with mental illness is not necessarily any more likely to be violent than a person without mental illness (Steadman et al., 1998; Swanson et al., 1990).

As we shall see below, the treatment of individuals with mental illness throughout recorded history has not generally been good, and this has contributed to their stigmatization, to the extent that they have often been brutalized and shunned by society. Torturous treatments have been described to the public as miracle cures, and even today, terms such as "crazy," "insane," "retard," and "schizo" are tossed about without thought of the people who actually suffer from mental illnesses and for whom these insults and the intensely distressing feelings and behaviors they refer to are a reality of daily life. The cases of Jack and Felicia illustrate how hurtful using such careless and mean-spirited names can be. In the 1970s, attempts were made to correct deplorably overcrowded conditions in mental hospitals by releasing many patients. But this was done without having appropriate aftercare programs in place; as a result, over a third of the homeless population in the United States would qualify for diagnosis of a mental illness of some sort (see Chapter 17).

Sadly, mental illness remains one of the most stigmatized of conditions in the twenty-first century, despite advances in the public's knowledge regarding the origins of mental disorders (Hinshaw, 2006). In 1999, David Satcher, then Surgeon General of the United States, wrote that stigma is the "most formidable obstacle to future progress in the arena of mental illness and mental health" in his groundbreaking report on mental illness (U.S. Department of Health and Human Services, 1999).

Throughout this book, we hope to fight this stigma by showing you the latest evidence about the nature, causes, and treatments for these disorders, dispelling myths and other misconceptions as we go. But you will have to help in this fight, for the mere acquisition of knowledge does not ensure the end of stigma (Penn, Chamberlin, & Mueser, 2003). As part of this effort, we will try to put a human face on mental disorders, by including descriptions of actual people with these disorders in the chapters that follow.

In this chapter, we first discuss what we mean by the term *abnormal behavior*. Then we look briefly at how our view of abnormality and mental illness has evolved through history to the more scientific perspectives of today. We will conclude with a discussion of the current mental health professions.

What Is Abnormal Behavior?

A difficult but fundamental task facing those in the field of abnormal psychology is to define **abnormal behavior**, because the concept of abnormal behavior is central to current thinking about psychological disorders. The best current definition of abnormal behavior, and by extension, mental disorder, is one that contains several characteristics. The definition of mental disorder presented in the current American diagnostic manual, the *Diagnostic and Statistical Manual of Mental Disorders*, Fourth Edition, Text Revision (DSM-IV-TR), includes a number of characteristics essential to the concept of abnormal behavior. In DSM-IV-TR, mental disorder is defined as

> *A clinically significant behavioral or psychological syndrome or pattern that occurs in an individual and that is associated with present distress (e.g., a painful symptom) or disability (i.e., impairment in one or more important areas of functioning) or with a significantly increased risk of suffering, death, pain, disability, or an important loss of freedom. In addition, this syndrome or pattern must not be merely an expectable and culturally sanctioned response to a particular event, for example, the death of a loved one. Whatever its original cause, it must currently be considered a manifestation of a behavioral, psychological, or biological dysfunction in the individual (American Psychological Association, APA, 2000, p. xxxi).*

In the following sections, we consider in more detail some of the key characteristics that are highlighted by the DSM-IV-TR definition, including disability, distress, violation of social norms, and dysfunction. We will see that no single characteristic can fully define the concept, although each has merit and each captures some part of what might be a full definition. Consequently, abnormality is usually determined based on the presence of several characteristics at one time, as the DSM-IV-TR definition exemplifies.

Clinical Case: José

José didn't know what to think about his nightmares. Ever since he returned from the war, he couldn't get the bloody images to stay out of his head. He woke up nearly every night with nightmares about the carnage he witnessed as a soldier stationed in Falluja. Even during the day, he would have flashbacks to the moment his Humvee was nearly sliced in half by a rocket-propelled grenade. Watching his friend die sitting next to him was the worst part; even the occasional pain from shrapnel still embedded in his shoulder was not as bad as the recurring dreams and flashbacks. He seemed to be sweating all the time now, and whenever he heard a loud noise, he jumped out of his chair. Just the other day, his grandmother stepped on a balloon left over from his "welcome home" party. To José, it sounded like a gunshot, and he immediately dropped to the ground.

His grandmother was worried about him. She thought he must have *ataque de nervios*, just like her father had back home in Puerto Rico. She said her father was afraid all the time and felt like he was going crazy. She kept going to Mass and praying for José, which he appreciated. The army doctor said he had posttraumatic stress disorder, or PTSD. José was supposed to go to the Veterans Administration (VA) hospital for an evaluation, but he didn't really think there was anything wrong with him. Yet, his buddy Jorge had been to a group session at the VA, and he said it made him feel better. Maybe he would check it out. He wanted these images to get out of his head.

Personal Distress

One characteristic used to define some forms of abnormal behavior is personal distress—that is, a person's behavior may be classified as abnormal if it causes him or her great distress. Felicia felt distress about her difficulty with paying attention and the social consequences of this difficulty—that is, being called names by other schoolgirls. Personal distress also characterizes many of the forms of abnormality considered in this book—people experiencing anxiety disorders and depression suffer greatly. But not all abnormal behaviors cause distress. For example, an individual with antisocial personality disorder may treat others coldheartedly and violate the law without experiencing any guilt, remorse, anxiety, or other type of distress. And not all behavior that causes distress is abnormal—for example, the distress of hunger due to religious fasting or the pain of childbirth.

Personal distress can be part of the definition of abnormal behavior. In its expression, it resembles grief (shown in the photo), which is an expected response to losing a loved one, but unlike grief, psychopathological distress is not expected in the given situation. (AFP/Corbis Images.)

Disability

Disability, that is, impairment in some important area of life (e.g., work or personal relationships) can also be used to characterize abnormal behavior. For example, substance-related disorders are defined in part by the social or occupational disability (e.g., serious arguments with one's spouse or poor work performance) created by substance abuse. Being rejected by peers, as Felicia was, is also an example of this characteristic. Phobias can produce both distress and disability—for example, if a severe fear of flying prevents someone living in California from taking a job in New York. Like distress, however, disability alone cannot be used to define abnormality, because some, but not all, disorders involve disability. For example, the disorder bulimia nervosa involves binge eating and compensatory purging (e.g., vomiting) in an attempt to control weight gain but does not necessarily involve disability. Most individuals with bulimia lead lives without impairment, while bingeing and purging in private. Other characteristics that might in some circumstances be considered disabilities—such as being short if you want to be a professional basketball player—do not fall within the domain of abnormal psychology. As with the characteristic of statistical infrequency, we do not have a rule that tells us which disabilities belong in our domain of study and which do not.

Violation of Social Norms

In the realm of behavior, social norms are widely held standards (beliefs and attitudes) that people use consciously or intuitively to make judgments about where behaviors are situated on such scales as good–bad, right–wrong, justified–unjustified, and acceptable–unacceptable. Behavior that violates social norms might be classified as abnormal. For example, the repetitive rituals performed by people with obsessive-compulsive disorder (see Chapter 5) and the conversations with imaginary voices that some people with schizophrenia engage in (see Chapter 11) are behaviors that violate social norms. José's dropping to the floor at the sound of a popping balloon does not fit within most social norms. Yet this way of defining abnormal behavior is both too broad and too narrow. For example, it is too broad in that criminals and prostitutes violate social norms but are not usually studied within the domain of psychopathology; and it is too narrow in that highly anxious people typically do not violate social norms but are a focus of psychopathologists.

Also, of course, social norms vary a great deal across cultures and ethnic groups, so behavior that clearly violates a social norm in one group may not do so at all in another. For example, in some cultures but not in others it violates a social norm to directly disagree with someone. In Puerto Rico, José's behavior would not likely have been interpreted in the same way as it would be in the United States. Throughout this book, we will address this important issue of cultural and ethnic diversity as it applies to the descriptions, causes, and treatments of mental disorders.

Dysfunction

In an influential and widely discussed paper, Wakefield (1992) proposed that mental disorders could be defined as **harmful dysfunction**. It is important to note that this definition has two parts: a value judgment ("harmful") and an objective, scientific component—the "dysfunction". A judgment that a behavior is harmful requires some standard, and this standard is likely to depend on social norms and values, the characteristic just described. Dysfunctions are said to occur when an internal mechanism is unable to perform its natural function—that is, the function that it evolved to perform. By grounding this part of the definition of mental disorder in evolutionary theory, Wakefield hoped to give the definition scientific objectivity.

Numerous critics have argued that the dysfunction component of Wakefield's definition is not so easily and objectively identifiable in relation to mental disorders (e.g., Houts, 2001; Lilienfeld & Marino, 1999). One difficulty is that the internal mechanisms involved in mental disorders are largely unknown; thus, we cannot say exactly what may not be functioning properly. Wakefield (1999) has tried to meet this objection by, in part, referring to plausible dysfunctions rather than proven ones. In the case of Jack, for example, hallucinations (hearing voices) could be construed as a failure of the mind to "turn off" unwanted sounds. Nevertheless, we have a situation in which we judge a behavior or set of behaviors to be harmful and then decide that the behavior represents a mental disorder because we believe it is caused by a dysfunction of some unknown internal mechanism. Clearly, like the other definitions of abnormality, Wakefield's concept of harmful dysfunction has its limitations.

The broader concept of dysfunction as indicated in the DSM-IV-TR definition of mental disorder refers to behavioral, psychological, or biological dysfunctions that are supported by our current body of evidence. This broadening does not entirely avoid the problems that Wakefield's definition suffers from, but it is an attempt that formally recognizes the limits of our current understanding.

Indeed, it is crucial to keep in mind that our text presents human problems that are currently considered abnormal and are therefore called mental disorders. Over time, because the field is continually evolving, the disorders discussed in books like this will undoubtedly change, and so will the definition of abnormality. It is also quite possible that we will never be able to arrive at a definition that captures abnormality in its entirety and for all time. Nevertheless, at the current time, the characteristics that are included in the DSM-IV-TR definition constitute a useful partial definition, but keep in mind that they are not equally or invariably applicable to every diagnosis. Figure 1.2 shows the different characteristics of the definition of mental disorder.

Figure 1.2   Key characteristics in the DSM-IV-TR definition of mental disorder.

Quick Summary

The focus of this book will be on the description, causes, and treatments of a number of different mental disorders. It is important to note at the outset that the personal impact of our subject matter requires us to make a conscious, determined effort to remain objective. Stigma remains a central problem in the field of abnormal psychology and mental disorders. Stigma has four components that involve the labels for mental illness and their uses. Even the use of everyday language terms such as "crazy" or "schizo" can contribute to the stigmatization of the mentally ill.

Abnormal behavior is at the center of mental disorders, but defining abnormality remains difficult. A number of different definitions have been offered, but none can entirely account for the full range of abnormality. Whether or not a behavior causes personal distress can be a char-

acteristic of abnormality. But not all abnormal behavior that we consider to be part of mental disorders causes distress. Behaviors that cause a disability or are unexpected can be considered abnormal. But again, some abnormal behaviors do not cause disability nor are they unexpected. Behavior that violates social norms is also considered abnormal. However, not all such behavior is considered part of a mental disorder, and some behaviors that are part of mental disorders do not necessarily violate social norms. Harmful dysfunction involves both a value component and a scientific component. Like the other definitions, however, it cannot fully account for what we study in psychopathology. Taken together, each definition of abnormal behavior has something helpful to offer in the study of psychopathology.

Check Your Knowledge 1.1 (answers are at the end of the chapter)

1. Characteristics of stigma include all of the following *except*:
   a. The label reflects desirable characteristics.
   b. Discrimination against those with the label.
   c. Focus on differences between those with and without the label.
   d. Labeling a group of people who are different.
2. Which of the following definitions of abnormality is currently thought best?
   a. Statistical infrequency.
   b. Harmful dysfunction.
   c. Norm violation.
   d. None of the above.
3. The DSM-IV-TR definition of mental disorder is perhaps the best current definition because:
   a. It includes information about both violation of social norms and dysfunction.
   b. It includes many components, none of which can alone account for mental disorder.
   c. It is part of the current diagnostic system.
   d. It recognizes the limits of our current understanding.

History of Psychopathology

Many textbooks begin with a chapter on the history of the field. Why? It is important to consider how concepts and approaches have changed (or not) over time, because we can learn not to make the same mistakes made in the past and because we can see that our current concepts and approaches are likely to change in the future.

As psychopathologists we are interested in the causes of mental disorders. This search for causes has gone on for a considerable period of time. At different periods in history, explanations for mental disorders have been supernatural, biological, and psychological. As we quickly travel through these different periods, ask yourself what level of explanation was operating at different times.

Early Demonology

Before the age of scientific inquiry, all good and bad manifestations of power beyond human control—eclipses, earthquakes, storms, fire, diseases, the changing seasons—were regarded as supernatural. Behavior seemingly outside individual control was also ascribed to supernatural causes. Many early philosophers, theologians, and physicians who studied the troubled mind believed that disturbed behavior reflected the displeasure of the gods or possession by demons.

Christ driving the evil spirits out of a possessed man. (Archivo Iconografico, S.A./Corbis Images.)

The doctrine that an evil being or spirit can dwell within a person and control his or her mind and body is called **demonology**. Examples of demonological thinking are found in the records of the early Chinese, Egyptians, Babylonians, and Greeks. Among the Hebrews, abnormal behavior was attributed to possession of the person by bad spirits, after God in his wrath had withdrawn protection. The New Testament includes the story of Christ curing a man with an unclean spirit by casting out the devils from within him and hurling them onto a herd of swine (Mark 5:8–13).

The belief that abnormal behavior was caused by possession led to treating it by **exorcism**, the ritualistic casting out of evil spirits. Exorcism typically took the form of elaborate rites of prayer, noisemaking, forcing the afflicted to drink terrible-tasting brews, and on occasion more extreme measures, such as flogging and starvation, to render the body uninhabitable to devils.

Early Biological Explanations

In the fifth century B.C., Hippocrates (460?–377? B.C.), often called the father of modern medicine, separated medicine from religion, magic, and superstition. He rejected the prevailing Greek belief that the gods sent serious physical diseases and mental disturbances as punishment and insisted instead that such illnesses had natural causes and hence should be treated like other, more common maladies, such as colds and constipation. Hippocrates regarded the brain as the organ of consciousness, intellectual life, and emotion; thus he thought that deviant thinking and behavior were indications of some kind of brain pathology. Hippocrates is often considered one of the earliest proponents of the notion that something wrong with the physical body disturbs thought and action.

Hippocrates classified mental disorders into three categories: mania, melancholia, and phrenitis, or brain fever. Further, Hippocrates believed that normal brain functioning, and therefore mental health, depended on a delicate balance among four humors, or fluids of the body, namely, blood, black bile, yellow bile, and phlegm. An imbalance produced disorders. If a person was sluggish and dull, for example, the body supposedly contained a preponderance of phlegm. A preponderance of black bile was the explanation for melancholia; too much yellow bile explained irritability and anxiousness; and too much blood, changeable temperament.

Through his teachings, the phenomena associated with mental disorders became more clearly the province of physicians than of priests. The treatments Hippocrates suggested were quite different from exorcism. For melancholia, for example, he prescribed tranquility, sobriety, care in choosing food and drink, and abstinence from sexual activity. Because Hippocrates believed in natural rather than supernatural causes, he depended on his own keen observations and made valuable contributions as a clinician. He also left behind remarkably detailed records clearly describing many of the symptoms now recognized in epilepsy, alcoholic delusion, stroke, and paranoia.

The Greek physician Hippocrates held a biological view of abnormal behavior, considering psychopathology a disease of the brain. (Archivo Iconografico, S.A./Corbis Images.)

Hippocrates' ideas, of course, did not withstand later scientific scrutiny. However, his basic premise—that human behavior is markedly affected by bodily structures or substances and that abnormal behavior is produced by some kind of physical imbalance or even damage—did foreshadow aspects of contemporary thought. In the next seven centuries, Hippocrates' naturalistic approach to disease and disorder was generally accepted by other Greeks as well as by the Romans, who adopted the medicine of the Greeks after their empire became the major power in the ancient European world.

The Dark Ages and Demonology

Historians have often pointed to the death of Galen (A.D. 130–200), the second-century Greek who is regarded as the last great physician of the classical era, as the beginning of the so-called Dark Ages in western European medicine and in the treatment and investigation of psychological disorders. Over several centuries of decay, Greek and Roman civilization ceased to be. The churches gained in influence, and the papacy was declared independent of the state. Christian monasteries, through their missionary and educational work, replaced physicians as healers and as authorities on mental disorder.[1]

The monks in the monasteries cared for and nursed the sick, and a few of the monasteries were repositories for the classic Greek medical manuscripts, even though the monks may not have made use of the knowledge within these works. Monks cared for the mentally disordered by praying over them and touching them with relics; they also concocted fantastic potions for them to drink in the waning phase of the moon. Many of the mentally ill roamed the countryside, destitute and progressively becoming worse. During this period, there was a return to a belief in supernatural causes of mental disorders.

The Persecution of Witches   Beginning in the thirteenth century, in response to widespread social unrest and recurrent famines and plagues, people in Europe turned to demonology to explain these disasters. They became obsessed with the devil. Witchcraft, now viewed as instigated by Satan, was seen as a heresy and a denial of God. Then, as today, when faced with inexplicable and frightening occurrences, people tended to seize on whatever explanation seemed most plausible. The times conspired to heap enormous blame on those regarded as witches, who were persecuted with great zeal.

In 1484, Pope Innocent VIII exhorted the clergy of Europe to leave no stone un- turned in the search for witches. He sent two Dominican monks to northern Germany as

inquisitors. Two years later they issued a comprehensive and explicit manual, *Malleus Maleficarum* ("the witches' hammer"), to guide the witch hunts. This legal and theological document came to be regarded by Catholics and Protestants alike as a textbook on witchcraft. Those accused of witchcraft should be tortured if they did not confess; those convicted and penitent were to be imprisoned for life; and those convicted and unre- pentant were to be handed over to the law for execution. The manual specified that a person's sudden loss of reason was a symptom of demonic possession and that burning was the usual method of driving out the supposed demon. Records of the pe- riod are not considered reliable, but it is thought that over the next several centuries hundreds of thousands of people, partic- ularly women and children, were accused, tortured, and put to death.

Investigators initially believed that many of the people ac- cused of being witches during the later Middle Ages were men- tally ill (Zilboorg & Henry, 1941). The basis for this belief was the confessions of the accused, who sometimes reported having had intercourse with the devil and having flown to sabbats, the secret meetings of their cults. Some investigators have interpreted these confessions as delusions or hallucinations, indicating that these so-called witches were mentally ill.

In the dunking test, if the woman did not drown, she was considered to be in league with the devil (and punished accordingly); this is the ultimate no-win situation. (Corbis-Bettmann.)

More detailed research into this historical period, however, indicates that many of the accused were not mentally ill, despite such confessions. Careful analyses of the witch hunts reveal that more sane than insane people were tried. Confessions like those described above were typically obtained during brutal torture, having been suggested to the accused witches both by their accusers and by the prevailing beliefs of the times. Indeed, in England, where torture was not allowed, the confessions did not usually contain descriptions resembling delusions or hallucinations (Schoeneman, 1977).

---

[1] The teachings of Galen continued to be influential in the Islamic world. For example, the Persian physician al-Razi (865–925) established a facility for the treatment of the mentally ill in Baghdad and was an early practitioner of psychotherapy.

Lunacy Trials   Evaluations of other sources of information also indicate that mental illness was not primarily ascribed to witchcraft. From the thirteenth century on, as the cities of Europe grew larger, hospitals began to come under secular jurisdiction. Municipal authorities, gaining in power, tended to supplement or take over some of the activities of the church, one of these being the care of the mentally ill. The foundation deed for the Holy Trinity Hospital in Salisbury, England, dating from the mid-fourteenth century, specified the purposes of the hospital, among them that the "mad are kept safe until they are restored of reason." English laws during this period allowed both the dangerously insane and the incompetent to be confined in a hospital. Notably, the people who were confined were not described as being possessed (Allderidge, 1979).

Beginning in the thirteenth century, lunacy trials to determine a person's sanity were held in England. The trials were conducted under the Crown's right to protect the mentally impaired, and a judgment of insanity allowed the Crown to become guardian of the lunatic's estate (Neugebauer, 1979). The defendant's orientation, memory, intellect, daily life, and habits were at issue in the trial. Usually, strange behavior was attributed to physical illness or injury or to some emotional shock. In all the cases that Neugebauer examined, only one referred to demonic possession. Interestingly, the term *lunacy* comes from a theory espoused by the Swiss physician Paracelsus (1493–1541), who attributed abnormal behavior to a misalignment of the moon and stars (the Latin word for moon is *luna*). This lunar explanation, even if unsubstantiated, was a welcome alternative to explanations involving demons or witches. Even today, many people believe that a full moon is linked to abnormal behavior; however, there is no scientific evidence to support this belief.

Development of Asylums

Until the end of the Crusades in the fifteenth century, there were very few mental hospitals in Europe. However, there were many hospitals for lepers—for example, in the twelfth century, England and Scotland had 220 leprosy hospitals serving a total population of a million and a half. After the principal Crusades, leprosy gradually disappeared from Europe, probably because with the end of the wars came a break with the eastern sources of the infection. With hospitals now underused, attention seems to have turned to the mentally ill.

Confinement of the mentally ill began in earnest in the fifteenth and sixteenth centuries. Leprosariums were converted to **asylums**, refuges for the confinement and care of the mentally ill. Many of these asylums took in a mix of mentally disturbed people and beggars. Beggars were regarded as a great social problem at the time; in sixteenth-century Paris, the population of fewer than 100,000 included 30,000 beggars (Foucault, 1965). These asylums had no specific regimen for their inmates other than to have them work. During the same period, however, hospitals geared more specifically to the confinement of the mentally ill also emerged.

Bethlehem and Other Early Asylums   The Priory of St. Mary of Bethlehem was founded in 1243. Records indicate that in 1403 it housed six mentally ill men. In 1547, Henry VIII handed it over to the city of London, thereafter to be a hospital devoted solely to the confinement of the mentally ill. The conditions in Bethlehem were deplorable. Over the years the word bedlam, the popular name for this hospital, came to mean a place or scene of wild uproar and confusion. Bethlehem eventually became one of

In this eighteenth-century painting by Hogarth, two upper-class women find amusement in touring St. Mary's of Bethlehem (Bedlam). (Corbis-Bettmann.)

London's great tourist attractions, by the eighteenth century rivaling both Westminster Abbey and the Tower of London. Even as late as the nineteenth century, viewing the violent patients was considered entertainment, and people bought tickets to see them. Similarly, in the Lunatics Tower, which was constructed in Vienna in 1784, patients were confined in the spaces between inner square rooms and the outer walls, where they could be viewed by passersby.

Obviously, confining the mentally ill in hospitals and placing their abnormal behavior in the domain of medicine did not necessarily lead to more humane and effective treatment. Medical treatments were often crude and painful. Benjamin Rush (1745–1813), for example, began practicing medicine in Philadelphia in 1769 and is considered the father of American psychiatry. Yet he believed that mental disorder was caused by an excess of blood in the brain, for which his favored treatment was to draw great quantities of blood from disordered individuals (Farina, 1976). Rush also believed that many "lunatics" could be cured by being frightened. Thus, one of his recommended procedures was for the physician to convince the patient that death was near! A New England doctor of the nineteenth century implemented this procedure in an ingenious manner: "On his premises stood a tank of water, into which a patient, packed into a coffin-like box pierced with holes, was lowered. He was kept under water until the bubbles of air ceased to rise, after which he was taken out, rubbed, and revived—if he had not already passed beyond reviving!" (Deutsch, 1949, p. 82).

Pinel's Reforms   Philippe Pinel (1745–1826) has often been considered a primary figure in the movement for humanitarian treatment of the mentally ill in asylums. In 1793, while the French Revolution raged, he was put in charge of a large asylum in Paris known as La Bicêtre. A historian described the conditions at this particular hospital:

> [The patients were] shackled to the walls of their cells, by iron collars which held them flat against the wall and permitted little movement. They could not lie down at night, as a rule. Oftentimes there was a hoop of iron around the waist of the patient and in addition chains on both the hands and the feet. These chains [were] sufficiently long so that the patient could feed himself out of a bowl, the food usually being a mushy gruel—bread soaked in a weak soup. Since little was known about dietetics, [no attention] was paid to the type of diet given the patients. They were presumed to be animals and not to care whether the food was good or bad. (Selling, 1940, p. 54)

Many texts assert that Pinel removed the chains of the people imprisoned in La Bicêtre, an event that was memorialized in well-known paintings. Pinel is said to have begun to treat the inmates as sick human beings rather than as beasts. Many who had been

The freeing of the patients at La Bicêtre (supposedly by Pinel, as pictured here) is often considered to mark the beginning of more humanitarian treatment of people with mental illness. (Stock Montage, Inc.)

completely unmanageable became calm. Patients formerly considered dangerous now strolled through the hospital and grounds without creating disturbances or harming anyone. Light and airy rooms replaced dungeons. Some patients who had been incarcerated for years were apparently restored to health and eventually discharged from the hospital.

Historical research, however, indicates that it was not Pinel who released the patients from their chains. Rather, it was a former patient, Jean-Baptiste Pussin, who had become an orderly at the hospital. In fact, Pinel was not even present when the patients were released (Weiner, 1994). Several years later, though, Pinel did praise Pussin's efforts and began to follow the same practices.

Consistent with the egalitarianism of the new French Republic, Pinel came to believe that the mental patients in his care were essentially normal people who should be approached with compassion and understanding and treated with dignity as individual human beings. He surmised that if their reason had left them because of severe personal and social problems, it might be restored to them through comforting counsel and purposeful activity.

Pinel did much good for people with mental illness, but he was no paragon of enlightenment and egalitarianism. He reserved the more humanitarian treatment for the upper classes; patients of the lower classes were still subjected to terror and coercion as a means of control, with straitjackets replacing chains.

Moral Treatment   For a time, mental hospitals established in Europe and the United States were relatively small, privately supported, and operated along the lines of the humanitarian changes at La Bicêtre. In England, a prominent merchant and Quaker, William Tuke (1732–1822), shocked by the conditions at York Asylum, proposed to the Society of Friends that it found its own institution. In 1796, York Retreat was established on a country estate. It provided mentally ill patients with a quiet and religious atmosphere in which to live, work, and rest. Patients discussed their difficulties with attendants, worked in the garden, and took walks through the countryside.

In the United States, the Friends' Asylum, founded in 1817 in Pennsylvania, and the Hartford Retreat, established in 1824 in Connecticut, were patterned after the York Retreat. Other U.S. hospitals were influenced by the sympathetic and attentive treatment provided by Pinel and Tuke. In accordance with this approach, which became known as **moral treatment**, patients had close contact with attendants, who talked and read to them and encouraged them to engage in purposeful activity; residents led lives as close to normal as possible and in general took responsibility for themselves within the constraints of their disorders. Further, there were to be no more than 250 patients in a given hospital (Whitaker, 2002).

Despite these seemingly positive features, two less favorable findings emerged from a review of detailed case records of the York Retreat from 1880 to 1884 (Renvoize & Beveridge, 1989). First, drugs were the most common treatment, including alcohol, cannabis, opium, and chloral hydrate (knockout drops). Second, the outcomes were not very favorable; fewer than one-third of the patients were discharged as improved or recovered.

Moral treatment was largely abandoned in the latter part of the nineteenth century. Ironically, the efforts of Dorothea Dix (1802–1887), a crusader for improved conditions for people with mental illness who fought to have hospitals created for their care, helped effect this change. Dix, a Boston schoolteacher, taught a Sunday-school class at the local prison and was shocked at the deplorable conditions in which the inmates lived. Her interest spread to the conditions at mental hospitals and to mentally ill people who had nowhere to go for treatment. She campaigned vigorously to improve the lot of people with mental illness and personally helped see that 32 state hospitals were built. These large, public hospitals took in many of the patients whom the private hospitals could not accommodate. Unfortunately, the small staffs of these new hospitals were unable to provide the individual attention that was a hallmark of moral treatment (Bockhoven, 1963). Moreover, the hospitals came to be administered by physicians, most of whom were interested in the biological aspects of illness and in the physical, rather than the psychological well-being of mental patients. The

In the nineteenth century, Dorothea Dix played a major role in establishing more mental hospitals in the United States. (Corbis Images.)

Focus on Discovery 1.1

The Mental Hospital Today

In the 1970s concerns about the restrictive nature of confinement in a mental hospital led to the so-called deinstitutionalization of a large number of patients with mental illness. Budget cuts beginning in the 1980s and continuing today have caused this trend to continue. But the problems of the chronically ill patient, who cannot be deinstitutionalized, have yet to be handled adequately (as we will discuss in more detail in Chapter 17). Treatment in public mental hospitals is primarily custodial in nature. Patients live in a protected environment, but they may receive little treatment; their existence is monotonous and sedentary for the most part.

Today, public mental hospitals in the United States are usually funded either by the federal government or by the state where they are located. Many Veterans Administration hospitals and general medical hospitals also contain psychiatric wards.

In addition, there are private mental hospitals. Sheppard and Enoch Pratt near Baltimore, Maryland, and McLean Hospital, in Belmont, Massachusetts, are two of the most prominent. The physical facilities and professional care in private hospitals tend to be superior to those of public hospitals for one reason: the private hospitals have more money. The costs to patients in these private institutions can exceed $1,000 per day, with individual therapy sessions with a member of the professional staff costing extra! Although many patients have medical insurance, it usually has a 90-day stay limit, so such hospitals are clearly beyond the means of most patients with mental disorders.

A somewhat specialized mental hospital, sometimes called a forensic hospital, is reserved for people who have been arrested and judged unable to stand trial and for those who have been acquitted of a crime by reason of insanity (see p. 565). Although these patients have not been sent to prison, armed guards and tight security regiment their lives. Treatment of some kind is supposed to take place during their incarceration.

Most hospitals require patients to attend group therapy—here, a general term indicating only that at least two patients are supposed to

Most dormitory rooms at state mental hospitals are bleak and unstimulating. (Eric Roth/Index Stock.)

relate to each other and to a group leader in a room for a specific period of time. Some patients have a few sessions alone with a professional therapist. For the most part, however, traditional hospital treatment over the past 40 years has been oriented toward dispensing drugs rather than offering psychotherapy. The institutional setting itself is used as a way to provide supportive care, to try to ensure that patients take their medication, and to protect and look after patients whose conditions make it virtually impossible for them to care for themselves or that render them an unreasonable burden or threat to others (Paul & Menditto, 1992).

money that had once paid the salaries of personal attendants now paid for equipment and laboratories. (See Focus on Discovery 1.1 for an examination of whether the conditions in today's mental hospitals have improved.)

Quick Summary

Early concepts of mental illness included demonology (possession by demons) but also biological approaches as evidenced by the ideas of Hippocrates. During the Dark Ages, some people with mental illness were cared for in monasteries, but many simply roamed the countryside. Some were persecuted as witches, but this was relatively rare (later analyses indicated that many of the people accused of being witches were not mentally ill). Treatments for the mentally ill have changed over time. Exorcisms did not do much good. Treatments in asylums could also be cruel and unhelpful, but pioneering work by Pinel, Dix, and others made asylums more humane places for treatment. Unfortunately, their good ideas did not last as the mental hospitals became overcrowded and understaffed.

Check Your Knowledge 1.2

True or false?
1. Benjamin Rush is credited with beginning moral treatment in the United States.
2. The most recent historical research has found that nearly all of the individuals persecuted as witches were mentally ill.
3. Hippocrates was one of the first to propose that mental illness had a biological cause.
4. The term lunatic is derived from the ideas of Paracelsus.

The Evolution of Contemporary Thought

Galen was a Greek physician who followed Hippocrates's ideas and is regarded as the last great physician of the classical era. (Corbis Images.)

Contemporary developments in biological and psychological approaches to the causes and treatments of mental disorders were heavily influenced by theorists and scientists working in the late nineteenth and early twentieth centuries. We will discuss, compare, and evaluate these approaches more fully in Chapter 2. In this section, we review the historical antecedents of these more contemporary approaches, beginning with the important advances made in the classification of mental disorders.

Recall that in the West, the death of Galen and the decline of Greco-Roman civilization temporarily ended inquiries into the nature of both physical and mental illness. Not until the late Middle Ages did any new facts begin to emerge, thanks to an emerging empirical approach to medical science, which gathered knowledge by direct observation. For example, the Flemish anatomist and physician Vesalius (1514–1564) discovered that many aspects of Galen's presentation of human anatomy were incorrect. Galen had presumed that human physiology mirrored that of the monkeys he studied. It took more than 1,000 years for autopsy studies of humans—not allowed during his time—to begin finding where Galen was wrong. Further progress came from the efforts of the English physician Thomas Sydenham (1624–1689). Sydenham was particularly successful in advocating an empirical approach to classification and diagnosis, and this approach subsequently influenced those interested in mental disorders.

An Early System of Classification

One of those impressed by Sydenham's approach was the German physician Wilhelm Griesinger, who insisted that any diagnosis of mental disorder specify a biological cause, a clear return to the biological views first espoused by Hippocrates. A textbook of psychiatry written by Griesinger's well-known follower Emil Kraepelin (1856–1926) and first published in 1883 included a classification system that attempted to definitively establish the biological nature of mental illnesses.

Kraepelin discerned among mental disorders a tendency for groups of symptoms, called a *syndrome*, to appear together regularly enough to be regarded as having a biological cause, much as a particular medical disease may have an associated set of symptoms and may be attributed to a biological dysfunction. He regarded each type of mental illness as distinct from all others, with its own cause, symptoms, course, and outcome. Even though cures had not been worked out, at least the course of the disease could be predicted.

Kraepelin proposed two major groups of severe mental illnesses: dementia praecox (an early term for schizophrenia) and manic-depressive psychosis (an early term for bipolar disorder). He postulated a chemical imbalance as the cause of dementia praecox and an irregularity in metabolism as the explanation of manic-depressive psychosis. Kraepelin's classification scheme influenced the current diagnostic categories, which are described more fully in Chapter 3.

Biological Approaches

Discovering Biological Origins in General Paresis and Syphilis   The anatomy and workings of the nervous system were partially understood by the mid-1800s, but not enough was known to let investigators conclude whether the structural abnormalities presumed to cause various mental disorders were present or not. However, degenerative changes in brain cells associated with senile and presenile psychoses and some structural pathologies that accompany mental retardation were identified. Perhaps the most striking medical success was the elucidation of the nature and origin of syphilis, a venereal disease that had been recognized for several centuries.

The story of this discovery provides a good illustration of how an empirical approach, the basis for contemporary science, works. Since 1798 it had been known that a number of mentally ill patients manifested a syndrome characterized by a steady deterioration of both physical and mental abilities, including symptoms such as delusions of grandeur and progressive paralysis. Soon after these symptoms were recognized, investigators realized that these patients never recovered. In 1825, the presumed disease associated with this syndrome was given the name **general paresis**. In 1857, it was established that some patients with general paresis had earlier had syphilis, but there were many competing theories of the origin of paresis. For example, in attempting to account for the high rate of the disorder among sailors, some supposed that seawater might be the cause. And Griesinger, in trying to explain the higher incidence among men, speculated that liquor, tobacco, and coffee might be implicated.

In the 1860s and 1870s, Louis Pasteur established the germ theory of disease, which set forth the view that disease is caused by infection of the body by minute organisms. This theory laid the groundwork for demonstrating the relation between syphilis and general paresis. In 1897, Richard von Krafft-Ebing inoculated paretic patients with matter from syphilitic sores, and the patients did not develop syphilis, indicating that they had been infected earlier. Finally, in 1905, the specific microorganism that causes syphilis was discovered. For the first time, a causal link had been established between infection, destruction of certain areas of the brain, and a form of psychopathology (general paresis). If one type of psychopathology had a biological cause, so could others. Biological approaches gained credibility, and the search for more biological causes was off and running.

Genetics   In the early twentieth century, investigators became intrigued by the idea that mental illness may run in families, and beginning at that time, a number of studies documented the heritability of mental illnesses such as schizophrenia, bipolar disorder, and depression. These studies would set the stage for later theories about the causes of mental illness. (**Behavior genetics**, the study of individual differences in behavior that are attributable in part to differences in genetic makeup, is discussed in Chapter 2.)

Unfortunately, many of the early efforts in the United States to determine whether mental illness could be inherited were associated with the eugenics movement, whose advocates sought to eliminate undesirable characteristics from the population by restricting the ability to have children (e.g., by enforced sterilization). Among such "undesirable characteristics" was mental illness, and in a sad page from U.S. history, state laws were written in the late 1800s and early 1900s to prohibit marriage and force sterilization for the mentally ill in order to prevent them from "passing on" their illness. Such laws were upheld by the United States Supreme Court in 1927 (Chase, 1980), and it wasn't until the middle of the twentieth century that these abhorrent practices were halted. Nevertheless, much damage had been done: by 1945, over 45,000 mentally ill individuals in the United States had been forcibly sterilized (Whitaker, 2002).

Biological Treatments   The general warehousing of patients in mental hospitals earlier in the twentieth century, coupled with the shortage of professional staff, created a climate that allowed, perhaps even subtly encouraged, experimentation with radical interventions. In the early 1930s, the practice of inducing a coma with large dosages of insulin was introduced by Sakel (1938), who claimed that up to three-quarters of the patients with schizophrenia whom he treated showed significant improvement. Later findings by others were less encouraging, and insulin-coma therapy—which presented serious risks to health, including irreversible coma and death—was gradually abandoned.

In the early twentieth century, **electroconvulsive therapy (ECT)** was originated by two Italian physicians, Ugo Cerletti and Lucino Bini. Cerletti was interested in epilepsy and was seeking a way to induce seizures experimentally. The solution became apparent when he visited a slaughterhouse, where he saw seizures induced in animals by electric shocks administered to the head. Shortly thereafter he found that by applying electric shocks to the sides of the human head, he could produce full epileptic seizures. Then, in Rome in 1938, he used the technique on a patient with schizophrenia.

In the decades that followed, ECT was administered to patients with both schizophrenia and severe depression, usually in hospital settings. As we will discuss in Chapter 8 it is still used in some rare instances today for patients with severe depression. The introduction of medications with fewer side effects contributed to the decline in use of ECT. However, refinements in the ECT procedures made it less problematic.

In 1935, Egas Moniz, a Portuguese psychiatrist, introduced the *prefrontal lobotomy*, a surgical procedure that destroys the tracts connecting the frontal lobes to lower centers of the brain. His initial reports claimed high rates of success (Moniz, 1936), and for 20 years thereafter thousands of mentally ill patients underwent variations of psychosurgery. The procedure was used especially for those whose behavior was violent. Many patients did indeed quiet down and could even be discharged from hospitals. During the 1950s, however, this intervention fell into disrepute for several reasons. After surgery, many patients became dull and listless and suffered serious losses in their cognitive capacities—for example, becoming unable to carry on a coherent conversation with another person—which is not surprising given the destruction of parts of their brains believed responsible for thought.

Scene from *One Flew over the Cuckoo's Nest*. The character portrayed by Jack Nicholson was lobotomized in the film. (Photofest.)

Psychological Approaches

The search for biological causes dominated the field of abnormal psychology until well into the twentieth century, no doubt partly because of the stunning discoveries made about general paresis and genetics. But beginning in the late eighteenth century, various psychological points of view emerged, which attributed mental disorders to psychological malfunctions. These theories were first fashionable in France and Austria, and later in the United States, leading to the development of psychotherapeutic interventions based on the tenets of the individual theories.

Mesmer's procedure for manipulating animal magnetism was generally considered a form of hypnosis. (Jean-Loup Charnet/Photo Researchers.)

Mesmer and Charcot During the eighteenth century in western Europe, many people were observed to be subject to hysterical states; they suffered from physical incapacities, such as blindness or paralysis, for which no physical cause could be found. Franz Anton Mesmer (1734–1815), an Austrian physician practicing in Vienna and Paris in the late eighteenth century, believed that hysterical disorders were caused by a particular distribution of a universal magnetic fluid in the body. Moreover, he felt that one person could influence the fluid of another to bring about a change in the other's behavior.

Mesmer conducted meetings cloaked in mystery and mysticism, at which afflicted patients sat around a covered *baquet*, or wooden tub, with iron rods protruding through the cover from bottles underneath that contained various chemicals. Mesmer would enter the room, take various rods from the tub, and touch afflicted parts of his patients' bodies. The rods were believed to transmit animal magnetism and adjust the distribution of the universal magnetic fluid, thereby removing the hysterical disorder. Whatever we may think of this questionable explanation and strange procedure, Mesmer apparently helped many people overcome their hysterical problems.

Although Mesmer regarded hysterical disorders as having strictly biological causes, we discuss his work here because he is generally considered one of the earlier practitioners of modern-day hypnosis (the word *mesmerism* is a synonym for hypnotism; the phenomenon itself was known to the ancients of many cultures, as part of the sorcery and magic of conjurers, fakirs, and faith healers).

Mesmer was regarded as a quack by his contemporaries, but the study of hypnosis gradually became respectable. The great Parisian neurologist Jean Martin Charcot (1825–1893) also studied hysterical states, including anesthesia (loss of sensation), paralysis, blindness, deafness, convulsive attacks, and gaps in memory. Charcot initially espoused a biological point of view. One day, however, some of his enterprising students hypnotized a normal woman and, by suggestion, induced her to display certain hysterical symptoms. Charcot was deceived into believing that she was an actual hysterical patient. When the students showed him how readily they could remove the symptoms by waking the woman, Charcot changed his mind about hysteria and became interested in nonbiological interpretations of these very puzzling phenomena.

In this famous painting, the French psychiatrist Jean Charcot lectures on hysteria (note the woman suffering hysterical symptoms). Charcot was an important figure in reviving interest in psychological approaches. (Corbis-Bettmann.)

Breuer and the Cathartic Method   In the nineteenth century, a Viennese physician, Josef Breuer (1842–1925), treated a young woman with a number of hysterical symptoms, including partial paralysis, impairment of sight and hearing, and, often, difficulty speaking. She also sometimes went into a dreamlike state, or "absence," during which she mumbled to herself, seemingly preoccupied with troubling thoughts. During one treatment session Breuer hypnotized her and repeated some of her mumbled words back to her. Hypnosis led to her talking more freely and, ultimately, with considerable emotion about upsetting events from her past. Frequently, on awakening from a hypnotic session she felt much better. Breuer found that the relief of a particular symptom seemed to last longer if, under hypnosis, she was able to recall the event associated with the first appearance of that symptom and if she was able to express the emotion she had felt at the time. Reliving an earlier emotional trauma and releasing emotional tension by expressing previously forgotten thoughts about the event were called catharsis, and Breuer's method became known as the **cathartic method**. In 1895, Breuer and a younger colleague, Sigmund Freud (1856–1939), jointly published *Studies in Hysteria*, partly based on the case of this young woman (whose identity was disguised under the pseudonym Anna O.) and now considered a milestone in abnormal psychology.[2]

Josef Breuer, an Austrian physician and physiologist, collaborated with Freud in the early development of psychoanalysis. (Corbis-Bettmann.)

Freud and Psychoanalysis   The apparently powerful role played by factors of which patients seemed unaware led Freud to postulate that much of human behavior is determined by forces that are inaccessible to awareness. The central assumption of Freud's theorizing,

---

[2] The case of Anna O. has become one of the best-known clinical cases in all psychotherapeutic literature. However, there is controversy over whether Breuer and Freud reported the case correctly. Historical investigations by Henri Ellenberger (1972) indicate that the young woman was helped only temporarily by Breuer's talking cure. This is supported by Carl Jung, a renowned colleague of Freud's, who is quoted as saying that during a conference in 1925, Freud told him that Anna O. had never been cured. Hospital records discovered by Ellenberger confirmed that Anna O. continued to rely on morphine to ease the "hysterical" problems that Breuer is reputed to have removed by catharsis.

Sigmund Freud developed psychoanalytic theory, both as a theory of the structure and functions of the mind (including explanations of the causes of mental disorders) and as a new method of therapy. (Corbis-Images.)

often referred to as **psychoanalytic theory**, is that psychopathology results from unconscious conflicts in the individual. In the next sections, we take a detailed look at Freud's theory.

Structure of the Mind   Freud divided the mind, or the **psyche**, into three principal parts: id, ego, and superego. According to Freud, the **id** is present at birth and is the repository of all of the energy needed to run the psyche, including the basic urges for food, water, elimination, warmth, affection, and sex. Trained as a neurologist, Freud saw the source of the id's energy as biological, and he called this energy **libido**. The individual cannot consciously perceive this energy—it is **unconscious**, below the level of awareness.

The id seeks immediate gratification of its urges, operating on what Freud called the **pleasure principle**. When the id is not satisfied, tension is produced, and the id impels the individual to eliminate this tension as quickly as possible. For example, the infant feels hunger and is impelled to move about, sucking, in an attempt to reduce the tension arising from the unsatisfied drive. The individual may also attempt to obtain gratification by generating images—in essence, fantasies—of what is desired. For instance, the hungry infant imagines sucking at the mother's breast and thereby obtains some substitute, short-term satisfaction. Of course, fantasizing cannot really satisfy such urges. This is where the ego comes in.

The **ego** begins to develop from the id during the second 6 months of life. Unlike the contents of the id, those of the ego are primarily conscious. The id may resort to fantasy when seeking satisfaction, but the task of the ego is to deal with reality. The ego thus operates on what Freud termed the **reality principle** as it mediates between the demands of reality and the id's demands for immediate gratification. The ego's task, however, is complicated by the fact that the ego derives all its energies from the id; thus, it must direct what it is entirely dependent on for energy.

The **superego**—the third part of the psyche in Freud's theory—can be roughly conceived of as the individual's conscience. Freud believed that the superego develops throughout childhood, arising from the ego much as the ego arises from the id. As children discover that many of their impulses—for example, biting and bed-wetting—are not acceptable to their parents, they begin to incorporate parental values as their own in order to receive the pleasure of parental approval and avoid the pain of disapproval.

The behavior of human beings, as conceptualized by Freud, is a complex interplay of these three parts of the psyche, all vying for the achievement of sometimes irreconcilable goals. The interplay of these forces is referred to as the psychodynamics of the personality. Theorists who follow Freud's ideas (many different versions of Freudian theory have evolved over time) are therefore referred to as psychodynamic theorists. We will discuss more current psychodynamic theories in Chapter 2.

Stages of Psychosexual Development   Freud conceived of the personality as developing through a series of four distinct psychosexual stages. He used the term psychosexual because, at each stage, a different part of the body is the most sensitive to sexual excitation and therefore the most capable of satisfying the id.

The **oral stage** is the first stage of psychosexual development. From birth to about 18 months the demands of the infant's id are satisfied primarily by feeding and the sucking and biting associated with it. The body parts through which the infant receives gratification at this stage are the lips, mouth, gums, and tongue. During the **anal stage**, from about 18 months to 3 years of age, the child mainly receives pleasure via the anus, by passing and retaining feces. The **phallic stage** extends from age 3 to age 5 or 6; during this stage, maximum gratification of the id is obtained through genital stimulation. Between the ages of 6 and 12 the child is in a **latency period**; during these years the id impulses do not play a major role in motivating behavior. The final and adult stage is the **genital stage**, during which heterosexual interests predominate.

During each stage, the developing person must resolve the conflicts between what the id wants and what the environment will provide. How this is accomplished is believed to determine basic personality traits that last throughout the person's life. A person who

In Freud's theory, the first stage of psychosexual development is the oral stage, during which pleasure is obtained from feeding. (Laura Dwight/Corbis Images.)

experiences either excessive or deficient amounts of gratification at a particular stage develops a **fixation** and is likely to regress to that stage when stressed.

One crisis of development occurs during the phallic stage, around age 4. Freud asserted the child is overcome by a desire to receive genital pleasure from the parent of the opposite sex; at the same time, the child views the parent of the same sex as a rival—the child both experiences aggressive urges against that parent and fears retaliation. The threat of dire punishment from the parent of the same sex may cause the child to repress the entire conflict, pushing both the desire for gratification and the aggressive urges into the unconscious. This repressed conflict is referred to as the **Oedipus complex** in boys and as the **Electra complex** in girls. Usually, the child resolves the conflict through increased identification with the parent of the same sex and through the adoption of society's moral values—specifically, the prohibition against sex between child and parent.

According to Freud, too much or too little gratification during one of the psychosexual stages may lead to regression to this stage during stress. (Jennie Woodcock; Reflections Photolibrary/Corbis Images.)

Defense Mechanisms   According to Freud, and as elaborated by his daughter Anna (A. Freud, 1966), herself an influential psychoanalyst, discomforts experienced by the ego as it attempts to resolve conflicts and satisfy the demands of the id and superego can be reduced in several ways. A **defense mechanism** is a strategy used by the ego to protect itself from anxiety. Perhaps the most important defense mechanism is **repression**, the process of pushing impulses and thoughts unacceptable to the ego into the unconscious. Of course, for the strategy to work—that is, for the person to remain unaware of the existence of these unacceptable things—repression must itself take place unconsciously, out of the person's awareness. Examples of other defense mechanisms are presented in Table 1.1.

Psychoanalytic Therapy   Psychotherapy based on Freud's theory is called **psychoanalysis**, or psychoanalytic therapy. It is still practiced today, although not as commonly as it once was. In Chapter 2, we will present more recent therapies derived from classical

Table 1.1 Selected Defense Mechanisms

Defense Mechanism	Definition	Example
Repression	Keeping unacceptable impulses she has or wishes from conscious awareness	A professor starting a lecture she dreaded giving says, "In conclusion."
Denial	Keeping objective events from conscious awareness	A victim of incest in childhood cannot recall it as an adult.
Projection	Attributing to someone else one's own unacceptable thoughts or feelings	A man who hates members of a racial group believes that it is they who dislike him.
Displacement	Redirecting emotional responses from their real target to someone else	A child gets mad at her brother but instead acts angrily toward her friend.
Reaction formation	Converting an unacceptable feeling into its opposite	A person with sexual feelings toward children leads a campaign against child sexual abuse.
Regression	Retreating to the behavioral patterns of an earlier stage of development	An adolescent dealing with unacceptable feelings of social inadequacy might attempt to mask those feelings by seeking oral gratification.
Rationalization	Offering acceptable reasons for an unacceptable action or attitude	A parent berates a child out of impatience, then indicates that she did so to "build character."
Sublimation	Converting unacceptable aggressive or sexual impulses into socially valued behaviors	Someone who has aggressive feelings toward his father becomes a surgeon.

Table 1.2 Major Techniques of Psychoanalysis

Technique	Description
Free association	The patient tries to say whatever comes to mind without censoring anything.
Interpretation	The analyst points out to the patient the real meaning of certain of the patient's behaviors.
Analysis of transference	The patient responds to the analyst in ways that the patient has previously responded to other important figures in his or her life, and the analyst helps the patient understand and interpret these responses.

psychoanalysis. Here, we present some of the basic concepts of psychoanalysis as it was originally conceived.

Psychoanalysis attempts to help patients face childhood conflicts, gain insight into them, and resolve them in the light of adult reality. Early repressions may prevent the ego from developing in an adult fashion; facing and resolving the repressed conflicts is supposed to undo such repression and enable adult development to continue.

Freud developed a number of techniques in his efforts to help patients resolve repressed conflicts. With **free association**, the patient reclined on a couch, facing away from the analyst, and was encouraged to give free rein to his or her thoughts, verbalizing whatever comes to mind, without censoring anything. As the patient gradually mastered this skill, defenses built up over many years were eventually bypassed. The patient's verbalizations more and more directly related to the repressed material, and the patient learned to use those relationships to develop insight into the material.

Another key component of psychoanalytic therapy is the analysis of **transference**. Transference refers to the patient's responses to his or her analyst that seem to reflect attitudes and ways of behaving toward important people in the patient's past, rather than reflecting actual aspects of the analyst–patient relationship. For example, a patient might feel that the analyst is generally bored by what he or she is saying and as a result might struggle to be entertaining, and this pattern of response might reflect the patient's childhood relationship with a parent rather than what's actually going on between the patient and the analyst. Freud encouraged the development of transference by intentionally remaining a shadowy figure, sitting behind his patients and divulging little of his own personal life and feelings. Through careful observation and analysis of these transferred attitudes, Freud believed the analyst could gain insight into the childhood origins of the patient's repressed conflicts. In the example above, the analyst might find that the patient was made to feel boring and unimportant as a child and could only gain parental attention through humor.

As previously repressed material begins to appear in therapy, the technique of **interpretation** comes into play—the analyst points out to the patient the meanings of certain of the patient's behaviors. Defense mechanisms are a principal focus of interpretation. For instance, a man who appears to have trouble with intimacy may look out the window and change the subject whenever anything touches on closeness during the course of a session. The analyst will attempt at some point to interpret the patient's behavior, pointing out its defensive nature in the hope of stimulating the patient to acknowledge that he is in fact avoiding the topic (see Table 1.2 for a summary of psychoanalysis techniques).

Neo-Freudian Psychodynamic Perspectives Several of Freud's contemporaries met with him periodically to discuss psychoanalytic theory and therapy. As often happens when a brilliant leader attracts brilliant followers and colleagues, disagreements arose about many general issues, such as the relative importance of id versus ego, of biological versus sociocultural forces on psychological development, of unconscious versus conscious processes, and of childhood versus adult experiences; whether sexual urges drive behaviors that are not

Carl Jung was the founder of analytical psychology, a blending of Freudian and humanistic concepts. (Topham/The Image Works.)

obviously sexual; and the role of reflexlike id impulses versus that of purposive behavior governed primarily by conscious ego deliberations. We discuss two influential historical figures here: Carl Jung and Alfred Adler.

Jung and Analytical Psychology   Carl Gustav Jung (1875–1961), a Swiss psychiatrist originally considered Freud's heir apparent, broke with Freud in 1914 on many issues, after a 7-year period of intense correspondence about their disagreements. Jung proposed ideas radically different from Freud's, ultimately establishing **analytical psychology**, a blend of Freudian psychology and humanistic psychology (see Chapter 16 for more on humanistic psychology).

Jung hypothesized that in addition to the personal unconscious postulated by Freud, there is a **collective unconscious**, the part of the unconscious that is common to all human beings and that consists primarily of what Jung called *archetypes*, or basic categories that all human beings use in conceptualizing about the world. In addition, Jung asserted that each of us has masculine and feminine traits that are blended and that people's spiritual and religious urges are as basic as their id urges. Jung also catalogued various personality characteristics; perhaps most important among them are extraversion (an orientation toward the external world) versus introversion (an orientation toward the inner, subjective world). This personality dimension continues to be regarded as very important, and we will encounter it again in our discussion of the personality disorders in Chapter 12.

Jung also wrote at length on religious symbolism and the meaning of life, and as a consequence became popular among certain mystics, novelists, and poets. Finally, whereas Freud regarded current and future behavior as determined primarily by the past, Jung focused on purposiveness, decision making, and goal setting. To understand people, according to Jung, one has to appreciate their hopes and aspirations, not just the effects of their past experiences, as important as those may be (Jung, 1935).

Adler and Individual Psychology   Alfred Adler (1870–1937), also an early adherent of Freud's theories, came to be even less dependent on Freud's views than was Jung, and Freud remained quite bitter toward Adler after their relationship ended. Adler had grown up as a sickly child in Vienna and had had to strive mightily to overcome feelings of inferiority. His theory, which came to be known as **individual psychology**, emphasized striving for superiority, but not in an asocial sense. Indeed, he regarded people as inextricably tied to their society because he believed that fulfillment was found in doing things for the social good. Like Jung, he stressed the importance of working toward goals, and also like Jung, much of his theorizing anticipated later developments in humanistic therapy (Adler, 1930).

A central element in Adler's work was his focus on helping individual patients change their illogical and mistaken ideas and expectations; Adler believed that feeling and behaving better depend on thinking more rationally, an approach that anticipated contemporary developments in cognitive behavior therapy (discussed in Chapter 2). Adler's interest in growth, in the prevention of problems, and in the betterment of society influenced the development of child guidance centers and parent education.

Alfred Adler was the founder of individual psychology and is well known for originating the notion of the inferiority complex. (Corbis-Bettmann.)

Quick Summary

The nineteenth and twentieth centuries saw a return to biological explanations for mental illness. Developments outside the field of psychopathology, such as the germ theory of disease and the discovery of the cause of syphilis, illustrated how the brain and behavior were linked. Early investigations into the genetics of mental illness led to a tragic emphasis on eugenics and the enforced sterilization of many thousands of mentally ill individuals. Such biological approaches to treatment as induced insulin coma, electroconvulsive therapy, and lobotomy eventually gave way to drug treatments. Psychological approaches to psychopathology evolved from Mesmer's manipulation of "animal magnetism" to treat hysteria (late eighteenth century) through Breuer's conceptualization of the cathartic method in his treatment of Anna O. (late nineteenth century) and culminated in Freud's psychoanalytic theories and treatment techniques (early twentieth century). Jung and Adler took Freud's basic ideas in a variety of different directions. Freud's theorizing, though often criticized, introduced a number of concepts that are still discussed today, including defense mechanisms and the importance of the early environment in the development of psychological problems.

Check Your Knowledge 1.3

Fill in the blank.

1. _____ was a French neurologist who was influenced by the work of _____.
2. _____ developed the cathartic method, which _____ later built on in the development of psychoanalysis.
3. The _____ is driven by the pleasure principle, but the _____ is driven by the reality principle.
4. In psychoanalysis, _____ refers to interpreting the relationship between therapist and client as indicative of the client's relationship to others.
5. _____ developed the concept of the collective unconscious; _____ developed the technique of free association; _____ is associated with individual psychology.

John B. Watson, an American psychologist, was the major figure in establishing behaviorism; he defined psychology as the study of observable behavior rather than as the investigation of subjective experience. (Underwood & Underwood/Corbis Images.)

Humanistic and Existential Psychology   Humanistic and existential psychological theories arose in the mid-twentieth century. They placed greater emphasis than Freudian theories did on the person's freedom of choice, regarding free will as the person's most important characteristic, and seldom focused on how psychological problems develop. Their main focus was on therapeutic intervention, and we cover these contributions more fully in Chapter 16.

The Rise of Behaviorism   As exemplified by Freud and his followers, psychology in the early twentieth century was dominated by a structuralist approach, which held that the proper subject of study was mental functioning. The goal of psychology, then a very new discipline, was to learn more about what went on in the mind by analyzing its elementary constituents. Through painstaking introspection, self-observation, and reporting about mental processes, psychologists hoped to discover the structure of consciousness.

After some years, many in the field began to lose faith in this approach. The problem was that different laboratories were yielding conflicting data. This dissatisfaction was brought to a head by John B. Watson (1878–1958), who in 1913 revolutionized psychology with his views.

To replace introspection, Watson looked to the experimental procedures of the psychologists who were investigating learning in animals. Because of his efforts, the dominant focus of psychology switched from thinking to learning. **Behaviorism** can be defined as an approach that studies learning by focusing on observable behavior rather than on consciousness. We will look at three types of learning that influenced the behaviorist approach in the early and middle parts of the twentieth century and that continue to be influential today: classical conditioning, operant conditioning, and modeling.

Ivan P. Pavlov, a Russian physiologist and Nobel laureate, made important contributions to the research and theory of classical conditioning. His influence is still very strong in Russian psychology. (Culver Pictures, Inc.)

Classical Conditioning   Around the turn of the twentieth century, the Russian physiologist and Nobel laureate Ivan Pavlov (1849–1936) discovered **classical conditioning**, quite by accident. As part of his study of the digestive system, Pavlov gave a dog meat powder to make it salivate. Before long, Pavlov's laboratory assistants became aware that the dog began salivating when it saw the person who fed it. As the experiment continued, the dog began to salivate even earlier, when it heard the footsteps of its feeder. Pavlov was intrigued by these findings and decided to study the dog's reactions systematically. In the first of many experiments, a bell was rung behind the dog and then the meat powder was placed in its mouth. After this procedure had been repeated a number of times, the dog began salivating as soon as it heard the bell and before it received the meat powder.

In this experiment, because the meat powder automatically elicits salivation with no prior learning, the powder is termed an **unconditioned stimulus (UCS)** and the response of salivation an **unconditioned response**

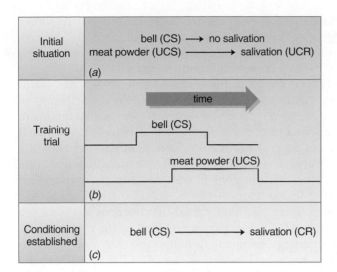

Figure 1.3 The process of classical conditioning. (*a*) Before learning, the meat powder (UCS) elicits salivation (UCR), but the bell (CS) does not. (*b*) A training or learning trial consists of presentations of the CS, followed closely by the UCS. (*c*) Classical conditioning has been accomplished when the previously neutral bell elicits salivation (CR).

(**UCR**). When the offering of meat powder is preceded several times by a neutral stimulus, the ringing of a bell, the sound of the bell alone (the **conditioned stimulus, or CS**) is able to elicit the salivary response (the **conditioned response, or CR**) (see Figure 1.3). The CR may differ somewhat from the UCR (e.g., Rescorla, 1988), but such differences need not concern us here. As the number of paired presentations of the bell and the meat powder increases, the number of salivations elicited by the bell alone increases. What happens to an established CR if the CS is no longer followed by the UCS—for example, if repeated soundings of the bell are not followed by meat powder? The answer is that fewer and fewer CRs (salivations) are elicited, and the CR gradually disappears. This is termed **extinction**.

Classical conditioning can even instill pathological fear. A famous but ethically questionable experiment conducted by John Watson and Rosalie Rayner (1920) involved introducing a white rat to an 11-month-old boy, Little Albert. The boy showed no fear of the animal and appeared to want to play with it. But whenever the boy reached for the rat, the experimenter made a loud noise (the UCS) by striking a steel bar behind Albert's head. This caused Little Albert great fright (the UCR). After five such experiences, Albert became very frightened (the CR) by the sight of the white rat, even when the steel bar was not struck. The fear initially associated with the loud noise had come to be elicited by the previously neutral stimulus, the white rat (now the CS). This study suggests a possible relationship between classical conditioning and the development of certain emotional disorders, in this instance a phobia. It is important to note that this type of study could never be done today because it breaches ethical standards.

Operant Conditioning   In the 1890s, Edward Thorndike (1874–1949) began work that led to the discovery of another principal type of learning. Rather than investigate the association between stimuli, as Pavlov did, Thorndike studied the effects of consequences on behavior. He had observed that caged alley cats, in their efforts to escape, would accidentally hit the latch that freed them. Recaged again and again, they would soon come to touch the latch immediately and purposefully. Thorndike formulated what was to become an extremely important principle, the **law of effect**: behavior that is followed by consequences satisfying to the organism will be repeated, and behavior that is followed by noxious or unpleasant consequences will be discouraged.

Important changes in these ideas were made by B. F. Skinner (1904–1990). Skinner introduced the concept of **operant conditioning**, so called because it applies to behavior that operates on the environment. He reformulated the law of effect by shifting the

B. F. Skinner originated the study of operant conditioning and the extension of this approach to education, psychotherapy, and society as a whole. (Kathy Bendo.)

focus from the linking of stimuli and responses to the relationships between responses and their consequences or contingencies. The distinction is subtle, but it reflects Skinner's contention that stimuli do not so much get connected to responses as they become the occasions for responses to occur, if in the past they have been reinforced.

Renaming Thorndike's "law of effect" the "principle of reinforcement," Skinner distinguished two types of reinforcement. **Positive reinforcement** refers to the strengthening of a tendency to respond by virtue of the presentation of a pleasant event, called a positive reinforcer. For example, a water-deprived pigeon will tend to repeat behaviors (operants) that are followed by the availability of water. **Negative reinforcement** also strengthens a response, but it does so via the removal of an aversive event, such as the cessation of electric shock. Extrapolating his extensive work with pigeons to complex human behavior (his book *Walden Two* is one of the better-known utopian novels, describing an ideal society governed by his principles of reinforcement), Skinner argued that freedom of choice is a myth and that all behavior is determined by the reinforcers provided by the environment.

In a prototypical operant-conditioning experiment, a hungry rat might be placed in a box, known as a Skinner box, that has a lever located at one end. The rat will explore its new environment and by chance come close to the lever. The experimenter may then drop a food pellet into the receptacle located near the lever. After a few such rewards the animal will come to spend more and more time in the area around the lever. But now the experimenter may drop a pellet into the receptacle only when the rat happens to touch the lever. After capitalizing on a few chance touches, the rat begins to touch the lever frequently. With lever touching well established, the experimenter can make the criterion for reward more stringent—the animal must now actually press the lever. Thus the desired operant behavior, lever pressing, is gradually achieved by **shaping**, that is, by rewarding a series of responses, called successive approximations, that more and more closely resemble the desired response. The number of lever presses increases as soon as they become the criterion for the release of pellets and decreases, or extinguishes, when the pellet is no longer dropped into the receptacle after a lever press.

As an example of how operant conditioning can contribute to the development of psychopathology, let us consider a key feature of conduct disorder (see Chapter 14), a high frequency of aggressive behavior. Aggression is often rewarded, as when one child beats up another to secure the possession of a toy (getting the toy is the reinforcer). Parents may also unwittingly reinforce aggression by giving in when the child becomes angry or threatens violence to achieve some goal, such as staying up late to watch TV.

Skinner boxes are often used in studies of operant conditioning to demonstrate how behavior can be shaped by reinforcing it. (Index Stock.)

Aggressive responses in children are often rewarded, which makes them more likely to occur in the future. In this photo, the more aggressive child gets to keep the toy. (Ken Cavanagh/Photo Researchers.)

Modeling   Learning often goes on even in the absence of reinforcers. We all learn by watching and imitating others, a process called **modeling**. In the 1960s, experimental work demonstrated that witnessing someone perform certain activities can increase or decrease diverse kinds of behavior, such as sharing, aggression, and fear. For example, Bandura and Menlove (1968) used a modeling treatment to reduce fear of dogs in children. After witnessing a fearless model engage in various activities with a dog, initially fearful children showed a decided increase in their willingness to approach and handle a dog. Similarly, modeling may explain the acquisition of abnormal behavior. Children of parents with phobias or substance-abuse problems may acquire similar behavior patterns, in part through observation.

Behavior Therapy   **Behavior therapy** emerged in the 1950s. In its initial form, this therapy applied procedures based on classical and operant conditioning to alter clinical problems. Sometimes the term *behavior modification* is used as well, and therapists who employ operant conditioning as a means of treatment often prefer that term. Behavior therapy was an attempt to change abnormal behavior, thoughts, and feelings by applying in a clinical context the methods used and the discoveries made by experimental psychologists in their study of both normal and abnormal behavior.

One behavior therapy technique developed during this time is called **counterconditioning**, which refers to eliciting a new response to a particular stimulus—that is, a response (R_1) to a given stimulus (S) can be eliminated by eliciting a new response (R_2) to that stimulus (see Figure 1.4). For example, in an early and now famous demonstration, Mary Cover Jones successfully treated a young boy's fear of rabbits by feeding him in the presence of a rabbit. The animal was at first kept several feet away and then gradually moved closer on successive occasions. In this way the fear (R_1) produced by the rabbit (S) was replaced by the stronger positive feelings evoked by eating (R_2).

The counterconditioning principle is behind an important behavior therapy technique that is still used to treat phobias and anxiety today called **systematic desensitization**. This technique was developed by Joseph Wolpe in 1958, and it includes two components: (1) deep muscle relaxation; and (2) gradual exposure to a list of feared situations, starting with those that arouse minimal anxiety and progressing to those that are the most frightening. Wolpe hypothesized that counterconditioning underlies the efficacy of desensitization: a state or response antagonistic to anxiety is substituted for anxiety as the person is exposed gradually to stronger and stronger doses of what he or she fears. We will cover this technique in more detail in Chapter 2, as it remains an important part of current forms of behavior therapy.

Another type of counterconditioning, **aversive conditioning**, also played an important historical role in the development of behavior therapy. In aversive conditioning, a stimulus attractive to the patient is paired with an unpleasant event, such as a drug that produces nausea or a painful electric shock applied to the hand, in the hope of endowing it with negative properties. For example, a problem drinker who wishes to stop drinking might be asked to smell alcohol while he or she is being made nauseous by a drug. Aversive techniques have been employed to reduce smoking, drug use, and socially inappropriate attractions such as the sexual arousal that children produce in pedophiles.

Aversion therapy has been controversial for ethical reasons because it involves inflicting pain and discomfort on people. Currently, it is rarely used as the only treatment for a particular problem. For example, in treating a problem drinker, the aversion treatment may help to temporarily reduce the problem behavior while the client is taught new ways of coping with stress.

Modeling was also included in behavior therapy starting in the 1960s. For example, people reduced their fear of snakes by viewing both live and filmed encounters in which other people gradually approached and successfully handled snakes (Bandura, Blanchard, & Ritter, 1969). Fears of surgery and dental work have also been treated in a similar manner (Melamed & Siegel, 1975).

Figure 1.4 Schematic diagram of counterconditioning, whereby an original response (R_1) to a given stimulus (S) is eliminated by evoking a new response (R_2) to the same stimulus.

Quick Summary

Behaviorism began its ascendancy in the 1920s and continues to be an important part of various psychotherapies. John Watson built on the work of Ivan Pavlov in showing how some behaviors can be conditioned. B. F. Skinner, building on the work of Edward Thorndike, emphasized the contingencies associated with behavior, showing how positive and negative reinforcement could shape behavior. Research on modeling helped to explain how people can learn even when no obvious reinforcers are present. Early behavior therapy techniques included counterconditioning techniques such as systematic desensitization and aversion therapy as well as modeling.

Check Your Knowledge 1.4

True or false?
1. Positive reinforcement refers to increasing a desired behavior, while negative reinforcement refers to eliminating an undesirable behavior.
2. Among the different techniques in behavior therapy, aversion therapy has been criticized on ethical grounds.

3. A cat comes running at the sound of a treat jar rattling, and his human friend then gives him a treat. The conditioned stimulus in this example is the sound of the jar rattling.

The Mental Health Professions

As views of mental disorders and abnormal behavior have evolved, so, too, have the professions associated with the field. Professionals authorized to provide psychological services include clinical psychologists, counseling psychologists, psychiatrists, psychoanalysts, and social workers. In this section, we discuss these different types of clinicians, the different types of training they receive, and a few related issues.

Clinical psychologists (such as the authors of this textbook) must have a Ph.D. or Psy.D. degree, which entails 4 to 7 years of graduate study. Training for the Ph.D. in clinical psychology is similar to that in other psychological specialties, such as developmental or cognitive neuroscience. It requires a heavy emphasis on research, statistics, neuroscience, and the empirically based study of human and animal behavior. As in other fields of psychology, the Ph.D. is basically a research degree, and candidates are required to write a dissertation on a specialized topic. But candidates in clinical psychology learn skills in two additional areas, which distinguishes them from other Ph.D. candidates in psychology. First, they learn techniques of assessment and diagnosis of mental disorders; that is, they learn the skills necessary to determine whether a person's symptoms or problems indicate a particular disorder. Second, they learn how to practice **psychotherapy**, a primarily verbal means of helping troubled individuals change their thoughts, feelings, and behavior to reduce distress and to achieve greater life satisfaction. Students take courses in which they master specific techniques under close professional supervision; then, during an intensive internship, they gradually assume increasing responsibility for the care of patients.

Other graduate programs are more focused on clinical practice than are the traditional Ph.D. programs. One of these is counseling psychology. **Counseling psychologists** originally dealt mostly with vocational issues; their focus today may be quite similar to those in clinical psychology. There is also the relatively new degree of Psy.D. (doctor of psychology), for which the curriculum is similar to that required of Ph.D. students, but with less emphasis on research and more on clinical training. The thinking behind this approach is that clinical psychology has advanced to a level of knowledge and certainty that justifies—even requires—intensive training in specific techniques of assessment and therapeutic intervention rather than combining practice with research.

Psychiatrists hold an M.D. degree and have had postgraduate training, called a residency, in which they have received supervision in the practice of diagnosis and pharmacotherapy (administering psychoactive medications). By virtue of the medical degree, and in contrast with psychologists, psychiatrists can function as physicians—giving physical examinations, diagnosing medical problems, and the like. Most often, however, the only aspect of medical practice in which psychiatrists engage is prescribing **psychoactive medications**, chemical compounds that can influence how people feel and think. Psychiatrists may receive some training in psychotherapy as well, though this is not a strong focus of training.

There has recently been a lively and sometimes acrimonious debate about whether to allow clinical psychologists with suitable training to prescribe psychoactive medications. Such a move is opposed not only by psychiatrists, whose turf would be invaded, but also by many psychologists, who view it as an ill-advised dilution of the basic behavioral science focus of psychology. Also at issue is the question of whether a non-M.D. can learn enough about neurobiology and neurochemistry to monitor the effects of drugs and protect patients from adverse side effects and drug interactions. This debate will undoubtedly continue for some time before any resolution is reached.

A **psychoanalyst** receives specialized training at a psychoanalytic institute. The program usually involves several years of clinical training as well as the in-depth psychoanalysis of the trainee. Until recently, most U.S. psychoanalytic institutes required of their graduates an M.D. and a psychiatric residency. Nowadays, one need not even have a doctoral degree in psychology to gain admission. It can take up to 10 years of graduate work to become a psychoanalyst.

Social workers have an M.S.W. (master of social work) degree. Training programs are shorter than Ph.D. programs, typically requiring 2 years of study. The focus of training is on psychotherapy. Those in social work graduate programs do not receive training in psychological assessment.

A highly diverse group of people can be called **psychopathologists**. These people conduct research into the nature and development of the various disorders that their therapist colleagues try to diagnose and treat. Psychopathologists may come from any number of disciplines; some are clinical psychologists, but the educational backgrounds of others range from neuroscience to developmental psychology. What unites them is their commitment to the study of how mental disorders develop. Since we still have much to learn about psychopathology, the diversity of backgrounds and interests is an advantage, for it seems clear that major advances will be made in many areas.

Summary

- The study of psychopathology is a search for the reasons why people behave, think, and feel in abnormal—unexpected, sometimes odd, and possibly self-defeating—ways. Unfortunately, people who exhibit abnormal behavior or have a mental illness are often stigmatized. Reducing the stigma associated with mental illness remains a great challenge for the field.

- In evaluating whether a behavior is abnormal, psychologists consider several different characteristics, including personal distress, disability, violation of social norms, and dysfunction. Each characteristic tells us something about what can be considered abnormal, but none by itself provides a fully satisfactory definition. The DSM-IV-TR definition includes all of these characteristics.

- Since the beginning of scientific inquiry into abnormal behavior, supernatural, biological, and psychological points of view have vied for attention. More supernatural viewpoints included early demonology, which posited that mentally ill people are possessed by demons or evil spirits, leading to treatments such as exorcism. Early biological viewpoints originated in the writings of Hippocrates. After the fall of Greco-Roman civilization, the biological perspective became less prominent in western Europe, and demonological thinking gained ascendancy, as evidenced by the persecution of so-called witches. Beginning in the fifteenth century, mentally ill people were often confined in asylums, such as Bethlehem; treatment in asylums was generally poor or nonexistent, until various humanitarian reforms were instituted. Early systems of classifying mental disorders led to a reemergence of the biological perspective in the eighteenth and nineteenth centuries. In the twentieth century, genetics and mental illness became an important area of inquiry, though the findings from genetic studies were used to the detriment of the mentally ill during the eugenics movement.

- Psychological viewpoints emerged in the nineteenth century from the work of Charcot and the seminal writings of Breuer and Freud. Freud's theory emphasized stages of psychosexual development and the importance of unconscious processes, such as repression and defense mechanisms, that are traceable to early-childhood conflicts. Therapeutic interventions based on psychoanalytic theory make use of techniques such as free association and the analysis of transference in attempting to overcome repressions so that patients can confront and understand their conflicts and find healthier ways of dealing with them. Later theorists such as Jung and Adler made various modifications in Freud's basic ideas and emphasized different factors in their perspectives on therapy.

- Behaviorism suggested that behavior develops through classical conditioning, operant conditioning, or modeling. B. F. Skinner introduced the ideas of positive and negative reinforcement and showed that operant conditioning can shape behavior. Behavior therapists try to apply these ideas to change undesired behavior, thoughts, and feelings.

- There are a number of different mental health professions, including clinical psychologist, counseling psychologist, psychiatrist, psychoanalyst, social worker, and psychopathologist. Each involves different training programs of different lengths and with different emphasis on research, psychological assessment, psychotherapy, and psychopharmacology.

Answers to Check Your Knowledge Questions

1.1 1. a; 2. d; 3. b
1.2 1. F; 2.F; 3. T; 4. T

1.3 1. Charcot, Mesmer, 2. Breuer, Freud; 3. id, ego; 4. transference; 5. Jung, Freud, Adler
1.4 1. F; 2. T; 3. T

Key Terms

abnormal behavior
anal stage
analytical psychology
asylums
aversive conditioning
behavior genetics
behaviorism
behavior therapy
cathartic method
classical conditioning
clinical psychologist
collective unconscious
conditioned response (CR)
conditioned stimulus (CS)
counseling psychologist
counterconditioning

defense mechanism
demonology
ego
electra complex
electroconvulsive therapy (ECT)
exorcism
extinction
fixation
free association
general paresis
genital stage
harmful dysfunction
id
individual psychology
interpretation
latency period

law of effect
libido
modeling
moral treatment
negative reinforcement
oedipus complex
operant conditioning
oral stage
phallic stage
pleasure principle
positive reinforcement
psyche
psychiatrist
psychoactive medications
psychoanalysis
psychoanalyst

psychoanalytic theory
psychopathologist
psychopathology
psychotherapy
reality principle
represssion
shaping
social worker
stigma
superego
systematic desensitization
transference
unconditioned response (UCR)
unconditioned stimulus (UCS)
unconscious

2 Current Paradigms in Psychopathology

Learning Goals

1. Be able to describe the essentials of the genetic, neuroscience, psychoanalytic, cognitive behavioral, and diathesis–stress paradigms.
2. Be able to describe the concept of emotion and how it may be relevant to psychopathology.
3. Be able to explain how culture, ethnicity, and social factors figure into the study and treatment of psychopathology.
4. Be able to recognize the limits of adopting any one paradigm and the importance of integration across multiple levels of analysis.

As we noted in Chapter 1, we face an enormous challenge to remain objective when trying to understand and study abnormal behavior and mental illness scientifically. Science is a human enterprise that is bound by scientists' human limitations; it is also bound by the current state of scientific knowledge. We cannot ask questions or investigate phenomena that go beyond what human beings can understand, and it is very difficult even to go beyond what we currently understand. Our view is that every effort should be made to study abnormal behavior according to scientific principles. But science is not a completely objective and certain enterprise. Rather, as suggested by philosopher of science Thomas Kuhn (1962), subjective factors as well as our human limitations enter into the conduct of scientific inquiry.

Central to scientific activity, in Kuhn's view, is the notion of a **paradigm**, a conceptual framework or approach within which the scientist works—that is, a set of basic assumptions, a general perspective, that defines how to conceptualize and study a subject, how to gather and interpret relevant data, even how to think about a particular subject.[1] A paradigm has profound implications for how scientists operate at any given time. Paradigms specify what problems scientists will investigate and how they will go about the investigation. In perceptual terms a paradigm may be likened to a general perspective or approach, a tendency to focus on certain factors and not on others.

In this chapter we consider current paradigms of psychopathology and treatment. We present four paradigms that guide the study and treatment of psychopathology: genetic, neuroscience, psychodynamic, and cognitive behavioral. We also consider the important role of emotion and sociocultural factors in psychopathology. These factors cut across all of the paradigms and are significant in terms of the description, causes, and treatments of all the disorders we will discuss in this book.

---

[1] William O'Donohue (1993) has criticized Kuhn's use of the concept of paradigm, noting that he was inconsistent in its definition. The complexities of this argument are beyond the scope of this book. Suffice it to say that we find it useful to organize our thinking about abnormal behavior around the paradigm concept. We use the term to refer to the general perspectives that constrain the way scientists collect and interpret information in their efforts to understand the world.

Current thinking about psychopathology is multifaceted. The work of clinicians and researchers is informed by an awareness of the strengths and limitations of a number of paradigms. For this reason, current views of psychopathology and its treatment typically integrate several paradigms. At the end of this chapter we describe another paradigm—diathesis–stress—which provides the basis for an integrative approach.

For researchers and clinicians, the choice of a paradigm has some very important consequences for the way in which they define, investigate, and treat abnormal behavior. Our discussion of paradigms will lay the groundwork for the examination of the major categories of disorders and of intervention that makes up the rest of the book. It is important to note at the outset that no one paradigm offers the "complete" conceptualization of psychopathology. Rather, for most disorders, each paradigm offers some important information with respect to etiology and treatment, but only part of the picture.

The Genetic Paradigm

> *. . . the more we lift the lid on the genome, the more vulnerable to experience genes appear to be (Ridley, 2003, p. 4).*

In 2003, we celebrated the fiftieth anniversary of the discovery of human DNA's double helix structure. That has been coupled with the virtual explosion of information regarding human genetics in just the past 5 or 6 years. The **genetic paradigm** has guided a number of discoveries regarding genes and human behavior since the early part of the twentieth century. However, the changes that have occurred recently have transformed the way we think about genes and behavior. We no longer have to wonder, "Is it nature or nurture that is responsible for human behavior?" We now know (a) almost all behavior is heritable to some degree (i.e., involves genes); and (b) despite this, genes do not operate in isolation from the environment. Instead, throughout the life span, the environment shapes how our genes are expressed, and our genes also shape our environments (Plomin et al., 2003; Rutter & Silberg, 2002; Turkheimer, 2000).

The more contemporary way to think about genes and the environment is cast as "nature via nurture" (Ridley, 2003). In other words, researchers are learning how environmental influences, such as stress, relationships, and culture (the nurture part), influence which of our genes are turned on or off and how our genes (the nature part) influence our bodies and brain. These new discoveries make clear that nature and nurture work together, not in opposition to one another, and that we cannot conclude that nature is responsible for this behavior and nurture for that behavior. Instead, we know that without the genes, a behavior might not be possible. But without the environment, genes could not express themselves and thus contribute to the behavior. Genes are remarkably flexible at responding to different types of environments. In turn, human beings are quite good at adapting to different environments.

In the year 2001, two different groups of researchers announced that the human genome consisted of around 30,000 genes. At first, this news was surprising, since researchers had been thinking the human genome consisted of closer to 100,000 genes. After all, the mere fruit fly has around 14,000 genes—researchers had thought that surely human beings were several times more complex than that! As it turns out, however, one of the exciting things about this discovery was the revelation from dozens of other genetic labs that the number of genes was not all that important. Instead, it is the sequencing or ordering of these genes as well as the expression of these genes that make us unique. Genes are essentially responsible for making proteins that in turn make the body and brain work. Some of these proteins switch or turn on and off other genes, a process called **gene expression**. Learning about the flexibility of genes and how they switch on or off has closed the door on beliefs about the inevitability of the effects of genes, good or bad. As we will illustrate throughout this book, the data do not often support the supposition that if you have the gene for *x*, you will necessarily get *x*. With respect to most mental illnesses, there will likely not be just one gene that contributes vulnerability. Instead, psychopathology will be **polygenic**, meaning several genes, perhaps operating at different times during the course of development, will be the essence of genetic vulnerability.

An important term that will be used throughout the book is **heritability**. Heritability refers to the extent to which variability in a particular behavior (or disorder) in a population can be accounted for by genetic factors. This term can be easily misused or misunderstood. There are two important points about heritability to keep in mind.

1. It is a *population* statistic, ranging from 0.0 to 1.0. The higher the number, the greater the heritability. It is only relevant for a large population of people, not a particular individual. Thus, it is incorrect to talk about any one person's heritability for a particular behavior or disorder. Knowing that the heritability of attention-deficit/hyperactivity disorder (ADHD) is around .70 does not mean that 70 percent of Jane's ADHD is because of her genes and 30 percent is due to other factors. It means that in a population (e.g., a large sample in a study), the variation in ADHD is understood as being attributed to 70 percent genes and 30 percent environment.

2. It is a measure of what *varies* in a population, not what determines a behavior in a population.

Other terms that are important in genetic research involve environmental factors. **Shared environment** factors include those things that members of a family have in common, such as family income level, child-rearing practices, and parents' marital status and quality. **Nonshared environment** factors are those things believed to be distinct among members of family, such as relationships with friends or specific events unique to a person (e.g., being in a car accident or on the swim team), and these are believed to be important in understanding why two siblings from the same family can be so different. Research suggests that the *effect* nonshared environmental events have on siblings is what matters most for understanding genetic variability among siblings, not the specific types of events (Turkheimer & Waldron, 2000). Consider an example. Jason is a 34-year-old man who is dependent on alcohol and struggling to keep his job. His sister Joan is a 32-year-old executive in a computer company in San Jose and has no alcohol or drug problems. Jason did not have many friends as a child; Joan was one of the most popular girls in high school. Peer relationships may have differentially affected Jason and Joan and thus differently impacted gene expression and other environment selection between these two siblings, contributing to their different adult outcomes.

We now turn to review two broad approaches in the genetic paradigm, including behavior genetics and molecular genetics. We then discuss the exciting evidence on the ways in which genes and environments interact. This sets the stage for our discussion of an integrative paradigm later in this chapter.

Behavior Genetics

When the ovum, the female reproductive cell, is joined by the male's spermatozoon, a zygote, or fertilized egg, is produced. It has 46 chromosomes, the number characteristic of a human being. Each chromosome is made up of thousands of **genes**, the carriers of the genetic information (DNA) passed from parents to child.

Behavior genetics is the study of individual differences in behavior that are attributable in part to differences in genetic makeup. To be clear, behavior genetics is not the study of how genes determine behavior. Instead, it is the study of how genes vary. The total genetic makeup of an individual, consisting of inherited genes, is referred to as the **genotype** (physical sequence of DNA), which is an individual's unobservable genetic constitution. In contrast, the totality of observable, behavioral characteristics, such as level of anxiety, is referred to as the **phenotype**. The genotype should not be viewed as a static entity. Genes controlling various features of development switch off and on at specific times, for example,

Behavior genetics studies the degree to which characteristics, such as physical resemblance or psychopathology, are shared by family members because of shared genes. (Tony Freeman/ PhotoEdit.)

to control various aspects of development. Indeed, genetic programs are quite flexible—they respond in remarkable ways to things that happen to us.

The phenotype changes over time and is generally viewed as the product of an interaction between the genotype and the environment. For example, an individual may be born with the capacity for high intellectual achievement, but whether he or she develops this genetically given potential depends on such environmental factors as upbringing and education. Hence any measure of intelligence is best viewed as an index of the phenotype. A recent study by Turkheimer and colleagues confirmed this proposition (Turkheimer et al., 2003). A number of studies have demonstrated high heritability for IQ (e.g., Plomin, 1999). What Turkheimer et al. found, though, was that heritability depended on environment. The study included 319 twin pairs of 7-year-olds (114 identical, 205 fraternal). Many of the children were living in families either below the poverty line or with a low family income. Among the families of lower socioeconomic status (SES), 60 percent of the variability in children's IQ was attributable to the environment. Among the higher SES families, the opposite was found. That is, variability in IQ was more attributable to genes than environment. Thus, being in an impoverished environment may have deleterious effects on IQ whereas being in a more affluent environment may not help out all that much. It is important to point out that these interesting findings deal with IQ scores, a measure of what psychologists consider to be intelligence, and not achievement (we discuss this more in Chapters 3 and 14).

It is critical to recognize that various mental disorders are disorders of the phenotype, not of the genotype. Thus it is not correct to speak of the direct inheritance of schizophrenia or anxiety disorders; at most, only the genotypes for these disorders can be inherited. Whether these genotypes will eventually engender the phenotypic behavior disorder will depend on environment and experience; a predisposition, also known as a **diathesis**, may be inherited, but not the disorder itself. A genetic diathesis is a tendency that can be expressed or not, depending on environmental circumstances.

Molecular Genetics

Molecular genetics studies seek to find out what exactly is heritable by identifying particular genes and their functions. Recall that a human being has 46 chromosomes and that each chromosome is made up of thousands of genes. Different forms of the same gene are called **alleles**. The alleles of a gene are found at the same location or locus of a chromosome pair. A genetic **polymorphism** refers to a difference in DNA sequence that has occurred in a population.

What genes do is a complicated process still under investigation. We know that genes consist of DNA that is transcribed to RNA. In some cases, the RNA is then translated into amino acids, which then form proteins, and proteins make cells (see Figure 2.1).

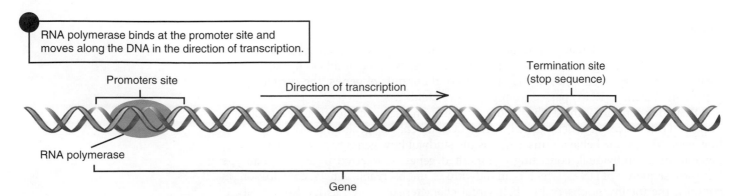

Figure 2.1 This figure shows the process by which DNA is transcribed to RNA. In some cases, the RNA is then translated into amino acids, which then form proteins, and proteins make cells.

The expression of genes also involves particular types of DNA called *promoters*. These promoters are recognized by particular proteins called *transcription factors*. Promoters and transcription factors are the focus of much new research in molecular genetics and psychopathology. All of this is a remarkably complex system, and variations along the way, such as different combinations or sequences of events, lead to different outcomes.

Researchers studying animals can actually manipulate specific genes and then observe the effects on behavior. This is a major area of molecular genetic work. Linking the findings from these animal studies to humans remains a challenge for the field, however. Specific genes can be taken out of mice DNA—these studies are often called "knockout studies." For example, the gene that is responsible for a specific receptor for the neurotransmitter serotonin called 5-HT_{1A} has been knocked out in mice before their birth. As adults, they show what could be described as an anxious phenotype. Interestingly, one study that employed a novel technique to only temporarily knockout this gene found that the restoration of it early in development prevented the development of anxious behavior in the adult mice (e.g., Gross et al., 2002).

One method of molecular genetics that is used with humans is called **linkage analysis**. The method typically studies families in which a disorder is heavily concentrated and collects diagnostic information and blood samples from affected individuals and their relatives. The blood samples are used to study the inheritance pattern of characteristics whose genetics are fully understood, referred to as **genetic markers**. If the occurrence of a form of psychopathology among relatives goes along with the occurrence of another characteristic whose genetics are known (the genetic marker), it is concluded that the gene predisposing to the psychopathology is on the same chromosome and in a similar location on that chromosome (i.e., it is linked) as the gene controlling the other characteristic. We will see several examples of linkage analysis in subsequent chapters, especially when we discuss mood disorders (Chapter 8) and schizophrenia (Chapter 11), though "breakthrough" findings have often failed to be replicated. The greatest success of the method thus far has been in identifying specific genes on several chromosomes that are extremely important in Alzheimer's disease (see Chapter 15). Linkage analysis will be most successful with disorders for which a single gene is involved, like Huntington's disease (Plomin & McGuffin, 2003). As we noted above, the disorders we cover in this book undoubtedly involve many, many genes.

Another method of molecular genetics that is used with humans is called association studies. In these studies, researchers compute the correlation between some allele and some trait or behavior in the population. For example, as we will discuss in Chapter 15, a particular allele called APOE-4 is more often found among adults with later onset Alzheimer's disease than those without it. Not all people with Alzheimer's have this, and not all people who have APOE-4 develop Alzheimer's. Still, there is a strong association between this allele and Alzheimer's disease (Williams, 2003).

Gene–Environment Interactions

As we noted above, we know now that genes and environments work together. Life experience shapes how our genes are expressed, and our genes guide us in behaviors that lead to the selection of different experiences. A **gene–environment interaction** means that a given person's sensitivity or reaction to an environmental event is influenced by genes.

Adoption studies can be a method for studying gene–environment interaction. For example, one study found that adoptees who had a biological parent with antisocial personality disorder (APD) and were raised in an unhealthy adoptive family (e.g., parental conflict, abuse, alcohol/drugs in the adoptive family) were more likely to develop APD than two other groups of adoptees: (1) adoptees who had a biological parent with APD but were raised in a healthy family; and (2) adoptees who had no biological parent with APD but were raised in an unhealthy adoptive family (Cadoret et al., 1995b). Thus, genes (APD in a biological parent) and environment (unhealthy adoptive family) worked together to increase the risk for developing antisocial personality disorder.

More recent research has concentrated on the ways in which specific genes interact with the environment to influence behavior and psychopathology. Take a simple (and made-up) example. If a person has gene XYZ, he or she might respond to a snakebite by developing a fear of snakes. A person without the XYZ gene would not develop a fear of snakes after being bitten by a snake. This simple relationship involves both genes (the XYZ gene) and an environmental event (snakebite).

A different (and true) example of a gene–environment interaction involves depression. In one longitudinal study, a large sample of children in New Zealand was followed across time from the age of five until their mid-twenties (Caspi et al., 2003). Across this time, the researchers assessed a number of variables, including early childhood maltreatment (abuse) and depression as an adult. They also measured a particular gene called the **serotonin transporter gene** (5-HTT). This gene has a polymorphism such that some people have two short alleles, some have two long alleles, and some have one short and one long allele. They found that those individuals who had either the short-short allele or the short-long allele combinations of the 5-HTT gene *and* were maltreated as children were more likely to have depression as adults than either those people who had the same gene combination but no childhood maltreatment or those people who were maltreated as children but had the long-long allele combination of the gene (see Figure 2.2). Thus, having the gene was not enough to predict depression, nor was the presence of early life stress. Rather, it was the specific combination of the gene configuration and environmental events that predicted depression. They found the same gene–environment interaction for having at least one short allele of the gene and reports of stressful life events. That is, those people who reported a good deal of stressful life events and had at least one short allele of the 5-HTT gene were at greater risk of developing depression.

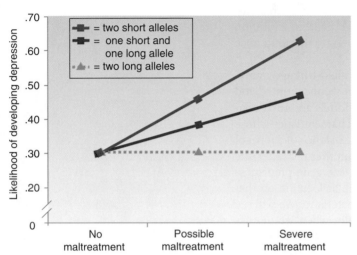

Figure 2.2   A gene–environment interaction is illustrated here. Having both the short allele of the 5-HTT gene and childhood maltreatment were associated with the greatest probability of developing depression as an adult. Adapted from Caspi et al. (2003).

Other exciting developments in this area have been done with animals. In these studies, different environments are manipulated and then changes in behavior and gene expression are measured. The study of how the environment can alter gene expression or function is called *epigenetics*.

In a series of fascinating studies with rats, Darlene Francis has shown that parenting behaviors can be passed on to offspring in a nongenetic way. Good parenting among rats consists of a lot of licking and grooming (LG) and what is called arched-back nursing (ABN). Mothers differ in the extent to which they do these LG-ABN behaviors, but mothers who do it more tend to have pups that grow up to be less reactive to stress. Francis and colleagues (1999) found that pups who were born to mothers who were low in this LG-ABN behavior but were raised by mothers high in LG-ABN (called a cross-fostering adoptee method, discussed in more detail in Chapter 4) grew up to be low in stress reactivity and as mothers themselves exhibited the high LG-ABN style. And, when they had their own pups, these "grandpups" were also low in stress reactivity and became high LG-ABN mothers. Thus, this parenting style was transmitted across two generations after an adoption. Does this suggest that genes are not important? The adoptive parent's behavior was what was transmitted across generations, not the biological parent's behavior, which would suggest that this is an environmental effect.

Baby rats who are raised by a mother who does a lot of licking are more likely to do this when they grow up to be mothers, even if they were raised by an adoptive mother. (Courtesy Darlene Francis.)

However, a later study showed that this transmission of good mothering was due in part to the fact that it triggered an increase in the expression of a certain gene among the adopted offspring (Weaver et al., 2004). In this study, pups of high LG-ABN mothers showed increased expression of a certain gene (glucocorticoid receptor) that pups of low LG-ABN mothers did not. (The reason for this increase in gene expression had to do with differences between the high and low LG-ABN pups in the regulation of DNA promoter regions.) Using cross-fostering again, pups with a low LG-ABN biological mother who were raised by a high LG-ABN mother had increases in gene expression in the same way that the pups with a biological high LG-ABN mother did. And finally, they found a drug that could be administered to the adult rats that had the same effect on gene expression. That is, adult rats that were raised by a low LG-ABN mother but were given the drug as adults were then able to express the glucocorticoid receptor gene to the same level that rats of high LG-ABN mothers did. The environment (mothering) was responsible for turning on (or turning up) the expression of a particular gene. Once it was on, the mothering style seemed to continue across generations.

These kinds of studies have also been done with other animals. For example, Steve Suomi has studied rhesus monkeys and has shown that babies born to highly stress reactive mothers but who are raised by calmer mothers grow up to be calmer themselves. This seems to operate by turning on a particular serotonin gene (Suomi, 1999, 2000).

We will continue to see these types of studies in animals and humans. Understanding how environments influence the expression of genes will be important for the study of psychopathology.

Reciprocal Gene–Environment Interactions

Another important way in which genes are important in psychopathology is in how they may promote certain types of environments. This is called a **reciprocal gene–environment interaction** (Plomin et al., 2003; Rutter & Silberg, 2002). The basic idea is that genes may predispose us to seek out certain environments that then increase our risk for developing a particular disorder. For example, studies suggest that a genetic risk for alcohol dependence may predispose persons to life events that put them in high risk situations for alcohol abuse, such as being in trouble with the law (Kendler & Karkowski-Shuman, 1997). Another study found that genetic vulnerability to depression may promote certain life events, such as breaking up with a boyfriend or difficulties with parents, that can trigger depression among adolescent girls (Silberg et al., 1999).

Evaluating the Genetic Paradigm

Our discussion of each paradigm will conclude with an evaluation section. For the most part these sections will focus on etiology—the factors that contribute to the development of a disorder—rather than on treatment. Treatments will be evaluated in the chapters dealing with specific disorders as well as in Chapter 16.

Genetics is an important part of the study of psychopathology, and there are many ways in which genes might be involved in psychopathology. However, genes do not typically operate without influence from the environment. The models that will help us understand how genes are implicated in psychopathology are the ones that take the contemporary view that genes do their work *via* the environment. Perhaps the biggest challenge facing scientists working within the genetic paradigm is to specify exactly how genes and environments reciprocally influence one another. This is more easily done in tightly controlled laboratory studies with animals. Making the leap to understanding how genes interact with complex human environments throughout the course of development is of course a greater challenge. Nevertheless, this is an exciting time for genetics research, and important discoveries about genes, environments, and psychopathology are being made at a rapid rate.

Quick Summary

The genetic paradigm focuses on questions such as whether certain disorders are heritable and if so, what is actually inherited. Heritability is a population statistic, not a metric of the likelihood a particular person will inherit a disorder. Environmental effects can be classified as shared and nonshared. Molecular genetics studies involve linkage analysis and association studies.

Research has emphasized the importance of gene–environment interactions. Genes do their work via the environment in most cases. Re-

cent examples of genetic influence being manifested only under certain environmental conditions (e.g., poverty and IQ; early maltreatment and depression) make clear that we must not just look for the genes associated with mental illness, but also for the conditions under which these genes may be expressed.

Check Your Knowledge 2.1

1. The process by which genes are turned on or off is referred to as:
   a. Heritability.
   b. Gene expression.
   c. Polygenic.
   d. Gene switching.
2. Sam and Sally are twins raised by their biological parents. Sam excelled in music and was in the high school band; Sally was the star basketball player on the team. They both received top notch grades, and they both had part-time jobs at the bagel store. An example of a shared environment variable would be _____; whereas an example of a nonshared environment variable would be _____.
   a. school activities; their parent's relationship.
   b. band for Sam; basketball for Sally.
   c. their parent's relationship; work.
   d. their parent's relationship; school activities.
3. _____ refers to different forms of the same gene; _____ refers to different genes contributing to a disorder.

   a. allele; polygenic.
   b. polygenic; allele.
   c. allele; polymorphism.
   d. polymorphism; allele.
4. In the Caspi et al. (2003) gene–environment interaction study of depression, those who were at highest risk for developing depression were
   a. those who were maltreated as children and had a biological parent with depression.
   b. those who were maltreated as children and had at least one long allele of the 5-HTT gene.
   c. those who were maltreated as children and had at least one short allele of the 5-HTT gene.
   d. those who were not maltreated as children but had at least one short allele of the 5-HTT gene.

The Neuroscience Paradigm

The **neuroscience paradigm** holds that mental disorders are linked to aberrant processes in the brain. Considerable literature, both research and theory based, deals with the brain and psychopathology. For example, some depressions are associated with neurotransmitter problems within the brain; anxiety disorders may be related to a defect within the autonomic nervous system that causes a person to be too easily aroused; dementia can be traced to impairments in structures of the brain. Those working with the neuroscience paradigm assume that answers to puzzles of psychopathology will be found within the brain. In this section, we look at four components of this paradigm in which the data are particularly interesting: neurons and neurotransmitters, brain structure and function, the autonomic nervous system, and the neuroendocrine system. We then consider some of the key treatments that follow from the paradigm.

Neurons and Neurotransmitters

The nervous system is comprised of billions of neurons. Although neurons differ in some respects, each **neuron** has four major parts: (1) the cell body; (2) several dendrites, the short and thick extensions; (3) one or more axons of varying lengths, but usually only one long and thin axon that extends a considerable distance from the cell body; and (4) terminal buttons on the many end branches of the axon (Figure 2.3). When a neuron is appropriately stimulated at its cell body or through its dendrites, a **nerve impulse**, which is a change in the electric potential of the cell, travels down the axon to the terminal endings. Between the terminal endings of the sending axon and the cell membrane of the receiving neuron there is a small gap, the **synapse** (Figure 2.4).

For a nerve impulse to pass from one neuron to another and for communication to occur, the impulse must have a way of bridging the synaptic gap. The terminal buttons of each axon contain synaptic vesicles, small structures that are filled with **neurotransmitters**, chemical substances that allow a nerve impulse to cross the synapse. As the neurotransmitter flows into the synapse, some of the molecules reach the receiving, or postsynaptic, neuron. The cell membrane of the postsynaptic cell contains proteins, called receptor sites, which are configured so that specific neurotransmitters can fit into them. When a neurotransmitter fits into a receptor site, a message can be sent to the postsynaptic cell. What actually happens to the postsynaptic neuron depends on integrating thousands of similar messages. Sometimes these messages are excitatory, leading to the creation of a nerve impulse in the postsynaptic cell; at other times the messages are inhibitory, making the postsynaptic cell less likely to fire.

Once a presynaptic neuron (the sending neuron) has released its neurotransmitter, the last step is for the synapse to be returned to its normal state. Not all of the released neurotransmitter has found its way to postsynaptic receptors. Some of what remains in the synapse is broken down by enzymes, and some is taken back into the presynaptic cell through a process called **reuptake**.

Several key neurotransmitters have been implicated in psychopathology, including **dopamine**, **norepinephrine**, and **serotonin**. Norepinephrine is a neurotransmitter that communicates with the sympathetic nervous system, where it is involved in producing states of high arousal and thus may be involved in the anxiety disorders and other stress-related conditions. Both serotonin and dopamine may be involved in depression and schizophrenia. Another important brain transmitter is **gamma-aminobutyric acid (GABA)**, which inhibits nerve impulses throughout most areas of the brain and may be involved in the anxiety disorders.

Early theories linking neurotransmitters to psychopathology sometimes proposed that a given disorder was caused by either too much or too little of a particular transmitter (e.g., mania is associated with too much norepinephrine, anxiety disorders too little GABA). Later research has uncovered the details behind these ideas. Neurotransmitters are synthesized in the neuron through a series of metabolic steps, beginning with an amino acid. Each reaction along the way to producing an actual neurotransmitter is catalyzed by an enzyme. Too much or too little of a particular neurotransmitter could result from an error in these metabolic pathways. Similar disturbances in the amounts of specific transmitters could result from alterations in the usual processes by which transmitters are deactivated after being released into the synapse. For example, a failure to pump leftover neurotransmitter back into the presynaptic cell (reuptake) would leave excess transmitter in the synapse. Then, if a new nerve impulse causes more neurotransmitter to be released into the synapse, the postsynaptic neuron would, in a sense, get a double dose of neurotransmitter, making it more likely for a new nerve impulse to be created.

More recent research has focused to a large extent on the possibility that the neurotransmitter receptors are at fault in some psychopathologies. If the receptors on the postsynaptic neuron were too numerous or too easily excited, the result would be akin to having too much transmitter released. There would simply be more sites available with which the

Figure 2.3 The neuron, the basic unit of the nervous system.

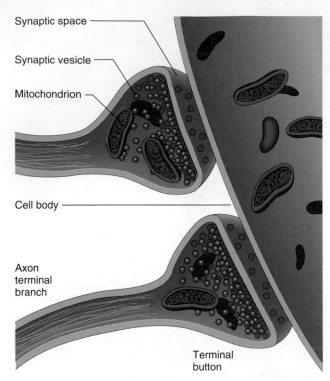

Synaptic space

Synaptic vesicle

Mitochondrion

Cell body

Axon
terminal
branch

Terminal
button

Figure 2.4 A synapse, showing the terminal buttons of two axon branches in close contact with a very small portion of the cell body of another neuron.

neurotransmitter could interact, increasing the chances that the postsynaptic neuron would be stimulated. The delusions and hallucinations of schizophrenia, for example, may result from an overabundance of dopamine receptors.

Many mechanisms control the sensitivity of postsynaptic neurons. For example, if a receptor has been activated extensively over time, the cell may retune the sensitivity of the receptors so that it becomes more difficult to fire. When a cell has been firing more frequently, this receptor releases **second messengers** (see Figure 2.5). Once second messengers are released, they play a role in adjusting the sensitivity of postsynaptic receptors to dopamine, norepinephrine, or serotonin (Duman, Heninger, & Nestler, 1997; Shelton, 2000; Shelton, Mainer, & Sulser, 1996). One can think of second messengers as helping a neuron adjust receptor sensitivity when it has been overly active. Current research on depression suggests that antidepressant medications may be effective in part due to their ability to impact second messengers (see p. 256 in Chapter 8).

One method that investigators use to study how neurotransmitters are working in the brain is to have people take a drug that stimulates a particular neurotransmitter's receptors. This kind of drug is referred to as an **agonist**. A serotonin agonist, for example, is a drug that stimulates serotonin receptors to produce the same effects as serotonin does naturally. By contrast, an **antagonist** is a drug that works on a neurotransmitter's receptors to dampen the activity of that neurotransmitter. For example, many drugs used to treat schizophrenia are dopamine antagonists that work by blocking dopamine receptors (see p. 363 in Chapter 11).

Structure and Function of the Human Brain

The brain is located within the protective coating of the skull and is enveloped with three layers of nonneural tissue, membranes referred to as meninges. Viewed from the top, the brain is divided by a midline fissure into two mirror-image cerebral hemispheres; together they constitute most of the cerebrum. The major connection between the two hemispheres is a band of nerve fibers called the **corpus callosum**. Figure 2.6 shows the surface of one of the cerebral hemispheres. The upper, side, and some of the lower surfaces of the hemispheres form the cerebral cortex. The cortex consists of six layers of tightly packed neuron cell bodies with many short, unsheathed interconnecting processes. These neurons, estimated to number 10 to 15 billion, make up a thin outer covering, the so-called **gray matter** of the brain. A measure of gray matter is in essence a measure of the number of brain cells. The cortex is vastly convoluted; the ridges are called gyri, and the depressions between them sulci, or fissures. If unfolded, the cortex would be about the size of a formal dinner napkin. These sulci are used to define different regions of the brain, much like guide points on a map. Deep fissures divide the cerebral hemispheres into several distinct areas called lobes. The **frontal lobe** lies in front of the central sulcus; the **parietal lobe** is behind it and above the lateral sulcus; the **temporal lobe** is located below the lateral sulcus; and the **occipital lobe** lies behind the parietal and temporal lobes (see Figure 2.6). Different functions tend to be associated with particular areas of the lobes: vision with the occipital; discrimination of sounds with the temporal; reasoning, problem solving, working memory, and other executive processes plus the regulation of fine voluntary movement with the frontal; initiation of movements of the skeletal musculature in a band in front of the central sulcus; receipt of sensations of touch, pressure, pain, temperature, and body position from skin, muscles, tendons, and joints in a band behind the central sulcus.

The two hemispheres of the brain also have different functions. The left hemisphere, which generally controls the right half of the body by a crossing over of motor and sensory fibers, is responsible for speech and, according to some neuropsychologists, for analytical thinking in right-handed people and in a fair number of left-handed people as well. The right hemisphere controls the left side of the body and discerns spatial relations and patterns. But language and analytical thinking cannot be located exclusively in the left hemisphere or spatial relations in the right. Moreover, the two hemispheres communicate with each other constantly via the corpus callosum. Localization of these different mental functions is not as clear-cut as it once was thought to be.

If the brain is sliced in half, separating the two cerebral hemispheres (see Figure 2.7), additional important features can be seen. The gray matter of the cerebral cortex does not extend throughout the interior of the brain. Much of the interior is **white matter**, made up of large tracts or bundles of myelinated (sheathed) fibers that connect cell bodies in the cortex with those in the spinal cord and in other centers lower in the brain. In certain areas, called *nuclei*, sets of nerves converge. The nuclei serve both as way stations, connecting tracts from the cortex with other ascending and descending tracts, and as integrating motor and sensory control centers. Some cells from the cortex project fibers all the way down to motor neurons in the spinal cord, but others project only an inch or less, down to these nuclei. One important area, collectively referred to as the *basal ganglia*, is located deep within each hemisphere. This area helps regulate starting and stopping both motor and cognitive activity. Also deep within the brain are cavities called **ventricles**. These ventricles are filled with cerebrospinal fluid. Cerebrospinal fluid circulates through the brain through these ventricles, which are connected with the spinal cord.

The **thalamus** is a relay station for all sensory pathways except the olfactory. The nuclei making up the thalamus receive nearly all impulses arriving from the different sensory areas of the body before passing them on to the cortex, where they are interpreted as conscious sensations. The **brain stem** comprises the *pons* and the *medulla oblongata* and functions primarily as a neural relay station. The pons contains tracts that connect the cerebellum with the spinal cord and with motor areas of the cerebrum. The medulla oblongata serves as the main line of traffic for tracts ascending from the spinal cord and descending from the higher centers of the brain. The **cerebellum** consists primarily of two deeply convoluted hemispheres with an exterior cortex of gray matter and an interior of white tracts. The cerebellum receives sensory nerves from the vestibular apparatus of the ear and from muscles, tendons, and joints. The information received and integrated relates to balance and posture and equilibrium and to the smooth coordination of the body when in motion.

In addition, a set of deeper, mostly subcortical structures are often implicated in different forms of psychopathology. There is a long history of referring to different groupings of these structures as the *limbic system*, a term that most contemporary neuroscientists consider outdated. These structures, shown in Figure 2.8, are continuous with one another in the lower cerebrum and developed earlier than the mammalian cerebral cortex. These structures control the visceral and physical expressions of emotion—quickened heartbeat and respiration, trembling, sweating, and alterations in facial expressions— and the expression of appetitive and other primary drives,

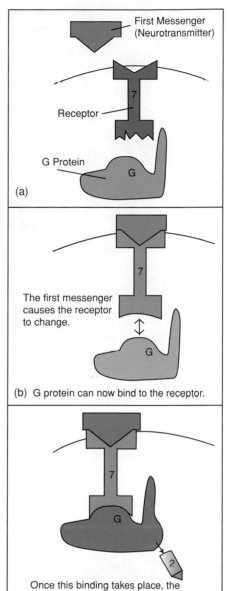

Figure 2.5   The process by which a second messenger is released.

(a) First Messenger (Neurotransmitter) / Receptor / G Protein

(b) The first messenger causes the receptor to change. G protein can now bind to the receptor.

(c) Once this binding takes place, the second messenger will be released.

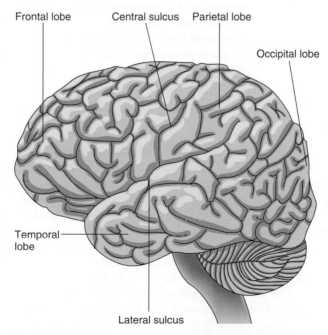

Frontal lobe   Central sulcus   Parietal lobe

Occipital lobe

Temporal lobe

Lateral sulcus

Figure 2.6   Surface of the left cerebral hemisphere, indicating the lobes and the two principal fissures of the cortex.

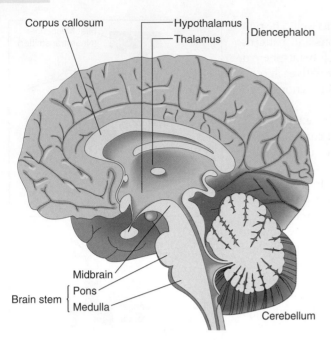

Figure 2.7   Slice of brain through the medial plane, showing the internal structures.

Anterior cingulate

Septal area

Hypothalamus

Amygdala

Hippocampus

Figure 2.8   Subcortical structures of the brain.

namely, hunger, thirst, mating, defense, attack, and flight. Important structures are the anterior portion of the cingulate gyrus stretching about the corpus callosum, called the **anterior cingulate**; the **septal area**, which is anterior to the thalamus; the long, tubelike **hippocampus**, which stretches from the septal area into the temporal lobe; the **hypothalamus**, which regulates metabolism, temperature, perspiration, blood pressure, sleeping, and appetite; and the **amygdala**, which is embedded in the tip of the temporal lobe. The amygdala is also an important area for attention to emotionally salient stimuli and memory for emotionally relevant memories. This is one of the key brain structures for psychopathology researchers given the ubiquity of emotion problems in the psychological disorders. For example, people with depression show more activity in the amygdala when watching pictures of emotional faces than do people without depression (Sheline et al., 2001).

The development of the human brain is a complex process that begins early in the first trimester and continues into early adulthood. It has been estimated that about a third of our genes are expressed in the brain, and many of these genes are responsible for laying out the structure of the brain. The development of the cells and migration of these cells to the appropriate layers of cortex are an intricate dance. Unfortunately, missteps can happen and current thinking about a number of disorders, such as schizophrenia, places the beginnings of the problem in these early developmental stages. Brain development continues throughout childhood, adolescence, and even into adulthood. What is happening during this time is cell development and a honing of the connections between cells and brain areas. The gray matter of the brain continues to develop, filling with cells, until early adolescence. Then, somewhat surprisingly, a number of synaptic connections begin to be eliminated—a process called **pruning**. Throughout early adulthood, the connections in the brain may become fewer, but they also become faster. The areas that develop the quickest are areas linked to sensory processes, like the cerebellum and occipital lobe. The area that develops last is the frontal cortex.

We will discuss a number of these brain areas throughout the book. For example, patients with schizophrenia have been found to have enlarged ventricles of the brain (Chapter 11); the size of the hippocampus is reduced among some patients with posttraumatic stress disorder, perhaps due to overactivity of their stress response systems (Chapter 5); brain size among some children with autism expands at a much greater rate than it should in typical development (Chapter 14).

The Autonomic Nervous System

Because the autonomic nervous system is especially important in the study of emotional behavior and thus psychopathology, it will be useful to review its principal characteristics. The mammalian nervous system can be divided into two relatively separate functional parts: the **somatic** (or voluntary) **nervous system** and the **autonomic** (or involuntary) **nervous system (ANS)**.

Skeletal muscles, such as those that move our limbs, are innervated, or stimulated, by the voluntary nervous system. Much of our behavior, however, is dependent on a nervous system that operates very quickly, generally without our awareness, and that has traditionally been viewed as beyond voluntary control; hence the term *autonomic*.

The autonomic nervous system innervates the endocrine glands, the heart, and the smooth muscles that are found in the walls of the blood vessels, stomach, intestines, kidneys, and other organs. This nervous system is itself divided into two parts, the **sympathetic nervous system** and the **parasympathetic nervous system** (Figure 2.9), which work sometimes in opposition to each other, sometimes in unison. The sympathetic portion of the ANS, when energized, accelerates the heartbeat, dilates the pupils, inhibits intestinal

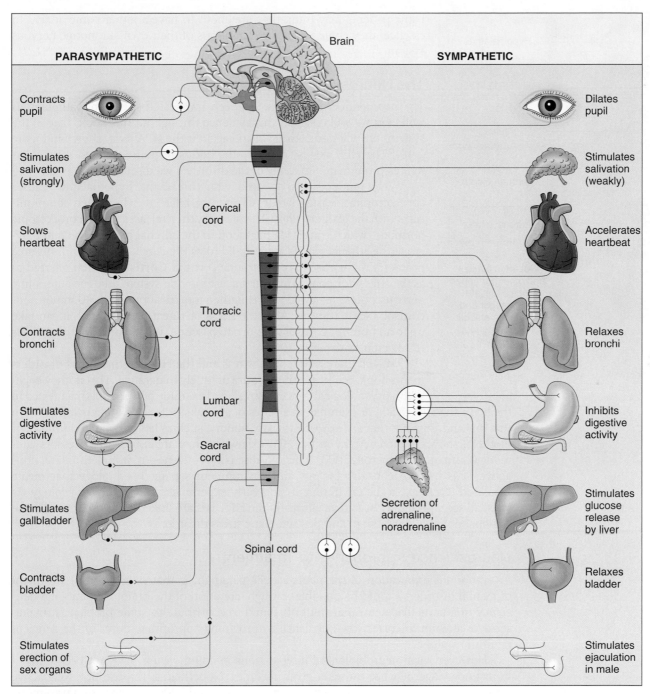

Brain

PARASYMPATHETIC   **SYMPATHETIC**

Contracts pupil   Dilates pupil

Stimulates salivation (strongly)   Stimulates salivation (weakly)

Cervical cord

Slows heartbeat   Accelerates heartbeat

Thoracic cord

Contracts bronchi   Relaxes bronchi

Stimulates digestive activity   Inhibits digestive activity

Lumbar cord

Stimulates gallbladder   Secretion of adrenaline, noradrenaline

Sacral cord   Stimulates glucose release by liver

Spinal cord

Contracts bladder   Relaxes bladder

Stimulates erection of sex organs   Stimulates ejaculation in male

Figure 2.9   The autonomic nervous system.

activity, increases electrodermal activity, and initiates other smooth-muscle and glandular responses that prepare the organism for sudden activity and stress. Some physiologists view the sympathetic nervous system as primarily excitatory and view the other division, the parasympathetic, as responsible for maintenance functions and more quiescent behavior, such as deceleration of the heartbeat, constriction of the pupils, and acceleration of intestinal contractions. Division of activities is not quite so clear-cut, however, for it is the parasympathetic system that increases blood flow to the genitals during sexual excitement.

The autonomic nervous system figures prominently in many of the anxiety disorders, such as panic disorder and posttraumatic stress disorder. For example, people with panic disorder tend to misinterpret normal changes in their nervous system, such as shortness of breath after running up a flight of stairs. Instead of attributing this to being out of shape,

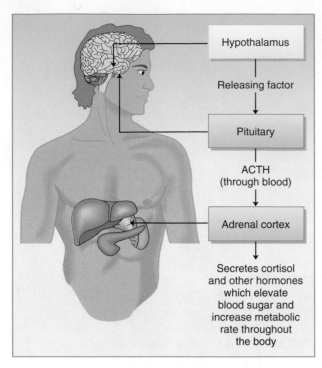

Figure 2.10 The HPA axis.

panic patients may think they are about to have another panic attack. In essence, they come to fear the sensations of their own autonomic nervous system.

The Neuroendocrine System

The neuroendocrine system has been implicated in psychopathology as well, and we will consider this evidence throughout this book. One of the systems we will return to again and again is the **HPA axis** (shown in Figure 2.10). The HPA axis is central to the body's response to stress, and stress figures prominently in many of the disorders we discuss in this book.

When under stress or faced with threat, the hypothalamus causes corticotropin-releasing factor (CRF) to be released, which then communicates with the *pituitary gland*. The pituitary then releases adrenocorticotropic hormone, which travels via the blood to the adrenal glands. The outer layers of the adrenal glands are referred to as the *adrenal cortex*, and this area promotes the release of the hormone cortisol. **Cortisol** is often referred to as the stress hormone. This is not a fast moving system, like the autonomic nervous system reviewed above. Rather, it takes about 20 to 40 minutes for cortisol release to peak. After the stress or threat has remitted, it can take up to an hour for cortisol to return to baseline (i.e., before the stress) levels (Dickerson & Kemeny, 2004).

We will discuss the role of stress and the HPA axis in several disorders in this book. Studies in this area are uniquely integrative. That is, they begin with a psychological concept, stress, and examine how stress is manifested in the body, the HPA axis. For example, in a series of animal studies, researchers have shown that rats and primates that are exposed to early trauma, such as being separated from their mothers, show elevated activity in the HPA axis when they are exposed to stressors later in life (Gutman & Nemeroff, 2003). Like our discussion of gene–environment interactions above, it is hard to consider biology and environment separately—biology may create increased reactivity to the environment, and early experiences may influence biology. As we shall see, chronic stress and its effects on the HPA axis are linked to disorders as diverse as schizophrenia, depression, and posttraumatic stress disorder.

Neuroscience Approaches to Treatment

An important implication of the neuroscience paradigm is that prevention or treatment of mental disorders should be possible through alteration of the brain. Certainly if a deficiency in a particular neurotransmitter is found to contribute to some problem, it makes sense to attempt to correct the imbalance by providing appropriate doses of the deficient neurotransmitter.

However, most neurobiological interventions in common use have not been derived from knowledge of what causes a given disorder. Nonetheless, the use of psychoactive drugs has been increasing. For example, between 1988 and 2000 antidepressant use among adults nearly tripled (National Center for Health Statistics, 2004). Benzodiazepines, such as Xanax, can be effective in reducing the tension associated with some anxiety disorders, perhaps by stimulating GABA neurons to inhibit other neural systems that create the physical symptoms of anxiety. Antidepressants, such as Prozac, increase neural transmission in neurons that use serotonin as a neurotransmitter by inhibiting the reuptake of serotonin. Antipsychotic drugs, such as Olanzapine, used in the treatment of schizophrenia, reduce the activity of neurons that use dopamine as a neurotransmitter by blocking their receptors and also impact serotonin. Stimulants are often employed in treating children with attention-deficit/hyperactivity disorder; they increase the levels of several neurotransmitters that help children pay attention.

It should be noted that a person could hold a neuroscience view about the nature of a disorder yet recommend psychological intervention. Recall from Chapter 1 that Hippocrates proposed nonbiological treatments—rest for melancholia, for example—to deal with mental disorders that he considered somatic in origin. Contemporary scientists and clinicians also appreciate that nonbiological interventions can have beneficial and reciprocal effects. For example, preventing a person from performing a compulsive ritual, which is an effective and widely used behavioral treatment for obsessive-compulsive disorder, has measurable effects on brain activity (Baxter et al., 2000).

Evaluating the Neuroscience Paradigm

Over the past three decades neuroscientists have made great progress in elucidating brain–behavior relationships. Neuroscience research on both causes and treatment of psychopathology is proceeding at a rapid rate, as we will see when we discuss specific disorders in later chapters. Although we view these developments in a positive light, we also want to caution against reductionism, a position taken by some neuroscientists.

Reductionism refers to the view that whatever is being studied can and should be reduced to its most basic elements or constituents. In the case of mental disorders the position proposes reducing complex mental and emotional responses to biology. Using this logic, the argument could be taken even further to propose that biology be reduced to atomic physics. In its extreme form, reductionism asserts that psychology and psychopathology will ultimately be nothing more than biology.

Although reductionism is an influential viewpoint among some biological psychiatrists, in philosophical circles it has been severely criticized. Once basic elements, such as individual nerve cells, are organized into more complex structures or systems, such as neural pathways or circuits, the properties of these systems cannot be deduced from the properties of the constituents. The whole is greater than the sum of its parts. A good example is provided by the geological theory of plate tectonics. The earth's outer shell is made up of about a dozen large plates and several smaller ones. Movement of the plates at their boundaries is what causes most earthquakes. Although the earth's plates are made up of rock and the rock of atoms, tectonic movement cannot be accounted for at all by our knowledge of atoms. A different example is that of computers. Students writing papers for their courses use word processing programs like Word or WordPerfect. These software programs consist of many levels of code that communicate with the computer or hardware. The word processing program necessarily involves low-level communication with the computer, involving a series of 0's and 1's and even electronics. Yet we don't conceptualize the program in terms of binary digits or electrical impulses. If the spell-checker stopped working, our first place to begin repairs would not be with the computer chips. Instead, we would want the programmer to fix the bug in the program. To be sure, the program would not run without the computer, but the program is more than just the impulses sent by the chips. In the same way, although a complex behavior like a hallucination necessarily involves the brain and nerve impulses, it is not likely that we can capture this by knowing specific nerve impulses.

Certain phenomena emerge only at certain levels of analysis and will be missed by investigators who focus only at the molecular level. In the field of psychopathology, problems such as delusional beliefs, dysfunctional attitudes, and catastrophizing cognitions may well be impossible to explain neurobiologically, even with a detailed understanding of the behavior of individual neurons (Turkheimer, 1998).

Quick Summary

The neuroscience paradigm is concerned with the ways in which the brain contributes to psychopathology. Neurotransmitters such as serotonin, norepinephrine, dopamine, and GABA have been implicated in a number of disorders. A number of different brain areas are also a focus of research. The autonomic nervous system, which includes the sympathetic and parasympathetic nervous systems, is also implicated in the manifestations of some disorders. The sympathetic nervous system prepares us for sudden activity and stress. The parasympathetic helps us to calm down, though these distinctions are not always so clear-cut. The HPA axis is responsible for the body's response to stress and thus is relevant for several stress-related disorders. Biological treatments, primarily medications, are effective treatments for different disorders, but these treatments are not necessarily treating the cause of the problems. Although the brain plays an important role in our understanding of the causes of psychopathology, we must be careful to avoid reductionism.

Check Your Knowledge 2.2

Fill in the blanks.

1. The so-called limbic system of the brain includes the following brain areas: _____, _____, _____, _____, and _____.
2. The _____ matter of the brain consists of the tracts of myelinated fibers that connect cells; the _____ matter of the brain refers to the brain's cells or neurons.
3. Heart rate deceleration is linked with the _____ nervous system, while heart rate acceleration is linked with the_____ nervous system.
4. The HPA axis consists of the _____, _____, and_____.

The Psychoanalytic Paradigm

The central assumption of the psychoanalytic theory that Sigmund Freud developed (see Chapter 1) was that psychopathology resulted from unconscious conflicts in the individual. More specifically, Freud believed that the various forms of psychopathology resulted from the presence of strong drives or id instincts, which set the stage for the development of unconscious conflicts linked to a particular psychosexual stage. For example, he proposed that obsessive-compulsive disorder was traced to the anal stage, with the urge to soil or to be aggressive transformed by reaction formation into compulsive cleanliness.

In his early writings and lectures, Freud postulated that his patients' maladies were caused by environmental events (e.g., abuse). However, he later came to believe that many of his patients' accounts were fantasies (Masson, 1984). This change had a profound impact on the development of psychoanalysis, for it directed the search for the causes of psychopathology away from the environment and toward the patient and his or her fantasies. Furthermore, the emphasis on fantasy was crucial to Freud's conception of the Oedipal conflict, a cornerstone of psychoanalytic thought. So important was this emphasis on fantasy that in a letter to Jeffrey Masson, a well-known critic of psychoanalysis, Anna Freud wrote that without it there would have been no psychoanalysis.

Psychoanalysis and its later variants are the essence of the **psychoanalytic paradigm**. Although psychoanalysis and other psychodynamic therapies are based on a theory about the causes of abnormal behavior, very little research has been conducted to support the theory. Part of the reason for this is that the theory does not lend itself easily to empirical scrutiny. However, psychoanalysis was also based largely on observations of a select group of patients. Even later followers of Freud were not as concerned with empirically verifying the theory as they were with treating patients. Thus, the major contribution of this paradigm is in treatment, not in understanding the causes of psychopathology.

Although traditional psychoanalysis is still practiced today, it is more rare than other forms of psychotherapy, and psychodynamic therapies are more common than traditional psychoanalysis. (See Focus on Discovery 2.1 for a discussion of what psychotherapy is.) As we reviewed in Chapter 1, a number of Freud's followers altered psychoanalysis and developed variants on this treatment. In the next sections we review these more contemporary changes to psychoanalysis.

Ego Analysis

After Freud's death a group of practitioners generally referred to as ego analysts introduced some important modifications to psychoanalytic theory. The major figures in this loosely formed movement include Karen Horney (1942), Anna Freud (1946), Erik Erikson (1950), David Rapaport (1951), and Heinz Hartmann (1958).

Although Freud did not ignore the interactions of the person with the environment, his view was essentially a push model, in which people's behavior is largely driven by

Focus on Discovery 2.1

What Is Psychotherapy?

Shorn of its theoretical complexities, any **psychotherapy** is a social interaction in which a trained professional tries to help another person, the client or patient, behave and feel differently. The therapist follows procedures that are to a greater or lesser extent prescribed by a certain theory or school of thought. The basic assumption is that particular kinds of verbal and nonverbal exchanges in a trusting relationship can achieve goals such as reducing anxiety and eliminating self-defeating or dangerous behavior.

Basic as this definition may seem, there is little general agreement about what really constitutes psychotherapy. A person's next-door neighbor might utter the same words of comfort as a clinical psychologist, but should we regard this as psychotherapy? In what way is psychotherapy different from such nonprofessional reassurance? Is the distinction made on the straightforward basis of whether the dispenser of reassurance has a particular academic degree or license? Does it relate to whether the giver of information has a theory that dictates or at least guides what he or she says? Does it depend on how sound the basic assumptions of the theory are? These are difficult questions, and as in other areas of abnormal psychology, there is less than complete agreement among professionals.

It is important to note that the people who seek or are sent for professional help have probably tried nonprofessional avenues to feeling better and have failed to obtain relief. Before most individuals go to a therapist, they have confided in friends or in a spouse, perhaps spoken to the family doctor, consulted with a member of the clergy, or maybe tried several of the vast number of self-help books and programs that are so popular. For most people in psychological distress, one or more of these options provide enough relief, and they seek no further help. But for others such attempts fall short, and these individuals are left feeling helpless, often hopeless. These are the people who go to mental health clinics, university counseling centers, and the private offices of independent practitioners.

Insight therapies, such as psychoanalysis, assume that behavior, emotions, and thoughts become disordered because people do not adequately understand what motivates them, especially when their needs and drives conflict. The point of insight therapies is to help people discover the true reasons they behave, feel, and think as they do. The premise is that greater awareness of motivations will yield greater control over and subsequent improvement in thought, emotion, and behavior. In the behavioral therapies the focus is on changing behavior; insight is often a peripheral benefit. The cognitive therapies place greater emphasis on certain kinds of insights.

Theories and psychotherapies are great in number. There are scores, perhaps hundreds, each with its enthusiastic supporters. We will review the data on how effective these different types of therapies are with particular types of disorders throughout this book, and we will examine the methods for evaluating *how* psychotherapy works in Chapter 16.

intrapsychic urges. Those who subscribe to **ego analysis** place greater emphasis on a person's ability to control the environment and to select the time and the means for satisfying basic drives. Their fundamental contention is that the individual is as much ego as id. In addition, they focus more on the individual's current living conditions than did Freud, although they sometimes advocate delving deeply into the historical causes of an individual's behavior. Generally, they employ most of the psychoanalytic techniques described in Chapter 1, but with far less emphasis on transference.

An important assumption for the ego analysts is that there is a set of ego functions that are primarily conscious, are capable of controlling both id urges and the external environment, and, significantly, do not depend on the id for energy. Ego analysts assume that these ego functions and capabilities are present at birth and then develop through experience. They contend that ego functions were underemphasized by Freud and that they have energies and gratifications of their own, usually separate from the gratification of id impulses. Also, whereas Freud viewed the relationship of the individual to society as a struggle to overcome social inhibitions and achieve unfettered gratification of id urges, the ego analysts hold that an individual's social interactions can provide their own special kind of gratification.

Brief Psychodynamic Therapy

Although many laypeople assume that patients usually spend many months, even years, in psychodynamic psychotherapy, most courses of therapy last fewer than 10 sessions (Garfield, 1978). Among the many reasons for the short duration of therapy is that people today are less likely to consider the ambitious examination of the past as the best way to deal with today's realities—the essence of classical psychoanalytic therapy. Indeed, most patients expect therapy to be fairly short term and targeted to specific problems in their everyday lives. These expectations contributed to the design of briefer forms of dynamic therapy.

No doubt, insurance companies have also played a role both in shortening the duration of treatment and in encouraging analytically oriented workers to adapt their ideas to brief therapy. Insurance companies have become increasingly reluctant to cover more than a limited number of psychotherapy sessions—say, 25, in a given calendar year—and have set limits as well on reimbursement amounts.

All these factors, combined with the growing acceptability of psychotherapy in the population at large, have set the stage for **brief therapy**. Time-limited psychodynamic therapies share several common elements (Koss & Shiang, 1994):

- Assessment tends to be rapid and early.
- The therapist takes a more active role than a traditional psychoanalyst.
- It is made clear right away that therapy will be limited and that improvement is expected within a small number of sessions, from 6 to 25.
- Goals are concrete and focused on the amelioration of the patient's worst symptoms, on helping the patient understand what is going on in his or her life, and on enabling the patient to cope better in the future.
- Interpretations are directed more toward present life circumstances and patient behavior than on the historical significance of feelings.
- Development of transference is not encouraged, but some positive transference to the therapist is fostered to encourage the patient to follow the therapist's suggestions and advice.
- There is a general understanding that psychotherapy does not cure, but that it can help troubled individuals learn to deal better with life's inevitable stressors.

Evaluating the Psychoanalytic Paradigm

Many of the criticisms leveled at the psychoanalytic paradigm are criticisms of Freud's original ideas and methods. For example, Freud conducted no formal research on the causes and treatments of mental illness; rather he believed that the information obtained from therapy sessions was enough to validate his theory and demonstrate the effectiveness of the therapy. This remains one of the main criticisms today: because they are based on anecdotal evidence gathered during therapy sessions, contemporary psychoanalytic theories are not grounded in objectivity and therefore are not scientific.

Furthermore, Freud's patients were not merely a small sample; they were largely affluent, educated, and Viennese. Many individuals who receive psychoanalysis today are also affluent since most insurance companies will not often reimburse for this kind of treatment. It is easy to believe that a theory of personality development or structure of the mind based on such a restricted group of individuals might not be generally applicable. On the other hand, much of contemporary psychological research is based on college students in the United States, and thus one could question the generalizability of these findings as well (Sue, 1999).

The case reports used by Freud and his followers can also be assailed on the grounds of the reliability of Freud's perceptions in those therapy sessions and his ability to recall them accurately, since he did not take careful notes. However, as we discuss in Chapter 4, case studies conducted today are a valuable research method that can set the stage for later systematic research.

Despite these criticisms, the psychoanalytic paradigm continues to have an impact on the field of psychopathology, albeit indirectly (Westen, 1998). This influence is most evident in the following three commonly held assumptions:

1. *Childhood experiences help shape adult personality.* Contemporary clinicians and researchers still view childhood experiences and other environmental events as crucial. They seldom focus on the psychosexual stages about which Freud wrote, but some emphasize problematic parent–child relationships in general and how they can influence later adult relationships in negative ways.

2. *There are unconscious influences on behavior.* In Focus on Discovery 6.2 (p. 168) we review research showing that people can be unaware of the causes of their behavior. However, most current researchers and clinicians do not think of an unconscious or view it as a repository of id instincts.

3. *The causes and purposes of human behavior are not always obvious.* Freud and his followers sensitized generations of clinicians and psychopathologists to the nonobviousness of the causes and purposes of human behavior. Contemporary psychoanalysis continues to caution us against taking everything at face value. A person expressing disdain for another, for example, may actually like the other person very much yet be fearful of admitting positive feelings. This tendency to look under the surface, to find hidden meanings in behavior, is perhaps the best known legacy of Freud.

The Cognitive Behavioral Paradigm

The **cognitive behavioral paradigm** traces its roots to behavior therapy (and the learning principles on which this treatment is based) and cognitive science. As we shall see, the principles from classical and operant conditioning and the therapies that derive from them are important in cognitive behavioral views.

Influences from Behavior Therapy

One of the key influences from behaviorism is the notion that problem behavior is likely to continue if it is reinforced. Generally, problem behavior is thought to be reinforced by four possible consequences: getting attention, escaping from tasks, generating sensory feedback (such as results from the hand flapping often seen in children with autistic disorder), and gaining access to desirable things or situations (Carr et al., 1994). Once the source of reinforcement has been identified, treatment is then tailored to alter the consequences of the problem behavior. For example, if it was established that the problem behavior was reinforced by getting attention, the treatment might be to ignore the behavior. Alternatively, the problem behavior could be followed by **time-out**—the person is sent for a period of time to a location where positive reinforcers are not available.

Another technique is making positive reinforcers contingent on behavior, which is used to increase the frequency of desirable behavior. For example, a socially withdrawn child could be reinforced for playing with others. Similarly, positive reinforcement has been used to help children with autistic disorder develop language, to remediate learning disabilities, and to help children with mental retardation develop necessary living skills. Other problems treated with these methods include bed-wetting, aggression, hyperactivity, tantrums, and social withdrawal (Kazdin, 1994).

The **token economy** is a procedure in which tokens (such as stickers) are given for desired behavior; the tokens can later be exchanged for desirable items and activities (Staats & Staats, 1963). This procedure is still used today, particularly with children. For example, each time a child completes her homework or remains seated during class, she receives a sticker; the stickers can then be traded in for items or activities, such as a new Game Boy cartridge, a DVD, computer time, or time outside.

We introduced the technique called systematic desensitization in Chapter 1. Recall that this involves two components: (1) deep muscle relaxation; and (2) gradual exposure to a list of feared situations, starting with those that arouse minimal anxiety and progressing to those that are the most frightening. The still-influential contribution from this behavioral approach is the **exposure** component of this treatment. The basic idea was that the anxiety will extinguish if the person can face the object or situation for long enough with no actual harm occurring. Sometimes, this exposure can be conducted "**in vivo**"—that is, in real-life situations. For example, if someone has a fear of flying, you might have him or her take an actual flight. At times, exposure cannot be conducted in real life, so *imaginal exposure* will be used to address fears, such as rape, trauma, or contamination. In other situations, both types of exposure are used.

Time-out is a behavioral therapy technique based on operant conditioning; the consequence for misbehavior is removal to an environment with no positive reinforcers. (Jeff Greenberg/PhotoEdit.)

To illustrate exposure and systematic desensitization, consider a person who suffers from a fear of spiders. The person is taught to relax deeply. Next, the person develops a list of situations with spiders that vary in how frightening or anxiety producing they are. Examples of hierarchy items for someone who has a specific phobia of spiders might include

- You hear the word spider.
- You look at an illustration of a spider in a children's book.
- You look at a photo of a spider.
- You look at a nature program on DVD about spiders.
- You look at a spider in a glass case at the zoo.
- You look at a live spider from several feet away.
- You look at a live spider up close.

Step-by-step, while relaxed, the person imagines the graded series of situations with spiders. The relaxation tends to inhibit any anxiety that might otherwise be elicited by the imagined scenes of spiders. The fearful person becomes able to tolerate increasingly more difficult imagined situations as he or she climbs the hierarchy over a number of therapy sessions.

Exposure continues to be a centrally important component of many forms of cognitive behavior therapy today. In the years since exposure treatments such as systematic desensitization were first developed, much has been learned about them. For instance, exposure to the real thing (in vivo exposure), when practical, is more effective than imagining situations. Also, even though relaxation training does help people experience less arousal when they first face the feared stimulus, there is no evidence that such training is required for good outcomes; as a result, it has been possible to develop briefer psychological treatments that do not include relaxation training.

As influential as these behavior therapy techniques were and still are, behaviorism and behavior therapy were often criticized for minimizing the importance of two important factors: thinking and feeling. In other words, the way we think and feel about things undoubtedly influences our behavior. Yet behaviorists did not often take this into account when conceptualizing or treating psychological problems. These limitations of behavioral points of views, plus the explosion of research in the 1960s and 1970s in cognitive science, led some behavioral researchers and clinicians to include cognitive variables in their analyses of psychopathology and therapy.

Cognitive Science

Cognition is a term that groups together the mental processes of perceiving, recognizing, conceiving, judging, and reasoning. Cognitive science focuses on how people (and animals as well) structure their experiences, how they make sense of them, and how they relate their current experiences to past ones that have been stored in memory.

At any given moment we are bombarded by far more stimuli than we can possibly respond to. How do we filter this overwhelming input, put it into words or images, form hypotheses, and arrive at a perception of what is out there?

Cognitive scientists consider the learning process much more complex than the passive formation of new stimulus–response associations. Even classical conditioning is viewed by cognitive psychologists as an active process by which organisms learn about relationships among events rather than as an automatic stamping in of associations between stimuli (Rescorla, 1988). Moreover, cognitive scientists regard the learner as an active interpreter of a situation, with the learner's past knowledge imposing a perceptual funnel on the experience. The learner fits new information into an organized network of already accumulated knowledge, often referred to as a **schema**, or cognitive set (Neisser, 1976). New information may fit the schema; if not, the learner reorganizes the schema to fit the information or construes the information in such a way as to fit the schema. The following situation illustrates how a schema may alter the way in which information is processed and remembered.

The man stood before the mirror and combed his hair. He checked his face carefully for any places he might have missed shaving and then put on the conservative tie he had decided to wear. At breakfast, he studied the newspaper carefully and, over coffee, discussed the possibility of buying a new washing machine with his wife. Then he made several phone calls. As he was leaving the house he thought about the fact that his children would probably want to go to that private camp again this summer. When the car didn't start, he got out, slammed the door and walked down to the bus stop in a very angry mood. Now he would be late. (Bransford & Johnson, 1973, p. 415)

Now read the excerpt again, but add the word "unemployed" before the word "man." Now read it a third time, substituting "stockbroker" for "man." Notice how differently you understand the passage. Ask yourself what parts of the newspaper these men read. If you were asked on a questionnaire to recall this information and you no longer had access to the excerpt, you might answer "the want ads" for the unemployed man and "the financial pages" for the stockbroker. Since the passage does not specify which part of the paper was read, these answers are wrong, but in each instance the error would have been a meaningful, predictable one.

Other important contributions from cognitive science include the study of attention. As we shall see, people with disorders as diverse as anxiety disorders, mood disorders, and schizophrenia have problems in attention. For example, individuals with anxiety disorders tend to focus their attention on threatening or anxiety-producing events or situations in the environment. People with schizophrenia have a hard time concentrating their attention for a period of time.

One of the ways in which researchers have studied attention is with the Stroop task. In this task, the participant sees a set of color words printed in different colors and must name the color of each word as rapidly as possible (see Figure 2.11). To do this, participants have to resist the natural impulse to say the printed word. For example, a participant might see the word blue written in the green ink. The participant is instructed to name the ink color (green) as fast as possible without making mistakes (saying the word blue). It is difficult to say green and "inhibit" the more natural tendency to say blue. Interference, measured as a lengthening of response time, occurs because the words are more "attention grabbing" than the ink color.

The Stroop task has been modified to focus on emotion rather than colors. In this emotion Stroop task, participants are still instructed to name the color of the ink rather than saying the word. However, the list of words are now emotion words instead of color words. So, for example, words such as threat, danger, happy, or anxious are written in different ink colors. In such an emotion Stroop task, individuals with anxiety disorders find that some of the emotion words are so attention grabbing, the impulse to say the word is especially strong. As in the original Stroop task, the more attention grabbing the word is, the more interference and the slower the response. Research has shown that people with anxiety disorders show more interference for threatening words (i.e., they say these words more slowly) than nonthreatening words, and this is used as evidence of an attention bias toward threatening information (see Chapter 5).

Of course, the concepts of schema and attention are related to one another. If a person has a particular set or schema about the world (e.g., the world is dangerous), that person may be more likely to pay attention to threatening or dangerous things in the environment. Furthermore, this person may be more likely to interpret ambiguous things in the environment as threatening. For example, seeing a stranger standing on a front porch may be interpreted as a sign of danger to someone with such a "danger" schema. For someone without such a schema, this person may be viewed simply as the person who lives in that house.

Cognitive explanations are now central in the search for the causes of psychopathology and for new methods of intervention. A widely held view of depression, for example, places the blame on a particular cognitive set, namely, the individual's overriding sense of hopelessness (see p. 248). Many people who are depressed believe that they have no important effect on their surroundings regardless of what they do. Their destiny seems to them to be out of their hands, and they expect their future to be negative. If depression does

Black	Pink
Red	White
Blue	Red
Green	**Black**
Yellow	Purple
Blue	Green
Red	Blue
White	Yellow

Figure 2.11 In the Stroop task, participants must name the color of the ink instead of reading the words.

develop from a sense of hopelessness, this fact could have implications for how clinicians treat the disorder. Cognitive theorizing will be included in discussions of most of the disorders presented in subsequent chapters.

Cognitive Behavior Therapy

Cognitive behavior therapy (CBT) incorporates theory and research on cognitive processes. Cognitive behavior therapists pay attention to private events—thoughts, perceptions, judgments, self-statements, and even tacit (unconscious) assumptions—and have studied and manipulated these processes in their attempts to understand and modify overt and covert disturbed behavior. **Cognitive restructuring** is a general term for changing a pattern of thought that is presumed to be causing a disturbed emotion or behavior. This restructuring is implemented in several ways by cognitive behavior therapists.

Beck's Cognitive Therapy Psychiatrist Aaron Beck, one of the leading cognitive behavior therapists, developed a cognitive therapy for depression based on the idea that depressed mood is caused by distortions in the way people perceive life experiences (Beck, 1976; Salkovskis, 1996). For example, a depressed person may focus exclusively on negative happenings and ignore positive ones. Imagine that a woman's romantic partner both praises and criticizes her. If the woman attends to the praise and remembers it the next day, she is likely to feel happy. But if she focuses on the criticism and continues to dwell on it the next day, she is likely to feel unhappy. Beck proposed that the attention, interpretation, and recall of negative and positive information were biased in depression. These effects on attention and memory are called "information-processing biases." Beck's therapy, which we examine in detail in Chapter 8, addresses these biases by trying to persuade patients to change their opinions of themselves and the way in which they interpret life events. When a depressed person expresses feelings that nothing ever goes right, for example, the therapist offers counterexamples, pointing out how the client has overlooked favorable happenings. The general goal of Beck's therapy is to provide patients with experiences, both inside and outside the consulting room, that will alter their negative schemas, enabling them to have hope rather than despair.

Aaron Beck developed a cognitive theory of depression and a cognitive therapy for the cognitive biases of people with depression. (Courtesy Dr. Aaron T. Beck.)

Ellis's Rational-Emotive Behavior Therapy Albert Ellis developed a different type of cognitive behavior therapy. His principal thesis is that sustained emotional reactions are caused by internal sentences that people repeat to themselves; these self-statements reflect sometimes unspoken assumptions—irrational beliefs—about what is necessary to lead a meaningful life. In Ellis's rational-emotive therapy (RET), now renamed **rational-emotive behavior therapy (REBT)** (Ellis, 1993a, 1995), the aim is to eliminate self-defeating beliefs. A person with depression, for example, may say several times a day, "What a worthless jerk I am." Ellis proposes that people interpret what is happening around them, that sometimes these interpretations can cause emotional turmoil, and that a therapist's attention should be focused on these beliefs rather than on historical causes or, indeed, on overt behavior.

Ellis used to list a number of irrational beliefs that people can harbor. More recently, Ellis (1991; Kendall et al., 1995) has shifted from a cataloguing of specific beliefs to the more general concept of "demandingness," that is, the musts or shoulds that people impose on themselves and on others. Thus, instead of wanting something to be a certain way, feeling disappointed, and then perhaps engaging in some behavior that might bring about the desired outcome, the person demands that it be so. It is this unrealistic, unproductive demand, Ellis hypothesizes, that creates the kind of emotional distress and behavioral dysfunction that bring people to therapists.

Albert Ellis, a cognitive behavior therapist and founder of rational-emotive behavior therapy, has focused on the role of irrational beliefs as causes of psychopathology. (Courtesy Michael A. Fenichel, Ph.D.)

Evaluating the Cognitive Behavioral Paradigm

The concepts on which the cognitive behavioral paradigm is based (e.g., schema, attention) are somewhat slippery and not always well-defined. Furthermore, cognitive explanations of psychopathology do not always explain much. That a person with depression has a negative schema tells us that the person thinks gloomy thoughts. But such a pattern of thinking is actually part of the diagnosis of depression. What is distinctive in the cognitive behavioral paradigm is that the thoughts are given causal status; that is, the thoughts are regarded as causing the other features of the disorder, such as sadness. Left unanswered is the question of where the negative schema came from in the first place. Cognitive behavioral explanations of psychopathology tend to focus more on current determinants of a disorder and less on its historical antecedents.

Is the cognitive behavioral paradigm basically different and separate from the behavioral or learning point of view? Much of what we have just said suggests that it is. But the growing field of cognitive behavior therapy gives us pause, for its workers study the complex interplay of beliefs, expectations, perceptions, and attitudes on the one hand and overt behavior on the other. For example, Albert Bandura (1977), a leading cognitive behavioral theorist, argued that different therapies produce improvement by increasing people's sense of *self-efficacy*, a belief that they can achieve desired goals. But, at the same time, he argues that changing behavior through behavioral techniques is the most powerful way to enhance self-efficacy. Therapists such as Ellis, in contrast, emphasize direct alteration of cognitions through argument, persuasion, Socratic dialogue, and the like to bring about improvements in emotion and behavior. Complicating matters still further, cognitive behavior therapists also place considerable importance on homework assignments that require clients to behave in ways in which they have been unable to behave because they have been hindered by negative thoughts. Therapists identified with cognitive behavior therapy work at both the cognitive and behavioral levels, and most of those who use cognitive concepts and try to change beliefs with verbal means also use behavioral procedures to alter behavior directly.

This issue is reflected in the terminology used to refer to people such as Beck and Ellis. Are they cognitive therapists or cognitive behavior therapists? For the most part we will use the latter term because it denotes both that the therapist regards cognitions as major determinants of emotion and behavior and that he or she maintains the focus on overt behavior that has always characterized behavior therapy. Nonetheless, it is important for the reader to know that Beck, even though he assigns many behavioral tasks as part of his therapy, is usually referred to as the founder of cognitive therapy (CT), and that Ellis's rational-emotive therapy (RET) used to be spoken of as something separate from behavior therapy. Table 2.1 compares the basic assumptions of the psychoanalytic and cognitive behavioral paradigms.

Table 2.1 Comparison of Psychoanalytic and Cognitive Behavioral Paradigms

Psychoanalytic	Cognitive Behavioral
We don't always say what we mean.	We usually say what we mean or at least we are able to quite readily.
We don't always know what we mean.	We usually know what we mean.
We can have strongly inconsistent feelings about things, desires, and fears.	We do have strongly inconsistent conflicting feelings, but such conflicts are not emphasized.
What lies on the surface is not (always) the most important aspect of ourselves; in fact, it seldom is.	What lies on the surface is usually the most important aspect of ourselves. Yet looking for controlling variables can take cognitive-behaviorists into the realm of causes.
Our earliest life experiences are pivotal, especially with our parents and parent figures.	Current factors in one's life are at least as important as past experiences.
We can come to fear our own desires and experience conflict about expressing them.	Fear of our own desires is emphasized less.
We often/always desire or fear what is nonnormative, unconventional, bizarre, taboo.	People's wishes and fears are much more prosaic. There is little presumption of taboo concerns.
"The truth shall set you free." Insight into one's actual motivations has, in itself, curative properties.	Insight can be helpful, but it is to be found more in current thoughts than the past. It facilitates control over our fears and desires.

Quick Summary

The psychoanalytic paradigm derives from the work of Freud and his followers. The contribution of the paradigm has been primarily in treatment. Although Freud's early work is often criticized, this paradigm has been influential in the study of psychopathology in that it has made clear the importance of early experiences, the notion that we can do things without conscious awareness, and the point that the causes of behavior are not always obvious.

The cognitive behavioral paradigm reflects influences from behavior therapy and cognitive science. Treatment techniques designed to alter the consequences or reinforcers of a behavior, such as in time-out or a token economy, are still used today. Exposure is still a key component to cognitive behavioral treatments of anxiety. Cognitive science focuses on concepts such as schemas (a network of accumulated knowledge or set), attention, and memory, and these concepts are part of cognitive behavioral theories and treatments of psychopathology. Cognitive behavior therapy uses behavior therapy techniques and cognitive restructuring. Aaron Beck and Albert Ellis are two influential cognitive behavior therapists. The boundary between what is behavioral and what is cognitive is not always so clear in the cognitive behavioral paradigm.

Factors That Cut across the Paradigms

Two important sets of factors that we will consider throughout this book are relevant for all the paradigms. These are emotion and sociocultural factors. Some type of disturbance in emotion can be found in nearly all the mental disorders. In addition, we shall see that gender, culture, ethnicity, and social relationships bear importantly on the descriptions, causes, and treatments of the different disorders. In the next sections, we introduce these concepts and give some examples of why they are so important in psychopathology, regardless of what paradigm has been adopted.

Emotion and Psychopathology

Emotions influence how we respond to problems and challenges in our environment; they help us organize our thoughts and actions, both explicitly and implicitly, and they guide our behavior. Perhaps because our emotions exert such widespread influence, we spend a good deal of time trying to regulate how we feel and how we present our emotions to others. Given their centrality, it is not surprising that emotion disturbances figure prominently in many different forms of psychopathology. By one analysis, as many as 85 percent of psychological disorders include disturbances in emotional processing of some kind (Thoits, 1985).

What is emotion? The answer to that question could fill an entire textbook on its own. Emotions are believed to be fairly short-lived states, lasting for a few seconds, minutes, or at most hours. Sometimes the word *affect* is used to describe short-lasting emotional feelings. Moods, on the other hand, are emotional experiences that endure for a longer period of time.

Most contemporary emotion theorists and researchers suggest that emotions are comprised of a number of components—including (but not limited to) expressive, experiential, and physiological components—that are typically coordinated within the individual. The expressive or behavioral component of emotion typically refers to facial expressions of emotion. For example, anger expression is an important variable in studies of heart disease. Many patients with schizophrenia do not display very many facial expressions. The experience or subjective feeling component of emotion refers to how someone reports they feel at any given moment or in response to some event. For example, learning that you received an A on your midterm might elicit feelings of happiness, pride, and relief. Learning you received a grade of C might elicit feelings of anger, concern, or embarrassment. The physiological component of emotion involves changes in the body, such as those due to the autonomic nervous system activity

Emotion consists of many components, including expression (shown here), experience, and physiology. (Rachel Epstein/PhotoEdit.)

that accompanies emotion. For example, if a car almost runs you down as you are crossing the street, you may show a frightened look on your face, feel fear, and experience an increase in your heart rate, breathing rate, and skin conductance.

When we consider emotional disturbances in psychopathology, it will be important to consider which of the emotion components are affected. In some disorders, all emotion components may be disrupted, whereas in others, just one might be problematic. For example, people with schizophrenia do not readily express their emotions outwardly, but they report feeling emotions very strongly. People with panic disorder experience excessive fear and anxiety when no actual danger is present. People with depression may experience prolonged sadness and other negative feelings. A person with antisocial personality disorder does not feel empathy. We will try to be clear in the book as to what component of emotion is being considered.

The study of emotion figures prominently in the work of neuroscientists who are examining the ways in which the brain contributes to the different emotion components. Geneticists have also begun to examine how tendencies to experience a lot of positive or negative emotion may run in families. Emotions such as anger figured prominently in Freud's views; more contemporary psychodynamic treatments also focus on changing emotion. Even cognitive behavioral therapies consider how emotion influences thinking and behavior. As noted above, emotion is the starting point for Ellis' theory. Emotion thus cuts across the paradigms and can be studied from multiple perspectives depending on the paradigm that is adopted.

Sociocultural Factors and Psychopathology

A good deal of research has focused on the ways in which sociocultural factors, such as culture, ethnicity, gender, and social relationships, can contribute to different psychological disorders. Researchers who study such sociocultural factors and psychopathology all share the premise that environmental factors can trigger, exacerbate, or maintain the symptoms that make up the different disorders. But the range of variables considered, and the ways of studying those variables, cover a lot of ground.

Epidemiological studies have been an increasingly popular approach to studying the role of environmental factors. We will describe these studies further in Chapter 4, but the basic goal of such studies is to study a group of people specifically sampled to mirror the demographic characteristics of the underlying population. These studies often involve thousands of participants and allow researchers a chance to examine sociocultural variables like poverty and unemployment. An increasing number of such studies look at the role of culture and ethnicity by conducting multinational studies. In addition, these studies have shown that some disorders affect men and women differently. For example, depression is nearly twice as common among women as it is men. On the other hand, antisocial personality disorder and alcohol dependence are more common among men than women. Childhood disorders, such as attention-deficit/hyperactivity disorder, affect boys more than girls, but some researchers question whether this reflects a true difference between boys and girls or a bias in the diagnostic criteria.

Beyond epidemiological studies, thousands of articles have been published on how the quality of relationships influences different disorders. Family and marital relationships, social support, and even the amount of casual social contact all play a role in influencing the course of disorders. Within relationships, researchers have looked for ways to capture the relative closeness and support offered, but also the degree of hostility. In addition, current research is looking beyond whether men and women differ in the prevalence rates of certain disorders to asking questions about risk factors that may differentially impact men and women in the development of certain disorders. For example, father to son genetic transmission appears to be an important risk factor in the development of alcohol dependence for men, whereas sociocultural standards of thinness may be a risk factor in the development of eating disorders for women.

One tradition involves examining problem-solving interactions of the family members to try to capture key dimensions in relationships. In a typical family interaction task, researchers might ask family members to discuss a topic that has been a source of concern, like whether the family is spending enough time together. An interviewer talks with each family member independently to capture the basics of his or her position. Then, in a family meeting, the interviewer briefly summarizes each person's perspective, and asks the family to discuss the area for 10 to 15 minutes and try to come to some resolution. Researchers then might code various dimensions from watching videotapes, like how family members share power, express positive sentiments, or deal with negative emotions.

Other researchers are interested in understanding the role of trauma, serious life events, and stress in psychopathology. We will describe some of the ways people measure life events in the next chapter. But the influence of stress within the context of social relationships plays a role in just about all the disorders we will consider.

Cultural and ethnic factors in psychopathology must be examined more closely. Some questions, such as whether or not the disorders we diagnose and treat in the United States are observed in other parts of the world, have been fairly well studied. This research has demonstrated that a number of disorders are indeed observed in diverse parts of the world. Indeed, no country or culture is without psychopathology of some sort. For example, Murphy (1976) examined whether schizophrenia symptoms could be observed in cultures as diverse as Eskimo and Yoruba. She found that both cultures have a concept of being "crazy" that is quite similar to the Western definition of schizophrenia. The Eskimo's *nuthkavihak* includes talking to oneself, refusing to talk, delusional beliefs, and bizarre behavior. The Yoruba's *were* encompasses similar symptoms. Notably, both cultures also have shamans but draw a clear distinction between their behavior and that of crazy people. In Chapter 5, we discuss a number of anxiety conditions across the world that look very similar to the symptoms of panic disorder. In Chapter 9, we will consider the evidence that eating disorders are specific to Western culture. As we discuss in the next chapter, the current diagnostic system includes cultural factors in the discussion of every category of disorder, and this may be an important step toward increasing research in this area.

Even though there are some cross-cultural similarities in the presence of mental illnesses across cultures, there are also a number of profound cultural influences on the symptoms expressed in different disorders, the availability of treatment, and the willingness to seek treatment. We will consider these issues throughout this book.

We must also consider the role of ethnicity in psychopathology. Some disorders, such as schizophrenia, are diagnosed more often among African-Americans than whites. Does this mean schizophrenia occurs more often in this group or does it mean that some type of ethnic bias might be operating in diagnostic assessments? Drug use and abuse and their effects vary by ethnicity. Whites are more likely to use or abuse many drugs, such as nicotine, hallucinogens, methamphetamine, prescription pain killers, and, depending on the age group, alcohol. Yet African-American smokers are more likely to die from lung cancer. Eating disturbances and body dissatisfaction are greater among white women than black women, particularly in college, but differences in actual eating disorders, particularly bulimia, do not appear to be as great. The reasons for these differences are not yet well understood and are the focus of current research.

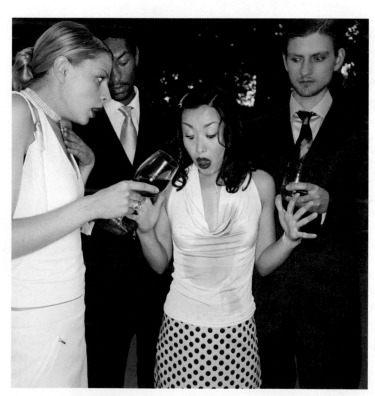

Culture and ethnicity play an important role in the descriptions, causes, and treatments of mental disorders. (Betsie Van der Meer/Stone/Getty Images.)

Although sociocultural factors have not traditionally been the focus of many studies in genetics or neuroscience, they have become more prominent in recent years. For example, *social neuroscience* seeks to understand what happens in the brain during complex social situations. Gene–environment interaction studies are uncovering the ways in which the social environment in combination with certain genes can increase the risk for disorders, as illustrated by the Caspi et al. (2003) study discussed earlier. Psychoanalysis and cognitive behavior traditions have tended to focus more on the individual rather than how the individual interacts with the social world. However, this too is changing. New efforts are underway, for example, to develop cognitive behavior therapy for people from different cultures and ethnicities.

Quick Summary

Emotion disturbances figure prominently in psychopathology, but the ways in which emotions can be disrupted varies quite a bit. Emotions guide our behavior and help us to respond to problems or challenges in our environment. It is important to distinguish between components of emotion, including expression, experience, and physiology. In addition, mood can be distinguished from emotion. Psychological disorders have different types of emotion disturbances, and thus it is important to consider which of the emotion components are affected. In some disorders, all emotion components may be disrupted, whereas in others, just one might be problematic. Emotion is an important focus in the paradigms.

Sociocultural factors, such as culture, ethnicity, gender, social support, and relationships are important factors in the study of psychopathology. Some disorders appear to be universal across cultures, like schizophrenia or anxiety, yet their manifestations may differ somewhat and the ways in which society regards them may also differ. Some disorders are more frequently diagnosed in some ethnic groups compared to others. It is not clear that this reflects a true difference in the presence of disorder or perhaps a bias on the part of diagnosticians. Social relationships can be important buffers against stress and have benefits for physical and mental health. Current research is also examining whether risk factors associated with various disorders differ for men and women. Sociocultural factors have recently become the focus of people working in the other paradigms, and this trend will continue.

Check Your Knowledge 2.3

True or false?
1. One of the current contributions of the psychoanalytic paradigm is the recognition that the unconscious is not important.
2. Beck's theory suggests that emotions are caused by irrational thoughts, whereas Ellis' theory suggests that people have distortions in the way they perceive life's experiences.
3. In the Stroop task, interference is measured by how long it takes to name the color of the ink in a list of words.
4. Emotion consists of at least three components: expression, experience, and physiology.
5. Sociocultural factors such as gender, culture, ethnicity, and social relationships are less important to consider from the neuroscience paradigm.

Diathesis–Stress: An Integrative Paradigm

Psychopathology is much too diverse to be explained or treated adequately by any one of the current paradigms. It is probably advantageous that psychologists do not agree on which paradigm is the best. We know far too little to make hard-and-fast decisions on the exclusive superiority of any one paradigm, and there is enough important work to go around. We will see, too, that often a plausible way of looking at the data is to assume multiple causation. Most of the disorders we will discuss in this book likely develop through an interaction of neurobiological defects and environmental factors, a view that we turn to next.

The **diathesis–stress** paradigm is an integrative paradigm that links neurobiological, psychological, and environmental factors. It is not limited to one particular school of thought, such as cognitive behavioral, genetic, or psychoanalytic. The diathesis–stress concept was introduced in the 1970s as a way to account for the multiple causes of schizophrenia (Zubin & Spring, 1977). Its appeal continues today for many disorders, however, because, like the gene–environment interaction models reviewed above, it is a model that focuses on the interaction between a predisposition toward disease—the **diathesis**—and environmental, or life, disturbances—the stress. Diathesis refers most precisely to a constitutional predisposition toward illness, but the term may be extended to any characteristic or set of characteristics of a person that increases his or her chance of developing a disorder.

In the realm of neurobiology, for example, a number of disorders considered in later chapters appear to have a genetically transmitted diathesis. Although the precise nature of these genetic diatheses is currently unknown (e.g., we don't know exactly what is inherited that makes one person more likely than another to develop bipolar disorder), it is clear that a genetic predisposition is an important component of many disorders. Other neurobiological diatheses include oxygen deprivation at birth, poor nutrition, and a maternal viral infection or smoking during pregnancy. Each of these conditions may lead to changes in the brain that predispose the individual toward psychopathology.

In the psychological realm, a diathesis for depression may be the cognitive set already mentioned, the chronic feeling of hopelessness sometimes found in depressed people. Other psychological diatheses include the ability to be easily hypnotized, which may be a diathesis for dissociative identity disorder (formerly called multiple personality disorder), and an intense fear of becoming fat, which predisposes an individual toward eating disorders.

These diatheses can arise for a variety of reasons. Some, such as hypnotizability, are personality characteristics that are probably in part genetically determined. Others, such as a sense of hopelessness, may result from childhood experiences with harshly critical parents. Sexual or physical abuse during childhood produces psychological changes as well as changes in the brain that seem to predispose people to develop a number of different disorders. Sociocultural influences also play an important role; for instance, cultural standards of what is beautiful may lead to an intense fear of being fat and thus predispose some people to eating disorders. The diathesis–stress paradigm is integrative because it draws on all these diverse sources of information about the causes of diatheses. In later chapters we will see that concepts from the major paradigms we have already discussed are differentially applicable to different disorders. For example, a genetic diathesis plays a major role in attention-deficit/hyperactivity disorder. Cognitive diatheses, in contrast, are more influential in the anxiety disorders and depression. A diathesis–stress paradigm allows us to draw on concepts from many sources and to make more or less use of them depending on the disorder being considered.

Possessing the diathesis for a disorder increases a person's risk of developing it but does not by any means guarantee that a disorder will develop. The stress part of diathesis–stress is meant to account for how a diathesis may be translated into an actual disorder. In this context stress generally refers to some noxious or unpleasant environmental stimulus that triggers psychopathology. Psychological stressors include major traumatic events (e.g., becoming unemployed, divorce, death of a spouse) as well as more mundane happenings, which many of us experience (e.g., being stuck in traffic). By including these environmental events, the diathesis–stress model goes beyond the major paradigms we have already discussed.

The key point of the diathesis–stress model is that both diathesis and stress are necessary in the development of disorders. Some people, for example, have inherited a predisposition that places them at high risk for schizophrenia (see Chapter 11); given a certain amount of stress, they stand a good chance of developing schizophrenia. Other people, those at low genetic risk, are not likely to develop schizophrenia, regardless of how difficult their lives are.

Another major feature of the diathesis–stress paradigm is that psychopathology is unlikely to result from the impact of any single factor. Like our discussion of the reciprocal relationships between genes and the environment above, a genetically transmitted diathesis may be necessary for some disorders, but it is embedded in a network of other factors that also contribute to the disorder. These factors could include genetically transmitted diatheses for other personality characteristics; childhood experiences that shape personality, the development of behavioral competencies, and coping strategies; stressors encountered in adulthood; cultural influences; and numerous other factors.

Stressors that may activate a diathesis range from minor, such as having a flat to major such as the aftermath of a hurricane. (Top photo: Corbis Images; bottom photo: AFP/Getty Images.)

Finally, we should note that within this framework the data gathered by researchers holding different paradigms are not incompatible with one another. For example, stress may be needed to activate a predisposition toward a problem in neurotransmitter systems. Some of the differences between the paradigms also appear to be more linguistic than substantive. A cognitive behavioral theorist may propose that maladaptive cognitions cause depression, whereas a neurobiological theorist may speak of the underactivity of a certain neural pathway. The two positions are not contradictory, but merely reflect different levels of description, just as we could describe a table as pieces of wood in a particular configuration or as a collection of atoms.

Multiple Perspectives on a Clinical Problem

To provide a concrete example of how it is possible to conceptualize a clinical case using multiple paradigms, we present a case and discuss how information provided is open to a number of interpretations, depending on the paradigm adopted.

Clinical Case: Arthur

Arthur's childhood had not been a particularly happy one. His mother died suddenly when he was only 6, and for the next 10 years he lived either with his father or with a maternal aunt. His father drank heavily, seldom managing to get through any day without some alcohol. His father's income was so irregular that he could seldom pay bills on time or afford to live in any but the most run-down neighborhoods. At times Arthur's father was totally incapable of caring for himself, let alone his son. Arthur would then spend weeks, sometimes months, with his aunt in a nearby suburb.

Despite these early life circumstances, Arthur completed high school and entered college at a nearby state university. He qualified for student loans and other financial aid, but he also needed to wait tables and tend bar to make ends meet. During these college years, he felt an acute self-consciousness with people who he felt had authority over him—his boss, his professors, and even some of his classmates, with whom he compared himself unfavorably.

Like many kids in college, Arthur attended his fair share of parties. He pledged a fraternity at the end of his freshman year, and this was the source of most of his socializing. It was also the source of a lot of alcohol. He drank heavily at the weekend parties. By his senior year, however, he was drinking daily, often as a way to deal with the stress of being in school and working at the same time.

Two years after college, Arthur married his college girlfriend. Arthur could never quite believe that his wife, as intelligent as she was beautiful, really cared for him. As the years wore on, his doubts about himself and about her feelings toward him would continue to grow. He felt she was far brighter than he and he worried that she would make more money than he would.

After college, Arthur began a job at a publishing company, serving as an assistant editor. This job proved to be even more stressful than college. The deadlines and demands of the senior editors were difficult. He constantly questioned whether he had what it took to be an editor. Like his father, he often drank to deal with this stress.

Several years later, when it seemed that life should be getting easier, he found himself in even greater turmoil. Now 32 years old, with a fairly secure job that paid reasonably well, he and his wife were arguing more often. She continually complained about his drinking; he denied that there was a problem. After all, he was only drinking four beers a night. His wife wanted to start a family, but he was not sure if he wanted to have this additional stress in his life. His brooding over his marriage led him to drink even more heavily until finally one day, he realized he was drinking too much and needed to seek help.

Depending on the paradigm you adopt, your conceptualization of this case may differ. If you hold a genetic point of view, you are attentive to the family history, noting that Arthur's father had similar difficulties with alcohol. You are probably aware of the research (to be reviewed in Chapter 10) that suggests a genetic factor in substance-related disorders such as alcohol dependence. You do not discount environmental contributions to Arthur's problems, but you hypothesize that some inherited defect predisposes him to react poorly to stress, which may in turn increase the likelihood that he will turn to alcohol to cope. After all, not everyone who experiences a difficult childhood and adolescence develops a drinking problem.

A psychoanalytic point of view casts Arthur in yet another light. Believing that events in early childhood are of great importance in later patterns of adjustment, you may hypothesize that Arthur is still grieving for his mother and has blamed his father for her early death. Such strong anger at the father has been repressed, and this plus the death of his mother is negatively impacting his adult relationships with others. For treatment you may choose interpersonal therapy to work on Arthur's relationships and to deal openly and consciously with his hitherto buried anger toward his father.

Now suppose that you are committed to a cognitive behavioral perspective, which encourages you to analyze human behavior in terms of reinforcement patterns as well as cognitive variables. You may focus on Arthur's self-consciousness at college, which seems related to the fact that compared with his fellow students, he grew up with few advantages. Economic insecurity and hardship may have made him unduly sensitive to criticism and rejection. Alcohol has been his escape from such tensions. But heavy drinking, coupled with persistent doubt about his own worth as a human being, has worsened an already deteriorating marital relationship, further undermining his confidence. As a cognitive behavior therapist, you may employ systematic desensitization, in which you teach Arthur to relax deeply as he imagines a hierarchy of situations in which he is being evaluated by others. Or you may decide on cognitive behavior therapy to convince Arthur that he need not obtain universal approval for every undertaking.

If you adopt a diathesis–stress perspective, you might follow more than one of these strategies. You would acknowledge the likely genetic contribution to Arthur's alcohol dependence, but you would also identify key triggers (e.g., job stress) that might lead to greater bouts of drinking. You would likely employ many of the therapeutic techniques noted above.

Summary

● Scientific inquiry is limited by scientists' human limitations and by the limited state of our knowledge: people see only what they are able to see, and other phenomena go undetected because scientists can discover things only if they already have some general idea about them.

● A paradigm is a conceptual framework or general perspective. Because the paradigm within which scientists and clinicians work helps to shape what they investigate and find, understanding paradigms helps us to appreciate subjective influences that may affect their work.

● Several major paradigms are current in the study of psychopathology and therapy. The choice of a paradigm has important consequences for the way in which abnormal behavior is defined, investigated, and treated.

● The genetic paradigm holds that psychopathology is caused or at least influenced by heritable factors. Recent genetic findings show how genes and the environment interact, and it is this type of interaction that will figure most prominently in psychopathology.

● The neuroscience paradigm emphasizes the role of the brain, neurotransmitters, and other systems, such as the HPA axis. Biological treatments attempt to rectify the specific problems in the brain or to alleviate symptoms of disorders, often using drugs to do so.

● The psychoanalytic paradigm derives from the work of Sigmund Freud. The more contemporary contributions of this paradigm are primarily in treatment, including ego analysis and brief therapy. Although Freud has been criticized, the psychoanalytic paradigm continues to influence the field by highlighting the importance of childhood experiences, the unconscious, and the fact that the causes of behavior are not always obvious.

● The cognitive behavioral paradigm emphasizes schemas, attention, and irrational interpretations and their influence on behavior as major factors in psychopathology. In both practice and theory, the cognitive behavioral paradigm has usually blended cognitive findings with the behavioral in an approach to intervention that is referred to as cognitive behavioral. Cognitive behavior therapists such as Beck and Ellis focus on altering patients' negative schemas and interpretations.

● Emotion plays a prominent role in a number of disorders. It is important to distinguish among components of emotion that may be disrupted, including expression, experience, and physiology. Emotion disturbances are the focus of study across the paradigms.

● Sociocultural factors, including culture, ethnicity, gender, social support, and relationships, are also important in conceptions of psychopathology. The prevalence and meaning of disorders may vary by culture and ethnicity; men and women may have different risk factors for different disorders; and social relationships can be an important buffer against stress. Sociocultural factors are now being considered in the work of geneticists, neuroscientists, psychoanalysts, and cognitive behaviorists.

● Because each paradigm seems to have something to offer to our understanding of mental disorders, it is important to develop more integrative paradigms. The diathesis–stress paradigm, which integrates several points of view, assumes that people are predisposed to react adversely to environmental stressors. The diathesis may be genetic, neurobiological, or psychological and may be caused by early-childhood experiences, genetically influenced personality traits, or sociocultural influences, among other things.

Answers to Check Your Knowledge Questions

2.1 1. b; 2. d; 3. a; 4. c

2.2 1. hypothalamus, anterior cingulate, septal area, hippocampus, amygdala; 2. white, gray; 3. parasympathetic, sympathetic; 4. hypothalamus, pituitary gland, adrenal cortex

2.3 1. F; 2. F; 3. T; 4. T; 5. F

Key Terms

agonist
allele
amygdala
antagonist
anterior cingulate
autonomic nervous system (ANS)
behavior genetics
brain stem
brief therapy
cerebellum
cognition
cognitive behavior therapy (CBT)
cognitive behavioral paradigm
cognitive restructuring
corpus callosum
cortisol
diathesis
diathesis–stress
dopamine

ego analysis
emotion
exposure
frontal lobe
gamma-aminobutyric acid (GABA)
gene–environment interaction
gene expression
genes
genetic markers
genetic paradigm
genotype
gray matter
heritability
hippocampus
HPA axis
hypothalamus
in vivo
linkage analysis

molecular genetics
nerve impulse
neuron
neuroscience paradigm
neurotransmitters
nonshared environment
norepinephrine
occipital lobe
paradigm
parasympathetic nervous system
parietal lobe
phenotype
polygenic
polymorphism
pruning
psychoanalytic paradigm
psychotherapy
rational-emotive behavior therapy (REBT)

reciprocal gene–environment interaction
reuptake
schema
second messengers
septal area
serotonin
serotonin transporter gene
shared environment
somatic nervous system
sympathetic nervous system
synapse
temporal lobe
thalamus
time-out
token economy
ventricles
white matter

3 Diagnosis and Assessment

Learning Goals

1. Be able to describe the purposes of diagnosis and assessment.
2. Be able to distinguish the different types of reliability and validity.
3. Be able to identify the basic features, strengths, and weaknesses of the DSM-IV-TR.
4. Be able to describe the goals, strengths, and weaknesses of psychological and neurobiological approaches to assessment.
5. Be able to discuss the ways in which culture and ethnicity impact diagnosis and assessment.

Clinical Case: Aaron

Hearing the sirens in the distance, Aaron realized that someone must have called the police. He didn't mean to get upset with the people sitting next to him at the bar, but he just knew that they were talking about him and plotting to have his special status with the CIA revoked. He could not let this happen again. The last time people conspired against him he wound up in a mental hospital. He did not want to go to the hospital again and endure all of the evaluations. Different doctors would ask him all sorts of questions about his work with the CIA, which he simply was not at liberty to discuss. They asked other odd questions, such as whether he heard voices or believed others were putting thoughts into his head. He was never sure how they knew that he had those experiences, but he suspected that there were electronic bugging devices in his room at his parents' house, perhaps in the electrical outlets.

Just yesterday, Aaron began to suspect that someone was watching and listening to him through the electrical outlets. He decided that the safest thing to do was to stop speaking to his parents. Besides, they were constantly hounding him to take his medication. But, when he took this medication, his vision got blurry and he had trouble sitting still. He reasoned that his parents must somehow be part of the group of people trying to remove him from the CIA. If he took this medication, he would lose his special powers that allowed him to spot terrorists in any setting, and the CIA would stop leaving messages for him in phone booths or in the commercials on Channel 2. Just the other day, he found a tattered paperback book in a phone booth, which he interpreted to mean that a new assignment was imminent. The voices in his head were giving him new clues about terrorist activity. They were currently telling him that he should be wary of people wearing the color purple, as this was a sign of a terrorist. If his parents were trying to sabotage his career with the CIA, he needed to keep out of the house at all costs. That was what led him to the bar in the first place. If only the people next to him wouldn't have laughed out loud and looked toward the door. He knew this meant that they were about to expose him as a CIA operative. If he didn't yell at them to stop, his cover would have been blown.

Diagnosis and assessment are the critically important "first steps" in the study and treatment of psychopathology. In the case of Aaron, a clinician may begin treatment by determining whether Aaron meets the diagnostic criteria for a mood disorder, schizophrenia, or perhaps a substance-related disorder. Having a correct diagnosis will allow the clinician to describe base rates, causes, and treatment for Aaron and his family, all of which are important aspects of good clinical care. More broadly, diagnosis enables clinicians and scientists to communicate accurately with one another about cases or research. Without agreed-on definitions and categories, our field would face a situation like the Tower of Babel (Hyman, 2002), in which different scientists and clinicians would be unable to understand each other. In order to find the causes or treatments for a disorder, we need to be able to classify disorders and then to diagnose disorders in people.

Diagnosis is also important for research on causes and treatments. Sometimes researchers discover unique causes and treatments associated with a certain set of symptoms. For example, only a few decades ago, bipolar disorder (defined by an episode of mania) was not typically distinguished from depression. Without this distinction, the medication lithium probably would not have been recognized as an effective treatment.

Diagnosis also can be the first major step in good clinical care. Imagine if your doctor told you, "There is no diagnosis for what you have." Rather than this alarming scenario, hearing a label can provide relief in several different ways. Often, a diagnosis can help a person begin to understand why certain symptoms are occurring. Many disorders are extremely common, such as depression, anxiety, and substance abuse—knowing that his or her diagnosis is common can help a person feel less unusual. Understanding the causes of symptoms can also be a relief.

To help make the correct diagnosis, clinicians and researchers use a variety of assessment procedures, beginning with a clinical interview followed by other psychological and neurobiological assessment methods. Broadly speaking, all clinical assessment procedures are more or less formal ways of finding out what is wrong with a person, what may have caused problems, and what can be done to improve the person's condition. Assessment procedures can help to make a diagnosis, and they can also provide information beyond a diagnosis. Indeed, a diagnosis is only a starting point. In the case of Aaron, for example, many other questions remain to be answered. Why does Aaron behave as he does? Why does he believe he is working for the CIA? What can be done to resolve his conflicts with his parents? Has he performed up to his intellectual potential in school and in his career? What obstacles might interfere with treatment? These are also the types of questions that mental health professionals address in their assessments.

In this chapter, we will describe the official diagnostic system used by many mental health professionals, as well as the strengths and weaknesses of this system. We will then turn to a discussion of the most widely used assessment techniques, including interviews, psychological assessment, and neurobiological assessment. We then conclude this chapter with an examination of a sometimes neglected aspect of assessment, the role of cultural bias.

Before considering diagnosis and assessment in detail, however, we begin with a discussion of two concepts that play a key role in diagnosis and assessment: reliability and validity.

Cornerstones of Diagnosis and Assessment

The concepts of reliability and validity are the cornerstones of any diagnostic or assessment procedure. Without them, the usefulness of our methods is seriously limited. That said, these two concepts are quite complex. There are several kinds of each, and an entire subfield of psychology—psychometrics—exists primarily for their study. Here, we provide a general overview.

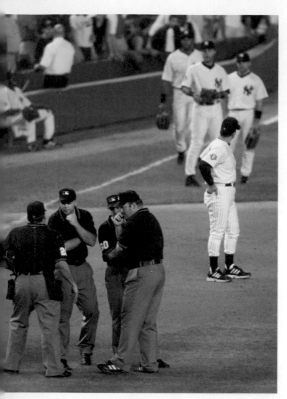

Reliability is an essential property of all assessment procedures. One means of determining reliability is to find if different judges agree, as happens when two umpires witness the same event in a baseball game. (Reuters/ NewMedia Inc./Corbis Images.)

Reliability

Reliability refers to consistency of measurement. An example of a reliable measure would be a wooden ruler, which produces the same value every time it is used to measure an object. In contrast, an unreliable measure would be a flexible, elastic-like ruler whose length changes every time it is used. Several types of reliability exist, and we will discuss here the types most central to assessment and diagnosis.

Interrater reliability refers to the degree to which two independent observers agree on what they have observed. To take an example from baseball, the third-base umpire may or may not agree with the home-plate umpire as to whether a line drive down the left-field line is fair or foul.

Test-retest reliability measures the extent to which people being observed twice or taking the same test twice, perhaps several weeks or months apart, receive similar scores. This kind of reliability makes sense only when we can assume that people being observed will not change appreciably between test sessions on the underlying variable being measured; a prime example of a situation in which this type of reliability is typically high is in evaluating intelligence tests (see p. 84). On the other hand, we cannot expect people to be in the same mood at a baseline and a follow-up 4 weeks later.

Sometimes psychologists use 2 forms of a test rather than giving the same test twice, perhaps when there is concern that test takers will remember their answers from the first round of taking the test and aim merely to be consistent. This approach enables the tester to determine **alternate-form reliability**, the extent to which scores on the two forms of the test are consistent.

Finally, **internal consistency reliability** assesses whether the items on a test are related to one another. For example, one would expect the items on an anxiety questionnaire to be interrelated, or to correlate with one another, if they truly tap anxiety. A person who reports a dry mouth in a threatening situation would be expected to report increases in muscle tension as well, since both are common characteristics of anxiety.

Validity

Validity is a complex concept, generally related to whether a measure measures what it is supposed to measure. For example, if a questionnaire is supposed to measure a person's hostility, does it do so? Before we describe types of validity, it is important to note that validity is related to reliability—unreliable measures will not have good validity. Because an unreliable measure does not yield consistent results (recall our example of a ruler whose length is constantly changing), an unreliable measure will not relate very strongly to other measures. For example, an unreliable measure of coping is not likely to relate well to how a person adjusts to a stressful life experience. Reliability, however, does not guarantee validity. Height can be measured very reliably, but height would not be a valid measure of anxiety.

Content validity refers to whether a measure adequately samples the domain of interest. For example, later in this chapter we will describe an interview that is often used to make an Axis I diagnosis. It has excellent content validity because it contains questions about all the symptoms that are involved in Axis I diagnoses. As another example, consider a measure of life stress that we will examine in more detail below. It consists of a list of 43 life experiences. Respondents indicate which of these experiences—for example, losing one's job—they have had in some time period, for example, the past year. Content validity is less certain here because many people may have life experiences that do not appear on the questionnaire. If you read the experiences in Table 3.5, you will likely think of stressors that are not on the list (e.g., the serious illness of someone close to you).

Criterion validity is evaluated by determining whether a measure is associated in an expected way with some other measure (the criterion). If both variables are measured at the same point in time, the resulting validity is referred to as **concurrent validity**. For example, we will describe a measure below of the distorted thoughts that are believed to play an important role in depression (see p. 87). Criterion validity for this measure of distorted thoughts could be established by showing that people with depression score higher on the test than do people without depression. Alternatively, criterion validity can be assessed by evaluating the ability of the measure to predict some other variable that is measured at some point in the future, often referred to as **predictive validity**. For example, IQ tests were originally developed to predict future school performance. Similarly, the measure of distorted thinking could be used to predict the development of depression in the future. In summary, concurrent and predictive validity are both types of criterion validity.

Construct validity is a more complex concept. It is relevant when we want to interpret a test as a measure of some characteristic or construct that is not observed simply or overtly (Cronbach & Meehl, 1955). A construct is an inferred attribute, such as anxiousness or distorted cognition. Consider an anxiety-proneness questionnaire as an example. If the questionnaire has construct validity, people who obtain different scores on our test really will differ in anxiety proneness. Just because we call our test a measure of anxiety proneness, and the items seem to be about the tendency to become anxious ("I find that I become anxious in many situations"), it is not certain that the test is a valid measure of the construct of anxiety proneness.

Construct validity is evaluated by looking at a wide variety of data from multiple sources (compare this to criterion validity, where a test is typically evaluated against just one other piece of data). For example, people diagnosed as having an anxiety disorder and people without such a diagnosis could be compared on their scores on our self-report measure of anxiety proneness. The self-report measure would achieve some construct validity if the people with anxiety disorders scored higher than the people without anxiety disorders. Greater construct validity would be achieved by showing that the self-report measure was related to other measures thought to reflect anxiety, such as observations of fidgeting and trembling, and physiological indicators, such as increased heart rate and rapid breathing. When the self-report measure is associated with these multiple measures (diagnosis, observational indicators, physiological measures), its construct validity is increased.

More broadly, construct validity is related to theory. For example, we might hypothesize that being prone to anxiety is in part caused by a family history of anxiety. We could then obtain further evidence for the construct validity of our questionnaire by showing that it relates to a family history of anxiety. At the same time, we would have also gathered support for our theory of anxiety proneness. Thus, construct validation is an important part of the process of theory testing.

Construct validity is also centrally important to diagnostic categories. Below, we consider in more detail the issue of construct validity and the DSM-IV-TR.

Classification and Diagnosis

Clinical Case: Roxanne

Roxanne is a middle-aged woman who was brought to the local psychiatric emergency room by the police. They had found her running through a crowded street, laughing loudly and running into people. Her clothes were dirty and torn. When they questioned her, she was speaking very rapidly, and she was hard to follow. At the ER, she wrestled free of the police and began running down the hallway. She knocked over two staff members during her flight, while bellowing at the top of her lungs "I am the resurrection! Come follow me!" Police brought her back to the exam room, and the staff began to form hypotheses. Clearly, she was full of energy. Had she been through some trauma? She believed she had special religious powers—could this be a delusion? Unfortunately, the staff were unable to gain much information from an interview due to her rapid and pressured speech. Rather, Roxanne sat restlessly, breathing heavily, and occasionally laughing and shouting; treatment could not proceed without understanding the reason for her unusual behavior. When efforts to calm Roxanne failed, police helped the staff to contact family members, who were relieved to hear that Roxanne was safe. She had disappeared from home the day before. Family members described a long history of bipolar disorder (formerly known as manic depression). Treatment was able to proceed based on the idea that Roxanne was experiencing a new manic episode of her long-standing bipolar disorder.

In this section, we focus on the official diagnostic system used by mental health professionals, the **Diagnostic and Statistical Manual of Mental Disorders**, now in its fourth edition, commonly referred to as **DSM-IV-TR**. After reviewing the major components of DSM-IV-TR, we will describe the strengths of the DSM-IV-TR, and then review some criticisms of this system as well as of diagnosis in general.

The Diagnostic System of the American Psychiatric Association (DSM-IV-TR)

In 1952, the American Psychiatric Association published its Diagnostic and Statistical Manual (DSM). The publication of the DSM was informed by earlier systems of classification (for a review, see Focus on Discovery 3.1), and it has been revised five times since 1952. DSM-IV was published in 1994, and in June 2000, a "text revision," DSM-IV-TR, followed. Almost no changes were made to the diagnostic categories and criteria in the 2000 revision. Rather, DSM-IV-TR provided a summary of new research findings on prevalence rates, course, and etiology (causes).

The DSM-IV-TR includes several key features: the use of separate dimensions, or axes, to rate people; discrete diagnostic categories; and more focus on cultural issues.

DSM-IV-TR is the official diagnostic system of the American Psychiatric Association. (Courtesy American Psychiatric Association.)

Five Axes of Classification   As shown in Table 3.1, DSM-IV-TR includes five axes. This **multiaxial classification system**, by requiring judgments on each of the five axes, forces the diagnostician to consider a broad range of information.

Axis I includes all diagnostic categories except the personality disorders and mental retardation, which make up Axis II. Thus Axes I and II cover the classification of abnormal behavior. A complete listing of the DSM-IV-TR categories of Axes I and II appears inside the front cover of this book. (We will describe many of these disorders throughout the rest of this book.) Most people consult a mental health professional for an Axis I condition, such as depression or an anxiety disorder. But beyond Axis I conditions, clients might have a long-standing Axis II condition, such as dependent personality disorder. Axes I and II are separated to encourage clinicians to be attentive to the possibility of an Axis II disorder. The presence of an Axis II disorder along with an Axis I disorder generally means that a person's problems will be more difficult to treat.

Axes III, IV, and V are designed to capture the broader life context of the disorder. On Axis III, the clinician indicates any general medical conditions. For many diagnoses, the DSM includes a provision for indicating that the disorder is due to a medical condition or substance abuse. For example, depression resulting from an endocrine gland dysfunction would be diagnosed on Axis I but listed as caused by a medical problem. Therefore, clinicians must be sensitive to possible medical causes of symptoms.

On Axis IV, the clinician codes psychosocial problems that may contribute to the disorder, including occupational problems, economic problems, or interpersonal difficulties. Finally, on Axis V, the clinician indicates the person's current level of adaptive functioning, using the Global Assessment of Functioning (GAF) scale (see Table 3.1) to consider social relationships, occupational functioning, and use of leisure time.

Table 3.1 DSM-IV-TR Multiaxial Classification System

Axis I

Disorders Usually First Diagnosed in Infancy, Childhood, or Adolescence
Delirium, Dementia, Amnesic and Other Cognitive Disorders
Substance-Related Disorders
Schizophrenia and Other Psychotic Disorders
Mood Disorders
Anxiety Disorders
Somatoform Disorders
Factitious Disorders
Dissociative Disorders
Sexual and Gender Identity Disorders
Eating Disorders
Sleep Disorders
Impulse Control Disorders Not Elsewhere Classified
Adjustment Disorders

Axis II

Mental Retardation
Personality Disorders

Axis III

General Medical Conditions

Axis IV Psychosocial and Environmental Problems

Check:
_____Problems with primary support group.
Specify:
_____Problems related to the social environment.
Specify:
_____Educational problem.
Specify:
_____Occupational problem.
Specify:
_____Housing problem.
Specify:
_____Economic problem.
Specify:
_____Problems with access to health care services.
Specify:
_____Problems related to interaction with the legal system/crime.
Specify:
_____Other psychosocial and environmental problems.
Specify:

Axis V Global Assessment of Functioning Scale (GAF Scale)

Consider psychological, social, and occupational functioning on a hypothetical continuum of mental health/illness. Do not include impairment in functioning due to physical (or environmental) limitations.

Code

100 Superior functioning in a wide range of activities, life's problems never seem to get out of hand, is sought out by others because of many positive qualities. No symptoms.

90 Absent or minimal symptoms (e.g., mild anxiety before an exam), good functioning in all areas, interested and involved in a wide range of activities, socially effective, generally satisfied with life, no more than everyday problems or concerns (e.g., an occasional argument with family members).

80 If symptoms are present, they are transient and expectable reactions to psychosocial stressors (e.g., difficulty concentrating after family argument); no more than slight impairment in social, occupational, or school functioning (e.g., temporarily falling behind in schoolwork).

70 Some mild symptoms (e.g., depressed mood and mild insomnia) OR some difficulty in social, occupational, or school functioning (e.g., occasional truancy, or theft within the household), but generally functioning pretty well, has some meaningful interpersonal relationships.

60 Moderate symptoms (e.g., flat affect and circumstantial speech, occasional panic attacks) OR moderate difficulty in social, occupational, or school functioning (e.g., no friends, unable to keep a job).

50 Serious symptoms (e.g., suicidal ideation, severe obsessional rituals, frequent shoplifting) OR any serious impairment in social, occupational, or school functioning (e.g., no friends, unable to keep a job).

40 Some impairment in reality testing or communication (e.g., speech is at times illogical, obscure, or irrelevant) OR major impairment in several areas, such as work or school, family relations, judgment, thinking, or mood (e.g., depressed man avoids friends, neglects family, and is unable to work; child frequently beats up younger children, is defiant at home, and is failing at school).

30 Behavior is considerably influenced by delusions or hallucinations OR serious impairment in communication or judgment (e.g., sometimes incoherent, acts grossly inappropriately, suicidal preoccupation) OR inability to function in almost all areas (e.g., stays in bed all day; no job, home, or friends).

20 Some danger of hurting self or others (e.g., suicide attempts without clear expectation of death, frequently violent, manic excitement) OR occasionally fails to maintain minimal personal hygiene (e.g., smears feces) OR gross impairment in communication (e.g., largely incoherent or mute).

10 Persistent danger of severely hurting self or others (e.g., recurrent violence) OR persistent inability to maintain minimal personal hygiene OR serious suicidal act with clear expectation of death.

0 Inadequate information.

Focus on Discovery 3.1

A Brief History of Classification and Diagnosis

By the end of the nineteenth century as people recognized that different illnesses required different treatments, medical diagnostic procedures were improved. During the same period, other sciences, such as botany and chemistry, advanced after classification systems were developed. Impressed by these successes, investigators of mental illness sought to develop classification schemes. Unfortunately, progress in classifying mental disorders was not gained easily.

Early Efforts at Classification of Mental Illness

From the end of the nineteenth century through the first half of the twentieth century, a series of mental health classification systems were developed by the Royal Medico-Psychological Association in the United Kingdom, the Congress of Mental Science in Paris, and the forerunner of the American Psychiatric Association in the United States. Unfortunately, none of these systems were widely adopted.

Development of the WHO and DSM Systems

In 1939 the World Health Organization (WHO) added mental disorders to the International List of Causes of Death (ICD). In 1948 the list was expanded to become the International Statistical Classification of Diseases, Injuries, and Causes of Death, a comprehensive listing of all diseases, including a classification of abnormal behavior. Unfortunately, the mental disorders section was not widely accepted. Even though American psychiatrists had played a prominent role in the WHO effort, the American Psychiatric Association published its own Diagnostic and Statistical Manual (DSM) in 1952.

In 1969 the WHO published a new classification system, which was more widely accepted. In the United Kingdom, a glossary of definitions was produced to accompany the WHO system (General Register Office, 1968). A second version of the American Psychiatric Association's DSM, DSM-II (1968), was similar to the WHO system. But true consensus still eluded the field. Even though DSM-II and the British Glossary of Mental Disorders specified some symptoms of diagnoses, the two systems defined different symptoms for a given disorder! Thus diagnostic practices still varied widely.

In 1980 the American Psychiatric Association published an extensively revised diagnostic manual, DSM-III, and a somewhat revised version, DSM-III-R, followed in 1987. In 1988 the American Psychiatric Association began work on DSM-IV. Thirteen working groups, which included many psychologists, were established to critique DSM-III-R, to review literature, analyze previously collected data, and collect new data. The committee adopted an important new approach—the reasons for changes in diagnoses would be explicitly stated and supported by data. In previous versions of the DSM, the reasons for diagnostic changes had not always been explicit.

Improvements in the DSM   Beginning with the third edition of DSM and continuing today, an effort was made to create more reliable and valid diagnostic categories. Major improvements include the following:

1. Specific diagnostic criteria—the symptoms for a given diagnosis are spelled out precisely, and clinical symptoms are defined in a glossary. Table 3.2 compares the descriptions of a manic episode given in DSM-II with the diagnostic criteria given in DSM-IV-TR. Notice how DSM-IV-TR is much more detailed and concrete.

2. The characteristics of each diagnosis in Axes I and II are described much more extensively than they were in DSM-II. For each disorder there is a description of essential features, then of associated features, such as laboratory findings (e.g., enlarged ventricles in schizophrenia) and results from physical exams (e.g., electrolyte imbalances in people who have eating disorders). Next, a summary of the research literature provides information about age of onset, course, prevalence and sex ratio, familial pattern, and differential diagnosis (i.e., how to distinguish similar diagnoses from each other).

3. With each revision of the DSM, the number of diagnostic categories has increased to cover most people's concerns and symptoms (see Table 3.3). For example, autism was added in DSM-III. Below, we discuss some of the implications of so many diagnostic categories. Although the number of diagnostic categories has increased over the years, some categories have been dropped because they no longer have research to support their validity (e.g., homosexuality).

4. Beginning with DSM-IV, a special section is provided on diagnoses and axes that need more study to decide whether they should become part of the diagnostic system (see Focus on Discovery 3.2). This type of information was not provided in previous versions of DSM, which sometimes meant that the reasons for diagnostic changes were not clear.

Table 3.2 Description of Mania in DSM-II versus DSM-IV-TR

DSM-II (1968, p. 36)

Manic-depressive illness, manic type. This disorder consists exclusively of manic episodes. These episodes are characterized by excessive elation, irritability, talkativeness, flight of ideas, and accelerated speech and motor activity. Brief periods of depression sometimes occur, but they are never true depressive episodes.

DSM-IV-TR (2000, p. 362)

Diagnostic Criteria for a Manic Episode

A. A distinct period of abnormally and persistently elevated, expansive, or irritable mood, lasting at least 1 week (or any duration if hospitalization is necessary).

B. During the period of mood disturbance, three (or more) of the following symptoms have persisted (four if the mood is only irritable) and have been present to a significant degree:
  1. inflated self-esteem or grandiosity
  2. decreased need for sleep (e.g., feels rested after only 3 hours of sleep)
  3. more talkative than usual or pressure to keep talking
  4. flight of ideas or subjective experience that thoughts are racing
  5. distractibility (i.e., attention too easily drawn to unimportant or irrelevant external stimuli)
  6. increase in goal-directed activity (either socially, at work or school, or sexually) or psychomotor agitation
  7. excessive involvement in pleasurable activities that have a high potential for painful consequences (e.g., engaging in unrestrained buying sprees, sexual indiscretions, or foolish business investments)

C. The symptoms do not meet criteria for a Mixed Episode.

D. The mood disturbance is sufficiently severe to cause marked impairment in occupational functioning or in usual social activities or relationships with others, or to necessitate hospitalization to prevent harm to self or others, or there are psychotic features.

E. The symptoms are not due to the direct physiological effects of a substance (e.g., a drug of abuse, a medication, or other treatment) or a general medical condition (e.g., hyperthyroidism).

Note: DSM-IV-TR material reprinted with permission from the DSM-IV-TR, copyright 2000, American Psychiatric Association.

Ethnic and Cultural Considerations in DSM-IV-TR   Mental illness is universal. There is not a single culture in which people are free of mental illness. But there are many different cultural influences on the risk factors for mental illness (e.g., social cohesion, poverty, access to drugs of abuse, and stress), the types of symptoms experienced, the willingness to seek help, and the treatments available. Sometimes, these differences across cultures are profound. For example, although mental health care is widely available in the United States, it is estimated that there is only one psychiatrist for every 2 million people living in sub-Saharan Africa (WHO, 2001).

Cultural differences do not always play out in the way one might expect. For example, even with the access to medical care in the United States, a major study found that outcomes for schizophrenia were more favorable in Nigeria, India, and Colombia than in more industrialized countries, including the United States (Sartorius et al., 1986). People who immigrate from Mexico to the United States are about half as likely to meet criteria for mental illness than native born citizens in the United States initially, but over time, they and their children begin to show an increase in certain disorders, such as substance abuse, such that their risk for disorder begins to approximate that of people born in the United States (Vega et al., 1998). If we hope to understand how culture defines risk, symptom expression, and outcomes, we need a diagnostic system that can be applied reliably and validly in different countries and cultures.

Previous editions of the DSM were criticized for their lack of attention to cultural and ethnic variations in psychopathology. DSM-IV-TR attempts to enhance cultural sensitivity in three ways: (1) by providing a general framework for evaluating the role of culture and ethnicity; (2) by describing cultural factors and ethnicity for each disorder; and (3) by listing culture-bound syndromes in an appendix.

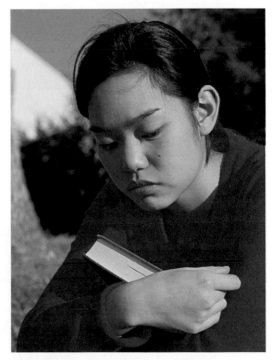

The core symptoms of depression appear to be similar cross-culturally. (Richard Nowitz/Photo Researchers.)

Focus on Discovery 3.2

Issues and Possible Categories in Need of Further Study

One of DSM-IV-TR's appendixes is entitled "Criteria Sets and Axes Provided for Further Study." It contains several proposals for new categories that the DSM-IV task force considers promising but not sufficiently supported by data to merit inclusion in DSM-IV. By describing these potential categories, the DSM task force hopes to encourage professionals to consider whether a future DSM should contain any of these syndromes or axes officially.

Possible New Syndromes

Here is a sampling of the more than two dozen categories described as meriting further study.

Caffeine Withdrawal.   Symptoms include headache, fatigue, anxiety, depression, nausea, and impaired thinking. Significant distress or impairment in occupational or social functioning must result from not drinking accustomed levels of beverages containing caffeine. Inclusion of caffeine withdrawal as a new category would certainly swell the ranks of the mentally disordered.

Premenstrual Dysphoric Disorder.   This proposed syndrome is marked by depression, anxiety, anger, mood swings, and decreased interest in usually pleasurable activities. The symptoms occur a week or so before menstruation for most months in a given year and are severe enough to interfere with social or occupational functioning. This category is to be distinguished from premenstrual syndrome, which is experienced by many more women and is not nearly as debilitating.

Arguments abound for and against this possible category. On the plus side, inclusion might alert people to the hormonal bases of monthly mood changes linked to the menstrual cycle and thereby foster more tolerance and less blame. On the minus side, listing such mood changes in a manual of mental disorders would seem to convey the message that women who experience these psychological changes are mentally disordered.

Passive-Aggressive Personality Disorder (Negativistic Personality Disorder).   This personality disorder was present in DSM-III and DSM-III-R but was moved to the appendix in DSM-IV. Symptoms include resenting, resisting, and opposing demands and expectations by means of passive activities, such as lateness, procrastination, forgetfulness, and intentional inefficiency. The inference is that the person expresses anger or resentment by not doing certain things rather than by more direct expression, such as assertiveness or aggressiveness. Such people often feel mistreated, cheated, or underappreciated.

Depressive Personality Disorder.   In lay terms, symptoms of this personality disorder include gloominess, lack of cheer, and a tendency to worry a lot. This traitlike, long-term disorder may be a precursor to a full-blown major depressive disorder. One concern is that it is very difficult to distinguish between depressive personality disorder and other depressive disorders.

In the general framework, clinicians are cautioned not to diagnose symptoms unless they are atypical and problematic within a person's culture. People vary in the degree to which they identify with their cultural or ethnic group. Some value assimilation into the majority culture, whereas others wish to maintain close ties to their cultural background. In general, clinicians are advised to be constantly mindful of how culture and ethnicity influence diagnosis and treatment. We will return to this topic when we cover assessment tools.

Much more attention is paid now to how culture can shape the symptoms of a given disorder. For example, the symptoms of both schizophrenia (e.g., delusions and hallucinations) and depression (e.g., depressed mood and loss of interest or pleasure in activities) are similar cross-culturally (Draguns, 1989). But as we will discuss in Chapter 5, it is more likely in Japan than in the United States for anxiety to be focused around fears of offending others (Kirmayer, 2001).

In evaluating symptoms, clinicians also need to be aware that cultures may shape the language used to describe distress. Many cultures, for example, describe grief or anxiety in physical terms—"I am sick in my heart" or "My heart is heavy"—rather than in psychological terms.

The DSM includes 25 culture-bound syndromes in the appendix. Culture-bound syndromes are diagnoses that are likely to be seen within specific regions. It is important to note that these culture-bound syndromes are not just found in cultures outside the United States. For example, some argued for listing eating disorders as a Western culture-bound syndrome, a topic we return to in more detail in Chapter 9. The following are some examples of syndromes listed in the appendix.

- *amok.*   A dissociative episode in which there is a period of brooding followed by a violent and sometimes homicidal outburst. The episode tends to be triggered by an

---

Table 3.3 Number of Diagnostic Categories per Edition of DSM

Edition of DSM	Number of Categories
DSM I	106
DSM-II	182
DSM-III	265
DSM-III-R	292
DSM-IV-TR	297

Source: From Pincus et al., 1992.

Clinical Case: Lola: An Example of a Multiaxial Diagnosis

Lola is a 17-year-old high school junior. She moved to the United States from Mexico with her parents and brother when she was 14 years old. A few months after they arrived, Lola's father returned to Mexico to attend the funeral of his brother. He was denied reentry to the United States due to a problem with his visa, and he has been unable to reunite with the family for nearly 3 years. Lola's mother has found it difficult to make ends meet on her salary as a bookkeeper, and the family was forced to move to a rougher neighborhood a year ago. Lola's English was fairly good when she came to the United States, and she has picked up many of the nuances of the language from watching television. For the past 2 years, she has been dating a boy in her school. They have been fairly constant companions, and she describes him as the one person who she would turn to if she were feeling upset. If her mother had any concern about Lola, it was that she seemed to rely on her boyfriend too much—she asked for his advice with small and large decisions, and she seemed wary of social interactions when he wasn't present. Lola's mother stated "It is as though she is afraid to think for herself." Lola's mother noted that she had always been a bit shy and had tended to count on her brother for decisions and social support a lot when she was younger.

With little warning, her boyfriend announced that he wanted to break up with her. Lola was extremely distressed by this change and reported that almost immediately she was unable to sleep or eat. She lost weight rapidly and found herself unable to concentrate on her school work. Friends complained that she no longer wanted to talk during lunch or by phone. After 2 weeks of steadily feeling worse, Lola left a suicide note and disappeared. Police found her the next day in an abandoned home, holding a bottle of medicines. She reported that she had been sitting there all night, considering ending her life. Lola's mother reported that she had never seen her this distressed, but that a few other family members had what she called bouts of sadness. Still, these family members in Mexico had not made suicide attempts nor had they received any formal treatment. Instead, the family learned to give these family members support and time to heal on their own. After the police found Lola, she was hospitalized for intensive treatment.

Multiaxial Diagnosis of Lola

Axis I   Major Depressive Disorder

Axis II   Dependent Personality Disorder

Axis III None

Axis IV   Problems with primary support group (Father not with family); Problems related to social environment (acculturation stress; relationship with boyfriend)

Axis V   GAF: 25

insult and is found primarily among men. Persecutory delusions are often present as well. The term is Malaysian and is defined by the dictionary as a murderous frenzy. You may have heard the phrase "run amok."

- *dhat.*   A term used in India to refer to severe anxiety about the discharge of semen.

- *ghost sickness.*   An extreme preoccupation with death and those who have died found among certain Native American tribes.

- *koro.*   Reported in south and east Asia, an episode of intense anxiety about the possibility that the penis or nipples will recede into the body, possibly leading to death.

- *shenjing shuairuo* (neurasthenia).   A common diagnosis in China, this syndrome is characterized by fatigue, dizziness, headaches, pain, poor concentration, sleep problems, and memory loss.

- *taijin kyofusho.*   The fear that one could offend others through inappropriate eye contact, blushing, a perceived body deformation, or one's own foul body odor. This disorder is most common in Japan, but cases have been reported in the United States. Japanese cultural norms appear to proscribe more careful attention to social appropriateness and hierarchy, perhaps intensifying the risk of these symptoms (Fabrega, 2002).

A therapist must be mindful of the role of cultural differences in the ways in which patients describe their problems. (Rhoda Sidney/PhotoEdit.)

Some have argued that we should try to identify broad syndromes that can be identified across cultures, and in this light have argued against the inclusion of culturally bound syndromes (Lopez-Ibor, 2003). In support of this position, they point toward a number of culturally bound syndromes that are not so different from the main DSM-IV-TR diagnoses. For example, Kleinman (1986) interviewed 100 Chinese people who had been diagnosed with *shenjing shauiro* and found that 87 percent of them met criteria for major depressive disorder. Many of those responded to antidepressant medications. Suzuki and colleagues (2003) have pointed out that the symptoms of *taijin kyofusho* overlap with social phobia (excessive fear of social interaction and evaluation) and body dysmorphic disorders (the mistaken belief that one is deformed or ugly), which are more commonly diagnosed in the United States. Other syndromes may reflect the common concerns of anxiety and distress, with the content shaped by life circumstances and values (Lopez-Ibor, 2003). Hence, some researchers believe it is important to look for commonalities across cultures. In contrast, others believe that culture-bound syndromes are central, as local and personal meanings are a key issue in understanding mental illness (Gaw, 2001). Researchers already are considering various approaches to culture and diagnosis for DSM-V (Kupfer, First, & Regier, 2002).

Quick Summary

Diagnosis provides the first step in thinking about the causes of symptoms, and so is the first step in planning treatment. Because psychopathology is diagnosed on the basis of symptoms, clinical interviews are used to make diagnoses.

The interview is only one of a set of assessment tools used by psychologists, and with all assessments, the reliability (the consistency of measurement) and validity (whether an assessment measures what it is designed to measure) should be evaluated. Reliability can be estimated by examining how well raters agree, how consistent test scores are over time, how alternate forms of a test compare, or how well items correlate with each other. There are many different forms of validity, including content, criterion, and construct validity.

Diagnostic systems for mental illness have changed a great deal in the past 100 years. Currently, the system in use in the United States is the DSM-IV-TR, a multiaxial classification system that includes approximately 300 different diagnostic categories. Most consider the DSM to be a tremendous achievement. One of the most heartening features of the DSM is the explicit rules for diagnosis. This clarity has improved reliability and provides a systematic foundation to study whether each diagnosis is valid. In several different ways, the system guides clinicians to be more sensitive to the role of culture and ethnicity in evaluating mental health.

Check Your Knowledge 3.1

1. Key problems with early mental health classification systems included (circle all that apply):
   a. personality disorders were given too much emphasis
   b. the systems were not widely adopted
   c. criteria for diagnoses were not well-defined
   d. symptoms were not defined
2. Match each axis with its function.

   _____ Axis I
   _____ Axis II
   _____ Axis III
   _____ Axis IV
   _____ Axis V

   a. Most major mental illnesses, with the exception of personality disorders and mental retardation
   b. Functioning
   c. Problems with the social environment
   d. Personality disorders and mental retardation
   e. Medical conditions

3. Which type of reliability or validity is tested with the following procedures?

   _____ A group of high school students is given the same IQ test 2 years in a row.

   _____ A group of high school students is given an IQ test, and their scores are correlated with a different IQ test they took the year before.

   _____ A measure of the tendency to blame onself is developed, and researchers then test whether it predicts depression, whether it is related to childhood abuse, and whether it is related to less assertiveness in the workplace.

   _____ Patients are interviewed by two different doctors. Researchers examine whether the doctors agreed about the diagnosis.

   a interrater reliability
   b test-retest reliability
   c criterion validity
   d construct validity

Specific Criticisms of the DSM

Some specific questions and concerns have been raised about the current version of the DSM. We review some of these concerns in the following sections.

Too Many Diagnoses? DSM-IV-TR contains almost 300 different diagnoses. Some have critiqued the burgeoning number of diagnostic categories (see Table 3.3). The DSM-IV-TR even includes an all-encompassing category for "Other conditions that may be a focus of clinical attention." This category comprises conditions that are not regarded as mental disorders per se but still may be a focus of professional attention or treatment, including academic problems, relational problems, bereavement, religious doubt, and noncompliance with treatment.[1] This category seems to exist, perhaps, so that anyone entering the mental health system can be categorized. Should a problem such as religious doubt be considered a mental disorder? The DSM-IV includes a category for acute stress disorder, to capture symptoms in the first month after a severe trauma. Should these relatively common reactions to trauma be pathologized by diagnosing them as a mental illness (Harvey & Bryant, 2003)? By expanding its coverage, the authors of the DSM seem to have made too many problems into psychiatric disorders, without good justification for doing so.

Others argue that the system includes too many minute distinctions based on small differences in symptoms. One side effect of the huge number of diagnostic categories is a phenomenon called **comorbidity**, which refers to the presence of a second diagnosis. When diagnosticians use DSM-IV-TR, comorbidity is the norm rather than the exception. Among people who meet criteria for at least one psychiatric diagnosis, 45 percent will meet criteria for at least one more psychiatric diagnosis (Kessler et al., 2005). Some argue that this overlap is a sign that we are dividing syndromes too finely. Others praise the careful specificity.

To beginning students of abnormal psychology, the emphasis on small distinctions to make a diagnosis can seem tedious. For example, anxiety in social situations—being extremely tense around others—is a symptom of both social phobia and avoidant personality disorder. Avoidant personality disorder is characterized by more general lack of social contact, though. This fine distinction might seem like hairsplitting. But as we will discuss later, the key issue is whether the distinction is useful.

A more subtle issue about the large number of diagnostic criteria is that many risk factors seem to trigger more than one disorder. For example, early trauma, dysregulation of stress hormones, tendencies to attend to and remember negative information about the self, and neuroticism all seem to increase risk for a broad range of anxiety disorders as well as mood disorders (A.G. Harvey et al., 2004). Similarly, selective serotonergic reuptake inhibitors (SSRIs), such as Prozac, often seem to relieve symptoms of anxiety as well as depression (Van Ameringen et al., 2001). Does this mean that we should lump anxiety and depressive disorders into one category? Beliefs about this differ. Some think we should lump, others think we should keep these finer distinctions.

Categorical Diagnoses versus Continuum In the DSM, Axes I and II rely on **categorical** (yes–no) **classification**. Does the patient have schizophrenia or not? This type of classification does not consider continuity between normal and abnormal behavior. For example, in Table 3.2 we see that the diagnosis of mania requires the presence of three symptoms from a list of seven, or four if the person's mood is irritable. But why require three symptoms rather than two or five? A categorical system forces clinicians to define one threshold as "diagnosable." As many as 20–50 percent of people seeking treatment fall into the not otherwise specified category (Helmuth, 2003); that is, many people have mild symptoms that appear to fall just below the threshold for a diagnosis. Categorical diagnoses foster a false impression of discontinuity.

---

[1] Many of these conditions will not be covered in this book, although malingering is discussed in Chapter 6, therapy for marital problems in Chapter 16, and physical and sexual abuse in Chapters 6 and 13.

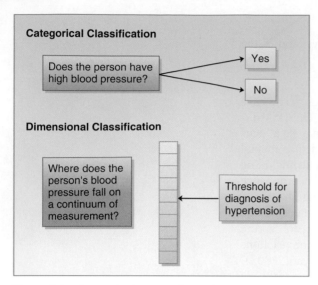

Figure 3.1 Categorical versus dimensional systems of diagnosis.

Consider an illustration of a problem with categorical systems. A central feature of narcissistic personality disorder is grandiosity. As Drew Westen quipped, "Anyone who has been on a bad blind date knows that narcissism and grandiosity are fairly common" (Helmuth, 2003, p. 809). If you were considering a blind date, you might rather know how much grandiosity was present, rather than whether grandiosity was present at all. Because anxiety, depression, and many personality disorder symptoms are common, it may be more helpful to know their severity rather than if they are present.

In contrast to categorical diagnostic systems, **dimensional diagnostic systems** describe the *degree* of an entity that is present (e.g., a 1-to-10 scale of anxiety, where 1 represents minimal and 10 extreme). Diagnosis involves a profile on several dimensions. (See Figure 3.1 for an illustration of the difference between dimensional and categorical approaches.) A dimensional system can subsume a categorical system by specifying a threshold. This capability is a potential advantage of the dimensional approach.

One reason why categorical systems are popular is that they define a threshold for treatment. Consider high blood pressure (hypertension), a topic discussed at length in Chapter 7. Blood-pressure measurements form a continuum, which clearly fits a dimensional approach; yet by defining a threshold for high blood pressure, doctors can feel more certain about when to offer treatment. Similarly, a threshold for clinical depression may help demarcate a point where treatment is recommended. Although the cutoffs are likely to be somewhat arbitrary, they can provide helpful guidance.

In sum, the discrete entity versus continuum issue is not resolved. In any categorical approach, there will be questions about thresholds for diagnosis.

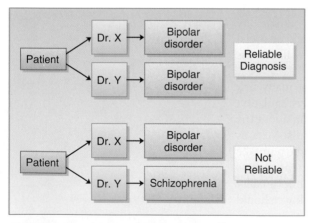

Figure 3.2 Interrater reliability. In this example, the diagnosis of the first patient is reliable—both clinicians diagnose bipolar disorder—whereas the diagnosis of the second is not reliable.

Reliability of the DSM Suppose you were concerned about your mental health, and you went to see two psychologists. Consider the distress you would feel if the two psychologists disagreed—one told you that you suffered from schizophrenia, and the other labeled you with bipolar disorder. Diagnostic systems must have high interrater reliability to be useful. Before DSM-III, reliability for DSM diagnoses was poor, mainly because the criteria for making a diagnosis were not clear (see Figure 3.2 for an illustration of interrater reliability).

The increased explicitness of the DSM criteria has improved reliability. Nonetheless, because clinicians might not rely on the criteria precisely, the reliability of the DSM in everyday usage may be a bit lower than that seen in research studies. Even when following criteria, there is some room for disagreement in DSM-IV-TR. Consider again the criteria for manic syndrome in Table 3.2. What does it mean to say that mood is abnormally elevated? Or when is "involvement in pleasurable activities with high potential for painful consequences" excessive? Such judgments set the stage for the insertion of cultural biases as well as the clinician's own personal ideas of what the average person should be doing at a given stage of life. Because different clinicians may adopt different definitions for symptoms like "elevated mood," achieving high reliability is likely to be a challenge.

How Valid Are Diagnostic Categories? Construct validity is considered the most important type of validity for diagnosis. The diagnoses of DSM are referred to as constructs because they are inferred, not proven, entities. Every diagnosis is based on a pattern of symptoms. With the exception of IQ tests for mental retardation or polysomnography for sleep disorders, we have no laboratory tests, neurobiological markers, or genetic indicators to use in making diagnoses. A diagnosis of schizophrenia, then, does not have the same status as a diagnosis of diabetes, where we have laboratory tests.

One way of thinking about diagnosis is to ask whether the system helps organize different observations (see Figure 3.3 for one example of how a diagnosis might help organize different observations). Diagnoses have construct validity if they help make accurate predictions. What types of predictions should a good diagnostic category facilitate? One would hope that a diagnosis would inform us about related clinical characteristics, such as poor social skills in people with schizophrenia. Similarly, one would hope that a diagnosis would inform us about what to expect next—the likely course of the disorder and response to different treatments. Perhaps most importantly, one would hope that the diagnosis relates to possible causes of the disorder, for example, a genetic predisposition or a biochemical imbalance. A diagnosis with strong construct validity should help predict a broad range of characteristics (see Figure 3.3).

The central question, then, is whether diagnoses made with the DSM criteria reveal anything useful about patients. We have organized this book around the major DSM diagnostic categories because we believe that they do indeed possess some construct validity. Certain categories have greater validity than others, however, and we will discuss some gaps in the validity of specific diagnostic categories in later chapters.

General Criticisms of Diagnosing Mental Illness

Although we described many advantages of diagnosis in the beginning of this chapter, it is also clear that diagnoses can have negative effects on a person. Consider how your life might be changed by receiving the diagnosis of schizophrenia. You might become worried that someone will recognize your disorder. Or you might fear the onset of another episode. You might worry about your ability to deal with new challenges. The fact that you are a "former mental patient" could have a stigmatizing effect. Friends and loved ones might treat you differently, and employment might be hard to find.

There is little doubt that diagnosis can have negative consequences. Research shows that many people view mentally ill patients negatively, and patients and their families often encounter stigma against mental illness (Wahl, 1999). As we discussed in Chapter 1, stigma of mental disorders remains a huge problem.

Another concern about diagnosis is that it can result in a loss of information about that person, because once classified by a diagnostic category, we may lose sight of the uniqueness of that person. Because of this concern, the American Psychological Association recommends that people avoid using words like "schizophrenic" or "depressive" to describe patients. Consider that we do not call people with medical illnesses by their disease (e.g., you aren't likely to hear someone with cancer described as the "canceric"). Rather, psychologists are encouraged to use phrases such as "a person with schizophrenia."

Even with more careful language, some maintain that diagnosis shapes us to focus on illnesses, and in doing so, to ignore important differences among people. Unfortunately, this criticism ignores a fundamental truth: It is human nature to categorize whenever we think about anything. Some would argue, then, that if we use categories anyway, it is best to systematically develop the categories. If one accepts this perspective, then the question is how well the current system does in grouping similar illnesses.

(a)

(b)

Figure 3.3 Construct validity: An example of the types of information a diagnosis might help predict.

Quick Summary

Despite the major improvements in the DSM, a number of problems remain. Some argue that there are too many diagnoses, and others challenge the use of a categorical rather than a dimensional approach to diagnoses. Reliability is substantially higher than it was for DSM-II, but there is still some disagreement across clinicians regarding some symptoms and diagnoses. Reliability in everyday usage may be lower than what is seen in formal research studies. Finally, the field as a whole faces a huge challenge; researchers are focused on validating this diagnostic system, by trying to identify the causal patterns, symptom patterns, and treatment that can be predicted by a given diagnosis. As research findings accumulate on whether each category has construct validity, this

is likely to shape the next edition of the DSM (see Focus on Discovery 3.3 for a discussion of likely changes in DSM-V). In sum, although the DSM is continually improving, it is far from perfect. We can expect more changes and refinements over the next several years. Regardless of the diagnostic system used, there are certain problems inherent in diagnosing people with mental illness; it is important to be aware of the potential stigma associated with diagnoses, or the tendency to ignore a person's strengths when focusing on diagnoses. APA recommends using phrases such as "person with schizophrenia" rather than "schizophrenic" as one way to be conscious that a person is much more than their diagnosis.

Check Your Knowledge 3.2

1. Some researchers have argued that we should "lump" diagnoses so that we have fewer categories. List three reasons why some think we should lump diagnoses.
2. Most of the axes in DSM-IV-TR are categorical, but one is dimensional. Which one is dimensional?

3. List three broad types of characteristics that a valid diagnosis should help predict:

    _____ _____ _____

4. In clinical practice, diagnostic reliability may be (higher or lower) than in research studies.

    _____

Psychological Assessment

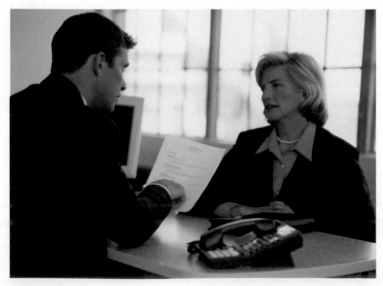

Although it is illegal to discriminate based on mental illness, many employers do so. Stigma must be considered when giving a person a psychiatric diagnosis. (Ryan McVay/PhotoDisc, Inc./Getty Images.)

In order to diagnose a mental disorder, mental health professionals can use a variety of assessment measures and tools, especially psychological ones. Beyond making a diagnosis, psychological assessment techniques are used in other important ways. For example, assessment methods are often used to identify appropriate therapeutic interventions. And repeated assessments are very useful in monitoring the effects of treatment over time. In addition, assessments are fundamental to conduct research on the causes of disorder.

We will see that beyond the basic interview, which is used in various guises almost universally, many of the assessment techniques stem from the paradigms presented in Chapter 2. We discuss here clinical interviews, measures for assessing stress, personality tests, including objective and projective tests, intelligence tests, and behavioral and cognitive assessment techniques. Although we present these methods individually, a complete psychological assessment of a person will often entail several assessment techniques. The data from the various techniques complement each other and provide a more complete picture of the person. In short, there is no one best assessment measure. Rather, using multiple techniques and multiple sources of information will provide the best assessment.

Focus on Discovery 3.3

Possible Changes for DSM-V

DSM-V is not likely to appear before 2010. But researchers are already considering possible changes. Some of the proposals are described below (Helmuth, 2003; Kupfer et al., 2002).

Personal Health Index. DSM-V may include a place to list the strengths of a patient.

Reorganizing Categories Based on Overlap. Currently, some diagnoses overlap so much that people have wondered whether they should be separated. For example, depression and anxiety often strike the same people, share many risk factors, and respond similarly to antidepressant medication. Do they still belong in separate categories? As well, overlap is a particular issue for personality disorders and disorders usually first diagnosed in infancy, childhood, or adolescence.

Dimensional Approach to Diagnoses. As described in the text, some have argued against a categorical approach to diagnosis. The next round of DSM may include specific dimensions for clinicians to evaluate. This approach is receiving considerable attention as a way to think about personality disorders.

Organizing Diagnoses by Causes. Currently, DSM-IV-TR defines diagnoses entirely on the basis of symptoms. Some have argued that recent advances in neuroscience and behavioral approaches to psychology could help us rethink this approach. For example, schizophrenia and schizotypal personality disorder share a great deal of genetic overlap; could these ties be reflected in the diagnostic system? Others have proposed organizing diagnoses based on parallels in neurotransmitter activity, temperament, emotion dysregulation, or social triggers. Most, however, agree that we still need much more knowledge to be able to use this type of system.

Defining Disability. DSM-IV-TR requires the presence of disability for a diagnosis to be made. Some have argued that we should be considering symptoms and disability separately, so that we can begin to understand what types of variables predict disability in the face of symptoms.

It isn't clear whether any of these changes will be adopted; substantial debate and research are likely to occur between then and now. Ongoing updates will be posted at http://dsm5.org/index.cfm. Some have argued that changes in the next round should be minor, and that science supports most of the current diagnoses.

Clinical Interviews

Most of us have probably been interviewed at one time or another, although the conversation may have been so informal that we did not regard it as an interview. To the layperson the word interview connotes a formal, highly structured conversation as in a job interview, but we find it useful to construe the term as any interpersonal encounter, conversational in style, in which one person, the interviewer, uses language as the principal means of finding out about another, the interviewee. There are both formal, structured clinical interviews as well as informal and less structured clinical interviews that are used in psychopathological assessment.

Characteristics of Clinical Interviews   One way in which a **clinical interview** is perhaps different from a casual conversation is the attention the interviewer pays to how the respondent answers questions—or does not answer them. For example, if a client is recounting marital conflicts, the clinician will generally be attentive to any emotion accompanying the comments. If the person does not seem upset about a difficult situation, the answers probably will be understood differently from how they would be interpreted if the person were crying or agitated while relating the story.

The interviewer's choice of paradigm influences the type of information sought, how it is obtained, and how it is interpreted. A psychoanalytically trained clinician is likely to remain skeptical of verbal reports because the analytic paradigm holds that the most significant aspects of a disturbed person's developmental history are repressed into the unconscious. By the same token, the cognitive behavioral clinician is likely to focus on current environmental conditions that can be related to changes in the person's behavior—for example, the circumstances under which the person becomes anxious as well as the thoughts the person articulates about the anxiety. Thus the informal clinical interview does not follow one prescribed course but varies with the paradigm adopted by the interviewer.

Great skill is necessary to carry out good clinical interviews, for they are usually conducted with people who are under considerable stress. Clinicians, regardless of their theoretical orientation, recognize the importance of establishing rapport with the client. The interviewer must obtain the trust of the person; it is naive to assume that a client will easily reveal information to another, even to an authority figure with the title "Doctor." Even a client who sincerely, perhaps desperately, wants to recount intensely personal problems to a professional may not be able to do so without help.

Most clinicians empathize with their clients in an effort to draw them out and to encourage them to elaborate on their concerns. An accurate summary statement of what the client has been saying can help sustain the momentum of talk about painful and possibly embarrassing events and feelings, and an accepting attitude toward personal disclosures dispels the fear that revealing "secrets of the heart" (London, 1964) to another human being will have disastrous consequences.

Interviews vary in the degree to which they are structured. In practice, most clinicians probably operate from only the vaguest outlines. Exactly how information is collected is left largely up to the particular interviewer and depends, too, on the responsiveness and responses of the interviewee. Through years of training and clinical experience, each clinician develops ways of asking questions with which he or she is comfortable and that seem to draw out the information that will be of maximum benefit to the client. Thus, to the extent that an interview is unstructured, the interviewer must rely on intuition and general experience. As a consequence, reliability for unstructured clinical interviews is probably lower than for structured interviews; that is, two interviewers may reach different conclusions about the same patient.

Structured Interviews   At times mental health professionals need to collect standardized information, particularly for making diagnostic judgments based on the DSM. To meet that need, investigators have developed structured interviews, such as the Structured Clinical Interview (SCID) for Axis I of DSM-IV (Spitzer, Gibbon, & Williams, 1996), which assists researchers and clinicians in making diagnostic decisions. A **structured interview** is one in which the questions are set out in a prescribed fashion for the interviewer.

The SCID is a branching interview, that is, the client's response to one question determines the next question that is asked. It also contains detailed instructions to the interviewer concerning when and how to probe in detail and when to go on to questions about another diagnosis. Most symptoms are rated on a three-point scale of severity, with instructions in the interview schedule for directly translating the symptom ratings into diagnoses. The initial questions pertaining to obsessive-compulsive disorder (discussed in Chapter 5) are presented in Figure 3.4. The interviewer begins by asking about obsessions. If the responses elicit a rating of 1 (absent), the interviewer turns to questions about compulsions. If the patient's responses again elicit a rating of 1, the interviewer is instructed to go to the questions for posttraumatic stress disorder. On the other hand, if positive responses (2 or 3) are elicited about obsessive-compulsive disorder, the interviewer continues with further questions about that problem.

Results of several studies demonstrate that the SCID achieves good interrater reliability for most diagnostic categories (see Table 3.4). Reliabilities are fair for schizophrenia, some anxiety disorders, and depressive personality disorders. Other structured interviews with good reliability have been developed for diagnosing personality

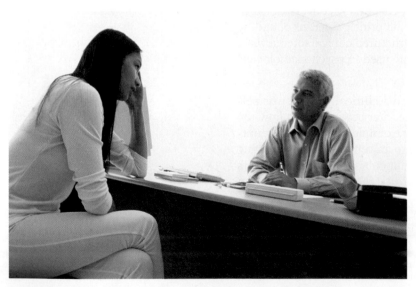

Structured interviews are widely used to make reliable diagnoses. (BSIP/Phototake.)

disorders and for more specific disorders, such as the anxiety disorders, and for diagnosing disorders of childhood (DiNardo et al., 1993; Shaffer et al., 2000). With adequate training, interrater reliability for structured interviews is generally good (Blanchard & Brown, 1998).

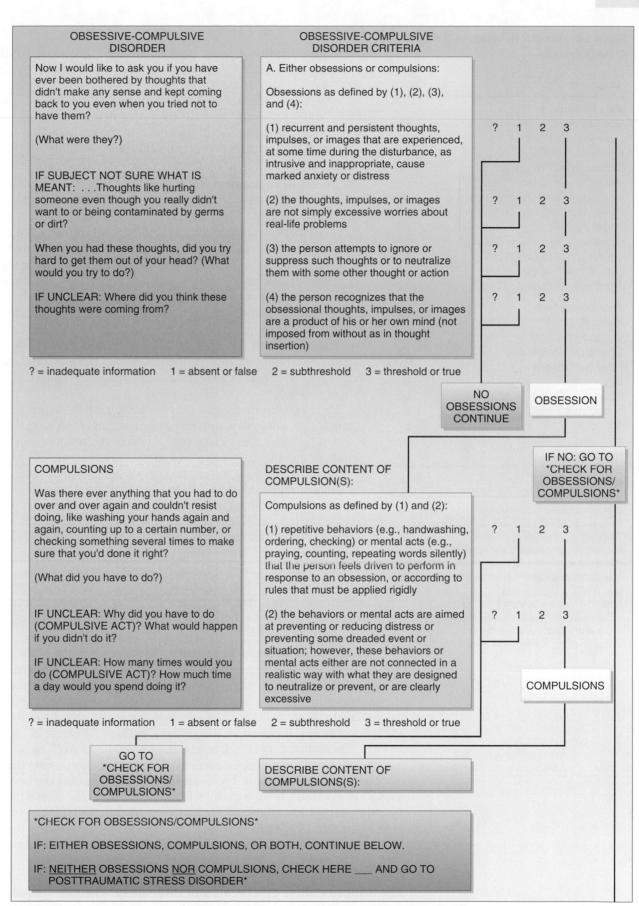

Figure 3.4 Sample item from the SCID. Reprinted by permission of New York State Psychiatric Institute Biometrics Research Division. Copyright © 1996 by the Board of Trustees of the Leland Stanford Junior University.

Table 3.4 Interrater Reliability of Selected DSM Diagnoses

Diagnosis	Kappa
Axis I disorders	
Major Depressive Disorder	.80
Dysthymic Disorder	.76
Bipolar Disorder	.84
Schizophrenia	.79
Alcohol Dependence/Abuse	1.0
Other Substance Dependence/Abuse	1.0
Panic Disorder	.65
Social Phobia	.63
Obsessive-Compulsive Disorder	.57
Generalized Anxiety Disorder	.63
Posttraumatic Stress Disorder	.88
Any Eating Disorder	.77
Axis II disorders	
Avoidant	.97
Dependent	.86
Obsessive-Compulsive	.83
Passive-Aggressive	.91
Depressive	.65
Paranoid	.93
Schizotypal	.91
Schizoid	.91
Histrionic	.92
Narcissistic	.98
Borderline	.91
Antisocial	.95

Source: Estimates for bipolar disorder are based on a study using DSM-III-R criteria (J. B. W. Williams et al., 1992), which are largely comparable to DSM-IV-TR. Estimates for schizophrenia are drawn from Flaum et al. (1998). Other Axis I estimates are drawn from Zanarini et al. (2000), and Axis II estimates are based on Maffei et al. (1997).

Note: The numbers here are a statistic called kappa, which measures the proportion of agreement over and above what would be expected by chance. Generally, kappas over .70 are considered good.

Assessment of Stress

Given the centrality of stress to nearly all the disorders we consider in this book, measuring stress is clearly important in the total assessment picture. Unfortunately, stress is difficult to define with precision. Broadly, **stress** can be conceptualized as the subjective experience of distress in response to perceived environmental problems. Various scales and methods have been developed to measure life stress. Here we examine three: the Social Readjustment Rating Scale, the Assessment of Daily Experience, and the Life Events and Difficulties Schedule.

The Social Readjustment Rating Scale   In the 1960s two researchers, Holmes and Rahe (1967), asked a large group of men in the military to describe life events they had encountered. Then they gave that list of life events to a large group of people and asked them to rate each item according to its intensity and the amount of time they thought they would need to adjust to it. Marriage was arbitrarily assigned a stress value of 500; all other items were then evaluated using this reference point. For example, an event twice as stressful as marriage would be assigned a value of 1,000, and an event one-fifth as stressful as marriage would be assigned a value of 100. The average ratings assigned to the events by the respondents in Holmes and Rahe's study are shown in Table 3.5. From this study Holmes and Rahe created the Social Readjustment Rating Scale (SRRS). A respondent checks off the life events experienced during the time period in question. Ratings are then totaled for all the events actually experienced to produce a Life Change Unit (LCU) score, a weighted sum of events.

The SRRS has been criticized because it contains items that are both the outcomes and the antecedents of stress with no attempt to separate the two. For example, the item "change in financial status" could be the result of a lost job after a factory closing or it could cause additional stress. Moreover, the SRRS was developed over 35 years ago based on the experiences of one group of men, rendering some of the original ratings of stressful life events potentially out of sync with the times. Two recent studies have given the 43 original events on the SRRS to community residents and found that indeed a number of the ratings changed compared to the original ratings from the 1960s, with some items being rated as less stressful (e.g., changing jobs), and others being rated as more stressful (e.g., change in financial status) (Miller & Rahe, 1997; Scully, Tosi, & Banning, 2000). Another criticism of the SRRS is that it relies on a retrospective method, asking participants to recall the stressful life events that they experienced over some past time period. Retrospective reports are subject to considerable distortion and forgetting.

Assessment of Daily Experience   Problems with the SRRS led Stone and Neale (1982) to develop a new assessment of stress called the Assessment of Daily Experience (ADE). Rather than relying on retrospective reports across long periods of time, the ADE allows persons to record and rate their daily experiences so that researchers can trace whether day-to-day stressors predict changes in symptoms. Retrospective recall of moods, thoughts, or experiences over time may be inaccurate. Consider, for example, how difficult it would be for you to recall accurately the exact thoughts you had a week earlier when you received a speeding ticket. Memory researchers have shown not only that simple forgetting leads to inaccurate retrospective recall, but also that recalled information can be biased. For example, a report of a person's mood is overly influenced by moods the person has experienced most recently or most strongly (e.g., Fredrickson & Kahneman, 1993). In the ADE, a day is used as the unit of analysis because a thorough characterization of this period should be possible without major retrospective-recall bias. Part of the ADE is shown in Figure 3.5. We will discuss how this measure relates to health in Chapter 7.

The Bedford College Life Events and Difficulties Schedule   Another assessment technique that is widely used to study life stressors and psychopathology is the Bedford

College Life Events and Difficulties Schedule (LEDS; Brown & Harris, 1978). The LEDS includes an interview, which covers over 200 different kinds of stressors. Because the interview is only semistructured, there is room to capture events that might only occur to a small number of people. The interviewer and the interviewee work collaboratively to produce a calendar of each of the major events within a given time period (see Figure 3.6 for an example). After the interview, raters evaluate the severity and several other dimensions of each stressor. The LEDS was designed to address a number of problems in life stress assessment, including the need to evaluate the importance of any given life event in the context of a person's life circumstances. For example, pregnancy might have quite a different meaning for an unmarried 14-year-old woman compared to a 38-year-old woman who has been trying to conceive for a long time. A second goal of the LEDS is to exclude life events that might just be consequences of symptoms. For example, if a person misses work because they are too depressed to get out of bed, consequences for job stability should really be seen as the symptoms of disorder rather than a triggering life event. Finally, the LEDS includes a set of strategies to carefully date when a life stressor happened. Using this more careful assessment method, researchers have found that life stressors are robust predictors of episodes of anxiety, depression, schizophrenia, and even the common cold (Brown & Harris, 1989a; Cohen et al., 1998).

Personality Tests

Psychological tests further structure the process of assessment. The two most common types of psychological tests are personality tests and intelligence tests. Here, we will examine the two types of personality tests: self-report personality inventories and projective personality tests.

Self-Report Personality Inventories   In a **personality inventory**, the person is asked to complete a self-report questionnaire indicating whether statements assessing habitual tendencies apply to him or her. When these tests are developed, they are typically administered to many people to analyze how certain kinds of people tend to respond. Statistical norms for the test can thereby be established. This process is called **standardization**. The responses of a particular person can then be compared with the statistical norms.

Perhaps the best known of these tests is the **Minnesota Multiphasic Personality Inventory (MMPI)**, developed in the early 1940s by Hathaway and McKinley (1943) and revised in 1989 (Butcher et al., 1989). Intended to serve as an inexpensive means of detecting psychopathology, the MMPI is called multiphasic because it was designed to detect a number of psychological problems. Over the years the MMPI has been widely used to screen large groups of people for whom clinical interviews are not feasible.

In developing the test, the investigators used several steps. First, many clinicians provided statements that they considered indicative of various mental problems. Second, patients diagnosed with particular disorders and people with no diagnoses were asked to rate whether hundreds of statements described them. Items were selected for the final version of the test if patients in one clinical group responded to them more often in a certain way than did those in other groups.

Table 3.5 Social Readjustment Rating Scale (SRRS)

Rank	Life Event	Mean Value
1	Death of spouse	100
2	Divorce	73
3	Marital separation	65
4	Jail term	63
5	Death of close family member	63
6	Personal injury or illness	53
7	Marriage	50[a]
8	Fired from work	47
9	Marital reconciliation	45
10	Retirement	45
11	Change in health of family member	44
12	Pregnancy	40
13	Sex difficulties	39
14	New family member	39
15	Business readjustment	39
16	Change in financial state	38
17	Death of close friend	37
18	Change to different line of work	36
19	Change in number of arguments with spouse	35
20	Mortgage over $10,000[b]	31
21	Foreclosure of mortgage or loan	30
22	Change in responsibilities at work	29
23	Child leaving home	29
24	Trouble with in-laws	29
25	Outstanding personal achievement	28
26	Spouse begins or stops work	26
27	Begin or end school	26
28	Change in living conditions	25
29	Revision of personal habits	24
30	Trouble with boss	23
31	Change in work hours or conditions	20
32	Change in residence	20
33	Change in schools	20
34	Change in recreation	19
35	Change in church activities	19
36	Change in social activities	18
37	Mortgage or loan less than $10,000[b]	17
38	Change in sleeping habits	16
39	Change in number of family get-togethers	15
40	Change in eating habits	15
41	Vacation	13
42	Christmas	12
43	Minor violations of the law	11

Source: From Holmes and Rahe, 1967.

[a]Marriage was arbitrarily assigned a stress value of 500; no event was found to be any more than twice as stressful. Here the values are reduced proportionally and range up to 100.

[b]In the mid-1960s, a mortgage like this was considered very large.

Reprinted from Holmes, T.H. and Rahe, R.H. (1967). The social readjustment rating scale. *Journal of Psychosomatic Research*,[11] 213–218 with permission from Elsevier.

WORK-RELATED ACTIVITIES

Concerning Boss, Supervisor, Upper Management, etc.

► Praised for a job well done ☐○○△ 01

► Criticism for job performance, lateness, etc. ☐○○△ 02

Concerning Co-workers, Employees, Supervisees, and/or Clients

► Positive emotional interactions and/or happenings with co-workers, employees, supervisees, and/or clients (work-related events which were fulfilling, etc.) ☐○○△ 03

► Negative emotional interactions and/or happenings with co-workers, employees, supervisees, and/or clients (work-related events which were frustrating, irritating, etc.) ☐○○△ 04

► Firing or disciplining (by Target) ☐○○△ 05

► Socializing with staff, co-workers, employees, supervisees, and/or clients ☐○○△ 06

General Happenings Concerning Target at Work

► Promotion, raise ☐○○△ 07

► Fired, quit, resigned ☐○○△ 08

► Some change in job (different from the above, i.e., new assignment, new boss, etc.) ☐○○△ 09

► Under a lot of pressure at work (impending deadlines, heavy workload, etc.) ☐○○△ 10

Figure 3.5 Sample page from the Assessment of Daily Experience scale (Stone & Neale, 1982). Respondents indicate whether an event occurred by circling the arrows to the left of the list of events. If an event has occurred, it is then rated on the dimensions of desirability, change, meaningfulness, and control using the enclosed spaces to the right.

Life Event Calendar

2005   J   F   M   12th   A   M   J

New Year's Day

January 23rd heard father was diagnosed with lung cancer

February 12th went to stay with father for his first radiation treatment

Valentine's Day

On March 20 heard that father not responding well to treatment

May 17th father died

Figure 3.6 Example of a life events timeline. The LEDS interview is designed to capture the major stressors a person has encountered in the past year.

With additional refinements, sets of these items were established as scales for determining whether a respondent should be diagnosed in a particular way. If a person answered a large number of the items in a scale in the same way as had a certain diagnostic group, his or her behavior was expected to resemble that of the particular diagnostic group. The 10 scales are described in Table 3.6.

The revised MMPI-2 (Butcher et al., 1989) has several changes designed to improve its validity and acceptability. The original sample of 60 years ago lacked representation of ethnic minorities, including African-Americans and Native Americans; its standardization sample was restricted to white men and women—essentially to Minnesotans. The new version was standardized using a sample that was much larger and more representative of 1980 U.S. census figures. Several items containing allusions to sexual adjustment, bowel and bladder functions, and excessive religiosity were removed because they were judged in some testing contexts to be needlessly intrusive and objectionable. Sexist wording was eliminated, along with outmoded idioms. Several new scales deal with substance abuse, Type A behavior (see p. 202), and marital problems.

Aside from these differences, MMPI-2 is otherwise quite similar to the original, having the same format, yielding the same scale scores and profiles (Ben-Porath & Butcher, 1989; Graham, 1988), and in general providing continuity with the vast literature already existing on the original MMPI (Graham, 1990). An extensive research literature shows that the MMPI-2 is reliable and has adequate criterion validity when it is related to diagnoses made by clinicians and to ratings made by spouses (Ganellan, 1996; Vacha-Hasse et al., 2001).

Like many other personality inventories, the MMPI-2 can now be administered by computer, and there are several commercial MMPI-2 services that score the test and provide narratives about the respondent. Of course, the validity and usefulness of the printouts are only as good as the program, which in turn is only as good as the competency and experience of the psychologist who wrote it. Figure 3.7 shows a hypothetical profile. Such profiles can be used in conjunction with a therapist's evaluation to help diagnose a client, assess personality functioning and coping style, and identify likely obstacles to treatment.

You may wonder whether it would be easy to fake answers that suggest no psychopathology. For example, a superficial knowledge of contemporary abnormal psychology could alert someone that in order to be regarded as psychologically healthy, he or she must not admit to worrying a great deal about hearing voices emanating from microwave ovens.

As shown in Table 3.6, the test designers have included as part of the MMPI-2 several so-called validity scales designed to detect deliberately faked responses. In one of these, the lie scale, a series of statements sets a trap for the person who is trying to look too good. An item on the lie scale might be, "I read the newspaper editorials every day." The assumption is that few people would be able to endorse such a statement honestly. Persons who endorse a large number of the statements in the lie scale might be attempting to present

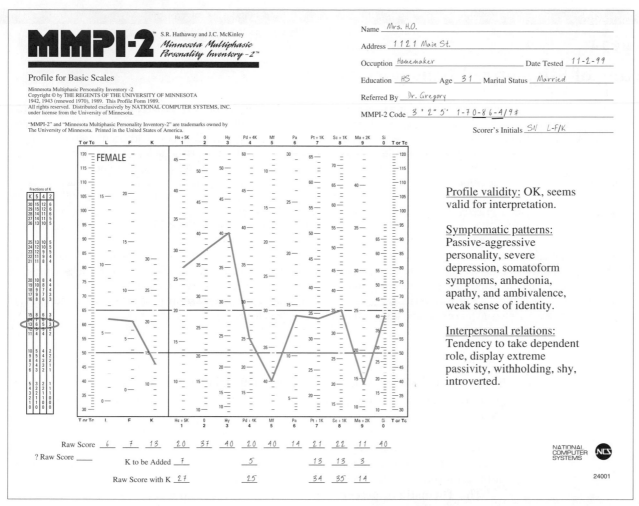

MMPI-2™ S.R. Hathaway and J.C. McKinley
Minnesota Multiphasic Personality Inventory-2™

Profile for Basic Scales

Minnesota Multiphasic Personality Inventory -2
Copyright © by THE REGENTS OF THE UNIVERSITY OF MINNESOTA
1942, 1943 (renewed 1970), 1989. This Profile Form 1989.
All rights reserved. Distributed exclusively by NATIONAL COMPUTER SYSTEMS, INC.
under license from the University of Minnesota.

"MMPI-2" and "Minnesota Multiphasic Personality Inventory-2" are trademarks owned by
The University of Minnesota. Printed in the United States of America.

Name _Mrs. H.O._
Address _1121 Main St._
Occupation _Homemaker_ Date Tested _11-2-99_
Education _HS_ Age _31_ Marital Status _Married_
Referred By _Dr. Gregory_
MMPI-2 Code _3 ' 2 " 5 ' 1-7 0-8 6-4/9 #_
Scorer's Initials _SN L-F/K_

FEMALE

Profile validity: OK, seems valid for interpretation.

Symptomatic patterns: Passive-aggressive personality, severe depression, somatoform symptoms, anhedonia, apathy, and ambivalence, weak sense of identity.

Interpersonal relations: Tendency to take dependent role, display extreme passivity, withholding, shy, introverted.

	L	F	K	Hs+5K 1	D 2	Hy 3	Pd+4K 4	Mf 5	Pa 6	Pt+1K 7	Sc+1K 8	Ma+2K 9	Si 0	
Raw Score	6	7	13	20	37	40	20	40	14	21	22	11	40	
K to be Added				7			5			13	13	3		
Raw Score with K				27			25			34	35	14		

? Raw Score ____

NATIONAL COMPUTER SYSTEMS NCS

24001

Figure 3.7 Hypothetical MMPI-2 profile.

themselves in a good light. High scores on the F scale also discriminate between people trying to fake psychopathology and real patients (Bagby et al., 2002). If a person obtains high scores on the lie or F scale, their profile might be viewed with skepticism. People who are aware of these validity scales, however, can effectively fake a normal profile (Baer & Sekirnjak, 1997; Walters & Clopton, 2000). In most testing circumstances, however, people do not want to falsify their responses, because they want to be helped. Focus on Discovery 3.4 discusses other issues surrounding the validity of self-report questionnaires.

Projective Personality Tests A **projective test** is a psychological assessment tool in which a set of standard stimuli—inkblots or drawings—ambiguous enough to allow variation in responses is presented to the person. The assumption is that because the stimulus materials are unstructured and ambiguous, the person's responses will be determined primarily by unconscious processes and will reveal his or her true attitudes, motivations, and modes of behavior. This notion is referred to as the **projective hypothesis**.

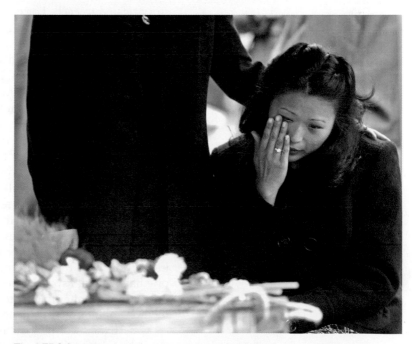

The LEDS focuses on major stressors, such as deaths, job losses, and romantic breakups. (Bob Falcetti Reportage/Getty Images News and Sport Services.)

Focus on Discovery 3.4

Underreporting of Stigmatized Behaviors

A survey of self-reported drug use, sexual behavior, and violence high-lights the importance of the setting in establishing the validity of what people will tell about their actions and attitudes (Turner et al., 1998). Findings from self-report questionnaires were compared with results from a novel self-report method—boys and young men (ages 15 to 19) listened by themselves through headphones to questions probing risky, often stigmatized behavioral practices and then indicated whether they had engaged in those behaviors by pressing keys on a computer keyboard labeled Yes and No.

Compared to a matched control group who responded to the same items on a paper-and-pencil questionnaire, many more of the computer respondents admitted to having engaged in a range of high risk behaviors. For example, they were almost 14 times more likely to report having sexual intercourse with an intravenous drug user (2.8 percent versus 0.2 percent), more than twice as likely to have been paid for sex (3.8 percent versus 1.6 percent), and almost twice as likely to have used cocaine (6.0 percent versus 3.3 percent). (One can safely assume that the differences would have been even greater if the boys had been interviewed by an adult researcher facing them across a table, another method that has been used to collect such survey data.) No differences showed up on questions directed at nonstigmatized or legal behaviors such as having sexual intercourse with a female in the preceding year (47.8 percent for computer users versus 49.6 percent for paper-and-pencil question-naires) or drinking alcohol in the past year (69.2 percent versus 65.9 percent).

If these findings show nothing else, they suggest strongly that the frequencies of problematic behavior as determined by questionnaire or interview studies may be gross underestimates and that social problems such as needle sharing and unsafe sex may be considerably more serious than most people believe.

If a patient reports seeing eyes in an ambiguous inkblot, for example, the projective hypothesis might be that the patient tends toward paranoia. As you might have guessed, projective techniques are derived from the psychoanalytic paradigm. The use of projective tests assumes that the respondent would be either unable or unwilling to express his or her true feelings if asked directly. Psychoanalytically oriented clinicians often favor such tests, a tendency that is consistent with the psychoanalytic assumption that people defend against unpleasant thoughts and feelings by repressing them into the unconscious.

The **Thematic Apperception Test (TAT)** is a well-known projective test. In this test a person is shown a series of black-and-white pictures one by one and asked to tell a story related to each. For example, a patient seeing a picture of a boy observing a youth baseball game from behind a fence may tell a story that contains angry references to the boy's parents. The clinician may, through the projective hypothesis, infer that the patient harbors resentment toward his or her parents.

The **Rorschach Inkblot Test** is perhaps the best-known projective technique. In the Rorschach test, a person is shown 10 inkblots (for similar inkblots, see Figure 3.8), one at a time, and asked to tell what the blots look like. Half the inkblots are in black, white, and shades of gray, two also have red splotches, and three are in pastel colors.

Exner (1978) designed one commonly used system for scoring the Rorschach test, which concentrates more on the perceptual and cognitive patterns in a person's responses (Exner, 1978). The person's responses are viewed as a sample of how he or she perceptually and cognitively organizes real-life situations (Exner, 1986). For example, Erdberg and Exner (1984) concluded from the research literature that respondents who express a great deal of human movement in their Rorschach responses (e.g., "The man is running to catch a plane.") tend to use inner resources when coping with their needs, whereas those whose Rorschach responses involve color ("The red spot is a kidney.") are more likely to seek interaction with the environment. Rorschach suggested this approach to scoring in his original manual, *Psychodiagnostics: A Diagnostic Test Based on Perception* (1921), but he died only 8 months after publishing his 10 inkblots and his immediate followers devised other methods of interpreting the test.

The Exner scoring system for the Rorschach test yields scores that can then be validated by relating them to what they are supposed to predict, for example, the schizophrenia index to schizophrenia or the depression index to depression. The system also has norms, although the sample on which they are based was rather small and did not

Table 3.6 Typical Clinical Interpretations of Items Similar to Those on the MMPI-2

Scale	Sample Item	Interpretation
? (cannot say)	This is merely the number of items left unanswered or marked both true and false.	A high score indicates evasiveness, reading difficulties, or other problems that could invalidate the results of the test. A very high score could also suggest severe depression or obsessional tendencies.
L (Lie)	I approve of every person I meet. (True)	Person is trying to look good, to present self as someone with an ideal personality.
F (Infrequency)	Everything tastes sweet. (True)	Person is trying to look abnormal, perhaps to ensure getting special attention from the clinician.
K (Correction)	Things couldn't be going any better for me. (True)	Person is guarded, defensive in taking the test, wishes to avoid appearing incompetent or poorly adjusted.
1. Hs (Hypochondriasis)	I am seldom aware of tingling feelings in my body. (False)	Person is overly sensitive to and concerned about bodily sensations as signs of possible physical illness.
2. D (Depression)	Life usually feels worthwhile to me. (False)	Person is discouraged, pessimistic, sad, self-deprecating, feeling inadequate.
3. Hy (Hysteria)	My muscles often twitch for no apparent reason. (True)	Person has somatic complaints unlikely to be due to physical problems; also tends to be demanding and histrionic.
4. Pd (Psychopathy)	I don't care about what people think of me. (True)	Person expresses little concern for social mores, is irresponsible, has only superficial relationships.
5. Mf (Masculinity–Femininity)	I like taking care of plants and flowers. (True, female)	Person shows nontraditional gender characteristics (e.g., men with high scores tend to be artistic and sensitive; women with high scores tend to be rebellious and assertive).
6. Pa (Paranoia)	If they were not afraid of being caught, most people would lie and cheat. (True)	Person tends to misinterpret the motives of others, is suspicious and jealous, vengeful and brooding.
7. Pt (Psychasthenia)	I am not as competent as most other people I know. (True)	Person is overanxious, full of self-doubts, moralistic, and generally obsessive-compulsive.
8. Sc (Schizophrenia)	I sometimes smell things others don't sense. (True)	Person has bizarre sensory experiences and beliefs, is socially reclusive.
9. Ma (Hypomania)	Sometimes I have a strong impulse to do something that others will find appalling. (True)	Person has overly ambitious aspirations and can be hyperactive, impatient, and irritable
10. Si (Social Introversion).	Rather than spend time alone, I prefer be around other people. (False)	Person is very modest and shy, preferring solitary activities.

Source: Hathaway and McKinley (1943); revised by Butcher et al. (1989).

Note: The first four scales assess the validity of the test; the numbered scales are the clinical or content scales.

represent different ethnicities and cultures well. Though many clinical practitioners still rely on the projective hypothesis in analyzing Rorschach responses, Exner's work has attracted a good deal of attention from academic researchers. Regarding its reliability and validity, this work has enthusiastic supporters as well as equally harsh critics (e.g., Hunsley & Bailey, 1999; Lilienfeld, Wood, & Garb, 2000). Perhaps trying to make a blanket statement about the validity of the Exner system for scoring the Rorschach is not the right approach. It may have more validity in some issues than in others. For example, some evidence suggests that the Rorschach may have validity in identifying schizophrenia (Lilienfeld et al., 2000). The utility of the Rorschach in this case can probably be attributed to the fact that a person's responses on the test are highly related to the communication disturbances that are an important symptom of schizophrenia. In this case, however, it is unclear whether the Rorschach provides information that could not be obtained more simply—for example, through an interview.

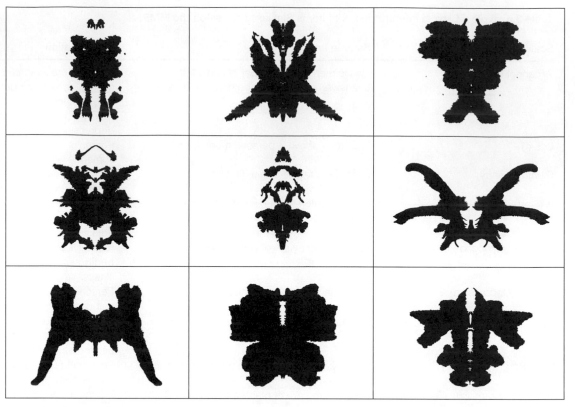

Figure 3.8 In the Rorschach test the client is shown a series of inkblots and is asked what the blots look like.

During a ride in the country with his two children, Hermann Rorschach (1884–1922), Swiss psychiatrist, noticed that what they saw in the clouds reflected their personalities. From this observation came the famous inkblot test. (Courtesy National Library of Medicine.)

Intelligence Tests

Alfred Binet, a French psychologist, originally constructed mental tests to help the Parisian school board predict which children were in need of special schooling. Intelligence testing has since developed into one of the largest psychological industries. An **intelligence test**, often referred to as an IQ test, is a way of assessing a person's current mental ability. Individually administered tests, such as the Wechsler Adult Intelligence Scale, 3rd edition (WAIS-III), the Wechsler Intelligence Scale for Children, 3rd edition (1991) (WISC-III), and the Stanford–Binet, 4th edition (SB:IV) are all based on the assumption that a detailed sample of a person's current intellectual functioning can predict how well he or she will perform in school. Like personality inventoriers, intelligence tests are standardized.

Beyond predicting school performance, intelligence tests are also used in other ways:

- in conjunction with achievement tests, to diagnose learning disabilities and to identify areas of strengths and weaknesses for academic planning;
- to help determine whether a person is mentally retarded;
- to identify intellectually gifted children so that appropriate instruction can be provided them in school;
- as part of neuropsychological evaluations, for example, periodically testing a person believed to be suffering from a degenerative dementia so that deterioration of mental ability can be followed over time.

IQ tests tap several functions asserted to constitute intelligence, including language skills, abstract thinking, nonverbal reasoning, visual-spatial skills, attention and concentration, and speed of processing. Scores on most IQ tests are standardized so that 100 is the mean and 15 or 16 is the standard deviation (a measure of how scores are dispersed above and below the average). Approximately 65 percent of the population receives scores between 85 and 115. Those with a score below 70 are two standard deviations below the mean of the population and are considered to have "significant subaverage general intellectual functioning." Those with scores above 130 (two standard deviations above the mean) are considered "intellectually gifted." Approximately 2.5 percent of the population falls at each of these extremes. In Chapter 14 we discuss people whose IQ falls at the low end of the distribution.

IQ tests are highly reliable (e.g., Canivez & Walkins, 1998) and have good criterion validity. For example, they distinguish between people who are intellectually gifted and those with mental retardation and between people with different occupations or levels of educational attainment (Reynolds et al., 1997). They also predict educational attainment and occupational success (Hanson, Hunsley, & Parker, 1988), at least among Caucasians (see below for a discussion of cultural bias in assessment). Though the correlations between IQ scores and school performance are statistically significant, IQ tests explain only a small part of school performance; much more is unexplained by IQ test scores than is explained.

Regarding construct validity, it is important to keep in mind that IQ tests measure only what psychologists consider intelligence. Factors other than what we think of as pure intelligence play an important role in how people will do in school, such as family and circumstances, motivation to do well, levels of performance anxiety, and difficulty of the curriculum. Another factor relevant to IQ test performance is called stereotype threat. It suggests that the social stigma of poor intellectual performance borne by some groups (e.g., African Americans do poorly on IQ tests; women perform more poorly than men on mathematics tests) actually interferes with their performance on these tests. In one study demonstrating this phenomenon, groups of men and women were given a difficult mathematics test. In one condition the participants were told that men scored higher than women on the test they were going to take (stereotype threat condition), while in the other condition they were told there were no gender differences in performance on the test. Only when the test was described as yielding gender differences did the women perform more poorly than men (Spencer, Steele, & Quinn, 1999).

Unfortunately, awareness of these stereotypes develops early. For example, a recent study revealed that children develop awareness of stereotypes regarding ethnicity and ability between the ages of 6 and 10, with 93 percent of children being aware of such stereotypes by age 10 (McKown & Weinstein, 2003). Evidence for stereotype threat among children has also been found. In the McKown and Weinstein (2003) study, children were also asked to complete a puzzle task. Half of the children received instructions that the task reflected their ability (stereotype threat condition), and half the children received instructions that the test did not reflect their ability. Looking only at African-American children who were aware of the stereotype about ethnicity and ability yielded evidence of stereotype threat. Specifically, those children who received the ability instructions performed more poorly on the puzzle task than the children who did not, suggesting that the instructions activated the stereotype and thus influenced their performance.

John Exner developed the most widely used scoring system for the Rorschach test (Courtesy Dr. John E. Exner.)

Behavioral and Cognitive Assessment

Thus far, we have discussed assessment methods that measure underlying personality structures and intellectual ability. Behavioral and cognitively oriented clinicians assess other characteristics, including:

- aspects of the environment that might contribute to symptoms (e.g., an office location next to a noisy hallway might contribute to concentration problems),
- characteristics of the person (e.g., a client's fatigue may be caused in part by a cognitive tendency toward self-deprecation manifested in such statements as "I never do anything right, so what's the point in trying?"),
- the frequency and form of problematic behaviors (e.g., procrastination taking the form of missing important deadlines), and
- consequences of problem behaviors (e.g., when a client avoids a feared situation, his or her partner offers sympathy and excuses, thereby unwittingly keeping the client from facing up to his or her fears).

The French psychologist Alfred Binet developed the first IQ test to predict how well children would do in school. (Courtesy Psychology Archive, University of Akron.)

Behavioral assessment often involves direct observation of behavior, as in this case, where the observer is behind a one-way mirror. (Jeff Greenberg/PhotoEdit.)

The hope is that understanding these aspects of cognition and behavior will guide the clinician toward more effective intervention targets.

The information necessary for a behavioral or cognitive assessment is gathered by several methods, including direct observation of behavior in real life as well as in contrived settings, interviews and self-report measures, and various other methods of cognitive assessment (Bellack & Hersen, 1998). We turn to these now.

Direct Observation of Behavior It is not surprising that behavior therapists have paid considerable attention to careful observation of overt behavior in a variety of settings, but it should not be assumed that they simply go out and observe. Like other scientists, they try to fit events into a framework consistent with their points of view. In formal **behavioral observation**, the observer divides the sequence of behavior into various parts that make sense within a learning framework, including such things as the antecedents and consequences of particular behaviors. Behavioral observation is also often linked to intervention (O'Brien & Haynes, 1995). The behavioral clinician's way of conceptualizing a situation typically implies a way to try to change it.

It is difficult to observe most behavior as it actually takes place, and little control can be exercised over where and when it may occur. For this reason, many therapists contrive artificial situations in their consulting rooms or in a laboratory so they can observe how a client or a family acts under certain conditions. For example, Barkley (1981) had a mother and her hyperactive child spend time together in a laboratory living room, complete with sofas and a television set. The mother was given a list of tasks for the child to complete, such as picking up toys or doing arithmetic problems. Observers behind a one-way mirror watched the proceedings and reliably coded the child's reactions to the mother's efforts to control as well as the mother's reactions to the child's compliant or noncompliant responses. These **behavioral assessment** procedures yielded data that could be used to measure the effects of treatment.

Self-Observation Behavior therapists and researchers have also asked individuals to observe and track their own behavior and responses. This approach is called **self-monitoring**. Self-monitoring is used to collect a wide variety of data of interest to both clinicians and researchers, including moods, stressful experiences, coping behaviors, and thoughts (Hurlburt, 1979; Stone et al., 1998).

Another method of self-observation is called **ecological momentary assessment** or **EMA**. EMA involves the collection of data in real time as opposed to the more usual methods of having people reflect back over some time period and report on recently experienced thoughts, moods, or stressors. The methods for implementing EMA range from having people complete diaries at specified times during the day (perhaps signaled by a wristwatch that beeps at those times) to supplying them with PDAs (personal data assistants, like the Palm Pilot) that not only signal when reports are to be made but also allow them to enter their responses directly into the computer (Stone & Shiffman, 1994).

Given the problems in retrospective recall, some theories in the field of psychopathology can best be tested using EMA. For example, current theories of both anxiety disorders and depression propose that emotional reactions to a stressor are determined by thoughts that the stressor elicits. It is unlikely, however, that these thoughts can be recalled accurately in retrospect.

EMA also may be useful in clinical settings, revealing information that traditional assessment procedures might miss. For example, Hurlburt (1997) describes a case of a man with severe attacks of anxiety. In clinical interviews, the patient reported that his life was going very well, that he loved his wife and children, and that his work was both financially and personally rewarding. No cause of the anxiety attacks could be discerned. The man was asked to record his thoughts as he went about his daily routine. Surprisingly, about a third of his thoughts were concerned with annoyance with his children (e.g., "He left the fence gate open again and the dog got out").

> *Once the high frequency of annoyance thoughts was pointed out to him, he . . . accepted that he was in fact often annoyed with his children. However, he believed that anger at his children was sinful and felt unfit as a father for having such thoughts and feelings. . . . [He] entered into brief therapy that focused on the normality of being annoyed by one's children and on the important distinction between being annoyed and acting out aggressively. Almost immediately, his anxiety attacks disappeared. (Hurlburt, 1997, p. 944)*

Although some research indicates that self-monitoring or EMA can provide accurate measurement of such behavior, considerable research indicates that behavior may be altered by the very fact that it is being self-monitored—that is, the self-consciousness required for self-monitoring affects the behavior (Haynes & Horn, 1982). The phenomenon wherein behavior changes because it is being observed is called **reactivity**. In general, desirable behavior, such as engaging in social conversation, often increases in frequency when self-monitored (Nelson, Lipinski, & Black, 1976), whereas behavior the person wishes to reduce, such as cigarette smoking, diminishes (McFall & Hammen, 1971). Therapeutic interventions can take advantage of the reactivity that is a natural by-product of self-monitoring. Smoking, anxiety, depression, and health problems all have undergone beneficial changes in self-monitoring studies (Febbraro & Clum, 1998).

Cognitive-Style Questionnaires Cognitive questionnaires tend to be used to help plan appropriate targets for treatment as well as to determine whether clinical interventions are helping to change overly negative thought patterns. In format, some of these questionnaires are similar to the personality tests we have already described.

Self-monitoring generally leads to increase in desirable behaviors and decreases in undesirable ones. (Courtesy invivodata, Inc.)

One self-report questionnaire that was developed based on Beck's theory is the Dysfunctional Attitude Scale (DAS). The DAS contains items such as "People will probably think less of me if I make a mistake" (Weissman & Beck, 1978). Supporting construct validity, researchers have shown that they can differentiate between depressed and nondepressed people on the basis of their scores on this scale and that scores decrease (i.e., improve) after interventions that relieve depression. Furthermore, the DAS relates to other aspects of cognition in ways consistent with Beck's theory. For example, it correlates with another self-report instrument called the Cognitive Bias Questionnaire (Krantz & Hammen, 1979), which measures the ways in which people distort information to be more negative. A body of data is helping to establish both the validity and the reliability of these questionnaires (Glass & Arnkoff, 1997).

Capturing Thoughts in a Specific Situation As mentioned, people's responses to inventories and to questions asked by interviewers about their thoughts in past situations may well be different from what they would report were they able to do so in the immediate circumstance. The Articulated Thoughts in Simulated Situations (ATSS) method of Davison and his associates (Davison, Robins, & Johnson, 1983) is one way to assess immediate

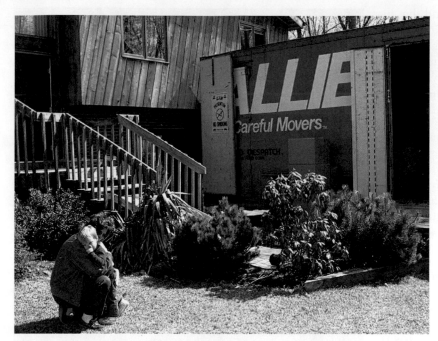

Cognitive assessment focuses on the person's perception of a situation, realizing that the same event can be perceived differently. For example, moving could be regarded as a very negative event or a very positive one, resulting in very different levels of stress. (Renata Hiller.)

thoughts in specific situations. In this procedure, a person pretends that he or she is in a situation, such as listening to a teaching assistant criticize a term paper. Presented on audiotape, the scene pauses every 10 or 15 seconds. During the ensuing 30 seconds of silence, the participant talks aloud about whatever is going through his or her mind in reaction to the words just heard. One taped scene in which the participant overhears two pretend acquaintances criticizing him or her includes the following segments.

First acquaintance: He certainly did make a fool of himself over what he said about religion. I just find that kind of opinion very closed-minded and unaware. You have to be blind to the facts of the universe to believe that. [Thirty-second pause for subject's response.]

Second acquaintance: What really bugs me is the way he expresses himself. He never seems to stop and think, but just blurts out the first thing that comes into his head. [Thirty-second pause.]

Participants readily become involved in the pretend situations, regarding them as credible and realistic. Furthermore, the responses of participants can be reliably coded (Davison et al., 1983). Using this method, research has shown that socially anxious therapy patients articulate thoughts of greater unfounded negativity (e.g., "Oh God, I wish I were dead. I'm so embarrassed.") than do nonanxious controls (e.g., Davison & Zighelboim, 1987). In a study that directly compared ATSS data with overt behavior (Davison, Haaga, et al., 1991), the more anxiously subjects behaved on a timed behavioral checklist measure of public-speaking anxiety, the less capable they felt they were while articulating thoughts in a stressful, simulated speech-giving situation. These and related findings (Davison, Navarre, & Vogel, 1995) indicate that this method ferrets out people's thinking about both inherently bothersome and "objectively" innocuous situations.

Table 3.7   Major Psychological Assessment Methods

Interviews	Clinical interviews	The clinician attempts to learn about the patient's problems through conversation. The paradigm of the interviewer shapes the content of the interview.
	Structured interviews	Questions to be asked are spelled out in detail in a booklet; most often used for gathering information to make a diagnosis.
Stress measures		Self-report scales or interviews that assess stressful events and responses to these events
Psychological tests	Personality tests	Self-report questionnaires, used to assess either a broad range of characteristics, as in the MMPI-2, or a single characteristic, such as dysfunctional attitudes.
	Projective tests	Ambiguous stimuli, such as inkblots (Rorschach test), are presented and responses are thought to be determined by unconscious processes.
	Intelligence tests	Assessments of current mental functioning. Used to predict school performance and diagnose mental retardation.
Direct observation		Used by behavioral clinicians to identify problem behaviors as well as antecedents and consequences. Also used to assess cognition, as in the Articulated Thoughts in Simulated Situations technique.
Self-observation		Individuals monitor and keep records of their own behavior; as in ecological momentary assessment.

Quick Summary

The psychological assessments we have described are summarized in Table 3.7. A comprehensive psychological assessment draws on many different methods and tests. Clinicians often begin with an interview, particularly to help form a diagnosis. These can be structured, with the questions predetermined and followed in a certain order, or unstructured to follow more closely what the client tells the interviewer. Structured interviews are more reliable. Rapport is important to establish regardless of the type of interview.

Stress can be assessed via a checklist of life events as in the SRRS, by assessing daily reports of thoughts and feelings such as with the Assessment of Daily Experience (ADE), or by a semistructured interview that captures the importance of any given life event in the context of a person's life circumstances, as in the LEDS.

The MMPI-2 is a standardized and objective personality inventory. The test has good reliability and validity and is widely used. Projective personality tests, like the Rorschach or TAT, are not as widely used today, likely due to their poor validity. Reliability can be achieved using scoring systems such as Exner's.

Intelligence tests have been used for a number of years and are quite reliable. Like any test, there are limits to what an IQ test can tell a clinician or researcher. Further, cultural bias is a salient issue with these tests, perhaps due to stereotypes about ethnicity and intelligence.

Direct observation of behavior can be very useful in assessment, though it can take more time than a self-report inventory. Other behavioral and cognitive assessment methods include ecological momentary assessment (EMA) and the Articulated Thoughts in Simulated Situations (ATSS). All assessment instruments have advantages and disadvantages, including considerations of reliability, ease of administration and scoring, and relevance to the particular clinical problem.

Check Your Knowledge 3.3

True or false?
1. If conducted properly, a psychological assessment typically includes just one measure most appropriate to the client.
2. Unstructured interviews may have poor reliability, but they can still be quite valuable in a psychological assessment.
3. The MMPI-2 contains scales to detect whether someone is faking their answers.
4. The projective hypothesis is based on the idea that a person does not really know what is bothering him or her; thus a subtler means of assessment is needed.
5. Intelligence tests are highly reliable.
6. EMA is a method to assess unwanted impulses.

Neurobiological Assessment

For many years researchers and clinicians have attempted to study the functioning of the brain and other parts of the nervous system in their efforts to understand both normal and abnormal psychological functioning. Recall from Chapters 1 and 2 that throughout history people interested in psychopathology have assumed, quite reasonably, that some abnormal behavior is likely to be due to or at least reflected in malfunctions of the brain. We turn now to contemporary work in neurobiological assessment. We'll look at four areas in particular: brain imaging, neurotransmitter assessment, neuropsychological assessment, and psychophysiological assessment (see Table 3.8 for a summary of these methods).

Brain Imaging: "Seeing" the Brain

Because many behavioral problems can be brought on by brain dysfunction, neurological tests, such as checking the reflexes, examining the retina for any indication of blood-vessel damage, and evaluating motor coordination and perception, have been used for many years to identify brain dysfunction. More recently, devices have become available that allow clinicians and researchers a much more direct look at both the structure and functioning of the brain.

Table 3.8 Neurobiological Assessment Methods

Brain imaging	CT and MRI scans reveal the structure of the brain. PET reveals brain function and to a lesser extent, brain structure. fMRI is used to study both brain structure and brain function.
Neurotransmitter assessment	Includes postmortem analysis of neurotransmitters and receptors, assays of metabolites of neurotransmitters, and PET scans of receptors.
Neuropsychological assessment	Behavioral tests such as the Halstead–Reitan and Luria–Nebraska assess abilities such as motor speed, memory, and spatial ability. Deficits on particular tests help point to an area of brain dysfunction.
Psychophysiological assessment	Includes measures of electrical activity in the autonomic nervous system, such as skin conductance, or in the central nervous system, such as the EEG.

These two CT scans show a horizontal slice through the brain. The one on the left is normal; the one on the right has a tumor on the left side. (Dan McCoy/Rainbow.)

Computerized axial tomography, the **CT** or **CAT scan**, helps to assess structural brain abnormalities (and is able to image other parts of the body for medical purposes). A moving beam of X-rays passes into a horizontal cross section of the person's brain, scanning it through 360 degrees; the moving X-ray detector on the other side measures the amount of radioactivity that penetrates, thus detecting subtle differences in tissue density. A computer uses the information to construct a two-dimensional, detailed image of the cross section, giving it optimal contrasts. Then the person's head is moved, and the machine scans another cross section of the brain. The resulting images can show the enlargement of ventricles (which signals degeneration of tissue) and the locations of tumors and blood clots.

Newer computer-based devices for seeing the living brain include **magnetic resonance imaging**, also known as **MRI**, which is superior to the CT scan because it produces pictures of higher quality and does not rely on even the small amount of radiation required by a CT scan. In MRI the person is placed inside a large, circular magnet, which causes the hydrogen atoms in the body to move. When the magnetic force is turned off, the atoms return to their original positions and thereby produce an electromagnetic signal. These signals are then read by the computer and translated into pictures of brain tissue. This technique provides an enormous advance. For example, it has allowed physicians to locate and remove delicate brain tumors that would have been considered inoperable without such sophisticated methods of viewing brain structures.

Functional magnetic resonance images (fMRI). [From J. E. McDowell et al., *Biological Psychiatry,* 51, 216–223 (2002).]

More recently, a modification called **fMRI (functional MRI)** has been developed that allows researchers to measure both brain structure and brain function. This technique takes MRI pictures so quickly that metabolic changes can be measured, providing a picture of the brain at work rather than of its structure alone. For example, researchers can measure how brain activity changes while a person is doing different tasks, such as viewing an emotional film, completing a memory test, looking at a visual puzzle, or hearing and learning a list of words. fMRI measures blood flow in the brain, and this is called the **BOLD** signal, which stands for blood oxygenation level dependent. As neurons fire, blood flow increases to that area. Therefore, blood flow in a particular region of the brain is a reasonable proxy for neural activity in that brain region.

Positron emission tomography, the **PET scan**, a more expensive and invasive procedure, also allows measurement of both brain structure and brain function, although the measurement of brain structure is not as precise as with MRI or fMRI and the time period captured is longer. A substance used by the brain is labeled with a short-lived radioactive isotope and injected into the bloodstream. The radioactive molecules of the substance emit a particle called a positron, which quickly collides with an electron. A pair of high-energy light particles shoot out from the skull in opposite directions and are detected by the scanner. The computer analyzes millions of such recordings and converts them into a picture of the functioning brain. The images are in color; fuzzy spots of lighter and warmer colors are areas in which metabolic rates for the substance are higher. Because this is more invasive than fMRI, it is now used less often as a measure of brain function.

Visual images of the working brain can indicate sites of epileptic seizures, brain tumors, strokes, and trauma from head injuries, as well as the distribution of psychoactive drugs in the brain. fMRI, and to a lesser extent PET, is being used to study possible abnormal brain processes that are linked to various disorders, such as the failure of the frontal cortex of patients with schizophrenia to become activated while they attempt to perform a cognitive task. It is important to keep in mind, however, that these techniques do not allow us to manipulate brain activity and then measure a change in behavior. Rather, we can manipulate behavior of some sort (e.g., ask a person to remember a list of words or show an emotionally evocative picture) and then measure blood flow in the brain (Feldman Barrett, 2003).

The PET scan on the left shows a normal brain; the one on the right shows the brain of a patient with Alzheimer's disease. (Dr. Robert Friedland/Photo Researchers.)

Neurotransmitter Assessment

It might seem that assessing the amount of a particular neurotransmitter or the quantity of its receptors in the brain would be straightforward. But as we began to discuss in Chapter 2, it is not. Most of the research on neurotransmitters and psychopathology—of increasing importance in recent years—has relied on indirect assessments.

In postmortem studies, the brains of deceased patients are removed and the amount of specific neurotransmitters in particular brain areas can then be directly measured. Different brain areas can be infused with substances that bind to receptors, and the amount of binding can then be quantified; more binding indicates more receptors. In Chapter 11 we will discuss how this method has been used to study the dopamine theory of schizophrenia.

In studies of participants who are alive, one common method of neurotransmitter assessment involves analyzing the metabolites of neurotransmitters that have been broken down by enzymes. A **metabolite**, typically an acid, is produced when a neurotransmitter is deactivated. These by-products of the breakdown of neurotransmitters such as norepinephrine, dopamine, and serotonin are found in urine, blood serum, and cerebrospinal fluid (CSF; the fluid in the spinal column and in the brain's ventricles). For example, the major metabolite of dopamine is homovanillic acid; of serotonin, 5-hydroxyindoleacetic acid. A high level of a particular metabolite indicates a high level of a neurotransmitter, and a low level indicates a low level of the transmitter.

But there is a problem with measuring metabolites from blood or urine: such measures are not direct reflections of levels of neurotransmitters in the brain; metabolites measured in this way could reflect neurotransmitters anywhere in the body. A more specific measure can be taken of metabolites in the cerebrospinal fluid drawn from a person's spinal cord. Even with cerebrospinal fluid, however, metabolites may reflect activity throughout the brain and spinal cord, rather than regions that are more directly involved in psychopathology. We will see in Chapter 8 (see p. 239) that some people with depression have low levels of the main metabolite of serotonin—a fact that has played an important role in the serotonin theory of depression.

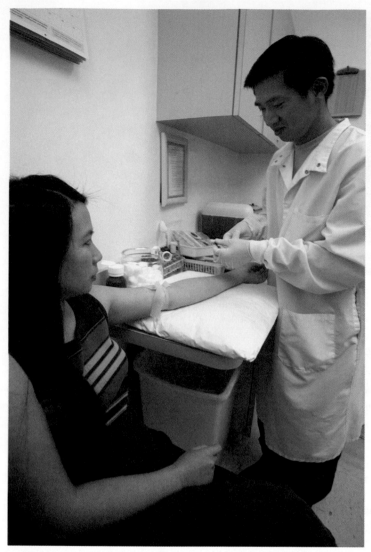

Measures of neurotransmitter metabolites based on blood or urine levels do not provide a very accurate index of neurotransmitter levels in the brain. (Spencer Grant/Photo Researchers, Inc.)

Another problem with metabolite studies is that they are correlational. In Chapter 4, we discuss the limits of correlational research, including the fact that causation cannot be determined from a correlational study. That is, when researchers find that neurotransmitter levels are low during a particular disorder such as depression, this could be because neurotransmitter levels cause depression, because depression causes neurotransmitter changes, or because a third variable causes shifts in both neurotransmitters and depression. For example, dopamine, norepinephrine, and serotonin levels change in response to stress. To test whether neurotransmitter levels could cause symptoms, experimental evidence is needed.

To provide more experimental data on whether these neurotransmitter systems actually help cause psychopathology, one strategy is to administer drugs that increase or decrease the brain levels of neurotransmitters. For example, a drug that raises the level of serotonin should alleviate depression; one reducing it should trigger depressive symptoms. This strategy also has its problems, though. One might wonder about whether it is ethical to do these studies if the goal of an experiment is to produce symptoms. On this front, it is reassuring that most studies find very temporary effects of these medications; neurotransmitter systems quickly return to normal levels, allowing for recovery from these brief mood periods. Another issue is that drugs that change levels of one neurotransmitter often tend to influence other neurotransmitter systems. We will see examples of these types of studies throughout this book.

Clinicians and researchers in many disciplines are currently using brain imaging and neurotransmitter assessment techniques both to discover previously undetectable brain problems and to conduct inquiries into the neural and chemical contributions to thought, emotion, and behavior. It is a very lively and exciting area of research and application. Indeed, one might reasonably assume that researchers and clinicians, with the help of such procedures and technological devices as fMRI, could observe the brain and its functions more or less directly and thus assess all brain abnormalities. Results to date, however, are not strong enough for these methods to be used in diagnosing psychopathology. Moreover, many brain abnormalities involve alterations in structure so subtle or slight in extent that they have thus far eluded direct examination. Furthermore, the problems in some disorders are so widespread, finding the contributing brain dysfunction is a daunting task. Take, for example, schizophrenia, which affects thinking, feeling, and behavior. Where in the brain might there be dysfunction? Looking for areas that influence thinking, feeling, and behavior requires just about the entire brain.

Neuropsychological Assessment

It is important at this point to note a distinction between neurologists and neuropsychologists, even though both specialists are concerned with the study of the central nervous system. A **neurologist** is a physician who specializes in medical diseases that affect the nervous system, such as muscular dystrophy, cerebral palsy, or Alzheimer's disease. A **neuropsychologist** is a psychologist who studies how dysfunctions of the brain affect the way we think, feel, and behave. As the term implies, a neuropsychologist is trained as a psychologist, but with a focus on how abnormalities of the brain affect thought, emotion, and behavior in deleterious ways. Both kinds of specialists contribute much to each other as they work in different ways, often collaboratively, to learn how the nervous system functions and how to ameliorate problems caused by disease or injury to the brain.

Neuropsychological tests assess behavioral disturbances caused by brain dysfunctions. The tests are often used in conjunction with the brain imaging techniques just described. The evidence indicates that these tests have some validity in both detecting brain damage and in localizing it in specific areas of the brain (Garb & Schramke, 1996). Neuropsychological tests are based on the idea that different psychological functions (e.g., motor speed, memory, language) are localized in different areas of the brain. Thus, for example, neuropsychological testing might help identify the extent of brain damage suffered during a stroke, and it can provide clues about where in the brain damage may exist. The concept of using a battery of tests, each tapping a different function, is critical, for only by studying a person's pattern of performance can an investigator adequately judge whether the person is brain damaged and where the damage is located. There are numerous neuropsychological tests used in psychopathology assessment. Here, we highlight two widely used batteries of tests.

One neuropsychological test is Reitan's modification of a battery or group of tests previously developed by Halstead. The following are three of the tests included in the Halstead–Reitan battery.

1. **Tactile Performance Test—Time.** While blindfolded, the patient tries to fit variously shaped blocks into spaces of a form board, first using the preferred hand, then the other, and finally both.

2. **Tactile Performance Test—Memory.** After completing the timed test, the participant is asked to draw the form board from memory, showing the blocks in their proper location. Both this and the timed test are sensitive to damage in the right parietal lobe.

3. **Speech Sounds Perception Test.** Participants listen to a series of nonsense words, each comprising two consonants with a long e sound in the middle. They then select the "word" they heard from a set of alternatives. This test measures left-hemisphere function, especially temporal and parietal areas.

Extensive research has demonstrated that the battery is valid for detecting behavior changes linked to brain dysfunction resulting from a variety of conditions, such as tumors, stroke, and head injury.

The Luria–Nebraska battery (Golden, Hammeke, & Purisch, 1978), based on the work of the Russian psychologist Aleksandr Luria (1902–1977), is also widely used (Moses & Purisch, 1997). The battery includes 269 items divided into 11 sections designed to determine basic and complex motor skills, rhythm and pitch abilities, tactile and kinesthetic skills, verbal and spatial skills, receptive speech ability, expressive speech ability, writing, reading, arithmetic skills, memory, and intellectual processes. The pattern of scores on these sections, as well as on the 32 items found to be the most discriminating and indicative of overall impairment, helps reveal potential damage to the frontal, temporal, sensorimotor, or parietal-occipital area of the right or left hemisphere.

The Luria–Nebraska battery can be administered in $2\frac{1}{2}$ hours and can be scored in a highly reliable manner (e.g., Kashden & Franzen, 1996). It also has an alternate form. Criterion validity has been established by findings such as a correct classification rate of over 86 percent when used with a sample of neurological patients and controls (Moses et al., 1992). A particular advantage

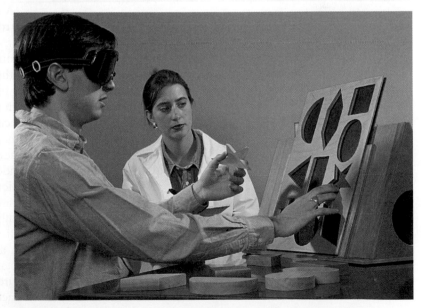

Neuropsychological tests assess various performance deficits in the hope of detecting a specific area of brain malfunction. Shown here is the Tactile Performance Test. (Richard Nowitz/Photo Researchers.)

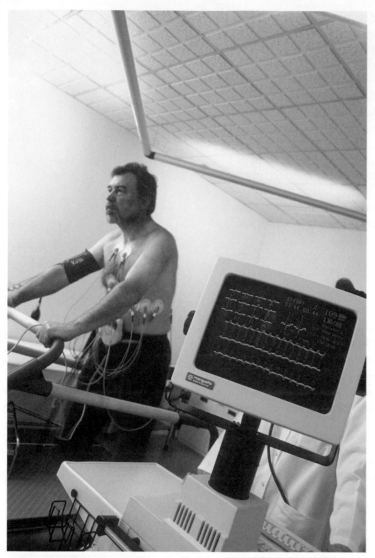

In psychophysiological assessment, physical changes in the body are measured. The electrocardiograph is one such assessment. (BSIP/Phototake.)

of the Luria–Nebraska tests is that one can control for educational level so that a less-educated person will not receive a lower score solely because of limited educational experience (Brickman et al., 1984). Finally, a version for children ages 8 to 12 (Golden, 1981a,b) has been found useful in diagnosing brain damage and in evaluating the educational strengths and weaknesses of children (Sweet et al., 1986).

Psychophysiological Assessment

The discipline of **psychophysiology** is concerned with the bodily changes that are associated with psychological events or characteristics. Experimenters have used measures such as heart rate, tension in the muscles, blood flow in various parts of the body, and brain waves to study physiological changes when people are afraid, depressed, asleep, imagining, solving problems, and so on. Like the brain-imaging methods we have already discussed, the assessments we describe here are not sensitive enough to be used for diagnosis. They can, however, provide important information. For example, in using exposure to treat a patient with an anxiety disorder, it would be useful to know the extent to which the patient shows physiological arousal when exposed to the stimuli that create anxiety. Patients who show higher levels of physiological arousal may be experiencing higher levels of fear, which predict more benefit from the therapy (Foa et al., 1995).

The activities of the autonomic nervous system (also discussed in Chapter 2) are often assessed by electrical and chemical measurements in attempts to understand the nature of emotion. One important measure is heart rate. Each heartbeat generates electrical changes, which can be recorded by electrodes placed on the chest, which convey signals to an electrocardiograph or a polygraph. The signal is graphically depicted in an **electrocardiogram (EKG)**, which may be seen as waves on a computer screen or a roll of graph paper.

A second measure of autonomic nervous system activity is **electrodermal responding**, or skin conductance. Anxiety, fear, anger, and other emotions increase activity in the sympathetic nervous system, which then boosts sweat-gland activity. Increased sweat-gland activity increases the electrical conductance of the skin. Conductance is typically measured by determining the current that flows through the skin when a known small voltage derived from an external source is passed between two electrodes on the hand. This current shows a pronounced increase after activation of the sweat glands. Since the sweat glands are activated by the sympathetic nervous system, increased sweat-gland activity indicates sympathetic autonomic excitation and is often taken as a measure of emotional arousal. These measures are widely used in research in psychopathology.

Advances in technology allow researchers to track changes in physiological processes, such as blood pressure in vivo, as people go about their normal business. Participants wear a portable device that automatically records blood pressure many times during the day. Combining these measures with self-reports recorded by the participants in specially designed diaries, researchers have been able to study how people's changing moods affect blood pressure—of interest to understanding hypertension (Kamarck et al., 1998; see Chapter 7).

Brain activity can be measured by an **electroencephalogram (EEG)**. Electrodes placed on the scalp record electrical activity in the underlying brain area. Abnormal patterns of electrical activity can indicate epilepsy or help in locating brain lesions or tumors.

As with the brain-imaging techniques reviewed earlier, a more complete picture of a human being is obtained when physiological functioning is assessed while the person is engaging in some form of behavior or cognitive activity. If experimenters are interested in psychophysiological responding in patients with obsessive-compulsive disorder, for example, they would likely study the patients while presenting stimuli, such as dirt, that would elicit the problematic behaviors.

A Cautionary Note about Neurobiological Assessment

A cautionary note regarding neurobiological assessment methods is in order here. Inasmuch as psychophysiology and brain imaging employ highly sophisticated electronic machinery, and many psychologists aspire to be as scientific as possible, researchers sometimes believe uncritically in these apparently objective assessment devices without appreciating their real limitations and complications. Many of the measurements do not differentiate clearly among emotional states. Skin conductance, for example, increases not only with anxiety but also with other emotions—among them, happiness. In addition, being in a scanner is itself an emotional experience. Thus, the investigator interested in measuring brain changes associated with emotion using fMRI must also take the scanning environment into account.

Neither is there a one-to-one relationship between a score on a given neuropsychological test or a finding on an fMRI scan on the one hand and psychological dysfunction on the other. The reasons for these sometimes loose relationships have to do with such factors as how the person has, over time, reacted to and coped with the losses brought about by the brain dysfunction. And the success of coping, in turn, has to do with the social environment in which the person has lived, for example, how understanding parents and associates have been or how well the school system has provided for the special educational needs of the person. Furthermore, the brain has also changed in response to these psychological and socioenvironmental factors over time. Therefore, in addition to the imperfect nature of the neurobiological assessment instruments themselves and our incomplete understanding of how the brain actually functions, clinicians and researchers must consider these environmental factors that operate over time to contribute to the clinical picture. In other words, a complete assessment must include multiple methods (clinical interviews, psychological and neurobiological methods).

A final caution is reflected in the simple yet often unappreciated fact that in attempting to understand the neurocognitive consequences of any brain dysfunction, one must understand the preexisting abilities that the patient had prior to diagnosis with a mental disorder. This straightforward truth brings to mind the story of the man who, recovering from an accident that has broken all the fingers in both hands, earnestly asks the surgeon whether he will be able to play the piano when his wounds heal. "Yes, I'm sure you will," says the doctor reassuringly. "That's wonderful," exclaims the man, "I've always wanted to be able to play the piano."

Quick Summary

Recent advances in technology have allowed clinicians and researchers to "see" the living brain. Different imaging techniques, such as CT, MRI, and fMRI, have the potential to show areas of the brain that might not be working optimally. Direct assessment of neurotransmitters is not done often. Rather, examinations of the metabolites of neurotransmitters provide a window within which we can estimate how neurotransmitters are functioning. Another approach is to administer drugs that increase or decrease the levels of a neurotransmitter. Postmortem exams also allow for measurements of neurotransmitters, particularly receptors. Neuropsychological tests are tests that have been developed to show how changes in behavior may reflect damage or disturbance with particular areas of the brain. Psychophysiological assessment methods can show how behaviors and cognitions are linked to changes in nervous system activity, such as heart rate, skin conductance, or brain activity. These methods are sometimes considered more scientific because they involve complicated instrumentation. They have as many or more limitations as other assessment measures, however, and the key concepts of reliability and validity are just as relevant with neurobiological assessment as with other forms of assessment.

Check Your Knowledge 3.4

True or false?
1. MRI is a technique that shows both structure and function of the brain.
2. Neurotransmitter assessment is most often done using indirect methods.

3. A neuropsychologist is a psychologist who studies how dysfunctions of the brain affect the way we think, feel, and behave.
4. Brain activity can be measured with the psychophysiological method called EKG.

Cultural and Ethnic Diversity and Assessment

Studies of the influences of culture and ethnicity on psychopathology and its assessment have proliferated in recent years. As you read about some of this research, it is critical to keep in mind that there are typically more differences within cultural and ethnic groups than there are between them. Remembering this important point can help avoid the dangers of stereotyping members of a culture.

We should also note that the reliability and validity of various forms of psychological assessment have been questioned on the grounds that their content and scoring procedures reflect the culture of white European Americans and so may not accurately assess people from other cultures. In this section we discuss problems of cultural bias and what can be done about them.

Cultural Bias in Assessment

The issue of cultural bias in assessment refers to the notion that a measure developed for one culture or ethnic group may not be equally reliable and valid with a different cultural or ethnic group. Some tests that were developed in the United States have been translated into different languages and used in different cultures successfully. For example, a Spanish-language version of the WAIS has been available for over 30 years (Wechsler, 1968) and can be useful in assessing the intellectual functioning of people from Hispanic or Latino cultures (Gomez, Piedmont, & Fleming, 1992). Additionally, the MMPI-2 has been translated into more than two dozen languages (Tsai et al., 2001). Simply translating words into a different language, however, does not ensure that the meaning of those words will be the same across different cultures. Several steps in the translation process, including working with multiple translators, back-translating, and testing with multiple native speakers can help to ensure that the test is similar in different languages. This approach has been successful in achieving equivalence across different cultures and ethnic groups for some instruments, such as the MMPI-2 (Arbisi, Ben-Porath, & McNulty, 2002). Even with the MMPI-2, however, there are cultural differences that are not likely attributable to differences in psychopathology. For example, among Asian Americans who are not heavily assimilated into American culture, scores on most MMPI-2 scales are higher than those of Caucasians (Tsai & Pike, 2000). This is unlikely to be due to higher levels of emotional disturbance among Asians.

Despite these efforts, the field has a ways to go in reducing cultural and ethnic bias in clinical assessment. Furthermore, these cultural assumptions or biases may cause clinicians to over- or underestimate psychological problems in members of other cultures (Lopez, 1989, 1996). African American children are overrepresented in special-education classes, which may be a result of subtle biases in the tests used to determine such placement (Artiles & Trent, 1994). At least since the 1970s, studies have found that African Americans are more likely to receive a diagnosis of schizophrenia than are Caucasian Americans, but it is still unclear if this reflects an actual difference or a form of ethnic bias on the part of clinicians (Arnold et al., 2004; Trierweiler et al., 2000). Yet take the example of an Asian

American man who is very emotionally withdrawn. Should the clinician consider that lower levels of emotional expressiveness in men are viewed more positively in Asian cultures than in Euro-American culture? A clinician who quickly attributes the behavior to a cultural difference may overlook an emotional problem that he or she would be likely to diagnose if the patient were a white male.

How do such biases come about? Cultural factors may affect assessment in various ways. Language differences, differing religious and spiritual beliefs, the alienation or timidity of members of ethnic groups when being assessed by clinicians of the Euro-American culture—all these factors can play a role. For example, clinicians who encounter clients claiming to be surrounded by spirits might view this belief as a sign of schizophrenia. Yet in Puerto Rican cultures such a belief is common; therefore, believing that one is surrounded by spirits should probably not be taken as a sign of schizophrenia in a Puerto Rican person (Rogler & Hollingshead, 1985).

Cultural and ethnic differences in psychopathology must be examined more closely. Unfortunately, the cultural and ethnic biases that can creep into clinical

Assessment must take the person's cultural background into account. Believing in possession by spirits is common in some cultures and thus should not always be taken to mean that the believer is psychotic. (Tony Savino/The Image Works.)

assessment do not necessarily yield to efforts to compensate for them. There is no simple answer. DSM-IV-TR's inclusion of cultural factors in the discussion of every category of disorder may well sensitize clinicians to the issue, a necessary first step. When practitioners were surveyed, they overwhelmingly reported taking culture into account in their clinical work (Lopez, 1994), so it appears that the problem, if not the solution, is clearly in focus.

Strategies for Avoiding Cultural Bias in Assessment

Clinicians can—and do—use various methods to minimize the negative effects of cultural biases when assessing patients. Perhaps the place to begin is with graduate training programs. Lopez (2002) has noted three important issues that should be taught to graduate students in clinical psychology programs. First, students must learn about basic issues in assessment, such as reliability and validity. Second, students must become informed about the specific ways in which culture or ethnicity may impact assessment rather than more global stereotypes about a particular cultural or ethnic group. Third, students must learn to consider that culture or ethnicity may not impact assessment in every individual case.

Assessment procedures can also be modified to ensure that the person truly understands the requirements of the task. For example, suppose that a Native American child performed poorly on a test measuring psychomotor speed. The examiner's hunch is that the child did not understand the importance of working quickly and was overly concerned with accuracy instead. The test could be administered again after a more thorough explanation of the importance of working quickly without worrying about mistakes. If the child's performance improves, the examiner has gained an important understanding of the child's test-taking strategy and avoids diagnosing psychomotor-speed deficits.

Cultural differences can lead to different results on an aptitude or IQ test. For example, Native American children may lack interest in the individualistic, competitive nature of IQ tests because of the cooperative, group-oriented values instilled by their culture. (Lawrence Migdale/Photo Researchers.)

Finally, when the examiner and client have different ethnic backgrounds, the examiner may need to make an extra effort to establish a rapport that will result in the person's best performance. For example, when testing a shy, Hispanic preschooler, one of the authors was unable to obtain a verbal response to test questions. However, the boy was overheard talking in an animated and articulate manner to his mother in the waiting room, leading to a judgment that the test results did not represent a valid assessment of the child's language skills. When testing was repeated in the child's home with his mother present, advanced verbal abilities were observed.

As Lopez (1994) points out, however, "the distance between cultural responsiveness and cultural stereotyping can be short" (p. 123). To minimize such problems, clinicians are encouraged to be particularly tentative about drawing conclusions with patients from different cultural and ethnic backgrounds. Rather, they are advised to make hypotheses about the influence of culture on a particular client, entertain alternative hypotheses, and then test those hypotheses.

In a case from our files, a young man was suspected of having schizophrenia. One prominent symptom he reported was hearing voices. However, he claimed that he heard voices only while meditating and that within his (Buddhist) culture this experience was normative. To test this hypothesis the examiner (with the permission of the client) contacted the family's religious leader. The Buddhist priest indicated that the symptom reported by this young man was very unusual, and it turned out that the religious community to which he belonged was quite concerned about his increasingly bizarre behavior. Thus, the hypothesis that his symptom should be attributed to cultural factors was refuted, and an error of failing to detect psychopathology was avoided.

Summary

In gathering diagnosis and assessment information, clinicians and researchers must be concerned with both reliability and validity. Reliability refers to whether measurements are consistent and replicable; and validity, to whether assessments are tapping into what they are meant to measure. Assessment procedures vary greatly in their reliability and validity. Certain diagnostic categories are more reliable than others.

Diagnosis

● Diagnosis, the process of assessing whether a person meets criteria for a mental disorder, is a critical aspect of the field of abnormal psychology. Having an agreed-on diagnostic system allows clinicians to communicate effectively with each other and facilitates the search for causes and treatments. Clinically, diagnosis provides the foundation for treatment planning.

● The Diagnostic and Statistical Manual of Mental Disorders (DSM), published by the American Psychiatric Association, is an official diagnostic system widely used by mental health professionals. A revision of the fourth edition of the manual, referred to as DSM-IV-TR, was published in 2000. An important feature of the current DSM is its multiaxial organization. In the multiaxial classification system of DSM, Axes I and II make up the mental disorders per se; Axis III lists any physical disorders believed to bear on the mental disorder in question; Axis IV is used to indicate the psychosocial and environmental problems that the person has been experiencing; and Axis V rates the person's current level of adaptive functioning.

● Some critics of the DSM argue against diagnosis in general. They point out that diagnostic classifications may ignore important information and may also increase stigma. Specific shortcomings of the DSM have also been identified. These include the high rates of comorbidity, the reliance on a categorical classification system, limited reliability for some disorders, and questions about the validity of a few of the diagnostic categories. Most researchers and clinicians, though, recognize that the DSM is an enormous advance compared to historical systems.

Assessment

● Clinicians rely on several modes of psychological and neurobiological assessment in trying to find out how best to describe a client, search for the reasons the patient is troubled, arrive at an accurate diagnosis, and design effective preventive or remedial treatments. Regardless of what assessment method is used, it inevitably reflects the paradigm of the clinician. The best assessment involves multiple types of methods.

● Psychological assessments include clinical interviews, assessments of stress, psychological tests, and behavioral and cognitive assessments.

● Clinical interviews are structured or relatively unstructured conversations in which the clinician probes the patient for information about his or her problems. Assessing stress is key to the field of abnormal psychology. A number of useful methods for assessing stress have been developed, including the LEDS and ADE.

- Psychological tests are standardized procedures designed to assess personality or measure performance. Personality assessments range from empirically derived self-report questionnaires, such as the Minnesota Multiphasic Personality Inventory, to projective tests in which the patient interprets ambiguous stimuli, such as the Rorschach test. Intelligence tests, such as the Wechsler Adult Intelligence Scale, evaluate a person's intellectual ability and predict how well he or she will perform academically.
- Behavioral and cognitive assessment is concerned with how people act, feel, and think in particular situations. Approaches include direct observation of behavior; interviews and self-report measures that are situational in their focus; and specialized, think-aloud cognitive assessment procedures that attempt to uncover beliefs, attitudes, and thinking patterns related to specific situations.

- Neurobiological assessments include imaging techniques—such as fMRI—that enable us to see various structures and access functions of the living brain; neurochemical assays that allow clinicians to make inferences about levels of neurotransmitters; neuropsychological tests, such as the Halstead–Reitan, which seek to identify brain defects based on variations in responses to psychological tests; and psychophysiological measurements, such as heart rate and skin conductance, which are associated with certain psychological events or characteristics.
- Cultural and ethnic factors play a role in clinical assessment. Assessment techniques developed on the basis of research with Caucasian populations may be inaccurate when used with clients of differing ethnic or cultural backgrounds, for example. Clinicians can have biases when evaluating ethnic minority patients, which can lead to minimizing or exaggerating a patient's psychopathology. Clinicians use various methods to guard against the negative effects of cultural biases in assessment.

Answers to Check Your Knowledge Questions

3.1 1. b, c, and d; 2. a, d, e, c, b; 3. b, c, d, a

3.2 1. high comorbidity, many different diagnoses are related to the same causes, symptoms of many different diagnoses respond to the same treatments; 2. Axis V; 3. course, treatment, etiology; 4. lower

3.3 1. F; 2. T; 3. T; 4. T; 5. T; 6. F

3.4 1. F; 2. T; 3. T; 4. F

Key Terms

alternate-form reliability
behavioral assessment
behavioral observation
BOLD
categorical classification
clinical interview
comorbidity
concurrent validity
construct validity
content validity
criterion validity
CT or CAT scan

Diagnostic and Statistical Manual of Mental Disorders (DSM-IV-TR)
dimensional diagnostic systems
ecological momentary assessment (EMA)
electrocardiogram (EKG)
electrodermal responding
electroencephalogram (EEG)
functional magnetic resonance imaging (fMRI)
intelligence test
internal consistency reliability
interrater reliability

magnetic resonance imaging (MRI)
metabolite
Minnesota Multiphasic Personality Inventory (MMPI)
multiaxial classification system
neurologist
neuropsychological tests
neuropsychologist
personality inventory
PET scan
predictive validity
projective hypothesis
projective test

psychological tests
psychophysiology
reactivity
reliability
Rorschach Inkblot Test
self-monitoring
standardization
stress
structured interview
test-retest reliability
Thematic Apperception Test (TAT)
validity

4

Research Methods in the Study of Psychopathology

Our ability to conceptualize and treat mental illness has improved vastly over the past 50 years. Nonetheless, there are still important unanswered questions about the causes and treatments of these disorders. It is precisely because facts about mental disorders are still emerging that it is important to pursue new discoveries using scientific research methods. This chapter discusses the methods that are applied in psychopathology research.

Science and Scientific Methods

The term science comes from the Latin *scire*, "to know." At its core, science is a way of knowing. More formally, science is the systematic pursuit of knowledge through observation. Science involves forming a theory and then systematically gathering data to test the theory.

A **theory** is a set of propositions meant to explain a class of observations. Usually, the goal of scientific theories is to understand cause–effect relationships. A theory permits the generation of more specific **hypotheses**—expectations about what should occur if a theory is true. For example, if the classical-conditioning theory is valid, people with phobias should be more likely than those in the general population to have had traumatic experiences with the situations they fear, such as flying. By collecting such data, you could test your hypothesis.

People sometimes assume that a scientist formulates a theory by simply considering data that were previously collected and then deciding, in a rather straightforward fashion, that one way of thinking about the data is the most useful. Although some theory building follows this course, not all does. Theory building often involves creativity—a theory sometimes seems to leap into the scientist's head in a wonderful moment of insight. New ideas suddenly occur, and connections that were overlooked before are grasped. Formerly obscure observations might make a new kind of sense within the framework of the new theory (see Focus on Discovery 4.1).

Focus on Discovery 4.1

Chaos Theory and Limits on Prediction

> *... the Butterfly Effect—the notion that a butterfly stirring the air today in Peking can transform storm systems next month in New York. (Gleick, 1987, p. 8)*

This quotation captures the essence of chaos theory, which suggests that major events (such as a storm system) may be affected by seemingly trivial events (the air turbulence created by a flying butterfly). The chaos theory perspective argues against the ability of scientists to predict with any confidence the long-term outcomes of apparently tiny changes in events (Gleick, 1987). The world is almost unfathomably complex, and we are inherently limited in what we can predict and explain. We have all experienced frustration with weather reports—it is a standing joke to blame the meteorologist for favorable forecasts that turn out to be wrong. But an appreciation of the many factors that enter into the development of a storm system justifies more tolerance of the limitations of forecasters.

In the human sciences it seems especially appropriate to view our task in terms of chaos theory (e.g., Duke, 1994), or, as some would term it more broadly, complexity studies (Mahoney & Moes, 1997). Even if we knew all the variables controlling behavior—and no one would claim that we do—our ability to predict would be limited by many unexpected and uncontrollable factors that are likely to affect a person over a period of time. People do not behave in a social vacuum. Consequently, simple cause–effect statements are exceedingly difficult to construct with confidence.

As we review the theories and evidence about the causes of and treatments for abnormal behavior, we will often encounter the complexities and shortcomings in the research literature. Our discussions of intervention in particular should be informed by the chaos perspective. Therapists have limited contact with their patients, all of whom live moment-to-moment in exquisitely complex interaction with others who themselves are affected on a moment-to-moment basis by hundreds of factors that are nigh impossible to anticipate, let alone to influence. We are not embracing chaos as a goal—we are not scientific nihilists; rather, we want to counsel humility, even awe, in an enterprise that tries to understand how things go awry with the human condition.

Chaos theory suggests that major weather events, such as the series of hurricanes that hit the coast of Florida in 2004, can be influenced by seemingly trivial events, such as air's being disturbed by the flight of a butterfly thousands of miles away.

What makes a good theory? A scientific approach requires that ideas be stated clearly and precisely. This is needed for scientific claims to be exposed to systematic tests that could negate the scientist's expectations. That is, regardless of how plausible a theory seems, it must be subject to disproof. Science proceeds by disproving theories, never by "proving theories." Because of this, it is not enough to assert that traumatic experiences during childhood cause psychological maladjustment in adulthood. This is no more than a possibility. According to a scientific point of view, a hypothesis must be amenable to systematic testing that could show it to be false. That is, the focus of testing is on disproving rather than proving a theory.

In testing a theory, each scientific observation must be replicable. Each facet of a study must be carefully defined, so that findings can be replicated. Much of this depends on using assessments with strong reliability and validity, as discussed in Chapter 3. Beyond choosing measures carefully, though, researchers in psychopathology choose among a set of different types of research designs. We turn to a discussion of the strengths and weaknesses of the most common types of research methods next.

Approaches to Research on Psychopathology

In this section we describe the most common research methods in the study of abnormal behavior: the case study, correlational methods, and experimental methods. These methods will be seen in the studies described throughout this book. Table 4.1 shows a summary of the strengths and weaknesses of each.

The Case Study

The **case study**, perhaps the most familiar method of observing human behavior, involves recording detailed information about one person at a time. The clinical cases described in the last chapter are examples of case studies. A comprehensive case study would cover family history and background, medical history, educational background, jobs held, marital history, and details concerning development, adjustment, personality, the current situation, and experiences in therapy across the life course.

Case studies lack the control and objectivity of other research methods. That is, the validity of the information gathered in a case study is sometimes questionable. Focus on Discovery 4.2 describes a famous case history of dissociative identity disorder (formerly known as multiple personality disorder). This case history provided immeasurably rich information about a rare disorder; nonetheless, the major treatment successes its authors described were later disputed by the client, who published an account describing major deterioration after her treatment.

The objectivity of case studies is limited because the clinician's paradigm will shape the kinds of information reported in a case study. To take one example, case studies by psychodynamic clinicians typically contain more information about the client's early childhood and parental conflicts than reports by behavioral clinicians do.

Despite their relative lack of control, case studies still play an important role in the study of abnormal behavior. Specifically, the case study can be used:

1. to provide a rich description of a clinical phenomenon;
2. to disprove an allegedly universal hypothesis;
3. to generate hypotheses that can be tested through controlled research (Davison & Lazarus, 1994).

We discuss each of these uses next.

Table 4.1 Research Methods in Psychopathology

Method	Description	Evaluation
Case study	Collection of detailed biographical information	Excellent source of hypotheses
		Can provide information about novel cases or procedures
		Can disconfirm a relationship that was believed to be universal
		Cannot provide causal evidence, because cannot rule out alternative hypotheses
		May be biased by observer's theoretical viewpoint
Correlation	Study of the relationship between two or more variables; measured as they exist in nature	Used widely because we often cannot manipulate risk variables or diagnosis in psychopathology research
		Epidemiologists often use the correlational method to study the incidence, prevalence, and risk factors of disorders in a representative sample
		Behavioral genetic studies often use the correlational method to study the heritability of different psychological disorders
		Cannot determine causality because of the directionality and third-variable problems
Experiment	Includes a manipulated independent variable, a dependent variable, preferably at least one control group, and random assignment	Most powerful method for determining causal relationships
		Used often in studies of treatment effectiveness
		Also used in analogue studies of the risk factors for mental illness
		Single case experimental designs are also common, but can have limited external validity

The Case Study as a Rich Description   Because it focuses on a single person, the case study can include much more detail than other research methods typically do. This is particularly helpful when a report covers a rare clinical phenomenon. Another typical use is to provide a detailed description of how a new intervention works.

The Case Study Can Disprove, but Not Prove a Hypothesis   Case histories can provide examples that contradict an assumed universal relationship. Consider, for example, the proposition that depressive episodes are always preceded by life stress. Finding even a single case of non-stress-related depression would negate the theory.

Even though case studies can disprove a hypothesis, case studies do not provide good evidence in support of a particular theory, because they do not provide the means for ruling out alternative hypotheses. To illustrate this problem, consider a clinician who develops a new treatment for depression, tries it out on a client, and finds that the depression lifts after 10 weeks of the therapy. Although it would be tempting to conclude that the therapy is effective, such a conclusion cannot be drawn legitimately because other factors could have produced the change. A stressful situation in the patient's life may have resolved or the client's depression might have been naturally time limited (most are). Thus several plausible rival hypotheses could account for the clinical improvement. The data yielded by the case study do not allow us to determine the true cause of the change.

Generating Hypotheses   Although the case study may not provide valid support for hypotheses, it does help generate hypotheses. As they hear the life histories of many different clients, clinicians may notice patterns and then formulate important hypotheses that they could not have formed otherwise. For example, in his clinical work, Kanner (1943) noticed that some disturbed children showed a similar constellation of symptoms, including failure to develop language and extreme isolation from other people. He therefore proposed a new

Focus on Discovery 4.2

An Example of the Advantages and Disadvantages of Case Studies

In 1954, psychiatrists Thigpen and Cleckley described a patient, Eve White, who seemed to have three very distinct personalities. Their book, *The Three Faces of Eve*, describes how new personalities emerged and functioned.

Eve White had been seen in psychotherapy for several months because she was experiencing severe headaches accompanied by blackouts. Her therapist, Dr. Thigpen, described her as a quiet, gentle, and conventional woman. One day during the course of an interview, however, she changed abruptly and in a surprising way.

> As if seized by sudden pain, she put both hands to her head. After a tense moment of silence, both hands dropped. There was a quick, reckless smile, and, in a bright voice that sparkled, she said, "Hi there, Doc!" The demure and constrained posture of Eve White had melted into buoyant repose.... This new and apparently carefree girl spoke casually of Eve White and her problems, always using she or her in every reference, always respecting the strict bounds of a separate identity.... When asked her name, she immediately replied, "Oh, I'm Eve Black." (Thigpen & Cleckley, p. 137)

After this rather startling revelation, Eve was observed for 14 months in a series of interviews that ran to almost 100 hours. A very important part of Eve White's therapy was to help her learn about Eve Black, her other, infectiously exuberant self, who added seductive and expensive clothing to her wardrobe and lived unremembered episodes of her life.

During this period a third personality, Jane, emerged while Eve White was recollecting a childhood incident in which she had been painfully scalded by water from a wash pot. Jane, who from then on knew all that happened to the two Eves, although they did not know of her existence, was "far more mature, more vivid, more boldly capable, and more interesting than Eve White." Jane also developed a deep and revering affection for the first Eve, who was considered somewhat a ninny by Eve Black. Jane knew nothing of Eve White's earlier life except what she learned through Eve's memories.

Some 11 months later, in a calamitous session with all three personalities present at different times, Eve Black emerged and reminisced for a moment about the many good times she had had in the past but then remarked that she did not seem to have real fun anymore. She began to sob, the only time Dr. Thigpen had seen her in tears. She told him that she wanted him to have her red dress to remember her by. All expression left her face and her eyes closed. Eve White opened them. When Jane was summoned a few minutes later, she soon realized that there was no longer any Eve White either and began to remember a terrifying event from childhood. "No, no!...Oh no, Mother...I can't...Don't make me do it," she cried. Jane, who earlier had known nothing of Eve's childhood, was 5 years old and at her grandmother's funeral. Her mother was holding her high off the floor and above the coffin and saying that she must touch her grandmother's face. As she felt her hand leave the clammy cheek, the young woman screamed so piercingly that Dr. Cleckley, Dr. Thigpen's associate, came running from his office across the hall.

The two physicians were not certain who confronted them. In the searing intensity of the remembered moment a new personality had been welded. Their transformed patient did not at first feel herself as apart, and as sharply distinct a person, as had the two Eves and Jane, although she knew a great deal about all of them. When her initial bewilderment lessened, she tended to identify herself with Jane. But the identification was not sure or complete, and she mourned the absence of the two Eves as though they were lost sisters. This new person decided to call herself Mrs. Evelyn White.

Chris Sizemore was the subject of the famous "three faces of Eve" case. She subsequently claimed to have had 21 separate personalities. (AP/Wide Word Photos.)

The case of Eve White, Eve Black, Jane, and eventually Evelyn constitutes a valuable classic in the literature because it is one of only a few detailed accounts of a rare phenomenon, multiple personality, now known as dissociative identity disorder. This intriguing and controversial disorder is discussed in Chapter 6. In addition to illustrating the phenomenon itself, the Thigpen and Cleckley report provides valuable details about the interview procedures they followed and how the treatment progressed in this one case of multiple personality.

Since publication of the original account, major questions have been raised about how successful this treatment actually was. The real Eve, a woman named Chris Sizemore, wrote a book that challenged Thigpen and Cleckley's account of her case (Sizemore & Pittillo, 1977). She claimed that after therapy with them, her personality continued to fragment. In all, 21 separate and distinct strangers inhabited her body at one time or another. Eventually her personality changes were so constant and numerous that she might become her three persons in rapid switches resembling the flipping of television channels. The debilitating round-robin of transformations filled her entire life. After realizing finally that her alternate personalities were true aspects of herself rather than strangers from without, Chris Sizemore decided to reveal her story to help deal with her ordeals.

diagnosis—infantile autism—which was subsequently confirmed by larger-scale research and adopted into the DSM (see pp. 485).

The Correlational Method

A great deal of psychopathology research relies on the **correlational method**. Correlational studies address questions of the form "Do variable *X* and variable *Y* vary together (co-relate)?". In correlational research, variables are measured as they exist in nature. This is distinct from experimental research (discussed on pp. 111–117), in which the researcher manipulates variables.

To illustrate the difference, consider that the role of stress in hypertension can be assessed with either a correlational or an experimental design. In a correlational study, we might measure stress levels by interviewing people about their recent stressful experiences. Stress would then be correlated with blood-pressure measurements collected from these same people. In an experimental study, in contrast, the experimenter might create stress in the laboratory; for example, some participants might be asked to give a speech to an audience about the aspect of their personal appearance they find least appealing (see Figure 4.1). The key difference between these methods is whether or not a variable is manipulated. Psychopathologists will rely on correlational methods when there are ethical reasons not to manipulate a variable; for example, no researcher would try to manipulate genes, trauma, or neurobiological deficits.

Numerous examples of **correlation** can be drawn from mental health research. For example, depression tends to correlate with anxiety; people who feel depressed tend to report feeling anxious. It is worth highlighting that comparisons of people with and without a diagnosis can be correlational as well. See Table 4.2 for a description of how such data might be coded. For example, two diagnostic groups may be compared to see how much stress was experienced before the onset of their disorders. In other words, questions are asked about relationships between a given diagnosis and some other variable; for example, "Is schizophrenia related to social class?" or "Are anxiety disorders related to neurotransmitter levels?"

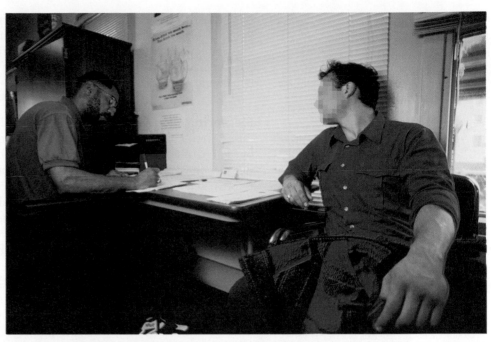

Although the information yielded by a case study does not fare well as a source of evidence, it is an important source of hypotheses. (Greg Smith/Cortis Images.)

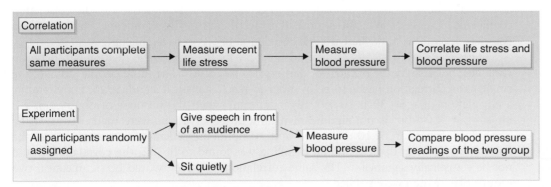

Figure 4.1 Correlational versus experimental studies.

Table 4.2 Data for a Correlational Study with Diagnosis

Participant Number	Diagnosis	Stress Score
1	1	65
2	1	72
3	0	40
4	1	86
5	0	72
6	0	21
7	1	65
8	0	40
9	1	37
10	0	28

Note: Diagnosis—having an anxiety disorder or not, with having an anxiety disorder designated as 1 and not as 0—is correlated with an assessment of recent life stress on a 0–100 scale. Higher scores indicate greater recent stress. To make the point clearly, we present a smaller sample of cases than would be used in an actual research study. Notice that diagnosis is associated with recent life stress. Patients with an anxiety disorder tend to have higher stress scores than people without an anxiety disorder. In this example, the correlation between stress and anxiety scores = + .60.

Table 4.3 Data for Determining a Correlation

	Height	Weight in Pounds
John	5′10″	170
Asher	5′10″	140
Eve	5′4″	112
Gail	5′3″	105
Jerry	5′10″	177
Gayla	5′2″	100
Steve	5′8″	145
Margy	5′5″	128
Gert	5′6″	143
Sean	5′10″	140
Kathleen	5′4″	116

Note: For these figures $r = + .88$

In the next sections, we discuss how to measure the relationship (correlation) between two variables, how to test whether the relationship is statistically and clinically significant, and some issues in determining whether variables are causally related. Then, we discuss two specific domains of research that tend to use correlational designs: epidemiology and behavioral genetics.

Measuring Correlation   The first step in determining a correlation is to obtain pairs of observations of the variables in question. One example would be the height and weight of each participant. Another example would be the intelligence of mothers and daughters. Once such pairs of measurements are obtained, the strength of the relationship between the two sets of observations can be computed to determine the **correlation coefficient**, denoted by the symbol r. This statistic may take any value between -1.00 and $+1.00$, and measures both the magnitude and the direction of a relationship. The higher the absolute value of r, the stronger the relationship between the two variables. That is, an r of either $+1.00$ or -1.00 indicates the strongest possible, or perfect, relationship, whereas an r of .00 indicates that the variables are unrelated. If the sign of r is positive, the two variables are said to be positively related; in other words, as the values for variable X increase, those for variable Y also tend to increase. Table 4.3 shows data for a correlation of $+.88$ between height and weight, indicating a very strong positive relationship; as height increases, so does weight. Conversely, when the sign of r is negative, variables are said to be negatively related; as scores on one variable increase, those for the other tend to decrease. For example, the number of hours spent watching television is negatively correlated with grade point average.

One way to think about how strong a correlation is is to plot the two variables. In Figure 4.2, each point represents the scores for a given person on variable X and variable Y. In a perfect correlation, all the points fall on a straight line; if we know the value of only one of the variables for a person, we can know the value of the other variable. Similarly, when the correlation is relatively large, there is only a small degree of scatter about the line of perfect correlation. The values tend to scatter increasingly far from the line as the correlations become lower. When the correlation reaches .00, knowledge of a person's score on one variable tells us nothing about his or her score on the other.

Statistical and Clinical Significance   Thus far we have established that the magnitude of a correlation coefficient tells us the strength of a relationship between two variables. But scientists use **statistical significance** for a more rigorous test of the importance of a relationship. (Significance is considered with many different statistics, but here we focus on correlation coefficients.) A statistically significant correlation is unlikely to have occurred by chance. A nonsignificant correlation may have occurred by chance, so does not provide evidence for an important relationship.

A statistical finding usually is considered significant if the probability that it is a chance finding is 5 or less in 100. This level of significance is called the .05 level, commonly written as $p < .05$ (the p stands for probability). In general, as the absolute size of the correlation coefficient increases, the result is more likely to be statistically significant. For example, a correlation of .80 is more likely than a correlation of .40 to be significant.

Statistical significance is influenced not only by the size of the relationship between variables, but also by the number of participants in a study. The more people studied, the smaller the correlation needs to be in order to reach statistical significance. For example, a correlation of $r = .30$ is statistically significant when the number of observations is large—say, 300—but is not significant if only 20 observations were made. Thus, if the alcohol consumption of 10 depressed and 10 nondepressed men were studied and the correlation between depression and drinking was found to be .32, the correlation would not be statistically significant. The same correlation, however, would be significant if two groups of 150 men were studied.

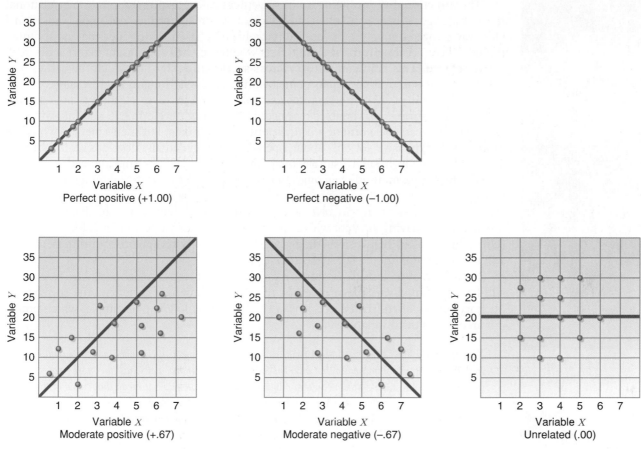

Figure 4.2 Scatter diagrams showing various degrees of correlational relationship.

In a survey as large as the United States Census Bureau, almost every correlation you could conceive of would be statistically significant. Because of this issue, researchers also attend to whether a correlation is large enough to be of **clinical significance**. For example, one might want to see that a risk factor has a moderately strong relationship with the severity of symptoms. Clinical significance is also considered with statistics other than correlations. For a treatment effect to be considered clinically significant, a researcher might want to see that symptoms in the active treatment condition were decreased by 50 percent or that patients appeared comparable to those without disorder at the end of treatment. In other words, researchers should evaluate whether an effect is statistically significant (Jacobson et al., 1999), but also whether the effect is large enough to be meaningful in predicting or treating a clinical disorder.

Problems of Causality Even though it is commonly used, the correlational method has a critical drawback: It does not allow determination of cause–effect relationships. A large correlation between two variables tells us only that they are related to each other, but we do not know if either variable is the cause of the other. For example, a correlation has been found between the diagnosis of schizophrenia and social class; lower-class people are diagnosed with schizophrenia more often than middle- and upper-class people are. One possible explanation is that the stresses of living in the lowest social class cause an increase in the prevalence of schizophrenia. But a second hypothesis has been supported. It may be that the disorganized behavior patterns of persons with schizophrenia cause them to perform poorly in their occupational endeavors and thus to become impoverished.

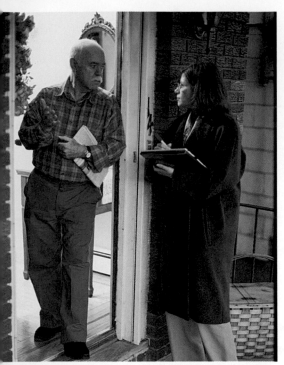

In some epidemiological research, interviewers go door-to-door to conduct interviews. (R. Lord/ The Image Works.)

Epidemiological research has shown that mood disorders, anxiety disorders, and substance abuse are extremely common. (Stone/Getty Images.)

The **directionality problem**, as it is sometimes called, is present in most correlational research designs—hence the often-cited dictum "Correlation does not imply causation." One way of overcoming the directionality problem is based on the idea that causes must precede effects. A **longitudinal design** tests whether causes are present before a disorder has developed. This is in contrast to a **cross-sectional design**, in which the causes and effects are measured at the same point of time. A classic longitudinal design to study the development of schizophrenia, for example, would involve selecting a large sample of babies, measuring risk variables repeatedly throughout development, and following the sample for 45 years to determine who develops schizophrenia. But such a method would be prohibitively expensive, for only about 1 person in 100 eventually develops schizophrenia. The yield of data from such a simple longitudinal study would be small indeed.

The **high-risk method** overcomes this problem; with this approach, only people with above average risk of developing schizophrenia would be studied. For example, several current research programs involve studying people who have a parent diagnosed with schizophrenia (having a parent with schizophrenia increases a person's risk for developing schizophrenia). The high-risk method is also used to study several other disorders, and we will examine these findings in subsequent chapters.

Even if a high-risk study identifies a variable that precedes schizophrenia, a researcher still faces the **third-variable problem**; a third factor may have produced the correlation. Such factors are often labeled as *confounds*. Consider the following example, which points out an obvious third variable.

> One regularly finds a high positive correlation between the number of churches in a city and the number of crimes committed in that city. That is, the more churches a city has, the more crimes are committed in it. Does this mean that religion fosters crime, or does it mean that crime fosters religion? It means neither. The relationship is due to a particular third variable—population. The higher the population of a particular community, the greater...the number of churches and ... the frequency of criminal activity. (Neale & Liebert, 1986, p. 109)

Psychopathology research offers numerous examples of third variables. Biochemical differences between patients with schizophrenia and those with no psychiatric disorder often are reported. These differences could reflect the influence of medications for the schizophrenia, or even dietary differences between groups; the differences do not reveal anything about the nature of schizophrenia. Are there ways to resolve the third-variable problem? Although some strategies can help reduce it, the solutions are only partially satisfactory. Take the example of diet as a potential confound in biochemical differences in schizophrenia. Researchers can try to control for diet in statistical analyses, but they may not measure the most important aspects of diet. It is not feasible to measure every possible confound. Because of the third-variable problem, causal inferences cannot be made from correlational data.

One Example of Correlational Research: Epidemiological Research   Epidemiology is the study of the distribution of disorders in a population. That is, data are gathered about the rates of a disorder and its possible correlates in a large sample. This provides a picture of a disorder and how many people it affects. Epidemiological research focuses on three features of a disorder:

1. **Prevalence**. The proportion of people with the disorder either currently or during their lifetime;
2. **Incidence**. The proportion of people who develop *new* cases of the disorder in some period, usually a year;
3. **Risk factor**. Variables that are related to the likelihood of developing the disorder.

Epidemiological studies of risk factors are usually correlational studies, because they examine how variables relate to each other without including a manipulation of the independent variable.

Epidemiological studies are designed to be *representative* of the population being studied—researchers use a set of strategies to test a group of people that matches the population on key characteristics, like gender, economic status, and ethnicity. Unfortunately, much of mental health research does not follow these principles, but rather draws on samples that are not representative. For example, many studies use undergraduate samples. Undergraduates are likely to be wealthier and more educated than the general population. If we only studied undergraduates with anxiety disorders, we could end up concluding that people with anxiety disorders are above average in intelligence. Other studies use samples drawn from treatment centers; people who seek treatment may be those with the more severe forms of disorders. These types of bias can skew our perceptions of how risk factors relate to mental disorders. Epidemiological studies, then, are needed to carefully identify risk variables.

Table 4.4 Lifetime Prevalence Rates of Selected Diagnoses

Disorder	Male	Female	Total
Major depressive disorder	12.7	21.3	16.6
Bipolar I or II disorder	1.6	1.7	3.9
Dysthymia	4.8	8.0	2.5
Panic disorder	2.0	5.0	4.7
Agoraphobia without panic	3.5	7.0	1.4
Social phobia	11.1	15.5	12.1
Specific phobia	6.7	15.7	12.5
Generalized anxiety disorder	3.6	6.6	5.7
Alcohol abuse	20.1	8.2	13.2
Drug abuse	5.8	1.2	7.9

Source: From data collected in the National Comorbidity Survey (Kessler et al., 2005).

The National Comorbidity Survey–Replication is an example of one large-scale national survey that used structured interviews to collect information on the prevalence of several diagnoses (Kessler et al., 2005). Table 4.4 shows some data from this study. The table presents lifetime prevalence rates—the proportion of people who experienced a disorder during their lifetime. From the table, we can see that major depression, alcoholism, and anxiety disorders are very common—so common, in fact, that as many as half (46.4 percent) of the people in the United States describe meeting criteria for a mental disorder at some point during their life. Knowing that mental disorders will strike one out of every two people should help reduce stigma. People who experience the disorders may take comfort in knowing that so many other people struggle with similar issues.

Knowledge about risk factors may give clues to the causes of disorders. For example, depression is about twice as common in women as in men. Thus, gender is a risk factor for depression. In Chapter 8, we will review theories about this gender difference. The results of epidemiological research may inform us about risk factors (like gender and social class) that can be more thoroughly investigated using other research methods.

Another Example of Correlational Research: Behavior Genetics   Research on behavior genetics has relied on three basic methods to uncover whether a genetic predisposition for psychopathology is inherited—comparison of members of a family, comparison of pairs of twins, and the investigation of adoptees. In each case, researchers are interested in whether patterns of disorder in one group of people are correlated with patterns of disorder in relatives.

The **family method** can be used to study a genetic predisposition among members of a family because the average number of genes shared by two blood relatives is known. Children receive a random sample of half their genes from one parent and half from the other, so on average siblings and parents and children share 50 percent of their genetic background. People who share 50 percent of their genes with a given person are called first-degree relatives of that person. Relatives not as closely related share fewer genes. For example, nephews and nieces share 25 percent of the genetic makeup of an uncle, and are called second-degree

Studies of college students with mild symptoms may not provide a good analogue for major mental illness. (B. Daemmrich/The Image Works.)

relatives. If a predisposition for a mental disorder can be inherited, a study of the family should reveal a relationship between the number of shared genes and the *concordance* of the disorder in relatives (that is, whether the relatives are matched on presence or absence of a disorder).

The starting point in such investigations is the collection of a sample of persons with the diagnosis in question. These people are referred to as **index cases,** or **probands**. Then relatives are studied to determine the frequency with which the same diagnosis might be applied to them. If a genetic predisposition to the disorder being studied is present, first-degree relatives of the index cases should have the disorder at a rate higher than that found in the general population. This is the case with schizophrenia: about 10 percent of the first-degree relatives of index cases with schizophrenia can be diagnosed as having this disorder, compared with about 1 percent of the general population.

In the **twin method** both **monozygotic (MZ) twins** and **dizygotic (DZ) twins** are compared. MZ, or identical, twins develop from a single fertilized egg and are genetically the same. DZ, or fraternal, pairs develop from separate eggs and are on average only 50⁻percent alike genetically, no more alike than are any two siblings. MZ twins are always the same sex, but DZ twins can be either the same sex or opposite in sex. Twin studies begin with diagnosed cases and then search for the presence of the disorder in the other twin. When the twins are similar diagnostically they are said to be concordant. To the extent that a predisposition for a mental disorder can be inherited, **concordance** for the disorder should be greater in genetically identical MZ pairs than in DZ pairs. When the MZ concordance rate is higher than the DZ rate, the characteristic being studied is said to be heritable. We will see in later chapters that the concordance for many forms of psychopathology is higher in MZ twins than in DZ twins.

Although the methodology of family and twin studies is clear, the data they yield are not always easy to interpret. For example, children of parents with agoraphobia—people suffering from a fear of being in places where it would be hard to escape if they were to become highly anxious—are themselves more likely than average to have agoraphobia. Does this mean that a predisposition for this anxiety disorder is genetically transmitted? Not necessarily. The greater number of family members with agoraphobia could reflect the child-rearing practices and modeling of the phobic parents. In other words, family and twin studies show that agoraphobia runs in families, but not necessarily that a genetic predisposition is involved.

The ability to offer a genetic interpretation of data from twin studies hinges on what is called the "equal environment assumption." Psychopathology is a phenotypic characteristic, that is, psychopathology is a result of both genetic and environmental factors. For whatever diagnosis is being studied, the equal environment assumption is that the environmental factors that are partial causes of concordance are equally influential for both MZ pairs and DZ pairs. This does not mean that the environments of MZ and DZ twins are equal in all respects; the assumption of equality applies only to factors that are plausible environmental causes of psychopathology. For example, the equal environment assumption would assert that MZ pairs and DZ pairs have equivalent numbers of stressful life experiences. In general, the equal environment assumption seems to be reasonable, although it is clearly in need of further study (Kendler, 1993).

The **adoptees method** studies children who were adopted and reared completely apart from their biological parents. Though infrequent, this method has the benefit of eliminating the influence of being raised by parents with a disorder. If a high frequency of agoraphobia were found in children reared apart from their parents who also had agoraphobia, we would have convincing support for the theory that a genetic predisposition figures in the disorder. Another adoptee method is called **cross-fostering**. In this method, children are adopted and reared completely apart from their biological parents. In this case, however, the adoptive parent has a particular disorder, not the biological parent.

The study of MZ twins reared completely apart would also be valuable, but this situation occurs so rarely that there is almost no research using this method to study psychopathology. However, research involving separated twins does exist in the study of the inheritance of personality traits.

Quick Summary

Science is the systematic pursuit of knowledge through observation. The first step of science is to define a theory and related hypotheses. A good theory is precise and could be disproven.

The case study is an excellent way of examining the behavior of a single person in rich detail and of generating hypotheses that can be evaluated by controlled research. Some cases provide evidence that goes against a universal law, or illustrate a rare disorder or technique. But findings from a case study may or may not be valid—they may be biased by the observer's theories, and the patterns observed in one case may not apply to others. Furthermore, the case study cannot provide satisfactory evidence concerning cause–effect relationships because alternative hypotheses are not examined.

Correlational studies allow a researcher to gather data about variables and to see if these variables covary. No variables are manipulated; rather the experimenter assesses whether a naturally occurring relationship is large enough to appear statistically significant and clinically meaningful. Psychopathologists are forced to make heavy use of the correlational method because there are many key variables, including diagnosis, genes, trauma, and neurobiological deficits, that they do not have the freedom to manipulate. But correlational findings are clouded by third-variable and directionality problems.

Studies of epidemiology and behavioral genetics often use correlational designs. Researchers use epidemiological studies to assess how common disorders are (incidence and prevalence), and what risk factors are associated with disorders. Behavior genetic research uses the family method, looking to see how the presence of a disorder varies by the amount of genes shared by family members; the twin method, comparing monozygotic and dizygotic twins to see whether twins with more shared genes are at greater risk for developing a disorder; and the adoptees method to help separate gene and environmental effects.

Check Your Knowledge 4.2

1. Which of the following are good uses of case studies (circle all that apply):
   a. to illustrate a rare disorder or treatment
   b. to show that a theory does not fit for everyone
   c. to prove a model
   d. to show cause and effect
2. Correlational studies involve
   a. manipulating the independent variable
   b. manipulating the dependent variable
   c. manipulating the independent and dependent variable
   d. none of the above
3. The most central problem that is unique to correlational studies, regardless of how carefully a researcher designs a study, is
   a. findings are qualitative rather than statistical
   b. it is impossible to know which variable changes first
   c. third variables may explain a correlation

d. findings may not generalize
4. Incidence refers to:
   a. the number of people who will develop a disorder during their lifetime
   b. the number of people who report a disorder at the time of an interview
   c. the number of people who develop a disorder during a given time period
   d. none of the above
5. In studies of behavior genetics, researchers can rule out the influence of parenting variables most carefully if they conduct studies using the:
   a. correlational method
   b. family method
   c. twin method
   d. adoptee method

The Experiment

The **experiment** is the most powerful tool for determining causal relationships. It involves the **random assignment** of participants to conditions, the manipulation of an **independent variable**, and the measurement of a **dependent variable**. In the field of psychopathology the experiment is most often used to evaluate the effects of therapies.

As an introduction to the basics of experimental research, consider a study of how emotional expression relates to health (Pennebaker, Kiecolt-Glaser, & Glaser, 1988). In this experiment, 50 undergraduates came to a laboratory for 4 consecutive days. On each of the 4 days, half the students wrote a short essay about a past traumatic event. They were instructed as follows:

> *During each of the four writing days, I want you to write about the most traumatic and upsetting experiences of your entire life. You can write on different topics each day or on the same topic for*

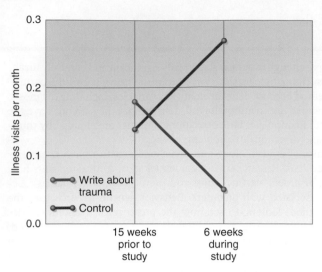

Figure 4.3 Health-center illness visits for the periods before and during the experiment. Visits for students who wrote about past traumas went down while visits for those who wrote about mundane events actually rose. After Pennebaker et al. (1988).

all four days. The important thing is that you write about your deepest thoughts and feelings. Ideally, whatever you write about should deal with an event or experience that you have not talked with others about in detail.

The remaining students also came to the laboratory each day but wrote essays describing topics like their daily activities, a recent social event, the shoes they were wearing, and their plans for the rest of the day.

Information about how often the participants used the university health center was available for the 15-week period before the study began and for the 6 weeks after it had begun. Figure 4.3 shows these data. Members of the two groups had visited the health center about equally before the experiment. After writing the essays, however, the number of visits declined for students who wrote about their emotions and increased for the remaining students. (This increase may have been due to seasonal variation in rates of visits to the health center. The second measure of number of visits was taken in February, just before midterm exams.) From these data the investigators concluded that expressing emotions has a beneficial effect on health.

Basic Features of Experimental Design The emotional expression study illustrates many of the basic features of an experiment.

1. The investigator manipulates an independent variable. In this study, the independent variable was the writing topic.
2. Participants are assigned to the two conditions (emotions versus mundane happenings) by random assignment.
3. The researcher measures a dependent variable, which is expected to vary with conditions of the independent variable. The dependent variable in this study was the number of visits to the health center.
4. Differences between conditions on the dependent variable are called the **experimental effect**.

Table 4.5 Results of a Hypothetical Study Comparing Cognitive Therapy to No Treatment for Depression

Cognitive Treatment Participants	Depression Score at End of Study	No. Therapy Participants	Depression Score at End of Study
Participant 1	8	Participant 11	22
Participant 2	6	Participant 12	14
Participant 3	12	Participant 13	26
Participant 4	4	Participant 14	28
Participant 5	3	Participant 15	19
Participant 6	6	Participant 16	27
Participant 7	18	Participant 17	6
Participant 8	14	Participant 18	32
Participant 9	7	Participant 19	21
Participant 10	5	Participant 20	23
Group Average	**8.3**		**21.7**

Note: Low scores indicate less depression following treatment.

To illustrate, consider a hypothetical study of the effectiveness of cognitive therapy in reducing depression among 20 depressed patients. (In actual research, 20 patients would be regarded as a very small sample; we present a small number of cases so the example is easier to follow.) The independent variable is cognitive therapy versus no treatment; 10 patients are randomly assigned to receive cognitive therapy and 10 are randomly assigned to a no-treatment control group. The dependent variable is the score on a standardized measure of the severity of depression, assessed after 12 weeks of treatment or no treatment; higher scores reflect more severe depression. Table 4.5 presents data for the hypothetical patients in each group. Note that the average scores of the two groups differ considerably (8.3 for the cognitive-therapy group and 21.7 for the no-treatment group). This difference between groups, called the experimental effect, is an index of whether the independent variable influences the dependent variable. To evaluate the importance of an experimental effect, as with correlations, researchers determine statistical significance.

Internal Validity Internal validity refers to the extent to which the experimental effect can be attributed to the independent variable. For example, for a treatment study to have internal validity, the researchers must include at least one **control group** that does not receive the experimental treatment. That is, a control group is needed to claim that the effects of an experiment are due to the independent variable. In the Pennebaker study, the control group wrote about mundane happenings. In the cognitive-therapy example, the control group received no treatment. The data from a control group provide a standard against which the effects of an independent variable can be assessed.

To illustrate the importance of a control group with another example, consider a study of the effectiveness of a particular therapy in reducing anxiety. Let us assume that persons with high anxiety receive therapy to remedy their condition. With no control group against which to compare the improvement, we cannot argue that changes are due to the treatment or that this study is an experiment. The improvement in anxiety from the beginning of the treatment to the end could have been due to factors other than the treatment, such as the resolution of difficult stressors, the passage of time, or support from friends. Without a control group, any changes during treatment are difficult to interpret.

In the example just outlined, including a control group would improve internal validity. For example, a control group might consist of persons with equally severe anxiety who do not receive the treatment. The effects of the independent variable could be assessed by comparing changes in anxiety of the treatment and control groups. If the treatment group experiences more relief from anxiety than the control group, we can be relatively confident that this difference is attributable to the treatment. See Focus on Discovery 4.3 for a discussion of some special considerations when a control group includes a **placebo**.

The inclusion of a control group does not always ensure internal validity, however. Consider another therapy study involving two psychiatric inpatient units. An investigator may decide to select one inpatient unit to receive an experimental treatment and the other unit as a control. In this study, the researcher cannot claim that group differences are the result of treatment, because a competing hypothesis cannot be disproven: patients in the two units might have differed because staff on the two units might offer care that differs in many ways. Without true random assignment, potential confounds make results hard to interpret. This study design is poor because the researchers did not use random assignment. To randomly assign participants in a two-group experiment, for example, the researchers could toss a coin for each participant. If the coin turned up heads, the participant would be assigned to one group; if tails to the other group. Random assignment helps ensure that groups are similar on variables other than the independent variable.

External Validity   **External validity** is defined as the extent to which results can be generalized beyond the study. If investigators find that a particular treatment helps a particular group of patients, they will want to conclude that this treatment will be effective for other similar patients, at other times, and in other places. For example, Pennebaker and his colleagues would hope that their findings would generalize to other instances of emotional expression (e.g., confiding to a close friend), to other situations, and to people other than the study participants.

Determining the external validity of the results of an experiment is extremely difficult. For example, participants in studies often behave in certain ways because they are being observed, and thus results that are produced in the laboratory may not automatically be produced in the natural environment. External validity may also be threatened by including only a select group of persons in a study, such as college students (Coyne, 1994) or Caucasian middle-class Americans (Hall, 2001). Many treatment studies have recruited participants who only suffer from the illness being considered and excluded people who have additional mental illnesses. Because many people suffer from more than one mental illness, participants in these treatment studies may not mirror patients in the real world. Researchers must be alert to the extent to which they can claim findings are likely to generalize to people and instances not studied. Often, they must perform similar studies in new settings to test the generalizability of a finding.

Focus on Discovery 4.3

The Placebo Effect

Research on the effects of treatment—psychological or biological—should consider the **placebo effect**. This term refers to an improvement in physical or psychological condition that is due to a patient's expectations of help rather than to any active ingredient in a treatment. The classic example of a placebo effect occurs when a doctor prescribes a sugar pill but describes the pill as a proven treatment, and the patient reports symptom relief. J. D. Frank (1978) related placebo effects to faith healing in nonscientific societies. For centuries, suffering people have made pilgrimages to sanctified places and ingested sometimes foul-smelling concoctions in the belief that these efforts would improve their condition. Sometimes they did.

In psychotherapy research, patients in such groups receive support and encouragement, but do not receive the active ingredient in the kind of therapy under study. For example, in a cognitive therapy study, the person in the placebo control condition would not get help with changing self-critical thoughts.

The effects of pilgrimages to shrines, such as Fatima, may be placebo effects. (Hans Georg Roth/Corbis Images.)

The effects of placebos are significant and sometimes even long lasting. For example, a meta-analysis of 75 research studies revealed that 29.7 percent of patients with depression improved after they received a placebo (Walsh et al., 2002). Among depressed patients who respond to antidepressant medication, many may actually be showing a placebo response (Kirsch, 2000). To know whether a treatment is effective because of the active chemical ingredients or a placebo response, medication trials have often included a placebo control group.

In most medication studies with a placebo control group, a **double-blind procedure** is used. That is, researchers and patients are not told whether the patient receives active medication or placebo, so as to reduce bias in evaluating outcomes. A double-blind procedure can be hard to implement. Researchers and patients may figure out who is getting the active treatment because medications are much more likely to produce side effects than placebos are (Salamone, 2000).

The use of placebo control has become hotly contested. First, it raises ethical issues because effective treatment is being withheld from some patients. Second, for ethical reasons, potential participants must be informed about the details of the study in which they are being asked to participate (see p. 595), including if they have a chance of being assigned to a placebo condition. What does this knowledge do to the possibility of experiencing a placebo effect? Can the findings be generalized if people who feel an intense need for an active treatment won't sign up for a study?

Problems such as these have led the World Medical Association (Rothman & Michels, 1994; World Medical Association, 2000) to suggest that placebo and no-treatment control groups should only be used if the experimenter can justify the need for such groups scientifically, and if the study does not include people who might be irreversibly harmed by the lack of treatment (e.g., people who are acutely suicidal). Instead of a placebo control, they recommend comparing an experimental treatment to the currently standard treatment. Of course, this approach can only be used if there is a standard treatment. In sum, there is considerable pressure against the use of placebo trials.

Others have argued that placebo control groups are vital for testing how treatments work (Charney et al., 2002). For example, consider recent studies of St.-John's-wort, an herbal remedy which many people believed could be helpful for depression. In a recent study, St.-John's-wort performed comparably to a standard antidepressant in producing relief from depressive symptoms (Hypericum Depression Trial Group, 2002). If no placebo control group were included, the conclusion of the study would have seemed supportive of St.-John's-wort. But the researchers also included a placebo control group, and they showed that neither St.-John's-wort nor the standard antidepressant treatment fared better than placebo. These results, then, suggest that St.-John's-wort is not an effective treatment. The inclusion of the placebo control group changes the conclusions of the study rather dramatically!

The debate continues over whether or not to use placebo control groups. The answers are not easy, and they are likely to vary for different disorders, different patients, and different researchers.

Analogue Experiments   The experimental method is the most telling way to determine cause–effect relationships. Even though experiments are typically used to test treatments, there are many situations in which the experimental method cannot be used to understand the causes of abnormal behavior. Why?

Suppose that a researcher has hypothesized that a child's emotionally charged, overly dependent relationship with his or her mother causes generalized anxiety disorder. An experimental test of this hypothesis would require assigning infants randomly to either of two groups of mothers. The mothers in one group would undergo an extensive training program to ensure that they would be able to create a highly emotional atmosphere and foster overdependence in children. The mothers in the second group would be trained not to create such a relationship with their children. The researcher would then wait until the participants in each group reached adulthood and determine how many of them had developed generalized anxiety disorder.

Beyond the pragmatic barriers, such an experimental design contains obvious ethical problems. Would the potential scientific gain of proving that an overly dependent relationship with a person's mother brings on generalized anxiety disorder outweigh the suffering that would be imposed on some of the participants? In almost any person's view, it would not. (Ethical issues are considered in detail in Chapter 17.)

In an effort to take advantage of the power of the experimental method, researchers sometimes use an **analogue experiment**. Investigators attempt to bring a related phenomenon, that is, an analogue, into the laboratory for more intensive study. Because a true experiment is conducted, results with good internal validity can be obtained. The problem of external validity arises, however, because the researchers are no longer studying the actual phenomenon of interest.

In one type of analogue study, temporary symptoms are produced through experimental manipulations. For example, lactate infusion can elicit a panic attack, hypnotic suggestion can produce blindness similar to that seen in conversion disorder, and threats to self-esteem can produce anxiety or sadness. If mild symptoms can be experimentally induced by such manipulations, this may provide clues into the causes of more severe symptoms.

In another type of analogue study, participants are selected because they are considered similar to people with certain diagnoses. Thousands of studies, for example, have been conducted with college students who received high scores on questionnaire measures of anxiety or depression.

A third type of analogue study involves using animals as a way to understand human behavior. For example, researchers found that dogs who were exposed to electrical shocks that they could not control developed many of the symptoms of depression, including seeming despair and passivity (Seligman, Maier, & Geer, 1968). Similarly, researchers interested in studying anxiety disorder in humans sometimes study how animals become conditioned to fear previously unthreatening stimuli (Grillon, 2002). Such animal models have helped to understand more about the neurotransmitter systems that may be involved in depression and anxiety disorders in humans.

The key to interpreting such studies lies in the validity of the analogue. Is a stressor encountered in the laboratory fundamentally similar to the death of a parent or other serious stressors? Are distressed college students similar to people with clinically diagnosable depression? Are lethargy and decreased eating in mice akin to depressive symptoms in humans? Some would argue against such approaches overall, even when researchers are careful to discuss the limits of generalizability. For example, Coyne (1994) has argued that clinical depression is caused by different processes than those that cause common distress. He would argue that analogue studies with undergraduates have poor external validity.

We believe that analogue studies can be very helpful, but that findings from these types of studies must be considered conjointly with studies that do not rely on analogues. Science often depends on comparing the results of experimental analogue studies to those of longitudinal correlational studies. For example, analogue studies have shown that people with depression respond more negatively to laboratory stressors (an analogue of life stress), and correlational studies have shown that major life events predict the onset of clinical levels of depression. Because the findings from correlational and analogue studies complement each other, this provides a strong level of support for life event models of depression. Analogue studies can provide the precision of an experiment (high internal validity) whereas correlational studies provide the ability to study very important

Harlow's famous analogue research examined the effects of early separation from the mother on infant monkeys. Even a cloth surrogate mother is better than isolation for preventing subsequent emotional distress and depression. (Martin Rogers/Woodfin Camp & Associates.)

influences that cannot be manipulated, like the influence of death and trauma (high external validity).

Single-Subject Experiments   We have been discussing experimental research with groups of participants, but experiments do not always have to be conducted on groups. In **single-subject experimental design**, the experimenter studies how each person responds to manipulations of the independent variable. Unlike the traditional case studies described above, single-subject experimental designs can have high internal validity.

Chorpita, Vitali, and Barlow (1997) provide an example of how single case studies can provide well-controlled data. They describe their treatment of a 13-year-old girl with a phobia (intense fear) of choking, such that she was no longer able to eat solid foods. At times, her fear was so intense that she would experience fast heart rate, chest pain, dizziness, and other symptoms. She reported that the most frightening foods were hard foods, such as raw vegetables.

A behavioral treatment was designed based on exposure. During the first 2 weeks, baseline ratings were taken of the amount of different foods eaten, along with her level of discomfort in eating those foods. Discomfort ratings were made on a "subjective units of distress scale" (SUDS) ranging from 0 to 9. Figure 4.4 shows her SUDS ratings and eating behavior over time for each food group. During the third week, she was asked to begin eating foods she described as less threatening—crackers and cookies—in three 4-minute blocks each day. The authors hoped that exposure to feared foods would reduce her anxiety, a common strategy for treating anxiety.

Despite this intervention, though, the patient's SUDS ratings and food consumption did not improve. When the therapist talked with the client and her parents, he discovered that the patient was eating only the absolute minimum of foods, such that she was not getting enough exposure to the feared stimulus. To increase her exposure to foods, reinforcement was added to the program—her parents were instructed to give her ice cream at the end of any day in which the patient had consumed at least three servings of the target food. Within a week, she reported being able to consume crackers and cereals without distress. Gradually, she was asked to begin eating more frightening foods. One week, she was asked to begin consuming soft vegetables, pasta, and cheese, followed the next week by meat, and the next week by raw vegetables, salad, and hard fruit. As shown by the graphs, with the introduction of exposure to each new food group, the client experienced a reduction in SUDS ratings within the next week; effects do not look like they were due to just simply time or maturation, as anxiety was only reduced after the client began exposure for the new food group. The repeated decrements in anxiety are hard to explain using any variable other than treatment. Gains were maintained through a 19-month follow-up.

In one form of single-case design, referred to as a **reversal design** or **ABAB** design, the participant's behavior must be carefully measured in a specific sequence:

1. An initial time period, the baseline (A);
2. A period when a treatment is introduced (B);
3. A reinstatement of the conditions of the baseline period (A);
4. A reintroduction of the experimental manipulation (B).

If behavior in the experimental period is different from that in the baseline period, reverses when the treatment is removed, and re-reverses when the treatment is again introduced, there is little doubt that the manipulation, rather than chance or uncontrolled factors, has produced the change. Hence, even though there is no control group, there are time periods that serve as control comparisons for the experimental manipulation (Hersen & Barlow, 1976).

The reversal technique cannot always be employed, however, because the initial state of a participant may not be recoverable. Remember that most treatments aim to produce

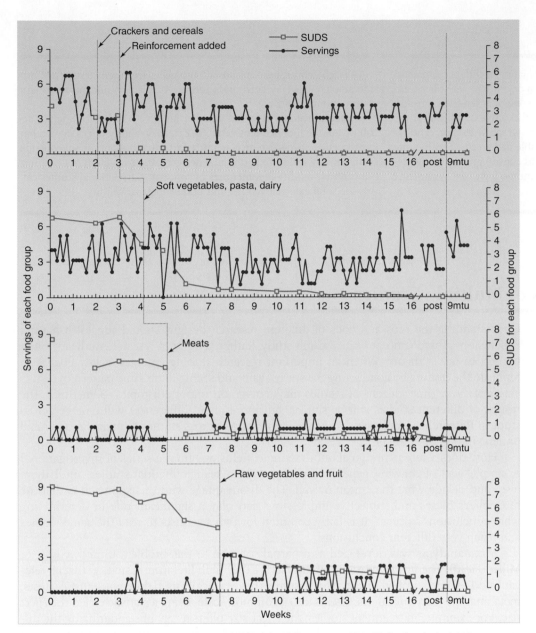

Figure 4.4   Effects of exposure treatment (E) and reinforcement (E + R) for food phobia in a single-subject design. Note the rapid shifts in SUDS ratings as exposure for each new food group is introduced. Reprinted from *Journal of Behavior Therapy and Experimental Psychiatry, 28,* Chorpita et al., "Behavioral treatment of choking phobia in an adolescent: An experimental analysis," 307–315, copyright 1997, with permission from Elsevier.

enduring change, so just removing an intervention may not return a person to the pre-treatment state. This type of design, then, is most applicable when a researcher believes that the effects of their manipulation are temporary.

Perhaps the biggest drawback of single-case designs is the potential lack of external validity. The fact that a treatment works for a single person does not necessarily imply that it will be effective for others. Findings may relate to a unique aspect of the one person whose behavior has been explored. Often researchers will present data from a small series of cases. Even then, it is important to consider whether results can be generalized to other people. Results of single-case experimental studies may help investigators to decide whether research with larger groups is warranted.

Quick Summary

The experimental method entails the manipulation of independent variables and the measurement of their effects on dependent variables. Generally, participants are randomly assigned to one of at least two groups: an experimental group, which experiences the active condition of the independent variable; and a control group, which does not. The researcher tests to see if the independent variable had an effect by looking for differences between the experimental and control groups on the dependent variable. Treatment studies are a common form of experimental research.

Placebo control groups are often used in treatment research. Considerable controversy surrounds the use of placebo and no-treatment control groups.

Internal validity refers to whether an effect can be confidently attributed to the independent variable. External validity refers to whether experimental effects can be generalized to situations and people outside of this specific study. Experimental designs can provide internal validity, but external validity is sometimes of concern. Correlational studies can provide solid external validity, but poorer internal validity.

Integrating the Findings of Multiple Studies

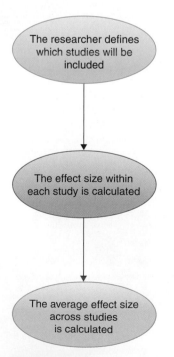

Figure 4.5 Steps in conducting a meta-analysis.

Understanding the pros and cons of different research designs should suggest a natural conclusion—there is no perfect research study. Rather, a body of research studies is often needed to test a theory. When an important research finding emerges, a key goal is to replicate the finding by conducting the study again and seeing if the same pattern of results emerges. Over time, dozens of studies may emerge on important topics. Sometimes, the results of different studies will be similar, but more often, differences will emerge across studies. Researchers must synthesize the information across studies to arrive at a general understanding of findings.

How does a researcher go about drawing conclusions from a series of investigations? A simple way of drawing general conclusions is to read individual studies, mull them over, and decide what they mean overall. The disadvantage with this approach is that the researcher's biases and subjective impressions can play a significant role in determining what conclusion is drawn. It is fairly common for two scientists to read the same studies and reach very different conclusions.

Meta-analysis was developed as a partial solution to this problem (Smith, Glass, & Miller, 1980). The first step in a meta-analysis is a thorough literature search, so that all relevant studies are identified. Because these studies have typically used different statistical tests, meta-analysis then puts all the results into a common scale, using a statistic called the *effect size*. For example, in treatment studies, the effect size offers a way of standardizing the differences in improvement between a therapy group and a control group so that the results of many different studies can be averaged. Figure 4.5 summarizes the steps in a meta-analysis.

In their often-cited report, Smith et al. (1980) meta-analyzed 475 psychotherapy outcome studies involving more than 25,000 patients and 1,700 effect sizes; they came to conclusions that have attracted considerable attention and some controversy. Most importantly, they concluded that psychotherapies produce more improvement than does no treatment. Specifically, treated patients were found to be better off than almost 80 percent of untreated patients. Subsequent meta-analyses by other authors have confirmed that therapy appears effective (Lambert & Ogles, 2004).

Meta-analysis has been criticized by a number of researchers. The central problem is that researchers sometimes include studies that are of poor quality in a meta-analysis. Smith and colleagues gave equal weight to all studies, so that a poorly controlled outcome study (such as one that did not evaluate what the therapists actually did in each session) received as much weight as a well-controlled one (such as a study in which therapists used a manual that specified what they did with each research participant). When Smith and colleagues attempted to address this problem by comparing effect sizes of good versus poor studies and found no differences, they were further criticized for the criteria they employed in separating the good from the not so good (Rachman & Wilson, 1980)! O'Leary and Wilson

(1987) concluded that the ultimate problem is that someone has to make a judgment of good versus poor quality in research and that others can find fault with that judgment. A good meta-analysis, though, will be clear about the criteria for including or excluding studies.

Check Your Knowledge 4.3

1. In an experimental design, the researcher manipulates:
   a. the independent variable
   b. the dependent variable
2. Dr. Jones is interested in whether a new treatment for autism will be helpful. She recruits 30 participants, and she randomly assigns 15 to receive drug *x* and 15 to receive a placebo. After 3 weeks of treatment, she measures social engagement. In this study, the independent variable is
   a. medication condition
   b. drug *x*
   c. social engagement
   d. autism
3. The dependent variable is
   a. treatment

   b. drug *x*
   c. social engagement
   d. autism
4. Single-case experimental designs may lack
   a. internal validity
   b. external validity
5. Correlational studies may lack
   a. internal validity
   b. external validity
6. The step in meta-analysis that has received extensive criticism is
   a. defining which studies should be included
   b. calculating the effect size of each study
   c. calculating the average effect size across studies
   d. none of the above

Summary

Science and Scientific Methods

- Science involves forming a theory and then systematically gathering data to test the theory. It is important for researchers to replicate findings from a given study, which requires being precise about the methods used.

Approaches to Research on Psychopathology

- Common methods for studying abnormal behavior include case studies, correlational studies, and experimental studies. Each method has strengths and weaknesses.
- Clinical case studies provide detailed descriptions of rare or unusual phenomena or novel procedures. Case studies can disconfirm that a relationship is universal and can generate hypotheses that can be tested through controlled research. Case studies, however, may not always be valid, and they are of limited value in providing evidence to support a theory.
- Correlational methods are the most common way to study the causes of abnormal behavior, because we cannot manipulate most of the key risk variables that we believe cause disease, nor can we manipulate diagnosis.
- Conclusions drawn from cross-sectional correlational studies cannot be interpreted in cause–effect terms, because of the directionality. Longitudinal studies help address which variable came first, but can still suffer from the third-variable problems.
- One form of correlational study, epidemiological research, involves gathering information about the prevalence and incidence of disorders

in populations and about risk factors that relate to higher probability of developing a disorder. Epidemiological studies avoid the sampling biases seen in studies of people drawn from undergraduate psychology classes or from treatment clinics.
- Studies of behavioral genetics often rely on correlational techniques as well. The most common behavioral genetic methods include the family method, the twin method, and the adoptees method.
- In the experimental method, the researcher randomly assigns people to an experimental group or a control group. Effects of the independent variable, or experimental condition, on a dependent variable are then tested. Treatment studies are a common example of experimental research. Some controversy has arisen about the use of placebos. Many different forms of analogue studies are conducted in psychopathology research. Single-case experimental designs can provide well-controlled data.
- Generally, experimental methods help enhance internal validity, but correlational methods sometimes offer greater external validity.

Integrating the Findings of Multiple Studies

- Meta-analysis is an important tool for reaching general conclusions from a group of research studies. It entails putting the statistical comparisons from single studies into a common format—the effect size—so the results of many studies can be averaged.

Answers to Check Your Knowledge Questions

4.1 1. F; 2. F
4.2 1. a and b; 2. d; 3. c; 4. c; 5. d

4.3 1. a; 2. a; 3. c; 4. b; 5. a; 6. a

Key Terms

adoptees method
analogue experiment
case study
clinical significance
concordance
control group
correlation
correlation coefficient
correlational method
cross-fostering
cross-sectional design

dependent variable
directionality problem
dizygotic (DZ) twins
double-blind procedure
epidemiology
experiment
experimental effect
external validity
family method
high-risk method
hypothesis

incidence
independent variable
index cases (probands)
internal validity
longitudinal design
meta-analysis
monozygotic (MZ) twins
placebo
placebo effect
prevalence
random assignment

reversal (ABAB) designs
risk factors
single-subject experimental
   design
statistical significance
theory
third-variable problem
twin method

5 Anxiety Disorders

Learning Goals

1. Be able to describe the clinical features of the anxiety disorders, and how the anxiety disorders tend to co-occur with each other.
2. Be able to describe how gender and culture influence the prevalence of anxiety disorders.
3. Be able to recognize commonalities in etiology and treatment across the anxiety disorders.
4. Be able to describe etiological factors and treatment approaches that are specific to each of the anxiety disorders.

Clinical Case: Jenny

Jenny was a 23-year-old student completing her first year of medical school. The year had been a difficult one, not only because of the long hours and academic challenges of medical school, but also because her mother had developed cancer. One day, while attending rounds, Jenny found herself feeling light-headed and dizzy. During rounds, the attending physician would ask students to diagnose and explain a given case, and on that day Jenny became extremely worried about whether she would be able to answer these questions when her turn came. As she thought about this, her heart began to pound, and her palms began to sweat. Overwhelmed by a deep sense of fear that something was horribly wrong, she abruptly left the room without explaining her departure. Later in the day, she thought about how to explain leaving rounds, but could not figure out how to describe the situation to the attending physician. That night, she could not sleep, wondering what had happened and worrying about whether it would happen again. She worried about how this would affect her ability not only to take part in rounds but also to perform well in other roles, such as leading a small research group and meeting with other medical staff and clients. One week later while driving to school, she experienced a sudden attack of similar symptoms, which forced her to pull off to the side of the road. She took the day off from school. Over the next several weeks, she began to avoid public situations as much as possible because she feared being humiliated by the return of these symptoms. She avoided study groups and going out with friends, and she turned down opportunities for training that involved public interviews of patients. Although she had enjoyed being part of a choir for several years, she resigned from the choir. Despite her withdrawal, she experienced three more attacks, each in unexpected situations. She began to think that maybe medical school was a poor choice for her, because she had such deep fears about experiencing another attack during rounds. After she read about panic disorder in one of her textbooks, she decided to visit a psychologist. The psychologist confirmed that she was experiencing an anxiety disorder called panic disorder, and they started cognitive behavioral treatment.

Very few of us go through even a week of our lives without experiencing anxiety or fear. In this chapter, we focus on a group of disorders called *anxiety disorders*. Both anxiety and fear play a significant role in these disorders, and so it is important to understand some of the similarities and differences between these two emotions.

Anxiety is defined as apprehension over an anticipated problem. In contrast, **fear** is defined as a reaction to immediate danger. Psychologists focus on the "immediate" aspect of fear versus the "anticipated" aspect of anxiety—fear tends to be about a threat that's happening now, whereas anxiety tends to be about a future threat. Thus, a person facing a bear experiences fear, whereas a college student concerned about the possibility of low wages after graduation experiences anxiety.

Both anxiety and fear can involve arousal, or sympathetic nervous system activity. Anxiety often involves moderate arousal, and fear involves higher arousal. At the low end, a person experiencing anxiety may feel no more than restless energy and physiological tension; at the high end, a person experiencing fear may sweat profusely, breathe rapidly, and feel an overpowering urge to run.

Anxiety and fear are not necessarily "bad"—in fact, both are adaptive. Fear is fundamental for "flight or fight" reactions—that is, fear triggers rapid changes in the sympathetic nervous system that prepare the body for escape or fighting. In the right circumstance, fear saves lives. (Imagine a person who faces a bear and experiences no impulse to flee, no surge in energy, and no marshalling of that energy to run quickly!) In some anxiety disorders, though, the fear system seems to misfire—a person experiences fear at a time when there is no danger in the environment (see the discussion of panic attacks later in this chapter).

Anxiety is adaptive in helping us notice and plan for future threats—that is, to increase our preparedness, to help people avoid potentially dangerous situations, and to think through potential problems before they happen. In laboratory studies first conducted 100 years ago and since verified many times over, a small degree of anxiety has been found to improve performance on laboratory tasks (Yerkes & Dodson, 1908). Ask anyone with extreme test anxiety, though, and they will tell you that too much anxiety interferes with performance. Anxiety, then, provides a classic example of a U-shaped curve with performance—a little anxiety is adaptive, a lot of anxiety is detrimental.

In this chapter, we examine the **anxiety disorders** included in DSM-IV-TR: specific phobias, social phobia, panic disorder (along with agoraphobia), generalized anxiety disorder, obsessive-compulsive disorder, and posttraumatic stress disorder (along with acute stress disorder). Anxiety disorders as a group are the most common type of psychiatric diagnosis. For example, in one study of over 8,000 adults in the United States, approximately 28 percent of people reported having experienced symptoms at some point during their life that met the DSM-IV-TR criteria for diagnosis of an anxiety disorder (Kessler et al., 2005-11-06). Phobias are particularly common. As a group, anxiety disorders are very costly to society and to people with the disorders. These disorders are associated with twice the average rate of medical costs (Simon et al., 1995), with difficulties in employment (APA, 2004), and with serious interpersonal concerns (Zatzick et al., 1997).

We begin by defining the symptoms of the anxiety disorders. Then we turn to the common themes in the etiology and treatment for these disorders as a group. Finally, we consider the etiology and treatment of the specific types of anxiety disorders. Like most disorders, many different paradigms have helped shed light on the anxiety disorders. Hence, throughout our discussions of etiology and treatment we look at issues from various perspectives, with particular focus on genetic, neurobiological, personality, cognitive, and behavioral research.

Clinical Descriptions of the Anxiety Disorders

The anxiety disorders all share excessively high or frequent levels of anxiety. Panic disorder and phobias are distinguished by high levels of fear as well as anxiety (Cox, Clara, & Enns, 2002). Each disorder, though, is defined by a different set of symptoms related to anxiety or

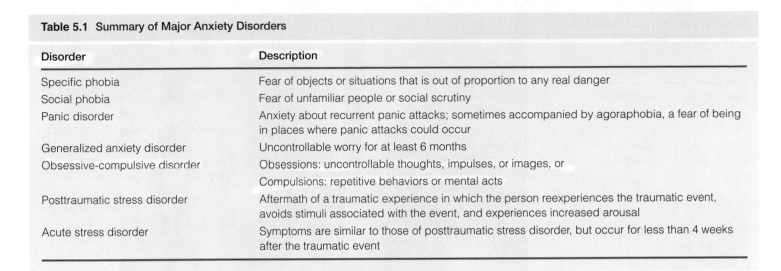

Table 5.1 Summary of Major Anxiety Disorders

Disorder	Description
Specific phobia	Fear of objects or situations that is out of proportion to any real danger
Social phobia	Fear of unfamiliar people or social scrutiny
Panic disorder	Anxiety about recurrent panic attacks; sometimes accompanied by agoraphobia, a fear of being in places where panic attacks could occur
Generalized anxiety disorder	Uncontrollable worry for at least 6 months
Obsessive-compulsive disorder	Obsessions: uncontrollable thoughts, impulses, or images, or
	Compulsions: repetitive behaviors or mental acts
Posttraumatic stress disorder	Aftermath of a traumatic experience in which the person reexperiences the traumatic event, avoids stimuli associated with the event, and experiences increased arousal
Acute stress disorder	Symptoms are similar to those of posttraumatic stress disorder, but occur for less than 4 weeks after the traumatic event

fear (see Table 5.1 for a brief summary). In each disorder, criteria specify that these anxieties or fears must interfere with functioning or cause marked distress to be diagnosed.

Phobias

DSM-IV-TR defines a **phobia** as a disruptive fear of a particular object or situation that is out of proportion to any danger posed. The person recognizes that the fear is excessive but still goes to great lengths to avoid the feared object or situation. The symptoms are so intense that they cause distress or interfere with the person's social or occupational activities. Here, we discuss two types of phobias: specific phobias and social phobia. (We will discuss agoraphobia below, in the context of panic disorder.)

Specific Phobias   A **specific phobia** is an unwarranted fear caused by the presence of a specific object or situation. Some examples of specific phobias are fear of flying, fear of snakes, and fear of heights. The names for these fears consist of a Greek word for the feared object or situation followed by the suffix *-phobia* (derived from the name of the Greek god Phobos, who frightened his enemies). Two of the more familiar phobias are claustrophobia (fear of closed spaces) and acrophobia (fear of heights). Table 5.2 describes potential names of some highly unlikely phobias. Despite this array of possible phobias, the actual occurrence of specific phobias tends to cluster around a small number of feared objects and situations. DSM-IV-TR categorizes specific phobias according to these sources of fear (see Table 5.3).

DSM-IV-TR Criteria for Specific Phobia

- Marked, persistent fear triggered by objects or situations
- Exposure to the trigger leads to intense anxiety
- The person recognizes the fear is unrealistic
- The object or situation is avoided or endured with intense anxiety

Clinical Case: Jan

Jan was a 42-year-old woman who was offered a high-paying job in Florida. She was considering turning the position down because it would force her to live in an area known for having snakes. Before making this decision, she decided to see a therapist. She described avoiding nature programs that might show snakes, asking her husband to read nature books to her children just in case they contained pictures of snakes, and avoiding outdoor activities because of this fear. Although she had been able to cope without too many negative consequences so far, the idea of living in an area with snakes had greatly increased her apprehension. Aside from her phobia, Jan reported that she had always been a bit of a nervous person, like her mother.

A person with one type of specific phobia is very likely to have another type of specific phobia as well—that is, there is high **comorbidity** of specific phobias (Kendler et al., 2001).

Table 5.2 Words Used to Describe Highly Unlikely Phobias

Fear	Phobia
Anything new	Neophobia
Asymmetrical things	Asymmetriphobia
Books	Bibliophobia
Children	Pedophobia
Dancing	Chorophobia
Englishness	Anglophobia
Garlic	Alliumphobia
Peanut butter sticking to the roof of the mouth	Arachibutyrophobia
Technology	Technophobia
Mice	Musophobia
Pseudoscientific terms	Hellenophobia

Source: Drawn from *www.phobialist.com.*

DSM-IV-TR Criteria for Social Phobia

- Marked, persistent fear triggered by exposure to unfamiliar people or social scrutiny
- Exposure to the trigger leads to intense anxiety about being humiliated or embarrassed
- The person recognizes the fear is unrealistic
- Trigger situations are avoided or endured with intense anxiety

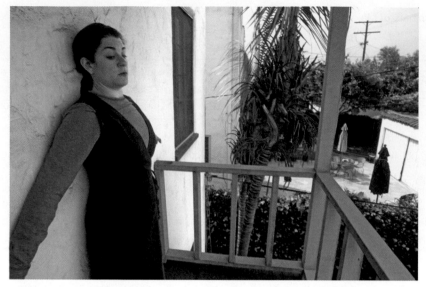

Fear and avoidance of heights is classified as a specific phobia. Other specific phobias include fears of animals, injections, and enclosed spaces. (Bill Aron/PhotoEdit.)

Phobias also are often comorbid with physical disorders—for example, in one study of men, those with high levels of phobic symptoms were three times more likely to develop coronary heart disease than those with low levels of phobic symptoms (Kawachi et al., 1994).

Social Phobia   A **social phobia** is a persistent, unrealistically intense fear of social situations that might involve being scrutinized by, or even just exposed to, unfamiliar people. The term "social anxiety disorder" has been proposed as a more appropriate label for this disorder because the problems caused by it tend to be much more pervasive and to interfere much more with normal activities than the problems caused by other phobias (Liebowitz et al., 2000). People with a social phobia usually try to avoid situations in which they might be evaluated, show signs of anxiety, or behave in embarrassing ways. Although this may sound like shyness, people with social phobia avoid more social situations, feel more discomfort socially, and experience these symptoms for longer periods of their life than people who are shy (Turner, Beidel, & Townsley, 1990). They often fear that they will blush or sweat excessively. Speaking or performing in public, eating in public, using public lavatories, or engaging in virtually any activity in the presence of others can cause extreme anxiety. People with social phobia often work in occupations far below their talents because of their extreme social fears. Better to resign oneself to a less rewarding job with limited social demand than deal with social situations every day.

Table 5.3 Types of Simple Phobias

Type of Phobia	Source of Fear	Associated Characteristics
Animal	Animals (e.g., snakes, insects)	Generally begins during childhood
Natural environment	Aspects of the natural environment (e.g., storms, heights, water)	Generally begins during childhood
Blood, injection, injury	Blood, injury, injections, or other invasive medical procedures	Clearly runs in families
Situational	Specific situations (e.g., public transportation, tunnels, bridges, elevators, flying, driving, closed spaces)	Tends to begin either in childhood or in mid-20s.
Other	Fear of choking, fear of contracting an illness, etc.; children's fears of loud sounds, clowns, etc.	—

Clinical Case: Maureen

Maureen, a 30-year-old accountant, sought psychotherapy after reading a newspaper notice advertising group therapy for people with difficulties in social situations. Maureen appeared nervous during the interview and described deep distress over the amount of anxiety she experienced in conversations with others. She described the problem as becoming worse over the years, to the point where she no longer interacted socially with anyone other than her husband. She would not even go to the supermarket for fear of having to interact with others. Maureen explained that she was afraid of interacting with others because she would feel extreme shame if others thought that she was stupid or could not express herself well. This fear made Maureen so nervous that she would often stammer or forget what she was going to say while talking to others, thus adding to her apprehension that others would see her as stupid and creating a vicious cycle of ever-increasing fear.

Among people with a social phobia, at least a third also meet the DSM-IV-TR criteria for diagnosis of avoidant personality disorder (see p. 403; Chavira, Stein, & Malcarne, 2002). Although symptoms of the two conditions overlap a great deal, avoidant personality disorder is considered a more severe disorder with an earlier onset and more pervasive symptoms (Heimberg, 1996). See Figure 5.1 for one way of thinking about shyness, social phobia, and avoidant personality disorder. Social phobia generally begins during adolescence, when social interactions become more important, but social phobia is sometimes found in children as well. Without treatment, social phobia tends to be chronic.

Social phobia is diagnosed as either generalized or specific, depending on the range of situations that the person fears and avoids. For example, a person who is anxious about writing in public, but is not anxious about other social situations would be diagnosed with specific social phobia. In contrast, a person who fears most social situations would be diagnosed with generalized social phobia. The generalized type is associated with an earlier age of onset, more comorbidity with other disorders, such as depression and alcohol abuse, and more negative effects on the person's social and occupational activities (Wittchen, Stein, & Kessler, 1999).

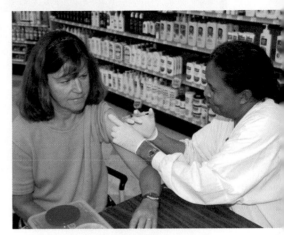

One form of specific phobia is an intense fear of blood, injection, or injuries. (David Young-Wolf/PhotoEdit.)

Panic Disorder and Agoraphobia

Panic disorder is characterized by frequent panic attacks that are unrelated to specific situations, and worry about having more panic attacks (see the case of Jenny, described in the beginning of this chapter). A **panic attack** is a sudden attack of intense apprehension, terror, and feelings of impending doom, accompanied by symptoms such as labored breathing, heart palpitations, nausea, chest pain, feelings of choking and smothering, dizziness, sweating, and trembling. Other symptoms that may occur during a panic attack include **depersonalization** (a feeling of being outside one's body), **derealization** (a feeling of the world's not being real), and fears of losing control, of going crazy, or even of dying. Not surprisingly, people often report that they have an intense urge to flee whatever situation they are in when a panic attack occurs. The symptoms tend to come on very rapidly and reach a peak of intensity within 10 minutes.

We can think about a panic attack as a misfire of the fear system—physiologically, the person experiences sympathetic nervous system arousal appropriate to an immediate threat to life. Because the symptoms are inexplicable, the person tries to make sense of the experience. If they begin to think that they are dying, losing control, or going crazy, they are likely to feel even more fear. Among people with panic disorder, 90 percent report just these types of beliefs when panic attacks occur.

When panic attacks occur unexpectedly, they are called *uncued* attacks. Uncued attacks can even happen when a person is relaxing or sleeping. When panic attacks are clearly triggered by specific situations, such as driving a car, they are referred to as *cued* panic attacks. People who only have cued attacks most likely suffer from a phobia. According to DSM-IV-TR criteria, for a diagnosis of panic disorder, a person must experience recurrent uncued panic attacks. They also must worry about the attacks or change their behavior

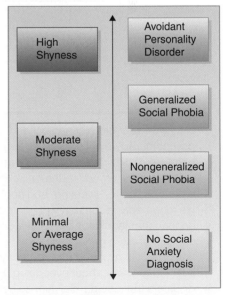

Figure 5.1 A spectrum model of shyness, social phobia, and avoidant personality disorder. [Adapted from Chavira, Stein & Malcarne (2002).]

Social phobia typically begins in adolescence and interferes with developing friendships with peers. (Spencer Grant/PhotoEdit.)

because of the attacks for at least 1 month—hence, the response to panic attacks is as important as the attacks themselves in making this diagnosis.

In DSM-IV-TR, there are two types of panic disorder: with agoraphobia and without agoraphobia. **Agoraphobia** (from the Greek *agora*, meaning "marketplace") is defined by anxiety about situations in which it would be embarrassing or difficult to escape if panic symptoms occurred. Often, the person fears public places where it would be embarrassing to experience a panic attack. Commonly feared situations include driving, being on bridges, being in grocery stores, malls, and churches, and being in crowds. Many people with agoraphobia are unable to leave their house, and even those who can leave their home do so only with great distress. Agoraphobia can also be diagnosed in the absence of panic disorder. In such a case, the person's fears still focus on developing panic-like symptoms (e.g., dizziness) in a place from which it would be hard to escape.

Panic disorder typically begins in adolescence, and over time it can take a heavy toll; for example, as many as one-quarter of people with panic disorder report being unemployed for more than 5 years (Leon, Portera, & Weissman, 1995). Among people with panic disorder, those with agoraphobia tend to have much more chronic symptoms. In a 22-month follow-up study, only 18 percent of those diagnosed with panic disorder with agoraphobia recovered from these symptoms, compared to 43 percent of those without agoraphobia (Keller et al., 1994).

Remember that the criteria for panic disorder specify that panic attacks must be recurrent. But it is fairly common for people to experience a single panic attack—in some studies, as many as 30 percent of people in the United States report that they have experienced at least one panic attack during their lifetime, and 3–5 percent report a panic attack in the past year (Norton, Cox, & Malan, 1992). As Table 5.4 shows, though, many fewer people develop full-blown panic disorder.

DSM-IV-TR Criteria for Panic Disorder

- Recurrent unexpected panic attacks
- At least 1 month of concern about the possibility of more attacks, worry about the consequences of an attack, or behavioral changes because of the attacks

Generalized Anxiety Disorder

One of the central features of **generalized anxiety disorder (GAD)** is worry. People with GAD are persistently worried, often about minor things. The term worry refers to the cognitive tendency to chew on a problem, to be unable to let go of it (Mennin, Heimberg, & Turk, 2004). Often, worry continues because a person cannot settle on a solution to the problem.

Clinical Case: Joe

Joe, a 24-year-old mechanic, had been referred for psychotherapy by his physician, whom he had consulted because of dizziness and difficulty falling asleep. He was quite visibly distressed during the entire initial interview, gulping before he spoke, sweating, and continually fidgeting in his chair. He repeatedly requested water to slake a seemingly unquenchable thirst. Although he described his physical concerns first, a general picture of pervasive anxiety soon emerged. He reported that he nearly always felt tense. He seemed to worry about everything. He was apprehensive of disasters that could befall him as he interacted with other

people and worked, and he described worrying much of the time about his ability to form a relationship, his finances, and other issues. He reported a long history of difficulties relating to others, which had led to his being fired from several jobs. As he put it, "I really like people and try to get along with them, but it seems like I fly off the handle too easily. Little things they do upset me too much. I just can't cope unless everything is going exactly right." Joe reported that he had always felt more nervous than other people, but that his anxiety had become much worse after a romantic breakup 1 year ago.

Most of us worry from time to time, but the worries of people with GAD are excessive, uncontrollable, and long lasting (per the DSM-IV-TR criteria). Other symptoms of GAD include difficulty concentrating, tiring easily, restlessness, irritability, and muscle tension. A person must have symptoms for at least 6 months to qualify for a diagnosis of GAD. Also, GAD is not diagnosed if a person only worries about concerns driven by another Axis I disorder; for example, a person with claustrophobia who only worried about being in closed spaces would not meet the criteria for GAD. The worries of people with GAD are similar in focus to those of most people—they worry about relationships, health, finances, and daily hassles (Roemer, Molina, & Borkovec, 1997)—but they worry more about these issues, and these persistent worries interfere with daily life.

GAD typically begins in adolescence, though many people who have generalized anxiety disorder report having had a tendency to worry all their lives (Barlow et al., 1986). GAD is often chronic; in one study, about half of people with GAD reported ongoing symptoms 5 years after an initial interview (Yonkers et al., 2000).

Obsessive-Compulsive Disorder

Obsessive-compulsive disorder (OCD) is characterized by persistent and uncontrollable thoughts or urges (obsessions) and by the need to repeat certain acts again and again (compulsions). Of course, most of us have unwanted thoughts from time to time, like an advertising jingle that gets stuck in our mind. And most of us also have urges now and then to behave in ways that would be embarrassing or dangerous. But few of us have thoughts or urges that are persistent and intrusive enough to qualify us for a diagnosis of OCD. For a diagnosis of OCD, the obsessions and compulsions must either cause marked distress or interfere with functioning.

Clinical Case: Bernice

Bernice was a 46-year-old woman. This was her fourth time seeking outpatient therapy, and she had been hospitalized twice previously. Her obsessive-compulsive disorder had begun 12 years earlier, shortly after the death of her father. Since then it had waxed and waned but currently was as severe as ever.

Bernice was obsessed with a fear of contamination, a fear she developed after her father's death from pneumonia (which she related to germs). Although she reported that she was afraid of nearly everything because germs could be anywhere, she was particularly afraid of touching wood, "scratchy objects," mail, canned goods, silver embossing on a greeting card, eyeglass frames, shiny appliances, and silverware. She was unable to state why these particular objects were sources of possible contamination.

To try to reduce her discomfort, Bernice engaged in a variety of compulsive rituals that took up almost all her waking hours. In the morning, she spent 3 to 4 hours in the bathroom, washing and rewashing herself. Before each washing, she scraped away the outside layer of her bar of soap so that it would be free of germs. Mealtimes lasted for hours because of rituals designed to decontaminate her food, such as eating three bites of food at a time and chewing each mouthful 300 times. Her rituals had taken over her life—she did almost nothing else. Because of her fear of contamination, she would not leave the house, do housework, or even talk on the telephone.

Obsessions are intrusive and recurring thoughts, images, or impulses that come unbidden to the mind, are uncontrollable (i.e., the person cannot stop the thoughts from happening), and usually appear irrational to the person experiencing them. For Bernice and others with OCD, obsessions have such force and frequency that they interfere with normal activities. The most frequent obsessions concern fears of contamination, sexual or aggressive impulses, and body problems (Jenike, Baer, & Minichiello, 1986). People with obsessions may also be prone to extreme doubts, procrastination, and indecision.

Compulsions are repetitive, clearly excessive behaviors or mental acts that the person feels driven to perform to reduce the anxiety caused by obsessive thoughts or to prevent

In agoraphobia, a person is afraid of being in shopping malls, crowds, and other public situations where escape would be difficult if anxiety symptoms occurred; people with agoraphobia can become housebound. (Frank Siteman/Stone/Getty Images.)

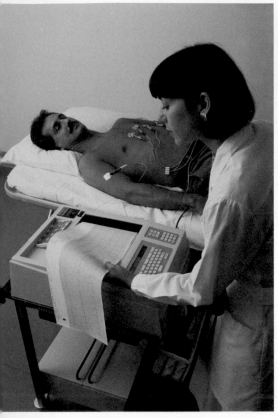

People with panic disorder often seek cardiac tests because they are frightened by changes in their heart rate. (David Joel/Stone/Getty Images.)

some calamity from occurring. Bernice's rituals while washing and eating, for example, fit this definition. A person with such a compulsion fears dire consequences if the act is not performed. The sheer frequency with which such an act, overt or mental, is repeated may be staggering (remember that Bernice chewed each mouthful of food 300 times). Commonly reported compulsions include the following:

- Pursuing cleanliness and orderliness, sometimes through elaborate rituals;
- Performing repetitive, magically protective acts, such as counting, or touching a body part;
- Repeatedly checking to ensure that certain acts are carried out—for example, returning seven or eight times in a row to see that lights, gas jets, or faucets were turned off, windows fastened, and doors locked.

We often hear people described as compulsive gamblers, compulsive eaters, and compulsive drinkers. Even though people may report irresistible urges to gamble, eat, and drink, clinicians do not regard these behaviors as compulsions because they are often experienced as pleasurable. In one study, 78 percent of people with compulsions viewed their rituals as "rather silly or absurd" even though they were unable to stop performing them (Stern & Cobb, 1978).

Obsessive-compulsive disorder tends to begin either before age 10 or else in late adolescence early adulthood (Conceicao do Rosario-Campos et al., 2001). It has been described in children as young as age 2 (Rapoport, Swedo, & Leonard, 1992). Early onset is more common among men; later onset is more frequent among women and is often linked with cleaning compulsions (Noshirvani et al., 1991). OCD is a chronic disorder—a 40-year follow-up study of people hospitalized for OCD in the 1950s showed that only 20 percent had recovered completely (Skoog & Skoog, 1999).

Obsessive-compulsive disorder often has a bad impact on close relationships. People saddled with the irresistible need to wash their hands every 10 minutes, to touch every doorknob they pass, or to count every tile in a bathroom floor are likely to cause concern and even resentment in family members, friends, and co-workers.

A crowd is likely to be very distressing to people with agoraphobia, because escape would be difficult if a panic attack occurred (Cosmo Siteman/Stone/Getty Images.)

Posttraumatic Stress Disorder and Acute Stress Disorder

Posttraumatic stress disorder (PTSD) was introduced as a diagnosis in DSM-III. It entails an extreme response to a severe stressor, including increased anxiety, avoidance of stimuli associated with the trauma, and a general numbing of emotional responses. Although people have known for many years that the stresses of combat can have powerful adverse effects on soldiers, the aftermath of the Vietnam War spurred the development of this diagnosis.

Clinical Case: John

John was a 54-year-old man who was referred for treatment by his physician at the VA hospital. John had recently separated from his wife, was currently unemployed, and reported having no close friends. He stated that he had felt haunted by images of the Vietnam War ever since he had returned from military service decades before. More recently, these symptoms had become worse when he began seeing coverage of the Iraq War on TV. He reported that he frequently experienced nightmares about a particular scene in the jungle in Vietnam, and he would wake up with his heart pounding. He tried to avoid reminders of the war, including parades, political conversations, and helicopters, but this was not doable—he often stumbled into reminders unexpectedly. When he did, he found that he was quickly overwhelmed by emotional horror and physical shakiness. He reported feeling hopeless ever since returning from war.

He had had many separations from his wife, who would often respond with angry outbursts when she was unable to take his emotional distance. He believed that his wife loved him, but when asked if he wanted to work toward a reunion with her, he stated that he wasn't sure what he felt about her and that he had not really felt emotionally engaged with her since the war.

Like other disorders in the DSM, PTSD is defined by a cluster of symptoms, but unlike other disorders, one criterion for diagnosis is exposure to a specific type of situation—a traumatic event. The person must have experienced or witnessed an event that involved actual or threatened death, serious injury, or a threat to the physical integrity of self or others. The trauma must have created intense fear, horror, or a sense of helplessness. As noted above, war veterans often have been exposed to these sorts of severe traumas. For women, rape is the most common type of trauma preceding PTSD (Creamer, Burgess, & McFarlane, 2001), with at least one-third of women meeting criteria for PTSD after a rape (cf. Breslau et al., 1999).

The symptoms for PTSD are grouped into three major categories:

Kim Basinger, the Oscar winning actress, is reported to have suffered from panic disorder with agoraphobia, as well as social phobia. (Matthew Simmons/Getty Images News and Sport Services.)

- *Reexperiencing* the traumatic event. The person often recalls the event or has nightmares about it. The person may be intensely upset by reminders of the event (e.g., helicopter sounds that remind a veteran of the battlefield; darkness that reminds a woman of a rape).
- *Avoidance* of stimuli associated with the event or a general numbing of responsiveness. Some may try to avoid all reminders of the event. For example, a Turkish earthquake survivor stopped sleeping indoors after he was buried alive at night (McNally, 2003b). Other people try to avoid thinking about the trauma; some may only remember disorganized fragments of the event. *Numbing* refers to a decreased interest in others, a sense of estrangement from others, and an inability to feel positive emotions. These symptoms may seem contradictory to reexperiencing symptoms; generally, the person goes back and forth between reexperiencing and numbing.
- Symptoms of *increased arousal*. These symptoms include difficulty falling asleep or staying asleep, difficulty concentrating, hypervigilance, and an exaggerated startle response. Laboratory studies have confirmed these clinical symptoms by documenting the heightened physiological responses of people with PTSD to images of combat (e.g., Orr et al., 2003).

DSM-IV-TR Criteria for PTSD

- Exposure to a traumatic event causing extreme fear, helplessness, or horror
- The event is reexperienced
- The person avoids stimuli associated with the trauma or has a numbing of responsiveness
- Increased arousal
- Duration of symptoms is more than 1 month

DSM-IV-TR Criteria for Acute Stress Disorder

- Exposure to a traumatic event causing extreme fear, helplessness, or horror
- During or after the event, the person experiences dissociative symptoms.
- The event is reexperienced intrusively
- The person avoids stimuli associated with the trauma
- Increased arousal or anxiety
- Symptoms occur within the first month after the trauma

Extreme fear of contamination triggering abnormally frequent hand washing is common in obsessive-compulsive disorder. (Bill Aron/PhotoEdit.)

Table 5.4 12-Month Prevalence of Anxiety Disorders in the General Population in Germany (*N* = 4181)

Anxiety Disorder	Male (percent)	Female (percent)	Total (percent)
Panic disorder	1.7	3.0	2.3
Any phobia	7.5	17.7	12.6
Generalized anxiety disorder	1.0	2.1	1.5
Obsessive-compulsive disorder	0.6	0.9	0.7

Source: Jacobi, et al. (2004). Prevalence, co-morbidity and correlates of mental disorders in the general population: Results from the German Health Interview and Examination Survey. *Psychological Medicine*, 34. 597–611.

Suicidal thoughts are common among people with PTSD, as are incidents of explosive anger and stress-related physical symptoms, such as low back pain, headaches, and gastrointestinal disorders (Hobfoll et al., 1991).

In addition to PTSD, DSM-IV-TR includes a diagnosis for **acute stress disorder (ASD)**. According to DSM-IV-TR, if symptoms occur between 2 days and 1 month after a trauma, acute stress disorder (ASD) is diagnosed. Other than duration, the symptoms of ASD are fairly similar to PTSD. The ASD diagnosis is not as well accepted as the PTSD diagnosis. Some have criticized the ASD diagnosis because it seems to pathologize short-term reactions to serious traumas, even though these are quite common (Harvery & Bryant, 2002). The number of people who experience symptoms of ASD varies with the type of trauma. For example, after a rape, as many as 90 percent of women report at least some (subsyndromal) symptoms (Rothbaum et al., 1992); in contrast, among people who have been exposed to a mass shooting, approximately one-third develop symptoms of ASD (Classen et al., 1998). One main reason to consider this diagnosis, though, is that more than two-thirds of those diagnosed with ASD develop PTSD within 2 years (Harvey & Bryant, 2002).

Comorbidity in Anxiety Disorders

More than half of people with one anxiety disorder meet the criteria for another anxiety disorder during their life (T.A. Brown et al., 2001). **Subthreshold symptoms** of other anxiety disorders—that is, symptoms that do not meet full diagnostic criteria—are also common. For example, more than 80 percent of people diagnosed with an anxiety disorder other than panic disorder also experience panic attacks (Barlow et al., 1985). Comorbidity within anxiety disorders arises for two primary reasons:

- The symptoms used to diagnose the various anxiety disorders overlap; for example, somatic signs of anxiety (e.g., perspiration, fast heart rate) are among the diagnostic criteria for panic disorder, phobias, and posttraumatic stress disorder.
- Some etiological factors, like certain neurobiological or personality characteristics, may increase risk for more than one anxiety disorder. (See the next section for discussion of some of these risk factors.)

Anxiety disorders are also highly comorbid with other disorders. Three-quarters of people with an anxiety disorder meet the diagnostic criteria for at least one other disorder (Kessler et al., 1997). Approximately 60 percent of people in treatment for anxiety disorders also meet the diagnostic criteria for major depression (T. A. Brown et al., 2001). Findings from a 15-year follow-up study suggest that in most cases, depression develops after the anxiety disorder, perhaps because the severe problems related to anxiety disorders engender feelings of hopelessness and despair that lead to depression (Merikangas et al., 2003). Other conditions commonly comorbid with anxiety disorders include substance abuse (Jacobsen, Southwick, & Kosten, 2001) and personality disorders (Johnson, Weissman, & Klerman,

1990), especially avoidant, dependent, and histrionic personality disorders (see p. 388). As with many disorders, comorbidity is associated with greater severity and poorer outcomes of both the anxiety disorder(s) and the comorbid condition(s), probably because there are simply more problems to address (Newman et al., 1998).

Gender and Sociocultural Factors in the Anxiety Disorders

It is well-known that gender and culture are closely tied to the risk for anxiety disorders, as well as the specific types of symptoms that a person develops. As you will see, there are still some puzzles about why these differences exist.

Gender

As Table 5.4 shows, the German Health Interview and Examination Survey indicated that women are at least twice as likely as men to be diagnosed with an anxiety disorder (de Graaf et al., 2002). The gender disparity is particularly evident for agoraphobia. Among people exposed to a trauma, women are twice as likely to develop PTSD as men are (Breslau et al., 1999). OCD is the only anxiety disorder that is equally common in women and men.

There are many different theories about why women are more likely to develop anxiety disorders than men are. Women may be more likely to report their symptoms. Psychological differences also might help explain these gender gaps. For example, men may be raised to believe more in their personal control over situations, a variable we will discuss later as protective against anxiety disorders. Sociocultural explanations, like gender roles, are also likely to play a role. For example, men may experience more social pressure than women to face fears—as you will see below, facing fears may be the base for one of the most effective treatments available. Although the gender gap is not fully understood, it is an important phenomenon.

Culture

People in every culture seem to experience problems with anxiety disorders. But the focus of these problems appears to vary by culture. For example, in Japan a syndrome called *taijin kyofusho* involves fear of displeasing or embarrassing others; people with this syndrome typically fear such things as making direct eye contact, blushing, having body odor, or having a bodily deformity. The symptoms of this disorder overlap with those of social phobia, but the focus on other's feelings is distinct. Perhaps this focus is related to characteristics of traditional Japanese culture that encourage extreme concern for the feelings of others and discourage the direct communication of one's own feelings (McNally, 1997).

Kayak-angst, a disorder similar to panic disorder, occurs among the Inuit people of western Greenland; seal hunters who are alone at sea may experience intense fear, disorientation, and concerns about drowning. And *ataque de nervios*, originally identified in Puerto Rico, involves physical symptoms and fears of going crazy in the aftermath of severe stress and thus is similar to PTSD.

Other syndromes, such as *koro* (a sudden fear that one's genitals will recede into the body—reported in southern and eastern Asia), *shenkui* (intense anxiety and somatic symptoms attributed to the loss of semen as through masturbation or excessive sexual activity—reported in China and similar to other syndromes reported in India and Sri Lanka), and *susto* (fright-illness, the belief that a severe fright has caused the soul to leave the body—reported in Latin America and among Latinos in the United States), also involve symptoms similar to those of the anxiety disorders defined in DSM-IV-TR.

Disorders similar to panic attacks occur cross-culturally. Among the Inuit, kayak-angst is defined by intense fear in lone hunters. (B & C Alexander/Photo Researchers.)

As with the Japanese syndrome *taijin kyofusho*, it seems that the objects of anxiety and fear in these syndromes relate to beliefs and attitudes that are prevalent in the cultures where the syndromes occur. In other words, culture seems to influence what people come to fear (Kirmayer, 2001). (See p. 68 for more discussion of culturally specific syndromes.)

Beyond culturally specific syndromes, the prevalence of DSM-IV anxiety disorders varies across cultures. This is not surprising given that cultures differ with regard to factors such as attitudes toward mental illness, stress levels, the nature of relationships within families, and the prevalence of poverty—all of which are known to play a role in the occurrence or reporting of anxiety disorders. For example, in Taiwan and Japan, the prevalence of anxiety disorders seems to be quite low; however, this may reflect a strong stigma associated with having mental problems, which could lead to underreporting in those countries (Kawakami et al., 2004; Weissman et al., 1997). In Cambodia and among Cambodian refugees, very elevated rates of panic disorder (often diagnosed traditionally as *kyol goeu*, or "wind overload") have been reported, perhaps because of the extreme stress experienced by Cambodians over the past several decades (Hinton et al., 2000; Hinton, Um, & Ba, 2001). In the United States, where trauma exposure is often elevated among nonwhites, a study of over 14,000 people found higher rates of PTSD symptoms among people of color (Ritsher et al., 2002).

When researchers consider the more specific symptoms that comprise the anxiety disorders, research becomes more controversial. For some time, researchers have thought that people from different cultures express symptoms of psychological distress and anxiety in different ways, but new research questions how major those cultural differences are. At one time, many researchers believed that somatic (physical) expressions of distress were more common in "collectivistic" cultures—that is, in cultures where, in some sense, the group is held to be more important than the individual (supposedly in contrast to "individualistic" Western cultures). It now seems, however, that this conclusion might reflect sampling problems—that is, researchers often studied anxiety and depression in psychological clinics in the United States but in medical clinics in other cultures. One can imagine that a person seeing a medical doctor might be likely to emphasize somatic concerns! Indeed, many people, regardless of culture, tend to describe anxiety and depression initially in terms of bodily sensations when visiting a medical clinic. When researchers interview people in similar settings, the ratio of somatic to psychological expression of symptoms appears much more similar across cultures (Kirmayer, 2001).

Check Your Knowledge 5.1

Match the word to the definition.
1. fear
2. anxiety
3. worry
4. panic
5. obsession
6. compulsion
7. specific phobia
   a. an intense state of fear, accompanied by somatic symptoms, often in the absence of any clear danger
   b. an emotional response to immediate danger

c. an excessive fear of a specific object or situation that causes distress or impairment
d. a state of apprehension, often accompanied by autonomic arousal
e. an intrusive and distressing thought that is hard to dispel and often does not make sense to the person
f. thinking about potential problems, often without settling on a solution
g. a behavior that the person feels must be repeated again and again

8. PTSD is defined by symptoms of (circle all that apply):
   a. intense worry
   b. high levels of arousal
   c. excessive sleeping
   d. numbing and avoidance
   e. intrusive thoughts and memories regarding the initial trauma
9. GAD is defined by:
   a. worry
   b. panic attacks
   c. fear of situations in which escape would be difficult
   d. obsessions and compulsions

10. A person with one anxiety disorder has about a xx percent chance of developing a second disorder, and about a xx percent chance of developing major depressive disorder.
    a. 35, 25
    b. 55, 35
    c. 75, 60
    d. 90, 60
11. The odds that a person will develop an anxiety disorder sometime during his or her lifetime are approximately:
    a. 1 in 10
    b. 1 in 5
    c. 1 in 4
    d. 1 in 2

Common Risk Factors across the Anxiety Disorders

In this section, we consider factors associated with a range of anxiety disorders. The existence of such risk factors may help explain why people with one anxiety disorder are likely to develop a second anxiety disorder—that is, some risk factors increase the odds of more than one anxiety disorder. For example, the factors that increase risk for social phobia may also increase risk for PTSD. Psychoanalytic models dominated the field until the 1960s (see Focus on Discovery 5.1). Today, however, researchers have focused more on biology, personality, cognition, and life events. Table 5.5 summarizes the factors that researchers have related to a broad range of anxiety disorders.

Genetic Factors: Are Genes a Diathesis for Anxiety Disorders?

Twin studies suggest a heritability of 20–40 percent for phobias, GAD, and PTSD and 48 percent for panic disorder (Hettama, Neale, & Kendler, 2001; True et al., 1993). Some genes may indicate elevated risk for several different types of anxiety disorder, while the presence of other genes may indicate elevated risk for a specific type of anxiety disorder (Cox et al., 2002). For example, having a family member with phobia seems to increase the risk of developing not only a phobia but also other anxiety disorders (Kendler et al., 2001).

Neurobiological Factors: The Fear Circuit and the Activity of Neurotransmitters

A set of brain structures, called the **fear circuit**, tends to be activated when people are feeling anxious or fearful (Malizia, 2003). The fear circuit, shown in Figure 5.2, appears to be especially active among people with anxiety disorders. One part of the fear circuit that seems centrally involved in anxiety disorders is the amygdala. The amygdala is a small almond-shaped structure in the temporal lobe that appears to be involved in assigning emotional significance to stimuli. In animals, the amygdala has been shown to be critical for the conditioning of fear. The amygdala sends signals to a range of different brain structures involved in the fear circuit (see Figure 5.2). Studies suggest that when shown pictures of sad or angry faces, people with several different anxiety disorders respond with greater activity in the amygdala than do people without anxiety disorders (Thomas et al., 2001). Hence, elevated activity in the fear circuit, and particularly the amygdala, may help explain many different anxiety disorders.

Table 5.5 Factors That May Increase Risk for More than One Anxiety Disorder

Genetic vulnerability

Increased activity in the fear circuit of the brain

Decreased functioning of GABA and serotonin; increased norepinephrine activity

Behavioral inhibition

Neuroticism

Cognitive factors, including attention to cues of threat and low perception of control

Negative life events

Focus on Discovery 5.1

Psychoanalytic Perspective: Anxiety and Defense Mechanisms

Many years ago, psychoanalytic theories of anxiety disorders dominated the field. Psychoanalysts provided a number of early case reports using the then-current diagnostic category neurosis. **Neurosis** included both anxiety and depression and was distinguished from *psychosis*, a disorder in which a person loses insight into reality.

The prevailing idea was that anxiety resulted from conflicts between the id and the ego, triggered by intense sexual or aggressive impulses from the id. Anxiety was seen as a signal to the ego that renewed efforts to defend against expression were needed. The ego feared punishment if these urges were expressed and used defense mechanisms to keep the urges under control. When defense mechanisms were overworked, the result might be frequent or chronic feelings of anxiety, like the worry seen in GAD; that is, the anxiety "signal" would persist because the defense mechanisms were unable to completely repress the urges. More specific types of anxiety would be determined by the developmental stage when the conflict began, the specific defense mechanisms used by the ego,

and how well those defense mechanisms were working. For example, a fixation in the anal stage of development (a time when toilet-training is occurring and there is a focus on defecation) could promote intense conflict between whether to control impulses or not. Impulses to soil could be transformed into a desire to be compulsively neat, clean, and orderly (note the parallel with symptoms of OCD). When defense mechanisms break down, the person might experience the aggressive or sexual urge as an intrusive obsessive thought.

Attaching the anxiety to a specific object might result in a phobia. For example, Freud reported on the case of Little Hans, who was afraid of encountering horses if he went outside. Hans described "black things around horses' mouths and the things in front of their eyes." To Freud, this seemed parallel with the image of Hans' father, who had a mustache and eyeglasses. He theorized that Hans had an underlying Oedipal fear of his father. The fear was too intense for Hans to manage, so Hans had symbolically transformed it into a fear of horses.

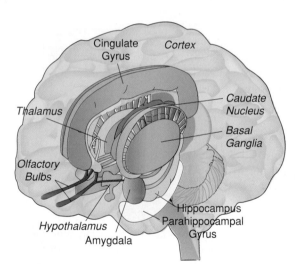

Figure 5.2 Fear and anxiety appear to be related to a set of structures in the brain called the fear circuit.

Many of the neurotransmitters involved in the fear circuit are involved in anxiety disorders. For instance, anxiety disorders seem to be related to poor functioning of the serotonin system (Chang, Cloak, & Ernst, 2003; Stein, 1998) and higher than normal levels of norepinephrine (Geracioti et al., 2001). GABA appears to be involved in inhibiting activity throughout the brain, and one of its effects is decreased anxiety (Sinha, Mohlman, & Gorman, 2004). Poor GABA function, then, could contribute to anxiety.

Personality: Behavioral Inhibition and Neuroticism

Some infants show the trait of **behavioral inhibition**, a tendency to become agitated and cry when faced with novel toys, people, or other stimuli. This behavior pattern, which has been described in infants as young as 4 months old, may be inherited and may set the stage for the later development of anxiety disorders. One study followed infants from 14 months through 7.5 years; 45 percent of those who showed elevated behavioral inhibition levels at 14 months showed symptoms of anxiety at age 7.5, compared to only 15 percent of those who had shown low behavioral inhibition levels (Kagan & Snidman, 1999). Behavioral inhibition appears to be a particularly strong predictor of social phobia: Thirty percent of infants showing elevated behavioral inhibition levels developed social anxiety by adolescence (Biederman, 1990).

Neuroticism is a personality trait defined by the tendency to react to events with greater than average negative affect. How does neuroticism relate to anxiety disorders? In a sample of 7,076 adults, neuroticism predicted the onset of both anxiety disorders and depression (de Graaf et al., 2002). People with high levels of neuroticism were more than twice as likely to develop an anxiety disorder as those without high neuroticism.

Cognitive Factors: Perceived Control and Attending to Threat

People with anxiety disorders often report believing that bad things are likely to happen. For example, people with panic disorder might believe that they will die when their heart begins to pound, whereas people with social phobia might believe that they will suffer humiliating rejection if they blush. As pointed out by David Clark and colleagues (1999), the key issue is not why people think so negatively initially, but rather, how are these beliefs sustained? For example, by the time a person survives 100 panic attacks, you might expect the belief "this attack means I am about to die" would fade. One reason these beliefs might be sustained is that people think and act in ways that maintain these beliefs. Researchers have focused on several separate cognitive aspects of anxiety disorders. Here, we focus on two: a lack of control and attention to signs of threat.

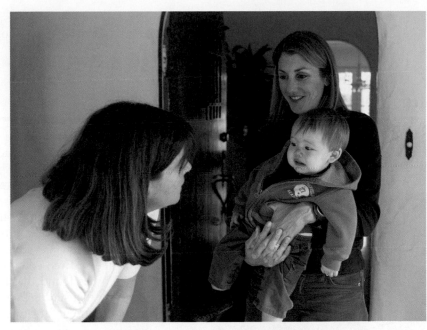

Infants and toddlers showing behavioral inhibition—high levels of anxiety about novel situations and people—are at greater risk of developing anxiety disorders during their lifetime. (David Young-Wolff/PhotoEdit.)

Perceived Control   People who think that they lack control over their environment appear to be at greater risk for a broad range of anxiety disorders than people who do not have that feeling. For example, people with anxiety disorders report experiencing little sense of control over their surroundings (Mineka & Zinbarg, 1998). Childhood experiences, such as traumatic events (Hofmann et al., 2001) and punitive, restrictive parenting (Chorpita, Brown, & Barlow, 1998) could promote a sustained view that life is not controllable.

Animal studies have illustrated that a lack of control over the environment can promote anxiety. For example, Insel et al. (1988) randomly assigned monkeys to one of two conditions. One group of monkeys grew up with the ability to choose whether and when they would receive treats. A second group of monkeys had no control over whether and when they received treats—that is, a given monkey in this second group was given a treat whenever a given monkey in the first group received a treat. In the third year of life, monkeys who had grown up without control behaved in ways that looked anxious when facing new situations and interacting with other monkeys; monkeys who had grown up with control did not show the same levels of anxiety. In short, animal and human studies both point toward the importance of a perception of lack of control in the development of anxiety disorders.

Attention to Threat   People with anxiety disorders have been found to pay more attention to negative cues in their environment. Many research studies have tested for attention patterns like these among people with anxiety disorders, using measures such as the emotion Stroop task (see Figure 2.11) (Williams et al., 1997). Generally, such studies provide evidence that anxiety disorders are associated with greater attention toward threatening stimuli (Williams et al., 1997). For example, Vietnam veterans with PTSD have been found to selectively attend to words related to war (e.g., "body bags"), whereas people with snake phobias attend to cues related to snakes (McNally et al., 1990; Öhman, Flykt, & Esteves, 2001). Researchers have also shown that this attention to threatening stimuli happens automatically and very quickly—before people are even consciously aware of the stimuli (Öhman & Soares, 1994). In sum, anxiety disorders are associated with selective attention to signs of threat.

The Social Environment: Actual Threats

Negative life events, particularly those involving danger of something bad happening in the future, often precede the onset of anxiety disorders (Kendler, Prescott et al., 2003). For example, as many as 80 percent of people with panic disorder report experiencing a severe stressor before the onset of the disorder (Barlow, 2004). More broadly, about 70 percent of people report a severe stressor before the onset of an anxiety disorder (Finlay-Jones, 1989).

Common Aspects of Treatments for the Anxiety Disorders

Only a small proportion of people with anxiety disorders seek treatment. Although public awareness campaigns and pharmaceutical company advertising have increased treatment-seeking, a community survey of 5,877 participants suggested that fewer than 20 percent of people with anxiety disorders receive minimally adequate treatment (Wang, Demler, & Kessler, 2002). One reason for the lack of treatment-seeking may be the chronic nature of symptoms; a person suffering from an anxiety disorder might think "I'm just an anxious person" and not realize that treatment could help. Many seek treatment only when a change in life circumstances forces them to confront a previously avoided situation, like Jan described above. Even when people do seek treatment, many will only visit a family doctor. Research has found that family physicians are less effective than psychiatrists in prescribing drugs that successfully treat anxiety disorders, mostly due to insufficient doses or insufficient duration of treatment (Roy-Byrne et al., 2001).

In the most frequent type of therapy for phobias, clients are exposed to what they fear most—here, an enclosed space. (Mimi Forsyth.)

Commonalities across Psychological Treatments

Effective psychological treatments for anxiety disorders share a common focus: exposure— that is, the person must face what he or she deems too terrifying to face. Therapists from varying perspectives all agree that we must face up to the source of our fear or, as an ancient Chinese proverb puts it, "Go straight to the heart of danger, for there you will find safety." Although exposure is a core aspect of many treatments, treatments do differ in how they include exposure. Even psychoanalysts, who believe that the unconscious sources of anxiety are in the buried past and who therefore delay direct confrontation, eventually encourage it (Zane, 1984).

Cognitive approaches to treatment of anxiety disorders typically focus on challenging a person's beliefs about the likelihood of negative outcomes if he or she faces an anxiety-provoking object or situation. For example, a person with a phobia of flying might overestimate the odds that a plane will crash. A therapist might review how small the odds are of a plane crash. Such approaches have been found to be helpful in the treatment of social phobia, panic disorder, generalized anxiety disorder, and obsessive-compulsive disorder.

Medications That Reduce Anxiety

While the psychological treatments focus on helping a person face fears, conventional medication treatments are used to quell the symptoms of anxiety pharmacologically. Drugs that reduce anxiety are referred to as sedatives, minor tranquilizers, or **anxiolytics** (the suffix *-lytic* comes from a Greek word meaning "to loosen or dissolve"). See Table 5.6 for an overview of the medications used in treating anxiety disorders and the neuro-transmitter systems that they influence. Two types of medications are most commonly used for the treatment of anxiety disorders: **benzodiazepines** (e.g., Valium and Xanax) and **antidepressants**, including **tricyclic antidepressants** and **selective serotonin reuptake inhibitors** (SSRIs). Researchers also are beginning to examine other drugs as potential anxiolytics, including buspirone (BuSpar), gabapentin (Neurontin), and clomipramine (Anafranil).

Because several different types of medications help relieve anxiety symptoms, the choice of drugs is often guided by concerns about side effects and withdrawal symptoms. All anxiolytics have side effects. Many people report being surprised by the extent of side

Table 5.6 Medications Commonly Used to Treat Anxiety Disorders

Drug Category	Generic Names	Trade Names	Uses	Neurotransmitter Systems Influenced
Benzodiazepines	Diazepam, alprazolam	Valium, Xanax	Anxiety disorders other than OCD	GABA
Selective serotonin reuptake inhibitors (SSRIs)	Paroxetine, fluoxetine, sertraline	Paxil, Prozac, Zoloft	All anxiety disorders	Serotonin
Tricyclic antidepressants	Imipramine	Tofranil	Panic disorder, GAD, OCD, PTSD	Dopamine and norepinephrine
Azaspirodecanediones	Buspirone	BuSpar	GAD	Serotonin and dopamine
Anticonvulsants	Gabapentin	Neurontin	Social phobia	GABA
Serotonin reuptake inhibitors (SRIs)	Clomipramine	Anafranil	OCD	Serotonin and norepinephrine

effects and wishing they had known more about what to expect (Haslam et al., 2004). Benzodiazepines can have significant cognitive and motor side effects, such as memory lapses and difficulty driving. Also, people may experience severe withdrawal symptoms (Schweizer et al., 1990), so it can be difficult to stop using benzodiazapenes—that is, they can be addictive. Antidepressants tend to have fewer side effects than benzodiazapexer. Nonetheless, as many as half of people discontinue tricyclic antidepressants because of side effects like jitteriness, weight gain, elevated heart rate, and high blood pressure (cf. Taylor, Hayward, et al., 1990). Compared to tricyclic antidepressants, SSRIs tend to have fewer side effects, but some of their side effects may be significant, such as interference with sexual functioning (Rauch & Jenike, 1998).

This leads us to the key problem: most people relapse once they stop taking medications (Herbert, 1995). Hence, medications are only effective during the time when they are taken.

Quick Summary

As a group, anxiety disorders are the most common type of mental illness. The DSM-IV-TR defines seven anxiety disorders. As Table 5.1 shows, the specific anxiety disorders are each defined by a different type of key symptom. That is, specific phobia is defined by an intense fear of an object or situation, social phobia by an intense fear of strangers or social scrutiny, panic disorder by anxiety about recurrent panic attacks, generalized anxiety disorder by worries lasting at least 6 months, and obsessive-compulsive disorder by either obsessions or compulsions. Posttraumatic stress disorder and acute stress disorder are both severe reactions to trauma; acute stress disorder occurs 2 days to 4 weeks after a trauma, and posttraumatic stress disorder lasts for more than 4 weeks after a trauma.

People with one anxiety disorder are very likely to experience a second anxiety disorder during their life. About 60 percent of people will experience an episode of major depression during their life. Women are much more likely than men to report an anxiety disorder. Culture influences the focus of fears, the ways that symptoms are expressed, and even the prevalence of different anxiety disorders.

Genetic research suggests that genes increase risk for anxiety disorders. Neurobiological research on anxiety focuses on elevated levels of activity in the brain's fear circuit. Anxiety disorders also appear to involve poor functioning of the GABA and serotonin systems, and high levels of norepinephrine. The personality traits of behavioral inhibition and neuroticism both are related to the development of anxiety disorders. From the cognitive perspective, anxiety disorders are associated with negative beliefs that intensify the experience of anxiety. These beliefs may be sustained because people hold long-standing beliefs that life is uncontrollable, and because they tend to pay attention to negative stimuli. Severe negative life events often precede the development of an anxiety disorder.

Psychological treatments often focus on exposure. Cognitive treatments often include an exposure component, but add a specific set of interventions to challenge the negative beliefs about what will happen when a person faces their fears. Benzodiazapenes and antidepressants are commonly used to treat anxiety disorders, but anxiety symptoms typically return once a person stops taking medications.

Check Your Knowledge 5.2

1. Research suggests that _____ percent of the variance in anxiety disorders other than panic disorder can be explained by genes.
   a. 0–20 percent
   b. 20–40 percent
   c. 40–60 percent
   d. 60–80 percent
2. _____ is a personality trait characterized by a tendency to react to events with intense negative affect.
   a. extraversion
   b. neurosis
   c. neuroticism
   d. psychosis
3. Cognitive factors found to correlate with anxiety disorders include (circle all that apply):
   a. low self-esteem
   b. belief that bad things are likely to occur

   c. attention to signs of threat
   d. hopelessness
   e. lack of perceived control
4. A key structure in the fear circuit is the:
   a. basal ganglia
   b. amygdala
   c. occipital cortex
   d. inferior colliculi
5. Which of the following are the most common treatment approaches to anxiety disorders? (Circle all that apply.)
   a. supportive listening
   b. benzodiazapenes
   c. barbituates
   d. antidepressants
   e. exposure

Etiology and Treatment of Specific Anxiety Disorders

In the following sections, we look at the various approaches to the etiology and treatment specific to each of the anxiety disorders. Above, we discussed genetic, neurobiological, cognitive, and behavioral research on factors that might set the stage for development of anxiety disorders in general. Here, we turn to the question of how each of the specific anxiety disorders arise and how they are best treated. That is, why does one person develop a specific phobia while another person develops generalized anxiety disorder? We also look at how psychotherapy and pharmacotherapy can be tailored to these specific anxiety disorders. Even though exposure treatment is used with each anxiety disorder, how can it be tailored to specific anxiety disorders? What is the first choice of medication for a given anxiety disorder? Keep in mind the common etiological factors and treatment approaches already described and think about how these commonalities relate to and combine with the specifics described next.

Etiology of Specific Phobias

Much of the behavioral research on phobias focuses on traumatic experiences and conditioning. The heart of this model focuses on the idea that people develop phobias after exposure to an aversive stimulus. As you read this section, keep in mind that many of the people who are exposed to aversive stimuli don't develop phobias. The risk factors described above, such as heritability and neuroticism, probably operate as a diathesis—a vulnerability factor that shapes whether or not a phobia will develop in the context of a conditioning experience (Mineka & Öhman, 2002).

Behavioral Factors: Conditioning of Specific Phobias Behavioral theories of specific phobias focus on conditioning, based on **Mowrer's two-factor model** (see Figure 5.3). This model suggests two steps in phobic conditioning (Mowrer, 1947):

1. Through *classical conditioning*, a person learns to fear a neutral stimulus (the CS) that is paired with an intrinsically aversive stimulus (the UCS).
2. Through *operant conditioning*, the person gains relief from this conditioned fear, by avoiding the CS. The avoidant response is maintained by its reinforcing consequence of reducing the amount of fear the person experiences.

Let's consider an example. Imagine that a man is bitten by a dog and then develops a phobia of dogs. Through classical conditioning, he has learned to associate dogs (the CS) with painful bites (the UCS). This corresponds to step 1 above. In step 2, the man reduces his experience of fear by avoiding dogs as much as possible; the avoidant behavior is reinforced by the reduction in fear. This lets us see why the phobia isn't extinguished. With repeated exposure to dogs that don't bite, the man should lose his fear, but by avoiding dogs, the man gets little or no such exposure. (See p. 22 for more detailed discussions of classical and operant conditioning and for a description of a 1920 experiment in which a young child, referred to as Little Albert, was classically conditioned to fear white rats.)

We should note that Mowrer's early version of the two-factor model does not actually fit the evidence very well; several extensions of this model, which we look at next, have been developed

Figure 5.3   Two-factor model of conditioning.

that fit the evidence better (Mineka & Zinbarg, 1998). One extension of the model has been to consider different ways that conditioning could take place (Rachman, 1977). These include:

- by direct experience, like the conditioned fear of dogs in the example above;
- by seeing another person harmed by a stimulus (e.g., seeing a dog bite a man) or by seeing a stimulus inspire fear in another person (e.g., seeing a man show fear of dogs). This type of learning is called modeling (Fredrikson, Annas, & Wik, 1997);
- by verbal instruction—for example, by a parent warning a child that dogs are dangerous.

Current theory suggests that phobias *could* be conditioned by any of these types of experiences: direct trauma, modeling, or verbal instruction. But do most people with a phobia report one of these types of conditioning experiences? In one study, 1,937 people were asked whether they had had these types of conditioning experiences before the onset of their phobias (Kendler, Myers, & Prescott, 2002). Although conditioning experiences were common, about half of the people in the study could not remember any such experiences (see Table 5.7). Obviously, if many phobias start without a conditioning experience, this is a big problem for the behavioral model. But proponents of the behavioral model argue that people may forget some conditioning experiences (Mineka & Öhman, 2002). Because of memory gaps, simple surveys of how many people remember a conditioning experience do not provide very accurate evidence about the behavioral model.

Another extension of the model considers the types of stimuli that become feared. Mowrer's original two-factor model suggests that people could be conditioned to be afraid

Little Albert, shown here with Watson and Rayner, was classically conditioned to develop a fear of a white rat. (Courtesy Benjamin Harris.)

Table 5.7   Percent of People Reporting Conditioning Experiences Before the Onset of a Phobia

Type of Fear	Direct Trauma	Observed Trauma or Fear in Others	Taught Fear	No Memory of Conditioning Experience
Agoraphobia	27.0	3.4	4.6	65.1
Social	23.3	4.6	7.3	65.0
Animal	48.1	9.1	11.6	31.2
Situational	32.7	8.1	6.36	48.8
Blood/injection/injury	46.7	15.0	7.0	52.9

Source: From a survey of 1,937 people conducted by Kendler, Myers, and Prescott (2002).

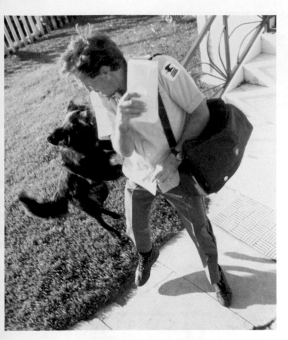

Many people report that they develop a phobia after a traumatic event. Debate exists about why some people don't report a traumatic event before the onset of their phobia. (Bruce Herman/Stone/Getty Images.)

of all types of stimuli. But people with phobias tend to fear certain types of stimuli. Typically, people do not develop phobias of flowers, lambs, or lamp shades! But, phobias of insects or other animals, natural environments, and blood are particularly common. As many as half of women report a fear of snakes; moreover, many different types of animals also show fear in response to snakes (Öhman & Mineka, 2003). Researchers have suggested that during the evolution of our species, people learned to react especially strongly to stimuli that could be life-threatening, including naturally dangerous environments such as heights, animals such as snakes, and angry humans (Seligman, 1971). Perhaps our fear circuit has evolved to respond especially rapidly and automatically to these types of stimuli. That is, our fear circuit may have been "prepared" by evolution to learn fear of certain stimuli; hence, this type of learning is called **prepared learning**. As researchers have tested this model, some have discovered that people can be initially conditioned to fear many different types of stimuli (McNally, 1987). Fears to most types of stimuli fade quickly with ongoing exposure, though, whereas fears of naturally dangerous stimuli are sustained in most studies (Dawson, Schell, & Banis, 1986).

Prepared learning also is relevant to modeling, as indicated by a study involving four groups of rhesus monkeys (Cook & Mineka, 1989). Each group of monkeys was shown a videotape of a monkey exhibiting intense fear, but for each group, clever videotape editing was used to make the feared object appear to be different: a toy snake, a toy crocodile, flowers, or a toy rabbit. Only the monkeys exposed to the tapes showing a monkey who expressed fear of a toy snake or toy crocodile acquired fear of the object shown, suggesting that, with rhesus monkeys as with people, it is easier to condition fear of potentially life-threatening stimuli than of neutral stimuli.

Despite a great deal of research on conditioning models of phobia, controversy remains. Some authors have suggested that at least some fears might be biologically preprogrammed, such that no conditioning experience is required (Menzies & Clarke, 1995). For example, monkeys raised with no exposure to other monkeys still display fear when they are shown pictures of another monkey expressing anger. Similarly, infants tend to show fear of water and of strangers even if they have no previous exposure to these stimuli. This type of finding suggests that conditioning models of phobias will need to be integrated with biological models of the fear system.

Etiology of Social Phobia

In this section, we review behavioral and cognitive factors related to social phobia. The trait of behavioral inhibition, discussed above, may also be important in the development of social phobia.

Behavioral Factors: Conditioning of Social Phobia   Behavioral perspectives on the causes of social phobia are similar to those on specific phobias, insofar as they are based on a two-factor conditioning model. That is, a person could have a negative social experience (directly, through modeling, or through verbal instruction), and become classically conditioned to fear similar situations, which the person then avoids. Through operant conditioning, this avoidance behavior is maintained because it reduces the amount of fear the person experiences. The conditioned fear is not extinguished by participation in social situations that don't have negative consequences, because the person tends to avoid social situations in general. Even when the person interacts with others, he or she may show avoidant behavior in smaller ways that have been labeled as *safety behaviors*. Examples of safety behaviors include avoiding eye contact, disengaging from conversation, and standing apart from others. There is research evidence that people with social phobia avoid looking at social stimuli, and even pictures of faces (Chen et al., 2002). Unfortunately, other people tend to disapprove of these types of avoidant behaviors, which then intensifies the problem (Wells, 1998). (Think about how you might respond if you were trying to talk to someone who looks at the floor, fails to answer your questions, and leaves the room in the middle of the conversation.)

Cognitive Factors: Too Much Focus on Negative Self-Evaluations   Researchers have described several different ways in which cognitive processes might intensify social anxiety (Clark & Wells, 1995). First, people with social anxiety appear to hold much higher standards for their performance and to have unrealistically negative beliefs about the consequences of their social behaviors—for example, they may believe that others will reject them if they blush or pause while speaking. Second, they attend more to how they are doing in social situations than other people do, which means reduced attention to other people. They are particularly likely to think about how others might be perceiving them ("He must think I'm an idiot"), and they are harsher than other people would be in evaluating their performance (Woody & Rodriguez, 2000). They often form powerful negative visual images of how others will react to them (Hirsch & Clark, 2004). The resultant anxiety interferes with their ability to perform well socially, creating a vicious cycle—for example, the person doesn't pay enough attention to others, who then perceive the person as not interested in them, which leads the person to perceive others as judging her or him negatively (in this case, an accurate perception).

There is plenty of evidence that people with social anxiety think more negatively about their social performance than other people do even if they are not actually more socially awkward (Stopa & Clark, 2000). For example, in one study, researchers assessed blushing in people with and without social phobia. Participants were asked to estimate how much they would blush during different tasks, such as singing a children's song. Then they were asked to engage in these different tasks. Participants with social phobia overestimated how much they would blush (Gerlach et al., 2001). Therefore, people with social phobia may be unfairly harsh in the way they evaluate their performance.

How might all this fit together when we consider a person with social phobia, like Maureen (described above)? Maureen is likely to have inherited some tendency to be anxious when faced with new people. As she grew up, this may have interfered with her chances to acquire social skills and to gain self-confidence. Her fear of other people's opinions and her own negative thoughts about her social abilities create a vicious cycle in which her intolerable anxiety leads her to avoid social situations, and then the avoidance leads to increased anxiety.

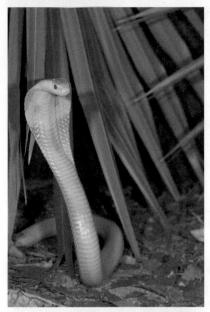

Treatment of Phobias

Behavioral and Cognitive Approaches   Exposure to the feared object or situation is the predominant behavioral approach to the treatment of phobias, with many different types of exposure treatments having been developed. Systematic desensitization was the first widely used behavioral treatment for phobias (Wolpe, 1958). In this treatment, the client first is taught relaxation skills. Then, the client uses these skills to relax while undergoing exposure to a list of feared situations developed with the therapist—starting with the least feared and working up to the most feared (see p. 47 for a more detailed description). Evidence indicates that this technique is effective in reducing the fear and anxiety associated with phobias (Barlow, Raffa, & Cohen, 2002). Remember Jan (see before), who had a fear of snakes. In systematic desensitization, Jan's exposure treatment might consist of relaxing while first, imagining a snake in a cage, then imagining her therapist holding a snake, and finally, imagining that she herself is holding a snake.

Over time, exposure treatments have become more and more efficient and now often include *in vivo* (real life) exposure to feared objects. For phobias involving fear of animals, injections, or dental work, very brief treatments lasting only a couple of hours have been found to be highly effective—most people experience relief from phobic symptoms. Many studies indicate that the effects of exposure therapy last for at least a year (Ost, Ferebee, & Furmark, 1997); however, one study found that many people experienced at least some return of fear over a 12-year period (Lipsitz et al., 1999).

Exposure also appears to be an effective treatment for social phobia; such treatments often begin with role playing or practicing with the therapist or in small therapy groups before undergoing exposure in more public social situations (Marks, 1995). With prolonged exposure, anxiety typically extinguishes (Hope, Heimberg, & Bruch, 1995). Social skills

The notion of prepared learning suggests that we have evolved to pay special attention to signs of danger, including angry people, threatening animals, and dangerous natural environments. (Top to bottom: Digital Vision/Getty Images; Gail Shumway/Taxi/Getty Images; S. F. Vincent/Taxi/Getty Images.)

Susan Mineka's research showed that when monkeys observe another monkey display fear of a snake, they also acquire the fear. This indicates that modeling may play a role in the etiology of phobias. (Courtesy of Susan Mineka.)

Social phobia is often treated in groups, which provide exposure to social threats and provide opportunities to practice new skills. (David Harry Stewart/Stone/Getty Images.)

training, in which a therapist might provide extensive modeling of behavior, can help people with social phobia who may not know what to do or say in social situations. Remember that safety behaviors, like avoiding eye contact, are believed to interfere with the extinction of social anxiety (Clark & Wells, 1995). Consistent with this idea, the effects of exposure treatment seem to be enhanced when people with social phobia are taught to stop using safety behaviors (Kim, 2005). That is, not only are people asked to engage in social activities, but while doing so, they are asked to make direct eye contact, to engage in conversation, and to be fully present. All in all, several studies attest to the effectiveness of exposure approaches (Turk, Heimberg, & Hope 2001).

Most studies have found that cognitive approaches to therapy for specific phobias are not as effective as exposure treatment; in addition, there is not much evidence to suggest that outcomes are better when cognitive therapy is added to exposure (Antony & Barlow, 2004). The reason for this may be that cognitive therapy aims at getting the person to recognize that the phobic fear is excessive or unreasonable, but this is something that most people with specific phobias already know.

With social phobia, however, some though not all studies indicate that cognitive therapy added to exposure therapy is better than exposure alone (Turk et al., 2001). Cognitive approaches may include challenging the person's belief that others are appraising him or her negatively (e.g., probably, a frown from a teacher is not directed at the person but is a response to something else on the teacher's mind) and helping the person not to rely on approval from others for a sense of self-worth (e.g., being criticized doesn't imply worthlessness). Richard Heimberg and colleagues (1990) have developed a cognitive therapy of social phobia, and studies suggest that treatment based on this manual is more effective than supportive psychotherapy (Telch et al., 1993).

As described above, people with social phobia often form very negative images of how others will react to them. David Clark and his colleagues have developed a different cognitive treatment approach that is specifically designed to combat these negative images. This cognitive therapy has performed more effectively than fluoxetine or self-guided exposure treatment (Clark et al., 2003).

Social phobia appears to be harder to treat than specific phobias are. Research suggests that treatment for social phobia is helpful, but for many people treatment leads to only a partial reduction of anxiety (DeRubeis & Crits-Christoph, 1998). Nevertheless, that partial reduction is meaningful for most clients.

Medications Benzodiazepenes and antidepressants have been found to provide relief from phobic symptoms, as they do with symptoms of most anxiety disorders. Within the antidepressants, SSRIs have shown promise in reducing anxiety in both specific and social phobia (Van Ameringen et al., 2001). Paroxetine (Paxil), an SSRI, is the first medication specifically approved by the Food and Drug Administration (FDA) for the treatment of social phobia. In one study, about 55 percent of people with a social phobia responded to paroxetine (Stein et al., 1998). Some research also supports the efficacy of the anti-convulsant gabapentin (Neurontin) for the treatment of social phobia (Ashton & Young, 2003).

Beta blockers block some of the effects of adrenaline on the body, such as increased heart rate, one part of the experience of anxiety. For this reason, beta blockers are among the most commonly prescribed medications for social phobia. Despite their common use, research doesn't indicate that beta blockers are effective in treating this disorder (Hofmann & Barlow, 2004).

Combining Medications with Psychological Treatment In general, adding anxiolytics to exposure treatment actually leads to worse outcomes than exposure treatment without anxiolytics, perhaps because people do not get the same chance to face their fears. In one interesting study, Kerry Ressler and colleagues (2004) examined a different type of drug—one that enhances learning as a way to bolster exposure treatment for acrophobia (fear of heights). In this study, all 28 patients were treated using two sessions of virtual reality exposure to heights. Half of the patients were randomly assigned to receive the medicine

D-cycloserine (DCS) while they completed the exposure sessions; the other half received placebo. The patients who received DCS were less afraid of heights at the end of treatment and 3 months later than the patients were who did not receive DCS. The authors suggested that a medication that enhances learning might help people respond more quickly to a psychotherapy based on conditioning principles.

Etiology of Panic Disorder

In this section, we look at current thinking about the etiology and treatment of panic disorder, from neurobiological, behavioral, and cognitive perspectives. It is interesting to note that the neurobiological, behavioral, and cognitive perspectives each focus on how people respond to somatic (bodily) changes like increased heart rate.

Neurobiological Factors   Neurobiological studies of panic disorder have focused on the role of the locus ceruleus and on experiments involving triggering panic attacks. We'll begin by describing the research on the locus ceruleus. Remember that a panic attack seems to reflect a misfire of the fear circuit, with a concomitant surge in activity in the sympathetic nervous system. We have seen that the fear circuit appears to play an important role in many of the anxiety disorders. Now we will see that a particular part of the fear circuit seems to be especially important in panic disorder: the **locus ceruleus** (see Figure 5.4). The basis for this is that the locus ceruleus is the major source of the neurotransmitter norepinephrine in the brain, and norepinephrine plays a major role in triggering sympathetic nervous system activity.

Monkeys exposed to feared stimuli, such as snakes, show high levels of activity in the locus ceruleus. Further, when activity in the locus ceruleus is triggered using an electrical signal, monkeys behave as if they were having a panic attack (Redmond, 1977). In humans, drugs that increase activity in the locus ceruleus can trigger panic attacks, and drugs that decrease activity in the locus ceruleus, including clonidine and some antidepressants, decrease the risk of panic attacks.

Other than research on the locus ceruleus, a great deal of research has focused on triggering panic attacks experimentally. That is, for more than 75 years, researchers have been conducting studies that involve the use of drugs to induce panic attacks in the laboratory, in hopes that finding particular drugs that induce panic attacks might point toward the neurobiological systems involved in panic disorder. For the most part, however, researchers have found that such drugs are more likely to induce panic in people who already have a history of panic attacks (Zinbarg et al., 2001). That is, whatever mechanism is triggered by these drugs, it only seems to operate for people vulnerable to the disorder.

One giant puzzle arising from these studies is that more than a dozen different types of drugs can trigger panic attacks, including serotonergic drugs, those that increase norepinephrine levels, those that decrease GABA levels, caffeine, and even sodium lactate (a chemical released during exercise) (Swain et al., 2003). Furthermore, drugs that have opposite effects can even set off panic attacks! In one study, for example, 20 people with panic disorder were given either adrenaline (a drug that increases sympathetic nervous system activity) or acetylcholine (a drug that increases parasympathetic nervous system activity). The sympathetic and parasympathetic nervous systems work in opposition to each other.

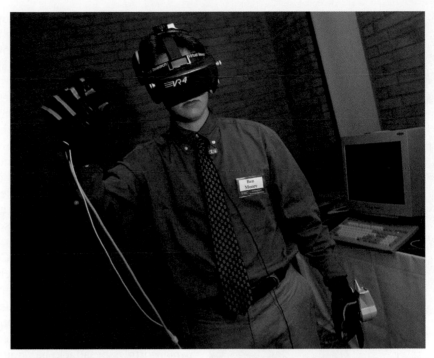

Virtual reality technology is sometimes used to facilitate exposure to feared stimuli. (Kim Kulish/Corbis Images.)

Figure 5.4   Locus ceruleus. [Drawn from Martin, J. H. (1996). Neuroanatomy Text and Atlas, second edition. NY-McGraw-Hill Professions Division. With permission, McGraw-Hill Companies.]

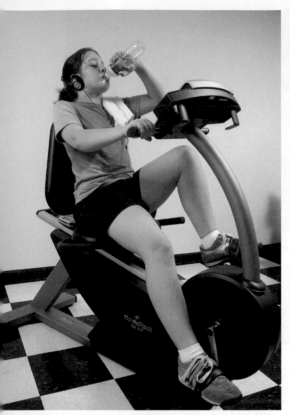

Panic attacks can be experimentally triggered by a variety of agents that change body sensations, including drugs and even exercise. (Robin Nelson/PhotoEdit.)

With either drug, about half of people had a panic attack (Lindemann & Finesinger, 1938). Even exercise alone, simple relaxation, or the physical sensations caused by an illness such as inner ear disease can induce panic attacks (Asmundson, Larsen, & Stein, 1998). In short, drugs with many different effects and even other body sensations can trigger panic attacks (Barlow, 2004).

This could mean that all these different agents (drug and nondrug) activate some underlying neurobiological abnormality in patients with panic disorder, but this conclusion is opposed by the fact that the physiological responses of people with panic disorder to these agents are very similar to those of people without panic disorder (Gorman et al., 2001). People who do and do not develop panic attacks after being exposed to these agents seem to vary only on one characteristic—the extent to which they find the body changes frightening (Margraf, Ehlers, & Roth, 1986). This seems consistent with the idea that people who experience panic attacks are overly fearful about somatic changes—a topic we will return to when we discuss the cognitive contributions to panic disorder.

Behavioral Factors: Classical Conditioning The behavioral perspective on the etiology of panic disorder focuses on classical conditioning. Theory suggests that panic attacks may be classically conditioned responses to either the situations that trigger anxiety or the internal bodily sensations of arousal (Bouton, Mineka, & Barlow, 2001). Classical conditioning of panic attacks in response to bodily sensations has been called **interoceptive conditioning**: a person experiences somatic signs of anxiety, which are followed by the person's first panic attack; panic attacks then become a conditioned response to the somatic changes (see Figure 5.5). This classical conditioning model is supported by studies in which people with panic disorder kept records indicating that anxiety and physical sensations often occurred before a panic attack (Kenardy & Taylor, 1999).

Cognitive Factors Cognitive perspectives on the causes of panic disorder focus on the person's sense of control and on catastrophic misinterpretations of somatic changes.

Perceived Control The importance of a person's sense of control in panic disorder was demonstrated by a study in which people with the disorder breathed air mixed with higher levels of carbon dioxide, which has been shown to induce panic attacks for many people (Sanderson, Rapee, & Barlow, 1989). Participants were told that when a light came on they could turn a dial to reduce the concentration of carbon dioxide. For half the participants, the light was on continuously; for the other half, the light never came on. In either case, turning the dial had no actual effect on carbon dioxide levels—that is, the study aimed at investigating the effects of perceived control, not actual control. Eighty percent of the people with no perceived control over carbon dioxide levels had a panic attack, compared with only 20 percent of the people with perceived control. These findings suggest that perceived control over somatic changes could play a crucial role in whether or not a person develops a panic attack.

Fear of Bodily Sensations Another cognitive perspective on the cause of panic disorder focuses on the catastrophic misinterpretation of bodily sensations (Clark, 1996). According to this model, panic attacks develop when a person interprets bodily sensations as signs of impending doom. For example, the person may interpret the sensation of an increase in heart rate as a sign of an impending heart attack. Obviously, such thoughts will increase the person's anxiety, which produces more physical sensations, creating a vicious cycle.

In an important test of this model, people with a history of panic attacks were exposed to air with high levels of carbon dioxide. Before breathing the air, some people were given a full explanation regarding the physical sensations they were likely to experience, and others were given no explanation. After breathing the air, those who received a full explanation reported that they had fewer catastrophic interpretations of their bodily sensations, and they were much less likely to have a panic attack than those who did not receive an explanation

Figure 5.5 Interoceptive conditioning.

(Rapee, Mattick, & Murrell, 1986). A key question, though, is whether the propensity toward catastrophic interpretations can be detected before panic disorder develops. Many researchers have used a test called the **Anxiety Sensitivity Index**, which measures the extent to which people respond fearfully to their bodily sensations (Telch, Shermis, & Lucas, 1989). (Sample items from the questionnaire used in this study are shown in Table 5.8.) In one study, college students with no history of panic attacks were divided into high and low scorers on the Anxiety Sensitivity Index (Telch & Harrington, 1992). All the participants went through two trials. In one trial they breathed room air, and in the other they breathed air with a higher-than-usual concentration of carbon dioxide. Before the trials, they were told that they would be breathing air with a high concentration of carbon dioxide. Half the participants in each trial were told that the carbon dioxide would be relaxing, and half were told that it would produce symptoms of high arousal. The frequency of panic attacks in each group is shown in Table 5.9. Note that panic attacks did not occur among people breathing room air. In the condition involving increased carbon dioxide, panic attacks were most common among people who feared their bodily sensations, particularly if they did not expect breathing carbon dioxide to be arousing. This result is exactly what the model predicts: unexplained physiological arousal in someone who is fearful of such sensations leads to panic attacks.

Another study bearing on this theory of panic disorder followed 1,296 Air Force recruits as they went through the stressful experiences of basic training (Schmidt, Lerew, & Jackson, 1999). Each participant completed the Anxiety Sensitivity Index. Consistent with the model, high scores on the Anxiety Sensitivity Index predicted the development of panic attacks during basic training.

Agoraphobia and the Fear-of-Fear Hypothesis   As mentioned earlier, panic disorder is often accompanied by agoraphobia. The principal cognitive model for the etiology of agoraphobia is the **fear-of-fear hypothesis** (Goldstein & Chambless, 1978), which suggests that agoraphobia is driven by negative thoughts about the consequences of having a panic attack in public. There is evidence that people with agoraphobia think about places where panic attacks could occur or places where the consequences of a panic attack would be horrible. People with panic disorder without agoraphobia do not seem to worry as much about specific places, so spend less time avoiding specific places (Clark, 1997).

Treatment of Panic Disorder and Agoraphobia

There are both cognitive behavioral and medication treatments available for panic disorder. Analysis of the more than 40 studies of treatments for panic disorder indicated that treatment is better than no treatment and that cognitive behavioral treatments yield the best results (Gould, Otto, & Pollack, 1995).

Cognitive Behavioral Approaches   Like the behavioral treatments for phobias already discussed, cognitive behavioral treatments for panic disorder focus on exposure (White & Barlow, 2004). One well-validated treatment approach called **panic control therapy** (**PCT**; Craske & Barlow, 2001) is based on the tendency of people with panic disorder to overreact to bodily sensations (as discussed above).

Table 5.8 Sample Items from the Anxiety Sensitivity Index

Unusual body sensations scare me.
When I notice that my heart is beating rapidly, I worry that I might have a heart attack.
It scares me when I feel faint.
It scares me when I feel "shaky" (trembling).

Source: Peterson & Reiss, 1987.
Note: People respond to each item on a 0 (very little) to 4 (very much) scale.

Table 5.9 Frequency of Panic Attacks as a Function of Breathing Room Air versus Breathing Air with Carbon Dioxide, Fear of Bodily Sensations, and Expectations

Inhale	High Fear of Bodily Sensations		Low Fear of Bodily Sensations	
	Expect Relaxation	Expect Arousal	Expect Relaxation	Expect Arousal
Room air	0	0	0	0
Carbon dioxide	52	17	5	5

In PCT, the therapist uses exposure techniques—that is, he or she persuades the client to deliberately elicit the sensations associated with panic. For example, a person whose panic attacks begin with hyperventilation is asked to breathe rapidly for 3 minutes; or someone whose panic attacks are associated with dizziness might be requested to spin in a chair for several minutes. When sensations such as dizziness, dry mouth, light-headedness, increased heart rate, and other signs of panic begin, the person experiences them under safe conditions; in addition, the person uses previously learned coping tactics (e.g., breathing from the diaphragm to avoid hyperventilation).

With practice and encouragement from the therapist, the person learns to stop seeing internal sensations as signals of loss of control and to see them instead as intrinsically harmless sensations that can be controlled. The person's ability to create these physical sensations and then cope with them makes them seem more predictable and less frightening (Craske, Maidenberg, & Bystritsky, 1995).

The Multisite Comparative Study for the Treatment of Panic Disorder (Barlow et al., 2000) compared the effects of PCT, the drug imipramine, PCT plus imipramine, and placebo. Initial treatment was offered once a week for 3 months, and if it was working, treatment was then continued for 6 months. Throughout treatment, both PCT and imipramine each provided better results than the placebo. Moreover, adding imipramine to PCT did not yield better results than PCT alone. Six months after treatment ended, relapse was significantly more common among people who had taken imipramine alone than among those given PCT alone. That is, medication was protective only while people continued treatment, but PCT offered protection even after treatment was finished.

Numerous studies have shown that 70–80 percent of people with panic disorder who are treated with cognitive behavioral therapy are free of panic at the end of treatment (DeRubeis & Crits-Cristoph, 1998). Other studies have shown that therapeutic gains generally are maintained after 2 years and are superior in this respect to drug treatment with imipramine (Tofranil; Clark et al., 1994). Cognitive behavioral treatment is one of the most successful treatments available for panic disorder.

A similar cognitive treatment has been developed for panic disorder (Clark, 1996). This treatment focuses on helping a person identify thoughts that may make physical sensations threatening (see Figure 5.6 for an example of one patient's thoughts). The therapist then helps a person challenge those beliefs. For example, if a person with panic disorder imagines that he or she will collapse, the therapist might help the person to examine the evidence for this belief, and to develop a different image of the consequences of a panic attack. This treatment has been shown to work well in at least seven research studies, with specific evidence that this form of treatment is more helpful than relaxation or pure exposure, and that few people drop out of treatment (Clark et al., 1999). A seven-session version is also available (Clark et al., in press).

Among people with panic disorder, those with severe agoraphobic symptoms do worse than those without such symptoms (Williams & Falbo, 1996). Cognitive behavioral approaches to the treatment of agoraphobia also focus on exposure—specifically, on systematic exposure to feared situations. A series of studies support the efficacy of this approach (DeRubeis & Crits-Cristoph, 1998). Married people who suffer primarily from agoraphobia have benefited from family-oriented treatments in which the nonphobic spouse is encouraged to stop catering to the phobic partner's avoidance of leaving the home. Exposure treatment of agoraphobia is more effective when the spouse is involved (Cerny et al., 1987).

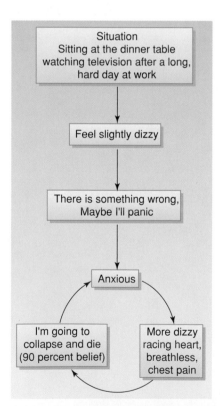

Figure 5.6 An example of catastrophic misinterpretation of bodily cues. Drawn from Clark, D. M. (1997). Panic disorder and social phobia. [In D. M. Clark and C. G. Fairburn (Eds.), *Science and Practice of Cognitive Behaviour Therapy* (pp. 121–153). With permission, Oxford University Press.]

Medications When people with panic disorder first seek treatment, they usually consult a physician, so medications are typically the first and sometimes the only kind of treatment people get. The vigorous marketing of antipanic medications is probably also a factor in the prevalence of drug treatments. This is unfortunate, because as mentioned above, medications do not offer protection once a person discontinues them. Many studies, however, confirm that medications for panic disorder do work while they are taken, including SSRI antidepressants such as fluoxetine (Prozac), tricyclic antidepressants such as imipramine (Tofranil), and benzodiazepines such as alprazolam (Xanax) (Roy-Byrne & Cowley, 1998; White & Barlow, 2004). SSRIs are often prescribed because they have fewer side effects, but they do not seem as effective as tricyclic antidepressants.

Quick Summary

Behavioral perspectives on specific and social phobias are based on a two-factor model (classical conditioning followed by operant conditioning). Many people describe exposure to conditioning experiences prior to developing specific phobias, but many people don't, perhaps because the conditioning experience has been forgotten. Prepared learning refers to the fact that people are likely to sustain conditioned responses to fear stimuli that have some evolutionary significance. Cognitive factors are also considered significant in the maintenance of social phobia, and the trait of behavioral inhibition may play a role as well.

Exposure treatment is the bedrock of psychological treatment for specific and social phobias. For specific phobias, these treatments can work quite quickly. Social phobia is harder to treat, and cognitive components may be a helpful addition to exposure treatment. Antidepressants and anxiolytics medications are helpful for as long as they are taken, but do not help when added to exposure treatment. One new approach involves providing D-cycloserine during exposure treatment for phobia.

Neurobiological research demonstrates high levels of activity in the locus ceruleus associated with panic attacks. Studies have found that many different types of drugs, as well as nonpharmacological agents, can induce panic attacks, but many believe that these studies provide evidence for the role of cognitions—people with panic disorder overreact to bodily sensations. Behavioral models emphasize the possibility that people could become classically conditioned to experience panic attacks in response to external situations or internal somatic signs of anxiety. Conditioning to somatic signs is called interoceptive conditioning. Cognitive perspectives focus on a lack of perceived control and on catastrophic misinterpretations of somatic symptoms.

The most effective treatments for panic disorder include exposure to somatic sensations, along with some cognitive techniques to challenge catastrophic misinterpretations of those symptoms. Medications, such as antidepressants and benzodiazepenes, do help quell panic symptoms and are often the only treatment that is provided. Unfortunately, panic symptoms tend to return once medications are stopped.

Etiology of Generalized Anxiety Disorder

Generalized anxiety disorder (GAD) tends to co-occur with other anxiety disorders and with depression. Because the comorbidity is so high, researchers believe that many of the factors involved in predicting anxiety disorders in general are particularly important for understanding GAD. For example, deficits in the functioning of the GABA system, which are important for many anxiety disorders, appear to be involved in GAD (Tiihonen et al., 1997). Beyond these general risk factors, recent research has focused on cognitive factors.

Cognitive Factors: Why Do People Worry?   Cognitive factors may help answer why some people worry more than others. Tom Borkovec and colleagues focus on the main symptom of GAD, worry, in their cognitive model (Borkovec & Newman, 1998). Worry would seem so unpleasant that one might ask why anyone would worry a lot. Borkovec and colleagues have marshaled evidence that worry is actually reinforcing because it distracts people from more powerful negative emotions and images. The key to understanding this argument is to realize that worry does not involve powerful visual images and does not produce the physiological changes that usually accompany emotion. Indeed, worrying actually seems to decrease psychophysiological signs of arousal (Freeston, Dugas, & Ladoceur, 1996). Thus, by worrying, people with GAD may be avoiding unpleasant emotions that would be more powerful than worry. But as a consequence of this avoidance, their underlying anxiety about these images does not extinguish (just as avoidance prevents the extinction of fear and anxiety in phobias—see p. 138). What kinds of anxiety-evoking images might people with GAD be avoiding? A possible answer comes from studies showing that people with GAD report high rates of past trauma involving death, injury, or illness (Borkovec & Newman, 1998). It may be that worry distracts people with GAD from the distress of remembering these past traumas. Others may find that worry, because it tends not to involve images, protects from horrifying images of potential future stressors such as a husband in a car crash.

Treatment of Generalized Anxiety Disorder

In the past few years, behavioral, cognitive, and pharmacological approaches to the treatment of GAD have all had some success. Also, people with GAD increasingly have been seeking treatment (Salzman et al., 2001), perhaps in response to extensive public health campaigns and advertising for medications. Regardless of the type of treatment, however,

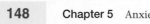

success rates are generally lower than they are for other anxiety disorders (Roemer, Orsillo & Barlow, 2004).

Behavioral and Cognitive Approaches   A prominent behavioral approach to the treatment of GAD involves relaxation training, in which the therapist teaches the person strategies for behaving in ways that promote calmness. These strategies can involve relaxing muscle groups one-by-one or generating mental pictures of relaxing images. With practice, clients typically become able to relax rapidly. Studies suggest that relaxation training is more effective than nondirective treatment or no treatment (DeRubeis & Crits-Christoph, 1998).

Studies also suggest that cognitive behavioral treatment is effective compared to treatment with a placebo (Gould et al., 2004), and there is some evidence that cognitive behavioral treatment is more effective than benzodiazepine treatment (Power et al., 1990). Most studies of cognitive behavioral treatment are based on an approach that involves challenging the person's negative thoughts about potential threats or losses of control (Beck & Emery, 1985). Almost all studies have included several cognitive or behavioral components, such as training in detecting cues of anxiety, relaxation training, and strategies to counter negative thoughts (Roemer et al., 2004).

One study tested a version of cognitive therapy that included helping people tolerate uncertainty, as people with GAD seem to be more distressed by uncertainty than are those without GAD (Ladoceur et al., 2000). Tom Borkovec and colleagues also have designed a supplement to cognitive behavioral treatment; their supplement focuses on reducing worry with innovative strategies that include asking people to worry only during scheduled times, asking people to test whether worry "works" by keeping a diary of the outcomes of worrying, helping people focus their thoughts on the present moment instead of worrying, and helping people address core fears that they may be avoiding through worry (Borkovec, Alcaine, & Behar, 2004).

Medications   Current research indicates that several types of medications can be effective in treating GAD: benzodiazepines, buspirone (BuSpar), tricyclic antidepressants, and SSRIs (Pollack et al., 2001). Hundreds of studies confirm that medications benefit GAD clients more than placebos do (Roemer et al., 2004). Overall, about 70 percent of people experience relief from the symptoms of GAD while taking medication (Lydiard & Monnier, 2004). Tricyclic antidepressants have become the preferred drugs for treating GAD because they have fewer side effects than benzodiazepenes (Lydiard & Monnier, 2004). Antidepressants are also helpful because people with GAD often suffer from major depression as well.

Etiology of Obsessive-Compulsive Disorder

We now turn to neurobiological, behavioral, and cognitive perspectives on the etiology of obsessive-compulsive disorder (OCD). Brain imaging studies of OCD provide an excellent example of how neurobiology can help us understand mental illness; behavioral and cognitive models tend to provide distinct explanations for compulsions versus obsessions.

Neurobiological Factors: Hyperactive Regions of the Brain   Brain imaging studies indicate that three closely related areas of the brain are unusually active in people with OCD (see Figure 5.2): the **orbitofrontal cortex** (an area of the frontal lobe located just above the eyes), the caudate nucleus (part of the basal ganglia), and the **anterior cingulate** (Micallef & Blin, 2001). When people with OCD are shown objects that tend to cause symptoms (such as a soiled glove for a person who fears contamination), activity in these three areas increases (McGuire et al., 1994). Overall, evidence is fairly strong that the symptoms of OCD are tied to overactivity in these three brain areas. It is less clear whether these patterns of neurobiological activity drive symptoms, or vice versa, that symptoms drive neurobiological activity. Studies indicate that when symptoms of OCD decrease with either medication or psychological treatment, neurobiological deficits normalize (Baxter et al., 2000).

Behavioral Factors in Compulsions   Behavioral models consider compulsions to be operantly conditioned responses. That is compulsions are reinforced because they reduce anxiety (Meyer & Chesser, 1970). For example, compulsive hand washing would provide immediate relief from the anxiety associated with obsessions about germs. Similarly, checking the stove may provide immediate relief from the anxiety associated with the thought that the house will catch on fire. Consistent with this view, compulsive behavior is followed by drops in self-reported anxiety and even psychophysiological arousal (Carr, 1971).

Cognitive Factors in Compulsions: Lack of Confidence in Memory   A cognitive explanation of one type of compulsion—checking behaviors—proposes that this behavior results from a lack of confidence in memory. For example, the thought "maybe I just think I turned off the stove" could cause someone to check, and having that thought repeatedly could cause repeated checking. A meta-analysis examined how memory relates to checking in 794 people who had taken part in 22 studies (Woods et al., 2002). By summarizing across studies, the authors were able to provide an accurate estimate of effects. This analysis revealed that people with checking symptoms did worse than people without such symptoms at recalling stimuli that had been presented to them in experiments; generally, though, the actual memory deficits were very small. The analysis did suggest, though, that people with OCD are unduly concerned about gaps in their memory. This concern could lead to a lack of confidence in memory that could, as suggested above, lead to repeated checking.

Cognitive Factors in Obsessions: Attempts to Suppress Thoughts   At least 80 percent of people experience brief intrusive thoughts from time to time—a song that gets stuck in your head, or an image you prefer not to see appears again and again in your mind's eye (Rachman & deSilva, 1978). Because intrusive thoughts are so common, much of the cognitive research has focused on why such thoughts persist, rather than on why such thoughts happen in the first place. After all, we don't diagnose OCD until intrusive thoughts are so persistent that they cause real distress or impairment.

One model suggests that people with OCD may try harder to suppress their obsessions than other people, and in doing so, may actually make the situation worse. Several researchers have shown that people with OCD tend to believe that thinking about something can make it more likely to occur (Rachman, 1997). People with OCD are also likely to describe especially deep feelings of responsibility for what occurs (Ladoceur et al., 2000). As a consequence of these two factors, they are more likely to attempt **thought suppression** (Salkovskis, 1996).

Unfortunately, it is hard to suppress thoughts. One study looked at what happens when people are asked to suppress a thought (Wegner et al., 1987). Two groups of college students were asked either to think about a white bear or not to think about one; they were also told to ring a bell every time they thought about a white bear. The study indicated that attempts to avoid thinking about the white bear did not work—students thought about the bear more than once a minute when trying not to do so. Beyond that, there was a rebound effect—after students tried to suppress thoughts about the bear for 5 minutes, they thought about the bear much more often during the next 5 minutes. Trying to suppress a thought may have the paradoxical effect of inducing preoccupation with it.

Most studies look at the effects of suppression over a matter of minutes, but the effects of trying to suppress a thought can continue for days. In one study, for example, people were asked to identify a recent intrusive thought and then were told to pay attention to the thought, were told to suppress the thought, or were given no instructions about the thought (Trinder & Salkoviskis, 1994). The people recorded how often they had the intrusive thought and how uncomfortable the experience was for the next 4 days. People told to suppress the thought had more frequent intrusions of the thought and rated the intrusions as more uncomfortable over the 4-day period.

Beyond these studies of how hard it is to suppress thoughts, there is some evidence that thought suppression does actually play a role in OCD—namely, people with OCD tend to give more reasons why they should try to suppress thoughts than do people without OCD. For example, people who say they believe that bad things will happen if you think about them are more likely to try to suppress thoughts, and people who report more thought suppression also report more obsessive symptoms (Rassin et al., 2000). Research also indicates, however, that people with a wide range of anxiety disorders worry that bad things will happen if you think about them. So it is not clear if thought suppression gives us an explanation of OCD in particular or if it just relates to anxiety disorders in general (Rassin et al., 2001).

Treatment of Obsessive-Compulsive Disorder

Behavioral Approach: Exposure and Ritual Prevention Exposure and ritual prevention (ERP), pioneered in England by Victor Meyer (1966), is the most widely used and generally accepted behavioral treatment of OCD. OCD sufferers often hold an almost magical belief that their compulsive behavior will prevent awful things from happening. With ERP, people expose themselves to situations that elicit the compulsive act and then refrain from performing the compulsive ritual—for instance, the person touches a dirty dish and then refrains from washing his or her hands. The reasoning behind this approach goes like this:

1. The ritual is negatively reinforcing because it reduces anxiety.
2. Not performing the ritual exposes the person to the full force of the anxiety provoked by the stimulus.
3. The exposure results in the extinction of the conditioned response (the anxiety).

Studies suggests that ERP is at least partially effective for more than half of people with OCD (Stanley & Turner, 1995), including children and adolescents (Franklin & Foa, 1998). Even though most people experience a clinically significant reduction in symptoms (Franklin et al., 2000), some symptoms are likely to remain (Steketee & Frost, 1998).

The first study of ERP as a treatment for OCD involved creating a controlled environment at Middlesex Hospital in London (Meyer, 1966). These days, the therapist guides exposure to feared stimuli in the home, often with help from family members (Foa & Franklin, 2001).

In the short term, refraining from performing a ritual is extremely unpleasant for people with OCD. (To get some idea of how unpleasant, try delaying for a minute or two before scratching an itch.) Typically, ERP involves refraining from performing rituals during sessions lasting upwards of 90 minutes, with 15 to 20 sessions within a 3-week period, and with instructions to practice between sessions as well. Initially, treatment often involved physical coercion to prevent people from performing rituals (Meyer, 1966), but contemporary treatments emphasize encouragement and support from the therapist and significant others (Foa & Franklin, 2001). Nevertheless, up to 25 percent of clients refuse ERP treatment (Foa & Franklin, 2001). Clients with OCD tend to fear changes, and these tendencies create special problems for behavior therapy and medication approaches (Jenike & Rauch, 1994).

Cognitive Therapy Cognitive approaches to OCD focus on challenging a person's beliefs about what will happen if they do not engage in rituals (Van Oppen et al., 1995). Eventually, to help test such beliefs, these approaches will include exposure. Several studies suggest that cognitive approaches perform as well as ERP (DeRubeis & Crits-Cristoph, 1998).

Medications One particular class of antidepressants that is closely related to SSRIs, the serotonin reuptake inhibitor (SRIs), appear particularly effective in the treatment of OCD but a broad range of studies have shown other antidepressants to be helpful in treating OCD as well (Steketee & Barlow, 2004). The most commonly prescribed SRI for OCD is clomipramine (Anafranil; McDonough & Kennedy, 2002). In one multisite study, clomipramine led to an approximately 50 percent reduction in symptoms (Mundo, Maina, & Uslenghi, 2000). Without a doubt, this was a major improvement; nevertheless, most

Exposure treatment for OCD can include confronting one's worst fears, such as contamination by dirty objects. (Copyright John Wiley & Sons, Inc.)

people still had some ongoing symptoms after treatment. Also, people are likely to relapse if they stop taking the medications (Koran et al., 2002). Because ERP provides protection even after treatment ends, it is considered the first-line approach (McDonough & Kennedy, 2002). Plus, it seems that adding clomipramine to ERP is not more effective than ERP alone (Kozak, Liebowitz, & Foa, 2000).

Quick Summary

Generalized anxiety disorder (GAD) has been related to deficits in the GABA system. One cognitive model emphasizes that worry might actually protect people from intensely disturbing emotional images. Cognitive behavioral treatment focuses on helping a person challenge their thoughts about potential threats or loss of control, coupled with relaxation therapy. Antidepressants and benzodiazepenes are often used to treat GAD, but appear less effective than psychological treatment.

Obsessive-compulsive disorder (OCD) is characterized by higher activity in the orbitofrontal cortex, the caudate nucleus, and the anterior cingulate. Behavioral models of compulsions focus on the relief provided by performing these acts, which could act as a reinforcer. Cognitive models of checking symptoms focus on a decreased confidence in memories. Cognitive models of obsessions focus on thought suppression.

Exposure and ritual prevention is an effective behavioral treatment for OCD. Treatments that integrate cognitive components to this exposure-based treatment have been found to perform similarly. OCD symptoms tend to be relieved by the SRI clomipramine, as well as other antidepressants.

Etiology of Posttraumatic Stress Disorder

As with other anxiety disorders, **posttraumatic stress disorder (PTSD)** tends to occur more often among people with childhood experiences of trauma, people with other anxiety or depressive disorders, people who are high in neuroticism (Breslau, Davis, & Andreski, 1995), and women (McNally, 2003b). Also, as with other anxiety disorders, people with PTSD tend to show high levels of brain activity in areas of the fear circuit, such as the amygdala (Rauch et al., 2000). Keeping these things in mind, in this section we focus on factors that are uniquely associated with PTSD. Even among people who experience traumas, not everyone develops PTSD. Thus, a great deal of research has been conducted on aspects of the trauma and the person that help predict the onset of PTSD. We begin by describing aspects of the trauma, and then turn to individual differences.

Nature of the Trauma: Severity Matters   The severity of the trauma influences whether or not a person will develop PTSD. Consider the case of people who are exposed to war. About 20 percent of American fighters wounded in Vietnam developed PTSD, contrasted with 50 percent of those who were prisoners of war there (Engdahl et al., 1997). During Operation Desert Storm (in the 1990–1991 conflict following the Iraqi invasion of Kuwait), among those assigned to collect, tag, and bury scattered body parts of the dead, 65 percent developed PTSD (Sutker et al., 1994). During World War II, doctors believed that 98 percent of men would develop psychiatric problems with 60 days of continuous combat (Grossman, 1995).

The occurrence of PTSD among residents of Manhattan, in New York City, following the terrorist attack on the World Trade Center on September 11, 2001, showed a similar correspondence with the severity of the trauma. Based on a telephone survey after the attack, researchers determined that 7 percent of the adults living south of 110th Street in New York City (but well north of the World Trade Center) reported symptoms that would have warranted a diagnosis of PTSD, but 20 percent of those living south of Canal Street (close to the disaster site) reported such symptoms (Galea et al., 2002). In short, among people who have been exposed to traumas, those exposed to the most severe traumas seem most likely to develop PTSD.

Survivors of natural disasters, such as the tsunami at the end of 2004, are at risk for PTSD. (NAMAS BHOJANI/Bloomberg News/Landov LLC.)

Neurobiological Factors: Hippocampus and Hormones   The hippocampus is an area in the brain known for its role in memory, including memories related to emotions (see

Focus on Discovery 5.2

Perspectives on Memory: Integrating Neurobiology and Cognition

Memory is a hot topic in research on PTSD. People with PTSD seem to have more frequent intrusions of memories, cued by sensory stimuli. This is consistent with findings that surges of norepinephrine, which are typically present during periods of extreme stress, lead to stronger memory formation, particularly for the central aspects of a threatening experience. Now consider the fact that people with PTSD often report fragmented and disjointed memories of their trauma, making it difficult for them to construct a coherent narrative about the event. How can we account for both facts at once—that memories occur more often but are also disjointed?

Some researchers propose that cognitive avoidance strategies limit the time spent thinking about the trauma—that is, intrusive memories may occur frequently, but the person may respond to each one by quickly suppressing it, ensuring that the memories remain fragmented and disjointed (Koutstaal & Schacter, 1997).

Other researchers, though, have begun to think about the different systems involved in memory, and how they may operate in PTSD. Brewin and Holmes (2003) theorize that PTSD may involve deficits in ability to access memories verbally, yet preserve ability to access memories using cues such as smells, sounds, and other sensory stimuli. Bremner and colleagues highlight the possible relation of hippocampal damage to this fragmentation of verbal memory (Bremner et al., 2003). The hippocampus plays a central role in our ability to locate autobiographical memories in space, time, and context, letting us give clear, organized descriptions of them. Perhaps people with decreased hippocampal volume are less able to organize their verbal memories. Other brain systems may play a more central role in **nonverbal memories**—that is, memories based on a link between sensory stimuli and external events. Hence, poor functioning of the hippocampus may not have the same influence on people's ability to access nonverbal memories as on their ability to organize memories verbally. This could explain why smells, sounds, and other sensory stimuli continue to trigger recall among people with PTSD, regardless of hippocampal volume. Thus, a person may be prone toward powerful memories, often triggered by sensory stimuli, but not be able to consolidate and organize those memories verbally in a way that allows for effective coping and decreased anxiety. Many clinicians find this notion helpful, but some researchers have criticized it, noting that, in fact, it is extremely unusual for a person to form nonverbal memories without also forming consolidated verbal memories (McNally et al., 2003b).

Figure 5.2). Brain-imaging studies show that, in people with PTSD, the hippocampus has a smaller volume than in people who do not have PTSD (Bremner et al., 2003). A study of multiple pairs of identical twins, one of whom was a Vietnam veteran and the other not, is especially revealing of how hippocampal volume and PTSD are related (Gilbertson et al., 2002). As in previous studies of veterans with PTSD, smaller hippocampal volume was associated with PTSD symptoms, but this study went on to find an additional important pattern. Nonveteran twins with small hippocampal volume were more likely to have twins who developed PTSD after military service. That is, there was a consistent relationship between hippocampal volume in the nonveteran twins and the likelihood of PTSD in the veteran twins. This suggests that smaller-than-average hippocampal volume probably precedes the onset of disorder. These findings are among the first that point toward brain characteristics that might precede the onset of an anxiety disorder. See Focus on Discovery 5.2 for more perspectives on how these findings regarding the hippocampus can be integrated with cognitive models to understand memory complaints in PTSD.

Other neurobiological research has indicated that PTSD is associated with an increased sensitivity of receptors to the stress hormone, cortisol (Golier & Yehuda, 1998; see p. 42 for a description of cortisol). One consequence of this elevated sensitivity may be the high levels of norepinephrine (a stress-related neurotransmitter) found in PTSD (Geracioti et al., 2001).

Behavioral Factors: The Two-Factor Model   Like phobias, PTSD has been related to the two-factor model of conditioning. In this model, the initial fear in PTSD is assumed to arise from classical conditioning (Keane, Zimering, & Caddell, 1985). For example, a woman may come to fear walking in the neighborhood (the CS) where she was raped (the UCS). This classically conditioned fear is so intense that the woman avoids the neighborhood as much as possible. This avoidance behavior (the CR) is operantly conditioned; the avoidance is reinforced by the reduction of fear that comes from not being in the presence of the CS. And as we have seen before, the avoidant behavior interferes with chances for the fear to extinguish.

Psychological Factors: Cognition and Coping   From the cognitive perspective, it is important to consider how a person thinks about the event, and particularly his or her sense of perceived control (Brewin & Holmes, 2003). For example, among people who survived political imprisonment and torture, those who had believed they had some ability to control the torture were less likely to develop PTSD (Basoglu & Mineka, 1992).

People who cope with a trauma by trying to avoid thinking about it are more likely than others to develop PTSD (Sharkansky et al., 2000). People who had symptoms of **dissociation** (including depersonalization, derealization, amnesia, and out-of-body experiences) at the time of the trauma also are more likely to develop PTSD, as are people who try to suppress memories of the trauma (Ehlers, Mayou, & Bryant, 1998). Dissociation and memory suppression may play a role in maintaining the disorder, as they keep the person from confronting memories of the trauma. A compelling study of dissociation assessed rape victims within 2 weeks of the assault (Griffin, Resick, & Mechanic, 1997). The women talked about the rape and about neutral topics; while talking, the women reported when they felt stress and were measured for psychophysiological arousal. Based on their responses to questions about dissociation during the rape (e.g., "Did you feel numb?" "Did you have moments of losing track of what was going on?"), the women were divided into a high-dissociation group and a low-dissociation group. Women in the high-dissociation group were much more likely to have PTSD symptoms than women in the low-dissociation group. Furthermore, even though the women in the high-dissociation group reported emotional stress while talking about being raped, they actually showed less physiological arousal than did the women in the low-dissociation group. A range of studies now show that women who report symptoms of dissociation shortly after being raped are more likely than others to develop PTSD (Brewin & Holmes, 2003). We will discuss dissociation more in the chapter on dissociative disorders.

Other factors may help a person cope with severe traumas more adaptively. Two that seem particularly important include high intelligence (Macklin et al., 1998) and strong social support (Brewin, Andrews, & Valentine, 2000). Having greater intellectual ability to make sense of horrifying events, and more friends and family members to help with that process, seems to help people avoid symptoms after traumatic events.

Rescue workers, such as this fireman who was at the World Trade Center in the aftermath of the 9/11 terrorist attack, could be vulnerable to PTSD. (AFP/Getty Images.)

Quick Summary

Posttraumatic stress disorder (PTSD) can be diagnosed only in people who have experienced a severe trauma; even among people who have been traumatized, though, the likelihood that a person will develop PTSD depends on the severity of the trauma. Neurobiological research has found people with small hippocampal volume are more likely to develop PTSD. Other neurobiological research has found that PTSD is associated with elevated sensitivity to the stress hormone, cortisol. Studies from the cognitive perspective indicate that people who are able to maintain some sense of control during the trauma are less likely to develop PTSD. After exposure to trauma, people who rely on dissociative coping strategies (i.e., who avoid thinking about the trauma) seem more likely to develop PTSD than people who rely on other strategies. The behavioral perspective focuses on the same two-factor model used to explain phobias: classical conditioning of fear, followed by operant conditioning of avoidant behavior that prevents the fear from extinguishing.

Treatment of Posttraumatic Stress Disorder

As with the other anxiety disorders, treatment of PTSD—regardless of the therapist's theoretical orientation—involves exposure to fear-provoking stimuli. But in the case of PTSD,

Eye Movement Desensitization and Reprocessing

In 1989, Francine Shapiro began to promulgate an approach to trauma treatment called **eye movement desensitization and reprocessing (EMDR)**. In this procedure, the person imagines a situation related to the trauma, such as seeing a horrible automobile accident. Keeping the image in mind, the person visually tracks the therapist's fingers as the therapist moves them back and forth about a foot in front of the person's eyes. This process continues for a minute or so, or until the person reports that the image is becoming less painful. At this point, the therapist tells the person to say whatever negative thoughts he or she is having, while continuing to track the therapist's fingers. Finally, the therapist tells the person to think a positive thought (e.g., "I can deal with this") and to hold this thought in mind, still tracking the therapist's fingers. This treatment, then, consists of classic imaginal exposure techniques, along with the extra technique of eye movement. Studies in which EMDR was used to treat people with PTSD have reported dramatically rapid symptom relief; EMDR proponents argue that combining eye movements with thoughts about the feared event promotes rapid extinction of the conditioned fear and correction of mistaken beliefs about fear-provoking stimuli (Shapiro, 1999). [1]

EMDR is controversial to a degree not often found in science. Some studies that meet current standards for psychotherapy research suggest that EMDR is more effective than placebo, standard care, or no treatment (DeRubeis & Crits-Cristoph, 1998), but many other studies of EMDR have been criticized for being poorly designed or conducted—for ex-

ample, for relying on people's statements that they have improved after EMDR treatment, without also assessing improvement more objectively (Lohr, Lilienfeld, Tolin, & Herbert, 1999). In some of the more careful studies, results indicate that EMDR is not more effective than control treatments, like attention from a therapist who is not following a particular treatment manual (Goldstein et al., 2000). Further, in longer-term follow-up studies, many of the initial gains from EMDR treatment do not appear to be maintained. For example, one study found that many people treated with EMDR relapsed over a 5-year period (Macklin et al., 2000).

Beyond critiques of the quality of the evidence, several studies have indicated that the eye movement component of treatment is not necessary. For example, one researcher developed a version of EMDR that included all its techniques except eye movement (Pitman, 1996) and then conducted a study in which people were randomly assigned to receive either a version without eye movement or a version with eye movement. The two groups achieved similar levels of symptom relief, and several teams of researchers have replicated these findings. In sum, even if we accept the evidence that this therapy works, there is no evidence that it works any better than exposure therapy or cognitive therapy (McNally, 1999). Some investigators have argued that EMDR should not be offered as a first line treatment for PTSD because the eye movement component is not supported either by studies or by adequate theoretical explanations (cf. Goldstein et al., 2000).

---

the exposure is to memories and reminders of the original trauma, with the person being encouraged to confront the trauma to gain mastery and extinguish the anxiety. Where possible, the person is directly exposed to reminders of the trauma—for example, by returning to the scene of the event. In other cases, imaginal exposure is used—the person deliberately remembers the event. Despite the success of this approach, recent years have seen a great deal of controversy over other treatments of PTSD. See Focus on Discovery 5.3 for more discussion of these controversies.

Exposure Treatment   Evidence indicates that exposure to trauma-related events, either in imagination or directly, is more effective in treating PTSD than medication or supportive unstructured psychotherapy (Foa & Meadows, 1997). Many different exposure techniques have been used. In one study, for example, Vietnam veterans with PTSD were assigned either to receive no treatment (the control group) or to take part in an **imaginal exposure** treatment that involved visualizing trauma-related scenes for extended periods of time. The exposure treatment led to significantly greater reductions in depression, anxiety, reexperiencing of the trauma, startle reactions, and irritability than did no treatment (Keane et al., 1989). Exposure therapy is difficult for both the patient and the therapist, however, because it requires such intense contact with traumatizing events. For example, women who have developed PTSD after rape might be asked to relive the fearsome events of the attack, imagining them in vivid detail (Rothbaum & Foa, 1993). The patient's symptoms may even increase temporarily in the initial stages of therapy, and therapists may become upset when they hear about their patient's horrifying experiences (Keane et al., 1992).

---

[1] Recently, the claims of dramatic efficacy have extended to disorders other than PTSD, including attention-deficit hyperactivity disorder, dissociative disorders, panic disorder, public-speaking fears, test anxiety, and specific phobias (Lohr et al., 1998).

Focus on Discovery 5.4

Critical Incident Stress Debriefing

Critical incident stress debriefing (CISD) involves immediate treatment of trauma victims within 72 hours of the traumatic event (Mitchell & Everly, 2000). Unlike cognitive behavioral treatment, the therapy is usually limited to one long session and is given regardless of whether the person has developed symptoms. Therapists encourage people to remember the details of the trauma and to express their feelings as fully as they can. Therapists who practice this approach often visit disaster sites immediately after events—sometimes invited by local authorities (as in the aftermath of the World Trade Center attack) and sometimes not; they offer therapy both to victims and to their families.

Like EMDR, CISD is highly controversial. A review of six studies, all of which included randomly assigning clients to receive CISD or no treatment, found that those who received CISD tended to fare worse (Litz et al., 2002). No one is certain why harmful effects occur, but it may be that immediately after a disaster, people do best when supported by family members and friends, rather than by strangers; at such times, no matter how gently strangers offer support, people may experience them as coercive and intrusive, and such experiences may be harmful to people who have just been traumatized (Gist & Woodall, 2000).

It is important to recall that many people who experience a trauma do not develop PTSD. Many experts are dubious about the idea of providing therapy for people who have not developed a disorder. Some researchers raise the objection to CISD that a person's natural coping strategies may work better than those recommended by someone else (Bonanno et al., 2002).

Therapists have also used virtual reality (VR) technology to treat PTSD, because this technology can provide more vivid exposure than some clients may be able to generate in their imaginations (virtual reality technology also has been used to treat phobias). In one study, Vietnam veterans with PTSD benefited from taking a VR helicopter trip replete with the sounds of battle (Rothbaum et al., 1999).

As described above, the behavioral view of exposure is that it works by extinguishing the fear response. A cognitive view has also been proposed (by Edna Foa and colleagues) that exposure can change the meaning which stimuli have for people—namely, that it can help people correct their mistaken beliefs about what they fear. In this view, exposure relieves symptoms by allowing people to realize that, contrary to their beliefs, they can tolerate situations that remind them of their trauma without fear or loss of control (Foa & Meadows, 1997, p. 462). Cognitive therapy for PTSD, which helps address a person's thoughts about their ability to cope with the initial trauma, has been shown to fare well as an intervention for PTSD (Ehlers et al., 2003), even when patients are experiencing comorbid conditions (Gillespie et al., 2002). Cognitive processing therapy for rape victims has received some empirical support (Resick et al., 2002). In this work, the rape victim is encouraged to dispute any tendency to attribute the blame to herself and to consider fully those aspects of the attack that were beyond her control.

Medications   Psychoactive drugs used with PTSD clients include benzodiazepenes and antidepressants; among the antidepressants, SSRIs have been found most effective (Brady et al., 2000). Sometimes, medication is used to deal with conditions comorbid with PTSD, such as depression. Nevertheless, medication tends to be less effective than exposure treatment in PTSD (Keane & Barlow, 2004).

Treatment of Acute Stress Disorder   Is it possible to prevent the development of PTSD by offering treatment to people who have developed acute stress disorder (ASD)? Short-term (five or six session) cognitive behavioral approaches that include exposure appear to do so. For example, Richard Bryant and colleagues found that early intervention decreased the risk that ASD would develop into PTSD (Bryant et al., 1999)—specifically, they found that exposure therapy reduced the risk of PTSD to 14 percent, compared to 67 percent among people who received unstructured support from therapists. Unfortunately, not all approaches to prevention seem to work this well (see Focus on Discovery 5.4).

Check Your Knowledge 5.3

Match the theory to the model of etiology:
1. Panic disorder
2. GAD
3. OCD
4. PTSD
5. Specific phobias
   a. anxiety sensitivity
   b. overly sensitive cortisol receptors and small hippocampus
   c. prepared learning
   d. increased activity in the orbitofrontal cortex, caudate nucleus, and anterior cingulate
   e. avoidance of powerful negative emotions
6. The first step in Mowrer's two-factor model includes _____ conditioning, and the second step involves _____ conditioning.
   a. operant, operant
   b. classical, classical
   c. classical, operant
   d. operant, classical
7. Prepared learning refers to:
   a. humans are preprogrammed to be fearful
   b. animals and humans have evolved to learn certain fears more quickly
   c. People have to be taught what to fear.
   d. none of the above

8. Major risk factors for PTSD include (circle all that apply):
   a. decreased hippocampal volume
   b. being male
   c. dissociation
   d. decreased dopamine functioning
   e. low self-esteem
9. In vivo exposure is generally more effective than imaginal exposure, but often cannot be done for _____:
   a. social phobia
   b. panic disorder
   c. most anxiety disorders
   d. PTSD
10. Cognitive therapy when added to behavioral exposure bolsters symptom relief for _____, but not _____.
   a. social phobia, specific phobia
   b. specific phobia, social phobia
   c. PTSD; any other anxiety disorders
   d. GAD; PTSD
11. Which of the following is true?
   a. Anxiolytic medications work better than CBT.
   b. Anxiety symptoms often return when a person stops taking anxiolytic medications.
   c. Antidepressants are addicting.
   d. Side effects are no longer a concern with modern anxiolytics.

Summary

Clinical Descriptions of the Anxiety Disorders

● As a class, anxiety disorders are the most common type of mental illness.

● DSM-IV-TR lists seven principal diagnoses: specific phobia, social phobia, panic disorder (with and without agoraphobia), generalized anxiety disorder, obsessive-compulsive disorder, posttraumatic stress disorder, and acute stress disorder. Anxiety is common to all the anxiety disorders, but phobias and panic also involve fear as a clinical feature.

● Phobias are intense, unreasonable fears that interfere with functioning. Social phobia is defined by: intense fear of unknown people or social scrutiny. Specific phobias include fears of animals, heights, enclosed spaces, and blood, injury, or injections.

● A patient with panic disorder has recurrent, inexplicable attacks of intense fear. Panic attacks alone are not sufficient for the diagnosis; a person must be worried about the potential of having another attack. Panic attacks sometimes lead to fear and avoidance of being in places where escape would be difficult if another attack were to occur, known as agoraphobia.

● In generalized anxiety disorder, the person is beset with virtually constant tension, apprehension, and worry which lasts for at least 6 months.

● People with obsessive-compulsive disorder have intrusive, unwanted thoughts and feel pressured to engage in rituals to avoid overwhelming levels of anxiety.

● Posttraumatic stress disorder is diagnosed in some people who have experienced a traumatic event that would evoke extreme distress in most people. It is marked by symptoms of reexperiencing the trauma, arousal, and emotional numbing. Acute stress disorder is defined by similar symptoms, but lasts less than 1 month.

Gender and Sociocultural Factors in the Anxiety Disorders

● Anxiety disorders are much more common among women than men.
● The focus of anxiety, the prevalence of anxiety disorders, and the specific symptoms expressed may be shaped by culture.

Common Risk Factors across the Anxiety Disorders

● The psychoanalytic view of anxiety disorders is that they are a defense against repressed conflicts.

● Genes increase risk for a broad range of anxiety disorders. Beyond this general risk for anxiety disorders, there may be more specific heritability for certain anxiety disorders. Beyond genetic diatheses, other factors that appear to be involved in a range of anxiety disorders include elevated activity in the fear circuit, poor regulation of several neurotransmitter systems (GABA, serotonin, and norepinephrine), lack of perceived control, a tendency to pay closer attention to signs of potential danger, and negative life events.

Common Aspects of Treatment for the Anxiety Disorders

● Behavior therapists focus on exposure to what is feared. Systematic desensitization and modeling may be used as parts of exposure therapy. For some disorders, including social phobia, GAD, OCD and panic disorder, cognitive components may also be helpful in therapy.

● Antidepressants and benzodiazepenes are most commonly used for anxiety disorders, but new research also has begun to focus on medications like the anticonvulsant medication gabapentin (Neurontin). The effects of medications are often not as long-lasting as those seen for psychotherapy. There are some concerns that benzodiazapenes are subject to abuse, and discontinuing medications usually leads to relapse.

Etiology and Treatment of Specific Anxiety Disorders

● Behavioral models of phobias typically emphasize two stages of conditioning. The first stage involves classical condition, in which a formerly innocuous object is paired with a feared object. This can occur through direct exposure, modeling, or cognition. Fears of objects with evolutionary significance may be more sustained after conditioning. The second stage involves avoidance. Because not all people with negative experiences develop phobias, diatheses must be important. Exposure treatment for specific phobia tends to work quickly and well. Social phobia is harder to treat and adding cognitive components to behavioral treatments may help.

● Neurobiological models of panic disorder have focused on the locus ceruleus, the brain region responsible for norepinephrine release. Many different drugs have been found to trigger panic attacks in laboratory studies among people with a history of panic attacks. The key trigger is probably not a shift in a given neurotransmitter, but rather, how a person interprets changes in their body. Behavioral theories of panic attacks have posited that the attacks are classically conditioned to internal bodily sensations. Cognitive theories suggest that such sensations are more frightening due to catastrophic misinterpretation of somatic cues. CBT treatment appears more effective than medication treatment of panic disorder.

● Cognitive behavioral theories hold that GAD results from distorted cognitive processes. One model suggests that worry actually helps people avoid more intense emotions. Neurobiological approaches focus on the neurotransmitter GABA, which may be deficient in those with the disorder. Relaxation and cognitive approaches may be helpful, as are medication approaches.

● OCD symptoms have been robustly linked to activity in the orbitofrontal cortex, the caudate, and the anterior cingulate. In behavioral accounts, compulsions are considered avoidance responses that are reinforced because they provide relief. Checking behaviors may be intensified by doubts about memories. Obsessions may be intensified by attempts to inhibit unwanted thoughts, in part because people with OCD seem to feel that thinking about something is as bad as doing it. ERP is a well-validated approach that involves exposure. The SRI, clomipramine, also appears helpful, as do other antidepressant medications.

● Research and theory on the causes of posttraumatic stress disorder focus on risk factors such as small hippocampal volume, the severity of the event, dissociation, and other factors that may influence the ability to cope with stress, such as social support and intelligence. Psychological treatment involves exposure, but often, imaginal exposure is used.

Answers to Check Your Knowledge Questions

5.1 1. b; 2. d; 3. f; 4. a; 5. e; 6. g; 7. c; 8. b, d, e; 9. a; 10. c; 11. c
5.2 1. b; 2. c; 3. b, c, e; 4. b; 5. b, d, e

5.3 1. a; 2. e; 3. d; 4. b; 5. c; 6. c; 7. b; 8. a and c; 9. d; 10. a; 11. b

Key Terms

acute stress disorder (ASD)
agoraphobia
anterior cingulate
antidepressants
anxiety
anxiety disorders
Anxiety Sensitivity Index
anxiolytics
behavioral inhibition
benzodiazepines
beta blockers
comorbidity
compulsion

critical incident stress debriefing (CISD)
depersonalization
dissociation
derealization
eye-movement desensitization and reprocessing (EMDR)
exposure and ritual prevention
fear
fear circuit
fear-of-fear hypothesis
generalized anxiety disorder (GAD)

imaginal exposure
interoceptive conditioning
locus ceruleus
Mowrer's two-factor model
neuroses
neuroticism
nonverbal memories
obsessions
obsessive-compulsive disorder (OCD)
orbitofrontal cortex
panic attack
panic control therapy (PCT)

panic disorder
phobia
posttraumatic stress disorder (PTSD)
prepared learning
selective serotonin reuptake inhibitor (SSRI)
social phobia
specific phobia
subthreshold symptoms
thought suppression
tricyclic antidepressants

6 Somatoform Disorders and Dissociative Disorders

Learning Goals

1. Be able to define the symptoms of the somatoform and dissociative disorders.
2. Be able to explain the psychoanalytic and sociocultural perspectives on conversion disorder.
3. Be able to discuss neurobiological and cognitive behavioral models of other somatoform disorders.
4. Be able to summarize current debate regarding the etiology of dissociative identity disorders.
5. Be able to describe the goals and issues in available treatments for somatoform and dissociative disorders.

Clinical Case

A 27-year-old man was brought to a hospital emergency room by the police because he had lain down in the middle of a busy intersection. He said that he wanted to die and was very depressed. He had no memory of any events before being picked up by the police—he could not tell the hospital staff his name or anything else about himself.

Neurological tests revealed no abnormality. After the first week in the hospital, his memory returned. He had just come to town to look for work. Two men had approached him and asked if he wanted a job. All three then had left in a pickup truck. Later, after smoking some marijuana, the other men had forced him at gunpoint to have sex with them. (Adapted from Kaszniak et al., 1988.)

In this chapter, we discuss the somatoform disorders and the dissociative disorders. In early versions of the DSM, these disorders and the anxiety disorders were all classified together as neuroses, because anxiety was considered the predominant cause of these symptoms. Signs of anxiety, however, are not always observable in the somatoform and dissociative disorders, whereas anxiety is always clearly present in the anxiety disorders. Starting with DSM-III, in which classification is based on observable symptoms instead of presumed etiology, the diagnostic category of neurosis was abandoned, and the somatoform and dissociative disorders became diagnostic categories separate from each other and from the anxiety disorders.

We cover somatoform disorders and dissociative disorders together in this chapter because the onset of disorders of both classes is hypothesized to be related to some stressful experience, yet symptoms do not involve direct expressions of anxiety or distress. In the somatoform disorders, the person complains of bodily symptoms that suggest a physical defect or dysfunction—sometimes dramatic in nature—for which no physiological basis can be found. In the dissociative disorders, the person experiences disruptions of consciousness—they lose track of self-awareness, memory, and identity.

Researchers know less about the somatoform disorders or the dissociative disorders compared to other psychological conditions, and there is a great deal of controversy about the risk factors for these disorders, as well as the best treatments. To some, this controversy may seem daunting; we believe, however, that issues like this make a fascinating focus, as researchers strive to untangle a complex puzzle. Because so little is known about most of these disorders, though, we will focus on two of these disorders in more depth: conversion disorder and dissociative identity disorder.

Somatoform Disorders

In **somatoform disorders**, psychological problems take a physical form (*soma* means "body")—that is, the person experiences bodily symptoms that have no known physical cause. These disorders are not under voluntary control, nor are they intentionally produced by the person. People with these disorders tend to seek medical treatment, sometimes at great expense, and are typically distressed and confused when doctors are unable to provide a physiological explanation for their complaints.

In this section, we begin by briefly considering the less well understood somatoform disorders—pain disorder, body dysmorphic disorder, hypochondriasis, and somatization disorder; we then take an in-depth look at one other somatoform disorder—conversion disorder. Table 6.1 provides brief clinical descriptions of the somatoform disorders; the table also lists two related disorders (malingering and factitious disorder) that we discuss in Focus on Discovery 6.1.

Pain Disorder

In **pain disorder**, psychological factors play a major role in the onset, maintenance, and severity of physical pain (see DSM criteria). The pain causes significant distress or impairment; for example, the patient may be unable to work or may become dependent on

 DSM-IV-TR Criteria for Pain Disorder

- Pain that is severe enough to warrant clinical attention
- The pain causes significant distress or impairment
- Psychological factors are thought to be important to the onset, severity, or maintenance of pain
- The pain is not intentionally produced or faked
- The pain is not explained by another psychological condition

Table 6.1 Summary of Somatoform and Related Disorders

Disorder	Description
Pain disorder	Pain that is brought on and maintained to a significant extent by psychological factors
Body dysmorphic disorder	Preoccupation with imagined or exaggerated defects in physical appearance
Hypochondriasis	Preoccupation with fears of having a serious illness
Somatization disorder	Recurrent, multiple physical complaints that have no biological basis
Conversion disorder	Sensory or motor symptoms without any physiological cause
Malingering	Physical incapacity faked to avoid responsibility
Factitious disorder	Intentionally produced symptoms

Focus on Discovery 6.1

Malingering and Factitious Disorder

In DSM-IV-TR, **malingering** is classified among the "Other Conditions That May Be a Focus of Clinical Attention" (see p. 71). In malingering, a person intentionally fakes an incapacity to avoid a responsibility, such as work or military duty, or to achieve some goal, such as being awarded an insurance settlement. Thus, it is related to the somatoform disorders, in which people also show symptoms that have no physical basis.

In distinguishing between malingering and conversion disorder, clinicians try to determine whether the symptoms have been consciously or unconsciously adopted; in malingering, the conversion-like symptoms are under voluntary control, which is not thought to be the case in conversion disorder. Insurance companies often go to great lengths to show that a person is faking symptoms and can actually function well outside of doctors' offices. When such detective work fails, though, it is often difficult, if not impossible, to know with any degree of certainty whether behavior is consciously or unconsciously motivated. An aspect of behavior that can sometimes help distinguish the two disorders is known as **la belle indifférence**, which is characterized by a relative lack of concern or a blasé attitude toward the symptoms that is out of keeping with their severity and supposedly long-term consequences. Patients with conversion disorder sometimes demonstrate this behavior; they also appear willing and eager to talk endlessly and dramatically about their symptoms, but often without the concern one might expect. In contrast, malingerers are likely to be more guarded and cautious, perhaps because they consider interviews a threat to the success of the lie. But this distinction is not foolproof, for only about one-third of people with conversion disorder show la belle indifférence (Stephens & Kamp, 1962). Furthermore, a stoic attitude that resembles la belle indifférence is sometimes found among patients with actual medical diseases.

Factitious disorder, which is listed in a category of its own in DSM-IV-TR, is also related to the somatoform disorders. In factitious disorder, as in malingering, people intentionally produce physical symptoms (or sometimes psychological ones). They may make up symptoms, for example, reporting acute pain, or may inflict injuries on themselves. In contrast to malingering, however, the symptoms in factitious disorder

are less obviously linked to a recognizable goal; that is, the motivation for adopting the symptoms is much less clear. The person, for some unknown reason, wants to assume the role of a patient.

Factitious disorder may also be diagnosed in a parent who creates physical illnesses in a child; in this case it is called *factitious disorder by proxy* or *Munchausen syndrome by proxy*. In one extreme case, a 7-year-old girl was hospitalized over 150 times and experienced 40 surgeries at a cost of over $2 million. Her mother caused her illnesses by using drugs and even contaminating her feeding tube with fecal material (*Time*, 1996). The motivation in a case such as this appears to be a need to be regarded as an excellent parent who is tireless in seeing to the child's needs.

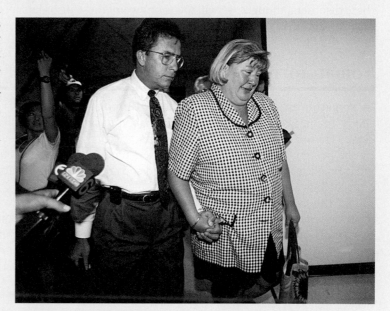

Kathleen Bush is taken into custody, charged with child abuse and fraud for deliberately causing her child's illnesses. (© Sun-Sentinel.)

painkillers. As seen above, the pain may begin or intensify after some conflict or stress. To an outside observer, it may seem that the person is using the pain to avoid some unpleasant activity or to get attention and sympathy, but people with pain disorder have no sense of this—they experience their pain as a completely physical symptom.

Accurate diagnosis is difficult because pain is a subjective experience—there is no way to objectively measure someone's pain. To some degree, however, people with pain disorder may describe their pain differently from people whose pain is clearly linked to a physical problem, who tend to localize pain more specifically, give more detailed descriptions of their pain sensations, and more clearly describe factors that increase or decrease their pain (Adler et al., 1997). Understanding the potential psychological aspects of pain, though, is important, because millions of Americans experience chronic pain, accounting for billions of dollars of lost work time and incalculable personal and familial suffering (Turk, 2001). Traditional medical treatments seldom help with pain disorder.

Clinical Case

A 29-year-old married woman was referred to a psychiatrist after extensive medical tests failed to identify a source for her pain. Four months before the interview, she and her husband had been involved in a car accident. During the accident, she was thrown forward but did not hit the window or dashboard. Her neck, arms, back, and legs began to ache 3 days later, and she had experienced pain on a daily basis since that time.

During the interview, she completed all neurological tests carefully, and described her pain in vivid detail. All neurological tests were within normal limits. She reported no history of psychological disorder. She and her husband had been married for 4 years, and they had enjoyed a smooth marriage with the exception of complaints from her husband that he would like more frequent and "imaginative" sex. Two weeks before the accident, the patient had discovered a woman's phone number in her husband's wallet. When she confronted him, he admitted that he had seen several women during the past year for "sexual release." They argued for the 2 weeks before the accident. After the accident, they had made a renewed commitment to the marriage and had agreed to begin working on their sexual relationship. The patient's pain, though, interfered with her ability to engage in sexual activity. Because the pain seemed to be genuine, malingering and factitious disorder were not diagnosed. But because the pain seemed to offer some protection from facing difficult marital issues, pain disorder was diagnosed. (Adapted from Spitzer et al., 1994.)

Body Dysmorphic Disorder

People with **body dysmorphic disorder** are preoccupied with an imagined or exaggerated defect in their appearance. Women tend to focus on their skin (like Joann in the clinical case), hips, breasts, and legs, whereas men are more likely to focus on their height, penis size, or body hair (Perugi et al., 1997). Some patients with the disorder spend hours each day compulsively looking at themselves in mirrors to check on their defect. Others try to avoid being reminded of the defect by camouflaging the defect—for example, by wearing very loose clothing to cover the imagined flaw (Albertini & Phillips, 1999). Some people become housebound to keep others from seeing their imagined defect. The symptoms are extremely distressing—as many as half of people with this disorder report that they have thought about committing suicide (Altamura et al., 2001), and as many as a quarter have plastic surgery (Phillips et al., 2001). Unfortunately, plastic surgery does little to allay their concerns (Veale, 2000), and many people report wanting to sue or hurt their physicians after the surgery because they are so disappointed.

DSM-IV-TR Criteria for Body Dysmorphic Disorder

- Preoccupation with an imagined defect or markedly excessive concern over a slight defect in appearance
- Preoccupation causes significant distress or impairment
- Preoccupation is not explained by another mental disorder, like anorexia nervosa

Clinical Case: Joann

Joann was a 23-year-old woman who sought psychotherapy after losing her job as a salesclerk for a record store because she had been taking very long breaks. At the first therapy session, she seemed extremely uncomfortable; she huddled in her coat and told her story while looking at the floor. She said that she took long breaks at work because she was uncomfortable when customers were in the store—she had the feeling they were staring at her. When asked why she thought that, she said that she knew they were looking at her skin, which was far too dark. She described feeling compelled to spend hours a day in her home examining her appearance in the mirror, and she described those hours as torture. She would spend all morning getting dressed and putting on makeup, but never felt satisfied with the results. Throughout the day, she would think about how her skin, nose, and lips were repulsively ugly. She often avoided leaving her home, and when in public, she was paralyzed by extreme anxiety when others looked at her. She said that these symptoms had come and gone since adolescence, but had become much worse over the last 2 years.

Social and cultural factors surely play a role in how people decide whether they are attractive. Among college students, concerns about body appearance appear to be more common in American students than in European students—as many as 74 percent of American

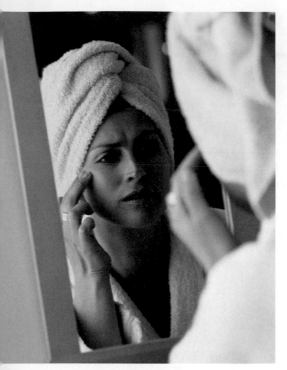

People with body dysmorphic disorder may spend hours a day checking on their appearance. (Tony Latham/Stone/Getty Images.)

students report at least some concern about their body image, with women being more likely than men to report dissatisfaction (Bohne et al., 2002). Most of these concerns, though, are not extreme enough to be characterized as psychological disorders. The person with body dysmorphic disorder experiences agonizing distress over their perceived physical flaws.

There is some evidence that body dysmorphic disorder occurs slightly more often in women than in men, but even among women it is relatively rare, with a prevalence of less than 1 percent (Otto et al., 2001). Among women seeking plastic surgery, however, about 5–7 percent meet the diagnostic criteria for this disorder (Altamura et al., 2001). Body dysmorphic disorder typically begins in late adolescence.

Nearly all people with body dysmorphic disorder meet the diagnostic criteria for another disorder. The most common comorbid disorders include major depressive disorder, social phobia, obsessive-compulsive disorder, substance abuse, and personality disorders (Gustad & Phillips, 2003). Some comorbidity may be explained by similarity of symptoms used in making different diagnoses—body dysmorphic disorder and obsessive-compulsive disorder share symptoms of repetitive unwanted thoughts and checking behaviors.

Hypochondriasis

The main feature of **hypochondriasis** is a preoccupation with fears of having a serious disease. To meet the DSM criteria for diagnosis, these fears must persist for at least 6 months despite medical reassurances that no serious disease is present. The disorder typically begins in early adulthood, and it tends to be chronic. In one study, over 60 percent of people who had been diagnosed still met the criteria 4 or 5 years later (Barsky et al., 1998). The diagnosis is rarely used, but people who do receive it are frequent—and dissatisfied—consumers of medical services, like Denise above. They often view their physicians as incompetent and uncaring (Persing et al., 2000).

Clinical Case: Denise

Denise was a 60-year-old woman whose husband had died of cancer a year before she first came for therapy. After her husband's death, she had begun calling her children repeatedly to describe her own physical symptoms and concerns. For example, if she felt light-headed, she would believe that she had a brain tumor. She had always had more health concerns than most people, but these became much more severe after her husband's death. In response to her symptoms, she had seen more than 15 doctors during the year. She would dismiss the negative results of her medical tests, stating that the doctors were clearly unable to understand her rare disorders. She was not interested in therapy, but she agreed to come at the urging of her children after her medical bills had tallied up to more than her annual income.

DSM-IV-TR Criteria for Hypochondriasis

- Preoccupation with fears about having a serious disease
- The preoccupation continues despite medical reassurance
- Not explained by a delusional disorder or body dysmorphic disorder
- Symptoms last at least 6 months
- Symptoms cause significant distress or functional impairment

Hypochondriasis often co-occurs with anxiety and mood disorders, which has led some researchers to conclude that it is not a discrete disorder but a symptom of other disorders (Noyes, 1999). In addition, hypochondriasis is not well differentiated from somatization disorder (see below), which is also characterized by a long history of complaints of medical illnesses. The key difference is that the person with hypochondriasis is concerned that their symptoms are a sign of a very serious disease.

Somatization Disorder

In 1859 the French physician Pierre Briquet described a syndrome that was then called *Briquet's syndrome* and is now known as **somatization disorder**. As illustrated by the case history of Maria, this disorder is defined by multiple, recurrent somatic complaints that have no apparent physical explanation but still cause the person to seek treatment. To qualify for the diagnosis, a person must have several different kinds of physical symptoms and the symptoms must cause impairment.

People with somatization disorder tend to make frequent visits to physicians, to visit several different physicians for a given symptom, and to try many different medications. Hospitalization and even surgery are common. Patients typically express their complaints in a histrionic, exaggerated fashion or as part of a long and complicated medical history—like Maria—and many believe that they have been ailing all their lives.

Clinical Case: Maria

Maria, a 32-year-old woman, was referred to a psychological clinic by her physician. Over a period of about 6 months, her physician had seen Maria 23 times. Maria had dwelt on a number of rather vague complaints—general aches and pains, bouts of nausea, fatigue, irregular menstruation, and dizziness. But various tests—complete blood workups, X-rays, spinal taps, and so on—had not revealed any pathology.

On meeting her therapist, Maria immediately let him know that she was a somewhat reluctant client: "I'm here only because I trust my doctor and she urged me to come. I'm physically sick and don't see how a psychologist is going to help." But when Maria was asked to describe the history of her physical problems, she quickly warmed to the task. According to Maria, she had always been sick. As a child she had had episodes of high fever, frequent respiratory infections, convulsions, and her first two operations, an appendectomy and a tonsillectomy. As she continued her account, her descriptions of her problems became more and more colorful: "Yes, when I was in my early twenties I had some problems with vomiting. For

weeks at a time I'd vomit up everything I ate. I'd even vomit up liquids, even water. Just the sight of food would make me vomit. The smell of food cooking was absolutely unbearable. I must have been vomiting every 10 minutes." During her twenties Maria had gone from one physician to another. She had seen several gynecologists for her menstrual irregularity and dyspareunia (pain during intercourse) and had undergone dilation and curettage (scraping the lining of the uterus). She had been referred to neurologists for her headaches, dizziness, and fainting spells, and they had performed EEGs, spinal taps, and even a CT scan. Other physicians had ordered X-rays to look for the possible causes of her abdominal pain and EKGs for her chest pains. Doctors responding to her desperate pleas for a cure had performed rectal and gallbladder surgery.

When the interview shifted away from Maria's medical history, it became apparent that she was highly anxious in many situations, particularly those in which she thought she might be evaluated by other people. Indeed, some of her physical complaints could be regarded as consequences of anxiety.

Somatization disorder typically begins in early adulthood (Cloninger et al., 1986). It may not be as stable as the DSM-IV-TR diagnostic criteria imply, though, for in one study only one-third of patients with the disorder still met the criteria when reassessed 12 months later (Simon & Gureje, 1999). People with somatization disorder often report a host of behavioral and interpersonal problems, such as truancy, poor work history, and marital difficulties. Comorbidity is high with anxiety disorders, mood disorders, substance abuse, a number of personality disorders (Golding, Smith, & Kashner, 1991; Kirmayer, Robbins, & Paris, 1994), and conversion disorder (see below; Ford & Folks, 1985).

The lifetime prevalence of somatization disorder is estimated at less than 0.5 percent of the U.S. population; it is more frequent among women, especially African American and Hispanic women (Escobar et al., 1987), and among patients who are in medical treatment. Prevalence is also higher in some parts of the world, including South America and Puerto Rico (Tomasson, Kent, & Coryell, 1991). DSM-IV-TR notes that the specific symptoms of the disorder may vary across cultures. For example, burning pains in the hands and the sensation of ants crawling under the skin are more frequent in Asia and Africa than in North America. Furthermore, the disorder is thought to be most frequent in cultures that discourage the overt display of emotion (Ford, 1995).

Interpreting these cultural differences is not straightforward (Kirmayer & Young, 1998). There is some evidence that doctors are more likely to miss a true medical problem in people from sociocultural backgrounds different from their own. Thus, some of the higher rates of somatization disorder could reflect misdiagnosis (Schuepback et al., 2002), but this is not likely to be the whole explanation of cultural differences. The Western

DSM-IV-TR Criteria for Somatization Disorder

- History of many physical complaints over several years
- At least four pain symptoms, as well as at least two gastrointestinal symptoms, one sexual symptom, and one pseudoneurological symptom
- Symptoms are not due to a medical condition or are excessive given a medical condition the person may be experiencing
- Symptoms cause significant distress or functional impairment

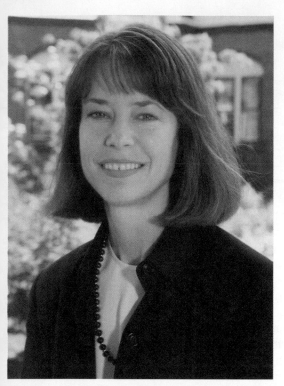

Katherine Phillips has conducted extensive research on body dysmorphic disorder. (Courtesy of Katherine Phillips, Butler Hospital, Brown University.)

perspective sometimes suggests that physical presentation of psychological problems is somehow primitive or unsophisticated. But this distinction between physical and psychological is not necessarily made in non-Western medical traditions (e.g., in Chinese medicine). Culture provides people with a concept of how distress should be communicated, and so culture may influence how and when people seek treatment for symptoms. Furthermore, as we have noted previously (see p. 132), researchers now realize that many of our ideas about these issues were based on faulty comparisons. That is, people in other countries usually explained their symptoms to medical doctors and would probably tend to put their explanations in physical terms, whereas more people in the United States sought help in psychiatric clinics and would probably tend to use psychological terms (Kirmayer, 2001).

Conversion Disorder

In **conversion disorder**, sensory or motor symptoms, such as a sudden loss of vision or sudden paralysis, suggest an illness related to neurological damage, but medical examinations and tests indicate that the bodily organs and nervous system are fine. People may experience partial or complete paralysis of arms or legs; seizures and coordination disturbances; a sensation of prickling, tingling, or creeping on the skin; insensitivity to pain; or **anesthesia**—the loss of sensation. Vision may be seriously impaired; the person may become partially or completely blind or have *tunnel vision*, in which the visual field is constricted as it would be if the person were peering through a tube. *Aphonia*, loss of the voice other than whispered speech, and *anosmia*, loss of the sense of smell, can also be symptoms of conversion disorder. Some people with conversion disorder seem complacent or even serene, are not particularly eager to part with their symptoms, and do not connect their symptoms with whatever stressful situation they may be in.

Conversion disorder has a long history, dating back to the earliest writings on abnormal behavior. *Hysteria* was the term originally used to describe the disorder, which the Greek physician Hippocrates considered to be an affliction limited to women and brought on by the wandering of the uterus through the body. (The Greek word *hystera* means "womb"; the wandering uterus symbolized the longing of the woman's body for the production of a child.) The term "conversion" originated with Sigmund Freud, who thought that anxiety and psychological conflict were converted into physical symptoms.

Clinical Case: Anna O.

As described in the initial case report, Anna O. was sitting at the bedside of her seriously ill father when she dropped off into a waking dream. She saw a black snake come toward her sick father to bite him. She tried to ward it away, but her arm had gone to sleep. When she looked at her hand, her fingers seemed to turn into little snakes with death's heads. The next day, when a bent branch recalled her hallucination of the snake, her right arm became rigidly extended. After that, whenever some object revived her hallucination, her arm responded in the same way—with rigid extension. Later, her symptoms extended to paralysis and anesthesia of her entire right side.

Drawn from Breuer and Freud (1895/1982)

Symptoms of conversion disorder usually develop in adolescence or early adulthood, typically after some life stress. An episode may end abruptly, but sooner or later the disorder is likely to return, either in its original form or with a different symptom. The prevalence of conversion disorder is less than 1 percent, and more women than men are given the diagnosis (Faravelli et al., 1997). During World War I, however, a large number of men in combat developed symptoms resembling those in conversion disorder (Ziegler, Imboden, & Meyer, 1960). Among soldiers in World War II, conversion disorder was less common, and occurred mainly in elite combat units (e.g., paratroopers) whose subculture prohibited psychological expressions of distress (Marlowe, 2001). Conversion disorder is often comorbid with other

Axis I disorders—for example, major depressive disorder and substance abuse—and with personality disorders, notably borderline and histrionic personality disorders (Binzer & Kullgren, 1996; Rechlin, Loew, & Joraschky, 1997).

It is important to distinguish the symptoms of conversion disorder, such as a paralysis or a sensory dysfunction, from similar symptoms that have a true neurological basis. Sometimes this task seems easy, as when the paralysis does not make anatomical sense, but even then the diagnostician has to be careful. Consider, for instance, the classic example of "glove anesthesia," a rare symptom of conversion disorder in which the person experiences little or no sensation in the part of the hand and lower arm that would be covered by a glove (see Figure 6.1). For years this was considered a textbook illustration of anatomical nonsense because the nerves run continuously from the hand up the arm. Yet even in this case it now appears that misdiagnosis can occur if the person has carpal tunnel syndrome, a relatively recently recognized disease that can produce symptoms similar to those of glove anesthesia. Nerves in the wrist run through a tunnel formed by the wrist bones and membranes. The tunnel can become swollen and may pinch the nerves, leading to tingling, numbness, and pain in the hand. People who sit at computer keyboards for many hours a day seem to be at risk for this condition.

Since the majority of paralyses, analgesias, and sensory failures do have neurological causes, true neurological problems may indeed sometimes be misdiagnosed as conversion disorder. Follow-up studies conducted during the 1960s indicated that many patients diagnosed with conversion disorder may have been misdiagnosed. One of these studies found that 9 years after diagnosis, an alarming number—60 percent—of these people had either died or developed further symptoms of neurological disease (Slater & Glithero, 1965)! Fortunately, with technological advances in detecting neurological problems (such as MRI), the percentage of apparent conversion-disorder patients who go on to develop a neurological problem seems to be much lower now (Moene et al., 2000).

DSM-IV-TR Criteria for Conversion Disorder

- One or more symptoms affecting motor or sensory functioning and suggesting a neurological or medical condition
- Symptoms are related to conflict or stress
- Symptoms are not intentionally produced and cannot be explained by a medical condition
- Symptoms cause significant distress or functional impairment or warrant medical evaluation

---

Check Your Knowledge 6.1

Match the case description to the disorder, assuming that the symptoms cause significant distress or impairment.

1. Paula, a 24-year-old librarian, sought psychological assessment on the advice of her sister because of her deep fears about medical conditions. In daily phone calls with her sister, she had described worries that she had cancer, a brain tumor, diabetes, or a thyroid condition. She had seen doctors several times per month for several years, but when they reassured her that she was healthy, she became annoyed with them, criticized the insensitivity of their medical tests, and sought a new consultant.

2. Jan, a 41-year-old woman, was referred by her husband. He was worried because she spent hours and hours in the bathroom each day, crying while looking in the mirror at her hairline. She was convinced that her face and hairline were horribly asymmetrical, and that others would dislike her as a result. She had visited two doctors to inquire about getting hair implants along her forehead, but both doctors felt that this was not advised, as they saw no evidence that her hairline was in any way atypical.

3. John, a 35-year-old man, was referred for psychological treatment by his surgeon. In the past 5 years, John had sought a stunning array of medical treatments and tests for complaints about stomach distress, itching, frequent urination, and any number of other complaints. By the time he was referred, he had received 10 MRIs, an uncountable number of X-rays, and had seen 15 different specialists. Each test had been negative.

4. Thomas, a 50-year-old man, was referred for psychological treatment by an ophthalmologist. He reported that 2 weeks before, he had suddenly become blind. Extensive medical tests had failed to reveal any reason for his blindness.

   a. pain disorder
   b. hypochondriasis
   c. somatization disorder
   d. conversion disorder
   e. body dysmorphic disorder
   f. cannot be determined based on this information.

Etiology of Conversion Disorder

Much of the work on the etiology of somatoform disorders has been directed toward understanding conversion disorder. In this section, we begin by discussing psychoanalytic views of conversion disorder and then consider biological and sociocultural factors.

People with somatization disorder may undergo unnecessary surgeries in hopes of finding a cure for their medical symptoms. (Michelle Del Guercio/Photo Researchers, Inc.)

Psychoanalytic Perspective   Conversion disorder occupies a central place in psychoanalytic theory, for its symptoms provide a clear example of the role of the unconscious. Consider trying to diagnose a woman who says that she awakened one morning with a paralyzed left arm. Assume that a series of neurological tests reveal no neurological disorder. Perhaps she has decided to fake paralysis to achieve some end—this would be an example of malingering (see Focus on Discovery 6.1). But what if you believe her? You would almost be forced to conclude that unconscious processes were operating. On a conscious level, she is telling the truth; she believes that her arm is paralyzed. On an unconscious level, some psychological factor is at work, making her unable to move her arm despite the absence of any physical cause.

Freud (1895/1982) developed a psychoanalytic model of conversion disorder by drawing on cases like that of Anna O. Freud and his colleague Josef Breuer proposed that a conversion disorder results when a person experiences an emotionally arousing event, but the emotion is not expressed and the memory of the event is cut off from consciousness. In later writings Freud theorized that conversion disorder in women is rooted in an unresolved Electra complex. The young female child has sexual feelings toward her father, and if her parents respond to these feelings in a harshly disapproving manner, the feelings are repressed. The result is an unconscious preoccupation with sex coupled with a conscious avoidance of it. Later in life, sexual excitement or some other circumstance reawakens her repressed impulses, creating anxiety, which is then converted into physical symptoms. Thus, the conversion disorder lets the woman avoid her unresolved Electra complex. In addition, as Freud pointed out, the symptoms could also let the person avoid an unpleasant life situation or obtain attention. This theory of conversion disorder is intriguing, but there is no empirical support for it.

A more recent psychodynamic interpretation of one form of conversion disorder, hysterical blindness, is based on a review of two case studies of hysterically blind teenage women (Sackeim, Nordlie, & Gur, 1979). In one case, a young woman who reported being blind performed more poorly on a vision test than would a person who was actually blind (i.e., she performed below chance levels). In the other case, a teenage girl reported that she could not see to

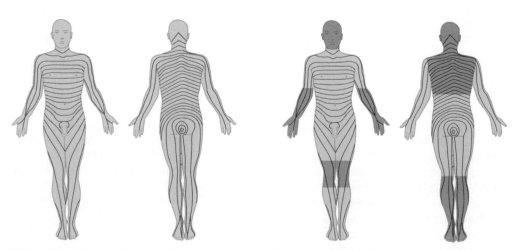

Figure 6.1   The anesthesias of conversion disorder can be distinguished from neurological dysfunctions. The patterns of neural innervation are shown on the left. Typical areas of anesthesias in conversion disorder are superimposed on the right. The anesthesias of conversion disorder do not make anatomical sense. [Adapted from an original painting by Frank H. Netter, M.D. From *The CIBA Collection of Medical Illustrations*, copyright © by CIBA Pharmaceutical Company, Division of CIBA-GEIGY Corporation.]

read, but tests showed that she could readily identify objects of various sizes and shapes and count fingers at a distance of 15 feet.

Drawing on these cases, Sackeim and colleagues (1979) proposed a two-stage model to account for the discrepancies between the women's vision tests and their reports of blindness. The first stage focuses on the idea that people can process visual information outside of their conscious awareness. Research on patients with lesions in the visual cortex supports this idea. These patients are missing some of the key cells in the visual system of the brain and believe they are blind, but they can perform well on some specific types of visual tests (their condition is called **blindsight**). So it is possible for people to claim truthfully that they cannot see, even when tests suggest that they can. More generally, many different studies show that perceptions formed outside of consciousness can influence behavior (see Focus on Discovery 6.2). Hence, because some perceptual abilities may be unconscious (outside of awareness), hysterically blind persons are able to genuinely say that they cannot see, even when visual stimuli clearly influence their behavior.

The second stage of this model focuses on motivation—that is, some people, perhaps because of their personality, are motivated to appear blind. Such people would be expected to perform below chance levels on visual tests. Support for the importance of motivation comes from a study in which a man with hysterical blindness had his vision tested over a large number of sessions. The man was given different motivational instructions in different sessions, and motivation was found to influence performance (Bryant & McConkey, 1989).

The degree to which people need to be considered blind (their motivation) will shape how much they show signs of being able to see. In sum, recent psychoanalytic models of conversion disorder focus on the idea that people could be unconscious of certain perceptions, and be motivated to have certain symptoms. Unfortunately, despite the fact that case studies can set the stage for further empirical work, this work has not yet been done.

Research on Possible Genetic Factors   Some investigators have proposed that genetic factors are important in conversion disorder, but research does not support this proposal. One study investigated concordance rates in 12 identical (MZ) and 12 fraternal (DZ) pairs of twins (Slater, 1961). One twin in each pair had been diagnosed with conversion disorder, but none of the co-twins in either of the two groups showed any symptoms.

Social and Cultural Factors   Over the past century, there has been an apparent decrease in the incidence of conversion disorder, which suggests a possible role for social and cultural factors. During the nineteenth century, Jean-Martin Charcot and Freud (who studied with Charcot) seemed to have an abundance of female patients with symptoms of conversion disorder, but contemporary clinicians rarely see anyone with such problems. Several hypotheses have been proposed to explain this apparent decrease. For example, therapists with a psychoanalytic bent point out that in the second half of the nineteenth century, when the incidence of these problems was apparently high in France and Austria, repressive sexual attitudes may have contributed to the increased prevalence of the disorder. The decrease in the incidence of such symptoms, then, may be attributed to a general relaxing of sexual mores and to the greater psychological and medical sophistication of contemporary culture, which is more tolerant of anxiety than it is of dysfunctions that do not make physiological sense.

Support for the role of social and cultural factors also comes from studies showing that conversion disorder is more common

Some psychoanalysts believe that the high frequency of conversion disorder in nineteenth-century Europe was due to the repressive sexual attitudes of the time. (Hulton-Archive/Stone/Getty Images.)

Focus on Discovery 6.2

Evidence for the Unconscious

We are unaware of much that goes on in our minds as we perceive our environment—that is, much of the working of the mind proceeds outside consciousness (awareness). We can find a good deal of support for this idea in studies by cognitive psychologists. Consider these examples.

- In one study, participants were presented with different shapes for 1 millisecond (one-thousandth of a second) (Kunst-Wilson & Zajonc, 1980). Later they showed virtually no ability to recognize the shapes they had seen, but when they rated how much they liked the shapes, they preferred the ones they had been shown to other ones. It is known that familiarity affects judgments of stimuli; people tend to like familiar stimuli more than unfamiliar ones. This indicates that some aspects of the stimuli must have been absorbed, even though participants said that they did not recognize the shapes.

- Similarly, when people are presented with pictures of fearful faces for 33 milliseconds, they report no awareness of seeing the faces, but show increased activity in the amygdala, a brain region involved in responding to emotionally relevant stimuli (Whalen et al., 1998).

These experiments—and others like them—have begun to document that humans do have an unconscious. But the modern cognitive perspective understands the unconscious processes in a different way from psychoanalysis. Freud postulated that the unconscious was a repository of instinctual energy and repressed conflicts and impulses. Contemporary researchers reject the notions of an energy reservoir and of repression, holding more simply that we are not aware of everything going on around us or even everything in our mind. While the original psychoanalytic view of the unconscious emphasized aggressive and sexual motivations, the newer cognitive perspective focuses on the brain as a highly efficient machine, in which some tasks are conducted automatically without entering consciousness.

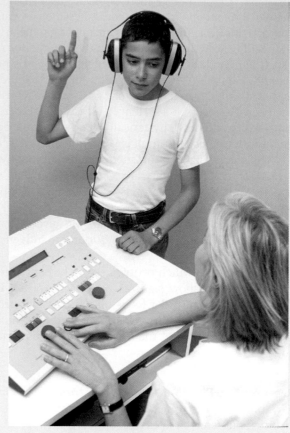

A child participates in a dichotic listening experiment. Although he attends to information presented to only one ear, the information reaching the unattended ear can affect behavior. (Phanie/Photo Researchers, Inc.)

among people from rural areas and people of lower socioeconomic status (Binzer/Kullgen, 1996). Studies show that the diagnosis of hysteria has declined in Western societies such as the United States and England (Hare, 1969), but has remained more common in countries that may place less emphasis on "psychologizing" distress, such as Libya (Pu et al., 1986), China, and India (Tseng, 2001). These results are difficult to interpret. They could mean that increasing sophistication about medical and psychological concepts leads to decreased prevalence of conversion disorder. But they might instead indicate that diagnostic practices vary from country to country, producing the different rates. A cross-national study conducted by diagnosticians trained to follow the same procedures in each country is needed.

Etiology of Somatoform Disorders Other Than Conversion Disorder

Now that we've considered conversion disorder in depth, let's look at various perspectives on the etiology of the other somatoform disorders. We begin by briefly discussing genetic research on somatoform disorders and neurobiological risk factors for body dysmorphic disorder. Then we consider cognitive behavioral models used to explain a range of somatoform disorders, since these reflect the dominant perspective on somatoform disorders other than conversion disorder.

Genetic Research on Somatoform Disorders   Torgersen (1986) reported the results of a twin study of somatoform disorders that included 10 cases of conversion disorder, 12 of somatization disorder, and 7 of pain disorder. No co-twin had the same diagnosis as his or her proband! Even the overall concordance for somatoform disorders was no higher in the identical (MZ) twins than in the fraternal (DZ) twins. Genetic factors, then, from the studies so far, seem to be of no importance for most somatoform disorders, with the possible exception of body dysmorphic disorder, discussed next.

Neurobiology of Body Dysmorphic Disorder   Above, we described some parallels in the symptoms of body dysmorphic disorder and obsessive-compulsive disorder. These two disorders often are comorbid as well. Some researchers have suggested that body dysmorphic disorder does not warrant a specific diagnosis or that it may be a special form of obsessive-compulsive disorder. For example, the rates of obsessive-compulsive disorder are higher than average in the family members of people with body dysmorphic disorder (Gustad & Phillips, 2003), and both disorders are associated with changes in the volume of the caudate nucleus region of the brain (Rauch et al., 2003). Thus, some of the neurobiological risk factors for obsessive-compulsive disorder may be involved in the genesis of body dysmorphic disorder.

Cognitive Behavioral Models   Cognitive behavioral models suggest that a number of different mechanisms contribute to somatoform disorders. Figure 6.2 illustrates one model of how these mechanisms could fit together for somatoform disorders other than body dysmorphic disorder. The process is believed to start with a physiological symptom, as a result of either a medical illness or a nonpathological change in physiological functioning (e.g., increased heart rate from effort). For body dysmorphic disorder, the process is thought to begin when a person notices a physical anomaly. Because physical symptoms are so common, these models tend to focus on cognitive and behavioral processes that guide responses to physical symptoms.

Everybody experiences physical sensations and pays a certain amount of attention to their appearance, but people who are prone to somatoform disorders appear to have a cognitive style characterized by paying much greater attention to these things. In one study, researchers used the emotion Stroop task (see p. 49) to examine attention to cues of physical health problems among patients with somatoform disorder, depression, or panic disorder (Lim & Kim, 2005). When asked to name the color of words, patients with somatoform disorder were slow to name the color of words that were related to physical health (a sign of increased attention to these words), while other patients were not slower to name such colors. When they were asked to remember words later in the session, patients with somatoform disorder also remembered more physical health-related words than other patients did. Hence, people with somatoform disorder may automatically focus on cues of physical health problems.

Once people with somatoform disorder notice physical symptoms, they also seem to make more negative attributions about them. (Remember that an attribution is a person's idea about why something is happening.) The specific attributions will vary with the specific somatoform disorder. For example, a woman with hypochondriasis might interpret a red blotch as a sign of skin cancer (MacLeod, Haynes, & Sensky, 1998). Or a man with body dysmorphic disorder might focus obsessively on unnoticeable facial wrinkles, convinced that they make him look old and ugly. The exact form of the cognitive bias may vary, but most somatoform disorders seem to be characterized by worry about health and a tendency to catastrophize the symptoms (i.e., to interpret them in the worst possible way). Once these negative thoughts begin, elevated anxiety and cortisol reactivity may exacerbate somatic symptoms and distress over those symptoms (Rief & Auer, 2001).

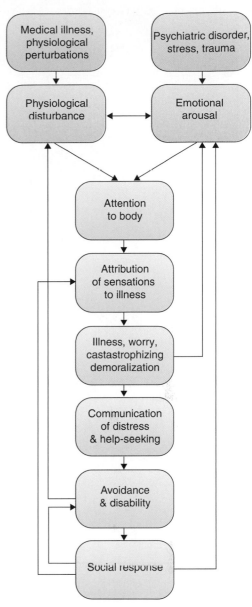

Figure 6.2   Mechanisms involved in somatoform disorders. [From Looper and Kirmayer (2002).]

In Chapter 5, we described a very similar cognitive process as part of panic disorder (see p. 144). That is, people with panic disorder are likely to overreact to physiological symptoms. In panic disorder, the person often believes that the symptoms are a sign of an immediate threat (e.g., a heart attack), whereas in hypochondriasis, the person believes the symptoms are a sign of an underlying long-term disease (e.g., cancer or AIDS). The types of physical cues that a person focuses on also differ for people with panic disorder compared to hypochondriasis. The person with panic disorder often focuses on symptoms that will actually become worse as they become more anxious—for example, a fast heart rate, shortness of breath, or sweaty palms. In contrast, a patient with hypochondriasis cannot, for example, increase the size of a spot on the skin by misconstruing it as cancer.

The tendency to believe that one is physically ill may have evolved from early experiences of medical symptoms or from family attitudes that became internalized. Consistent with the idea of developmental influences on cognitive biases, people with somatoform disorders report missing school for illness more often than others report that they did as children (Barsky et al., 1995).

Fear that a bodily sensation signifies illness or one's physical appearance signifies ugliness is likely to have two behavioral consequences. First, the person may assume the role of being sick and avoid work and social tasks, and this can intensify symptoms by limiting exercise and other healthy behaviors. Second, the person may seek reassurance, both from doctors and from family members, and this help-seeking behavior may be reinforced if it results in the person getting attention or sympathy. Often, people with these disorders tend to have trouble eliciting socially reinforcing interactions in other ways. For example, people with the symptoms of somatoform disorders do have trouble identifying their emotions and describing them directly (Bankier, Argner, & Bach, 2001), so they may find such attention and sympathy particularly reinforcing. Beyond this type of attention, people may receive other types of behavioral reinforcers for somatoform symptoms—for example, people receive disability payments based on the amount that symptoms interfere with their daily activities.

Treatment of Somatoform Disorders

Somatoform disorders are rarer than most other types of mental health problems, so there has been little controlled research on the relative efficacy of different treatments. Indeed, one of the major obstacles to such research may be that most people with somatoform disorders do not want to consult mental health professionals. They resent referrals from their physician to "shrinks" because they interpret such a referral as a sign that the doctor thinks the illness is "all in their head." Innovative programs in which general practitioners help people think less negatively about symptoms, or insurance companies work with comprehensive teams to offer psychological and medical care, are likely to be needed.

Short-term psychodynamic treatment has been found to be effective in alleviating the symptoms of somatoform disorders (Junkert-Tress et al., 2001), but there have been few controlled studies comparing psychodynamic treatment to other treatments (see the discussion of the treatment of pain disorder for one exception). In this section, therefore, we focus mainly on cognitive behavioral treatments and on the use of antidepressant medications.

Cognitive behavioral therapists have applied many different techniques in trying to help people with somatoform disorders. Generally, these include helping people (1) identify and change the emotions that trigger their somatic concerns, (2) change their cognitions regarding their somatic symptoms, and (3) change their behaviors so they stop playing the role of a sick person and gain more reinforcement for engaging in other types of social interactions (Looper & Kirmayer, 2002).

Cognitive strategies involve training people to pay less attention to their body. Alternatively, cognitive strategies might help a person to identify and challenge negative thoughts about their body.

Behavioral techniques might involve helping people resume healthy activities and decrease their reliance on playing the sick role. For example, a therapist might use operant-conditioning approaches with family or friends to reduce the amount of attention they give the person who is displaying somatic symptoms.

Focus on Discovery 6.3

The Management of Pain

We know enough about pain to appreciate the fact that there is no one-to-one relationship between a stimulus that is capable of triggering pain, referred to as nociceptive stimulation, and the actual sensation of pain. Soldiers in combat can be wounded by a bullet and yet be so involved in their efforts to survive and inflict harm on the enemy that they do not feel any pain until later. This well-known fact hints at ways of controlling pain: if one is distracted from a nociceptive stimulus, one may not experience as much pain as when one attends to the stimulation (Turk, 2001). In addition to distraction, other factors that reduce pain are lowered anxiety, feelings of optimism and control (Geer, Davison, & Gatchel, 1970), and a sense of meaning and purpose in activities (Gatchel, Baum, & Krantz, 1989).

Researchers have drawn on basic research on pain to develop treatment programs that help people manage pain and its consequences for their lifestyle. These programs typically begin by providing information about the nature of pain, including the fact that being in a negative mood can make the pain worse (Morley, 1997). Often, treatment programs include training in the use of distraction and cognitive techniques for controlling pain, as illustrated next.

The patient may be encouraged to alter the focus of their attention to the pain without switching attention directly away from the pain. In this instance, the subject may be asked to focus on the sensory qualities of the pain and transform it to a less threatening quality. For example, a young man with a severe "shooting" pain was able to reinterpret the sensory quality into an image which included him shooting at goal in a soccer match. As a result of this transformation, the impact of the pain was greatly reduced although its shooting quality remained. (Morley, 1997, p. 236)

Treatment programs also tend to distinguish between pain per se—that is, the perception of nociceptive stimulation—and suffering and pain behaviors. Suffering refers to the emotional response to nociception. Pain behaviors refer to observable behaviors associated with pain or suffering; examples include moaning, clenching teeth, irritability, and avoidance of activity (Turk, Wack, & Kerns, 1985). Pain programs often focus on reducing suffering and pain behaviors. The emphasis is on restoring a lifestyle by toughing it out, rather than allowing oneself to be incapacitated by pain. The goal is increased activity and function, which can sometimes even reduce the actual experience of pain.

The negative emotions that accompany anxiety and depressive disorders often trigger physiological symptoms and intensify the symptoms of somatoform disorders (Simon, Goreje, & Fullerton, 2001). Indeed, as shown in Chapters 5 and 8, concern about physical health is common among people suffering from anxiety or depression. It should therefore come as no surprise that treating anxiety and depression often reduces somatoform concerns (Smith, 1992).

Pain Disorder There is evidence from a number of double-blind experiments that low doses of some antidepressant drugs, most especially imipramine (Tofranil), are superior to a placebo in reducing chronic pain and distress (Fishbain et al., 2000). Interestingly, these antidepressants reduce pain even when, in the low dosages given, they don't alleviate the associated depression (Simon, 1998).

Current thinking suggests that, in conducting psychotherapy, it is fruitless to make a sharp distinction between psychogenic pain and medically caused pain, such as pain resulting from injury to muscle tissue. Typically, clinicians assume that pain has physical and psychological components. Effective treatments for pain disorder tend to include the following ingredients:

- Validating that the pain is real, not just "in the patient's head"
- Relaxation training
- Rewarding the person for less focus on pain and more focus on life (toughing it out).

In general, it is advisable to focus less on what the patient cannot do because of pain and more on teaching the patient how to deal with stress, encouraging the patient to engage in more activities, and helping the patient gain a greater sense of control. The cognitive behavioral techniques used to do this are described in greater detail in Focus on Discovery 6.3. In addition to cognitive behavioral treatment, one study reported that a form of short-term psychodynamic therapy called *psychodynamic body therapy*, was effective in reducing patients' pain, and these gains were maintained over the long term (Monsen & Monsen, 2000).

Body Dysmorphic Disorder   At least four trials have been conducted in which people with body dysmorphic disorder were randomly assigned to receive either a cognitive behavioral treatment or a control treatment. In each study, cognitive behavioral treatment was shown to produce a major decrease in symptoms of the disorder (Looper & Kirmayer, 2002).

Given the parallels between body dysmorphic disorder and obsessive-compulsive disorder, the treatment of choice for obsessive-compulsive disorder—exposure and response prevention (ERP, see p. 150)—has been modified to address the symptoms of body dysmorphic disorder. For example, for response prevention, people may be asked to avoid checking their appearance in mirrors and other reflective surfaces. Cognitive behavioral approaches that include response prevention have been found to reduce symptoms of body dysmorphic disorder (Veale, Boocock, Gournay et al., 1996). Also parallel with treatment for obsessive-compulsive disorder, fluoxetine (Prozac) and clomipramine (Anafranil), two serotonergic reuptake inhibitors, have been shown to reduce symptoms of body dysmorphic disorder (Phillips, Li, & Zhang, 2002).

Hypochondriasis   Cognitive behavioral treatment for people with hypochondriasis aims at reducing their excessive attention to bodily sensations, challenging their negative thoughts about those sensations, and discouraging them from seeking reassurance from doctors (Warwick & Salkovskis, 2001). The behavioral components of the treatment focus on keeping people from repetitively checking on their health, increasing their engagement in healthy activities, and decreasing their focus on seeking treatment. Cognitive behavioral approaches have proved effective in reducing health concerns, symptoms of depression and anxiety, and health care utilization (Looper & Kirmayer, 2002). For example, in one trial of cognitive behavioral treatment, patients were able to reduce worrying about their physical concerns from approximately 50 percent of their time to about 15 percent of their time (Warwick et al., 1996).

Somatization Disorder   In a widely accepted approach to somatization disorder, the physician does not dispute the validity of the person's physical complaints, but minimizes the use of diagnostic tests and medications, maintaining contact with the person regardless of whether he or she is complaining of illness (Monson & Smith, 1983). A study of this approach found that it resulted in less frequent use of health care services (Rost, Kashner, & Smith, 1994).

It is also possible to direct the person's attention to sources of anxiety and depression that may underlie the unexplained somatic symptoms, rather than allowing the person to focus excessively on minor aches and pains. Techniques such as relaxation training and various forms of cognitive treatment have proved useful in this regard (Payne & Blanchard, 1995). Biofeedback, which entails gaining control over physiological processes (see Chapter 8), has turned out to be effective in reducing catastrophizing cognitions in people suffering from somatization disorder—even more so than relaxation training (Nanke & Rief, 2000).

Cognitive behavioral therapists often focus on addressing the social concerns associated with somatization disorder. Maria, the woman described above, revealed that she was extremely anxious about her shaky marriage and about situations in which other people might judge her.

Biofeedback can be a helpful treatment for somatization. (Michael Newman/ PhotoEdit.)

Techniques such as exposure and cognitive restructuring could address her interpersonal fears, which might help lessen her somatic complaints. Assertion training and social skills training—for example, coaching Maria in effective ways to approach and talk to people, to maintain eye contact, to give compliments, to accept criticism, and to make requests—could be useful in helping her have healthier interpersonal interactions that do not focus on her physical illness.

More specific to her concerns about physical symptoms, cognitive treatment could help her monitor her negative cognitions about her physical symptoms and help her evaluate the accuracy of those cognitions. She could also practice focusing less on physical symptoms. Behavioral approaches could help change her reliance on playing the role of a sick person. If the people who live with Maria have adjusted to her infirmity and are reinforcing her avoidance of normal adult responsibilities, family therapy might help. Maria and the members of her family might be able to change relationships to support her movement toward greater autonomy and away from a focus on physical complaints.

Conversion Disorder   To date, there have been no controlled trials of psychological treatment for conversion disorder. Traditional long-term psychoanalysis and psychoanalytically oriented psychotherapy have not been demonstrated to be useful with conversion disorder, except perhaps to reduce the patient's concern about the disabling problems by taking a gentle, supportive approach (Simon, 1998). Case studies suggest that it is usually not a good idea to try to convince people with conversion disorder that their symptoms are related to psychological factors. Case studies have also suggested that reinforcing a person for being able to function better can be helpful.

Quick Summary

The somatoform disorders are defined by physical symptoms that are believed to be related to psychological causes. Somatoform disorders include body dysmorphic disorder, pain disorder, hypochondriasis, somatization, and conversion disorder. In pain disorder, psychological factors are believed to create or intensify pain. In body dysmorphic disorder, a person experiences distress and impairment over their imagined ugliness or physical flaws. Hypochondriasis is characterized by belief in a severe disease, despite evidence to the contrary. Conversion disorder is characterized by sensory and motor dysfunctions that suggest neurological impairments, but that cannot be explained by medical tests. In somatization disorder, multiple physical complaints, not adequately explained by physical disorder or injury, eventuate in frequent visits to physicians, hospitalization, and even unnecessary surgery. The symptoms of somatoform disorders seem to serve some psychological purpose; for example, they may arise suddenly in stressful situations, allowing the person to avoid some activity or responsibility.

Psychoanalytic theories of conversion disorder have focused on the idea that people can be unaware of their perceptions and abilities, and that some people may be motivated to have symptoms. Body dysmorphic disorder is often comorbid with obsessive-compulsive disorder, and these two disorders may be related to some of the same genetic and neurobiological risk factors. Cognitive behavioral models of somatoform disorders focus on two risk factors: cognitive beliefs that promote negative responses to bodily sensations and appearance, and reinforcement of help-seeking behaviors. Generally, little systematic research is available on the etiology of somatoform disorders, in part because of the relatively low prevalence of these disorders.

One of the primary issues in treating somatoform disorders is that few people will want to see a mental health provider for their physical symptoms. Nonetheless, cognitive behavioral techniques to help people address emotions more directly, change their cognitive responses to physical symptoms, and shift from assuming the sick role have been found to be helpful. Beyond these cognitive behavioral approaches, some other techniques have been found to be helpful for specific somatoform disorders. For pain disorder, short-term psychodynamic treatment and low levels of antidepressant medication may be helpful. For body dysmorphic disorder, cognitive behavioral techniques that are highly parallel with those used to treat obsessive-compulsive disorder are helpful. For somatization disorder, physicians can reduce health care utilization by minimizing the use of diagnostic tests.

Dissociative Disorders

The **dissociative disorders** defined in DSM-IV-TR include dissociative amnesia, dissociative fugue, dissociative identity disorder (formerly known as multiple personality disorder), and depersonalization disorder. The dissociative disorders are all presumed to be caused

Check Your Knowledge 6.2

True or false?

1. Conversion disorder is highly heritable.
2. Conversion disorder is disproportionately common among the wealthy.
3. The two-stage psychodynamic model of conversion disorder emphasizes unconscious perceptions and motivation for having symptoms.
4. The risk factors for pain disorder may overlap substantially with the risk factors for obsessive-compulsive disorder.

by a common mechanism, **dissociation**, which results in some aspects of cognition or experience being inaccessible consciously. Thus, dissociation involves the failure of consciousness to perform its usual role of integrating our cognitions, emotions, motivations, and other aspects of experience in our awareness. The concept of dissociation was first popularized by the French neurologist Pierre Janet (1859–1947). Some mild dissociative states are very common—for example, in one example of a loss of self-awareness, a preoccupied person may miss a turn on the road home when thinking about problems. Today, both psychoanalytic and behavioral theorists generally consider pathological dissociation to be an avoidance response that protects the person from consciously experiencing stressful events. In studies of people undergoing very intense stressors, such as advanced military survival training, most participants report moments of dissociation (Morgan et al., 2001). In contrast to common dissociative experiences like these, dissociative disorders are thought to result from extremely high levels of dissociation.

People with these disorders may be unable to recall important personal events, may temporarily forget their identity or assume a new identity, or may wander far from their usual surroundings. Few high-quality studies have been done of prevalence of the dissociative disorders; perhaps the best study to date found lifetime prevalences of 7.0 percent, 2.4 percent, and 0.2 percent for dissociative amnesia, depersonalization disorder, and dissociative fugue, respectively (Ross, 1991). Table 6.2 presents brief descriptions of the dissociative disorders, and Focus on Discovery 6.4 discusses some issues in the way DSM-IV-TR classifies these disorders and conversion disorder.

Because these disorders are so rare, there is very little research on the etiology and treatment of dissociative amnesia, depersonalization disorder, and fugue states. For this reason, we focus on etiology and treatment only when we discuss dissociative identity disorder (DID).

Table 6.2 Summary of Dissociative Disorders

Disorder	Description
Dissociative amnesia	Memory loss, typically of a stressful experience
Dissociative fugue	Memory loss accompanied by leaving home and establishing a new identity
Depersonalization disorder	Alteration in the experience of the self
Dissociative identity disorder	At least two distinct personalities that act independently of each other

Dissociation and Memory

Dissociative disorders raise fundamentally important questions about how memory works under stress. Some have suggested that in dissociative disorders, traumatic events are forgotten (i.e., dissociated) because of their aversiveness. Cognitive scientists have questioned how this could happen, because research on both animals and humans shows that high levels of stress usually enhance rather than impair memory (Shobe & Kihlstrom, 1997). For example, children who go through extremely painful medical procedures have accurate, detailed memories of the experience. The nature of attention and memory, however, does change during periods of intense stress. Memory for emotionally relevant stimuli is enhanced by stress, while memory for neutral stimuli is impaired (Jelicic et al., 2004). People under stress tend to focus on the central features of the threatening situation and to stop paying attention to peripheral features (McNally, 2003b). For example, people might remember every detail about a gun that was trained on them, yet be unable to remember the face of the person who held the gun. On recall, then, they are likely to be unable to connect up all aspects of the stressful situation into a coherent whole. Given that the usual response to trauma is enhanced memory of the central features of the threat, how does the stress-related loss of memory arise that we seem to see in the dissociative disorders?

One answer might be that dissociative disorders involve unusual ways of responding to stress—for example, extremely high levels of stress hormones could interfere with memory formation in some way (Howe, 1998). Some theorists believe that as the intensity and frequency of dissociations increase, they can interfere with memory. That is, in the face of severe trauma, memories may be stored in such a way that they are not later accessible to awareness when the person has returned to a more normal state (Kihlstrom, Tataryn, & Hoyt, 1993). Dissociative disorders are considered an extreme outcome of this process. Debate continues about how to understand memory in the context of trauma and dissociation (see Focus on Discovery 6.5).

Focus on Discovery 6.4

Classification of Conversion Disorder and Dissociative Disorders

Conversion disorder and the dissociative disorders are separately classified in DSM-IV-TR—conversion disorder as a somatoform disorder because it involves physical symptoms and the dissociative disorders as a distinct category because they involve disruptions in consciousness. John Kihlstrom (1994), a leading researcher in the study of these disorders, has argued that this separation is a mistake. He believes that conversion disorder also involves disruption in the normal controlling functions of consciousness, in this case affecting perception. As in the dissociative disorders, stimuli that are not consciously seen, heard, or felt nevertheless affect behavior. Thus, we might consider conversion disorder to be a disruption in explicit perception affecting the sensory

and motor systems (the cases we described of hysterical blindness make this point clearly). Empirical support for Kihlstrom's idea comes from research showing that dissociative symptoms are common in patients with conversion disorder (Roelofs et al., 2002).

As we noted in Chapter 3, DSM-III and DSM-IV classify abnormal behavior based on symptoms. Kihlstrom's position on conversion disorder and the dissociative disorders illustrates that classification on the basis of dysfunctional mechanisms may also make sense, as opposed to a system based entirely on symptoms; a symptom-based system could be misleading in separating disorders that are caused by similar dysfunctions.

Some basic research has examined how dissociation influences memory. The widely used Dissociative Experiences Scale assesses a person's propensity to dissociate; questions cover changes in time sense, the sensation of watching events from outside the body, or losing track of events because of spaciness. Researchers asked college students with high and low scores on the Dissociative Experiences Scale to complete an emotion Stroop task (see p. 49)—that is, participants were asked to name the color of words, some of which were emotionally charged, as quickly as possible when they appeared on a screen (DePrince & Freyd, 1999). After the task, participants were asked to remember the words. People with high scores on the Dissociative Experiences Scale remembered fewer of the emotionally charged words than did those with low scores. That is, people who dissociated seemed to be able to block out the emotionally charged words. In a test of whether people who dissociated could use this skill deliberately, these researchers asked high and low dissociators to view a list of words and to deliberately forget some of them. High dissociators were better at forgetting words related to trauma when asked to do so than the low dissociators were (DePrince & Freyd, 2004). In sum, dissociation does seem related to less recall of emotionally relevant words, a phenomenon that could help us understand how people organize and make sense of negative experiences.

This type of cognitive research, however, is needed with people who have dissociative disorders or who have experienced traumas, to determine how well these phenomena generalize (McNally, 2003b). One group failed to replicate the DePrince and Freyd (2004) effect in those whom one might think would exhibit it most strongly: adults who report having recovered memories of childhood sexual abuse after many years of not having thought about their abuse (McNally, Ristuccia, & Perlman, 2005). Until we have more evidence, it is probably safest to regard these theories of dissociation and memory as tentative, awaiting confirmation that the same processes can explain the onset of full-blown disorders (Shobe & Kihlstrom, 1997).

Dissociative Amnesia

As illustrated in the clinical case in the opening of this chapter, the person with **dissociative amnesia** is unable to recall important personal information, usually information about some traumatic experience. The holes in memory are too extensive to be explained by ordinary forgetfulness. The information is not permanently lost, but it cannot be retrieved during the episode of amnesia, which may last for as short a period as several hours or as long as several years. The amnesia usually disappears as suddenly as it came on, with complete recovery and only a small chance of recurrence.

 DSM-IV-TR Criteria for Dissociative Amnesia

- One or more episodes of inability to remember important personal information, usually of a traumatic experience, that is too extensive to be ordinary forgetfulness
- The amnesia occurs outside of other dissociative disorders, PTSD or acute stress disorder, or somatization disorder, and is not explained by other medical or psychological conditions
- The symptoms cause significant distress or impairment

Focus on Discovery 6.5

Debates about Repression: Recovered Memories of Abuse in Childhood

A history of severe abuse in childhood is thought to be an important cause of DID and other psychological disorders. It is estimated that 13.5 percent of women and 2.5 percent of men have experienced some form of childhood sexual abuse (CSA; Molnar, Buka, & Kessler, 2001), and more have experienced other forms of abuse. Although these estimates of the frequency of abuse have been derived from retrospective reports and thus could be distorted, most researchers assume that they are fairly accurate.

Here we focus on recovered memories of childhood abuse—that is, on cases in which a person had no memory of being abused as a child but then "recovered" the memory. Few issues are more hotly debated in psychology than whether these recovered memories are real. Memory researchers caution against a blanket acceptance of memories of sexual or physical abuse recovered during therapy (Loftus, 1997).

This is an important issue, because recovered memories of abuse have assumed importance in court cases (Pope, 1998). In a typical scenario, a woman recovers a memory during psychotherapy, accuses one or both of her parents of having abused her during childhood and brings charges against them. For most crimes, plaintiffs must file suit within a certain number of years of a crime. In the 1980s, courts in more than 30 states increased the time allowed for filing suit in cases where plaintiffs claimed to have recovered memories of CSA (Brown, Scheflin, & Whitfield, 1999). By the late 1990s, however, the tide had turned, and many appellate courts refused to allow testimony based on recovered memories (Piper, Pope, & Borowiecki, 2000). More than 100 former patients have sued therapists for malpractice, claiming that the therapists implanted false memories of abuse (McNally, 2003b).

What does the research evidence say about repression? In laboratory studies of memory, researchers have asked people to forget information, such as a list of words, and have shown that people can do so. Indeed, the more they practice forgetting the words, the less they are able to retrieve them when asked (Anderson & Green, 2001). This study demonstrates that people can deliberately forget material, but other evidence does not support the idea that this forgetting extends to trauma. When people who were exposed to CSA are asked to ignore or forget cues related to their traumas, they do not show any superior ability (McNally, Clancy et al., 2004).

Other researchers have focused on trying to understand memory for trauma outside of the laboratory setting. In one careful study of whether memories of abuse can be repressed, Williams (1995) interviewed women known to have been abused as children. Fully 38 percent of these women were unable to recall the abuse when they were asked about it almost two decades later. In line with these findings, many women who report abuse say that there were times when they did not remember having been abused.

Would a simple failure to remember mean that repression has occurred? Perhaps not—women may actively try to keep these thoughts out of mind because they are distressing, or they might not want to discuss such distressing events during an interview. Perhaps the abuse happened before the time of their earliest memories (generally around age 3 or 4). With certain traumas, brain injury or loss of consciousness could explain gaps in memory. Thus, a failure to think about and describe a memory may not be the same thing as repression.

There is also plenty of evidence suggesting that memories are sometimes inaccurate. Memory is not like a video recorder, and cognitive psychologists have shown that it is possible for people to firmly believe in an inaccurate memory. For example, in a study of people's memories of the explosion of the space shuttle *Challenger* on January 28, 1986, participants were interviewed the day after the disaster and then 2 years later (Neisser & Harsch, 1991). No later accounts were entirely accurate, and many were way off the mark, despite the fact that participants reported still having vivid memories of the event. This would lead us to suppose that, at least in some cases, memories are not accurate.

Where could recovered memories come from, if not from actual experiences? A leading researcher suggests several possibilities (Loftus, 1993):

1. **Popular writings.** *The Courage to Heal* (Bass & Davis, 1994) is an extremely popular guide for victims of CSA. It repeatedly suggests to readers that they were probably abused and offers as signs of abuse low self-esteem, feeling different from others, substance abuse, sexual dysfunction, and depression. The problem is that symptoms such as these can result from many factors other than CSA.

Studies of memory show that recall of even a major event such as the explosion of the space shuttle *Challenger* can be considerably distorted. (AP/Wide World Photos.)

2. **Therapists' suggestions.** By their own accounts (Poole et al., 1995), many therapists who genuinely believe that many adult disorders result from abuse directly suggest to their clients that they were probably sexually abused as children; sometimes, the therapist does this with the assistance of hypnotic age regression and guided imagery (Poole et al., 1995). Unfortunately, techniques like hypnosis may actually contribute to the development of false memories (Lynn et al., 2003). Guided imagery, in which a person closes their eyes and tries to imagine an event occurring, tends to increase confidence that a false memory actually occurred. One group of researchers found that with guided imagery, at least 55 percent of college students were able to develop at least a partial memory for a childhood event that never occurred, such as getting lost or being hurt (Porter, Yuille, & Lehman, 1999).

3. Suggestions from other experts can also influence memories. For example, in one study, people who were witnesses to a bomb explosion were interviewed (Nourkova, Bernstein, & Loftus, 2004). At follow-up, interviewers used the following suggestion: "When you were taking part in our study, you mentioned a wounded animal. Could you tell us about it?" Even though there was actually no mention of any animal during the first interview, more than 10 percent of people responded to the question with details about the wounded animal. Studies like this one indicate that expert suggestions can lead to memory distortions.

Not only do memory distortions occur, but once they do, they hold emotional power. In one study, researchers interviewed people who reported having been abducted by space aliens (a presumably false memory). While participants talked about the experience, the researchers recorded heart rate, sweating, and other signs of arousal. People describing their abduction demonstrated just as much arousal as others do when they recount experiences of war or trauma (McNally, Lasko et al., 2004). Even false memories, then, can be associated with a lot of pain!

There is little doubt that abuse occurs. But we must be wary of uncritically accepting reports of abuse. Social scientists and the courts share a heavy responsibility in deciding whether a given recovered memory is an accurate reflection of a criminal event. Erring in either direction could result in an injustice to either the accused or the accuser.

Most often the memory loss involves information about some part of a traumatic experience, such as witnessing the sudden death of a loved one. It is presumed that the person was able to initially form the memory (e.g., that they were not so overwhelmed and disorganized from the traumatic experience to preclude being aware of and encoding the traumatic event). More rarely the amnesia is for entire events during a circumscribed period of distress, is continuous from a traumatic event to the present, or is total, covering the person's entire life (Coons & Milstein, 1992). During the period of amnesia the person's behavior is otherwise unremarkable, except that the memory loss may cause some disorientation. With total amnesia the person does not recognize other people, not even close relatives and friends, but retains the ability to talk, read, and reason and also retains talents and previously acquired knowledge of the world and how to function in it.

The pattern of memory deficits highlights an important distinction. Typically, dissociative disorders involve deficits in explicit memory, but not implicit memory. **Explicit memory** involves the conscious recall of experiences—for example, explicit memory would be involved in describing a bicycle that you had as a child. **Implicit memory** underlies behaviors based on experiences that are not consciously recalled—for example, implicit memory of how to ride a bike underlies the behavior of actually riding one. There are numerous examples of patients with dissociative disorders whose implicit memory remains intact (Kihlstrom, 1994). One woman, for example, became amnesic after being victimized by a practical joke. She had no explicit memory of the event, but she became terrified when passing the location of the incident (implicit memory). We will discuss some recent intriguing tests of implicit memory when we discuss the etiology of dissociative identity disorder.

Memory loss is also common in many brain disorders, as well as in substance abuse, but these types of memory loss can be fairly easily distinguished from dissociative amnesia. In degenerative brain disorders, memory fails slowly over time, is not linked to stress, and is accompanied by other cognitive deficits, such as an inability to learn new information. Memory loss after a brain injury or substance abuse can be linked to the time of the injury or to the substance being abused.

In *Spellbound*, Gregory Peck played a man with amnesia. Dissociative amnesia is typically triggered by a stressful event, as it was in the film. (Springer/Corbis-Bettmann.)

DSM-IV-TR Criteria for Dissociative Fugue

- Sudden, unexpected travel away from home or work
- An inability to recall one's past
- Confusion about identity or assumption of a new identity
- Symptoms are not explained by another medical or psychological disorder
- Symptoms cause significant distress or impairment

Dissociative Fugue

In **dissociative fugue** (from the Latin *fugere*, "to flee") the memory loss is more extensive than in dissociative amnesia. Like Gene described below, the person not only becomes totally amnesic but suddenly leaves home and work and assumes a new identity. Sometimes the person takes a new name, a new home, a new job, and even a new set of personality characteristics. The person may even succeed in establishing a fairly complex social life. More often, however, the new life does not crystallize to this extent, and the fugue is of relatively brief duration, consisting for the most part of limited but apparently purposeful travel, during which social contacts are minimal or absent. Recovery is usually complete, although it takes varying amounts of time; after recovery, the person does not recollect what took place during the fugue.

Fugues can occur after a person has experienced some severe stress, such as marital quarrels, personal rejections, financial or occupational difficulties, war service, or a natural disaster, but not all fugues seem to immediately follow traumatic triggers (Hacking, 1998). It should also be noted that even in samples of people who have experienced intense trauma, such as imprisonment in a concentration camp, dissociative amnesia and fugue are extremely rare (Merckelbach et al., 2003).

Clinical Case: Burt/Gene

A 42-year-old male was brought to the emergency room by the police after he was involved in a fight at the diner where he worked. When the police arrived, the patient had given his name as Burt Tate but was unable to provide any identification. Several weeks before the fight, Burt had arrived in town and begun working as a short-order cook. He had no memory of where he had worked or lived before he had arrived in town.

At the emergency room, Burt could answer questions about the date and his location, but could not remember anything about his previous life. He was not concerned by his memory gaps. There was no evidence that alcohol, drugs, head trauma, or any medical condition could explain the gaps in his memory.

A missing person search revealed that he fit the description of a man named Gene who had disappeared a month before from a city about 200 miles away. Gene's wife was contacted, and she was able to confirm that "Burt" was her husband. Gene's wife described that he had been experiencing considerable stress in his job as a manager at a manufacturing plant for 18 months leading up to his disappearance. Two days before his disappearance, Gene had a violent fight with his adolescent son who called him a failure and moved out of the home. Gene claimed not to recognize his wife. (Adapted from Spitzer et al., 1994.)

Depersonalization Disorder

In **depersonalization disorder**, the person's perception or experience of the self is disconcertingly and disruptively altered. Unlike the other dissociative disorders in DSM-IV-TR, it involves no disturbance of memory. In a depersonalization episode, which is typically triggered by stress, people rather suddenly lose their sense of self. This involves unusual sensory experiences. For example, their limbs may seem drastically changed in size or their voices may sound strange to them. They may have the impression that they are outside their bodies, viewing themselves from a distance. Sometimes they feel mechanical, as though they and others are robots, or they move as though the world has lost its reality.

Depersonalization disorder usually begins in adolescence and has a chronic course—that is, it lasts a long time. Comorbid personality disorders are frequent, as are anxiety disorders and depression (Simeon et al., 1997). As in the case of Mrs. A., childhood trauma is often reported.

Diagnostic criteria for depersonalization disorder do specify that the depersonalization cannot be explained by another disorder, so it is important to rule out disorders that commonly involve depersonalization, including schizophrenia, panic disorder, posttraumatic stress disorder, and borderline personality disorder (Maldonado, Butler, & Spiegel, 1998). Depersonalization also can be triggered by hyperventilation, a common symptom of panic attacks. It should be noted that some have criticized the existence of a diagnosis for depersonalization, pointing out that depersonalization disorder requires just one symptom for diagnosis, whereas diagnosis of most other disorders requires a cluster of symptoms (McNally, 2003b).

Clinical Case: Mrs. A.

Mrs. A was a 43-year-old woman who lived with her mother and son and worked at a clerical job. She had experienced symptoms of depersonalization several times per year for as long as she could remember. "It's as if the real me is taken out and put on a shelf or stored somewhere inside of me. Whatever makes me me is not there. It is like an opaque curtain...like going through the motions and having to exert discipline to keep the unit together." She had found these symptoms to be extremely distressing. She had experienced panic attacks for 1 year when she was 35 and also had been diagnosed with self-defeating personality disorder. She described a childhood trauma history that included nightly genital fondling and frequent enemas by her mother from earliest memory to age 10 (Simeon et al., 1997, p. 1109).

Dissociative Identity Disorder

Consider what it would be like to have **dissociative identity disorder (DID)**. People tell you about things you have done that seem out of character, events of which you have no memory. You have been waking up each morning with the remains of a cup of tea by your bedside—and you do not like tea. How can you explain these happenings?

Clinical Description of DID   Dissociative identity disorder has nothing to do with the common experience of feeling not quite like ourselves. Rather, according to DSM-IV-TR, a diagnosis of dissociative identity disorder (DID) requires that a person have at least two separate personalities, or alters—different modes of being, thinking, feeling, and acting that exist independently of each other and that come forth at different times. Each determines the person's nature and activities when it is in command. Sometimes there is one primary personality, and this is typically the alter that seeks treatment. Usually, there are two to four alters at the time a diagnosis is made, but over the course of treatment others may emerge. Gaps in memory are also common, because in most cases at least one alter has no contact with the others—for example, the primary alter may be totally unaware that the other alters exist and may have no memory of what those other alters do and experience when they are in control. The diagnosis also requires that the existence of different alters be chronic; it cannot be a temporary change resulting from the ingestion of a drug, for example.

 DSM-IV-TR Criteria for Dissociative Identity Disorder

- Presence of two or more personalities (alters)
- At least two of the alters recurrently take control of behavior
- Inability of at least one of the alters to recall important personal information

Each alter may be quite complex, with its own behavior patterns, memories, and relationships. Usually the personalities of the different alters are quite different from one another, even polar opposites. They may have different handedness, wear glasses with different prescriptions, and have allergies to different substances. The original and subordinate alters are all aware of lost periods of time, and the voices of the others may sometimes echo in an alter's consciousness, even though the alter does not know to whom these voices belong.

DID usually begins in childhood, but it is rarely diagnosed until adulthood. It is more severe and extensive than the other dissociative disorders, and recovery may be less complete. It is much more common in women than in men. Other diagnoses—in particular, posttraumatic stress disorder, major depressive disorder, substance abuse, phobias, border-line personality disorder, sexual dysfunction, and somatization disorder—are often present (Boon & Draijer, 1993a,b; Loewenstein, 1991). DID is commonly accompanied by other symptoms such as headaches, hallucinations, suicide attempts, and self-abusive behavior, as well as by other dissociative symptoms such as amnesia and depersonalization (Scroppo et al., 1998).

Clinical Case: Gina

In December 1965, Dr. Robert Jeans was consulted by a woman named Gina Rinaldi, who had been referred to him by her friends. Gina, single and 31 years old, lived with another single woman and was working successfully as a writer at a large educational publishing firm. She was considered to be efficient, businesslike, and productive, but her friends had observed that she was becoming forgetful and sometimes acted out of character. The youngest of nine siblings, Gina reported that she had been sleepwalking since her early teens; her present roommate had told her that she sometimes screamed in her sleep.

Gina described her 74-year-old mother as the most domineering woman she had ever known. She reported that as a child she had been a fearful and obedient daughter. At age 28 she had an "affair," her first, with a former Jesuit priest, although it was apparently not sexual in nature. Then she became involved with T. C., a married man who assured her he would get a divorce and marry her. She indicated that she had been faithful to him since the start of their relationship. T. C., however, fell out of her favor as he did not come through with his promised divorce and stopped seeing Gina regularly. By analyzing one of her dreams, Jeans concluded that Gina was uncomfortable about being a woman, particularly when a close, sexual relationship with a man might be expected of her.

After several sessions with Gina, Jeans began to notice a second personality emerging. Mary Sunshine, as she came to be called by Jeans and Gina, was quite different from Gina. She seemed more childlike, more traditionally feminine, ebullient, and seductive. Gina felt that she walked like a coal miner, but Mary certainly did not. Some quite concrete incidents indicated Mary's existence. Sometimes while cleaning her home Gina found cups that had had hot chocolate in them—neither Gina nor her roommate liked hot chocolate. There were large withdrawals from Gina's bank account that she could not remember making. She even discovered herself ordering a sewing machine on the telephone, although she disliked sewing; some weeks later she arrived at her therapy session wearing a new dress, which Mary had sewn. At work, Gina reported, people were finding her more pleasant to be with, and her colleagues took to consulting her on how to encourage people to work better with one another. All these phenomena were entirely alien to Gina. Jeans and Gina came to realize that sometimes Gina was transformed into Mary.

More and more often, Jeans witnessed Gina turning into Mary in the consulting room. T. C. accompanied Gina to a session during which her posture and demeanor became more relaxed, her tone of voice warmer. When T. C. explained that he really cared for her, Gina, or rather, Mary, said warmly, "Of course, T., I know you do." At another session Mary was upset and, as Jeans put it, chewed off Gina's fingernails. Then the two of them started having conversations with each other in front of Jeans.

A year after the start of therapy an apparent synthesis of Gina and Mary began to emerge. At first it seemed that Gina had taken over entirely, but then Jeans noticed that Gina was not as serious as before, particularly about "getting the job done," that is, working extremely hard on the therapy. Jeans encouraged Gina to talk with Mary. The following is that conversation:

I was lying in bed trying to go to sleep. Someone started to cry about T. C. I was sure that it was Mary. I started to talk to her. The person told me that she didn't have a name. Later she said that Mary called her Evelyn.... I was suspicious at first that it was Mary pretending to be Evelyn. I changed my mind, however, because the person I talked to had too much sense to be Mary. She said that she realized that T. C. was unreliable but she still loved him and was very lonely. She agreed that it would be best to find a reliable man. She told me that she comes out once a day for a very short time to get used to the world. She promised that she will come out to see you [Jeans] sometime when she is stronger. (Jeans, 1976, pp. 254–255)

Throughout January, Evelyn appeared more and more often, and Jeans felt that his patient was improving rapidly. Within a few months she seemed to be Evelyn all the time; soon thereafter this woman married a physician. Now, years later, she has had no recurrences of the other personalities.

(Drawn from the account, "The Three Faces of Evelyn," which appeared in 1976 in the *Journal of Abnormal Psychology*.)

Cases of dissociative identity disorder are sometimes mislabeled in the popular press as schizophrenia (see Chapter 11), which derives part of its name from the Greek root *schizo*, which means "splitting away from"—hence the confusion. A split into two or more fairly separate and coherent systems of being that exist alternately in the same person is quite different from the symptoms of schizophrenia. People with DID do not show the thought disorder and behavioral disorganization characteristic of schizophrenia.

The inclusion of DID as a diagnosis in DSM-IV-TR is a matter of some controversy. For example, in a survey of board-certified psychiatrists, two-thirds reported reservations about the presence of DID in the DSM (Pope et al., 1999). Students and the public often ask, "Does DID exist"? Clinicians can describe DID reliably; it "exists" in this sense. As we will discuss later, though, controversy swirls about the reasons these symptoms occur.

Check Your Knowledge 6.3

1. Dissociative fugue differs from dissociative amnesia in the following ways (circle all that apply):
   a. longer periods of no memory
   b. assumption of a new identity
   c. symptoms often triggered by a trauma
   d. typically triggered by drug use
2. Most typically, dissociative amnesia involves being unable to remember:
   a. the entire life

b. childhood
c. a trauma
d. life up until a trauma

3. In the context of dissociative identity disorder, *alter* refers to:
   a. extreme splitting
   b. a distinct personality
   c. the host personality
   d. the bridge between different personalities

The Epidemiology of DID: Major Increases Over Time   DID was first mentioned in the nineteenth century. A review of the literature identified a total of 77 cases, most of which had been reported in the period between 1890 and 1920 (Sutcliffe & Jones, 1962). After 1920, reports of DID declined until the 1970s, when they increased markedly, not only in the United States but also in countries such as Japan (Uchinuma & Sekine, 2000). More formal data on the prevalence of DID were collected on samples of adults in Winnipeg, Canada, and in Sivas, Turkey (Akyuez et al., 1999; Ross, 1991). Prevalence was 1.3 percent in the Canadian study and 0.4 percent in the Turkish one. Although these prevalence figures may not seem high, they are; prevalence was earlier thought to be about 1 in a million.

What has caused the vast increases in the rates of the DID diagnosis over time? It is possible that more people began to experience symptoms of DID. But another possible explanation is that in DSM-III, which was published in 1980, the diagnostic criteria for DID were spelled out clearly for the first time, causing more cases to be recognized (Putnam, 1996). Another factor of possible relevance to the increase in DID diagnoses was the 1973 publication of *Sybil*, which presented a dramatic case with 16 personalities (Schreiber, 1973). This extremely popular book spawned much interest in the disorder, and a series of other case reports were also published. Some critics hypothesize that this heightened interest led some therapists to suggest strongly to clients that they had DID, sometimes using hypnosis to probe for alters. It even has been claimed that in Sybil's case, the alters were created by a therapist who gave substance to Sybil's different emotional states by giving them names (Borch-Jacobsen, 1997). The case of Eve White, popularized in the book *The Three Faces of Eve* as well as a movie, was at one time the most detailed report of DID available. Like the case of Sybil, there has been significant controversy about this case as well (see p. 104).

In the film version of *Sybil*, about a famous case of dissociative identity disorder, the title role was played by Sally Field. (Jerry Ohlinger's Movie Material Store.)

Clinical Case: Elizabeth, An Example of Unwarranted Diagnosis

Elizabeth Carlson, a 35-year-old married woman, was referred to a psychiatrist after being hospitalized for severe depression. Elizabeth reported that soon after treatment began, her psychiatrist suggested to her that perhaps her problem was the elusive, often undiagnosed condition of multiple personality disorder [now referred to as DID]. Her psychiatrist reviewed "certain telltale signs of MPD. Did Carlson ever 'zone out' while driving and arrive at her destination without remembering how she got there? Why yes, Carlson said. Well, that was an alter taking over the driving and then vanishing again, leaving her,

the 'host' personality, to account for the blackout. Another sign of MPD, Humenansky said, was 'voices in the head.' Did Carlson ever have internal arguments—for example, telling herself, 'Turn right' and then 'No, turn left'? Yes, Carlson replied, that happened sometimes. Well, that was the alters fighting with each other inside her head. Carlson was amazed and embarrassed. All these years, she had done these things, never realizing that they were symptoms of a severe mental disorder" (Acocella, 1999, p. 1).

Roseanne Barr has talked about her history of dissociative identity disorder. (Frederick M. Brown/Getty Images News and Sport Services.)

Etiology of DID   There are two major theories of DID: the **posttraumatic model** and the **sociocognitive model**. As we will see, there is considerable debate between proponents of these two approaches.

The posttraumatic model assumes that DID begins in childhood as a result of severe physical or sexual abuse. Almost all patients with DID report severe childhood abuse. There is also evidence that children who are abused are at risk for developing dissociative symptoms, although whether these symptoms reach diagnosable levels is less clear (Chu et al., 1999). It is important to note, though, that the reports of child abuse in patients with DID are often not corroborated (see Focus on Discovery 6.5).

Since not everyone who experiences child abuse develops DID, it is further proposed that a diathesis is present among those who do develop DID. That is, some people are particularly likely to use dissociation to cope with trauma, and this is seen as a key factor in causing people to develop alters after trauma (Gleaves, 1996). There is evidence that children who dissociate are more likely to develop some psychological symptoms after trauma (Kisiel & Lyons, 2001). But because DID is so rare, no prospective studies have focused on dissociative coping styles and the development of DID.

The other theory, the sociocognitive model, considers DID to be the result of learning to enact social roles. According to this model, alters appear in response to suggestions by therapists, exposure to media reports of DID, or other cultural influences (S.O. Lilienfeld et al., 1999; Spanos, 1994). An important implication of this model, then, is that DID could be created within therapy. This does not mean, however, that DID is viewed as conscious deception; the issue is not whether DID is real, but how it develops.

A leading advocate of the idea that DID is basically a role-play suggests that people with trauma histories may be particularly likely to have a rich fantasy life, to have had considerable practice at imagining they are other people, and to have a deep desire to please others (Spanos, 1994). According to this theory, people adopt the DID role when given suggestions by a therapist or when provided with inducements to behave as though a previous bad act had been committed by another personality. S.O. Lilienfeld and colleagues (1999) note that many of the therapeutic techniques being used with DID reinforce clients for identifying different alters; this researcher argues that repeated probing and reinforcement for describing alters may promote these symptoms within vulnerable people. The clinical case of Elizabeth provides an extreme example of a therapist who unwittingly encourages her client to adopt a diagnosis of DID when it isn't really justified by the symptoms. Each of the symptoms described are common experiences; indeed, none of the symptoms listed are actual diagnostic criteria for DID. Like the posttraumatic model, the sociocognitive model assumes that child abuse may set the stage for DID.

We will never have experimental evidence for either the posttraumatic model or the sociocognitive model, since it would be unethical to intentionally reinforce dissociative symptoms. Given this, what kinds of evidence have been raised in this debate?

DID Symptoms Can Be Role-Played It has been established that people are capable of role-playing the symptoms of DID. One relevant study was conducted in the 1980s after the trial of a serial murderer in California known as the Hillside strangler (Spanos, Weekes, & Bertrand, 1985). The accused murderer, Ken Bianchi, unsuccessfully pled not guilty by reason of insanity, claiming that the murders had been committed by an alter, Steve. (For discussion of the insanity defense, see p. 572.) In the study, undergraduate students were told that they would play the role of an accused murderer and that despite much evidence of guilt, a plea of not guilty had been entered. They also were told that they were to participate in a simulated psychiatric interview that might involve hypnosis. Then the students were taken to another room and introduced to the "psychiatrist," actually an experimental assistant. After a number of standard questions, the students were assigned to one of three experimental conditions. In the most important of these, the Bianchi condition, students were given a rudimentary hypnotic induction and were then instructed to let a second personality come forward, just as had happened when Bianchi had been hypnotized.

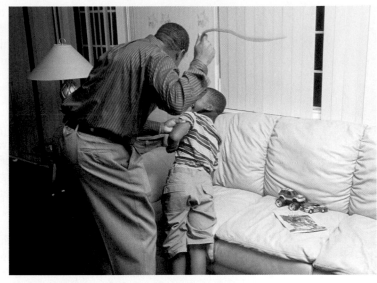
Physical or sexual abuse in childhood is regarded as a major cause of dissociative disorders. (Patrick Olear/PhotoEdit.)

After the experimental manipulations, the possible existence of a second personality was probed directly by the "psychiatrist." In addition, students were asked questions about the facts of the murders. Finally, in a second session, those who acknowledged another personality were asked to take personality tests twice—once for each of their two personalities. Eighty-one percent of the students in the Bianchi condition adopted a new name, and many of these admitted guilt for the murders. Even the personality test results of the two personalities differed considerably.

Clearly, then, when the situation demands, people can adopt a second personality. We should remember, however, that this demonstration illustrates only that such role-playing is possible; it in no way demonstrates that DID results from role-playing. Furthermore, the impact of such role-playing studies depends on how compelling the role-play is as an analogue of DID. Critics have pointed out that DID is a complex disorder involving many symptoms, including auditory hallucinations, time loss, and depersonalization. None of these symptoms has been produced in role-playing studies (Gleaves, 1996).

Patients with DID Do Not Show Deficits in Some Forms of Implicit Memory Several studies suggest that even though different alters report being unable to share memories, they actually do share a fair amount of information, as revealed by subtle tests. For example, one group of researchers tested two different alters of a woman with DID (Nissen et al., 1988). If one alter, Alice, learned word lists, the other alter, Bonnie, could not repeat them to an experimenter (a test of explicit memory). But after Alice had been asked to focus on the word "lullaby," Bonnie was quicker than normal to identify "lullaby" as the word that filled in the puzzle "l_l_a_y" (a test of implicit memory).

Other researchers obtained similar results from testing a group of people with DID (Huntjen et al., 2003). Each person was tested first as one alter and then as a second alter. Of the 31 people with DID who were tested, 21 claimed at the second testing session that they had no memory of the first session, but these 21 people performed comparably to people without DID on tests of implicit memory. That is, word lists learned during the first session had a variety of subtle effects on performance during the second session, when a different alter was tested. The researchers interpreted the findings as supportive of a role-playing explanation of DID—people with DID had demonstrated more accurate memories than they had acknowledged.

It should be noted, however, that even cognitive scientists disagree on whether implicit memory deficits actually exist in DID. Some authors have suggested that only certain types

Ken Bianchi, a serial killer known as the Hillside strangler, unsuccessfully attempted an insanity defense. The jury decided that he was faking the symptoms of DID. (AP/Wide World Photos.)

of implicit memory seem to transfer between alters. In two studies, memories that required complex verbal processing were less likely to be transferred between alters than were memories that were less verbal, such as those involving pictures (Eich et al., 1997; Elzinga et al., 2003). Studies like this support the idea that DID involves deficits in certain forms of implicit memory, even though some aspects of implicit memory appear to be preserved. So, controversy continues.

The Detection of DID Differs by Clinician   A small number of clinicians contribute most of the diagnoses of DID within a given time period. For example, a survey conducted in Switzerland found that 66 percent of the diagnoses of DID were made by fewer than 10 percent of the psychiatrists who responded (Modestin, 1992). Therapists who are most likely to diagnose DID tend to use hypnosis, to urge clients to try to unbury unremembered abuse experiences, or to name different "alters." Proponents of the sociocognitive model would argue that the extremes in diagnosis rates support the idea that certain clinicians are likely to elicit the symptoms of DID in their patients. Proponents of the posttraumatic model, however, point out that people with DID may be referred to clinicians who specialize in treating this condition (Gleaves, 1996). Once again, the data are inconclusive.

Many DID Symptoms Emerge after Treatment Starts   Do people develop DID in childhood, before entering therapy? If symptoms only emerge after treatment begins, this might provide critical evidence against the posttraumatic model. Studies have shown that when patients with DID enter therapy, they are usually unaware of having alters. But as treatment progresses, they tend to become aware of alters, and they report a rapid increase in the number of alters they can identify. This pattern is consistent with the idea that treatment is evoking the DID symptoms (S.O. Lilienfeld et al., 1999). Proponents of posttraumatic theory, however, explain this pattern by suggesting that most alters began their existence during childhood and that therapy just allows the person to become aware of and describe alters. Still, in most cases, even when people with DID say they had alters during childhood, there is no corroborating evidence, and we should be cautious about uncritically accepting these self-reports.

One study, however, has provided evidence regarding childhood onset in cases of DID (Lewis et al., 1997), although it has been criticized by proponents of the sociocognitive model (S.O. Lilienfeld et al., 1999). The study, which was conducted over a period of two decades, involved detailed examination of 150 convicted murderers. Fourteen of them were found to have DID. Twelve of the 14 people had long-standing psychological symptoms that preceded their incarceration: 8 had experienced trances during childhood, 9 had had auditory hallucinations, and 10 had had imaginary companions (which is frequently reported by people with DID). Each of these symptoms was corroborated by at least three outside sources (e.g., by interviews with family members, teachers, and parole officers). Furthermore, several of the people with DID had shown distinctly different handwriting styles (indicating the existence of alters) well before committing their crimes (see Figure 6.3). The results of this study, then, support the idea that DID does begin in childhood for some people even if other people only develop symptoms after treatment begins.

Treatment of DID   There seems to be widespread agreement on several principles in the treatment of dissociative identity disorder, whatever the clinician's orientation (Kluft, 1994; Ross, 1989). These include an empathic and gentle stance, with the goal of helping the client function as one wholly integrated person. The goal of treatment should be to convince the person that splitting into different personalities is no longer necessary to deal with traumas. In addition, assuming that DID is in some measure a means of escaping from severe stress, treatment can help teach the person to cope better with present-day challenges. Often, people with DID are hospitalized to help them stabilize and avoid self-harm and to begin the treatment in a more intensive fashion.

Figure 6.3 Handwriting samples from 4 DID cases. (From Lewis et al., 1997. Reprinted with permission from the *American Journal of Psychiatry*, Copyright 1997. American Psychiatric Association.)

Psychoanalytic treatment is probably used more for DID and the other dissociative disorders than for any other psychological disorders. The goal of this treatment is to overcome repressions, using basic psychoanalytic techniques (MacGregor, 1996). DID, like posttraumatic stress disorder (PTSD), is widely believed to arise from traumatic events that the person is trying to block from consciousness.

Psychoanalysis had its beginnings in hypnosis (see Chapter 1), and through the years, psychoanalytic practitioners have continued to use hypnosis with patients diagnosed with

Check Your Knowledge 6.4

True or false?
1. Prevalence of DID is currently at an all-time high.
2. Most people with DID report childhood abuse.
3. The sociocognitive model of DID emphasizes role enactment.

Quick Summary

Dissociative disorders are defined on the basis of disruptions in consciousness or memory. Dissociative amnesia is diagnosed based on the inability to recall important personal information, usually about a traumatic experience. Dissociative fugue is more severe than amnesia, because the person not only has an inability to recall important information, but also moves and assumes a new identity. In depersonalization disorders, the person's perception of the self is altered; he or she may experience being outside the body or perceive changes in the size of body parts. The person with dissociative identity disorder has two or more distinct personalities, each with unique memories, behavior patterns, and relationships.

Relatively little research is available concerning the causes of these disorders. Considerable debate exists about the causes of DID. The post-traumatic model suggests that DID is the result of extreme abuse, coupled with a tendency to use dissociation as a coping strategy. The sociocognitive model suggests that DID is caused by role-playing of symptoms among patients with a history of abuse and a deep need to satisfy authority figures like therapists. Debate about these two viewpoints has focused on the dramatic shifts in diagnosis over time, the differences between clinicians in the recognition of disorder, the ability of undergraduates to role-play symptoms of DID, the indications on subtler memory tests of alters sharing information that they deny conscious awareness of, and indications that many people only develop symptoms after treatment begins.

dissociative disorders as a means of helping them gain access to repressed material (Putnam, 1993). DID patients are unusually hypnotizable (Butler et al., 1996). Typically, the person is hypnotized and encouraged to go back in his or her mind to traumatic events in childhood—a technique called *age regression*. The hope is that accessing these traumatic memories will allow the person to realize that childhood threats are no longer present and that adult life need not be governed by these ghosts from the past (Grinker & Spiegel, 1944). It has been cautioned, however, that there is little evidence that age regression relieves symptoms. Indeed, treatment involving recovered memories may be harmful and could result in a worsening of DID symptoms (Fetkewicz, Sharma, & Merskey, 2000; Powell & Gee, 2000).

Some mental health specialists have proposed strategies for treating DID that are reminiscent of the strategies used in treating PTSD. For example, in the safe, supportive context of therapy, patients are encouraged to think back to the traumatic events that are believed to have triggered their problems and to view those events with the expectation that they can come to terms with the horrible things that happened to them.

Because of the rarity of diagnosed cases of DID, there are no controlled studies of the results of treatment. Nearly all the reports come from the clinical observations of one highly experienced therapist, Richard Kluft (1994). The greater the number of alters, the longer the treatment lasted (Putnam et al., 1986); in general, therapy took almost 2 years and upwards of 500 hours per patient. Years after treatment started, Kluft (1994) reported that 84 percent of an original 123 patients had achieved stable integration of alters and another 10 percent were at least functioning better. In a different follow-up study of 12 patients, 6 patients achieved full integration of their alters within a 10-year period (Coons & Bowman, 2001).

DID is often comorbid with anxiety and depression, which can sometimes be lessened with antianxiety or antidepressant medications. These medications have no effect on the dissociative identity disorder itself, however (Simon, 1998).

Summary

Somatoform Disorders

- In somatoform disorder, biological explanations for physical symptoms cannot be found. The major somatoform diagnoses include pain disorder, body dysmorphic disorder, hypochondriasis, conversion disorder and somatization disorder.
- Psychoanalytic theory proposes that in conversion disorder, repressed impulses are converted into physical symptoms. Sackeim has proposed a two-stage model of conversion disorder that focuses on lack of conscious awareness of perceptions as well as motivation for symptoms. Cultural factors that influence how people think about and express distress may shape the rates of disorder as well.
- Data regarding other somatoform disorder are less available. Most somatoform disorders do not appear to be inherited. There may be some neurobiological overlap between body dysmorphic disorder and obsessive-compulsive disorder. Cognitive behavioral models emphasize that some people may have a cognitive style that leads them to overly attend to physical symptoms or problems, and to make negative attributions about these symptoms and their implications. The form of the cognitive bias may differ for the various somatoform disorders. Behavioral reinforcement may maintain help-seeking behavior.
- Antidepressants have been shown to be effective for some somatoform disorders. In psychoanalytic treatments for somatoform disorders, analysts try to help the client face the repressed impulses. Cognitive behavioral treatments, which have received a great deal of support, try to

address the maladaptively negative cognitions about physical symptoms, to reduce anxiety, and to reinforce behavior that is not consistent with the sick role.

Dissociative Disorders

- Dissociative disorders are defined by disruptions of consciousness, memory, and identity.
- The dissociative disorders include dissociative amnesia, dissociative fugue, depersonalization disorder, and dissociative identity disorder.
- Most of the writing about the causes of dissociative disorders focuses on dissociative identity disorder. Psychoanalytic theory regards dissociative disorders as instances of massive repression of some undesirable event or aspect of the self. People with dissociative identity disorder very often report severe physical or sexual abuse during childhood. One model, the posttraumatic model, suggests that extensive reliance on dissociation to fend off overwhelming feelings from abuse puts people at risk for developing dissociative identity disorder. The sociocognitive model, though, raises the question of whether some of these symptoms are elicited by treatment. Proponents of the sociocognitive model point out that abuse in childhood may result in high levels of suggestibility, that some therapists use strategies that suggest such symptoms to people, and that most people do not recognize the presence of any alters until after they see a therapist.

- Regardless of theoretical orientation, all clinicians focus their treatment efforts on helping a person cope with anxiety, face fears more directly, and operate in a manner that integrates their memory and consciousness.

- Psychoanalytic treatment is perhaps the most commonly used treatment for dissociative disorders, but some of the techniques involved, such as hypnosis and age regression, may make symptoms worse.

Answers to Check Your Knowledge Questions

6.1 1. b; 2. e; 3. c; 4. d
6.2 1. F; 2. F; 3. T; 4. F

6.3 1. b; 2. c; 3. b
6.4 1. T; 2. T; 3. T

Key Terms

anesthesia
blindsight
body dysmorphic disorder
conversion disorder
depersonalization disorder
dissociation

dissociative amnesia
dissociative disorders
dissociative fugue
dissociative identity disorder
 (DID)
explicit memory

factitious disorder
hypochondriasis
implicit memory
la belle indifférence
malingering
pain disorder

posttraumatic model
sociocognitive model
somatization disorder
somatoform disorders

7

Stress and Health

Learning Goals

1. Be able to distinguish the definitions of stress, coping, and social support.
2. Be able to understand the theories of the stress–illness link as well as concept of allostatic load and the basic components of the immune system.
3. Be able to describe how psychological factors impact cardiovascular disorders, asthma, and AIDS.
4. Be able to delineate the importance of gender, socioeconomic status, and ethnicity in health.
5. Be able to describe the major psychological treatments for psychophysiological disorders, including psychological approaches to reduce anger, anxiety, and depression, stress management, and biofeedback.

Clinical Case: Mark

Mark Howard was 38. After earning an M.B.A. he had joined the marketing division of a large conglomerate and had worked his way up the corporate ladder. His talent and long hours of work had recently culminated in a promotion to head of his division. The promotion had left him with mixed feelings. On the one hand, it was what he had been working so hard to achieve; but on the other hand, he had never been comfortable giving orders to others and he especially dreaded the staff meetings he would have to run.

Soon after the promotion, during a routine checkup, Mark's physician discovered that Mark's blood pressure had moved into the borderline hypertension range, around 150 over 100. Before implementing any treatment, the physician asked Mark to wear an ambulatory monitor for a few days so that his blood pressure could be assessed as he went about his usual routine. The device was programmed to take blood pressure readings 20 times a day.

On the first day of monitoring, Mark had a staff meeting scheduled for 10 o'clock. While he was laying out the marketing plans for a new product, the cuff inflated to take his blood pressure. A couple of minutes later he checked the reading. It was 195 over 140—not a borderline reading, but seriously high blood pressure. The next day he signed up for a yoga class and consulted a therapist for help with stress management. He also went to a trainer to help redesign his exercise plan and diet. He hoped that with these behavioral changes, he could continue in his managerial role and reduce the stress associated with the position.

A number of disorders characterized by genuine physical symptoms are caused by or can be worsened by stress. These disorders include those that we focus on in this chapter—cardiovascular disorders (including essential hypertension and coronary heart disease), asthma, and AIDS—as well as other, perhaps less serious but extremely common conditions such as headache and gastritis. These disorders are often referred to as **psychophysiological disorders**. The term "psychophysiological disorders" is preferred today to a term that was once used, *psychosomatic disorders*, which was intended to convey the idea that the mind (psyche) was having an undesirable effect on the body (soma).

Psychophysiological disorders as such do not appear in DSM-IV-TR, as they did in some earlier versions of the DSM. Rather, DSM-IV-TR covers these disorders under the rubric **psychological factors affecting medical condition**, in the broad section "Other Conditions That May Be a Focus of Clinical Attention." The psychological or behavioral factors that may be involved in the diagnosis include Axis I and II disorders; personality traits, such as neuroticism; coping styles, such as holding anger in rather than expressing it; and behavioral factors, such as failing to exercise regularly.

The new approach to diagnosis in DSM-IV-TR is also broader in scope than in previous versions of the DSM. Formerly, psychophysiological disorders were generally thought to include only some diseases (such as ulcers, headaches, asthma, and hypertension). The new approach makes the diagnosis applicable to any disease, as it is now known that any disease can be influenced by psychological factors. Furthermore, the diagnosis includes cases in which psychological or behavioral factors influence the course or treatment of a disorder, not just cases in which it influences the onset, again broadening the application. If, for example, a person with high blood pressure continues to drink alcohol while knowing that alcohol increases blood pressure, or if a patient fails to take prescribed medication regularly, their disorders may be diagnosed as psychophysiological.

What is the evidence for the view that any illness may be in part affected by psychological factors such as stress? For years it has been known that various diseases can be produced or enhanced in laboratory animals through exposure to stressors. For example, researchers induced tumors in mice and then studied the impact of stress—uncontrollable electric shocks—on growth of the tumors (Sklar & Anisman, 1979). In animals exposed to electric shock the tumors grew more rapidly, and these animals died earlier. Similarly, a 20-year follow-up of veterans of the Vietnam War revealed unusually high rates of a broad range of diseases involving the circulatory, respiratory, digestive, musculoskeletal, endocrine, and nervous systems (Boscarino, 1997). The stress of war was thought to be a factor in the severity of the diseases, if not also in their onset.

The many demonstrations of the pervasive role of psychological factors in health form the basis for the fields of **behavioral medicine** and **health psychology**. Since the 1970s these fields have dealt with the role of psychological factors in all facets of health and illness. Beyond examining the role that stress can play in the onset or severity of illness, researchers in these fields study psychological treatments (e.g., biofeedback for headache) and the health care system itself (e.g., how better to deliver services to underserved populations) (Appel et al., 1997; Stone, 1982).

Prevention is also a major focus of health psychology. As the twentieth century progressed and infectious diseases were brought under better control, people were dying more often from such illnesses as coronary heart disease (CHD). The causes of CHD involve behavior—people's lifestyles—such as smoking, eating too much, and excessive alcohol use. Thus, it is believed that changing unhealthy lifestyles can prevent many cases of CHD. Health psychologists are at the forefront of these preventative efforts, some of which we describe later in this chapter.

Health psychology and behavioral medicine are not restricted to a set of techniques or to particular principles of changing behavior. Clinicians in the field employ a wide variety of techniques—from contingency management, to stress reduction, to cognitive behavioral approaches—all of which share the goal of altering unhealthy living habits, distressed psychological states, and aberrant physiological processes in order to bring about health benefits.

We begin our discussion by reviewing general findings on the relationship between stress and health, as well as theories about how stress can produce illness. Then we turn to an in-depth examination of three types of disorders—cardiovascular disorders, asthma, and AIDS. Next we look at relationships between health and gender, socioeconomic status, and

> **DSM-IV-TR Criteria for Psychological Factors Affecting Medical Condition**
>
> - A medical illness is present
> - Psychological factors have influenced the course of the condition, interfered with treatment, increased health risks, or exacerbated symptoms

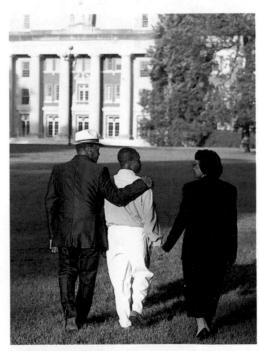

Experiencing major life events such as starting school is associated with increased risk of illness. (Will McIntyre/Photo Researchers.)

ethnicity. Finally, we consider various approaches to the treatment of psychophysiological disorders.

What Is Stress?

To understand the role of stress, we must first be able to define and measure it. Neither task is simple, as we discussed in Chapter 3. Stress has been defined in many ways. Perhaps one of the more influential antecedents to our current conceptualizations of stress was the work by the physician Hans Selye. He introduced the term *general adaptation syndrome* (GAS) to describe the biological response to sustained and high levels of stress. In Selye's model there are three phases of the response (see Figure 7.1):

Figure 7.1 Selye's general adaptation syndrome.

1. During the first phase, the alarm reaction, the autonomic nervous system is activated by the stress. If the stress is too powerful, gastrointestinal ulcers form, the adrenal glands become enlarged, and the thymus undergoes atrophy (wasting away).

2. During the second phase, resistance, the organism tries to adapt to the stress through available coping mechanisms.

3. If the stressor persists or the organism is unable to adapt effectively, the third phase, exhaustion, follows, and the organism dies or suffers irreversible damage (Selye, 1950).

In Selye's syndrome, the emphasis was on the body's response, not the environmental events that trigger that response. Psychological researchers later broadened Selye's concept to account for the diverse stress responses that people exhibited, including emotional upset, deterioration of performance, or physiological changes such as increased skin conductance or increases in the levels of certain hormones. The problem with these response-focused definitions of stress is that the criteria are not clear-cut. Physiological changes in the body can occur in response to a number of things that we would not consider stressful (e.g., anticipating a pleasurable event). Other researchers defined stress as a stimulus, often referred to as a stressor, rather than a response, and identified stress with a long list of environmental conditions, such as electric shock, boredom, uncontrollable stimuli, catastrophic life events, daily hassles, and sleep deprivation. Stimuli that are considered stressors can be major (the death of a loved one), minor (daily hassles, such as being stuck in traffic), acute (failing an exam), or chronic (a persistently unpleasant work environment). For the most part they are experiences that people regard as unpleasant, but they can also be pleasant events.

Like response-based definitions of stress, stimulus-based definitions present problems. Stipulating exactly what constitutes a stressor is difficult. It is not merely negativity, for marriage, generally a positive event, is regarded as a stressor because it requires adaptation. Furthermore, people vary widely in how they respond to life's challenges. A given event does not elicit the same amount of stress in everyone. For example, a family that has lost its home in a flood but has money enough to rebuild and strong social support from a network of friends nearby will experience less stress from this event than will a family that has neither adequate money to rebuild nor a network of friends to provide social support.

One way of addressing the limitations associated with defining stress as either a response or a stimulus is to consider them both. In addition, cognitive aspects of stress are an important part of current conceptualizations of stress. Specifically, researchers have emphasized that how we perceive or appraise the environment determines whether a stressor is present. When a person determines that the demands of a situation exceed his or her resources, the person experiences stress (Lazarus, 1966). Stress is perhaps most completely conceptualized as the subjective experience of distress in response to perceived environmental problems. A final exam that is merely challenging to some students may be

An exam, may be appraised as an interesting challenge or as an event that is extremely stressful. (Borrfdon/Photo Researchers.)

highly stressful to others who do not feel equipped to take it (whether their concerns are realistic or not).

Coping and Health

Relevant to individual differences in perceptions of potentially stressful situations is the concept of **coping**, or how people try to deal with problems, including the problem of handling the typically negative emotions stress produces. Even among those who perceive a situation as stressful, the effects of the stress may vary depending on how the individual copes with it. Researchers have identified two broad dimensions of coping (Lazarus & Folkman, 1984):

- *Problem-focused coping* involves taking direct action to solve the problem or seeking information that will be relevant to the solution. An example would be developing a study schedule covering an entire semester in order to reduce end-of-semester pressure.
- *Emotion-focused coping* involves efforts to reduce the negative emotional reactions to stress—for example, by distracting oneself from the problem, relaxing, or seeking comfort from others.

Coping researchers also refer to *avoidance coping,* which involves aspects of both problem-focused and emotion-focused coping (Carver & Scheier, 1999). The essence of avoidance coping is either attempting to avoid admitting that there is a problem to deal with (e.g., by distraction or denial) or neglecting to do anything about the problem (e.g., by giving up or just wishing the problem would go away).

The role of positive emotions in coping is an area of current interest to researchers (Folkman & Moskowitz, 2000). Positive emotions may co-occur with negative emotions during stressful situations, and they can provide some benefit. For example, positive emotions can "undo" some of the ill effects of negative emotions, particularly the physiological effects (Fredrickson & Levenson, 1998). In one study, individuals who expressed genuine smiling and laughter when talking about their relationship with a spouse who had died 6 months earlier had fewer grief-related symptoms and better relationships with others 2 years after the loss (Bonanno & Keltner, 1997; Keltner & Bonanno, 1997). Another study found that individuals who were able to find positive meaning, such as spiritual growth or an appreciation of life, following a traumatic event were able to respond to a laboratory stressor in a more adaptive fashion (Epel, McEwen, & Ickovics, 1998).

Effective coping often varies with the situation. Distraction may be an effective way of dealing with the emotional upset produced by impending surgery, for example, but it would be a poor way to handle the upset produced by the discovery of a lump on the breast (Lazarus & Folkman, 1984). Similarly, persistently trying to solve a problem that is unsolvable leads to increases in frustration, rather than providing any psychological benefit (Terry & Hynes, 1998). In some cases, avoidance coping (e.g., giving up) may be a practical approach—for example, a person who has repeatedly been denied admission to graduate school may do best by giving up on this endeavor and instead focusing on pursuing a different career path. In general, however, evidence indicates that avoidance coping is the least effective method of dealing with most problems (Roesch & Weiner, 2001).

Studies Using the Assessment of Daily Experience (ADE)   As discussed in Chapter 3, one of the currently effective methods for measuring stress and its relationship to health is the Assessment of Daily Experience (ADE; see p. 78). Recall that the ADE does not rely on retrospective reports as much as other measures of stress do. Studies using the ADE ask people for responses at the end of the day for several days. Although the events reported on a day will generally be less severe than those reported over a longer time period, there is now direct evidence that comparatively minor events are related to illness (Jandorf et al., 1986).

Researchers used the ADE to study the relationship between events in daily life and the onset of respiratory illness, which occurs with sufficient frequency to be analyzed as a distinct outcome (Stone, Reed, and Neale, 1987). After reviewing the data, the researchers identified 30 people who had experienced episodes of infectious illness during

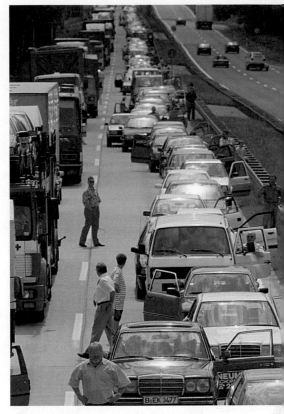

Daily hassles can be upsetting and increase risk for illness. (Herve Donnezan Photo Researchers.)

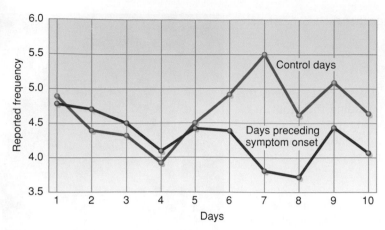

Figure 7.2   Mean number of desirable events in the 10 days preceding an episode of respiratory infection. [After Stone et al. (1987)].

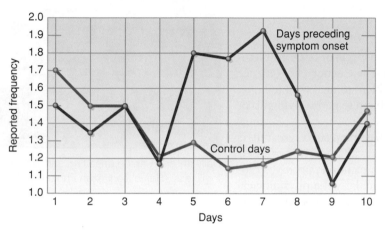

Figure 7.3   Mean number of undesirable events in the 10 days preceding an episode of respiratory infection. [After Stone et al. (1987).]

Researchers have found that changes in the frequency of daily life events precede the onset of episodes of respiratory infection. The mechanism may be a stress-induced lowering of sIgA. (Michael P. Gadomski/Photo Researchers.)

the assessment period. Next, they examined the daily frequency of undesirable and desirable events during a period of 1 to 10 days before the start of an episode. For each person, they also selected a set of control days without an episode, matching that set to the days examined before the start of an episode, to control for the higher ratio of desirable versus undesirable events typically reported on weekends. Results of this analysis are shown in Figure 7.2 and Figure 7.3. As expected, prior to the onset of illness, there were significant decreases in the number of desirable events and significant increases in the number of undesirable events.

These results, which have been replicated (Evans & Edgerton, 1990), were the first to show a relationship between life events and health with both factors measured daily over a period of several days. By carefully controlling for relevant factors, this study lets us come much closer to asserting with confidence that negative life events can make people more vulnerable to episodes of infectious illness.

One of the most revealing aspects of the pattern of events preceding illness in this study is that there was a peak in undesirable events and a trough in desirable ones several days prior to onset, yet the 2 days just before onset had average rates of both types of events. Thus, it is unlikely that the results were caused by individuals' feeling poorly long before actually getting sick, which might influence their perception of events; that is, a bias like this would undoubtedly show up also during the 2 days just prior to illness.

Studies Using the COPE Scale   The relationship between health and ways of coping is most often assessed by means of questionnaires that ask respondents to indicate how much they used various ways of coping to handle a recent stressor. One such measure, the COPE (Coping Orientations to Problems Experienced) scale, is presented in Table 7.1.

As with the relationship between stress and health, the best way to examine links between coping and health is by means of longitudinal study. Breast cancer, which strikes about one woman in nine and is the second most deadly cancer among women (behind lung cancer), has been investigated in this way. Breast cancer is a major stressor on many levels: it is life-threatening; surgical interventions are often disfiguring and thus have serious implications for psychological well-being; and both radiation therapy and chemotherapy often have very unpleasant side effects.

In one study, the coping methods of women who had just been diagnosed with breast cancer were assessed several times during the year following the diagnosis (Carver et al., 1993). Women who accepted their diagnosis and retained a sense of humor had lower levels of distress. Avoidant coping methods, such as denial and behavioral disengagement (see Table 7.1), were associated with higher levels of distress, and this negative relationship between denial and adjustment to breast cancer has been replicated (Heim, Valach, & Schaffner, 1997). Another longitudinal study of several types of cancer found that avoidant coping ("I try not to think about it") predicted greater progression of the disease at a 1-year follow-up (Epping-Jordan, Compas, & Howell, 1994). These results show that how a person reacts to a stressor is as crucial as the stressor itself in predicting its physical and emotional effects. In the case of cancer, reducing stress by ignoring the problem is not a good idea.

Social Support and Health

In the discussions so far, we have shown that life events are related to the onset and course of illness, but important questions remain. We have already noted that the same life experience apparently can have different effects on different people. This raises the possibility that other factors, too, can moderate the general stress–illness relationship. One such factor that can significantly reduce the negative effects of stress is social support.

There are various types of social support. **Structural social support** refers to a person's basic network of social relationships, which includes such factors as marital status and number of friends. **Functional social support** refers more to the quality of a person's relationships—for example, whether the person believes he or she can call on friends in a time of need (Cohen & Wills, 1985).

Structural support is a well-established predictor of mortality. People with few friends or relatives tend to have a higher mortality rate than those with a higher level of structural support (Kaplan et al., 1994). Similarly, unmarried people have a higher mortality rate than married people, and this is particularly true for men (N. J. Johnson et al., 2000). In one study, people with more diverse social networks were found to be less likely to develop a cold following exposure to a virus (S. Cohen et al., 1997). Higher levels of functional support have been found to be related to lower rates of atherosclerosis (clogging of the arteries) (Seeman & Syme, 1987), to an increased ability among women to adjust to chronic rheumatoid arthritis (Goodenow, Reisine, & Grady, 1990), and to less distress among women following surgery for breast cancer (Alferi et al., 2001).

How does social support exert its beneficial effects? One possibility is that people with higher levels of social support are more likely to have healthy lifestyles—for example, eating right, not smoking, and not drinking alcohol to excess. Another possibility is that social support (or the lack of it) could have a direct effect on physiological processes (Uchino, Cacioppo, & Kiecolt-Glaser, 1996). For example, low levels of social support are related to an increase in negative emotions (Kessler & McLeod, 1985), which may affect some hormone levels and the immune system (Cohen et al., 1997; Kiecolt-Glaser et al., 1984). In fact, both psychological and physiological mechanisms are at work, and theories that take both into account are able to account for the link between social support and health most completely. For example, research on the relationship between marriage and health has suggested that social support can affect health by impacting the married couple's relationship and each partner's emotions, cognitions, and physiology.

Social support has also been studied in the laboratory, where cause and effect can be more readily established than is possible in the naturalistic studies already described. In one such study, college-aged women were required to complete a challenging task while experiencing high or low stress with or without social support (Kamarck, Annunziato, & Amateau, 1995). Stress was created by having the experimenter behave coldly and impersonally as she told the women to improve their performance on the task. Social support was created by having a close friend "silently cheer on" each woman while sitting close to her and placing a hand on her wrist. The researchers measured each woman's blood pressure while she performed the task. As Figure 7.4 shows, high stress led to higher blood pressure, but this effect was much greater in women who experienced the stress alone, without social support. This shows that social support can have a causal effect on a physiological process. Subsequent research indicated that such results were produced only when the support came from a friend, and not when it came from a stranger (Christenfeld et al., 1997), but further research showed that support from a female stranger can in fact produce the blood-pressure benefits for both men and women, whereas support from a male stranger has no effect (Glynn, Christenfeld, & Gerin, 1999). Apparently, the presence of either a friend or a nonfriend female, but not a nonfriend male, can lead both men and women to appraise a stressful situation as less threatening.

A recent review of a number of laboratory studies of marital conflict discussions concluded that these interactions, which are full of negative emotions and cognitions, have a negative impact on cardiovascular reactivity, the immune system, and the endocrine system (Robles & Kiecolt-Glaser, 2004). These short-term psychological and physiological effects of marital conflict have prospectively predicted cardiovascular and

Table 7.1 Scales and Sample Items from the COPE

Active Coping
I've been concentrating my efforts on doing something about the situation I'm in.

Suppression of Competing Activities
I've been putting aside other activities in order to concentrate on this.

Planning
I've been trying to come up with a strategy about what to do.

Restraint
I've been making sure not to make matters worse by acting too soon.

Use of Social Support
I've been getting sympathy and understanding from someone.

Positive Reframing
I've been looking for something good in what is happening.

Religion
I've been putting my trust in God.

Acceptance
I've been accepting the reality of the fact that it happened.

Denial
I've been refusing to believe that it has happened.

Behavioral Disengagement
I've been giving up the attempt to cope.

Use of Humor
I've been making jokes about it.

Self-Distraction
I've been going to movies, watching TV, or reading, to think about it less.

Source: From Carver et al., 1993.

Figure 7.4 Stress led to increased blood pressure, but less so for people who experienced the stressor with a friend. DBP, diastolic blood pressure; SBP, systolic blood pressure. [From Kamarck et al. (1995).]

Seeking comfort or social support from others is an example of emotion-focused coping. (Bruce Ayers/Stone/Getty Images.)

blood-pressure dysregulation (Baker et al., 2000) and divorce (Kiecolt-Glaser et al., 2003).

A possible neurobiological mechanism for the stress-reducing effects of social support is suggested by some research with animals. A hormone called oxytocin, which is released during social interaction, decreases activity of the sympathetic nervous system and promotes relaxation, perhaps thereby lessening the physiological effects of a stressor (Carter, DeVries, & Getz, 1995; Uvnas-Moberg, 1997, 1999). Although oxytocin is released during stress in both male and female animals, evidence suggests that this response is even greater among females (Jezova et al., 1996).

Not all research has found that social support has positive effects. With very severe stressors the person may be so overwhelmed that support does no good. This point was well made in a study of social support and breast cancer, in which social support did not lead to reduced distress or less physical impairment (Bolger et al., 1996).

Check Your Knowledge 7.1

Multiple choice.
1. Which of the following describes the phases of Selye's general adaptation syndrome:
   a. Alarm, resistance, exhaustion
   b. Alarm, adapt, change
   c. Stress, react, move on
   d. Stress, resist, adapt
2. Problem-focused coping differs from emotion-focused in that:
   a. Problem-focused coping emphasizes reducing emotions problems cause; emotion-focused coping emphasizes acting on emotions, particularly negative emotions.
   b. Problem-focused coping emphasizes taking action to solve a problem; emotion-focused coping emphasizes reducing negative feelings.
   c. Both are forms of structural social support.
   d. None of the above.
3. Which of the following statements is incorrect regarding the relationship between social support and health?
   a. People with social support may do more healthy behaviors.
   b. Social support may buffer against negative emotions, which can influence the immune system.
   c. Social support is not always beneficial.
   d. All of the above are correct.

Theories of the Stress–Illness Link

In considering the etiology of psychophysiological disorders, we are confronted with three questions:

1. Why does stress produce illness in only some people who are exposed to it?
2. Why does stress sometimes cause a psychophysiological disorder and not a psychological disorder?
3. When stress produces a psychophysiological disorder, what determines the disorder produced?

Theories in this domain are invariably diathesis–stress in nature—that is, theories that focus on individual vulnerabilities to stress. They differ primarily in whether the diatheses are described in psychological or biological terms. However, most theories involve both psychological and biological factors, and our descriptions of these theories should not be construed as implying that they are incompatible with one another.

A persistent problem with much of the research on the etiology of psychophysiological disorders is that it has attempted to link stress to *self-reports* of illness, and as we have already noted, self-reports may not always be accurate. For example, an extensive review of the literature concluded that an apparent association between negative emotional states and health was actually only a relationship between negative emotions and illness reporting (Watson & Pennebaker, 1989). Another study similarly noted that neuroticism predicted reports of higher numbers of somatic complaints of all kinds (recall our discussion of hypochondriasis and somatization disorder) but did not predict "hard endpoints," such as death or verified coronary artery disease (Stone and Costa, 1990). Because of such problems, we will focus mainly on research that includes more than self-reports of illness.

In addition, the effects of stress are probably indirect. For example, stress may lead to health changes that are not directly due to biological or psychological factors but to changes in health-related behaviors. High stress may result in increased smoking, disrupted sleep, increased alcohol consumption, and altered diet (the opposite of what we saw with social support). These behavioral changes may then increase the risk of illness. For example, low socioeconomic status (often thought of as a stressor) has been shown to be related to greater mortality from several diseases, and this relationship is accounted for by a higher incidence among poor people of such behaviors as smoking and excessive use of alcohol (Lynch et al., 1996). In addition, high stress may result in changes in cardiovascular reactivity to stress or in changes in the immune system, such as an increase in cytokine production (see p. 197). These physiological changes may then increase the risk of illness. Thus, the stress–illness association is real but is likely to be mediated through changes in health behaviors or in physiology rather than to be a direct effect of stress.

Theories That Focus on Biological Factors

Biological responses are a healthy and regular part of responding to stress. It is only when biological responses to stress are continuously activated or when other biological processes do not bring the body's systems back to their pre-stress levels within a reasonable amount of time that physiological damage can occur. The major biological responses to stress involve activation of the sympathetic nervous system and the HPA axis (see Figure 2.10, p. 42).

In this section, we discuss theories that attribute particular psychophysiological disorders mainly to biological factors. The factors focused on in such theories have included specific organ weaknesses and an overactivity of particular organ systems in responding to stress. An organ-weakness theory would posit that prior illnesses, poor diet, and the like could disrupt a particular organ system, making it weak and vulnerable to stress—for instance, a congenitally weak respiratory system might predispose the individual to develop asthma after stress. By contrast, a theory involving overactivity of particular organ systems would hold that individuals respond to stress in idiosyncratic ways, and the individual's most responsive organ system becomes a likely candidate for the locus of a subsequent psychophysiological disorder—for example, someone whose circulatory system is highly reactive to stress (manifested as elevated blood pressure) may be more susceptible to essential hypertension.

More recent theories about the ways in which stress impacts health take more specific factors into consideration, such as different kinds of stressors and differences among individuals' responses to stress, appraisals of stressful situations, and perceptions of control (Kemeny, 2003). We will discuss two biological systems that have been the focus of much research—stress hormones (the endocrine system) and the immune system. Before we begin, however, we should note that these systems do not respond to stress in isolation—indeed, we now know that the autonomic nervous system, the endocrine system, and the immune system all impact one another. We present research about them separately here for ease of explanation, not because they are separate or independent biological responses to stress.

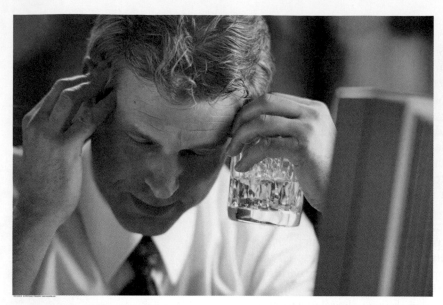

Stress may indirectly increase the risk of illness by causing people to engage in behaviors such as increased consumption of alcohol. (MTPA Stock/Masterfile.)

Allostatic Load: Prolonged Exposure to Stress Hormones   The body pays a price if it must constantly adapt to stress, and this price can be expressed in terms of what is referred to as **allostatic load**. For example, if the body is exposed to high levels of stress hormones such as cortisol and becomes susceptible to disease because of altered immune system functioning, we can view this as an effect of a high allostatic load. Furthermore, high levels of cortisol can have direct effects on the brain—for example, by damaging cells in the hippocampus, which regulates the secretion of cortisol. The result may be that, over time, the allostatic load makes the person even more susceptible to the effects of stress.

Individuals can manifest allostatic load in different ways (McEwen & Seeman, 1999). Some people may have high levels of stress hormones simply because they experience frequent stress, whereas high levels in other people may be due to some difficulty in adapting to stress. For example, some people may have a genetically slow-to-adapt biological stress reaction. Other people may have learned behaviors that interfere with adaptation (such as poor eating habits, too little exercise, smoking, and excessive alcohol consumption), or some combination of factors. Still others may have trouble "shutting down" the biological stress response (e.g., they may exhibit an unusually high level of cortisol secretion even after the stress has abated). And some may have a weakened biological stress response, reflected by low levels of cortisol release in response to stress, which in turn causes other parts of the immune system to overrespond.

A real-world example of the way in which stress can interfere with our biological systems involves public speaking. Most people react to the stress of public speaking with an increase in cortisol secretion. After repeated exposure to such a stress (i.e., many public speaking experiences), most people adapt to the stress, and the amount of cortisol secreted declines. However, about 10 percent of people show no adaptation and even increase their secretion of cortisol (Kirschbaum, Prussner, & Stone, 1995), and these are the individuals at risk for health problems. A study measuring the presumed effects of allostatic load on the body (e.g., elevated blood pressure, cholesterol levels, and cortisol secretion) found that higher allostatic load effects predicted greater risk for cardiovascular disease 2 1/2 years later (Seeman et al., 1997).

Stress and the Immune System   Stressors have multiple effects on the body—on the autonomic nervous system, on hormone levels, and on brain activity. One major area of current interest is the immune system, which is an important consideration in infectious diseases, cancer, and allergies as well as in autoimmune diseases, such as rheumatoid arthritis, in which the immune system attacks the body. The field that studies how psychological factors impact the immune system is called **psychoneuroimmunology**. Recent reviews of nearly 300 studies confirmed that a wide range of stressors produce problematic changes in the immune system, including medical-school examinations, depression and bereavement, marital discord and divorce, job loss, caring for a relative with Alzheimer's disease, and the Three Mile Island nuclear disaster, among others (Kiecolt-Glaser et al., 2002; Segerstrom & Miller, 2004).

In the past 10 years, much progress has been made toward answering a key question: whether such immune-system changes are great enough to actually increase the risk of disease, leading to outcomes such as early death from cancer or the onset of arthritis. For example, we now know that stress-induced changes to the immune system can hasten the progression of AIDS (see the more detailed discussion later in this chapter). Recent studies that examine the body's response to different types of vaccines (e.g., flu and herpes vaccines) show that people exposed to stress are slower to develop antibodies in response to vaccines than those not exposed to stress. This slower response could increase the chance of illness. In addition, exposure to stress also slows the process of wound healing, which relies on the immune system (Kiecolt-Glaser et al., 2002). Across a number of studies, age appears to be a factor—that is, older adults are more likely than younger adults to show a deleterious immune response to stress.

Brief Overview of the Immune System   The immune system involves a broad array of cells and proteins that respond when the body is infected or invaded. A useful way of thinking about the immune system is to consider two broad types of immunity, natural and specific (Segerstrom & Miller, 2004).

Natural immunity is the body's first and quickest line of defense against infectious microorganisms or other invaders. A number of

Figure 7.5   Components of the immune system.

different cells, such as macrophages and natural killer cells, are unleashed on the invaders and begin to destroy them. Inflammation or swelling is a sign of these natural immunity cells at work. Activation of macrophages in turn stimulates the release of substances called **cytokines**, which help initiate such bodily responses to infection as fatigue, fever, and activation of the HPA axis. Although unpleasant, fever is actually a sign that the body is responding as it should to an infection.

Specific immunity involves cells that respond more slowly to infection, such as lymphocytes, which are involved in responding to specific pathogens or invading agents. Lymphocytes include T-helper cells and B cells. T-helper cells promote the release of cytokines; B cells release antibodies that deal with specific pathogens.

Figure 7.5 shows the components of the immune system. In the following sections, we illustrate the role of stress and immune system changes in infectious diseases by discussing two components of specific immunity—secretory immunity and cytokines—in some detail.

Secretory Immunity   The secretory component of the immune system exists in the secretions that bathe the mucosal surfaces of the body—that is, in tears and saliva and in gastrointestinal, vaginal, nasal, and bronchial secretions. The antibodies produced by this component prevent viruses and bacteria from infecting mucosal tissues.

An antibody called **secretory immunoglobulin A (sIgA)** has been fairly well studied with regard to the relationship between changes in the number of sIgA antibodies and changes in mood. In a study conducted over an 8-week period, a group of dental students came to the laboratory three times a week to have their saliva collected and to undergo a brief psychological assessment (Stone, Cox et al., 1987). On days when the assessment indicated that the students were experiencing relatively high levels of negative mood, fewer sIgA antibodies were present in their saliva than on days when the students had low levels of negative mood. Similarly, antibody levels were higher on days with higher levels of positive mood. Importantly, this link between mood and levels of sIgA antibodies has been replicated (Stone et al., 1994).

These studies let us postulate the following mechanism by which stress could increase a person's risk of infection. Research has shown that daily events affect mood (Stone & Neale, 1984). An increased number of negative daily events and a decreased number of positive events could put a person in a negative mood. This negative mood could then be reflected in lower numbers of sIgA antibodies. And lower levels of these antibodies could increase the person's risk of infection if exposed to a virus or other pathogen (see Figure 7.6).

Figure 7.6 Mechanism through which stress could increase the risk of viral infection.

Several studies have confirmed that there is indeed a relationship between stress and respiratory infection. In each of them, volunteers took nasal drops containing a mild cold virus and also completed a battery of measures of recent stress. The advantage of this method was that exposure to the virus was under experimental control. Researchers found that stress was clearly linked to developing a cold (Cohen, Tyrell, & Smith, 1991; Stone et al., 1992) and that the stressors most often implicated were interpersonal problems and work difficulties (Cohen et al., 1998). These findings illustrate the complex interplay between psychological and biological factors in the etiology of psychophysiological disorders.

Cytokines   Evidence indicates that stress can trigger the release of cytokines such as interleukin-1 and interleukin-6, as if the body were fighting off an infection (Maier & Watkins, 1998). Why is this important for health? **Interleukin-6 (IL-6)** is often called a pro-inflammatory cytokine because it promotes inflammation in response to infection. Inflammation and higher levels of IL-6 have been linked to a number of diseases in older adults, such as coronary heart disease, arthritis, multiple myeloma, non-Hodgkin's lymphoma, osteoporosis, and type 2 diabetes. Thus, if stress increases the release of IL-6, the impact on health is likely to be negative.

Theories That Focus on Psychological Factors

Psychological theories try to account for the development of psychophysiological disorders by focusing on such factors as unconscious emotional states, personality traits, cognitive appraisals, and specific styles of coping with stress. Like the biological theories discussed above, most of these theories integrate psychological and biological factors.

Psychoanalytic Theories   Psychoanalytic theories propose that specific conflicts and their associated negative emotional states give rise to psychophysiological disorders. Of the psychoanalytic theorists who have studied psychophysiological disorders, Franz Alexander has had the greatest impact. In his view, undischarged hostile impulses create the chronic negative emotional state that impacts health.

> *The damming up of hostile impulses will continue and will consequently increase in intensity. This will induce the development of stronger defensive measures in order to keep pent-up aggressions in check. Because of the marked degree of their inhibitions, these patients are less effective in their occupational activities and for that reason tend to fail in competition with others . . . envy is stimulated and hostile feelings toward more successful, less inhibited competitors are further intensified. (Alexander, 1950, p. 150)*

Alexander formulated this theory of unexpressed-anger, or **anger-in theory**, on the basis of his observations of patients undergoing psychoanalysis. Although this theory has not received much empirical support per se, the role of anger expression as a psychological factor in essential hypertension and coronary heart disease continues to be investigated, as discussed in the sections below on those disorders.

The Role of Cognition and Personality   We experience stress in relation to a wide variety of conditions and situations. Physical threats obviously create stress, but so do negative emotions such as resentment, regret, and worry, which often do not easily pass and which cannot be fought against or escaped from as readily as can physical threats. Negative emotions stimulate sympathetic nervous system activity and may keep the body's stress systems aroused and the body in a continual state of emergency, sometimes for far longer than it can bear, as suggested by the notion of allostatic load. The higher mental capacities that have evolved in humans create the potential for distressing thoughts and the resulting negative emotions, which can subject our bodies to physical storms they were not built to withstand.

In our general discussion of stress, we saw that the appraisal of a potential stressor is central to how it affects the person. People who continually appraise life events and experiences as exceeding their resources may be chronically stressed and at risk for the development of a psychophysiological disorder. We have also seen that how people cope with stress can be relevant. In addition, personality traits are implicated in several disorders, most notably cardiovascular disease. People who chronically experience high levels of negative emotions are at increased risk for the development of heart problems.

Personality traits have also been linked to immune system functioning. For example, the predisposition to experience negative emotions has been linked to slowed antibody production following a flu vaccine (Rosenkranz et al., 2003). In a study of first-year law school students, optimism predicted better mood and a stronger immune system (Segerstrom et al., 1998). This link between optimism and immune functioning was mediated in part by students' cognitive appraisals of stress—that is, optimistic students appraised law school as less aversive than did nonoptimistic students, which presumably made school less stressful and led to better immune system functioning.

Quick Summary

Psychophysiological disorders are disorders with genuine physical symptoms that can be caused or worsened by psychological factors. DSM-IV-TR covers such disorders under "psychological factors affecting medical condition," which can be applied to just about any illness. The fields of health psychology and behavioral medicine are dedicated to the study of how psychological factors and associated stress impact health.

Stress can be viewed as a response to a stimulus or as the stimulus itself, but neither view is without problems. Different people experience different degrees of stress in relation to the same stimuli. These differences relate to ways in which people perceive or appraise events and to people's coping styles, some of which are beneficial for health whereas others are not. Longitudinal studies using the Assessment of Daily Experience have shown a link between stress and respiratory infections, and longitudinal studies using the COPE scale have shown a link between coping styles and breast cancer. People with structural social support have better health, and much research is aimed at understanding why this is so.

Theories about the ways in which stress impacts health are diathesis–stress theories that involve both psychological and biological factors. One biological factor is the allostatic load that results when stress results in high levels of stress hormones. Some people may have high levels of stress hormones because they experience frequent stress, whereas high levels in other people may be due to some difficulty in adapting to stress. Another biological factor is the effect of stress on the immune system. The field that studies how psychological factors impact the immune system is called psychoneuroimmunology. A wide range of stressors produce problematic changes in the immune system, and this can impact disease, for example, in hastening the progression of AIDS. Cytokines help initiate such bodily responses to infection as fatigue, fever, and activation of the HPA axis. Inflammation and higher levels of the cytokine IL-6 have been linked to a number of diseases in older adults. Fewer sIgA antibodies are associated with negative mood and these two factors could increase the risk for infection. Psychological factors can include unexpressed anger and high levels of negative emotions, both of which can increase stress, and optimism, which then can reduce stress.

Check Your Knowledge 7.2

True or false?
1. Allostatic load refers to the body's need to adapt to stress.
2. The body's first line of defense against infection involves lymphocytes.
3. Cytokines may mediate the relationship between stress and illness.
4. Anger-in refers to expressing the experience of anger.

Cardiovascular Disorders

Cardiovascular disorders (collectively referred to as "cardiovascular disease") are diseases involving the heart and blood-circulation system. Cardiovascular disease accounts for almost half the deaths in the United States each year, is one of the leading killers of men and women from all ethnicities, and affects nearly 65 million Americans. In 2001, it accounted for 1 of every 2.6 deaths in the United States. In 2004, the estimated costs associated with cardiovascular disease, including health care and reductions in productivity, amounted to $368.4 billion dollars (American Heart Association, 2004).

In this section we focus on two forms of cardiovascular disease that appear to be adversely affected by stress—essential hypertension and coronary heart disease. Of all the cardiovascular disorders, coronary heart disease causes the greatest number of deaths. Experts generally agree that many of the deaths resulting from cardiovascular disorders could be prevented or delayed by dealing with known risk factors, many of which are behavioral in nature.

Essential Hypertension

Hypertension, commonly called high blood pressure, increases the risk of atherosclerosis (clogging of the arteries), heart attacks, and strokes; it can also cause death through kidney failure. Hypertension without an evident biological cause is called **essential hypertension** (or sometimes *primary hypertension*), and no more than 10 percent of all cases of hypertension in the United States have an evident biological cause—thus, essential hypertension accounts for about 90 percent of all cases. According to recent estimates, varying degrees of hypertension are found in about 20 percent of the adult population of the United States; it is twice as frequent in African-Americans as in whites. As many as 10 percent of American college students have hypertension, and most of them are unaware of their illness. Around the world, hypertension affects between 25 and 33 percent of the adult population (Kearney et al., 2004). People who do not have their blood pressure checked may go for years without knowing that they are hypertensive, which is why this disease is known as the silent killer.

Clinical Description   Blood pressure is measured by two numbers, one for systolic pressure (arterial pressure when the ventricles contract and the heart is pumping) and the other for diastolic pressure (arterial pressure when the ventricles relax and the heart is resting). Normal blood pressure in a young adult is about 120 (systolic) over about 80 (diastolic). High blood pressure is defined as 140 or higher (systolic) over 90 or higher (diastolic).

Etiology   Essential hypertension is viewed as a heterogeneous condition—that is, a condition brought on by some combination of the many possible disturbances in bodily systems responsible for regulating blood pressure. Such risk factors for hypertension include genes, which play a substantial role in blood pressure; obesity; excessive intake of alcohol; and excessive salt consumption. In addition, blood pressure may be elevated by increased cardiac output (the amount of blood leaving the left ventricle of the heart), by increased resistance to the passage of blood through the arteries (vasoconstriction), or by both. The physiological mechanisms that regulate blood pressure interact in an extremely complex manner—activation of the sympathetic nervous system is a key factor, but hormones, salt metabolism, and central nervous system mechanisms are all involved—and many of these physiological mechanisms can be affected by psychological stress. Over the long term, according to current thinking, frequent elevations in blood pressure lead the arterial walls to thicken, resulting in sustained hypertension (National Heart, Lung, and Blood Institute, 1998).

The Role of Psychological Stress   Various stressful real-world conditions have been examined to determine their role in the etiology of essential hypertension. Stressful interviews, natural disasters such as earthquakes, and job stress have all been found to produce short-term elevations in blood pressure (Niedhammer et al., 1998).

It is also relatively easy to produce increased blood pressure in the laboratory. The induction of various emotional states, such as anger, fear, and sadness, increases blood pressure (Caccioppo et al., 1998). Similarly, challenging tasks such as mental arithmetic, mirror drawing, putting a hand in ice water (known as the cold pressor test), and giving a speech in front of an audience all lead to increased blood pressure (Manuck, Kaplan, & Clarkson, 1983; Tuomisto, 1997). A classic series of studies used a reaction-time task in which participants were told that they would receive an electric shock if they did not respond quickly enough but that good performance would lead to a monetary reward (Obrist et al., 1978). This reaction-time task yielded significant increases in both heart rate and systolic blood pressure.

For ethical reasons, no experimental work has been done with human beings to determine whether short-term increases in blood pressure will develop into prolonged hypertension and actual structural changes in the cardiovascular system. In research done on animals, sustained hypertension has proved difficult to induce. In many studies using electric shock as a stressor, blood pressure increased during the period when the animal was stressed but returned to normal when the stressor was removed. Studies that have used more natural stressors, such as competing with other animals for food (Peters, 1977), have proved somewhat more successful in producing long-term blood-pressure elevations. But the overall picture indicates that some predisposing factor or factors, such as the activation of the sympathetic nervous system by anger, are required if stress is to bring on essential hypertension.

Although the results from laboratory studies are interesting, ultimately we must understand blood-pressure increases in people's natural environments. Therefore, researchers have also undertaken studies of ambulatory blood pressure, wherein participants wear a blood-pressure cuff that takes readings as they go about their daily lives. Many of these studies have asked participants about their emotional state at the time a blood-pressure reading is taken. The general finding has been that both positive and negative emotional states are associated with higher blood pressure (Jacob et al., 1999; Kamarck et al., 1998). There is also some indication that anger is the negative emotion most strongly linked to elevated blood pressure (Faber & Burns, 1996; Schwartz, Warren, & Pickering, 1994).

Other ambulatory monitoring studies have examined environmental conditions associated with blood pressure. For example, a series of studies examined the effects of stress on blood pressure among paramedics (Shapiro, Jamner, & Goldstein, 1993). In one of these analyses, ambulance calls were divided into high- and low-stress types. As expected, the high-stress calls

In a study of paramedics, high-stress ambulance calls, as when the victim had to be revived, led to greater blood pressure increases than low-stress calls. (Bruce Ayres/Stone/Getty Images.)

were associated with higher blood pressure. Even more interesting were the results when the paramedics were divided into groups on the basis of personality-test measures of anger and defensiveness. The groups did not differ in blood pressure during the low-stress calls. However, during the high-stress calls, paramedics high in anger and defensiveness had higher blood pressure. In another study, participants rated job strain each time blood-pressure readings were taken (Kamarck et al., 1998). Blood pressure was lower at times when participants felt in control of their work environment—for example, when they felt they could exercise choice over what they were working on. Still another ambulatory blood pressure study found that, for women, the combination of job strain and family responsibilities was associated with increases in systolic and diastolic blood pressure (Brisson et al., 1999).

In the ambulatory monitoring studies just described, the overall amount of blood-pressure increase associated with emotional states or environmental conditions was rather small. But it was also consistently found that a subset of participants had large increases,

Among men, the expression of anger has been linked to coronary heart disease. (Stone/Getty Images.)

One characteristic of the Type-A behavior pattern is feeling under time pressure and consequently trying to do several things at once. (Claudia Kunin/Stone/Getty Images.)

suggesting that only people who have some predisposition, or diathesis, will experience large blood-pressure increases that over time may lead to sustained hypertension. Next, we discuss three possible diatheses, including anger, the Type A behavior pattern, and cardiovascular reactivity.

Anger   Anger per se is not bad for our cardiovascular health; rather, it is excessive or inappropriate anger that is linked to ill health (Mayne, 2001). What is less clear is the relative importance of different aspects of anger: becoming angry easily, becoming angry and not expressing it, or having a cynical or suspicious attitude toward others. Recent research has not totally resolved this issue, but the evidence suggests that being easily angered may be the most important factor (e.g., Raikkonen et al., 1999).

Complicating the picture further, anger may function differently in men and women, depending on the situation. With respect to cardiovascular health, expressing anger has been related to increased blood-pressure reactivity in men, whereas suppressing anger has been linked to increased blood-pressure reactivity in women (Faber & Burns, 1996; Shapiro, Goldstein, & Jamner, 1995). Sex differences have also been found in the relationship between becoming angry easily and ambulatory blood pressure. Among men, but not among women, this trait is related to higher blood pressure (Guyll & Contrada, 1998). We return to this issue in our discussion of myocardial infarction (see p. 205).

Type A Behavior Pattern   In 1958, two cardiologists, Meyer Friedman and Ray Rosenman, identified a behavior pattern called **Type A behavior pattern** (Friedman, 1969; Rosenman et al., 1975). A structured interview identifies three components of the Type A behavior pattern. *Achievement striving/competitiveness* characterizes someone with an intense and competitive drive for achievement and advancement. *Time urgency/impatience* characterizes someone with an exaggerated sense of urgency—of time passing and of the need to hurry. *Hostility* captures someone who exhibits considerable aggressiveness and hostility toward others. The Type A behavior pattern has been most often studied as a risk factor for coronary heart disease, but it has also been examined as a predisposing factor for hypertension.

A large, prospective, and longitudinal study called the Coronary Artery Risk Development in Young Adults Study (CARDIA) examined whether the three components of Type A could predict the development of hypertension among black and white men and women. The study began in 1985 with over 5,000 participants between the ages of 18 and 30. Fifteen years later, a team of investigators examined Type A and hypertension among 3,308 of these original participants (Yan et al., 2003). They found that the time urgency/impatience and hostility components from the Type A structured interview predicted a twofold increase in risk of developing hypertension. The findings for time urgency/impatience were stronger for men than women; the findings for hostility were just about equally strong for both men and women. Achievement striving/competitiveness was a predictor of later hypertension for white men only. These findings provide strong support for the role of psychological factors like these in hypertension.

Cardiovascular Reactivity   In the past 15 years or so there has been a great deal of interest in cardiovascular reactivity as a risk factor for hypertension (and coronary heart disease as well). *Cardiovascular reactivity* refers to the extent to which blood pressure and heart rate increase in response to stress. Typically, researchers assess cardiovascular reactivity to a laboratory stressor (or, even better, a battery of stressors) among people who are not currently hypertensive and then assess the participants again some years later to determine whether the reactivity measure (usually, the amount by which the stressor causes change from a baseline condition) predicts blood pressure.

In one study, cardiovascular reactivity was measured while participants performed a laboratory reaction-time task in which they were threatened with shock if their responses were slow (Light et al., 1992). A follow-up 10 to 15 years later found that heart-rate reactivity was the strongest predictor of blood pressure. Importantly, these reactivity measures predicted subsequent blood pressure over and above the contribution of standard clinical predictors such as family history of hypertension. Other research has shown that cardiovascular reactivity is related to other known risk factors for hypertension, such as socioeconomic status and race (Gump, Matthews, & Räikkönen, 1999; Jackson et al., 1999).

These findings concern levels of blood pressure but not the actual disease of hypertension. A different study entailed a 4-year follow-up of 508 Finnish men whose blood-pressure reactivity had been assessed as they anticipated a bicycle exercise test (Everson et al., 1996). Men whose systolic blood pressure increased by 30 points or more were almost four times more likely to have developed hypertension 4 years later. One limitation of this study is that reactivity was assessed in an unusual situation. Thus, we can't be sure that the results would generalize to the more usual tests that have been used to assess reactivity.

Further support for the importance of cardiovascular reactivity comes from high-risk research comparing individuals with and without a family history of hypertension (Adler & Ditto, 1998; Lovallo & Al'Absi, 1998). People with such a history show greater blood-pressure reactivity to various stressors. Coupled with research showing the heritability of hypertension, these findings suggest that blood-pressure reactivity is a good candidate for a genetically transmitted diathesis. But what exactly is inherited?

Research has focused on genes linked to the neurotransmitter serotonin. This evidence suggests that individuals with one or two long alleles in the promoter region of the serotonin transporter gene (see Chapter 2, p. 34) show greater cardiovascular reactivity in response to tasks involving mental arithmetic (R. B. Williams et al., 2001) and are at greater risk for myocardial infarction (Fumeron et al., 2002). Needed next are studies that examine how stress interacts with the presence of a long allele on this gene. This type of work has been done for depression: recall from our discussions in Chapter 2 that having one or two *short* alleles in this gene was associated with an increased risk of depression, but only among those individuals who had experienced early life stress.

Coronary Heart Disease

Coronary heart disease (CHD) takes two principal forms, angina pectoris and myocardial infarction, or heart attack.

Clinical Description   The symptoms of **angina pectoris** are periodic chest pains, usually located behind the sternum and frequently radiating into the back and sometimes the left shoulder and arm. The major cause of these severe attacks of pain is an insufficient supply of oxygen to the heart, called *ischemia*, which in turn is due to coronary atherosclerosis, a narrowing or plugging of the coronary arteries by deposits of cholesterol, a fatty material, or to constriction of these blood vessels. In many patients with coronary artery disease, episodes of ischemia do not cause pain, so these are called episodes of silent ischemia. Both angina and episodes of silent ischemia are precipitated by physical exertion or emotional stress and are commonly relieved by rest or medication. Angina and silent ischemia rarely result in serious physical damage to the heart, because blood flow to the heart is reduced but not cut off. If, however, the narrowing of one or more coronary arteries progresses to the point of producing a total blockage, a myocardial infarction, or heart attack, is likely to occur.

Myocardial infarction is a much more serious disorder; it is the leading cause of death in the United States today. Like angina pectoris, it is caused by an insufficient supply of oxygen to the heart. But unlike angina, a heart attack usually results in permanent damage to the heart.

Etiology   Several factors increase the risk of CHD; the risk generally increases with the number and severity of these factors:

age

cigarette smoking

diabetes

elevated blood pressure

elevated serum cholesterol

excessive use of alcohol

increase in the size of the left ventricle of the heart

long-standing pattern of physical inactivity

obesity

sex (males are at greater risk)

A combination of particular risk factors has been named the **metabolic syndrome**. It is defined by the presence of a number of related metabolic factors, including abdominal obesity, insulin resistance, high blood pressure, low HDL cholesterol, and heightened inflammation as indexed by the presence of a protein called CRP (Grundy et al., 2004). Adults with the metabolic syndrome are more likely to die from CHD than those without it (Malik et al., 2004).

Although these risk factors are clearly important, they leave at least half the instances of CHD unexplained (Jenkins, 1976). Also unexplained is why, in earlier decades, the incidence of CHD and related cardiovascular diseases was much lower than now, even though people then paid less attention to risk factors such as obesity, poor exercise habits, consumption of fatty foods, and smoking than they do now. And why is the incidence of CHD relatively low in France, despite the prevalence of heavy smoking and a fat-rich diet there?

In the next three sections, we examine research on psychological and biological risk factors for CHD. As with research on the links between stress and health, this research typically involves both psychological and biological factors, and we discuss them separately only for simplicity of presentation. Psychological and biological risk factors are intertwined, and a complete explanation of the etiology of CHD must include both.

Stress and Myocardial Infarction   In the short term, physical exertion can trigger a myocardial infarction, as can episodes of anger (Mittleman et al., 1997). Acute stress is another short-term factor—the frequency of myocardial infarction, for example, increased among residents of Tel Aviv on the day of an Iraqi missile attack (NHLBI, 1998). Death from myocardial infarction did not increase following the September 11, 2001 terrorist attacks in the United States (Chi et al., 2003); however, there were almost twice as many heart arrhythmias among people who had a cardiac defibrillator implanted (Steinberg et al., 2004). Over the longer term, more chronic stressors, such as marital conflict and financial worries, are also relevant.

One of the most studied chronic stressors is job strain (Karasek, 1979), an employment situation in which the person experiences a high level of demand—too much work and too little time in which to do it—coupled with a lack of control over decision making and lack of opportunity to make full use of skills on the job.

Several studies have found that a high level of job strain is associated with increased risk for myocardial infarction. In one study, over 10,000 British civil servants were assessed for the degree of control they could exercise on their jobs. They were then followed for about 5 years to determine the incidence of CHD. As in earlier studies, more CHD was found at follow-up among workers in lower-status jobs (e.g., clerical work). This result, in turn, was related to these workers' reports of having little control on the job (Marmot et al., 1997). In a large-scale study conducted in Finland, a high level of job demands was related to the progression of atherosclerosis (Lynch, Kaplan et al., 1997) and to cardiovascular disease mortality and morbidity (Lynch, Krause et al., 1997).

Other Psychological Risk Factors   Contemporary evidence linking CHD to psychological risk factors stems from the early investigations of the Type A behavior pattern. Initial support for the idea that the Type A pattern predicts CHD came from the classic Western Collaborative Group Study (WCGS) (Rosenman et al., 1975). In this double-blind, prospective investigation, 3,154 men aged 39 to 59 were followed over a period of 8 1/2 years. Individuals who had been identified as Type A by interview were more than twice as likely to develop CHD as were Type B men (Type B behavior pattern is characterized by a less driven and less hostile way of life). Traditional risk factors, such as high levels of cholesterol, were also found to be related to CHD, but even when these factors were controlled for, Type A individuals were still twice as likely to develop CHD.

More recent research, however, has not supported the predictive utility of Type A behavior (e.g., Eaker, Pinsky, & Castelli, 1992; Orth-Gomer & Unden, 1990). There are several reasons for these conflicting results. One is that later investigators used different methods of assessing Type A (e.g., questionnaires) that may not have been adequate. Second, it became apparent that not all aspects of the Type A behavior pattern were truly related to CHD.

For example, in further analyses of the WCGS data, anger and hostility emerged as the major predictors of CHD (Hecker et al., 1988). A longitudinal study also found that difficulty controlling one's anger is related to higher rates of CHD (Kawachi et al., 1996). Anger and hostility are also related to several other variables that play a role in CHD. For example, high levels of anger and hostility are related to greater blood-pressure reactivity to stress, higher levels of cholesterol, abnormal deposits of calcium on the walls of coronary arteries, cigarette smoking and alcohol use, the metabolic syndrome among adolescents, and greater activation of platelets, which play a major role in the formation of blockages in the coronary arteries (Fredrickson et al., 2000; Iribarren et al., 2000; Räikkönen, Matthews, & Salomen, 2003; Weidner et al., 1989).

Anger and hostility may be differentially related to CHD risk for men and women. For example, researchers found that indirect expressions of anger were associated with CHD risk for women, whereas overt expressions of anger were related to CHD risk for men (Siegman et al., 2000). These findings are similar to those discussed earlier showing that expression of anger was related to increased blood-pressure reactivity in men, but the suppression of anger was related to increased blood-pressure reactivity in women (Faber & Burns, 1996; Shapiro et al., 1995).

Other findings suggest that cynicism (an approach to life that involves hostility) is an important component of the Type A behavior pattern (Almada, 1991). For example, the amount of coronary-artery blockage was especially high in Type A participants who had earlier given responses to MMPI items reflecting a cynical or hostile attitude (e.g., agreeing with the statement "Most people will use somewhat unfair means to gain profit or advantage, rather than lose it"). An earlier follow-up study of medical students who had been healthy when they took the MMPI 25 years earlier found a higher rate of CHD and death in those whose answers had indicated cynicism toward others (Barefoot, Dahlstrom, & Williams, 1983). More recently, cynicism was found to predict atherosclerosis, myocardial infarctions, and death from CHD in the large Finnish study mentioned earlier (Everson et al., 1997; Kamarck et al., 1997). Cynicism also prospectively predicted a broad array of cardiovascular disorders (angina, stroke, heart attack) among older adults, and the link between cynicism and disease was accounted for in part by the presence of the metabolic syndrome among participants (Nelson, Palmer, & Pederson, 2004).

What is not yet clear is the best way to think about these results concerning anger, hostility, and cynicism. Are they the same or different? Is one more important than another in predicting cardiovascular disease? The answers to these questions remain unanswered at this point.

Research has also examined the relationship between other negative emotions—particularly anxiety and depression—and CHD. For example, anxiety has been shown to be related to the onset of CHD in humans (Kawachi et al., 1994; Kubansky & Kawachi, 2000), and animal research has shown that inducing anxiety in animals with atherosclerosis can precipitate a heart attack (Carpeggiani & Skinner, 1991). Similarly, research has found that depression is related to the development of CHD (reviewed by Suls & Bunde, 2005).

In addition, cardiac patients who also have a depressive disorder are over five times more likely than others to die within 6 months of a heart attack (Glassman & Shapiro, 1998).

It is almost certain that these factors interact with biological factors to produce their effects on CHD. Anxiety, for example, is associated with activation of the sympathetic nervous system, which can lead to both hypertension and atherosclerosis. Research has also shown that depression is linked to a greater tendency for platelets to aggregate and thus produce obstructions in the arteries. Furthermore, depression is often associated with increases in steroidal hormones, which increase blood pressure and damage cells in arteries (Musselman, Evans, & Nemeroff, 1998).

Despite these results, it is worth noting that not all studies find that anxiety and depression predict mortality from CHD (e.g., Lane et al., 2001; Matthews et al., 1998). The reasons for inconsistencies may reflect differences in the measures used in different studies. More generally, a number of questions remain to be addressed in additional research. For example, must one have a diagnosed mood or anxiety disorder to be at risk for CHD, or is having mood or anxiety symptoms sufficient? And how severe must the symptoms be? Another set of questions concerns behavior. For example, do depressed individuals who have had a heart attack eat poorly, exercise less, smoke more, or engage in other unhealthful behaviors and thereby increase their risk for CHD?

Biological Risk Factors   Like research on hypertension, research on biological risk factors for myocardial infarction has focused on reactivity. Excessive changes in heart rate and the consequent alterations in the force with which blood is pumped through the arteries may injure them, increasing risk for a myocardial infarction. Heart-rate reactivity has been related to CHD in several research contexts. A series of experimental studies investigated monkeys who were on a special diet designed to promote atherosclerosis. On the basis of a stress test, the animals were divided into high versus low heart-rate reactors. Subsequently, the high heart-rate reactors developed twice as much atherosclerosis as did the low reactors (Kaplan et al., 1994). In another investigation by the same group, stress was experimentally created by changing the monkeys' living groups every 3 months. The type of monkeys in this study form hierarchically ordered social groups, with some animals dominant and others submissive. Thus, changing living groups stresses the animals because they are continually forced to reestablish a dominance hierarchy. In an earlier study, this manipulation had been found to promote atherosclerosis in dominant monkeys. This time, some animals were given drugs to reduce the sympathetic activation that the stress was expected to produce. Animals treated with the drugs did not show an increase in atherosclerosis.

In studies of humans, heart-rate reactivity and ischemia elicited by laboratory stressors have predicted the development of CHD (Jiang et al., 1996; Keys et al., 1971). Thus, cardiovascular reactivity is a plausible candidate for a biological diathesis, and as we have already seen, it is associated with the psychological risk factors of anger and hostility.

Interest is also growing in another possible biological factor—heart-rate variability, which is thought to provide an index of activation of the parasympathetic division of the autonomic nervous system. Parasympathetic activation can reduce excess sympathetic activity and also protects the heart from fibrillating (a state in which the muscles in the ventricles fail to contract in a coordinated manner, so that no blood is pumped out of the heart). In patients who had experienced a heart attack, higher heart-rate variability was indeed predictive of a lower death rate (NHLBI, 1998).

Check Your Knowledge 7.3

Fill in the blank.

1. _____ hypertension has no known biological cause.
2. Type A behavior pattern is linked to the disorders _____ and _____.

3. Cardiovascular reactivity is linked to changes in _____ in laboratory studies, but its link to _____ is less well established.

Asthma

Asthma, a disorder of the respiratory system (see Figure 7.7), afflicts over 30 million people in the United States (NHIS, 2003). In 2000, the economic costs of asthma in the United States, including both medical expenditures and lost productivity, amounted to $14.5 billion (NHLBI, 2001). The prevalence of asthma increased 74 percent from 1984 to 1994, but it seems to have remained stable since 1997, perhaps due to the fact that the survey is now more reliable (NHLBI, 2003). Of the over 30 million Americans with asthma, nearly one-third are children. During childhood, asthma is more common among boys than among girls. But by age 18 it becomes more prevalent in women and remains so until after age 45, when men again predominate (NHLBI, 2004). Asthma is more common among smokers, people who are obese, and people of lower socioeconomic status (Gwynn, 2004).

Clinical Case: Tom

During his childhood Tom had frequent asthma attacks. His asthma was triggered principally by pollen, and each year he went through a particularly bad period that included several trips to the emergency room of a local hospital. He also seemed to get more than his share of colds, which frequently developed into bronchitis. As he reached his teenage years, the attacks of asthma mysteriously vanished, and he was symptom free for the next 20 years. But at age 34 the attacks returned with a vengeance following a bout of pneumonia. In contrast to his childhood attacks, emotional stress now appeared to be the major precipitant. This hypothesis was confirmed when his physician asked Tom to keep a diary for 2 weeks in which he recorded how he had been feeling and what had been going on before each attack. He had four attacks over the period, three preceded by unpleasant interactions with his boss at work and one by an argument with his wife over an impending visit by her parents.

Clinical Description

In an asthma attack, the air passages in the lungs become narrowed, causing extremely labored and wheezy breathing (particularly exhalation). In addition, activity of the immune system during asthma attacks leads to inflammation of lung tissue, resulting in an increase in mucus secretion and edema (accumulation of fluid in the tissues) (Moran, 1991).

Asthma attacks occur intermittently, sometimes almost daily and sometimes separated by weeks or months, and vary in severity. For unknown reasons, attacks are most frequent in early morning hours. The frequency of attacks may increase seasonally, when certain pollens are present. The airways are not continuously blocked; rather, the respiratory system returns to normal or near normal either spontaneously or after treatment, and this differentiates asthma from chronic respiratory problems such as emphysema (Creer, 1982). Symptoms may last an hour or may continue for several hours or sometimes even for days.

For individuals with exercise-induced asthma, the attacks follow strenuous exercise. Although some athletes are debilitated by the attacks, others are able to perform at the highest level despite their asthma—for example, Jackie Joyner-Kersee, a six-time Olympic medalist in track and field.

Most often, asthma attacks begin suddenly. During an asthma attack, a person will take a longer time than normal to exhale, and whistling sounds, referred to as rales, can be detected throughout the chest. Between attacks, there may be no detectable abnormal signs when the individual is breathing normally, but forced, heavy expiration often allows the rales to be heard through a stethoscope. A severe attack is a frightening experience and may cause a panic attack (Carr, 1998, 1999), which exacerbates the asthma. People with asthma have immense difficulty getting air into and out of the lungs and feel as though they

Asthma attacks are often treated by using a nebulizer to spray a fine mist of a bronchodilator into the bronchial tubes. (Hattye Young/Photo Researchers.)

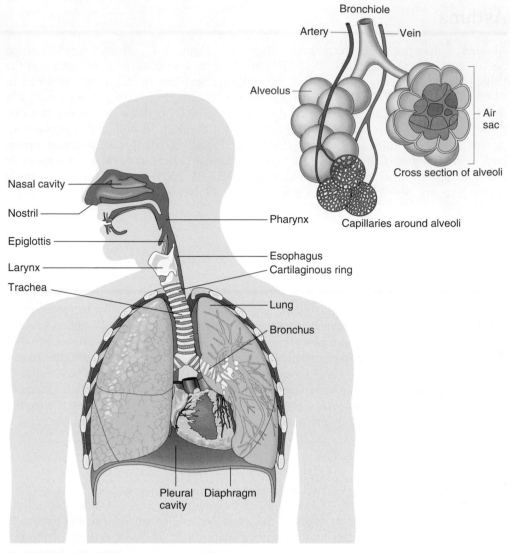

Figure 7.7 Major structures of the respiratory system—trachea, lungs, bronchi, bronchioles, and alveoli—and the ancillary organs. In asthma, the air passages, especially the bronchioles, become constricted and fluid and mucus build up in the lungs.

are suffocating; the raspy, harsh noise of the gasping, wheezing, and coughing compounds the terror. After an attack, a person may become exhausted by the exertion and fall asleep as soon as breathing is more normal.

Etiology

Asthma attacks seem to be brought on by a very wide variety of factors, including allergens, other environmental toxins, viral infections, cold, exercise, and psychological factors. Air pollution is known to be a contributing factor—for example, emergency room visits for asthma declined considerably in urban Atlanta during the 1996 Olympic games when automobile traffic was severely restricted (Friedman et al., 2001). As you will see from the discussions below, a diathesis–stress perspective seems to provide the best explanation for the etiology of asthma. That is, once the respiratory system is predisposed to asthma, any number of stressors can interact with the diathesis to produce the disease.

A now classic study divided the various possible causes into three categories: allergic, infective, and psychological (Rees, 1964). In this study, 388 asthmatic children from Cardiff, Wales, were divided into groups according to the causes of their attacks, as shown in

Table 7.2. This study also showed that the different causes of asthma varied in importance depending on the age of the individual. For asthmatic individuals younger than 5 years of age, the infective factors predominated. From ages 6 to 16 the infective factors still predominated, but psychological variables increased in importance. As is shown in the table, psychological factors were considered a dominant cause in 37 percent of the cases, and in 30 percent of the cases psychological variables were regarded as totally unimportant, a finding that strongly suggests that psychological factors do not always play a role in asthma. This study also found that 86 percent of the asthmatic individuals had had a respiratory infection before asthma developed, compared with only 30 percent of a control group, suggesting that infection may weaken the lungs, making them vulnerable to stress.

Table 7.2 Relative Importance (percent) of Allergic, Infective, and Psychological Factors in the Etiology of Asthma

Causal Factors	Dominant	Subsidiary	Unimportant
Allergic	23	13	64
Infective	38	30	32
Psychological	37	33	30

Source: From Rees, 1964.

Stressful Life Events and Negative Emotions   The importance of psychological factors in the development of asthma is a topic of debate. Psychological factors that may disturb the functioning of the respiratory system and thus bring on an asthma attack include stressful life events, anxiety, anger, depression, the tension produced by frustration, and the anticipation of pleasurable excitement. Even when asthma is originally induced by an infection or allergy, psychological stress can precipitate an attack. One prospective study asked children ages 6 to 13 and their parents to keep daily records for 18 months (Sandberg et al., 2004). The daily records consisted of asthma symptom reports and peak expiratory flow measures, which is an assessment of airway obstruction obtained by having the child take a deep breath and then exhale as hard as possible into a device that measures the force of the air expelled. The parents and children were also interviewed about stressful life events during the period of the study. The investigators found that the children were nearly five times as likely to have an asthma attack if they experienced a stressful life event 1 or 2 days before the attack. In addition, the children who experienced stressful life events were more likely to have another attack 5 to 7 weeks later.

Because of the link between the autonomic nervous system (ANS) and the constriction and dilation of the airways, and the connection between the ANS and emotions, most research has focused on heightened experience and expression of negative emotions. Research has generally found higher levels of negative emotional experience and expression in people with asthma (Lehrer, Isenberg, & Hochron, 1993; Mrazek, Schuman, & Klinnert, 1998). Asthma patients report that many attacks are precipitated by emotions such as anxiety (Rumbak et al., 1993). In both laboratory and real-life settings, individuals with asthma show greater constriction of the bronchial tubes in response to stressors (Affleck et al., 2000; Miller & Wood, 1994).

Negative emotions have also been found to be directly related to reports of asthma symptoms and to peak expiratory flow. One study assessed people with asthma over a period of several days (Smyth et al., 1999). Five times each day the participants were signaled to measure their peak expiratory flow and to record in a diary any asthma symptoms they were experiencing, their level of stress, and the mood they were in. Reports of higher levels of stress and negative emotions were related to lower peak flow and more reports of asthma symptoms. Another study found that reports of sadness following a sad film predicted greater bronchial constriction among children with asthma (Miller & Wood, 1997).

In interpreting these results it is probably reasonable to assume that some of this heightened negative emotional experience is a reaction to having a chronic disease. But some research also shows that negative emotions precede asthma attacks, indicating that negative emotion does play a role in precipitating attacks (Hyland, 1990). In contrast, pleasant emotions predict better lung functioning among individuals with asthma (Apter et al., 1997).

Role of the Family   Sources of psychological stress associated with asthma include parent–child interactions and other family-related factors. One investigation looked at 150 pregnant

Olympic medalist Jackie Joyner-Kersee suffers from exercise-induced asthma. (AP/Wide World Photos.)

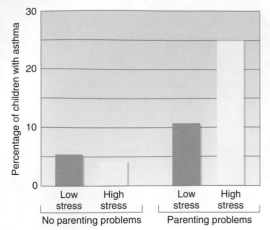

Figure 7.8 The effects of parenting problems and mothers' prior stress on the frequency of asthma in their children. Children whose mothers had been under a high level of stress and who were raised in families with parenting problems had high rates of asthma. [From Klinnert et al. (1994).]

women who had asthma (Klinnert, Mrazek, & Mrazek, 1994). The investigators intended to study the mothers' offspring, who were at genetic risk, and to assess parental characteristics as well. Both parents were interviewed 3 weeks after the child's birth to determine their attitudes toward the infant, their sensitivity to the infant, their strategy for sharing parenting duties, and the presence of any emotional disturbances. The amount of stress experienced by the mother in the past year was also assessed. The children were closely monitored over the next 3 years, and the frequency of asthma was then related to the parental characteristics noted earlier. Results showed a high rate of asthma among children whose mothers had high levels of stress and whose families were rated as having problems (see Figure 7.8).

Not all research, however, has found that parent–child relationships figure in asthma (Eiser et al., 1991; Sawyer et al., 2001). One group of investigators studied young asthmatic children and their mothers through a battery of questionnaires and interviews and by making observations in the home (Gauthier et al., 1977, 1978). Most of the children and their mothers were well adjusted. The children's levels of development were normal for their age, and they were independent and successful at coping with their surroundings.

Another study used cross-sectional and prospective analyses of the link between family factors and (re)hospitalization for asthma (Chen et al., 2003). The cross-sectional analyses revealed that a higher level of family conflict and strain was associated with an increased number of hospitalizations for asthma among children in the family. Although this factor did not prospectively predict rehospitalization among the children, parental reports of less mastery and less emotional concern over their child's illness were predictive of later rehospitalization. These cross-sectional findings, however, do not tell us about the direction of the effects—that is, family stress could be greater due to having a serious illness in the family, or the severity of the asthma could be greater due to family stress. Nevertheless, the longitudinal prospective findings suggest that higher levels of family stress do not cause an exacerbation in asthma, at least not with respect to rehospitalization, whereas lower levels of parental mastery and emotional concern do seem to predict a later exacerbation.

The research we have reviewed is thus not completely consistent regarding the role that the home life of people with asthma plays in their illness. Even if we allow that family relationships are consequential in asthma, we cannot always tell whether the various family-related factors are causal or maintaining agents. It may be that certain negative emotional factors in the home are important in eliciting early asthmatic attacks in some children, but in others who originally develop the illness for nonfamilial reasons, it may be that their parents then unwittingly reward various symptoms of the syndrome. For example, parents may cater to asthmatic children by giving them special treatment. Given how debilitating and frightening asthma episodes can be, it is not surprising that some parents may be a bit overprotective of children with this condition.

Biological Factors   Diatheses leading to asthma might include the effects of respiratory infections, as mentioned in relation to the study discussed earlier (Rees, 1964) and as seems to have been the case with Tom.

Allergies, too, can predispose people to this disorder. When asthma is caused primarily by allergens, the cells in the respiratory tract are especially sensitive to one or more substances (allergens), such as pollen, molds, fur, cockroaches, air pollution, smoke, and dust mites, which bring on an attack. Individuals whose asthma is primarily allergic may have an inherited hypersensitivity of the respiratory mucosa, which then overresponds to one or more of such usually harmless substances. Asthma does run in families, which is consistent with genetic transmission of a diathesis (Konig & Godfrey, 1973). Recent studies are narrowing in on how genes may interact with environmental factors to produce asthma (e.g., Cookson & Moffatt, 1997, 2000). Finally, two studies (reviewed by Lehrer et al., 1993) have found that asthmatic persons, but not people without asthma, respond to gory films with bronchoconstriction, suggesting that their respiratory systems respond to stress in a way that may induce an asthma attack.

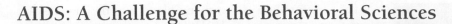

AIDS: A Challenge for the Behavioral Sciences

AIDS (acquired immunodeficiency syndrome) is a major public health concern. This invariably fatal illness has two unique, interrelated characteristics that make it appropriate for discussion in an abnormal psychology textbook: (1) it can arise from behavior that is apparently irrational and self-defeating; and (2) it can be prevented by psychological means.

In the United States, AIDS was originally proclaimed a disease of gay men, but it never was exclusively a "gay disease." Indeed, there are indications that the disease is increasing among heterosexual men and women in the United States. In Africa and parts of Latin America, AIDS is found primarily among heterosexuals, and throughout the world HIV-positive women [i.e., women who are infected with HIV (human immunodeficiency virus), which causes AIDS] give birth to HIV-positive babies. The following statistics give some sense of the scope of the problem (CDC, 2004; Kalichman, 1995; Maugh, 1998a,b; San Francisco Department of Health, 2002; UNAIDS, 2000):

- Since the start of the epidemic, more than 20 million people worldwide have died of AIDS.
- Nearly 40 million people worldwide are now HIV positive. Of these, 25 million live in sub-Saharan Africa. In seven countries in Africa, at least one in five adults is infected.
- There were 3 million deaths from HIV/AIDS in 2003.
- There were nearly 5 million new cases worldwide in 2003. This is the largest number of new cases in any 1 year since the epidemic began.
- Worldwide, women now account for nearly 50 percent of people infected with HIV.
- Incidence is rising sharply in Asia, especially in India and China, and most of these new cases result from heterosexual activity.
- In 2002, 42,000 Americans became HIV positive; 50 percent of these were African-Americans.
- In the United States, African-American and Hispanic women are 17 times more likely than white women to become infected.
- In the United States, AIDS is the fifth leading cause of death among all adults ages 25 to 44, a remarkable statistic given that it wasn't even included as a cause of death just over 20 years ago. It is the third leading cause of death among African-American men ages 25–54 and African-American women ages 35–44.

Clinical Description

The medical complexities of AIDS are beyond the scope of this book, but it is important to understand a few fundamentals. AIDS is a disease in which the body's immune system is severely compromised by HIV, putting the individual at high risk for fatal diseases such as Kaposi's sarcoma, rare forms of lymph cancer, and a wide range of dangerous fungal, viral, and bacterial infections. The term *opportunistic* is often used to describe these illnesses, which are seldom found in people with healthy immune systems, because we can say that these diseases take advantage of the opportunity afforded by a weakened immune system (Kalichman, 1996). Strictly speaking, people do not die of AIDS but of the diseases to which AIDS makes them vulnerable.

Spread of the Disease

HIV is most often transmitted from one person to another through unsafe sexual practices, regardless of sexual orientation. HIV is present in blood, semen, and vaginal secretions and can be transmitted only when infected fluids get into the bloodstream. It cannot be transmitted through casual social contact. Among intravenous drug users, sharing unsterilized

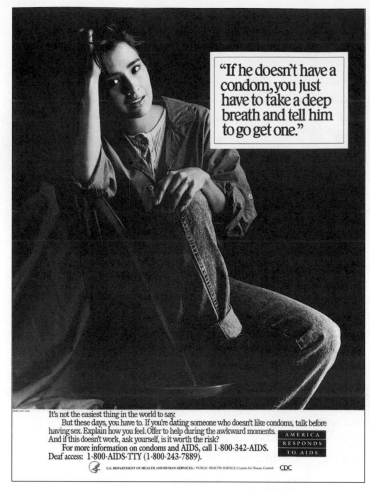

"If he doesn't have a condom, you just have to take a deep breath and tell him to go get one."

It's not the easiest thing in the world to say.
   But these days, you have to. If you're dating someone who doesn't like condoms, talk before having sex. Explain how you feel. Offer to help during the awkward moments. And if this doesn't work, ask yourself, is it worth the risk?
   For more information on condoms and AIDS, call 1-800-342-AIDS.
Deaf access: 1-800-AIDS-TTY (1-800-243-7889).

AMERICA RESPONDS TO AIDS

U.S. DEPARTMENT OF HEALTH AND HUMAN SERVICES / PUBLIC HEALTH SERVICE/Centers for Disease Control   CDC

Encouraging assertiveness in sex is a key component to AIDS prevention efforts. This advertisement emphasizes the importance of insisting on condom use. (Courtesy of US Department of Health and Human Service and the Center for Disease Control.)

needles can introduce HIV-carrying blood into the bloodstream of another. Infants born to HIV-positive mothers are at risk, for the virus can cross the placental barrier and infect the developing fetus.

Risk is elevated in people who abuse drugs, including drugs that are not injected, perhaps because the effects of drugs can compromise a person's ability or willingness to consider the consequences of behavior. Another possible mechanism is a risk-taking disposition, for which frequent drug use is a marker; that is, engaging in unprotected sex may be another sign of a tendency to take risks (Chesney, Barrett, & Stall, 1998). Whatever the reasons, ample evidence shows that unsafe sex is associated with the frequent use of many kinds of drugs, including alcohol and methamphetamine (Colfax et al., 2004; Halkitis, Parsons, & Stirratt, 2001).

AIDS Prevention Efforts

Despite promising advances in drug treatment (e.g., AZT and saquinavir), there is widespread agreement that by far the best strategy is prevention through behavioral changes. For example, scientists generally agree that needle exchange programs or the free distribution of needles and syringes reduces needle sharing and thereby the spread of infectious diseases associated with intravenous drug use (Gibson, 2001; Yoast et al., 2001). The primary focus in preventing sexually transmitted AIDS is on changing sexual practices. Early efforts in this regard were successful. For example, in the 1980s, when prevention efforts focused on encouraging the use of condoms during every sexual contact, new cases of HIV dropped in many large cities, from an annual infection rate among gay men of around 10 percent or more to 1 or 2 percent. But more recent data have indicated that younger gay men are engaging in more unprotected sexual behaviors than are older gay men (CDC, 2001; Boxall, 1995).

Why might this be happening? Perhaps young gay men do not see as many of their age cohort infected as do older gay men, and so they don't consider AIDS as much of a threat for themselves as it is for others. It has also been suggested that the introduction of new drugs in the mid-1990s increased the hope that a cure was going to be discovered soon. After the Food and Drug Administration permitted direct marketing of AIDS medicines to consumers in 1997, ads from drug companies began to appear that portrayed HIV-positive men as healthy, active, robust, and happy and as engaging in all sorts of activities and sports; such ads may have given the impression that these drugs can cure AIDS. Even if such ads accurately portrayed some small percentage of HIV-positive men, their relevance for women seems doubtful. Moreover, many HIV-positive men are not as healthy and active as the ads suggested. More importantly, these drugs can neither cure AIDS nor reduce its transmission. The FDA has since ordered that such ads be discontinued.

Other prevention efforts focus on encouraging monogamous relationships. One can eliminate the possibility of exposure by being in a monogamous relationship with a partner who tests negative for HIV. However, monogamous relationships are rare among young people and are not invariably found among married people or those in other committed relationships.

Furthermore, rationality does not always prevail in a committed relationship. A study of gay male couples who had been in their relationship at least 6 months (the average length was almost 4 years) found that engaging in unsafe sex symbolized trust, love, and commitment, whereas safer sex was seen negatively by partners and as possibly threatening the closeness of a committed relationship (Appleby, Miller, & Rothspan, 1999). Further, suggestions by a partner that safer sex should be practiced were viewed with suspicion, as a sign of infidelity. There is no reason to expect the views of heterosexual couples to be any different.

Thus, although advocating monogamous relationships remains a prevalent approach in the public health arena, prevention is best directed at encouraging sexually active people to use condoms, which are about 90 percent effective in preventing HIV infection. Avoiding sex after using alcohol or drugs is also prudent because, as noted, use of these substances increases the tendency to engage in risky sex (e.g., Colfax et al., 2004). The safest strategy is to use condoms in a monogamous relationship.

How can changes be brought about, especially in generations of sexually active people? Social psychological and cognitive behavior therapy theory and research suggest strategies that can form the basis of effective preventive interventions (Chernoff, 1998; Kalichman, 1995; Kelly, 1995):

- Provide accurate information about HIV transmission. Such information is readily available online or in pamphlets from the Centers for Disease Control and from local AIDS organizations.
- Explain clearly what the person's risks are (e.g., people with many sexual partners are at higher risk, regardless of sexual orientation; sharing needles with other intravenous drug users is very risky).
- Identify cues to high-risk situations (e.g., drinking alcohol in a sexually provocative situation is associated with higher-risk sexual behavior).
- Provide instruction in condom use (and, as appropriate, needle cleaning and exchanging), including "eroticizing" the use of condoms (suggesting ways in which a condom can be experienced as sexually exciting). Also, emphasize that using condoms gives individuals some degree of control over their health.
- Provide social skills training that includes sexual assertiveness skills (e.g., resisting pressure to have sex or insisting that safer sex be practiced) and other communication skills that can help preserve relationships while reducing the risk of infection with HIV.
- Work at the community level to generate large-scale social support for making safer sex the expected thing, creating a "we're all in this together" atmosphere.

A review (Chernoff, 1998) revealed that interventions implementing these principles often, but do not always, lead to increases in sexual assertiveness, reductions in unprotected anal intercourse, and increased use of condoms in gay and bisexual men (Kelly et al., 1989, 1990; Roffman et al., 1998), low-income minority women (Auerbach et. al., 1994), African-American gay and bisexual men (Peterson et al., 1996), Mexican American gay and bisexual men (Zimmerman et al., 1997), female prostitutes (Bhave et al., 1995), substance abusers (Kotranski et al., 1998), and mentally ill adults (Susser et al., 1998). School-based efforts to get young adolescents (in middle or junior high school) to forgo sexual activity or to use condoms if they are sexually active have not been particularly successful (e.g., Siegel et al., 1995). Somewhat greater success has been achieved with high school (Smith & Katner, 1995) and college students (Reeder, Pryor, & Harsh, 1997). Only mixed success has been reported in discouraging intravenous drug use to reduce HIV exposure (Auerbach et al. 1994).

An especially noteworthy study involved over 3,700 heterosexual men and women at the highest risk for HIV infection in 37 sexually transmitted disease (STD) clinics across the United States (NIMH Multisite HIV Prevention Trial Group, 1998). In this study, three-quarters of the participants were African-American and the rest were Latino; most were unemployed and single. All met one or more of the following high-risk criteria: having sex with multiple partners, being infected with an STD, having sex with someone known to have multiple partners, having sex with an intravenous drug user, and having sex with someone known to be HIV positive. A 4-week behavioral intervention applying several of the principles mentioned here, compared with a one-session information-only control group, led to significantly more reduction in unprotected sex, with some indications also of fewer cases of STDs over a 12-month period following the intervention. In addition, the estimated cost per person in the 4-week behavioral intervention was less than $300, which is equivalent to the cost of about 1 week of treatment with the newest AIDS drugs (protease inhibitors).

An additional large study, called the EXPLORE study, conducted across six U.S. cities included nearly 4,300 men who have sex with men. The men were randomly assigned to either a prevention intervention group or a standard group. Men in the standard group received counseling two times a year on the risks associated with unprotected sex, as recommended by the Centers for Disease Control. Men in the prevention intervention group received 10 individual counseling sessions that focused on individual and social factors that contribute to risky sexual behaviors, such as alcohol and drugs, mood states, communication issues, and pleasure associated with risky sexual behavior. Counselors followed a treatment manual for each of the 10 sessions. At both 12 and 18 months following the interventions, men in the prevention intervention group tended to be less likely than men in the standard group to have been infected with HIV; however, the difference between the two groups in HIV infection rates was not statistically significant. Does this mean the intervention was not successful? Not necessarily. The men in the prevention intervention group engaged in fewer risky sexual behaviors, such as unprotected anal receptive sex and unprotected sex with an HIV-positive partner (EXPLORE study team, 2004).

Unfortunately, prevention efforts aimed at women have been less successful. A meta-analysis of all such studies found that despite an abundance of findings on social and contextual risk factors associated with women and HIV, there are few prevention intervention studies designed to address them. The studies that have been done to date do not yield very promising results (Logan, Cole, & Leukefeld, 2002). This is clearly an area in need of research, as women account for about half of the HIV infections worldwide, and the rates of HIV infection among women of color in the United States are much higher than among men or white women.

A Cautionary Note on the Role of Knowledge about AIDS in AIDS Prevention

The most widely adopted strategy in AIDS prevention is the provision of accurate information about the nature of the disease, how it is transmitted, and how to reduce risk by changing behavior. However, we know that AIDS-prevention programs, all of which seek to increase knowledge about the disease and how to avoid it, are far from completely effective. Why isn't it enough just to tell people what's what, especially if a given course of action is very dangerous? It's obvious even to the casual observer of human behavior that knowing that something is bad for us is far from a guarantee that we will refrain from partaking of it.

The strong emphasis in prevention programs on educational messages about HIV rests on the assumption that people are rational beings and that they will usually act in their own best interests. This assumption has been challenged by two social psychologists who reviewed studies showing that knowledge about the mode of transmission of HIV and ways to prevent its transmission is by no means a guarantee that people will protect themselves (Helweg-Larsen & Collins, 1997). Indeed, many surveys indicate that knowledge about HIV transmission and preventive behaviors is quite high among people who engage in high-risk behavior, including intravenous drug users (Calsyn et al., 1992), heterosexual adolescents (DiClemente et al., 1990), and gay men (Aspinwall et al., 1991).

Another thing to consider is that when people are in a heightened state of autonomic arousal, especially sexual arousal, they are not exactly paragons of rational thinking. Thinking too much, analyzing things, making deliberate and careful decisions—these tend to interfere with sexual enjoyment. It is reasonable to assume that when people are drinking alcohol or taking drugs such as methamphetamine, they are similarly not operating on an entirely rational level.

The focus on providing information about HIV transmission can overlook how people feel about the knowledge they have. For example, adolescents can understand that a condom will markedly reduce HIV risk and yet avoid using one because it is a reminder of disease, hardly something one wants to have in mind in sexual situations. Or they might believe that their immune systems are strong enough to repel HIV.

In some ways, knowledge can actually be a hindrance; that is, under some conditions knowledge may have negative consequences (Helweg-Larsen & Collins, 1997). Consider, for example, "AIDS information saturation," a state of irritation that results from being overwhelmed by a constant barrage of warnings about HIV and by exhortations to refrain from high-risk behaviors. In one study, college students judged to be affected by this information overload reported weaker intentions to engage in safer sexual behavior than did students who did not feel overwhelmed by information (Berrenberg et al., 1993, as cited in Helweg-Larsen & Collins, 1997). Repeatedly telling people what they already know can apparently make them less likely to act on that knowledge. Furthermore, as mentioned earlier, introducing condoms into an existing, ostensibly monogamous relationship can engender suspicion and lack of trust.

Another consideration often overlooked in public education campaigns about HIV involves the skills needed to act on knowledge. For example, a young man or woman may understand the benefits of using condoms but may be embarrassed about purchasing them (the ability to purchase condoms from vending machines should lessen this embarrassment). Indeed, there are examples of successful prevention efforts that go beyond providing information. For example, as part of a broad-based program designed to prevent HIV infection among urban women, researchers provided women with a "condom credit card" that allowed them to receive free condoms and spermicide from a local pharmacy for a year (Hobfoll et al., 1994). In another program targeting urban women, investigators provided not only information and education about risk, but also training in condom use, assertiveness training, peer support, group support in developing problem solving skills, and help with identifying triggers for risky sexual behavior. Women who received this intervention increased their use of condoms from 26 percent of the time to 56 percent of the time, and they developed better and more effective sexual communication and negotiation skills and behavior (Kelly et al., 1994).

Quick Summary

The reasons why individuals have hypertension are not well understood, but psychological factors such as Type A behavior pattern and anger as well as behavioral factors such as diet and exercise play a key role. Laboratory and naturalistic studies have shown that stress, anger, Type A, and cardiovascular reactivity all contribute to short-term increases in blood pressure. There is less research showing how these factors are linked to hypertension.

Type A behavior pattern has predicted CHD in some studies but not others. Researchers have looked at more specific components of Type A, and evidence suggests that anger, hostility, and cynicism may be important predictors of CHD. Anxiety and depression are also related to CHD. Cardiovascular reactivity and heart rate variability are possible biological risk factors for CHD.

Asthma involves severe constriction of the airways; the air passages in the lungs become narrowed, causing extremely labored and wheezy breathing. There are many causes of asthma, several involve allergens or air pollutants. Psychological factors, such as stressful life events, negative emotions, and family conflict may trigger attacks.

AIDS remains an epidemic worldwide, with over half of the 40 million people with HIV living in sub-Saharan Africa. In the United States, AIDS is increasing among heterosexual women of color and younger gay men. Prevention has been a key focus of psychological researchers since the disease can be prevented with changes in behavior. Much work has been done to change risky sexual behaviors among gay and straight men, and straight women. These programs have been effective in the short term, but no longer term follow-ups have yet been conducted. Additional work is needed to develop effective prevention programs for adolescents.

Gender and Health

Clinical Case: Juana

Juana was a 58-year-old veterinarian. She was slightly overweight but exercised regularly, did not smoke, and had only an occasional glass of wine with dinner. She had been happily married for 22 years, and her children were both in college. She enjoyed her job quite a bit, despite the long hours and the after-hours calls she often received from worried pet owners.

For several weeks, Juana had been experiencing fatigue and had found herself taking short naps during the day. She had had increasingly frequent bouts of indigestion, and occasionally she had become dizzy or light headed. She wondered if these were the beginning signs of menopause. She consulted with her doctor, who examined her and concluded that the symptoms probably would resolve on their own. If they didn't go away in a few weeks, the doctor said, Juana should

contact her again. About a week later, Juana began to experience shortness of breath. Then, on a long hike with her husband, she had a fainting spell. Thinking it was the heat, she dismissed it. The next night, she awoke from sleep feeling nauseous and sweaty. She was sure this was a symptom of menopause until she felt a shooting pain in her arm. She awakened her husband, and he took her to the hospital. An electrocardiogram revealed that Juana had had a small heart attack. The next day, Juana had an angiogram that showed three completely occluded coronary arteries. She would need bypass surgery. Beyond her concerns about her health, Juana was quite surprised by this turn of events—didn't heart attacks and heart disease affect men more than women, and shouldn't her doctor have diagnosed her condition?

At every age from birth to 85 and older, more men die than women. Men are more than twice as likely to die in automobile accidents and of homicides, cirrhosis, heart disease, lung cancer and other lung diseases, and suicide. Women, however, have higher rates of morbidity. That is, general poor health is more frequent among women, and women have a higher incidence of several specific diseases. For example, women have higher rates of diabetes, anemia, gastrointestinal problems, systemic lupus erythematosus, and rheumatoid arthritis; and they report more visits to physicians, use more prescription drugs, and account for two-thirds of all surgical procedures performed in the United States. Further, in recent years, women's mortality advantage has been decreasing. For example, the death rate from cardiovascular disease declined among men in the late twentieth century but stayed about the same in women (Rodin & Ickovics, 1990); also, death from cardiovascular disease is more common among African-American women than white women (Casper et al., 2000).

What are some of the possible reasons for the differences in mortality and morbidity rates in men and women? It might be that women have some biological mechanism that protects them from certain life-threatening diseases. For example, epidemiological and observational studies have suggested that estrogen may offer protection from cardiovascular disease. Based on this evidence, many women began hormone replacement therapy (HRT) following menopause in an attempt to reduce the risk of cardiovascular disease. However, the first randomized clinical trial of HRT for postmenopausal women, called the Heart and Estrogen/Progestin Replacement Study, failed to find a reduced risk with respect to one type of cardiovascular disease—coronary heart disease (CHD) (Hulley et al., 1998).

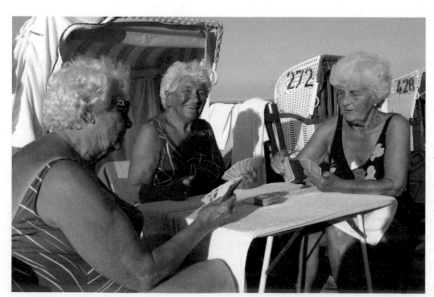

Research shows that women live longer than men but women have more health problems than men. (Thomas Langreder VISUM/The Image Works.)

A later study, called the Women's Health Initiative (WHI), began in 1993 with a sample of over 150,000 women. It is a large, prospective study designed to examine the effects of HRT as possible protective factors against osteoporosis, CHD, and cancer. One group of women was randomly assigned to receive estrogen plus progesterone therapy (combined therapy), another group was randomly assigned to receive estrogen only, and a third group was randomly assigned to receive a placebo. The study originally planned to follow women prospectively for 9 years. However, the study was stopped for women in the combined therapy group after 5 years because the data suggested that the combined treatment was *increasing* the risk of CHD, stroke, and breast cancer (WHI, 2002). The estrogen-only portion of the study was similarly discontinued after 7 years because there was no evidence for a decreased risk of CHD or breast cancer, though there was a protective effect for hip fractures, which are related to osteoporosis (WHI, 2004). These findings may not be the last word on HRT. The WHI study was limited in that most of the women were postmenopausal, leaving open the possibility that HRT during the period of transition to menopause could afford some health benefits.

Early evidence suggested that women are less likely than men to exhibit the Type A behavior pattern and are also less hostile than men (Waldron, 1976; Weidner & Collins, 1993). Researchers have hypothesized that the Type A pattern is part and parcel of a rigid commitment to the traditional masculine gender role, which emphasizes achievement, mastery, competitiveness, not asking for help or emotional support, an excessive need for control, and the tendency to become angry and to express anger when frustrated (Eisler & Blalock, 1991). They link these attributes to the tendency for men to be more prone to cardiovascular disease and other stress-related health risks, such as hypertension (Harrison, Chin, & Ficarrotto, 1989).

Increasing evidence, however, indicates that anger is not necessarily more commonly experienced and expressed by men (Kring, 2000; Lavoie et al., 2001). Moreover, increased hostility and both the suppression and expression of anger are associated with risk factors for CHD among women (Matthews et al., 1998; Rutledge et al., 2001). In addition, anxiety and depression are more common among women than men (see Chapters 5 and 8) and are also linked to cardiovascular disease (e.g., Suls & Bunde, 2005). Thus, many questions remain about the role of these psychological factors in differences between the mortality from cardiovascular disease in men and women.

Another question concerns why the gap between mortality rates in men and women is decreasing. In the early twentieth century, most deaths were due to infectious diseases, but now most deaths result from diseases that are affected by lifestyle. One possibility, then, is that lifestyle differences between men and women account for the sex difference in mortality and that these lifestyle differences are decreasing. For example, men smoke more than women and consume more alcohol, and these differences are likely contributors to men's higher mortality from cardiovascular disease and lung cancer. In recent years, however, women have begun to smoke and drink more, and these changes have been paralleled by increases in lung cancer and by the failure of the mortality rate for cardiovascular disease to decrease among women. Since 1987, lung cancer has been the leading cause of cancer death among women. In 2001, the surgeon general recommended a number of measures to stop smoking among women in the United States. In 2004, a report issued by the National Women's Law Center and the Oregon Health and Sciences University called "Making the Grade: A National and State-by-State Report Card" showed that 39 states received a failing grade in their efforts to curb smoking among women. Only one state, Utah, received a semi-satisfactory grade (Waxman et al., 2004).

Other explanations focus on the identification and treatment of disease in women. For example, even though cardiovascular disease is the number one killer of women, there is still a widespread belief that men should be more concerned with heart disease than women. Furthermore, a common diagnostic procedure for heart disease risk, the so-called stress test, which involves measuring heart rate while on a treadmill, is not a good predictor of problems among women (Mora et al., 2003). In addition, a low dose of aspirin does not appear to prevent myocardial infarction in women as it does in men (though it does appear to prevent stroke in women, which is not true for men) (Ridker et al., 2005). Other research shows that women are less likely to be referred to a cardiovascular rehabilitation program following a heart attack, perhaps contributing to their persistent rates of mortality (Abbey & Stewart, 2000).

There are several possible explanations for the difference in morbidity of men and women. First, because women live longer than men, they may be more likely to experience certain diseases that are associated with aging. Second, women may be more attentive to their health than are men and thus may be more likely to visit physicians and be diagnosed. Third, women are exposed to more stress than men and they rate stress as having a greater impact on them, particularly stress related to major life events (Davis, Matthews, & Twamley, 1999). Fourth, physicians tend to treat women's health concerns and complaints less seriously than men's concerns (Weisman & Teitelbaum, 1985). Finally, evidence indicates that women's morbidity differs depending on socioeconomic and demographic variables, such as income, education, and ethnicity. For example, having more education and a higher income are associated with fewer risk factors for cardiovascular disease, including obesity, smoking, hypertension, and reduced amounts of exercise. In the United States, women tend to have lower income than men. Also, 16.5 million women in the United States do not have health insurance. However, even after controlling for differences in income level and education, a recent study found that Mexican American and African American women still had a greater likelihood of having more risk factors for CHD than men (Winkleby et al., 1999).

The tendency to exclude women from research studies has probably compromised the scientific validity of data on how best to minimize women's risk for a number of illnesses. Women have been understudied in research on health and stress (Rodin & Ickovics, 1990; Taylor et al., 2000). Not only have women been excluded from such studies, but many researchers have simply assumed that men and women respond similarly to stress and thus will have similar stress-related health problems. Other researchers have called this assumption into question and proposed that women may respond differently to stress, both behaviorally and biologically (Taylor et al., 2000). Future studies need to include equal samples of men and women, to consider that men and women may respond differently to stress, and to focus on the special health concerns of women. The WHI, described above, is a promising step in this direction. Other parts of the WHI investigation include examining why women with low socioeconomic status are at high risk for various diseases and studying psychosocial factors such as life stress and personality that increase risk for these diseases (Matthews et al., 1997; WHI study group, 1998). Other findings from this large study suggested that neither form of hormone replacement therapy reduced the risk of dementia and that the combined therapy actually seemed to increase the risk (Shumaker et al., 2003, 2004).

Socioeconomic Status, Ethnicity, and Health

Low socioeconomic status (SES) is associated with higher rates of health problems and mortality from all causes. A number of explanations have been proposed for the correlation between SES and poor health and mortality, but many of these are still in need of empirical support. Recent research attempts to trace the connections between health and SES, encompassing economic, societal, relationship, individual, and biological factors. For example, one pathway to poor health among individuals has to do with environmental factors that reinforce poor health behaviors. Poorer neighborhoods often have high numbers of liquor stores, grocery stores offering fewer healthy food choices, and fewer opportunities for exercise at health clubs. Given these environmental constraints, it is perhaps not surprising to learn that lower SES people are more likely than higher SES people to engage in behaviors that increase the risk of disease, such as smoking, eating a high-fat diet, and drinking more alcohol (Lantz et al., 1998).

Other pathways include limited access to health services and greater exposure to stressors. Recall our earlier discussion of allostatic load, the bodily effects of repeated and chronic stress. In a longitudinal study, researchers found that the most economically disadvantaged individuals had the highest allostatic load (Singer & Ryff, 1999). These investigators also found that, regardless of SES, individuals who reported having poor relationships with parents or negative relationships with spouses had a higher allostatic load than individuals with positive parental and spousal relationships. Not surprisingly, the combination of lower SES and negative relationships had the greatest effect on allostatic load. These findings indicate that lower SES is a likely source of chronic stress that impacts the body. They also illustrate the complicated relationship between individual, social, and economic factors and health.

Certainly discrimination and prejudice are likely sources of chronic stress, and these abhorrent social conditions continue to affect people of color as well as people of lower SES. Since people of color are found in high numbers among lower SES groups, ethnicity has also been a feature of research into the relationship of SES to health. Consider, for example, that the mortality rate for African Americans is nearly two times as high as it is for whites in the United States (Williams, 1999). Why might this be? The reasons are complex and not completely understood. Some research suggests that certain risk factors for disease are more common in people of color. For example, risk factors for cardiovascular disease (such as smoking, obesity, hypertension, and reduced exercise) are higher among women from ethnic minorities than among white women. This finding holds even when members of the two groups are comparable in SES (Winkleby et al., 1998). The increased prevalence of some of these risk factors shows up in studies of children as young as 6 to 9 years of age. For example, African American and Mexican American girls in this age range have higher body mass indexes and higher fat intake than do non-Hispanic white girls (Winkleby et al., 1999). Other studies have found that increased stress associated with discrimination is linked to cardiovascular reactivity among African American women (Guyll, Matthews, & Bromberger, 2001). Consideration of SES at multiple levels, including the individual, family, and neighborhood, is also important. For example, lower family SES and neighborhood SES were found to be associated with greater cardiovascular reactivity for African American children and adolescents, but only lower family SES was associated with greater cardiovascular reactivity among white children and adolescents (Gump et al., 1999). In sum, both social class and ethnicity are clearly very important factors in health.

Ethnicity is also an important factor in how people cope with cancer, and it is associated with detection of illness, adherence to treatment regimens, survival, and quality of life (these relationships were examined in a review by Meyerowitz et al., 1998). Among the many ethnicity-related findings based on data from the National Cancer Institute are the following:

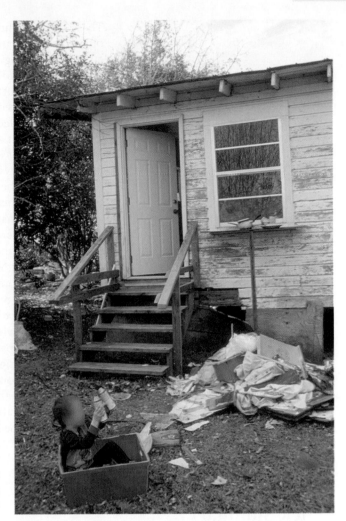

Poverty is stressful and is associated with poor health. (Jeff Greenberg/PhotoEdit.)

- African Americans have the highest rates of cancer overall, as a result of very high rates of lung and prostate cancer among men.
- Although African American women have lower breast cancer rates than do white women, their mortality rates 5 years after diagnosis are the same because their survival rates are lower.
- Latino men and women have low rates of cancer in general, but Latina women have high rates of cervical cancer.
- Asian Americans have low rates for all cancers except stomach cancer.

These and other findings are illustrative of ethnic differences in the incidence and outcomes of cancer. What might account for these differences? The answers appear to lie less with ethnic and biological factors than with social and psychological factors such as access to and willingness to seek out medical care (e.g., Bach et al., 1999).[1]

As one might expect, the ability to afford skilled health care is not uniform across ethnic and socioeconomic lines. Based on the review cited above, researchers argue that ethnicity may affect detection of illness, survival, and quality of life by virtue of SES and knowledge about and attitudes toward the detection and treatment of cancer (Meyerowitz et al., 1998). For example, African Americans who are poor are not likely to have health insurance and therefore have less access to health care than do those who come from the middle classes; they tend to have less information on steps to take to detect the illness (e.g., breast self-examination), and then, if a potential problem is detected, they may delay seeing a physician for financial reasons (though in general African American women are more likely than white women to get Pap smears and just as likely to have mammogram screenings). Cultural beliefs about cancer are also relevant. For example, thinking that chiropractic is an effective treatment or believing that cancer is spread through the air are predictors of advanced-stage breast cancer (Lannin et al., 1998).

The years of research on SES and health have clearly demonstrated that there is a linear relationship between morbidity/mortality and SES: the higher the SES, the better the health. But the reasons why this is so are less clear. Taken together, the explanations posited above can account for part of the relationship between SES and health, but not all. Investigators are now proposing models that cut across these different explanations in an effort to do a better job of accounting for the SES–health link. For example, researchers have proposed a testable model that includes SES; health outcomes; stress reactivity; negative emotional states such as hostility, anxiety, and depression; and negative cognitions such as hopelessness (Gallo and Matthews, 2003). Future research will tell us if this model can do what it hopes to do.

Quick Summary

Women live longer than men, yet women have poorer health than men. Researchers wondered if sex hormones might protect women from death, but studies of estrogen replacement failed to show that it decreased risk for CHD. Men may be more likely than women to exhibit the Type A behavior pattern, but there are few gender differences in anger, and women are more likely to experience anxiety and depression. The identification and treatment of CHD differs between men and women. Even though CHD is the number one killer of women, diagnostic procedures such as the stress test and preventative measures, such as aspirin therapy, are not as effective for women as they are for men. Women may have poorer health than men because they live longer. Lower socioeconomic status (SES) is associated with poorer health, and women are more likely than men to have lower SES.

The reasons why lower SES is linked to poorer health are many and include environmental factors such as limited resources in poorer neighborhoods, greater stress associated with lower SES, less social support, discrimination, and less access to health care. Ethnicity impacts some diseases, such as cancer, but the reasons for this are not well understood. Some differences attributed to ethnicity may have more to do with SES.

---

[1] Of course, biological factors, including genetic factors, have to be taken into consideration, and some of these variables may be linked to ethnicity. As researchers have pointed out (Meyerowitz et al., 1998), for example, African American women have a higher incidence of a particularly lethal type of tumor than do white women (Stanford & Greenberg, 1989). However, there is mounting evidence that when biological differences exist in the incidence of illness, they are sometimes a function of (mediated by) behavioral factors (Anderson, Kiecolt-Glaser, & Glaser, 1994). For example, as Asians living in the United States have adopted the eating habits of Americans, their previously low cancer rates have risen to levels comparable to those of non-Hispanic whites (Whittemore et al., 1990). Thus, being Japanese appears not to be important; rather, it is the diet (and perhaps also the general lifestyle) that affects rates of illness.

Check Your Knowledge 7.4

True or false?
1. Asthma is caused by psychological factors in nearly 50 percent of cases.
2. The number of HIV infections reached an all-time low in 2003.

3. HIV prevention programs have shown promise in the short term, except among young adolescents.
4. Among the reasons women may have poorer health than men is that their concerns are not taken as seriously by doctors.
5. Higher SES is associated with greater allostatic load.

Treatment of Psychophysiological Disorders

Any treatment of psychophysiological disorders calls for close consultation with a physician. Whether high blood pressure is biologically caused or, as in essential hypertension, linked to psychological stress, a number of medications can reduce it. Asthma attacks can also be alleviated by medications, taken either by inhalation or injection, that dilate the bronchial tubes. The help drugs provide in ameliorating damage and discomfort in particular bodily systems cannot be underestimated. They are frequently lifesaving. Mental health and medical professionals recognize, however, that most drug interventions do not address the fact that the person is reacting to psychological stress.

Therapists of all persuasions agree that reducing anxiety, depression, and anger is the best way to alleviate suffering from psychophysiological disorders. The particular disorder—whether essential hypertension, cardiovascular disease, or asthma—is considered to be adversely affected, if not actually caused, by these emotions.

Treating Hypertension and Reducing the Risk of Coronary Heart Disease

Before the advent of effective drugs for treating hypertension in the late 1950s, physicians generally advised patients basically to "take it easy," lose weight, and restrict salt intake—all reasonably helpful measures. It is noteworthy that simple verbal reassurance was also considered important and was even demonstrated to be helpful in an early study (Reiser et al., 1950) in which non-psychiatrically trained internists (physicians specializing in internal medicine, which includes the diagnosis and treatment of hypertension) provided what we today call nonspecific supportive psychotherapy. Clinically significant reductions in blood pressure were observed after 2 years of regular albeit infrequent contact.

The advent of effective drugs to lower blood pressure shifted the direction of treatment strongly toward their use from the 1960s onward. But over time the undesirable side effects of these medications—drowsiness, light-headedness, and in men, erectile difficulties—as well as the growth of behavioral approaches to treatment, led many investigators to explore nonpharmacological treatments for borderline essential hypertension. Successful nonpharmacological efforts have been directed at weight reduction, restricting salt intake, giving up cigarettes, exercising regularly, and reducing alcohol consumption. Still, those with more severe hypertension usually have to take drugs to control its deleterious long-term effects.

Two of three Americans over the age of 60 have high blood pressure, and more than half of them take costly and sometimes risky hypertensive medication (risky because all drugs pose particularly serious risks to older people). As just mentioned, the importance of losing weight and reducing salt intake has been recognized for many years as useful in keeping blood pressure under control, but until recently there was little optimism that diet and weight loss could play a positive role in older adults, who often have had undesirable dietary habits for a lifetime.

A 1998 report from TONE, the controlled Trial of Nonpharmacologic Interventions in the Elderly (Whelton et al., 1998), indicated for the first time that significant benefits can be achieved by people between the ages of 60 and 80 who are obese and who are taking blood-pressure medication. Specifically, half the overweight people in the study who reduced their salt intake by 25 percent and lost as little as 8 pounds over the course of 3 months were able to come off their antihypertensive medications and maintain normal blood pressure. The ability to maintain normal blood pressure was achieved by 31 percent of the patients who reduced their salt intake, 36 percent of those who lost weight, and more than half of those who reduced both their salt intake and their weight. Furthermore, these results—the dietary and weight changes as well as the maintenance of normal blood pressure without medication—lasted for more than 3 years.

Research has shown that increasing exercise—for example, walking up stairs rather than using an elevator, and walking short distances rather than driving—yields as much benefit as a structured program of aerobic exercise (Whelton et al., 2002). Other research indicates that people with essential hypertension, as well as those whose blood pressure is within the normal range, should adopt regular exercise habits, such as walking briskly almost every day for about half an hour or engaging in other aerobic exercise that raises the heart and respiration rates (Whelton, He, et al., 2002). Most people can engage in such activity without even checking with their physician if the activity is not so strenuous that it prevents them from carrying on a conversation at the same time. In fact, the research suggests that people with high blood pressure and no other health complications should try exercise for about a year before turning to drugs to lower their blood pressure. For those already taking antihypertension drugs, a regular and not necessarily strenuous exercise regimen can sometimes reduce or even eliminate their dependence on medication. Decreases of 10 points in both systolic and diastolic blood pressure—a significant reduction—can be achieved by most people after just a few weeks. All these beneficial results may be mediated by the favorable effects that exercise has on stress, weight, and blood cholesterol. And if the sense of well-being that accompanies regular exercise and weight loss generalizes to the adoption of other health-enhancing habits, such as stopping smoking and avoiding drinking to excess, the positive effects on blood pressure will be stronger and more enduring.

Exercising regularly can also reduce mortality from cardiovascular disease (Blumenthal et al., 2002; Wannamethee, Shaper, & Walker, 1998). One study compared a stress-management intervention with an exercise intervention for men who had a history of CHD (Blumenthal et al., 2002). Patients were randomly assigned to either a weekly stress-management group, an aerobic exercise group, or a no-treatment group. The interventions lasted for 4 months. These men were followed up 5 years after the intervention, and the findings revealed that the men who had received stress-management training or exercise were significantly less likely to have had another cardiac problem than the men who did not receive treatment. Focus on Discovery 7.1 describes a major effort to prevent cardiovascular disease.

Evidence suggesting the importance of cognitive change, as well as the role of anger, has been reported. Borderline hypertensive patients who achieved significant reductions in angry thoughts showed decreases in blood pressure—as their articulated thoughts became less angry, their blood pressure became lower (Davison, Haaga, et al., 1991). This finding is consistent with the research discussed earlier linking anger with hypertension.

Biofeedback

All learning depends on feedback—that is, knowledge of the consequences of our actions guides our behavior. So the notion that feedback affects what we think, feel, and do is not at all remarkable. But a type of feedback called **biofeedback** is noteworthy because it lets people acquire control over behaviors commonly regarded as not being under voluntary control, such as muscle activity, brain waves, heart rate, skin temperature, blood pressure, and other bodily functions. The key is that the person knows immediately, through an

Exercise, such as walking briskly, can help to reduce blood pressure. (Ariel Skelley/Corbis Images.)

Focus on Discovery 7.1

Community Psychology—Preventing Cardiovascular Disease

Most of our discussions of therapy have focused on situations in which professionals make themselves available to clients in offices, clinics, or hospitals. This type of service delivery, referred to as the *waiting mode* (Rappaport & Chinsky, 1974), is characteristic of traditional therapy, whether inpatient or outpatient. **Community psychology**, in contrast, operates in the *seeking mode*; community psychologists, rather than waiting for people to initiate contact, seek out problems, or even potential problems. In addition, community psychologists often focus on prevention, in contrast to the more usual focus on trying to reduce the severity or duration of an already existing problem. Here we describe a program aimed at the prevention of cardiovascular disease.

Using Mass Media to Reduce Cardiovascular Disease

The risk of premature cardiovascular diseases is increased by the common lifestyle in an affluent, industrialized society, a lifestyle in which there is little need for physical exertion and plenty of high-calorie food rich in fat. One way to try to change harmful lifestyles is to use the mass media to inform people of what they can do to reduce their risks for such illnesses. A group of researchers in the Stanford Heart Disease Prevention Program undertook such a task (Maccoby & Altman, 1988). For their Three Communities Project, they chose a media campaign and a direct, intensive instructional program.

Three towns in northern California were the subjects of their investigation. Watsonville and Gilroy were the two experimental towns, and Tracy was the control town. For 2 years, both experimental towns were bombarded by a mass-media campaign to inform citizens about cardiovascular disorders. The campaign consisted of television and radio spots, weekly newspaper columns, and newspaper advertisements and stories urging people to stop smoking, exercise more, and eat foods low in cholesterol. Posters in buses and in stores conveyed briefly and graphically such vital information as the desirability of eating fewer eggs, since yolks are rich in cholesterol. In addition, a sample of Watsonville residents at high risk for heart disease received intensive instruction in group sessions and individual home counseling over a 10-week period. The researchers wanted to examine whether information (e.g., how to select and prepare foods low in fat and cholesterol) and exhortations to alter lifestyle delivered face to face might add to whatever positive benefits derived from the mass-media campaign. The control town, Tracy, had media services that were quite different from those of the two experimental towns. Tracy is separated from Watsonville and Gilroy by a range of low mountains and therefore, at the time, had entirely separate local television stations. The inhabitants of Tracy were not, of course, imprisoned in their hometown for the duration of the 2-year study, but for the most part they did not receive through their media the messages that were conveyed to the citizens of the two experimental towns. Because all three towns had a sizable Spanish-speaking population, all media messages were in Spanish as well as in English.

The findings revealed that citizens of Watsonville and Gilroy significantly increased their knowledge of cardiovascular risk factors; people in the control town did not gain in such knowledge. Egg consumption was reduced more in Watsonville and Gilroy than in Tracy, and clinically significant decreases in blood pressure were observed in the two experimental towns, in contrast with small increases in the control town. The high-risk residents of Watsonville who participated in the special intensive-instruction program reaped even greater benefits in lower egg consumption and lower blood pressure. Finally, the researchers considered the townspeople's overall measure of risk, a weighted average of the several known physical risk factors—high blood levels of cholesterol, smoking cigarettes, and not exercising enough. They found highly significant drops in risk in the people in the experimental towns, an important result, since we know from previous research that elevated risk scores predict reasonably well the incidence of heart disease over a 12-year period.

These positive findings led to a more ambitious and larger-scale program called the Stanford Five City Project, which extended face-to-face instructional programs to a variety of community settings, such as schools, community colleges, hospitals, and work sites, and involved many more people across a broader age range. An important goal was to embed the educational programs in existing community organizations so that any beneficial effects might persist well after the researchers had left the scene (Altman, Flora, & Farquhar, 1986). The outcome variables included actual illness and death from cardiovascular disorders. The program began in 1978 and continued well into the 1990s, with results that supported the efficacy of the interventions in significantly reducing several risk factors, including cigarette smoking, elevated cholesterol levels, low levels of physical activity, and high blood pressure (Farquhar, 1991; Farquhar et al., 1990; Jackson et al., 1991; Maccoby & Altman, 1988; Schooler, Flora, & Farquhar, 1993). The work of the Stanford group and similar projects in Finland (Tuomilehto et al., 1986) and South Africa (Farquhar et al., 1990) are important as community psychology efforts, for they demonstrate that people can learn from properly designed and delivered mass-media and other large-scale educational programs how to reduce their overall risk for cardiovascular disorders. The multiyear span of these studies is considerable and highly unusual as far as experiments in psychology are concerned. But in terms of the serious health problems that can develop through certain long-standing detrimental behavior patterns, 5 or 10 or more years is not a very long time at all. There is great potential for such community-based programs to reduce the incidence and seriousness of many medical illnesses beyond what is achievable by strictly medical practices, for it is increasingly accepted that people's physical health is primarily in their own hands and that changing one's lifestyle is often the best means of reducing the risk of illness (Bandura, 1986). However, such efforts are up against a formidable counterforce, namely, the vigorous promotion of unhealthy food, alcohol, and other negative lifestyle factors, which is much more prevalent than the promotion of healthful changes in behavior (Altman & Goodman, 2001).

auditory or visual signal, whether the somatic activity of interest is increasing or decreasing. For example, to teach a person to raise her skin temperature, we need to be able to let her know whether her skin temperature is increasing, and sensitive instrumentation can be used to provide such feedback.

Because anxiety has generally been viewed as a state involving the autonomic nervous system, and because psychophysiological disorders often afflict organs innervated by this system, researchers and clinicians have been intrigued by biofeedback aimed at giving people control over autonomic functions.

A series of classic studies at Harvard Medical School demonstrated that human volunteers could use biofeedback to achieve significant short-term changes in blood pressure and heart rate (Shapiro, Tursky, & Schwartz, 1970; Schwartz, 1973). They found that some people could even be trained to increase their heart rate while decreasing their blood pressure. Achievement of such fine-grained control lent impetus to biofeedback work and awakened hope that certain clinical disorders might be alleviated in this new way.

Unfortunately, later research using biofeedback to treat patients with essential hypertension has been somewhat encouraging, but results have not been certain enough to establish biofeedback as a standard treatment for the disease (Blanchard, 1994). Moreover, several investigators believe that relaxation training, which is often given along with biofeedback, does more than the biofeedback to reduce blood pressure (Emmelkamp, 1986; Reed, Katkin, & Goldband, 1986). In addition, biofeedback is not particularly effective for asthma (Ritz, Dahme, & Roth, 2004).

Reducing Anger and Hostility, Depression, and Social Isolation

Reducing anger and hostility has been a focus of behavioral medicine interventions for many years, especially in hypertension and coronary heart disease. The reason is straightforward, as explained earlier in this chapter: studies indicated that excessive anger and hostility are risk factors in these illnesses. These studies generally involved men who had suffered a myocardial infarction (heart attack), and the focus was on reducing the likelihood that they would have a second one.

One of the most comprehensive of these studies was the Recurrent Coronary Prevention Project (Friedman et al., 1982), which served as a model for later research. In this study, men were assigned to receive either Type A counseling or cardiological counseling. The cardiological counseling consisted of information about CHD. Those receiving the Type A counseling practiced talking more slowly and listening to others more closely. They also learned to reduce the demands placed on them so they could relax more and, in general, take a less time-pressured and less hostile approach to everyday challenges. In addition, participants were encouraged to lend less credence to beliefs identified as common among people with Type A behavior pattern—the belief that many events represent direct personal threats and the belief that a high level of mental and emotional intensity is essential to success.

This study found that Type A behavior can be changed. After 3 years of treatment, men who had received Type A counseling had cut their risk of a second heart attack almost in half (Friedman et al., 1984; Friedman & Ulmer, 1984; Powell et al., 1984; Thoresen et al., 1985). Reductions in hostility may have been particularly significant, consistent with its increasing importance in Type A research and in psychophysiological disorders generally (Haaga, 1987b).

In recent years, focus has shifted away from Type A to other psychological targets, most especially to hostility (Williams, 2001) and to the desirability of teaching people to, in general, lead more healthful and less stressful lives. The focus on anger and hostility has been widened to include depression and social isolation, also discovered to be risk factors in cardiovascular disorders as well as in other illnesses. In one study, men who had experienced myocardial infarction were randomly assigned to a hostility reduction treatment or an information-only treatment. Men who received the hostility treatment reported less hostility, were rated as less hostile, and evidenced a decrease in diastolic blood pressure (Gidron, Davidson, & Bata, 1999). The Enhancing Recovery in Coronary Heart Disease (ENRICHD) project targeted depression and social isolation among individuals recovering from myocardial infarction. Although the treatment was successful in reducing depression and social isolation, those in the treatment group did not have better heart health at the end of the study compared to the control group (Writing Committee for the ENRICHD Investigators, 2003).

See Focus on Discovery 7.2 for a discussion of coping with cancer.

Stress Management

Stress management is a set of techniques for helping people who are seldom labeled as patients (e.g., hospital personnel, factory workers, and students) to cope with the challenges that life poses for all of us. Stress management has also been used successfully for several specific diseases, including tension headaches, cancer, hypertension, AIDS, coronary heart disease, and chronic pain (e.g., Antoni et al., 2000; Cruess et al., 2000). For CHD, stress management is most effective when the intervention focuses on behavioral targets, such as quitting smoking, exercising regularly, and reducing blood pressure (Dusseldorp et al., 1999).

Stress management encompasses a variety of techniques, and more than one is typically used in any given instance (Davison & Thompson, 1988; Lehrer & Woolfolk, 1993; Steptoe, 1997). Techniques include

- *Arousal reduction.* In arousal reduction the person is trained in muscle relaxation. Teaching people to relax deeply and to apply these skills to real-life stressors can be helpful in lowering their stress levels. There is also evidence that the immune function can be improved by relaxation training (Jasnoski & Kugler, 1987; Kiecolt-Glaser et al., 1985), although enduring benefits are doubtful unless relaxation is practiced regularly over a long period of time (Davison & Thompson, 1988; Goldfried & Davison, 1994; Zakowski et al., 1992). Because stress can be seen as a reaction to situations perceived by the person as unpredictable, uncontrollable, or both, relaxation training may work by enhancing the individual's sense of self-efficacy, the belief that one is not merely a pawn at the mercy of uncontrollable forces that are not always benign (Bandura, 1997).

- *Cognitive restructuring.* Cognitive restructuring includes approaches such as those of Ellis (1962) and Beck (1976). The focus is on altering people's belief systems and improving the logical clarity of their interpretations of experience, on the assumption that people's intellectual level can affect how they feel and behave. Providing information to reduce uncertainty and enhance the person's sense of control has also been helpful in reducing stress.

- *Behavioral-skills training.* Because it is natural to feel overwhelmed if one lacks the skills to execute a challenging task, stress management often includes instruction and practice in necessary skills as well as in general issues such as time management and effective prioritizing. Included also under this rubric is training in assertion skills—expressing likes and dislikes without encroaching on the rights of others.

- *Environmental-change approaches.* Whereas the other individual strategies aim at helping the person deal with a particular environment, environmental-change approaches take the position that sometimes the environment is the problem and that efforts are best directed at altering it. One kind of environmental approach draws on research on the positive role of social support on health (see p. 192). If social support helps keep people healthy or helps them cope with illnesses, then it is reasonable to assume that enhancing such support can only be beneficial. Another kind of environmental change involves the workplace. Altering management practices or providing greater privacy and fewer interruptions can reduce stress in the world where people work and live for a significant portion of their waking hours (Murphy et al., 1995).

Cognitive Behavioral Interventions

Cognitive behavioral interventions have shown some initial success. For asthma sufferers, behavioral treatments that emphasize breathing training are associated with taking less

A community psychology approach to stress management focuses on the environment rather than on the person. To reduce stress, an office can be redesigned with partitions to provide some privacy for employees. (Dick Luria/Photo Researchers, Inc.)

Focus on Discovery 7.2

Coping with Cancer

An optimistic, upbeat attitude can be important in combating illness, including illnesses as serious as cancer (Carver et al., 1993) and HIV-positive status (Taylor et al., 1992). The mechanism by which an optimistic attitude helps people with life-threatening illnesses may be its link to adaptive coping. Optimistic people may be more likely to engage in risk-reducing behaviors such as avoiding risky sex or engaging in prescribed regular exercise following coronary-bypass surgery (Scheier & Carver, 1987).

Psychological Interventions to Help People Cope

Problem-solving therapy (PST) has shown its value in helping cancer patients cope with the myriad life challenges facing them, from daily hassles to dealing with isolation and depression (Nezu et al., 1997). An important component of PST is that it gives patients an enhanced sense of control, which seems to be particularly important for people with a life-threatening illness who are experiencing the side effects of treatment. PST has also been shown to be helpful for caregivers, who have to cope with the patient's many cancer-related problems, such as fatigue and hair loss (Bucher et al., 1999).

The stressfulness of a cancer diagnosis and its treatment makes stress-management approaches relevant, like those described earlier. Clear information about the treatment procedures themselves, including what the patient is likely to experience during and following treatment, as well as training in relaxation and hypnosis, can be helpful in reducing anxiety both prior to and following various cancer treatments. It is especially important that patients understand that fatigue is a natural accompaniment of many treatments for cancer, especially radiation and

chemotherapy. A common side effect is conditioned food aversions that result from associating certain foods with nausea from chemotherapy or radiation (Chambers & Bernstein, 1995).

Interventions to Encourage Prevention

Psychological interventions in a community psychology model also focus on preventing cancer by encouraging healthy behaviors and discouraging unhealthy ones. For example, research programs to help people stop smoking are discussed in Chapter 10. Other interventions are aimed at getting women to perform breast self-examination (BSE). The main hurdle in accomplishing this is that BSE significantly raises the probability of an aversive consequence, that is, finding a lump. Logically, it is better to take this risk than not, but the fact is that the fear of learning something unpleasant is a major deterrent to doing the exam (Mahoney, 1977). For the same reason, many high-risk women (those with first-degree relatives who had breast cancer) do not have regular mammograms (Vogel et al., 1990).

In an effort to develop ways to help women perform BSE regularly, researchers compared two pamphlets on BSE (Meyerowitz & Chaiken, 1987). One contained persuasive arguments for performing BSE while emphasizing the negative consequences of not performing BSE; the other emphasized the positive consequences of performing BSE. Both pamphlets also contained factual information about breast cancer and instructions about how to do BSE. In the following examples from these pamphlets, words in parentheses were included in the positive condition, those in brackets in the negative.

medications, but they do not really improve lung functioning significantly (Ritz & Roth, 2003). For men and women with AIDS, group-based cognitive behavioral treatments have been effective in reducing distress, increasing coping and perceived social support, and reducing depression (Lechner et al., 2003; Lutgendorf et al., 1997). Bereavement group therapy for HIV-positive gay men who had lost a partner or close friend to AIDS was beneficial in decreasing distress and viral load, a biological predictor of the progression to AIDS (Goodkin et al., 2001).

Check Your Knowledge 7.5

True or False?

1. Biofeedback has been shown to be an effective treatment for a number of psychophysiological disorders.
2. Behavioral interventions aimed at reducing salt intake and increasing exercise are effective in reducing CHD risk.
3. Stress management involves arousal reduction, cognitive restructuring, behavioral-skills training, and environmental change.
4. Cognitive behavioral approaches have been shown to be effective with chronic pain, AIDS, and to a lesser extent, asthma.

*By [not] doing BSE now, you (can) [will not] learn what your
normal healthy breasts feel like so that you will be (better) [ill]
prepared to notice any small, abnormal changes that might occur
as you get older.*

*Research shows that women who (do) [do not do] BSE have
(an increased) [a decreased] chance of finding a tumor in the early,
more treatable stage of the disease. (p. 504)*

The groups given the different pamphlets did not differ in their attitudes toward BSE immediately after reading the pamphlets. However,
4 months later, women who had received the negatively framed information were more likely to have
engaged in BSE. This effect may have occurred because those who do not engage in regular BSE take
an ignorance-is-bliss attitude, but by making the
possible negative consequences of not doing BSE
more salient, the pamphlet made doing the exam
more acceptable. This finding is particularly important because most pamphlets intended to help
women do BSE stress the positive rather than the
negative.

Other researchers extended this work by asking whether messages of the kind that were found
effective in encouraging BSE—sometimes referred to
as "loss-frame" communications—might under certain circumstances be less effective than messages
that emphasize the benefits of a certain behavior
(referred to as "gain-frame" messages). The results
from two experiments suggest that loss-frame communications are superior when people are being encouraged to detect signs of illness, while gain-frame
communications are better when people are being
encouraged to prevent illness (Rothman & Salovey,
1997).

Encouraging women to perform
breast self-examination (BSE) can
lead to earlier detection of cancer
and better treatment outcomes.
Shown here is an advertisement from
the American Cancer Society
demonstrating how to perform BSE.

What is the difference? BSE and mammography are designed to
detect signs of illness. The person lacks information about whether she
has an illness and has to decide whether to engage in behavior that
could provide information on her status, in this case, whether she might
have breast cancer. In contrast, a person going to the beach has a choice
about putting on sunscreen with a protection factor of 15 or greater,
the strength recommended to reduce the chances of getting skin cancer in the future. Such behavior is preventive in nature, that is, it is
designed to have a direct effect on reducing the
chances of getting skin cancer.

In a study that replicated the findings of
Meyerowitz and Chaiken, women told of the risks
arising from not taking a mammography exam—the
loss-frame approach—were more likely to have a
mammogram than were women told of the benefits
of doing so (Banks et al., 1995). In a later study,
sunbathers at a beach who were told of the benefits
of using sunscreen—a gain-frame communication—
were more likely to use sunscreen after reading a
communication that emphasized the benefits of such
preventive health behavior than were those who read
something that focused on the risks of not using sunscreen (Detweiler et al., 1999).

The implications of these studies are important.
If one wants to foster healthful detection-related behaviors, one should emphasize the risks associated
with not taking a certain action that could detect
a problem. But if one wants to foster healthful preventive behaviors, it is best to emphasize the benefits
that arise from doing something that can forestall a
problem.

Summary

- Psychophysiological disorders are physical diseases produced or influenced in part by psychological factors, including stress, social support,
and negative emotions.

- Psychophysiological disorders no longer appear as a diagnostic category in the DSM. Instead, the diagnostician can make a diagnosis of
psychological factors affecting a medical condition and then note the
condition on Axis III. This change reflects the growing realization that
life stress is relevant to all diseases and is not limited to those previously
considered psychosomatic.

- In attempting to understand the complex stress–illness relationship,
researchers have focused on precisely defining what stress is; on assessing differences in how people cope with perceived stress; and on how
social support impacts the stress–illness relationship.

- Theories of the etiology of psychophysiological disorders are
diathesis–stress in nature but differ in whether the diathesis is de-

scribed in psychological or biological terms. Theories positing a biological diathesis emphasize the effects of allostatic load or changes in the
immune system that are caused by stress. Theories positing a psychological diathesis focus on such factors as emotional states, personality traits,
cognitive appraisals, and specific styles of coping with stress. The most
successful accounts of etiology are those that integrate psychological and
biological factors.

- Cardiovascular disorders, which involve the heart and circulatory system, include essential hypertension and coronary heart disease
(CHD). While both conditions are complex and multifaceted, their etiologies appear to include a tendency to respond to stress with increases
in blood pressure or heart rate. Anger, hostility, cynicism, anxiety, and
depression are linked to these conditions.

- Individuals with asthma tend to have respiratory systems that over-respond to allergens or that have been weakened by prior infection. Psychological factors such as anxiety, anger, depression, stressful life events, and family conflict may trigger an asthma attack.

- Acquired immunodeficiency syndrome (AIDS) has psychological elements in that it usually arises from behavior that appears irrational and generally is preventable by psychological means. The primary focus of prevention is to change people's behavior—specifically, to encourage safer sex and to discourage the sharing of needles in intravenous substance abuse.

- Because psychophysiological disorders represent true physical dysfunctions, treatment usually includes medication. The general aim of psychotherapies for these disorders is to reduce stress, anxiety, depression, or anger.

- Researchers in the field of behavioral medicine try to find psychological interventions that can improve patients' physiological state by changing unhealthy behaviors and reducing stress. They have developed ways of helping people relax, smoke less, eat fewer fatty foods, and engage in behaviors that can prevent or alleviate illnesses, such as encouraging breast self-examination and adhering to medical treatment recommendations.

- Stress management interventions help people without diagnosable problems avail themselves of techniques that allow them to cope with the inevitable stress of everyday life and thereby ameliorate the toll that stress can take on the body.

Answers to Check Your Knowledge Questions

7.1 1. a; 2. b; 3. d
7.2 1. T; 2. F; 3. F; 4. F
7.3 1. essential or primary; 2. hypertension, CHD; 3. blood pressure, hypertension

7.4 1. F; 2. F; 3. T; 4. T; 5. F
7.5 1. F; 2. T; 3. T; 4. T

Key Terms

AIDS (acquired immune deficiency syndrome)
allostatic load
anger-in theory
angina pectoris
asthma
behavioral medicine

biofeedback
cardiovascular disorders
community psychology
coping
coronary heart disease (CHD)
cytokines
essential hypertension

functional social support
health psychology
interleukin-6 (IL-6)
metabolic syndrome
myocardial infarction
psychological factors affecting medical condition

psychoneuroimmunology
psychophysiological disorders
secretory immunoglobulin A (sIgA)
stress management
structural social support
Type A behavior pattern

8 Mood Disorders

Learning Goals

1. Be able to describe the symptoms of depression and mania, the diagnostic criteria for depressive disorders and bipolar disorders, and the epidemiology of these disorders.
2. Be able to discuss the genetic, neurobiological, social, and psychological factors that contribute to the symptoms of mood disorders.
3. Be able to identify the medication and psychological treatments of depressive and manic symptoms, and the current views of electroconvulsive therapy.
4. Be able to explain the epidemiology of suicide, the neurobiological, social, and psychological risk factors associated with suicide, and methods for preventing suicide.

Clinical Case: Mary

Mary M., a 38-year-old mother of four children, had been deeply depressed for about 2 months when she first went to see a psychologist. Three years earlier, she had returned to work when health care bills made it hard for her family to get by on her husband's income as a high school teacher. About 7 months before her visit to the psychologist, she was laid off from her job as an administrative assistant, which was a serious blow to the family's finances. She felt guilty about the loss of her job and became preoccupied with signs of her overall incompetence. Each night, she struggled for more than an hour to fall asleep, only to wake up frequently throughout the night. She had little appetite and as a result had lost 10 pounds. She also had little energy for and no interest in activities that she had enjoyed in the past. Household chores became impossible for her to do, and her husband began to complain. Their marriage had already been strained for 2 years, and her lack of energy and negativity contributed to further arguments. Finally, realizing that something serious had happened to his wife, Mr. M. cajoled her into making an appointment with a psychologist. (You will read about the outcome of Mary's treatment later in this chapter.)

Mood disorders involve disabling disturbances in emotion—from the extreme sadness and disengagement of depression to the extreme elation and irritability of mania. In this chapter, we begin by discussing the clinical description and the epidemiology of the different mood disorders. Next, we consider various perspectives on the etiology of these disorders, and then consider approaches to treating them. We conclude with an examination of suicide, an action far too often associated with mood disorders.

Clinical Descriptions and Epidemiology of Mood Disorders

DSM-IV-TR recognizes two broad types of **mood disorders**: those that involve only depressive symptoms, and those that involve manic symptoms (bipolar disorders). We begin by considering the signs of depression, the formal criteria for diagnosis of the depressive disorders (including major depressive disorder and dysthymic disorder), and the epidemiology and consequences of depressive disorders. Then, we turn to bipolar disorders. There, we describe the signs of mania, followed by the formal criteria for diagnosing bipolar I disorder, bipolar II disorder, and cyclothymic disorder, and then the epidemiology and consequences of bipolar disorders. Table 8.1 presents a summary of the symptoms of each of these disorders. After covering the basic diagnostic categories, we describe DSM-IV-TR subtypes that are used to further define depressive disorders and bipolar disorders.

Depressive Disorders

The cardinal symptoms of depression include profound sadness and/or an inability to experience pleasure. Most of us experience sadness during our lives, and most of us say that we are "depressed" at one time or another. But most of these experiences do not have the intensity and duration to be diagnosable. The author William Styron (1992) wrote about his depression, "Like anyone else I have always had times when I felt deeply depressed, but this was something altogether new in my experience—a despairing, unchanging paralysis of the spirit beyond anything I had ever known or imagined could exist."

When people develop a depressive disorder, their heads may reverberate with self-recriminations. Like Mary, described in the clinical case, they may become focused on their flaws and deficits. Paying attention can be so exhausting that they have difficulty absorbing what they read and hear. They often view things in a very negative light, and they tend to lose hope.

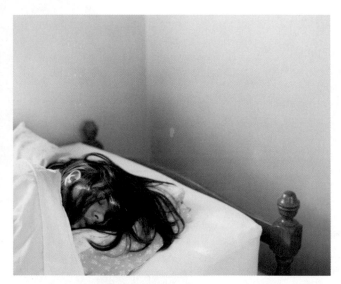

Some people with depression have trouble falling asleep and staying asleep. Others find themselves sleeping for more than 10 hours, but still feeling exhausted. (Shannon Fagan/Stone/Getty Images.)

Physical symptoms of depression are also common, including fatigue and low energy, as well as physical aches and pains. These symptoms can be profound enough to convince afflicted persons that they must be suffering from some serious medical condition, even though the symptoms have no apparent physical cause (Simon et al., 1999). Although people with depression typically feel exhausted, they may find it hard to fall asleep and may wake up frequently. Other people sleep throughout the day. They may find that food tastes bland or that their appetite is gone, or they may experience an increase in appetite. Sexual interest disappears. Some may find their limbs feel heavy. Thoughts and

Table 8.1 A Summary of the Mood Disorder Diagnoses

Depressive Disorders	Diagnostic Criteria	Bipolar Disorders	Diagnostic Criteria
Major depressive disorder	Sad mood or loss of pleasure for 2 weeks, along with at least 4 other symptoms	Bipolar I disorder	At least one lifetime manic or mixed episode
		Bipolar II disorder	At least one lifetime episode of hypomania and episodes of major depression
Dysthymic disorder	Mood is down and other symptoms are present at least 50 percent of the time for at least 2 years	Cyclothymic disorder	Recurrent mood changes from high to low, without hypomanic or manic episodes for at least 2 years

movements may slow for some (*psychomotor retardation*), but others cannot sit still—they pace, fidget, and wring their hands (*psychomotor agitation*).

Beyond these cognitive and physical symptoms, initiative may disappear. Withdrawal from others is common; many prefer to sit alone and remain silent. Some people with depression neglect their appearance. When people become utterly dejected and hopeless, thoughts about suicide are common.

Major Depressive Disorder   The DSM-IV-TR diagnosis of **major depressive disorder (MDD)** requires depressive symptoms to be present for at least 2 weeks. These symptoms must include either depressed mood or loss of interest and pleasure. As shown in the DSM-IV-TR criteria, at least four additional symptoms must be present, such as changes in sleep, appetite, attention, feelings of worthlessness, suicidality, psychomotor agitation, or retardation.

MDD is called an **episodic disorder**, because symptoms tend to be present for a period of time and then clear. A depressive episode tends to dissipate over time, but an untreated episode may stretch on for 5 months or even longer. For a small percentage of people, the depression becomes chronic—the person does not completely snap back to the prior level of functioning. Even among those who improve enough that they no longer meet the criteria for diagnosis of MDD, subclinical depression can remain for years (Judd et al., 1998).

Major depressive episodes tend to recur—once a given episode clears, a person is likely to experience another episode. About two-thirds of people with an episode of major depression will experience at least one more episode during their lifetime (Solomon et al., 2000). The average number of episodes is about four (Judd, 1997). With every new episode that a person experiences, his or her risk for experiencing another episode goes up by 16 percent (Solomon et al., 2000). DSM-IV-TR distinguishes people with a single episode from those with recurrent MDD.

There is controversy about whether a person with five symptoms lasting 2 weeks (i.e., someone who meets the criteria for diagnosis with MDD) is distinctly different from someone who has only three symptoms for 10 days (i.e., someone who meets the criteria for so-called *subclinical depression*). A study of twins found that subclinical depression predicted the occurrence of future episodes of MDD and even the diagnosis of MDD in a co-twin. That is, when one twin had subclinical depression, both twins were likely to have future episodes of major depression (Kendler & Gardner, 1998). Another study found that people with subclinical depression had as much trouble functioning normally in their everyday activities as did people who met the criteria for diagnosis of MDD (Gotlib, Lewinsohn, & Seeley, 1995). Evidence from studies like these might lead to a change of criteria for the diagnosis of MDD in DSM-V.

Dysthymic Disorder   People with **dysthymic disorder** (also called *dysthymia*) are chronically depressed—more than half of the time for at least 2 years, they feel blue or derive little pleasure from usual activities and pastimes. In addition, they have at least two of the other symptoms of depression. DSM-IV-TR distinguishes dysthymia from MDD by the duration, type, and number of symptoms. Compare the diagnostic criteria for MDD and dysthymic disorder—note that one of the diagnostic criteria for dysthymia is that the person does not have enough symptoms to warrant a diagnosis of MDD.

Epidemiology and Consequences of Depressive Disorders   MDD is one of the most prevalent psychiatric disorders, leading some to dub this "the common cold of mental illness." One large-scale epidemiological study in the United States estimated that 16.2 percent of people meet the criteria for diagnosis of MDD at some point in their lives (Kessler et al., 2005). Dysthymia is rarer than MDD: about 2.5 percent of people meet criteria for dysthymia during their lives (Kessler et al., 2005).

MDD is approximately two times more common in women than in men (see Focus on Discovery 8.1 for a discussion of possible reasons for this gender difference in rates of MDD). Socioeconomic status also matters—that is, MDD is three times as common among people who are impoverished compared to those who are not (Kessler et al., 2003).

DSM-IV-TR Criteria for Major Depressive Disorder

Sad mood or loss of pleasure in usual activities.
At least four of the following:

- Difficulties in sleeping (insomnia): trouble falling asleep; not returning to sleep after awakening during the night, waking too early; or, prolonged duration of sleep
- Psychomotor retardation or agitation
- Poor appetite and weight loss, or increased appetite and weight gain
- Loss of energy
- Feelings of worthlessness
- Difficulty concentrating, thinking, or making decisions
- Recurrent thoughts of death or suicide

Symptoms are present nearly every day, most of the day, for at least 2 weeks.
Symptoms cause significant distress or functional impairment.
The symptoms are not due to normal bereavement.

DSM-IV-TR Criteria for Dysthymic Disorder

Depressed mood more than half of the time for 2 years
At least two of the following during that time:

- poor appetite or overeating
- sleeping too much or too little
- low energy
- poor self-esteem
- trouble concentrating or making decisions
- hopelessness

The symptoms do not clear for more than 2 months at a time
No major depressive episode was present during the first 2 years of symptoms
Symptoms cause significant distress or functional impairment

Focus on Discovery 8.1

Gender Differences in Depression

Major depression occurs about twice as often in women as in men, with the exception of certain groups. For example, this gender difference does not hold between Jewish adults, because depression is more common among Jewish men than among men in general (Levav et al., 1997). But for most ethnic and cultural groups, a clear gender difference in MDD begins to emerge during early adolescence and is documented consistently by late adolescence. Several factors may help explain this gender difference (Nolan-Hoeksema, 2001):

- Twice as many girls as boys are exposed to childhood sexual abuse.
- During adulthood, women are more likely than men to be exposed to chronic stressors such as poverty and are more likely to have primary responsibility for taking care of children and sick family members.
- Acceptance of established social roles among girls may intensify self-critical attitudes about appearance.

- Social roles may interfere with pursuit of some potentially rewarding activities that are not considered "feminine."
- Exposure to childhood and chronic stressors, as well as the effects of female hormones, could change the reactivity of the HPA axis, a biological system guiding reactions to stress.
- A focus on gaining approval and closeness within interpersonal relationships, which is more commonly endorsed by women, may intensify reactions to major losses.
- Social roles promote emotion-focused coping among women, which may then extend the duration of sad moods after major stressors.

In all likelihood, gender differences in depression are related to multiple factors. Identifying these factors and understanding how they work continues to be a major focus of research.

The gender difference in depression does not emerge until adolescence. At that time, young women encounter many stressors and more pressure concerning social roles and body image, and they tend to ruminate about the resulting negative feelings. (Jeff Greenberg/Photo Researchers.)

The prevalence of depression varies considerably across cultures. In a major cross-cultural study using the same diagnostic criteria and structured interview in each country, prevalence of MDD varied from a low of 1.5 percent in Taiwan to a high of 19 percent in Beirut, Lebanon (Weissman et al., 1996). Another study yielded the intriguing result that people who have moved to the United States from Mexico have lower rates of MDD and other psychiatric disorders than do people of Mexican descent who were born in the United States (Vega et al., 1998). Why? People have speculated that traditional Mexican values may help protect against depression, or that the resiliency of people who are able to immigrate could be protective. Symptoms of depression also show some cross-cultural variation, probably resulting from differences in cultural standards of acceptable expressions of emotional distress. For example, complaints of nerves and headaches are common in Latino culture, and reports of weakness and fatigue are common among some Asian cultures.

In most countries, the prevalence of MDD increased steadily during the mid to late twentieth century (Klerman, 1988); at the same time, the age of onset decreased. Figure 8.1 shows that the age of onset has become lower for each recent generation of people in the United States: among people in their 60s, less than 5 percent reported that they had experienced an episode of MDD by age 20, whereas among people ages 18–29, almost 10 percent reported that they had experienced an episode of MDD by age 20. The median age of onset is now the late teens to early twenties. One possible explanation for the increasing depression rates lies in the social changes that have occurred over the past 100 years. Support structures—such as a tightly knit extended family and marital stability—that were a more central part of society in the past—are often absent for people today. Yet, there are no clear

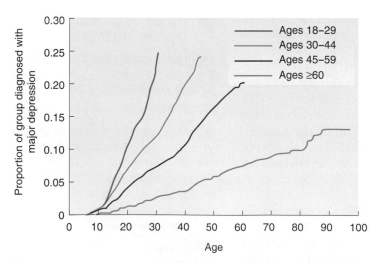

Figure 8.1 With each generation, the median age of onset for major depression gets younger. [Adapted from Kessler et al. (2003). JAMA, 289, 3095–3105.]

data about why depression seems to strike earlier and earlier. Beyond the prevalence rates, the symptoms of depression vary somewhat across the life span. Depression in children often results in somatic complaints, such as headaches or stomachaches (see p. 468). In older adults, depression is often characterized by distractibility and complaints of memory loss (see p. 514).

Both MDD and dysthymia are often associated, or comorbid, with other psychological problems. The most common comorbid conditions include anxiety disorders, substance-related disorders, sexual dysfunctions, and personality disorders. As many as two-thirds of people who meet the criteria for diagnosis of MDD during their lifetime will also meet the criteria for diagnosis of an anxiety disorder at some point (Mineka, Watson, & Clark, 1998).

Depression has many serious consequences. As we will discuss later, suicide is a real risk. MDD is also one of the world's leading causes of disability (Murray & Lopez, 1996); it is estimated that MDD is associated with $31 billion per year in lost productivity in the United States (Stewart et al., 2003). Although the diagnostic criteria for dysthymia require fewer symptoms than for MDD, do not make the mistake of thinking that dysthymia is a less severe disorder than MDD. Unlike MDD, dysthymia is chronic, and this takes a toll. Indeed, a study following patients for 5 years found that people with dysthymia were more likely to require hospitalization, were more likely to attempt suicide, and were more impaired in their functioning than people with MDD (Klein et al., 2000).

Bipolar Disorders

DSM-IV-TR recognizes three forms of bipolar disorders: bipolar I disorder, bipolar II disorder, and cyclothymia. Manic symptoms are the defining feature of each of these disorders. Like depressive disorders, the bipolar disorders are differentiated by how severe and long-lasting the manic symptoms are.

These disorders are labeled "bipolar" because most people who experience symptoms of mania will also experience symptoms of depression during their lifetime (mania and depression are considered opposite poles). An episode of depression is not required for a diagnosis of bipolar I, but it is required for a diagnosis of bipolar II disorder. Most people seeking treatment for bipolar I disorder are likely to have experienced depressive episodes (Johnson & Kizer, 2002).

Mania is a state of intense elation or irritability accompanied by other symptoms shown in the diagnostic criteria. During a manic episode, people may become louder and make an incessant stream of remarks, sometimes full of puns, jokes, rhymes, and interjections about nearby stimuli that have attracted their attention (like Wayne in the Clinical Case). These remarks may be difficult to interrupt and may shift rapidly from topic to topic, reflecting an underlying **flight of ideas**. During mania, people may become sociable to a point of intrusiveness. Unfortunately, they can be oblivious to the potentially disastrous consequences of their behavior, which can include imprudent sexual activities, overspending, and reckless driving. Attempts by others to curb such excesses can quickly bring anger and even rage. Mania usually comes on suddenly over a period of a day or two.

Most manic episodes are "purely" manic, but sometimes, people experience **mixed episodes**, characterized by severe symptoms of both mania and depression within the same week. DSM-IV-TR also includes criteria for **hypomania** (see diagnostic criteria for mania and hypomania). *Hypo-* comes from the Greek for "under"; hypomania is "under"—less extreme than—mania.

Bipolar I Disorder   In DSM-IV-TR, the criteria for diagnosis of **bipolar I disorder** (formerly known as manic-depressive disorder) include a single episode of mania or a single mixed episode during the course of a person's life. It is important to note, then, that a person who is diagnosed with bipolar I disorder may or may not be experiencing current symptoms of mania. In fact, even if they experienced only 1 week of manic symptoms years ago, they are still diagnosed with bipolar I disorder. Even more than MDD, bipolar disorders tend to recur. Over 50 percent of people with bipolar I disorder have four or more episodes (Goodwin & Jamison, 1990).

DSM-IV-TR Criteria for Manic and Hypomanic Episodes

Distinctly elevated or irritable mood
At least three of the following (four if mood is irritable):

- Increase in goal-directed activity or physical restlessness
- Unusual talkativeness; rapid speech
- Flight of ideas or subjective impression that thoughts are racing
- Decreased need for sleep
- Inflated self-esteem; belief that one has special talents, powers, or abilities
- Distractibility; attention easily diverted
- Excessive involvement in pleasurable activities that are likely to have undesirable consequences, such as reckless spending, sexual behavior, or driving

For a manic episode:

- Symptoms last for 1 week or require hospitalization
- Symptoms cause significant distress or functional impairment

For a hypomanic episode:

- Symptoms last at least 4 days
- Functioning is unequivocally different, but not markedly impaired

Clinical Case: Wayne

Wayne, a 32-year-old insurance appraiser, had been married for 8 years. He and his wife and their two children lived comfortably and happily in a middle-class neighborhood. He had not experienced any clear symptoms until age 32. One morning, Wayne told his wife that he was bursting with energy and ideas, that his job was unfulfilling, and that he was just wasting his talent. That night he slept little, spending most of the time at a desk, writing furiously. The next morning he left for work at the usual time but returned home at 11:00 A.M., his car overflowing with aquariums and other equipment for tropical fish. He had quit his job, then withdrawn all the money from the family's savings account and spent it on tropical-fish equipment. Wayne reported that the previous night he had worked out a way to modify existing equipment so that fish "won't die anymore. We'll be millionaires." After unloading the paraphernalia, Wayne set off to canvass the neighborhood for possible buyers, going door-to-door and talking to anyone who would listen.

Wayne reported that no one in his family had been treated for bipolar disorder. But his mother had gone through periods when she would be extremely adventurous and stop sleeping. For the most part, the family had regarded these episodes as unproblematic, but during one period, she had set off across the country without the children and had returned only after spending a major amount of money.

The following bit of conversation indicates Wayne's incorrigible optimism and provocativeness:

Therapist: Well, you seem pretty happy today.
Wayne: Happy! Happy! You certainly are a master of understatement, you rogue! [Shouting, literally jumping out of his seat.] Why, I'm ecstatic! I'm leaving for the West Coast today, on my daughter's bicycle. Only 3,100 miles. That's nothing, you know. I could probably walk, but I want to get there by next week. And along the way I plan to contact a lot of people about investing in my fish equipment. I'll get to know more people that way—you know, Doc, "know" in the biblical sense [leering at the therapist seductively]. Oh, God, how good it feels. It's almost like a nonstop orgasm.

DSM-IV-TR Criteria for Cyclothymic Disorder

For at least 2 years:

- numerous periods with hypomanic symptoms that do not meet criteria for a manic episode.
- numerous periods with depressive symptoms that do not meet criteria for a major depressive episode

The symptoms do not clear for more than 2 months at a time.
Symptoms cause significant distress or functional impairment.

Bipolar II Disorder DSM-IV-TR also includes a milder form of bipolar disorder, called **bipolar II disorder**. To be diagnosed with bipolar II disorder, a person must have experienced at least one major depressive episode and at least one episode of *hypomania*.

Cyclothymic Disorder **Cyclothymic disorder** (also called *cyclothymia*) is a second chronic mood disorder (the other is dysthymic disorder). As with diagnosis of dysthymic disorder, DSM-IV-TR requires that symptoms be present for at least 2 years (see diagnostic criteria). In cyclothymic disorder, the person has frequent but mild symptoms of depression, alternating with mild symptoms of mania. Although the symptoms do not reach the severity of full-blown manic or depressive episodes, people with the disorder and those close to them typically notice the ups and downs. During lows, a person may be sad, feel inadequate, withdraw from people, and sleep for 10 hours a night. During highs, a person may be boisterous, overly confident, socially uninhibited and gregarious, and need little sleep.

Epidemiology and Consequences of Bipolar Disorders Conducting community studies on bipolar disorders is a challenge—many people with a history of manic symptoms do not realize that they have had these symptoms, so estimates of prevalence may be underestimates. Bipolar I disorder is much rarer than MDD—about 1 percent of people will meet the criteria for bipolar I disorder (Weissman et al., 1996). It is hard to know with certainty, but researchers estimate that about 4 percent of people experience some bipolar I or bipolar II disorder (Kessler et al., 2005), and perhaps another 4 percent experience cyclothymic disorder (Regeer et al., 2004). The average age of onset of bipolar disorders is in the twenties, but these conditions are being seen with increasing frequency among children and adolescents (Kessler et al., 2005). Bipolar disorders occur equally often in men and women, but women experience episodes of depression more commonly than do men (Leibenluft, 1996).

Bipolar I disorder is among the most severe forms of mental illnesses. One-third of people remain unemployed a full year after hospitalization for mania (Harrow et al., 1990). Suicide rates are high for both bipolar I and bipolar II disorders (Angst et al., 2002). People with bipolar disorders are at high risk for a range of other medical conditions, including cardiovascular disease, diabetes mellitus, obesity, and thyroid disease (Kupfer, 2005). The sad consequences of bipolar disorders are not offset by evidence that hypomania is associated with creativity and achievement (see Focus on Discovery 8.2).

People with cyclothymia are at elevated risk for developing episodes of mania and major depression. Even if full-blown manic episodes do not emerge, the chronicity of cyclothymic symptoms takes a toll.

Check Your Knowledge 8.1

Fill in the blank.

1. Major depressive disorder is diagnosed based on at least_____ symptoms lasting at least_____ weeks.
2. Approximately_____percent of people will experience depression during their lifetime.
3. As many as _____percent of people with an episode of depression will experience another episode.
4. The average age of onset for MDD is _____.
5. Depressive symptoms must last for at least _____ years to qualify for a DSM-IV-TR diagnosis of dysthymia.
6. Approximately _____ out of every 100 people will experience a manic episode during their lifetime.
7. Bipolar I disorder is diagnosed on the basis of _____ or _____ episodes, and bipolar II disorder is diagnosed on the basis of_____ episodes.

Subtypes of Depressive Disorders and Bipolar Disorders

The mood disorders are highly heterogeneous—that is, people who have been diagnosed with the same disorder may show very different symptoms. DSM-IV-TR deals with this by providing criteria for dividing MDD and bipolar disorders into a number of subtypes, based on either specific symptoms or the pattern of symptoms over time.

DSM-IV-TR states that MDD, bipolar I disorder, and bipolar II disorder qualify as **seasonal** if episodes happen regularly at a particular time of the year. Therapy for "winter depressions" involves exposing the patients to bright white light (Wirz-Justice et al., 1993). Bipolar I disorder and bipolar II disorder qualify as **rapid cycling** if the person has experienced at least four episodes within the past year (see Figure 8.2).

Other subtypes are applied to a given episode of MDD or mania. These include subtypes to label the presence of **psychotic features** (delusions or hallucinations), **catatonic features** (extreme physical immobility or excessive peculiar physical movement), or a **postpartum onset** (onset within 4 weeks postpartum).

Although psychotic, catatonic, and postpartum subtypes can be applied to both depressed and manic episodes, the term **melancholic** is used only for episodes of depression. As described in DSM-IV-TR, a person suffering from depression with melancholic features finds no pleasure in any activity and does not feel better even temporarily when good things happen, and also experiences at least three other symptoms of depression such as a distinct quality of mood, depressive symptoms that are worse in the morning than at other times of

Figure 8.2 The rapid cycling subtype of bipolar disorder is defined by at least four mood episodes per year, as shown in this case.

Mike Wallace, an internationally recognized anchorman, has talked openly about his struggles with major depressive disorder. (AP/Wide World Photos.)

Creativity and Mood Disorders

Mood disorders are common among artists and writers. Tchaikovsky and Gauguin (shown here in a self-portrait) were affected, and so is Axl Rose. (Top photo: Photo Researchers; bottom photo: Timothy A. Clary/AFP/Getty Images News and Sport Services.)

In her book *Touched with Fire: Manic-Depressive Illness and the Artistic Temperament* (1992), Kay Jamison, an expert on bipolar disorders and herself a longtime sufferer with bipolar I disorder, assembled much evidence linking mood disorders, especially bipolar disorder, to artistic creativity. Of course, most people with mood disorders are not particularly creative, and most creative people do not have mood disorders—but the list of visual artists, composers, and writers who seem to have experienced mood disorders is impressive, including Michelangelo, van Gogh, Tchaikovsky, Schumann, Gauguin, Tennyson, Shelley, and Whitman, among others.

Self-portrait by Paul Gauguin. He is but one of the many artists and writers who apparently suffered from a mood disorder. (Paul Gauguin/SUPERSTOCK.)

Many people assume that the manic state itself fosters creativity through elated mood, increased energy, rapid thoughts, and a heightened ability to make connections among seemingly unrelated events. Extreme mania, however, lowers creative output, and even if people produce more work during a manic period, the quality of that work might suffer, as seems to have been the case for the composer Robert Schumann (Weisberg, 1994). Moreover, studies have shown that people who have experienced episodes of mania tend to be less creative than those who have had the milder episodes of hypomania, and both groups tend to produce less than non ill family members (Richards et al., 1988). These findings are important, because many people with bipolar disorder worry that taking medications may lower their creativity. Rather, reducing manic symptoms should help, rather than hurt, creativity.

day, waking at least 2 hours too early, loss of appetite, psychomotor retardation or agitation, or guilt. Studies of the distinction between depressions with or without melancholic features have not always supported the validity of this subtype. One study, for example, suggested that MDD with melancholic features may just be a more severe type of depression—that is, people with melancholic features have more comorbidity (e.g., with anxiety disorders), more frequent episodes of depression, and more impairment in everyday activities (Kendler, 1997).

Quick Summary

DSM-IV-TR contains two broad types of mood disorders: depressive disorders and bipolar disorders. Depressive disorders include major depressive disorder and dysthymic disorder, and bipolar disorders include bipolar I disorder, bipolar II disorder, and cyclothymic disorder. Major depression is characterized by severe episodes lasting at least 2 weeks, whereas dysthymia is characterized by milder symptoms that last at least 2 years. Bipolar I disorder is diagnosed on the basis of a single lifetime manic or mixed episode, and bipolar II disorder is diagnosed on the basis of hypomania and major depression. Cyclothymia is defined by frequent shifts between mild depressive and manic symptoms that last at least 2 years. Subtypes of mood disorders are used to differentiate different patterns of symptoms. These subtypes include distinctions based on a seasonal pattern, rapid cycling, psychotic features, catatonic features, postpartum onset, and for depression, melancholia. MDD is one of the most common disorders, whereas bipolar I disorder affects approximately 1 percent of the population. Most people with MDD will experience another episode. Bipolar disorder is even more recurrent— about 50 percent of people with bipolar I disorder experience four or more episodes.

Etiology of Mood Disorders

When we think of the profound extremes embodied in the mood disorders, it is natural to ask why these happen. How can we explain Mary sinking into the depths of depression? What factors combined to drive Wayne into his frenzied state of unrealistic ambitions? Studies of etiology focus on why these disorders unfold. No single cause can explain mood disorders. A number of different factors combine to explain the onset of the disorders.

While the diagnostic criteria specify several different depressive disorders and bipolar disorders, the research on etiology and treatment has tended to focus on major depressive disorder and bipolar I disorder. For simplicity, we refer to these conditions as depression and bipolar disorder through the remainder of this chapter.

We begin by discussing neurobiological factors involved in depression and bipolar disorder. We discuss psychosocial predictors of depression, then turn to psychosocial models of bipolar disorder.

Neurobiological Factors in Mood Disorders

As Table 8.2 shows there are many different approaches to understanding the neurobiological factors involved in mood disorders. Here, we will discuss genetic, neurotransmitter, brain imaging, and neuroendocrine research.

Genetic Factors A meta-analysis of a set of studies found that, on average, the more careful studies of MZ (identical) and DZ (fraternal) twins yield heritability estimates of 37 percent for MDD (Sullivan, Neale, & Kendler, 2000). That is, about 37 percent of the variance in whether or not a person will develop depression is explained by genes (see p. 109 for more detail about genetic research). Heritability estimates are higher when researchers study more severe samples (e.g., when the people in the study are recruited in inpatient hospitals rather than outpatient clinics; Kendler, Vale et al., 1992). Beyond the twin studies, several small-scale adoption studies also support the modest heritability of MDD (Wender et al., 1986).

Noted psychologist Kay Redfield Jamison has experienced episodes of mania and therefore would be regarded as having bipolar I disorder. She has written vivid accounts of her experiences, as well as scientific books about the disorders. (Courtesy of Kay Redfield Jamison.)

Table 8.2 Summary of Neurobiological Hypotheses about Major Depression and Bipolar Disorder

	Genetic Contribution	Neurotransmitter Dysfunction	Cortisol	Brain Imaging
Major depressive disorder	Modest	Serotonin-receptor dysfunction	High	Changes in the dorsolateral prefrontal cortex, amygdala, hippocampus, and dorsal anterior cingulate
		Possible change in the dopamine receptors within the reward system		
Bipolar disorder	High	Serotonin-receptor dysfunction	High	Changes in the dorsolateral prefrontal cortex, amygdala, hippocampus, and dorsal anterior cingulate;
		Possible involvement of dopamine receptors in the reward system		Loss of volume in the raphe nucleus, where serotonin is produced

Seasonal depression is one of the subtypes of major depressive disorder. This woman is having light therapy, which is an effective treatment for patients whose seasonal depression occurs during the winter. (Griffin/The Image Works.)

Figure 8.3 Serotonin and dopamine pathways are widespread in the brain.

Bipolar disorder is among the most heritable of disorders. Much of the evidence for this comes from studies of twins. If one twin has bipolar disorder, the odds are about 70 percent that an MZ twin will have bipolar disorder (a 70 percent concordance rate), and the odds are about 25 percent that a fraternal twin will have bipolar disorder (Kelsoe, 1997). Based on differences in the concordance rates for MZ and DZ twins, heritability estimates as high as 85 percent have been obtained for bipolar disorder (McGuffin et al., 2003). Stated differently, genes seem to account for as much as 85% of the variance in whether or not a person will develop mania. Adoption studies also confirm the importance of heritability in bipolar disorder (e.g., Wender et al., 1986). Genetic models, however, do not explain the timing or severity of manic symptoms.

As we have noted, people who experience manic episodes are likely also to experience depressive episodes, and there is evidence that this pattern has a genetic basis. That is, family members of people with a history of mania are at higher risk for depression than the general population. Twin studies also suggest that the risk for mania is related to a higher risk for depression (McGuffin et al., 2003).

Linkage analysis (see p. 33) has also been applied to bipolar I disorder. A widely reported linkage study of the Old Order Amish found evidence favoring the hypothesis that bipolar disorder results from a dominant gene on chromosome 11 (Egeland et al., 1987). These findings generated a great deal of excitement, but several attempts to replicate the Egeland study failed, leading many researchers to conclude that chromosome 11 is not involved in bipolar disorder (Kelsoe, 1997). Research on linkage continues and has broadened to focus on genes on other chromosomes, especially on chromosomes 13 and 22 (Badner & Gershon, 2002).

Because the mood disorders are characterized by so many different symptoms, most researchers think that these disorders will eventually be related to a set of genes, rather than to any single gene. Even if we can identify the genes involved in mood disorders, many questions still remain about how they will work. It is unlikely that genes will simply control whether or not a person develops depression. Rather, as we will discuss later, genes may guide the way people regulate emotions or respond to life stressors. As such, they may set the stage for mood disorders to occur when other conditions are present.

Neurotransmitters   Three neurotransmitters have been studied the most in terms of their possible role in mood disorders: **norepinephrine**, **dopamine**, and **serotonin**. Each of these neurotransmitters is present in many different areas of the brain. Figure 8.3 illustrates how widespread serotonin and dopamine pathways are in the brain.

Original models suggested that depression would be tied to low levels of norepinephrine and dopamine, and mania would be tied to high levels of norepinephrine and dopamine. Mania and depression also were both posited to be tied to low levels of serotonin, a neurotransmitter which is believed to help regulate norepinephrine and dopamine (Thase et al., 2002). Researchers initially believed that mood disorders would be explained by absolute levels of neurotransmitters in the synaptic cleft that were either too high or too low. Emerging evidence, however, did not completely support the idea that levels of neurotransmitters were important in the mood disorders.

Studies of antidepressants were one source of contradictory evidence. On the one hand, these studies do suggest that depression is related in some way to these neurotransmitters. For example, effective antidepressants promote an immediate increase in levels of serotonin, norepinephrine, and/or dopamine. See Figure 8.4 for an overview of these immediate effects. But when researchers studied the time course of how antidepressants change neurotransmitter levels, they began to realize that depression could not be explained just by the absolute level of the neurotransmitters. Antidepressants take 7 to 14 days to relieve depression, and by that time, the neurotransmitter levels have already returned to their previous state. It would seem, then, that a simple change in norepinephrine, dopamine, or serotonin levels is not a good explanation for why the drugs alleviate depression.

Other evidence also indicates that absolute levels of neurotransmitters did not tell the whole story. For decades, researchers studied the metabolites of neurotransmitters as an index of how much of a neurotransmitter was being released into the synaptic cleft. Recall that after a neurotransmitter is released into the synaptic cleft, enzymes begin to break down the neurotransmitter that is not reabsorbed by the cell. Metabolite studies, then, assess how much neurotransmitter has been broken down and carried into the cerebrospinal fluid, the blood, or the urine. Although some people with mania or depression showed the expected high or low levels of metabolites, findings from these studies were not consistent, suggesting that many people with depression did not have disturbances in the absolute levels of neurotransmitters; similarly, many people with mania did not have disturbances in the absolute levels of neurotransmitters (Placidi et al., 2001; Ressler & Nemeroff, 1999).

Given this inconsistent evidence, researchers began to focus on the idea that mood disorders might be related to the sensitivity of postsynaptic receptors that detect the presence of neurotransmitter in the synaptic cleft. How can researchers test models of high or low receptor sensitivity? If receptors are more or less sensitive, one might expect people to react differently to drugs that influence the level of a given neurotransmitter. For example, receptors that are overly sensitive may respond to even the smallest amount of a neurotransmitter in the synaptic cleft. Researchers have focused more on dopamine and serotonin in these studies than on norepinephrine. Among people with bipolar disorder, several different drugs that increase dopamine levels have been found to trigger manic symptoms, suggesting that dopamine receptors may be overly sensitive in bipolar disorder (Anand et al., 2000). Other research has shown that people with depression respond differently than other people do to drugs that increase dopamine levels (Naranjo et al., 2001). Some theories suggest that we will need to look at dopamine receptors within specific regions of the brain, a topic we will return to when we discuss brain imaging below.

In addition to links between dopamine and mania, studies focused on depression and receptor sensitivity to serotonin. Researchers have conducted a set of studies that involve experimentally lowering serotonin levels. By raising or lowering serotonin levels, researchers can check how sensitive receptors are to fluctuations. A person who has insensitive receptors is expected to experience depressive symptoms as levels drop. To lower serotonin levels, researchers deplete levels of **tryptophan**, the major precursor of serotonin. Tryptophan can be depleted with a drink that contains high levels of 15 amino acids, but no tryptophan. As a control condition, people can be given a similar-tasting drink that has no effect on tryptophan. Studies show that depleting tryptophan (and so lowering serotonin levels) causes temporary depressive symptoms among people with a

(a) Postsynaptic neuron

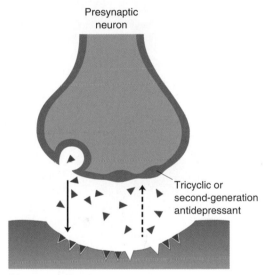

(b) Postsynaptic neuron

Figure 8.4 (*a*) When a neuron releases norepinephrine or serotonin into a synapse, a pumplike reuptake mechanism immediately begins to recapture some of the neurotransmitter molecules before they are received by the postsynaptic (receptor) neuron. (*b*) Tricyclic drugs block this reuptake process, enabling more norepinephrine or serotonin to reach and stimulate the postsynaptic (receptor) neuron. Selective serotonin reuptake inhibitors act more selectively on serotonin. [Adapted from Snyder (1986), p. 106.]

history of depression or a family history of depression (Benkelfat et al., 1994; Moore et al., 2000). Current thinking is that people who are vulnerable to depression may have less sensitive serotonin receptors, so that they respond more dramatically to lower levels of serotonin.

Researchers are also beginning to study how medications influence receptor sensitivity. These types of studies are being conducted for both mania and depression. For example, one line of research is examining whether antidepressants alter chemical messengers called **second messengers** (see Figure 2.5), which then adjust postsynaptic receptor sensitivity. Another area of current research focuses on **G-proteins** (guanine nucleotide-binding proteins), which play an important role in modulating activity in the postsynaptic cell. High levels of G-proteins have been found in patients with mania and low levels in patients with depression (Avissar et al., 1997, 1999). Some have argued that the therapeutic effects of lithium, the most effective pharmacological treatment for mania, may result from its ability to regulate G-proteins (Manji et al., 1995).

Brain Imaging Studies Two different types of brain-imaging studies are commonly used in research on mood disorders. *Structural studies* focus on whether there are fewer cells or connections within a given region of the brain. *Functional activation studies* focus on whether there is a change in the activity of a brain region. Structural studies can indicate whether a person has lost connections between brain cells; functional studies are used to gain information on how people use the cells they have. Deficits found in structural studies may be more permanent than those found in functional studies.

Brain-imaging studies suggest that episodes of MDD are associated with changes in many of the brain systems that are activated when a person without symptoms of depression experiences strong emotions (Davidson, Pizzagalli, & Nitschke, 2002). As one might expect, many different brain structures become involved when a person experiences emotion: the person needs to attend to and interpret the stimuli that are causing the emotion and then must make plans to deal with those stimuli (Phillips et al., 2003). Because these brain systems are so complex, researchers are still working to understand how depression relates to brain activity. We will provide a brief overview of current theory (see Davidson et al., 2002 for more detail).

Table 8.3 shows the four primary brain structures involved in depression: the **amygdala**, the **hippocampus**, the **prefrontal cortex**, and the **anterior cingulate** (Figure 8.5). The amygdala helps a person to assess how emotionally important a stimulus is. For example, animals with damage to the amygdala fail to react with a fear response to threatening stimuli, and also fail to respond positively to food. In humans, the amygdala has been shown to respond when people are shown pictures of threatening stimuli. The other structures help a person retrieve previous memories of this type of stimulus (hippocampus), and then focus on the situation and execute appropriate plans (the prefrontal cortex and the anterior cingulate). Taken together, then, these brain structures function to assess how emotionally important a stimulus is, to focus effectively, and to make plans based on emotionally relevant cues.

Functional activation studies show elevated activity of the amygdala among people with MDD. For example, when shown sad or angry faces, people with current MDD have a more intense and sustained reaction in the amygdala than people with no MDD do (Sheline et al., 2001). Similarly, when shown negative words, people with current MDD have a more sustained reaction in the amygdala than people with no MDD do (Siegle et al., 2002). Functional studies also show that MDD is associated with diminished activation of certain areas of the anterior cingulate, the prefrontal cortex, and the hippocampus during exposure to emotional stimuli (Davidson et al., 2002). Structural studies of people with depression also find diminished volume of the prefrontal cortex, and for people who have had depression for many years, diminished volume of the hippocampus (Sheline, 2000).

How might these findings fit together? One theory is that the overactivity in the amygdala during depression causes oversensitivity to emotionally relevant stimuli. At the same time, systems involved in weighing rewards and costs, making decisions, and systematically pursuing goals in the face of emotions appear less active (the anterior cingulate, the hippocampus, and the prefrontal cortex). In response to emotionally relevant stimuli, then, a person with depression may react with increased emotion, but decreased ability to plan (Davidson et al., 2002).

Given this pattern of findings related to greater emotional reactivity, one might expect that people who are vulnerable to depression would show a robust shift in brain activity in the context of a sad mood. One study found just that (Liotti et al., 2002). That is, people with current major depression, with a history of major depression, and with no current or previous depression were asked to think about sad events in their lives and to try to place themselves in a sad mood. All three groups reported a similar level of sadness after this induction. Before and after the sad mood induction, PET scans were taken to measure brain activity. Among people with either current or previous major depression, activity of the orbitofrontal cortex decreased after the sadness induction compared to baseline; activity of the orbitofrontal cortex did not change among people with no current or previous depression. Stated differently, as people with current depression become sad, they display less activity in brain regions that are involved with planning and executing

Table 8.3 Brain Structures Involved in Major Depression

Brain Structure	Functional Activation Studies
Prefrontal cortex (dorsolateral portion)	Diminished
Anterior cingulate (dorsal portion)	Diminished
Hippocampus	Diminished
Amygdala	Elevated

A) Orbital prefrontal cortex(green) and the ventromedial prefrontal cortex(red)

B) Dorsolateral prefrontal cortex(blue)

C) Hippocampus(purple) and amygdala(orange)

D) Anterior cingulate cortex(yellow)

Figure 8.5 Key brain structures involved in major depressive disorder. (Reprinted with permission from the *Annual Review of Psychology*, Vol. 53, © 2002 by Annual Reviews, www.annualreviews.org.)

goals. The findings of this study indicate that these patterns of brain activity can be seen even when the depression has cleared; such patterns may be part of the vulnerability to depression.

Many of the same brain structures appear to be involved in bipolar disorder as in MDD. In functional studies, bipolar I disorder is associated with elevated responsiveness in the amygdala, along with diminished activity of the hippocampus and prefrontal cortex (cf. Kruger et al., 2003). In structural studies, bipolar disorder is associated with a loss of volume in the prefrontal cortex, basal ganglia, hippocampus, and anterior cingulate, and some studies report an increase in the volume of the amygdala (Phillips et al., 2003). Beyond these deficits that appear entirely similar to those seen in depression, bipolar I disorder is also associated with diminished volume of the raphe nucleus, a brain structure involved in the production of serotonin. This may contribute to even more dysregulation of serotonin in bipolar disorder than in depression.

Other functional imaging studies (using PET and other techniques, see p. 90) allow researchers to study the receptors for a specific neurotransmitter. Studies using these imaging techniques suggest changes in serotonin receptor sensitivity associated with mood disorders (Stockmeier, 2003). Similar brain-imaging studies have allowed researchers to focus on a more specific part of the dopamine system. Remember that depressive symptoms include decreased pleasure, motivation, and energy, and manic symptoms include increased pleasure, motivation, and energy. Some researchers think that symptoms like these could be explained by changes in the sensitivity of the **reward system** in the brain (Depue & Iacono, 1989). That is, changes in this brain structure could help explain why people seem less motivated to pursue rewards during depression and overly focused on possible rewards during mania. Although findings are not entirely consistent, many researchers are studying one part of the reward system, the basal ganglia, to see if dopamine receptors in this area are involved in depression and mania (Meyer et al., 2001; Neumeister et al., 2001).

The Neuroendocrine System: Cortisol Dysregulation and Depression   The **HPA axis** (hypothalamic–pituitary–adrenocortical axis—see Figure 2.10, p. 42), the biological system that manages reactivity to stress, may be overly active when people have MDD. As described above, there is evidence that the amygdala is overly reactive in people with MDD. The HPA axis receives input from structures related to the amygdala, and so may also be overly active in people with MDD. The HPA axis triggers the release of **cortisol**, the main "stress hormone." Cortisol is secreted at times of stress and triggers changes that help the body prepare for threats.

Various findings link depression to high cortisol levels. For example, people with **Cushing's syndrome**, which causes oversecretion of cortisol, frequently experience depressive symptoms. A second line of research with animals has shown that when chemicals that increase cortisol release are injected into the brain, many of the classic symptoms of depression are produced, including decreased interest in sex, decreased appetite, and sleep disturbances (Gutman & Nemeroff, 2003). In animals and humans, then, too much cortisol seems to produce depressive symptoms.

Even among people who are depressed but do not have Cushing's syndrome, cortisol levels are often poorly regulated—that is, the system does not seem to respond well to signals to decrease cortisol levels (Garbutt et al., 1994). The dexamethasone suppression test is used to measure cortisol regulation. In people who do not have a mood disorder, dexamethasone suppresses cortisol secretion over the course of the night. In contrast, in some people with mood disorders, dexamethasone does not suppress cortisol secretion, particularly in people whose disorder has psychotic features (Nelson & Davis, 1997). This lack of cortisol suppression is seen as a sign of poor regulation of the HPA axis during episodes of MDD. Challenging the HPA system even further by administering both dexamethasone and corticotropin-releasing hormone (which increases cortisol levels) results in subtle deficits in the regulation of cortisol in 80 percent of people with depression (Heuser, Yassouridis, & Holsboer, 1994). These deficits in regulation would be expected to explain prolonged elevations of cortisol during depression. These abnormal responses to dexamethasone, though, normalize when the depressive episode ends.

Although cortisol helps mobilize beneficial short-term stress responses, prolonged high levels of cortisol can cause harm to body systems. For example, long-term excesses of cortisol have been linked to damage to the hippocampus—studies have found smaller-than-normal hippocampi among people who have experienced depression for years (e.g., Duman et al., 1997).

Although less is known, cortisol levels are also believed to be dysregulated in people with bipolar disorder (Goodwin & Jamison, 1990). It is worth noting, however, that high levels of cortisol are seen in many different psychiatric disorders, and that this makes sense when one considers that many different psychiatric disorders involve extreme stress.

Quick Summary

Bipolar disorder is highly heritable, and major depression is modestly heritable. Neurotransmitter models focus on serotonin, dopamine, and norepinephrine. Researchers have begun to focus on receptor sensitivity rather than levels of neurotransmitters. Consistent with this idea, studies which involve experimentally manipulating levels of neurotransmitters provide support for the role of poor serotonin sensitivity in depression. Neuroimaging studies suggest that depression is associated with changes in regions of the brain that are involved in emotion. These changes seem consistent with a greater emotional reactivity (heightened activity of the amygdala), but less planful thinking in the face of emotion (diminished activity of the prefrontal cortex, hippocampus, and dorsal anterior cingulate). Many people who are depressed also show poor regulation of cortisol.

Generally, the neurobiological dysfunctions associated with depression also are observed in bipolar disorder. Beyond the shifts in the amygdala, prefrontal cortex, hippocampus, and anterior cingulate, bipolar disorder does appear specifically related to a loss of volume in the raphe nucleus, a brain region which produces serotonin. Researchers are also examining dopamine and mania.

Check Your Knowledge 8.2

1. Estimates of heritability are approximately _____ percent for MDD and _____ percent for bipolar I disorder.
   a. 60, 85
   b. 20, 100
   c. 37, 85
   d. 10, 59
2. Which of the following neurotransmitters is **not** believed to be involved in depression and mania:
   a. acetylcholine
   b. serotonin
   c. dopamine
   d. norepinephrine
3. Recent models suggest that depression is
   a. related to absolute levels of neurotransmitters
   b. related to changes in receptor sensitivity for neurotransmitters
   c. unrelated to neurotransmitter systems
4. In depression, overactivity of the HPA axis is shown by:
   a. hypersensitivity of the pituitary gland
   b. failure to suppress cortisol by dexamethasone
   c. too little cortisol
   d. elevated parasympathetic nervous system activity
5. One brain region that appears to be overly active among people with mood disorders is the:
   a. hippocampus
   b. prefrontal cortex
   c. cerebellum
   d. amygdala

Social Factors in Depression: Life Events and Interpersonal Difficulties

Data summarized indicate that neurobiological factors influence whether or not a person develops a mood disorder. Does this mean that social and psychological theories are irrelevant or useless? Not in the least. For example, neurobiological theories are consistent with vulnerability to stressors among people with mood disorders. Neurobiological factors, then, may be *diatheses* (p. 55) that increase risk for mood disorders in the context of other triggers or stressors.

The role of stressful life events in triggering episodes of depression is well established (Kendler et al., 1999). A great deal of research has focused on cause–effect relationships: do life events cause depression, or does depression cause life events? Prospective studies are particularly important since they should be able to shed light on whether depression or life events came first. Even with a prospective study, though, it remains possible that some life events are caused by early symptoms of depression that have not yet developed into a full-blown disorder. Remember the case of Mary, who developed symptoms after she was laid off from her job. Maybe Mary lost her job because she was sleeping too much and then arriving at work late; trouble sleeping can be a sign of depression.

Even after stressful life events that could have been caused by mild depressive symptoms are excluded, there is much evidence that stress can cause major depressive disorder. In careful prospective studies, 42–67 percent of people report that they experienced a very serious life event (that was not caused by symptoms) in the year before their depression began. Common events include losing a job, a key friendship, or a romantic relationship. These findings have been replicated in at least 12 studies, conducted in six different countries (Brown & Harris, 1989b). Certain types of life events, such as loss and humiliation, appear particularly likely to trigger depressive episodes (Kendler, Hettema, et al., 2003). Above and beyond the people who report stressful life events that happened suddenly, many people with depression report that they had been experiencing long-term chronic stressors before the depression, such as poverty (Brown & Harris, 1989b).

Although many depressions follow a stressful life event, most people do not become depressed after such an event. Why do some people become depressed after stressful life events and others do not? The obvious answer is that some people must be more vulnerable to stress than others. In the previous section, we described neurobiological systems involved in depression; many of these systems could be involved in reactivity to stress. Psychological and cognitive vulnerabilities also appear important. The most common models, then, are diathesis–stress models—that is, models that consider both preexisting vulnerabilities (diatheses) and stressors.

One diathesis may be a lack of social support. People who are depressed tend to have sparse social networks and to regard those networks as providing little support (Keltner & Kring, 1998). Low social support may lessen a person's ability to handle stressful life events and make the person vulnerable to depression. One study showed that women experiencing a severely stressful life event without support from a confidant had a 40 percent risk of developing depression, whereas those with a confidant's support had only a 4 percent risk (Brown & Andrews, 1986). Social support, then, seems to minimize the effects of major stressors.

There is also some evidence that interpersonal problems within the family are particularly likely to trigger depression. A long line of research has focused on **expressed emotion**, defined as critical or hostile comments or emotional overinvolvement by a family member toward the person with depression. High expressed emotion strongly predicts relapse in depression. Indeed, one review of six studies found that 69.5 percent of patients in families with high levels of expressed emotion relapsed within 1 year, compared to 30.5 percent of patient in families with low levels of expressed emotion (Butzlaff & Hooley, 1998). In a community study, marital discord also predicted the onset of depression (Whisman & Bruce, 1999).

Clearly, interpersonal problems can trigger the onset of depressive symptoms, but it is also important to consider the flip side of the coin. Once depressive symptoms emerge, they can create interpersonal problems—that is, depressive symptoms seem to elicit negative reactions from others (Coyne, 1976). For example, roommates of depressed college students rated social contacts with them as less enjoyable, and they reported feeling aggressive and rejecting toward them (Joiner, Alfano, & Metalsky, 1992).

What is it about the person who is depressed that elicits these negative reactions? Researchers have studied this aspect of depression by coding how people with depression interact with their spouses and with strangers, and then doing studies in which people mimic key depressive behaviors. The following signs of depression seem to elicit negative reactions in others: slow speech, silences, negative self-disclosures, negative affect, poor eye contact, and fewer positive facial expressions (Gotlib & Robinson, 1982; Gottman & Krokoff, 1989). People who are depressed also tend to make more frequent hostile comments to their spouses than nondepressed people do (Biglan, Hops, & Sherman, 1988).

More recent research has explored the effects of constant reassurance seeking on others (Joiner, 1995). More than most, people who are depressed seek reassurance that others truly care. But even when others express support, they are only temporarily satisfied. Their negative self-concept causes them to doubt the positive feedback, and their constant efforts to obtain reassurance come to irritate others. Ultimately, people experiencing depression actually elicit negative feedback (e.g., by asking questions like "how do you *truly* feel about me?" after the other person has given a supportive response); other people's responses typically confirm the person's negative self-concept. Ultimately, the depressed person's excessive reassurance seeking can lead to rejection (Joiner and Metalsky, 1995).

Many of the negative social behaviors, such as excessive reassurance seeking, could be the direct result of depressive symptoms. If some of these same social problems are present before symptoms appear, can the problems increase the risk for depression? Research suggests that the answer is yes. Among a group of undergraduates who were not initially depressed, those who were high in reassurance-seeking were more likely to develop depressive symptoms over a 10-week period (Joiner & Metalsky, 2001). Similarly, research using high-risk samples, identified before the onset of depression, suggests that interpersonal problems may precede depression. For example, the behavior of elementary-school children of depressed parents was rated negatively by both peers and teachers (Weintraub, Prinz, & Neale, 1978); low social competence predicted the onset of depression among elementary-school children (Cole et al., 1990); and poor interpersonal problem-solving skills predicted increases in depression among adolescents (Davila et al., 1995). It seems clear that interpersonal problems are one risk factor for depression.

Psychological Factors in Depression

Many different psychological factors may play a role in depressive disorders. In this section, we discuss Sigmund Freud's psychoanalytic views, which emphasize the unconscious conflicts associated with grief and loss; personality factors, such as neuroticism and positive and negative affectivity; and cognitive factors, such as thoughts about the self and life events. These theories describe different diatheses to answer the question, what are the characteristics of people who respond to negative life events with a depressive episode?

Freud's Theory   In his celebrated paper "Mourning and Melancholia," Freud (1917/1950) drew from clinical observations to develop a model of depression. He theorized that the potential for depression is created early in childhood, during the oral period. If the child's needs are insufficiently or overly gratified, the person becomes fixated in the oral stage (see p. 18). This arrest in development may cause the person to become excessively dependent on other people for the maintenance of self-esteem.

Why do people with this childhood history come to suffer from depression? Freud hypothesized that after the loss of a loved one, whether by death, separation, or withdrawal of affection, the mourner first *introjects* the lost person; that is, the mourner identifies with the lost one, perhaps in a fruitless attempt to undo the loss. Freud asserted that the mourner unconsciously resents being deserted and feels anger toward the loved one for the loss. In addition, the mourner feels guilt for real or imagined sins against the lost person. According to the theory, the mourner's anger toward the lost one becomes directed inward, developing into ongoing self-blame and depression. In this view, depression can be described as anger turned against oneself. Overly dependent persons are believed to be particularly susceptible to this process, and as noted above, people fixated in the oral stage are overly dependent on others.

Not much research has been carried out to test this theory, but the little information available does not strongly support it. Contrary to the idea that depression is a result of anger turned inward, people with depression express anger much more than nondepressed people do (Biglan et al., 1988). Despite this, it is important to note that some of his basic suppositions continue to influence the models described next. For example, Freud also maintained that depression could be triggered by the loss of a loved one. As we have seen, a large body of evidence indicates that episodes of MDD are precipitated by stressful life events, which often involve losses. We will see below that people who are high in dependency are prone to depressive symptoms after a rejection (Nietzel & Harris, 1990), a finding that also is congruent with Freud's theory. Although some of Freud's ideas still influence theories of depression, researchers have gone far beyond the clinical observations that were the foundation of his ideas.

Affect and Neuroticism   Current personality research has focused on the propensity to experience negative and positive affect as a risk factor for mood disorders. To understand the personality research, though, it is helpful to understand a bit about how depression and anxiety disorders relate to negative and positive affect.

As we have noted, major depression and anxiety disorders frequently co-occur. How can we differentiate anxiety and depression? One model conceptualizes depression and anxiety along three broad dimensions (see Table 8.4): **negative affect** (distress and worry), **positive affect** (happiness and contentment), and **somatic arousal** (sweaty palms, fast heart rate, etc.). Anxiety and depression are both expected to involve negative affect. Anxiety, but not depression, is expected to involve somatic arousal (Clark, Watson, & Mineka, 1994). And depression, but not anxiety, is expected to involve low levels of positive affect. People who show high negative affect, low positive affect, and high somatic arousal may be at risk for comorbid anxiety and depressive disorders.

Table 8.4 Affective Dimensions in Depressive Disorders and Anxiety Disorders

	Negative Affect	Positive Affect	Somatic Arousal
Depressive disorders	high	low	moderate
Anxiety disorders	high	moderate	high
Comorbid anxiety disorders and depressive disorders	high	low	high

According to this model, depressive disorders should be differentiated from anxiety disorders by the lack of positive affect. Many of the symptoms of depression seem closely related to lack of positive affect—a loss of interest in pleasurable activities, and even symptoms like lack of appetite and lack of interest in sex. Other than the clinical symptoms, what is the evidence? Studies of responses to positive pictures and films suggest that people with MDD show fewer positive facial expressions and report less pleasant emotion in response to positive stimuli than do people without depression (Berenbaum & Oltmanns, 1992; Sloan, Strauss, & Wisner, 2001). Researchers using a psychophysiological method called *electrocortical potential* found that people with MDD responded less strongly to positive (but not negative) stimuli than did people without depression (Deldin et al., 2001). Other researchers found that people with MDD responded less strongly to a chance to earn money (a positive stimulus) than people without depression did (Henriques & Davidson, 2000). Research then does support the idea that episodes of MDD are characterized by high negative affect and low positive affect.

Can high negative affect and low positive affect be used to predict depression? Studies of personality help address this question. Several longitudinal studies suggest that **neuroticism**, a personality trait that involves the tendency to react to events with greater than average negative affect, predicts the onset of depression (Jorm et al., 2000). (As you would expect, neuroticism is associated with anxiety too—see p. 134.) A major study of twins suggests that neuroticism explains at least part of the genetic vulnerability to depression (Fanous, Prescott, & Kendler, 2004). In fact, neuroticism is the personality trait most strongly associated with depression. Thus, there is good evidence that people who tend to experience negative affect are at elevated risk for developing depression.

The evidence for positive affect is not as clear. For example, **extraversion** is a personality trait associated with frequent experiences of positive affect. Some, but not all studies, suggest that low extraversion predicts the onset of depression (Klein et al., 2002). How would this fit with the idea that once a person is depressed, they experience less positive affect? Some people might be fairly happy until the depressive symptoms kick in, at which point their level of happiness might decrease. Other people might be prone to less happiness, and this could increase their risk of depression.

In sum, neuroticism predicts both anxiety and depression. But low extraversion doesn't always precede depression. Once people are depressed, though, they seem to experience more negative affect and less positive affect than do people with no disorder, and less positive affect than those with anxiety disorders.

Cognitive Theories   In some theories, negative thoughts and beliefs are seen as major causes of depression. One can easily think of people who interpret life events differently; some people seem to see the down side of events much more easily than others do. Because cognitive theories are the most common focus of research on depression, we discuss two of them: Beck's theory and hopelessness theory.

Beck's Theory   The most important cognitive theory of depression is that of Aaron Beck (1967). His thesis is that people develop depression because their thinking is negative (see Figure 8.6). That is, Beck proposed that depression is associated with the **negative triad**: negative views of the self, the world, and the future. The "world" part of the depressive triad refers to the person's own corner of the world—the situations he or she faces. For example, the person might think, "I cannot possibly cope with all these demands and responsibilities," as opposed to thinking, "The world has been going south since the American League adopted the designated hitter rule" (Haaga, Dyck, & Ernst, 1991, p. 218).

According to this model, in childhood, people with depression acquired negative **schemata**—tendencies to see the world negatively—through such stressful life events as loss of a parent, the social rejection of peers, or the depressive attitude of a parent. Schemata are different from conscious thoughts—they are an underlying set of beliefs, which operate outside of a person's awareness to shape the way a person makes sense of their experiences. The negative schema is activated whenever the person encounters situations similar to those that originally caused the schema to form.

Once activated, negative schemata are believed to cause **cognitive biases**, or tendencies to process information in certain negative ways (Kendall & Ingram, 1989). That is, Beck suggested that people with depression might be overly attentive to negative feedback about themselves and more likely to remember such negative information than other people are. Likewise, they might fail to notice or to remember positive feedback about themselves. A person with an underlying ineptness schema might readily notice signs that they are inept and remember feedback that they are inept. Signs that they are competent, though, are not noted or remembered. Their conclusions are consistent with the underlying schema, which then maintains the schema (a vicious cycle).

According to Beck, the person with depression is also likely to make the following types of cognitive errors to maintain their schemata:

- *Arbitrary inference*—drawing a conclusion in the absence of sufficient evidence. For example, a man concludes that he is worthless because it is raining the day he hosts an outdoor party.
- *Selective abstraction*—drawing a conclusion by focusing on one element while ignoring many other elements. For example, a worker feels worthless when a product fails to function, even though she is only one of many people who contributed to its creation.
- *Overgeneralization*—drawing a sweeping conclusion on the basis of a single, perhaps trivial, event. For example, a student regards his poor performance in a single class on one particular day as proof of his worthlessness.

How has Beck's theory been tested? One widely used instrument in studies of Beck's theory is a self-report scale called the Dysfunctional Attitudes Scale (DAS), which includes items concerning whether people would consider themselves worthwhile or loveable. Hundreds of studies have shown that people do demonstrate negative thinking on scales like the

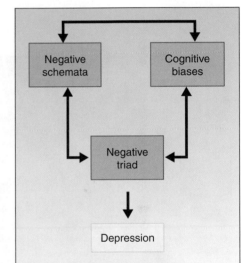

Figure 8.6 The interrelationships among different kinds of cognitions in Beck's theory of depression.

Aaron Beck's cognitive theory suggests that depression is caused by negative thinking about the self, world, and future. (Courtesy of Dr. Aaron T. Beck.)

DAS during depression (Haaga et al., 1991). In studies of how people process information, depression is associated with a tendency to pay more attention to negative stimuli more than to positive stimuli (Gotlib & Krasnoperova, 1998), and to remember negative information more than positive information (Matt, Vazquez, & Campbell, 1992).

Despite the clear evidence that cognition is negative during a depressive episode, the greatest challenge for cognitive theories of depression is to resolve questions of cause and effect—that is, can certain cognitive styles cause depression, or do depressive symptoms cause those cognitive styles? Several studies suggest that people with negative cognitive styles are at elevated risk for developing depression. For example, a study of 1,507 adolescents found that very high scores on the DAS in combination with negative life events predicted the onset of MDD (Lewinsohn, Joiner, & Rohde, 2001). Other researchers found that high scores on the DAS predicted relapse for several years after treatment for depression (Segal et al., 1999). Some of the items on the DAS focus on an excessive need for approval, and a series of longitudinal studies suggest that people high in need for approval are more likely to become depressed after an interpersonal loss or rejection (Nietzel & Harris, 1990). Cognitive biases in the way people process positive and negative information have also been found to predict depression over a 12- to 18-month period in a large sample of undergraduate students (Rude et al., 2003).

Hopelessness Theory   In this section we discuss the evolution of an influential cognitive theory of depression—the hopelessness theory. The initial version of this theory was called learned helplessness; it was then modified to incorporate attributions and then modified again to emphasize hopelessness (see Figure 8.7).

Martin Seligman (1974) formulated **learned helplessness theory** to explain the behavior of dogs given electric shocks that they could not escape from. After receiving repeated shocks, the dogs seemed to give up and passively accept the painful stimulation. Later, when the experimental conditions were changed and the shocks could be avoided, these dogs were less likely to learn an avoidance response than dogs that had been able to escape from shocks. Rather, after a shock, most of them would lay down in a corner and whimper. Seligman proposed that animals acquire a sense of helplessness when confronted with uncontrollable aversive situations. This sense of helplessness then impairs their performance in controllable aversive situations. Animals exposed to uncontrollable shocks also developed symptoms that look like depressive symptoms, such as decreased appetite. On the basis of a set of studies on the neurobiological and behavioral effects of uncontrollable stress, Seligman concluded that learned helplessness in animals could provide a model for human depression.

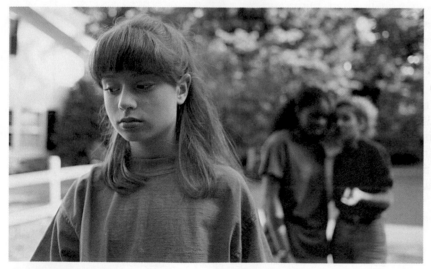

Being rejected by peers may lead to the development of the negative schema that, according to Beck's theory, plays a key role in depression. (Richard Hutchings/ Photo Researchers.)

As researchers began to apply this research to humans, they found that aversive experiences triggered helplessness in some people but not others. To deal with this problem, researchers revised the learned helplessness model to incorporate cognition (Abramson, Seligman, & Teasdale, 1978). The revised theory focused on three key dimensions of **attributions**—the explanations a person forms about why a stressor has occurred (Weiner et al., 1971):

1. Internal (personal) versus external (environmental) causes.
2. Stable (permanent) versus unstable (temporary) causes.
3. Global (relevant to many life domains) versus specific (limited to one area) causes.

Table 8.5 illustrates these dimensions by considering how different people might explain their low score on the Graduate Record Examination (GRE). This revised model suggests

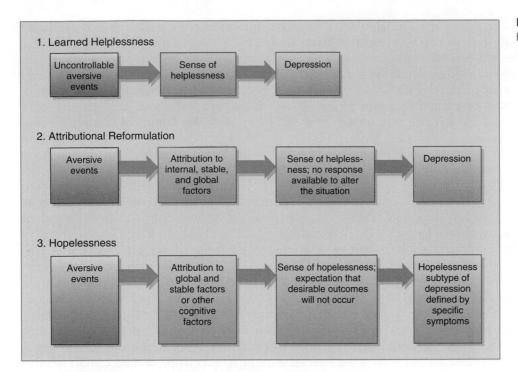

Figure 8.7 The three helplessness/hopelessness theories of depression.

that people whose **attributional style** leads them to believe that negative life events are due to internal, stable, and global causes are likely to become depressed.

Attributional style predicts increases in depressive symptoms (Peterson, Maier, & Seligman, 1993), but it is unclear whether attributional style predicts full diagnoses of MDD. For instance, attributional style has predicted the onset of MDD in studies of children (Nolen-Hoeksema, Girgus, & Seligman, 1986), but some studies have found that attributional style did not predict the onset of diagnosable MDD in adolescents (Lewinsohn et al., 2001) or adults (Barnett & Gotlib, 1988).

The current version of the theory, **hopelessness theory** (Abramson, Metalsky, & Alloy, 1989), suggests that cognitive processes explain only one type of depression (hopelessness depression). Symptoms of hopelessness depression include decreased motivation, sadness, suicidality, decreased energy, psychomotor retardation, sleep disturbances, poor concentration, and negative cognitions. In this view, the most important trigger of this type of depression is hopelessness, an expectation that (1) desirable outcomes will not occur and that (2) the person has no responses available to change this situation. As in the revised model incorporating attributions, hopelessness can be triggered by negative attributions about the causes of stressors. In this revision of the theory, a person who attributes negative life events to stable and global factors is more likely to become hopeless and therefore depressed. But the model also suggests that there are many different ways in which a person can become hopeless, including through low self-esteem and through the belief that negative life events will have severe negative consequences.

Table 8.5 An Example of Attributions: Why I Failed My GRE Math Exam

| | Internal (Personal) | | External (Environmental) | |
	Stable	Unstable	Stable	Unstable
Global	I lack intelligence.	I am exhausted.	These tests are all unfair.	It's an unlucky day, Friday the 13th.
Specific	I lack mathematical ability.	I am fed up with math.	The math tests are unfair.	My math test was numbered "13."

In 1993, Gerald Metalsky and colleagues conducted the first test of hopelessness theory, early in the semester, college students taking a course in introductory psychology completed the Attributional Style Questionnaire (ASQ), as well as questionnaires to assess their grade aspirations, their depressive symptoms, hopelessness, and self-esteem. These measures were used to predict the persistence of depressive symptoms after a test among the students whose grades were below their expectations. Those who attributed the grade to global and stable factors experienced more hopelessness, but this pattern was found only among students whose self-esteem was low. Hopelessness predicted depressive symptoms. Clearly, these results support the hopelessness theory. Also, a similar study conducted with children in the sixth and seventh grades yielded almost identical results (Robinson, Garber, & Hillsman, 1995).

One study has assessed several different aspects of cognitive theories of depression. In the Temple-Wisconsin Cognitive Vulnerability to Depression study, both the DAS and the ASQ were used to predict the development of MDD and also the hopelessness subtype of MDD. In this study, high- and low-risk groups were defined based on scores on the DAS and the ASQ and then followed for 2 1/2 years. The 173 students in the upper 25 percent of the distributions for both measures were classified as high risk; the 176 students in the bottom 25 percent of the distributions were classified as low risk. Findings from this study provided support for cognitive theories: students in the high-risk group were more likely to develop MDD than were students in the low-risk group. Unfortunately, though, because both the DAS, a measure used to test Beck's theory, and the ASQ, the measure used in tests of the hopelessness theory, were used to define the high-risk group, we do not know whether this finding supports the hopelessness theory, Beck's theory, or both. Findings did provide support for one part of the hopelessness model, in that the cognitive measures predicted the specific symptoms defined as hopelessness depression (Alloy et al., 2000).

Fitting Together the Etiological Factors in Depressive Disorders

Research integrating the neurobiological and psychosocial etiology of depressive disorders is increasingly common—for example, studies of the serotonin transporter gene, which is involved in modulating serotonin levels. Researchers are particularly interested in this gene in regard to depression, as antidepressants that target reuptake of serotonin are very effective. In rhesus monkeys, the presence of a polymorphism (at least one short allele) in this gene is associated with poor serotonergic function. A study found that people with this polymorphism (at least one short allele) were at greater risk for depression after a stressful life event than those without the polymorphism (Caspi et al., 2003). That is, having at least one short allele was associated with elevated reactivity to stress (see Figure 8.8). Thus, some people seem to inherit a propensity for a weaker serotonin system, which then is expressed as a greater likelihood to experience depression after a major stressor. This type of neuro-biological vulnerability could set the stage for depressive disorder after major negative life events. Intriguingly, a polymorphism in the serotonin transporter gene has also been related to elevated activity of the amygdala (Hanri et al., 2005). This type of work, drawing together genetic and neurobiological risk factors with social and psychological variables, is increasingly common. By considering the set of variables together, researchers can begin to develop more precise models of who is likely to become depressed under what circumstances.

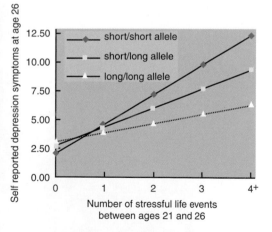

Figure 8.8 Life events interact with the serotonin transporter gene to predict symptoms of depression. [Adapted from Caspi et al. (2003). *Science*, 301, 387.]

Social and Psychological Factors in Bipolar Disorder

Most people who experience a manic episode during their life will also experience a major depressive episode—but not everyone will. Given this, researchers often try to study the triggers of manic and depressive episodes separately within bipolar disorder.

Depression in Bipolar Disorder   The triggers of depressive episodes in bipolar disorder appear quite similar to the triggers of major depressive episodes (Johnson & Kizer, 2002). As in MDD, negative life events appear important in precipitating depressive episodes in bipolar disorder (Johnson & Miller, 1997). Similarly, neuroticism (Lozano & Johnson, 2001), negative cognitions (Reilly-Harrington et al., 1999), and lack of social support (S. L. Johnson et al., 1999) predict depressive symptoms in bipolar disorder.

Mania   There are two different models of the kinds of psychological factors that could trigger mania. In the first, the **manic defense** model, mania is seen as a protection against a painful psychological state. The case of Joel illustrates why many theorists think that the manic state serves a protective function.

Clinical Case: Joel

Joel, a 42-year-old man, was experiencing his third manic episode. During each episode he had exhibited the classic pattern of manic symptoms, with much of his manic behavior centered on a grandiose delusion that he was the world's greatest businessman. "Did you know that I've already bought 20 companies today?" he stated at the beginning of a therapy session. "Not even Bill Gates has anything on me." From sessions between episodes it was apparent that success in business was indeed one of Joel's central concerns. But he was far from successful. His parents had lent him money to start several companies, but each had gone bankrupt. He was obsessed with matching the business successes of his wealthy father, but as the years passed his opportunities to do so were slipping away. According to the manic defense theory, his manic grandiosity was protecting him from facing his lack of business success.

According to the manic defense theory, mania results from an attempt to defend against painful admissions about the self. Yet studies indicate that people with remitted bipolar disorder describe themselves in a way that is not overly confident nor self-effacing when asked directly to evaluate their selves (Johnson & Kizer, 2002). Does this mean that they hold truly healthy self views during remission or that they are not presenting their true state? If a person is defending against negative views of the self, standard self-esteem scales would be invalid, and researchers would need to use subtler ways to measure thoughts about the self. Some studies have found that people with bipolar disorder in remission do tend to make more blaming attributions for stressors (Winters & Neale, 1985) and to pay more attention to negative stimuli (Lyon, Startup, & Bentall, 1999). That is, there is some evidence for a pattern of standard responses when asked directly about views of the self, but more negative responses to subtler questions. This might indicate that people with bipolar disorder think more negatively about themselves than they admit (Winters & Neale, 1985). In a study that supports that negative thoughts might help trigger manic symptoms, a negative attributional style and dysfunctional attitudes in combination with negative life events were found to predict an increase in hypomanic symptoms among undergraduate students (Reilly-Harrington et al., 1999).

In contrast to the manic defense model, the second model of the psychological triggers of mania hypothesizes that mania reflects a disturbance in the reward system of the brain (Depue, Collins, & Luciano, 1996). Researchers have demonstrated that people with bipolar disorder describe themselves as highly responsive to reward on a self-report measure (Meyer et al., 2001). In addition, a study found that a particular kind of life event predicted an increase in manic symptoms in people with bipolar I disorder over a 2-year period (Johnson et al., 2000)—specifically, life events that involved attaining goals, such as gaining acceptance to graduate school or getting married.

How could successes like these promote increases in symptoms? In studies that have provided (false) success feedback, people with a history of mild hypomanic symptoms seem to develop more confidence after an initial success compared to those with no history of hypomanic symptoms (Stern & Berrenberg, 1979). Thus, researchers have proposed that life events involving success may trigger cognitive changes in confidence, which then spiral into excessive goal pursuit (Johnson, 2005). This excess goal pursuit may help trigger manic symptoms among people with bipolar disorder.

Quick Summary

Research strongly supports the role of life events as a trigger for MDD. Because many people do not become depressed after a life event, researchers have studied diatheses that could explain vulnerability to life events. Interpersonal research highlights the role of low social support, high expressed emotion, high need for reassurance, and poor social skills as risk factors for depression. Once a person becomes depressed, increases in negativity and reassurance-seeking may lead to more negativity and rejection from other people, potentially prolonging the episodes.

Beyond social factors, researchers have focused on psychological factors. Freud's theory, that depression was due to anger turned inward, has not obtained much support. But other psychological risk factors can help explain why some people become depressed. People do tend to experience high negative affect and low positive affect when depressed;

evidence suggests that neuroticism, which involves high negative affect, predicts the onset of depression. Cognitive factors include a negative schema; negative beliefs about the self, world, and future; biases to attend to and recall negative rather than positive information; stable, global, and internal attributions for stressors; and hopelessness.

Less psychological research is available on bipolar disorder. Nonetheless, many of the variables that predict MDD also appear to predict depressive symptoms within bipolar disorder. For mania, two psychosocial models have been proposed. One model suggests that mania may be a defense against negative feelings (and hence provoked by low self-esteem and negative life events). A different model suggests that mania may arise after life events involving goal attainment and excess involvement in pursuing goals.

Treatment of Mood Disorders

Most episodes of depression end after a few months, but the time may seem immeasurably longer to people with depression and to those close to them. With mania, even a few days of acute symptoms can create troubles for relationships and jobs. Moreover, suicide is a risk for people with mood disorders. Thus it is important to treat mood disorders.

A major public health goal is to increase the number of people who receive treatment. For example, surveys suggest that three-quarters of people do not receive effective treatments for MDD (Young et al., 2001). The first treatment with either psychotherapy or antidepressant medications is likely to help about 50–70 percent of people with MDD. Why do up to half of people not get relief? Many people stop treatment early, and others are not provided with enough medication or therapy.

In this section, we cover current psychological treatments of depressive disorders and bipolar disorder. Then we turn to biological treatments of depressive disorders and bipolar disorder.

Psychological Treatment of Depression

Several different forms of psychological treatment have been shown to help relieve depression. As with studies of etiology, most of the research has focused on MDD. We note when treatments have been shown to be effective in the treatment of dysthymia.

Here, we review treatments that have been shown to perform well in comparison with placebo. For this reason, we do not discuss traditional psychoanalytic therapy—a report from the American Psychiatric Association (1993) concluded that there is no reliable evidence indicating that long-term psychoanalysis is effective in treating depression.

Interpersonal Psychotherapy In contrast to traditional psychoanalytic treatment of depression, a treatment known as **interpersonal psychotherapy (IPT)**, which draws on some psychoanalytic ideas, has fared well in clinical trials. IPT builds on the idea that depression is closely tied to interpersonal problems (Klerman et al., 1984). But unlike the psychoanalytic focus on repressed problems stemming from the person's childhood, the focus in IPT is on the person's current life. The core of the therapy is to examine major interpersonal problems, such as role transitions, interpersonal conflicts, bereavement, and interpersonal isolation. Typically, the therapist and the patient focus on one or two such issues, with the goal of helping the person identify his or her feelings about these issues, make important decisions, and make changes to resolve problems related to these issues. To facilitate problem resolution, the person might be taught how to improve communication with others in order to meet his or her needs better, have more satisfying social interactions, and get more support. Like cognitive behavioral treatments, IPT is typically short term (e.g., 16 sessions or so). Techniques include fairly nondirective discussion of interpersonal problems, exploration of negative feelings and encouragement to express them, improving both verbal and nonverbal communications, problem solving, and suggesting new and more satisfying modes of behavior.

Several studies have found that IPT is effective in relieving MDD (Elkin et al., 1989; described in more detail below) and that it appears to prevent relapse when treatment is continued after recovery (Frank et al., 1990). In addition, studies indicate that IPT can be effective in treating MDD in the elderly (Reynolds et al., 1999), in adolescents (Mufson et al., 1999), and in postpartum women (Zlotnick et al., 2001). In a study among villagers in Uganda, group sessions of IPT provided highly effective relief from depressive symptoms (Bolton et al., 2003). IPT has also been found to be effective in the treatment of dysthymia (Markowitz, 1994). Overall, then, IPT appears helpful across a broad range of people.

Cognitive Therapy   In keeping with their theory that depression is caused by negative schemata and cognitive biases, Beck and associates devised a **cognitive therapy** aimed at altering maladaptive thought patterns. The therapist tries to help the depressed person to change his or her opinions about events and the self. When a person states that he or she is worthless because "nothing goes right; and everything I try to do ends in a disaster," the therapist helps the person look for evidence that contradicts this overgeneralization, such as abilities that the person is overlooking or discounting. The therapist also teaches the person to monitor private monologues and to identify thought patterns that contribute to depression. The therapist then teaches the person to challenge negative beliefs and to learn strategies that promote making realistic and positive assumptions. Beck's emphasis is on cognitive restructuring (i.e., persuading the person to think less negatively about theirself).

Clinical Case: An Example of Challenging a Negative Thought in Cognitive Therapy

The following dialogue is an example of one way that a therapist might begin to challenge a person's negative thoughts in cognitive therapy, although it would take several sessions to help a client learn the cognitive model and to identify overly negative thoughts. It should be noted that the therapist and client are likely to challenge thoughts in several different ways over the course of treatment. Another example of thought restructuring with this client is described in Chapter 16.

> *Therapist: You said that you are a "loser" because you and Roger got divorced. Now we already defined what it is to be a loser—not to achieve anything.*
> *Patient: Right. That sounds really extreme.*
> *Therapist: OK. Let's look at the evidence for and against the thought that you have achieved something. Draw a line down the center of the page. On the top I'd like you to write, "I have achieved some things".*
> *Patient: [draws line and writes statement]*
> *Therapist: What is the evidence that you have achieved some things?*
> *Patient: I graduated from college, I raised my son, I worked at the office, I have some friends, and I exercise. I am reliable. I care about my friends.*

> *Therapist: OK. Let's write all of that down. Now in the right column let's write down evidence against the thought that you have achieved some things.*
> *Patient: Well, maybe it's irrational, but I would have to write down that I got divorced.*
> *Therapist: OK. Now in looking at the evidence for and against your thought that you have achieved some things, how do you weigh it out? 50–50? Differently than 50–50?*
> *Patient: I'd have to say it's 95% in favor of the positive thought.*
> *Therapist: So, how much do you believe now that you have achieved some things?*
> *Patient: 100%*
> *Therapist: And how much do you believe that you are a failure because you got divorced?*
> *Patient: Maybe I'm not a failure, but the marriage failed. I'd give myself about 10%.*
> Quoted from Leahy, 2003.

Note: As is typical, this dialog challenges some, but not all, negative thoughts. Future sessions are likely to examine other negative thoughts.

This type of cognitive therapy was developed independently of Ellis's rational-emotive therapy (see p. 50), but the therapies are similar in some ways. For example, Beck suggests that people who are depressed are likely to consider themselves totally inept and incompetent if they make a mistake; similarly, Ellis maintains that such people are likely to hold the **irrational belief** that they must be competent in all things to be worthwhile.

Beck also includes a behavioral technique in his therapy called **behavioral activation (BA)**, in which people are given activity assignments to provide them with successful experiences and to allow them to think well of themselves. For example, the therapist encourages patients to do things that increase the opportunity to have positive experiences, such as getting out of bed in the morning, going for a walk, and talking with friends.

Considerable research has been conducted on Beck's therapy, beginning with a widely cited study indicating that cognitive therapy was more successful than the tricyclic antidepressant imipramine (Tofranil) in alleviating depression (Rush et al., 1977). Many other studies have confirmed the efficacy of cognitive therapy for relieving symptoms of MDD and preventing subsequent bouts of depression (Hollon, Thase, & Markowitz, 2002). With modifications, early results show promise of CT in the treatment of dysthymia (Hollon et al., 2002). Below we examine a widely cited study comparing Beck's therapy with IPT and with antidepressant medication.

A recent adaptation of cognitive therapy called **mindfulness-based cognitive therapy (MBCT)** focuses on relapse prevention after successful treatment for recurrent episodes of major depression (Segal et al., 2001). MBCT is based on the assumption that a person becomes vulnerable to relapse because of repeated associations between sad mood and patterns of negative, self-devaluative, hopeless thinking during major depressive episodes. As a result, when people who have recovered from depression become sad, they begin to think as negatively as they had when they were severely depressed. These reactivated patterns of thinking in turn maintain and intensify the sadness (Teasdale, 1988). Thus, in people with a history of major depression, sadness is more likely to escalate, which may contribute to further major depressive episodes.

The goal of MBCT is to teach people to recognize when they start to become depressed and to try adopting what can be called a "decentered" perspective, viewing their thoughts merely as "mental events" rather than as core aspects of the self or as accurate reflections of reality. For example, the person might say to himself or herself such statements as "thoughts are not facts" and "I am not my thoughts" (Teasdale et al., 2000, p. 616). In other words, using a wide array of strategies, including meditation, the person is taught over time to develop a detached relationship to depression-related thoughts and feelings. This perspective, it is believed, can prevent the escalation of negative thinking patterns that may cause depression.

A multisite study (Teasdale et al., 2000) compared relapse rates of formerly depressed patients randomly assigned to MBCT or to "treatment as usual" (e.g., patients were instructed to seek help from their family doctor or other sources, as they normally would). Results of this study showed that MBCT was more effective than "treatment as usual" in reducing the risk of relapse in people with three or more previous major depressive episodes. MBCT does not appear to protect against relapse among people with only one or two previous major depressive episodes (Ma & Teasdale, 2004). This treatment, then, shows promise for patients with highly recurrent major depression.

Social Skills Training   Since depression is so closely tied to interpersonal difficulties, behavioral treatments focus on helping patients improve social interactions. Evidence supports the effectiveness of enhancing overt social behaviors by such techniques as assertiveness training and **social skills training** (Hersen et al., 1984; Lewinsohn & Gotlib, 1995). A recent review concluded that treatments based on social skills training are effective in alleviating depression (Segrin, 2000), but few of these studies focused on people with severe levels of depression (Hollon et al., 2002).

Behavioral Activation Therapy   As we noted above (see p. 254), some studies have focused on a treatment that uses just the behavioral activation component of Beck's therapy. Behavioral activation (BA) therapy (Jacobson & Gortner, 2000) is related to social skills training in its distinctly behavioral approach. Inactivity, withdrawal, and inertia are common symptoms of depression. From a behavioral activation perspective, however, the *function* of these behaviors is crucial. Proponents of BA contend that these behaviors will diminish the already low levels of positive reinforcement associated with depression. Consequently, BA seeks to increase participation in positively reinforcing activities, so as to disrupt the spiral of depression.

BA has received a great deal of attention after positive findings in a study of which ingredients in Beck's therapy are most effective (Gortner et al., 1998). These findings suggested that the BA component of Beck's therapy performed as well as the full package in the treatment of MDD and the prevention of relapse over a 2-year follow-up period. This challenged the notion that people must directly modify their negative thinking in order to alleviate depression and suggested instead that having people engage in rewarding activities may be enough.

Behavioral Marital Therapy   As described above, depression is often tied to interpersonal problems, including marital and family distress. Drawing on these findings, researchers have studied behavioral marital therapy as a treatment for depression. In this approach, researchers work with both members of a couple to improve communication and marital satisfaction. The findings indicate that when a person with depression is also experiencing marital distress, **behavioral marital therapy** is as effective in relieving depression as individual cognitive therapy is (Jacobson et al., 1991). As one might expect, marital therapy has the advantage that it is more likely to relieve marital distress than individual cognitive therapy is.

Psychological Treatment of Bipolar Disorder

Medication is considered a necessary part of treatment for bipolar disorder, but psychological treatments can supplement medications. Psychological treatments show promise in dealing with many of the social and cognitive problems associated with bipolar disorder (Johnson & Leahy, 2002).

Educating people about their illness is a common component to treating many disorders, including bipolar disorder and schizophrenia. **Psychoeducational approaches** typically help people learn about the symptoms of the disorder, the expected time course of symptoms, the biological and psychological triggers for symptoms, and treatment strategies. A small number of empirical studies confirm that careful education about bipolar disorder can help people adhere to treatment with medications such as lithium (Colom et al., 2003). This is an important goal, because as many as half of people being treated for bipolar disorder do not take medication consistently (Regier et al., 1993). A friend of one of the authors put it like this: "Lithium cuts out the highs as well as the lows. I don't miss the lows, but I gotta admit that there were some aspects of the highs that I do miss. It took me a while to accept that I had to give up those highs. Wanting to keep my job and my marriage helped!" A drug alone does not address this kind of concern.

Studies have begun to suggest that psychotherapies designed to offer more than just education also can help reduce symptoms in bipolar disorder. For example, cognitive therapy like that offered for MDD appears effective as a supplement to medications (Lam et al., 2000). Not surprisingly, however, cognitive treatment seems to relieve symptoms of depression more than mania.

Expressed emotion (see p. 244) predicts faster relapse in bipolar I disorder (Miklowitz et al., 1996). This points to the need for family interventions. **Family-focused treatment (FFT)** focuses on educating the family about the illness, enhancing communication in the family, and developing problem-solving skills (Miklowitz & Goldstein, 1997). FFT leads to lower rates of relapse compared to medication with crisis management (Miklowitz et al., 2003).

Biological Treatment of Mood Disorders

A variety of biological therapies are used to treat depression and mania. The two most common are electroconvulsive therapy and drugs.

Electroconvulsive Therapy for Depression Perhaps the most dramatic and controversial treatment for MDD is **electroconvulsive therapy (ECT)** (see p. 16). For the most part now, ECT is only used to treat MDD that has not responded to medication. ECT entails the deliberate induction of a seizure and momentary unconsciousness by passing a current of 70–130 volts through the patient's brain. Formerly, electrodes were placed on each side of the forehead, a method known as *bilateral ECT*. Today, *unilateral ECT,* in which the current passes through the nondominant (typically the right) cerebral hemisphere only, is more common. In the past, the patient was usually awake until the current triggered the seizure, and the electric shock often created frightening contortions of the body, sometimes even causing bone fractures. Now the patient is given a short-acting anesthetic and a strong muscle relaxant before the current is applied. The convulsive spasms of the body muscles are barely perceptible to onlookers, and the patient awakens a few minutes later remembering nothing about the treatment. Typically, patients receive between 6 and 12 treatments, spaced several days apart.

Even with these improvements in procedures, inducing a seizure is drastic treatment. Why should anyone agree to undergo such radical therapy? The answer is simple. ECT is the most reliable treatment available for depression with psychotic features (Sackheim et al., 2001), even though we don't know why it works. Most professionals acknowledge that people undergoing ECT face some risks of short-term confusion and memory loss. It is fairly common for patients to have no memory of the period during which they received ECT and, sometimes, for the weeks surrounding the procedure. Unilateral ECT, however, produces fewer cognitive side effects than bilateral ECT does (Sackeim et al., 2001). A long-term follow-up study of people treated with ECT during adolescence showed no lasting memory impairment (Cohen et al., 2000). In addition, some evidence suggests that the cognitive side effects of ECT can be minimized by using thyroid hormone as part of the treatment (Tremont & Stern, 2000). In any case, clinicians typically resort to ECT only if less drastic treatments have failed. Given that suicide is a real possibility among people who are depressed, many experts regard the use of ECT after other treatments have failed as a responsible approach.

Medications for Depressive Disorders Drugs are the most commonly used and best-researched treatments—biological or otherwise—for depressive disorders (and, as we will see, for bipolar disorders as well). Table 8.6 shows the three major categories of antidepressant drugs: **monoamine oxidase (MAO) inhibitors**, **tricyclic antidepressants**, and **selective serotonin reuptake inhibitors (SSRIs)** and their side effects. These medications do not work for all people. A number of double-blind studies have shown these medications to be effective in treating depressive disorders, with 50–70 percent of people who complete treatment showing improvement (Depression Guideline Panel, 1993; Nemeroff & Schatzberg, 1998). A meta-analysis summarizing across many different studies of antidepressants has shown that the clinical effectiveness of all three classes of drugs is about the same (Depression Guideline Panel, 1993). These medications have been found to be effective in treating dysthymia as well as major depression (Hollon, Thase, & Markowitz, 2002).

One major problem with drug treatments is that many people stop taking their medications, often because they find the side effects unpleasant (Thase & Rush, 1997). The MAO inhibitors are the least used antidepressants because of their potentially life-threatening side effects. The SSRIs have become the most commonly prescribed antidepressants because they tend to produce fewer side effects than the other classes of antidepressants (Enserink, 1999).

Electroconvulsive therapy is an effective treatment for depression that has not responded to medication. Using unilateral shock, anesthetics, and muscle relaxants has reduced its undesirable side effects. (Will & Deni McIntyre/Photo Researchers.)

Table 8.6 Medications for Treating Mood Disorders

Category	Generic Name	Trade Name	Side Effects
MAO inhibitor antidepressants	tranylcypromine	Parnate	Possibly fatal hypertension, dry mouth, dizziness, nausea, headaches
Tricyclic antidepressants	imipramine amitriptyline	Tofranil, Elavil	Heart attack, stroke, hypotension, blurred vision, anxiety, tiredness, dry mouth, constipation, gastric disorders, erectile dysfunction, weight gain
Selective serotonin reuptake inhibitor (SSRI) antidepressants	fluoxetine sertraline	Prozac, Zoloft	Nervousness, fatigue, gastrointestinal complaints, dizziness, headaches, insomnia, suicidality
Mood stabilizers	lithium	Lithium	Tremors, gastric distress, lack of coordination, dizziness, cardiac arrhythmia, blurred vision, fatigue, death (in rare cases)
Anticonvulsants	divalproex sodium	Depakote	Pancreatitis
Antipsychotics	olanzapine	Zyprexa	Hyperglycemia, diabetes, and in elderly patients, cardiovascular problems, neuroleptic malignant syndrome, tardive dyskinesia

In March 2004, however, the Food and Drug Administration asked manufacturers to include packaging information warning people that there have been case reports of suicidality associated with SSRIs. These reports suggest that suicidality may be greater during the early phases of treatment or after increases in dosage. There is particular concern about the potential for suicidality in children and adolescents, and researchers continue to look at this important issue, as findings have been controversial. Such effects seem rare, but the FDA approach is designed to protect against risk, even if that risk is faced by only a small number of people.

Although the various antidepressants hasten recovery from an episode of depression, relapse is common after the drugs are withdrawn (Reimherr et al., 2001). This is not to dismiss the advantages of temporary relief, given the potential for social problems, suicide, and hospitalization as depression continues. Results from one meta-analysis of 31 different drug trials suggest that continuing antidepressants after remission lowers the risk of recurrence from approximately 40 percent to about 20 percent (Geddes et al., 2003). Treatment guidelines recommend continuing antidepressant medications for at least 6 months after a depressive episode ends, and longer if a person has experienced several episodes. But many people do not receive long-term dosages that are in the recommended treatment ranges; to prevent recurrence, medication doses should be as high as those offered during the acute treatment period.

Combining psychotherapy and antidepressant medications does not bolster the odds of recovery by more than 10–20 percent above either psychotherapy or medications alone for most depressed patients, but each treatment offers unique advantages (Hollon, Thase, & Markowitz, 2002). Antidepressants work more quickly than psychotherapy, thus providing immediate relief. Psychotherapy may take longer but may help people learn skills that they can use after treatment is finished to protect against recurrent depressive episodes.

Research Comparing Medications and Psychological Treatment for Major Depressive Disorder   In 1977 the National Institute of Mental Health (NIMH) undertook a large and complex three-site study called the Treatment of Depression Collaborative Research Program (TDCRP; Elkin et al., 1985). Because it is a widely cited and controversial study, and because it illustrates a number of issues in treatment research, we will describe it in detail.

In this study, 240 patients diagnosed with MDD were randomly assigned to receive cognitive therapy (CT), interpersonal psychotherapy (IPT), pharmacotherapy, or a placebo. All treatments lasted about 16 weeks. For pharmacotherapy, patients received imipramine (Tofranil), a well-tested, commonly used antidepressant medication; guidelines for dosages were developed but were flexible enough to allow for clinical judgment. Both the placebo condition and the pharmacotherapy condition included clinical management. Clinical

Clinical Case: Treatment Decisions for Mary

Mary, the woman described in the beginning of this chapter, reported increasing problems because of her depression. Given this, her therapist referred her to a psychiatrist who prescribed Prozac (fluoxetine). Both the psychologist and the psychiatrist agreed that medication might help by quickly relieving her symptoms. But after 2 weeks, Mary decided she did not want to continue taking Prozac because she found the side effects uncomfortable and did not like the idea of taking medication over the long term. She had not gotten much relief, but she also explained that she had missed many doses because of her concerns.

With so many different types of treatment available, determining the best therapy for each client can be a challenge. Mary had experienced a major life event and transition, suggesting that interpersonal psychotherapy might fit. But she was blaming herself for her job loss and other issues, suggesting that cognitive therapy (CT) might help. Marital conflicts suggest behavioral marital therapy could be appropriate. How does a therapist choose which approach to use? Sometimes, this decision reflects personal preferences and training of the therapist. Ideally, it incorporates the treatment preferences of the client as well. Her therapist began CT, in the belief that Mary's tendency to blame herself excessively when things went wrong was a key force in her depression. CT helped her learn to identify and challenge irrationally negative cognitions about herself. Therapy began by helping her identify times in day-to-day life when her sad moods could be explained by overly negative conclusions about small events. For example, when her children would misbehave, Mary would quickly assume this was evidence that she was a bad mother. Over time, Mary began to examine and challenge long-held beliefs about her lack of competence. By the end of 16 weeks of treatment, she had obtained relief from her symptoms of depression.

management did not include any explicit psychotherapy, but it did involve close monitoring and a supportive doctor–patient relationship; researchers regarded this almost as supportive therapy (Elkin et al., 1985). That is, the placebo condition involved more care than is typical in some studies.

Many findings emerged from this study (Elkin et al., 1996; Shea et al., 1992). Here are some of the major ones:

- In the first few weeks of treatment, imipramine reduced depressive symptoms more quickly than the other treatments.
- Among the patients with less severe MDD, those who received the placebo were doing as well as those receiving the three active treatments on some measures at the time treatment ended.
- Among the patients with more severe MDD: imipramine performed better than CT, IPT, or placebo; IPT performed better than placebo; CT did not perform better than placebo at the time treatment ended.
- In some analyses, imipramine performed better than CT at the time treatment ended (Klein & Ross, 1993).
- Only 20–30 percent of the patients who had markedly improved by the end of treatment remained free of depressive symptoms 18 months later.

The comparisons of imipramine and CT in this study have been particularly controversial. Klein and others (Elkin et al., 1996) argued that medications are more effective for severe MDD than either CT or IPT, and others have disagreed. Some of this controversy centers about the 33 percent of the imipramine patients who dropped out before completing treatment. If one considers both treatment dropout and lingering symptoms to be poor outcomes, far more people in the medication condition had poor outcomes than in the CT condition (Jacobson & Hollon, 1996). Newer selective serotonin reuptake inhibitors, such as fluoxetine (Prozac), have fewer side effects, which might have minimized dropouts (Klein, 1996).

Researchers also argued that the TDCRP study might not have offered a fair test of CT (Jacobson & Hollon, 1996). They point out that this study is the only one indicating that pharmacotherapy is more effective than CT for even severe MDD. They also note that the differences between imipramine and the two psychotherapy treatments were not consistent across the three treatment sites—differences in therapists across sites could have influenced the findings.

In response to the unanswered questions, researchers designed a new clinical trial (Hollon & DeRubeis, 2003). They wanted to more carefully examine whether therapist differences influenced the success of CT and to examine the longer-term consequences of treatment, particularly for severe depression. They randomly assigned 240 patients with severe depression to receive antidepressant medication, CT, or a placebo for 4 months. Those who recovered were followed for another 12 months. The researchers found that CT was at least as effective as antidepressant medication for severe depression. They also found that experienced therapists were more effective than therapists without CT experience. Although both CT and medication helped people recover from depression more than a placebo did, CT had an advantage over the long term in that it helped protect against relapse once treatment was finished. The researchers also noted that CT was less expensive than treatment with medication.

Formal medical guidelines for practitioners have been extensively influenced by the TDCRP study, despite the controversies over some of its findings. For instance, guidelines now often suggest that antidepressants should always be used for severely depressed patients (APA, 2000). Like the findings of the study described above (Hollon & DeRubeis, 2003), however, several other findings suggest that CT and IPT are just as effective (Jarrett et al., 1999), with the added benefits that there are no side effects and that these psychotherapies offer more protection after treatment stops than medications do (Persons, Thase, & Crits-Christoph, 1996).

Medications for Bipolar Disorder   Medications that reduce manic symptoms are called *"mood-stabilizing medications."* **Lithium**, a naturally occurring chemical element, was the first mood stabilizer identified. Up to 80 percent of people with bipolar I disorder experience at least some benefit from taking this drug (Prien & Potter, 1993). Even though symptoms may become milder with medications, most patients continue to experience at least some manic and depressive symptoms. The median time to relapse on lithium is approximately 1 year (Keller et al., 1992). Lithium is more effective in preventing manic episodes than depressive episodes, but does help somewhat with depression.

Because of possibly serious, even fatal, side effects, lithium has to be prescribed and used very carefully. When serum levels of lithium get too high, lithium toxicity can result, so patients taking lithium must have regular blood tests. Signs of lithium toxicity range from mild symptoms like tremor, nausea, blurred vision, vertigo, and confusion, to quite severe symptoms, including cardiac dysrhythmias, seizures, coma, and even death. It is recommended that lithium be used continually for the person's entire life (Bowden et al., 2000), but many patients discontinue treatment (Maj et al., 1998).

Several new medications have been tested as treatments for bipolar I disorder. Two classes of medications other than lithium have been FDA-approved for the treatment of acute mania: anticonvulsant (antiseizure) medications such as divalproex sodium (Depakote), and antipsychotic medications such as Olanzapine (Zyprexa). Lithium is still recommended as the first choice, but both new types of treatments are recommended for people who are unable to tolerate lithium's side effects. In addition, several other medications show early promising results.

Typically, lithium is used in combination with other medications. Because lithium takes effect gradually, therapy typically begins with both lithium and an antipsychotic medication, such as Haldol, which has an immediate calming effect.

Many people continue to experience depression even when taking a mood-stabilizing medication like lithium. For these people, an antidepressant medication is often added to the regimen (Sachs & Thase, 2000). It is important that an antidepressant be administered in combination with a mood stabilizer; without a mood stabilizer, an antidepressant can actually trigger manic symptoms for as many as one-quarter of people with bipolar I disorder (Ghaemi, Boiman, & Goodwin, 2000). Because of the risk of mania, treatment guidelines have recommended stopping antidepressant medications after depressive symptoms have been absent for 6 months. Recent findings, though, have called this strategy into question. One study focused on people who had obtained relief from depressive episodes in bipolar disorder using antidepressants. The risk of a new episode of depression in the next year doubled for people who stopped antidepressant medications (Altshuler et al., 2003). A major focus of current research is on identifying the best treatments for depression in bipolar disorder, and some of these studies indicate that the anticonvulsant medication lamictal (lamotrigine) might be effective (Calabrese et al., 1999).

Depression and Primary Care

Most treatments for depressive disorders are tested in university specialty settings, but many people with depression first seek help from their primary care physician—for example, about half of all antidepressant prescriptions are written by primary care physicians. Research has shown that primary care doctors, perhaps because of time pressure, often fail to diagnose episodes of depression, and even when they offer treatment, these treatments tend to be too short, medication doses tend to be too small, and opportunities for psychotherapy tend to be limited. In HMO settings, too, time pressures may interfere with optimal care. One group of researchers studied antidepressant treatment at an HMO and found that only about half of the patients received an adequate regimen of drug therapy (Simon et al., 2001).

Researchers are studying how to improve the quality of care offered by primary care physicians or within HMOs. Simply telling doctors to diagnose and treat depression does not work very well; studies of written treatment guidelines and workshops for doctors do not show much effect on treatment practices (Gilbody et al., 2003). More intensive programs, however, do seem to help. For example, promising results have been obtained with telephone follow-ups, increased nursing care, or specific guidelines that help physicians identify patients who should receive more intensive care (Gilbody et al., 2003).

A Final Note on the Treatment of Depression

Some of the most exciting research today is focused on how treatments work. Researchers have shown that successful treatments, whether with psychotherapy, medications, or ECT, change activity in the brain regions related to depression (Brody et al., 2001; Goldapple et al., 2004; Martin et al., 2001; Nobler et al., 2001). Intriguingly, antidepressant medications and ECT both stimulate growth of neurons in the hippocampus in rats (Duman, Nakagawa, & Malberg, 2001), and the effects of antidepressants, at least in animals, appear to depend on whether these neurons grow (Santarelli et al., 2003). Understanding more about how psychological and medication treatments change underlying neurobiological processes may help us refine treatments for the future.

Quick Summary

Many different treatments are available for depression. The most-researched psychological treatments include cognitive therapy and interpersonal psychotherapy, but social skills training, behavioral activation treatment, and behavioral marital therapy have also received support. The three forms of antidepressants have been found to be similarly effective; SSRIs have become more popular because they have fewer side effects than MAO inhibitors and tricyclic antidepressants. One major study found that cognitive therapy was not as powerful as imipramine in relieving severe MDD, which led to treatment guidelines recommending use of antidepressant medication for severe MDD. Nonetheless, newer research has found strong support for CT in the treatment of even severe MDD.

Medication treatment is the first line of defense against bipolar disorder. The best-researched mood stabilizer is lithium, but anticonvulsants, antidepressants, and antipsychotic medications are also used. Some psychological treatments may provide supplements to medications for the treatment of bipolar disorder. These include psychoeducational approaches, cognitive therapy, and family therapy. These treatments appear particularly helpful in improving adherence to medication and relieving depressive symptoms within bipolar disorder.

Check Your Knowledge 8.4

1. A first round of psychotherapy or medication for MDD is likely to produce recovery for at least _____ percent of people.
   a. 25
   b. 50
   c. 75
   d. 90
2. The most effective treatment for MDD with psychotic features is
   a. Prozac
   b. any antidepressant medication
   c. ECT
   d. psychotherapy
3. Selective serotonin reuptake inhibitors (SSRIs) are more popular than other antidepressants because:
   a. they are more effective
   b. they have fewer side effects
   c. they are cheaper

Suicide

Suicide, and stigmatizing attitudes toward suicide, have been societal issues for thousands of years. Suicide was not condemned in Western thought until the fourth century, when Saint Augustine proclaimed it a crime because it violated the Sixth Commandment, "Thou shalt not kill" (Shneidman, 1973). As late as 1823, anyone in London who committed suicide was buried with a stake pounded through the heart, and not until 1961 did suicide cease to be a criminal offense in the United Kingdom. In the United States today, some states categorize suicide attempts as misdemeanors, although these offenses are seldom prosecuted (Shneidman, 1987).

We will focus on quantitative research on suicide, but suicidologists learn from many different sources. Many philosophers have written searchingly on the topic, including Descartes, Voltaire, Kant, Heidegger, and Camus. In addition, novelists such as Herman Melville and Leo Tolstoy have provided insights on suicide, as have writers who have killed themselves, such as Virginia Woolf (see p. 262 for her note) and Sylvia Plath.

It is important to begin by differentiating suicidal ideation, suicide attempts, and suicide. Suicidal ideation refers to thoughts of killing oneself and is much more common than attempted successful suicide. Suicide attempts involve behaviors that are intended to cause death but do not result in death. **Suicides** involve behaviors that are intended to cause death and actually do so.

Suicide rates may be grossly underestimated because some deaths are ambiguous—for example, seemingly accidental death may involve suicidal intentions. Nonetheless, it has been estimated that, on average, every 20 minutes someone in the United States commits suicide (Arias et al., 2003).

No other kind of death leaves friends and relatives with such long-lasting feelings of distress, shame, guilt, puzzlement, and general disturbance as does suicide (Gallo & Pfeffer, 2003). Survivors have an especially high mortality rate in the year after the suicide of a loved one.

Epidemiology of Suicide and Suicide Attempts

Studies on the epidemiology of suicidality suggest the following.

- The overall suicide rate in the United States is about 11 per 100,000. In the United States, it is estimated that approximately 1 in 20 suicide attempts results in death (Moscicki, 1995).
- About 10–20 percent of people report suicidal ideation at least once in their lives, and 3–5 percent have made at least one suicide attempt (Weissman et al., 1999).
- Men are four times more likely than women to kill themselves (Arias et al., 2003).
- Three times as many women as men make suicide attempts that do not result in death.

Writers who killed themselves, such as Sylvia Plath, have provided insights into the causes of suicide. (Corbis-Bettmann.)

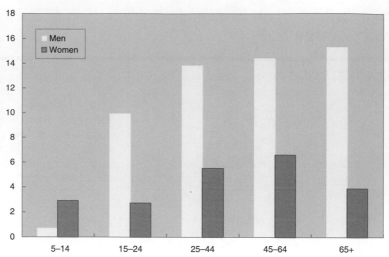

Figure 8.9 Deaths due to suicides per 100,000 people. [Arias, E., Andress, R. N., Kung, H. C., Murphy, S. L., Kochanek., K. (2003). *Deaths: Final Data for 2001*. Hyattsville, Maryland: National Center for deals Statistics, 52.]

On March 28, 1941, at the age of 59, Virginia Woolf drowned herself in the river near her Sussex home. Two suicide notes were found in the house, similar in content; one may have been written 10 days earlier, and it is possible that she may have made an unsuccessful attempt then, for she returned from a walk soaking wet, saying that she had fallen. The first was addressed to her sister Vanessa and the second to her husband, Leonard. To him, she wrote:

Dearest, I feel certain I am going mad again. I feel we can't go through another of those terrible times. And I shan't recover this time. I begin to hear voices, and I can't concentrate. So I am doing what seems the best thing to do. You have given me the greatest possible happiness. You have been in every way all that anyone could be. I don't think two people could have been happier till this terrible disease came. I can't fight it any longer. I know that I am spoiling your life, that without me you could work. And you will I know. You see I can't even write this properly. I can't read. What I want to say is I owe all the happiness of my life to you. You have been entirely patient with me and incredibly good. I want to say that—everybody knows it. If anybody could have saved me it would have been you. Everything has gone from me but the certainty of your goodness. I can't go on spoiling your life any longer. I don't think two people could have been happier than we have been. V.

Quoted from pp. 400–401, Briggs, J. (2005). Virginia Woolf: An Innter Life. Orlando, Fl: Harcourt, Inc.

English novelist and critic Virginia Woolf (1882–1941). (Photo by George C. Beresford/Getty Images.)

- Guns are by far the most common means of committing suicide in the United States (Arias et al., 2003), accounting for about 60 percent of all suicides. Men usually choose to shoot or hang themselves; women are more likely to use pills, a less lethal method, which may account for their lower rate of completed suicide.
- The suicide rate increases in old age. The highest rates of suicide in the United States are for white males over age 50.
- The rates of suicide for adolescents and children in the United States are increasing dramatically, but are still far below the rates of adults (see Figure 8.9). Some estimates suggest that at least 40 percent of children and adolescents experience suicidal ideation at least once. Because young people are less likely to die from other causes, suicide ranks as the third leading cause of death among those aged 10 to 24.
- Being divorced or widowed elevates suicide risk four- or fivefold.

Models of Suicide

Suicide is such a complex and multifaceted act that no single model can hope to explain it. Myths about suicide abound, highlighting the need for careful research (see Table 8.7). The study of suicide involves many different ethical questions and forces people to consider their own views on life and death. As an example of how complex these questions can be, Focus on Discovery 8.3 discusses physician-assisted suicide.

Psychological Disorders Suicide is discussed in this chapter because many persons with mood disorders have suicidal thoughts and some engage in suicidal behaviors. Researchers believe that more than half of those who try to kill themselves are depressed at the time of the act (Henriksson et al., 1993) and that as many as 15 percent of people who have been hospitalized with depression ultimately commit suicide (Angst et al., 2002). Other mental illnesses also are important in understanding suicide: as many as 90 percent of people who attempt suicide are suffering from a mental illness. Among people hospitalized for schizophrenia, bipolar I disorder, or bipolar II disorder, 10–12 percent commit suicide eventually (Angst et al., 2002; Roy, 1982). Even less severe mental disorders, such as panic disorder, eating disorders, and, among men, alcoholism are associated with suicide (Linehan, 1997; Schmidt, Woolaway-Bickel, & Bates, 2000). Although understanding suicide within the context of mental disorders is extremely important, most people with mental illnesses do not commit suicide.

Table 8.7 Myths about Suicide

Common Myth	Contrary Evidence
People who discuss suicide will not actually commit suicide.	Up to three-quarters of those who take their own lives communicate their intention beforehand.
Suicide is committed without warning.	People usually give many warnings, such as saying that the world would be better off without them or making unexpected and inexplicable gifts of highly valued possessions.
Suicidal people want to die.	Most people who commit suicide appear to be ambivalent about their own deaths. Most people are grateful after suicide is prevented.
People who attempt suicide by low-lethal means are not serious about killing themselves.	Many people are not well informed about pill dosages or human anatomy. Because of this, people who really want to die sometimes make nonlethal attempts.

Drawn from Fremouw et al., 1990 and Shneidman, 1973.

Within most disorders, suicides are most likely when a person is experiencing comorbid depression (Angst et al., 2002; Linehan, 1997; Schmidt et al., 2000). A significant number of people who are not depressed, however, make suicidal attempts or successfully commit suicide—most notably, people who have been diagnosed with borderline personality disorder (Linehan, 1997; see p. 394).

Neurobiological Models   Studies suggest that suicide risk is partially heritable (Baldessarini & Hennen, 2004). That is, MZ twins have a substantially higher concordance for suicidality than DZ twins do. Also, adoption studies suggest that the adopted-away biological relatives of a person who commits suicide are at elevated risk for suicide.

Research has established that, just as low levels of serotonin appear related to depression, there is a connection between serotonin and suicide. Low levels of serotonin's major metabolite, 5-HIAA, have been found in people who committed suicide (van Praag, Plutchik, & Apter, 1990). Particularly low 5-HIAA levels have been found in cases of violent and impulsive suicide (Roy, 1994; Winchel, Stanley, & Stanley, 1990). Neuroimaging studies suggest that genes modulating serotonin, such as the serotonin transporter gene or a specific type of serotonin receptor, the serotonin-2A receptor within the dorsal prefrontal cortex, may play a role in the predisposition to suicide (Mann et al., 2000).

Beyond the serotonin system, other research has found that among patients with MDD, those who had an abnormal dexamethasone suppression test response had very high rates of suicide several years later (Coryell & Schlesser, 2001). This is consistent with the idea that the HPA axis is overly reactive to stress among these people.

Sociocultural Models   Some of the strongest evidence for the role of the social environment in suicide comes from the strong effects of media reports of suicide. In one example of these effects, suicides rose 12 percent the month after Marilyn Monroe's death (Phillips, 1985). A review of 293 studies found that media coverage of a celebrity suicide is much more likely to spark an increase in suicidality than coverage of a noncelebrity suicide (Stack, 2000). Media reports of natural deaths of famous people are not followed by increases in suicide, suggesting that it is not grief per se that is the influential factor (Phillips, 1974). These statistics suggest that sociocultural factors matter.

Emile Durkheim (1897, 1951) developed a broader sociological model of suicide. Based on analysis of suicide cases from different countries, he developed a theory of three different kinds of suicide: egoistic, altruistic, and anomic.

Egoistic suicide is committed by people who have few ties to family, society, or community.

The suicide of Nirvana's lead singer, Kurt Cobain, triggered an increase in suicide among teenagers. (Kevin Estrada.)

Focus on Discovery 8.3

Physician-Assisted Suicide

Decisions not to resuscitate terminally ill patients are made every day in hospitals. About 15 percent of physicians in the United States report that they have written at least one prescription to hasten death (Meier et al., 1998). Are these examples of physician-assisted suicide? Physician-assisted suicide is a highly charged issue that came to the fore in the early 1990s when a Michigan physician, Jack Kevorkian, helped a 54-year-old Oregonian woman in the early stages of Alzheimer's disease commit suicide. Kevorkian designed a machine to inject a drug that induced unconsciousness and a lethal dose of potassium chloride (Egan, 1990), and then he helped the Woman press a button on the machine. For almost 10 years Kevorkian assisted upwards of a hundred terminally ill people in taking their lives. At the same time, he steadfastly provoked a searching discussion about the ethical issues involved in considering whether a physician may take the life of a dying patient. Kevorkian was brought to trial several times on charges both of murder and of professional misconduct but was not convicted until 1999, when he was found guilty of murder and sentenced to prison.

Passionate arguments pro and con continue. Among powerful groups opposing assisted suicide are the American Medical Association and the Catholic Church. In contrast, others, such as the American Civil Liberties Union, believe that terminally ill people should have the right to end their suffering and that the state should not intrude in such decisions.

Oregon became the first state to have a law—the Death with Dignity Act, originally approved by voters in 1994 and reaffirmed by an even greater margin in 1997—that made physician-assisted suicide legal. This law permits a patient diagnosed by two physicians as hav-

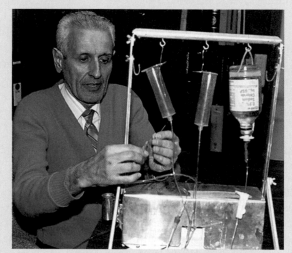

Jack Kevorkian, a Michigan physician, assisted many patients in taking their own lives. The controversy stimulated by his actions focused attention on the moral and ethical issues surrounding physician-assisted suicide. (Blake Discher/Corbis Sygma.)

ing less than 6 months to live to seek a doctor's prescription for a lethal dose of barbiturates. But the law also requires that the prescribing physician determine that the patient is not suffering from mental illness and that there be a waiting period of 15 days before the prescription can be filled.

Since the law went into effect, there have been two interesting developments. First, there has been no increase in such suicides. Second, there has been an increase in the use of morphine to ease the pain of terminally ill patients. This practice is in contrast to other states, where physicians often undermedicate for pain. Indeed, nearly 90 percent of physicians reported knowingly prescribing too little pain medication for cancer patients (Rubin, 1998b), probably because of potential legal charges for hastening death. The Oregon law has relieved physicians there of this concern.

In 2001, then Attorney General John Ashcroft attempted to overturn Oregon's Death with Dignity Act, declaring that assisted suicide is not an appropriate practice for physicians. The state of Oregon responded by filing suit (*State of Oregon v. Attorney General John Ashcroft*), and in April 2002, a federal judge ruled that a federal agency cannot usurp powers relegated to the states without specific authority from Congress, thus leaving the Oregon law in place. The Death with Dignity Act was upheld in a federal appeals court in 2004. The Supreme Court was considering a case involving physician-assisted suicide at the time this book went to press.

Altruistic suicide is committed because the person believes it will be for the good of society. Examples of this type of suicide include the self-immolations of Buddhist monks and nuns to protest the Vietnam War, hara-kiri among the Japanese, and more recently, suicide bombings.

Anomic suicide is triggered by a sudden change in a person's relation to society. That is, societies experiencing serious changes can promote anomie and even suicidality. One pattern that possibly illustrates anomic suicide has emerged in rural China. China is one of the most quickly changing countries in the world economically, leading to vast migrations of people from rural to urban areas. In rural China, suicide has become one of the leading causes of death (Phillips et al., 2002).

A rural Brazilian tribe, the Guarani, experienced a surge of anomic suicide after a sudden change in their living conditions—losing most of their ancestral lands to industrialization. Communities that had lived by hunting and fishing were now crowded onto reservations too small to support that way of life. Nearby cities tempted the Guarani with consumer goods that they could not afford. These changes significantly affected economic, family, and religious life (Long, 1995). Their suicide rate increased markedly in 1995 to 160 per 100,000 (more than 14 times higher than the U.S. rate!).

Without a doubt, when trying to understand suicide, it is important to consider social factors. But as with all sociological theories, Durkheim's hypotheses do not account for how different people react to the same societal conditions. For example, most of the Guarani people did not attempt suicide, even though their lifestyle had changed so dramatically. Durkheim, aware of this problem, suggested that psychological factors would interact with the social causes of suicide.

Psychological Models   Suicide has been viewed as retaliation, intended to induce guilt in others; as an effort to force love from others; as an effort to make amends for wrongs; as an effort to rid oneself of unacceptable feelings; as an expression of a desire to rejoin a dead loved one; and as an expression of a desire to escape from emotional pain or emotional vacuum. Undoubtedly, the psychological variables involved in suicide vary across people, but a number of researchers have attempted to identify factors that will help predict who is at highest risk.

The high suicide rate among the Guarani, who were forced onto crowded reservations, illustrates Durkheim's concept of anomic suicide. (Rogerio Reis/Black Star.)

One theory holds that some suicides arise from a strong desire to escape from aversive self-awareness (Baumeister, 1990). According to this theory, people are at risk when they set unattainable goals and then blame themselves for their failure to achieve those goals. Research is consistent with the idea that failure to attain goals and self-blame are correlates of suicidality. For example, suicide rates are often higher in countries and subgroups with high expectations for achievement. Perfectionism (one personality trait related to high expectations for the self) is known to be a risk factor for suicidality.

Other researchers relate suicide to difficulties in problem solving (Linehan & Shearin, 1988). Problem-solving deficits do predict suicide attempts prospectively (Dieserud et al., 2003). Problem-solving deficits also relate to the seriousness of previous suicide attempts, even after controlling for severity of depression, age, and overall intellectual functioning (Keilp et al., 2001).

One might expect that a person who has trouble resolving problems would be more vulnerable to hopelessness. Hopelessness, which can be defined as the expectation that life will be no better in the future than it is now, is strongly tied to suicidality. High levels of hopelessness are associated with a fourfold elevation in the risk of suicide (Brown et al., 2000), and hopelessness seems important even after considering depression levels (Beck, Kovacs, & Weissman, 1975).

Beyond these negative characteristics (e.g., failure to achieve goals, poor problem solving, hopelessness), positive qualities may motivate a person to live and help a clinician build a case for choosing life (Malone et al., 2000). One line of research builds on Marsha Linehan's Reasons for Living (RFL) Inventory (Linehan et al., 1983). Items on this inventory tap into what is important to the person, such as responsibility to family and concerns about children. People with more reasons to live tend to be less suicidal than those with few reasons to live (Ivanoff et al., 1994).

Another factor that has been studied is life satisfaction. A recent prospective study in Finland found that people who expressed relatively high life satisfaction on a simple

After a broken engagement at age 31, Abraham Lincoln developed symptoms of depression that were so severe that his friends feared that he would hurt himself, and they removed any sharp objects from his room. "I am now the most miserable man living," he confessed. "Whether I shall ever be better I can not tell; I awfully forebode I shall not. To remain as I am is impossible; I must die or be better." (Cited in Goodwin, 2003.) (Granger Collection.)

four-item questionnaire at the beginning of the study were significantly less likely to have attempted or committed suicide up to 20 years later. For example, men with the highest levels of life dissatisfaction were 25 times more likely to commit suicide than men with the lowest levels (Koivuma-Honkanen et al., 2001).

Preventing Suicide

Many people worry that talking about suicide will make it more likely to happen. Rather, clinicians learn that it is helpful to talk about suicide openly and matter-of-factly. Giving a person permission to talk about suicide may relieve a sense of secrecy and isolation, and it allows for a better assessment of risk. The therapist treating a suicidal person must be prepared to devote more energy and time than usual, even compared to time spent with patients who are psychotic. The therapist is likely to become a singularly important figure in the suicidal person's life.

Most people are ambivalent about their suicidal intentions, and they will communicate their intentions in some way. "The prototypical suicidal state is one in which a person cuts his or her throat, cries for help at the same time, and is genuine in both of these acts . . . . Individuals would be happy not to do it, if they didn't have to" (Shneidman, 1987, p. 170). This ambivalence gives the clinician an important foothold.

Treating the Associated Mental Disorder   One way to look at the prevention of suicide is to bear in mind that most people who kill themselves are suffering from a mental disorder. Thus, when a therapist following Beck's cognitive approach successfully lessens a patient's depression, that patient's prior suicidal risk is reduced. Marsha Linehan's dialectical behavior therapy with borderline patients provides another example of a treatment that is designed for a specific disorder, but provides protection from suicide (p. 409). Most studies of treatment for acute disorders, though, exclude people who are highly suicidal, a fact that sadly limits our knowledge (Linehan, 1997).

Community studies, however, have found that medications for mood disorders reduce the risk of suicidality three- to fourfold (Angst et al., 2002). Specifically, lithium appears effective in suicide prevention for people with bipolar disorder (Goodwin et al., 2003), and antidepressants reduce suicidality among elderly people who have been diagnosed with depressive disorders (Bruce et al., 2004). Risperidone (Clozapine), an antipsychotic medication, also appears to reduce the risk of suicide attempts among people with schizophrenia (Meltzer, 2003). Findings like these highlight the importance of helping people with mental illnesses to obtain appropriate care.

Treating Suicidality Directly   Edwin Shneidman is a pioneer in the development of suicide prevention interventions. His general strategy of suicide prevention (1987) is threefold.

1. Reduce the intense psychological pain.
2. Help the person see options other than continued suffering.
3. Encourage the person to pull back even a little from the self-destructive act.

The clinical case below illustrates how this strategy worked with one college student.

Because few people die from suicide in any given year, most intervention studies tend to focus on reducing suicide attempts and suicidal ideation. Cognitive behavioral approaches

Clinical Case: An Example of Suicide Prevention

A wealthy college student was single, pregnant, and suicidal, with a clearly formed plan. The only solution she could think of besides suicide was never to have become pregnant, even to be virginal again. Edwin Shneidman (1987, p. 171) describes his approach with this young woman:

> I took out a sheet of paper and began to widen her blinders. I said something like, "Now, let's see: You could have an abortion here locally." She responded, "I couldn't do that." I continued, "You could go away and have an abortion." "I couldn't do that." "You could bring the baby to term and keep the baby." "I couldn't do that." "You could have the baby and

adopt it out." Further options were similarly dismissed. When I said, "You can always commit suicide, but there is obviously no need to do that today," there was no response. "Now," I said, "let's look at this list and rank them in order of your preference, keeping in mind that none of them is optimal."

Shneidman reports that just drawing up the list had a calming effect. The student's drive to kill herself receded, and she was able to rank the list even though she found something wrong with each item. But an important goal had been achieved: she had been pulled back from the brink.

---

that emphasize social problem solving appear to be the most promising for reducing suicidal ideation (van der Sande, 1997), but not all results have been positive (Tyrer et al., 2003). In a study of people with anxiety and depression symptoms, researchers found that treatment focused on coping with emotion and solving problems led to significant reductions in suicidal ideation compared to treatment as usually offered in the community (Joiner, Voelz, & Rudd, 2001).

Professional organizations such as the American Psychiatric Association, the National Association of Social Workers, and the American Psychological Association charge their members with protecting people from suicide even if doing so requires breaking the confidentiality of the therapist–patient relationship. Therapists are expected to take reasonable precautions when they learn a patient is suicidal (Roy, 1995). It is not easy to agree about what constitutes reasonable precaution. One approach to keeping a person alive is to hospitalize them. Although many people worry about ethics of confining patients through involuntary hospitalization, it often is used as a short-term means of keeping people safe while helping them begin to consider ways of improving their life and resolving their intense emotions. Focus on Discovery 8.4 discusses the controversial views of psychiatrist Thomas Szasz on the ethical dilemma facing those involved in trying to prevent people from committing suicide.

Suicide Prevention Centers   There are more than 200 **suicide prevention centers** in the United States, plus others abroad (Lester, 1995). These centers typically aim to provide 24-hour phone hotline support to people in suicidal crises. Staff members assess the likelihood that the caller will make a serious suicide attempt (Shneidman, Farberow, & Litman, 1970). For example, a caller would be regarded as a lethal risk if he were male, middle-aged, divorced, and living alone, and he had a history of previous suicide attempts. The more detailed and concrete the suicide plan, the higher the risk. The most important goal is to show empathy and dissuade the caller from suicide.

It is exceedingly difficult to do controlled research on suicide prevention, and outcome studies have yielded inconsistent results. A meta-analysis of five studies on the effectiveness of suicide prevention centers failed to demonstrate that suicide rates decline after the implementation of services (Dew et al., 1987). A similarly negative finding was reported from Canada (Leenaars & Lester, 1995). Other research, however, has found that suicide rates declined in the years after suicide prevention centers were started in several cities (Lester, 1991) and that older people referred to a telephone support service demonstrated lower rates of suicide than the local population (De Leo, Buono, & Dwyer, 2002). Thus, we are left with conflicting evidence. Human lives are precious, though, and since many people who contact prevention centers weather a suicidal crisis successfully, these efforts will continue.

Community mental health centers often provide a 24-hour-a-day hotline for people who are considering suicide. (Mark Antman/The Image Works.)

Focus on Discovery 8.4

An Argument against Coercive Suicide Prevention

Boldly and controversially, Thomas Szasz (1999) argues that it is impractical and immoral to prevent a person from committing suicide. It is impractical because we cannot really force people to live if they are intent on committing suicide (even hospitalized patients manage to take their own lives). It is immoral because people should be free to make choices. Szasz does make an exception for "impulsive suicide"—when people are temporarily agitated and need to be protected for a short while from their uncontrollable impulses. (Presumably he would broaden this protection to children and adolescents, whose problem-solving abilities and control over impulsive acts are not as well developed as those of

adults.) He is also not opposed to treating problems such as depression that might be behind self-destructive thinking.

Like the other arguments about freedom and responsibility that Szasz has made over the years (see p. 570 for a discussion of his writings on mental illness and legal responsibility for crimes), his analysis is radical but worth consideration. In our view, his principal omissions are that treatment and hospitalization often do deter people from suicide, and most people who are prevented from killing themselves are grateful afterward for another chance at life. There are no easy answers here, but it is important to raise the questions.

Check Your Knowledge 8.5

True or False?
1. Men have higher rates of suicide than women.
2. Men have higher rates of suicide attempts than women.
3. Adolescents have higher rates of suicide than older adults do.
4. Dopamine dysfunction is implicated in suicidality.
5. Most people with MDD will make a suicide attempt.

Summary

Clinical Descriptions and Epidemiology

● There are two broad types of mood disorders: depressive disorders and bipolar disorders.
● Depressive disorders include major depression and dysthymia, and bipolar disorders include bipolar I disorder, bipolar II disorder, and cyclothymia.
● Bipolar I disorder is defined by mania or mixed episodes. Bipolar II disorder is defined by hypomania and episodes of depression. Major depressive disorder, bipolar I disorder, and bipolar II disorder are episodic. Recurrence is very common in these disorders.
● Dysthymia and cyclothymia are characterized by low levels of symptoms that last for at least 2 years.
● Major depression is one of the most common psychiatric disorders, affecting as many as 16.2 percent of people during their lifetime. Rates of depression are twice as high in women as in men. Bipolar I disorder is much more rare, affecting approximately 1 percent of people.

Etiology

● Genetic studies provide evidence that bipolar disorder is strongly heritable, and that depression is somewhat heritable.
● Neurobiological research has focused on the sensitivity of postsynaptic receptors rather than on the amount of various transmitters, with

the strongest evidence for changes in serotonin receptors in depression, and potential changes in the dopamine receptors within the reward system as related to mania and depression.
● Bipolar and unipolar disorders seem tied to elevated activity of the amygdala, and diminished activity in regions of the prefrontal cortex, the hippocampus, and the anterior cingulate.
● Overactivity of the hypothalamic–pituitary–adrenal axis is also found among depressive patients, manifested by high levels of cortisol and poor suppression of cortisol by dexamethasone.
● Socioenvironmental models focus on the role of negative life events, lack of social support, and family criticism as triggers for episodes, but also consider ways in which a person with depression may elicit negative responses from others. People with less social skill and those who tend to seek more excessive reassurance are at elevated risk for the development of depression.
● Psychological theories of depression include psychoanalytic, emotion and personality, and cognitive models. Psychoanalytic formulations focus on anger turned inward, but this idea has not been supported. Neuroticism appears to predict the onset of depression. Beck's cognitive theory ascribes causal significance to negative schemata and cognitive biases. According to hopelessness theory, low self-esteem or beliefs that an event will have long-term meaningful consequences can instill a sense of hopelessness, which is expressed in a specific set of depressive symptoms called hopelessness depression.

- Psychological theories of depression in bipolar disorder are similar to those proposed for unipolar depression. Some researchers have proposed that mania may arise after negative experiences, but others suggest that because of dysregulation in the reward system in the brain, mania can be triggered by life events involving success and unrealistically positive cognitions about future goals.

Treatment

- Several psychological therapies are effective for depression, including interpersonal therapy, cognitive therapy, social skills therapy, behavioral activation therapy, and behavioral marital therapy.
- The major approaches that have been found to help as adjuncts to medication for bipolar disorder include psychoeducation, family therapy, and cognitive therapy.
- Electroconvulsive shock and several antidepressant drugs (tricyclics, selective serotonin reuptake inhibitors, and MAO inhibitors) have proved their worth in lifting depression. Lithium is the best-researched treatment for prevention of mania, but antipsychotic and anticonvulsant medications also help decrease manic symptoms.

Suicide

- Men, elderly people, and people who are divorced or widowed are at elevated risk for suicide. Most people who commit suicide meet diagnostic criteria for psychiatric disorders, with more than half experiencing depression. Suicide is at least partially heritable, and neurobiological models focus on serotonin and overactivity in the HPA. Social changes are common precedents to anomic suicide. Individual vulnerability may be tied to difficulty achieving high goals, poor problem solving, hopelessness, lack of reasons to live, and low life satisfaction.
- Several approaches have been taken to prevention. For people with a mental illness, psychological treatments and medications to quell symptoms help reduce suicidality. Many people believe it is important to address suicidality more directly, though. Problem-solving therapy has shown promise in reducing suicidal behavior, but not all results have been positive. Suicide hotlines are found in most cities, but it has been hard to conduct research demonstrating that these work.

Answers to Check Your Knowledge Questions

8.1 1. 5 (including mood), 2; 2. 16; 3. 66; 4. late teens to early twenties; 5. 2; 6. 1; 7. manic, mixed, hypomanic
8.2 1. c; 2. a; 3. b; 4. b; 5. d
8.3 1. T; 2. F; 3. T; 4. F
8.4 1. b; 2. c; 3. b
8.5 1. T; 2. F; 3. F; 4. F; 5. F

Key Terms

altruistic suicide
amygdala
anomic suicide
anterior cingulate
attributional style
attributions
behavioral activation (BA) therapy
behavioral marital therapy
bipolar I disorder
bipolar II disorder
catatonic features
cognitive biases
cognitive therapy
cortisol
Cushing's syndrome
cyclothymic disorder
dopamine

dysthymic disorder
egoistic suicide
electroconvulsive therapy (ECT)
episodic disorder
expressed emotion (EE)
extraversion
family-focused treatment (FFT)
flight of ideas
G-proteins
hippocampus
hopelessness theory
HPA axis
hypomania
interpersonal psychotherapy (IPT)
irrational belief
learned helplessness theory

lithium
major depressive disorder (MDD)
mania
manic defense
melancholic
mindfulness-based cognitive therapy
mixed episode
monoamine oxidase (MAO) inhibitors
mood disorder
negative affect
negative triad
neuroticism
norepinephrine
positive affect
postpartum onset

prefrontal cortex
psychoeducational approaches
psychotic features
rapid cycling
reward system
schema
seasonal
second messengers
selective serotonin reuptake inhibitors (SSRIs)
serotonin
social skills training
somatic arousal
suicide
suicide prevention centers
tricyclic antidepressants
tryptophan

9

Eating Disorders

Learning Goals

1. Be able to distinguish the symptoms associated with anorexia, bulimia, and binge eating disorder and be able to distinguish among the different eating disorders.
2. Be able to describe the neurobiological, sociocultural, and psychological factors implicated in the etiology of eating disorders.
3. Be able to discuss the issues surrounding the growing epidemic of obesity in the United States.
4. Be able to describe the methods of treatment for eating disorders and the evidence supporting their effectiveness.

Clinical Case: Lynne

Lynne, a 24-year-old Caucasian woman, was admitted to the psychiatric ward of a general hospital for treatment of anorexia nervosa. Although she didn't really think anything was wrong with her, her parents had consulted with a psychiatrist, and the three of them had confronted her with a choice of admitting herself or being committed involuntarily.

At the time Lynne was 5 feet, 5 inches and weighed only 78 pounds. She hadn't menstruated for 3 years and had a variety of medical problems—hypotension, irregularities in her heartbeat, and abnormally low levels of potassium and calcium.

Lynne had experienced several episodes of dramatic weight loss, beginning at age 18 when she first left home for college. But none of the prior episodes had been this severe, and she had not sought treatment before. She had an intense fear of becoming fat, and although she had never really been overweight she felt that her buttocks and abdomen were far too large. (This belief persisted even when she weighed 78 pounds.) During the periods of weight loss she severely restricted food intake and used laxatives heavily. She had occasionally had episodes of binge eating, typically followed by self-induced vomiting so that she would not gain any weight.

Many cultures are preoccupied with food. In the United States today, gourmet restaurants abound, and numerous magazines and television shows are devoted to food preparation. At the same time, many people are overweight. Dieting to lose weight is common, and the desire of many people, especially women, to be thinner has created a multibillion-dollar-a-year business. Given this intense interest in food and eating, it is not surprising that this aspect of human behavior is subject to disorder.

Although clinical descriptions of eating disorders can be traced back many years, particularly for anorexia nervosa, these disorders appeared in the DSM for the first time in 1980 as one subcategory of disorders beginning in childhood or adolescence. With the publication of DSM-IV the eating disorders became a distinct category, reflecting the increased attention they have received from clinicians and researchers over the past three decades.

Clinical Descriptions of Eating Disorders

We begin by describing anorexia nervosa and bulimia nervosa. The diagnoses of these two disorders share several clinical features. We then discuss binge eating disorder; a disorder not yet in the current diagnostic system but that has generated a good deal of attention due to its association with obesity.

Anorexia Nervosa

Lynne, the woman just described, had **anorexia nervosa**. The term *anorexia* refers to loss of appetite, and *nervosa* indicates that the loss is due to emotional reasons. The term is something of a misnomer because most individuals with anorexia nervosa actually do not lose their appetite or interest in food. On the contrary, while starving themselves, most individuals with the disorder become preoccupied with food; they may read cookbooks constantly and prepare gourmet meals for their families.

Lynne met all four features required for the diagnosis.

> **Diagnostic Criteria for Anorexia Nervosa**
>
> - Refusal to maintain normal body weight
> - Body weight less than 85 percent of normal
> - Intense fear of weight gain
> - Body image disturbance
> - In women, amenorrhea

1. **Refusal to maintain normal body weight.** This is usually taken to mean that the person weighs less than 85 percent of what is considered normal for that person's age and height. Weight loss is typically achieved through dieting, although purging (self-induced vomiting, heavy use of laxatives or diuretics) and excessive exercise can also be part of the picture.

2. **Intense fear of gaining weight and being fat.** This fear is not reduced by weight loss. There is no such thing as "too thin."

3. **Distorted body image or sense of their body shape.** Even when emaciated, those with anorexia nervosa maintain that they are overweight or that certain parts of their bodies, particularly the abdomen, buttocks, and thighs, are too fat. To check on their body size, they typically weigh themselves frequently, measure the size of different parts of the body, and gaze critically at their reflections in mirrors. Their self-esteem is closely linked to maintaining thinness.

4. **Amenorrhea (loss of menstrual period).** In females, this is caused by extreme emaciation. Of the four diagnostic criteria, amenorrhea seems least important; few differences have been found between women who meet all four criteria and those who meet the other three but not amenorrhea (Garfinkel et al., 1996).

The distorted body image that accompanies anorexia nervosa has been assessed in several ways, most frequently by a questionnaire such as the Eating Disorders Inventory (Garner, Olmsted, & Polivy, 1983). Some of the items on this questionnaire are presented in Table 9.1. In another type of assessment, individuals with anorexia nervosa are shown line drawings of women with varying body weights and asked to pick the one closest to their own and the one that represents their ideal shape (see Figure 9.1). Individuals overestimate their own body size and choose a thin figure as their ideal. Despite this distortion in body size, individuals with anorexia nervosa are fairly accurate when reporting their actual weight (McCabe et al., 2001), perhaps because they weigh themselves frequently.

DSM-IV-TR distinguishes two types of anorexia nervosa. In the *restricting type*, weight loss is achieved by severely limiting food intake; in the *binge-eating–purging type*, as illustrated in Lynne's case, the person has also regularly engaged in binge eating and purging. Initial research indicated a number of differences between these two subtypes, thus supporting the validity of this distinction. For example, studies have shown that individuals with the binging–purging subtype exhibit more personality disorders, impulsive behavior, stealing,

Despite being thin, women with anorexia believe that parts of their bodies are too fat and spend a lot of time critically examining themselves in front of mirrors. (Susan Rosenberg/Photo Researchers.)

Table 9.1 Subscales and Illustrative Items from the Eating Disorders Inventory

Drive for thinness	I think about dieting.
	I feel extremely guilty after overeating.
	I am preoccupied with the desire to be thinner.
Bulimia	I stuff myself with food.
	I have gone on eating binges where I have felt that I could not stop.
	I have the thought of trying to vomit in order to lose weight.
Body dissatisfaction	I think that my thighs are too large.
	I think that my buttocks are too large.
	I think that my hips are too big.
Ineffectiveness	I feel inadequate.
	I have a low opinion of myself.
	I feel empty inside (emotionally).
Perfectionism	Only outstanding performance is good enough in my family.
	As a child, I tried hard to avoid disappointing my parents and teachers.
	I hate being less than best at things.
Interpersonal distrust	I have trouble expressing my emotions to others.
	I need to keep people at a certain distance (feel uncomfortable if someone tries to get too close).
Interoceptive awareness	I get confused about what emotion I am feeling.
	I don't know what's going on inside me.
	I get confused as to whether or not I am hungry.
Maturity fears	I wish that I could return to the security of childhood.
	I feel that people are happiest when they are children.
	The demands of adulthood are too great.

Source: From Garner et al., 1983.
Note: Responses use a six-point scale ranging from always to never.

Anorexia nervosa can be a life-threatening condition. It is especially prevalent among young women who are under intense pressure to keep their weight low. Gymnast Christy Henrich died from the condition in 1994 at age 22. (AP/Wide World Photos.)

alcohol and drug abuse, social withdrawal, and suicide attempts than do individuals with the restricting type of anorexia (e.g., Herzog et al., 2000; Pryor, Wiederman, & McGilley, 1996). However, recent longitudinal research suggests the distinction between subtypes may not be all that useful (Eddy et al., 2002). Nearly two-thirds of women who initially met criteria for the restricting subtype had switched over to the binge-eating–purging type 8 years later. Furthermore, this study found few differences in substance abuse or personality disturbances between the two subtypes.

Anorexia nervosa typically begins in the early to middle teenage years, often after an episode of dieting and the occurrence of a life stress. Lifetime prevalence of anorexia is less than 1 percent, and it is at least 10 times more frequent in women than in men (Hoek & van Hoeken, 2003). When anorexia nervosa does occur in men, symptomatology and other characteristics, such as reports of family conflict, are generally similar to those reported by women with the disorder (Olivardia et al., 1995). As we discuss more fully later, the gender difference in the prevalence of anorexia most likely reflects the greater cultural emphasis on women's beauty, which has promoted a thin shape as the ideal over the past several decades.

Women with anorexia nervosa are frequently diagnosed with depression, obsessive-compulsive disorder, phobias, panic disorder, alcoholism, and various personality disorders (Godart et al., 2000; Ivarsson et al., 2000). Men with anorexia nervosa are also likely to have a diagnosis of a mood disorder, schizophrenia, or substance dependence (Striegel-Moore et al., 1999b).

Physical Changes in Anorexia Nervosa Self-starvation and use of laxatives produce numerous undesirable biological consequences in people with anorexia nervosa. Blood

Figure 9.1 In this assessment of body image, respondents indicate their current shape, their ideal shape, and the shape they think is most attractive to the opposite sex. The figure actually rated as most attractive by members of the opposite sex is shown in both panels. Ratings of women who scored high on a measure of distorted attitudes toward eating are shown in (a); ratings of women who scored low are shown in (b). The high scorers overestimated their current size and ideally would be very thin. [From Zellner, Harner, and Adler (1989).]

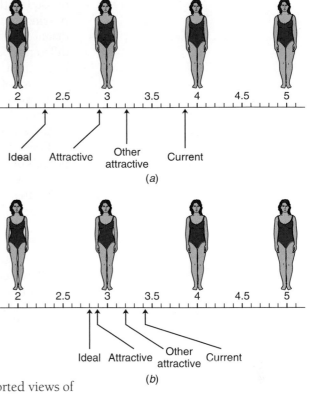

pressure often falls, heart rate slows, kidney and gastrointestinal problems develop, bone mass declines, the skin dries out, nails become brittle, hormone levels change, and mild anemia may occur. Some individuals lose hair from the scalp, and they may develop lanugo, a fine, soft hair, on their bodies. As in Lynne's case, levels of electrolytes, such as potassium and sodium, are altered. These ionized salts, present in various bodily fluids, are essential to neural transmission, and lowered levels can lead to tiredness, weakness, cardiac arrythmias, and even sudden death. EEG abnormalities and neurological impairments are frequent in individuals with anorexia (Garner, 1997; Lambe et al., 1997). Structural brain changes, such as enlarged ventricles or sulcal widening, can also occur, but can be reversed (Hoffman et al., 1989; Lambe et al., 1997).

Prognosis About 70 percent of patients with anorexia eventually recover. However, recovery often takes 6 or 7 years, and relapses are common before a stable pattern of eating and maintenance of weight is achieved (Strober, Freeman, & Morrell, 1997). As we discuss later, changing these patients' distorted views of themselves is very difficult, particularly in cultures that value thinness.

Anorexia nervosa is a life-threatening illness; death rates are 10 times higher among individuals with the disorder than among the general population and twice as high as among individuals with other psychological disorders. Death most often results from physical complications of the illness—for example, congestive heart failure—and from suicide (Herzog et al., 2000; Sullivan, 1995).

Clinical Case: Jill

Jill was the second child born to her parents. Both she and her brother became intensely involved in athletics at an early age, Jill in gymnastics and her brother in Little League baseball. At age 4 Jill was enrolled in gymnastics school, where she excelled. By the time she was 9 her mother had decided that Jill had outgrown the coaching abilities of the local instructors and began driving her to a nationally recognized coach several times a week. Over the next few years, Jill's trophy case swelled and her aspirations for a place on the Olympic team grew. As she reached puberty, though, her thin frame began to fill out, raising concerns about the effects of weight gain on her

performance as a gymnast. She began to restrict her intake of food but found that after several days of semistarvation she would lose control and go on an eating binge. This pattern of dieting and binging lasted for several months, and Jill's fear of becoming fat seemed to increase during that time. At age 13, she hit on the solution of self-induced vomiting. She quickly fell into a pattern of episodes of binging and vomiting three or four times per week. Although she maintained this pattern in secret for a while, eventually her parents caught on and initiated treatment for her.

Bulimia Nervosa

Jill's behavior illustrates the features of **bulimia nervosa**. *Bulimia* is from a Greek word meaning "ox hunger." This disorder involves episodes of rapid consumption of a large amount of food, followed by compensatory behavior, such as vomiting, fasting, or excessive exercise, to prevent weight gain. The DSM defines a *binge* as eating an excessive amount of food within less than 2 hours. Bulimia nervosa is not diagnosed if the binging and purging occur only in the context of anorexia nervosa and its extreme weight loss; the diagnosis in such a case is anorexia nervosa, binge-eating–purging type. Indeed, one striking difference between anorexia and bulimia is weight loss: individuals with anorexia nervosa lose a tremendous amount of weight whereas individuals with bulimia nervosa do not. A summary of the diagnostic criteria for both anorexia nervosa and bulimia nervosa appears in the margins.

In bulimia, binges typically occur in secret; they may be triggered by stress and the negative emotions it arouses, and continue until the person is uncomfortably full (Grilo, Shiffman, & Carter-Campbell, 1994). In the case of Jill, she was likely to binge following periods of stress associated with being an elite athlete. Foods that can be rapidly consumed, especially sweets such as ice cream and cake, are usually part of a binge. A recent study found that women with bulimia nervosa were more likely to binge while alone and during the morning or afternoon. In addition, avoiding a craved food on one day was associated with a binge episode the next morning (Waters, Hill, & Waller, 2001). Other studies show that a binge is likely to occur after a negative social interaction, or at least the perception of a negative social exchange (Steiger et al., 1999).

Research suggests that individuals with bulimia nervosa sometimes ingest enormous quantities of food during binges, often more than what a normal person eats in an entire day; however, binges are not always as large as the DSM implies, and there is wide variation in the caloric content consumed by individuals with bulimia nervosa during binges (e.g., Rossiter & Agras, 1990). Patients report that they lose control during a binge, even to the point of experiencing something akin to a dissociative state, perhaps losing awareness of their behavior or feeling that it is not really they who are binging. They are usually ashamed of their binges and try to conceal them.

After the binge is over, disgust, feelings of discomfort, and fear of weight gain lead to the second step of bulimia nervosa—purging to attempt to undo the caloric effects of the binge. Individuals with bulimia most often stick fingers down their throats to cause gagging, but after a time many can induce vomiting at will without gagging themselves. Laxative and diuretic abuse (which do little to reduce body weight) as well as fasting and excessive exercise are also used to prevent weight gain.

Although many people binge occasionally and some people also experiment with purging, the DSM diagnosis of bulimia nervosa requires that the episodes of binging and purging occur at least twice a week for 3 months. Is twice a week a well-established cut-off point? Probably not. Few differences are found between patients who binge twice a week and those who do so less frequently, suggesting that we are dealing with a continuum of severity rather than a sharp distinction (Garfinkel, Kennedy, & Kaplan, 1995).

Like those with anorexia nervosa, individuals with bulimia nervosa are afraid of gaining weight, and their self-esteem depends heavily on maintaining normal weight. Whereas people without eating disorders typically underreport their weight and say they are taller than they actually are, individuals with bulimia nervosa are more accurate in their reports (Doll & Fairburn, 1998; McCabe et al., 2001). Yet individuals with bulimia nervosa are also likely to be highly dissatisfied with their bodies. At this point, it remains somewhat unclear if this body dissatisfaction is uniquely related to bulimia nervosa or if it is more strongly linked to comorbid depression or cultural ideas on thinness (Keel et al., 2001; Wiederman & Pryer, 2000).

As with anorexia, two subtypes of bulimia nervosa are distinguished: a *purging type* and a *nonpurging type* in which the compensatory behaviors are fasting or excessive exercise. And, as with anorexia, evidence for the validity of this distinction is mixed. In some studies, people diagnosed with nonpurging bulimia were heavier, binged less frequently, and showed less psychopathology than did people with purging-type bulimia (e.g., Mitchell, 1992). But in other research, few differences emerged between the two types (e.g., Tobin, Griffing, & Griffing, 1997). Given the limited validity of these two subtypes, researchers have investigated other possible subtypes. Three different studies have now validated two different subtypes: a *dietary subtype*, which is characterized by dietary restraint, and a *dietary-depressive subtype*, which is characterized by both dietary restraint and persistent

Diagnostic Criteria for Bulimia Nervosa

- Recurrent episodes of binge eating
- Recurrent compensatory behaviors to prevent weight gain, for example, vomiting
- Body shape and weight are extremely important for self-evaluation

negative affect (Stice & Fairburn, 2003). Dietary restraint refers to rigid and strict patterns of eating that is very restrictive with respect to what, when, and how much to eat. Individuals with the dietary-depressive subtype are more likely to have comorbid mood and anxiety disorders, personality disorders, more severe bulimia, social impairment, more persistent binge eating, and a poor response to cognitive behavioral treatment (Stice & Agras, 1999; Stice & Fairburn, 2003). These two subtypes appear to have greater validity than the purging/nonpurging types, and perhaps they will be included in the next version of DSM.

Bulimia nervosa typically begins in late adolescence or early adulthood. About 90 percent of cases are women, and prevalence among women is thought to be about 1 to 2 percent of the population (Hoek & van Hoeken, 2003). Many people with bulimia nervosa were somewhat overweight before the onset of the disorder, and the binge eating often started during an episode of dieting.

Bulimia nervosa is comorbid with numerous other diagnoses, notably depression, personality disorders, anxiety disorders, substance abuse, and conduct disorder (discussed in Chapter 12) (Godart et al., 2000; Lilenfeld et al., 1997; Stice, Burton, & Shaw, 2004). Men with bulimia are also likely to be diagnosed with a mood disorder or substance dependence (Striegel-Moore et al., 1999). Suicide rates are much higher among people with bulimia nervosa than in the general population (Favaro & Santonastaso, 1997). Suicide attempts among bulimia nervosa patients are comparable to suicide attempts among patients with major depression and anorexia nervosa (Bulik, Sullivan, & Joyce, 1999).

A prospective study examined the relationship between bulimia and depression symptoms among adolescent girls (Stice et al., 2004). This study found that bulimia symptoms predicted the onset of depression symptoms. However, the converse was also true: depression symptoms predicted the onset of bulimia symptoms. Thus, it appears each disorder increases the risk for the other.

Physical Changes in Bulimia Nervosa   Like anorexia, bulimia is associated with several physical side effects. Although less common than in anorexia, menstrual irregularities, including amenorrhea, can occur, even though bulimia patients typically have a normal **body mass index (BMI)** (Gendall et al., 2000). [The BMI is calculated by dividing weight in kilograms by height in meters squared and is considered a more valid estimate of body fat than many others. For women, a normal BMI is between 20 and 25.] In addition, frequent purging can cause potassium depletion. Heavy use of laxatives induces diarrhea, which can also lead to changes in electrolytes and cause irregularities in the heartbeat. Recurrent vomiting has been linked to menstrual problems and may lead to tearing of tissue in the stomach and throat and to loss of dental enamel as stomach acids eat away at the teeth, which become ragged. The salivary glands may become swollen. Bulimia nervosa, like anorexia, is a serious disorder with many unfortunate medical consequences (Garner, 1997). However, mortality appears to be much less common in bulimia nervosa than in anorexia nervosa (Herzog et al., 2000; Keel & Mitchell, 1997).

Prognosis   Long-term follow-ups of individuals with bulimia nervosa reveal that about 70 percent recover, although about 10 percent remain fully symptomatic (Keel et al., 1999; Reas et al., 2000). Intervening soon after a diagnosis is made (i.e., within the first few years) is linked with an even better prognosis (Reas et al., 2000). Individuals with bulimia nervosa who binge and vomit more, and have comorbid substance abuse or a history of depression, have a poorer prognosis than patients without these factors (Wilson et al., 1999).

Binge Eating Disorder

DSM-IV-TR includes **binge eating disorder** as a diagnosis in need of further study rather than as a formal diagnosis. This disorder includes recurrent binges (two times per week for at least 6 months), lack of control during the binging episode, and distress about binging, as well as other characteristics, such as rapid eating and eating alone. It is distinguished from anorexia nervosa by the absence of weight loss and from bulimia nervosa by the absence of compensatory behaviors (purging, fasting, or excessive exercise). Most often, individuals with binge eating disorder are **obese**. A person with a BMI of greater than 30 is considered obese. With the current explosion in the prevalence of obesity in the United States, it is perhaps not surprising that research on binge eating disorder continues to increase (Yanovski, 2003). It is important to point out, however, that not all obese people meet criteria for binge eating disorder. Indeed, only those who have binge episodes and report feeling a loss of control over their eating will qualify, which amounts to anywhere from 2 to 25 percent of obese individuals (Yanovski, 2003). For further discussion of obesity, see Focus on Discovery 9.1.

Though it did not meet the threshold for inclusion in the current DSM (Fairburn, Welsh, & Hay, 1993), binge eating disorder has several features that support its validity. It is associated with obesity and a history of dieting (Kinzl et al., 1999; Pike et al., 2001). It is linked to impaired work and social functioning, depression, low self-esteem, substance abuse, and dissatisfaction with body shape (Spitzer et al., 1993; Striegel-Moore et al., 1998, 2001). Risk factors for developing binge eating disorder include childhood obesity, critical comments regarding being overweight, low self-concept, depression, and childhood physical or sexual abuse (Fairburn et al., 1998).

Binge eating disorder appears to be more prevalent than either anorexia nervosa or bulimia nervosa, particularly among individuals seeking treatment for weight control. In a community sample it was found in 6 percent of successful dieters (those who had kept their weight off for more than 1 year) and in 19 percent of unsuccessful dieters (Ferguson & Spitzer, 1995). Though few epidemiological studies have been done, research suggests that binge eating disorder is more common in women than men, although the gender difference is not as great as it is in anorexia or bulimia. In addition, black or white individuals seem to be equally likely to have binge eating disorder (Striegel-Moore & Franco, 2003).

One advantage of including this disorder as a diagnosis is that it would apply to many people who are now given the vague diagnosis of "eating disorder not otherwise specified" because they do not meet criteria for anorexia or bulimia (Spitzer et al., 1993).

Nevertheless, some researchers do not view binge eating disorder as a discrete diagnostic category but rather as a less severe version of bulimia nervosa. The reason is that few differences are found between women with binge eating disorder and the nonpurging form of bulimia nervosa (Hay & Fairburn, 1998; Joiner, Vohs, & Heatherton, 2000; Striegal-Moore et al., 2001). Making this distinction even more difficult is the fact that the nonpurging type of bulimia nervosa is quite rare, so that large sample comparisons are difficult to conduct (Striegal-Moore et al., 2001).

Quick Summary

Anorexia nervosa has four characteristics: refusal to maintain a normal body weight, an intense fear of gaining weight and being fat, a distorted body image, and amenorrhea. Anorexia usually begins in the early teen years and is more common in women than men. Bodily changes that can occur following severe weight loss can be serious and life threatening. About 70 percent of women with anorexia eventually recover, but it can take many years.

Bulimia nervosa involves both binging and purging. Binging often involves sweet foods, and is more likely to occur when someone is alone, following a negative social encounter, and in the morning or afternoon. One striking difference between anorexia and bulimia is weight loss: individuals with anorexia nervosa lose a tremendous amount of weight whereas individuals with bulimia nervosa do not. Bulimia typ-

ically begins in late adolescence and is more common in women than men. Depression often co-occurs with bulimia; each condition appears to be a risk factor for the other. Dangerous changes to the body can also occur as a result of bulimia, such as menstrual problems, tearing in the stomach and throat, and swelling of the salivary glands.

Binge eating disorder is characterized by several binges, and most (but not all) individuals are obese (defined as having a BMI greater than 30). Not all obese people meet criteria for binge eating disorder; only those who have binge episodes and report feeling a loss of control over their eating qualify. Binge eating disorder is more common than anorexia and bulimia and is more common in women than men, though the gender difference is not as great as it is in anorexia and bulimia.

Neurobiological Factors

The hypothalamus is a key brain center in regulating hunger and eating. Research on animals with lesions to the lateral hypothalamus indicates that they lose weight and have no appetite (Hoebel & Teitelbaum, 1966). Thus, it is not surprising that the hypothalamus has been proposed to play a role in anorexia. The level of some hormones regulated by the hypothalamus, such as cortisol, are indeed abnormal in individuals with anorexia. Rather than causing the disorder, however, these hormonal abnormalities occur as a result of self-starvation, and levels return to normal following weight gain (Doerr et al., 1980; Stoving et al., 1999). Furthermore, the weight loss of animals with hypothalamic lesions does not parallel what we know about anorexia. These animals appear to have no hunger and become indifferent to food, whereas individuals with anorexia continue to starve themselves despite being hungry and having an interest in food. Nor does the hypothalamic model account for body-image disturbance or fear of becoming fat. A dysfunctional hypothalamus thus does not seem highly likely as a factor in anorexia nervosa.

Endogenous opioids are substances produced by the body that reduce pain sensations, enhance mood, and suppress appetite. Opioids are released during starvation and have been hypothesized to play a role in both anorexia and bulimia. Starvation among individuals with anorexia may increase the levels of endogenous opioids, resulting in a positively reinforcing euphoric state (Marrazzi & Luby, 1986). Furthermore, the excessive exercise seen among some patients with eating disorders would increase opioids and thus be reinforcing (Davis, 1996; Epling & Pierce, 1992). Researchers have hypothesized that bulimia is mediated by low levels of endogenous opioids, which are thought to promote craving; a euphoric state is then produced by the ingestion of food, thus reinforcing binging (Hardy & Waller, 1988).

Some research supports the theory that endogenous opioids play a role in eating disorders, at least in bulimia. For example, two studies both found low levels of the endogenous opioid beta-endorphin in individuals with bulimia (Brewerton et al., 1992; Waller et al., 1986). In one of these studies, the researchers observed that the individuals with more severe cases of bulimia had the lowest levels of beta-endorphin (Waller et al., 1986). It is important to note, however, that these findings demonstrate that low levels of opioids are seen concurrently with bulimia, not that such levels are seen before the onset of the disorder. Changes in food intake could affect the opioid system rather than the reverse. Therefore, it is unclear whether the opioid system is directly or indirectly involved in the etiology of bulimia.

Finally, some research has focused on neurotransmitters related to eating and satiety (feeling full). Animal research has shown that serotonin promotes satiety. Therefore, it could be that the binges of individuals with bulimia result from a serotonin deficit that causes them not to feel satiated as they eat. Animal research has also shown that food restriction interferes with serotonin synthesis in the brain. Thus, in individuals with anorexia, the severe food intake restrictions could interfere with the serotonin system.

Researchers have examined levels of serotonin and other neurotransmitters or their metabolites in individuals with anorexia and bulimia. With respect to anorexia, several studies have reported low levels of serotonin metabolites in individuals with anorexia (e.g., Kaye et al., 1984). Lower levels of a neurotransmitter's metabolites are one indicator that the neurotransmitter activity is underactive. In addition, people with anorexia who have not been restored to a healthy weight show a poorer response to serotonin agonists (i.e., a drug that stimulates serotonin receptors) than those people who have regained a good portion of their weight, again suggesting an underactive serotonin system (Attia et al., 1998; Ferguson et al., 1999). Other studies, however, find evidence of increased serotonin metabolites in individuals with anorexia (Kaye et al., 1991), and so the role of serotonin in anorexia is not entirely clear. The evidence appears to be more consistent in bulimia, with most findings suggesting a decrease in serotonin metabolites (e.g., Carrasco et al., 2000; Jimerson et al., 1992; Kaye et al., 1998). Individuals with bulimia also show smaller responses to serotonin agonists (Jimerson et al., 1997; Levitan et al., 1997). Furthermore, when individuals who had recovered from bulimia nervosa had their serotonin levels reduced, they showed an increase in cognitions related to eating disorders, such as feeling fat (Smith, Fairburn, & Cowan, 1999).

Other research supports the idea that a serotonin deficit might be related to anorexia and bulimia. The antidepressant drugs that are often effective treatments for anorexia and bulimia (discussed later) are known to increase serotonin activity, adding to the possible importance of serotonin. Finally, serotonin could be linked to the comorbid depression often found in anorexia and bulimia and to the impulsive behavior of individuals with bulimia nervosa.

Table 9.2 The Restraint Scale Used to Select Participants for Studies of Factors Controlling Eating in Dieters

1. How often are you dieting? Never; rarely; sometimes; often; always.
2. What is the maximum amount of weight (in pounds) you have ever lost within 1 month? 0–4; 5–9; 10–14; 15–19; 20+.
3. What is your maximum weight gain within a week? 0–1; 1.1–2; 2.1–3; 3.1–5; 5.1+.
4. In a typical week, how much does your weight fluctuate? 0–1; 1.1–2; 2.1–3; 3.1–5; 5.1+.
5. Would a weight fluctuation of 5 pounds affect the way you live your life? Not at all; slightly; moderately; very much.
6. Do you eat sensibly in front of others and splurge alone? Never; rarely; often; always.
7. Do you give too much time and thought to food? Never; rarely; often; always.
8. Do you have feelings of guilt after overeating? Never; rarely; often; always.
9. How conscious are you of what you are eating? Not at all; slightly; moderately; extremely.
10. How many pounds over your desired weight were you at your maximum weight? 0–1; 1–5; 6–10; 11–20; 21+.

Source: From Polivy, Herman, & Howard, 1980.

Researchers have recently begun to more closely examine the role of the neurotransmitter dopamine in eating behavior. Studies with animals have shown that dopamine is linked to the hedonic or pleasurable aspects of food that compels an animal to go after food (e.g., Szczypka et al., 2001), and brain-imaging studies in humans have shown how dopamine is linked to the motivation to obtain food (Volkow et al., 2002). In one study with healthy individuals, participants were presented with smells and tastes of food while undergoing a PET scan (Volkow et al., 2002). The participants also filled out a measure of dietary restraint (see Table 9.2). Individuals who scored higher on dietary restraint exhibited greater dopamine activity in the dorsal striatum area of the brain during the presentation of food. This finding suggests that restrained eaters may be more sensitive to cues of food, since one of the functions of dopamine is to signal the saliency of particular stimuli. Whether or not these findings will be relevant to individuals with eating disorders remains to be seen.

Though we can expect further neurotransmitter research in the future, it is important to keep in mind that much of this work focuses on brain mechanisms relevant to hunger, eating, and satiety and does little to account for other key features of both disorders, in particular, the intense fear of becoming fat. Furthermore, as suggested, the evidence accumulated to date does not show that brain changes predate the onset of eating disorders. Sociocultural factors appear to play a role in the faulty perceptions and eating habits of those with eating disorders, and it is to these influences that we now turn.

Sociocultural Factors

Throughout history the standards societies have set for the ideal body—especially the ideal female body—have varied greatly. Think of the famous nudes painted by Rubens in the seventeenth century: according to modern standards these women are chubby. Over the past 40 years, the American cultural ideal has progressed steadily toward increasing thinness. *Playboy* centerfolds became thinner between 1959 and 1978, for example (Garner et al., 1980); and beauty pageant contestants also became thinner through 1988. More recent studies show that this trend continues. A study that calculated the body mass index (BMI) of *Playboy* centerfolds from 1985 to 1997 (Owen & Laurel-Seller, 2000) found that all but one of the *Playboy* centerfolds had a BMI of less than 20, which is considered to be a low weight, and almost half of the centerfolds had a BMI of less than 18, which is considered to be severe underweight. Of course, *Playboy* centerfolds are not necessarily the standard to which Western women compare themselves. Still, this study indicates that thin—at least, for women—is still very much "in."

For men, the situation appears somewhat different. In a study parallel to the studies examining *Playboy* centerfolds, researchers analyzed the BMI of *Playgirl* male centerfolds from 1973 to 1997 (Leit, Pope, & Gray, 2001). They found that the centerfolds' BMI increased over the period and that their muscularity, assessed using a fat to muscle estimate, increased even more. A different study analyzed the content of several men's magazines and found that the frequency of articles on weight loss, although lower in men's than in women's magazines, increased during the time period studied (Nemeroff et al., 1994). It would probably be incorrect to assume from these studies, however, that we are about to witness an explosion of eating disorders in men. It is more plausible that the articles focus attention on the masculine ideal of normal body weight or on increased muscle mass (Mishkind et al., 1986).

Somewhat paradoxically, as cultural standards were moving in the direction of thinness over the later part of the twentieth century, more and more people were becoming over-weight. The prevalence of obesity has doubled since 1900 (see Focus on Discovery 9.1). Currently, nearly 30 percent of Americans are obese (BMI greater than 30), setting the stage for greater conflict between the cultural ideal and reality.

As society has become more health and fat conscious, dieting to lose weight has become more common; the number of dieters increased from 7 percent of men and 14 percent of women in 1950 to 29 percent of men and 44 percent of women in 1999 (Serdula et al., 1999). The focus on cutting carbohydrates, so widespread during the past few years, added yet another craze to dieting. For example, the sale of low carb foods yielded nearly 30 billion dollars in 2004; more than 1,500 new, low carb foods were introduced in a 2-year period; the number of low carb diet books increased from 15 to 194 between 1999 and 2004; and 26 million people in the United States were on a diet that severely limited carbohydrate consumption in 2004 (*Time* Magazine, May 3, 2004). Like many diet fads, the "low carb" craze has quieted a bit since 2004. Finally, surgeries such as liposuction (vacuuming out fat deposits just under the skin) and gastroplasty (surgically changing the stomach so it cannot digest as much food) are becoming more common despite their risk (Brownell & Horgen, 2003).

The percentages above indicate that women are more likely than men to be dieters. Dieting to lose weight is especially common among white, upper socioeconomic status women—the same group with the highest rate of anorexia nervosa. The onset of eating disorders is typically preceded by dieting and other concerns about weight, supporting the idea that social standards stressing the importance of thinness play a role in the development of these disorders (Killen et al., 1994; Stice, 2001).

It is likely that women who either are actually overweight or fear being fat are also dissatisfied with their bodies. Not surprisingly, studies have found individuals with both a high BMI and body dissatisfaction are at higher risk for developing eating disorders (Fairburn et al., 1997; Killen et al., 1996). Body dissatisfaction is also a robust predictor of the development of eating disorders among adolescent girls (Killen et al., 1996). In addition, preoccupation with being thin or feeling pressure to be thin predicts an increase in body dissatisfaction among adolescent girls, which in turn predicts more dieting and feelings of negative emotions. Preoccupation with thinness and body dissatisfaction both predict greater eating disorder pathology (Stice, 2001), and these factors were operating in the case of Jill, presented earlier. Finally, exposure to media portrayals of unrealistically thin models can influence reports of body dissatisfaction. One study reviewed results from 25 experiments that presented thin model images to women and then asked the women to report on their body satisfaction. Perhaps not surprisingly, results from these studies showed that women reported a decline in body satisfaction after viewing these images (Groesz, Levine, & Murnen, 2002). For men, the ideal may have more to do with muscularity than thinness. Another study found that men's body dissatisfaction, as indexed by a greater discrepancy between actual and ideal self muscularity, increased after viewing images of muscular men (Leit, Gray, & Pope, 2002).

The sociocultural ideal of thinness is a likely vehicle through which people learn to fear being or even feeling fat, and this was probably influential in the cases of both Lynne and Jill. In addition to creating an undesired physical shape, fat has negative connotations, such as being unsuccessful and having little self-control. Obese people are viewed by others as less smart and are stereotyped as lonely, shy, and greedy for the affection of others (DeJong & Kleck, 1986). Even more disturbing, health professionals who specialize in obesity have also exhibited beliefs that obese people are lazy, stupid, or worthless (Schwartz et al., 2003).

Cultural standards regarding the ideal feminine shape have changed over time. Even in the 1950s and 1960s, the feminine ideal was considerably heavier than what it became in the 1970s, 1980s, 1990s, and today. (Corbis Images, Eve Arnold/Magnum Photos, Inc., Maria C. Valentino/Corbis Sygma.)

Reducing the stigma associated with being overweight will be beneficial to those with eating disorders as well as obesity.

As society's negative attitudes about being overweight have become stronger, the prevalence of eating disorders as well as obesity has increased. In an epidemiological study conducted in Switzerland, the incidence of anorexia nervosa quadrupled from the 1950s to the 1970s (Willi & Grossman, 1983). Although the incidence continued to increase slightly in Switzerland from the 1970s to the 1990s, the increase was nowhere near as dramatic, leading the authors to suggest that women in their country had become accustomed to the images of thinness portrayed in the media (Milos et al., 2004). Similar increases have been found in other countries (Eagles et al., 1995).

Gender Influences   We have discussed the fact that eating disorders are more common in women than in men. One primary reason for the greater prevalence of eating disorders among women is likely due to the fact that Western cultural standards about thinness have changed over the past 40 years, today reinforcing the desirability of being thin for women more than for men.

Another sociocultural factor has remained remarkably resilient to change—namely, the objectification of women's bodies. Women's bodies are often viewed through a sexual lens; and in effect, women are defined by their bodies whereas men are esteemed more for their accomplishments. According to objectification theory (Fredrickson & Roberts, 1997), the saturation of objectification messages in Western culture (in television, advertisements, and so forth) has led some women to "self-objectify," which means that they see their own bodies through the eyes of others. Research has shown that self-objectification causes women to feel more shame about their bodies. The emotion of shame is most often elicited in situations where an individual's ideal falls short of a cultural ideal or standard. Thus, women are likely experiencing body shame when they see a mismatch between their ideal self and the cultural (objectified) view of a woman. Research has also shown that both self-objectification and body shame are associated with disordered eating (Fredrickson et al., 1998; McKinley & Hyde, 1996; Noll & Fredrickson, 1998).

The risk for eating disorders among groups of women who might be expected to be particularly concerned with their weight, for example, models, dancers, and gymnasts, as in the case of Jill, appears to be especially high (Garner et al., 1980).

Cross-Cultural Studies   Evidence for eating disorders across cultures depends on the disorder. Anorexia has been observed across a number of cultures and countries besides the United States; for example, in Hong Kong, China, Taiwan, England, Korea, Japan, Denmark, Nigeria, South Africa, Zimbabwe, Ethiopia, Iran, Malaysia, India, Pakistan, Australia, The Netherlands, and Egypt (Keel & Klump, 2003). Furthermore, cases of anorexia have been documented in cultures with very little Western culture influence. However, an important caveat must be made. The anorexia observed in these diverse cultures does not always include the intense fear of gaining weight or being fat that is part of the DSM-IV-TR criteria. Thus, intense fear of fat likely reflects an ideal more widely espoused in more westernized cultures. For example, Lee (1994) has described a disorder similar to anorexia nervosa that exists in several nonindustrialized Asian countries (India, Malaysia, the Philippines). This disorder involves severe emaciation, food refusal, and amenorrhea, but not a fear of becoming fat. Is this a cultural variant of anorexia or a different disorder, such as depression? This question is but one of the challenges that face cross-cultural researchers (Lee et al., 2001). Indeed, in some other cultures, higher weight among women is especially valued and considered a sign of fertility and healthiness (Nasser, 1988). The wide variation in the clinical presentation of anorexia across cultures provides a window on the importance of culture in establishing realistic versus potentially disordered views of one's body.

Another feature of eating disorders that may be heavily influenced by Western ideals of beauty and thinness is body image. In a study supporting the notion of cross-cultural differences in body image perception, Ugandan and British college students rated the attractiveness of drawings of nudes ranging from very emaciated to very obese (Furnham &

Al Roker had surgery to accomplish weight loss. (Evan Agostini/Getty Images News and Sport Services.)

Baguma, 1994). Ugandan students rated the obese females as more attractive than did the British students.

Bulimia nervosa appears to be more common in industrialized societies, such as the United States, Canada, Japan, Australia, and Europe, than in nonindustrialized nations. In addition, as cultures undergo social changes associated with adopting the practices of more westernized cultures, the incidence of bulimia appears to increase (Abou-Saleh, Younis, & Karim, 1998; Nasser, 1997). Indeed, a recent comprehensive review of research on culture and eating disorders could not find evidence of bulimia outside of a westernized culture (Keel & Klump, 2003). Studies have also found that when women from cultures with low prevalence rates of eating disorders move into cultures with higher prevalence rates, their prevalence rate goes up (Nasser, 1986; Yates, 1989).

Cross-cultural variation in prevalence of eating disorders thus remains an important area for further study. Another concerns the role of the individual in relation to family and society in cross-cultural studies of eating disorders.

Ethnic Differences   In the United States, it was reported at one time that the incidence of anorexia was eight times greater in white women than in women of color (Dolan, 1991). More recent studies confirm greater eating disturbances and body dissatisfaction among white women than black women (Perez & Joiner, 2003), but differences in actual eating disorders, particularly bulimia, do not appear to be as great (Wildes, Emery, & Simons, 2001). In addition, the greatest differences between white and black women in eating disorder pathology appear to be most pronounced in college student samples; fewer differences are observed in either high school or nonclinical community samples (Wildes et al., 2001).

Differences have been observed in the United States in some areas, however. Studies show that white teenage girls diet more frequently than do African American teenage girls and are more likely to be dissatisfied with their bodies (Fitzgibbons et al., 1998; Striegel-Moore et al., 2000). Both white and Hispanic college students reported greater body dissatisfaction than African American students (Perez & Joiner, 2003). The relationship between BMI and body dissatisfaction also differs by ethnicity. Compared with African American adolescents, white adolescents become more dissatisfied with their bodies as their BMI rises (Striegel-Moore et al., 2000). As already noted, both dieting and body dissatisfaction are related to an increased risk for developing an eating disorder. Indeed, a recent study found that white women with binge eating disorder were more dissatisfied with their bodies than African American women with binge eating disorder, and the white women were more likely to have a history of bulimia nervosa than the African American women (Pike et al., 2001).

Ethnic group membership is not the only critical variable in observed differences. Socioeconomic status may also be important (Caldwell, Brownell, & Wilfley, 1997; French et al., 1997). The emphasis on thinness and dieting has now begun to spread beyond white upper- and middle-socioeconomic status women to women of lower socioeconomic status as has the prevalence of eating disorder pathology (e.g., Story et al., 1995; Striegel-Moore et al., 2000). In addition, acculturation, the extent to which someone assimilates their own culture with a new culture, may be another important variable to consider. This process can at times be quite stressful. A recent study found that the relationship between body dissatisfaction and bulimia symptoms was stronger for African American and Hispanic college students who reported higher levels of acculturative stress compared to those students who reported lower levels of this type of stress (Perez et al., 2002).

Finally, very little is known about the prevalence of eating disorders among Latina or Native American women, and this remains a much-needed research focus. Beyond the study of racial or ethnic differences in eating disorders, attention should also be paid to stereotyped beliefs about race and eating disorders. One study found that college students who read a fictional case study about a woman with eating

Another indication of our society's preoccupation with thinness is what happened with Miss Universe of 1996, Alicia Machado. When, after winning the title, she gained a few pounds, some people became outraged and suggested she give up her crown. (AP/Wide World Photos.)

Standards of beauty vary cross-culturally as shown by Gaugain's painting of Tahitian women. (Musee d'Orsay, Paris/Lauris-Giraudon, Paris/SUPERSTOCK.)

disorder symptoms were more likely to ascribe an eating disorder to the woman if her race was presented as Caucasian rather than African American or Hispanic (Gordon, Perez, & Joiner, 2002). In other words, the symptoms were only rated as clinically significant for the white case presentation and not for the African American or Hispanic ones, even though the details were identical. Although it remains to be seen if mental health professionals would also exhibit the same stereotypes when making clinical judgments, it suggests that symptoms may be more easily overlooked among non-Caucasian women.

Quick Summary

Genetic factors appear to play a role in both anorexia and bulimia. Both disorders tend to run in families, and twin studies support the role of genetics in the actual disorders and particular characteristics of the disorders, such as body dissatisfaction, preoccupation with thinness, and binge eating. The hypothalamus does not appear to be directly involved in eating disorders, and low levels of endogenous opioids are seen concurrently with bulimia, but not before the onset of the disorder. Thus, changes in food intake could affect the opioid system instead of changes in the opioid system affecting food intake. Research findings on the role of serotonin in anorexia are mixed. Serotonin may play a role in bulimia, with studies finding a decrease in serotonin metabolites, smaller responses to serotonin agonists, and an increase in cognitions related to eating disorders, such as feeling fat, among formerly bulimic individuals who had their serotonin levels reduced. Newer research suggests dopamine may play a role in restrained eating, a characteristic that is found in people with eating disorders. The neurobiological factors do not do a particularly good job of accounting for some key features of anorexia and bulimia, in particular, the intense fear of becoming fat.

Sociocultural factors, including society's preoccupation with thinness may play a role in eating disorders. This preoccupation is linked to dieting efforts, and dieting precedes the development of eating disorders among many people. In addition, the preoccupation with thinness, as well as media portrayals of thin models, predicts an increase in body dissatisfaction, which also precedes the development of eating disorders. Stigma associated with being overweight also contributes. Women are more likely to have eating disorders than men, and the ways in which women's bodies are objectified may lead some women to see their bodies as others do (self-objectify) which in turn may increase body dissatisfaction and eating pathology. Anorexia appears to occur in many cultures; bulimia appears to be more common in industrialized and westernized societies. Eating disorders are slightly more common among white women than women of color, with the difference being most pronounced in college student samples. Eating disorders used to be more common among women of higher socioeconomic status, but this is less true today.

Psychodynamic Views

Many psychodynamic theories of eating disorders propose that the core cause is to be found in disturbed parent–child relationships and that certain core personality traits, such as low self-esteem and perfectionism, are found among individuals with eating disorders. As we will see in what follows, these personality characteristics are not solely the province of psychodynamic theorists. Psychodynamic theories also propose that the symptoms of an eating disorder fulfill some need, such as increasing one's sense of personal effectiveness by being successful in maintaining a strict diet or avoiding growing up sexually by being very thin and thus not achieving the usual female shape (Goodsitt, 1997).

One view holds that anorexia nervosa is an attempt by children who have been raised to feel ineffectual to gain competence and respect and to ward off feelings of helplessness, ineffectiveness, and powerlessness (Bruch, 1980). This sense of ineffectiveness is believed to be created by a parenting style in which the parents' wishes are imposed on the child without consideration of the child's needs or wishes. For example, parents may arbitrarily decide when the child is hungry or tired, failing to perceive the child's actual state. Children reared in this way do not learn to identify their own internal states and do not become self-reliant. Facing the demands of adolescence, the child seizes on the societal emphasis on thinness and turns dieting into a means of acquiring control and identity. Moreover, negative self-perceptions about weight become the broad lens through which the child sees other aspects of the self, thus contributing to an overall poor self-evaluation.

Another psychodynamic theory, described by Goodsitt (1997), proposes that bulimia nervosa in women stems from a failure to develop an adequate sense of self because of a conflict-ridden mother–daughter relationship. Food becomes a symbol of this failed relationship. The daughter's binging and purging represent the conflict between the need for the mother and the desire to reject her.

Although interesting theories, the evidence in favor of many psychodynamic views is limited. Independent of these psychodynamic theories, studies of personality characteristics of patients with eating disorders and studies of the characteristics of their families have revealed interesting relationships between these variables and eating disorders. But it is difficult to reach definitive conclusions in either area of research because the disorder itself may have resulted in changes in personality or in the patient's family.

Personality and Eating Disorders

We have already seen that neurobiological changes occur as a result of an eating disorder. It is also important to keep in mind that an eating disorder itself can affect personality. A study of semistarvation in male conscientious objectors conducted in the late 1940s supports the idea that the personality of patients with eating disorders, particularly those with anorexia, is affected by their weight loss (Keys et al., 1950). For a period of 6 weeks the men were given two meals a day, totaling 1,500 calories, to simulate the meals in a concentration camp. On average, the men lost 25 percent of their body weight. They all soon became preoccupied with food; they also reported increased fatigue, poor concentration, lack of sexual interest, irritability, moodiness, and insomnia. Four became depressed, and one developed bipolar disorder. This research shows vividly how severe restriction of food intake can have powerful effects on personality and behavior, which we need to consider when evaluating the personalities of patients with anorexia and bulimia.

In part as a response to the findings just mentioned, some researchers have collected retrospective reports of personality before the onset of an eating disorder. This research describes individuals with anorexia as having been perfectionistic, shy, and compliant before the onset of the disorder. The description of individuals with bulimia includes the additional characteristics of histrionic features, affective instability, and an outgoing social disposition (Vitousek & Manke, 1994). It is important to remember, however, that retrospective reports in which patients and their families recall what the person was like before diagnosis can be inaccurate and biased by awareness of the patient's current problem.

Additional research has taken a closer look at the link between perfectionism and anorexia. Perfectionism is multifaceted and may be self-oriented (setting high standards for oneself), other-oriented (setting high standards for others), or socially oriented (trying to conform to the high standards imposed by others). A multinational study found anorexia patients scored higher on self- and other-oriented types of perfectionism than nonpatient controls (Halmi et al., 2000). Researchers have also distinguished between normal perfectionism (striving for success) and neurotic perfectionism (setting impossibly high standards). The poor body image of individuals with eating disorders is related to high scores on both forms of perfectionism (Davis, 1997). Finally, mothers of girls with anorexia score higher on perfectionism than mothers of girls without anorexia, suggesting that perfectionism contains a genetic component that may put girls at risk for developing anorexia (Woodside et al., 2002). This intriguing finding needs to be replicated, but it suggests that what is genetically transmitted in anorexia could be a personality characteristic like perfectionism that increases the vulnerability for the disorder rather than the disorder per se.

Numerous studies have also measured the current personality of individuals with eating disorders, relying on results from established personality questionnaires such as the MMPI. Both patients with anorexia and patients with bulimia are high in neuroticism and anxiety and low in self-esteem. They also score high on a measure of traditionalism, indicating strong endorsement of family and social standards. Some differences emerged between the two groups on the MMPI; patients with anorexia nervosa reported depression, social isolation, and anxiety, whereas patients with bulimia nervosa exhibited more diffuse and serious psychopathology, scoring higher than the anorexia patients on several of the MMPI scales (Vitousek & Manke, 1994).

Prospective studies examine personality characteristics before an eating disorder is present. In one study, more than 2,000 students in a suburban Minneapolis school district completed a variety of tests for three consecutive years. Among the measures were assessments of personality characteristics as well as an index of the risk for developing an eating disorder based on the Eating Disorders Inventory. During year 1 of the study, cross-sectional predictors of disordered eating included body dissatisfaction, a measure of interoceptive awareness, which is the extent to which people can distinguish different biological states of their bodies (see Table 9.1 for items that assess interoceptive awareness), and a propensity to experience negative emotions (Leon et al., 1995). At year 3, these same variables were found to have prospectively predicted disordered eating (Leon et al., 1999). A more recent study found that perfectionism prospectively predicted the onset of anorexia in young adult women (Tyrka et al., 2002).

Patients with eating disorders consistently report that their family life was high in conflict. (Penny Tweedie/Stone/Getty Images.)

Characteristics of Families

Studies of the characteristics of families of individuals with eating disorders have yielded variable results. Some of the variation stems, in part, from the different methods used to collect the data and from the sources of the information. For example, self-reports of patients consistently reveal high levels of conflict in the family (e.g., Bulik, Sullivan, et al., 2000; Hodges, Cochrane, & Brewerton, 1998). However, reports of parents do not necessarily indicate high levels of family problems.

Disturbed family relationships do seem to characterize the families of some individuals with eating disorders, with one of the most often observed characteristics being low levels of support. However, these family characteristics could be a result of the eating disorder and not necessarily a cause of it. Moreover, some of these same characteristics of family disturbance have been observed in families with other types of psychopathology, including depression and personality disorders. Thus, these family patterns may not be specific to eating disorder pathology but may be common among families in which a member suffers from psychopathology more generally (e.g., Wonderlich & Swift, 1990).

Family characteristics may contribute to the risk for developing an eating disorder; however, eating disorders also likely have an impact on family functioning. One study assessed both eating-disordered patients and their parents on tests designed to measure rigidity, closeness, emotional overinvolvement, critical comments, and hostility (Dare et al., 1994). The families showed considerable variation in whether parents were overinvolved with their children; the families were also quite low in conflict (low levels of criticism and hostility). A family study in which assessments were conducted before and after treatment of the patient found that ratings of family functioning improved after treatment (Woodside et al., 1995). Finally, one study examined identical twins discordant for bulimia (i.e., one twin had the disorder; the other didn't). The twin who developed bulimia reported greater family discord than the twin who did not develop the disorder. Because these studies rely on retrospective self-report, it remains unclear whether the family discord was a contributory factor or consequence of the eating disorder.

To better understand the role of family functioning, it will be necessary to study these families directly by observational measures rather than by self-reports alone. Although a child's perception of his or her family's characteristics is important, we also need to know how much of reported family disturbance is perceived and how much is consistent with others' perceptions. In one of the few observational studies conducted thus far, parents of children with eating disorders did not appear to be very different from control parents. The two groups did not differ in the frequency of positive and negative messages given to their children, and the parents of children with eating disorders were more self-disclosing than were the controls. The parents of eating-disordered children did lack some communication skills, however, such as the ability to request clarification of vague statements (van den Broucke, Vandereycken, & Vertommen, 1995). Observational studies such as this, coupled with data on perceived family characteristics, would help determine whether actual or perceived family characteristics are related to eating disorders.

Despite the equivocal findings on how the family may impact individuals with eating disorders, family therapy is a common form of treatment for eating disorders, particularly for anorexia nervosa. One influential theorist in this area is Salvador Minuchin.

Minuchin and colleagues propose that the symptoms of an eating disorder are best understood by considering both the patient and how the symptoms are embedded in a dysfunctional family structure. In this view, often referred to as *family systems theory*, the child is seen as vulnerable (although the precise nature of this vulnerability is unspecified), and the child's family has several characteristics that promote the development of an eating disorder. Also, the child's eating disorder plays an important role in helping the family avoid other conflicts. Thus the child's symptoms are a substitute for other conflicts within the family.

According to the theory proposed by Minuchin et al. (1975), the families of children with eating disorders exhibit the following characteristics.

- *Enmeshment.* Families have an extreme form of overinvolvement and intimacy in which parents may speak for their children because they believe they know exactly how they feel.
- *Overprotectiveness.* Family members have an extreme level of concern for one another's welfare.
- *Rigidity.* Families have a tendency to try to maintain the status quo and avoid dealing effectively with events that require change (e.g., the demand that adolescence creates for increased autonomy).
- *Lack of conflict resolution.* Families either avoid conflict or are in a state of chronic conflict.

In Minuchin's theory, the family member with an eating disorder deflects attention away from underlying conflicts in family relationships. Although this theory is the basis for a form of family therapy that we discuss later, few empirical studies have been conducted to support the major tenets of the theory.

Child Abuse and Eating Disorders

Some studies have indicated that self-reports of childhood sexual abuse are higher among individuals with eating disorders than among individuals without eating disorders, especially those with bulimia nervosa (Deep et al., 1999; Webster & Palmer, 2000). Since, as discussed in Chapter 7, some research indicates that reports of abuse may be created in therapy, it is notable that high rates of sexual abuse have been found among individuals with eating disorders who have not been in treatment as well as those who have (Romans et al., 2001; Wonderlich et al., 1996, 2001). Still, the role of childhood sexual abuse in the etiology of eating disorders remains uncertain. Furthermore, high rates of childhood sexual abuse are found among people in many diagnostic categories, so if it plays some role, it may not be highly specific to eating disorders (Fairburn, Cooper, et al., 1999; Romans et al., 2001).

Research has also found higher rates of childhood physical abuse among individuals with eating disorders. These data suggest that future studies should focus on a broad range of abusive experiences. Furthermore, it has been suggested that the presence or absence of abuse may be too general a variable. Abuse at a very early age, involving force, and by a family member may bear a stronger relationship to eating disorders than abuse of any other type (Everill & Waller, 1995).

Cognitive Behavioral Views

Anorexia Nervosa Cognitive behavioral theories of anorexia nervosa emphasize fear of fatness and body-image disturbance as the motivating factors that make self-starvation and weight loss powerful reinforcers. Behaviors that achieve or maintain thinness are negatively reinforced by the reduction of anxiety about becoming fat. Furthermore, dieting and weight loss may be positively reinforced by the sense of mastery or self-control they create (Fairburn, Shafran, & Cooper, 1999; Garner, Vitousek, & Pike, 1997). Some theories also include personality and sociocultural variables in an attempt to explain how fear of fatness and body-image disturbances develop. For example, perfectionism and a sense of personal inadequacy may lead a person to become especially concerned with his or her appearance, making dieting a potent reinforcer. Similarly, seeing portrayals in the media of thinness as an ideal, being overweight, and tending to compare oneself with especially attractive others all contribute to dissatisfaction with one's body (Stormer & Thompson, 1996).

The fear of being fat, which is so important in eating disorders, is partly based on society's negative stereotypes about overweight people. (The Copyright Group/SUPERSTOCK.)

Another important factor in producing a strong drive for thinness and a disturbed body image is criticism from peers and parents about being overweight (Paxton et al., 1999). In one study supporting this conclusion, adolescent girls aged 10 to 15 were evaluated twice, with a 3-year interval between assessments. Obesity at the first assessment was related to being teased by peers and at the second assessment was linked to dissatisfaction with their bodies. Dissatisfaction was in turn related to symptoms of eating disorder.

It is known that binging frequently results when diets are broken (Polivy & Herman, 1985). Thus, when a lapse occurs in the strict dieting of a person with anorexia nervosa, the lapse is likely to escalate into a binge. The purging following an episode of binge eating can again be seen as motivated by the fear of weight gain that the binge elicited. Individuals with anorexia who do not have episodes of binging and purging may have a more intense preoccupation with and fear of weight gain (Schlundt & Johnson, 1990) or may be more able to exercise self-control.

Bulimia Nervosa Individuals with bulimia nervosa are also thought to be overconcerned with weight gain and body appearance; indeed, they judge their self-worth mainly by their weight and shape. They also have low self-esteem, and because weight and shape are somewhat more controllable than are other features of the self, they tend to focus on weight and shape, hoping their efforts in this area will make them feel better generally. They try to follow a pattern of restrictive eating that is very rigid, with strict rules regarding how much to eat, what kinds of food to eat, and when to eat. These strict rules inevitably are broken, and the lapse escalates into a binge. After the binge, feelings of disgust and fear of becoming fat build up, leading to compensatory actions such as vomiting (Fairburn, 1997). Although purging temporarily reduces the anxiety from having eaten too much, this cycle lowers the person's self-esteem, which triggers still more binging and purging, a vicious circle that maintains desired body weight but has serious medical consequences (see Figure 9.2 for a summary of this theory).

Figure 9.2   Schematic of cognitive behavioral theory of bulimia nervosa.

One group of researchers developed the Restraint Scale (see Table 9.2, p. 280), a questionnaire measure of concerns about dieting and overeating, to study in the laboratory people who are dieting and have distorted attitudes about eating (Polivy et al., 1980). These studies are generally conducted under the guise of being taste tests. One such study was described as an assessment of the effects of temperature on taste (Polivy, Heatherton, & Herman, 1988). To achieve a "cold" condition, some participants first drank a 15-ounce chocolate milk shake (termed a *preload* by the investigators) and were then given three bowls of ice cream to taste and rate for flavor. Participants were told that once they had completed their ratings they could eat as much of the ice cream as they wanted. The researchers then measured the amount of ice cream eaten.

In laboratory studies following this general design, people who scored high on the Restraint Scale ate more than nondieters after a fattening preload, even when the preload was only perceived as fattening but was actually low in calories (e.g., Polivy, 1976) and even when the food was relatively unpalatable (Polivy, Herman, & McFarlane, 1994). Thus, people who score high on the Restraint Scale show a pattern similar to that of individuals with bulimia nervosa, albeit at a much less intense level.

Several additional conditions have been found to increase further the eating of restrained eaters following a preload, most notably various negative mood states, such as anxiety and depression (e.g., Herman et al., 1987). The increased consumption of restrained eaters is especially pronounced when their self-image is threatened (Heatherton, Herman, & Polivy, 1991) and if they have low self-esteem (Polivy et al., 1988). Finally, when restrained eaters are given false feedback indicating that their weight is high, they respond with increases in negative emotion and increased food consumption (McFarlane, Polivy, & Herman, 1998).

The eating pattern of individuals with bulimia is similar to, but more extreme than, the behavior highlighted in the studies of restrained eaters. Patients with bulimia nervosa typically binge when they encounter stress and experience negative affect. The binge may therefore function as a means of regulating the negative affect (Stice & Agras, 1999). Evidence also supports the idea that anxiety is relieved by purging. Patients with bulimia report increased levels of anxiety when they eat a meal and are not allowed to purge (Leitenberg et al., 1984), and these self-reports have been validated by physiological measures, such as skin conductance (e.g., Williamson et al., 1988). Similarly, anxiety levels decline after purging (Jarrell, Johnson, & Williamson, 1986), again supporting the idea that purging is reinforced by anxiety reduction. Given the similarities between people who score high on the Restraint Scale and people with bulimia nervosa, we might expect that restrained eating would play a central role in bulimia. In fact, a study of the naturalistic course of bulimia (i.e., the course of bulimia left untreated) has found that the relationship between concern over shape and weight and binge eating was partially mediated by restrained eating (Fairburn et al., 2003). In other words, concerns about body shape and weight predicted restrained eating which in turn predicted an increase in binge eating across 5 years of follow-up assessments. Other studies have failed to find this relationship (Burne & McLean, 2002), however, and thus additional research will need to sort out the ways in which restraint is linked with the symptoms of bulimia.

Quick Summary

Psychodynamic theories focus on disturbed parent–child relationships and personality characteristics. There is not much research support for these views, but other research on personality characteristics finds that perfectionism may play a role. Personality characteristics that predicted disordered eating across 3 years include body dissatisfaction, the extent to which people can distinguish different biological states of their bodies, and a propensity to experience negative emotions.

Disturbed family relationships are fairly common among individuals with eating disorders, but this could be a result of the eating disorder and not necessarily a cause of it. Minuchin developed a family therapy for individuals with eating disorders. The therapy is based on his theory, which is in need of research support, and suggests that families exhibit characteristics such as enmeshment, overprotectiveness, rigidity, and lack of conflict resolution.

High rates of sexual and physical abuse are found among individuals with eating disorders, but these are not risk factors specific to the development of eating disorders.

Cognitive behavioral theories focus on body dissatisfaction and preoccupation with thinness. The Restraint Scale measures concerns about dieting and overeating, and high scores are linked to binge eating among individuals without eating disorders. The eating pattern of individuals with bulimia is similar to, but more extreme than, the behavior highlighted in the studies of restrained eaters. Studies have found that concerns about body shape and weight predicted restrained eating which in turn predicted an increase in binge eating.

Check Your Knowledge 9.2

True or false?

1. The brain structure linked to the cause of eating disorders is the hypothalamus.
2. Prospective studies of personality and eating disorders indicate that the tendency to experience negative emotions is related to disordered eating.
3. The concept of enmeshment refers to families being underinvolved and unconcerned with the family member who has an eating disorder.
4. Child abuse appears to be a specific causal factor for eating disorders.
5. Cognitive behavioral views of bulimia suggest that women judge their self-worth by their weight and shape.

Treatment of Eating Disorders

It is often difficult to get individuals with eating disorders into treatment because they typically deny the problem. For this reason, the majority of individuals with eating disorders—up to 90 percent of them—are not in treatment (Fairburn et al., 1996).

Hospitalization, sometimes involuntary commitment, is frequently required to treat people with anorexia so that their ingestion of food can be gradually increased and carefully monitored. This was necessary for Lynne. Weight loss can be so severe that intravenous feeding is necessary to save the patient's life. The medical complications of anorexia, such as electrolyte imbalances, also require treatment. For both anorexia and bulimia, both medications and psychological treatments have been employed.

Medications

Because bulimia nervosa is often comorbid with depression, it has been treated with various antidepressants. Interest has focused on fluoxetine (Prozac). In one multicenter study, 387 women with bulimia were treated as outpatients for 8 weeks. Fluoxetine was shown to be superior to a placebo in reducing binge eating and vomiting; it also decreased depression and lessened distorted attitudes toward food and eating. Findings from most studies, including double-blind studies with placebo controls, confirm the efficacy of a variety of antidepressants in reducing purging and binge eating, even among patients who had not responded to prior psychological treatment (Walsh et al., 2000; Wilson & Fairburn, 1998; Wilson & Pike, 2001).

On the negative side, many more patients drop out of drug treatment conditions in studies on bulimia than drop out of the kind of cognitive behavioral treatments discussed later (Fairburn, Agras, & Wilson, 1992). In the multicenter fluoxetine study cited, almost one-third of the patients dropped out before the end of the 8-week treatment, primarily because of the side effects of the medication; this figure compares with drop-out rates of under 5 percent with cognitive behavioral therapy (Agras et al., 1992). Moreover, most patients relapse when various kinds of antidepressant medication are withdrawn (Wilson & Pike, 2001), as is the case with most psychoactive drugs. There is some evidence that this tendency to relapse is reduced if antidepressants are given in the context of the kind of cognitive behavioral therapy described below (Agras et al., 1994).

Medications have also been used in attempts to treat anorexia nervosa. Unfortunately, they have not been very successful. There has been very limited success with drugs leading to significant weight gain, changed core features of anorexia, or even added significant benefit to a standard inpatient treatment program (Attia et al., 1998; Johnson, Tsoh, & Varnado, 1996). Recent case reports have suggested that the antipsychotic medication, Olanzapine (Zyprexa), might help with weight gain and reductions in anxiety among anorexia patients (Bosanac, Burrows, & Norman, 2004; Malina et al., 2003). As we discuss in Chapter 11, weight gain is a common side effect reported by schizophrenia patients who take this medication. However, these reports do not provide information as to whether or not patients develop other troubling side effects that can occur with these medications, and thus it is difficult to ascertain whether this will be a viable treatment strategy at this time.

Psychological Treatment of Anorexia Nervosa

Little in the way of controlled research exists on psychological treatments for anorexia nervosa, but we will present what appear to be the most promising of the psychotherapeutic approaches to this life-threatening disorder.

Therapy for anorexia is generally believed to be a two-tiered process. The immediate goal is to help the patient gain weight in order to avoid medical complications and the possibility of death. The patient is often so weak and physiological functioning so disturbed that hospital treatment is medically imperative (in addition to being needed to ensure that the patient ingests some food). Operant conditioning behavior therapy programs have been somewhat successful in achieving weight gain in the short term (Hsu, 1990). However, the second goal of treatment—long-term maintenance of weight gain—remains a challenge for the field.

Beyond immediate weight gain, psychological treatment for anorexia often enlists the participation of family members. Family therapy is the principal form of psychological treatment for anorexia, based on theorists such as Minuchin who suggest that interactions among members of the patient's family can play a role in the disorder.

To treat anorexia, Minuchin attempts to redefine it as interpersonal rather than individual and to bring the family conflict to the fore. In this way, he theorizes, the symptomatic family member is freed from having to maintain his or her problem, for it no longer deflects attention from the dysfunctional family.

How is this accomplished? The therapist sees the family at a family lunch session, since the conflicts related to anorexia are believed to be most evident at mealtime. These lunch sessions have three major goals:

Family therapy is a main form of treatment for anorexia nervosa. (Michael Newman/PhotoEdit.)

1. Changing the patient role of the person with anorexia
2. Redefining the eating problem as an interpersonal problem
3. Preventing the parents from using their child's anorexia as a means of avoiding conflict

One strategy is to instruct each parent to try individually to force the child to eat. The other parent may leave the room. The individual efforts are expected to fail. But through this failure and frustration, the mother and father may now work together to persuade the child to eat. Thus, rather than being a focus of conflict, the child's eating will produce cooperation and increase parental effectiveness in dealing with the child (Rosman, Minuchin, & Liebman, 1975).

Like many other treatments, family therapy has not yet been sufficiently studied for its long-term effects. One report suggested that as many as 86 percent of 50 anorexic daughters treated with their families were still functioning well when assessed at times ranging from 3 months to 4 years after treatment (Rosman, Minuchin, & Liebman, 1976). A newer family therapy, based largely on Minuchin's theorizing, was recently developed in England, and preliminary evidence suggests that it is effective (Lock & LeGrange, 2001; Lock et al., 2001).

Psychological Treatment of Bulimia Nervosa

Cognitive behavior therapy (CBT) is the best validated and most current standard for the treatment of bulimia (Fairburn, 1985; Fairburn, Marcus, & Wilson, 1993). In CBT, individuals with bulimia are encouraged to question society's standards for physical attractiveness. Patients must also uncover and then change beliefs that encourage them to starve themselves to avoid becoming overweight. They must be helped to see that normal body weight can be maintained without severe dieting and that unrealistic restriction of food intake can often trigger a binge. They are taught that all is not lost with just one bite of high-calorie food and that snacking need not trigger a binge, which will be followed by induced vomiting or taking laxatives that will lead to still lower self-esteem and depression. Altering this all-or-nothing thinking can help patients begin to eat more moderately. They are also taught assertiveness skills to help them cope with unreasonable demands placed on them by others, and they learn as well more satisfying ways of relating to people.

The overall goal of treatment in bulimia nervosa is to develop normal eating patterns. Patients need to learn to eat 3 meals a day and even some snacks between meals without sliding back into binging and purging. Regular meals control hunger and thereby, it is hoped, the urge to eat enormous amounts of food, the effects of which are counteracted by purging. To help patients develop less extreme beliefs about themselves, the cognitive behavior therapist gently but firmly challenges such irrational beliefs as "No one will respect me if I am a few pounds heavier than I am now" or "Eric loves me only because I weigh 112 pounds and would surely reject me if I ballooned to 120 pounds." A generalized assumption underlying these and related cognitions for female patients might be that a woman has value only if she is a few pounds underweight—a belief that is put forth in the media and advertisements.

One intervention that is sometimes used in the cognitive behavioral treatment approach has the patient bring small amounts of forbidden food to eat in the session. Relaxation is employed to control the urge to induce vomiting. Unrealistic demands and other cognitive distortions—such as the belief that eating a small amount of high-calorie food means that the patient is an utter failure and doomed never to improve—are continually challenged. The therapist and patient work together to determine events, thoughts, and feelings that trigger an urge to binge and then to learn more adaptive ways to cope with these situations. In the case of Jill, she and her therapist discovered that binging often took place after she was criticized by her coach. Therapy included the following:

- Encouraging Jill to assert herself if the criticism is unwarranted
- Teaching her that it is not a catastrophe to make a mistake and it is not necessary to be perfect, even if the coach's criticism is valid
- Desensitizing her to social evaluation and encouraging her to question society's standards for ideal weight and the pressures on women to be thin—not an easy task by any means

The outcomes of cognitive behavioral therapies are rather promising, both in the short term and over time. A meta-analysis showed that CBT yielded better results than antidepressant drug treatments (Whittal, Agras, & Gould, 1999), and therapeutic gains were maintained

Actress Mary-Kate Olsen has been treated for an eating disorder. (Peter Kramer/Getty Images News and Sport Services.)

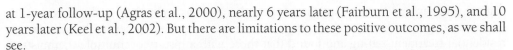

at 1-year follow-up (Agras et al., 2000), nearly 6 years later (Fairburn et al., 1995), and 10 years later (Keel et al., 2002). But there are limitations to these positive outcomes, as we shall see.

Findings from a number of studies indicate that CBT often results in less frequent binging and purging, with reductions ranging from 70 to more than 90 percent; extreme dietary restraint is also reduced significantly, and there is improvement in attitudes toward body shape and weight (Compas et al., 1998; Richards et al., 2000). However, if we focus on the patients themselves rather than on numbers of binges and purges across patients, we find that at least half of those treated with CBT improve very little (Wilson, 1995; Wilson & Pike, 1993). And if we look at how patients who do improve significantly are doing at 6- and 12-month follow-ups, we find that only about one-third are maintaining their treatment gains (Fairburn, Jones, et al., 1993). Clearly, while CBT may be the most effective treatment available for bulimia, it still has room for improvement!

To better understand how it works and how it might be improved, some investigators are conducting what are called component analyses of the CBT therapy package just described. One important aspect that has been examined is the exposure and ritual prevention (ERP) component (recall this aspect of the cognitive behavioral treatment of obsessive-compulsive disorder in Chapter 5). This ERP component involves discouraging the patient from purging after eating foods that usually elicit an urge to vomit. Indications are that this is an important component; CBT without ERP does not appear to be as effective as when they are a combined treatment package, at least in the short term (e.g., Fairburn et al., 1995). The ERP component may have its strongest effect early in treatment, and this is likely important for early treatment gains. A recent research review found that about 70 percent of the total improvement in frequency of binging and vomiting is evident by the third week of treatment (Wilson & Pike, 2001). ERP may not continue to be an advantage over the long term, however. One study examined outcome 3 years after treatment for patients who had received CBT either with or without ERP. They found similar outcomes for the two groups (Carter et al., 2003). That is, 85 percent of patients did not meet criteria for bulimia 3 years after treatment, regardless of which treatment they received.

Patients who are successful in overcoming their urge to binge and purge also improve in associated problems such as depression and low self-esteem. This result is not surprising. If a person is able to achieve normal eating patterns after viewing bulimia as an uncontrollable problem, the person can be expected to become less depressed and to feel generally better about himself or herself. One last finding from the empirical CBT literature is that self-help groups that follow a manual based on Fairburn's treatment model and are minimally supervised by a mental health professional can achieve significant benefits (Cooper, Coker, & Fleming, 1994).

Are outcomes better when CBT is combined with antidepressant medication? Adding drug treatment to CBT sometimes does and sometimes does not enhance the effectiveness of CBT, and CBT alone is more effective than any available drug treatment (Compas et al., 1998; Thase, 2000; Walsh et al., 1997). Adding antidepressant drugs, however, may be useful in alleviating the depression that often occurs with bulimia (Keel et al., 2002; Wilson & Fairburn, 1998).

In several other studies (Fairburn et al., 1991; Fairburn, Jones, et al., 1993), interpersonal therapy (IPT) fared well in comparisons with CBT, though it did not produce results as quickly. The two modes of intervention were equivalent at 1-year follow-up in effecting change across all four of the specific aspects of bulimia: binge eating, purging, dietary restraint, and maladaptive attitudes about body shape and weight (Wilson, 1995). This pattern—CBT superior to IPT immediately following treatment but IPT catching up at follow-up—was replicated in a later study (Agras et al., 2000).

Although the outcomes from these two leading psychological treatments, especially the cognitive behavioral one, appear to be superior to those from other modes of intervention, including drugs, a good deal more remains to be learned about how best to treat bulimia nervosa. Part of the reason at least half of the patients in the controlled studies do not recover may be that significant numbers of the patients in these studies have psychological disorders in addition to eating disorders, such as borderline personality disorder, depression, anxiety, and marital distress (Wilson, 1995). Such patients show less improvement from cognitive behavioral therapy and from other therapies as well. One study, for example, examined cognitive behavioral therapy outcomes among 464 women with bulimia in a residential-treatment setting and found that those with a history of multiple therapists or hospitalizations, suicide attempts, and sexual abuse derived significantly less benefit from therapy than did those without such backgrounds (Gleaves & Eberenz, 1994). The poor therapeutic outcomes could have resulted because such patients simply have more pervasive and more serious psychopathology.

Quick Summary

Antidepressant medications have shown some benefit for the treatment of bulimia, but not anorexia. However, patients are more likely to discontinue the medication than therapy. Psychological treatment of anorexia must first focus on weight gain. Family therapy is common for anorexia, but studies are needed to demonstrate whether this is effective. The most effective psychological treatment for bulimia is cognitive behavior

therapy. CBT involves changing a patient's beliefs and thinking about thinness, being overweight, dieting, and restriction of food, with the overall goal being to reestablish normal eating patterns. Exposure plus ritual prevention is one CBT component that is effective early in treatment. CBT alone is more effective than medication treatment, though antidepressants can help lessen comorbid depression.

Preventive Interventions for Eating Disorders

A different approach to treating eating disorders involves prevention. Intervening with children or adolescents before the onset of eating disorders may help to prevent these disorders from ever developing. Broadly speaking, three different types of preventive interventions have been developed and implemented:

1. *Psychoeducational Approaches.* The focus is on educating children and adolescents about eating disorders in order to prevent them from developing the symptoms;
2. *De-emphasizing Sociocultural Influences.* The focus here is on helping children and adolescents resist or reject sociocultural pressures to be thin;
3. *Risk Factor Approach.* The focus here is on identifying individuals with known risk factors for developing eating disorders (e.g., weight and body concern, dietary restraint) and intervening to alter these factors.

A recent study examined all such prevention studies conducted between 1980 and 2003 (Stice & Shaw, 2004), and they found modest support for some of these prevention approaches. Overall, these programs did very little to reduce the risk for developing an eating disorder, with the psychoeducational approaches being the least effective type of prevention program. On the other hand, preventive interventions that were interactive rather than didactic, included adolescents age 15 or older, included all females, and contained multiple sessions rather than just one session were the most effective, with some effects lasting as long as 2 years. These findings point to the importance of continuing to develop and implement prevention programs.

Check Your Knowledge 9.3

Fill in the blank:
1. Research suggests that _____ therapy is an effective treatment for bulimia, both in the short and long term.
2. For anorexia, _____ may be required to get the patient to gain weight. There are not many _____ that have been shown to be

effective; the most common type of therapy used to treat anorexia is _____.
3. Research on prevention programs has shown that _____ approaches were the least effective.

Summary

Clinical Descriptions

- The two main eating disorders are anorexia nervosa and bulimia nervosa. Binge eating disorder is being studied for possible inclusion in the DSM-V. The symptoms of anorexia nervosa include refusal to maintain normal body weight, an intense fear of being fat, a distorted sense of body shape, and, in women, amenorrhea. Anorexia typically begins in the midteens, is 10 times more frequent in women than in men, and is comorbid with several other disorders, notably depression. Its course is not favorable, and it can be life threatening. The symptoms of bulimia nervosa include episodes of binge eating followed by purging, fear of being fat, and a distorted body image. Like anorexia, bulimia begins in adolescence, is much more frequent in women than in men, and is comorbid with other diagnoses, such as depression. Prognosis is somewhat more favorable than for anorexia.

Etiology

- Research in the eating disorders has examined genetics and brain mechanisms. Evidence is consistent with a possible genetic diathesis. Endogenous opioids and serotonin, both of which play a role in mediating hunger and satiety, have been examined in eating disorders. Low levels of both these brain chemicals have been found in such patients, but evidence that these cause eating disorders is limited. Dopamine is also involved with eating, but its role in eating disorders is less well studied.

- As sociocultural standards changed to favor a thinner shape as the ideal for women, the frequency of eating disorders increased. The objectification of women's bodies also exerts pressure for women to see themselves through a sociocultural lens. The prevalence of eating disorders is higher in industrialized countries, where the cultural pressure to be thin is strongest. White women tend to have greater body dissatisfaction and general eating disturbances than African American women, though the prevalence rates for actual eating disorders are not markedly different between these two ethnic groups.

- On a psychological level several factors play important roles. Psychodynamic theories of eating disorders emphasize parent–child relationships and personality characteristics. Research on characteristics of families with an eating-disordered child have yielded different data depending on how the data were collected. Reports of patients show high levels of conflict, but actual observations of the families do not find them especially deviant. Studies of personality have found that patients with eating disorders are high in neuroticism and perfectionism and low in self-esteem. Many women with eating disorders report being abused as children, but early abuse does not appear to be a specific risk factor for eating disorders.

- Cognitive behavioral theories of eating disorders propose that fear of being fat and body-image distortion make weight loss a powerful reinforcer. Among patients with bulimia nervosa, negative affect and stress precipitate binges that create anxiety, which is then relieved by purging.

Treatment

- The main neurobiological treatment of eating disorders is the use of antidepressants. Although somewhat effective, drop-out rates from drug-treatment programs are high and relapse is common when patients stop taking the medication. Treatment of anorexia often requires hospitalization to reduce the medical complications of the disorder. Providing reinforcers for weight gain, such as visits from friends, has been somewhat successful, but no treatment has yet been shown to produce long-term maintenance of weight gain.

- Cognitive behavioral treatment for bulimia focuses on questioning society's standards for physical attractiveness, challenging beliefs that encourage severe food restriction, and developing normal eating patterns. Outcomes are promising, both in the short and long term.

Answers to Check Your Knowledge Questions

9.1 1. c; 2. d; 3. d
9.2 1. F; 2. T; 3. F; 4. F; 5. T

9.3 1. cognitive behavior therapy; 2. hospitalization; medications; family therapy; 3. psychoeducational.

Key Terms

anorexia nervosa	body mass index (BMI)	obese
binge eating disorder	bulimia nervosa	

10 Substance-Related Disorders

From prehistoric times, humankind has used various substances in the hope of reducing physical pain or altering states of consciousness. Almost all peoples use one or more intoxicants that affect the central nervous system, relieving physical and mental anguish or producing euphoria. Despite the often devastating consequences of taking such substances into the body, their initial effects are usually pleasing, a factor that is perhaps at the root of **substance-related disorders**.

Clinical Descriptions, Prevalence, and Effects of Substance-Related Disorders

The United States is a drug culture. Americans use drugs to wake up (coffee or tea) and stay alert throughout the day (cigarettes, soft drinks), as a way to relax (alcohol), and to reduce pain (aspirin). The widespread availability and frequent use of various drugs sets the stage for the potential abuse of drugs, the topic of this chapter.

In 2003, nearly 20 million people over the age of 12 in the United States reported having used an illicit drug. Over 15 million people abused prescription drugs such as pain medication in 2003, more than double the number that did so in 1992 (National Center on Addiction and Substance Abuse, 2005). In addition, 119 million Americans over the age of 12 reported alcohol use of some kind, and 54 million Americans reported at least one episode of binge drinking (defined as having five or more drinks) in the last 30 days [Substance Abuse and Mental Health Services Administration (SAMHSA), 2004]. Recent data on the frequency of use of several drugs, legal and illegal, are presented in Table 10.1. These figures do not represent the frequency of abuse or dependence but simply provide an indication of the pervasiveness of drug use in the United States.

Drug use by youth is considerable. By the eighth grade, nearly 40 percent of adolescents have tried an illicit drug; by the time of high school graduation, over half have tried at least one (Johnston, O'Malley, & Bachman, 2001b). After steady declines in the use of many illicit drugs in the late 1980s and early 1990s, use appears to be once again increasing, perhaps reflecting a generational shift in beliefs about the risks associated with drug use (Johnston, O'Malley, & Bachman, 2001a). Use of illicit drugs was nearly eight times higher among youths who smoked cigarettes; nearly 75 percent of youths who both drank alcohol and smoked cigarettes used illicit drugs, compared with 3 percent of youths who did not drink or smoke (SAMHSA, 2004).

The pathological use of substances falls into two categories: substance abuse and substance dependence. **Substance dependence**, also referred to as **addiction**, is characterized by DSM-IV-TR as the presence of many problems related to taking the substance. These include using more of the substance than intended, trying unsuccessfully to stop, having physical or psychological problems made worse by the drug, and experiencing problems at work or with friends.

Substance dependence typically involves either tolerance or withdrawal. **Tolerance** is indicated by either (a) larger doses of the substance being needed to produce the desired effect or (b) the effects of the drug becoming markedly less if the usual amount is taken. **Withdrawal** symptoms (i.e., negative physical and psychological effects) develop when the person stops taking the substance or reduces the amount. An example of substance withdrawal is alcohol withdrawal delirium, commonly known as the DTs (delirium tremens). The person may also use the substance to relieve or avoid withdrawal symptoms. Some investigators argue that withdrawal should be mandatory for the diagnosis of substance dependence (Langenbucher et al., 2000). In general, being dependent on a drug is associated with more severe problems (Schuckit, Smith, et al., 1998).

For the less serious diagnosis of **substance abuse** the person must experience problems such as failure to meet obligations at work or within the family. Use of the substance may also expose the person to physical dangers, as in driving while intoxicated. Social relationships may be strained, and legal problems may be frequent.

In 2003, over 21 million people in the United States met the diagnostic criteria for substance abuse or dependence. This figure represents over 9 percent of the U.S. population—not a trivial number. Of this large number of people, the majority (nearly 15 million) met criteria for alcohol abuse or dependence. Close to 4 million met the criteria for drug abuse or dependence, and another 3 million met the criteria for both drug and alcohol problems (SAMHSA, 2004).

The DSM-IV-TR section on substance-related disorders includes other diagnoses. *Substance intoxication* is diagnosed when the ingestion of a substance affects the central nervous system and produces maladaptive cognitive and behavioral effects. If a person who is addicted to a drug is denied it and then experiences withdrawal, that person receives a diagnosis of both substance dependence and substance withdrawal.

Drug and alcohol dependence are serious and prevalent mental disorders. Yet they are also among the most stigmatized of disorders. Terms such as "addict" or "alcoholic" are tossed about carelessly, as if these words capture the essence of people and not the disorder that they suffer from. Historically, drug and alcohol problems have been viewed as moral lapses rather than as conditions in need of treatment. Unfortunately, such attitudes persist today. Yet there is convincing evidence that becoming dependent on drugs or alcohol is not, in fact, a personal choice. True, people make decisions about whether or not to try alcohol or drugs, but the ways in which these decisions and the substances involved interact with an individual's makeup, neurobiology, social setting, culture, and other environmental factors all conspire to create dependence. Such factors put some people at higher risk for substance dependence than others; it is a mistake to consider substance-related disorders as somehow solely the result of moral failing or personal choice. But, it is also a mistake to consider those dependent on drugs or alcohol as being without recourse to change the course of their disorder. Treatment and behavioral change can work in this sphere in much the same way they can work for medical disorders such as diabetes, where individuals can change the course of their disease with insulin and diet control.

We turn now to an overview of the major substance-related disorders, those involving alcohol, nicotine, marijuana, opiates, stimulants, and hallucinogens.

Table 10.1 Percentage of U.S. Population Reporting Drug Use in Past Month (2003)

Substance	Percentage Reporting Use
Alcohol	50.1
Cigarettes	29.8
Marijuana	6.2
Nonmedical psychotherapeutics	2.7
Cocaine	1.0
Hallucinogens	0.4
Inhalants	0.2

Source: Substance Abuse and Mental Health Services Administration, 2004. "Nonmedical psychotherapeutics" includes pain relievers, stimulants, sedatives, and tranquilizers.

DSM-IV-TR Criteria for Substance Dependence

Three or more of the following:

- Tolerance
- Withdrawal
- Substance taken for a longer time or in greater amounts than intended
- Desire or efforts to reduce or control use
- Much time spent trying to obtain the substance
- Social, recreational, or occupational activities given up or reduced
- Continued use despite knowing problems caused by substance

DSM-IV-TR Criteria for Substance Abuse

Maladaptive use of a substance shown by 1 of the following:

- Failure to meet obligations
- Repeated use in situations where it is physically dangerous
- Repeated substance-related legal problems
- Continued use despite problems caused by the substance

Alcohol Abuse and Dependence

Clinical Case: Alice

Alice was 54 years old and living alone when her family finally persuaded her to check into an alcohol rehabilitation clinic. She had taken a bad fall while drunk, and it may have been this event that finally got her to admit that something was wrong. Her drinking had been out of control for several years. She began each day with a drink, continued through the morning, and was totally intoxicated by the afternoon. She seldom had any memory for events after noon of any day. Since early adulthood she had drunk regularly, but rarely during the day and never to the point of drunkenness. The sudden death of her husband in an automobile accident two years earlier had triggered a quick increase in her drinking, and within six months she had slipped into a pattern of severe alcohol dependence. She had little desire to go out of her house and had cut back on social activities with family and friends. Repeated efforts by her family to get her to curtail her intake of alcohol had only led to angry confrontations.

The term "alcoholic" is familiar to most people, yet it does not have a precise meaning. DSM-IV-TR distinguishes between alcohol dependence and alcohol abuse, but this distinction is not always made in the research literature, with the term "abuse" often being used to refer to both aspects of the excessive and harmful use of alcohol. People who meet DSM-IV-TR criteria for alcohol abuse experience negative social and occupational effects from the drug. However, they do not show tolerance, withdrawal, or a compulsive pattern of abuse.

People who are dependent on alcohol generally have more severe symptoms of the disorder, such as tolerance or withdrawal, than do people who only abuse alcohol without being dependent (Schuckit et al., 1998). The effects of the abrupt withdrawal of alcohol in a chronic, heavy user may be rather dramatic because the body has become accustomed to the drug. Subjectively, the person often feels anxious, depressed, weak, restless, and unable to sleep. Tremors of the muscles, especially of the small musculatures of the fingers, face, eyelids, lips, and tongue, may be marked, and pulse, blood pressure, and temperature are elevated.

In relatively rare cases a person who has been drinking heavily for a number of years may also experience **delirium tremens (DTs)** when the level of alcohol in the blood drops suddenly. The person becomes delirious as well as tremulous and has hallucinations that are primarily visual but may be tactile as well. Unpleasant and very active creatures—snakes, cockroaches, spiders, and the like—may appear to be crawling up the wall or over the person's body or they may fill the room. Feverish, disoriented, and terrified, the person may claw frantically at his or her skin to get rid of the vermin or may cower in the corner to escape an advancing army of fantastic animals. The delirium and physiological paroxysms caused by withdrawal of alcohol indicate that the person is addicted.

Although changes in the liver enzymes that metabolize alcohol can account to a small extent for tolerance, research suggests that the central nervous system is responsible as well. Some research suggests that tolerance results from changes in the number or sensitivity of GABA or glutamate receptors (Tsai et al., 1998). Withdrawal may result because some neural

An etching showing the vivid portrayal of delirium tremens in a scene in a play. (Culver Pictures, Inc.)

pathways increase their level of activation to compensate for alcohol's inhibitory effects in the brain.

Both alcohol abuse and dependence are often part of **poly-drug abuse**, abusing more than one drug at a time. It is estimated, for example, that 80 to 85 percent of alcohol abusers are smokers. In addition, alcohol serves as a cue for smoking; smoking is twice as frequent in situations where a person is also drinking (Shiffman et al., 1994). This very high level of comorbidity may occur because alcohol and nicotine are cross-tolerant; that is, nicotine can induce tolerance for the rewarding effects of alcohol and vice versa. Thus, consumption of both drugs may be increased to maintain their rewarding effects (Rose et al., 2004).

Polydrug abuse can create serious health problems because the effects of some drugs when taken together are synergistic—their effects combine to produce an especially strong reaction. For example, mixing alcohol and barbiturates is a common means of suicide, intentional and accidental. Alcohol is also believed to contribute to deaths from using heroin, for it can reduce the amount of the narcotic needed to make a dose lethal.

Polydrug abuse involves the abuse of multiple drugs. Alcohol and nicotine are a frequent combination, although most people who smoke and drink in social situations do not become substance abusers. (Timothy Shonnard/Stone/Getty Images.)

Prevalence of Alcohol Abuse   The prevalence of alcohol abuse and dependence in the United States varies according to such factors as gender, age, region, ethnicity, and education level.

In a recent U.S. epidemiological study, lifetime prevalence rates for alcohol dependence defined by DSM criteria were greater than 25 percent, and lifetime prevalence rates for alcohol abuse were over 13 percent (Kessler et al., 2005). In the 2001–2002 National Epidemiologic Survey on Alcohol and Related Conditions (NESARC), 8.5 percent of Americans met DSM-IV-TR criteria for either current alcohol abuse or alcohol dependence (NESARC, 2005). Rates of alcohol dependence among young women are approaching those of men, although it is still more prevalent among men. The prevalence of alcohol dependence declines for both men and women with advancing age, both because of early death among long-term abusers and because many manage to stop drinking (Wilsnack & Wilsnack, 1995; Vaillant, 1996).

Alcohol use is especially frequent among college-aged adults. This is true for binge drinking, defined as having five drinks in a short period of time (e.g., within an hour), and heavy use drinking, defined as having five drinks on the same occasion five or more times in a 30 day period. Among both male and female college students, binge and heavy use prevalence rates were 43.5 and 17.6 percent, respectively (SAMHSA, 2004). Binge drinking even occurs with high frequency among high school students. In a recent survey, for example, 30 percent of twelfth graders reported binging in the previous two weeks [Johnston et al., 2001b; National Institute on Alcohol Abuse and Alcoholism (NIAAA), 1997]. Generally speaking, the prevalence of binge drinking is highest among individuals aged 18 to 25, with a peak prevalence at age 21 (SAMHSA, 2004).

Within the college population, binge drinking is often associated with sorority and fraternity life. One study found that sorority and fraternity members reported drinking more often than college athletes; those students who were involved in both sorority or fraternity life and college athletics reported drinking the most and were more likely to engage in binge drinking (Meilman, Leichliter, & Presley, 1999). Other evidence suggests that although being affiliated with a sorority or fraternity is indeed associated with heavier drinking during college, it is not associated with continued heavy drinking after college (Sher, Bartholow, & Nanda, 2001).

Regardless of whether college students are members of sororities or fraternities, binge drinking can have serious consequences. Estimates suggest that as many as 1,400 college students die from alcohol-related incidents (e.g., driving under the influence, toxicity) each year. An additional 600,000 are assaulted by other students who have been drinking, and as many as 70,000 students are sexually assaulted (NIAAA, 2002).

The prevalence of alcohol problems differs by ethnicity and education level as well. White adolescents and adults are more likely to abuse alcohol than African American adolescents and adults. Among whites and Latinos, the rates of alcohol abuse or dependence are highest in those aged 18 to 29. For African Americans, the highest rate is among 30- to 44-year-olds. However, the gap between whites and African Americans narrows considerably among individuals who drop out of high school (Barr et al., 1993; Paschall, Flewelling, & Faulkner, 2000). Dropping out of high school is associated with greater drug use in general, among both white and African American individuals (Obot & Anthony, 1999, 2000). Binge and heavy use drinking is lowest among Asian Americans (SAMHSA, 2004).

Alcohol abuse is common in some Native American tribes and is associated with 40 percent of deaths and with virtually all crimes committed by Native Americans (Yetman, 1994). Native American youth have higher rates of alcohol abuse than other ethnic groups. It is important to note, however, that over half of the population in some Native American communities completely abstains from alcohol (Weisner, 1984).

Problem drinking is comorbid with several personality disorders, mood disorders, anxiety disorders, as well as with other drug use, and with schizophrenia (Kessler et al., 1997; Morgenstern et al., 1997; Skinstad & Swain, 2001). According to the Substance Abuse and Mental Health Services Administration, 21.3 percent of people suffering from alcohol or drug dependence or abuse also have at least one other mental disorder (SAMHSA, 2004).

Course of the Disorder   At one time the life histories of alcohol abusers were thought to share a common, downhill progression. A study in the 1950s based on a survey of 2,000 members of Alcoholics Anonymous described the male alcohol abuser as passing through four stages, beginning with social drinking and progressing to a stage at which the person lives only to drink (Jellinek, 1952). This stage model implied that the person dependent on alcohol follows an inevitable decline, with no possibility of returning to an earlier stage.

This model has been widely cited, but the available evidence does not really corroborate it. Some alcohol-dependent people do indeed show a progression from alcohol abuse to alcohol dependence (Langenbucher & Chung, 1995), but many others show considerable fluctuations in their drinking patterns, from heavy drinking at some times to abstinence or lighter drinking at others (Schuckit et al., 2001; Schuckit, Tip, & Smith, 1997; Vaillant, 1996).

In addition, the great majority of people who meet criteria for alcohol abuse do not go on to develop alcohol dependence. For example, one prospective study found that only 3.5 percent of persons meeting DSM-IV-TR criteria for alcohol abuse had developed alcohol dependence five years later, a number not significantly greater than the 2.5 percent of the population who developed alcohol dependence for the first time over the same five-year period (Schuckit et al., 2001). And prospective studies also indicate that almost one-third of individuals dependent on alcohol and over half of individuals who abuse alcohol fail to show any alcohol-related problems one to five years later, further refuting the idea of an inevitable decline (Hasin et al., 1997; Schuckit et al., 2001). Put simply, there is no single pattern of problem drinking.

Alcohol is often implicated in vehicular accidents. The driver of this New York subway train, which derailed, killing five and injuring over 100 people, was intoxicated. (Corbis Images.)

Costs of Alcohol Abuse and Dependence   Expenditures on health care for problem drinkers have been estimated to be over $26 billion annually (NIAAA, 2001). Alcohol-related traffic fatalities are a serious problem (Alonso-Zaldivar, 1999), and the highest-risk drivers are young men. Through vigorous law-enforcement efforts and educational campaigns such as those waged by MADD (Mothers Against Drunk Driving), the situation has improved in recent years. Alcohol-related traffic fatalities declined 5 percent between 1993 and 2003, and another 2.4 percent between 2003 and 2004. Still, there were 16,694 deaths from drinking-related driving in 2004, which was nearly 4 out of every 10 traffic fatalities that year. [National Highway Transportation & Safety Administration (NHTSA), 2003, 2005]. More men than women died in alcohol-related fatalities in 2003, and the highest percentage of fatalities with blood alcohol contents of greater than .08 (the legal limit in many states) was among adults aged 21–24 (NHTSA, 2003; SAMHSA, 2004).

Short-Term Effects of Alcohol   How does alcohol produce its short-term effects? After being swallowed and reaching the stomach, alcohol begins to be metabolized by enzymes. Most of it goes into the small intestine and from there is absorbed into the blood. It is then broken down, primarily in the liver, which can metabolize about one ounce of 100-proof (50 percent alcohol) liquor per hour. Quantities in excess of this amount remain in the bloodstream. Whereas absorption of alcohol can be very rapid, removal is always slow.

The effects of alcohol vary with the level of concentration of the drug in the bloodstream, which in turn depends on the amount ingested in a particular period of time, the presence of food in the stomach (food retains the alcohol and reduces its absorption rate), the height and weight of the individual, and the efficiency of the liver. Two ounces of alcohol will thus have a different effect on a 180-pound man who has just eaten than on a 110-pound woman with an empty stomach. However, women achieve higher blood alcohol concentrations even after adjustment for differences in body weight, perhaps due to differences in body water content between men and women.

Because drinking alcoholic beverages is accepted in most societies, alcohol is rarely regarded as a drug, especially by those who drink. But it is indeed a drug, and it has what is referred to as a *biphasic effect*. The initial effect of alcohol is stimulating; the drinker experiences an expansive feeling of sociability and well-being as his or her blood-alcohol level rises. But after the blood-alcohol level peaks and begins to decline, alcohol acts as a depressant, and the person may experience increases in negative emotions. Large amounts of alcohol interfere with complex thought processes; motor coordination, balance, speech, and vision are also impaired. At this stage of intoxication some individuals become depressed and withdrawn. Alcohol is also capable of blunting pain and, in larger doses, of inducing sedation, sleep, and even death.

Alcohol produces its effects through its interactions with several neural systems in the brain. It stimulates GABA receptors, which may account for its ability to reduce tension. (GABA is a major inhibitory neurotransmitter; the benzodiazepines, such as Valium, have an effect on GABA receptors similar to that of alcohol.) Alcohol also increases levels of serotonin and dopamine, and this may be the source of its ability to produce pleasurable effects. Finally, alcohol inhibits glutamate receptors, which may cause the cognitive effects of alcohol intoxication, such as slowed thinking and memory loss.

A novel study examined the effects of alcohol on both the brain and behavior. Participants were given different doses of alcohol while in an fMRI scanner performing a simulated driving test (Calhoun, Pekar, & Pearlson, 2004). The low dose (.04 blood alcohol content) led to just a small impairment in motor functioning, but the high dose (.08 blood alcohol content) led to more significant motor impairment that interfered with driving ability. Furthermore, the effects of the alcohol in the brain were in areas associated with monitoring errors and making decisions, namely, the anterior cingulate and orbitofrontal cortex, which suggested to the researchers that individuals at the legal limit of alcohol may make poor decisions about driving and not realize they are making mistakes.

Long-Term Effects of Prolonged Alcohol Abuse   Chronic drinking not only causes psychological deterioration but also has severe deleterious effects on the body. Almost every tissue and organ of the body is adversely affected by prolonged consumption of alcohol. For example, alcohol provides calories—a pint of 80-proof spirits supplies about half a day's caloric requirements—so heavy drinkers often reduce their intake of food. But the calories provided by alcohol are empty; they do not supply the nutrients essential for health, and the result can be severe malnutrition. Alcohol also contributes directly to malnutrition by impairing the digestion of food and absorption of vitamins. In older chronic alcohol abusers, a deficiency of B-complex vitamins can cause amnestic syndrome, a severe loss of memory for both recent and long-past events. These memory gaps are often filled in by reporting imaginary events (confabulation).

Prolonged alcohol use plus reduction in the intake of proteins contributes to the development of cirrhosis of the liver, a disease in which some liver cells become engorged with fat and protein, impeding their function; some cells die, triggering an inflammatory process, and when scar tissue develops, blood flow is obstructed. Taken together, chronic liver disease and cirrhosis rank 12th among causes of death in the United States, with 27,257 deaths in 2002 (Kochanek et al., 2004).

Other common changes to the body due to drinking include damage to the endocrine glands and pancreas, heart failure, erectile dysfunction, hypertension, stroke, and capillary hemorrhages, which are responsible for the swelling and redness in the face, and especially the nose, of chronic alcohol abusers. Prolonged use of alcohol appears to destroy brain cells; a 5-year longitudinal study found significant loss of gray matter from the temporal lobes (Pfefferbaum et al., 1998). In fact, chronic heavy drinking is associated with damage to many areas of the brain, many of which are implicated in memory functions. Even shorter-term abuse may affect cognitive performance: alcohol-abusing college students show impairment on neuropsychological tests (Sher et al., 1997).

Heavy alcohol consumption by the mother during pregnancy is the leading known cause of mental retardation. The growth of the fetus is slowed, and cranial, facial, and limb anomalies can be produced, a condition known as **fetal alcohol syndrome (FAS)**. Even moderate drinking can produce undesirable, if less severe, effects on the fetus, leading the National Institute on Alcohol Abuse and Alcoholism to counsel total abstention during pregnancy as the safest courses. Research with children who did not have FAS but whose mothers drank moderately (i.e., about one drink per day) during the first trimester revealed that these children had impairments in learning and memory (Willford et al., 2004) and exhibited growth deficits (such as smaller head size and lower height and weight) at age 14 (Day et al., 2004). Newer research is beginning to solve the puzzle of why some fetuses exposed to alcohol will not develop any problems, whereas others will have profound problems. For example, by six months of age, infants exposed to alcohol prenatally may exhibit problems in attention that can then contribute to the development of other cognitive problems later in childhood (Kable & Coles, 2004). The news is not all bad. Animal research has shown that some of the problems associated with prenatal alcohol exposure, such as deficits in learning and memory, can be turned around (Klintsova et al., 2002). Intervention studies with children are currently underway to see if cognitive training can make up for some of the problems associated with prenatal alcohol exposure. In addition, research suggests that growth deficits associated with prenatal alcohol exposure can be mitigated if children are raised in a more stable and healthy environment, indicating that the biological effects of early alcohol exposure are sensitive to environmental conditions (Day & Richardson, 2004).

Although it is appropriate and accurate to concentrate on the deleterious effects of alcohol, tantalizing evidence suggests positive health benefits for some people. Light drinking, especially of red wine, has been related to decreased risk for coronary heart disease and stroke (Sacco et al., 1999; Theobald et al., 2000). Not all researchers, however, accept this finding at face value, because some people who abstain may do so for health reasons, for example, because of hypertension. Comparing these less healthy abstainers to light drinkers could result in misleading conclusions. If alcohol does have a beneficial effect, it could be either physiological (e.g., acetate, a metabolite of alcohol, increases coronary blood flow) or psychological (a less-driven lifestyle and decreased levels of hostility).

Research on this topic was stimulated by the so-called French paradox—despite diets rich in saturated fats, the French have relatively low cholesterol levels. Some hypothesize that consumption of low to moderate amounts of red wine may lower cholesterol levels.

Heavy drinking during pregnancy can cause fetal alcohol syndrome. Children with this disorder can have facial abnormalities and mental retardation. (Courtesy of James W. Hanson.)

Indirect evidence for this hypothesis has recently been found in an animal study, where researchers discovered that pigment substances in red wine called polyphenols interfered with the synthesis of a peptide called endothelin-1, which is believed to contribute to atherosclerosis (Corder et al., 2001). Of course, the French lifestyle has other characteristics that may result in lower risk of heart disease: the French eat more fresh foods and get more daily exercise than Americans (e.g., by walking instead of driving to work). Given these factors, there does not appear to be much of a paradox.

Check Your Knowledge 10.1

True or false?

1. The diagnosis of substance dependence requires both tolerance and withdrawal.
2. Research suggests that nicotine can enhance the rewarding properties of alcohol.
3. Research has shown that alcohol dependence follows more or less distinctive stages.
4. Even moderate drinking by pregnant women can cause learning and attention problems in their children.

Nicotine and Cigarette Smoking

Not long after Columbus's first commerce with Native Americans, sailors and merchants began to imitate the Native Americans' smoking of rolled leaves of tobacco, with the result that they too experienced an increasing craving for it. When not smoked, tobacco was—and is—chewed or ground into small pieces and inhaled as snuff.

Nicotine is the addicting agent of tobacco. The neural pathways that become activated stimulate the dopamine neurons in the mesolimbic area that seem to be involved in producing the reinforcing effects of most drugs (E. A. Stein et al., 1998). Some idea of the addictive qualities of tobacco can be appreciated by considering how much people have sacrificed to maintain their supplies. In sixteenth-century England, for example, tobacco was exchanged for silver, ounce for ounce. Poor people squandered their meager resources for their several daily pipefuls. In Turkey during the seventeenth century, Sultan Murad IV instituted the public tortures and executions as punishment for using tobacco, but this did not dissuade those of his subjects who were addicted to it (Brecher, 1972).

Prevalence and Health Consequences of Smoking   The threat to health posed by smoking has been documented convincingly by the Surgeon General of the United States in a series of reports since 1964. It is estimated that more than 440,000 American tobacco users die prematurely each year [U.S. Department of Health and Human Sources (USD-HHS) 2004)]. Cigarette smoking is responsible in some way for one of every six deaths in the United States, killing more than 1,100 people each day. It remains the single most preventable cause of premature death in the United States as well as other parts of the world. Since the first Surgeon General's report in 1964 that definitively stated that tobacco caused cancer, more than 12 million Americans have died from tobacco-related illnesses. Cigarette smoking kills more Americans each year than AIDS, car accidents, cocaine, crack, heroin, homicide, and suicide combined. Lung cancer kills more people than any other cancer, and cigarette smoking is probably the cause of as many as 87 percent of lung cancers. The health risks of smoking are less for cigar and pipe smokers because they seldom inhale the smoke into their lungs; however, these smokers increase their risk for cancers of the mouth.

Among the other medical problems associated with, and almost certainly caused or exacerbated by, long-term cigarette smoking are emphysema; cancers of the larynx and of the esophagus, pancreas, bladder, cervix, and stomach; complications during pregnancy; sudden infant death syndrome; periodontitis; and a number of cardiovascular disorders (US-DHHS, 2004). The most probable harmful components in the smoke from burning tobacco

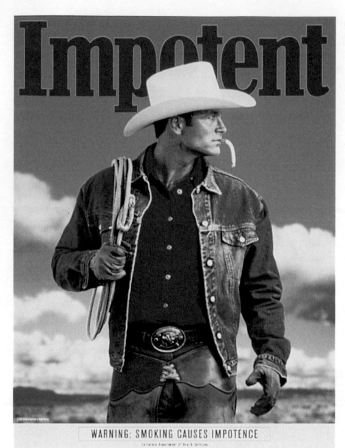

WARNING: SMOKING CAUSES IMPOTENCE

California's Tobacco Education Media Campaign parodies tobacco ads to illustrate health risks associated with smoking and to attack pro-tobacco influences. (Courtesy of California Department of Health Services.)

are nicotine, carbon monoxide, and tar, which consists primarily of certain hydrocarbons, many of which are known carcinogens (Jaffe, 1985).

Reports from the Surgeon General (USDHHS, 1989, 1990, 2004), the Centers for Disease Control and Prevention (2004), and the Substance Abuse and Mental Health Services Administration (SAMSHA, 2004), as well as other publications (Jansen, Glynn, & Howard, 1996; Johnston et al., 2001a) draw several conclusions from more than 40 years of focused efforts by the federal government to discourage cigarette smoking.

- The prevalence of habitual smoking among American adults decreased from a little over 40 percent in 1965 to about 25 percent in 1997, a hefty 25 percent decrease; almost half of all living adults who had ever smoked quit. But 46 million Americans still smoked regularly in 2001, and 60 million Americans over age 12 reported smoking at least once in the past month during 2003. Smoking rates are higher still in Asia and South America. In the United States, the rate of quitting from 1987 to the present more than doubled the rate of quitting between 1965 and 1985.
- Rates of smoking have, however, increased through the 1990s to reach a level equal to that found in 1977, at least among white adolescents (Johnston et al., 2001a). There is some evidence of a decline in smoking among high school students between the years of 1991 and 2003, with current and frequent smoking prevalence rates declining from 12.7 percent to 9.7 percent. In 2003, nearly 4 million youths between the ages of 12 and 17 reported using a tobacco product (cigarette, cigar, smokeless tobacco, pipe). Smoking is more prevalent among white and Hispanic adolescents than among African American adolescents, but the prevalence rate among African American youth has gone up alarmingly since the early 1990s following years of decline.
- Prevalence remains high among Native Americans, blue-collar workers, and less educated people generally. Prevalence is lowest among college graduates and those over the age of 75.
- In general, smoking is more prevalent among men than women. However, prevalence among girls and boys between ages of 12 and 17 is the same.
- People begin to smoke primarily in childhood and adolescence; the age at which smoking begins is decreasing, especially among young women.
- Of the more than 1,000 children and adolescents who begin smoking every day, 750 will die prematurely from a preventable, smoking-related disease.
- The Surgeon General's report in 2004 estimated that the costs of smoking in the United States exceeded $157 billion a year, with half of that reflecting medical costs and the other half reflecting costs of lost productivity.

Research demonstrates the significance of ethnicity in nicotine addiction, as well as the intricate interplay among behavioral, social, and biological factors (Leischow, Ranger-Moore, & Lawrence, 2000). It has been known for years that African American cigarette smokers are less likely to quit and are more likely, if they continue to smoke, to get lung cancer. Why? It turns out that they retain nicotine in their blood longer than do whites, that is, they metabolize it more slowly (Mustonen et al. 2005). Another reason has to do with the type of cigarette smoked. African Americans prefer menthol cigarettes, and research shows that people who smoke menthol inhale more deeply and hold the smoke in for longer, thus providing more opportunity for deleterious effects (Celebucki et al. 2005).

Mortality rates also differ between whites and African Americans, with the latter more likely to die from lung-related or cardiovascular illnesses associated with smoking. Indeed, the 1998 Surgeon's General Report on ethnic minorities and tobacco use indicated that the health burdens associated with smoking are greatest among African Americans. At a broader societal level, African Americans are more likely to live in poverty and less likely to have health insurance than whites and thus are likely to have less access to health care and to treatment programs that might help them quit smoking.

Recent research has found that Chinese Americans metabolize less nicotine from cigarettes than either white or Latino smokers (Benowitz et al., 2002). In general, lung cancer rates are lower among Asians than whites or Latinos. The relatively lower metabolism of nicotine among Chinese Americans may help explain why lung cancer rates are lower in this group.

Cigarettes are not the only form of nicotine that is hazardous to health. Smokeless tobacco is particularly popular among younger men, with prevalence estimates of around 9 percent for men aged 18 to 24 (USDHHS, 1996). The image of the major league baseball player spitting out tobacco juice from a wad of chewing tobacco bulging in his cheek is almost an American archetype. Because of its popularity among athletes, the NCAA banned the use of chewing tobacco during practice and competition in its collegiate sports. So far, compliance with this rule, implemented in 1995, appears to be fairly good, with an estimated 77 percent of schools complying (Chakravorty, Ahmed, & Buchanan, 2000).

Health Consequences of Secondhand Smoke   As we have known for many years, the health hazards of smoking are not restricted to those who smoke. The smoke coming from the burning end of a cigarette, so-called **secondhand smoke**, or environmental tobacco smoke (ETS), contains higher concentrations of ammonia, carbon monoxide, nicotine, and tar than does the smoke actually inhaled by the smoker. Environmental tobacco smoke is blamed for close to 40,000 deaths a year in the United States. In 1993 the Environmental Protection Agency classified ETS as a hazard on a par with asbestos and radon. The National Institute of Health has classified ETS as a known carcinogen, indicating that evidence has established a cause–effect relationship between ETS and cancer. Effects of ETS include the following:

Parental smoking greatly increases the chances that children will begin to smoke. (Peter Poulides/Stone/Getty Images.)

- Nonsmokers can suffer lung damage, possibly permanent, from extended exposure to cigarette smoke. Those living with smokers are at greatest risk. Precancerous lung abnormalities have been observed in those living with smokers, and nonsmokers are at greater risk for developing cardiovascular disease and lung cancer. In addition, some nonsmokers have allergic reactions to the smoke from burning tobacco.
- Babies of women exposed to secondhand smoke during pregnancy are more likely to be born prematurely, to have lower birth weights, and to have birth defects.
- Children of smokers are more likely to have upper-respiratory infections, asthma, bronchitis, and inner ear infections than are their peers whose parents do not smoke.

The Surgeon General has stated that the best form of prevention for exposure to secondhand smoke is to promote smoke-free environments. In recent years various local governments have passed ordinances regulating cigarette smoking in public places and work settings. Smoking is banned in many supermarkets, buses, hospitals, and government buildings and on all domestic U.S. airline flights. Restaurants must often post signs indicating whether they have an area for nonsmokers, and in many states, such as California, New York, Delaware, Connecticut, Massachusetts, Rhode Island, and Maine, smoking is banned altogether in restaurants. Indeed, smoking is banned in nearly all public places in these seven states, and it is likely that more states will adopt similar regulations.

Children of mothers who smoke are at increased risk for respiratory infections, bronchitis, and inner ear infections. (Jennie Woodcock, Reflections Photolibrary/Corbis Images.)

Recreational use of hashish in a fashionable apartment in New York City in the nineteenth century. An 1876 issue of the *Illustrated Police News* carried this picture with the title "Secret Dissipation of New York Belles: Interior of a Hasheesh Hell on Fifth Avenue." (Culver Pictures, Inc.)

Marijuana

Marijuana consists of the dried and crushed leaves and flowering tops of the hemp plant, *Cannabis sativa*. It is most often smoked, but it may be chewed, prepared as a tea, or eaten in baked goods. **Hashish**, much stronger than marijuana, is produced by removing and drying the resin exudate of the tops of cannabis plants.

Originally the hemp plant was extensively cultivated in the United States not for smoking but for its fibers, which were used in the manufacture of cloth and rope. By the nineteenth century the medicinal properties of cannabis resin had been noted, and it was marketed by several drug companies as a treatment for rheumatism, gout, depression, cholera, and neuralgia. It was also smoked for pleasure, though this was little seen in the United States until 1920. At that time, the passage of the Eighteenth Amendment prohibiting the sale of alcohol prompted some people to begin smoking marijuana brought across the border from Mexico. Unfavorable reports in the press attributing crimes to marijuana use led to the enactment of a federal law against the sale of the drug in 1937. Today marijuana use is illegal in most countries.

Prevalence of Marijuana Use   The use of marijuana peaked in 1979, declined for the next decade, rose between 1991 and 1997, and has shown little change since then (see Figure 10.1 for data on youth from 1985 to 2000) (Kozel & Adams, 1986; *Marijuana Research Findings*, 1980; Johnston et al., 2001a; NIDA, 1998). In 2003, about 8 percent of youths aged 12–17 reported using marijuana during the past month. Although prevalence is higher among men than women, the data suggest that use by women increased more rapidly in the 1990s (Greenfield & O'Leary, 1999). Marijuana use is generally greater in the United States, Australia, and New Zealand than in the European Union, Africa, Asia, South America, and Canada (Rey, Martin, & Krabman, 2004).

Effects of Marijuana   As with most other drugs, marijuana use has its risks. Generally, the more we learn about a drug, the less benign it turns out to be, and marijuana is no exception (see Focus on Discovery 10.1).

Psychological Effects   The intoxicating effects of marijuana, like those of most drugs, depend in part on its potency and the size of the dose. Smokers of marijuana find it makes them feel relaxed and sociable. Large doses have been reported to bring rapid shifts in emotion, to dull attention, to fragment thoughts, to impair memory, and to give the sense that time is moving more slowly. Extremely heavy doses have sometimes been found to induce hallucinations and other effects similar to those of LSD, including extreme panic, sometimes arising from the belief that a frightening experience will never end. Dosage can be difficult to regulate because it may take up to half an hour after smoking marijuana for its effects to appear; many users thus get much higher than intended.

The major active chemical in marijuana is named delta-9-tetrahydrocannabinol (THC). The amount of THC in marijuana is variable, but in general marijuana is more potent now than it was two decades ago (Zimmer & Morgan, 1995). In addition, users smoke more now than in the past (e.g., a "blunt" contains more cannabis than a joint). In the early 1990s, cannabis receptors were discovered in the brain; shortly thereafter it was found that the body produces its own cannabis-like substance, anandamide, named for the Sanskrit word for bliss (Sussman et al., 1996).

An abundance of scientific evidence indicates that marijuana interferes with a wide range of cognitive functions. Laboratory studies conducted for the most part in the late 1960s found that a number of tests—substituting symbols for numbers, reaction-time tests, repeating series of digits forward and backward, arithmetic calculations, reading comprehension and speech tests—revealed intellectual impairment in those under the influence of marijuana (*Marijuana Research Findings*, 1980). Of special significance are findings that show loss of short-term memory. One recent prospective study assessed IQ scores at multiple time points among users between the ages of 17 and 23 and found a decline of about 4 points in current users (Fried et al., 2002).

Figure 10.1   Trends in adolescents' annual use of marijuana.

Focus on Discovery 10.1

Is Marijuana a Gateway Drug?

The so-called stepping-stone, or gateway, theory of marijuana use has been around for a long time. According to this view, marijuana is dangerous not only in itself but also because it is a first step for young people on the path to becoming addicted to other drugs, such as heroin. In the late 1960s, when information on the harmfulness of marijuana was scant, the issue was basically political and generational. People in their teens and college years believed that the older generation, lacking scientific evidence that marijuana was bad for you, had concocted the gateway theory, which also lacked empirical support, to justify harsh legal penalties for the use and sale of marijuana. Since there was little doubt that hard drugs were very harmful, marijuana was said to be so too because it was a first step to a lifetime of abusing these drugs.

Studies done since that time have established several specific dangers from using marijuana, as described in the text. But is marijuana a gateway to more serious substance abuse? First of all, there is little evidence to suggest that this theory applies to African Americans. Furthermore, about 40 percent of regular marijuana users do not go on to use such drugs as heroin and cocaine (Stephens, Roffman, & Simpson, 1993). So if by "gateway" we mean that escalation to a more serious drug is inevitable, then marijuana is not a gateway drug. As mentioned, however, we do know that many, but far from all, who abuse heroin and cocaine began their drug experimentation with marijuana. And at least in the United States and New Zealand, users of marijuana are more likely than nonusers to experiment later with heroin and cocaine (Fergusson

Most people who use marijuana do not go on to use heroin, but many heroin users do begin their drug use with marijuana. (Richard Hutchings/Photo Researchers.)

& Horwood, 2000; Kandel, 2002; Miller & Volk, 1996). Another study found that use of marijuana predicted later use of other drugs even if there was no genetic factor at play (Lynskey et al., 2003). Marijuana is part of the picture, but only one of many factors contributing to the use of other harmful drugs.

Several studies have demonstrated that being high on marijuana impairs complex psychomotor skills necessary for driving. Highway fatality and driver-arrest figures indicate that marijuana plays a role in a significant proportion of accidents and arrests (Brookoff et al., 1994). Marijuana has similarly been found to impair manipulation of flight simulators. Poor performance after smoking one or two marijuana cigarettes containing two percent THC can persist for up to eight hours after a person believes he or she is no longer high, creating the very real danger that people will attempt to drive or fly when they are not functioning adequately.

Does chronic use of marijuana affect intellectual functioning even when the person is not using the drug? Unfortunately, there are not many well-controlled studies that have been conducted to address this question. Collectively, current evidence suggests that long-term users may exhibit a slight impairment in learning and memory, but there is not strong evidence to suggest such impairments persist after discontinuation of use (Rey et al., 2004).

Bodily Effects   The short-term effects of marijuana include bloodshot and itchy eyes, dry mouth and throat, increased appetite, reduced pressure within the eye, and somewhat raised blood pressure.

There is no evidence that smoking marijuana has untoward effects on a normal heart. The drug apparently poses a danger to people with already abnormal heart functioning, however, for it elevates heart rate, sometimes dramatically. As a report from the National Institute on Drug Abuse suggests, this effect may be of particular concern as present smokers grow older. The relatively healthy 30-year-old marijuana users of today are the 50-year-olds of tomorrow, with a statistically greater chance of having a cardiovascular system impaired for other reasons, such as atherosclerosis. If they are still using the drug then, their hearts will be more vulnerable to its effects. It is also possible that long-term use of marijuana, like the chronic use of tobacco, may be harmful in ways that cannot be predicted from the short-term effects studied so far.

We do know that the long-term use of marijuana seriously impairs lung structure and function (Grinspoon & Bakalar, 1995). Even though marijuana users smoke far fewer cigarettes than do tobacco smokers, most inhale marijuana smoke more deeply and retain it in their lungs for much longer periods of time. Since marijuana has some of the same carcinogens found in tobacco, its harmful effects are much greater than would be expected were only the absolute number of cigarettes or pipefuls considered. For example, one marijuana cigarette smoked in the typical way is the equivalent of five tobacco cigarettes in carbon monoxide intake, four in tar intake, and ten in terms of damage to cells lining the airways (Sussman et al., 1996).

How does marijuana affect the brain? In the early 1990s, researchers identified two cannabinoid brain receptors, called CB1 and CB2 (Matsuda et al., 1990; Munro et al., 1993). CB1 receptors are found throughout the body and the brain, with a particularly high number in the hippocampus, an important region of the brain for a number of learning and memory abilities. Based on accumulating evidence, researchers have concluded that the well-documented short-term memory problems associated with marijuana use are linked to the effects of marijuana on these receptors in the hippocampus (e.g., Sullivan, 2000).

In addition, a PET study found that smoking marijuana was associated with increased blood flow to regions in the brain often associated with emotion, including the amygdala and the anterior cingulate gyrus. Decreased blood flow was observed in regions of the temporal lobe that have been associated with auditory attention, and participants in this study who were high on marijuana performed poorly on a listening task (O'Leary et al., 2000). These findings might help explain some of the psychological effects associated with marijuana use, including changes in emotion and attentional capabilities.

Is marijuana addictive? Contrary to widespread earlier belief, it may be. The development of tolerance began to be suspected when U.S. service personnel returned from Vietnam accustomed to concentrations of THC that would be toxic to domestic users. Controlled observations have confirmed that habitual use of marijuana does produce tolerance (Compton, Dewey, & Martin, 1990). Whether long-term users experience withdrawal when accustomed amounts of marijuana are not available is less clear, though surveys and laboratory studies conducted in the past 10 years suggest that withdrawal symptoms do occur (Rey et al., 2004).

The question of addiction to marijuana is complicated by what is termed *sensitization*. A person addicted to heroin needs greater and greater amounts to achieve the same effects. In contrast, experienced smokers need only a few puffs to become high from a marijuana cigarette, whereas less experienced users must puff many times to reach a similar state of intoxication.

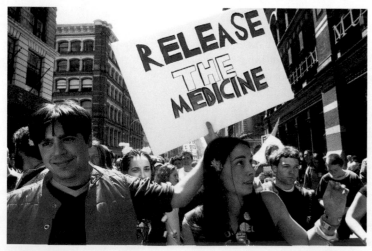

Demonstrators in New York advocate the legalization of marijuana for medical purposes. (Spencer Platt/Liaison Agency, Inc./Getty Images.)

Therapeutic Effects Ironically, therapeutic uses of marijuana came to light just as the negative effects of regular and heavy usage of the drug were being uncovered. In the 1970s several double-blind studies showed that THC and related drugs could reduce the nausea and loss of appetite that accompany chemotherapy for some cancer patients (e.g., Salan, Zinberg, & Frei, 1975). Later findings confirmed this result (Grinspoon & Bakalar, 1995). Marijuana often appears to reduce nausea when other antinausea agents fail. Marijuana is also a treatment for the discomfort of AIDS (Sussman et al., 1996).

Animal studies confirm these clinical observations. For example, the active ingredient of marijuana, THC, has been demonstrated to relieve pain by blocking pain signals from injuries or inflammation (as in arthritis) and thereby preventing them from reaching the brain. The analgesic effects have been shown with both injections of THC and by direct application to an affected area (Li et al., 1999; Richardson, Kilo, & Hargreaves, 1998).

In 1998, the potential benefits of smoking marijuana were confirmed in a report by a panel of experts to the National Institutes of Health (NIH); the report suggested that these benefits be taken more seriously by medical researchers and clinicians (Ad Hoc Advisory Group of Experts, 1998). The NIH agreed to fund research on the subject, including research on whether the benefits from taking THC in pill form are comparable to what patients report from smoking marijuana. (Most people report more beneficial effects from smoking than from swallowing THC in capsule form; this may be due to other compounds than THC in marijuana leaves that are separate from THC.) The report warned, however, that undesirable effects from smoking marijuana, such as suppression of immune function, had to be considered, especially with people whose immune system is already compromised, as with AIDS.

In 1999, positive findings were again confirmed by a committee of the Institute of Medicine, a branch of the National Academy of Sciences (Institute of Medicine, 1999). The report of this committee recommended that patients with "debilitating symptoms" or terminal illnesses be allowed to smoke marijuana under close medical supervision for up to 6 months; the rationale for smoking was based on the just-mentioned findings that THC swallowed by mouth does not provide the same level of relief. But the Institute of Medicine report also emphasized the dangers of smoking per se and urged the development of alternative delivery systems, such as inhalers.

The recommendations of medical experts represent sharp disagreement with the federal government. A controversial law, Proposition 215, passed in California in 1996, made it legal for physicians to recommend marijuana to help AIDS patients and other seriously ill individuals cope with pain and relieve nausea from medications used in treating their illnesses. Federal authorities took issue with the California law, and the U.S. Supreme Court ruled in May 2001 that federal law prohibits the dispensing of marijuana for those medical purposes. Interestingly, this ruling did not expressly forbid the *use* of the drug to alleviate pain and nausea. In November 2004, the U.S. Supreme Court heard arguments in another case from California and was asked to decide whether the use of marijuana for medical purposes was in violation of federal law even though the voters of California approved it. In June 2005, the Supreme Court ruled that the federal government could indeed prohibit the use of marijuana for medical purposes even though the voters in California approved it. California is not the only state to approve the use of marijuana for medical purposes— voters in 11 other states have approved laws similar to California's—so this ruling will likely extend beyond California. State officials in these 12 states will not prosecute individuals for using medical marijuana even though federal officials may do so. It seems likely that the debate on this issue will continue for years to come.

Quick Summary

Alcohol and drug use is common in the United States. The DSM-IV-TR lists substance dependence, which typically includes either tolerance or withdrawal, and substance abuse as two major categories of substance-related disorders.

Withdrawal from alcohol can involve hallucinations and delirium tremens. People who abuse or are dependent on alcohol are likely to use other drugs, particularly nicotine. Alcohol dependence, once thought to follow distinct stages, can have quite a variable course. Alcohol use is particularly high among college students; men are more likely to drink alcohol than women, and differences in use, abuse, and dependence by ethnicity have been observed. Even light or moderate drinking during pregnancy can be associated with later problems in learning for the child.

Smoking remains prevalent, though it has been on the decline. Cigarette smoking causes a number of illnesses, including several can-

cers, heart disease, and other lung diseases. Although more men smoke than women, the rates are the same among adolescent boys and girls. The ill effects of tobacco are greater for African Americans. Secondhand smoke, called environmental tobacco smoke, also is linked to a number of serious health problems.

Marijuana makes people feel relaxed and sociable, but it can also interfere with attention, memory, and thinking. In addition, it has been linked to lung-related problems. It remains among the most prevalently used drugs, particularly among youth. Men use it more than women. Users can develop tolerance to marijuana; it is less clear whether withdrawal symptoms occur after users stop smoking it. Marijuana also has therapeutic benefits, particularly for those suffering from the side-effects of chemotherapy and for patients with AIDS.

Check Your Knowledge 10.2

Fill in the blank.

1. People who try _____ are more likely to become dependent on it than either _____, _____, or _____.
2. List three types of cancer that are caused by smoking.
3. Marijuana can have _____ effects on learning and memory; it is less clear if there are _____ effects.
4. List three of the therapeutic benefits of marijuana.

Opiates

Addiction to drugs was disapproved of but tolerated in the United States until the early 1900s. One of the concerns at that time was the opiate drugs. In 1909, President Theodore Roosevelt called for an international investigation of opium and the other opiates, and in 1914, the Harrison Narcotics Act made the unauthorized use of various drugs illegal and those addicted to them criminals. The **opiates**, which fall under the broader category of *sedatives*, include opium and its derivatives morphine, heroin, and codeine. Synthetic barbiturates and tranquilizers, such as secobarbital (Seconal) and diazepam (Valium), are also considered sedatives.

The opiates are a group of addictive sedatives that in moderate doses relieve pain and induce sleep. Foremost among them is **opium**, originally the principal drug of illegal international traffic; it was known to the people of the Sumerian civilization, dating as far back as 7000 B.C. They gave the poppy that supplied this drug the name opium, meaning "the plant of joy."

In 1806 the alkaloid **morphine**, named after Morpheus, the Greek god of dreams, was separated from raw opium. This bitter-tasting powder proved to be a powerful sedative and pain reliever. Before its addictive properties were noted, it was commonly used in patent medicines. In the middle of the nineteenth century, when the hypodermic needle was introduced in the United States, morphine began to be injected directly into the veins to relieve pain. Many soldiers wounded in battle and those suffering from dysentery during the Civil War were treated with morphine and became addicted to the drug.

Concerned about administering a drug that could disturb the later lives of patients, scientists began studying morphine. In 1874 they found that morphine could be converted

Clinical Case: James

James was a 27-year-old man who had been addicted to heroin for seven years. He first tried heroin during his time in the Marine Corps. Unable to control his habit, he was dishonorably discharged from the Marines a year later. He lived with his family for a short time, but after stealing money and valuables to support his habit, he was asked to leave the house. He then began living on the street, panhandling for money to support his habit. He also donated blood platelets when he was physically able. Over the years, James lost a tremendous amount of weight and became quite malnourished. He was over six feet tall, but he weighed only 150 pounds. Food wasn't a priority on most days, though he was usually able to gather a meal of scraps from the local diner. James tried to get into several rehabilitation programs, but they required that James remain free of heroin for at least a week before he could be admitted.

James was able to resist for a day or two, but then withdrawal symptoms would begin, making it too painful to continue without the drug. A friend from the streets, formerly addicted to heroin, had recently helped James get to a methadone clinic. James tried methadone for a few weeks, but was unable to tolerate the long waits outside the clinic each morning and the shame of being stared at by people passing on their way to work. Still, having been free of heroin for over a week, James gained admittance to a residential treatment program. One of the physicians at the program prescribed a newly approved medication called Suboxone that eased the discomfort of heroin withdrawal while also replacing the cravings for heroin. James no longer needed to go to the methadone clinic, and he was getting job training at the treatment program. He was hopeful that he would shake his habit for good.

into another powerful pain-relieving drug, which they named **heroin**. Used initially as a cure for morphine addiction, heroin was substituted for morphine in cough syrups and other patent medicines. So many maladies were treated with heroin that it came to be known as G.O.M., or "God's own medicine" (Brecher, 1972). However, heroin proved to be even more addictive and more potent than morphine. Today, heroin is most often injected, though it can also be smoked, snorted, or taken orally.

More recently, opiates prescribed as pain medications, including **hydrocodone** and **oxycodone** have become drugs of abuse [National Drug Intelligence Center (NDIC), 2001]. Hydrocodone is most often combined with other drugs, such as acetaminophen (the active agent in Tylenol) to create prescription pain medicines such as Vicodin, Zydone, or Lortab. Oxycodone is found in medicines such as Percodan, Tylox, and OxyContin. Vicodin is one of the most commonly abused drugs containing hydrocodone, and OxyContin is one of the most commonly abused drugs containing oxycodone.

Prevalence of Opiate Abuse   There are enormous difficulties in gathering data, but the considered opinion is that there are more than a million people addicted to heroin in the United States, with an estimated 119,000 users in 2003 alone (NIDA, 2000; SAMHSA, 2004).

Heroin used to be confined to poor neighborhoods and urban environments. In the early 1990s, it became popular among middle- and upper-middle-class college students and young professionals. Among seniors in high school the prevalence rose from 1 percent to 1.6 percent in the year 2000 (Johnston et al., 2001b). From 1995 to 2002, rates of use among adults 18 to 25 increased from 0.8 percent to 1.6 percent. Furthermore, between 1991 and 1998, the number of people seen in emergency rooms after injecting or snorting heroin more than doubled, rising from 35,898 to 73,846 (NIDA, 2000). In Baltimore, Boston, and Newark, heroin accounted for between 62 and 82 percent of drug-related hospital admissions in 2003. Deaths attributable to heroin in Baltimore, Chicago, Detroit, and Philadelphia ranged from 275 to nearly 500 in the year 2003 [Community Epidemiology Work Group (CEWG), 2003].

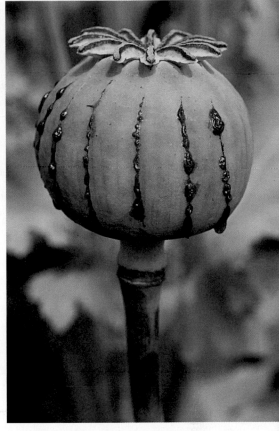

An opium poppy. Opium is harvested by slitting the seed capsule, which allows the raw opium to seep out. (Dr. Jeremy Burgess/Photo Researchers.)

Some of the increases in drug casualties are due to the nature of the heroin now available. In the early 1980s, for example, the heroin sold in southern California was in powder form that was less than 5 percent pure. By the mid-1990s, heroin ranged from 25 to 50 percent pure and was being sold in a gummy form that is difficult to dilute, or step down; this means that users, especially the less experienced, are more likely to overdose (Corwin, 1996). New forms of heroin that need not be injected are believed to be responsible for the increased use by high school students.

From 1990 to 1997, reports of hydrocodone abuse increased by 173 percent in the United States, and between 2002 and 2003, use of hydrocodone among individuals 12 and older increased from 4.5 million to 5.7 million. Reports of oxycodone abuse increased 43 percent in just 1 year, from 1997 to 1998 (SAMHSA, 2004). Prescriptions for OxyContin, a drug containing oxycodone, jumped 1,800 percent between 1996 and 2000 [Drug Enforcement Administration (DEA, 2001)]; between 2002 and 2003, use of OxyContin among individuals 12 and older increased from 1.9 million to 2.8 million (SAMHSA, 2004). The illicit supply seems to come largely from prescriptions that are forged, stolen, or diverted to dealers on the black market. As prescribed, OxyContin comes in a pill format with polymer coating. Unfortunately the pills can easily be dissolved into a form that can then be injected or snorted by abusers. The legitimate sales price of a 40 milligram OxyContin pill ranges from $.50 to $1.00, but pills sell on the street for $25.00 to $40.00 each. Abuse of OxyContin appears to be more prevalent in rural areas, but it is rapidly spreading to large metropolitan areas (DEA, 2001; Meier, 2003). OxyContin's effects are quite similar to those of heroin, so health professionals are concerned that individuals dependent on OxyContin who can no longer afford its hefty street price will turn to heroin, which is less expensive. As shown in Figure 10.2,

Heroin was synthesized from opium in 1874 and was soon being added to a variety of medicines that could be purchased without prescription. This ad shows a teething remedy containing heroin. It probably worked. (National Library of Medicine/Photo Researchers.)

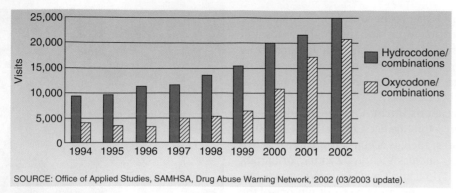

SOURCE: Office of Applied Studies, SAMHSA, Drug Abuse Warning Network, 2002 (03/2003 update).

Figure 10.2 Emergency room visits following overdoses of hydrocodone and oxycodone have increased dramatically in less than 10 years.

visits to hospital emergency rooms following overdoses of hydrocodone and oxycodone have been steadily increasing since 1994, with nearly 48,000 such visits in 2002 (Ball & Lehder Roberts, 2004).

Psychological and Physical Effects Opiates produce euphoria, drowsiness, reverie, and sometimes a lack of coordination. Heroin and OxyContin also produce a "rush," a feeling of warm, suffusing ecstasy immediately following an intravenous injection. The user sheds worries and fears and has great self-confidence for four to six hours. However, the user then experiences a severe letdown, bordering on stupor.

Opiates produce their effects by stimulating neural receptors of the body's own opioid system (the body naturally produces opioids, called endorphins and enkephalins). Heroin, for example, is converted into morphine in the brain and then binds to opioid receptors, which are located throughout the brain. Some evidence suggests that a link between these receptors and the dopamine system is responsible for opiates' pleasurable effects. However, evidence from animal studies suggests that opiates may achieve their pleasurable effects via their action in the area of the brain called the nucleus accumbens, perhaps independently from the dopamine system (Koob et al., 1999).

Opiates are clearly addicting, for users develop tolerance and show withdrawal symptoms. Withdrawal from heroin may begin within eight hours of the last injection, at least after high tolerance has built up. During the next few hours after withdrawal begins, the individual typically has muscle pain, sneezes, sweats, becomes tearful, and yawns a great deal. The symptoms resemble those of influenza. Within 36 hours the withdrawal symptoms become more severe. There may be uncontrollable muscle twitching, cramps, chills alternating with excessive flushing and sweating, and a rise in heart rate and blood pressure. The person is unable to sleep, vomits, and has diarrhea. These symptoms typically persist for about 72 hours and then diminish gradually over a five- to ten-day period.

Opiate abusers face serious problems. In a 29-year follow-up of 500 people addicted to heroin, about 28 percent had died by age 40; half of these deaths were from homicide, suicide, or accident, and one-third were from overdose (Hser, Anglin, & Powers, 1993). Deaths caused by OxyContin overdose have also been reported, for example, 19 OxyContin-related deaths occurred in Pike County, Kentucky, during the year 2000 (NDIC, 2001). The social consequences of using an illegal drug are also serious. The drug and obtaining it become the center of the abuser's existence, governing all activities and social relationships. The high cost of drugs—users must often spend upwards of $200 per day for opiates—often drives users into acquiring money through illegal activities, such as theft, prostitution, or selling drugs. The correlation between opiate addiction and crime is thus rather high, undoubtedly contributing to the popular notion that addiction per se causes crime.

An additional problem associated with intravenous drug use is exposure, through sharing needles, to infectious agents such as the human immunodeficiency virus (HIV) which causes AIDS (see p. 211). Notably, there is good consensus among scientists that needle exchange programs and the free distribution of needles and syringes reduce needle sharing and the spread of infectious agents associated with intravenous drug use (Gibson, 2001; Yoast et al., 2001). Contrary to popular political rhetoric, such programs in combination with methadone treatment (discussed later in this chapter) do not lead to an increase in either initial or continued use of drugs. In 2004, California adopted a law that allows pharmacists to sell up to 10 syringes without a prescription.

Synthetic Sedatives **Barbiturates** were first synthesized in 1903 as aids for sleeping and relaxation. Since then, hundreds of different barbiturates have been synthesized. These drugs were initially prescribed frequently, but in the 1940s a campaign was mounted against them because they were discovered to be addicting. Physicians then began to prescribe barbiturates less frequently. From 1975 to the early 1990s use steadily declined, but now appears to be on the rise (Johnston, O'Malley, & Bachman, 2001c).

Other types of synthetic sedatives are also part of this upward trend. Benzodiazepines, such as Valium, are commonly used and abused. Ketamine, an anesthetic used with both animals and humans, has become part of the club scene.

In the United States, synthetic sedatives are manufactured in vast quantities—enough, it is estimated, to supply each man, woman, and child with 50 pills per year. Much is shipped legally to Mexico and then brought back into the United States and trafficked illegally. Many polydrug abusers choose a barbiturate or other sedative as one of their drugs, sometimes to come down from a stimulant or to reduce withdrawal effects.

Synthetic sedatives relax the muscles, reduce anxiety, and in small doses produce a mildly euphoric state. Like alcohol, they are thought to produce these psychological effects by stimulating the GABA system. With excessive doses, however, speech becomes slurred and gait unsteady. Judgment, concentration, and ability to work may be extremely impaired. The user loses emotional control and may become irritable and combative before falling into a deep sleep. Very large doses can be fatal because the diaphragm muscles relax to such an extent that the individual suffocates. Many users accidentally kill themselves by drinking alcohol, which magnifies the depressant effects of sedatives. Not surprisingly, prolonged excessive use can damage the brain.

Increased tolerance follows prolonged use of synthetic sedatives. The withdrawal reactions after abrupt termination are particularly severe and long lasting and can cause sudden death. The delirium, convulsions, and other symptoms resemble the symptoms that follow abrupt withdrawal from alcohol.

Stimulants

Stimulants act on the brain and the sympathetic nervous system to increase alertness and motor activity. The amphetamines are synthetic stimulants; cocaine is a natural stimulant extracted from the coca leaf. Focus on Discovery 10.2 discusses a less risky and more prevalent stimulant, caffeine.

Amphetamines   In the 1920s, seeking a treatment for asthma, the Chinese American pharmacologist Ku Kuei Chen studied ancient Chinese descriptions of drugs. He found that the leaves of a desert shrub called *mahuang* (genus *Ephedra*) had been commended again and again as an effective remedy. After systematic effort, Chen was able to isolate an alkaloid, *ephedrine,* from this plant that did indeed prove highly effective in treating asthma. But relying on the shrub for the drug was not viewed as efficient, and so efforts to develop a synthetic substitute began. **Amphetamines** were the result of these efforts (Snyder, 1974).

The first amphetamine, benzedrine, was synthesized in 1927, and other amphetamines were synthesized soon after. Almost as soon as benzedrine became commercially available in the early 1930s as an inhalant to relieve stuffy noses, the public discovered its stimulating effects, and physicians soon began to prescribe it and the other amphetamines to control mild depression and appetite. During World War II, soldiers on both sides were supplied with amphetamines to ward off fatigue.

Amphetamines such as benzedrine, dexedrine, and methedrine produce their effects by causing the release of norepinephrine and dopamine and blocking the reuptake of these neurotransmitters. Amphetamines are taken orally or intravenously and can be addicting. Wakefulness is heightened, intestinal functions are inhibited, and appetite is reduced— hence their use in dieting. The heart rate quickens, and blood vessels in the skin and mucous membranes constrict. The individual becomes alert, euphoric, and outgoing and is possessed with seemingly boundless energy and self-confidence. Larger doses can make a person nervous, agitated, and confused; other symptoms include palpitations, headaches, dizziness, and sleeplessness. Sometimes heavy users become extremely suspicious and

Focus on Discovery 10.2

Our Tastiest Addiction—Caffeine

What may be the world's most popular drug is seldom viewed as a drug at all, and yet it has strong effects, produces tolerance in people, and even subjects habitual users to withdrawal (Hughes et al., 1991). Users and nonusers alike joke about it, and most readers of this book have probably had some this very day. We are, of course, referring to **caffeine**, a substance found in coffee, tea, cocoa, cola and other soft drinks, some cold remedies, and some diet pills.

Two cups of coffee, containing between 150 and 300 milligrams of caffeine, affect most people within half an hour. Metabolism, body temperature, and blood pressure all increase; urine production goes up, as most of us will attest; there may be hand tremors, appetite can diminish, and, most familiar of all, sleepiness is warded off. Panic disorder can be exacerbated by caffeine, not surprising in light of the heightened sympathetic nervous system arousal occasioned by the drug. Extremely large doses of caffeine can cause headache, diarrhea, nervousness, severe agitation, even convulsions and death. Death, though, is virtually impossible unless the individual grossly

The caffeine found in coffee, tea, and soft drinks is probably the world's favorite drug. (Sepp Seitz/Woodfin Camp & Associates.)

overuses tablets containing caffeine, because the drug is excreted by the kidneys without any appreciable accumulation.

Although it has long been recognized that drinkers of very large amounts of regular (caffeinated) coffee daily can experience withdrawal symptoms when consumption ceases, people who drink no more than two cups of regular coffee a day can suffer from clinically significant headaches, fatigue, and anxiety if caffeine is withdrawn from their daily diet (Silverman et al., 1992), and these symptoms can interfere with social and occupational functioning. These findings are disturbing because more than three-quarters of Americans consume a little more than two cups of regular coffee a day (Roan, 1992). And although parents usually deny their children access to coffee and tea, they often do allow them to imbibe caffeine-laden soft drinks, hot chocolate, and cocoa, and to eat chocolate candy and chocolate and coffee ice cream. Thus our addiction to caffeine can begin to develop as early as six months of age, the form of it changing as we move from childhood to adulthood.

hostile, to an extent that they can be dangerous to others. Large doses taken over a period of time can induce a state quite similar to paranoid schizophrenia (see p. 358), including delusions.

Tolerance to amphetamines develops rapidly, so more and more of the drug is required to produce the stimulating effect. One study demonstrated tolerance after just 6 days of repeated use (Comer et al., 2001). As tolerance increases, users may stop taking pills and start injecting methedrine, the strongest of the amphetamines, directly into the veins. Users may give themselves repeated injections of the drug and maintain intense and euphoric activity for a few days, without eating or sleeping, after which, exhausted and depressed, they sleep, or crash, for several days. Then the cycle starts again. After several repetitions of this pattern, the physical and social functioning of the individual deteriorates considerably. Behavior becomes erratic and hostile, and users may become dangerous to themselves and others.

Amphetamine use in the workplace has increased as workers are under increased time pressure to produce. The mantra "do more with less" has led many workers to turn to amphetamines to stay awake, be more productive, and in general feel more energized, even euphoric. Although this may work in the short run, over time extreme irritability sets in and the person may take more and more of the addicting substance to combat the angry feelings. Sometimes the individual uses alcohol in the evening to wind down. The emotional and physical costs are steep as the individual's personal relationships begin to deteriorate along with job performance.

Clinical Case: Anton

Anton, a 37-year-old man, had just been arrested for a parole violation, stealing a package of string cheese from a convenience store. He was also found to be under the influence of methamphetamine. Two months earlier, he had been released from prison after serving time for petty theft and for purchasing methamphetamine. He was determined to remain out of prison, but his cravings for meth were so intense that he was unable to abide by the terms of his parole. He had been using meth since he was 26 years old, and he had been arrested numerous times for drug-related offenses, including prostitution (to get money to support his habit).

Methamphetamine   Abuse of an amphetamine derivative called **methamphetamine** skyrocketed in the 1990s. Some estimates indicate that as many as 4.7 million people in the United States have tried methamphetamine at some point (Anglin et al., 2000). Additionally, methamphetamine-related deaths nearly tripled between the years 1991 and 1994.

Hospital admissions for methamphetamine intoxication have also increased dramatically. From 1992 to 1993, admissions for methamphetamine use across 42 states increased 43 percent (Greenblatt, Gfroerer, & Melnick, 1995). In 1994 and 1995, 35 percent of admissions to California drug treatment centers were for methamphetamine abuse, compared with 27 percent for heroin and 24 percent for cocaine. The problem was, until recently, more serious in California than elsewhere in the United States because of the high concentration there of clandestine laboratories that manufacture this easily made and inexpensive drug. However, abuse is now becoming more widespread in the midwestern and southwestern United States.

Men tend to abuse methamphetamine more often than women in contrast with abuse of other amphetamines, where few gender differences occur. Among adolescents, however, abuse by both males and females has almost doubled since 1992 (Oetting et al., 2000). White males are the typical meth abusers, but recent studies suggest that use among Hispanic Americans and Native Americans is on the rise (Oetting et al., 2000).

Like other amphetamines, methamphetamine can be taken orally or intravenously. It can also be taken intranasally (i.e., by snorting). In a clear crystal form, the drug is often referred to as "crystal meth" or "ice." Craving for methamphetamine is particularly strong, often lasting several years after use of the drug is discontinued. Craving is also a reliable predictor of later use (Hartz, Fredrick-Osborne, & Galloway, 2001).

Several studies done with animals have indicated that chronic use of methamphetamine causes damage to the brain, affecting both the dopamine system and the serotonin system (Frost & Cadet, 2000). Recent neuroimaging studies have found similar effects in the human brain, particularly in the dopamine system. A recent study of chronic meth users who met DSM diagnostic criteria for dependence found a number with damage to the gray matter of the brain (see page 38), including the hippocampus (see Figure 10.3). The volume of the hippocampus was smaller among chronic meth users, and this correlated with poorer performance on a memory test (Thompson, Hayashi, et al., 2004). Another study reported that methamphetamine abusers who were currently clean of the substance, some for as long as 11 months, had a significant reduction in a dopamine transporter gene (a transporter gene is a gene that either lets a drug enter a cell or prevents a drug from entering a cell) (Volkow et al., 2001). In fact, in three of the patients studied, the reduction in dopamine reuptake was similar to that seen in the less severe stages of Parkinson's disease. Moreover, the methamphetamine abusers performed more slowly than a comparison group on several motor tasks, a finding similar to that seen with Parkinson's patients. Other studies have documented cognitive deficits associated with chronic methamphetamine use as well (e.g., Simon et al., 2000).

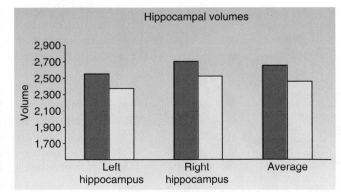

Figure 10.3   Results from an fMRI study showing that methamphetamine abusers (yellow bars) had smaller hippocampal volume (size) than those in the control group (blue bars) who did not abuse methamphetamine. Adapted from Thompson et al. (2004).

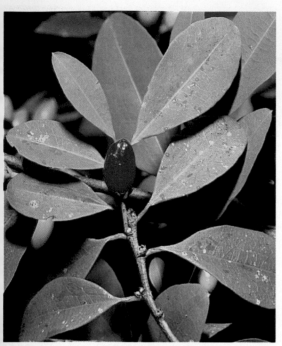

A coca plant. The leaves contain about 1 percent cocaine. (Dr. Morley Read/Photo Researchers.)

A caveat should be noted here. One difficulty with conducting these types of studies is finding participants who use only the drug of interest (in this case, methamphetamine) so that any observed effects can be linked to that drug and not others. However, it is difficult to find meth users who have not at some point used other substances, particularly alcohol and nicotine. For example, in one of the studies described above, the meth users did not differ from the control group in alcohol consumption, but they did smoke more (Thompson, Hayashi, et al., 2004). Nevertheless, it seems clear that the deleterious effects of methamphetamine are many and serious.

Chemicals for manufacturing methamphetamine, such as ephedrine, are readily available, though laws such as the Methamphetamine Control Act of 1996 have been passed to try to cut off the supply. When supplies of ephedrine became low, pseudoephedrine, a common substance in many over-the-counter decongestants, was substituted, but these substances are now also better regulated. Some chemicals used to make methamphetamine are highly volatile and dangerous to breathe, causing damage ranging from eye irritation and nausea to coma and death. They also create risks for fire and explosions.

Cocaine The inhabitants of the Andean uplands, where the coca shrub is native, chew the leaves. Europeans, introduced to coca by the Spanish conquistadors, chose instead to brew the leaves in beverages. The alkaloid **cocaine** was first extracted from the leaves of the coca shrub in the mid-1800s and has been used since then as a local anesthetic.

In 1884, while still a young neurologist, Sigmund Freud began using cocaine to combat his depression. Convinced of its wondrous effects, he prescribed it to a friend who had a painful disease. Freud published one of the first papers on the drug, "Song of Praise," which was an enthusiastic endorsement of the exhilarating effects he had experienced. Freud subsequently lost his enthusiasm for cocaine after nursing a physician friend to whom he had recommended the drug through a nightlong psychotic state brought on by it. Sherlock Holmes is perhaps the most famous fictional cocaine addict.

Cocaine has other effects, in addition to reducing pain. It acts rapidly on the brain, blocking the reuptake of dopamine in mesolimbic areas, and it is thought, yielding pleasurable states because dopamine left in the synapse facilitates neural transmission. Self-reports of pleasure induced by cocaine are strongly related to the extent to which cocaine has blocked dopamine reuptake (Volkow et al., 1997). Chronic use of cocaine is associated with a decrease in gray matter in various brain regions (Franklin et al., 2002). Cocaine increases sexual desire and produces feelings of self-confidence, well-being, and indefatigability. An overdose may bring on chills, nausea, and insomnia, as well as strong paranoid feelings and terrifying hallucinations of insects crawling beneath the skin. Chronic use can lead to heightened irritability, impaired social relationships, paranoid thinking, and disturbances in eating and sleeping (Scientific Perspectives on Cocaine Abuse, 1987). Some, but not all, users develop tolerance to cocaine, requiring a large dose to achieve the same effect. Other users may become more sensitive to cocaine's effects, which is believed to be a contributing factor in deaths after a fairly small dosage. Stopping cocaine use appears to cause severe withdrawal symptoms. Cocaine can take hold of people with as much tenacity as do other drugs.

Cocaine is a vasoconstrictor, causing the blood vessels to narrow. As users take larger and larger doses of the purer forms of cocaine now available, they are more often rushed to emergency rooms and may die of an overdose, often from a heart attack (NIDA, 2004a). Cocaine also increases a person's risk for stroke and causes cognitive impairments, such as difficulty paying attention and remembering. Because of its strong vasoconstricting properties, cocaine poses special dangers in pregnancy, for the blood supply to the developing fetus may be compromised.

Cocaine can be smoked, swallowed, injected, or snorted as shown here. (Mark Antman/The Image Works.)

Cocaine can be sniffed (snorted), smoked in pipes or cigarettes, swallowed, or even injected into the veins; some heroin users mix the two drugs. In the 1970s cocaine users in the United States began to separate, or free, a component of cocaine by heating it with ether. When purified by this chemical process the cocaine base—or freebase—produces very powerful effects because it is absorbed so rapidly. Like most drugs, the faster it is absorbed, the quicker and more intense the high. Freebase is usually smoked in a water pipe or sprinkled on a tobacco or marijuana cigarette. It is rapidly absorbed into the lungs and carried to the brain in a few seconds, where it induces an intense two-minute high, followed by restlessness and discomfort. The freebasing process is hazardous, however, because ether is flammable. Comedian Richard Pryor nearly died from the burns he suffered when the ether he was using ignited.

In the mid-1980s a new form of cocaine, called **crack**, appeared on the streets. Crack comes in a rock crystal form that is then heated, melted, and smoked. The name crack comes from the crackling sound the rock makes when being heated. The presence of crack brought about an increase in the number of users of cocaine and in casualties. Because it was available in small, relatively inexpensive doses ($10 for about 100 milligrams versus $100 per gram of cocaine), younger and less affluent buyers began to experiment with the drug and to become addicted (Kozel & Adams, 1986). Crack is now most often used in poorer urban areas.

Cocaine use in general soared in the 1970s and 1980s, increasing by more than 260 percent between 1974 and 1985. Men use cocaine and crack more often than women do. Although the use of cocaine dramatically decreased in the late 1980s and early 1990s, it began to rise again in the mid-1990s, particularly among high school and college students and young adults in general. Indeed, from 2000 to 2002, there were about a million new users per year. Among users, 25 percent met DSM criteria for cocaine dependence in 2003 (SAMHSA, 2004). The lifetime use of cocaine or crack among high school students declined from 3.6 percent to 2.7 percent between the years 2002 and 2003 (NIDA, 2004a). Still, the use of cocaine and crack in cities remains a problem. In 2003, 2.3 million people over the age of 12 reported using cocaine, and 604,000 reported using crack (SAMHSA, 2004). In major cities in 2002, there were more hospital emergency room (ER) visits for cocaine than any other drug. In Baltimore, the number of cocaine- or crack-related ER visits increased between 2001 and 2002; cities with the highest death rates from cocaine and crack between 2000 and 2002 included Detroit, Philadelphia, Miami, and Phoenix (CEWG, 2003). In short, cocaine and crack remain significant drugs of abuse. In U.S. West Coast cities during 2002, cocaine and crack use was greater than methamphetamine use.

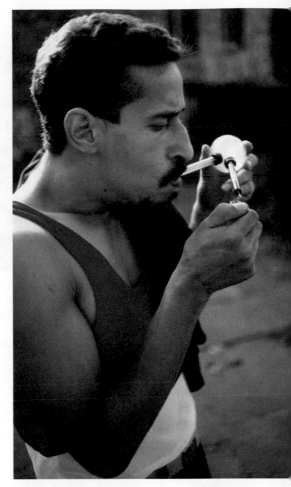

Crack use is highest in urban areas. (Wesley Bocxe/Photo Researchers, Inc.)

Hallucinogens, Ecstasy, and PCP

LSD and Other Hallucinogens   In 1943 the Swiss chemist Albert Hofmann recorded a description of an illness he had seemingly contracted.

> *Last Friday. . . I had to interrupt my laboratory work. . . I was seized with a feeling of great restlessness and mild dizziness. At home, I lay down and sank into a not unpleasant delirium, which was characterized by extremely exciting fantasies. In a semiconscious state with my eyes closed . . . fantastic visions of extraordinary realness and with an intense kaleidoscopic play of colors assaulted me. (Cited in Cashman, 1966, p. 31)*

Earlier in the day, Hofmann had manufactured a few milligrams of *d*-lysergic acid diethylamide, a drug that he had first synthesized in 1938. Reasoning that he might have unknowingly ingested some and that this was the cause of his unusual experience, he deliberately took a dose and confirmed his hypothesis.

On the basis of Hofmann's experiences with **LSD** in 1943, the drug was referred to as a *psychotomimetic* because it was thought to produce effects similar to the symptoms of a psychosis. Later, the term *psychedelic*, from the Greek words for "soul" and "to make manifest," was applied to emphasize the subjectively experienced expansion of consciousness reported by users of LSD and often referred to by them as a "trip." The term in current use for LSD and other drugs with similar effects is **hallucinogen**, which refers to the main effects of such drugs, hallucinations. Unlike the hallucinations in schizophrenia, however, these are usually recognized by the person as being caused by the drug.

The following description is of the general effects of LSD, but it also applies to the other hallucinogens:

Mescaline, obtained from the peyote cactus, is used in certain religious rites of Native American people of the American Southwest and northern Mexico. (Kal Muller/Woodfin Camp & Associates.)

Synesthesias, the overflow from one sensory modality to another, may occur. Colors are heard and sounds may be seen. Subjective time is also seriously altered, so that clock time seems to pass extremely slowly. The loss of boundaries [between one's sense of self and one's environment] and the fear of fragmentation create a need for a structuring or supporting environment; and in the sense that they create a need for experienced companions and an explanatory system, these drugs are "cultogenic." During the "trip," thoughts and memories can vividly emerge under self-guidance or unexpectedly, to the user's distress. Mood may be labile, shifting from depression to gaiety, from elation to fear. Tension and anxiety may mount and reach panic proportions. After about 4 to 5 hours, if a major panic episode does not occur, there may be a sense of detachment and the conviction that one is magically in control. . . . The user may be greatly impressed with the drug experience and feel a greater sensitivity for art, music, human feelings, and the harmony of the universe. (Jaffe, 1985, p. 564)

The effects of hallucinogens depend on a number of psychological variables in addition to the dose itself. A person's set—that is, attitudes, expectancies, and motivations with regard to taking drugs—is widely held to be an important determinant of his or her reactions to hallucinogens. The context in which the drug is experienced is also important.

Among the most prominent dangers of taking LSD is the possibility of developing a full-blown panic attack; this is far more likely to occur if taking the drug creates anxiety. Often the specific fear is of going crazy. These panics are usually short-lived and subside as the drug is metabolized. A minority of people, however, go into a psychotic state that can require hospitalization and extended treatment.

Flashbacks, recurrences of psychedelic experiences after the physiological effects of the drug have worn off, also sometimes occur, most frequently in times of stress, illness, or fatigue (Kaplan & Sadock, 1991). Flashbacks are not believed to be caused by drug-produced physical changes in the nervous system, in part because only 15 to 30 percent of users of hallucinogenic drugs are estimated ever to have flashbacks (Stanton & Bardoni, 1972). Moreover, there is no independent evidence of measurable neurological changes in drug users who experience flashbacks. Flashbacks seem to have a force of their own; they may come to haunt people weeks and months after they have taken the drug and are very upsetting for those who experience them.

Other hallucinogens include mescaline and psilocybin, whose effects are thought to be due to stimulating serotonin receptors. **Mescaline**, an alkaloid and the active ingredient of peyote, was isolated in 1896 from small, disklike growths of the top of the peyote cactus. The drug has been used for centuries in the religious rites of Native American peoples living in the Southwest U.S. and northern Mexico. **Psilocybin** is a crystalline powder that Hofmann isolated from the mushroom *Psilocybe mexicana* in 1958. In early Aztec and other Mexican cultures, this mushroom was called "God's flesh" and held sacred; some native peoples of Mexico still use them in their worship.

During the 1950s, LSD, mescaline, and psilocybin were given in research settings to study what were thought to be psychotic experiences. In 1960, Timothy Leary and Richard Alpert of Harvard University began an investigation of the effects of psilocybin on prisoners. The early results, although subject to several confounds, were encouraging: released prisoners who had taken psilocybin proved less likely to be rearrested. At the same time, the two investigators started taking trips themselves and soon had gathered around them a group of people interested in experimenting with psychedelic drugs. By 1962 their activities had attracted the attention of law-enforcement agencies. As the investigation continued, the situation became a scandal, culminating in Leary's and Alpert's departures from Harvard. The affair seemed to give tremendous impetus to the use of the hallucinogens, particularly since the manufacture of LSD and the extraction of mescaline and psilocybin are relatively

In the 1960s, Timothy Leary was one of the leading proponents of the use of hallucinogens to expand consciousness. (Corbis Images.)

Clinical Case: Tamara

Tamara tried Ecstasy (X) for the first time when she was a freshman in college. She went to her first rave, and a friend gave her a pill she thought was a Sweet Tart. Within a short period of time, she began to feel almost magical, as if she was seeing everything around her in a new light. She felt incredibly close to her friends and even to men and women she had just met. Hugging and close dancing were intensely pleasurable, in a completely new way. A few days after the party, she asked her friend about the "Sweet Tart" and found out how she could obtain more. But the next time she tried X, she was unable to achieve the same pleasurable feelings. Instead, she felt more subdued, even anxious. After several more times using X, she noticed that despite her enthusiasm and even craving for the effects, she found instead that she felt a little depressed and anxious, even several days after taking the drug.

easy and inexpensive. In 1966, the use of these substances was banned by Congress. Since then, little research has been done on their effects in humans.

The use of LSD and other hallucinogens peaked in the 1960s; by the 1980s only 1 or 2 percent of people could be classified as regular users. Even those who used hallucinogens did not indulge more than once or twice every two weeks (NIDA, 1982, 1983a). LSD use increased somewhat in the early 1990s (NIDA, 1998), but it seems to be once again on the decline among high school and college students as well as young adults (Johnston et al., 2001b,c). In 2003, the number of LSD users went down to 558,000 from 1 million in 2002 (SAMHSA, 2004). There is no evidence of withdrawal symptoms during abstinence, but tolerance appears to develop rapidly (McKim, 1991). Among youths between the ages of 12 and 17, African Americans are less likely to use hallucinogens than whites, Asian Americans, or Hispanics [Office of Applied Studies (OAS, 2002)].

Ecstasy and PCP   A newer hallucinogen-like substance, **Ecstasy**, became illegal in 1985. Ecstasy includes both MDA (methylenedioxyamphetamine) and MDMA (methylene-dioxymethamphetamine). **MDMA** was first synthesized in the early 1900s, and it was used as an appetite suppressant for World War I soldiers. Chemical precursors to MDMA are found in several commonly used spices, such as nutmeg, dill, saffron, and sassafras. Not until the 1970s were the psychoactive properties of MDMA reported in the scientific literature. **MDA** was first synthesized in 1910, but it was not until the 1960s that its psychedelic properties came to the attention of the drug-using, consciousness-expanding generation of the times.

Ecstasy is chemically similar to mescaline, but also to the amphetamines. It contains compounds from both the hallucinogen and amphetamine families, but its effects are sufficiently different from either that some have suggested putting it in its own category, called the "entactogens" (Morgan, 2000). Half of new users of Ecstasy are male. Today it remains popular on college campuses; in addition, use of Ecstasy increased precipitously in 1998 among high school students, being used more often than cocaine in this group (Johnston et al., 2001b). Across all ages, Ecstasy use seems to have peaked in 2001, with 1.8 million users. From 2002 to 2003, the number of users age 12 and over decreased from 676,000 to 470,000. Despite this general decline, use among Hispanics does not appear to be declining (SAMHSA, 2004).

Ecstasy acts primarily by activating the serotonin system via the serotonin transporter gene, contributing to both the release and the subsequent reuptake of serotonin (Huether, Zhou, & Ruther, 1997; Liechti et al., 2000; Morgan, 2000). It was believed at one time that the use of Ecstasy was relatively harmless, but accumulating scientific evidence suggests that it may have neurotoxic effects on the serotonin system (De Souza, Battaglia, & Insel, 1990; Gerra et al., 2000). It is difficult to say if these toxic effects are directly due to drug use, since no studies in humans to date have assessed serotonin functioning both before and after Ecstasy use. Studies with animals, however, have shown that a single dose of Ecstasy causes serotonin depletion, and prolonged use can damage serotonin axons and nerve terminals (Harkin et al., 2001; Morgan, 2000). Evidence of this alteration has been observed in

Ecstasy is a popular party drug, but like many drugs, is not free of ill effects. (Lynne Sobol/Montes De Oca & Associates.)

monkeys several years after use of the drug was discontinued (Hatzidimitriou, McCann, & Ricaurte, 1999). Other studies show that more extensive use of Ecstasy is associated with some impairments in learning and memory (Verkes et al., 2001) and that these impairments are correlated with serotonin reductions (Renemen et al., 2000). It is important to note, though, that many studies examining the cognitive effects of Ecstasy use have not shown that cognitive impairments can be attributed solely to Ecstasy, since many participants in those studies have used other drugs concurrently with or prior to using Ecstasy. For example, one study found that users of both marijuana and Ecstasy had impairments in memory, word fluency, and dexterity that were comparable to the impairments observed in users of marijuana alone (Croft et al., 2001).

Users report that Ecstasy enhances intimacy and insight, improves interpersonal relationships, elevates mood and self-confidence, and promotes aesthetic awareness. It can also cause muscle tension, rapid eye movements, jaw clenching, nausea, faintness, chills or sweating, and anxiety, depression, depersonalization, and confusion. Some evidence suggests that the subjective and physiological effects of Ecstasy, both pleasurable and adverse, may be stronger for women than men (Liechti et al., 2000). The Drug Enforcement Administration considers the use of Ecstasy and other so-called club drugs unsafe and a serious threat to health. Several deaths have been reported from accidental overdose (Climko et al., 1987). Focus on Discovery 10.3 discusses the use and effects of another club drug, nitrous oxide.

PCP, phencyclidine, often called *angel dust*, is another drug not easy to classify. Developed as a tranquilizer for horses and other large animals, it generally causes serious negative reactions, including severe paranoia and violence. Coma and death are also possible. PCP affects multiple neurotransmitters in the brain, and chronic use is associated with a variety of neuropsychological deficits. Abusers of PCP are likely to have used other drugs either prior to or concurrently with PCP, so it is difficult to sort out whether neuropsychological impairments are due solely to PCP, to other drugs, or to the combination. Use of PCP increased in the early to mid-1990s but was believed to be on the decline in the late 1990s. However, between 2000 and 2002, the number of arrests, emergency room visits, and treatment admissions linked to PCP increased in urban areas such as Chicago, Dallas, Los Angeles, Philadelphia, Phoenix, and Washington, D.C. (NIDA, 2004c).

Quick Summary

Opiates include heroin and other pain medications like hydrocodone and oxycodone. Abuse of prescription pain medications has risen dramatically, and overdoses are common. Heroin use has risen slightly in recent years, particularly among youth. Initial effects of opiates include euphoria; later, users experience a letdown. Death by overdose from opiates is a severe problem. Other problems include exposure to HIV and other infectious agents through the use of needles. Synthetic sedatives are prescribed less than they used to be. They relax the muscles, reduce anxiety, and can produce a mildly euphoric state. Large doses can be fatal. Withdrawal is severe for opiates and synthetic sedatives.

Amphetamines are stimulants that produce wakefulness, alertness, and euphoria. Men and women use these equally. Tolerance develops quickly. Methamphetamine is a synthesized amphetamine, and use has increased dramatically since the 1990s. Men use it more than women;

whites more than other ethnic groups. Methamphetamine can damage the brain, including gray matter and the hippocampus. Cocaine and crack remain serious problems. Cocaine increases sexual desire, well-being, and alertness, but chronic use is associated with problems in relationships, paranoia, and trouble sleeping among other things. The faster crack or cocaine is absorbed, the more quickly and intensely the person becomes high.

LSD was a popular hallucinogen in the 1960s and 1970s, often billed as a mind-expanding drug. The mind-expanding drug of the 1990s became Ecstasy. Although these drugs do not typically show signs of withdrawal symptoms, tolerance can develop. There is some indication that Ecstasy use may be on the decline, but not among all ethnic groups. PCP remains a problem in urban areas. This drug can cause severe paranoia and violence.

Focus on Discovery 10.3

Nitrous Oxide—Not a Laughing Matter

Nitrous oxide is a colorless gas that has been available since the nineteenth century. Within seconds it induces light-headedness and a state of euphoria in most people; for some, important insights seem to flood the mind. Clinical reports and some controlled research confirm that this gaseous mixture raises pain thresholds, perhaps by an induction of positive feelings that dull sensations that would normally be experienced as noxious (Devine et al., 1974). Many people find otherwise mundane events and thoughts irresistibly funny, hence the nickname "laughing gas."

Perhaps readers of this book have had nitrous oxide at a dentist's office to facilitate relaxation and otherwise make a potentially uncomfortable and intimidating dental procedure more palatable (and to make it easier for the dentist to work on the patient). A major advantage of nitrous oxide over other analgesics and relaxants is that the patient can return to the normal waking state within minutes of breathing enriched oxygen or normal air. An additional advantage is that patients can be taught to control how deep they go by taking a few breaths of regular air through the mouth (the gas is administered through a small mask that covers only the nose; otherwise the dentist could not work on the person's teeth). The experienced health professional can easily make continuing adjustments based on judgment of the patient's level of intoxication.

Nitrous oxide fits in the broader category of inhalants and has been used recreationally since it first became available, although it has been illegal for many years in most states except as administered by appropriate health professionals. As with the other drugs examined in this chapter, illegality has not prevented unsupervised use. It is one of the most prevalently used inhalants among teens (sniffing glue, gasoline, and paint are

more prevalent), with rates of use as high as 22 percent among those who use inhalants (Wu, Pilowsky, & Schlenger, 2004). More broadly, the use of inhalants among high school students increased in 2003 following years of decline (NIDA, 2004b). Sometimes called "hippie crack" or "whippets," nitrous oxide balloons are often combined with the use of Ecstasy and other drugs in parties with bright laser lights and loud dance music (i.e., at raves).

An important difference between the way in which dentists use nitrous oxide and the way in which it is used casually is that in the dental office the air mixture is seldom more than 80 percent nitrous oxide (the rest is oxygen). This mixture allows for the safe and effective use of the gas. When abused, nitrous oxide is often in much higher concentrations. Death by suffocation can occur with these higher concentrations, particularly if the drug is taken in an environment where oxygen is more limited. In addition, sniffing can cause heart failure and death in some cases; this is referred to as "sudden sniffing death" (NIDA, 2004b). Such was the case for three men who were found dead in the closed cab of a pickup truck in the early morning hours of March 6, 1992. They had apparently been asphyxiated by the nitrous oxide in an 80-pound industrial-sized canister that was lying across their laps. Evidence at the scene suggested that they had been filling balloons with the gas and had, perhaps inadvertently, allowed the gas to escape freely into the sealed cab. With little air from outside, the men had been breathing pure nitrous oxide and their own exhaled carbon dioxide—and very little oxygen.

Some of this material was taken from two Los Angeles Times articles: Connelly (1992) and Romero (1992).

Check Your Knowledge 10.3

True or False?

1. The use of heroin has been steadily decreasing since the 1960s and 1970s.
2. The use of OxyContin began in urban areas, but quickly spread to rural areas.
3. Methamphetamine is a less potent form of amphetamine, less likely to be associated with brain impairment.
4. Ecstasy contains compounds associated with hallucinogens and amphetamines.

Etiology of Substance-Related Disorders

In considering the causes of substance-related disorders, we must recognize that becoming substance dependent is generally a developmental process. The person must first have a positive attitude toward the substance, then begin to experiment with using it, then begin using it regularly, then use it heavily, and finally abuse or become dependent on it (see Figure 10.4). The general idea is that after prolonged heavy use some people become ensnared by the biological effects of tolerance and withdrawal.

Researchers have only recently begun to consider the nature of this process (Stice, Barrera, & Chassin, 1998). It appears that the factors that contribute to substance dependence

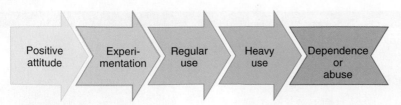

Figure 10.4 The process of becoming dependent on a drug.

may depend on the point in the process that is being considered. For example, developing a positive attitude toward smoking and beginning to experiment with tobacco are strongly related to smoking by other family members (Robinson et al., 1997). In contrast, becoming a regular smoker is more strongly related to smoking by peers and being able to acquire cigarettes readily (Robinson et al., 1997; Wang et al., 1997).

More generally, adopting a developmental approach to understanding the etiology of substance-related disorders requires the study of persons across time, beginning at the earliest sign of substance use. Studies of the trajectories of substance-related problems among adolescents are becoming more frequent, and the findings suggest, not surprisingly, that different adolescents follow different trajectories (Jackson, Sher, & Wood, 2000; Wills et al., 1999). For example, one study identified two typical trajectories toward alcohol abuse in adolescence: (1) a group that began drinking early in adolescence and continued to increase their drinking throughout high school and (2) a group that started drinking a lesser amount in early adolescence, and increased drinking at two peak points, one in middle school and another later in high school. Boys were more likely to follow the trajectory of the first group; girls were more likely to follow the trajectory of the second group, with even steeper trajectories in drinking than the boys (Li, Duncan, & Hops, 2001). Early deviant behavior predicted membership in the first group; peer encouragement predicted later drinking for both groups.

Other views incorporate what we know about the developing brain, particularly in adolescence. A recent review points to the fact that the area of the brain linked to judgment and decision making, novelty seeking, and impulse control, that is the frontal cortex, is still developing at the time when adolescents are beginning to experiment with drugs and alcohol (Chambers, Taylor, & Potenza, 2003). The neural systems believed to be important for reward, including dopaminergic, serotonergic, and glutamatergic pathways, all pass through the developing frontal cortex.

Although applicable in many cases, a developmental approach does not account for all cases of substance abuse or dependence. For example, there are documented cases in which heavy use of tobacco or heroin did not result in dependence. Furthermore, we must remember that we are not talking about an inevitable progression through stages. Some people have periods of heavy use of a substance—for example—alcohol, and then return to moderate use. In the following sections, we discuss sociocultural, psychological, and biological factors associated with substance-related disorders. It is important to keep in mind that these factors are likely to be differently related to different substances. Genetic factors, for example, may play some role in alcohol dependence but be less important in hallucinogen abuse.

Sociocultural Factors

Sociocultural factors play a widely varying role in drug abuse and dependence. From the effects of peers and parents to the influence of the media and what is considered acceptable behavior in a particular culture, the social world can affect people's interest in and access to drugs.

At the broadest level, for example, we can look at great cross-national variation in alcohol consumption. Some research suggests that there are commonalities in drug use across various countries. For example, a recent cross-national study of alcohol and drug use among high school students that included 36 countries worldwide found that alcohol was the most common substance used across countries, despite great variation in the proportions of students who consumed alcohol, ranging from 32 percent in Zimbabwe to 99 percent in Wales (Smart & Ogborne, 2000). In all but two of the countries studied, marijuana was the next most commonly used drug. In those countries where marijuana was used most often, with more than 15 percent of high school students having ever used marijuana, there were also higher rates of use of amphetamines, Ecstasy, and cocaine. Other research has found striking cross-national differences in alcohol consumption. For example, the highest consumption rates have typically been found in wine-drinking societies, such as those of France, Spain, and Italy, where drinking alcohol regularly is widely accepted (deLint, 1978). Cultural attitudes and patterns of drinking thus influence the likelihood of drinking heavily and therefore of abusing alcohol. One finding that seems quite similar across different cultures is that men consume more alcohol than women. An analysis conducted by the International Research Group on Gender and Alcohol, a collaboration of alcohol researchers across 35 countries, found that men drank more than women in an analysis of 10 countries, including Australia, Canada, the Czech Republic, Estonia, Finland, Israel, the Netherlands, Russia, Sweden, and the United States. Despite this consistency in gender differences, there was a large disparity across countries in the extent

Alcohol dependence is more prevalent in countries in which alcohol use is heavy, such as major wine-producing countries. Everyone is drinking wine in this French bar. (Eric Brissaud/Liaison Agency, Inc./Getty Images.)

to which men drank more than women. For example, men drank three times as much as women in Israel, but only one and a half times more than women in the Netherlands (Wilsnack et al., 2000). These findings suggest that cultural prescriptions about drinking by men and women are important to consider.

Not only do consumption patterns vary across countries, but the ways in which countries think about alcohol-related problems may differ. For example, in England, the laws regarding closing times for pubs changed in 2005 so that they are able to stay open longer. Instead of having to close at 11 P.M., they are allowed to stay open as long as they like. Will this promote greater drinking? Perhaps, but the rationale for the change was not to curb drinking as much as it was to reduce the problems that can go along with drinking. When people left the pubs after a 10:30 P.M. last call, they were not yet ready to go home, so they would hang out in the streets, sometimes getting into fights or causing other public disturbances. With pubs staying open later, the hope is that people will leave the pubs when they are ready to go home and thereby create fewer disturbances (*Los Angeles Times*, March 7, 2004).

Ready availability of the substance is also a factor. For example, in wine-drinking societies, wine is present in many settings, even in university cafeterias. Also, rates of alcohol abuse are high among bartenders and liquor store owners, people for whom alcohol is readily available (Fillmore & Caetano, 1980). In 2003, drug use among youths who had been approached by drug dealers was 35 percent, compared to just under 7 percent among youths who had not been approached (SAMHSA, 2004). With regard to smoking, if cigarettes are perceived as being easy to get and affordable, the rate of smoking increases (Robinson et al., 1997). This is one of the reasons states raise taxes on alcohol and cigarettes so frequently. Not only does this generate more revenue, but it also makes these substances less affordable for some and thereby less available. Of course, this tactic disproportionately affects the poor, which is not only unfair, but does not necessarily target all who would benefit from less available substances.

Family factors are important as well. For example, exposure to alcohol use by parents increases children's likelihood of drinking (Hawkins et al., 1997). Acculturation into American society may interact with family factors for people of other cultural and ethnic backgrounds. For example, a study of middle school Hispanic students in New York found that children who spoke English with their parents were more likely to smoke marijuana than children who spoke Spanish (Epstein, Botvin, & Diaz, 2001). Psychiatric, marital, or legal problems in the family are also related to drug abuse, and a lack of emotional support from parents is linked to increased use of cigarettes, marijuana, and alcohol (Cadoret et al., 1995a; Wills, DuHamel, & Vaccaro, 1995). Finally, longitudinal studies have shown that a lack of parental monitoring leads to increased association with drug-abusing peers and subsequent higher use of drugs (Chassin et al., 1996; Thomas et al., 2000).

The social setting in which a person operates can also affect substance abuse. For example, studies of smokers in daily life show that they are more likely to smoke with other smokers than with nonsmokers. In addition, smoking was more likely in bars, restaurants, or at home rather than in the workplace or in others' homes (Shiffman et al., 2002; Shiffman et al., 2004). Another study showed that having friends who smoke predicts smoking (Killen et al., 1997). In longitudinal studies, peer-group identification in the seventh grade predicted smoking in the eighth (Sussman et al., 1994), and in a three-year study it predicted increased drug use in general (Chassin et al., 1996). Peer influences are also important in promoting alcohol and marijuana use (Hussong et al., 2001; Stice, Barrera, & Chasin, 1998; Wills & Cleary, 1999).

These findings support the idea that social networks influence an individual's drug or alcohol behavior. However, other evidence indicates that individuals who are inclined to abuse substances may actually select social networks that conform to their own drinking or drug use patterns. Thus, we have two broad explanations for how the social environment is related to substance abuse: a social influence model and a social selection model. A longitudinal study of over 1,200 adults designed to test which model best accounted for drinking behavior found support for both models (Bullers, Cooper, & Russell, 2001). An individual's social network predicted individual drinking, but individual drinking also predicted subsequent social network drinking. In fact, the social selection effects were stronger, indicating that individuals often choose social networks with drinking patterns similar to their own. No doubt the selected networks then support or reinforce their drinking. Similar results have been found for adolescents (Farrell & Danish, 1993).

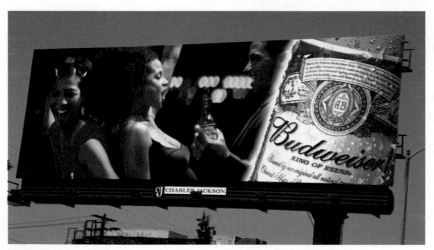

Advertising is one way that expectancies develop. (Bill Aron/PhotoEdit.)

Another variable to be considered is the media. Television commercials associate beer with athletic-looking males, bikini-clad women, and good times. Billboards equate cigarettes with excitement, relaxation, and being in style. An analysis of consumption in 17 countries between 1970 and 1983 supports the role of advertising in promoting alcohol use. Those countries that banned ads for alcohol had 16 percent less consumption than those that did not (Saffer, 1991). A recent study proposed that the narrowing gap between adolescent boys' and girls' drinking may be associated with advertising changes (Jernigan et al., 2004). Alcohol advertising in magazines has increased in recent years, and it seems that these ads are reaching girls more than boys. For example, between 2001 and 2002, exposure to alcohol ads for girls increased 216 percent, whereas exposure to such ads increased 46 percent for boys. Of course, this study does not show that ad exposure causes greater drinking among girls, only that there is a correlation. It could be that changes in magazine ads are driven by the increase in girls' drinking.

A particularly striking example of the pernicious role of the media was the Joe Camel campaign for Camel cigarettes. The number of smokers is declining, so the tobacco industry's profitability depends on recruiting new smokers to replace those who are quitting, and the obvious targets are elementary and high school students. Camel launched its campaign in 1988 with the Joe Camel character modeled after James Bond or the character played by Don Johnson in the television program *Miami Vice*, a popular show of the time. Prior to the campaign, in the period from 1976 to 1988, Camel was the preferred brand of less than 0.5 percent of seventh through twelfth graders. By 1991 Camel's share of this illegal market had increased to 33 percent (DiFranza et al., 1991)!

In March 1992, the surgeon general and the American Medical Association asked R. J. Reynolds, the manufacturer of Camel cigarettes, to drop Joe Camel from its ads because of this apparent appeal to youngsters. Billboard companies and print media were also requested to stop running the ads. The response from R. J. Reynolds? "We have no reason to believe that this campaign is causing anyone to begin smoking. If we thought it was causing young people to smoke, we'd pull it" (spokesperson for the company, quoted in Horovitz, 1992). The evidence indicates, however, that advertising does influence smoking. In a longitudinal study of nonsmoking adolescents, those who had a favorite cigarette ad were twice as likely subsequently to begin smoking or to be willing to do so (Pierce et al., 1998).

The days of Joe Camel and other cartoon characters that appeal to young people are over. On March 13, 1996, the Liggett Group, manufacturers of cigarettes, agreed to stop using such advertising tools and to take other steps to discourage smoking among minors. These actions were part of a settlement in a class action lawsuit against the U.S. cigarette industry that charged companies with manipulating nicotine levels to keep smokers addicted. Furthermore, the American Legacy Foundation was formed as part of the settlement that followed this class action lawsuit that included 46 states (www.americanlegacy.org). The goals of this group are to prevent smoking among young people, and to make sure information about smoking and how to stop smoking is equally accessible to all who want it. We will discuss the important efforts of this group later in the chapter when we discuss prevention.

Psychological Factors

In this section, we look at five types of psychological factors that contribute to the etiology of substance-related disorders. First, we consider the effects of drugs (particularly alcohol and nicotine) on mood; we examine the situations in which a tension-reducing effect occurs and the role of cognition in this process. Second, we consider people's expectancies about the effects of substances on behavior. Third, we examine people's beliefs about the prevalence with which a drug is used and about the health risks associated with using that drug. Fourth, we consider other psychological disorders and personality traits that may make it more likely for some people to use drugs heavily, and fifth, we examine cues and cravings for particular drugs that make use and abuse more likely.

F.T.C. Charges Joe Camel Ad Illegally Takes Aim at Minors

Internal Documents of R. J. Reynolds Are Cited by Agency

By JOHN M. BRODER

WASHINGTON, May 28 — In another blow to an industry under siege, the Federal Trade Commission charged today that the R. J. Reynolds Tobacco Company illegally aimed its Joe Camel advertising campaign at minors.

The agency asserted in an administrative complaint that the company violated Federal fair trade practice laws by promoting a lethal and addictive product to children and adolescents who could not legally purchase or use it.

This is the first time that the commission has accused the tobacco industry of peddling its products to minors. The complaint will be supported, agency officials said, by extensive citations from internal company documents.

The Government says it believes that R. J. Reynolds papers will prove that the company deliberately designed its cartoon-based advertising campaign in the mid-1980's to increase its shrinking market share among young smokers.

The complaint amounts to a civil indictment of a company for its issuing officials.

Linda Rosier for The New York Times

Advertising is an important factor in stimulating drug use. The Joe Camel campaign greatly increased Camel's share of the market among elementary and high school students. (New York Times.)

Mood Alteration   It is generally assumed that one of the principal psychological motives for using drugs is to alter mood—that is, drug use is reinforced because it enhances positive moods or diminishes negative ones. Things are more complex, however.

Early animal experiments (Conger, 1951) showed that alcohol impairs avoidance learning, which is usually regarded as being mediated by anxiety. Some later experiments with humans (Sher & Levenson, 1982) also indicated that alcohol reduces tension in people who are not yet alcohol abusers, but some conflicting findings emerged as well (Thyer & Curtis, 1984). For example, if alcohol reduces tension, it ought to have a specific effect on negative emotions associated with anxious or threatening situations. However, research has found that alcohol lessens both positive and negative emotions but does not have a selective effect on negative emotions in response to threatening cues (Curtin et al., 1998; Stritzke, Patrick, & Lang, 1995). Studies of the tension-reducing properties of nicotine have also yielded mixed findings, with some studies showing that nicotine reduces tension and other negative emotions and others failing to find tension reduction following nicotine ingestion (Kassel, Stroud, & Paronis, 2003). The reasons for the mixed findings may have to do with a failure to consider the stages of smoking. That is, tension reduction and negative affect seem to play more of a role in the initiation of smoking than in the maintenance of smoking or in relapse after treatment (Kassel et al., 2003).

Subsequent research to examine the reasons for these inconsistent results has focused on the situation in which alcohol or nicotine is consumed—specifically, a situation in which distraction is present. Findings indicate that alcohol may reduce tension by altering cognition and perception (Curtin et al., 1998; Steele & Josephs, 1988, 1990). Alcohol impairs cognitive processing and narrows attention to the most immediately available cues, resulting in "alcohol myopia" (Steele & Josephs, 1990). In other words, the intoxicated person has less cognitive capacity and tends to use that capacity to focus on an immediate distraction, if available, rather than on tension-producing thoughts, with a resultant decrease in anxiety. The benefits of distraction have also been documented for nicotine. Specifically, smokers who smoked in the presence of a distracting activity realized a reduction in anxiety, whereas smokers who smoked without a distracting activity did not experience a reduction in anxiety (Kassel & Shiffman, 1997; Kassel & Unrod, 2000). However, alcohol and nicotine may increase tension when no distractions are present. For example, a person drinking alone may focus all his or her limited cognitive capacity on unpleasant thoughts, begin brooding, and become increasingly tense and anxious, a situation reflected in the expression "crying in one's beer."

Another situational factor that influences the tension-reducing effects of alcohol and nicotine is the temporal relationship between consumption and stress—that is, whether alcohol or nicotine consumption precedes or follows stress. Most people believe that an increase in tension (e.g., because of a bad day at the office) leads to increased alcohol consumption to reduce the effects of the earlier stressor. Empirical support for this idea comes from studies showing that increases in life stress precede relapses (e.g., Brown et al., 1990). However, experimental research on the tension-reducing properties of alcohol has typically reversed the order of the two factors, by having subjects drink and then encounter a stressor. One study compared alcohol's effects in both orders (stress–alcohol versus alcohol–stress) and found tension reduction only in the alcohol–stress sequence (Sayette & Wilson, 1991). Similarly, a recent longitudinal study assessing the temporal relationship between stress and drinking did not find greater alcohol consumption following reports of greater life stress. Rather, greater alcohol consumption predicted later reductions in health stress and financial stress for women and later reductions in health stress for men (Brennan, Schutte, & Moos, 1999). Based on these results, we can say that alcohol may not be a potent tension reducer in many life situations when it is consumed after stress has already occurred.

With respect to smoking, some have argued that smoking causes increases in stress and tension, whereas others have argued that stress causes increases in smoking, at least the initiation of smoking and relapse after quitting smoking (Kassel et al., 2003; Shiffman & Waters, 2004). A recent longitudinal study of adolescent smokers found that increases in negative affect and negative life events were associated with increases in smoking. There was no evidence that increases in smoking caused increases in negative affect (Wills, Sandy, & Yaeger, 2002). More generally, the evidence points to a correlation between stress, negative affect, and smoking but does not show a strong causal link in any direction, largely because so few experimental studies have been done (Kassel et al., 2003).

Tension reduction is only one aspect of the possible effects of drugs on mood. Some people may use drugs to reduce negative affect, whereas others may use drugs to increase positive affect when they are bored or underaroused (Cooper et al., 1995). In both cases drug use could reflect a situation where other means of coping with emotional states haven't worked. But in the former case, a high level of negative affect plus expecting drugs to reduce tension leads to increased drug use, whereas in the latter case, increased drug use results from a high need for stimulation plus expectancies that drugs will promote increased positive affect. These patterns have been confirmed among alcohol and cocaine abusers (Ball, Carroll, & Rounsaville, 1994; Cooper et al., 1995; Hussong et al., 2001).

Expectancies about Alcohol and Drug Effects   If it is true that alcohol does not reduce stress when consumed after the fact, why do so many people who drink believe that it helps them unwind? Expectation may play a role here—that is, people may use alcohol after stress not because it actually reduces tension but because they expect it to do so. In support of this idea, studies have shown that people who expect alcohol to reduce stress and anxiety are those likely to be frequent users (Rather et al., 1992; Sher et al., 1991; Tran, Haaga, & Chambless, 1997). Furthermore, the level of drinking and positive expectancies about alcohol appear to influence each other. The expectation that drinking will reduce anxiety increases drinking, which in turn makes the positive expectancies even stronger (Smith et al., 1995).

Other research has shown that expectancies about a drug's effects—for example, the beliefs that a drug will stimulate aggression and increase sexual responsiveness, predict increased drug use in general (Stacy, Newcomb, & Bentler, 1991). In now classic experiments demonstrating these points, participants who believe they are consuming a quantity of alcohol when they are actually consuming an alcohol-free beverage subsequently become more aggressive (Lang et al., 1975) and report increased sexual arousal (Wilson & Lawson, 1976). Thus, as we have seen in other contexts, cognitions can have a powerful effect on behavior. Research also suggests a reciprocal relationship between expectancies and alcohol use: positive expectancies predict alcohol use, and alcohol use helps to maintain and strengthen positive expectancies (e.g., Sher et al., 1996).

Beliefs about Risks and Prevalence   The extent to which a person believes a drug is harmful and the perceived prevalence of use by others are also factors related to use. In general, the greater the perceived risk of a drug, the less likely it will be used. For example, in 2003, marijuana use among youths who perceived great risk was 1.8 percent, whereas use among youths who perceived no, little, or moderate risk was 11.2 percent (SAMHSA, 2004). Similarly, many smokers do not believe that they are at increased risk for cancer or cardiovascular disease (Ayanian & Cleary, 1999). Furthermore, alcohol and tobacco are used more frequently among people who overestimate the frequency with which these substances are used by others (Jackson, 1997).

There are also ethnic differences in beliefs about the risks associated with substance use. An analysis from the 1996 and 1997 National Household Surveys on Drug Abuse (SAMHSA, 1997a,b) found that whites reported less perceived risk associated with alcohol, cigarettes, marijuana, and cocaine than did African Americans and Hispanics (Ma & Shive, 2000). Not surprisingly, actual use of these substances was higher among whites than among either African Americans or Hispanics in 1996 and 1997, consistent with the notion that the lower the perceived risk, the greater the usage.

Psychopathology and Personality   Neither sociocultural factors nor mood-alteration theories can completely account for individual differences in drug use. Not all members of a particular culture or subculture are heavy users, nor do all who experience stress increase drug usage. Personality and other individual differences may help to explain why certain people are more likely to abuse or become dependent on drugs.

High levels of negative affect and a persistent desire for arousal and increased positive affect are two personality traits that have been studied in this context. In one study demonstrating these points, kindergarten children were rated by their teachers on several personality traits and were followed up several years later (Killen et al., 1997). Anxiety (e.g., worries about things, fear of new situations) and novelty seeking (e.g., being restless, fidgety) predicted the onset of getting drunk, using drugs, and smoking. Cross-sectional studies support the idea that both depression and anxiety are related to the initiation of smoking; however, prospective, longitudinal studies do not support such a link (Kassel et al., 2003). It may also be the case that smoking is a risk factor for depression, at least among adolescents.

An association has been found between drug use in general and antisocial personality disorder (Ball et al., 1994), where drug abuse may be part of thrill-seeking behavior in this disorder (see Chapter 12). Furthermore, alcohol use is comorbid with several personality disorders, most notably antisocial personality disorder for men and borderline personality disorder for women (Morgenstern et al., 1997). Rebelliousness and high levels of aggression are also related to substance abuse (Anderrson, Magnusson, & Wennberg, 1997; Masse & Trembley, 1997).

Attention deficit/hyperactivity disorder (ADHD) and conduct disorder in childhood (see Chapter 14) are also related to drug abuse. In a prospective study spanning more than

10 years, ADHD was a predictor of later alcohol abuse (Hechtman, Weiss, & Perlman, 1984). ADHD has also been associated with tobacco and cannabis use (Wills et al., 1995) and with cocaine abuse (Ball et al., 1994).

Cues and Cravings for a Particular Drug   Other research has examined the role that cues and cravings for a particular drug may play in maintaining or exacerbating drug or alcohol problems. These studies are not really testing etiological theories; rather, they seek to account for why people continue to use a drug. Newer treatment efforts (reviewed later) are aimed at curbing the cravings and reducing the cues associated with drug or alcohol use.

A number of laboratory stories have shown that cues for a particular drug can elicit responses not altogether unlike those associated with actual use of the drug. For example, those who were dependent on cocaine showed changes in physiological arousal, cravings, "high" feelings, and more negative emotions in response to cues of cocaine, which consisted of audio and videotapes of people preparing to inject or snort cocaine, than did individuals not dependent on cocaine (e.g., Robbins et al., 2000). Brain imaging studies have shown that cues for a drug, such as a needle or a cigarette, activate the reward and pleasure areas of the brain implicated in drug use.

Genetic Factors

Much research has addressed the possibility that there is a genetic predisposition for problem drinking and the abuse of other drugs. Evidence for a genetic predisposition for alcohol abuse is found in studies in which animals have been bred that greatly prefer alcohol to other beverages (Li et al., 1981). Data also indicate that problem drinking in human beings runs in families, suggesting a genetic component (but consistent also with social influence factors). Several studies have shown that relatives and children of problem drinkers have higher than expected rates of alcohol abuse or dependence (e.g., Chassin et al., 1999). Furthermore, family studies show that the relatives of substance abusers are at increased risk for abusing many substances, not just the one that was the basis for selecting the proband (Bierut et al., 1998; Merilkangas et al., 1998). Further evidence for a genetic diathesis comes from twin studies, which have revealed greater concordance in identical twins than in fraternal twins for alcohol abuse for men (McGue, Pickens, & Svikis, 1992), and for caffeine use (Kendler & Prescott, 1999), smoking (True et al., 1999), heavy use or abuse of marijuana (Kendler & Prescott, 1998), and drug abuse in general (Tsuang et al., 1998).

The role of genetics in alcohol dependence among women is less clear because there are fewer studies, and the findings are mixed. Some studies find evidence for a genetic component and others don't (Kendler et al., 1994; McGue et al., 1992). Data from the Collaborative Study on the Genetics of Alcoholism suggest that a low level of intoxication and body sway after alcohol ingestion (i.e., movement back and forth when standing still) may distinguish women with a family history of alcohol dependence from women without such a history (Schuckit et al., 2000).

The ability to tolerate alcohol may be an inherited diathesis for alcohol abuse or dependence. That is, to become a problem drinker, a person has to be able to drink a lot; in other words, the person must be able to tolerate large quantities of alcohol. Some ethnic groups, such as Asians, may have a low rate of alcohol abuse because of physiological intolerance, which is caused by an inherited deficiency in an enzyme involved in alcohol metabolism. About three-quarters of Asians experience unpleasant effects from small quantities of alcohol, which may protect them from alcohol abuse or dependence. Other evidence has found that individuals with a defect in a gene called CYP2A6, which is associated with the metabolism of nicotine, smoke fewer cigarettes and are less likely to become dependent on nicotine (Rao et al., 2000). This is an interesting example of a gene defect serving a protective function. It will be important to replicate this finding with other samples.

Animal research indicates that genetic components are at work both in how alcohol is metabolized and in how the central nervous system responds to alcohol (Schuckit, 1983). Corroborating this notion are findings from research using the high-risk method in humans, which have compared young, nonalcoholic adults with a first-degree alcohol-abusing relative to similar individuals without a positive family history for the disorder. Two factors predicted the development of alcohol abuse in men in a 10-year follow-up (Schuckit, 1994; Schuckit & Smith, 1996): (1) self-report of a low level of intoxication after a dose of alcohol and (2) less body sway (a measure of steadiness while standing) after drinking. Both findings indicate that alcohol abuse is more likely to occur in those on whom alcohol has little effect. Notably, these factors predict alcohol abuse among men with and without an alcohol-abusing father.[1]

The smaller response to alcohol in men who later became alcohol abusers may at first seem puzzling, but it fits with the notion that you have to drink a lot to become a problem drinker. A small response to alcohol may set the stage for heavier than normal drinking. The size of the response to alcohol is also related to our earlier discussion of alcohol's biphasic effects (p. 301). Follow-up studies found that the largest differences between sons of problem drinkers and controls occurred when their blood levels of alcohol were declining, suggesting that sons of alcohol abusers may experience fewer of the negative, depressing effects of alcohol (Schuckit & Smith, 1996). Other research indicates that sons of alcohol abusers experience greater effects of alcohol, for example, more tension reduction, as their blood-alcohol levels are on the rise (Newlin & Thomson, 1990). Thus, genetically predisposed individuals may receive more positive reinforcement and less punishment from alcohol (Newlin & Thomson, 1990).

Exciting research has also emerged on the mechanism through which genetics plays a role in smoking. Like most drugs, nicotine appears to stimulate dopamine release and inhibit its reuptake, and individuals who are more sensitive to these effects of nicotine are more likely to become regular smokers (Pomerleau et al., 1993). Research has examined a link between a gene that regulates the reuptake of dopamine and smoking. One form of this gene has been related to being less likely to begin smoking (Lerman et al., 1999) and to being more likely to have quit (Sabol et al., 1999). Recent research has found that genes contribute to the body's ability to metabolize nicotine, with some people able to do this quickly and others more slowly. Slower nicotine metabolism means that nicotine stays in the brain longer. A longitudinal study of seventh graders showed that those adolescents who had genes linked with slower nicotine metabolism were more likely to become dependent on it 5 years later (O'Loughlin et al., 2005).

Neurobiological Factors

You may have noticed that in our discussions of specific drugs, the neurotransmitter dopamine has almost always been mentioned. This is not surprising given that dopamine pathways in the brain are importantly linked to pleasure and reward. Drug use typically results in rewarding or pleasurable feelings, and it is via the dopamine system that these feelings are produced. Research with both humans and animals shows that nearly all drugs, including alcohol, stimulate the dopamine systems in the brain (see Figure 10.5), particularly the mesolimbic pathway (Camí & Farré, 2003). Researchers have wondered then if problems in the dopamine pathways in the brain might somehow account for why certain people become dependent on drugs. Some evidence suggests that individuals dependent on drugs or alcohol have a deficiency in the dopamine receptor DRD2 (Noble, 2003).

Investigators have proposed a neurobiological theory, referred to as an *incentive-sensitization theory*, that considers both the craving for drugs (what they term "wanting"), and the pleasure that comes with taking the drug (what they term "liking") (Robinson & Berridge, 1993, 2003). In their view, the dopamine system linked to reward, or liking, becomes supersensitive not just to the direct effects of drugs but also to the cues associated with drugs (e.g., needles, spoons, rolling paper). This sensitivity to cues induces craving,

---

[1] Interestingly, like the children of those dependent on alcohol, Native Americans do not report intense effects from a dose of alcohol. This contradicts the idea that the problems Native Americans have with alcohol result from some kind of heightened sensitivity to it (Garcia-Andrade, Wall, & Ehlers, 1997).

Figure 10.5 Reward pathways in the brain that are affected by different drugs. DA = Dopamine; GABA = gamma-aminobutyric acid; GLU = Glutamate; 5-HT = Serotonin. Adapted from Came and Farre (2003).

or wanting, and people go to extreme lengths to seek out and obtain drugs. Over time, the liking of drugs decreases, but the wanting remains very intense. These investigators argue that the transition from liking to powerful wanting, accomplished by the drug's effects on brain pathways involving dopamine, is what maintains the addiction.

Of course, neurobiological, genetic, and environmental factors do not operate in isolation. The most comprehensive explanations for substance-related disorders will be those that consider how environmental factors enable genetic or neurobiological factors to have their effects. Research with animals shows this quite clearly. For example, studies of mice that were separated from their mothers at birth (a very stressful occurrence, even for mice!) responded to injections of amphetamine or cocaine later in life very differently from mice that had not been separated but had experienced stress early in life (a lot of handling by humans). The investigators showed that these two types of early stress differently impacted the way in which the dopamine system developed in these animals, which then contributed to their drug responses (Meaney, Brake, & Gratton, 2002).

Quick Summary

A number of different etiological factors have been proposed to account for alcohol and drug dependence, and some have more support than others. Sociocultural factors play a role, including the culture, availability of a substance, family factors, social settings and networks, and advertising. There is support for both a social influence model and a social selection model.

Psychological factors have also been evaluated, and there is support for the idea that tension reduction plays a role, but only under certain circumstances, such as when distractions are present. Expectancies about the effects of drugs, such as reducing tension, increasing aggression, and increasing sexual prowess have been shown to predict drug and alcohol use. Expectancies about the effects of drugs are also powerful; the greater the perceived risk of a drug, the less likely it will be used. Perceived risks vary by ethnic group, however. Studies of individual differences in personality factors and other psychological disorders also

help us understand why some people may be more prone to abuse drugs and alcohol. Cues to certain drugs can evoke the same brain responses as if a person was actually using the drugs, and this is believed to help account for why people continue to use certain drugs.

Genetic factors play a role in alcohol dependence and perhaps also nicotine dependence. The ability to tolerate alcohol and metabolize nicotine may be what is passed on in the genes. Genetics have been less well studied with respect to other drugs, but broader theories about the role of genes that are important for the operation of the dopamine system suggest that this may be an important factor in explaining dependence across substances. The most-studied neurobiological factors are brain systems associated with dopamine pathways—the major reward pathways in the brain. The incentive-sensitization theory talks about how the brain is linked to liking (i.e., consuming) drugs and wanting (i.e., craving) drugs.

Check Your Knowledge 10.4

Multiple choice.

1. Which of the following is not one of the sociocultural factors implicated in the etiology of substance abuse or dependence?
   a. The media
   b. Gender
   c. Availability of a substance
   d. Social networks
2. Which of the following statements best captures the link between depression and smoking?
   a. Depression causes smoking

b. Smoking causes depression
c. It is likely that the effects are bidirectional
d. We just don't know yet

3. Genetic research on alcohol dependence indicates that:
   a. It may be less heritable among women
   b. Additional studies need to be done to determine heritability
   c. The dopamine receptor DRD1 may be faulty
   d. Twin studies show that the environment is just as important as genes

Treatment of Substance-Related Disorders

Many who work with those dependent on alcohol or drugs suggest that the first step to successful treatment is admitting there is a problem. To a certain extent, this makes sense. Why would someone get treatment for something that is not deemed a problem? Unfortunately, a number of treatment programs require more than just admitting a problem. They require individuals not only to admit a problem, but also to demonstrate their commitment to treatment by stopping their use of alcohol or drugs prior to beginning treatment. This requirement can exclude many who desire and need treatment. For example, James (in the case presented earlier) may not have been admitted to a residential program had he not been free of heroin for a week before trying to gain admission. Imagine if people with lung cancer were told they must demonstrate their commitment to treatment by stopping smoking before the cancer could be treated. In the next sections, we review treatments for alcohol-related problems, nicotine dependence, and other drug dependence.

Treatment of Alcohol Abuse and Dependence

The havoc created by problem drinking, for drinkers and for their families, friends, employers, and communities, makes this problem a serious public health issue in the United States and many other countries. Consequently, a great deal of research and clinical effort has gone into the design and evaluation of various treatments. In 2003 alone, over 1 million people over the age of 12 received treatment for alcohol abuse or dependence, with men being more likely to get treatment than women, perhaps since alcohol dependence is greater among men than women (SAMHSA, 2004). Unfortunately, an estimated 20 million people over the age of 12 were in need of treatment for alcohol or drug problems in 2003 who did not receive it. We have far to go in developing and providing effective treatments.

Inpatient Hospital Treatment   Public and private hospitals worldwide have for many years provided treatment for people dependent on alcohol, where individuals can avail themselves of a variety of individual and group therapies. Withdrawal from alcohol, **detoxification**, can be difficult, both physically and psychologically, and can take about 1 month. To help get through withdrawal, dependent drinkers also need carbohydrate solutions, B vitamins, and, sometimes, anticonvulsants. Many patients have to go through the detoxification process multiple times. Unfortunately, multiple previous detoxifications are associated with a poorer response to treatment (Malcolm et al., 2000). In recent years, the population served in detoxification centers has changed demographically: There have been large increases in admissions of women, African Americans, and Hispanics, as well as a decline in the mean age at admission and an increase in unemployed patients (McCarty et al., 2000). Alice, the woman described in the earlier case, would likely need hospital treatment, at least for detoxification.

The number of for-profit hospitals treating alcohol abuse increased dramatically until the mid-1990s, in part because such treatment was covered in large measure by both private insurance companies and the federal government (Holder et al., 1991). Annual costs run in the billions. Because inpatient treatment is much more expensive than outpatient treatment, its cost-effectiveness has been questioned. Is it worth the expense? Apparently not, at least in many cases. The therapeutic results of hospital treatment are not superior to those of outpatient treatment (Mundle et al., 2001; Soyka et al., 2001). In addition, short stays (less than 8 days) in detoxification hospitalizations may be as effective as longer stays (Foster, Marshall, & Peters, 2000). Some data even suggest that home detoxification may be a viable alternative to day hospital or inpatient treatment for selected groups of patients (Allan et al., 2000). However, an analysis of treatment for alcohol dependence concludes that an inpatient approach is probably necessary for people with few sources of social support who are living in environments that encourage the abuse of alcohol, especially individuals with serious psychological problems in addition to their substance abuse (Finney & Moos, 1998). Unfortunately, changes in health insurance in the United States over the past 10 years, including affordability, availability, and coverage, has made it more difficult for those dependent on alcohol to get hospital treatment when they need it. Between 2002 and 2003, the number of people receiving inpatient treatment at a hospital went from over 800,000 to just under 600,000 (SAMHSA, 2004).

Alcoholics Anonymous The largest and most widely known self-help group in the world is Alcoholics Anonymous (AA), founded in 1935 by two recovering alcoholics. It has well over 70,000 chapters and membership numbering more than two million people in the United States and in more than 100 other countries throughout the world. Each AA chapter runs regular and frequent meetings at which newcomers rise to announce that they are alcoholics, and older, sober members give testimonials relating the stories of their problem drinking and indicating how their lives are better now. The group provides emotional support, understanding, and close counseling for the problem drinker as well as a social network. Members are urged to call on one another around-the-clock when they need companionship and encouragement not to relapse into drinking. About 70 percent of Americans who have ever been treated for alcohol abuse have attended at least one AA meeting. Programs modeled after AA are available for other substance abusers, for example, Cocaine Anonymous and Marijuana Anonymous. There are even similar 12-step programs called Overeaters Anonymous and Gamblers Anonymous.

The AA program tries to instill in each AA member the belief that alcohol dependence is a disease that can never be cured and that continuing vigilance is necessary to resist taking even a single drink, lest uncontrollable drinking begin all over again. Even if the person has not consumed any alcohol for 15 years or more, the appellation "alcoholic" is still necessary according to the tenets of AA, since the person is always an alcoholic, always carrying the disease, even if it is currently under control.

The spiritual aspect of AA is apparent in the 12 steps of AA shown in Table 10.2, and there is evidence that belief in this philosophy is linked with achieving abstinence (Fiorentine & Hillhouse, 2000; Tonigan, Miller, & Connors, 2000). Other self-help groups do not have the religious overtones of AA, relying instead on social support, reassurance, encouragement, and suggestions for leading a life without alcohol. One such approach, termed *Rational Recovery*, focuses on the individual regaining self-reliance rather than developing reliance on a higher power (Trimpey, Velton, & Dain, 1993).

Two related self-help groups have developed from AA. The relatives of problem drinkers meet in Alanon Family Groups for mutual support in dealing with their family members and in realizing that it is exceedingly difficult to make them change their ways. Similarly,

Alcoholics Anonymous is the largest self-help group in the world. At their regular meetings, newcomers rise to announce their addiction and receive advice and support from others. (Hank Morgan/Photo Researchers.)

Alateen is for the children of alcohol abusers, who require support and understanding to help them overcome the sense that they are in some way responsible for their parents' problems and responsible also for changing them.

Claims made by AA about the effectiveness of its treatment have begun to be subjected to scientific scrutiny. Significant benefit from AA has been demonstrated (Ouimette, Finney, & Moos, 1997). However, AA has high drop out rates, and the dropouts are not always factored into the results of studies. In addition, until recently there has been only limited long-term follow-up of AA clients. One recent long-term follow-up study indicated that participation in AA was very effective (Timko et al., 2001). A large prospective study of over 2,000 men with alcohol dependence found that AA predicted a better outcome 2 years later (McKeller, Stewart, & Humphreys, 2003). In addition, becoming an AA member early in treatment and staying involved for a longer period of time is associated with a better outcome 8 years after treatment began (Moos & Humphreys, 2004). There have been no controlled studies testing the efficacy of Rational Recovery, though two findings from preliminary studies suggest that it may be effective (Schmidt, Carns, & Chandler, 2001).

Other evidence shows that frequent AA attendees differ from nonfrequent attendees in having histories of greater lifetime drug use, more arrests and treatment experiences, earlier age of initial alcohol use, and greater perceived helpfulness of 12-step programs (B. S. Brown et al., 2001). Among low-income individuals with alcohol dependence, it was found that African Americans and people with concurrent illicit drug problems do not prefer AA-type programs (Kingree, 2001). These findings can guide clinicians in making referrals to 12-step groups or alternative treatment programs.

Despite the difficulties associated with evaluating the effectiveness of self-help groups such as AA, they remain very widely used treatment programs. In 2003, for example, nearly two-thirds of people who received treatment for alcohol or drug dependence did so through a self-help program (SAMHSA, 2004).

Table 10.2 The 12 Steps of Alcoholics Anonymous

1. We admitted we were powerless over alcohol—that our lives had become unmanageable.
2. Came to believe that a power greater than ourselves could restore us to sanity.
3. Made a decision to turn our will and our lives over to the care of God as we understood Him.
4. Made a searching and fearless moral inventory of ourselves.
5. Admitted to God, to ourselves, and to another human being the exact nature of our wrongs.
6. Were entirely ready to have God remove all these defects of character.
7. Humbly asked Him to remove our shortcomings.
8. Made a list of all persons we had harmed, and became willing to make amends to them all.
9. Made direct amends to such people wherever possible, except when to do so would injure them or others.
10. Continued to take personal inventory and, when we were wrong, promptly admitted it.
11. Sought through prayer and meditation to improve our conscious contact with God as we understood Him, praying only for knowledge of His will for us and the power to carry that out.
12. Having had a spiritual awakening as the result of these steps, we tried to carry this message to alcoholics and to practice these principles in all our affairs.

Couples and Family Therapy   The intertwining of alcohol abuse and family conflict—the cause–effect relationship goes both ways (O'Farrell, 1993)—has led to the use of various kinds of couples and family therapy to help drinkers abstain or control their excessive drinking. Behaviorally oriented marital or couples therapy (O'Farrell & Fals-Stewart, 2000) has been found to achieve some reductions in problem drinking as well as some improvement in couples' distress generally (McCrady & Epstein, 1995). In addition, couples therapy is associated with reduced domestic violence (O'Farrell & Fals-Stewart, 2000; O'Farrell et al., 2000). One focus of this therapy is involving the spouse in helping the drinker take Antabuse on a regular basis. Couples therapy is also part of Nathan Azrin's community-reinforcement approach, which we discuss later.

The importance of a partner's support in the problem drinker's effort to deal with life's inevitable stresses is not to be underestimated. But also not to be underestimated is the difficulty of maintaining moderate drinking or abstinence at one- and two-year follow-ups regardless of the mode of marital intervention and its short-term positive effects (Baucom et al., 1998). It is thus interesting to note that 1-year follow-up data show that the gains associated with behaviorally oriented therapy discussed above are maintained (Fals-Stewart et al., 2000).

For adolescents, family treatments may also have preventative effects. Research in Iowa has shown that two different brief family interventions for the general population were associated with less initiation of alcohol use among teens (Spoth, Guyll, & Day, 2002). Other evidence suggests that the longer alcohol use is delayed, the less likely alcohol dependence will develop (Grant & Dawson, 1997), suggesting that preventive interventions can play a big role in keeping the prevalence of alcohol dependence down. Not only were these family interventions associated with less alcohol initiation among teens, but a cost-benefit analysis showed that the costs of the interventions were substantially less than the costs associated with higher rates of drinking.

Cognitive and Behavioral Treatments   Behavioral and cognitive behavioral researchers have been studying the treatment of alcohol abuse for many years—indeed, one of the earliest articles on behavior therapy concerned aversion therapy as a treatment for alcoholism (Kantorovich, 1930). In general, cognitive and behavioral therapies represent the most effective psychological treatments for alcohol abuse (Finney & Moos, 1998).

Aversion Therapy   In **aversion therapy** a person dependent on alcohol is shocked or made nauseous while looking at, reaching for, or beginning to drink alcohol. In one procedure, called *covert sensitization* (Cautela, 1966), the problem drinker is instructed to imagine being made violently and disgustingly sick by his or her drinking.

Despite some evidence that aversion therapy may slightly enhance the effectiveness of inpatient treatment (Smith, Frawley, & Polissar, 1991), some well-known behavior therapists discourage its use because it lacks empirical support and causes great discomfort (Wilson, 1991).

Contingency-Management Therapy   Contingency-management therapy for alcohol abuse involves teaching patients and those close to them to reinforce behaviors inconsistent with drinking—for example, taking Antabuse and avoiding situations that were associated with drinking in the past. It is based on the belief that environmental contingencies can play an important role in encouraging or discouraging drinking. This therapy also includes teaching job-hunting and social skills, as well as assertiveness training for refusing drinks. For socially isolated individuals, assistance and encouragement are provided to establish contacts with other people who are not associated with drinking. As noted earlier, this approach also includes couples therapy. Other effective contingency-based treatments include providing reinforcers for sobriety, such as opportunities to win prizes (Petry et al., 2000) and abstinence-contingent partial support for housing, food, recreational activities, and access to supportive therapy (Gruber, Chutuape, & Stitzer, 2000). Often referred to as the *community-reinforcement approach*, contingency-management therapy has generated very promising results (Azrin et al., 1982; Baucom et al., 1998; Sisson & Azrin, 1989; Smith & Meyers, 2000). A review of the literature shows that it is consistently found to be one of the most efficacious and cost-effective treatments available (Smith, Meyers, & Miller, 2001).

Moderation in Drinking   At least since the advent of Alcoholics Anonymous, many have believed that people dependent on alcohol had to abstain completely if they were to be successfully treated, for they were assumed to have no control over imbibing once they had taken that first drink. This continues to be the belief of Alcoholics Anonymous, but research mentioned earlier, indicating that drinkers' beliefs about themselves and alcohol may be as important as the physiological addiction to the drug itself, has called this assumption into question. Considering the difficulty in society of avoiding alcohol altogether, it may even be preferable to teach the problem drinker, at least the person who does not abuse alcohol in an extreme fashion, to imbibe with moderation. Drinkers' self-esteem will certainly benefit from being able to control a problem and from feeling in charge of their life.

The term **controlled drinking** was introduced into the domain of alcohol treatment by Mark and Linda Sobell (Sobell & Sobell, 1993). It refers to a pattern of alcohol consumption that is moderate, avoiding the extremes of total abstinence and inebriation. Findings of one well-known treatment program suggested that at least some alcohol abusers can learn to control their drinking and improve other aspects of their lives as well (Sobell & Sobell, 1976).

Mark and Linda Sobell introduced controlled drinking approaches to the treatment of alcohol abuse. (Courtesy of Mark Sobell; Courtesy of Linda Sobell.)

Controlled-drinking treatment programs were further developed to teach patients to respond adaptively to situations in which they might otherwise drink excessively. They learn various social skills to help them resist pressures to drink; they receive assertiveness, relaxation, and stress-management training, sometimes including biofeedback and meditation; and they are encouraged to exercise and maintain a healthy diet.

The Sobells' current approach to teaching moderation to problem drinkers has evolved even further. Termed *guided self-change*, this outpatient approach emphasizes personal responsibility and control. The basic assumption is that people have more potential control over their immoderate drinking than they typically believe and that heightened awareness of the costs of drinking to excess as well as of the benefits of abstaining or cutting down can be of material help. Patients are encouraged to view themselves as basically healthy people who have been making unwise, often self-destructive choices about how to deal with life's inevitable stresses, rather than as victims of an addiction.

In guided self-change, the therapist is empathic and supportive while making salient to the problem drinker the negative aspects of excessive drinking that the person may have been overlooking. For example, getting the person to delay 20 minutes before taking a second or third drink can help him or her reflect on the costs versus the benefits of drinking to excess. Evidence supports the effectiveness of this approach in helping problem drinkers moderate their intake and otherwise improve their lives (Sobell & Sobell, 1993).

The principles of controlled drinking have also been adopted by self-help groups such as Moderation Management (MM) (Nowinski, 1999). However, MM's approach to moderation states clearly that it is not intended for persons who are alcohol dependent. In addition, it recommends a period of abstinence prior to any attempts at moderation. Qualitative data indicate that MM involvement is often precipitated by a conscious rejection of the 12-step philosophy of AA and many other professional treatment programs (Klaw & Humphreys, 2000).

Whether abstinence or controlled drinking should be the goal of treatment remains controversial. This issue pits influential forces, such as AA, that uphold abstinence as the only proper goal for problem drinkers, against more recent researchers, such as the Sobells and those adopting their general approach, who have shown that moderation can work for many patients, including those with severe drinking problems. If the therapeutic means of achieving the goal of moderate drinking are available—and research strongly suggests that they are—then controlled drinking may be a more realistic goal even for a person dependent on alcohol. Controlled drinking is currently much more widely accepted in Canada and Europe than it is in the United States.

Alcohol researchers have been aware for some time that different treatment approaches are most likely appropriate for different kinds of drinkers (Mattson et al., 1994). The issue is which factors in the drinkers are important to align with which factors in treatment. A large-scale effort to address the question was Project MATCH, a multisite clinical trial designed to test the hypothesis that certain kinds of treatments are good matches for certain kinds of problem drinkers. This widely cited study is described in Focus on Discovery 10.4.

Medications   Medications are best viewed as adjunctive—that is, they may offer some benefit when combined with a psychological treatment. However, there has been less research involving the combination of medication with psychotherapy or the combinations of different medications (Myrick, Kathleen, & Malcolm, 2001). Moreover, such basic issues as the optimal dosing strategy and duration of treatment are unknown for the most common medications for alcohol dependence (Kranzler, 2000).

Some problem drinkers who are in treatment, inpatient or outpatient, take disulfiram, or **Antabuse**, a drug that discourages drinking by causing violent vomiting if alcohol is ingested. It blocks the metabolism of alcohol so that noxious by-products are created. As one can imagine, adherence to an Antabuse regimen can be a problem. The drinker must already be strongly committed to change. If an alcohol abuser is able and willing to take the drug every morning as prescribed, the chances are probably good that drinking will lessen because of the negative consequences of imbibing (Sisson & Azrin, 1989). However,

Antabuse is used to treat alcohol dependence, but is not a very effective treatment because many people stop taking it. (Mark Alberhasky/imagema.com.)

Focus on Discovery 10.4

Matching Patient to Treatment—Project MATCH

For many years, both practitioners and researchers have assumed that it is important to employ treatments that are suitable for particular patients. But Project MATCH, a large, 8-year, multisite study on alcohol abuse (Project MATCH Research Group, 1997), has become controversial in professional circles because of its failure to find what it was looking for—namely—a way to match particular kinds of alcohol-dependent patients with specific interventions.

Several factors that had been found in previous research to be associated with outcome of intervention were used to match patients with treatments. These factors included severity of alcohol dependency, severity of cognitive impairment, motivation to change, severity of psychological disturbance (referred to as "psychiatric severity"), support from one's social milieu for drinking, and sociopathic tendencies. There were three treatments:

- Twelve-step facilitation treatment (TSF) was designed to convert patients to the AA view of alcoholism as an incurable but manageable disease and to encourage their involvement in AA.
- Motivational-enhancement therapy (MET), based on William Miller's motivational interviewing approach (Miller et al., 1992), attempted to mobilize the person's own resources to reduce drinking. Part of this intervention involved highlighting for the person the ways in which current maladaptive behavior was interfering with the attainment of goals.
- Cognitive behavioral coping-skills therapy (CBT) presented to patients the idea that drinking is functionally related to problems in a person's life; this treatment taught patients skills for coping with situations that trigger drinking or for preventing relapse.

The researchers predicted that drinkers under heavy pressure to stop would do best with the TSF, that those with psychological problems would do best with CBT, and that those with low motivation to change would do best with MET.

All treatments were carefully administered in individual sessions by trained therapists over a 12-week period, following treatment manuals prepared for this study. Patients could not be dependent on other drugs and otherwise had to have reasonably stable lives. As in other efficacy studies, internal validity was quite good, but external validity—the generalizability of the findings to therapy as actually practiced—was apparently low.

The principal outcomes measured were percentage of days abstinent and drinks per drinking day during a 1-year posttreatment assessment period. Figure 10.a shows the main results of this study. Significant within-group improvement was observed—all treatments were very helpful on average, consistent with a subsequent study (Ouimette et al., 1997). But as noted at the outset of this discussion, predictions about which patients would benefit most from which therapy were not confirmed, except that patients in better psychological shape had more abstinent days after TSF than did patients who received CBT. However, patients in worse psychological condition did not fare differently across

the three treatments. And even this one significant finding did not hold up at the 1-year follow-up (Fuller & Allen, 2000).

Apparently, we have a long way to go before we can make statements with confidence about the kinds of patients who will benefit from particular treatments.

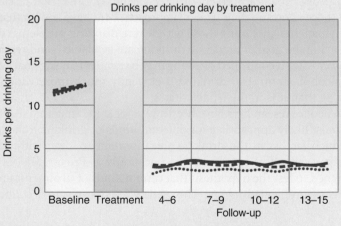

Figure 10.a   Monthly percentage of days abstinent and drinks per drinking day (DDD) for baseline (averaged over 3 months prior to treatment) and for each month of the posttreatment period (months 1–15).

in a large, multicenter study with placebo controls, Antabuse was not shown to have any specific benefit, and drop-out rates were as high as 80 percent (Fuller, 1988; Fuller et al., 1986).

The Food and Drug Administration approved the opiate antagonists naltrexone and naloxone (discussed in the section on treatment for heroin dependence), which block the activity of endorphins that are stimulated by alcohol, thus reducing the craving for it. Evidence is mixed regarding whether these drugs are more effective than a placebo in reducing drinking when they are the only treatment (Krystal et al., 2001). But they do appear to add to overall treatment effectiveness when combined with cognitive behavioral therapy (Streeton & Whelan, 2001; Volpicelli et al., 1995, 1997). As with most other drug treatments we have discussed, the benefits of naltrexone and naloxone continue only for as long as the person continues to take them, and long-lasting compliance with the treatment is difficult to achieve (Johnson & Ait-Daoud, 2000; O'Malley et al., 1996).

Acamprosate, which has been in regular use in Europe for 17 years under the brand name Campral, was approved by the FDA in July, 2004. Although its action is not completely understood, researchers believe that it impacts the glutamate and GABA neurotransmitter systems and thereby reduces the cravings associated with withdrawal. A recent review of data from all published double-blind, placebo-controlled clinical trials of acamprosate among alcohol-dependent outpatients suggests that it is highly effective (Mason, 2001). A meta-analysis comparing the effectiveness of acamprosate and naltrexone found them equally effective (Kranzler & Van Kirk, 2001). Newer pharmacological agents currently in development are targeting cravings rather than the drinking itself. In terms of incentive-sensitization theory (p. 337), the newer drugs are targeting wanting, not liking.

Though not specifically targeted to alcohol dependence, certain psychoactive drugs are used to treat problems that can co-occur with drinking. Thus, antidepressants may be used for depression and antianxiety medications for anxiety. By bringing about improvement in comorbid mental disorders which are often associated with problem drinking, these drugs can have a beneficial impact on alcohol dependence and abuse. For example, fluoxetine (Prozac) has produced improvement in depression and reduced drinking among alcohol abusers who are also depressed (Cornelius et al., 1997).

It should be noted that the use of drugs to treat alcohol-abusing patients carries some risk. Liver function is often impaired in these patients, and therefore the metabolism of the prescribed drug in the liver can be adversely affected, leading to undesirable side effects (Klerman et al., 1994). There is also the more general question of whether treating a substance abuse problem by giving another drug is necessarily a prudent strategy if one believes that some people come to rely on drugs in part because they are looking for a chemical solution to problems in their lives. Nevertheless, to the extent that medications are an effective treatment for alcohol dependence, disallowing them due to a concern over substituting one drug for another seems misguided.

Quick Summary

Inpatient hospital treatment for alcohol dependence is not as common today as it was in earlier years, primarily due to the cost. Detoxification from alcohol does often take place in hospitals, but treatment after this is more commonly done in outpatient settings.

Alcoholics Anonymous (AA) is the most common form of treatment for alcohol dependence. It is a group-based self-help treatment that instills the notion of alcohol dependence as disease. Though not widely studied, available research suggests that AA is an effective treatment.

There is some evidence that behavioral couples therapy is an effective treatment. Family interventions may be effective for preventing alcohol dependence among adolescents.

Aversion therapies, including administering shock or giving the medicine Antabuse, are not effective treatments in the long run. Non-compliance is a big problem. Contingency management therapy, which involves teaching patients and those close to them to reinforce behaviors inconsistent with drinking has shown some promise. Controlled drinking refers to a pattern of alcohol consumption that is moderate, avoiding the extremes of total abstinence and inebriation. The guided self-change treatment approach emphasizes control over moderate drinking, the costs of drinking to excess, and the benefits of abstaining.

Recently approved medications for alcohol dependence treatment include naltrexone and naloxone. It is not clear that they are effective on their own, but they do seem to be beneficial in combination with cognitive behavior therapy. Early evidence suggests that acamprosate may be an effective medication. Like all medications, these can have side effects and thus their use needs to be monitored.

Laws that have banned smoking in many places have probably increased the frequency of quitting. (Hugh Rogers.)

Treatment of Nicotine Dependence

The numerous laws that currently prohibit smoking in restaurants, trains, airplanes, and public buildings are part of a social context that provides incentives and support to stop smoking. We now know that smokers who quit before age 50 reduce their risk of dying in the following 15 years by half, as compared with those who continue to smoke (USDHHS, 1998b).

Some smokers who want to quit attend smoking clinics or consult with professionals for other specialized smoking-reduction programs. Even so, it is estimated that only about half of those who go through smoking-cessation programs succeed in abstaining by the time the program is over; only about 20 percent of those who have succeeded in the short term actually remain nonsmoking after a year. The greatest success overall is found among smokers who are better educated, older, or have acute health problems (USDHHS, 1998b).

Psychological Treatments This evidence does not belie the fact that a substantial minority of smokers can be helped; as with other efforts to change behavior, though, the task is not easy.

Many techniques have been tried. The idea behind some of them is to make smoking unpleasant, even nauseating. For a while in the 1970s there was considerable interest in rapid-smoking treatment, in which a smoker sits in a poorly ventilated room and puffs much faster than normal, perhaps as often as every 6 seconds (Lando, 1977). Newer variations include rapid puffing (rapid smoking without inhaling), focused smoking (smoking for a long period of time but at a normal rate), and smoke holding (retaining smoke in the mouth for several minutes but without inhaling). Although such treatments reduce smoking and foster abstinence more than no-treatment control conditions, they usually do not differ in effectiveness from each other or from other treatment approaches, showing high rates of relapse at follow-ups of several months to a year (Sobell, Toneatto, & Sobell, 1990).

Cognitively oriented investigators have tried to encourage more control in people who smoke; treatments aim at having people develop and use coping skills, such as relaxation and positive self-talk when confronted with tempting situations—for example, following a meal or sitting down to read a book. Results are not very promising, however (S.S. Smith et al., 2001).

In contrast, a review indicated that scheduled smoking shows real promise (Compas et al., 1998). The strategy is to reduce nicotine intake gradually over a period of a few weeks by getting smokers to agree to increase the time between cigarettes. For example, during the first week of treatment, a one-pack-a-day smoker would be put on a schedule allowing only 10 cigarettes per day; during the second week only five cigarettes a day would be allowed; and during the third week, the person would taper off to zero. The cigarettes would have to be smoked on a schedule provided by the treatment team, not when the smoker feels an intense craving. In this way, the person's smoking behavior is controlled by the passage of time rather than by urges, mood states, or situations. Smokers who are able to stay with the agreed-on schedule showed a 44 percent abstinence rate after one year, a very impressive outcome (Cinciripini et al., 1994).

Probably the most widespread psychological treatment consists of a physician telling the person to stop smoking. Each year millions of smokers are given this counsel—because of hypertension, heart disease, lung disease, or diabetes, on general grounds of preserving or improving health. Indeed, by age 65, most smokers have managed to quit (USDHHS, 1998b). There is some evidence that a physician's advice can get some people to stop smoking, at least for a while, especially when the person also chews nicotine gum (Law & Tang, 1995). But much more needs to be learned about the nature of the advice, the manner in which it is given, its timing, and other factors that must surely play a role in determining whether smokers are prepared and able to alter their behavior primarily on a physician's say-so (USDHHS, 1998b).

By age 18 about two-thirds of cigarette smokers regret having started smoking, one-half have already made an attempt to quit, and nearly 40 percent show interest in obtaining treatment for their dependence (Henningfield, Michaelides, & Sussman, et al., 2000).

Unfortunately, treatment in young people has not kept pace with the emerging need for treatment. A school-based program called Project EX includes training in coping skills and a psychoeducational component about the harmful effects of smoking. Two studies have found this program to be effective, both in the United States (Sussman, Dent, & Lichtman, 2001) and in China (Zheng et al., 2004), where the program was adapted to fit with Chinese culture and language.

Smoking reduction rather than cessation programs offer an alternative intervention for smokers who are not interested in quitting but wish to reduce the number of cigarettes they smoke. Currently there are no data on whether reduced smoking will reduce smoking risks. However, it appears that attempts at reduction do not undermine the probability of not smoking at all in the future. On the contrary, it appears that reduction promotes future cessation (Hughes, 2000).

People have trouble quitting for many different reasons, and diverse methods need to be developed to help them. Yet in their zeal to make an impact on the smoking problem, clinicians have until recently put smokers in standardized programs. Future efforts will no doubt require careful attention to the diverse psychological factors that are associated with continuing to smoke even knowing it is unhealthful to do so. A focus on the addicting nature of nicotine also merits attention, a topic to which we turn next.

Nicotine Replacement Treatments and Medications   Reducing a smoker's craving for nicotine by providing it in a different way is the goal of nicotine replacement treatments. Attention to nicotine dependence is clearly important because the more cigarettes people smoke daily, the less successful they are at quitting. Nicotine may be supplied in gum, patches, or inhalers. The idea is to help smokers endure the nicotine withdrawal that accompanies any effort to stop smoking. Although nicotine replacement alleviates withdrawal symptoms—which justifies its use in gum and in the nicotine patches to be described next—the severity of withdrawal is only minimally related to success in stopping smoking (Hughes et al., 1990; Hughes & Hatsukami, 1992).

Gum containing nicotine has been available in the United States since 1984 by doctor's prescription, and it is now available over the counter. The nicotine in gum is absorbed much more slowly and steadily than that in tobacco. The long-term goal is for the former smoker to be able to cut back on the use of the gum as well, eventually eliminating reliance on nicotine altogether.

This treatment involves some controversy, however. Ex-smokers can become dependent on the gum. Moreover, in doses that deliver an amount of nicotine equivalent to smoking one cigarette an hour, the gum causes cardiovascular changes, such as increased blood pressure, that can be dangerous to people with cardiovascular diseases. Nevertheless, some experts believe that even prolonged, continued use of the gum is healthier than obtaining nicotine by smoking, because at least the poisons in the smoke are avoided (de Wit & Zacny, 2000). The best results are obtained when the gum is combined with a behaviorally oriented treatment (Killen et al., 1990), although one well-controlled study showed no additional benefit from the gum over a behavioral treatment that emphasized education and environmental changes, such as the removal of ashtrays from home and work settings (Hill et al., 1994).

Nicotine patches became available in December 1991 with a doctor's prescription and in 1996 over the counter. A polyethylene patch taped to the arm serves as a transdermal (through the skin) nicotine delivery system that slowly and steadily releases the drug into the bloodstream and thence to the brain. An advantage of the patch over nicotine gum is that the person need only apply one patch each day and not remove it until applying the next patch, making compliance easier. Treatment usually lasts 10 to 12 weeks, with smaller and smaller patches used as treatment progresses. A drawback is that people who continue smoking while wearing the patch risk increasing the amount of nicotine in their body to dangerous levels.

Nicotine patches are available over the counter to help relieve withdrawal symptoms. (Jim Selby/Photo Researchers.)

Evidence suggests that the nicotine patch is superior to the use of a placebo patch in terms of both abstinence and subjective craving (Hughes & Hatsukami, 1992). However, as with nicotine gum, the patch is not a panacea. Abstinence rates are less than 40 percent immediately following the termination of treatment, and at nine-month follow-ups, differences between the drug and a placebo disappear. The manufacturers state that the patch is to be used only as part of a psychological smoking-cessation program and then for not more than 3 months at a time.

In nicotine replacement therapy involving an inhaler, the user inhales the nicotine through a plastic tube shaped like a cigarette holder. Unlike gum or patches, this method of nicotine delivery has some resemblance to smoking as the person handles the device and inhales. In a comparison of these inhalers with placebo inhalers that did not contain nicotine, one-year abstinence rates were 28 percent for the treatment group and 18 percent for the placebo group (Hjalmarson et al., 1997).

Research has shown that attempting to quit smoking can precipitate an episode of depression in someone who has previously been depressed, so researchers have also focused on the possible role of antidepressants in helping people quit. Thus far, the evidence shows that antidepressants that have strong effects on dopamine (and not on serotonin) do have some benefit, regardless of whether the person has a history of depression (Hall et al., 1998; Hurt, Sachs, & Glover, 1997). Patients are typically given an amount of the antidepressant that is less than would be used to treat depression. They take the drug for some period of time before trying to stop smoking and then continue taking the antidepressant for some amount of time (e.g., 7 weeks) as they try to give up smoking. One study combined brief counseling with either buprioprion (an antidepressant sold under the names of Wellbutrin and Zyban) or a placebo and found 1-year abstinence rates of 23 percent in the treated group and 12 percent in the placebo group (Hurt et al., 1997). Combining buprioprion and nicotine patches has yielded a 12-month abstinence rate of 35 percent, an impressive (albeit far from perfect) figure (Jorenby et al., 1999). Other promising non-nicotine pharmacotherapy for smoking cessation has included the antihypertensive drug clonidine and silver acetate (Benowitz & Peng, 2000), as well as glucose tablets (West, 2001).

Treatment of Illegal Drug Abuse and Dependence

Some factors involved in treatment for alcohol abuse are relevant also to treatment for drug abuse and dependence. Central to the treatment of people who use illegal drugs such as heroin and cocaine is detoxification—withdrawal from the drug itself. Heroin-withdrawal reactions range from relatively mild bouts of anxiety, nausea, and restlessness for several days to more severe and frightening bouts of delirium and panic, depending primarily on the purity of the heroin that the individual has been using. Withdrawal from amphetamines can be accomplished by appropriate dosages of one of the phenothiazines, a class of drugs used to treat schizophrenia (see p. 373), although it is important to remember that the person may also have been using other drugs in conjunction with amphetamines. Withdrawal reactions from barbiturates are especially severe, even life threatening; they begin about 24 hours after the last dose and peak 2 or 3 days later. They usually abate by the end of the first week but may last for a month if large doses were taken. Withdrawal from barbiturates is best undertaken gradually, not cold turkey (a term that derives from the goosebumps that occur during withdrawal, making the person's skin resemble that of a plucked turkey), and should take place under close medical supervision.

Detoxification is the first way in which therapists try to help an individual dependent on a drug, and it may be the easiest part of the rehabilitation process. Enabling the drug user to function without drugs after detoxification is extremely difficult—typically, both therapist and client experience more disappointment and sadness than success in this process. A variety of approaches to this task are available, including psychological treatments, drug substitution treatments, and medications.

Psychological Treatments Drug abuse and dependence are sometimes treated in the consulting rooms of psychiatrists, psychologists, and other mental health workers. Several kinds of psychotherapy are applied to drug-use disorders, often in combination with medication or drug substitution treatments aimed at reducing the physical dependence.

In the first direct comparison in a controlled study, the antidepressant medication desipramine and a cognitive behavioral treatment (CBT) were both found to be somewhat effective in reducing cocaine use as well as in improving abusers' family, social, and general psychological functioning (Carroll, Rounsaville, Gordon, et al., 1994; Carroll et al., 1995). In this 12-week study, desipramine was better than a placebo in patients with a low degree of dependence on cocaine, whereas CBT was better in patients with a high degree of dependence. This finding illustrates the significance of the psychological aspects of substance abuse.

In this study, patients receiving CBT learned how to avoid high-risk situations (e.g., being around people using cocaine), recognize the lure of the drug for them, and develop alternatives to using cocaine (e.g., recreational activities with nonusers). Cocaine abusers in this study also learned strategies for coping with the craving and for resisting the tendency to regard a slip as a catastrophe ("relapse prevention training," per Marlatt & Gordon, 1985). The more depressed the patient, the more favorable the outcome from both the antidepressant drug and CBT. Overall, the results for CBT were superior to those for the antidepressant drug in reducing cocaine use, and this pattern was maintained at a one-year follow-up (Carroll, Rounsaville, Nich, et al., 1994). The authors of the study take pains to point out that different treatments are probably necessary for different kinds of patients, a theme that is increasingly evident in the therapy literature. A more recent study testing the effectiveness of CBT for drug abuse in a community setting found that there was no difference in outcomes between CBT and standard substance-abuse counseling (Morgenstern et al., 2001). We have a ways to go in order to make our treatments more effective in community settings.

A treatment based more on operant conditioning has shown some promise. Vouchers are provided for not using cocaine or heroin (verified by urine samples), and the tokens are exchangeable for things that the person would like to have more of (Dallery et al., 2001; Katz et al., 2001; Silverman et al., 1996).

A treatment called *motivational interviewing* has also shown some promise. This treatment involves a combination of CBT techniques and techniques associated with the humanistic therapy of Carl Rogers (see p. 541). It was one of the treatments used in Project MATCH described in Focus on Discovery 10.4. A recent meta-analysis of this treatment found that it was effective for both alcohol and illegal drug dependence and abuse (Burke, Arkowitz, & Menchola, 2003).

Self-help residential homes are another psychological approach to treating heroin addiction and other types of drug abuse and dependence. Modeled after Synanon, a therapeutic community of people formerly addicted to drugs founded in 1958 by Charles Dederich in Santa Monica, California, these residences are designed to restructure radically the addict's outlook on life so that illicit drugs

Group therapy in residential settings is frequently used to treat heroin addiction. (David M. Grossman/Photo Researchers.)

no longer have a place. Daytop Village, Phoenix House, Odyssey House, and other drug-rehabilitation homes share the following features:

- Separation of patients from previous social contacts, on the assumption that these relationships have been instrumental in maintaining the drug dependence.
- A comprehensive environment in which drugs are not available and continuing support is offered to ease the transition from regular drug use to a drug-free existence.
- The presence of charismatic role models, people formerly dependent on drugs who appear to be meeting life's challenges without drugs.

- Direct, often brutal confrontation in group therapy, in which patients are goaded into accepting responsibility for their problems and for their drug habits and are urged to take charge of their lives.
- A setting in which patients are respected as human beings rather than stigmatized as failures or criminals.

There are several obstacles to evaluating the efficacy of residential drug-treatment programs. Since entrance is voluntary, only a small minority of dependent users enter such settings. Furthermore, because the drop-out rate is high, those who remain cannot be regarded as representative of the population of people addicted to illegal drugs; their motivation to stop using drugs is probably much stronger than that of the average addict. Any improvement participants in these programs make may reflect their uncommonly strong desire to rid themselves of the habit more than the specific qualities of the treatment program. Such self-regulating residential communities do, however, appear to help a large number of those who remain in them for a year or so (Institute of Medicine, 1990; Jaffe, 1985).

In 2000, voters in California approved Proposition 36, enacted into law in 2001 as the Substance Abuse and Crime Prevention Act (SACPA). The act allows nonviolent drug offenders to be sent to drug treatment rather than prison. Participation in this program is voluntary—someone meeting the criteria of SACPA has the choice of treatment or prison. In the first 2 years of the program, over 50,000 offenders were eligible and about 70 percent chose treatment over standard criminal justice proceedings. UCLA is in the midst of conducting a 5-year, prospective study of this program; thus far, findings from the first year suggest that the program is working, at least with respect to treatment completion. Just over one-third of those in treatment in year one completed the treatment. This may seem low, but it is actually quite favorable in comparison to completion rates of other programs, particularly those to which offenders are referred by the criminal justice system (Longshore et al., 2003). Time will tell if the program is successful in keeping individuals out of the criminal justice system.

Drug Replacement Treatments and Medications   Two widely used programs for heroin dependence involve the administration of *heroin substitutes*, drugs chemically similar to heroin that can replace the body's craving for it, or *opiate antagonists*, drugs that prevent the user from experiencing the heroin high. Recall from Chapter 2 (p. 38) that an antagonist is a drug that dampens the activity of neurotransmitters, and an agonist is a drug that stimulates neurotransmitters. The first category includes **methadone**, levomethadyl acetate, and bupreophine, synthetic narcotics designed to take the place of heroin. Since these drugs are themselves addicting, successful treatment essentially converts the individual's dependence on heroin into dependence on a different substance. This conversion occurs because these synthetic narcotics are **cross-dependent** with heroin; that is, by acting on the same central nervous system receptors, they become a substitute for the original dependency. Abrupt discontinuation of methadone results in its own pattern of withdrawal reactions, but because these reactions are less severe than those of heroin, methadone has potential for weaning the heroin users altogether from drug dependence (Strain et al., 1999).

Treatment with a heroin substitute usually involves going to a drug-treatment clinic and swallowing the drug in the presence of a staff member, once a day for methadone and three times a week for levomethadyl acetate and bupreophine. In some cases, the person receives treatment instead through weekly visits to a primary care physician, and there is some evidence that methadone maintenance carried out in this way is as effective as treatment in narcotic treatment programs (Fiellin et al., 2001). Some heroin users receiving methadone are able to hold jobs, commit no crimes, and refrain from using other illicit drugs (Eissenberg et al., 1997; Sees et al., 2000; Schottenfeld et al., 2000), but other users are unable to do so (Condelli et al., 1991). The effectiveness of methadone treatment is improved if a high (80–100 milligram) dose is used as opposed to the more typical 40–50 milligram dose (Strain et al., 1999) and if it is combined with regular psychological counseling (Ball & Ross, 1991). Drug treatment experts generally believe that treatment

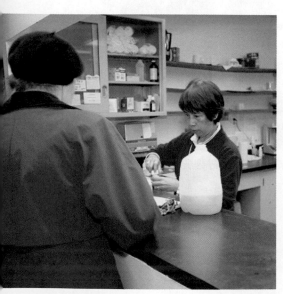

Methadone is a synthetic heroin substitute. People formerly addicted to heroin come to clinics each day and swallow their dose. (John Giordano/Corbis SABA.)

with heroin substitutes is best conducted in the context of a supportive social interaction and not merely as a medical encounter (Lilly et al., 2000).

Since methadone does not provide a euphoric high, many people will return to heroin if it becomes available to them. In addition, many people drop out of methadone programs, in part because of side effects such as insomnia, constipation, excessive sweating, and diminished sexual functioning. The stigma associated with going to methadone clinics is also linked to drop out rates, as illustrated in the case of James described above. Age of entry into treatment may be important—the older the individual, the greater the likelihood that he or she will stick with the treatment regimen (Friedmann, Lemon, & Stein, 2001).

Methadone programs may reduce the frequency of risky sexual behaviors: Some evidence suggests that methadone patients have fewer sexual partners as well as fewer high-risk sexual partners, and use condoms more than nonmethadone patients (Lollis et al., 2000; Sorensen & Copeland, 2000). A report from the Council on Scientific Affairs on methadone maintenance therapy confirms that it reduces heroin use and associated problems in a cost-effective manner without negative public health impacts (Yoast et al., 2001).

In treatment with the opiate or heroin antagonists such as naloxone or naltrexone, people are first gradually weaned from heroin. They then receive increasing dosages of one of these drugs, which prevents them from experiencing any high should they later take heroin. These drugs work because they have great affinity for the receptors to which opiates usually bind; their molecules occupy the receptors without stimulating them. This leaves heroin molecules with no place to go and therefore heroin does not have its usual effect on the user. As with methadone, however, treatment with heroin antagonists involves frequent and regular visits to a clinic, which requires motivation. In addition, patients do not lose the craving for heroin for some time. Both clinical effectiveness and treatment compliance can be increased by adding a contingency-management component to the therapy (Carroll et al., 2001). Giving patients vouchers that they can exchange for food and clothing in return for taking naltrexone and having drug-free urine samples markedly improves effectiveness.

Given the limitations of heroin substitutes such as methadone and other opiate antagonists, researchers have been searching for alternative medications. In 2003, a new prescription drug was introduced that may well revolutionize treatment of heroin dependence. Buprenorphine (trade name Suboxone) is a new prescription medication that actually contains two agents: buprenorphine and naloxone. Buprenorphine is a partial opiate agonist, which means it does not have the same powerfully addicting properties as heroin, which is a full agonist. Naloxone is one of the opiate antagonists described above. This unique combination in Suboxone does not produce an intense high, is only mildly addictive, and lasts for as long as three days. Heroin users do not need to go to a clinic to receive this medication since it can be prescribed to individual patients. Thus, this treatment avoids the stigma associated with visiting methadone clinics. Buprenorphine is effective at relieving withdrawal symptoms, and because it lasts longer than methadone, researchers are hopeful that relapse will be less likely. Still, some users may miss the more euphoric high associated with heroin, thus hastening a relapse.

Research continues to search for drugs that will ease the symptoms of withdrawal and perhaps also attack the cravings linked to cocaine addiction; the findings so far are mixed. For example, two similarly conducted double-blind experiments compared the tricyclic antidepressant desipramine (Norpramine) with a placebo. In the first study, cocaine abusers who used Norpramine did not show decreased use of cocaine at the end of 8 weeks of treatment (Kosten et al., 1992). In the second study, cocaine use was significantly greater in Norpramine users than in placebo patients at 3- and 6-month follow-ups after a 12-week treatment period (Arndt et al., 1992). Similarly, while imipramine (Tofranil) helped alleviate depression in cocaine abusers who were depressed, it did not help the patients achieve abstinence from cocaine (Nunes et al., 1998). However, desipramine fared better in another study, which will be discussed shortly (Carroll, Rounsaville, Gordon, et al., 1994). Researchers are also working on a possible vaccine to help stave off the cravings for cocaine. The vaccine contains tiny amounts of cocaine attached to otherwise harmless pathogens. The body's immune system responds to this invasion by developing antibodies that then squelch the cocaine. It is hoped that with repeated exposure, the antibodies will be able to keep a good deal of the cocaine taken by abusers from reaching the brain.

Developing effective treatments for methamphetamine dependence remains a challenge for the field. People like Anton described in the case earlier do not have many places to turn for treatment. The largest effort to date is a randomized controlled clinical trial conducted across eight different sites referred to as the Methamphetamine Treatment Project (Rawson et al., 2004). This study compared a multifaceted treatment called Matrix with treatment as usual. The Matrix treatment consisted of 16 cognitive behavior therapy group sessions, 12 family education sessions, 4 individual therapy sessions, and 4 social support group sessions. Treatment as usual (TAU) consisted of the best available treatment currently offered at the eight outpatient clinics. This varied quite a bit across the sites, with some offering individual counseling and others offering group counseling; some offering 4 weeks of treatment, others offering 16 weeks. Results of the study are somewhat supportive of the Matrix treatment. Compared to those in TAU, those people receiving Matrix stayed in treatment longer and were less likely to use methamphetamine during treatment (confirmed with urine analysis). However, at the end of treatment and at the 6-month follow-up, the Matrix treatment was no longer superior to TAU. That is, people who received Matrix were no less likely to have used methamphetamine than those in TAU. The good news is that all participants were less likely to use methamphetamine after 6 months, regardless of whether they received Matrix or TAU. Although these results are promising, additional work is clearly needed to develop effective treatments for methamphetamine abuse and dependence.

A final cautionary note. As successful as all these efforts are, the fact remains that most people who participate in drug-treatment programs do not achieve abstinence by the end of treatment, and of those who do, the majority fail to remain abstinent. Drug dependence remains a serious societal and health problem that resists even the most intensive therapeutic efforts. Building relapse prevention components into any treatment program can help increase the treatment's success, a topic we return to in the next section on prevention.

Quick Summary

Psychological treatments have not been all that effective for nicotine dependence. Scheduled smoking involves reducing nicotine intake gradually over a period of a few weeks, and it has shown some promise. Nicotine gum appears to be somewhat effective, though users can become dependent on the gum. Nicotine patches are more effective than placebo patches, but nine months after the treatment, abstinence differences between the drug and a placebo disappear. Adding buprioprion or therapy along with nicotine patches may be effective.

Detoxification is usually the first step in treatment for drug dependence. There is some evidence that CBT is an effective treatment for cocaine dependence. Motivational interviewing has shown promise for the treatment of alcohol and other drug dependence. Residential treatment homes have not been adequately evaluated for their efficacy though they are a common form of treatment.

The use of heroin substitutes, such as methadone, is an effective treatment for heroin dependence. Methadone can only be administered in a special clinic, and there is stigma associated with this type of treatment. A newly approved prescription drug called buprenorphine can be taken from home. Treating methamphetamine dependence remains a challenge.

Prevention of Substance-Related Disorders

From all that is known about the etiology of substance abuse, discouraging people from ever beginning to abuse drugs makes the most sense. It is difficult—often impossible—for people to stop using substances that create both psychological and physical dependency. We turn our attention next to prevention efforts in the realms of alcohol abuse, illegal drug abuse, and cigarette smoking.

Many prevention efforts have been aimed at adolescents because substance abuse in adulthood often follows experimentation in the teens and earlier. Programs, usually conducted in schools, have been directed at enhancing the young adolescent's self-esteem, teaching social skills, and encouraging the young person to say no to peer pressure. The results are mixed (Hansen, 1993; Jansen et al., 1996). Self-esteem enhancement has not demonstrated its effectiveness. In contrast, social skills training and resistance training (learning to say no) have shown some positive results, particularly with girls. A highly publicized program, Project DARE (Drug Abuse Resistance Education), which combines effective education and resistance training and is delivered by police officers in fifth- and sixth-grade classrooms, has shown disappointing results (Clayton, Catterello, & Walden, 1991; Ringwalt, Ennett, & Holt, 1991). Other preventive efforts, yet to be adequately evaluated, include the following:

- Parental involvement in school programs for their children.
- Warning labels on containers of alcoholic beverages (mandated by law in 1989).
- Informing consumers that drinking alcohol during pregnancy can cause birth defects in the fetus and that alcohol impairs driving a car and operating machinery.
- Cautionary announcements in the media about stiff legal penalties for driving under the influence of alcohol or other drugs and exhortations to arrange for designated drivers before imbibing at social occasions.
- Testing for alcohol and drugs in the workplace or schools.

Half of adult smokers began their habit before the age of 15, and nearly all before the age of 19 (USDHHS, 1998b). Thus, developing ways of discouraging young people from experimenting with tobacco has become a top priority among health researchers and politicians, with encouragement from the Surgeon General and funding from the National Cancer Institute, one of the National Institutes of Health. The American Legacy Foundation is an organization developed to prevent smoking among young people, and this organization was funded in part from the settlement that followed this class action lawsuit against tobacco companies in 1999.

The measures that hold promise for persuading young people to resist smoking may be useful also in dissuading them from trying illicit drugs and alcohol. Brief family interventions show such promise. In Iowa, the Iowa Strengthening Families Program and the five-session Preparing for the Drug Free Years Program have been found to forestall the onset of nicotine and alcohol use among teens (Spoth et al., 2004). These programs target families with early adolescents and include skills-based training in risk and protective factors linked to substance abuse.

Statewide comprehensive tobacco control programs, which include increasing taxes on cigarettes, restricting tobacco advertising, conducting public education campaigns, and creating smoke-free environments, appear to be an effective strategy for reducing teenage smoking (Wakefield & Chaloupka, 2000). In addition, recent years have seen scores of school-based programs aimed at preventing young people from starting to use tobacco. By and large, such programs have succeeded in delaying the onset of smoking (Sussman et al., 1995). These programs share some common components, not all of them shown to be effective (Evans, 2001; Hansen, 1992; Sussman, 1996):

- *Peer pressure resistance training.* Students learn about the nature of peer pressure and ways to say no. Overall, studies suggest that programs based on peer-pressure resistance training are effective in reducing the onset and level of tobacco use, as well as illegal drug use, in young people (Tobler et al., 2000).
- *Correction of beliefs and expectations.* Many young people believe that cigarette smoking is more prevalent (and by implication, more okay) than it actually is. Changing beliefs about the prevalence of smoking has been shown to be an effective strategy, perhaps because of the sensitivity young people have to what others their age do and believe. Establishing that it is not standard behavior to smoke cigarettes (or drink alcohol or use marijuana) appears to be significantly more effective than resistance training (Hansen & Graham, 1991).

- *Inoculation against mass-media messages*. Some prevention programs try to counter the positive images of smokers that have been put forth in the media (e.g., the Joe Camel ads mentioned earlier). Sophisticated mass-media campaigns, similar to the ones that have made tobacco a profitable consumer product, can be successful in discouraging smoking. For example, the *truth* campaign, instituted by the American Legacy Foundation, developed websites (www.thetruth.com and www.fairenough.com) and radio and television ads to tell youth about the health and social consequences of smoking and the ways in which the tobacco industry targets them so that they can make informed choices about whether to smoke. This campaign has been well-received among youth, and a recent study found that awareness and agreement with the *truth* messages were associated with less smoking among teens (Niederdeppe, Farrelly, & Haviland, 2004). These findings are particularly encouraging since we know that teenagers' receptivity to tobacco marketing is strongly related to whether or not they will actually smoke (Unger et al., 2001).

- *Information about parental and other adult influences*. Since it is known that parental smoking is strongly correlated with and most probably contributes to smoking by their children, some programs point out this fact and argue that this aspect of one's parents' behavior does not have to be imitated.

- *Peer leadership*. Most smoking and other drug-prevention programs involve peers of recognized status, which adds to the impact of the messages being conveyed.

- *Other components*. Additional features of preventive programs include information about the harmful effects of smoking or of drug use (a common element in adult smoking-cessation programs but not demonstrated to be effective with young people) and producing a public commitment not to smoke, such as making a commitment on videotape. Attention to other risk factors is also important because smoking prevalence is higher among children who are depressed or are having family or school problems (USDHHS, 1998b).

Relapse Prevention

Relapse prevention is an important part of any treatment for drug or alcohol dependence. Mark Twain quipped that stopping smoking was easy—he'd done it hundreds of times! In treating those dependent on alcohol, patients are taught—or more precisely, are encouraged to believe—that a lapse will not inevitably precipitate a total relapse and should be regarded as a learning experience rather than as a sign that the battle is lost, a marked contrast from the AA perspective (Marlatt & Gordon, 1985). This noncatastrophizing approach to relapse after therapy—falling off the wagon—is important because the overwhelming majority of problem drinkers who become abstinent do experience one or more relapses over a four-year period (Polich, Armor, & Braiker, 1980). Alcohol abusers examine sources of stress in their work, family, and relationships so that they can become active and responsible in anticipating and resisting situations that might lead them into excessive drinking (Marlatt, 1983; Sobell, Toneatto, & Sobell, 1990). And when they do lapse, as mentioned, they are encouraged not to see it as a sign that they are going to return to their earlier alcohol-dependent state.

Most smokers relapse within a year of stopping, regardless of the means used to stop. In a pattern we have already seen, people who smoked the most—and are presumably more addicted to nicotine—relapse more often and more quickly than moderate or light smokers. Frequent slips, younger age, nicotine dependence, low self-efficacy, weight concerns, and previous quitting attempts are all predictors of relapse (Ockene et al., 2000).

What factors contribute to success? Research results (and common sense) tell us that ex-smokers who do not live with a smoker do better at follow-up than those who do live with a smoker (McIntyre-Kingsolver, Lichtenstein, & Mermelstein, 1986). So-called booster or maintenance sessions help, but in a very real sense they represent a continuation of treatment; when they stop, relapse is the rule (Brandon, Zelman, & Baker, 1987). Intensive interventions, such as a telephone counseling (Brandon et al., 2000), also helps; however, they reach relatively few smokers. Brief relapse prevention interventions during medical visits are cost-effective and could potentially reach most smokers but are not consistently delivered (Ockene et al., 2000). On a positive note, there is considerably more social support for not smoking than there was just 10 years ago, at least in the United States. Perhaps as time goes on, societal sanctions against smoking will help those who have succeeded in quitting remain abstinent. (It is certainly more difficult to find a place to light up nowadays.)

One specific approach to the relapse problem is to focus on the cognitions of ex-smokers (Baer & Lichtenstein, 1988). Using the articulated thoughts paradigm (see p. 87), a study found that recent ex-smokers who tended to think of smoking without prompting relapsed more readily 3 months later (Haaga, 1989). However, if ex-smokers learned some effective ways of countering these smoking-related thoughts, such as distracting themselves, their abstinence was better months later. Using a questionnaire measure, a study found that ex-smokers' self-efficacy in facing their most difficult challenge—for example, not smoking while having coffee and dessert following a pleasant dinner—was a good predictor of abstinence a year later (Haaga, 1990). These and related studies indicate that the prediction of continued abstinence or relapse is enhanced by measuring the cognitions of ex-smokers. Such information may help therapists design programs that will improve the ability of a specific person to remain a nonsmoker (Compas et al., 1998).

Check Your Knowledge 10.5

Matching—match the treatment approach to the type of substance(s).

Treatment
1. Suboxone
2. AA
3. Couples therapy
4. opiate antagonist
5. antidepressant
6. patch
7. Matrix

Substance
a. alcohol
b. heroin
c. cocaine
d. nicotine
e. methamphetamine

Summary

Clinical Descriptions

- Using substances to alter mood and consciousness is a human characteristic, and so too is the tendency to abuse them. DSM-IV-TR distinguishes between substance dependence and substance abuse. Dependence refers to a compulsive pattern of substance use and consequent serious psychological and physical impairments, often including tolerance and withdrawal. In the less serious disorder, substance abuse, drug use leads to failure to meet obligations and to interpersonal and legal problems.

- Alcohol has a variety of short-term and long-term effects on human beings, ranging from poor judgment and impaired motor coordination to chronic health problems.

- People can become dependent on nicotine, most often via smoking cigarettes. Despite somberly phrased warnings from public-health offi-

cials, it continues to be used. Medical problems associated with long-term cigarette smoking include many cancers, emphysema, and cardiovascular disease. Moreover, the health hazards of smoking are not restricted to those who smoke, for secondhand (environmental) smoke can also cause lung damage and other problems.

- Recent trends indicate that marijuana use declined in the 1980s, increased in the 1990s, and has leveled off since then. When used regularly, marijuana can damage the lungs and cardiovascular system and lead to cognitive impairments. Constituents of marijuana may also adversely affect heart function in people who already have coronary problems, and pulmonary function. Further, tolerance to marijuana can develop. Ironically, just as the possible dangers of marijuana began to be uncovered, it was found to have therapeutic effects, easing the nausea of cancer patients undergoing chemotherapy, and easing discomfort associated with AIDS.

● Opiates slow the activities of the body and, in moderate doses, are used to relieve pain and induce sleep. Heroin has been a focus of concern because usage is up and stronger varieties have become available. Another group is the synthetic sedatives and tranquilizers. Barbiturates have been implicated in both intentional and accidental suicides; they are particularly lethal when taken with alcohol.

● Stimulants, which include amphetamines and cocaine, act on the brain and the sympathetic nervous system to increase alertness and motor activity. Tolerance and withdrawal are associated with all these drugs. Methamphetamine abuse, a derivative of amphetamine, has risen dramatically since the 1990s.

● The hallucinogens—LSD, mescaline, and psilocybin—alter or expand consciousness. Their use reflects humankind's desire not only to escape from unpleasant realities but also to explore inner space. Use of the hallucinogen-like drug Ecstasy has dramatically risen, and it is also considered a threat to health. PCP use often leads to violence.

Etiology

● Several factors are related to the etiology of substance abuse and dependence. Sociocultural variables, such as attitudes toward the substance, peer pressure, and how the substance is portrayed by the media, are all related to how frequently a substance is used. Many substances are used to alter mood (e.g., to reduce tension or increase positive affect), and people with certain personality traits, such as those high in negative affect or psychopathy, are especially likely to use drugs. Cognitive variables, such as the expectation that the drug will yield positive effects, are also important. Finally, neurobiological factors, most notably a genetic predisposition or diathesis and the brain's reward pathways, appear to play a role in the use of some substances.

Treatment

● Treatments of all kinds have been used to help people refrain from the use of both legal drugs (e.g., alcohol and nicotine) and illegal drugs (e.g., heroin and cocaine). Biological treatments have attempted to release users from their dependency often by substituting another drug. Some benefits have been observed for treatments using such drugs as clonidine, naltrexone, and methadone. Nicotine replacement via gum, patches, or inhalers has met with some success in reducing cigarette smoking. None of these approaches appears to lead to enduring change, however, unless accompanied by psychological treatments with such goals as helping patients resist pressures to indulge, cope with normal life stress, control emotions without relying on chemicals, and make use of social supports, such as Alcoholics Anonymous.

● Since it is far easier never to begin using drugs than to stop using them, considerable effort has been expended in recent years to prevent substance abuse by implementing educational and social programs to equip young people to develop their lives without a reliance on drugs.

Answers to Check Your Knowledge Questions

10.1 1. F; 2. T; 3. F; 4. T

10.2 1. nicotine, heroin, cocaine, alcohol; 2. lung, larynx, esophagus, pancreas, bladder, cervix, stomach; 3. short-term, long-term; 4. pain relief, reduce nausea, increase appetite, relief from the discomfort from AIDS

10.3 1. F; 2. F; 3. F; 4. T

10.4 1. b; 2. c; 3. a

10.5 1. b; 2. a; 3. a; 4. b; 5. a, c, d; 6. d; 7. e

Key Terms

addiction	detoxification	MDMA	polydrug abuse
amphetamines	Ecstasy	mescaline	psilocybin
Antabuse	fetal alcohol syndrome (FAS)	methadone	secondhand smoke
aversion therapy	flashback	methamphetamine	stimulants
barbiturates	hallucinogen	morphine	substance abuse
caffeine	hashish	nicotine	substance dependence
cocaine	heroin	nitrous oxide	substance-related disorders
controlled drinking	hydrocodone	opiates	tolerance
crack	LSD	opium	withdrawal
cross-dependent	marijuana	oxycodone	
delirium tremens (DTs)	MDA	PCP	

11 Schizophrenia

Learning Goals

1. Be able to describe the clinical symptoms of schizophrenia, including positive, negative, and disorganized symptoms.

2. Be able to differentiate the genetic factors, both behavioral and molecular, in the etiology of schizophrenia.

3. Be able to discuss how the brain has been implicated in schizophrenia, both in studies of etiology and in treatment.

4. Be able to describe the role of stress and other psychosocial factors in the etiology and relapse of schizophrenia.

5. Be able to distinguish the medication treatments and psychological treatments for schizophrenia.

All of a sudden things weren't going so well. I began to lose control of my life and, most of all, myself. I couldn't concentrate on my schoolwork, I couldn't sleep, and when I did sleep, I had dreams about dying. I was afraid to go to class, imagined that people were talking about me, and on top of that I heard voices. I called my mother in Pittsburgh and asked for her advice. She told me to move off campus into an apartment with my sister.

After I moved in with my sister, things got worse. I was afraid to go outside and when I looked out of the window, it seemed that everyone outside was yelling, "Kill her, kill her." My sister forced me to go to school. I would go out of the house until I knew she had gone to work; then I would return home. Things continued to get worse. I imagined that I had a foul body odor and I sometimes took up to 6 showers a day. I recall going to the grocery store one day, and I imagined that the people in the store were saying, "Get saved, Jesus is the answer." Things worsened—I couldn't remember a thing. I had a notebook full of reminders telling me what to do on that particular day. I couldn't remember my schoolwork, and I would study from 6:00 P.M. until 4:00 A.M. but never had the courage to go to class on the following day. I tried to tell my sister about it, but she didn't understand. She suggested that I see a psychiatrist, but I was afraid to go out of the house to see him.

One day I decided that I couldn't take this trauma anymore, so I took an overdose of 35 Darvon pills. At the same moment, a voice inside me said, "What did you do that for? Now you won't go to heaven." At that instant I realized that I didn't really want to die. I wanted to live, and I was afraid. I got on the phone and called the psychiatrist whom my sister had recommended. I told him I had taken an overdose of Darvon and that I was afraid. He told me to take a taxi to the hospital. When I arrived at the hospital, I began vomiting, but I didn't pass out. Somehow, I just couldn't accept the fact that I was really going to see a psychiatrist. I thought that psychiatrists were only for crazy people, and I definitely didn't think I was crazy. As a result, I did not admit myself right away. As a matter of fact I left the hospital and ended up meeting my sister on the way home. She told me to turn right back around because I was definitely going to be admitted. We then called my mother, and she said she would fly down the following day. (O'Neil, 1984, pp. 109–110)

The young woman described in this case study was diagnosed as having schizophrenia. The diagnosis of schizophrenia has existed now for over a century, and this serious mental disorder has spawned more research than any other, but we are far from understanding it.

Schizophrenia is a disorder characterized by disturbances in thought, emotion, and behavior—disordered thinking, in which ideas are not logically related; faulty perception and attention; a lack of emotional expressiveness or at times, inappropriate expressions; and disturbances in movement and behavior, such as a shuffling gait or a disheveled appearance. Patients with schizophrenia may withdraw from people and from everyday reality, often into a life of odd beliefs (delusions) and hallucinations. Given that schizophrenia is associated with such widespread disruptions in the person's life, we should not be surprised that it has proved difficult to uncover the causes of the disorder and develop methods to treat it. We still have a long way to go before we fully understand the multiple factors that trigger schizophrenia and have treatments that are both effective and free of unpleasant side effects.

The symptoms of schizophrenia have a profound effect not just on patients' lives, but also on the lives of families and friends. Delusions and hallucinations may cause considerable distress, both to patients and others, compounded by the fact that hopes and dreams have been shattered. Other symptoms make stable employment difficult, often leading to impoverishment and homelessness. Strange behavior and social skills deficits lead to loss of friends, a solitary existence, and sometimes ridicule and persecution. Substance-abuse rates are high (Fowler et al., 1998), perhaps reflecting an attempt to achieve some relief from negative emotions (Blanchard et al., 1999). Little wonder, then, that the suicide rate among patients with schizophrenia is high.

Schizophrenia is one of the most severe psychopathologies we will describe in this book. Its lifetime prevalence is slightly less than 1 percent, and it affects men and women about equally. Schizophrenia is diagnosed more frequently among some groups, such as African Americans, though it remains unclear whether this reflects an actual difference among groups or bias among clinicians (USDHHS, 2001a). Schizophrenia sometimes begins in childhood, but it usually appears in late adolescence or early adulthood, and usually somewhat earlier in men than in women. Age of onset appears to have been decreasing over recent last decades (DiMaggio, Martinez, & Menard, 2001). People with schizophrenia typically have a number of acute episodes of their symptoms and less severe but still very debilitating symptoms between episodes. Comorbid substance abuse occurs in about 50 percent of patients with schizophrenia and so it is a major problem (Kosten & Ziedonis, 1997).

In this chapter, we first describe the clinical features of schizophrenia followed by discussions of the etiology of schizophrenia and treatments for the disorder.

Clinical Descriptions of Schizophrenia

The range of symptoms in the diagnosis of schizophrenia is extensive, although patients typically have only some of these problems at any given time. The DSM determines for the diagnostician how many problems must be present, in what degree, and for what duration to justify the diagnosis (see DSM-IV-TR criteria).

No single essential symptom must be present for a diagnosis of schizophrenia. Thus, patients with schizophrenia can differ from one another quite a bit. The heterogeneity of schizophrenia suggests that it may be appropriate to subdivide patients into types that manifest particular constellations of problems, and we examine several recognized types later in this chapter. But first we present the main categories of symptoms of schizophrenia.

About 30 years ago, symptoms were divided into two categories called positive and negative (Crow, 1980; Strauss, Carpenter, & Bartko, 1974). Subsequently, the original category of positive symptoms was divided into two categories—positive (hallucinations and delusions) and disorganized (disorganized speech and behavior) (Lenzenwenger, Dworkin,

Table 11.1 Summary of the Major Symptom Dimensions in Schizophrenia

Positive Symptoms	Negative Symptoms	Disorganized Symptoms
Delusions, hallucinations	Avolition (apathy), alogia (poverty of speech, poverty of content of speech), anhedonia, flat affect, asociality	Disorganized behavior, disorganized speech

& Wethington, 1991). The distinction between positive, negative, and disorganized symptoms has been very useful in research on etiology and treatment of schizophrenia—even more useful than the DSM-IV-TR subtypes that we describe later. Table 11.1 shows the symptoms that comprise these categories.

In the following sections, we describe in some detail the individual symptoms that make up the positive, negative, and disorganized categories. We also describe some symptoms that do not fit neatly into these three categories.

Positive Symptoms

Positive symptoms comprise excesses and distortions, such as hallucinations and delusions. For the most part, acute episodes of schizophrenia are characterized by positive symptoms.

Delusions   No doubt all of us at one time or another have been concerned because we believed that others thought ill of us. Some of the time this belief may be justified. After all, who is universally loved? Consider, though, the anguish that you would feel if you were firmly convinced that many people did not like you—indeed, that they disliked you so much that they were plotting against you. Imagine that your persecutors have sophisticated listening devices that let them tune in on your most private conversations and gather evidence in a plot to discredit you. Those around you, including your loved ones, are unable to reassure you that people are not spying on you. Even your closest friends are gradually joining forces with your tormentor. Anxious and angry, you begin taking counteractions against the persecutors. You carefully check any new room you enter for listening devices. When you meet people for the first time, you question them at great length to determine whether they are part of the plot against you.

Such **delusions**, which are beliefs held contrary to reality and firmly held in spite of disconfirming evidence, are common positive symptoms of schizophrenia. Persecutory delusions such as those just related were found in 65 percent of a large, cross-national sample of people diagnosed with schizophrenia (Sartorius, Shapiro, & Jablonsky, 1974). Delusions may take several other forms as well, which were described by the German psychiatrist Kurt Schneider (1959). The following descriptions of these delusions are drawn from Mellor (1970):

- The patient may believe that thoughts that are not his or her own have been placed in his or her mind by an external source.

  A twenty-nine-year-old housewife said, "I look out of the window and I think the garden looks nice and the grass looks cool, but the thoughts of Eamonn Andrews come into my mind. There are no other thoughts there, only his. He treats my mind like a screen and flashes his thoughts on it like you flash a picture." (p. 17)

- Patients may believe that their thoughts are broadcast or transmitted, so that others know what they are thinking.

  A twenty-one-year-old student [found that], "As I think, my thoughts leave my head on a type of mental ticker-tape. Everyone around has only to pass the tape through their mind and they know my thoughts." (p. 17)

- Patients may think their thoughts are being stolen from them, suddenly and unexpectedly, by an external force.

  A twenty-two-year-old woman [described such an experience]. "I am thinking about my mother, and suddenly my thoughts are sucked out of my mind by a phrenological vacuum extractor, and there is nothing in my mind, it is empty." (pp. 16–17)

- Some patients believe that their feelings or behaviors are controlled by an external force.

  A twenty-nine-year-old shorthand typist described her [simplest] actions as follows: "When I reach my hand for the comb it is my hand and arm which move, and my fingers pick up the pen, but I don't control them. I sit there watching them move, and they are quite independent, what they do is nothing to do with me. I am just a puppet who is manipulated by cosmic strings. When the strings are pulled my body moves and I cannot prevent it." (p. 17)

Although delusions are found among more than half of people with schizophrenia, they are also found among patients with other diagnoses, particularly bipolar disorder, depression with psychotic features, and delusional disorder. In contrast to delusions among such patients, however, the delusions of patients with schizophrenia are highly implausible, as shown by the descriptions above (Junginger, Barker, & Coe, 1992).

Hallucinations and Other Disturbances of Perception   Patients with schizophrenia frequently report that the world seems somehow different or even unreal to them. A patient may mention changes in how his or her body feels, or the patient may become so depersonalized that his or her body feels as though it is a machine. As in the case at the beginning of this chapter, some people report difficulties in attending to what is happening around them:

> *I can't concentrate on television because I can't watch the screen and listen to what is being said at the same time. I can't seem to take in two things like this at the same time especially when one of them means watching and the other means listening. On the other hand I seem to be always taking in too much at the one time, and then I can't handle it and can't make sense of it. (McGhie & Chapman, 1961, p. 106)*

The most dramatic distortions of perception are **hallucinations**, sensory experiences in the absence of any relevant stimulation from the environment. They are more often auditory than visual; 74 percent of one sample of schizophrenia patients reported having auditory hallucinations (Sartorius et al., 1974). Like delusions, hallucinations can be very frightening experiences.

Some types of hallucinations are thought to be particularly important diagnostically because they occur more often in patients with schizophrenia than in other psychotic patients. These types of hallucinations include the following (taken from Mellor, 1970):

- Some patients with schizophrenia report hearing their own thoughts spoken by another voice.

  [The] thirty-two-year-old housewife complained of a man's voice speaking in an intense whisper from a point about two feet above her head. The voice would repeat almost all the patient's goal-directed thinking—even the most banal thoughts. The patient would think, "I must put the kettle on," and after a pause of not more than one second the voice would say, "I must put the kettle on." It would often say the opposite, "Don't put the kettle on." (p. 16)

- Some patients claim that they hear voices arguing.

  A twenty-four-year-old male patient reported hearing voices coming from the nurse's office. One voice, deep in pitch and roughly spoken, repeatedly said, "G. T. is a bloody paradox," and another higher in pitch said, "He is that, he should be locked up." A female voice occasionally interrupted, saying, "He is not, he is a lovely man." (p. 16)

- Some patients hear voices commenting on their behavior.

> *A forty-one-year-old housewife heard a voice coming from a house across the road. The voice went on incessantly in a flat monotone describing everything she was doing with an admixture of critical comments. "She is peeling potatoes, got hold of the peeler, she does not want that potato, she is putting it back, because she thinks it has a knobble like a penis, she has a dirty mind, she is peeling potatoes, now she is washing them." (p. 16)*

For many patients, these hallucinations are experienced negatively. In one study of nearly 200 patients, those who had hallucinations that were longer, louder, more frequent, and experienced in the third person found them unpleasant. Hallucinations that were believed to come from a known person were experienced more positively (Copolov, Mackinnon, & Trauer, 2004).

Recent neuroimaging studies have examined what happens in the brain during auditory hallucinations. Some theorists propose that patients misattribute their own voice as being someone else's voice. Behavioral studies have shown that schizophrenia patients with hallucinations are more likely to misattribute recordings of their own speech to a different source than are patients without hallucinations or nonpatient controls (Allen et al., 2004). Studies using brain-imaging methods have also found greater activity in Broca's area, the productive language area of the brain, when patients hear voices (McGuire, Shah, & Murray, 1993). Why might patients make this misattribution? Other studies suggest that there is a problem in the connections between the frontal lobe areas that enable the production of speech and the temporal lobe areas that enable the understanding of speech. Studies using both psychophysiological (Ford et al., 2002) and brain-imaging methods (McGuire, Silbersweig, & Frith 1996; Shergill et al., 2000) support this idea.

Negative Symptoms

The **negative symptoms** of schizophrenia consist of behavioral deficits, such as avolition, alogia, anhedonia, flat affect, and asociality, all of which we describe below. These symptoms tend to endure beyond an acute episode and have profound effects on the lives of patients with schizophrenia. They are also important prognostically; the presence of many negative symptoms is a strong predictor of a poor quality of life (e.g., occupational impairment, few friends) 2 years following hospitalization (Ho et al., 1998).

When assessing negative symptoms it is important to distinguish among those that are truly symptoms of schizophrenia and those that are due to some other factor (Carpenter, Heinrichs, & Wagman, 1988). For example, flat affect (a lack of emotional expressiveness) can be a side effect of antipsychotic medication. Observing patients over extended time periods is probably the only way to address this issue.

Avolition   Apathy, or **avolition**, refers to a lack of energy and a seeming absence of interest in or an inability to persist in what are usually routine activities. Patients may become inattentive to grooming and personal hygiene, with uncombed hair, dirty nails, unbrushed teeth, and disheveled clothes. They have difficulty persisting at work, school, or household chores and may spend much of their time sitting around doing nothing.

Alogia   **Alogia** can take several forms. In *poverty of speech*, the sheer amount of speech is greatly reduced. In *poverty of content of speech*, the amount of speech is adequate, but it conveys little information and tends to be vague and repetitive as shown by the following excerpt:

> *Interviewer: O.K. Why is it, do you think, that people believe in God?*
> *Patient: Well, first of all because, He is the person that is their personal savior. He walks with me and talks with me. And uh, the understanding that I have, a lot of peoples, they don't really know their personal self. Because they ain't, they all, just don't know their personal self. They don't know that He uh, seems to like me, a lot of them don't understand that He walks and talks with them. And uh, show 'em their way to go. I understand also that, every man and every lady, is not*

just pointed in the same direction. Some are pointed different. They go in their different ways. The way that Jesus Christ wanted 'em to go. Myself. I am pointed in the ways of uh, knowing right from wrong, and doing it, I can't do any more, or not less than that. (American Psychiatric Association, 1987, pp. 403–404)

Anhedonia A loss of interest in or a reported lessening of the experience of pleasure is called **anhedonia**. When asked about hypothetical situations or activities that are pleasurable to most people (e.g., good food, recreational activities, sex) on an anhedonia questionnaire, schizophrenia patients report that they derive less pleasure from these sorts of activities than people without schizophrenia. However, when patients are presented with actual pleasant activities, such as amusing films, they report experiencing as much pleasure as do people without schizophrenia (Kring & Earnst, 1999). How can patients report anhedonia yet still derive pleasure from positive things? One possibility is that patients do not *anticipate* that situations will be pleasurable. Thus, patients may score low on anhedonia questionnaires that require them to estimate how much pleasure they would experience in a variety of activities. But when in the presence of pleasurable things or situations, patients do get in-the-moment pleasure (Kring, 1999).

Flat Affect In patients with **flat affect** virtually no stimulus can elicit an emotional expression. The patient may stare vacantly, the muscles of the face flaccid, the eyes lifeless. When spoken to, the patient answers in a flat and toneless voice. Flat affect was found in 66 percent of a large sample of patients with schizophrenia (Sartorius et al., 1974).

The concept of flat affect refers only to the outward expression of emotion and not to the patient's inner experience, which may not be impoverished at all. In one study, patients with schizophrenia and a control group of people without schizophrenia watched excerpts from films while their facial reactions and skin conductance were recorded (Kring & Neale, 1996). After each film clip, participants self-reported on the emotions the films had elicited. As expected, the patients were much less facially expressive than were the people without schizophrenia, but they reported about the same amount of emotion and were even more physiologically aroused (as measured by skin conductance).

Asociality Some patients with schizophrenia have severe impairments in social relationships, referred to as **asociality**. They have few friends, poor social skills, and little interest in being with other people. Indeed, as will be seen later, these manifestations of schizophrenia are often the first to appear, beginning in childhood before the onset of other symptoms.

Disorganized Symptoms

Disorganized symptoms include disorganized speech and disorganized behavior.

Disorganized Speech Also known as *formal thought disorder*, **disorganized speech** refers to problems in organizing ideas and in speaking so that a listener can understand.

> *Interviewer*: Have you been nervous or tense lately?
>
> *Patient*: No, I got a head of lettuce.
>
> *Interviewer*: You got a head of lettuce? I don't understand.
>
> *Patient*: Well, it's just a head of lettuce.
>
> *Interviewer*: Tell me about lettuce. What do you mean?
>
> *Patient*: Well ... lettuce is a transformation of a dead cougar that suffered a relapse on the lion's toe. And he swallowed the lion and something happened. The ... see, the ... Gloria and Tommy, they're two heads and they're not whales. But they escaped with herds of vomit, and things like that.
>
> *Interviewer*: Who are Tommy and Gloria?
>
> *Patient*: Uh, ... there's Joe DiMaggio, Tommy Henrich, Bill Dickey, Phil Rizzuto, John Esclavera, Del Crandell, Ted Williams, Mickey Mantle, Roy Mantle, Ray Mantle, Bob Chance ...

Interviewer: Who are they? Who are those people?

Patient: Dead people . . . they want to be fucked . . . by this outlaw.

Interviewer: What does all that mean?

Patient: Well, you see, I have to leave the hospital. I'm supposed to have an operation on my legs, you know. And it comes to be pretty sickly that I don't want to keep my legs. That's why I wish I could have an operation.

Interviewer: You want to have your legs taken off?

Patient: It's possible, you know.

Interviewer: Why would you want to do that?

Patient: I didn't have any legs to begin with. So I would imagine that if I was a fast runner, I'd be scared to be a wife, because I had a splinter inside of my head of lettuce. (Neale & Oltmanns, 1980, pp. 103–104)

This excerpt illustrates the incoherence sometimes found in the conversation of individuals with schizophrenia. Although the patient may make repeated references to central ideas or themes, the images and fragments of thought are not connected; it is difficult to understand what the patient is trying to tell the interviewer.

Speech may also be disordered by what are called **loose associations**, or **derailment**, in which case the patient may be more successful in communicating with a listener but has difficulty sticking to one topic. Patients seem to drift off on a train of associations evoked by an idea from the past. Patients have themselves provided descriptions of this state.

> My thoughts get all jumbled up. I start thinking or talking about something but I never get there. Instead, I wander off in the wrong direction and get caught up with all sorts of different things that may be connected with things I want to say but in a way I can't explain. People listening to me get more lost than I do. My trouble is that I've got too many thoughts. You might think about something, let's say that ashtray and just think, oh yes, that's for putting my cigarette in, but I would think of it and then I would think of a dozen different things connected with it at the same time. (McGhie & Chapman, 1961, p. 108)

Disturbances in speech were at one time regarded as the principal clinical symptom of schizophrenia, and they remain one of the criteria for the diagnosis. But evidence indicates that the speech of many patients with schizophrenia is not disorganized, and the presence of disorganized speech does not discriminate well between schizophrenia and other disorders, such as some mood disorders (Andreasen, 1979). For example, patients in a manic episode exhibit loose associations as much as do patients with schizophrenia.

It would seem logical to expect disorganized speech to be associated with problems in language production, but this does not appear to be the case. Instead, disorganized speech is associated with problems in what is called *executive functioning*—problem solving, planning, and making associations between thinking and feeling. Disorganized speech is also related to the ability to perceive semantic information (i.e., the meaning of words) (Kerns & Berenbaum, 2002, 2003).

Disorganized Behavior   **Disorganized behavior** takes many forms. Patients may go into inexplicable bouts of agitation, dress in unusual clothes, act in a childlike or silly manner, hoard food, collect garbage, or engage in sexually inappropriate behavior such as masturbating in public. They seem to lose the ability to organize their behavior and make it conform to community standards. They also have difficulty performing the tasks of everyday living.

Other Symptoms

Several other symptoms of schizophrenia do not fit neatly into the categories we have just presented. Two important symptoms of this kind are catatonia and inappropriate affect.

An 1894 photo showing a woman with catatonic schizophrenia. She held this unusual posture for long periods of time. (The Burns Archive.)

Catatonia   Several motor abnormalities define **catatonia**. Patients may gesture repeatedly, using peculiar and sometimes complex sequences of finger, hand, and arm movements, which often seem to be purposeful. Some patients manifest an unusual increase in their overall level of activity, including much excitement, wild flailing of the limbs, and great expenditure of energy similar to that seen in mania. At the other end of the spectrum is **catatonic immobility**: patients adopt unusual postures and maintain them for very long periods of time. A patient may stand on one leg, with the other tucked up toward the buttocks, and remain in this position virtually all day. Catatonic patients may also have *waxy flexibility*—another person can move the patient's limbs into positions that the patient will then maintain for long periods of time.

Inappropriate Affect   Some people with schizophrenia show **inappropriate affect**—their emotional responses are out of context. Such a patient may laugh on hearing that his or her mother just died or become enraged when asked a simple question about how a new garment fits. These patients are likely to shift rapidly from one emotional state to another for no discernible reason. This symptom is quite rare, and it is relatively specific to schizophrenia.

Schizophrenia in DSM-IV-TR

The table in the margin (p. 351) presents the current diagnostic criteria for schizophrenia. In addition, DSM-IV-TR requires at least 6 months of disturbance for the diagnosis. The 6-month period must include at least 1 month of an acute episode, or active phase, defined by the presence of at least two of the following: delusions, hallucinations, disorganized speech, grossly disorganized or catatonic behavior, and negative symptoms. (Only one of these symptoms is required if the delusions are bizarre or if the hallucinations consist of voices commenting or arguing.) The remaining time required for the diagnosis can occur either before the active phase or after the active phase. This time criterion eliminates patients who have a brief psychotic episode and then recover quickly.

Are the DSM-IV-TR diagnostic criteria applicable across cultures? Evidence bearing on this question was collected in a World Health Organization study of both industrialized and developing countries (Jablonsky et al., 1994). The symptomatic criteria held up well cross-culturally. However, for reasons not yet fully understood, patients in developing countries have a more acute onset and a more favorable course than those in industrialized societies (Susser & Wanderling, 1994).

Categories of Schizophrenia in DSM-IV-TR   Although schizophrenia is much less broadly characterized than formerly (see Focus on Discovery 11.1), it continues to be a very heterogeneous disorder. The diverse array of symptoms has given rise to proposals concerning subtypes of the disorder. Yet, as we shall see, the validity of these subtypes is questionable.

Disorganized Schizophrenia   The subtype called **disorganized schizophrenia** in DSM-IV-TR is manifested by speech that is disorganized and difficult for a listener to follow. Patients may speak incoherently, stringing together similar-sounding words and even inventing new words, often accompanied by silliness or laughter. He or she may have flat affect or experience constant shifts of emotion, breaking into inexplicable fits of laughter and crying. The patient's behavior is also generally disorganized and not goal directed; for example, he or she may tie a ribbon around a big toe or move incessantly, pointing at objects for no apparent reason.

Catatonic Schizophrenia   The most obvious symptoms of **catatonic schizophrenia** are the catatonic symptoms described earlier. Patients typically alternate between catatonic

Focus on Discovery 11.1

History of the Concept of Schizophrenia

Two European psychiatrists, Emil Kraepelin and Eugen Bleuler, initially formulated the concept of schizophrenia. Kraepelin first described **dementia praecox**, his term for what we now call schizophrenia, in 1898. He differentiated two major groups of disorders that he asserted were endogenous, or internally caused: manic-depressive illness and dementia praecox. Dementia praecox included several diagnostic subtypes—dementia paranoides, catatonia, and hebephrenia—that had been regarded as distinct entities by clinicians in the previous few decades. Although these disorders were symptomatically diverse, Kraepelin believed that they shared a common core, and the term "dementia praecox" reflected what he believed was that core—an early onset (praecox) and a progressive, inevitable intellectual deterioration (dementia). The dementia in dementia praecox is not the same as the dementias we discuss in the chapter on late life (Chapter 15), which are defined principally by severe memory impairments. Kraepelin's term referred to a general "mental enfeeblement."

Bleuler broke with Kraepelin's description on two major points: he believed that the disorder did not necessarily have an early onset, and he believed that it did not inevitably progress toward dementia. Thus the label "dementia praecox" was no longer appropriate, and in 1908 Bleuler proposed his own term, *schizophrenia*, from the Greek words schizein ("to split"), and phren ("mind"), capturing what he viewed as the essential nature of the condition.

With age of onset and deteriorating course no longer considered defining features of the disorder, Bleuler faced a conceptual problem. The symptoms of schizophrenia could vary widely among patients, so he had to provide some justification for putting them into a single diagnostic category. That is, he needed to specify some common denominator, or essential property, that would link the various disturbances. The metaphorical concept that he adopted for this purpose was the "breaking of associative threads."

For Bleuler, associative threads joined not only words but also thoughts. Thus, goal-directed, efficient thinking and communication were possible only when these hypothetical structures were intact. The notion that associative threads were disrupted in patients with schizophrenia could then be used to account for the range of other disturbances. Bleuler viewed attentional difficulties, for example, as resulting from a loss of purposeful direction in thought, in turn causing passive responses to objects and people in the immediate surroundings. In a similar vein, he viewed blocking, the apparently total inability to hold a train of thought, as a complete disruption of the person's associative threads.

Kraepelin had recognized that a small percentage of patients with symptoms of dementia praecox

Emil Kraepelin (1856–1926), German psychiatrist, articulated descriptions of schizophrenia (then called dementia praecox) that have proved remarkably durable in the light of contemporary research. (Hueton Archive Getty Images.)

Eugen Bleuler (1857–1939), Swiss psychiatrist, contributed to our conceptions of schizophrenia and coined the term. (Corbis Bettmann.)

did not deteriorate, but he preferred to limit this diagnostic category to patients who had a poor prognosis. Bleuler's work, in contrast, led to a broader concept of the disorder. He diagnosed some patients with a good prognosis as having schizophrenia, and he also diagnosed schizophrenia in many patients who would have received different diagnoses from other clinicians.

The Broadened U.S. Concept

Bleuler had a great influence on the concept of schizophrenia as it developed in the United States. Over the first part of the twentieth century, the breadth of the diagnosis was extended considerably. In contrast, the concept of schizophrenia prevalent in Europe remained narrower.

The reasons for the increase in the frequency of diagnoses of schizophrenia in the United States are easily discerned. First of all, several prominent figures in U.S. psychiatry expanded Bleuler's already broad concept of schizophrenia even more. For example, patients who had a combination of both schizophrenia and affective symptoms were said to have a subtype of schizophrenia called *schizoaffective psychosis* in the DSM-I (1952) and DSM-II (1968). Also, U.S. clinicians tended to diagnose schizophrenia whenever delusions or hallucinations were present. Because these symptoms, particularly delusions, occur also in mood disorders, many patients with a DSM-II diagnosis of schizophrenia might actually have been diagnosed with a mood disorder (Cooper et al., 1972). Similarly, patients whom we would now diagnose as having a personality disorder (notably schizotypal, schizoid, borderline, and paranoid personality disorders, see Chapter 12) were diagnosed with schizophrenia.

Current Conceptions of Schizophrenia: A More Narrow Definition

Beginning with DSM-III (American Psychiatric Association, 1980) and continuing in DSM-IV (American Psychiatric Association, 1994) and DSM-IV-TR (American Psychiatric Association, 2000), the U.S. concept of schizophrenia has shifted considerably, narrowing the range of patients diagnosed with the disorder. This shift involved making the diagnostic criteria more detailed and explicit, creating separate categories of disorder for some conditions formerly considered subtypes of schizophrenia, and requiring at least 6 months of disturbance for a diagnosis (see the DSM-IV-TR diagnostic criteria for schizophrenia in the margin).

immobility and wild excitement, but one of these symptoms may predominate. The onset of catatonic symptoms may be more sudden than the onset of other symptoms of schizophrenia, although the person is likely to have previously shown some apathy and some withdrawal from reality.

Catatonic schizophrenia is seldom seen today, perhaps because medications work effectively on these disturbed motor processes. Alternatively, Boyle (1991) has argued that the apparent high prevalence of catatonia during the early part of the twentieth century reflected misdiagnosis. Specifically, the similarities between encephalitis lethargica (sleeping sickness) and catatonic schizophrenia suggest that many cases of the former were misdiagnosed as the latter. This idea was portrayed in the film *Awakenings*, which was based on the career and writings of Oliver Sacks.

Paranoid Schizophrenia   The key to the diagnosis of **paranoid schizophrenia** is the presence of prominent delusions. Delusions of persecution are most common, but patients may experience **grandiose delusions**, in which they have an exaggerated sense of their own importance, power, knowledge, or identity. The other delusions described earlier, such as being persecuted or spied on, may also be evident. Vivid auditory hallucinations may accompany the delusions. Patients with paranoid schizophrenia often develop **ideas of reference**: they incorporate unimportant events within a delusional framework and read personal significance into the trivial activities of others. For instance, they think that overheard segments of conversations are about them, that the frequent appearance of the same person on a street where they customarily walk means that they are being watched, and that what they see on television or read in magazines somehow refers to them. Individuals with paranoid schizophrenia can be agitated, argumentative, angry, and sometimes violent. They are emotionally responsive, although they may be somewhat stilted, formal, and intense with others. Their speech, although filled with references to their delusions, is not disorganized.

Additional subtypes   Additional subtypes included in DSM-IV-TR are **undifferentiated schizophrenia**, applied to patients who meet the diagnostic criteria for schizophrenia but not for any of the three main subtypes, and **residual schizophrenia**, used when the patient no longer meets the full criteria for schizophrenia but still shows some signs of the illness.

Evaluation of the Subtypes   Although the subtypes of schizophrenia in DSM-IV-TR form the basis of current diagnostic practices, their usefulness is often questioned. Actually, diagnosing the subtypes is extremely difficult, so diagnostic reliability is very low. Furthermore, the subtypes have little predictive validity; that is, the diagnosis of one or another form of schizophrenia provides little information helpful in either treating the disorder or predicting its course. There is also considerable overlap of symptoms among the subtypes. For example, patients with all subtypes of schizophrenia may have delusions.

Other Psychotic Disorders in the DSM-IV-TR

The DSM-IV-TR includes other categories of psychotic disorders besides schizophrenia. Many of these disorders used to be considered subtypes of schizophrenia, thus contributing to a very broad conception of schizophrenia in the United States (see Focus on Discovery 11.1). Today, these are considered distinct disorders, though most researchers and clinicians believe they are related to one another at the level of etiology.

Two brief psychotic disorders are **schizophreniform disorder** and **brief psychotic disorder**. The symptoms of schizophreniform disorder are the same as those of schizophrenia but last only from 1 to 6 months. Brief psychotic disorder lasts from 1 day to 1 month and is often brought on by extreme stress, such as bereavement. **Schizoaffective disorder** comprises a mixture of symptoms of schizophrenia and mood disorders.

A person with **delusional disorder** is troubled by persistent delusions of persecution or by delusional jealousy, the unfounded conviction that a spouse or lover is unfaithful. Other delusions seen in this disorder include delusions of being followed, delusions of erotomania (believing that one is loved by some other person, usually a complete stranger with a higher social status), and somatic delusions (believing that some internal organ is malfunctioning). Unlike the person with paranoid schizophrenia, the person with delusional disorder does not have hallucinations, and his or her delusions are less bizarre. Delusional disorder is quite rare and typically begins later in life than does schizophrenia. In most family studies it appears to be related to schizophrenia, perhaps genetically (Kendler & Diehl, 1993).

Quick Summary

Schizophrenia is a very heterogeneous disorder. It affects men and women about equally and typically begins in late adolescence or early adulthood. Symptoms can be distinguished as positive, negative, and disorganized. Positive symptoms include hallucinations and delusions. Negative symptoms include avolition, alogia, flat affect, anhedonia, and asociality. Disorganized symptoms include disorganized speech and disorganized behavior. No one of these symptoms is critical for the diagnosis of schizophrenia. The DSM-IV-TR subtypes include catatonic, paranoid,

disorganized, undifferentiated, and residual. Despite their presence in the DSM-IV-TR, they do not have a good deal of validity and are not that useful. Other psychotic disorders include schizophreniform disorder and brief psychotic disorder, which differ from schizophrenia in duration. Schizoaffective disorder involves symptoms of both schizophrenia and mood disorders. Delusional disorder involves delusions but no other symptoms of schizophrenia, and the delusions are less bizarre than those in schizophrenia.

Check Your Knowledge 11.1

List the symptom that each clinical vignette describes.
1. Charlie enjoyed going to movies. He particularly liked to see horror movies because they made him feel really scared. His sister was surprised to learn this, because when she went to movies with Charlie, he didn't gasp out loud or show fear on his face.
2. Marlene was convinced that Tom Cruise was sending her messages. In his movie *The Last Samurai*, his donning of the battle armor was a signal that he was prepared to fight for them to be together. That he ended his relationship with the actress Penelope Cruz also told her that he was trying to get in touch with her.
3. Sophia didn't want to go out to dinner with her family. She reasoned that these dinners were always the same food and conversation, so

why bother? After much encouragement from her father, she agreed to go. At dinner, Sophia remarked that this was a wonderful meal, perhaps the best she had had in a while. She laughed and enjoyed the stories her parents and cousins told during dinner. Later in the week, her mother mentioned that Sophia was not doing much around the house. Sophia said that nothing she could think of to do would be fun.
4. Jevon was talking with his doctor about the side effects of his medication. He talked about having dry mouth and then immediately began talking about cottonmouth snakes and jungle safaris and how hiking was good for your health but that Bill Clinton was in better shape than George Bush.

Etiology of Schizophrenia

What can explain the scattering and disconnection of thoughts, the lack of emotion expression, the odd delusions, and bewildering hallucinations of people with schizophrenia? Broad theoretical perspectives, such as psychoanalysis, have not had much of an impact in research on schizophrenia. Other perspectives, however, have yielded many interesting research results as we discuss in the following sections.

Genetic Factors

A good deal of research supports the idea that schizophrenia has a genetic component, as we discuss in the sections below on behavior genetics and molecular genetics research. The evidence is somewhat more convincing from behavior genetics studies, largely because they

Table 11.2 Summary of Major Family and Twin Studies of the Genetics of Schizophrenia

Relation to Proband	Percentage with Schizophrenia
Spouse	1.00
Grandchildren	2.84
Nieces/nephews	2.65
Children	9.35
Siblings	7.30
DZ twins	12.08
MZ twins	44.30

Source: After Gottesman, McGuffin, and Farmer, 1987.

have been well replicated. Many molecular genetics studies are still in need of replication to bolster confidence in their findings.

Behavior Genetics Research   The family, twin, and adoption methods employed in this research, as in other behavior genetics research projects, have led researchers to conclude that a predisposition to schizophrenia is inherited. It should be noted that many genetic studies of schizophrenia were conducted when the definition of schizophrenia was considerably broader then it is now. However, genetic investigators collected extensive descriptive data on their samples, allowing the results to be reanalyzed later using newer diagnostic criteria.

Family Studies   Table 11.2 presents a summary of the risk for schizophrenia in various relatives of index cases with schizophrenia. (In evaluating the figures, bear in mind that the risk for schizophrenia in the general population is a little less than 1 percent.) Quite clearly, relatives of patients with schizophrenia are at increased risk, and the risk increases as the genetic relationship between proband and relative becomes closer (Kendler, Karkowski-Shuman, & Walsh, 1996).

Furthermore, patients who have schizophrenia in their family histories have more negative symptoms than those whose families are free of schizophrenia (Malaspina et al., 2000), suggesting that negative symptoms may have a stronger genetic component. The relatives of patients with schizophrenia are also at increased risk for other disorders (e.g., schizotypal personality disorder) that are thought to be less severe forms of schizophrenia (Kendler, Neale, & Walsh, 1995).

The results of family studies thus support the notion that a predisposition for schizophrenia can be transmitted genetically. Yet the relatives of a person with schizophrenia share not only genes but also common experiences. Recall from Chapter 2 that genes do much of their work via the environment. Therefore, the influence of the environment cannot be discounted in explaining the higher risks among relatives.

Childhood photograph of the Genain quadruplets. Each of the girls developed schizophrenia later in life. (Courtesy of Monte S. Buchsbaum, M.D., Mt. Sinai School of Medicine, New York, NY.)

Twin Studies   Table 11.2 also shows the risk for identical (MZ) and fraternal (DZ) twins of people with schizophrenia. The risk for MZ twins (44.3 percent), although greater than that for DZ twins (12.08 percent), is still much less than 100 percent. Similar results have been obtained in more recent studies (Cannon et al., 1998; Cardno et al., 1999). The less-than-100-percent concordance in MZ twins is important: If genetic transmission alone accounted for schizophrenia and one twin had schizophrenia, the other twin would also have schizophrenia because MZ twins are genetically identical. The importance of genetic factors is supported, however, by the fact that the risk among MZ twins increases when the twin with schizophrenia is more severely ill (Gottesman & Shields, 1972). As with the family studies, twin study research suggests that negative symptoms may have a stronger genetic component than do positive symptoms (Dworkin & Lenzenweger, 1984; Dworkin, Lenzenweger, & Moldin, 1987).

As with family studies, of course, there is a critical problem in interpreting the results of twin studies. A common environment rather than common genetic factors could account for some portion of the increased risk. By common environment, we mean not only similar shared and nonshared environmental factors, such as child-rearing practices or peer relationships, but also a more similar intrauterine environment, for MZ twins are more likely than DZ twins to share a single blood supply.

A clever analysis supporting a genetic interpretation of the high risk found for identical twins was performed by Fischer (1971). She reasoned that if these rates indeed reflected a genetic effect, the twins without schizophrenia should be at high risk for the disorder. These nonschizophrenic MZ twins would presumably have the genotype for schizophrenia, even though it was not expressed behaviorally, and thus might pass along an increased risk for the disorder to their children. In agreement with this line of reasoning, the rate of schizophrenia and schizophrenia-like psychoses in the children of the nonschizophrenic twins was 9.4 percent, while the rate among the children of the twins with schizophrenia was only slightly and nonsignificantly higher, 12.3 percent. Both rates are substantially higher than the 1 percent prevalence found in the general population, and this lends further support to the importance of genetic factors in schizophrenia.

Adoption Studies The study of children whose mothers had schizophrenia but who were reared from early infancy by adoptive parents without schizophrenia has provided clearer confirmation of the role of genes in schizophrenia because such studies eliminate the possible effects of being reared in an environment where a parent has schizophrenia. In a now classic study, Heston (1966) followed up 47 people born between 1915 and 1945 to women with schizophrenia in a state mental hospital. The infants were separated from their mothers at birth and raised by foster or adoptive parents. Fifty control participants were selected from the same foundling homes that had placed the children of the women with schizophrenia.

The follow-up assessment revealed that 31 of the 47 children of mothers with schizophrenia (66 percent) were given a DSM diagnosis, versus only 9 of the 50 controls (18 percent). None of the controls was diagnosed with schizophrenia, versus 16.6 percent (five) of the offspring of women with schizophrenia.[1] Children of women with schizophrenia were also more likely to be diagnosed as mentally defective (i.e., mentally retarded, in today's terms), psychopathic, and neurotic (Table 11.3). They had been involved more frequently in criminal activity, had spent more time in prison, and had more often been discharged from the armed services for psychiatric reasons. This study provides strong support for the importance of genetic factors in the development of schizophrenia.

A similar study was carried out in Denmark (Kety et al., 1976, 1994), where researchers examined the records of children who had been adopted at a young age. All adoptees who had later been admitted to a psychiatric facility and diagnosed with schizophrenia were selected as the index cases. From the remaining cases the investigators chose a control group of people who had no psychiatric history and who were matched to the index group on such variables as sex and age. Both the adoptive and the biological parents and the siblings and half-siblings of the two groups were then identified, and a search was made to determine who among them had a psychiatric history. As might be expected if genetic factors figure in schizophrenia, the biological relatives of the group with schizophrenia were diagnosed with schizophrenia more often than were members of the general population; the adoptive relatives were not.

Another large sample of adopted offspring of mothers with schizophrenia was studied along with a control group of adopted children in Finland. In this study using DSM-IIIR criteria for schizophrenia, the age-corrected risk for developing schizophrenia among the 164 adoptees who had a biological parent with schizophrenia was 8.1 percent. The risk for the 197 control adoptees who did not have a biological parent with schizophrenia was significantly lower at 2.3 percent. The risk for other disorders, such as schizoaffective, schizophreniform, and schizotypal personality disorder, was also greater among the adoptees with a biological parent with schizophrenia than among the control adoptees (Tienari et al., 2000).

Table 11.3 Characteristics of Participants Separated from Their Mothers in Early Infancy

Characteristic	Offspring of Mothers with Schizophrenia	Control Offspring
Number of participants	47	50
Mean age at follow-up	35.8	36.3
Overall ratings of disability (low score indicates more pathology)	65.2	80.1
Number diagnosed with schizophrenia	5	0
Number diagnosed with mental defect	4	0
Number diagnosed with psychopathy	9	2
Number diagnosed with neurosis	13	7

Source: From Heston, 1966.

---

[1] The figure of 16.6 percent was age corrected—that is, the raw data were corrected to take into account the age of the participants. For example, if a person in Heston's sample was 24 years old when assessed as not having schizophrenia, he or she might still develop schizophrenia at some point later in life; the age-correction procedure attempts to account for this possibility.

Molecular Genetics Research   Knowing that schizophrenia has a genetic component is in many ways just the starting point for research. Understanding exactly what constitutes the genetic predisposition is the challenge faced by molecular genetics researchers. As with nearly all of the disorders we cover in this book, it does not appear that the predisposition for schizophrenia is transmitted by a single gene.

The results of linkage analysis studies (see p. 33), in which family pedigrees are studied to try to determine on which chromosome or chromosomes the schizophrenia genes are located, have been inconsistent. Studies have reported positive findings for linkage at locations on a number of different chromosomes, including 1, 5, 6, 8, 10, 11, 13, 15, 18, and 22 (Faraone, Taylor, & Tsuang, 2002). Although finding so many chromosomal locations to be possibly connected with schizophrenia is consistent with the idea that multiple genes are involved, the results of these studies are simply too varied to justify any firm conclusions. Also, such results have a history of not being replicated (DeLisi et al., 2002), possibly because these types of studies work better for conditions with a predisposition that is transmitted by a single gene or a small set of genes. It is also highly likely that schizophrenia is genetically heterogeneous—that is, the genetic diathesis may vary from case to case—mirroring the fact noted earlier that schizophrenia is certainly symptomatically heterogeneous.

Association studies (see p. 33) have begun to focus on specific genes associated with schizophrenia. In an association study, the goal is to establish how often a specific gene and a particular phenotype co-occur. As with the linkage studies, positive findings are often followed by failures to replicate. For example, research was initially focused on genes associated with the dopamine D2 receptor because, as we discuss below, this receptor is associated with the positive effectiveness of some medications used to treat schizophrenia. Although there are some positive findings (Glatt, Faraone, & Tsuang, 2003), a number of other studies are negative (Owen, Williams, & O'Donovan, 2004). Other studies have found associations with the serotonin receptor 5HT2 gene, though its role appears to be very small (Lohmueller et al., 2003; J. Williams et al., 1997).

Two promising candidate genes have received some recent support from association studies (Owen et al., 2004). One, a gene called DTNBP1, encodes a protein called dysbindin that is expressed throughout the brain, but it is not yet clear what the function is of either the gene or the protein. Nevertheless, five studies have replicated an association between DTNBP1 and schizophrenia. In addition, a postmortem study has shown that compared to people without schizophrenia, those with schizophrenia appear to have less dysbindin in a number of brain areas, including the frontal cortex, temporal cortex, hippocampus, and limbic system structures (Weickert et al., 2004). Another gene, NGR1, which has been linked to the neurotransmitter glutamate's receptors and is also helpful with the process of myelination (see p. 39), has also been found to be associated with schizophrenia. Time will tell if these results can be replicated.

Another approach to research on specific genes that may improve our understanding of schizophrenia is association studies that examine the relationship between genes and cognitive functions among people without psychopathology. For example, some research has found that a gene called COMT is associated with executive functions that rely on the **prefrontal cortex** (reviewed by Goldberg & Weinberger, 2004). A number of studies have demonstrated that schizophrenia patients have deficits in executive functions, which include planning, working memory, and problem solving, and other studies have shown problems in the prefrontal cortex (see below). A few association studies have implicated COMT in schizophrenia, but these are in need of replication (Harrison & Weinberger, 2004; Owen et al., 2004).

Evaluation of the Genetic Research   Research results indicate that genetic factors play an important role in the development of schizophrenia. Twin and family studies are difficult to interpret because they don't readily separate the effects of genes and environment. However, adoption studies have done a better job of separating genetic and environmental effects.

Despite this evidence, we cannot conclude that schizophrenia is a disorder completely determined by genetic transmission, for we must always keep in mind the distinction between phenotype and genotype (see p. 31). Like other mental disorders, schizophrenia is defined by behavior; it is a phenotype, and thus reflects the influence of both genes and environment. The diathesis–stress model introduced in Chapter 2 seems appropriate for guiding theory and research into the etiology of schizophrenia. Genetic factors can only predispose people to schizophrenia. Some kind of stress is required to cause this predisposition to be expressed as an observable pathology.

The genetic research in schizophrenia has some further limitations as well. First, as reviewed in the molecular genetics section above, it has not yet been possible to specify exactly how a predisposition for schizophrenia is transmitted. Second, the nature of the inherited diathesis remains unknown. What exactly is inherited that puts some people at risk for schizophrenia? One way of addressing this question is to study relatives of patients with schizophrenia. Although not necessarily disordered, these individuals, who are at increased risk for schizophrenia, may reveal signs of the genetic predisposition. One area of research has been the study of how well the eyes track a moving target, such as a pendulum. Patients with schizophrenia do poorly on this task, as do about 50 percent of their first-degree relatives (Holzman, 1985). The importance of eye tracking is supported by data showing that it is influenced by genetic factors (Iacono et al., 1992). Deficient eye tracking may reflect a problem in several areas of the brain, including the frontal and temporal lobes as well as the cerebellum (Chen et al., 1999). We will soon see that these brain areas are thought to be very important in schizophrenia.

This apparatus is used to assess a person's ability to track a moving target. This ability is impaired both in patients with schizophrenia and in their relatives, suggesting that eye tracking is a genetic marker for the disorder. (Courtesy of Dr. William Iacono, University of Minnesota.)

Despite the problems and loose ends, the results of genetics research represent an impressive body of evidence. The strong positive correlation between genetic relatedness and the prevalence of schizophrenia remains one of the strongest links in the chain of information about the causes of schizophrenia.

Neurotransmitters

Present research is examining several different neurotransmitters, such as norepinephrine, serotonin, and glutamate, to see what role they might play in the etiology of schizophrenia. The first neurotransmitter to receive substantial research attention was dopamine. We trace the history of this research here, highlighting how it has both helped and hindered efforts toward identifying causes and treatments for schizophrenia.

Dopamine Theory   The theory that schizophrenia is related to excess activity of the neurotransmitter dopamine is based principally on the knowledge that drugs effective in treating schizophrenia reduce dopamine activity. Researchers noted that antipsychotic drugs, in addition to being useful in treating some symptoms of schizophrenia, produce side effects resembling the symptoms of Parkinson's disease. Parkinsonism is known to be caused in part by low levels of dopamine in a particular nerve tract of the brain. It was subsequently confirmed that because of their structural similarities to the dopamine molecule, molecules of antipsychotic drugs fit into and thereby block postsynaptic dopamine receptors. The dopamine receptors that are blocked by antipsychotics are called D2 receptors. (As with receptors for other neurotransmitters, there are several subclasses of dopamine receptors that differ in the specifics of how they signal the postsynaptic neuron.) From this knowledge about the action of the drugs that help patients with schizophrenia, it was natural to conjecture that schizophrenia resulted from excess activity in dopamine nerve tracts.

Further indirect support for this **dopamine theory** of schizophrenia came from the literature on *amphetamine psychosis*. Amphetamines can produce a state that closely resembles paranoid schizophrenia, and they can exacerbate the symptoms of patients with schizophrenia (Angrist, Lee, & Gershon, 1974). The amphetamines cause the release of catecholamines, including norepinephrine and dopamine, into the synaptic cleft and prevent their inactivation. We can be relatively confident that the psychosis-inducing effects of amphetamines are a result of increasing activity of dopamine rather than of norepinephrine, because antipsychotics are effective in treating amphetamine psychosis.

Based on the evidence just reviewed, researchers at first assumed that schizophrenia was caused by an excess of dopamine. But as other studies progressed, this assumption did not gain support. For example, the major metabolite of dopamine, homovanillic acid (HVA), was not found in greater amounts in patients with schizophrenia (Bowers, 1974).

Such evidence, plus improved technologies for studying neurotransmitters in humans, led researchers to propose excess numbers of dopamine receptors or oversensitive dopamine receptors, rather than a high level of dopamine, as factors in schizophrenia. Research on the antipsychotics' mode of action suggests that the dopamine receptors are a more likely locus of disorder than the level of dopamine itself. Some postmortem studies of brains of schizophrenia patients, as well as PET scans of schizophrenia patients, have revealed that dopamine receptors are greater in number or are hypersensitive in some people with schizophrenia (Hietala et al., 1994; Tune et al., 1993; Wong et al., 1986). Having too many dopamine receptors would be functionally akin to having too much dopamine itself. The reason is that when dopamine (or any neurotransmitter) is released into the synapse, only some of it actually interacts with postsynaptic receptors. Having more receptors gives a greater opportunity for the dopamine that is released to stimulate a receptor.

An excess of dopamine receptors may not be responsible for all the symptoms of schizophrenia; such an excess appears to be related mainly to positive symptoms. (As with the genetics research, this work was done before positive symptoms were divided into two categories.) Amphetamines worsen positive symptoms. Antipsychotics lessen positive symptoms but have little or no effect on negative symptoms.

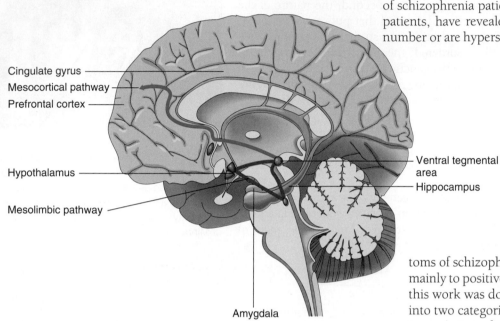

Cingulate gyrus
Mesocortical pathway
Prefrontal cortex
Hypothalamus
Mesolimbic pathway
Ventral tegmental area
Hippocampus
Amygdala

Figure 11.1 The brain and schizophrenia. The mesocortical pathway begins in the ventral tegmental area and projects to the prefrontal cortex. The mesolimbic pathway also begins in the ventral tegmental area, but projects to the hypothalamus, amygdala, hippocampus, and nucleus accumbens.

Subsequent developments in the dopamine theory (e.g., Davis et al., 1991) expanded its scope. The key change involved the recognition of differences among the neural pathways that use dopamine as a transmitter. The excess dopamine activity that is thought to be most relevant to schizophrenia is localized in the mesolimbic pathway (see Figure 11.1), and the therapeutic effects of antipsychotics on positive symptoms occur by blocking dopamine receptors in this neural system, thereby lowering dopamine activity.

The mesocortical pathway is another scene of dopamine activity. It begins in the same brain region as the mesolimbic pathway, but projects to the prefrontal cortex. The prefrontal cortex also projects to limbic areas that are innervated by dopamine. The dopamine neurons in the prefrontal cortex may be underactive and thus fail to exert inhibitory control over the dopamine neurons in the limbic area, with the result that there is dopamine overactivity in the pathways. Because the prefrontal cortex is thought to be especially relevant to the negative symptoms of schizophrenia, the underactivity of the dopamine neurons in this part of the brain may also be the cause of the negative symptoms of schizophrenia (see Figure 11.2). This proposal has the advantage of accounting for the simultaneous presence of positive and negative symptoms in the same patient with schizophrenia. Furthermore, because antipsychotics do not have major effects on the dopamine neurons in the prefrontal cortex, we would expect them to be relatively ineffective as treatments for negative symptoms, and they are. When we examine research on structural abnormalities in the brains of patients with schizophrenia, we will see some close connections between these two domains.

Evaluation of the Dopamine Theory Despite the positive evidence we have reviewed, the dopamine theory does not appear to be a complete theory of schizophrenia. For example, it takes several weeks for antipsychotics

Brain injury to prefrontal cortex

Dopamine neuron under-active in prefrontal cortex → Negative symptoms of schizophrenia

Release of mesolimbic dopamine neurons from inhibitory control → Positive symptoms of schizophrenia

Figure 11.2 Dopamine theory of schizophrenia.

to begin lessening the positive symptoms of schizophrenia, although they begin blocking dopamine receptors rapidly (Davis, 1978). This disjunction between the behavioral and pharmacological effects of antipsychotics is difficult to understand within the context of the theory. One possibility is that although antipsychotics do indeed block D2 receptors, their ultimate therapeutic effect may result from the effect this blockade has on other brain areas and other neurotransmitter systems (R. M. Cohen et al., 1997).

It is also puzzling that to be therapeutically effective, antipsychotics must reduce dopamine levels or receptor activity to below normal, in some cases producing Parkinsonian side effects. According to the theory, reducing dopamine levels or receptor activity to normal should be sufficient for a therapeutic effect.

In sum, although dopamine remains the most actively researched neurotransmitter in schizophrenia, it is not likely to provide a complete explanation of the etiology of schizophrenia. Schizophrenia is a disorder with widespread symptoms covering perception, cognition, motor activity, and social behavior. It is unlikely that a single neurotransmitter could account for all of them. Thus, schizophrenia researchers have cast a broader neurotransmitter net, moving away from an almost exclusive emphasis on dopamine.

Other Neurotransmitters   As we discuss later, newer drugs used in treating schizophrenia implicate other neurotransmitters, such as serotonin, in the disorder. These newer drugs partially block D2 receptors, but they also work by blocking the serotonin receptor 5HT2 (e.g., Burris et al., 2002). Dopamine neurons generally modulate the activity of other neural systems; for example, in the prefrontal cortex they regulate GABA neurons. Thus, it is not surprising that GABA transmission is disrupted in the prefrontal cortex of patients with schizophrenia (Volk et al., 2000). Similarly, serotonin neurons regulate dopamine neurons in the mesolimbic pathway.

Glutamate, a transmitter that is widespread in the human brain, may also play a role (Carlsson et al., 1999). Low levels of glutamate have been found in cerebrospinal fluid of patients with schizophrenia (Faustman et al., 1999), and postmortem studies have revealed low levels of the enzyme needed to produce glutamate (Tsai et al., 1995). The street drug PCP (p. 320) can induce both positive and negative symptoms in people without schizophrenia, and it produces this effect by interfering with one of glutamate's receptors (O'Donnell & Grace, 1998). Furthermore, a decrease in glutamate inputs from either the prefrontal cortex or the hippocampus (both of these brain structures are implicated in schizophrenia) to the corpus striatum (a temporal-lobe structure) could result in increased dopamine activity (O'Donnell & Grace, 1998).

Brain Structure and Function

The search for a brain abnormality that causes schizophrenia began as early as the syndrome was identified, but studies did not begin to yield consistent findings until fairly recently. The challenge of such a task is indeed daunting. Schizophrenia affects everything about us that makes us human—our thinking, feeling, and behaving. It is thus unlikely that a single type of brain abnormality can account for schizophrenia's wide array of symptoms. In the last two decades, however, spurred by a number of technological advances, research has yielded some promising results. Among the most well-replicated findings of brain abnormalities in schizophrenia are enlargement of the ventricles and dysfunction in the prefrontal cortex.

Enlarged Ventricles   Postmortem studies of the brains of patients with schizophrenia consistently reveal enlarged ventricles, which implies a loss of brain cells, although there are also contradictory findings. Findings from neuroimaging studies are even more impressive. Thus far, these studies have most consistently revealed that some patients, especially males (Nopoulos, Flaum, & Andreasen, 1997), have enlarged ventricles.[2] Further

MRI of the brain of a woman with schizophrenia (bottom) and the brain of a women without schizophrenia (top). Enlarged ventricles (the dark spaces at center of photos) are one of the best-validated biological features of schizophrenia. (Courtesy of J. Lieberman, American Journal of Psychiatry.)

---

[2] This difference between male and female schizophrenia patients prompts us to mention that there are other gender differences as well. For example, men with schizophrenia have an earlier age of onset and are more likely to express negative symptoms and to have a more deteriorating course than are women with schizophrenia (Salem & Kring, 1998).

evidence concerning enlarged ventricles comes from two MRI studies of pairs of MZ twins only one of whom had schizophrenia (McNeil, Cantor-Graae, & Weinberger, 2000; Suddath et al., 1990). In both studies the ill twin had larger ventricles than the well twin, and in one of the studies most of the twins with schizophrenia could be identified by simple visual inspection of the scan. Because the twins were genetically identical in these studies, these results suggest that the origin of these brain abnormalities may not be genetic.

Large ventricles in patients with schizophrenia are correlated with impaired performance on neuropsychological tests, poor adjustment prior to the onset of the disorder, and poor response to drug treatment (Andreasen et al., 1982; Weinberger et al., 1980). The extent to which the ventricles are enlarged, however, is modest, and many patients do not differ from people without schizophrenia in this respect. Furthermore, enlarged ventricles are not specific to schizophrenia, as they are also evident in the CT scans of patients with other disorders, such as bipolar disorder with psychotic features (Rieder et al., 1983). Such patients can show ventricular enlargement almost as great as that seen in schizophrenia (Elkis et al., 1995).[3]

Factors Involving the Prefrontal Cortex   A variety of evidence suggests that the prefrontal cortex is of particular importance in schizophrenia.

Differences in regional cerebral blood flow between patients with schizophrenia (bottom) and individuals without schizophrenia (top) for each hemisphere. The values shown were scored as the percentage change in cerebral blood flow while performing a control task to the Wisconsin Card Sort, that was expected to activate the prefrontal cortex. The participants without schizophrenia showed greater prefrontal cortical activation as indicated by the "hotter" color of this brain region. *Source*: Weinberger et al., 1988. (Courtesy of Daniel Weinberger, National Institute of Health.)

- The prefrontal cortex is known to play a role in behaviors such as speech, decision making, and goal-directed behavior, which are disrupted in schizophrenia.
- MRI studies have shown reductions in gray matter in the prefrontal cortex (Buchanan, Vladar, et al., 1998).
- Patients perform more poorly on neuropsychological tests designed to tap functions promoted by the prefrontal region, including working memory or the ability to hold bits of information in memory (Barch et al., 2002, 2003; Heinrichs & Zakzanis, 1998).
- In a type of functional imaging in which glucose metabolism is studied in various brain regions while patients perform psychological tests, patients with schizophrenia have shown low metabolic rates in the prefrontal cortex (Buchsbaum et al., 1984). Glucose metabolism in the prefrontal cortex has also been studied while patients are performing neuropsychological tests of prefrontal function. Because the tests place demands on the prefrontal cortex, glucose metabolism normally goes up as energy is used. Patients with schizophrenia, especially those with prominent negative symptoms, do poorly on the tests and also fail to show activation in the prefrontal region (Potkin et al., 2002; Weinberger, Berman, & Illowsky, 1988). Failure to show frontal activation has also been found using fMRI (Barch et al., 2001; MacDonald & Carter, 2003).

Failure to show frontal activation is related to the severity of negative symptoms (O'Donnell & Grace, 1998) and thus parallels the work on dopamine underactivity in the frontal cortex already discussed. Furthermore, this failure to show frontal activation is less pronounced

---

[3] Other findings also suggest that the schizophrenia and psychotic mood disorders should not perhaps be totally separate diagnostic categories. The disorders share some symptoms (notably, delusions) and some possible etiological factors (e.g., genetic factors, increased dopamine activity), and they respond similarly to medications. An important implication is that researchers would be well served to focus some of their efforts on psychotic symptoms in other disorders as well as in schizophrenia.

in the nonschizophrenic twin of discordant MZ pairs, again suggesting that this brain dysfunction may not have a genetic origin (Torrey et al., 1994).[4]

Despite the reduced volume of the gray matter in the prefrontal cortex (and also the temporal cortex), the number of neurons in this area does not appear to be reduced. More detailed studies indicate that what is lost may be what are called "dendritic spines" (Goldman-Rakic & Selemon, 1997; McGlashan & Hoffman, 2000). Dendritic spines are small projections on the shafts of dendrites where nerve impulses are received from other neurons (see Figure 11.3). The loss of these dendritic spines would mean that communication among neurons would be disrupted, resulting in what some have termed a "disconnection syndrome." One possible result of the failure of neural systems to communicate could be the speech and behavioral disorganization seen in schizophrenia.

Congenital and Developmental Factors   A possible cause of some of these brain abnormalities is damage during gestation or birth. Many studies have shown high rates of delivery complications in patients with schizophrenia; such complications could have resulted in a reduced supply of oxygen to the brain, resulting in loss of cortical gray matter (Cannon et al., 2002). These obstetrical complications do not raise the rate of schizophrenia in everyone who experiences them; rather, the risk for schizophrenia is increased in those who experience complications and have a genetic diathesis (Cannon & Mednick, 1993).

Although the data are not entirely consistent (Westergaard et al., 1999), another possibility is that a virus invades the brain and damages it during fetal development (Mednick, Huttonen, & Machon, 1994; Mednick et al., 1988). During a 5-week period in 1957, Helsinki, Finland experienced an epidemic of influenza virus. Researchers examined rates of schizophrenia among adults who had likely been exposed during their mothers' pregnancies. People who had been exposed to the virus during the second trimester of pregnancy had much higher rates than those who had been exposed in either of the other trimesters and much higher rates than in nonexposed control adults. This finding was intriguing because we know that the second trimester is a critical period for cortical development; however, only half of nearly 30 later studies were able to replicate this finding. And a recent study found evidence that mothers' exposure to the flu during the *first* trimester of pregnancy, as directly measured by the presence of flu antibodies in the blood, was associated with a sevenfold increase in the risk for schizophrenia among their children (Brown et al., 2004). Though the increase in risk sounds large, the difference from the control group was not quite statistically different, suggesting that it will be important to replicate this finding.

If, as the findings we have just reviewed suggest, the development of the brains of people with schizophrenia goes awry very early, why does the disorder begin many years later, in adolescence or early adulthood? The prefrontal cortex is a brain structure that matures late, typically in adolescence or early adulthood. Thus a problem in this area, even those that began early in the course of development, may not show itself in the person's behavior until the period of development when the prefrontal cortex begins to play a larger role in behavior (Weinberger, 1987). Notably, dopamine activity also peaks in adolescence, which may further set the stage for the onset of schizophrenia symptoms.

Another proposed explanation is that the development of symptoms in adolescence could reflect a loss of synapses due to excessive pruning, the elimination of synaptic connections. Pruning is a normal part of brain development that occurs at different rates in different areas of the brain. It is mostly complete in sensory areas by about 2 years of age but continues in the prefrontal cortex until mid-adolescence. If too extensive, pruning would result in the loss of necessary communication among neurons (McGlashan & Hoffman, 2000).

Figure 11.3   Micrograph of a neuron. The bumps on the dendrites are dendritic spines, which receive inputs from other neurons. Fewer dendritic spines may impair connections among neurons and may be a factor in schizophrenia. (BSIP/Sercomi/Photo Researchers, Inc.)

---

[4] This study consistently found that the well twin was indistinguishable from participants without schizophrenia on both structural and functional measures of the brain. The authors viewed this finding as evidence that these abnormalities are not genetically determined. However, the small number of participants in the study makes it difficult to statistically differentiate between groups. Furthermore, a large body of evidence has found neuropsychological impairments in the first-degree relatives of people with schizophrenia (e.g., Cannon et al., 1994). Therefore, it would be unwise to conclude that genes play no role in the brain dysfunction of schizophrenia.

Current Research Further work on the relationship of schizophrenia to brain structure and function is proceeding at a rapid rate. Recognizing that the symptoms of schizophrenia implicate many areas of the brain, researchers have moved away from trying to find some highly specific "lesion" and are beginning to examine neural systems and the ways in which different areas of the brain interact. This work is beginning to call attention to the possible roles of a wider range of brain structures, such as the thalamus and the cerebellum in schizophrenia (Byne et al., 2002; Gilbert et al., 2001). Research also shows a reduction in cortical gray matter in both the temporal and frontal regions (Gur et al., 2000) and reduced volume in basal ganglia (e.g., the caudate nucleus), hippocampus, and limbic structures (Chua & McKenna, 1995; Gur & Pearlson, 1993; Keshavan et al., 1998; Lim et al., 1998; Nelson et al., 1998; Velakoulis et al., 1999). A twin study found reduced hippocampus volume among twins with schizophrenia, but not among the twins without schizophrenia (van Erp et al., 2004). Recent attention has also turned to problems in the brain's connectivity using methods such as diffusion tensor imaging. In people with schizophrenia, the connections between the different areas of the brain (e.g., between the frontal cortex, temporal cortex, and limbic system) do not seem to be made as efficiently as in the brains of people without schizophrenia.

Psychological Stress

We have discussed several possible neurobiological diatheses for schizophrenia, but more than a diathesis is required to produce schizophrenia. Psychological stress plays a key role by interacting with a genetic or neurobiological vulnerability to produce this illness. Research shows that, as with many of the disorders we have discussed, increases in life stress increase the likelihood of a relapse (Ventura et al., 1989). Furthermore, individuals with schizophrenia appear to be very reactive to the stressors we all encounter in daily living. Groups of patients with psychotic disorders (92 percent with schizophrenia), their first-degree relatives, and controls participated in a 6-day ecological momentary assessment study in which they recorded stress and mood several times each day. Stress led to greater decreases in positive moods in both patients and their relatives compared with controls. Stress also led to greater increases in negative moods in the patients compared with both relatives and controls (Myin-Gremeys et al., 2001). Thus, patients with schizophrenia were particularly vulnerable to daily stress.

Much research on the role of life stress in the development and relapse of schizophrenia has focused on socioeconomic status and the family.

Socioeconomic Status For many years we have known that the highest rates of schizophrenia are found in urban areas inhabited by people of the lowest socioeconomic status or SES (Hollingshead & Redlich, 1958). The relationship between SES and schizophrenia is not such that the prevalence of schizophrenia goes up as SES goes down. Rather, there is a sharp upturn in the prevalence of schizophrenia in people of the lowest socioeconomic status. In a now classic 10-year study of SES and mental illness in New Haven, Connecticut, the rate of schizophrenia was found to be twice as high among those of the lowest SES as among those in the next lowest group (Hollingshead & Redlich, 1958). These findings have been confirmed cross-culturally by similar studies carried out in countries such as Denmark, Norway, and the United Kingdom (Kohn, 1968).

The correlation between SES and schizophrenia is consistent, but is difficult to interpret in causal terms. Some people believe that stressors associated with SES may cause or contribute to the development of schizophrenia—the **sociogenic hypothesis**. Degrading treatment by others of higher status, low levels of education, and lack of rewards and opportunities may, taken together, make very low SES so stressful that individuals who are predisposed to develop schizophrenia readily develop the disorder. Alternatively, these stressors could have neurobiological effects; for example, children of mothers whose nutrition during pregnancy was poor are at increased risk for schizophrenia (Susser et al., 1996).

Another explanation of the correlation between schizophrenia and low SES is the **social selection theory**, which reverses the direction of causality. The theory proposes that during the course of their developing illness, people with schizophrenia may drift into poor neighborhoods because their illness impairs their earning power and they cannot afford to live elsewhere.

One possible way of resolving the conflict between these opposing theories would be to study the social mobility of people with schizophrenia. However, results have been inconsistent (Dunham, 1965; Turner & Wagonfeld, 1967). One researcher suggested another way of examining this question (Kohn, 1968): Are the fathers of patients with schizophrenia also of the lowest SES? If they are, this could be considered evidence in favor of the sociogenic hypothesis that very low status is conducive to schizophrenia, for SES would be shown to precede schizophrenia. If the fathers are of a higher status, the social selection hypothesis would be the better explanation. Fathers were studied since they were the primary wage earners in the 1960s when this idea was proposed. Turner and Wagonfeld (1967) conducted such a study and found evidence for the social selection hypothesis. Of 26 patients of the lowest SES, only four had fathers of the lowest status.

A more recent study in Israel evaluated the two theories by investigating both SES and ethnic background (Dohrenwend et al., 1992). The rates of schizophrenia were examined in Israeli Jews of European ethnic background and in more recent immigrants to Israel from North Africa and the Middle East. The latter group experienced considerable racial prejudice and discrimination in Israel. The sociogenic hypothesis would predict that because they experienced high levels of stress regardless of socioeconomic status, the members of the disadvantaged ethnic group should have consistently higher rates of schizophrenia regardless of status. However, this pattern did not emerge, supporting the social selection theory.

In sum, research results are more supportive of the social selection theory than of the sociogenic hypothesis. But we should not conclude that the social environment plays no role in schizophrenia. For example, the prevalence of schizophrenia among Africans from the Caribbean who remain in their native country is much lower than among those who have emigrated to London (Hutchinson et al., 1996). This difference could well be caused by the stress associated with trying to assimilate into a new culture.

Family-Related Factors   Early theorists regarded family relationships, especially those between a mother and her son, as crucial in the development of schizophrenia. At one time the view was so prevalent that the term "schizophrenogenic mother" was coined for the supposedly cold and dominant, conflict-inducing parent who was said to produce schizophrenia in her offspring (Fromm-Reichmann, 1948). These mothers were characterized as rejecting, overprotective, self-sacrificing, impervious to the feelings of others, rigid and moralistic about sex, and fearful of intimacy. Controlled studies evaluating the schizophrenogenic-mother theory have not supported it. The damage done to families by this theory, however, was significant. For generations, parents blamed themselves for their child's illness, and until the 1970s, psychiatrists joined in this blame game.

How Do Families Influence Schizophrenia?   Other studies continued to explore the possibility that the family played some role in the etiology of schizophrenia. For the most part, the findings are only suggestive, not conclusive. For example, a few studies of families of individuals with schizophrenia have found that they communicate more vaguely with one another and have higher levels of conflict than families of individuals without schizophrenia. It is plausible, though, that the conflict and unclear communication are a response to having a young family member with schizophrenia.

Some other findings suggest that faulty communications by parents may play a role in the etiology of schizophrenia. One type of communication pattern studied is called *communication deviance (CD)*, which is characterized by hostility and poor communication. In a longitudinal study of adolescents with behavior problems, CD in the families was found to predict the later onset of schizophrenia (Norton, 1982). However, not all people who develop schizophrenia exhibit behavior problems as adolescents. Furthermore, it does not appear that CD is specifically associated with schizophrenia, since parents of patients with bipolar disorder are equally likely to show CD (Miklowitz, 1985).

Further evidence favoring some role for the family comes from the Finnish adoption study described above (Tienari et al., 2000). Various aspects of family life in the adoptive families were extensively studied and then related to the adjustment of the children (Tienari et al., 1994). The families were categorized into levels of maladjustment based on material from clinical interviews and psychological tests. More serious psychopathology was found among the adoptees reared in a disturbed family environment. Furthermore, among children reared in a disturbed family environment, those having a biological parent with schizophrenia showed more psychopathology than did the control participants. Although it is tempting to conclude that both a genetic predisposition and a noxious family environment are necessary to increase risk for psychopathology, a problem in interpretation remains: The disturbed family environment could be a response to a disturbed child. Thus we cannot firmly conclude that an etiological role for the family has been established.

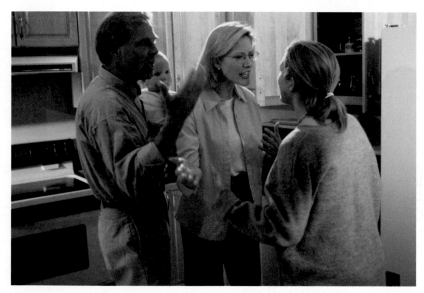

Expressed emotion, which includes hostility, critical comments, and emotional overinvolvement, has been linked with relapse in schizophrenia. (Lisette Le Bon/SUPERSTOCK.)

Families and Relapse A series of studies initiated in London indicate that the family can have an important impact on the adjustment of patients after they leave the hospital. In one study, investigators conducted a 9-month follow-up study of a sample of patients with schizophrenia who returned to live with their families after being discharged from the hospital (Brown et al., 1966). Interviews were conducted with parents or spouses before discharge and rated for the number of critical comments made about the patient and for expressions of hostility toward or emotional overinvolvement with the patient. The following is an example of a critical comment made by a father remarking on his daughter's behavior, in which he is expressing the idea that his daughter is deliberately symptomatic to avoid housework: "My view is that Maria acts this way so my wife doesn't give her any responsibilities around the house" (Weisman et al., 1998). On the basis of this variable, called **expressed emotion (EE)**, families were divided into two groups: those revealing a great deal of expressed emotion (high-EE families) and those revealing little (low-EE families). At the end of the follow-up period, only 10 percent of the patients returning to low-EE homes had relapsed, but 58 percent of the patients returning to high-EE homes had gone back to the hospital.

This research, which has since been replicated (see Butzlaff & Hooley, 1998, for a meta-analysis), indicates that the environment to which patients are discharged has great bearing on how soon they are rehospitalized. Researchers have also found that negative symptoms of schizophrenia are most likely to elicit critical comments, as in the example presented in the previous paragraph, and that the relatives who make the most critical comments are the most likely to view patients as being able to control their symptoms (Lopez et al., 1999; Weisman et al., 1998).

What is not yet clear is exactly how to interpret the effects of EE. Is EE causal, or does it reflect a reaction to the patients' behavior? For example, if the condition of a patient with schizophrenia begins to deteriorate, family concern and involvement may increase. Indeed, disorganized or dangerous behavior by the patient might seem to warrant limit setting and other familial efforts that could increase the level of EE. Research indicates that both interpretations of the operation of EE may be correct. Recently discharged patients with schizophrenia and their high- or low-EE families were observed as they engaged in a discussion of a family problem. Two key findings emerged (Rosenfarb et al., 1994).

1. The expression of unusual thoughts by the patients ("If that kid bites you, you'll get rabies") elicited a greater number of critical comments by family members who had previously been characterized as high in EE than by those characterized as low in EE.

2. In high-EE families, critical comments by family members led to increased expression of unusual thoughts by the patients.

Thus, this study found a bidirectional relationship in high-EE families: critical comments by family members elicited more unusual thoughts by patients; and unusual thoughts expressed by the patients led to increased critical comments.

How does stress, such as a high level of EE, increase the symptoms of schizophrenia and precipitate relapses? One answer to this question relates the effects of stress on the hypothalamic–pituitary–adrenal (HPA) axis (see p. 42) to the dopamine theory (Walker & DiForio, 1997). Stress activates the HPA axis, causing cortisol to be secreted. In turn, cortisol increases dopamine activity and may thereby increase the symptoms of schizophrenia. Furthermore, heightened dopamine activity itself can increase HPA activation, which may make a person overly sensitive to stress. Thus, the theory suggests that there is a bidirectional relationship between HPA activation and dopamine activity.

Developmental Studies

What are people who develop schizophrenia like before their symptoms begin? An early method of answering this question was to construct developmental histories by examining the childhood records of those who had later developed schizophrenia. In the 1960s, researchers found that children who later developed schizophrenia had lower IQs and were more often delinquent and withdrawn than did members of various control groups, usually comprising siblings and neighborhood peers (Albee, Lane, & Reuter, 1964; Lane & Albee, 1965; Berry, 1967). Other studies found that boys who later developed schizophrenia were rated by teachers as disagreeable; whereas, girls who later developed schizophrenia were rated as passive (Watt, 1974; Watt et al., 1970).

More recently, researchers have examined home movies before the onset of schizophrenia, made as part of normal family life (Walker, Davis, & Savoie, 1994; Walker et al., 1993). Compared with their siblings who did not later develop schizophrenia, preschizophrenic children showed poorer motor skills and more expressions of negative emotions.

As intriguing as these findings are, the major limitation of such developmental research is that the data were not originally collected with the intention of predicting the development of schizophrenia from childhood behavior. More specific information is required if developmental histories are to provide clear evidence regarding etiology.

The high-risk method can yield this information. The first such study of schizophrenia was begun in the 1960s (Mednick & Schulsinger, 1968). The researchers chose Denmark because Danish registries make it possible to keep track of people for long periods of time. The high-risk participants were 207 young people whose mothers had schizophrenia (The researchers decided that the mother should be the parent with the disorder because paternity is not always easy to determine.) Then, 104 low-risk participants, individuals whose mothers did not have schizophrenia, were matched to the high-risk subjects on variables such as sex, age, father's occupation, rural or urban residence, years of education, and institutional upbringing versus rearing by the family. In 1972 the now-grown men and women were followed up with a number of measures, including a battery of diagnostic tests. Fifteen of the high-risk participants were diagnosed with schizophrenia; none of the control participants was so diagnosed.

Additional analyses on the group of participants who were diagnosed with schizophrenia suggested that positive and negative symptoms of schizophrenia may have different etiologies (Cannon, Mednick, & Parnas, 1990). Patients with predominantly negative symptoms had a history of pregnancy and birth complications and a failure to show electrodermal responses to simple stimuli. By contrast, patients with predominantly positive symptoms had a history of family instability, such as separation from parents and placement in foster homes or institutions for periods of time.

In the wake of this pioneering study, several other high-risk investigations were undertaken, some of which have also yielded information concerning the possible causes of adult psychopathology, but not necessarily schizophrenia specifically. The New York High-Risk Study found that a composite measure of attentional dysfunction predicted behavioral

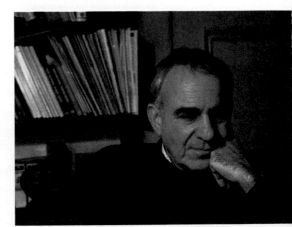

Sarnoff Mednick, a psychologist at the University of Southern California, pioneered the use of the high-risk method for studying schizophrenia. He has also contributed to the hypothesis that a maternal viral infection is implicated in this disorder. (Sarnoff Mednick.)

disturbance at follow-up (Cornblatt & Erlenmeyer-Kimling, 1985). Furthermore, low IQ was a characteristic of the first high-risk children to be hospitalized (Erlenmeyer-Kimling & Cornblatt, 1987). In an Israeli study, poor neurobehavioral functioning (poor concentration, poor verbal ability, lack of motor control and coordination) predicted schizophrenia-like outcomes, as did earlier interpersonal problems (Marcus et al., 1987).

A different type of high-risk study has been ongoing in Australia for the past several years, following people between the ages of 14 and 30 who were referred to a mental health clinic in the mid-1990s (Yung et al., 1995). None of the participants had schizophrenia when they entered the study, but many later exhibited varying degrees of schizophrenia symptoms and some had a biological relative with a psychotic disorder. Since the study began, 41 of the original 104 participants have developed some type of psychotic disorder (Yung et al., 2004). An MRI study of 75 of the 104 participants found that those people who later developed a psychotic disorder had lower gray matter volumes than those who had not developed a psychotic disorder (Pantelis et al., 2003). Recall that reduced gray matter volume has been found in schizophrenia patients; this study suggests that this characteristic may predate the onset of schizophrenia and other psychotic disorders.

Quick Summary

Given its complexity, a number of caused factors are likely contributing to schizophrenia. The genetic evidence is strong, with much of the evidence coming from family, twin, and adoption studies. Learning what is inherited remains a challenge for molecular genetics studies. Linkage studies have found linkage on several chromosomes, but these studies need to be replicated. Promising genes from association studies include DTNBP1, NGR1, and COMT, but replication is also needed here.

Neurotransmitters play a role in schizophrenia. For years, dopamine was the focus of study, but later findings led investigators to conclude that this one neurotransmitter could not fully account for schizophrenia. Other neurotransmitters are also the focus of study, such as serotonin, GABA, and glutamate. A number of different brain areas have been implicated in schizophrenia. One of the most widely replicated findings is of enlarged ventricles. Other research supports the role of the prefrontal cortex, particularly reduced activation of this area, in schizophrenia.

Research has examined the role of socioeconomic status in schizophrenia and generally this work supports the social selection theory more than the sociogenic hypothesis. Early theories blamed families, particularly mothers, for causing schizophrenia, but research does not support this view. Communication in families is important and could perhaps constitute the stress in the diathesis–stress theory for schizophrenia. Expressed emotion has also been found to predict relapse in schizophrenia.

Early developmental studies looked back at the childhood records of adults with schizophrenia and found that some adults with schizophrenia had lower IQs and were withdrawn and delinquent as children. Other studies found that adults who later developed schizophrenia expressed a lot of negative emotion and had poor motor skills. The problem with these studies is that the studies were not designed to predict the onset of schizophrenia. High-risk designs deal with this problem, and these studies have found that children at risk for adult psychopathology have difficulties with attention and motor control among other things.

Check Your Knowledge 11.2

Fill in the blank.
1. _____ and _____ studies do not do such a good job of teasing out genetic and environmental effects; _____ studies do a better job.
2. _____ and _____ are two genes that have recently been associated with schizophrenia.
3. Some studies showing the _____ area of the brain to be disrupted in schizophrenia also show that patients do poorly on tasks that rely on this area, such as planning and problem solving.
4. _____,_____, and _____ are the three components of expressed emotion.

Treatment of Schizophrenia

The history of psychopathology (see Chapter 1) is in many respects a history of humankind's efforts, often brutal and unenlightened, to deal with schizophrenia, arguably the most serious of the mental disorders. There seems little doubt that many of those thought mentally ill—or, for instance, possessed by demons—in earlier periods of history, would, if examined now, be given a diagnosis of schizophrenia. Today we know a good deal about the clinical descriptions and etiology of schizophrenia, and we can even treat its symptoms somewhat effectively, but a cure remains elusive.

For the most part, research indicates that hospital care does little to effect meaningful, enduring changes in the majority of patients with schizophrenia or other serious mental illnesses (but see Focus on Discovery 11.2). The overwhelming body of evidence shows rehospitalization rates of 40 to 50 percent after 1 year and upwards of 75 percent after 2 years (Paul & Menditto, 1992). Studies specifically designed to follow patients with schizophrenia after discharge from the hospital show generally poor outcomes as well (Robinson et al., 1999).

A problem with any kind of treatment for schizophrenia is that some patients with schizophrenia lack insight into their impaired condition and refuse any treatment at all (Amador et al., 1994). As they don't believe they have an illness, they don't see the need for professional help, particularly when it includes hospitalization or drugs. This may be especially true for those with paranoid schizophrenia, who may regard treatment as a threat from hostile outside forces. Family members therefore face a major challenge in getting their relatives into treatment, which is one reason they sometimes turn to involuntary hospitalization via civil commitment.

Before we examine the range of treatments for schizophrenia, it is important to point out that the appropriateness of a given treatment depends on the stage of illness that the patient is in. That is, when a patient is in an acutely psychotic phase of the illness, psychological interventions are not likely to be successful because the patient is too distracted, unable to concentrate on what the therapist is saying. In such a phase some sort of medication is likely necessary. Once the person becomes less psychotic, a psychological intervention can begin to have a beneficial impact, and the dosage of the medication can be reduced as the patient learns ways to reduce the stress that precipitated the episode (Kopelowicz, Liberman, & Zarate, 2002).

Medications

Without question the most important development in the treatment of schizophrenia was the advent in the 1950s of several medications collectively referred to as **antipsychotic drugs**, also referred to as *neuroleptics* because they produce side effects similar to the symptoms of a neurological disease.

Traditional Antipsychotic Drugs and Their Side Effects   One of the more frequently prescribed antipsychotic drugs, phenothiazine, was first produced by a German chemist in the late nineteenth century. But it was not until the discovery of the antihistamines, which have a phenothiazine nucleus, in the 1940s, that phenothiazines received much attention.

Reaching beyond their use to treat the common cold and asthma, the French surgeon Henri Laborit pioneered the use of antihistamines to reduce surgical shock. He noticed that they made his patients somewhat sleepy and less fearful about the impending operation. Laborit's work encouraged pharmaceutical companies to reexamine antihistamines in light of their tranquilizing effects. Shortly thereafter the French chemist, Paul Charpentier, prepared a new phenothiazine derivative, which he called chlorpromazine. This drug proved very effective in calming patients with schizophrenia. Phenothiazines derive their therapeutic properties by blocking dopamine receptors in the brain, thus reducing the influence of dopamine on thought, emotion, and behavior.

Chlorpromazine (trade name Thorazine) was first used therapeutically in the United States in 1954 and rapidly became the preferred treatment for schizophrenia. By 1970, more than 85 percent of all patients in state mental hospitals were receiving chlorpromazine or another phenothiazine. Other antipsychotics that have been used for years to treat schizophrenia include the butyrophenones (e.g., haloperidol, trade name Haldol) and the thioxanthenes (e.g., thiothixene, trade name Navane). Both types seem generally as effective as the phenothiazines and work in similar ways. These classes of drugs can reduce

Focus on Discovery 11.2

A Classic Behavior Therapy Project with Hospitalized Patients with Schizophrenia

In the 1960s, behavior therapists introduced an innovation known as the token economy into hospital settings (see Chapter 2). The most comprehensive and impressive of these efforts was reported by Gordon Paul and Robert Lentz (1977).

The long-term, seriously ill patients with schizophrenia in the program were the most severely ill, most debilitated hospitalized adults ever studied systematically. Some of these patients screamed for long periods, some were mute; many were incontinent, a few were assaultive. Most of them no longer used silverware, and some buried their faces in their food. The patients were matched for age, sex, socioeconomic background, symptoms, and length of hospitalization and then assigned to one of three wards—social learning (behavioral therapy), milieu therapy, and routine hospital management. Each ward had 28 residents. The first two wards offered treatment with ambitious objectives: to teach self-care, housekeeping, communication, and vocational skills; to reduce symptomatic behavior; and to release patients to the community. The characteristics of the three wards were as follows:

- *Social-learning ward.* Located in a new mental health center, the social-learning ward operated on a token economy that encompassed all aspects of the residents' lives. Tokens were a necessity, for they purchased meals as well as small luxuries. Residents' appearance had to pass muster in 11 specific ways each morning to earn a token. Well-made beds, good behavior at mealtime, classroom participation, and socializing during free periods were other means of earning tokens. Residents learned through modeling, shaping, prompting, and instructions. They were also taught to communicate better with one another, and they participated in problem-solving groups. In addition to living by the rules of the token economy, individuals received behavioral treatments tailored to their needs, for example, assertiveness training to deal with a specific interpersonal conflict they might be having with a staff member. Residents were kept busy 85 percent of their waking hours learning to behave more constructively.

- *Milieu-therapy ward.* The milieu-therapy ward, also located in the new center, operated according to the principles of a *therapeutic community* (Jones, 1953), an approach reminiscent of Pinel's moral treatment of the late eighteenth century (see p. 11). These residents, too, were kept busy 85 percent of their waking hours. Both individually and as a group they were expected to act responsibly and to participate in decisions about how the ward was to function. In general, they were treated more as nonpatients than as people with a serious mental illness. Staff members impressed on the residents their positive expectations and praised them for doing well. When patients behaved symptomatically, staff members stayed with them, making clear the expectation that they would soon behave more appropriately.

- *Routine hospital management.* Patients in this ward continued their usual hospital existence in an older state institution, receiving custodial care and heavy antipsychotic medication. Except for the 5 percent of their waking hours occupied by occasional activity,

and recreational, occupational, and individual and group therapies, these people were on their own.

Before the program began, the staffs of the two treatment wards were carefully trained to adhere to detailed instructions in therapy manuals; regular observations confirmed that they were implementing the principles of a social-learning or a milieu-therapy program. Over the 4 1/2 years of hospitalization and the 1 1/2 years of follow-up, the patients were carefully evaluated at regular 6-month intervals by structured interviews and by meticulous, direct behavioral observations.

The results? Both the social-learning and the milieu therapy reduced positive, negative, and disorganized symptoms, with social-learning therapy achieving better results than milieu therapy on a number of measures. The residents on the two therapy wards also acquired self-care, housekeeping, social, and vocational skills. The behavior of members of these two groups within the institution was superior to that of the residents of the hospital ward, and by the end of treatment more of them had been discharged—over 10 percent of the social-learning patients left the center for independent living; 7 percent of the milieu patients achieved this goal; and none of the hospital-treatment patients did.

An interesting finding also emerged concerning medication use. About 90 percent of the patients in all three groups were receiving antipsychotic drugs at the outset of the study. Over time, use among the routine-hospital-management group increased to 100 percent. In contrast, the percentage dropped to 18 percent in the milieu-therapy ward and 11 percent in the social-learning ward. This is a remarkable finding in itself, for the medical staff had assumed that if these patients did not get their medication they would be too difficult for the staff to manage. In addition, many patients from all three groups were discharged to community placements, such as residential treatment facilities and homes, where there was supervision but also considerably less restraint than they had experienced while hospitalized. Members of the social-learning group did significantly better at remaining in these community residences than did patients in the other two groups.

These results, though, should not be accepted as confirming the usefulness of token economies per se, for the social-learning therapy contained elements that went beyond operant conditioning of overt behavior. Staff provided information to residents about appropriate behavior and attempted verbally to clarify misconceptions. Paul (personal communication, 1981) relegated the token economy to a secondary, although not trivial, role. He saw it as a useful device for getting the attention of severely ill patients in the initial stages of treatment. The token economy created the opportunity for his patients to acquire new information or, in Paul's informal phrase, to "get good things into their heads."

Paul and Lentz never claimed that any one of these patients was cured. Although they were able to live outside the hospital, most continued to manifest many signs of mental disorder, and few of them had gainful employment or participated in the social activities that most people take for granted. Reports published since the Paul and Lentz study support the effectiveness of social-learning programs (see reviews by Mueser & Liberman, 1995, and Paul & Menditto, 1992; Paul, Stuve, & Cross, 1997).

the positive and disorganized symptoms of schizophrenia but have little or no effect on the negative symptoms.

Despite their effectiveness at reducing some of the symptoms of schizophrenia and allowing many patients to be released from the hospital, antipsychotics are not a cure. Furthermore, about 30 percent of patients with schizophrenia do not respond favorably to the traditional antipsychotics just discussed, although some of these patients may respond to newer drugs, such as clozapine, which we discuss later. Also, about half the patients who take antipsychotic drugs quit after 1 year and up to three-quarters quit before 2 years because the side effects are so unpleasant (Harvard Mental Health Letter, 1995; Lieberman et al. 2005).

Patients who respond positively to the antipsychotics are kept on so-called maintenance doses of the drug, just enough to continue the therapeutic effect. They take their medication and return to the hospital or clinic on occasion for adjustment of the dose level. Some patients who are maintained on medication may make only marginal adjustment to the community, however. For example, they may be unable to live unsupervised or to hold down the kind of job for which they would otherwise be qualified, and their social relationships may be sparse. And again, although the traditional antipsychotics keep positive and disorganized symptoms from returning, they tend to have little effect on negative symptoms, such as flat affect. The antipsychotics have significantly reduced long-term hospitalization, but they have also initiated the revolving-door pattern of admission, discharge, and readmission seen in some patients.

A promising procedure for reducing rehospitalization rates may now be available, however. In one study, patients were randomly assigned to maintenance treatment as usual (medication and supportive group therapy) or a new treatment involving the following components (Herz et al., 2000):

1. Educating patients about relapse and recognizing early signs of relapse
2. Monitoring early signs of relapse by staff
3. Weekly supportive group or individual therapy
4. Family educational sessions
5. Quick intervention, involving both increased doses of medication and crisis-oriented problem-solving therapy, when early signs of relapse were detected

Importantly, staff were able to accurately recognize early signs of relapse and implement procedures to deal with them. Over 18 months, the new treatment cut relapse rates in half and reduced rehospitalization rates by about 44 percent.

Commonly reported side effects of the antipsychotics include dizziness, blurred vision, restlessness, and sexual dysfunction. In addition, some particularly disturbing side effects, termed *extrapyramidal side effects*, stem from dysfunctions of the nerve tracts that descend from the brain to spinal motor neurons. Extrapyramidal side effects resemble the symptoms of Parkinson's disease. People taking antipsychotics usually develop tremors of the fingers, a shuffling gait, and drooling. Other side effects include dystonia, a state of muscular rigidity, and dyskinesia, an abnormal motion of voluntary and involuntary muscles, producing chewing movements as well as other movements of the lips, fingers, and legs; together they cause arching of the back and a twisted posture of the neck and body. Another side effect is akasthesia, an inability to remain still; people pace constantly and fidget. These perturbing symptoms can be treated by drugs used with patients who have Parkinson's disease.

In a muscular disturbance of older patients with schizophrenia, called *tardive dyskinesia*, the mouth muscles involuntarily make sucking, lip-smacking, and chin-wagging motions. In more severe cases the whole body can be subject to involuntary motor movements. This syndrome affects about 10 to 20 percent of patients treated with antipsychotics for a long period of time and is not responsive to any known treatment (Sweet et al., 1995). Finally, a side effect called *neuroleptic malignant syndrome* occurs in about 1 percent of cases. In this condition, which can sometimes be fatal, severe muscular rigidity develops,

Atypical antipsychotic drugs such as olanzapine may have fewer side effects than traditional antipsychotic drugs, but they still have side effects. (Copyright Eli Lilly and Company. All Rights Reserved. Used with permission.)

accompanied by fever. The heart races, blood pressure increases, and the patient may lapse into a coma.

Because of these serious side effects, some clinicians believe it is unwise to prescribe high doses of antipsychotics for extended periods of time. Current clinical practice calls for treating patients with the smallest possible doses of drugs. The clinician is put in a bind by this situation: if medication is reduced, the chance of relapse increases; but if medication is continued, serious and untreatable side effects may develop.

Atypical Antipsychotic Drugs and Their Side Effects In the decades following the introduction of the traditional antipsychotic drugs, there appeared to be little interest in developing new drugs to treat schizophrenia. This situation has changed in the last 15 years, with the introduction of clozapine (trade name Clozaril) in the United States, which can produce therapeutic gains in patients with schizophrenia who do not respond well to traditional antipsychotics (Kane et al., 1988). Some studies have found that clozapine has greater therapeutic gains in reducing positive and disorganization symptoms than traditional antipsychotics (Rosenheck et al., 1999; Wahlbeck et al., 1999). Patients who take clozapine are also less likely to drop out of treatment (Kane et al., 2001). In addition, clozapine produces fewer motor side effects than do traditional antipsychotics. Furthermore, maintenance of patients on clozapine reduces relapse rates (Conley et al., 1999). Although the precise mechanism of the therapeutic effects of clozapine is not yet completely understood, we do know that it has a major impact on serotonin receptors.

Clozapine does have serious side effects, however. It can impair the functioning of the immune system in a small percentage of patients (about 1 percent) by lowering the number of white blood cells, a condition called agranulocytosis, which makes patients vulnerable to infection and even death. For this reason, patients taking clozapine have to be carefully monitored with routine blood tests. It also can produce seizures and other side effects, such as dizziness, fatigue, drooling, and weight gain (Meltzer, Cola, & Way, 1993).

Nevertheless, the apparent success of clozapine stimulated drug companies to begin a more earnest search for other drugs that might be more effective than traditional antipsychotics. These drugs, including clozapine, are referred to as the **atypical antipsychotic drugs** because their mechanism of action was not like the typical or traditional antipsychotic medications. Two atypical antipsychotics developed after clozapine are olanzapine (trade name Zyprexa) and risperidone (trade name Risperdal). Early studies showed that olanzapine and risperidone produced fewer side effects than traditional antipsychotics, suggesting patients were somewhat less likely to discontinue treatment (Dolder et al., 2002). The atypical antipsychotics appear to be as effective as traditional antipsychotics in reducing positive and disorganized symptoms (Conley & Mahmoud, 2001), and they also appear to be superior to the traditional antipsychotics in reducing rehospitalization rates and relapse (Csernansky, Mahmoud, & Brenner, 2002; Leucht et al., 2003).

However, the news is not all good. A comprehensive randomized controlled clinical trial compared four atypical drugs (olanzapine, risperidone, ziprasidone and, guetiapine) and one traditional drug (perphenazine) against one another (Lieberman et al., 2005). Close to 1500 patients from all over the United States were in the study. Among the many findings from this study, three stand out. First, the atypical drugs were not more effective than the older, traditional drug. Second, the atypical drugs did not produce fewer unpleasant side effects. And third, nearly three-quarters of the patients stopped taking the medications before the 18 months of the study design had ended. Despite the early promise of atypical drugs, more work is needed to develop better treatments for schizophrenia.

In addition, other studies suggest that atypical antipsychotics may have unfortunate side effects of their own. For example, clozapine, and olanzapine have been related to the development of type 2 diabetes (Leslie & Rosenheck, 2004); however, it is not clear whether the medicine itself is increasing this risk, perhaps via side effect of weight gain, or whether patients were predisposed to developing diabetes independent of their medication usage. Other evidence suggests that these drugs may increase the risk for pancreatitis (Koller et al., 2003). Studies designed to examine these and other side effects more closely are currently underway.

A psychological approach to the study of the atypical antipsychotics examines fundamental aspects of cognition, such as attention and memory, that are known to be deficient in many patients with schizophrenia (Heinrichs & Zakzanis, 1998) and are associated with poor social adaptation (Green, 1996). A number of studies suggest that these medications may be more effective than the traditional drugs at improving cognitive functioning (P. D. Harvey, et al., 2003, 2004). For example, evidence suggests that risperidone improves short-term memory—involved in, for example, remembering a phone number long enough to be able to dial it—more than other antipsychotic drugs, apparently by reducing the activity of serotonin-sensitive receptors in the frontal cortex (Green et al., 1997). Research has also shown that improvements in memory are correlated with improvements in learning social skills in psychosocial rehabilitation programs (Green, 1996; Marder et al., 1999). More generally, the atypical antipsychotics may thus make possible more thoroughgoing changes in schizophrenia and its behavioral consequences than do drugs that do not have these cognitive effects. However, other evidence suggests that psychological treatments (reviewed below) are also effective, perhaps more so, at alleviating cognitive deficits.

Despite this relatively good news about the atypical antipsychotic medications, there is some evidence that they tend not to be used among ethnic minority patients. Two different studies recently found that African American patients were more likely to be prescribed the traditional antipsychotics and less likely to be prescribed the atypical antipsychotics (Kreyenbuhl et al., 2003; Valenti, Narendran, & Pristach, 2003). This is unfortunate for a number of reasons, but particularly since there is some evidence that African Americans may experience more side effects than whites in response to the traditional medications (Frackeiwicz et al., 1997). More broadly, these results echo the findings of the recent Surgeon General's supplement to his landmark report on mental health that elucidated a number of disparities in mental health treatment among members of ethnic minority groups (USDHHS, 2001a). Compared with other disorders reviewed in this book, there has been relatively less research on schizophrenia across different ethnic groups. This must be a focus of future research.

Development of New Drugs   Some patients do not respond to any of the available medications, suggesting the need for new medications to be developed. One exciting approach in this has been the MATRICS project. MATRICS (Measurement and Treatment Research to Improve Cognition in Schizophrenia) is a collaboration between psychologists, psychiatrists, pharmaceutical companies, the FDA, and the National Institute of Mental Health. One goal of this project is to develop a consensus battery of cognitive and neuropsychological tests that can be used to evaluate and compare the efficacy of medications to treat schizophrenia (Green et al., 2004). To achieve this goal, several systematic and transparent steps were followed, which included deciding on the most important cognitive domains to be studied, finding the best and most practical ways to measure these domains, and determining the extent to which improving performance in those domains is related to a better outcome in schizophrenia. Results from each step are made available to the public via a Web site (www.matrics. ucla.edu).

Evaluation of Drug Treatments   Antipsychotic drugs are an indispensable part of treatment for schizophrenia and will undoubtedly continue to be an important component. Furthermore, the recent success of clozapine, olanzapine, and risperidone has stimulated a continued effort to find new and more effective drug therapies for schizophrenia. Many other drugs are currently being evaluated, so we may be on the verge of a new era in the treatment of schizophrenia. See Table 11.4 for a summary of major drugs used to treat schizophrenia.

Table 11.4 Summary of Major Drugs Used in Treating Schizophrenia

Drug Category	Generic Name	Trade Name
Phenothiazine	Chlorpromazine	Thorazine
	Fluphenazine decanoate	Prolixin
Butyrophenone	Haloperidol	Haldol
Thioxanthene	Thiothixene	Navane
Tricyclic dibenzodiazepine	Clozapine	Clozaril
Thienbenzodiazepine	Olanzapine	Zyprexa
Benzisoxazole	Risperidone	Risperdal
Dibenzothiazepine	Quetiapine	Seroquel

Psychological Treatments

Our growing knowledge about neurobiological factors in schizophrenia and the continuing improvement in antipsychotic medications should not lead us to neglect the importance of psychosocial factors in both the etiology and treatment of schizophrenia. This is made clear in the following excerpt from a review of empirically supported psychological treatments for schizophrenia:

> *For veteran practitioners who have long considered only biological treatments as effective in protecting schizophrenic individuals from stress-induced relapse and disability . . . evidence [on reducing expressed emotion in families, reviewed later] that supports the protective value of psychosocial treatments . . . may serve as an antidote to the insidious biological reductionism that often characterizes the field of schizophrenia research and treatment . . . It is essential to view treatments of schizophrenia in their biopsychosocial matrix—leaving out any of the three components . . . will diminish the impact and efficacy of treatment. (Kopelowicz & Liberman, 1998, p. 192)*

Neglecting the psychological and social aspect of schizophrenia compromises efforts to help people and their families who are struggling with this illness. Indeed, the current treatment recommendations for schizophrenia as compiled by the schizophrenia Patient Outcomes Research Team (PORT) are medications plus psychosocial interventions (Lehman et al., 2004). The PORT recommendations are based on extensive reviews of treatment research. The following discussions of various psychological treatments of schizophrenia will help us appreciate both their limitations and their strengths.

Psychoanalytic Therapies   Freud did little, either in his clinical practice or through his writings, to adapt psychoanalysis to the treatment of patients with schizophrenia. He believed that they were incapable of establishing the close interpersonal relationship essential for analysis. It was Harry Stack Sullivan, an American psychiatrist, and later Frieda Fromm-Reichmann, a German psychiatrist who emigrated to the United States, who promoted the use of psychoanalysis with schizophrenic hospital patients.

In Sullivan's view, therapy required the patient to learn adult forms of communication and to achieve insight into the role the past has played in current problems. Sullivan advised the very gradual, nonthreatening development of a trusting relationship. After many sessions, and with the establishment of greater trust and support, the analyst begins to encourage the patient to examine his or her interpersonal relationships. Fromm-Reichmann treated patients with great patience and optimism, making it clear that they need not take her into their world or give up their sickness until they were completely ready to do so.

Despite these psychiatrists' enthusiasm and claims of success, research results do not support the efficacy of this treatment for schizophrenia. For some patients, it may do more harm than good (Katz & Gunderson, 1990; Mueser & Berenbaum, 1990; Stanton et al., 1984). A close consideration of the patients treated by Sullivan and Fromm-Reichmann indicates that many might not even have qualified for a diagnosis of schizophrenia by the strict DSM-IV-TR criteria for the disorder. Results from a long-term follow-up of patients bearing a diagnosis of schizophrenia and discharged after treatment between 1963 and 1976 at the New York State Psychiatric Institute showed that analytic approaches were largely unsuccessful with these patients (Stone, 1986).

More recent types of psychosocial treatments are more active, present-focused, and reality-oriented than psychoanalytic approaches, as therapists try to help patients and their families deal more directly with the everyday problems they face in coping with this disruptive and debilitating illness. Inherent to this work is the assumption that a good deal of the stress experienced by people with schizophrenia is due to their difficulties in negotiating everyday social challenges, including the pressures that arise in their families when they return home after hospitalization. We turn now to these newer and more effective approaches.

Social Skills Training   Social skills training   is designed to teach people with schizophrenia how to successfully manage a wide variety of interpersonal situations—

discussing their medications with their psychiatrist, ordering meals in a restaurant, filling out job applications, interviewing for jobs, saying no to drug dealers on the street, and reading bus schedules. Most of us take these skills for granted and give little thought to them in our daily lives, but people with schizophrenia cannot take them for granted—they need to work hard to acquire or reacquire such skills. Doing so enables them to partake more of the positive things that are available outside of institutional settings, enhancing their quality of life (Heinssen, Liberman, & Kopelowicz, 2000; Liberman et al., 2000).

In an early demonstration of social skills training, investigators provided social skills training that consisted of role-playing, modeling, and positive reinforcement of a variety of skills needed in different social situations (Bellack, Hersen, & Turner, 1976). This combination of approaches effected significant improvement in all three patients involved in the study, and there was even generalization to social situations that had not been worked on during the training. This study and others conducted with larger groups of patients indicate that schizophrenia patients can be taught new social behaviors that help them achieve fewer relapses, better social functioning, and a higher quality of life (Kopelowicz et al., 2002). Some of the studies are noteworthy in demonstrating benefits over a period of 2 years following treatment (Liberman et al., 1998; Marder et al., 1999), though not all results are positive (Pilling et al., 2002). Social skills training is usually a component of treatments for schizophrenia that go beyond the use of medications alone, including family therapies for lowering expressed emotion, which we discuss next.

Family Therapies That Reduce Expressed Emotion   Many patients with schizophrenia who are discharged from hospitals go home to their families. Earlier we discussed research showing that high levels of expressed emotion (EE) within the family, including being hostile, hypercritical, and overprotective, have been linked to relapse and rehospitalization. Based on this finding, a number of family therapies have been developed. These therapies may differ in length, setting, and specific techniques, but they have several features in common beyond the overall purpose of calming things down for the patient by calming things down for the family:

- *Educating family members about schizophrenia— specifically about the genetic or neurobiological factors that predispose some people to the illness, the cognitive problems associated with schizophrenia, the symptoms of schizophrenia, and the signs of impending relapse.* High-EE families are typically not well informed about schizophrenia, and giving them some basic information helps them be less critical of the relative with schizophrenia. Knowing, for example, that neurobiology has a lot to do with having schizophrenia and that the illness involves problems in thinking clearly and rationally might help family members be more accepting and understanding of the patient's inappropriate or ineffectual actions. Therapists encourage family members to lower their expectations of their relative with schizophrenia, and they make clear to family and patient alike that proper medication and therapy can reduce stress on the patient and prevent deterioration.

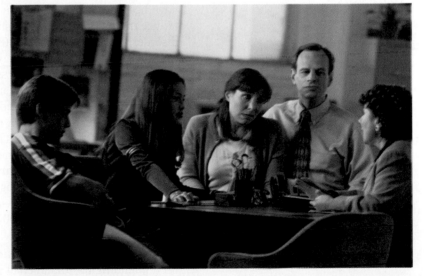

Family therapy can help educate patients and their families about schizophrenia and reduce expressed emotion. (Bruce Ayres/Stone/Getty Images.)

- *Informing patients and families about antipsychotic medication.* Therapists impress on both the family and the patient the importance of the patient's taking his or her antipsychotic medication, becoming better informed about the intended effects and the side effects of the medication, taking responsibility for monitoring the patient's response to medication, and seeking medical consultation rather than just discontinuing the medication if adverse side effects occur.

- *Helping families avoid blaming—specifically, encouraging family members to blame neither themselves nor the patient for the illness and for the difficulties all are having in coping with it.*

- *Improving communication and problem-solving skills within the family.* Therapists focus on teaching the family ways to express both positive and negative feelings in a constructive, empathic, nondemanding manner rather than in a finger-pointing, critical, or overprotective way. They focus as well on making personal conflicts less stressful by teaching family members ways to work together to solve everyday problems.

- *Encouraging patients and their families to expand their social contacts, especially their support networks.*

- *Instilling hope that things can improve, including the hope that the patient may not have to return to the hospital.*

Therapies use various techniques to implement these strategies. Examples include identifying stressors that could cause relapse, training families in communication skills and problem solving, and having high-EE family members watch videotapes of interactions of low-EE families (Penn & Mueser, 1996). Compared with standard treatments (usually just medication), family therapy plus medication has typically lowered relapse over periods of 1 to 2 years. This positive finding is evident particularly in studies in which the treatment lasted for at least 9 months (Falloon et al., 1982, 1985; Hogarty et al., 1986, 1991; Kopelowicz & Liberman, 1998; McFarlane et al., 1995; Penn & Mueser, 1996).

Cognitive Behavioral Therapies   At one time, researchers assumed that it was futile to try to alter the cognitive distortions, including delusions, of patients with schizophrenia. Now, however, a developing clinical and experimental literature demonstrates that the maladaptive beliefs of some patients can in fact be changed with cognitive behavioral interventions (Garety, Fowler, & Kuipers, 2000).

Some patients can be encouraged to test out their delusional beliefs in much the same way as people without schizophrenia do. Through collaborative discussions (and in the context of other modes of treatment, including antipsychotic drugs), some patients have been helped to attach a nonpsychotic meaning to paranoid symptoms and thereby reduce their intensity and aversive nature, similar to what is done for depression and panic disorder (Beck & Rector, 2000; Drury et al., 1996; Haddock et al., 1998). Researchers have found that cognitive behavioral therapy (CBT) can also reduce negative symptoms, for example, challenging belief structures tied to low expectations for success (anergia) and low expectations for pleasure (anhedonia) (Beck, Rector, & Stolar, 2004).

Findings from the few randomized controlled trials of CBT in schizophrenia suggest that this treatment, along with medication, can help reduce hallucinations and delusions (Bustillo et al., 2001). CBT has been used as an adjunctive treatment for schizophrenia in Great Britain for over 10 years, and the results are similarly positive, even in community settings (Sensky et al., 2000, Turkington, Kingdom, & Turner, 2002). One study has found that stress management training (discussed in Chapter 7) was effective in reducing stress among schizophrenia patients—a noteworthy outcome indeed, given the link between stress and relapse (Norman et al., 2002).

Therapies That Focus on Basic Cognitive Functions   In recent years researchers have been attending to fundamental aspects of cognition that are disordered in schizophrenia, in an attempt to improve these functions and thereby favorably affect behavior. The fact that positive clinical outcomes from risperidone are associated with improvements in certain kinds of memory (Green et al., 1997) lends support to the more general notion that therapies directed at basic cognitive processes—the kind that nonclinical cognitive scientists study—holds promise for improving the social and emotional lives of people with schizophrenia. This approach concentrates on trying to normalize such functions as attention and memory, which are known to be deficient in many patients with schizophrenia and are associated with poor social adaptation (Green et al., 2000).

Recently developed treatments that seek to enhance basic cognitive functions such as verbal learning ability are referred to as **cognitive enhancement therapy (CET)** or *cognitive training*. A 2-year randomized controlled clinical trial compared group-based CET with enriched supportive therapy (EST), an adaptation of personal therapy (see below). CET consisted of nearly 80 hours of computer-based training in attention, memory, and problem solving. Groups also worked on such daily-life, social-cognitive skills, as reading and understanding newspaper editorials, solving social problems, and starting and maintaining conversations. EST consisted of the supportive and educational elements of personal therapy. All patients were also taking medications. At the 1- and 2-year follow-up assessments, CET was more effective than EST in improving cognitive abilities in problem solving, attention, social cognition, and social adjustment, while symptom reduction was the same for both treatments (Hogarty et al., 2004). Patients who received CET were also rated as being more ready for employment and in fact, tended to be employed at the end of 2 years, largely driven by the fact that these patients were more likely to be in volunteer positions than those in the EST group. Thus, CET is effective at reducing symptoms and improving cognitive abilities, and it appears to be linked to good functional outcomes, such as employment.

A recent review of 17 other randomized trials of cognitive training therapies shows that these interventions, for the most part, improve cognitive abilities, whether the treatments focus on specific tasks (e.g., a memory test) or on broader strategies (e.g., problem solving) or whether done via computer-based training (Twamley, Jeste, & Bellack, 2003). Only a few of these studies included measures of symptoms and functional outcomes, such as employment or general functioning, but those that did generally found that cognitive training improved symptoms and functional outcomes. As promising as these findings are, nearly all of the studies to date have been with white men; thus, their generalizability remains to be established. And not all studies yield positive results (Pilling et al., 2002).

Personal Therapy   As encouraging as studies of family therapies directed at reducing EE were, most of the patients in those studies still returned to the hospital, and the clinical outcomes of those who managed to remain in the community left a lot to be desired (Hogarty et al., 1997a). Researchers asked what more could be done for patients with schizophrenia to increase their chances of being able to remain longer outside the hospital, whether or not they could do so within their family. This question led to a treatment called **personal therapy**, developed by one of the groups that had published positive, though limited, findings on treatments that reduce EE (Hogarty et al., 1995, 1997a,b).

Personal therapy is a broad spectrum cognitive behavioral approach to the multiplicity of problems of patients with schizophrenia who have been discharged from the hospital. It is conducted both one-on-one and in small groups (workshops). A key element in this approach, based on the finding in EE research that reduction of EE by family members leads to less relapse following hospital discharge, is teaching the patient how to recognize inappropriate affect. Patients are taught also to notice small signs of relapse, such as social withdrawal or inappropriate threats against others, and they learn skills to deal with these problems. The therapy also includes some cognitive restructuring to help patients avoid turning life's inevitable frustrations and challenges into catastrophes and thus to help them lower their stress levels.

In addition, patients are often taught muscle-relaxation techniques as an aid to learning to detect the gradual buildup of anxiety or anger and then to apply the relaxation skills in order to control these emotions better. There is also a strong focus on teaching specific social skills as well as on encouraging patients to continue to take their antipsychotic medication in a maintenance mode, that is, in a dose that is typically lower than what is necessary in an acute phase of the illness.

Personal therapy also includes nonbehavioral elements, especially warm and empathic acceptance of the patient's emotional and cognitive turmoil along with realistic but optimistic expectations that life can be better. In general, patients are taught that they are emotionally vulnerable to stress, that their thinking is not always clear, that they have to continue with their medication, and that they can learn a variety of skills to make the most of the hand that nature has dealt them. This is not a short-term treatment; it can extend over 3 years of weekly to biweekly sessions.

Note that the focus of much of this therapy is on the patient, not on the family. Whereas the focus in the family therapies was on reducing the EE in the patient's family—an environmental change from the point of view of the patient—the goal of personal therapy is teaching coping skills to the patient, new ways of thinking about and controlling affective reactions to whatever challenges are presented by the environment.

Also, important in this therapy is criticism management and conflict resolution, which refers to learning how to deal with negative feedback from others and how to resolve the interpersonal conflicts that are an inevitable part of dealing with others. Indications are that personal therapy can help many people with schizophrenia stay out of the hospital and function better, with the most favorable outcomes achieved by those who can live with their family of origin (Hogarty et al., 1997a,b).

Case Management   After large numbers of patients were discharged from hospitals (referred to as deinstitutionalization) in the 1960s, many patients with schizophrenia no longer resided in hospitals and thus had to fend for themselves in securing needed services. Lacking the centralized hospital as the site where most services were delivered, the mental health system became more complex. In 1977, fearing that many patients were not accessing services, the National Institute of Mental Health established a program giving grants to states to help patients cope with the mental health system. Out of this program, a new mental health specialty, the case manager, was created.

Initially, case managers were basically brokers of services; because they were familiar with the system, they were able to get patients into contact with providers of whatever services the patients required. As the years passed, different models of case management developed. The major innovation was the recognition that case managers often needed to provide direct clinical services and that services might best be delivered by a team rather than brokered out. The Assertive Community Treatment model (Stein & Test, 1980) and the Intensive Case Management model (Surles et al., 1992) both entail a multidisciplinary team that provides services in the community ranging from medication, treatment for substance abuse, help in dealing with stressors patients face regularly (such as managing money), psychotherapy, vocational training, and assistance to patients in obtaining housing and employment. Case managers hold together and coordinate the range of medical and psychological services that patients with schizophrenia need to keep functioning outside of institutions and with some degree of independence and peace of mind (Kopelowicz et al., 2002).

Indications are that this more intensive treatment is superior to less intensive methods in reducing time spent in the hospital, improving housing stability, and ameliorating symptoms (Mueser et al., 1998). However, more intensive case management has not shown positive effects in other domains, such as time spent out of jail or improvement in social functioning. The actual procedures that come under the rubric of case management vary a great deal from study to study. The services provided by a case management team will have positive effects only to the extent that those services are appropriate. In addition, in order for this approach to be effective, there have to be enough case managers for patients. Too often, the case loads of these mental health professionals are much too high.

Residential Treatment   Some people function too well to remain in a hospital and yet do not function well enough to live on their own or even within their family. For such individuals there are "halfway houses," or residential treatment homes. These are protected living units, typically located in large, formerly private residences. Here patients discharged from the hospital live, take their meals, and gradually return to ordinary community life by holding a part-time job or going to school. As part of what is called *vocational rehabilitation*, these patients learn marketable skills that can help them secure employment and thereby increase their chances of remaining in the community. Living arrangements may be relatively unstructured; some houses set up money-making enterprises that help train and support the residents.

The need in the United States for effective residential treatment cannot be underestimated, especially in light of the deinstitutionalization that has seen tens of thousands of patients discharged from hospitals. Of course, civil rights issues are very important here—patients must be shielded from ill-advised and even harmful detention (see Chapter 17), but discharge has all too often led to destitute former patients left to fend for themselves in the streets or being rehospitalized in what has been called the revolving-door syndrome. Discharge is a desirable goal, but patients with schizophrenia almost always need follow-up community-based services, and these are scarce. Indeed, today a large percentage of homeless people in the United States are mentally ill, including many people with schizophrenia. Social Security benefits are available to those with schizophrenia, but if they do not have an address, they often do not receive all the benefits to which they are entitled. Though there are good residential treatment programs available, there are not enough of them.

Depending on how well funded the residential treatment facility is, the staff may include psychiatrists or clinical psychologists or both. The most important staff members are paraprofessionals, often undergraduate psychology majors or graduate students in clinical psychology or social work who live at the facility and act both as administrators and as friends to the residents. Group meetings, at which residents talk out their frustrations and learn to relate to others in honest and constructive ways, are often part of the routine. There are many such programs across the United States that have helped thousands of patients, most of them with schizophrenia, make enough of a social adaptation to be able to remain out of the hospital. Integrating therapy with gainful employment is increasingly recognized as important in keeping people with schizophrenia (and also mental retardation; see Chapter 14) out of institutional settings (Kopelowicz & Liberman, 1998; Kopelowicz et al., 2002).

In the coming years, residential treatment programs are likely to pay increasing attention to preparing patients to obtain and retain employment for which they can qualify. For example, the U.S. government has begun to recognize the importance of employment by allowing people with mental disabilities such as schizophrenia to continue receiving Social Security benefits for up to 2 years while they are earning money from (low-paying) jobs that can increase their chances of living independently or at least outside of the hospital. This welcome change in policy (from one that terminated such benefits once the person began earning money) represents a recognition of the harmful effects of not working and not being able to live in a reasonably independent manner.

Still, obtaining employment can pose a major challenge because of bias against people with schizophrenia. Although the Americans with Disabilities Act of 1990 prohibits employers from asking applicants if they have a history of serious mental illness, people with schizophrenia still have a difficult time obtaining regular employment because their symptoms make negatively biased employers fearful of hiring them. Also a factor is how much leeway employers are willing to give people whose thinking, emotions, and behavior are usually unconventional to some degree.

Despite these difficulties, the trend seems to be to do whatever is necessary to assist people in working and living in as autonomous a manner as their physical and mental condition will allow (Kopelowicz & Liberman, 1998). Additional funding will be needed to create more residential treatment facilities with the hope of reducing the number of schizophrenia patients who are without treatment.

Remaining Challenges in the Treatment of Schizophrenia

It is increasingly recognized that early intervention is important and useful in affecting the course of schizophrenia over time. That is, getting patients onto the right medications and providing support and information to the family and appropriate psychotherapy to the patient can reduce the severity of relapses in the future (Drury et al., 1996). It is also important to teach patients social skills and more reality-based thinking so that they can function outside the hospital and probably reduce the EE encountered both inside and outside the home. Families affected by schizophrenia are encouraged to join support groups and formal organizations, such as the National Alliance for the Mentally Ill, to reduce the isolation and stigma associated with having a family member who has schizophrenia.

Despite the promise of these interventions, there is often a gap between what treatments are available and what treatments are actually received. This issue was highlighted in a study that involved interviewing over 700 patients and by reviewing their medical records (Lehman et al., 1998). As expected, almost 90 percent had been prescribed antipsychotic drugs, but of these patients only 62 percent received a dose in the recommended range. About 15 percent got too little, and the remainder too much. Further, although over 90 percent of patients were prescribed maintenance doses of drugs, only 29 percent of these received a dose in the recommended range; of the 71 percent who did not receive a recommended dose, about half were getting too much and half too little. African Americans were much more likely than whites to be prescribed maintenance doses that were too high.

Psychosocial treatments were also examined, but these were more difficult to evaluate because records or patient reports did not allow the researchers to know whether the treatment was one of those considered effective (such as family therapies or social skills training). Just in terms of whether any psychosocial treatments at all were prescribed for these patients, the study shows that some sort of individual or group therapy was provided for over 90 percent of inpatients. But for patients who had regular contact with their families, family treatment of some sort was prescribed for only about 40 percent. For unemployed patients, vocational rehabilitation (teaching job skills) was prescribed for only about 30 percent.

Conclusion? Many patients with schizophrenia are not getting anything near optimal therapy. Indeed, though the kind of integrated treatment we have been describing is promising, the sad fact is that it is not widely available or accessible to most patients and their families. The reasons for this are unclear (Baucom et al., 1998; Dixon et al., 1997).

Preventing substance abuse among patients with schizophrenia is largely an unmet challenge. The lifetime prevalence rate for substance abuse among people with schizophrenia is an astounding 50 percent (Kosten & Ziedonis, 1997); the rate is even higher among the homeless mentally ill population. Programs for treating substance abuse usually exclude people who are seriously mentally ill, and programs for treating people who are seriously mentally ill usually exclude substance abusers. In both instances the reason is that the comorbid condition is considered disruptive to the treatment (Mueser, Bellack, & Blanchard, 1992). This is a situation that simply must be turned around.

Check Your Knowledge 11.3

True or false?
1. Traditional antipsychotics include medications like Haldol or Prolixin; atypical antipsychotics include clozapine and olanzapine.
2. Atypical antipsychotics produce more motor side effects than traditional antipsychotics.
3. Cognitive behavior therapy, but not cognitive enhancement therapy, is effective for schizophrenia, if given along with medications.
4. One important focus of residential treatment programs is to help patients become employed.

Summary

Clinical Description

- The symptoms of schizophrenia involve disturbances in several major areas, including thought, perception, and attention; motor behavior; affect; and life functioning. Symptoms are typically divided into positive, negative, and disorganized categories. Positive symptoms include excesses and distortions, such as delusions and hallucinations. Negative symptoms are behavioral deficits, such as flat affect, avolition, alogia, and anhedonia. Disorganized symptoms include disorganized speech and behavior. Other symptoms include catatonia and inappropriate affect.

- The DSM-IV-TR includes several subtypes of schizophrenia, including disorganized, catatonic, and paranoid. These subtypes are based on the prominence of particular symptoms (e.g., delusions in the paranoid subtype) and reflect the variations in behavior found among people diagnosed with schizophrenia. However, there is considerable overlap among the subtypes, and they have little predictive validity.

Etiology

- The evidence for genetic transmission of schizophrenia is impressive. Family and twin studies suggest a genetic component; adoption studies show a strong relationship between having a schizophrenic parent and the likelihood of developing the disorder, typically in early adulthood. Molecular genetics studies are still in need of replication. The most promising findings to date seem to indicate genes such as DTNBP1, NGR1, and COMT.

- The genetic predisposition to develop schizophrenia may involve neurotransmitters. It appears that increased sensitivity of dopamine receptors in the limbic area of the brain is related to the positive symptoms of schizophrenia. The negative symptoms may be due to dopamine underactivity in the prefrontal cortex. Other neurotransmitters, such as serotonin, glutamate, and GABA, may also be involved.

- The brains of some patients with schizophrenia have enlarged ventricles and problems with the prefrontal cortex. Some of these structural abnormalities could result from maternal viral infection during the second trimester of pregnancy or from damage sustained during a difficult birth.

- The diagnosis of schizophrenia is most frequently applied to people of the lowest socioeconomic status, apparently because of downward social mobility created by the disorder. In addition, vague communications and conflicts are evident in the family life of patients with schizophrenia, though it is less clear if these contribute to their disorder. High levels of expressed emotion in families, as well as increases in general life stress, have been shown to be an important determinant of relapse. Developmental studies have identified problems in childhood that were there prior to the onset of schizophrenia, but these studies were not designed to predict schizophrenia, so it is difficult to interpret the findings. High-risk studies suggest that the causes of positive and negative symptoms may be different. Other studies have found cognitive problems in childhood to predict the onset of adult psychopathology, but not specifically schizophrenia.

Treatment

- Antipsychotic drugs, especially the phenothiazines, have been widely used to treat schizophrenia since the 1950s. Atypical antipsychotic drugs such as clozapine and risperidone are also effective and produce fewer motoric side effects, though they have their own set of side effects. Drugs alone are not a completely effective treatment, though, as patients with schizophrenia need to be taught or retaught ways of dealing with the challenges of everyday life.

- The efficacy of psychoanalytic treatments has not been supported by evidence. In contrast, family therapy aimed at reducing high levels of expressed emotion has been shown to be valuable in preventing relapse. In addition, social skills training and various cognitive behavioral therapies have helped patients meet the inevitable stresses of family and community living and lead more ordered and constructive lives within an institution. Recent efforts to change the thinking of people with schizophrenia are showing promise as well.

- The most promising approaches to treatment today emphasize the importance of both pharmacological and psychosocial interventions. Unfortunately, such integrated treatments are not widely available.

Answers to Check Your Knowledge Questions

11.1 1. flat affect; 2. delusion or ideas of reference; 3. anhedonia; 4. disorganized thinking or derailment.

11.2 1. family, twin, adoption; 2. DTNBP1, NGR1; 3. prefrontal; 4. hostility, critical comments, emotional overinvolvement.

11.3 1. T; 2. F; 3. F; 4. T

Key Terms

alogia
anhedonia
antipsychotic drugs
asociality
atypical antipsychotic drugs
avolition
brief psychotic disorder
catatonia
catatonic immobility
catatonic schizophrenia

cognitive enhancement therapy (CET)
delusional disorder
delusions
dementia praecox
disorganized behavior
disorganized speech
disorganized schizophrenia
disorganized symptoms
dopamine theory

expressed emotion (EE)
flat affect
grandiose delusions
hallucinations
ideas of reference
inappropriate affect
loose associations
negative symptoms
paranoid schizophrenia
personal therapy

positive symptoms
prefrontal cortex
residual schizophrenia
schizoaffective disorder
schizophrenia
schizophreniform disorder
social selection theory
social skills training
sociogenic hypothesis
undifferentiated schizophrenia

12 Personality Disorders

Learning Goals

1. Be able to explain the key features of each personality disorder, the issues in classifying these disorders, and alternative dimensional approaches to diagnosis.
2. Be able to describe the genetic, neurobiological, social, and other risk factors for personality disorders, and be able to discuss problems in the research on etiology.
3. Be able to describe the available medication and psychological treatments of personality disorders.

Clinical Case: Mary

Mary was single and 26 years old when she was first admitted to a psychiatric hospital. She had been in outpatient treatment with a psychologist for several months when her persistent thoughts of cutting, burning, and killing herself led her therapist to conclude that she could no longer be managed as an outpatient.

Mary's first experience with psychotherapy occurred when she was an adolescent. Her grades declined sharply in the eleventh grade, and her parents suspected she was using drugs. She began to miss curfews and, occasionally, to stay out all night. She often skipped school. Family therapy was started, and it seemed to go well at first. Mary was enthusiastic about the therapist and asked for additional, private sessions with him.

During the private sessions, Mary revealed she had used drugs extensively, including "everything I can get my hands on." She had been promiscuous and had prostituted herself several times to get drug money. Her relationships with her peers were changeable, to say the least. There was a constant parade of new friends, whom Mary at first thought to be the greatest ever but who soon disappointed her somehow and were cast aside, often in very unpleasant ways. Except for the one person with whom she was currently enamored, Mary had no friends. She said that she stayed away from others for fear that they would harm her in some way.

After several weeks of family therapy, Mary's parents noticed that Mary was angry and abusive toward the therapist. After several more weeks had passed, Mary refused to attend any more sessions. In a subsequent conversation with the therapist, Mary's father learned that she had behaved seductively toward the therapist during their private sessions and that her changed attitude coincided with his rejection of her advances, despite the therapist's attempt to mix firmness with warmth and empathy.

Mary managed to graduate from high school and enrolled in a local community college, but the old patterns returned. Poor grades, cutting classes, continuing drug use, and lack of interest in her studies finally led her to quit college in the middle of the first semester of her second year. After leaving school, Mary held a series of low-paying jobs. Most of them didn't last long, as her relationships with co-workers paralleled her relationships with her peers in high school. When Mary started a new job she would find someone she really liked, but something would come between them, and the relationship would end angrily. She was often suspicious of her co-workers and reported that she heard them plotting how to prevent her from getting ahead on the job. She was quick to find hidden meanings in their behavior, as when she interpreted being the last person asked to sign a birthday card to mean that she was the least liked person in the office. She indicated that she "received vibrations" from others and could tell when they really didn't like her even in the absence of any direct evidence.

Mary's frequent mood swings, with periods of depression and extreme irritability, led her to seek therapy several times. But after initial enthusiasm, her relationships with therapists always deteriorated, resulting in premature termination of therapy. By the time of her hospitalization, she had seen six therapists.

Personality disorders are a heterogeneous group of disorders defined by long-standing, pervasive, and inflexible patterns of behavior and inner experience that deviate from the expectations of a person's culture. These problematic patterns are manifested in at least two of the following areas: cognition, emotions, relationships, and impulse control. Like all other DSM-IV-TR disorders, personality disorders are not diagnosed unless they cause distress or functional impairment.

As we examine the personality disorders, some might seem to fit people we know, not to mention ourselves! This seems a good time to remind readers about the medical student syndrome, so called because medical students (and psychology students) have a tendency to see themselves or their families and friends in descriptions of the disorders they study. For example, suppose you hear a loud burst of laughter just as you enter a crowded room, and this makes you feel that you are the target of some joke and that people are talking about you. Such concerns would qualify as symptoms of paranoid personality disorder only if they occurred often enough and intensely enough to prevent you from developing close personal relationships. This illustrates a general point: from time to time and in varying degrees, we all behave, think, and feel in ways that look similar to symptoms of personality disorders, but an actual personality disorder is defined by the extreme, inflexible, and maladaptive ways in which these traits are expressed. The symptoms of personality disorders are pervasive and persistent.

It is also important to keep in mind that personality disorders, which are coded on Axis II of DSM-IV-TR, are often comorbid with Axis I disorders. When this comorbidity occurs, the personality disorder shapes the form of the Axis I symptoms. For example, a person diagnosed with an anxiety disorder on Axis I and obsessive-compulsive personality disorder on Axis II will express anxiety in perfectionistic and controlling ways. As one researcher put it, different personality disorders "evoke contrasting ways of perceiving and coping" with Axis I disorders, which means that clinicians should consider the 'context of personality' when dealing with Axis I disorders (Millon, 1996, p. vii). Comorbid personality disorders are associated with more severe symptoms and worse treatment outcomes for Axis I disorders. As a result, personality disorders are commonly encountered in treatment settings. Typically, though, patients seek help for the symptoms of an Axis I disorder (such as panic disorder), without initially emphasizing symptoms of personality disorders. Beginning with DSM-III, therefore, personality disorders were placed on a separate axis, Axis II, to ensure that clinicians would consider whether a personality disorder is also present.

In this chapter we begin by looking at how personality disorders are classified in the DSM, at classification-related issues, and at an alternative system of classification. Next we

Table 12.1 Key Features of the DSM-IV-TR Personality Disorders

Cluster A (odd/eccentric)

Paranoid	Distrust and suspiciousness of others
Schizoid	Detachment from social relationships and restricted range of emotional expression
Schizotypal	Lack of capacity for close relationships, cognitive distortions, and eccentric behavior

Cluster B (dramatic/erratic)

Antisocial	Disregard for and violation of the rights of others
Borderline	Instability of interpersonal relationships, self-image, and affect, and marked impulsivity
Histrionic	Excessive emotionality and attention seeking
Narcissistic	Grandiosity, need for admiration, and lack of empathy

Cluster C (anxious/fearful)

Avoidant	Social inhibition, feelings of inadequacy, and hypersensitivity to negative evaluation
Dependent	Excessive need to be taken care of, submissive behavior, and fears of separation
Obsessive-compulsive	Preoccupation with order, perfection, and control

turn to clinical descriptions of the personality disorders and to discussions of their etiology. We conclude with discussions of the treatment of personality disorders. Throughout, the extent of our coverage depends on how much is known about the specific personality disorder under consideration; for example, there have been few studies of histrionic personality disorder, but there is a vast literature on antisocial personality disorder.

Classifying Personality Disorders

There is considerable debate about the best way to classify personality disorders. We begin by providing an overview of the DSM-IV-TR approach, then turn to an alternate dimensional approach.

The DSM Approach to Classification

In DSM-IV-TR, the 10 different personality disorders are classified in three clusters, reflecting the idea that these disorders are characterized by odd or eccentric behavior (cluster A), dramatic, emotional, or erratic behavior (cluster B), or anxious or fearful behavior (cluster C). These clusters form a useful organizational framework for our discussions in this chapter. Table 12.1 presents the personality disorders, their key features, and their grouping in clusters. Here, we discuss how well the DSM-IV-TR system works in terms of giving clinicians a reliable way to identify stable, distinct patterns.

Table 12.2 Interrater Reliability for the Personality Disorders

Diagnosis	Interrater Reliability
Paranoid	.86
Schizoid	.69
Schizotypal	.91
Antisocial	.97
Borderline	.90
Histrionic	.83
Narcissistic	.88
Avoidant	.79
Dependent	.87
Obsessive-compulsive	.85

Source: Zanarini et al. (2000).

Diagnostic Reliability   Before DSM-III, the diagnosis of personality disorders was very unreliable—one clinician might diagnose a flamboyant patient with narcissistic personality disorder, whereas another might diagnose the patient with histrionic personality disorder. DSM-III began a trend toward improved reliability by including specific diagnostic criteria for personality disorders, as it did for other disorders (Coolidge & Segal, 1998). Structured interviews were also developed to assess personality disorders, and these, too, helped improve diagnostic reliability. Table 12.2 shows interrater reliabilities from a recent study of the DSM-IV personality disorders (Zanarini et al., 2000). Although diagnoses of most personality disorders have adequate or good reliability, schizoid personality disorder is still characterized by relatively low interrater reliability. This may be because clinicians differ in their thresholds for seeing a behavior as pathological.

When there is disagreement about how to apply diagnostic criteria, there is a potential for the personal biases of a clinician to influence decisions. Some have noted that clinicians tend to be more likely to decide that some behaviors are pathological for women more than they are for men. (See Focus on Discovery 12.1 for more discussion of gender bias in diagnosing personality disorders.)

Focus on Discovery 12.1

Gender and Personality Disorders

For many personality disorders, prevalence varies a great deal by gender (see Table 12.3). For example, women are more likely than men to be diagnosed with borderline, histrionic, and dependent personality disorders, and men are more likely than women to be diagnosed with antisocial, narcissistic, and obsessive-compulsive personality disorders. Before the publication of DSM-IV, some researchers argued that certain of the diagnostic criteria for personality disorders pathologized feminine traits (Kaplan, 1983). For example, histrionic personality disorder included criteria for emotional lability, a focus on physical appearance, and sexual seductiveness. Are these traits more reinforced, and therefore more common, among women? In response to these types of criticisms, DSM-IV refined such criteria to make them more gender neutral. For example, the criterion for a focus on physical appearance was modified to read as "consistently uses physical appearance to draw attention to self," and the text now includes descriptions of ways in which men might show macho behaviors that fit this criterion (Hartung & Widiger, 1998).

Despite these changes to the criteria, research has suggested that clinicians are still biased by gender stereotypes in the way they diagnose personality disorders. For example, clinicians might focus on different behaviors, depending on whether they are diagnosing a man or a woman. In a typical test of this issue, two different vignettes are written involving people with personality disorders. The versions are identical except that in one, the person in the vignette is named Joan, and in the other,

the person is named John. Clinicians read the vignettes and provide the most likely diagnosis. In these types of studies, clinicians are more likely to diagnose the person as having histrionic personality disorder if the vignette is about a woman and more likely to diagnose the person as having antisocial personality disorder if the vignette is about a man (Garb, 1997). These findings highlight how important it is for clinicians to be aware of biases.

Table 12.3 Rates of Personality Disorders in the Community

Disorder	Prevalence (%)	Gender Ratio
Paranoid	2	Males > Females
Schizoid	<2	Males > Females
Schizotypal	<1	Males > Females
Antisocial	2	Males > Females
Borderline	1	Females > Males
Histrionic	2	Females > Males
Narcissistic	<1	Males > Females
Avoidant	5	Males = Females
Dependent	1.5	Males < Females
Obsessive-compulsive	2	Males > Females

Source: Torgensen et al., 2001.

Interviews with people who know the patient well improve the reliability of diagnosis (Bernstein et al., 1997). However, fewer than 10 percent of published studies of personality disorders gather data from people other than the person being diagnosed (Bornstein, 2003), even though the diagnostic criteria often specify that people with personality disorders tend to see themselves in distorted ways (Thomas et al., 2003).

By definition, personality disorders are supposed to be more stable over time than episodic Axis I disorders (e.g., major depressive disorder). Therefore, studies of test-retest reliability—whether patients receive the same diagnosis at two assessments separated by some time interval—are an important test of the basic definition of the disorder. Figure 12.1 shows a summary of test-retest reliability (i.e., diagnostic stability) from one study (Shea et al., 2002). The figure indicates that diagnoses of personality disorders are much more stable than diagnoses for major depressive disorder; nevertheless, about half of the people initially diagnosed with a personality disorder did not receive the same personality disorder diagnosis when they were interviewed a year later. These results, then, indicate that many of the personality disorders may not be as enduring as the DSM asserts (of course, at the second assessment, many of the people in the study might still have had symptoms but not at the levels required for diagnosis).

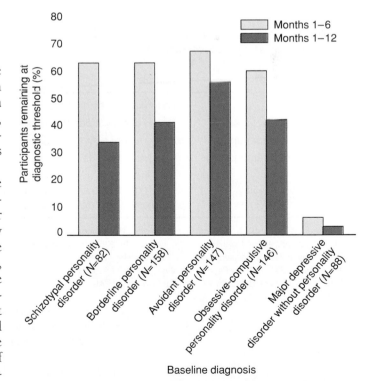

Figure 12.1 Test-retest stability for personality disorders and major depressive disorder after 1–6 months and after 6–12 months. (Drawn from Shea et al., 2002, *American Journal of Psychiatry*.)

DSM-IV-TR Criteria for Paranoid Personality Disorder

Presence of four or more of the following:

- Pervasive suspiciousness of being harmed, deceived, or exploited
- Unwarranted doubts about the loyalty or trustworthiness of friends or associates
- Reluctance to confide in others because of suspiciousness
- The tendency to read hidden meanings into the innocuous actions of others
- Bears grudges for perceived wrongs
- Angry reactions to perceived attacks on character or reputation
- Unwarranted suspiciousness of the fidelity of partner

Comorbidity A major problem in classifying personality disorders arises from their comorbidity with Axis I disorders and with each other. The Clinical Case of Mary illustrates this issue: Mary met the diagnostic criteria not only for borderline personality disorder but also for paranoid personality disorder, and she came close to meeting the criteria for schizotypal disorder as well. More than 50 percent of people diagnosed with a personality disorder meet the diagnostic criteria for another personality disorder, and more than two-thirds meet lifetime criteria for major depressive disorder (McGlashan et al., 2000). These facts are discouraging when we try to interpret the results of research that compares people who have a specific personality disorder with some control group. If, for example, we find that people with borderline personality disorder differ from normal people, is our finding specific to borderline personality disorder or related to personality disorders in general, or perhaps even applicable to Axis I disorders?

In sum, the categorical system of the DSM might not be ideal for classifying personality disorders, because of concerns about the lack of test-retest stability, the potential for gender bias, and the high rates of comorbidity. These types of concerns have led some authors to recommend shifting to a dimensional approach.

A Dimensional Approach to Personality: The Five-Factor Model

The personality traits used for classification form a continuum; that is, most of these traits are present in varying degrees in most people (see p. 71 for a discussion of dimensional versus categorical systems). When people with a personality disorder take a personality inventory, they endorse more extreme personality traits than those seen in the general population (Clark & Livesley, 2002). Thus, personality disorders might be defined by extremes of characteristics we all possess. A dimensional approach to the diagnosis of personality, then, might be more appropriate. A dimensional system was in fact considered for both DSM-III-R and DSM-IV, but consensus could not be reached on which dimensions to include (e.g., Livesley, Jang, & Vernon, 1998). In contemporary research, a major focus is on the **five-factor model** (McCrae & Costa, 1990), in which the five factors, or major dimensions, of personality are neuroticism, extraversion/introversion, openness to experience, agreeableness/antagonism, and conscientiousness. Table 12.4 presents questionnaire items that assess each of these dimensions; by reading the items, you can get a sense of what each dimension means. One interesting set of findings has shown that these dimensions of personality are moderately heritable (Jang et al., 2002).

Researchers have summarized the results of several studies linking these personality traits to schizoid, borderline, and avoidant personality disorders (Widiger & Costa, 1994). For example, people with schizoid personality disorder and those with avoidant personality disorder (two disorders that involve social aloofness) tend to be high in introversion but to differ in neuroticism—people with avoidant personality disorder tend to be higher in neuroticism than those with schizoid personality disorder. Rather than forcing each person into a discrete diagnostic category and then struggling with how to distinguish between the two disorders, the dimensional approach would simply describe each person's levels of neuroticism and introversion.

A recent meta-analysis shows that findings are fairly consistent across a range of studies that have mapped personality disorder diagnoses onto the dimensions of the five-factor model. Most personality disorders are characterized by high neuroticism and antagonism. High extraversion was tied to histrionic and narcissistic disorders (two disorders that involve dramatic behavior), whereas low extraversion was tied to schizoid, schizotypal, and avoidant disorders (Saulsman & Page, 2004).

Table 12.4 Sample Items from the Revised NEO Personality Inventory Assessing the Five-Factor Model

Personality Trait	Sample Items
Neuroticism	I often feel tense or jittery
Extraversion/introversion	I really like most people I meet
Openness to experience	I have a very active imagination
Agreeableness/antagonism	I tend to be cynical and skeptical of others' intentions (reverse scored)
Conscientiousness	I often come into situations without being prepared (reverse scored)

Reproduced by special permission of the Publisher, Psychological Assessment Resources, Inc., 16204 North Florida Avenue, Lutz, FL 33549, from the NEO Personality Inventory-Revised by Paul Costa and Robert McCrae, Copyright 1978, 1985, 1989, 1991, 1992 by Psychological Assessment Resources, Inc. (PAR). Further reproduction is prohibited without permission of PAR.

The five-factor model is not without its critics, however. In a study in which people with personality disorders completed a questionnaire assessing them on the basis of the five factors, the profiles of the various personality disorders turned out to be rather similar to one another (Morey et al., 2000). Some might say this is fine, and that fewer dimensions would simplify things. But proponents of the need to be more specific have responded to this difficulty by claiming that differentiating among the different personality disorders requires breaking down the five factors into their "facets" (Lynam & Widiger, 2001). Each of the five factors has six facets, or components; for example, the extraversion factor includes the facets of warmth, gregariousness, assertiveness, activity, excitement seeking, and positive emotionality. Differentiating among the personality disorders might require a more detailed assessment that includes these specific personality facets. Beyond the need to consider facets, it appears that some disorders, such as schizotypal personality disorder, are more distinct than being just extreme points along a dimension; statistical analyses suggest that people with these disorders tend to be qualitatively different from other people. For example, people with schizotypal personality disorder tend to experience perceptual oddities that others don't experience even in mild degrees (Haslam & Kim, 2002).

The five-factor model is certainly not a total solution to the problem of classifying personality disorders, but the important point is that a dimensional model has several distinct advantages. Most importantly, it handles the comorbidity problem, because comorbidity is a difficulty only in a categorical classification system like the one used in DSM-IV-TR. A dimensional system also links normal and abnormal personality, so findings on personality development in general become relevant to the personality disorders.

Problems with classifying personality disorders should not lead us to underestimate the importance of being able to identify them. Personality disorders are prevalent, and they cause severe impairments. Some of the problems with classification and diagnosis stem from the fact that these disorders have been the subject of serious research for less time than have most of the other disorders considered in this book. As research continues, the diagnostic categories will most likely be refined, and many of these problems might be solved. Bear these issues in mind, though, as we now turn to a review of the clinical description and etiology of the personality disorders in cluster A, cluster B, and cluster C.

Check Your Knowledge 12.1

True or false?
1. Most of the DSM-IV-TR personality disorders can be diagnosed with good interrater reliability.
2. Most people diagnosed with a personality disorder will still show that personality disorder 1 year later.
3. People who meet diagnostic criteria for a personality disorder are likely to meet diagnostic criteria for a second or third personality disorder as well.
4. Most studies of personality disorders include informants.
5. The seven-factor model is a popular approach to personality dimensions.

Odd/Eccentric Cluster

The odd/eccentric cluster of personality disorders includes paranoid personality disorder, schizoid personality disorder, and schizotypal personality disorder. The symptoms of these three disorders bear some similarity to types of bizarre thinking and experiences seen in schizophrenia. In personality disorders, though, the bizarre thinking and experiences are less severe than they are in schizophrenia.

Paranoid Personality Disorder

People with **paranoid personality disorder** are suspicious of others. This suspicion influences relationships with family, colleagues, and casual acquaintances. They expect to be mistreated or exploited and thus are secretive and continually on the lookout for signs of trickery and abuse. They are often hostile and react angrily to perceived insults. They might read hidden threatening messages into events—for example, they might believe that the newspaper boy with bad aim is actually trying to force them to walk into the yard in their bathrobe.

This disorder is different from paranoid schizophrenia because other symptoms of schizophrenia, such as hallucinations, are not present and there is less impairment in social and occupational functioning. Also absent is the cognitive disorganization that is characteristic of schizophrenia. It differs from delusional disorder because full-blown delusions are not present. Paranoid personality disorder co-occurs most often with schizotypal, border-line, and avoidant personality disorders (Bernstein, 1993).

Schizoid Personality Disorder

Like Joe (see Clinical Case), people with **schizoid personality disorder** do not desire or enjoy social relationships and usually have no close friends. They appear dull, bland, and aloof and have no warm, tender feelings for other people. They rarely experience strong emotions, are not interested in sex, and have few pleasurable activities. Indifferent to praise, criticism, and the sentiments of others, people with this disorder are loners, pursuing solitary interests. Comorbidity is highest for schizotypal, avoidant, and paranoid personality disorders, most likely because of the similar diagnostic criteria for the four disorders (see the DSM-IV-TR diagnostic criteria).

Clinical Case: Joe

Joe was a 53-year-old unmarried Vietnam veteran who was referred for treatment by his general practitioner, who was concerned about Joe's disconnection from life. Joe reluctantly agreed to see a therapist. He had not worked in several years and survived on a small disability pension from the Veterans Administration. He said that he found it unpleasant to shop for groceries because he didn't like having other people around him. The landlady at his boarding house persisted in trying to introduce him to women, even though he had declared his lack of interest in each and every one of the 10 women she had pestered him to meet. He stated that he did not like talking, and

in treatment he was often silent for long periods. He did talk about his sense that he had little connection with life and that he experienced little emotion other than mild irritability. Indeed, he was unable to describe a single person or activity that made him happy. After 6 weeks of treatment, Joe announced that he didn't think that he was a person who was going to feel any better from talking about things and that he had decided to spend his remaining savings to purchase a small cabin in a remote section of Maine. He seemed content with his decision, stating that by living there, he could avoid most interactions with people. He moved the next week.

Schizotypal Personality Disorder

The concept of the schizotypal personality grew out of Danish studies of the adopted children of schizophrenic parents (Kety et al., 1968). Some of these children developed schizophrenia as adults, but an even larger number developed what seemed to be an attenuated form of schizophrenia.

People with **schizotypal personality disorder** are often socially isolated, like people with schizoid personality, but they also show other, more eccentric symptoms, which are milder versions of the symptoms that define schizophrenia. (See the DSM-IV-TR diagnostic criteria for schizotypal personality disorder.) People with this disorder might have odd beliefs or magical thinking—for instance, the belief that they are clairvoyant and telepathic. It is also common for them to have ideas of reference (the belief that events have a particular and unusual meaning for them personally) and to show suspiciousness and paranoid ideation. They might also have recurrent illusions (inaccurate sensory perceptions), such as sensing the presence of a force or a person not actually there. In their speech, they might use words in an unusual and unclear fashion—for example, they might say "not a very talkable person" to mean a person not easy to talk to. Their behavior and appearance might also be eccentric—for example, they might talk to themselves or wear dirty and disheveled clothing. Their affect appears constricted and flat. A study of the relative importance of these symptoms for diagnosis found that paranoid ideation, ideas of reference, and illusions were most telling (Widiger, Frances, & Trall, 1987).

Comorbidity with other personality disorders is particularly high, even given the generally high comorbidity among personality disorders; on average, people with schizotypal personality disorder meet the diagnostic criteria for at least two other personality

DSM-IV-TR Criteria for Schizoid Personality Disorder

Presence of four or more of the following:

- Lack of desire for or enjoyment of close relationships
- Almost exclusive preference for solitude
- Little interest in sex with others
- Few if any pleasures
- Lack of friends
- Indifference to praise or criticism from others
- Flat affect, emotional detachment

disorders, the most likely being avoidant personality disorder and paranoid personality disorder, perhaps because of overlapping criteria (McGlashon et al., 2000).

Etiology of the Personality Disorders in the Odd/Eccentric Cluster

What causes the odd thinking, bizarre behavior, and interpersonal difficulties that appear in this cluster of personality disorders? The search for causes has been guided by the idea that these disorders are genetically linked to schizophrenia and might be less severe variants of that disorder.

The evidence for links with schizophrenia is stronger for schizotypal personality disorder than for the other disorders in the odd/eccentric cluster. Family studies have shown that the relatives of patients with schizophrenia are at increased risk for schizotypal personality disorder (Nigg & Goldsmith, 1994), as are adopted children of biological mothers with schizophrenia (Tienari et al., 2003). People with schizotypal personality disorder also have deficits in cognitive and neuropsychological functioning that are similar to those seen in schizophrenia (Cadenhead et al., 2002; Lenzenweger, 2001). Furthermore, and again paralleling findings from schizophrenia research, people with schizotypal personality disorder have enlarged ventricles and less temporal lobe gray matter (Dickey et al., 2002).

Family studies suggest that paranoid personality disorder is weakly related to schizophrenia and other psychotic disorders (Miller, 2001). No clear pattern has emerged from behavior-genetics research on schizoid personality disorder, although the prevalence of this disorder might be elevated among relatives of people with autism (Wolff, Narayan, & Moyes, 1988) and among those with schizotypal personality disorder (Battaglia et al., 1995). Overall, though, researchers don't know much about the etiology of paranoid personality disorder or schizoid personality disorder—as you can imagine, people with these disorders certainly aren't likely to be interested in completing lengthy research interviews.

In sum, we know more about the etiology of schizotypal personality disorder than of the other disorders in the odd/eccentric cluster. Schizotypal personality disorder appears tied to the neurobiological vulnerability to schizophrenia, as shown by genetic, neuropsychological, and brain-imaging studies.

DSM-IV-TR Criteria for Schizotypal Personality Disorder

Presence of five or more of the following:

- Ideas of reference
- Peculiar beliefs or magical thinking, e.g., belief in extrasensory perception
- Unusual perceptions, e.g., distorted feelings about one's body
- Peculiar patterns of speech
- Suspiciousness or paranoia
- Inappropriate or restricted affect
- Odd behavior or appearance
- Lack of close friends
- Anxiety around other people, which does not diminish with familiarity

---

Quick Summary

Personality disorders are defined by long-standing and pervasive ways of being that cause distress and impairment through their influence on cognition, emotions, relationships, and impulse control. Most people with personality disorders experience comorbid Axis I conditions as well as other personality disorders. In DSM-IV-TR, personality disorders are classified in three clusters, reflecting the idea that these disorders are characterized by odd or eccentric behavior (cluster A), dramatic, emotional, or erratic behavior (cluster B), or anxious or fearful behavior (cluster C). Interrater reliability of personality disorder diagnosis, particularly when clinicians use structured interviews, is strong. But despite the idea that personality disorders are long-standing, test-retest reliability is only modest. Concerns have also been raised about gender bias in diagnoses. Some have argued that we should be measuring personality traits as dimensions rather than attempting to classify people with personality disorders. A key issue is how many personality traits should be assessed to adequately differentiate the types of problems that are encountered in clinical settings, but much of current research focuses on five personality traits.

The odd/eccentric cluster of personality disorders (cluster A) includes paranoid personality disorder, schizoid personality disorder, and schizotypal personality disorder. People with paranoid personality disorder are suspicious of others, people with schizoid personality disorder are socially aloof, and people with schizotypal personality disorder are eccentric in their thoughts and behavior. Behavior-genetic studies indicate that schizotypal personality disorder and schizophrenia are related.

Dramatic/Erratic Cluster

The disorders in the dramatic/erratic cluster—borderline personality disorder, histrionic personality disorder, narcissistic personality disorder, and antisocial personality disorder—

DSM-IV-TR Criteria for Schizoid Personality Disorder

Presence of four or more of the following:

- Lack of desire for or enjoyment of close relationships
- Almost exclusive preference for solitude
- Little interest in sex with others
- Few if any pleasures
- Lack of friends
- Indifference to praise or criticism from others
- Flat affect, emotional detachment
- Symptoms not explained by schizophrenia, psychotic depression, or pervasive developmental disorder

Ted Kaczynski, the "unibomber," is believed to have schizoid personality disorder; he has a long history of extreme detachment from interpersonal relationships. (Ralf-Finn Hestoft/Corbis Images.)

are characterized by symptoms that range from highly inconsistent behavior to inflated self-esteem, exaggerated emotional displays, and rule-breaking behavior. Generally, more is known about the etiology of personality disorders in the dramatic/erratic cluster than those in the other clusters.

Borderline Personality Disorder

Borderline personality disorder (BPD) has been a major focus of interest for several reasons. Among these reasons, BPD is very common in clinical settings, very hard to treat, and associated with suicidality.

Clinical Description   The core features of **borderline personality disorder** (BPD) are impulsivity and instability in relationships and mood (see the summary of the DSM-IV-TR diagnostic criteria). For example, attitudes and feelings toward other people might vary considerably and inexplicably over short periods of time. Emotions are intense, erratic and can shift abruptly, particularly from passionate idealization to contemptuous anger. As in the case of Mary (see Clinical Case), the intense anger of people with BPD often damages relationships. Their unpredictable, impulsive, and potentially self-damaging behavior might include gambling, reckless spending, indiscriminate sexual activity, substance abuse, and eating sprees. People with BPD often have not developed a clear and coherent sense of self—they sometimes experience major swings in such basic aspects of identity as their values, loyalties, and career choices. They cannot bear to be alone, have fears of abandonment, demand attention, and experience chronic feelings of depression and emptiness. They may experience transient psychotic and dissociative symptoms when stressed.

BPD, which typically begins in adolescence or early adulthood, is the most common personality disorder in clinical settings (Paris, 1999). The prognosis is not favorable in the first decade of follow-up: in one 7-year follow-up, about 50 percent of people still had the disorder (Links, Heslegrave, & van Reekum, 1998). But over a 10- or 15-year period, as shown by a series of studies, as many as three-quarters of people with BPD no longer meet diagnostic criteria, and their functioning approximates that of the general population (Paris, 2003). Most people seem to no longer meet the diagnostic criteria by age 40 (Paris, 2002).

Suicidal behavior is a particular concern in BPD. One study found that, over a 20-year period, approximately 7.5 percent of people with BPD committed suicide (Linehan & Heard, 1999). In a study of 621 people with BPD, 15.5 percent were found to have engaged in at least one suicidal behavior within the previous year (Yen et al., 2003). People with BPD are also particularly likely to engage in *self-mutilating behavior*. For example, they might slice their legs with a razor blade or burn their arms with cigarettes—behaviors that are harmful but unlikely to cause death. At least two-thirds of people with BPD will engage in self-mutilation at some point during their lives (Stone, 1993).

People with BPD are highly likely to have a comorbid Axis I anxiety disorder (especially posttraumatic stress disorder) or mood disorder (McGlashan et al., 2000). They are also at risk for comorbid substance-related disorders and eating disorders, as well as with personality disorders from the odd/eccentric cluster (McGlashan et al., 2000).

A colorful account by Jonathan Kellerman, a clinical psychologist and successful mystery writer, gives a good sense of what people with BPD are like.

> They're the chronically depressed, the determinedly addictive, the compulsively divorced, living from one emotional disaster to the next. Bed hoppers, stomach pumpers, freeway jumpers, and sad-eyed bench-sitters with arms stitched up like footballs and psychic wounds that can never be sutured. Their egos are as fragile as spun sugar, their psyches irretrievably fragmented, like a jigsaw puzzle with crucial pieces missing. They play roles with alacrity, excel at being anyone but themselves, crave intimacy but repel it when they find it. Some of them gravitate toward stage or screen; others do their acting in more subtle ways....
>
> Borderlines go from therapist to therapist, hoping to find a magic bullet for the crushing feelings of emptiness. They turn to chemical bullets, gobble tranquilizers and antidepressants,

alcohol and cocaine. Embrace gurus and heaven-hucksters, any charismatic creep promising a quick fix of the pain. And they end up taking temporary vacations in psychiatric wards and prison cells, emerge looking good, raising everyone's hopes. Until the next letdown, real or imagined, the next excursion into self damage. (Kellerman, 1989, pp. 113–114)

Fortunately, research on new treatments for BPD, discussed later in the chapter, indicates a more positive outlook than Kellerman offers.

Etiology of Borderline Personality Disorder   There are several views concerning the causes of BPD. We discuss biological factors, social factors, object-relations theory, and Linehan's diathesis–stress theory.

Neurobiological Factors   Both twin studies and family studies support a strong heritability for BPD, with genes accounting for more than 60 percent of the variance in the development of this disorder. It has been suggested that genes contribute to the components of this disorder, such as impulsivity and emotional dysregulation, rather than to the disorder as a whole (Siever et al., 2002). Consistent with the idea that emotion dysregulation may be one of the components of this disorder, the parents of people with BPD are more likely than average to have mood disorders (Shachnow et al., 1997).

Deficits in sensitivity to the neurotransmitter serotonin are associated with impulsivity and emotional dysregulation. When patients with BPD were administered a drug to increase serotonin activity in the brain, they showed a smaller response than controls (Soloff et al., 2000). This finding indicates decreased functioning of the serotonin system in BPD.

In keeping with the idea that genes separately contribute to the components of this disorder, separable neurobiological findings may be related to impulsivity versus emotional dysregulation. The frontal lobes are thought to help control impulsiveness, and in some studies, people with BPD perform poorly on neurological tests of frontal lobe functioning (Bazanis et al., 2002). These findings, however, are not always replicated (Rogers, 2003), suggesting the need for more specificity in the kinds of tasks included on the tests. In brain-imaging studies, people with BPD show low levels of activity (Goyer et al., 1994) and structural changes (van Elst et al., 2001) in the frontal lobes.

Other neurobiological characteristics might be more closely related to emotional dysregulation. For example, people with BPD show increased activation of the amygdala (Herpetz et al., 2001a). Amygdala activation appears to be correlated with several disorders that involve intense emotions, including mood disorders and anxiety disorders, so it might be relevant for understanding the emotion dysregulation of BPD.

Social Factors: Childhood Abuse   Patients with BPD are much more likely to report a history of parental separation, verbal abuse, and emotional abuse during childhood than other Axis II patients are (Reich & Zanarini, 2001). Such abuse is believed to be more frequent among people with BPD than among people diagnosed with most other disorders (Herman, Perry, & van der Kolk, 1989), with the exception of dissociative identity disorder (see Chapter 6), which is also characterized by very high rates of childhood abuse. Given the frequency of dissociative symptoms in people with BPD, we can speculate that BPD and dissociative identity disorder might be related and that, in both, dissociation is caused by the extreme stress of child abuse. Indeed, one study found that people who dissociated after child abuse were more likely to develop symptoms of BPD (Ross et al., 1998). One note of caution is warranted: Considering how sensitive such people are to invalidating experiences as adults, it is conceivable that their recollections of past events are colored by their current psychological turmoil. Despite this issue, two major psychological models build on these high rates of reported abuse to explain how a person might come to develop the symptoms of BPD. We review these theories in the next two sections.

Object-Relations Theory   **Object-relations theory**, an important variant of psychoanalytic theory, focuses on the way children internalize (or *introject*) their images of the people

---

DSM-IV-TR Criteria for Schizotypal Personality Disorder

Presence of five or more of the following:

- Ideas of reference
- Peculiar beliefs or magical thinking, e.g., belief in extrasensory perception
- Unusual perceptions, e.g., distorted feelings about one's body
- Peculiar patterns of speech
- Suspiciousness or paranoia
- Inappropriate or restricted affect
- Odd behavior or appearance
- Lack of close friends
- Anxiety around other people, which does not diminish with familiarity
- Symptoms not explained by schizophrenia, psychotic depression, or pervasive developmental disorder

Figure 12.2 Marsha Linehan's diathesis–stress theory of borderline personality disorder.

who are important to them, such as their parents. In other words, the central topic is how children identify with people to whom they have strong emotional attachments. These internalized images (*object representations*) become part of the person's ego and influence how the person reacts to the world. But introjected values can come into conflict with the wishes and ideals of the adult—for example, when a college-age woman who has adopted her mother's notion of the proper role of a woman finds herself drawn to modern ideals of feminism.

The leading object-relations theorist is Otto Kernberg, who has written extensively about BPD. Kernberg (1985) proposed that adverse childhood experiences—for example, having parents who provide love and attention inconsistently, perhaps praising achievements but being unable to offer emotional support and warmth—cause children to internalize disturbed object representations that fail to integrate the loving and unloving aspects of the people who are close to them. As a result of these disturbed object relations, they develop insecure egos, a major feature of BPD.

Although people with BPD have weak egos and need constant reassuring, they retain the capacity to test reality. Despite being in touch with reality, though, they often engage in a defense mechanism called splitting—dichotomizing objects into all good or all bad and failing to integrate positive and negative aspects of another person or the self into a whole. This tendency causes extreme difficulty in regulating emotions because the people with BPD see the world, including themselves, in black-and-white terms. One week, they might see their therapist as a perfect human being, capable of saving them from pain and turmoil, but then might be scathingly angry the next week if the therapist is unavailable for some reason.

Linehan's Diathesis–Stress Theory Marsha Linehan proposes that BPD develops when people who have difficulty controlling their emotions because of a biological diathesis (possibly genetic) are raised in a family environment that is invalidating. That is, a diathesis of emotional dysregulation interacts with experiences of invalidation to promote the development of BPD.

In an invalidating environment, the person's feelings are discounted and disrespected—that is, the person's efforts to communicate feelings are disregarded or even punished. An extreme form of invalidation is child abuse, either sexual or nonsexual, where the abusive parent claims to love the child and yet hurts the child.

The two main hypothesized factors—emotional dysregulation and invalidation—interact with each other in a dynamic fashion (see Figure 12.2). For example, the emotionally dysregulated child makes enormous demands on his or her family. The exasperated parents ignore or even punish the child's outbursts, which leads the child to suppress his or her emotions. The suppressed emotions build up to an explosion, which then gets the attention of the parents. Thus, the parents end up reinforcing the very behaviors that they find aversive. Many other patterns are possible, of course, but what they have in common is a vicious circle, a constant back-and-forth between dysregulation and invalidation.

Histrionic Personality Disorder

The key feature of **histrionic personality disorder**, formerly called *hysterical personality*, is overly dramatic and attention-seeking behavior. People with this disorder often use their physical appearance, such as unusual clothes, makeup, or hair color, to draw attention to themselves. Despite displaying extravagant and intense emotions, they are thought to be emotionally shallow. For example, someone with this disorder might gush about a person and call them their best friend, only to have trouble remembering a conversation with them the next day. They are self-centered, overly concerned with their physical attractiveness, and uncomfortable when not the center of attention. They can be inappropriately sexually provocative and seductive and are easily influenced by others. Their speech is often impressionistic and lacking in detail. For example, they might state a strong opinion yet

---

DSM-IV-TR Criteria for Histrionic Personality Disorder

Presence of five or more of the following:

- Strong need to be the center of attention
- Inappropriately sexually seductive behavior
- Rapidly shifting expression of emotions
- Use of physical appearance to draw attention to self
- Speech that is excessively impressionistic
- Exaggerated, theatrical emotional expression
- Overly suggestible
- Misreads relationships as more intimate than they are

be completely unable to support it. (*Patient:* "She was absolutely the greatest." *Interviewer:* "What did you like best about her?" *Patient:* "Gosh, I'm not sure I could describe that."). Comorbidity of histrionic personality disorder with depression, borderline personality disorder, and medical problems is high (Nestadt et al., 1990).

Etiology of Histrionic Personality Disorder   Psychoanalytic theory proposes that the emotional display and seductiveness that are characteristic of this disorder are encouraged by parental seductiveness, especially a father's seductive behavior toward his daughter. The theory also proposes that people with this disorder were raised in a family environment in which parents talked about sex as something dirty yet behaved as though it was exciting and desirable. Such an upbringing might explain a preoccupation with sex, coupled with a fear of actually behaving sexually. Exaggerated displays of emotion are seen as symptoms of such underlying conflicts, whereas the need of people with this disorder to be the center of attention is seen as a way of defending against their low self-esteem (Apt & Hurlbert, 1994). Unfortunately, this theory has not been tested.

Narcissistic Personality Disorder

People with **narcissistic personality disorder** have a grandiose view of their abilities and are preoccupied with fantasies of great success. They are more than a little self-centered. They require almost constant attention and excessive admiration. Their interpersonal relationships are disturbed by their lack of empathy, by their arrogance coupled with feelings of envy, by their habit of taking advantage of others, and by their feelings of entitlement—they expect others to do special favors for them. People with this disorder are extremely sensitive to criticism and might become enraged when others do not admire them. They tend to seek out high-status partners whom they idealize, but when, inevitably, these partners fall short of their unrealistic expectations, they become angry and rejecting (like those with borderline personality disorder). They are also likely to change partners if given an opportunity to be with a person of higher status. This disorder most often co-occurs with borderline personality disorder (Morey, 1988).

> **DSM-IV-TR Criteria for Narcissistic Personality Disorder**
>
> Presence of five or more of the following:
>
> - Grandiose view of one's importance
> - Preoccupation with one's success, brilliance, beauty
> - Belief that one is special and can be understood only by other high-status people
> - Extreme need for admiration
> - Strong sense of entitlement
> - Tendency to exploit others
> - Lack of empathy
> - Envious of others
> - Arrogant behavior or attitudes

Clinical Case: Bob

Bob, a 50-year-old college professor, sought treatment only after urging from his wife. During the interview, Bob's wife noted a set of concerns, stating that he seemed so focused on himself and his own advancement that he often belittled others. Bob was dismissive of these concerns, stating that he had never been the sort of person to tolerate fools, and he could see no reason why he should begin offering such tolerance now—in rapid fire, he described his supervisor, his students, his parents, and a set of former friends as lacking the intelligence to merit his friendship. He willingly acknowledged working long hours, but stated that his research had the potential to change life for people, and that other activities could not be allowed to interfere with this success.

Etiology of Narcissistic Personality Disorder   In this section, we discuss the two most influential models of the etiology of this disorder: the self-psychology model and the social cognitive model. Both theories are attempts to understand how a person develops these traits.

Self-Psychology Model   Heinz Kohut established a variant of psychoanalysis known as *self-psychology,* which he described in his two books, *The Analysis of the Self* (1971) and *The Restoration of the Self* (1977). Kohut noted that the person with narcissistic personality disorder projects remarkable self-importance, self-absorption, and fantasies of limitless success on the surface. But Kohut theorizes that these characteristics mask a very fragile self-esteem.

Otto Kernberg, one of the leading object-relations theorists, has been very influential in the study of borderline personality disorder. (Courtesy Dr. Otto Kernberg.)

According to Kohut, the self emerges early in life as a bipolar structure with an immature grandiosity at one pole and a dependent overidealization of other people at the other. When parents respond to a child with respect, warmth, and empathy, they endow the youngster with a normal sense of self-worth. A failure to develop healthy self-esteem occurs when parents do not respond with approval to their child's displays of competency; that is, the child is valued as a means of fostering the parents' self-esteem but not for the child's own worth. The child will have trouble accepting their own shortcomings. These deficits in establishing a healthy sense of self drive the development of narcissistic personality disorder according to Kohut. As adults, people with narcissistic personality disorder strive to bolster their sense of self-worth through unending quests for love and approval from others. Although this model has been influential, there has been little research to test it.

Social Cognitive Model   A model of narcissistic personality disorder developed by Carolyn Morf and Frederick Rhodewalt (2001) is built around two basic ideas: first, that people with this disorder have fragile self-esteem, in part because they are trying to maintain the belief that they are special and second, that interpersonal interactions are important to them for bolstering self-esteem, rather than for gaining closeness or warmth. In other words, they are captive to the goal of maintaining a grand vision of themselves, and this goal pervades their experiences. The work of Morf and Rhodewalt is quite unusual in that they have designed laboratory and research studies aimed at elucidating the cognitive, emotional, and interpersonal processes associated with narcissistic personality disorder.

To assess the idea that people with narcissistic personality disorder are trying to maintain grandiose beliefs about themselves, they look at studies of biases in how people with this disorder rate themselves in various settings. For example, in laboratory studies, people with narcissistic personality disorder overestimate their attractiveness to others, and they overestimate their contributions to group activities. ("Others must be jealous of me, I've been responsible for the lion-share of our progress here today.") In some studies, researchers have provided people with feedback that they were successful on a task (regardless of their actual performance), then asked participants to rate the reasons why they were successful. In these types of studies, people with narcissistic personality disorder attribute successes to their abilities rather than chance or luck. So, a set of studies suggest that people with narcissistic personality disorder show cognitive biases that would help maintain grandiose self beliefs.

To assess whether people with narcissistic personality disorder have fragile self-esteem, Morf and Rhodewalt look at studies of how much their self-esteem depends on external feedback. For example, when falsely told they have failed an IQ test, they show much more reactivity than others do; similarly, they show more reactivity to being told they have succeeded at something. Morf and Rhodewalt argue that this vulnerability of their self-esteem to external feedback arises from their attempt to maintain an inflated view of themselves.

According to this theory, when people with narcissistic personality disorder interact with others, their primary goal is to bolster their own self-esteem. This goal influences how they act toward others in several ways. First, they tend to brag a lot; this often works well initially, but over time, repeated bragging comes to be perceived negatively by others (Paulhus, 1998). Second, when someone else performs better than they do on a task that is relevant to self-esteem, they will denigrate the other person, even if they have to do so to their face. That is, it is more important for them to be admired or to achieve competitive success than it is to have closeness with others. This framework makes it easy to understand why people with narcissistic personality disorder do things that alienate others; their major interest is in "winning," not in gaining or maintaining closeness.

Antisocial Personality Disorder and Psychopathy

Informally, the terms *antisocial personality disorder* and *psychopathy* (sometimes referred to as *sociopathy*) often are used interchangeably. Antisocial behavior, such as breaking laws,

Check Your Knowledge 12.2

1. Which personality disorder is most related to schizophrenia in family history studies?
   a. schizoid
   b. schizotypal
   c. antisocial
   d. borderline
2. Which of the following factors play a central role in Linehan's model of BPD (circle all that apply)?
   a. emotional dysregulation
   b. parental invalidation
   c. conflicts between introjected values and current needs
   d. splitting as a defense mechanism
3. Which personality disorder is most common in clinical settings?
   a. schizoid
   b. schizotypal
   c. antisocial
   d. borderline

is an important component of both, but there are important differences between the two disorders. One difference is that antisocial personality disorder is included in the DSM-IV-TR, whereas psychopathy is not. In this next section, we will review the definitions of these two highly related constructs, then discuss research on the etiology of these syndromes.

Clinical Case

A 19-year-old man with irregular breathing, a rapid pulse, and dilated pupils was brought to the hospital by a friend, who eventually admitted that they had been using a lot of cocaine before the symptoms began. The men didn't want to identify themselves, but eventually the medical team was able to get enough information to contact the patient's mother, who arrived at the hospital distraught and smelling of alcohol. When interviewed, she reported that her son had a long history of disobedience and disengagement from family activities. When she attempted to set rules, he became violently argumentative;

he often stayed out all night. She said that the father was not present to help with parenting. She believed that her son was a good student and a star basketball player, but both of these beliefs turned out to be false. Later research revealed, though, that her son was deeply involved in drugs and in drag racing, and he bragged that he typically consumed a case of beer per day. He used various schemes to get money for drugs, including stealing car radios and taking money from his mother. He denied that he had any problems and ended his first interview with a therapist early (adapted from Spitzer et al., 1994).

Antisocial Personality Disorder: Clinical Description   In DSM-IV-TR, the diagnostic criteria for **antisocial personality disorder** (APD) include two major components.

1. A pervasive pattern of disregard for the rights of others since the age of 15.
2. The presence of a conduct disorder (see Chapter 14) before the age of 15. Truancy, running away from home, frequent lying, theft, arson, and deliberate destruction of property are major symptoms of conduct disorder.

People with APD show irresponsible and antisocial behavior by working only inconsistently, breaking laws, being irritable and physically aggressive, defaulting on debts, being reckless and impulsive, and neglecting to plan ahead. They show little regard for truth and little remorse for their misdeeds.

In the United States, 3–5 percent of men and about 1 percent of women meet the diagnostic criteria for APD (Robins & Price, 1991). The disorder is more common among people of low socioeconomic status, and there is evidence that culture influences whether or not people develop this disorder—for example, rates of APD are higher in the United States than in Scotland (Cooke & Michie, 1999). Rates are also higher among younger adults than among older adults, and some people seem to mature out of the symptoms. In one study, people who had been hospitalized for APD were followed up 16 to 45 years later. About one-quarter of them no longer had APD, and another third had improved (Black, Baumgard, & Bell, 1995). About three-quarters of people with APD meet the diagnostic criteria for another disorder, with substance abuse being the most common comorbid disorder (Newman et al., 1998). Not surprisingly, then, high rates of APD are observed in drug and alcohol rehabilitation facilities (Sutker & Adams, 2001).

Psychopathy: Clinical Description   The concept of **psychopathy** predates the DSM-IV-TR diagnosis of antisocial personality disorder. In his classic book, *The Mask of Sanity* (1941/1976), Hervey Cleckley drew on his clinical experience to formulate diagnostic criteria for psychopathy. Unlike the DSM diagnostic criteria for APD, which focus on observable symptoms, Cleckley's criteria for psychopathy refer less to behavior per se and more to the person's thoughts and feelings.

In Cleckley's description, one of the key characteristics of psychopathy is poverty of emotions, both positive and negative: Psychopathic people have no sense of shame, and their seemingly positive feelings for others are merely an act. They are superficially charming and

DSM-IV-TR Criteria for Antisocial Personality Disorder

- Age at least 18
- Evidence of conduct disorder before age 15
- Pervasive pattern of disregard for the rights of others since the age of 15 and at least three of the following:
  1. Repeated law-breaking
  2. Deceitfulness, lying
  3. Impulsivity
  4. Irritability and aggressiveness
  5. Reckless disregard for own safety and that of others
  6. Irresponsibility as seen in unreliable employment history or not meeting financial obligations
  7. Lack of remorse

Narcissistic personality disorder draws its name from the Greek mythological figure Narcissus, who fell in love with his own reflection, was consumed by his own desire, and was transformed into a flower. (Kavaler/Art Resource.)

use that charm to manipulate others for personal gain. Their lack of anxiety might make it impossible for them to learn from their mistakes, and their lack of positive emotions leads them to behave irresponsibly and often cruelly toward others. Another key point in Cleckley's description is that the antisocial behavior of the psychopath is performed impulsively, as much for thrills as for a reason such as financial gain.

Robert Hare and associates (1990) developed a checklist to assess psychopathy. The checklist identifies two major clusters of psychopathic traits. The first, referred to as emotional detachment, describes a selfish, remorseless person who exploits others. The second describes an antisocial lifestyle marked by impulsivity and irresponsibility. Based on the Hare checklist, psychopathy occurs more among men than among women (Salekin, Rogers, & Sewell, 1997).

Diagnostic Controversies   As we have seen, APD and psychopathy are related but by no means identical. A recent study found that only about 20 percent of people with APD obtained high scores on the Hare checklist (Rutherford, Cacciola, & Alterman, 1999). Further, lack of remorse, a hallmark of psychopathy, is but one of seven DSM criteria for diagnosis of APD, and is not required to make the diagnosis. Therefore, a person can meet the DSM criteria for APD and not have the lack of remorse that is intrinsic to psychopathy.

The diagnostic criteria for APD have been criticized in several ways. The DSM criteria specify that these patterns of antisocial behavior must begin in childhood, with evidence of conduct disorder before the age of 15. Some researchers have criticized the DSM diagnostic criteria for APD because the onset-in-childhood criterion requires accurate reports of long-past events by people who are habitual liars (Hare, Hart, & Harpur, 1991). Other researchers believe that this early onset requirement is not justifiable. It is true that as many as 60 percent of children with conduct disorder later develop APD (Myers, Stewart, & Brown, 1998), but among people who meet the other criteria for APD, those who had conduct disorder in childhood appear quite similar to those who did not (Langbehn & Cadoret, 2001).

Furthermore, many researchers believe that diagnoses should not be synonymous with criminality. Nevertheless, 75–80 percent of convicted felons meet the DSM criteria for APD. In contrast, only 15–25 percent of convicted felons meet the criteria for psychopathy (Hart & Hare, 1989).

Etiology of Antisocial Personality Disorder and Psychopathy   In this section, we consider the etiology of APD and psychopathy. As we review the research in this area, keep in mind two issues that make findings a little hard to integrate. First, research has been conducted on persons diagnosed in different ways—some with APD and some with psychopathy. Second, most research on APD and psychopathy has been conducted on persons who have been convicted as criminals. Thus, the results of this research might not be applicable to psychopaths who are not criminals or who avoid arrest. Indeed, on cognitive and psychophysiological measures, psychopaths who have been convicted show more deficits than those who have not been caught (Ishikawa et al., 2001).

Genetic Factors   Research suggests that criminality (Gottesman & Goldsmith, 1994) and psychopathy (Taylor et al., 2003) are moderately heritable. Similarly, a large number of twin studies suggest a heritability of 40–50 percent for APD (Eley, Lichtenstein, & Moffitt, 2003), and adoption studies reveal higher than normal prevalence of antisocial behavior in adopted children of biological parents with APD and substance abuse (Cadoret et al., 1995b; Ge et al., 1996). Genetic risk for APD, conduct disorder, and substance abuse appear to be related; a person might inherit a general vulnerability for these types of symptoms, and then environmental factors might shape which of the symptoms evolve (Kendler, Prescoft, et al., 2003). Some genetic risk, however, is very specific—for example, some genes might influence aggressive behavior within APD (Eley et al., 2003).

Adoption research has also shown that genetic, behavioral, and family influences are very hard to disentangle (Ge et al., 1996). That is, the genetically influenced antisocial behavior of the child can provoke harsh discipline and lack of warmth, even in adoptive parents, and these parental characteristics in turn exacerbate the child's antisocial tendencies.

Social Factors: Family Environment   Since much psychopathic behavior violates social norms, many investigators focus on the primary agent of socialization, the family, in their search for the explanation of such behavior. Twin studies show that the family environment accounts for 20–30 percent of the variance in who develops APD. One such study, for example, showed that high negativity and low warmth predicted antisocial behavior (Reiss et al., 1995). The family environment might be particularly important when a child has an inherited tendency toward antisocial behavior. For example, in the adoption study referred to above (Cadoret et al., 1995b), an adverse environment in the adoptive home (such as marital problems and substance abuse) was related to the development of APD, particularly when the biological parents had APD.

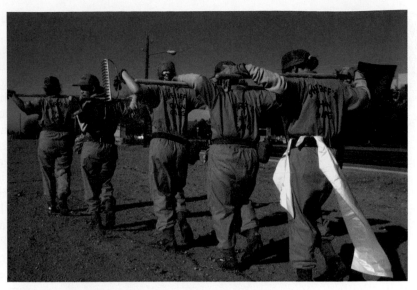

Three-quarters of convicted felons meet the DSM criteria for antisocial personality disorder. (Chris Steele-Perkins/Magnum Photos, Inc.)

Outside of twin studies, there is substantial prospective research to show that social factors, including poverty, exposure to violence, and parenting patterns, predict antisocial behavior in children (Loeber & Hay, 1997), even when children are not genetically at risk for APD (Jaffee et al., 2002). Parental inconsistency in discipline appears to be a consistent predictor of antisocial behavior in children (Marshall & Cooke, 1999), which might be related to antisocial symptoms in the fathers.

Emotion and Psychopathy   A large body of work has focused on understanding the emotional components of psychopathy. In defining the psychopathic syndrome, Cleckley pointed out the inability of psychopaths to profit from experience or even from punishment; they seem to be unable to avoid the negative consequences of social misbehavior. Many are chronic lawbreakers despite their experiences with jail sentences. They seem immune to the anxiety or pangs of conscience that keep most of us from breaking the law, lying, or injuring others, and they have difficulty curbing their impulses. In the terminology of learning theory, psychopaths do not learn to avoid certain behaviors because they are unresponsive to punishments for their antisocial behavior. Presumably, they do not experience conditioned fear responses when they encounter situations in which such responses would normally serve to inhibit antisocial behavior.

A classic study tested the idea that psychopaths have few inhibitions about committing antisocial acts because they experience little anxiety (Lykken, 1957). It is generally believed that anxiety mediates the ability to learn to avoid aversive stimuli, such as shocks. To determine whether psychopaths actually have low levels of anxiety, Lykken assessed how well psychopaths learned to avoid shock. Consistent with low anxiety, psychopaths were poorer than controls at learning to avoid shock.

Studies of the activity of the autonomic nervous system also have yielded results consistent with the idea that psychopaths respond to fear-eliciting stimuli with less anxiety than other people. At rest, psychopaths have lower than normal levels of skin conductance, and their skin conductance is less reactive when they are confronted with or anticipating an aversive stimulus (Herpertz et al., 2001b; Raine et al., 2000). Research using other methods of assessing emotion has also confirmed these results. One study measured the eye-blink component of the startle response, a good nonverbal indicator of whether a person is in a negative emotional state. When people are in a negative emotional state, they demonstrate a larger startle response in response to a sudden loud noise. Psychopaths do not show increased startle while they are viewing negative stimuli, like a picture of a gun or a horrible accident (Levenston et al., 2000), confirming the idea that psychopaths do not experience negative emotions (such as anxiety) in response to aversive stimuli.

Another startle-response study was conducted on four groups of penitentiary inmates selected with the Hare checklist. Remember that this checklist includes two subscales: antisocial behavior and emotional detachment. Persons who were high on both scales, high only on emotional detachment, high only on antisocial behavior, and high on both components were tested. Participants were first exposed to a baseline condition in which a simple visual cue was presented, sometimes with a blast of loud noise. Next they were told that they would view the visual cue and that the loud noise would occur when the visual cue disappeared. Marked differences emerged among the groups in the magnitude of their startle responses after the loud noise. Both the groups who were high on emotional detachment showed much smaller increases in their startle responses than the other two groups, indicating that less fear had been aroused. The pattern of results is important because it suggests that emotional detachment, not antisocial behavior, is driving the emotional deficits of psychopaths (Patrick, 1994).

The research we have described so far has been based on the idea that punishment does not arouse strong emotions in psychopaths and thus does not inhibit antisocial behavior. But some researchers believe that empathy, not punishment, is the critical agent of socialization. Empathy means being in tune with the emotional reactions of others; thus, empathizing with someone's distress could inhibit the tendency toward callous exploitation. From this perspective, one could argue that some features of psychopathy arise from a lack of empathy.

This idea has been tested by monitoring the skin conductance of psychopathic and nonpsychopathic men as they viewed slides showing three different types of pictures: threatening (e.g., gun, shark), neutral (e.g., book), and others' distress (e.g., a crying person). Unlike the results of the studies described above, the two groups did not differ in their responses to threatening stimuli, but the psychopaths were less responsive to the slides of others' distress (Blair et al., 1997)—that is, the psychopaths indeed appeared to show less empathy for the distress of others (see Figure 12.3). Similarly, when asked to identify the emotion conveyed in audiotaped statements from various strangers, psychopaths did very poorly in recognizing others' fear and sadness, even though they recognized other emotions well (Blair et al., 2002).

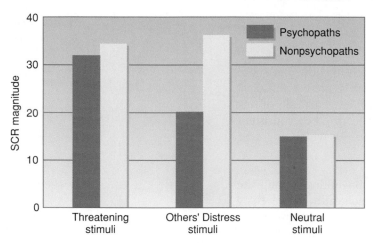

Figure 12.3 Skin-conductance response (SCR) of psychopathic and nonpsychopathic men to three types of stimuli. The psychopathic men showed less responsiveness to the distress stimuli, indicating a deficit in empathy (Blair et al., 1997).

Response Modulation, Impulsivity, and Psychopathy Impulsivity is defined as the tendency to pursue potential rewards without attending to potential threats. Remember that the frontal lobes appear involved in inhibiting impulsivity. Animals who have had parts of their brains destroyed—including the septum, hippocampus, and prefrontal cortex—show deficits in avoidance learning and a tendency to respond impulsively to immediate rewards. Some researches have suggested that impulsivity, related to deficits in the functioning of the frontal lobes, may drive psychopathy (Gorenstein & Newman, 1980). This idea is supported by studies showing that psychopaths perform poorly on neuropsychological tests of frontal lobe functioning and have less gray matter in the frontal lobes (Dinn & Harris, 2000; Raine et al., 2000).

Psychopaths also show impulsivity when presented with a task designed to test ability to modify responses depending on success or failure (Patterson & Newman, 1993). In one study demonstrating this phenomenon, participants viewed playing cards on a computer-generated video display (Newman, Patterson, & Kosson, 1987). If a face card appeared, the participant won 5 cents; if a nonface card appeared, the participant lost 5 cents. After each trial the participant had the opportunity to continue or stop the game. The probability of losing was controlled by the experimenter and started at 10 percent. Thereafter the probability of losing increased by 10 percent for every 10 cards played until it reached

A card guessing task that manipulates the odds of winning and losing was used to demonstrate psychopaths' impulsivity (Newman, et al., 1987). (Courtesy of Joseph Newman.)

100 percent. Psychopaths continued to play the game much longer than nonpsychopaths. Nine of twelve psychopaths never quit, even though they had lost money on 19 of the last 20 trials. That is, they did not quit pursuing reward even though they were being punished.

The same game was played again with one variation—a 5-second waiting period was imposed after feedback, thus delaying the decision about whether to play again. This dramatically reduced the number of trials for which psychopaths played the game. It seems that enforcing a delay might lead psychopaths to reflect on negative feedback and behave less impulsively. Insensitivity to feedback of many forms (particularly without a pause for reflection) appears to be a feature of psychopathy, as it has been shown even in situations that do not involve punishment (Newman, Schmitt, & Voss, 1997).

> ## Check Your Knowledge 12.3
>
> True or false?
> 1. Psychopathy and borderline personality disorder are tied to impulsivity.
> 2. Psychopathy is tied to increased amygdala activation.
> 3. Conduct disorder is not required for a DSM-IV-TR diagnosis of APD.

Quick Summary

The dramatic/erratic cluster (cluster B) includes borderline personality disorder, histrionic personality disorder, narcissistic personality disorder, and antisocial personality disorder. The key features of borderline personality disorder include intense emotionality, unstable identity, and impulsivity. Histrionic personality disorder is characterized by exaggerated emotional displays. Narcissistic personality disorder is characterized by highly inflated self-esteem but a deep need for admiration. Antisocial personality disorder is defined by violation of rules, and a disregard for others' feelings and social norms. Psychopathy is related to antisocial personality disorder, but is not defined in the DSM. Psychopathy criteria focus on internal experiences rather than behavior.

There is evidence that BPD is inherited, and that heritability might be particularly related to the greater emotional dysregulation and impulsivity. Consistent with the symptoms of impulsivity, some (but not all) research indicates low frontal lobe activity among people with BPD. Consistent with the greater emotionality, people with BPD also have been found to demonstrate increased activity in the amygdala and decreased functioning of the serotonin system. People with BPD report elevated rates of abuse.

Both object-relations theories and Linehan's model build on the high rates of abuse reported by people with BPD. Linehan's model also emphasizes the biological diathesis for emotional dysregulation. Object relations theory places an emphasis on conflicts between the internalized values drawn from major relationships and defense mechanisms such as splitting. Linehan's model focuses on emotional dysregulation coupled with parental invalidation.

Researchers know relatively little about the roots of histrionic personality disorder. This personality disorder is believed to be related to poor parenting.

According to self-psychology theory of narcissistic personality disorder, parents who are inconsistent and focused on their own worth fail to help the child develop a stable sense of self-worth. Social cognitive theory proposes that the behavior of the person with narcissistic personality disorder is shaped by their goal of maintaining specialness, and their belief that that the purpose of interpersonal interactions is to bolster self-esteem.

Antisocial personality disorder and psychopathy are both moderately heritable. Beyond genes, family and cultural environment seem to play a role in the development of this disorder. Inconsistent parental discipline is one well-documented risk variable.

Psychopaths have little anxiety. Their callous treatment of others might also be linked to their lack of empathy. Psychopaths are deficient in using negative feedback when pursuing reward—that is, they behave impulsively. This lack of anxiety and empathy, as well as their impulsivity, may drive misconduct without regret and thrill seeking without regard for rules.

Anxious/Fearful Cluster

The anxious/fearful cluster includes avoidant personality disorder, dependent personality disorder, and obsessive-compulsive personality disorder. Generally, people with these disorders are especially prone to worry and distress.

Avoidant Personality Disorder

People with **avoidant personality disorder** are so fearful of criticism, rejection, and disapproval that they will avoid jobs or relationships to protect themselves from negative feedback. In social situations they are restrained because of an extreme fear of saying something foolish, being embarrassed, blushing, or showing other signs of anxiety. They believe they are incompetent and inferior to others and are reluctant to take risks or try new activities.

Clinical Case: Leon

Leon was a 45-year-old man who sought treatment for depression, which he claimed to have experienced almost continuously since the first grade. During the interview, Leon described feeling uncomfortable socially for as long as he could remember. By age 5, he would experience intense anxiety with other children, and his mind would "go blank" if he had to speak in front of others. He grew up dreading birthday parties, having to answer in class, and meeting new children. Although he was able to play with some of the children in his neighborhood, he never had a "best friend," and he never went out on a date. Although he did well academically through high school, his grades worsened during college. He took a job at the post office after graduation because it involved little social interaction (adapted from Spitzer et al., 1994).

Check Your Knowledge 12.3

True or false?
1. Psychopathy and borderline personality disorder appear related to impulsivity.
2. Psychopathy appears related to increased amygdala activation.
3. Psychopathy appears related to decreased emotional reponsiveness.
4. Conduct disorder is not required for a DSM-IV-TR diagnosis of APD.

About 80 percent of people with avoidant personality disorder have comorbid major depression, as Leon did (see Clinical Case). Other common comorbid conditions include borderline personality disorder, schizotypal personality disorder, and alcohol abuse (McGlashan et al., 2000). The very high rate of comorbidity with generalized social phobia is probably a result of the fact that the diagnostic criteria for these two disorders are so similar; avoidant personality disorder might actually be a more chronic variant of generalized social phobia (Alden et al., 2002). See Figure 5.1 for one way of thinking about these two disorders.

Both avoidant personality disorder and social phobia are related to a syndrome called *taijin kyoufu* that occurs in Japan (*taijin* means "interpersonal" and *kyoufu* means "fear"). Like people with avoidant personality disorder and social phobia, those with *taijin kyoufusho* are overly sensitive in interpersonal situations and avoid interpersonal contact. But what they fear is somewhat different from the usual fears of those with the DSM diagnoses. Patients with *taijin kyoufusho* tend to be anxious or ashamed about how they affect or appear to others—for example, they fear that they are ugly or have body odor (Ono et al., 1996).

Dependent Personality Disorder

The core features of **dependent personality disorder** are an overreliance on others and a lack of self-confidence. People with dependent personality disorder have an intense need to be taken care of, which often leads them to feel uncomfortable when alone. They subordinate their own needs to ensure that they do not break up the protective relationships they have established. When a close relationship ends, they urgently seek another relationship to replace it. They see themselves as weak, and they turn to others for support and decision-making. The case history of Matthew (see Clinical Case) provides an example of how hard it can be for a person with dependent personality disorder to maintain different relationships that make conflicting demands.

Clinical Case: Matthew

Matthew was a 34-year-old man who sought treatment after breaking up with a girlfriend. His mother, with whom he lived, had disapproved of his marriage plans because his girlfriend came from a different religious background. Matthew felt that he could not marry his girlfriend without his mother's approval, because "blood is thicker than water." Although he cancelled the engagement, he was angry with his mother and feared that she would never approve of anyone he wanted to marry. He said that he feared disagreeing with his mother because he did not want to have to "fend for himself" (adapted from Spitzer et al., 2002).

The DSM diagnostic criteria for dependent personality disorder include some features that do not appear to be well supported by research. Specifically, the criteria portray people with dependent personality disorder as being very passive (e.g., having difficulty initiating projects or doing things on their own, not being able to disagree with others, allowing others to make decisions for them). Research indicates, however, that people with dependent personality disorder actually can do what is necessary to maintain a close relationship; this might involve being very deferential and passive, but it might equally well involve taking active steps to preserve the relationship (Bornstein, 1997).

The prevalence of dependent personality disorder is about 1.5 percent in the United States (Torgersen, Kringlen, & Cramer, 2001), but it is higher in India and Japan, perhaps because these societies encourage some behaviors that might be construed as dependent. Dependent personality disorder often co-occurs with borderline, schizoid, histrionic, schizotypal, and avoidant personality disorders, as well as with mood disorders, anxiety disorders, and bulimia.

Obsessive-Compulsive Personality Disorder

The person with **obsessive-compulsive personality disorder** is a perfectionist, preoccupied with details, rules, and schedules. People with this disorder often pay so much attention to detail that they fail to finish projects. They are more oriented toward work than pleasure. They have inordinate difficulty making decisions (lest they err) and allocating time (lest they focus on the wrong thing). Their interpersonal relationships are often poor because they are stubborn and demand that everything be done their way. They often become known as "control freaks." Generally, they are serious, rigid, formal, and inflexible, especially regarding moral issues. They are unable to discard worn-out and useless objects, even those with no sentimental value, and are likely to be excessively frugal, to a level that causes concern for those around them.

Obsessive-compulsive personality disorder is quite different from obsessive-compulsive disorder (OCD), despite the similarity in names. The personality disorder does not include the obsessions and compulsions that define the latter. Indeed, only a minority of people with OCD meet the diagnostic criteria for obsessive-compulsive personality disorder (Baer & Jenike, 1992). The disorder most frequently comorbid with obsessive-compulsive personality disorder is avoidant personality disorder.

Etiology of the Personality Disorders in the Anxious/Fearful Cluster

There has been little research on the causes of the personality disorders in the anxious/fearful cluster. We briefly review ideas about the etiology of avoidant personality disorders, then obsessive-compulsive personality disorder, followed by dependent personality disorder.

Much like the fears and phobias discussed in Chapter 5, avoidant personality disorder might reflect the influence of an environment in which the child is taught to fear people and situations that most of us regard as harmless. For example, one of the child's parents might have similar fears, which are transmitted by modeling. Alternatively, the fact that avoidant personality disorder runs in families might indicate a genetic diathesis (Tillfors et al., 2001).

Obsessive-compulsive personality traits were originally viewed by Freud as caused by fixation at the anal stage of psychosexual development. More contemporary psychodynamic theories emphasize a fear of loss of control, which is handled by overcompensation. For example, the man who is a compulsive workaholic might fear that his life will fall apart if he allows himself to relax and have fun.

Although there are no twin studies of dependent personality disorder as a category, twin studies are available that focus on dependency as a dimensional trait. There is at least some genetic influence on dependency, but environmental factors appear to be more important (O'Neill & Kendler, 1998).

 DSM-IV-TR Criteria for Dependent Personality Disorder

Presence of at least five of the following:

- Difficulty making decisions without excessive advice and reassurance from others
- Need for others to take responsibility for most major areas of life
- Difficulty disagreeing with others for fear of losing their support
- Difficulty doing things on own because of lack of self-confidence
- Doing unpleasant things as a way to obtain the approval and support of others
- Feelings of helplessness when alone because of lack of confidence in ability to handle things without others
- Urgently seeking new relationship when present one ends
- Preoccupation with fears of having to take care of self

 DSM-IV-TR Criteria for Obsessive-Compulsive Personality Disorder

Presence of at least four of the following:

- Preoccupation with rules, details, and organization to the extent that the major point of an activity is lost
- Extreme perfectionism interferes with task completion
- Excessive devotion to work to the exclusion of leisure and friendships
- Inflexibility about morals
- Difficulty discarding worthless items
- Reluctance to delegate unless others conform to one's standards
- Miserliness
- Rigidity and stubbornness

Investigators have argued that dependent personality disorder may result from an over-protective and authoritarian parenting style that prevents the development of feelings of self-efficacy (Bornstein, 1997). Dependent personality disorder might also be related to "attachment" problems (Livesley, Schroeder, & Jackson, 1990). Developmental psychologists regard attachment as one of the major influences on personality development. In healthy development, infants become attached to an adult and use the adult as a secure base from which to explore and pursue other goals. Separation from the adult leads to anger and distress. As development proceeds, children become less dependent on the presence of the attachment figure for security. It is possible that the abnormal attachment behaviors seen in dependent personality disorder reflect something gone wrong in the usual developmental process, such as a disruption of the early parent–child relationship caused by death, neglect, rejection, or overprotectiveness. Persons with dependent personality disorder engage in a number of tactics, originally established to maintain their relationship with their parents, to keep their relationships with other people at any cost—for example, agreeing to do unpleasant tasks to keep others happy (Stone, 1993).

Check Your Knowledge 12.4

You are the director of human resources for a major corporation. You are asked to review a set of situations in which employees had interpersonal and task-focused problems that were severe enough and persistent enough to raise concerns in the workplace. Name the most likely personality disorder for each of the following.

1. Jose refuses to meet with his boss; he says that the boss is stupid and that only the top guns could understand the type of brilliant ideas that he is generating. When asked to write his ideas down in a memo that could be shared, he refuses, stating that he doesn't have time for such petty exercises. When you sit down to meet with him, his first question is whether you are in a position of power to help him negotiate a higher salary.

2. Mariana refuses to meet with customers. She states that she is terrified that they will see that she does not know much. It turns out that she has called in sick the last three times her boss scheduled an appointment with her, and her colleagues barely know her name. When asked, she says that meeting with any of these people makes her feel horribly nervous about potential rejection of her ideas. She asks for a position that would involve little social contact.

3. Gary has had three employees request transfers. They each stated that he was too controlling, picked on small mistakes, and would not listen to any new ideas for solving problems. At the interview, he brought in a typed, 15-page chart of the goals he would like to execute for the company. Despite having an inordinate number of goals, he has failed to complete a single project during his first year with the company.

4. Seth, a 52-year-old man who has worked in the mail room for 10 years, has been the subject of complaints from many other staff members. They say that he seems cold and indifferent, even though they attempt to include him in conversations. Other mail room staff say they can't get him to talk. When you meet with Seth, he explains that he really has no interest in having friends or joining parties; socializing is just not part of his life in general. He is completely unenthusiastic about his colleagues, but he does his work without any other problems.

5. Police contact you to let you know that they have arrested Sam, one of your employees. He was caught at a bank trying to cash a $10,000 company check on which he had forged the signature. You learn that Sam had previously defrauded three other companies. When you meet with Sam, he laughs about how easy it was to get access to the checkbook, and he does not seem the least bit sorry.

Treatment of Personality Disorders

It is important to bear in mind that a therapist trying to address personality disorder symptoms typically is concerned with Axis I disorders as well. Indeed, many people with personality disorders enter treatment because of an Axis I disorder rather than a personality disorder. For example, a person with antisocial personality disorder might seek treatment of substance abuse problems; a person with avoidant personality disorder might seek treatment for a social phobia; and a patient with obsessive-compulsive personality disorder might seek help for depression. In this connection, it can be mentioned that people with Axis I disorders and personality disorders usually do not improve as much from various forms of psychotherapy as do people with Axis I disorders alone (Crits-Christoph & Barber, 2002). The reason seems pretty clear: people with both types of disorders are more seriously disturbed than are those with only Axis I disorders and therefore might require treatment that is both more intensive (because of the long-standing nature of personality disorders) and more extensive (i.e., focused on a broad range of psychological problems).

Medications are often used to treat personality disorders (Koenigsberg, Woo-Ming, & Siever, 2002), the choice of drug being determined by the Axis I problem that the personality disorder resembles. For example, patients with avoidant personality disorder can be prescribed antianxiety medications or antidepressants in hopes of reducing their social anxieties. When someone with a personality disorder also has depression, antidepressant medication can be helpful (Rinne et al., 2002). Given the connections noted earlier between schizophrenia and schizotypal personality disorder, it is not surprising that antipsychotic drugs (e.g., risperidone, trade name Risperdal) have shown some effectiveness with schizotypal personality disorder (Koenigsberg et al., 2003).

People with serious symptoms of personality disorders might attend a day treatment program that offers psychotherapy, in both group and individual formats, for several hours per day. Typically, psychotherapy sessions are interspersed with social and occupational therapy. The length of such programs varies, but some last several months. Programs tend to vary in their treatment approaches, with some offering psychodynamic approaches, others offering supportive approaches, and still others offering cognitive behavioral treatments. The early results do suggest that day treatment programs lead to improvements in symptoms and social functioning (Ogrodniczuk & Piper, 2001). Beyond day treatment programs, many patients are seen in individual outpatient psychological treatment. A recent review of 15 studies suggests that psychotherapy can be effective in treating personality disorders (Perry, Banon, & Ianni, 1999). For example, across studies, 52 percent of patients recovered within about 15 months of treatment.

Most of these studies of the effectiveness of either day treatment or psychotherapy, though, do not include a control group, but rather compare patients to those receiving standard medical care. This is of concern—Remember that many personality disorders seem to dissipate over time naturally (see Figure 12.1). Treatment studies also include a broad range of different personality disorders, treated with quite disparate approaches. In one trial that focused on more specific personality disorders, brief psychodynamic treatment was shown to be helpful in reducing symptoms of histrionic personality disorder and of personality disorders in the anxious/fearful cluster (Winston et al., 1994).

Psychodynamic therapists aim to alter the patient's present-day views of the childhood problems assumed to underlie the personality disorder. For example, they might guide a man with obsessive-compulsive personality disorder to the realization that his childhood quest to win his parents' love by being perfect need not be carried into adulthood—that he does not need to be perfect to win the approval of others, that it is possible to make mistakes without being abandoned by those whose love he seeks.

Cognitive behavioral therapists tend to break a personality disorder down into a set of separate problems. For example, a person diagnosed as having a paranoid personality disorder or avoidant personality disorder is extremely sensitive to criticism. This sensitivity might be treated by social skills training in how to address criticism, by systematic desensitization, or rational-emotive behavior therapy (Renneberg et al., 1990). Since the argumentativeness of people with paranoid personality disorder provokes counterattacks from others, the behavior therapist might help the person learn less antagonizing ways of relating to other people. Social skills training in a support group might encourage people with avoidant personality disorder to be more assertive with other people; one controlled study confirmed that this is a promising strategy (Alden, 1989).

In cognitive therapy for personality disorders, Aaron Beck and associates (1990) apply the same kind of analysis used in the treatment of depression (see p. 50). Each disorder is analyzed in terms of negative cognitive beliefs that could help explain the pattern of symptoms (see Table 12.5). For example, cognitive therapy for a perfectionistic person with obsessive-compulsive personality disorder entails first persuading the patient to accept the essence of the cognitive model—that feelings and behaviors are primarily a function of thoughts. Errors in logic are then explored, such as when the patient concludes that he or she cannot do anything right because of failing in one particular endeavor (an example of overgeneralization). The therapist also looks for dysfunctional assumptions or schemata

Children normally go through a phase in which separation from a parent is distressing. People with dependent personality disorder might be experiencing a similar phenomenon in their adult relationships. (Mary Kate Denny/PhotoEdit.)

Table 12.5 Examples of Maladaptive Cognitions Hypothesized to Be Associated with Each Personality Disorder

Personality Disorder	Maladaptive Cognitions
Avoidant	If people *know* the real me, they will reject me.
Dependent	I need people to survive and I need constant encouragement and reassurance.
Obsessive-compulsive	I know what's best.
	People *should* do better and try harder.
Paranoid	Don't trust anyone.
	Be on guard.
Antisocial	I am entitled to *break* rules.
	Others are exploitative.
Narcissistic	Since I am special, I *deserve* special rules.
	I am better than others.
Histrionic	People are there to serve or admire me.
Schizoid	Others are unrewarding.
	Relationships are messy and undesirable.

Source: Beck, A.T., & Freeman, A. (1990). *Cognitive therapy of personality disorders*. New York, NY: Guilford.

that might underlie the person's thoughts and feelings—for example, the belief that it is critical for every decision to be correct. Beyond challenging cognitions, Beck's approach to personality disorders incorporates a variety of other cognitive behavioral techniques.

The traits that characterize the personality disorders are probably too ingrained to change thoroughly. Instead, the therapist—regardless of theoretical orientation—might find it more realistic to change a disorder into a style or a more adaptive way of approaching life (Millon, 1996).

Treatment of Borderline Personality Disorder

Few patients pose a greater challenge to treatment than do those with borderline personality disorder, regardless of the type of treatment being used. Patients with borderline personality disorder tend to show their interpersonal problems toward therapists as much as they do in other relationships. Because these patients find it inordinately difficult to trust others, therapists find it inordinately difficult to develop and maintain the therapeutic relationship. The patient alternately idealizes and vilifies the therapist, demanding special attention and consideration one moment—such as therapy sessions at odd hours and countless phone calls during periods of particular crisis—and refusing to keep appointments the next; they beg the therapist for understanding and support but insist that certain topics are off-limits.

Suicide is always a serious risk, but it is often difficult for the therapist to judge whether a frantic phone call at 2:00 A.M. is a call for help or a manipulative gesture designed to test how special the patient is to the therapist and to what lengths the therapist will go to meet the patient's needs at the moment. As in the case of Mary (see the Clinical Case at the beginning of this chapter), hospitalization is often necessary when the threat of suicide cannot be handled without the degree of supervision possible only in the controlled setting of a mental hospital. Seeing such patients is so stressful that it is common for a therapist to regularly consult with another therapist for advice and for support in dealing with their own emotions as they cope with the extraordinary challenges of helping these patients.

A number of drugs have been tried in the treatment of people with borderline personality disorder, most notably antidepressant and antipsychotic medications. There is some evidence that fluoxetine (Prozac) decreases some of the aggressiveness and depression often found in these patients (Coccaro & Kavoussi, 1995) and that lithium can reduce some of their irritability, anger, and suicidality (Links et al., 1990). Similarly, antiseizure medications, which have been used to treat mood changes in bipolar disorder, appear helpful in the treatment of borderline personality disorder (Markovitz & Markovitz, 2004). Newer antipsychotic medications, such as olanzapine, seem to reduce the symptoms of borderline personality disorder (Bogenschutz & Nurnberg, 2004). Because such patients often abuse drugs and engage in suicidal behavior, extreme caution must be used in drug therapy (Waldenger & Frank, 1989).

Object-Relations Psychotherapy   Otto Kernberg developed a modified psychodynamic object-relations treatment, in which the overall goal is to strengthen the patient's weak ego so that he or she stops splitting (Kernberg et al., 1985). Splitting—seeing everything according to a simple good–bad dichotomy—is regarded as the result of an inability to form complex ideas of others (object representations). For example, the patient might begin by seeing the therapist as a godlike genius but then be furious when the therapist mentions that the patient is behind in therapy payments; in an instant the therapist becomes evil and incompetent. The therapist points out how the patient is allowing his or her emotions and behavior to be regulated by such defenses as splitting. Kernberg's approach is more directive than that of most analysts. In addition to interpreting defensive behavior, he recommends giving patients concrete suggestions for behaving more adaptively and hospitalizing patients whose behavior becomes dangerous.

A long-term study conducted at the world-famous analytically oriented Menninger Clinic suggested that classical psychoanalysis was not helpful for BPD (Stone, 1987). On the other hand, studies suggest that Kernberg's object-relations psychodynamic therapy (Trull, Stepp, & Durrett, 2003) and adaptations of this approach (Bateman & Fonagy, 2004) help relieve symptoms of borderline personality disorder. To date, however, researchers have not compared psychodynamic treatment to placebo or to treatment as usual.

Dialectical Behavior Therapy   Marsha Linehan (1987) introduced an approach that she called **dialectical behavior therapy (DBT)**, combining client-centered empathy and acceptance with cognitive behavioral problem-solving and social skills training. The concept of dialectics comes from the work of German philosopher Georg Wilhelm Friedrich Hegel (1770–1831). It refers to a constant tension between any phenomenon (any idea, event, etc., called the *thesis*) and its opposite (the *antithesis*), which is resolved by the creation of a new phenomenon (the *synthesis*). In DBT, the term *dialectical* is used in two main ways:

- In one sense, it refers to the seemingly opposite strategies that the therapist must use when treating patients with borderline personality disorder—accepting them as they are and yet helping them change. (For a closer look at the dialectic between acceptance and change, see Focus on Discovery 12.2.)
- In the other sense, it refers to the patient's realization that splitting the world into good and bad is not necessary; instead, one can achieve a synthesis of these apparent opposites. For example, instead of a friend being seen as either all bad (thesis) or all good (antithesis), the friend can have both kinds of qualities (synthesis). From this perspective, one goal of DBT is to teach the patient to adopt a dialectical view of the world, an understanding that things are not really all bad or all good.

DBT centers on the therapist's full acceptance of the client, combined with a matter-of-fact problem-solving attitude toward the client's dysfunctional behavior, including any suicidal behavior. The cognitive behavioral aspect of the treatment, conducted both individually and in groups, involves four stages. In the first stage, dangerously impulsive behaviors are addressed, with the goal of promoting greater control. In the second stage, the focus is on learning to modulate and control the extreme emotionality. This phase might involve coaching to help a person learn to tolerate emotional distress, but also skills for learning to trust emotions as important signs about the environment and one's thoughts. Stage three focuses on improving relationships and self-esteem. Stage four is designed to promote connectedness and happiness. Throughout, patients learn to solve problems, to acquire more effective and socially acceptable ways of handling their daily living problems and controlling their emotions. Basically, DBT involves giving patients cognitive behavioral therapy while simultaneously validating and accepting them for who they are.

Focus on Discovery 12.2

Acceptance in Dialectical Behavior Therapy

Marsha Linehan (1987) argues that a therapist treating patients with borderline personality disorder has to adopt a posture that might seem inconsistent to the Western mind. The therapist must work for change while at the same time accepting the real possibility that no changes are going to occur. Linehan's notions of acceptance are drawn from Zen philosophy and from Rogerian approaches to psychotherapy.

Marsha Linehan created dialectical behavior therapy, which combines cognitive behavioral therapy with acceptance. (Courtesy of Marsha M. Linehan.)

Linehan's reasoning is that people with borderline personality disorder are so sensitive to rejection and criticism that even gentle encouragement to behave or think differently can be misinterpreted as a serious rebuke, leading to extreme emotional reactions. When this happens, the therapist, who may have been revered a moment earlier, is suddenly vilified and spurned. Thus, while observing limits—"I would be very sad if you killed yourself, so I hope very much that you won't"—the therapist must convey to the patient that he or she is fully accepted. This is hard to do if the patient is threatening suicide, showing uncontrolled anger, or railing against imagined rebukes from the therapist.

Completely accepting the patient does not mean approving of everything the patient does; rather, it means that the therapist must accept the situation for what it is. And this acceptance, argues Linehan, must be real: the therapist must truly accept patients as they are; acceptance should not be in the service of change, an indirect way of encouraging patients to behave differently. "Acceptance can transform but if you accept in order to transform, it is not acceptance. It is like loving. Love seeks no reward but when given freely comes back a hundredfold. He who loses his life finds it. He who accepts, changes" (Linehan, personal communication, November 16, 1992). Full acceptance does not, in Linehan's view, preclude change. Indeed, she proposes the opposite—that it is the refusal to accept that precludes change.

Linehan's approach also emphasizes that the patients too must accept who they are and what they have been through. Patients are asked to accept that their childhood is now unchangeable, that their behaviors might have caused relationships to end, and that they feel emotions more intensely than others do. This approach, it is hoped, will provide a basis for understanding the self.

Linehan and associates (1991) were the first to publish the results of a randomized controlled study of a psychological treatment for borderline personality disorder. Patients were randomly assigned either to DBT or to treatment as usual, meaning any therapy available in the community (Seattle, Washington). After 1 year of treatment and again 6 and 12 months later, patients in the two groups were compared on a variety of measures (Linehan, Heard, & Armstrong, 1993). The findings immediately after treatment revealed that DBT was much superior to treatment as usual—patients showed less intentional self-injurious behavior, including fewer suicide attempts; dropped out of treatment less; and spent fewer days in the hospital. There were, however, no differences in self-reported depression and feelings of hopelessness between the two treatment groups. At the follow-ups, the superiority of DBT was maintained. Additionally, DBT patients had better work records, reported less anger, and were judged as overall better adjusted than the comparison therapy patients. But most patients were still feeling quite miserable at the 1-year follow-up, underscoring the extreme difficulty of treating such patients.

A second randomized controlled trial found that DBT provided more relief from depressive and other symptoms than did treatment as usual (Koons et al., 2001). A similarly designed study of women with borderline personality disorder who were also drug dependent found less substance abuse after DBT than after treatment as usual (Linehan et al., 1999).

There is widespread interest in this approach to treating borderline personality disorder; many outcome studies are in progress, and many treatment centers have begun to offer DBT. Results from some of these community centers do suggest that rates of hospitalization and emergency room visits decrease when programs begin to offer DBT (Robins & Chapman, 2004). Despite the encouraging interest in systematic treatment approaches for borderline personality disorder, to date, no study has compared DBT to a control group other than treatment as usual.

Treatment of Psychopathy

Experts of varying theoretical persuasions have asserted for years that it is pointless to try to alter the callous and remorseless nature of psychopaths (e.g., Cleckley, 1976). Even when behavioral change is observed—as with social skills training in prison—some argued that the apparent therapeutic gains might not last (Corrigan, 1991). That is, the psychopath might just play along with the therapist to derive some benefits, a manifestation of the manipulativeness that characterizes people with psychopathy. People who lie, who do not care about the feelings of others, who appear not to consider moral principles, and who lack motivation to obey society's laws were expected to be poor candidates for therapy.

These pessimistic views have been challenged in a comprehensive meta-analysis of 42 studies of the psychological treatment of psychopaths (Salekin, 2002). These studies had many methodological problems, but 17 of them, involving 88 psychopathic persons, found that psychoanalytic psychotherapy was very helpful in domains such as improving interpersonal relationships, increasing the capacity for feeling remorse and empathy, reducing the amount of lying, being released from probation, and holding down a job. Similar positive therapeutic effects were found in five studies employing cognitive behavioral techniques involving 246 psychopaths. Therapy was more beneficial for younger patients. To be at all effective, treatment had to be quite intensive—that is, four times a week for at least a year—a very heavy dose of psychosocial treatment whatever one's theoretical orientation. Another meta-analysis looked at the idea that people with high levels of psychopathy might actually get worse in treatment, but no good evidence emerged to support this idea (D'Silva, Duggan, & McCarthy, 2004).

These are remarkably positive findings given the widely held belief that psychopathy is basically untreatable. And yet, as optimistic as one researcher is about current and future treatment efforts for psychopaths, we find noteworthy his cautionary comment at the end of his article: ". . . research needs to make some attempt to determine whether clients are 'faking good' in treatment studies or whether the changes are genuine" (Salekin, 2002, p. 107).

Summary

- Coded on Axis II in DSM-IV-TR, personality disorders are defined as enduring patterns of behavior and inner experience that disrupt functioning. Personality disorders are grouped into three clusters in DSM-IV-TR: odd/eccentric, dramatic/erratic, and anxious/fearful.
- Personality disorders are usually comorbid with such Axis I disorders as depression and anxiety disorders, and they tend to predict poorer outcomes for these disorders.
- The high comorbidity of personality disorders with each other, and the fact that personality disorders are seen as the extremes of continuously distributed personality traits have led to proposals to develop a dimensional rather than a categorical approach to personality diagnoses.

Odd/Eccentric Cluster

- Specific diagnoses in the odd/eccentric cluster include paranoid, schizoid, and schizotypal.
- The major symptom of paranoid personality disorder is suspiciousness and mistrust; of schizoid personality disorder, interpersonal detachment; and of schizotypal personality disorder, unusual thought and behavior.
- Behavior-genetic research supports the idea that schizotypal personality disorder is related to schizophrenia.

Dramatic/Erratic Cluster

● The dramatic/erratic cluster includes borderline, histrionic, narcissistic, and antisocial personality disorders.

● The major symptom of borderline personality disorder is unstable, highly changeable emotion and behavior; of histrionic personality disorder, exaggerated emotional displays; and of narcissistic personality disorder, highly inflated self-esteem. Antisocial personality disorder and psychopathy overlap a great deal but are not equivalent. The diagnosis of antisocial personality focuses on behavior, whereas that of psychopathy emphasizes emotional deficits.

● There is evidence that much of the vulnerability to borderline personality disorder is inherited, and there are also (somewhat inconsistent) findings regarding deficits in frontal lobe functioning and regarding greater amygdala activation.

● Psychosocial theories of the etiology of borderline, histrionic, and narcissistic disorders focus on early parent–child relationships. It is clear that people with borderline personality disorder report extremely high rates of child abuse and parental separation compared to the general population.

● The object-relations theorist Kernberg and the self-psychologist Kohut have detailed proposals concerning borderline and narcissistic personality disorders, focusing on the child developing an insecure ego because of inconsistent love and attention from the parents. Linehan's cognitive behavioral theory of borderline personality disorder proposes an interaction between emotional dysregulation and an invalidating family environment.

● Antisocial personality disorder and psychopathy are moderately heritable.

● Psychopaths tend to have fathers who were antisocial, and discipline during their childhood was absent or inconsistent.

● Psychopathy is related to lack of response to punishment, poor empathy, and elevated impulsivity.

Anxious/Fearful Cluster

● The anxious/fearful cluster includes avoidant, dependent, and obsessive-compulsive personality disorders.

● The major symptom of avoidant personality disorder is fear of rejection or criticism; of dependent personality disorder, excessive reliance on others; and of obsessive-compulsive personality disorder, a perfectionistic, detail-oriented style.

● Theories of etiology for the anxious/fearful cluster focus on parenting. Avoidant personality disorder might result from the transmission of fear from parent to child via modeling. Dependent personality might be caused by disruptions of the parent–child relationship (e.g., through separation or loss) that lead the person to fear losing other relationships in adulthood. Dependency as a personality trait is only modestly heritable.

Treatment of Personality Disorders

● Although psychodynamic, behavioral and cognitive, and pharmacological treatments all are used for personality disorders, less research has been conducted for these disorders compared to Axis I disorders.

● Several medications appear to be helpful for quelling specific symptoms.

● Early research on day treatment programs is promising.

● Some promising evidence is emerging for the utility of dialectical behavior therapy for borderline personality disorder. This approach combines client-centered acceptance with a cognitive behavioral focus. Recent research suggests that even psychopathy, formerly considered virtually untreatable, might respond to intensive psychological treatment.

Answers to Check Your Knowledge Questions

12.1 1. T; 2. F; 3. T; 4. F; 5. F
12.2 1. b; 2. a, b; 3. d
12.3 1. T; 2. F; 3. F

12.4 1. narcissistic; 2. avoidant; 3. obsessive-compulsive; 4. schizoid; 5. antisocial

Key Terms

antisocial personality disorder	dialectical behavior therapy	object-relations theory	personality disorders
avoidant personality disorder	five-factor model	obsessive-compulsive personality disorder	psychopathy
borderline personality disorder	histrionic personality disorder	paranoid personality disorder	schizoid personality disorder
dependent personality disorder	narcissistic personality disorder		schizotypal personality disorder

13 Sexual and Gender Identity Disorders

S exuality is one of the most personal areas of a person's life. Each of us is a sexual being with preferences and fantasies that may surprise or even shock us from time to time. Usually these are part of normal sexual functioning. But when our fantasies or desires begin to affect us or others in unwanted or harmful ways, they begin to qualify as abnormal. In this chapter we consider the full range of human sexual thoughts, feelings, and actions that are listed in DSM-IV-TR as sexual and gender identity disorders (Table 13.1).

For perspective, we begin by briefly describing norms and healthy sexual behavior. Then, we divide our study of sexual disorders and problems into three major sections: **sexual dysfunctions**, disruptions in sexual functioning found in many people who are in otherwise good psychological health; **gender identity disorder**, a diagnosis used to describe people who believe they are of the opposite sex; and the **paraphilias**, in which people are attracted to unusual sexual activities or objects. We close this chapter with a discussion of rape. Although rape is not a diagnosis in DSM-IV-TR, we examine this issue because it is a harmful form of sexual behavior.

Sexual Norms and Behavior

Definitions of what is normal or desirable in human sexual behavior vary with time and place. Consider contemporary Western world views that *inhibition* of sexual expression causes problems. Contrast this with nineteenth and early twentieth century views that *excess* was the culprit; in particular, excessive masturbation in childhood was widely believed to lead to sexual problems in adulthood. Von Krafft-Ebing (1902) postulated that early masturbation damaged the sexual organs and exhausted a finite reservoir of sexual energy, resulting in diminished abilities to function sexually in adulthood. Even in adulthood, excessive sexual activity was thought to underlie problems such as erectile failure. The general Victorian view was that sexual appetite was basically dangerous and therefore had to be restrained. For example, to discourage handling of the genitals by children, metal mittens were promoted; and to distract adults from too much sex, outdoor exercise and a bland diet were recommended. In fact, Kellogg's Corn Flakes and graham crackers were developed as foods that would lessen sexual interest. They didn't.

Table 13.1 Sexual and Gender Identity Disorders

Sexual dysfunctions
    Sexual desire disorders
        Hypoactive sexual desire disorder
        Sexual aversion disorder
    Sexual arousal disorders
        Female sexual arousal disorder
        Male erectile disorder
    Orgasmic disorders
        Female orgasmic disorder
        Male orgasmic disorder
        Premature ejaculation
    Sexual pain disorders
        Dyspareunia
        Vaginismus
Gender identity disorder
Paraphilias
    Fetishism
    Transvestic fetishism
    Pedophilia
    Exhibitionism
    Voyeurism
    Frotteurism
    Sexual masochism
    Sexual sadism
    Paraphilias not otherwise specified (e.g., coprophilia, necrophilia)

Source: From DSM-IV-TR, 2000.

Other changes over time have influenced people's attitudes and experiences of sexuality. For example, technology is changing sexual experiences, as the number of people accessing sexual content on the Internet increases dramatically. Even as the accessibility of sexual content increases so dramatically, the spectre of AIDS and other sexually transmitted diseases changes the risks associated with sexual behavior. Other changes in sexual norms are occurring as well. As the population of the United States ages, a new-found emphasis on the right to a good sex life until the day of death has emerged, perhaps most visibly expressed in the barrage of television commercials for medications to improve erectile function among older men (Tiefer, 2003). Clearly, we must keep varying cultural norms in mind as we study human sexual behavior.

At the current point in time in our culture, what are the norms? Several major surveys have been conducted to assess typical levels of sexual activity. In one study that included a representative sample of almost 3,000 adults, Laumann and colleagues (1994) asked participants to describe their level of involvement in different sexual activities (see Table 13.2). Some of the findings were surprising. Although researchers had thought for some time that as many as 10 percent of people had engaged in sex with a same-sex partner, Laumann's study, which involved a more representative sample of participants, revealed much lower rates. In his study, approximately 5.1 percent of men and 3.3 percent of women reported that they had sex with a same-sex partner during their adult lives. On the other hand, about 30 percent of people reported that they would find a same-sex partner to be appealing. See Focus on Discovery 13.1 for a look at the complicated path taken by health professionals in response to changing attitudes toward sexual orientation.

Gender and Sexuality

Few topics raise as much political debate or personal turmoil as gender differences in sexuality. Across a wide range of indices, men report more engagement in sexual thought and behavior than do women. Of course, these are averages, there are going to be exceptions,

Table 13.2 Participation in Selected Sexual Behaviors in the Past Year

Behavior	Male (%)	Female (%)
Give oral sex		
Never	30	35.2
Occasionally	49.4	53.0
Always	20.7	11.8
Receive oral sex		
Never	30.5	33.2
Occasionally	50.4	52.2
Always	19.0	14.6
Number of sex partners		
0	9.9	13.6
1	66.7	74.7
2–4	18.3	10.0
5+	5.1	1.7
Frequency of sexual intercourse		
For Unmarried participants		
None	22.1	30.6
< 3x/month	38.9	36.6
1x/week+	38.9	32.8
For Married participants		
None	1.3	2.6
< 3x/month	31.4	33.9
1x/week+	67.3	63.5

Source: Laumann et al., 1994.

Focus on Discovery 13.1

Learning from History

Until 1973, homosexuality was listed in the DSM as one of the sexual disorders. In 1973 the Nomenclature Committee of the American Psychiatric Association, under pressure from professional and activist groups, recommended the elimination of the category "homosexuality" and the substitution of "sexual orientation disturbance." This new diagnosis was to be applied to gay men and women who are "disturbed by, in conflict with, or wish to change their sexual orientation." The change was approved, but not without vehement protests from several renowned psychiatrists who remained convinced that homosexuality reflects a fixation at an early stage of psychosexual development and is therefore inherently abnormal. Today, these protests would be considered misguided, prejudiced, and antiscientific.

In the 1980 publication of the DSM-III, the Nomenclature Committee waffled by adding a new category called *ego-dystonic homosexuality*, which referred to a person who is homosexually aroused, is persistently distressed by this arousal, and wishes to become heterosexual. In doing so, the crafters of DSM-III took an inconsistent position: a gay man or lesbian is abnormal if he or she has been persuaded by a prejudiced society that his or her sexual orientation is disordered. At the same time, according to DSM-III, homosexuality was not in itself abnormal!

In the years after publication of DSM-III, mental health professionals made very little use of the diagnosis of ego-dystonic homosexuality. By the time the American Psychiatric Association published DSM-III-R in 1987, the Nomenclature Committee dropped the category of ego-dystonic homosexuality. Instead, the catchall category of "sexual disorder not otherwise specified," which refers to "persistent and marked distress about one's sexual orientation" (p. 296), has been included in DSM-IV and DSM-IV-TR. It is noteworthy that the new category does not specify a sexual orientation, but rather, can be applied when a person is distressed over a heterosexual or homosexual orientation.

and most of these differences are small (Andersen et al., 2000). But compared to women, men report thinking about sex, masturbating, and desiring sex more often, as well as desiring more sexual partners and having more partners (Baumeister et al., 2001).

Beyond these differences in sex drive, Peplau and collegues (2003) have described several other ways in which the genders tend to differ in sexuality. For women, sexuality appears more closely tied to relationship status and social norms than for men (Baumeister, 2000). For example, women tend to engage less in sexual activities like masturbation when they are not in a relationship; men don't experience the same shift when a relationship ends. Some argue that the DSM pays too little attention to the relational components of human sexuality in describing sexual dysfunction, especially for women. Some propose that there should be a more women-centered definition that includes "discontent or dissatisfaction with any emotional, physical, or relational aspect of sexual experience" (Tiefer, Hall, & Tavris, 2002, pp. 228–229). Although there are many parallels in how men and women think about sex, men are more likely to think about their sexuality in terms of power than are women (Andersen et al., 1999). Men develop more sexual dysfunctions as they age, such as erectile dysfunctions; in contrast, sexually active older women report fewer sexual problems than younger women do (Laumann, Paik, & Rosen, 1999).

Debate continues about the reasons for these gender differences. Are they based on cultural prohibitions regarding women's sexuality? Are they based on biological differences? Are they tied to women's greater investment in parenting? It is hard to design research to tease apart cultural and biological influences on sexuality. Intriguingly, though, at least some research suggests that some gender differences seem to be remarkably consistent across cultures. In one study of more than 16,000 people (albeit mostly college students), men in 52 different countries reported that they wanted more partners over the course of a lifetime than did women (Schmitt et al., 2003). These findings suggest that biology may shape men's desire for many lifetime partners more than culture does. We know less about the basis for other gender differences in sexuality. There must be some reason for these

Norms about sexuality have fluctuated a great deal over time. In the early twentieth century, corn flakes were promoted as part of a bland diet to reduce sexual desire. (Corbis Images.)

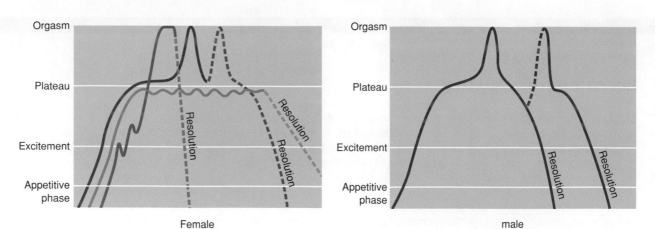

Figure 13.1 The sexual response cycle differs for women and men. Some women report no orgasms, others report one, and some report multiple orgasms. A single orgasm is the typical pattern for men, but a second orgasm may be possible after a refractory period.

differences, though—as Baumeister (2000) points out, in a perfect world, wouldn't men and women be well-matched on their sexual preferences?

Despite debate about gender differences in sexuality, we will see throughout this chapter that gender shapes sexual disorders in a number of ways. Women are much more likely to report symptoms of sexual dysfunction than men, but men are much more likely to meet diagnostic criteria for paraphilias. A better understanding of gender differences in sexuality is needed to understand why there are such major gender differences in sexual diagnoses.

The Sexual Response Cycle

Many researchers have focused on understanding the **sexual response cycle**. The Kinsey group made breakthroughs in the 1940s by interviewing people about their sexuality (Kinsey, Pomeroy, & Martin, 1948). Masters and Johnson created another revolution in research on human sexuality 40 years ago when they began to gather direct observations and physiological measurements of people masturbating and having sexual intercourse. Most contemporary conceptualizations distill proposals by Masters and Johnson (1966) and Kaplan (1974). Figure 13.1 shows the four phases in the human sexual response cycle typically identified for both men and women.

As portrayed in the movie *Kinsey*, Alfred Kinsey shocked people when he began to interview people to understand more about norms in sexual behavior. (Courtesy Kinsey Institute for Research in Sex, Gender, and Reproduction.)

1. **Appetitive phase**. Introduced by Kaplan (1974), this stage refers to sexual interest or desire, often associated with sexually arousing fantasies. Masters and Johnson omitted this stage because, we believe, they used well-functioning volunteers in their work; the people who were willing to be observed sexually did not report any concerns about a lack of sexual desire. This is a good example of how the nature of knowledge-gathering techniques—in this case, the kinds of people studied—constrains the kinds of information obtained.

2. **Excitement phase**. During this phase, men and women experience pleasure associated with increased blood flow to the genitalia (see Figure 13.2 for the sexual anatomy of men and women). Women also experience increased blood flow to the breasts. This flow of blood into tissues shows up in men as erection of the penis and in women as enlargement of the breasts and changes in the vagina, such as increased lubrication.

3. **Orgasm phase**. In this phase, sexual pleasure peaks in ways that have fascinated poets and the rest of us ordinary people for thousands of years. In men, ejaculation feels inevitable and indeed almost always occurs (in rare instances, men have an orgasm without ejaculating, and vice versa). In women, the outer walls of the vagina contract. In both sexes there is general muscle tension.

4. **Resolution phase**. This last stage refers to the relaxation and sense of well-being that usually follow an orgasm. In men there is an associated refractory period during which further erection and arousal are not possible. The duration of the refractory period

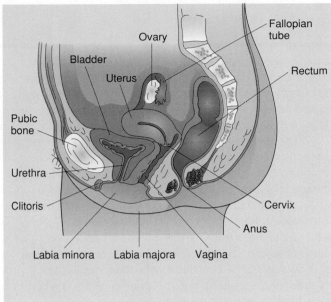

Figure 13.2   The male and female sexual anatomy.

varies across men and even in the same man across occasions. Women are often able to respond again with sexual excitement almost immediately, a capability that permits multiple orgasms.

Check Your Knowledge 13.1

1. Which of the following is **not** documented:
   a. Men report more sex drive than women do.
   b. Women's sexuality is more closely tied to relationship status than men's sexuality.
   c. Men describe their sexuality as more related to power than women do.
   d. Men are able to have more orgasms within a given sexual experience than are women.
2. Which of the following **is not** a phase of the human sexual response cycle?

   a. Appetitive
   b. Ejaculation
   c. Excitement
   d. Resolution
3. Gender differences in the desired number of lifetime partners appear tied to:
   a. culture
   b. biology
   c. personality
   d. this has never been tested.

Sexual Dysfunctions

Sexuality usually occurs in the context of an intimate personal relationship. At its best, it provides a forum for closeness and connection. For better or for worse, most of us base part of our self-concept on our sexuality. Do we please the people we love, do we gratify ourselves, or, more simply, are we able to enjoy the fulfillment and relaxation that can come from a pleasurable sexual experience? When sexual problems emerge, they can wreak havoc on our self-esteem and relationships. A marriage is likely to suffer as sexual dysfunctions become so severe that the intense satisfaction and tenderness of sexual activity is lost.

Clinical Case: Robert

Robert was a highly intelligent 25-year-old graduate student in physics at a leading East Coast university who consulted us for what he called "sexual diffidence." He was engaged to a young woman, and he said he loved his fiancée very much and felt compatible with her in every conceivable way except in bed. There, try as he might, and with apparent understanding from his fiancée, he found himself uninterested in initiating sexual contact or responding to it when initiated by her. Both parties had attributed these problems to the academic pressures he had sustained for the past 2 years, but a discussion with the therapist revealed that Robert had had little interest in sex—either with men or with women—for as far back as he could remember, and that he did not desire sex even when work pressures decreased. He asserted that he found his fiancée very attractive and appealing, but as with other women he had known, his feelings were not passionate.

He had masturbated very rarely in adolescence and did not begin dating until late in college, though he had had many female acquaintances. His general approach to life, including sex, was analytical and intellectual, and he described his problems in a very dispassionate and detached way to the therapist. He freely admitted that he would not have contacted a therapist at all were it not for the quietly stated wishes of his fiancée, who worried that his lack of interest in sex would interfere with their future marital relationship.

After a few individual sessions the therapist asked the young man to invite his fiancée to a therapy session, which the client readily agreed to do. During a conjoint session the couple appeared to be very much in love and looking forward to a life together, though the woman expressed concern about her fiancé's lack of interest in her sexually.

We turn now to sexual problems that interfere with sexual enjoyment for many people at some time during their life. We begin by describing the different types of sexual dysfunctions described in DSM-IV-TR. Then we discuss etiologies and treatments for these problems.

Clinical Descriptions of Sexual Dysfunctions

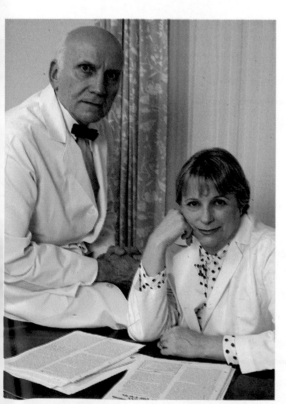

The pioneering work of the sex therapists William H. Masters and Virginia Johnson helped launch a candid and scientific appraisal of human sexuality. (Ira Wyman/Corbis Sygma.)

As Table 13.1 shows, DSM-IV-TR divides sexual dysfunctions into four categories: sexual desire disorders, sexual arousal disorders, orgasmic disorders, and sexual pain disorders. The dysfunction should be persistent and recurrent, a clinical judgment acknowledged in the DSM to entail some subjectivity. The dysfunction also should cause marked distress or interpersonal problems. A diagnosis of sexual dysfunction is not made if the problem is believed to be due entirely to a medical illness (such as advanced diabetes, which can cause erectile problems in men) or if it is due to another Axis I disorder (such as major depression).

One might not expect people to report problems as personal as sexual dysfunction in community surveys. But many people do report these symptoms, and the prevalence of occasional dysfunctions in sexual functioning is actually quite high. Table 13.3 presents data from a survey of approximately 3,000 men and women who were asked whether they had experienced various symptoms of sexual dysfunction for a period of a couple months over the past 12 months (Laumann et al., 1999). More women (43 percent) than men (31 percent) reported symptoms of sexual dysfunction.

Although a lot of people endorsed symptoms, it is important to note that clinical diagnoses are not made unless a person experiences distress or impairment from symptoms; distress or impairment were not assessed in the Laumann survey. In a study of over 1,000 women who were engaged in heterosexual relationships, Bancroft, Loftus, and Long (2003) found a very similar rate of women who reported symptoms of sexual dysfunction (44.3 percent). But when they asked women whether they were distressed by these symptoms, one-quarter of the women experiencing dysfunction reported distress. To be sure, 11 percent is still a relatively high prevalence rate, but it is important to note that most women experiencing a symptom did not meet criteria for a clinical diagnosis. Unfortunately, we have almost no data on how many people have experienced sexual dysfunctions at a diagnosable level (APA, 2000).

Although the diagnostic system for sexual dysfunction reflects the stages in the sexual cycle (see Figure 13.3), the problems often don't break out so cleanly in real life. Many people with problems in one phase of a sexual cycle will report problems in another phase

(Segraves & Segraves, 1991). Some of this may just be a vicious spiral. For example, women with low desire often have troubles with arousal and orgasms. Men who develop premature ejaculation may begin to worry about sex, and then experience problems with sexual desire or sexual arousal (Rowland, Cooper, & Slob, 1996). Beyond the consequences for the individual, sexual problems in one person may lead to sexual problems in the partner. Nonetheless, in the following section, we review the specific sexual dysfunction disorders defined by DSM-IV-TR.

Table 13.3 Self-Reported Rates of Experiencing Various Sexual Problems in the Past 12 Months

Problem	Men %	Women %
Lacked interest in sex	13–17	27–32
Unable to achieve orgasm	7–9	22–28
Climax too early	28–32	NA
Sex not pleasurable	6–8	17–24
Trouble maintaining/achieving erection	11–18	NA
Trouble lubricating	NA	18–27
Pain during sex	NA	8–15

Source: After Laumann et al., 1999.
Note: The ranges reflect the fact that rates vary according to age. NA, not applicable.

Sexual Desire Disorders DSM-IV-TR distinguishes two kinds of sexual desire disorders. **Hypoactive sexual desire disorder** refers to deficient or absent sexual fantasies and urges; **sexual aversion disorder** represents a more extreme disorder, in which the person actively avoids nearly all genital contact with another person. Among people seeking treatment for sexual dysfunctions, more than half complain of low desire. Diagnoses of hypoactive sexual desire increased in samples of men and women seeking treatment from the 1970s to the 1990s (Beck, 1995). As Table 13.3 shows, women are more likely than men to report at least occasional concerns about their level of sexual desire.

Of all the DSM-IV-TR diagnoses, the sexual desire disorders, often colloquially referred to as low sex drive (as illustrated in the case of Robert), seem the most subjective and influenced by cultural norms. How often should a person want sex? And with what intensity? Often, partners are the ones who encourage a person to see a clinician. The hypoactive desire category appeared for the first time in DSM-III in 1980 under the title of "inhibited sexual desire" and may owe its existence to the high expectations some people have about being sexual. Data attest to the significance of subjective and cultural factors in defining low sex drive; for example, hypoactive sexual desire disorder was reported more often by American men than by British (Hawton et al., 1986) or German men (Arentewicz & Schmidt, 1983) despite similar levels of sexual activity across these cultures. Cultural norms seem to influence perceptions of how much sex a person "should" want.

People with hypoactive sexual desire often meet criteria for other sexual dysfunctions, such as orgasmic disorder. Nonetheless, some people experience low sexual desire without other sexual dysfunctions. For example, women with low sexual desire show normal levels of sexual arousal to sexual stimuli in laboratory studies—most would not meet criteria for sexual arousal disorder (Kaplan, 1997).

Sexual Arousal Disorders Some people experience sexual desire but have difficulty attaining or maintaining sexual arousal, the next stage of the sexual response cycle. The two

 DSM-IV-TR Criteria for Hypoactive Sexual Desire Disorder

- Persistently deficient or absent sexual fantasies and desires
- Causes marked distress or interpersonal problems
- Not due to a medical illness, another Axis I disorder (except another sexual dysfunction), or the physiological effects of a drug

 DSM-IV-TR Criteria for Sexual Aversion Disorder

- Persistent avoidance of almost all sexual contact
- Causes marked distress or interpersonal problems
- Not due to another Axis I disorder (except another sexual dysfunction)

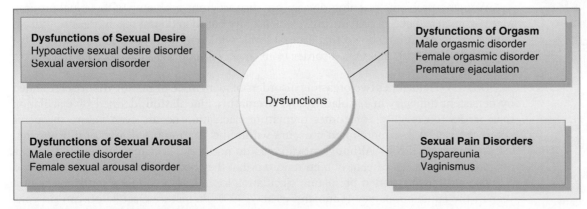

Dysfunctions of Sexual Desire
Hypoactive sexual desire disorder
Sexual aversion disorder

Dysfunctions of Orgasm
Male orgasmic disorder
Female orgasmic disorder
Premature ejaculation

Dysfunctions

Dysfunctions of Sexual Arousal
Male erectile disorder
Female sexual arousal disorder

Sexual Pain Disorders
Dyspareunia
Vaginismus

Figure 13.3 The sexual dysfunctions by phase of the sexual response cycle.

subcategories of arousal disorders are **female sexual arousal disorder** and **male erectile disorder**. The former used to be called *frigidity*, and the latter, *impotence*. These older names have been dropped because of their perjorative connotations.

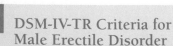

Clinical Case: Paul and Petula

Paul and Petula seek treatment at a sex therapy clinic. They are a young, middle-class couple who have been living together for 6 months and are engaged to be married. Petula reports that Paul "hasn't been able to keep his erection after he enters me" for the past 2 months. Paul experiences initial sexual arousal, but loses his erection almost immediately after he enters Petula. Although they enjoyed sexual intercourse in the beginning of

their relationship, the erectile problems started after they moved in together. During the interview, the psychiatrist learns that they have considerable conflict over time spent together and commitment, and at times, Petula has been violent toward Paul. Neither person is depressed, and no medical problems appear to be involved. (Drawn from Spitzer et al., 1994.)

 DSM-IV-TR Criteria for Female Sexual Arousal Disorder

- Persistent inability to attain or maintain sexual excitement (lubrication and swelling of the genitalia) adequate for completion of sexual activity
- Causes marked distress or interpersonal problems
- Not due to a medical illness, another Axis I disorder (except another sexual dysfunction), or the physiological effects of a drug

The diagnosis of arousal disorder is made for a woman when there is consistently inadequate vaginal lubrication for comfortable completion of intercourse and for a man when there is persistent failure to attain or maintain an erection through completion of the sexual activity. About 5 percent of men report at least occasional symptoms of erectile disorder (Laumann et al., 1999). Male erectile disorder increases greatly with age, with as many as 15 percent of men in their 70s reporting erectile disorder (Feldman et al., 1994), and as many as 70 percent reporting occasional erectile dysfunction (Kim & Lipshultz, 1997). The availability of new drugs for erectile dysfunction may change the rates at which we recognize these disorders. It is important to rule out biological explanations for these symptoms for both men and women. For example, laboratory tests of hormone levels are a routine part of assessment for postmenopausal women (Bartklik & Goldberg, 2000).

Orgasmic Disorders The DSM-IV-TR describes one kind of orgasmic disorder in women and two in men. **Female orgasmic disorder** refers to the persistent absence of orgasm after sexual excitement. Women have different thresholds for orgasm. Although some have orgasms quickly and without much clitoral stimulation, others seem to need intense and prolonged stimulation during sexual contact. Given this, it is not surprising that about two-thirds of women report that they do not consistently experience orgasms with their partners (Laumann et al., 1994). Female orgasmic disorder is not diagnosed unless the absence of orgasms is persistent and troubling. Beyond the distress some women feel about this issue, partners may come to believe they are unskilled or insensitive lovers, or that their partner no longer cares for them (both of which could be true). Worries about protecting a partner's feelings probably account for the fact that up to 60 percent of women report faking an orgasm on occasion (McConaghy, 1993).

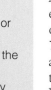 **DSM-IV-TR Criteria for Male Erectile Disorder**

- Persistent inability to attain or maintain an erection adequate for completion of sexual activity
- Causes marked distress or interpersonal problems
- Not due to a medical illness, another Axis I disorder (except another sexual dysfunction), or the physiological effects of a drug

Women's problems reaching orgasm are distinct from problems with sexual arousal. Many women achieve arousal during sexual activity but then do not reach orgasm. Indeed, laboratory research has shown that arousal levels while viewing erotic stimuli do not distinguish women with orgasmic disorder from those without orgasmic disorder (Meston & Gorzalka, 1996).

DSM-IV-TR includes two orgasmic disorders of men: **male orgasmic disorder**, defined by persistent difficulty in ejaculating, and **premature ejaculation**, defined by ejaculation that occurs too quickly. Sometimes premature ejaculation occurs even before the penis enters the vagina, but more often it occurs within the first minute or two of intromission (Strassberg et al., 1987). Although researchers do not know how many men meet formal diagnostic criteria, 10 percent of men reported that they had trouble reaching orgasm and 32 percent of men reported premature ejaculation for at least a couple months in the past year in the Laumann survey (Laumann et al., 1999). Premature ejaculation can provoke considerable anxiety.

Sexual Pain Disorders Two pain disorders associated with sex are listed in the DSM: dyspareunia and vaginismus. **Dyspareunia** is diagnosed when there is persistent or recurrent pain during sexual intercourse. Dyspareunia can be diagnosed in men and women. Some people report that the pain starts at entry, whereas others report pain only after penetration (Meana et al., 1997). A first step in making this diagnosis is ensuring that the pain is not caused by a medical problem, such as an infection (McCormick, 1999), or in women, to a lack of vaginal lubrication due to low desire or postmenopausal changes. Not surprisingly, women with dyspareunia show normal levels of sexual arousal to films of oral sex, but their arousal declines when they watch a depiction of intercourse (Wouda et al., 1998).

Vaginismus is marked by involuntary spasms of the outer third of the vagina to a degree that makes intercourse impossible. It can also occur in response to penetration by a finger or tampon, as well as during gynecological examinations. Despite not being able to have intercourse, women with vaginismus have normal sexual arousal and can have orgasms from manual or oral stimulation that does not involve penetration.

Prevalence rates for dyspareunia in women have been estimated to be as high as 15 percent (Laumann et al., 1994), but dyspareunia in men is rare. Estimates for vaginismus range from 12 to 17 percent of women seeking sex therapy (Rosen & Leiblum, 1995), and it is a very common complaint seen by gynecologists (Leiblum, 1997).

Etiology of Sexual Dysfunctions

Because sexuality can be so difficult to study, case studies have dominated the literature on the causes of sexual dysfunctions. Psychoanalytic case studies focus on underlying repressed conflicts as an explanation for sexual dysfunctions. For example, the theme of repressed aggression competing with the gratification of sexual needs pervades psychoanalytic writings. Thus a man who ejaculates so quickly that he frustrates his female partner could be expressing repressed hostility toward women, who remind him unconsciously of his mother. A woman with vaginismus could be expressing her hostility toward men, perhaps as a result of her husband's overbearing manner. Empirical evidence has failed to support these suppositions.

In 1970, Masters and Johnson (1970) published their widely acclaimed book, *Human Sexual Inadequacy*, which included a theory of why sexual dysfunctions develop based on case studies from their practice. Masters and Johnson used a two-tier model of current and historical causes to conceptualize the etiology of human sexual inadequacy (see Figure 13.4). The current causes can be distilled down to two: fears about performance and the adoption of a spectator role. Fear of performance refers to being overly concerned with how one is "performing" during sex. **Spectator role** refers to being an observer rather than a participant in a sexual experience. Both involve a focus on sexual performance that impedes the natural sexual responses. These current reasons for sexual dysfunctions were hypothesized to have one or more historical antecedents, such as sociocultural influences, biological causes, sexual traumas, or homosexual inclinations. Masters and Johnson's work set the tone for researchers to begin systematically studying risk factors for sexual dysfunction, much the same way case studies in other areas set the stage for empirical research. It is important to note, however, that many people who have one or more of the pathogenic factors discussed by Masters and Johnson do not develop sexual dysfunctions.

We turn now to studies on causes of sexual dysfunctions. Figure 13.5 summarizes factors related to increased and decreased risk of sexual dysfunctions. One thing is clear—sexual functioning is complex and multifaceted.

Biological Factors Biological causes of sexual dysfunctions can include diseases of the vascular (blood vessel) system such as atherosclerosis; diseases that affect the nervous system such as diabetes, multiple sclerosis, and spinal cord injury; low levels of testosterone or estrogen; heavy alcohol use before sex; chronic alcoholism; and heavy cigarette smoking (Bach, Wincze, & Barlow, 2001). Certain medications, such as antihypertensive drugs and especially the SSRI antidepressant drugs like Prozac and Zoloft, have effects on sexual

DSM-IV-TR Criteria for Female Orgasmic Disorder

- Persistent delay in or absence of orgasm after a normal period of sexual arousal Consideration given to woman's age, sexual experience, and adequacy of sexual stimulation she receives
- Causes marked distress or interpersonal problems
- Not due to a medical illness, another Axis I disorder (except another sexual dysfunction), or the physiological effects of a drug

DSM-IV-TR Criteria for Male Orgasmic Disorder

- Persistent delay in or absence of orgasm after a normal period of sexual arousal Consideration given to man's age and adequacy of sexual stimulation he receives
- Causes marked distress or interpersonal problems
- Not due to a medical illness, another Axis I disorder (except another sexual dysfunction), or the physiological effects of a drug

DSM-IV-TR Criteria for Premature Ejaculation

- Persistent ejaculation after minimal stimulation and before the man wishes it Consideration given to factors that affect the duration of excitement phase, such as the man's age, novelty of the situation or the partner, and recent frequency of sexual contacts
- Causes marked distress or interpersonal problems
- Not due exclusively to the direct effects of a drug

Figure 13.4 Distal and proximal causes of human sexual inadequacies, according to Masters and Johnson.

function, including delayed orgasm, decreased libido, and diminished lubrication (Segraves, 2003).

Some laboratory-based evidence exists that men with premature ejaculation are more sexually responsive to tactile stimulation than men who don't have this problem (Rowland et al., 1996). Perhaps, then, their penises are very sensitive, causing them to ejaculate more quickly.

Psychosocial Factors Some sexual dysfunctions can be traced to rape, childhood sexual abuse, or other degrading encounters. Sexual contact with an adult during childhood is associated with high rates of arousal disorder in women, and twice the rate of

DSM-IV-TR Criteria for Dyspareunia

- Recurrent genital pain associated with sexual intercourse
- Causes marked distress or interpersonal problems
- Not due vaginismus, or lack of vaginal lubrication, another Axis I disorder (except another sexual dysfunction), general medical illness or the direct physiological effects of a drug

DSM-IV-TR Criteria for Vaginismus

- Recurrent spasm of the outer third of the vagina such that conventional sexual intercourse is not possible
- Causes marked distress or interpersonal problems
- Not due to another Axis I disorder or to the direct physiological effects of a general medical illness

	Successful sexual functioning	Poor sexual functioning
Psychological factors	Good emotional health Attraction towards partner Positive attitude towards partner Positive sex attitude	Depression or anxiety disorders Focus on performance Routine Poor self-esteem Uncomfortable environment for sex Rigid, narrow attitude towards sex Negative thoughts about sex
Physical factors	Good physical health Regular appropriate exercise Good nutrition	Smoking Too much alcohol Cardiovascular problems Diabetes Neurological diseases Low physiological arousal SSRI medications Antihypertensive medication Other drugs
Social and sexual history factors	Positive sexual experiences in past Good relationship with partner Sexual knowledge and skills	Rape or sexual abuse Relationship problems, such as anger or poor communication Long periods of abstinence History of hurried sex

Figure 13.5 Predictors of sexual functioning. [Adapted from Enhancing Sexuality: A Problem-Solving Approach (1997), Graywind Publications.]

premature ejaculation and low sexual desire in men (Laumann et al., 1999). See Focus on Discovery 13.3, later in this chapter, for more discussion of childhood sexual abuse and its repercussions. Beyond the role of traumatic experiences, it is important to consider the benefits of previous positive experiences—many people with sexual problems lack knowledge and skill because they have not had opportunities to learn about their sexuality (LoPiccolo & Hogan, 1979).

Broader relationship problems can intrude into the sexual situation and thereby inhibit whatever arousal and pleasure might otherwise be found (Bach et al., 2001). As one might expect, people who are angry with their partners are less likely to want sex. Anger seems to be more detrimental to desire among men than among women (Beck & Bozman, 1995). Nonetheless, women with hypoactive sexual desire disorder also report that their communication with their husbands is poor and that they are unhappy with the way conflicts are resolved (Stuart, Hammond, & Pett, 1987). Even in couples who are satisfied in other realms of the relationship, poor communication can contribute to sexual dysfunction. For any number of reasons, including embarrassment, worry about the partner's feelings, or fear—one lover may not tell the other about preferences even if a partner is engaging in unstimulating or even aversive behaviors. After all, open discussions of sex by partners, among friends, in the media, and even in professional training programs are relatively recent phenomena.

Specific sexual experiences may shape premature ejaculation. Men with premature ejaculation also have longer periods of abstinence from climactic sex than do men who are not premature ejaculators (Spiess, Geer, & O'Donohue, 1984). It has also been proposed that men may acquire the tendency to ejaculate quickly as a result of having hurried sex because of not being in a private place and fearing detection (Metz et al., 1997).

Several psychological disorders are associated with increased risk of sexual dysfunctions. People who are depressed are more than twice as likely as nondepressed people (62 percent to 26 percent) to have a sexual dysfunction (Angst, 1998). People with a panic disorder, who are often fearful of physical sensations like rapid heart rate and sweating, are also at risk for sexual dysfunction (Sbrocco et al., 1997). Anxiety and depression are commonly comorbid with dyspareunia (Meana et al., 1998) and erectile disorder (Araujo et al., 1998).

Beyond evidence that depression and anxiety are detrimental, several studies suggest that low general physiological arousal can interfere with specific sexual arousal. Meston and Gorzalka (1995) looked at the role of arousal by assigning women to exercise or no exercise conditions, and then asked women to watch erotic films. Consistent with the positive role of higher arousal, exercise facilitated sexual arousal. No wonder, then, that exhausted couples, turning to sex after a full day of work, parenting, socializing, and other roles, can encounter problems with sexuality. Too much stress and exhaustion clearly impede sexual functioning (Morokoff & Gilliland, 1993).

Negative cognitions, such as worries about pregnancy or AIDS, negative attitudes about sex, or concerns about the partner, interfere with sexual functioning (e.g., Reissing, Binik, & Khalife, 1999). But as Masters and Johnson first suggested, cognitions concerning sexual performance are particularly important. Consider the idea that variability in sexual performance is common; a stressful day, a distracting context, a relationship concern, or any number of other issues may diminish sexual responsiveness. The key issue may be how people think about their diminished physical response when it happens. One theory is that people who blame themselves for decreased sexual performance will be more likely to develop recurrent problems.

In a test of the role of self-blame (cognitive attributions) and erectile dysfunction, Weisberg and colleagues (2001) asked 52 male participants to watch erotic videos. During the videos, their sexual arousal (penile circumference) was measured using a **penile plethysmograph** (see Figure 13.6). Regardless of their actual arousal, the men were given false feedback that the size of their erection was smaller than that typically measured among aroused men. Men were randomly assigned to receive two different explanations for this false feedback. In the first, they were told that the films did not seem to be working for most men (external explanation). In the second, they were told that the pattern of their responses on

Placed over penis

(a)

Photocell
Acrylic tube

(b)

Figure 13.6 Behavioral researchers use two genital devices for measuring sexual arousal. Both are sensitive indicators of vasocongestion (the flooding of the veins with blood) of the genitalia, a key physiological process in sexual arousal; both provide specific measurements of sexual excitement (e.g., Howes, 1998). (a) For men, the penile plethysmograph measures changes in the circumference of the penis by means of a strain gauge, consisting of a very thin rubber tube filled with mercury. As the penis enlarges with blood, the tube stretches, changing its electrical resistance. (b) For women, sexual arousal can be measured by a vaginal plethysmograph, such as the device invented by Sintchak and Geer (1975). Shaped like a tampon, this apparatus can be inserted into the vagina to measure the increased blood flow characteristic of female sexual arousal.

questionnaires about sexuality might help explain the low arousal (internal explanation). After receiving this feedback, the men were asked to watch one more film. The men who were given an internal explanation reported less arousal and also showed less physiological evidence of arousal during the next film than those given an external application. These results, then, support the idea that people who blame themselves when their body doesn't perform will diminish their subsequent arousal. Needless to say, men in this study were carefully debriefed after the experiment!

Masters and Johnson found that many of their sexually dysfunctional patients had learned negative views of sexuality from their social and cultural surroundings. For example, some religions and cultures may discourage sexuality for the sake of pleasure, particularly outside marriage. Other cultures may disapprove of sexual initiative or behavior among women, other than for the sake of procreation. When people learn such negative views about sexuality, it can affect how they behave sexually. One female patient suffering from hypoactive sexual desire, for example, had been taught as she was growing up not to look at herself naked in the mirror and that intercourse was reserved for marriage and then only to be endured for purposes of having children.

Quick Summary

Sexuality is profoundly shaped by culture and experience, so it is important to be aware of subjective biases in thinking about diagnoses. Gender also shapes sexuality: men report more frequent sexual thoughts and behaviors than do women. For men and women, four phases of the sexual response cycle have been recognized: appetitive, excitement, orgasm, and resolution.

In DSM-IV-TR, the sexual dysfunction disorders are divided into:

- the sexual desire disorders (hypoactive sexual desire disorder and sexual aversion disorder),
- the sexual arousal disorders (female sexual arousal disorder and male erectile disorder),
- the orgasmic disorders (female orgasmic disorder, male orgasmic disorder, and premature ejaculation), and
- the sexual pain disorders (dyspareunia and vaginismus).

Although there are no good estimates of how many people meet formal diagnostic criteria for sexual dysfunction disorders, in one major survey, 43 percent of women and 31 percent of men reported at least some symptoms of sexual dysfunction. People who experience one sexual dysfunction disorder often experience a comorbid sexual dysfunction disorder; for example, a man who is experiencing premature ejaculation may develop hypoactive sexual desire disorder. Before diagnosing sexual dysfunction, it is important to rule out medical explanations for a symptom. The key etiological variables involved in sexual dysfunctions appear to be previous sexual abuse, relationship problems, lack of sexual knowledge, psychological disorders like depression or anxiety or alcohol abuse, low arousal and exhaustion, and negative cognitions and attitudes about sexuality. For premature ejaculation, one possible cause is an overly sensitive penis.

Treatments of Sexual Dysfunctions

The pioneering work of Masters and Johnson (1970) in the treatment of sexual dysfunctions is described in Focus on Discovery 13.2. Over the past 30-plus years therapists and researchers have elaborated on Masters and Johnson's work and created new procedures. We will describe several of the procedures that extend the Masters and Johnson work. A therapist may choose only one technique for a given case, but the complex and multifaceted nature of sexual dysfunctions often requires the use of a combination of techniques. These approaches are suitable for treating sexual dysfunctions in homosexual as well as heterosexual individuals.

Anxiety Reduction   Well before the publication of the Masters and Johnson therapy program, behavior therapists appreciated that their sexually dysfunctional clients needed gradual and systematic exposure to anxiety-provoking aspects of the sexual situation. Wolpe's systematic desensitization and in vivo desensitization (desensitization by real-life encounters) have been employed with some success (Wolpe, 1958), especially when combined with skills training. For example, a woman with vaginismus might first be trained in relaxation and then practice inserting her fingers or dilators into her vagina, starting with

Focus on Discovery 13.2

Masters and Johnson's Therapy for Sexual Dysfunctions

In the 1970 publication of *Human Sexual Inadequacy*, Masters and Johnson reported on the successful results of one of the first sex therapy programs, which they had carried out with almost 800 sexually dysfunctional people. Each couple had traveled to St. Louis and spent 2 weeks attending intensive therapy during the day and completing sexual homework in a motel at night.

Many therapists continue to use the Masters and Johnson techniques, although success rates have tended to be lower than those originally reported (Segraves & Althof, 1998). Some believe that the lower success rates may be attributed more to the couples seeking treatment than to the therapy itself; as sex therapy has become more popular, more of the couples that clinicians see have poorer marital relationships than did those who sought treatment in the early years of sex therapy.

In the Masters and Johnson work, couples were always seen by one male therapist and one female therapist. For several days, couples completed an assessment of social history, sexual history, sexual values, and medical concerns. During the assessment and first couple of days of treatment, sexual intercourse was forbidden. Sometimes the couple discussed sex for the first time at the clinic. Therapists adopted a calm and open manner to help couples feel comfortable discussing sex.

On the third day the therapists began to offer interpretations about the sources of problems. If a person had negative attitudes toward sex, this would be addressed. But the basic emphasis was on relationship problems, not on individual difficulties of either partner. A premise of the therapy was that "there is no such thing as an uninvolved partner in any marriage in which there is some form of sexual inadequacy" (1970, p. 2). Whatever the problem, the couple was encouraged to see it as their mutual responsibility. At this time the clients were introduced to the idea of the spectator role. They were told, for example, that a male with erectile problems—and often his partner as well—usually worries about how well he is doing and that this pattern of observing the state of the erection, although totally understandable, blocks his natural responses and interferes with sexual enjoyment.

At the end of the third day, the couple was asked to engage in **sensate focus**. The couple was instructed to choose a time when both partners felt a sense of warmth and compatibility. They were to undress and give each other pleasure by touching each other's bodies. The co-therapists appointed one marital partner to do the first pleasuring; the partner who was "getting" was simply to be allowed to enjoy being touched. The one being touched was not required to feel a sexual response and was responsible for immediately telling the partner if something became uncomfortable. Then the roles were to be switched. The sensate-focus assignment usually promoted contact, constituting a first step toward reestablishing sexual intimacy.

Most of the time partners began to realize that their physical encounters could be intimate and pleasurable without necessarily being a prelude to sexual intercourse. On the next evening the partner being pleasured was instructed to give specific direction by guiding their partner's hand to regulate pressure and rate of stroking. The touching of genitals and breasts was now allowed, but still no intercourse. The partners were shown diagrams if they were uncertain about basic female and male anatomy. After 2 days of sensate focus, treatment began to be tailored to specific problems. To illustrate the process, we will outline the therapy for female orgasmic disorder.

After the sensate-focus exercises increased comfort, the woman was encouraged to focus on maximizing her own sexual stimulation without trying to have an orgasm. Her sexual excitement usually increased as a result. The therapists gave her partner explicit instructions about generally effective means of manually stroking the female genital area, although the female partner was encouraged to make decisions and express her wishes to her partner in the moment. At this stage it was emphasized that having orgasms was not the focus.

After the woman began to enjoy being pleasured by manual stimulation, she was told to place herself on top of the man, gently insert the penis, and simply tune in to her feelings. When she felt inclined, she could begin slowly to move her pelvis. She was encouraged to regard the penis as something for her to play with, something that could provide her with pleasure. The male could begin to thrust slowly. At all times, however, the woman was to decide what should happen next. When the couple was able to maintain this containment for minutes at a time, without the man thrusting forcefully toward orgasm, a major change had usually taken place in their sexual interactions: For perhaps the first time the woman was allowed to think sexually about her own pleasure. In their subsequent encounters, most couples began to have mutually satisfying intercourse.

A caveat about sensate focus is in order. As LoPiccolo (1992) pointed out, more and more people are aware that not getting an erection from sensate focus is at the same time expected and not expected! That is, although the instruction from the therapist is not to feel sexual, even a moderately knowledgeable man knows that at some point he is supposed to get an erection from this situation. Thus, rather than reducing performance anxiety and the spectator role, some men may experience a phenomenon called *metaperformance anxiety* during sensate focus, taking the form of self-statements such as, "Okay, I don't have any pressure to get an erection and have intercourse. Right. So now 10 minutes have passed, there's no pressure to perform, but I don't have an erection yet. When am I going to get an erection? And if I do, will I be able to maintain it long enough to insert it?" Sensate-focus treatment and other aspects of Masters and Johnson's sex therapy have elements of a paradoxical approach to treatment, which is based on the idea that telling people not to do something will reduce their anxiety about doing something (see p. 546).

small insertions and working up to larger ones (Leiblum, 1997). In vivo desensitization would appear to be the principal technique of the Masters and Johnson program, although additional components probably contribute to its overall effectiveness. Interestingly, simple psychoeducation programs about sexuality also appear to do a great deal to reduce anxiety, and accordingly, several studies have now shown minimal or no benefit of systematic desensitization compared to psychoeducation for male erectile disorder, female arousal disorder, and female inhibited orgasm disorder (Emmelkamp, 2004).

For the treatment of premature ejaculation, anxiety reduction techniques sometimes have a different focus. Anxiety about ejaculating too soon may be a natural result of an overemphasis on intercourse in sexual behavior among heterosexual couples. Sex therapists advise couples to expand their repertoire of activities to include techniques not requiring an engorged penis, such as oral or manual manipulation, so that gratification of the partner is possible after the man has climaxed. When the exclusive focus on penile–vaginal or penile–anal intercourse is removed, a couple's anxieties about sex usually diminish enough to permit greater ejaculatory control.

Directed Masturbation Directed masturbation was devised by LoPiccolo and Lobitz (1972) to enhance women's comfort with and enjoyment of their sexuality. The first step is for the woman to carefully examine her nude body, including her genitals, and to identify various areas with the aid of diagrams. Next, she is instructed to touch her genitals and locate areas that produce pleasure. Then, she increases the intensity of masturbation using erotic fantasies. If orgasm is not achieved, she is to use a vibrator in her masturbation. Finally, her partner enters the picture, first watching her masturbate, then doing for her what she has been doing for herself, and finally having intercourse in a position that allows him to stimulate the woman's genitals manually or with a vibrator. Directed masturbation appears to add significant effectiveness to the treatment of orgasmic disorder (O'Donohue, Dopke, & Swingen, 1997); it is also helpful in the treatment of sexual desire disorder (Renshaw, 2001). Directed masturbation with partner involvement has been found to be effective for 90 percent of women with a lifelong inability to experience orgasm (Riley & Riley, 1978).

Procedures to Change Attitudes and Thoughts In *sensory-awareness procedures*, clients are encouraged to tune in to the pleasant sensations that accompany even incipient sexual arousal. The sensate-focus exercises described in Focus on Discovery 13.2, for example, are a way of helping the person be more aware of and comfortable with sexual feelings. Rational-emotive behavior therapy tries to challenge self-demanding, perfectionistic thoughts that often cause problems for people with sexual dysfunctions. A therapist might try to reduce the pressure a man with erectile dysfunction feels by challenging his belief that intercourse is the only true form of sexual activity. Kaplan (1997) recommends several procedures to try to increase the attractiveness of sex. She has clients engage in erotic fantasies and gives them courtship and dating assignments, such as getting away for a weekend.

Skills and Communication Training To improve sexual skills and communication, therapists assign written materials and show clients explicit videotapes and films demonstrating sexual techniques (McMullen & Rosen, 1979). Encouraging partners to communicate their likes and dislikes to each other has been shown to be helpful for a range of sexual dysfunctions (Rosen, Leiblum, & Spector, 1994). Taken together, skills and communication training also expose partners to anxiety-provoking material—such as seeing one's partner naked—which allows for a desensitizing effect. Telling a partner one's preferences in sex is often made more difficult by tensions that go beyond the sexual relationship, which leads us to the next strategy.

Couples Therapy Masters and Johnson considered sexual dysfunctions as problems that could be treated directly, rather than as symptoms of other psychological or interpersonal difficulties. Many of the couples they treated had marriages that, in spite of sexual problems, were marked by caring and closeness. But as society changed and people became more comfortable seeking help, sex therapists began to see people whose relationships were seriously impaired. In current treatment settings, sexual dysfunctions are often embedded in a distressed relationship, and troubled couples usually need special training in nonsexual-communication skills (Rosen, 2000). Sex therapists now often work from a systems perspective, that is, the therapist appreciates that a sexual problem is embedded in a complex network of relationship factors (Wylie, 1997). Some therapists focus on nonsexual issues, such as difficulties with in-laws or with child rearing—either in addition to or instead of a Masters and Johnson type of sex therapy. For women with sexual dysfunctions in the context of marital distress, behavioral marital therapy has been found to improve many aspects of sexual functioning (Zimmer, 1987).

Medications and Physical Treatments   Sometimes medical treatments are used to correct an underlying physical condition. The current trend toward viewing sexual dysfunctions as medical problems may divert the attention of therapists and patients from the inherently interpersonal nature of sexual problems, giving rise to a quick-fix mentality that is probably ill-advised (Rosen & Leiblum, 1995). Medical approaches have been particularly criticized for women, given the strong links between sexuality and relationship satisfaction (Tiefer, 2001). Despite these caveats, medication treatments for sexual dysfunction have become increasingly popular. Antidepressant drugs have been found to be helpful when depression appears to contribute to diminished sex drive. Antianxiety medications also can be used as an adjunct to anxiety-reduction techniques. A complicating factor, though, is that some of these psychoactive drugs themselves interfere with sexual responsiveness. Sometimes, a second medication may be used to counteract the sexual side effects of the first; for example, buproprion (Wellbutrin) has been shown to help address the libido problems caused by SSRI medications (Segraves, 2003).

Premature Ejaculation   For the treatment of premature ejaculation, the squeeze technique is often used, in which a partner is trained to squeeze the penis in the area where the head and shaft meet to rapidly reduce arousal. This technique is practiced without insertion, and then during insertion, the penis is withdrawn and the squeeze is repeated as needed. Success rates initially tend to be high (60–90 percent), but there is some relapse when longer follow-up periods are used (Polonsky, 2000). Antidepressant drugs have also been found to be helpful in the treatment of premature ejaculation (Strassberg et al., 1999).

Erectile Dysfunction   A number of the medical procedures that were used previously to treat erectile dysfunction have declined in use since the advent of Viagra, described below. For example, a semirigid silicone rod can be implanted in a chronically flaccid penis, or a device can be implanted in the penis that can be stiffened with fluid from a reservoir and a small pump implanted in the scrotum. These surgical approaches have yielded mixed results in long-term follow-up studies (Tiefer, Pedersen, & Melman, 1988). A nonsurgical intervention entails placing the penis in a cylinder with a vacuum pump; when the air is removed from the cylinder, blood is drawn into the penis to create an erection (Skolnick, 1998). Drugs such as alprostadil and paparevine hydrochloride can be injected into the penis to dilate the arteries and thus produce an erection, even in the absence of sexual stimulation (Fallon, 1995). Not surprisingly, many men do not find this approach palatable (Rosen, 2000).

"YOU WANT A RAISE, BREWSTER? HOW ABOUT A VIAGRA PILL?"

(© Harley Schwadron.)

The aforementioned medical interventions for erectile dysfunction are being largely replaced by sildenafil (Viagra) and related medications [e.g., tadafil (Cialis) and vardenafil (Levitra)]. Viagra was approved by the FDA in March 1998 and in its first 3 months was prescribed over 3 million times. Viagra relaxes smooth muscles and thereby allows blood to flow into the penis during sexual stimulation, creating an erection. It is taken 1 hour before sex, and its effects last about 4 hours, allowing an erection to be maintained for a substantial time period. It is important to note that Viagra does not cause an erection in the absence of sexual stimulation; this means that the psychological dimension of erectile dysfunction must be attended to if this drug is to be effective (Rosen, 2000). Although promising, research reports indicate that between

16 and 44 percent of men do not derive much benefit from the drug (Bach et al., 2001). Viagra also produces side effects such as headaches and indigestion. Moreover, it may be dangerous for men with cardiovascular disease, and this is a concern since many of the older men who use Viagra are at risk for hypertension and coronary artery disease. Several trials of Viagra and related medicines have been conducted with women, but so far, the results are not promising, with the exception of Viagra for postmenopausal women who retain desire but have low arousal (Berman et al., 2003).

Quick Summary

Psychological treatments for sexual dysfunction include techniques to reduce anxiety, to increase knowledge and awareness of the body, to reduce negative thoughts about sexuality, to improve couples communication, and to reduce performance anxiety. Medical treatments are increasingly popular, despite some criticism. A number of physical approaches to erectile dysfunction, such as inflatable pumps, have become less common as new medications like Viagra and Cialis have become available. Antidepressant drugs can be helpful in the treatment of premature ejaculation.

Gender Identity Disorder

"Are you a man or a woman?" For virtually all people, the answer to such a question is obvious. And others would agree unequivocally with the answer. The sense of self as male or female, or **gender identity**, is so deeply ingrained from earliest childhood that the vast majority of people are absolutely certain of their gender. In contrast to gender identity, **sexual orientation** is the preference for the sex of a partner. Sexual orientation and gender identity are distinct. For example, a man may be attracted to men—a matter of sexual orientation—without believing he is a woman—a matter of gender identity. Here, we discuss gender identity disorder (formerly known as transsexualism).

Clinical Description of Gender Identity Disorder

People with gender identity disorder (GID) feel deep within themselves, usually from early childhood, that they are of the opposite sex. They are not persuaded by the presence of normal genitals, nor by others' perceptions of their gender. A man can look at himself in a mirror, see the body of a biological man, and yet experience that body as belonging to a woman. He may want to surgically alter his body to bring it in line with his gender identity. The diagnosis of GID is only applicable when the desire to be a member of the opposite sex causes significant distress or impairment. Persons who are comfortable perceiving themselves as a member of the opposite sex should not be diagnosed. In keeping with the distinctions between gender identity and sexual orientation, it is important to note that a person with GID may be attracted to people from the same or the opposite sex (Carroll, 2000).

The prevalence rates for GID are small: one in about 30,000 for men and one in 100,000 to 150,000 in women (American Psychiatric Association, 1994). The higher prevalence in men may reflect societal acceptance of women who choose to adopt a male role.

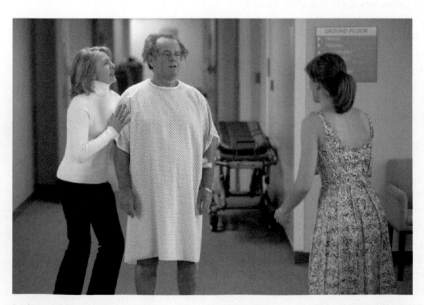

In the movie *Something's Gotta Give*, Jack Nicholson portrays a man whose use of Viagra complicates his cardiovascular treatment. (The Kobal Collection, Ltd.)

GID is one of the most debated categories in the DSM-IV. Few would argue that there are people with the intense belief that they are a member of the opposite sex. But should this be labeled as a disorder? Despite its controversial status, GID is still in the DSM-IV; it remains to be seen whether future versions of the DSM will be more sensitive to changing scientific and political opinions on this issue. Even for those who believe this should be classified as a disorder, there are controversies about the causes and treatment (Bailey, 2003). We turn to some of those concerns now. Some have argued that inclusion of this phenomenon as a diagnosis pathologizes a natural diversity. A lead spokesperson for this perspective is Joan Roughgarden (2004), a Stanford professor of biology. Dr. Roughgarden points to the tremendous diversity of gender roles in the animal kingdom. She describes countless examples of species in which biologically male animals will adopt behavior, courtship rituals, and mating strategies that parallel those seen by female animals. Dr. Roughgarden suggests that it does not make sense to conceptualize such universal behavior as a disorder, and that scientists should focus more on the adaptive consequences of gender role diversity.

One reason for the intense controversy about GID is that people who cross-dress are treated so harshly—disapproval and discrimination are rampant. Some worry that diagnosing these behaviors as a disorder will foster even more stigma. Negative attitudes in Western societies go back hundreds of years. For example, the *Malleus Maleficarum* (witches' hammer) was a religiously based diagnostic system of the fifteenth and sixteenth centuries and, among other things, labeled people who took on the persona of the opposite sex as witches and prescribed burning at the stake (Carroll, 2000). Other societies, though, have accorded high status to men who adopt feminine roles. For example, in some Native American cultures the "berdache" are considered a third gender, neither male nor female, and are not at all viewed in a negative light.

According to the DSM-IV-TR, GID can be diagnosed among children. GID in a child can be labeled in children as young as 2 to 4 years old (Green & Blanchard, 1995). GID is diagnosed on the basis of cross-gender behaviors, such as dressing in opposite-sex clothes, preferring opposite-sex playmates, and engaging in play that would usually be considered more typical of the opposite sex (e.g., a boy's playing with Barbie dolls), along with a persistently stated desire to be a member of the opposite sex.

The diagnosis of GID is more prevalent in children than in adults (Zucker & Bradley, 1995), perhaps because parents are more often upset by their children adopting different gender roles than are adults. Based on clinic referral rates, it appears to be about six times more frequent in boys than girls (Zucker, Bradley, & Sanikhani, 1997). Most children with GID grow up to be comfortable with their biological sex in adulthood, even without professional intervention (Zucker & Bradley, 1995). The vast majority of little boys engage in some traditional feminine play, and little girls in some traditional masculine play, with no identity conflicts whatsoever (Green, 1976). Aside from brief periods of play, about 1 percent of 4- or 5-year-old boys report wishing they were a girl at times, and about 5 percent of 4- or 5-year-old girls report wishing they were a boy (Bradley & Zucker, 1997). Cross-gender behaviors are so common that it should not be surprising that the vast majority of children with these behaviors do not grow up to be adults with GID. Because of the high rates of cross-gender behavior during childhood and the poor predictive validity of labelling this behavior, some argue that GID in childhood should be dropped from the DSM.

DSM-IV-TR Criteria for Gender Identity Disorder

Strong and persistent identification with the opposite sex
In children, presence of four or more of the following:

- Repeatedly stated desire to be or insistence that she or he is the other sex
- Preference for wearing opposite sex clothes
- Preference for cross-sex roles in play or persistent fantasies of being of the opposite sex
- Preference for stereotypical play of the opposite sex
- Preference for playmates of the opposite sex

In adolescents and adults, such symptoms as desire to be the opposite sex, passing as member of the opposite sex, desire to be treated as a member of the opposite sex, conviction that his or her emotions are typical of the opposite sex
Not concurrent with a physical intersex condition
Causes marked distress or impairment in functioning

Etiology of Gender Identity Disorder

Genetic, neurobiological, and psychosocial causes of GID have been proposed. In part because this condition is so rare, there are few studies of the causes.

Genetic Factors Some data suggest that gender identity may be at least partially genetic (see the case below of Joan/John for a discussion of this issue). Two twin studies suggest that some symptoms of gender identity during childhood are moderately heritable (Bailey, Dunne, & Martin, 2000; Coolidge, Thede, & Young, 2002). These studies have looked at people with cross-gender behaviors though, rather than those who met full diagnostic criteria for GID.

Clinical Case: Joan/John

As there is so little research on the prospective predictors of GID, many people have looked to other literature to understand how gender identity develops. In 1965, Linda Thiessen gave birth to twin boys. During a surgery to correct a problem with the foreskin, the penis of John, one of the twins, was destroyed. With advice from John Money, a well-known sex researcher at Johns Hopkins University, the Thiessens decided to castrate John, construct female genitals, and raise him as a girl named Joan.

Several years later, Money began to discuss the case with other health professionals, describing it as a total success and using it to buttress his theory that gender identity is determined by the environment. But the facts suggest instead that there is a strong biological influence on gender identity.

Despite having been instructed to encourage feminine behavior in Joan, her parents reported that Joan behaved in a very boyish way. At age 2 she ripped off her first dress; during her preschool years her play activities were clearly masculine. At age 11, Joan steadfastly held out against surgery to construct a more feminine vagina than the rudimentary one that had been created during the original surgery. By age 14, Joan decided to stop living as a girl. Given Joan's behavior and distress, Joan's physicians finally recommended that she be told the whole story. She immediately decided to reverse the earlier treatments and changed her name back to John. She took male hormones, had her breasts removed, and had an artificial penis constructed. At age 21, John had another operation to improve his artificial penis, and at age 25 he married a woman.

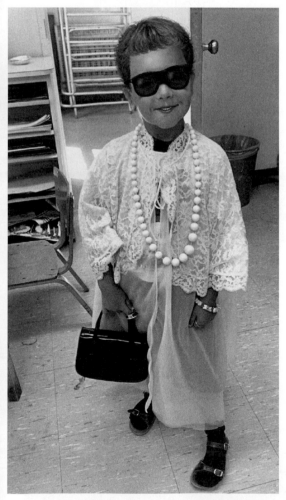

Although dressing up is common in childhood, most transsexuals trace their gender-identity disturbance to childhood and report dressing in gender- inappropriate clothes. (Francene Keery/ Stock, Boston.)

Neurobiological Factors Levels of sex hormones in adulthood and during the pregnancy have both been hypothesized as causal factors in GID. People with and without GID do not consistently differ in hormone levels during adulthood (Bosinski et al., 1997). Rather, most current research focuses on the role of hormones during gestation. Research with humans and primates shows that offspring of mothers who have taken sex hormones during pregnancy often behave like members of the opposite sex and have anatomical abnormalities. For example, a series of studies suggest that girls with high levels of androgen exposure in utero tend to display more masculine-typed behaviors and attitudes than girls without high levels of androgen exposure (Berenbaum, 1999). Young boys whose mothers ingested female hormones when pregnant were found to be less athletic and to engage less in rough-and-tumble play than their male peers (Yalom, Green, & Fisk, 1973). Despite the evidence that in utero hormone exposure can shape cross-gender behaviors, these children do not declare themselves to be of the opposite gender (Berenbaum, 1999). Hence, prenatal sex hormones only seem to explain some aspects of gender identity, rather than providing a full explanation.

The case of Joan/John and others like it demonstrate a strong biological underpinning for gender identity; despite not having a penis and being treated as a girl throughout childhood, John never developed a female gender identity (Colapinto, 1997). A recent study suggests similar conclusions. Reiner and Gearhart (2004) followed up 14 genetic males who for medical reasons had been surgically changed to females as young infants and then raised as girls. Of the 14, 8 had fully adopted a male identity by age 16, and all showed interests and activities that were typical of males. Even with the attempts to raise these children as girls, biology seemed to have influenced identity to a strong extent.

Social and Psychological Factors Masculinity and femininity are culturally shaped and defined, and heavily laden with value judgments and stereotyping. Our society is still sadly intolerant of boys who engage in activities more typical of girls. Girls can play games and dress in a manner more typical of boys and still conform to acceptable standards of behavior for girls (Williams, Goodman, & Green, 1985).

If gender-role behavior is environmentally shaped, some have suggested that GID could be shaped by environmental contingencies as well. One model of GID focuses on reinforcement of cross-gender behavior (Green, 1987). Most children engage in cross-gender behaviors at some point in time. Some parents and relatives may reinforce such behavior. Parents of children who show signs of GID often reveal that they did not discourage cross-dressing behavior in their children. This holds true especially for feminine boys—family members may have seen the behavior as cute. According to the reinforcement theory, such reactions on the part of the family to a child could contribute to the acquired gender identity (Zucker et al., 1993). As pointed out by Bailey (2003), though, family members and peers are often mercilessly cruel about cross-gender behavior—if environmental contingencies were powerful, one might expect these interpersonal punishments to dispel cross-gender behavior.

Treatments of Gender Identity Disorder

The most common treatment for GID is to change the body to suit the person's psychology. A few case studies are available of behavioral treatment designed to change the psychology to match the person's body.

Changing the Body   People seeking sex reassignment surgery are generally required to undergo 6 to 12 months of living as the desired gender and taking part in psychotherapy to address feelings about gender roles (Harry Benjamin International Gender Dysphoria Association, 1998). A range of physical procedures are used to change the person's body. For example, a man may have electrolysis to remove facial hair, surgery to reduce the size of the chin and Adam's apple, and training to raise the pitch of the voice. Female hormones promote breast growth and soften the skin of men (Schaefer, Wheeler, & Futterweit, 1997). Some men also have plastic surgery to attain a more feminine facial appearance, larger breasts, or more curvaceous hips. Some take the additional step of having sex-reassignment surgery. It is typically recommended that cosmetic changes be in place and that the person live as a member of the opposite sex for at least 1 year before surgery is conducted.

In **sex-reassignment surgery**, the existing genitalia are altered to be more similar to those of the opposite sex. The first sex-reassignment operation took place in Europe in 1930, but the surgery that attracted worldwide attention was performed on an ex-soldier, Christine (originally George) Jorgensen, in Copenhagen, Denmark, in 1952.

For male-to-female reassignment surgery, most of the penis is removed, but some of the tissue and nerves are used to form an artificial vagina, labia, and clitoris. Heterosexual intercourse is possible after reassignment surgery for men, with sensitivity of nerves to stimulation preserved.

The female-to-male reassignment process is more difficult in some ways and less difficult in others. On the one hand, the surgically constructed penis is small and not capable of normal erection; artificial supports are therefore needed for sexual intercourse. An operation extends the urethra into the newly constructed penis to allow the person the social comfort of being able to use public urinals. On the other hand, less cosmetic follow-up is needed than for male-to-female reassignment because the male hormones prescribed to women seeking sexual reassignment drastically alter fat distribution and stimulate the growth of facial and body hair. The relatively greater ease of the cosmetic female-to-male change may be due in part to society's lesser focus on the physical attributes of men. A small, soft-spoken man with a relatively high-pitched voice may be more acceptable to society than a 6-foot-tall deep-voiced woman. Nevertheless, sex-reassignment surgery is exercised by many more men than women.

Author and historian James Morris (in a 1960 picture), after sex-reassignment surgery, became Jan Morris (in a 1974 photograph). (Top photo: Corbis Images; bottom photo: Robin Laurence/New York Times Picture.)

How beneficial is sex-reassignment surgery? Over the years controversy has existed over its benefits, and the quality of the research itself is low (Carroll, 2000). A review by Green and Fleming (1990) of reasonably controlled outcome studies published between 1979 and 1989 with at least a 1-year follow-up drew favorable conclusions. Of 130 female-to-male surgeries, about 97 percent could be judged satisfactory; of 220 male-to-female surgeries, 87 percent were satisfactory. Preoperative factors that seemed to predict favorable postsurgery adjustment were (1) reasonable emotional stability, (2) successful adaptation in the new role for at least 1 year before the surgery, (3) adequate understanding of the actual limitations and consequences of the surgery, and (4) psychotherapy in the context of an established gender-identity program. The authors caution, however, that satisfactory ratings meant only that the patients reported that they did not regret having had the surgery. One report from

Check Your Knowledge 13.2

True or false?

1. A person who experiences a brief problem with sexual arousal, orgasm, or desire is likely to meet criteria for a sexual dysfunction.
2. The best treatment for premature ejaculation is Viagra.
3. Sex therapists may recommend that a woman with lack of orgasms practice masturbation without her partner present.
4. People with one sexual dysfunction tend to have other comorbid sexual dysfunctions.
5. Diagnostic criteria for GID include distress over sexual attraction to people of the same sex.

the University of Pennsylvania indicated that sexual responsiveness and sexual satisfaction increase dramatically after both male-to-female and female-to-male reassignments, with an overall high level of satisfaction with the results of the surgery (Lief & Hubschman, 1993). Finally, one long-term study found that young men who had undergone sex reassignment were no longer gender dysphoric, had no regrets about the procedures, and were otherwise functioning better than men who had been denied the hormonal treatment and surgery (Smith, van Goozen, & Cohen-Kettenis, 2001). Nonetheless, Michael Bailey (2003) cautions that few men who undertake surgery to become women are able to achieve their goal of establishing satisfying long-term partnerships.

Behavioral Treatment to Alter Gender Identity   A few case reports exist of behavioral treatment designed to alter sex-role behaviors. These treatments have included helping men to shape specific behaviors, such as mannerisms and interpersonal behavior, to be more masculine (Barlow, Reynolds, & Agras, 1973). In three cases, these treatments were successful in helping patients change sex-role behavior, and changes were sustained (Barlow, Abel, & Blanchard, 1979). This work demonstrates that sex-role behaviors may be amenable to change. But as the researchers pointed out even the limited success of this program might not be generalizable. Their clients might have been different from others with GID because they wanted treatment to change their gender identity. Most individuals are not interested in such treatment. For them, physically altering their bodies is the goal.

Quick Summary

GID is diagnosed when a person experiences long-term and intense discomfort with their gender identity. People with this disorder report that they feel like they are trapped in the wrong body. Prevalence rates are low: about one in 30,000 men and one in 100,000 women meet formal diagnostic criteria. There is major debate about whether diagnosing this experience pathologizes and stigmatizes naturally occurring diversity. There is also debate about the appropriateness of using this diagnosis during childhood. Because GID is so rare, researchers do not know much about the etiology. There is evidence that some cross-gender behavior is moderately heritable, but genetic studies do not focus on diagnos-

able levels of gender identity symptoms. Some evidence suggests a role for exposure to atypically high levels of hormones in utero. Behavioral theory focuses on possible reinforcement of cross-gender roles, but this theory does a poor job of taking into account the extreme punishment often provoked by cross-gender behavior.

Treatments for GID involve surgical and hormonal procedures that change the person's sexual anatomy to match their internal identity. Behavioral treatment has been used for a small number of cases to change cross-gender behavior, but even when a person changes the way they act, they may retain an internal sense of identity as the other gender.

Clinical Case: William

William is a twenty-eight-year-old computer programmer who sought treatment after being arrested for voyeurism. William grew up as the second of four children in a conservative, religious family living in a rural area. He began to masturbate at age fifteen, and did so while watching his sister urinate in their outhouse. Despite feeling very guilty, he continued to masturbate several times a week while having voyeuristic fantasies. A couple of times, he had masturbated while watching strangers undress.

As an adult, William was a timid, shy, and lonely man. He lived alone, and six months before the arrest, he had been rejected in a long-term relationship. In response, he withdrew from other social relationships and began drinking more

alcohol. As his self-esteem deteriorated, his voyeuristic fantasies became more and more urgent.

One summer night, William had been feeling lonely and depressed, and he had been drinking heavily at a lounge with a topless dancer. After leaving the bar, he had been driving through a suburban neighborhood when he noticed someone in an upstairs window. Without thinking much, he had parked, erected a ladder he found near the house, and climbed up to the window to peep. The residents called the police when they heard him, and William was arrested. He was very shocked at the arrest, but knew that his behavior was destructive and he was motivated to change (Rosen & Rosen, 1981, pp. 452–453, Reprinted by permission of McGraw-Hill Book Company).

The Paraphilias

In DSM-IV-TR the *paraphilias* are a group of disorders defined by sexual attraction to unusual objects or sexual activities. In other words, there is a deviation (*para*) in what the person is attracted to (*philia*). The fantasies, urges, or behaviors last at least 6 months. Attractions to parts of the body, such as feet, are not diagnosed. Indeed, surveys have shown that many people occasionally fantasize about some of the activities we will be describing (such as fantasizing about exhibiting the genitals to an unsuspecting stranger). For example, 50 percent of men report voyeuristic fantasies of peeping at unsuspecting naked women (Hanson & Harris, 1997). Diagnoses of paraphilias, though, are meant to capture sexual urges that are more problematic and long-lasting than the occasional fantasy or sexual experimentation. Paraphilias are not diagnosed unless the fantasies or behaviors are recurrent and cause marked distress or impairment.

 Accurate prevalence statistics are not available for the paraphilias. When responding to a community survey, many people with paraphilias may choose not to reveal their proclivities. As some persons with paraphilias seek nonconsenting partners or otherwise violate people's rights in offensive ways (as we shall see in exhibitionism and pedophilia), these disorders can have legal consequences. But statistics on arrests are likely to be underestimates because many crimes go unreported and some paraphilias (e.g., voyeurism) involve an unsuspecting victim. The data do indicate, though, that most people with paraphilias are male; even with masochism and pedophilia, which occur in noticeable numbers of women, men vastly outnumber women.

DSM-IV-TR differentiates the paraphilias based on the source of arousal, for example, providing one diagnostic category for people whose sexual attractions are focused on inanimate objects, and another diagnostic category for people whose attractions are focused on children (see Table 13.4). Here, we provide a clinical description of the paraphilias included in DSM-IV-TR. As we describe the symptoms, we describe the epidemiology of these disorders. Many people with paraphilias meet criteria for other paraphilias and for other DSM-IV-TR diagnoses, and we will discuss the most frequent comorbid conditions as we review epidemiology. Then, we will discuss models of the etiology and treatment of these disorders.

Table 13.4 Paraphilias Included in DSM-IV-TR

Paraphilia	Object of Sexual Attraction
Fetishism	an inanimate object
Transvestic Fetishism	cross-dressing
Pedophilia	children
Voyeurism	watching unsuspecting others undress or have sexual relations
Exhibitionism	exposing one's genitals to an unwilling stranger
Frotteurism	sexual touching of an unsuspecting person
Sadism	inflicting pain
Masochism	receiving pain

Fetishism

Fetishism involves a reliance on an inanimate object for sexual arousal. The person with fetishism, almost always a male, has recurrent and intense sexual urges toward nonliving objects, called fetishes (e.g., women's shoes), and the presence of the fetish is strongly preferred or even necessary for sexual arousal.

 Clothing (especially underwear), rubber products (like raincoats), and articles related to feet (stockings, women's shoes) are common fetishes. Some carry on their fetishism by themselves in secret by fondling, kissing, smelling, sucking, placing in their rectum, or merely gazing at the adored object as they masturbate. Others need their partner to don the fetish as a stimulant for intercourse. Some become interested in acquiring a collection of the desired objects, and they may even commit burglary week after week to add to their hoard.

 The person with fetishism feels a compulsive attraction toward the object; the attraction is experienced as involuntary and irresistible. It is the degree of the erotic focus—the exclusive and very special status the object occupies as a sexual stimulant—that distinguishes fetishisms from the ordinary attraction that, for example, high heels may hold for heterosexual men in Western cultures. The person with a boot fetish must see or touch a boot to become aroused, and the arousal is overwhelmingly strong when a boot is present.

 The disorder usually begins by adolescence, although the fetish may have acquired special significance even earlier, during childhood. People with fetishism often have other paraphilias, such as pedophilia, sadism, and masochism (Mason, 1997).

 DSM-IV-TR Criteria for Fetishism

- Recurrent and intense sexually arousing fantasies, urges, or behaviors involving the use of nonliving objects for at least 6 months
- Causes marked distress or impairment in functioning
- The sexually arousing objects are not limited to articles of female clothing used in cross-dressing or to devices designed to provide tactile genital stimulation, such as a vibrator

Transvestic Fetishism

Transvestic fetishism, or *transvestism*, refers to recurrent and intense sexual arousal from cross-dressing. The extent of transvestism varies from wearing women's underwear under conventional clothing to full cross-dressing. Some female impersonators in nightclubs cater to the delight that many people take in observing skilled cross-dressing. Unless the cross-dressing is associated with sexual arousal, however, these impersonators do not meet criteria for transvestic fetishism. Transvestism also should not be confused with the cross-dressing associated with gender identity disorder. Although they often dress in clothing typical of the opposite sex and may even report being uncomfortable with certain aspects of their masculinity, men with transvestism do not identify themselves as of the opposite sex.

Transvestic fetishism usually begins with partial cross-dressing in childhood or adolescence. Always men, most cross-dress episodically rather than regularly. They tend to be otherwise masculine in appearance and demeanor. Many are married and lead otherwise conventional lives. Cross-dressing usually takes place in secret. Men who engage in this behavior may feel guilt or shame about their behavior, and they sometimes hide their urges from their wives for years. The urge to cross-dress may become more frequent over time. Transvestism is often comorbid with other paraphilias, notably masochism (Zucker & Blanchard, 1997).

Pedophilia and Incest

According to the DSM, **pedophilia** (*pedos*, Greek for "child") is diagnosed when adults derive sexual gratification through physical and sexual contact with prepubertal children. DSM-IV-TR requires that the offender be at least 16 years old and at least 5 years older than the child. Despite these diagnostic criteria, some people with pedophilia also victimize adolescents (Marshall, 1997).

As in most paraphilias, a strong subjective attraction impels the behavior. Sometimes a man with pedophilia is content to stroke the child's hair, but he may also manipulate the child's genitalia, encourage the child to manipulate his, and, less often, attempt penile insertion. The molestations may be repeated over a period of weeks, months, or years if they are not discovered by other adults or if the child does not protest. Some people with pedophilia intentionally frighten the child by, for example, killing a pet and threatening further harm if the youngster tells his or her parents.

People with pedophilia generally molest children that they know, such as neighbors or friends of the family (Gebhard et al., 1965). Sadly, incidents abound involving scoutmasters, camp counselors, and in the past few years, clergy. In recent years, people with pedophilia have increasingly used the Internet to acquire child pornography and to contact potential victims (Durkin, 1997).

Most pedophilia does not involve violence other than the sexual act, although when it does it is often a focus of lurid stories in the media. A minority of people with pedophilia, who might also meet diagnostic criteria for sexual sadism, inflict serious bodily harm on the object of their passion. They may even murder them. These people fundamentally differ from other people with pedophilia by virtue of their wish to hurt the child physically at least as much as to obtain sexual gratification (Groth, Hobson, & Guy, 1982).

Because overt physical force is seldom used in pedophilia, the child molester often denies that he is actually forcing himself on his victim. Despite their distorted beliefs, it must be acknowledged that child sexual abuse inherently involves a betrayal of trust and other serious negative consequences (see Focus on Discovery 13.3 for a discussion of these consequences).

In discussing pedophilia, it is important to acknowledge that many men who are conventional in their sexual interests and behavior can be sexually aroused by erotic pictures of children. In a study using both self-report and penile plethysmographic measures, one-quarter of people drawn from a community sample showed or reported arousal when shown sexually provocative pictures of children (Hall et al., 1995). The investigators found that this arousal was correlated with conventional arousal, that is, men who were more aroused

Many people experiment with fetishes. Fetishism is not diagnosed unless the attraction to fetishes causes marked distress or impairment. (Cindy Charles/PhotoEdit.)

by adult heterosexual pictures were more aroused to the pedophilic pictures. Although this finding might seem disturbing, it highlights the importance of the distinction made by the DSM and by health professionals in general between fantasy and behavior. Pedophilia is diagnosed when adults either act on sexual urges toward children or are distressed by the urges.

A study of 11 men with pedophilia found that they were attracted to pictures of children that were not designed to be provocative. These men became aroused viewing widely available materials, such as television ads and clothing catalogs picturing young children in underwear. In other words, men with pedophilia were sexually stimulated from sources that are not stimulating to most (Howitt, 1995).

Incest is listed in DSM-IV-TR as a subtype of pedophilia. Incest refers to sexual relations between close relatives for whom marriage is forbidden. It is most common between brother and sister. The next most common form, which is considered more pathological, is between father and daughter.

The taboo against incest is virtually universal in human societies (Ford & Beach, 1951), with a notable exception of Egyptian pharaohs, who could marry their sisters or other females of their immediate families. In Egypt it was believed that the royal blood should not be contaminated by that of outsiders. The incest taboo makes sense according to present-day scientific knowledge. The offspring from a father–daughter or a brother–sister union have a greater probability of inheriting a pair of recessive genes, one from each parent. For the most part, recessive genes have negative biological effects, such as serious birth defects. The incest taboo, then, has adaptive evolutionary significance.

There is evidence that families in which incest occurs are unusually patriarchal, especially with respect to the subservient position of women relative to men (Alexander & Lupfer, 1987). Parents in these families also tend to neglect and remain emotionally distant from their children (Madonna, Van Scoyk, & Jones, 1991).

Typically, men who commit incest abuse their postpubertal daughters, whereas men with non-incestual pedophilia usually are interested in prepubertal children. Consistent with this difference in the age of victims, men who molest children within their families show greater penile arousal (as measured by penile plethysmography) to adult heterosexual cues than do men who molest children who are unrelated to them (Marshall, Barbaree, & Christophe, 1986).

What are the demographic characteristics of people who engage in pedophilia and incest? People with pedophilia can be straight or gay, though most are heterosexual. Most older heterosexual men with pedophilia are or have been married. Up to half of all child molestations, including those that take place within the family, are committed by adolescent males (Morenz & Becker, 1995). Consistent with this statistic, about half of adult offenders began their illegal behavior in their early teens. Academic problems are common, as are legal problems for a wide variety of lawbreaking (Becker & Hunter, 1997).

Psychologically, men with pedophilia demonstrate elevated levels of impulsivity and psychopathy compared to the general population (Ridenour et al., 1997). Not surprisingly, these men often meet criteria for comorbid conduct disorder and substance abuse, and molestations are more likely to occur when the person with pedophilia is intoxicated. Somewhat more surprisingly, depression and anxiety disorders are also common (Galli et al., 1999). Evidence also suggests that child molesters have sexual fantasies about children when their mood is negative, perhaps as a way to cope with their dysphoria; however, having the pedophilic fantasy appears to increase negative affect. Perhaps this downward spiral leads at some point to the person's acting on the impulse to molest a child (Looman, 1995).

Voyeurism

Now and then a man may happen to see a nude woman by chance without her knowledge. If his sex life is primarily conventional, he would not generally meet criteria for voyeurism. Similarly, voyeuristic fantasies are quite common in men but do not by themselves warrant a diagnosis (Hanson & Harris, 1997). **Voyeurism** involves an intense and recurrent desire to

DSM-IV-TR Criteria for Pedophilia

- Recurrent and intense, sexually arousing fantasies, urges, or behaviors involving sexual contact with a prepubescent child occur for at least 6 months
- Person has acted on these urges, or the urges and fantasies cause marked distress or interpersonal problems
- Person is at least 16 years old and 5 years older than the child

DSM-IV-TR Criteria for Voyeurism

- Recurrent and intense, sexually arousing fantasies, urges, or behaviors involving the observation of unsuspecting others who are naked or engaged in sexual activity occur for at least 6 months
- Person has acted on these urges, or the urges and fantasies cause marked distress or interpersonal problems

Focus on Discovery 13.3

The Effects of Pedophilia: Outcomes After Childhood Sexual Abuse

In one major community survey, 13.5 percent of women and 2.5 percent of men reported experiencing some form of **childhood sexual abuse (CSA)** (Molnar et al., 2001). How does this all-too-common experience affect mental health during childhood and beyond? What can be done to protect children and to help children heal from CSA?

Effects on the Child

About half of children who are exposed to CSA will develop symptoms, such as depression, low self-esteem, conduct disorder, and anxiety disorders like PTSD. On the other hand, almost half of children who are exposed to CSA do not appear to experience adverse short-term effects (Kuehnle, 1998). We have seen in previous chapters that a history of CSA is found among adults experiencing many different psychological disorders—notably, dissociative identity disorder, eating disorders, borderline personality disorder, major depressive disorder, sexual dysfunctions, and substance abuse (Litrownik & Castillo-Cañez, 2001).

What factors contribute to how CSA affects a child? One is the nature of the abuse itself. Consider, for example, the different consequences of a father repeatedly raping a 7-year-old girl compared to a woman inappropriately caressing a 12-year-old boy. The odds that CSA will produce negative reactions will be increased when a perpetrator threatens a child, the child blames his or her self, or the family is unsupportive (Kuehnle, 1998). Negative outcomes are more pronounced when the CSA involves sexual intercourse (Nelson et al., 2002).

The research linking CSA to mental disorders has been mired in methodological issues. For example, sampling biases appear important, in that studies of college students with a history of CSA typically find small effects of CSA (Rind, Tromovitch, & Bauserman, 1998), but studies of clients in treatment may overestimate the role of abuse. Understanding the effects of CSA will require conducting epidemiological studies of community samples that do not have these sampling biases.

A broader issue, though, is that families in which abuse happens often are experiencing a broad array of problems, such as alcoholism in one or both parents, which may be entangled with other genetic and environmental risks for psychopathology. Because of this, it is hard to isolate whether CSA is genuinely the factor that produces clinical disorder. Twin studies provide a unique way to disentangle these effects, particularly when one twin but not the other has been abused, because the twin who was not abused shares genetic, and at least some environmental, risk factors. In one study of almost 2,000 twin pairs, people with a history of CSA had substantially increased risk of depression, suicide, conduct disorder, alcohol dependence, social anxiety, rape during adulthood, and divorce compared to non-abused twins (Nelson et al., 2002).

The Issue of Betrayal

A molester is usually not a stranger. He may be a father, an uncle, a brother, a teacher, a coach, a neighbor, or even a cleric. Although difficult to accept, the child molester is often an adult whom the child knows and trusts. When the abuser is someone close to the child, the child is likely to be torn by allegiance to the abuser on the one hand, and on the other hand, by fear, revulsion, and the knowledge that what is happening is wrong.

The betrayal of this trust makes the crime more abhorrent than it would be if no prior relationship existed between molester and child. This type of betrayal is also experienced by adults and children who are sexually abused by clergy or other people related to religious organizations, like choir directors, religious school teachers, or church camp counselors.

During 2002–2003, more than 1,000 people filed claims accusing Catholic clergy of molesting children many years earlier (Sheler, 2003). As with childhood incest, molestation or sexual harassment by a religious authority figure violates trust and respect. The victim, whatever his or her age, cannot give meaningful consent. The power differential is just too great. Self-blame is likely to be strong in the victim because the offender is part of the person's religion. If the priest or minister or rabbi is doing this, how can it be wrong?

Prevention

CSA prevention efforts have focused on elementary schools. Programs vary, but common elements include teaching children to recognize

---

obtain sexual gratification by watching others in a state of undress or having sexual relations. For some men, voyeurism is their only sexual activity; for others, it is preferred but not absolutely essential for sexual arousal (Kaplan & Kreuger, 1997). As in the case of William earlier in this chapter, the looking, often called peeping, helps the person become sexually aroused and is sometimes essential for arousal. People with voyeurism achieve orgasm by masturbation, either while watching or later, remembering the peeping. Sometimes the person with voyeurism fantasizes about having sexual contact with the observed person, but it remains a fantasy; he or she seldom contacts the observed.

A true voyeur, almost always a man, does not find it particularly exciting to watch a woman who is undressing for his special benefit. The element of risk seems important, for the voyeur is excited by the anticipation of how the woman would react if she knew he was watching. As with all categories of illegal behavior, prevalence is difficult to assess since inappropriate adult behavior, resist inducements, leave the situation quickly, and report the incident to an appropriate adult (Wolfe, 1990). Children are taught to say no in a firm, assertive way when an adult talks to or touches them in a manner that makes them feel uncomfortable. Instructors may use comic books, films, and descriptions of risky situations to teach about sexual abuse and how children can protect themselves. Recently, policy makers have begun to consider how to prevent the burgeoning use of the Internet for CSA (Bowkett, 2003).

Evaluations of school programs suggest that they do increase awareness of sexual abuse, but researchers do not know whether children are able to translate what they have learned into overt behavior that reduces the problem (Wolfe, 1990). It is hoped that such interventions might empower children to tell their parents or guardians if an adult makes a sexual overture to them (Wurtele & Miller-Perrin, 1987).

Dealing with the Problem

When they suspect that something is awry, parents must raise the issue with their children; unfortunately, many adults are uncomfortable doing so. Physicians also need to be sensitized to signs of sexual abuse. Both sexual and nonsexual abuse are reportable offenses; professionals who suspect abuse are required by law to report their suspicions to the police or child protective agencies. When states first passed legislation requiring health care professionals and teachers to report suspected child abuse, confirmed cases skyrocketed 50 to 500 percent. For a child, reporting sexual abuse can be extremely difficult. We tend to forget how helpless and dependent the child feels, and it is difficult to imagine how frightening it would be to tell one's parents that one had been fondled by a brother or grandfather.

The vast majority of cases of sexual abuse do not leave any physical evidence, such as torn vaginal tissue. Furthermore, there is no behavioral pattern, such as anxiety, depression, or increased sexual activity which unequivocally indicates that abuse has occurred (Kuehnle, 1998). Therefore, the child's own report is the primary source of information about whether CSA occurred. The problem is that leading questions can produce some false reports. Great skill is required in questioning a child about possible sexual abuse to avoid biasing the youngster one way or the other. Some jurisdictions use innovative procedures to reduce the stress on the child while protecting the rights of the accused adult, for example, videotaped testimony, closed-courtroom trials, closed-circuit televised testimony, and special coaching sessions to explain what to expect in the courtroom (Wolfe, 1990).

Having the child play with anatomically correct dolls can be useful in getting at the truth, but it should be but one part of an assessment, because many nonabused children portray such dolls having sexual intercourse (Jampole & Weber, 1987).

Parents go through their own crisis when they become aware that someone has been molesting their child. If incest is involved, it is a true family crisis. Shame, guilt, fear, and anger abound. The incest victim's mother is in a particularly difficult situation, sometimes torn between her partner and her child, sometimes facing financial uncertainty should the father leave the home or be arrested. Decisions have to be made about how to protect the youngster from further sexual abuse. Sadly, a mother sometimes suspects what is happening to her child and yet allows it to continue—it can be incredibly hard to face these types of threats. It is impossible to know what percentage of incest cases are not reported to the police, but it is safe to say that it is sizable, perhaps the great majority (Finkelhor, 1983). Pedophilic offenses are more likely to be reported to police and prosecuted in court if the offender is not a family member.

Parents often need help in knowing how to respond to the child's allegations. A parent's strong emotional reaction, although understandable, is likely to make the child feel worse. It is important to remember that children construe things differently than adults, and although molestation of any kind is serious, preschool-age children may not understand the exact nature of what has been done to them.

Many children need professional attention (Litrownik & Castillo-Cañez, 2000). Like adult survivors of rape—and in a very real sense molested children are often rape victims—posttraumatic stress disorder (PTSD) can be a consequence. Many interventions are similar to those used for PTSD in adults; the emphasis is on exposure to memories of the trauma through discussion in a safe and supportive therapeutic atmosphere (Johnson, 1987). It is also important for children to learn that healthy human sexuality is not about power and fear (McCarthy, 1986). Inhibitions about bodily contact can be addressed in group therapy settings via structured, nonsexual hand-holding and back rubs (Wolfe, 1990). As with rape, it is important to externalize the blame for what happened, changing the person's attribution of responsibility from "I was bad" to "He/she was bad." Intervention varies with the person's age—a 14-year-old does not need dolls to recount what was done, and a 3-year-old is not an appropriate candidate for group therapy. As yet there has been no controlled research on these various and complex interventions, but uncontrolled studies are encouraging (E. M. Arnold et al., 2003).

most illegal activities are not reported to the police. Indeed, people with voyeurism are most often charged with loitering rather than with peeping itself (Kaplan & Kreuger, 1997).

Voyeurism typically begins in adolescence. People who meet diagnostic criteria for voyeurism often have other paraphilias, but they do not tend to have elevated rates of other psychological disorders.

Exhibitionism

Exhibitionism is a recurrent, intense desire to obtain sexual gratification by exposing one's genitals to an unwilling stranger, sometimes a child. It typically begins in adolescence. As with voyeurism, there is seldom an attempt to have actual contact with the stranger. Some exhibitionists, however, do get arrested for other crimes involving contact with a victim

DSM-IV-TR Criteria for Exhibitionism

- Recurrent, intense, and sexually arousing fantasies, urges, or behaviors involving showing one's genitals to an unsuspecting stranger occur for at least 6 months
- Person has acted on these urges, or the urges and fantasies cause marked distress or interpersonal problems

DSM-IV-TR Criteria for Frotteurism

- Recurrent and intense sexually arousing fantasies, urges, or behaviors involving touching and rubbing up against a nonconsenting person for at least 6 months
- Person has acted on these urges, or the urges and fantasies cause marked distress or interpersonal problems

DSM-IV-TR Criteria for Sexual Sadism

- Recurrent, intense, and occurring over a period of at least 6 months, sexually arousing fantasies, urges, or behaviors involving acts (not the fantasy) in which the humiliation or physical suffering of the other is sexually arousing
- Causes marked distress or impairment in functioning or the person has acted on these urges with a nonconsenting other

(Sugarman et al., 1994). Many exhibitionists masturbate either while fantasizing or even during the actual exposure. In most cases there is a desire to shock or embarrass the observer.

The urge to expose seems overwhelming and virtually uncontrollable to the exhibitionist and is apparently triggered by anxiety and restlessness as well as by sexual arousal. One exhibitionist persisted in his practices even after suffering a spinal cord injury that left him without sensation or movement from the waist down (DeFazio & Cunningham, 1987). Because of the compulsive nature of the urge, the exposures may be repeated often and even in the same place and at the same time of day. At the time of the act, the social and legal consequences are far from their mind (Stevenson & Jones, 1972). In the desperation and tension of the moment, they may experience headaches and palpitations and have a sense of unreality (also called derealization). After exposing themselves, exhibitions tend to flee and feel remorseful. Other paraphilias are very common in exhibitionists, notably voyeurism and frotteurism (see next section) (Freund, 1990).

Frotteurism

Frotteurism involves the sexually oriented touching of an unsuspecting person. The frotteur may rub his penis against a woman's thighs or buttocks or fondle her breasts or genitals. These attacks typically occur in places, such as a crowded bus or sidewalk, that provide an easy means of escape. Frotteurism has not been studied very extensively. It appears to begin in adolescence and typically occurs along with other paraphilias (Kreuger & Kaplan, 2000).

Sexual Sadism and Sexual Masochism

Sexual sadism is defined by an intense and recurrent desire to obtain or increase sexual gratification by inflicting pain or psychological suffering (such as humiliation) on another. **Sexual masochism** is defined by an intense and recurrent desire to obtain or increase sexual gratification through subjecting oneself to pain or humiliation. Some sadists achieve orgasm by inflicting pain, and some masochists achieve orgasm by being subjected to pain. For others, though, the sadistic and masochistic practices, such as spanking, are just one aspect of sexual intercourse.

Sadistic and masochistic behavior have become more accepted over time: 5 to 10 percent of the population has tried some form of sadomasochistic activity, such as blindfolding one's partner (Baumeister & Butler, 1997). Some clubs now cater to members seeking sadomasochistic partnerships. Most people who engage in sadomasochistic behaviors are relatively comfortable with their sexual practices (Spengler, 1977). Sadism and masochism are only diagnosed if the urges or behaviors cause distress or impairment.

Most sadists establish relationships with masochists to derive mutual sexual gratification. Although many people are able to take both dominant and submissive roles, masochists outnumber sadists. For this reason, bondage-and-discipline services may constitute a considerable portion of the business of prostitutes. The manifestations of sexual masochism are varied. Examples include restraint (physical bondage), blindfolding, spanking, whipping, electric shocks, cutting, humiliation (e.g., being urinated or defecated on, being forced to wear a collar and bark like a dog, or being put on display naked), and taking the role of slave and submitting to orders and commands. The term infantilism refers to a desire to be treated like a helpless infant and clothed in diapers. One particularly dangerous form of masochism, called hypoxyphilia, can result in death or brain damage; it involves sexual arousal by oxygen deprivation, which can be achieved using a noose, a plastic bag, chest compression, or a chemical that produces a temporary decrease in brain oxygenation by peripheral vasodilation (American Psychiatric Association, 1994).

A small percentage of sadists murder and mutilate; some sex offenders are imprisoned for torturing victims, mostly strangers, and deriving sexual satisfaction from doing so (Dietz, Hazelwood, & Warren, 1990). These aggressive sadists sometimes impersonate police officers, commit serial murders, tie up their victims, and conceal corpses (Gratzer & Bradford, 1995).

Sadism and masochism seem to begin by early adulthood. Both these disorders are found in straight and gay relationships. Surveys have found that 20 to 30 percent of the members of sadomasochistic clubs are female (Moser & Levitt, 1987), and it has been assumed that a similar gender ratio might be true of diagnosable sadism and masochism. The majority of sadists and masochists lead otherwise conventional lives, and there is some evidence that they are above average in income and educational status (Moser & Levitt, 1987). Alcohol abuse is common among sadists (Allnut et al., 1996).

Check Your Knowledge 13.3

Choose the diagnostic category that best fits each vignette. If not diagnosable, state so.

1. Joe is only able to obtain sexual arousal by rubbing his body against strangers. He has worked out a set of rituals to engage in this behavior; he knows which bus routes and times will be most crowded, chooses a bus that tends to have many women, and times his attacks so that he can leave the bus at a stop along with many other people.
2. Sam and Terry enjoy a good sexual relationship. They have mutually satisfying sex at least weekly. Occasionally, Terry likes to be tied down before sex, but she is able to enjoy sex without bondage as well. Most of their sex life involves no hint of pain or bondage.
3. Victor secretly enjoys wearing his wife's underwear. When she is away, he dresses up, watches himself in the mirror, and masturbates. He finds this activity to be the most exciting sexual activity he has ever engaged in, and despite an incredible sense of embarrassment and shame, feels he has no control over these urges. He fears that his wife would divorce him if she knew about his cross-dressing.
4. Matt only feels aroused when he is able to cause pain to someone before engaging in sex. Most of the time, he indulges in these activities at a sadomasochism club. He has not been able to sustain a relationship with any of the women he has met in clubs. He would like to form a more lasting partnership, but feels obsessed by sadism. He is deeply distressed by his inability to enjoy other forms of sexuality.
5. Ever since he was a small child, Dennis has felt like he was a girl. As a child, he would sneak into his mother's closet and dress up in her clothes. As he grew older, his belief that he was trapped in a boy's body became stronger. At age 20, he began taking female hormones, shaving his legs, dressing as a woman, and calling himself Deanna.
6. Barry is a 40-year-old single man who has never had a sustained dating relationship or sexual partner. Several times a week, Barry parks his car at the beach, masturbates, and then finds a way to lure a woman to his car, usually by asking for directions. He is unable to have an orgasm unless the woman notices his erection. He has been arrested three times for this behavior, but most women simply run away rather than press charges.

Etiology of the Paraphilias

Of the many theories about the etiology of the paraphilias, the principal ones come from biological, psychodynamic, and behavioral perspectives. Because many people do not want to talk about their paraphilias, researchers have few opportunities to understand the causes of paraphilias.

Neurobiological Factors   As the overwhelming majority of people with paraphilias are male, there has been speculation that androgens, or male hormones, play a role. Androgens regulate sexual desire, and sexual desire appears to be atypically high among people with paraphilias (Kafka, 1997). Findings of hormonal correlates of paraphilias are inconclusive, however. As to differences in the brain, a dysfunction in the temporal lobe may be relevant to a minority of cases of sadism and exhibitionism (Mason, 1997). If biology turns out to be important, it most likely will be but one factor in a complex network of causes that includes experience as a major player (Meyer, 1995).

Psychodynamic Perspectives   Psychodynamic theorists view paraphilias as a defense, guarding the ego from dealing with repressed fears and memories. The person with a paraphilia is seen as someone who is fearful of conventional heterosexual relationships, even when the relationships do not involve sex, because they are fixated at a pregenital stage of psychosexual development. Development is inadequate for social and sexual adult relationships (Lanyon, 1986). For example, fetishes, voyeurism, and pedophilia are seen as

DSM-IV-TR Criteria for Sexual Masochism

- Recurrent, intense, and occurring over a period of at least 6 months, sexually arousing fantasies, urges, or behaviors involving the act (not the fantasy) of being humiliated or beaten
- Causes marked distress or impairment in functioning

manifestations of intense castration anxiety that makes heterosexual sex with adult women too threatening. Castration anxiety leads the exhibitionist to reassure himself of his masculinity by showing his manhood (his genitals) to others (usually girls and women); it results in the sadist dominating others. Although many of the psychodynamic ideas have been influential, and some of these ideas have even been picked up and reformulated by cognitive theorists, there is little research available to test psychodynamic theory of paraphilias.

Psychological Factors   Most psychological theories of the paraphilias involve a set of risk factors, including conditioning experiences, relationship histories, and cognition. Some behavioral theorists view the cause of paraphilias as classical conditioning that by chance has linked sexual arousal with unusual or inappropriate stimuli. Though seldom acknowledged, this theory was first put forward in the famous Kinsey reports on sexual behavior in American men and women (Kinsey et al., 1948). For example, a young man may masturbate to images of women dressed in black leather boots. According to this theory, repetitions of these experiences make boots sexually arousing. Similar proposals have been made for transvestism, pedophilia, voyeurism, and exhibitionism. Although there is some minor support (e.g., Rachman, 1966), research has not supported most components of the orgasm-conditioning hypothesis (O'Donohue & Plaud, 1994). As described later, however, some innovative therapeutic strategies have been developed based on these ideas.

From an operant conditioning perspective, many paraphilias are considered an outcome of inadequate social skills or reinforcement of unconventionality by parents or relatives. Evidence does support poor social skills among men with pedophilia (Dreznick, 2003). Paraphilias such as exhibitionism may thus be activities that substitute for more conventional relationships and sexual activity. On the other hand, the fact that many pedophiles and exhibitionists have conventional social-sexual relationships indicates that the issue is more complex than a simple absence of nondeviant sexual outlets (Maletsky, 2000).

The childhood histories of people with paraphilias reveal that often they were exposed to physical abuse, sexual abuse, and poor parent–child relationships (Mason, 1997). These early experiences may contribute to the poor social skills and lack of intimate relationships often seen among those with paraphilias (Marshall, Serran, & Cortoni, 2000). But the widely accepted belief that sexual abuse in childhood predisposes people to paraphilic behavior (Worling, 1995) needs to be qualified by research showing that fewer than a third of adult sex offenders were sexually abused when they were below the age of 18 (Maletzky, 1993). Distorted parent–child relationships may also create hostility, negative attitudes, and lack of empathy toward women, which may increase the chances of victimizing a woman.

Alcohol and negative affect often are triggers of incidents of pedophilia, voyeurism, and exhibitionism. This is consistent with evidence that alcohol decreases inhibition. Deviant sexual activity, like alcohol use, may be a means of escaping from negative affect (Baumeister & Butler, 1997).

Cognitive distortions also play a role in the paraphilias. For example, a voyeur may believe that a woman who left her blinds up while undressing wanted someone to look at her (Kaplan & Kreuger, 1997). A person with pedophilia may believe that children want to have sex with adults (Marshall, 1997). Table 13.5 contains examples of the kinds of unwarranted beliefs that may be associated with pedophilia and exhibitionism. Rape, a topic dealt with later in this chapter, is also included in the table.

Treatments for the Paraphilias

Because many of the behaviors involved in paraphilias are illegal, many people diagnosed with them are imprisoned and court ordered into treatment. Outcomes for incarcerated juvenile and adult sex offenders are highly variable (Becker & Hunter, 1997; Maletzky, 2002). Published data on treatment are hard to interpret for several reasons. First, most researchers avoid using control groups who receive no treatment—many researchers consider it unethical to withhold treatment when the consequences of sexual offenses are so severe. Second, it is difficult to compare findings because studies vary greatly. Some programs select the most problematic prisoners for treatment, whereas others treat those with

Table 13.5 Examples of Cognitive Distortions and Justifications in Sexual Paraphilias

Category	Pedophilia	Exhibitionism	Rape
Misattributing blame	"She started it by being too cuddly."	"She kept looking at me like she was expecting it." "The way she was dressed, she was asking for it."	"She was saying no, but her body said yes." "I was always drinking when I did it."
Denying sexual intent	"I was just teaching her about sex … better from her father than from someone else.	"I was just looking for a place to pee." "My pants just slipped down."	"I was just trying to teach her a lesson; she deserved it."
Debasing the victim	"She'd had sex before with her boyfriend."	"She was just a slut anyway."	"The way she came on to me at the party, she deserved it."
Minimizing consequences	"She has always been real friendly to me, even afterward." "She was messed up even before it happened."	"I never touched her, so I couldn't have hurt her."	"She'd had sex with hundreds of guys before. It was no big deal."
Deflecting censure	"This happened years ago. Why can't everyone forget about it?"	"It's not like I raped anyone."	"I only did it once."
Justifying the cause	"If I wasn't molested as a kid, I'd never have done this."	"If I knew how to get dates, I wouldn't have to expose."	"If my girlfriend gave me what I want, I wouldn't be forced to rape."

Source: Maletzky, B. M. (2002). The paraphilias: Research and treatment. In P. E. Nathan and J. M. Gorman (Eds.), *A Guide to Treatments That Work* (pp. 525–558). New York: Oxford University Press.

the most promising prognoses, for example, first offenders. Some treatments have follow-up sessions after release, whereas others do not. Third, many studies do not evaluate treatment success over time, even though recidivism increases as the years go by, especially when 2 years have passed since termination of treatment (Maletzky, 2002).

Sex offenders often lack motivation to change their illegal behavior. They may deny the problem, minimize the seriousness of their problem, believe that their victims will not be credible witnesses, and feel confident that they can control their behavior without professional assistance. Some blame the victim—even a child—for being overly seductive. For these reasons, such people are often judged to be inappropriate for treatment programs (Dougher, 1988); when they do become involved, they often drop out (Knopp, 1984). To enhance motivation for treatment, a therapist can (Miller & Rollnick, 1991):

1. empathize with the offender's reluctance to admit that he is an offender and to seek treatment, thereby reducing defensiveness and hostility;

2. point out that treatments might help him control his behavior better;

3. emphasize the negative consequences of refusing treatment (e.g., transfer to a less attractive incarceration setting if the person is already in custody) and of offending again (e.g., stiffer legal penalties);

4. explain that there will be a psychophysiological assessment of the patient's sexual arousal, implying that this can reveal the patient's sexual proclivities without his admitting to them (Garland & Dougher, 1991).

With the foregoing as background, we now describe cognitive behavioral and biological treatments for the paraphilias. Then, we consider legal efforts to protect the public from sex offenders.

Cognitive Behavioral Treatment   In the earliest years of behavioral treatment, paraphilias were narrowly viewed as attractions to inappropriate objects and activities. Looking to experimental psychology for ways to reduce these attractions, researchers fixed on aversion therapy. Thus a person with boot fetishism would be given shock (on the hands or feet) or an emetic (a drug that produces nausea) when looking at a boot, a person with transvestism when cross-dressing, a person with pedophilia when gazing at a photograph of a nude child, and so on. A variation of aversion therapy based on imagery is covert sensitization, whereby the person imagines situations he finds inappropriately arousing and imagines also feeling sick or ashamed for feeling and acting this way. Versions of covert sensitization have been developed that pair the aversive imagery with a foul odor (Maletzky, 2000). Studies of covert sensitization have shown that it reduces deviant arousal, but little evidence is available that these techniques alone actually change the behavior (Maletzky, 2000).

Another aversion therapy technique is satiation, in which the man masturbates for a long time, typically after ejaculating, while fantasizing out loud about his deviant activity. The idea is that masturbation will continue for so long as to become aversive. Although aversion therapy may not completely eliminate the attraction, in some cases it provides the patient with a greater measure of control over the overt behavior (McConaghy, 1994).

Another technique entails imagining a typical deviant activity but changing its ending, as described in the following vignette.

> As you drive home one night you notice an attractive woman driver on your right in a van. She can see right into your car. You slow down and drive parallel with her as you begin to get aroused. You want to rub your penis and take it out to show her. However, the urge this time is weaker and you drive past her quickly without exposing. You feel good about yourself for being able to exert control. (Maletzky, 1997, p. 57)

Cognitive procedures are often used to counter the distorted thinking of people with paraphilias. Table 13.5 contains examples of cognitive distortions that would be targets for modification. For example, an exhibitionist might claim that the girls he exposes himself to are too young to be harmed by it. The therapist would counter this distortion by pointing out that the younger the victim, the worse the harm will be (Maletzky, 1997).

In general, cognitive and behavioral approaches have become more sophisticated and broader in scope since the 1960s, when the paraphilias were addressed almost exclusively in terms of sexual attraction that had been classically conditioned to inappropriate environmental stimuli. Now, treatment centers tend to combine aversive conditioning and cognitive interventions with broader approaches, such as social skills training and sexual impulse control training (Maletzky, 2002). Training in empathy toward others is another increasingly common cognitive technique; teaching the sex offender to consider how his or her behavior would affect someone else may lessen the tendency to engage in such activities. Relapse prevention, modeled after the work on substance abuse described in Chapter 10, is also an important component of many broader treatment programs. A therapist who uses relapse prevention techniques would help a person identify situations and emotions that might trigger symptomatic behavior.

Comprehensive programs that include aversion therapy combined with other types of psychological interventions, such as social skills training, have some beneficial effects on pedophilia, transvestism, exhibitionism, and fetishism (Maletzky, 2002). Overall, both institution-based and outpatient programs that follow a cognitive behavioral model with sex offenders reduce recidivism more than what would be expected were no treatment at all attempted (Maletzky, 2002). These outcomes are much better for people with pedophilia than for rapists. Although sex offenders evoke disgust and fear from many people, efforts to treat such people, even if only minimally effective, are not only cost-effective but stand the chance of protecting others after the person is released from prison (Prentky & Burgess, 1990).

Biological Treatment   A variety of biological interventions have been tried on sex offenders. Castration, or removal of the testes, was used a great deal in Western Europe two generations ago, with some apparent effectiveness in reducing the incidence of paraphilic behavior (e.g., Langeluddeke, 1963). Surgical castration is not a common treatment today, due to major ethical concerns.

On the other hand, several medications have been used to treat paraphilias, particularly among sex offenders. Typically, these medications are used as a supplement to psychological treatment. Among men, sexual drive and functioning are regulated by androgens (testosterone and dihydrotestoterone). Hence, hormonal agents that reduce androgens have been used to treat paraphilias, including medroxyprogesterone acetate (MPA, trade name Depo-Provera), cyproterone acetate (CPA, Cyprostat), and luteinizing hormone-releasing hormone agents (LHRH). Beyond drugs that influence hormones, SSRI antidepressants have been shown to reduce sexual arousal, as well as orgasmic and ejaculatory capacity. Across treatment trials, researchers tend to measure sexual fantasies to deviant objects, sexual behaviors, and legal offenses. In some studies, sexual arousal to deviant objects is measured using the plethysmograph. A range of clinical trials have found that SSRIs, MPA, and CPA are effective in reducing arousal (Hill et al., 2003). SSRIs have also been found to be helpful as an addition to psychological treatment (Hill et al., 2003).

Despite the promising findings, many ethical issues are raised about the indefinite use of hormonal agents. Long-term use of hormonal agents is associated with a number of negative side effects, including infertility, liver problems, osteoporosis, and diabetes (Gunn, 1993). Informed consent concerning these risks must be obtained, and many patients will not agree to use them or will drop out of treatment (Hill et al., 2003).

Efforts to Protect the Public: Megan's Law   The variable outcomes of treatment efforts and the rates of recidivism after prison release have led to public pressure to forbid sexual offenders from returning to the locales where they were arrested. A further trend is exemplified in laws that allow police to publicize the whereabouts of registered sex offenders if they are considered to be a potential danger. These laws also permit citizens to use a national network of computerized police records to determine whether sex offenders are living in their neighborhoods (Ingram, 1996; Kempster, 1996).

Referred to by some as Megan's law, this statute and others like it across the United States arose from public outrage at the brutal murder of a second grader in New Jersey who was kidnapped while walking home from school. The person convicted of this crime was a twice-convicted child molester. Sadly, some neighborhoods have responded to notification with vigilantism, as neighbors become aware of sex offenders in their neighborhoods (Younglove & Vitello, 2003). It should come as no surprise that civil rights groups are challenging these laws.

Check Your Knowledge 13.4

1. Which of the following has not been related to paraphilias?
   a. childhood abuse
   b. cognitive distortions
   c. permissive parenting
   d. negative affect
2. The most commonly used biological treatments to reduce sexual desire and paraphilic behaviors are
   a. surgical castration
   b. hormonal agents and antidepressants
   c. antianxiety medications
   d. none of the above

Quick Summary

Paraphilias are defined by a sexual attraction to an unusual sexual object or activity which lasts at least 6 months and causes significant distress or impairment. The DSM-IV-TR diagnostic criteria for paraphilias are distinguished based on the object of sexual attraction as shown in Table 13.4.

Researchers do not know the prevalence of these disorders, nor is much research available on the causes of paraphilias. Neurobiological factors that might be involved include excess levels of male hormones or for some, dysfunction in the temporal lobes. Psychodynamic theory emphasizes conflicts between the id and ego, based in early developmental experiences. Psychological theories focus on conditioning to inappropriate sexual objects, histories of physical and sexual abuse, poor parenting, hostility toward women, and cognitive distortions.

Treatment approaches must begin with a focus on engaging the client, which is often difficult to do. Cognitive behavioral approaches include various versions of aversion therapy, including covert sensitization and satiation. Cognitive techniques are used to challenge distorted beliefs about the consequences of sexual behaviors. Cognitive-behavioral therapists also use techniques to improve social skills, to help people control impulses, to increase empathy for potential victims, and to identify potential high-risk situations for the return of symptoms. The most common medication treatments involve antidepressants or medications that reduce male hormone levels such as Depo-Provera. Laws have been passed that allow the public to access information about where sexual offenders live, but civil rights groups are opposed to some aspects of these laws.

Rape

In legal terms, rape falls into two categories—forced and statutory. **Forced rape** is sexual intercourse with an unwilling partner. **Statutory rape** refers to sexual intercourse with a minor, someone under the age of consent (typically age 18). Because it is assumed that a person younger than the age of consent should not be held responsible for sexual activity with an older person, a charge of statutory rape can be made even if the minor reports consenting to sex willingly. Thus statutory rape need not involve force, only sex with a minor. We focus on forced rape in this section.

Twenty to 25 percent of American women will be raped during their lifetimes (Crowell & Burgess, 1996). The vast majority of women who are raped will experience symptoms of anxiety in the weeks after an attack (Rothbaum & Foa, 1993), and at least a third will develop PTSD (Breslau et al., 1999). More detail on PTSD and its treatment is provided in Chapter 5 (see p. 128 and p. 153).

Rape is an important issue on college campuses. Table 13.6 shows findings from one study which asked college-aged men and women the extent to which they had perpetrated and experienced physical coercion after people refused sexual contact. As shown, a discouraging 30 percent of female college students report that they have experienced the use of physical force, threats, or harm after they refused sexual contact with a person, with 8.7 percent reporting that they had experienced actual physical harm. In one survey of a representative sample of 4,446 women enrolled in college (Fisher, Cullen, & Turner, 2000),

Table 13.6 Behaviors That College Students Report after a Partner Refuses Sexual Contact

Tactic	Men experiencing the tactic N = 275 (%)	Women experiencing the tactic N = 381 (%)	Men perpetrating the tactic N = 275 (%)	Women perpetrating the tactic N = 381 (%)
Emotional manipulation and deception				
Repeatedly asking	36.9	65.8	29.2	13.9
Telling lies	21.5	42.4	16.2	3.1
Using authority of older age	8.7	13.4	0.7	0.3
Questioning target's sexuality	7.6	9.2	2.6	1.6
Threatening to break up	4.4	9.5	2.6	0.3
Using authority of position	3.3	5.3	1.1	0.5
Threatening self-harm	5.5	3.7	1.5	0.5
Threatening blackmail	3.6	2.4	1.5	0.8
One or more of the above	43.6	71.4	32.4	15.2
Exploitation of intoxication				
Taking advantage of a drunken target	29.5	42.1	12.9	5.0
Purposefully getting a target drunk	10.9	25.0	5.9	1.1
One or more of the above	30.5	43.8	13.1	5.2
Physical force or threats				
Blocking target's retreat	19.3	21.1	2.9	1.1
Using physical restraint	9.1	22.4	4.0	2.1
Using physical harm	6.2	8.7	1.1	0.5
Threatening physical harm	1.1	6.3	0.7	0.5
Tying up a target	3.6	0.8	1.1	1.1
Threatening with a weapon	1.1	1.8	0.7	0.3
One or more of the above	24.7	30.4	5.1	2.6

Note. Some percentages are based on less than the total *N* because of missing data.
Source: From Struckman.

2000), researchers provided carefully worded questions about rape. The authors coded forcible vaginal, oral, or anal insertion of the penis, fingers, tongue, or objects as rape. About 3 percent of women reported that they had experienced an attempted or completed rape in the 7 months before the study. Rape occurs far too often.

The Crime

The specifics of rape cases vary widely. Up to 70 percent of rapes are associated with intoxication (Crowell & Burgess, 1996). In a very small percentage of cases, rapists murder their victims. Although men can be victims of sexual assault, our discussion focuses on women, because more than 90 percent of rapes are committed by men against women (Crowell & Burgess, 1996). Younger women and girls are much more likely to be victims of rape than are older women (see Figure 13.7).

Approximately 70 percent of rapes are committed by someone known to the woman (National Center for Justice, 2003). People seem particularly likely to blame date-rape victims. This blame is wrong, though, because it overlooks the right to say no at any time. Willingness to have dinner, even to embrace and kiss, is not tantamount to consenting to anything more intimate.

Many believe rape should not be classified as a sexual crime, lest this terminology mask the violent nature of the act and create an atmosphere in which the sexual motives of the victim are questioned. In considering links between violence and rape, it is important to consider rape during wartime. The Crusaders raped their way across Europe on their holy pilgrimages in the eleventh through the thirteenth centuries; the Germans raped as they rampaged through Belgium in World War I; U.S. forces raped Vietnamese women and girls as they searched and destroyed; and Iraqi soldiers raped and brutalized women as they occupied Kuwait in 1990. In 2004, U.S. soldiers humiliated Iraqi prisoners through various torture tactics, including rape. Brownmiller (1975) contends that rape is actually expected in war. In March 1998, a Serbian soldier was found guilty of rape as a war crime (Associated Press, 1998). This is the first time sexual assault was treated as a war crime. Hopefully, this type of ruling will make it less likely that rape will be tacitly condoned during war.

The Rapist: Understanding the Etiology of Rape

Is the rapist primarily the psychopath who seeks the thrill of dominating and humiliating a woman through intimidation and often brutal assault? Is he an ordinarily unassertive man with a fragile ego who, feeling inadequate after disappointment and rejection in work or love, takes out his frustrations on an unwilling stranger? What types of characteristics distinguish rapists?

Many rapists probably share unusually high hostility toward women (Malamuth, 1998). Other studies have found that rapists tend to respond with more sexual arousal than nonsexual offenders to images of coercive sexual activity (Lalumiere & Quinsey,

Figure 13.7 Rates of sexual assault victimization among women by age group. From: National Center for Justice (2003). Unpublished document, National Center for Justice, Document NCJ, 206348.

This famous scene from *Gone with the Wind* illustrates one of the myths about rape—that despite initial resistance, women like to be "taken." (Everett Collection, Inc.)

Rape victims of the war in Bosnia. Rape often occurs during war, but only recently has sexual assault been considered a war crime. (Andrew Kaiser-G.A.F.F./Sipa Press.)

Quinsey, 1994). Sexually aggressive men tend to show antisocial and impulsive personality traits (Crowell & Burgess, 1996).

Beyond violent tendencies, rapists may have specific sexual difficulties. In one major community survey, men who had assaulted women sexually were 3.5 times as likely to report erectile dysfunction (Laumann et al., 1999). Rapists also appear to have high sex drive; across a range of samples, sex drive (as measured by frequency of sexual outlets) was correlated with sexual coercion (Kafka, 1997). Some rapists seem to have problems distinguishing friendliness from seductiveness and in accurately reading cues from a woman indicating that she wants intimacies to cease (Malamuth & Brown, 1994).

Although there has been a long history of belief that rapists have poor social skills, a recent meta-analysis of studies on this topic suggests that any social skills deficits are minor, and that they tend to be documented only among convicted rapists and not among those who escape legal charges (Dreznick, 2003). A more specific interpersonal skill though, may be deficient.

From a sociological perspective, the more a society accepts interpersonal violence as a way to handle conflict and solve problems, the higher the frequency of rape (Sanday, 1981). It seems worth noting that in a controlled experiment, male college students who stated that they regarded rape as unacceptable were aroused by video portrayals of rape if the woman was depicted as having an orgasm during the assault (Malamuth & Check, 1983). Since the time this study was conducted, eight experiments have been conducted in which men are asked to watch videos which contain either sexual activities with violence or sexual activities without violence. A meta-analysis of these studies suggested that after watching videos that contained violence, men were significantly more likely to report that violence toward women was acceptable (Allen et al., 1995). This research suggests that rape may be encouraged by pornography that depicts women enjoying violent sexual relations.

Psychological Treatment for Rapists

Treatment programs for incarcerated rapists are typically multidimensional. These programs often include cognitive techniques aimed at rapists' distorted beliefs and inappropriate attitudes toward women (such as the belief that women want to be raped—see Table 13.5), attempts to increase empathy with their victims, anger management, techniques to improve self-esteem, and efforts to reduce substance abuse. These methods are often implemented in confrontational group-therapy sessions that attempt to goad the rapist into taking responsibility for his aggressive behavior. As with the paraphilias, this therapy is sometimes supplemented with the use of biological treatments, like Depo-Provera, which reduce sex drive by lowering levels of male sex hormones.

Treatment studies are limited, in that they often measure legal charges rather than the rate of deviant sexual behavior, so probably underestimate relapse rates. Another issue is that these programs typically have not had adequate control groups. Despite these problems, meta-analyses have led to the conclusion that cognitive therapy and the biological interventions may lower recidivism somewhat, especially among men who complete treatment programs (Hanson & Bussiere, 1998). One study is notable for the inclusion of a control group in comparison to cognitive behavioral treatment (Marques et al., 1994). That study found that among 59 rapists, 9 percent of men in the treatment group committed an offense during the 5-year follow-up period, compared to 28 percent in the no-treatment group.

Reforming the Legal System

Estimates are that less than half of rapes are reported (National Center for Victims of Violent Crime, 2004). Interviews with half a million women indicated three reasons for reluctance to report rape:

1. Considering the rape a private matter;
2. Fearing reprisals from the rapist or his family or friends;
3. Believing that police would be ineffective or insensitive (Wright, 1991).

In recent years, several legal reforms have been enacted. For example, all states now allow for prosecution of rapes that occur within marriages; the laws in most states consider the likely absence of witnesses for such a private act; the definition of rape typically includes forced oral and anal entry as well as vaginal penetration; and perhaps most importantly, information about the victim's previous sexual behavior and history is no longer admissible. Despite these changes, trials remain very stressful. Only a very small percentage of rapists are ultimately convicted of their crimes. Any familiarity of the victim with her assailant makes conviction of the man more difficult to achieve. Even though many rapists rape hundreds of times, they are only occasionally imprisoned for an offense.

Summary

Sexual Norms

- Sexual behavior and attitudes are heavily influenced by culture, and so any discussion of disorders in sexuality must be sensitive to the idea that norms are likely to change over time and place. Currently, a great deal of research is focused on gender differences in sexuality.

Sexual Dysfunctions

- The DSM categorizes four kinds of sexual dysfunctions: sexual desire disorders, sexual arousal disorders, orgasmic disorders, and sexual pain disorders. Many people experience brief sexual symptoms, but these are not diagnosable unless they are recurrent; cause either distress or impairment; and are not explained by medical conditions.
- Research on the etiology of sexual dysfunctions is difficult to conduct, as surveys may be inaccurate and laboratory measures may be difficult to gather. Researchers have identified many different variables that can contribute to sexual dysfunctions, including biological variables, previous sexual experiences, relationship issues, psychopathology, affect and low arousal, and negative cognitions.
- Many effective interventions for sexual dysfunctions are available, most of them cognitive-behavioral. Sex therapy, aimed at reversing old habits and teaching new skills, was propelled into public consciousness by the Masters and Johnson work. Their method hinges on gradual, non-threatening exposure to increasingly intimate sexual encounters and the sanctioning of sexuality by credible therapists. Sex therapists also aim to educate patients in sexual anatomy and physiology; reduce anxiety; teach communication skills; and improve attitudes and thoughts about sexuality. Couples therapy is sometimes appropriate as well. Biological treatments such as Viagra also may be used, especially when the sex-

ual dysfunction is primarily due to physical rather than psychological causes, as in many cases of erectile dysfunction.

Gender Identity Disorder

- Gender identity disorder (GID) involves the deep and persistent conviction of the person that his or her anatomic sexual makeup and psychological sense of self as male or female are discrepant. Thus, a man with GID is physically male but considers himself a woman.
- Neurobiological models of GID emphasize genes and prenatal hormone exposure. Most research on neurobiology, though, has focused on sex-typed behavior and attitudes, rather than full-blown diagnoses, and even then, neurobiological variables account for only a certain amount of the variance. Another theory proposes that parents may have reinforced cross-gender behavior. This theory has been criticized, though, as peers are so harsh towards children who show cross-gender behaviors.
- The most common treatment for GID is sex-reassignment surgery to bring bodily features into line with gender identity. There are case reports that behavioral treatment can help a person minimize cross-gender behavior.

Paraphilias

- In the paraphilias, unusual imagery and acts are persistent and necessary for sexual gratification. The principal paraphilias are fetishism, transvestic fetishism, pedophilia, voyeurism, exhibitionism, frotteurism, sexual sadism, and sexual masochism.
- Efforts have also been made to detect hormonal anomalies in people with paraphilias, but the findings are inconclusive.

● According to the psychodynamic view, the person with a paraphilia is fearful of conventional heterosexual relationships; there is no empirical support for this idea. One behavioral view is that a fetishistic attraction to objects arises from accidental classical conditioning of sexual arousal, but this view has not received much empirical support. Another behavioral hypothesis posits deficiencies in social skills that make it difficult for the person to interact normally with other adults, but again, there is limited support for this idea. Cognitive distortions appear to be involved.

● The most promising treatments for the paraphilias are cognitive behavioral. One conditioning procedure is to pair the inappropriate sexual object with painful or aversive events. Cognitive methods focus on the cognitive distortions of the person with a paraphilia. Social skills and empathy training are also common. A range of studies suggest that psychological treatments do reduce rates of legal offenses. SSRIs and drugs that reduce testosterone levels have both been found to reduce sex drive and deviant sexual behaviors, but because of the side effects, there are ethical issues involved in the long-term use of hormonal drugs.

Rape

● Rape, although it is not separately diagnosed in DSM-IV-TR, results in considerable psychological trauma for the victim and is far too prevalent. Some estimates suggest that 20–25 percent of women will be raped during their lifetime. The nature of rapes varies a great deal; some people rape strangers, but most rapes are committed by someone known to the woman. The inclusion of rape in a discussion of human sexuality is a matter of some controversy, as many theorists regard rape as an act of aggressive violence rather than of sex.

● Although there is no single profile that fits all rapists, variables that appear to distinguish rapists include hostility toward women, antisocial and impulsive personality traits, and high rates of sexual dysfunction. Social skills do not seem to be poor, except in convicted rapists. Many have emphasized that the likelihood of rape is likely to be higher in societies that condone interpersonal violence.

● Psychological treatment programs focus on increasing empathy for victims, anger management, self-esteem, and substance abuse. Biological treatments, like those used for paraphilias, are used to decrease sex drive by lowering male hormone levels. Treatment has been shown to reduce the rate of recidivism. A major concern is that most rapes do not get reported to police, and so few rapists are convicted.

Answers to Check Your Knowledge Questions

13.1 1. d; 2. b; 3. b

13.2 1. F (explanation: unless the problem is recurrent and leads to distress or impairment, it cannot be diagnosed); 2. F; 3. T; 4. T; 5. F

13.3 1. frotterurism; 2. not a diagnosable disorder; 3. transvestic fetishism; 4. sadism; 5. gender identity disorder; 6. exhibitionism

13.4 1. c; 2. b

Key Terms

appetitive phase	frotteurism	pedophilia	sexual orientation
childhood sexual abuse(CSA)	gender identity	penile plethysmograph	sexual response cycle
dyspareunia	gender identity disorder	premature ejaculation	sexual sadism
excitement phase	hypoactive sexual desire disorder	resolution phase	spectator role
exhibitionism	incest	sensate focus	statutory rape
female orgasmic disorder	male erectile disorder	sex-reassignment surgery	transvestic fetishism
female sexual arousal disorder	male orgasmic disorder	sexual aversion disorder	vaginismus
fetishism	orgasm phase	sexual dysfunctions	voyeurism
forced rape	paraphilias	sexual masochism	

14 Disorders of Childhood

Learning Goals

1. Be able to describe the issues in the classification of psychopathology in children.

2. Be able to discuss the description, etiology, and treatments for externalizing problems, including ADHD and conduct disorder, and for internalizing problems, including depression and anxiety.

3. Be able to distinguish the distinctions between the different learning disabilities as well as our current understanding of the causes and treatments for dyslexia.

4. Be able to describe the different systems for classifying mental retardation and the current research on causes and treatments.

5. Be able to describe the symptoms, causes, and treatments for autism and Asperger's syndrome.

Clinical Case: Eric

"Eric. Eric? Eric!!" His teacher's voice and the laughter of his classmates roused the boy from his reverie. Glancing at the book of the girl sitting next to him, he noticed that the class was pages ahead of him. He was supposed to be answering a question about the Declaration of Independence, but he had been lost in thought, wondering about what seats he and his father would have for the baseball game they'd be attending that evening. A tall, lanky 12-year-old, Eric had just begun seventh grade. His history teacher had already warned him about being late to class and not paying attention, but Eric just couldn't seem to get from one class to the next without stopping for drinks of water or to investigate an altercation between classmates. In class, he was rarely prepared to answer when the teacher called on him, and he usually forgot to write down the homework assignment. He already had a reputation among his peers as an "airhead."

Eric's relief at the sound of the bell was quickly replaced by anxiety as he reached the playground for physical education. Despite his speed and physical strength, Eric was always picked last for baseball teams. His team was up to bat first, and Eric sat down to wait his turn. Absorbed in studying a pile of pebbles at his feet, he failed to notice his team's third out and missed the change of innings. The other team had already come in from the outfield before Eric noticed that his team was out in the field—too late to avoid the irate yells of his P.E. teacher to take his place at third base. Resolved to watch for his chance to field the ball, Eric nonetheless found himself without his glove on when a sharply hit ball rocketed his way; he had taken it off to toss it in the air in the middle of the pitch.

At home, Eric's father told him he had to finish his homework before they could go to the Dodgers game. He had only one page of math problems and was determined to finish them quickly. Thirty minutes later, his father emerged from the shower to find Eric building an elaborate Lego structure on the floor of his room; the math homework was half done. In exasperation, Eric's father left for the game without him.

At bedtime, frustrated and discouraged, Eric was unable to sleep. He often lay awake for what seemed like hours, reviewing the disappointments of the day and berating himself for his failures. On this night, he ruminated about his lack of friends, the frustration of his teachers, and his parents' exhortations to pay attention and "get it together." Feeling hopeless about doing better, despite his daily resolve, Eric's thoughts often turned to suicide. Tonight he reviewed his fantasy of wandering out into the street in front of a passing car. Although Eric had never acted on his suicidal thoughts, he frequently replayed in his mind his parents' sorrow and remorse, his classmates' irritation with him, and the concern of his teachers.

The disorders found in the DSM-IV-TR section entitled "Disorders Usually First Diagnosed in Infancy, Childhood, or Adolescence" cover a wide range of difficulties, from the attentional problems characteristic of attention-deficit/hyperactivity disorder, as in the case of Eric, to the sometimes serious intellectual deficits found in mental retardation, the gross and sometimes callous disregard for the rights of others found in conduct disorder, the disturbances in mood found in anxiety and depression, the learning problems characteristic of learning disorders, and the language impairment and social and emotional difficulties of autistic disorder. Children typically have access to fewer social, financial, and psychological resources than do adults in dealing with such problems. Thus, whether troubled children receive professional attention at all usually depends on the adults in their lives—parents, teachers, and school counselors.

Most psychological theories, whether psychodynamic, behavioral, cognitive, or neurobiological theories of childhood disorders consider childhood experience and development critically important to adult mental health. Most theories also regard children as better able to change than adults and thus as particularly suitable for treatment. Earlier research devoted little attention to childhood disorders, but recent years have seen a dramatic increase in professional interest in the nature, etiology, prevention, and treatment of child psychopathology. The number of children being diagnosed with and treated for different psychological disorders has also dramatically increased, but not without controversy (see Focus on Discovery 14.2).

In this chapter we discuss several of the disorders that are most likely to arise in childhood and adolescence. We first consider disorders involving attention and socially unacceptable behavior, followed by depression and anxiety disorders. Finally, we discuss disorders in which the acquisition of cognitive, language, motor, or social skills is disturbed. These include learning disabilities as well as the most severe of developmental disorders, mental retardation and pervasive developmental disorders (especially autism), which are usually chronic and often persist into adulthood.

Classification and Diagnosis of Childhood Disorders

To classify abnormal behavior in children, diagnosticians must first consider what is typical for a particular age. The diagnosis of children who lie on the floor kicking and screaming when they don't get their way would be assessed differently at two years old than at seven. The field of **developmental psychopathology** studies disorders of childhood within the context of normal life-span development, enabling us to identify behaviors that are considered appropriate at one stage but are disturbed at another.

Most childhood disorders, such as school phobia, are unique to children. Still others, such as attention-deficit/hyperactivity disorder, have been conceptualized primarily as childhood disorders but may continue into adulthood. The DSM description of the disorders we cover in this chapter are provided in the DSM tables in the margins. Table 14.1 lists the chapters where we discuss still other disorders that may occur in childhood but are primarily considered disorders of adulthood.

The more prevalent childhood disorders are often categorized in two broad domains, externalizing disorders and internalizing disorders. **Externalizing disorders** are characterized by more outward-directed behaviors, such as aggressiveness, noncompliance, overactivity, and impulsiveness; the category includes attention-deficit/ hyperactivity disorder, conduct disorder, and oppositional defiant disorder. **Internalizing disorders** are characterized by more inward-focused experiences and behaviors such as depression, social withdrawal, and anxiety; the category includes childhood anxiety and mood disorders. Children and adolescents may exhibit symptoms from both domains, as described in the case of Eric.

The behaviors that comprise externalizing and internalizing disorders are prevalent across many countries, including Switzerland (Steinhausen & Metzke, 1998), Australia (Achenbach, Hensley, et al., 1990), Puerto Rico (Achenbach, Hensley, et al., 1990), Kenya (Weisz et al., 1993), and Greece (MacDonnald et al., 1995). Externalizing behaviors are consistently found more often among boys and internalizing behaviors more often among girls, at least in adolescence, across cultures (Weisz et al., 1987). Focus on Discovery 14.1 discusses the possible role of culture in the prevalence of these problem behaviors in children.

Table 14.1 Chapters Where Disorders Are Discussed That Occur in Both Children and Adults
Substance-related disorders: Chapter 10
Schizophrenia: Chapter 11
Aftermath of child sexual abuse: Chapter 13
Somatoform disorders: Chapter 6
Dissociative disorders: Chapter 6
Eating disorders: Chapter 9
Parasomnias: Abnormal behavioral or physiological events occurring in association with sleep—for example, nightmare disorder, sleep terror disorder, and sleepwalking disorder (not covered in this text).

Attention-Deficit/Hyperactivity Disorder

The term *hyperactive* is familiar to most people, especially parents and teachers. The child who is constantly in motion, tapping fingers, jiggling legs, poking others for no apparent reason, talking out of turn, and fidgeting is often called hyperactive. Often, these children also have difficulty concentrating on the task at hand for an appropriate period of time. When such problems are severe and persistent enough, these children may meet the criteria for diagnosis of **attention-deficit/hyperactivity disorder (ADHD)**. Recognizing the impact of ADHD on children and families, Congress recently created a National ADHD Awareness Day, with the first such day being on September 7, 2004.

Clinical Descriptions, Prevalence, and Prognosis of ADHD

What distinguishes the typical range of hyperactive behaviors from a diagnosable disorder? When these behaviors are extreme for a particular developmental period, persistent across different situations, and linked to significant impairments in functioning, the diagnosis of ADHD may be appropriate (NIH Consensus Statement, 1998). The ADHD diagnosis does not properly apply to children who are rambunctious, active, or slightly distractible, for in the early school years children are often so (Whalen, 1983). Using the label simply because a child is more lively and more difficult to control than a parent or teacher would like is a serious mistake. The diagnosis of ADHD is reserved for truly severe and persistent cases.

Children with ADHD seem to have particular difficulty controlling their activity in situations that call for sitting still, such as in the classroom or at mealtimes. When told to be quiet, they appear unable to stop moving or talking. They are disorganized, erratic, tactless, obstinate, and bossy. Their activities and movements seem haphazard. They quickly wear out their shoes and clothing, smash their toys, and exhaust their families and teachers.

Many children with ADHD have inordinate difficulty getting along with peers and establishing friendships (Hinshaw & Melnick, 1995; Whalen & Henker, 1985), perhaps

Focus on Discovery 14.1

The Role of Culture in Internalizing and Externalizing Behavior Problems

The values and mores of a culture may play a role in whether a certain pattern of child behavior develops or is considered a problem. One study found that in Thailand, children with internalizing behavior problems, such as fearfulness, were the ones most likely to be seen in clinics, whereas in the United States, those with externalizing behavior problems, such as aggressiveness and hyperactivity, were more commonly seen (Weisz et al., 1987). The researchers attributed these differences to the fact that Buddhism, which disapproves of and discourages aggression, is widely practiced in Thailand. They also cautioned that their results were based on assessment measures that were normed on U.S. samples and that additional work needed to be done to ensure that the assessment measures were valid for Thai children (see Chapter 13 for more on the issue of culture and assessment).

Findings from a recent follow-up study suggest that the behavior problems described in the same terms may not really be exactly the same across Thai and U.S. cultures (Weisz et al., 2003). The researchers compared specific behavior problems (e.g., somatic complaints, aggressive behavior) and broad domains (internalizing, externalizing) using U.S. and Thai assessment measures. The broad domains of internalizing and externalizing behaviors were found to be fairly comparable across cultures, but more specific categories within those domains were not. Among boys, somatic complaints were seen consistently across cultures, but shyness was seen less consistently. Among girls, shyness was seen consistently across cultures but verbal aggressive behavior was not.

In this more recent study, the researchers modified their conclusion from their 1987 study (Weisz et al., 2003). Specifically, they now conclude that Thai children exhibit more internalizing behavior problems than U.S. children, but only for those problems that are identified in *both* the U.S. and Thai assessment measures.

These studies point to the importance of studying psychopathology across cultures. It is dangerous to assume that the measures we develop to assess psychopathology in the United States will work equally well across cultures. As the investigators cited above point out, our theories about the causes of psychopathology need to be able to account for cultural variation in such factors as parenting practices, beliefs and values, and the ways in which parents report on their child's behavior problems. This remains an urgent and important challenge for our field.

Thai teenagers serving as novices in a Buddhist temple. Buddhist culture may contribute to the relatively low prevalence of externalizing disorders in Thailand. (Paul Chesley/Stone/Getty Images.)

---

because their behavior is often aggressive and generally annoying and intrusive. Although these children are usually friendly and talkative, they often miss subtle social cues, such as noticing when playmates are tiring of their constant jiggling. They also frequently misinterpret the wishes and intentions of their peers and make inadvertent social mistakes, such as reacting aggressively because they assume that a neutral action by a peer was meant to be aggressive. (Such cognitive misattributions are also found in some children with conduct disorder.)

A study involving observation of children playing tabletop football demonstrated that children with ADHD, particularly those who are also aggressive, have different social goals than other children. The aggressive ADHD children approached the game with sensation-seeking goals, such as making trouble, achieving domination, and showing off, whereas the other children were more likely to have the goal of playing fair (Melnick & Hinshaw, 1996).

Children with ADHD can know what the socially correct action is in hypothetical situations but be unable to translate this knowledge into appropriate behavior in real-life social interactions (Whalen & Henker, 1985, 1991). Children with ADHD are often singled out very quickly and rejected or neglected by their peers. For example, in a study of previously unacquainted boys at a summer camp, boys with ADHD who exhibited a number of externalizing behaviors, such as overt aggression and noncompliance, were regarded quite negatively by their peers during the first day of camp, and these impressions remained unchanged throughout the 6-week camp period (Erhardt & Hinshaw, 1994; Hinshaw et al., 1997).

About 15 to 30 percent of children with ADHD have a learning disability in math, reading, or spelling (Barkley, DuPaul, & McMurray, 1990; Casey, Rourke, & Del Dotto, 1996), and about half of ADHD children are placed in special educational programs because of their difficulty in adjusting to a typical classroom environment (Barkley et al., 1990).

Because the symptoms of ADHD are varied, DSM-IV-TR includes three subcategories:

1. Predominantly Inattentive type: Children whose problems are primarily those of poor attention.
2. Predominantly Hyperactive-Impulsive type: Children whose difficulties result primarily from hyperactive/impulsive behavior.
3. Combined type: Children who have both sets of problems.

Eric, the boy described at the beginning of the chapter, most likely would meet criteria for the predominantly inattentive type. The combined type comprises the majority of children with ADHD. These children are more likely to develop conduct problems and oppositional behavior, to be placed in special classes for behavior-disordered children, and to have difficulties interacting with their peers (Faraone et al., 1998). Children with attentional problems but with otherwise developmentally appropriate activity levels appear to have more difficulties with focused attention or speed of information processing (Barkley, Grodzinsky, & DuPaul, 1992), perhaps associated with problems involving the neurotransmitter dopamine and certain areas of the brain including the prefrontal cortex (Krause et al., 2003). Accumulating evidence suggests that it may be best to think of two separate disorders, one of inattention and one involving both inattention and hyperactive/impulsive behavior (Barkley, 1998; Milich, Balentine, & Lynam, 2001). However, most of the theory and research on ADHD does not make this distinction. Moreover, it is not clear if some of the observed differences between the combined type and predominantly inattentive type apply to girls with ADHD (Biederman & Faraone, 2004; Hinshaw, 2002; Hinshaw et al., 2002).

A difficult differential diagnosis is between ADHD and conduct disorder, which involves gross violation of social norms. An overlap of 30 to 90 percent between the two categories (Hinshaw, 1987) has caused some researchers to assert that these two types of externalizing disorders are actually one and the same. There are some differences, however. ADHD is associated more with off-task behavior in school, cognitive and achievement deficits, and a better long-term prognosis. Children with conduct disorder act out in school and elsewhere and are likely to be much more aggressive and to have antisocial parents. Their home life is also usually marked by family hostility and low socioeconomic status, and they are much more at risk for delinquency and substance abuse in adolescence (Faraone et al., 1997; Hinshaw, 1987; Jensen, Martin, & Cantwell, 1997).

When these two disorders occur in the same child, the worst features of each are manifest. Such children exhibit the most serious antisocial behavior, are most likely to be rejected by their peers, have the worst academic achievement, and have the poorest prognosis (Hinshaw & Lee, 2003). It has been suggested that children with ADHD and conduct disorder form a distinct category highly likely to progress to the adult psychopathic patterns of antisocial personality disorder (Frick & Ellis, 1999; Lynam, 1998). It may be that ADHD comes first, with the child's aggravating behavior eliciting hostile reactions from peers and adults; then the situation escalates with more extreme attacks and counterattacks, finally resulting in the aggressive behaviors that are characteristic of conduct disorder. Indeed, having ADHD is associated with an earlier age of onset of conduct disorder symptoms (Hinshaw, Lahey, & Hart, 1993).

Internalizing disorders, such as anxiety and depression, also frequently co-occur with ADHD. Recent estimates suggest that as many as 30 percent of children with ADHD may

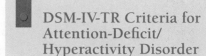

DSM-IV-TR Criteria for Attention-Deficit/ Hyperactivity Disorder

- Either A or B:
  A. Six or more manifestations of inattention present for at least 6 months to a maladaptive degree and greater than what would be expected, given person's developmental level, for example, careless mistakes, not listening well, not following instructions, easily distracted, forgetful in daily activities
  B. Six or more manifestations of hyperactivity-impulsivity present for at least 6 months to a maladaptive degree and greater than what would be expected, given person's developmental level, e.g., squirming in seat, running about inappropriately (in adults, restlessness), acting as if "driven by a motor," incessant talking
- Some of the above present before age 7
- Present in two or more settings, e.g., at home and at school or work
- Significant impairment in social, academic, or occupational functioning
- Not part of other disorders such as schizophrenia, an anxiety disorder, or a mood disorder

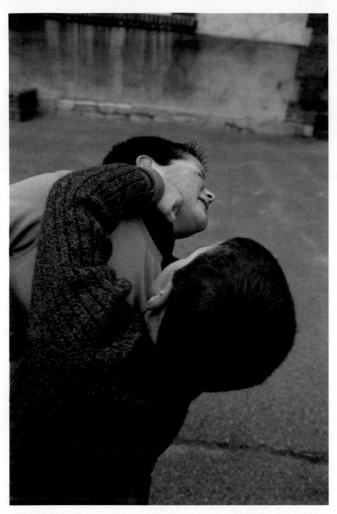

Aggression is not uncommon among boys with ADHD, and it contributes to them being rejected by peers. (Alamay Images.)

have comorbid internalizing disorders (e.g., Jensen et al., 1997; MTA Cooperative Group, 1999b).

The prevalence of ADHD has been difficult to establish because of varied definitions of the disorder over time and differences in the populations sampled. Estimates vary from 2 to 7 percent in the United States (August et al., 1996), New Zealand (Fergusson, Horwood, & Lynskey, 1993), and Germany (Esser, Schmidt, & Woerner, 1990), with somewhat higher rates found in India (Bhatia et al., 1991) and China (Leung et al., 1996). When similar criteria for ADHD are used across countries as diverse as the United States, Kenya, China, and Thailand, the prevalence rates are similar (Anderson, 1996); however, using the same criteria may not adequately capture cultural differences in ADHD (see Focus on Discovery 14.1). The consensus is that about 3 to 7 percent of school-age children worldwide currently have ADHD (DSM-IV-TR, 2000).

Much evidence indicates that ADHD is more common in boys than in girls, but exact figures depend on whether the sample is taken from clinic referrals or from the general population. Boys are more likely to be referred to clinics because of a higher likelihood of aggressive and antisocial behavior. Until recently, very few carefully controlled studies of girls with ADHD were conducted. Because so little research has been done with female samples, it is important to document the characteristics, correlates, comorbid disorders, and other social and cognitive deficits in a carefully selected sample of girls with ADHD. Two groups of researchers have recently conducted such studies (Biederman & Faraone, 2004; Hinshaw, 2002; Hinshaw et al., 2002). One research group examined a large and ethnically diverse sample of girls with and without ADHD and reported a number of key findings (Hinshaw et al., 2002):

- Girls with ADHD were more likely than other girls to have been adopted (see also Simmel et al., 2001).
- Similar to findings with male samples, girls with the combined type had more disruptive behavior symptoms than girls with the inattentive type.
- Girls with the combined type were more likely to have a comorbid diagnosis of conduct disorder or oppositional defiant disorder than girls without ADHD.
- Girls with ADHD were likely to be more anxious and depressed than were girls without ADHD.
- Girls with the combined type were viewed more negatively by peers than girls with the inattentive type and girls without ADHD; girls with the inattentive type were also viewed more negatively than girls without ADHD.
- Girls with ADHD exhibited a number of neuropsychological deficits, particularly in executive functioning (e.g., planning, solving problems), compared with girls without ADHD, replicating other findings (Castellanos et al., 2000).

At one time it was thought that ADHD simply went away by adolescence. However, this belief has been challenged by numerous longitudinal studies (Barkley et al., 2002; Biederman et al., 1996; Claude & Firestone, 1995; Weiss & Hechtman, 1993). Although some children show reduced severity of symptoms in adolescence (Hart et al., 1995), 65 to 80 percent of children with ADHD still meet criteria for the disorder in adolescence. Table 14.2 provides a catalogue of behaviors that are found more often among adolescents with ADHD than among adolescents without it. In addition, adolescents with ADHD are more likely to drop out of high school and develop antisocial behavior than are their peers. In adulthood, most are employed and financially independent, but some studies have found these individuals are generally at a lower socioeconomic level and change jobs more

Table 14.2 Behaviors in Adolescents with and without ADHD

Behavior	Percentage of Adolescents Who Show this Behavior	
	with ADHD	without ADHD
Blurts out answers	65.0	10.6
Distracted easily	82.1	15.2
Doesn't complete tasks before moving to another	77.2	16.7
Doesn't sustain attention	79.7	16.7
Doesn't follow instructions	83.7	12.1
Doesn't listen to others well	80.5	15.2
Engages in physically dangerous activities	37.4	3.0
Fidgets	73.2	10.6
Finds it hard to play quietly	39.8	7.6
Gets out of seat often	60.2	3.0
Interrupts others	65.9	10.6
Loses things needed for tasks	62.6	12.1
Talks a lot	43.9	6.1

Source: Adapted from Barkley et al., 1990.

frequently than is typical (Mannuzza et al., 1991; Weiss & Hechtman, 1993). A recent study on the persistence of ADHD into adulthood demonstrates quite dramatically that the rates of ADHD vary depending on the method of assessment (Barkley et al., 2002). Specifically, when ADHD in adulthood was assessed by self-reports of adults who had ADHD as children, only about 10 percent met criteria for ADHD. However, when ADHD was assessed by the parents of these same adults who had had ADHD as children, more than half met criteria for ADHD. Whose assessments are correct? This question is impossible to answer. It may be the case that the adults with ADHD were less aware of their symptoms, or it could be that the parents' reports were influenced by their memories of their children. It was noteworthy that the parents' ratings of ADHD were related to all eight measures of functioning included in the study (e.g., employer ratings, education level, number of friends), whereas the adult's self-reports were related only to two of these measures.

Etiology of ADHD

The search for causes of ADHD is complicated by the heterogeneity of children given this diagnosis; any factor found to be associated with the syndrome is perhaps linked with only some of those judged to have ADHD.

Genetic Factors   Research suggests that a genetic predisposition toward ADHD may play a role. When parents have ADHD, half of their children are likely to have the disorder (Biederman et al., 1995). Adoption studies (e.g., Sprich et al., 2000) and numerous large-scale twin studies (e.g., Levy et al., 1997; Sherman, Iacono, & McGue, 1997) indicate a genetic component to ADHD, with heritability estimates as high as 70 to 80 percent (Tannock, 1998). Molecular genetics studies that seek to identify genes linked to ADHD are underway. Some of the more promising findings involve genes associated with the neurotransmitter dopamine. Specifically, two different dopamine genes have been implicated in ADHD: a dopamine receptor gene called DRD4 (e.g., Faraone et al., 2001) and a dopamine transporter gene called DAT1 (Krause et al., 2003; Waldman et al., 1998). Even with these promising findings, most investigators agree that a single gene will not ultimately account for ADHD. Rather, several genes interacting with environmental factors will provide the most complete picture of the cause of ADHD.

Neurobiological Factors   Exactly what is inherited is as yet unknown, but recent studies suggest that brain function and structure differ in children with and without ADHD. Studies have documented that the frontal lobes of children with ADHD are underresponsive to stimulation (Rubia et al., 1999; Tannock, 1998), and cerebral blood flow is reduced (Sieg et al., 1995). Moreover, parts of the brains (frontal lobes, caudate nucleus, globus pallidus) of children with ADHD are smaller than normal (Castellanos et al., 1996; Filipek et al., 1997; Hynd et al., 1993). Evidence from other research shows that children with ADHD perform poorly on neuropsychological tests of frontal lobe functioning (such as inhibiting behavioral responses), providing further support for the theory that a basic deficit in this part of the brain may be related to the disorder (Barkley, 1997; Nigg, 1999, 2001; Tannock, 1998).

Perinatal and Prenatal Factors   Other neurobiological risk factors for ADHD include a number of perinatal and prenatal complications. Low birth weight, for example, is a quite specific predictor of the development of ADHD (e.g., Breslau et al., 1996; Whitaker et al., 1997). However, the impact of low birth weight on later symptoms of ADHD can be mitigated by greater maternal warmth (Tully et al., 2004). Other complications associated with childbirth, as well as mothers' use of substances such as tobacco (discussed below) and alcohol, are also predictive of ADHD symptoms (Tannock, 1998).

Environmental Toxins   Early theories of ADHD that were quite popular in the 1970s involved the role of environmental toxins in the development of hyperactivity. One theory of hyperactivity enjoyed much attention in the popular press for many years (Feingold, 1973). This researcher proposed that food additives upset the central nervous systems of hyperactive children, and he prescribed a diet free of them. However, well-controlled studies of the so-called Feingold diet have found that very few ADHD children respond positively to it (Goyette & Conners, 1977). Similarly, the popular view that refined sugar can cause ADHD has not been supported by careful research (Wolraich, Wilson, & White, 1995).

Although some evidence suggests that lead poisoning may be associated to a small degree with symptoms of hyperactivity and attentional problems (Thompson et al., 1989), most children with lead poisoning do not develop ADHD, and most children with ADHD do not show elevated levels of lead in the blood.

Nicotine—specifically, maternal smoking—is an environmental toxin that may play a role in the development of ADHD. One study found that 22 percent of mothers of children with ADHD reported smoking a pack of cigarettes per day during pregnancy, compared with 8 percent of mothers whose children did not develop ADHD (Milberger et al., 1996). This effect remained even after controlling for maternal depression and alcohol use (Chabrol et al., 1997). A recent twin study found that maternal smoking predicted ADHD symptoms even after controlling for genetic influences and other environmental risk factors (Thapar et al., 2003). Finally, a review of 24 studies examining the association between maternal smoking and ADHD found that exposure to tobacco in utero was associated with ADHD symptoms (Linnet et al., 2003). Several animal studies conducted since the 1980s indicate that chronic exposure to nicotine increases dopamine release in the brain and causes hyperactivity (e.g., Fung & Lau, 1989; Vaglenova et al., 2004). Furthermore, withdrawal from nicotine is associated with decreases in dopamine release in the brain and causes irritability. On the basis of these data, researchers hypothesize that maternal smoking can affect the dopaminergic system of the developing fetus, resulting in behavioral disinhibition and ADHD. It is important to note that all of the evidence in humans thus far shows a correlation between maternal smoking and ADHD, not a causal relationship.

Psychological Factors in ADHD   Although research results support neurological and genetic factors more than psychological factors in the etiology of ADHD, the parent–child relationship interacts with these neurobiological factors in a complex way to contribute to

Children born to mothers who smoked cigarettes during pregnancy have an increased risk for ADHD. (Richard Phelps/Photo Researchers.)

ADHD symptom expression (Hinshaw et al., 1997). Just as parents of children with ADHD may give them more commands and have negative interactions with them (Anderson, Hinshaw, & Simmel, 1994; Heller et al., 1996), so these children have been found to be less compliant and more negative in interactions with their parents (Barkley, Karlsson, & Pollard, 1985; Tallmadge & Barkley, 1983). Certainly, it must be difficult to parent a child who is impulsive, aggressive, noncompliant, and unable to follow instructions. As we will discuss shortly, stimulant medication has been shown to reduce hyperactivity and increase compliance in some ADHD children. Significantly, when such medication is used, either alone or in combination with behavioral treatment, the parents' commands, negative behavior, and ineffective parenting also decrease (Barkeley, 1990; Wells et al., 2000), suggesting that the child's behavior has at least some negative effect on the parents' behavior.

It is also important to consider a parent's own history of ADHD. As noted above, there appears to be a substantial genetic component to ADHD. Thus, it is not surprising that many parents of ADHD children have ADHD themselves. In one study that examined couples' parenting practices with their ADHD children, fathers who had a diagnosis of ADHD were less effective parents, suggesting that parental psychopathology may make parenting all the more difficult (Arnold, O'Leary, & Edwards, 1997). Family characteristics thus may well contribute to maintaining or exacerbating the symptoms and consequences of ADHD; however, there is little evidence to suggest that families actually cause ADHD (Johnston & Marsh, 2001).

Treatment of ADHD

ADHD is typically treated with medication and with behavioral therapies based on operant conditioning.

Stimulant Medications   Stimulant medications, in particular methylphenidate, or Ritalin, have been prescribed for ADHD since the early 1960s. Other medications approved by the FDA to treat ADHD include Adderall, Concerta, and Strattera; however, Ritalin is the most commonly prescribed medication. During the years 1996–2000, 11 million prescriptions of Ritalin were written each year in the United States, and 80 percent of them were for children diagnosed with ADHD (Drug Enforcement Agency, 2000). The prescription of these medications has sometimes continued into adolescence and adulthood in light of the accumulating evidence that the symptoms of ADHD do not usually disappear with the passage of time.

The drugs used to treat ADHD reduce disruptive behavior and improve ability to concentrate. Numerous controlled studies comparing stimulants with placebos in double-blind designs have shown short-term improvements in concentration, goal-directed activity, classroom behavior, and social interactions with parents, teachers, and peers and reductions in aggressiveness and impulsivity in about 75 percent of ADHD children (Spencer et al., 1996; Swanson et al., 1995).

The best designed randomized controlled clinical trial of treatments for ADHD was the Multimodal Treatment of Children with ADHD (MTA) study. Conducted at six different sites for 14 months with nearly 600 children with ADHD, the study compared standard community-based care and three other treatments: (1) medication alone, (2) medication plus intensive behavioral treatment, involving both parents and teachers, and (3) behavioral treatment alone. Across the 14-month period, children receiving medication alone had fewer ADHD symptoms than children receiving intensive behavioral treatment alone. The combined treatment was slightly superior to the medication alone and had the advantage of not requiring as high a dosage of Ritalin to reduce ADHD symptoms. In addition, the combined treatment yielded improved functioning in areas such as social skills more than did the medication alone. The medication alone and the combined treatment were superior to community-based care, though the behavioral treatment alone was not (MTA Cooperative Group, 1999a,b).

Ritalin is a commonly prescribed and effective drug treatment for ADHD. (Allan Tannenbaum/The Image Works.)

In secondary analyses undertaken to clarify the key findings from the MTA study, researchers reported that the behavioral treatment alone was superior to community-based care at three of the six sites, but not at the other three (Swanson et al., 2001). In addition, further comparisons of the combined treatment with treatment by medication alone suggested that 20 percent more children who received the combined treatment achieved an excellent treatment response. The combined treatment was also associated with fewer behavioral problems at school, and additional analyses suggest that this effect may be linked to a decrease in negative and ineffective parenting (Hinshaw et al., 2000). Finally, analyses that examined treatment effects by ethnicity indicated that white, African American, and Latino children benefited equally from treatment, particularly from the combined treatment (Arnold et al., 2003).

Despite the promising findings on the efficacy of stimulant medications for ADHD, other research indicates that these drugs may not improve academic achievement over the long haul (Weiss & Hechtman, 1993; Whalen & Henker, 1991). Further, stimulant medication can have side effects, such as transient loss of appetite and sleep problems. However, concerns that the use of stimulant medications among children would increase the risk of drug abuse have not been substantiated by research (see Focus on Discovery 14.2). For example, a prospective study of nearly 150 children with ADHD found that those treated with Ritalin were not at any greater risk of abusing or using drugs than were children not treated with Ritalin (Barkley et al., 2003).

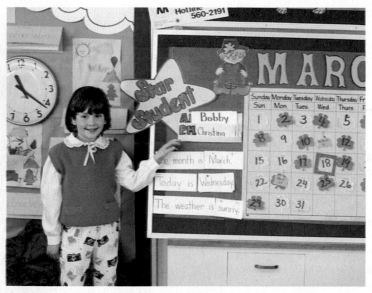

Point systems and star charts, which are common in classrooms, are particularly useful in the treatment of ADHD. (Lew Merrim/Photo Researchers.)

Psychological Treatment   Other than medication, the most promising treatments for ADHD involve parent training and changes in classroom management based on operant-conditioning principles. These programs have demonstrated at least short-term success in improving both social and academic behavior. In these treatments, children's behavior is monitored at home and in school, and they are reinforced for behaving appropriately—for example, for remaining in their seats and working on assignments. Point systems and star charts are typical components of these programs. Children earn points or stars for behaving in certain ways; the children can then spend their earnings for rewards. The focus of these operant programs is on improving academic work, completing household tasks, or learning specific social skills, rather than on reducing signs of hyperactivity, such as running around and jiggling. Accumulating evidence supports the efficacy of parent-training programs, although it is unclear whether they improve children's behavior beyond the effects of treatment with medication (Abikoff & Hechtman, 1996; Anastopoulos et al., 1993; MTA Cooperative Group, 1999a,b).

School interventions for children with ADHD include training teachers to understand the unique needs of these children and to apply operant techniques in the classroom (Welsh et al., 1997), providing peer tutoring in academic skills (DuPaul & Henningson, 1993), and having teachers provide daily reports to parents about in-school behavior, which are followed up with rewards and punishments at home (Kelley, 1990). Research has demonstrated that certain classroom structures can help children with ADHD. Ideally, teachers vary the presentation format and materials used for tasks, keep assignments brief and provide immediate feedback on whether they have been done correctly, have an enthusiastic and task-focused style, provide breaks for physical exercise, use computer-assisted drill programs, and schedule academic work during the morning hours. Such environmental changes are designed to accommodate the limitations imposed by this disorder rather than to change the disorder itself.

Finally, findings from the just-mentioned MTA study indicate that intensive behavioral therapies can be very helpful to children with ADHD. In that study, some of the children

Focus on Discovery 14.2

Controversies in the Diagnosis and Treatment of Children with Psychopathology

In recent years, the number of children diagnosed with psychological disorders has risen, as has the number of children taking psychoactive medications. These increases raise several questions:

Has there truly been an increase in the number of children with psychological disorders?

Have our diagnostic system and assessment measures improved enough to identify children once overlooked?

Are children being misdiagnosed and then treated for problems they do not have?

Are medications safe for children?

Will medication use lead to later drug use or abuse among children?

Here we briefly discuss some of the recent controversies and current evidence in some of these areas.

Bipolar Disorder in Children

For years, professionals thought bipolar disorders were very rare or even nonexistent among children. Today, however, professionals recognize bipolar disorders in children, and though they are still rare, they can be serious. One of the difficult diagnostic issues facing mental health professionals is distinguishing bipolar disorders from ADHD. Agitated behavior can be a sign of both, and only through careful and thorough assessments can the distinction be made. An additional controversy is whether the diagnostic criteria for bipolar disorders in children are the same as the criteria for bipolar disorders in adults. Some argue that the criteria for children should include explosive but brief outbursts of emotion and behavioral dysregulation (e.g., Biederman et al., 2000), but these are fundamentally different than the current DSM-IV-TR criteria for bipolar I disorder (see p. 233 in Chapter 8). Yet, the current DSM criteria apply mainly to adults and may not do a good job of characterizing bipolar disorders, particularly bipolar I disorder among children. Additional research on bipolar disorders in children is clearly needed to sort through these issues.

Antidepressant Medications

In 2002, physicians wrote close to 11 million prescriptions for antidepressant medications for children and adolescents (*New York Times*, September 15, 2004). In the fall of 2004, the Federal Drug Administration (FDA) held a series of hearings on the safety of treating children and adolescents with antidepressant medications. These hearings were prompted by research reports, one of which was kept quiet within the FDA, suggesting that children and adolescents with depression who were taking antidepressant medication were more likely to become suicidal than children who were not taking these medications. Earlier in 2004, Great Britain had prohibited the use of all antidepressants for the treatment of adolescent depression. This decision was based on a review of the research suggesting that the risk of suicide was greater for adolescents taking these medications than adolescents not taking them.

Concerns over the safety of the medications were joined by concerns that these medications were not all that effective in treating depression among children and adolescents. Findings from the TADS (Treatment of Adolescent Depression Study) study, perhaps the largest randomized controlled clinical trial of antidepressant treatment for adolescents to date, were reported in August 2004 (March et al., 2004). In this study, the most effective treatment was a combination of Prozac and cognitive behavioral therapy (CBT). Prozac alone was slightly better than CBT alone. However, the authors also reported that six adolescents taking Prozac attempted suicide, whereas only one receiving CBT attempted suicide. These seven were from a sample of over 400 and thus represented around 1.5 percent of the sample. The participants in the study were randomly assigned to treatment conditions, so it is less likely that the adolescents taking Prozac were more seriously ill or suicidal than the ones receiving CBT.

Antidepressants can take as long as 3–4 weeks to start working (see Chapter 8), and one analysis of adolescent suicide attempts and antidepressant use found that the risk for suicide was highest in the first 3–4 weeks of treatment. Thus, it could be the case that the medications did not have sufficient time to begin working in the adolescents who attempted suicide. It may also be true that the combined treatment in the TADS study was most effective because CBT began working earlier in the course of treatment. These sorts of issues will need to be sorted out in future studies.

At the end of the FDA hearings, the panel did not decide to withdraw authorization for physicians to prescribe antidepressants for children and adolescents. Instead, they recommended a "black box warning" to accompany information sent to physicians on their use with adolescents. This is the strongest safety warning the FDA can issue with medications. Additional research will need to be conducted to more fully sort out both the efficacy and safety of these medications with children and adolescents.

Stimulant Medications

Over the past two decades, the number of children taking stimulant medications such as Ritalin has risen dramatically (e.g., Angold et al., 2000). Does the use of stimulant medications lead to increases in illicit drug use among children? Two recent prospective, longitudinal studies suggest that the answer to this question is no. In one study, two groups of children with ADHD were studied for 13 years (Barkley et al., 2003). One group of children had been treated with stimulant medication for 3 1/2 years on average and the other group had never received stimulant medication. Consistent with a number of other studies, at follow-up in young adulthood, those who had taken stimulant medication were not more likely to have used illicit drugs than those who had not been treated with stimulant medication, with one exception—those who had taken stimulant medication were at great risk for having tried cocaine. However, after controlling for the severity of conduct disorder symptoms, the relationship between stimulant medication use and trying cocaine disappeared. This suggests that having severe conduct disorder symptoms accounts for the link between stimulant medication and trying cocaine, not the use of stimulant medication per se.

The second study followed into adulthood a group of children with reading disorders who had been treated with stimulant medications for 12 to 18 weeks and compared them to a group of children with reading disorders who had not received stimulant medication. Sixteen years after the medication treatment, the two groups did not differ in their use of illicit drugs (Mannuzza, Klein, & Moulton, 2003).

Autism: Diagnosis and Causes

The number of cases of autism has increased dramatically over the past 10 years. For example, the number of families seeking services for their children with autism tripled between 1987 and 1998 (*New York Times*, January 26, 2004). Why has there been such an increase? Are there that many more children with autism, or have mental health professionals gotten better at making a diagnosis? Autism wasn't formally recognized in the DSM until 1980. With the availability of formalized diagnostic criteria, mental health professionals are likely doing a better job now of identifying autism. In addition, the diagnostic criteria have broadened quite a bit between the publication of DSM-III in 1980 and the release of DSM-IV in 1994. More children meet the criteria for a diagnosis of

autism today under the broader criteria of DSM-IV than they did under the more narrow criteria of DSM-III (Gernsbacher, Dawson, & Goldsmith, 2005). Additionally, there is greater public awareness of autism, and this may spur families to seek out mental health professionals for a formal psychological assessment. Some children with autism may have been diagnosed with mental retardation in years past; it is likely that more children are now being correctly diagnosed. Also, the delay in or lack of language acquisition has become a widely recognized warning sign among parents and mental health professionals that autism may be a consideration.

With the increase in autism has come an increase in parents and families advocating for their children. Parents have been particularly worried that autism may be caused by vaccines routinely given to toddlers. The MMR vaccine (for measles, mumps, and rubella) is given to children right around the age when autism signs and symptoms begin to appear. A related concern is that the product used to preserve these vaccines, a substance called thimerosal that contains mercury, may be responsible for autism. To date, however, there is not much evidence to link autism with either the MMR vaccine or thimerosal. Vaccines have not been stored in thimerosal for the last several years, and even those vaccines that were stored in thimerosal contained very small amounts of mercury (CDC Web site). In May 2004, the Institute of Medicine published the results of their comprehensive review of the available evidence on the link between MMR and autistic disorder. This report concluded that the MMR vaccines are not responsible for autism (Institute of Medicine, 2004).

participated in an intensive eight-week summer program that included a number of validated behavioral treatments. At the end of the summer program, children receiving the combined treatment had very few significant improvements over children receiving the intensive behavioral treatment alone (L. E. Arnold et al., 2003; Pelham et al., 2000). This finding suggests that intensive behavioral therapy may be as effective as Ritalin combined with a less intensive behavioral therapy.

Check Your Knowledge 14.1

True or false?
1. The two broad domains of childhood psychopathology are internalizing disorders and externalizing disorders.
2. Girls with the combined type of ADHD have more severe problems than girls with the predominantly inattentive type, similar to findings with boys.
3. Dopamine has been investigated in ADHD, particularly genes for the DRD4 receptors.
4. The most effective treatment for ADHD is behavioral treatment without medication.

Conduct Disorder

Conduct disorder is another externalizing disorder. The DSM-IV-TR definition of conduct disorder focuses on behaviors that violate the basic rights of others and that violate major societal norms. Nearly all such behavior is also illegal. The behaviors considered symptomatic of conduct disorder must be frequent and severe enough to go beyond the mischief and pranks common among children and adolescents. These behaviors include aggression and cruelty toward people or animals, damaging property, lying, and stealing. Often the behavior is marked by callousness, viciousness, and lack of remorse, making conduct disorder one of the historical criteria for adult antisocial personality disorder (see p. 399).

A related but less well understood externalizing disorder in the DSM-IV-TR is **oppositional defiant disorder** (ODD). There is some debate as to whether ODD is distinct from conduct disorder, a precursor to it, or an earlier and milder manifestation of it (Hinshaw & Lee, 2003; Lahey, McBurnett, & Loeber, 2000). ODD is diagnosed if a child does not meet the criteria for conduct disorder—most especially, extreme physical aggressiveness—but exhibits such behaviors as losing his or her temper, arguing with adults, repeatedly refusing to comply with requests from adults, deliberately doing things to annoy others, and being angry, spiteful, touchy, or vindictive. The DSM also mentions that such children, most of them boys, seldom see their conflicts with others as their own fault; they justify their oppositional behavior by claiming that unreasonable demands are being placed on them.

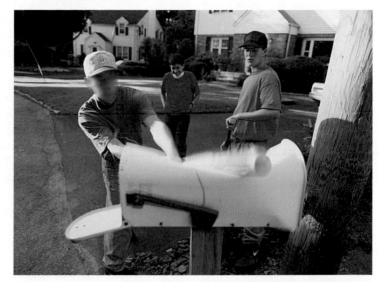

Commonly comorbid with ODD are ADHD, learning disorders, and communication disorders (p. 399), but ODD is different from ADHD in that the defiant behavior is not thought to arise from attentional deficits or sheer impulsiveness. One manifestation of difference is that ODD children are more deliberate in their unruly behavior than ADHD children. Although conduct disorder is three to four times more common among boys than among girls, research suggests that boys are only slightly more likely to have ODD, and some studies find no difference in prevalence rates for ODD between boys and girls (Loeber et al., 2000). Because of ODD's somewhat uncertain status, we will focus here on the more serious diagnosis of conduct disorder.

Conduct disorder is diagnosed among those who are aggressive, steal, lie, and vandalize property. (Ken Lax/Photo Researchers.)

Clinical Description, Prevalence, and Prognosis of Conduct Disorder

Perhaps more than any other childhood disorder, conduct disorder is defined by the impact of the child's behavior on people and surroundings. Schools, parents, peers, and the criminal justice system usually determine which externalizing behaviors constitute unacceptable conduct. Preadolescents and adolescents are often identified as conduct problems by legal authorities, in which case they might be considered juvenile delinquents—a legal, not a psychological, term.

Many children with conduct disorder display other problems as well. Substance abuse also commonly co-occurs with conduct disorder. The Pittsburgh Youth Study, a longitudinal investigation of conduct disorder in boys, found a strong association between substance use and delinquent acts (van Kammen, Loeber, & Stouthamer-Loeber, 1991). For example, among seventh graders who reported having tried marijuana, more than 30 percent had attacked someone with a weapon and 43 percent admitted breaking and entering; fewer than 5 percent of children who reported no substance use had committed these acts. Some research suggests that conduct disorder precedes substance use problems, but other findings suggest that conduct disorder and substance use occur concomitantly, with the two conditions exacerbating one another (Loeber et al., 2000). Further, some evidence indicates that comorbid conduct disorder and substance use portends a more severe outcome for boys than it does for girls (Whitmore et al., 1997).

Anxiety and depression are common among children with conduct disorder, with comorbidity estimates varying from 15 to 45 percent (Loeber & Keenan, 1994; Loeber et al., 2000). Girls with conduct disorder may be at higher risk for developing comorbid

DSM-IV-TR Criteria for Conduct Disorder

- Repetitive and persistent behavior pattern that violates the basic rights of others or conventional social norms as manifested by the presence of three or more of the following in the previous 12 months and at least one of them in the previous six months:
  A. Aggression to people and animals, e.g., bullying, initiating physical fights, physically cruel to people or animals, forcing someone into sexual activity
  B. Destruction of property, e.g., fire-setting, vandalism
  C. Deceitfulness or theft, e.g., breaking into another's house or car, conning, shoplifting
  D. Serious violation of rules, e.g., staying out at night before age 13 in defiance of parental rules, truancy before age 13
- Significant impairment in social, academic, or occupational functioning
- If person older than 18, criteria not met for antisocial personality disorder

disorders, including anxiety, depression, substance abuse, and ADHD, than are boys with conduct disorder (Loeber & Keenan, 1994).

A review of epidemiological studies indicates that conduct disorder is fairly common, with prevalence rates ranging from 4 to 16 percent for boys and 1.2 to 9 percent for girls (Loeber et al., 2000). As shown in Figure 14.1, both the incidence and the prevalence of serious lawbreaking peak sharply at around age 17 and drop precipitously in young adulthood (Moffitt, 1993). Not all the criminal acts represented in Figure 14.1 are marked by the viciousness and callousness that are often a part of conduct disorder, but the figure illustrates the problem of antisocial behavior in children and adolescents.

Moffitt (1993) has theorized that two different courses of conduct problems should be distinguished. Some individuals seem to show a "life-course-persistent" pattern of antisocial behavior, beginning to show conduct problems by age three and continuing to commit serious transgressions into adulthood. Others are "adolescence-limited"—they have typical childhoods, engage in high levels of antisocial behavior during adolescence, and return to nonproblematic lifestyles in adulthood. Moffitt proposed that the adolescence-limited form of antisocial behavior is the result of a maturity gap between the adolescent's physical maturation and his or her opportunity to assume adult responsibilities and obtain the rewards usually accorded such behavior.

There is some evidence supporting this distinction. For example, children with the life-course-persistent form of conduct disorder do indeed show an early onset of antisocial behavior that persists through adolescence, and these children have a number of other problems, such as academic underachievement, neuropsychological deficits, and comorbid ADHD (Moffitt & Caspi, 2001). Other evidence supports the notion that children with the life-course-persistent type have more severe neuropsychological deficits and family psychopathology, and these findings have been replicated across cultures (Hinshaw & Lee, 2003).

The original sample from which Moffitt and colleagues made the life-course-persistent and adolescent-limited distinction has now been followed into early adulthood (age 26). Those who were classified as life-course-persistent continue to have the most severe problems, including psychopathology, lower levels of education, partner and child abuse, and violent behavior. However, those classified as adolescent-limited, who were expected to "grow out" of their aggressive and antisocial behavior, have apparently not done so. The participants now in their mid 20s continue to have troubles with substance abuse and dependence, impulsivity, crime, and overall mental health (Moffitt et al., 2002). Additional follow-ups of this sample will help us learn whether or not these maladaptive patterns get better toward the later 20s or early 30s.

The prognosis for children diagnosed as having conduct disorder is mixed. Conduct disorder in childhood does not inevitably lead to antisocial behavior in adulthood, though it certainly is a predisposing factor. For example, a longitudinal study indicated that although about half of boys with conduct disorder did not fully meet the criteria for the diagnosis at a later assessment (1 to 4 years later), almost all of them continued to demonstrate some conduct problems (Lahey et al., 1995).

The ability to identify which youths are most likely to persist in their antisocial behavior would be important. Research shows that most boys who are very aggressive at an early age, including but not restricted to those with conduct disorder, do not persist in this aggressive behavior into and beyond adolescence (Moffitt et al., 2002; Nagin & Tremblay, 1999). One study found that boys with conduct disorder were much more likely to persist in their antisocial behavior if they had a parent with antisocial personality disorder or if they had low verbal intelligence (Lahey et al., 1995). Boys with higher verbal IQs and no antisocial parent apparently had a more transient form of the disorder. In this study, other factors, including socioeconomic status and ethnicity, did not predict which boys would continue to show conduct disorder over time. Other research, however, suggests that the interaction of individual factors, such as temperament,

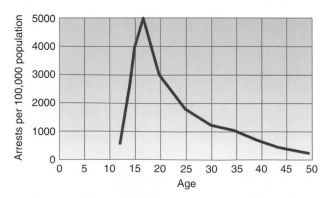

Figure 14.1 Arrest rates across ages for the crimes of homicide, forcible rape, robbery, aggravated assault, and auto theft. (From "Criminal Career Research: Its Value for Criminology," by A. Blumstein, J. Cohen, and D. P. Farrington, 1988. *Criminology*, *26*, p. 11. Copyright © 1988 by the American Society of Criminology. Adapted by permission.)

parent psychopathology, and dysfunctional parent–child interactions, with sociocultural factors, such as poverty and low social support, can increase the likelihood of early and persistent aggressive behavior (Campbell, 2002; DeKlyen & Speltz, 2001; Shaw, Bell, & Gilliom, 2000; Shaw et al., 2001).

Etiology of Conduct Disorder

Proposals for risk factors in the etiology of conduct disorder have included neurobiological factors, behavioral and cognitive factors, and sociocultural factors. A good deal of research has highlighted specific factors that increase the risk for conduct disorder and for antisocial/aggressive behavior, including parental psychopathology, parenting practices, and peer influences. It seems clear that multiple factors are involved in the etiology of conduct disorder, including genetic, neurobiological, psychological, and social factors that interact in a complex manner (Figure 14.2). A recent review concluded that the evidence favors an etiology

Children with the life-course-persistent type of conduct disorder continue to have trouble with the law into their mid 20s and perhaps even longer. (The Image Works.)

that includes heritable temperamental characteristics that interact with other neurobiological difficulties (e.g., neuropsychological deficits) as well as with a whole host of environmental factors (e.g., parenting, school performance, peer influences) (Hinshaw & Lee, 2003).

Genetic Factors The evidence for genetic influences in conduct disorder is mixed, although heritability likely plays a part. For example, a study of over 3,000 twin pairs indicated only modest genetic influence on childhood antisocial behavior; family-environment influences were more significant (Lyons et al., 1995). However, a study of over 2,600 twin pairs in Australia found a substantial genetic influence and almost no family-environment influence for childhood symptoms of conduct disorder (Slutske et al., 1997). The authors of the latter study point out that differences in the samples may have accounted for the different findings.

To date, three large-scale adoption studies, in Sweden, Denmark, and the United States, have been conducted, but two of them focused on the heritability of criminal behavior rather than conduct disorder (Simonoff, 2001). As with most traits, these studies indicate

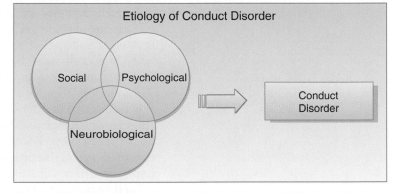

Figure 14.2 Neurobiological, psychological, and social factors all play a role in conduct disorder.

that criminal and aggressive behavior is accounted for by both genetic and environmental factors. Interestingly, despite different prevalence rates for boys and girls, the evidence favoring genetic and environmental contributions to conduct disorder and antisocial behavior does not differ between boys and girls.

Distinguishing types of conduct problems may help to clarify findings on the heritability of conduct disorder. Evidence from twin studies indicates that aggressive behavior (e.g., cruelty to animals, fighting, destroying property) is clearly heritable, whereas other delinquent behavior (e.g., stealing, running away, truancy) may not be (Edelbrock et al., 1995). Other evidence suggests that the time when antisocial and aggressive behavior problems begin is related to heritability. For example, aggressive and antisocial behaviors that begin in childhood, as in the case of Moffitt's life-course-persistent type, are more heritable than similar behaviors that begin in adolescence (Taylor, Iacono, & McGue, 2000).

A recent elegant study examined the interaction between genetic and environmental factors in predicting later adult antisocial behavior (Caspi et al., 2002). It examined the MAOA gene, which is located on the X chromosome and releases an MAO enzyme, which metabolizes a number of neurotransmitters, including dopamine, serotonin, and norepinephrine. This gene varies in its activity, with some people having high MAOA activity and others having low MAOA activity. Using a large sample of over 1,000 children from Dunedin, New Zealand (the same sample that was the basis for Moffitt's characterization of the life-course-persistent and adolescent-limited types of conduct disorder), the researchers measured MAOA activity and assessed the extent to which the children had been maltreated. Being maltreated as a child was not enough to predict later conduct disorder, nor was the presence of low MAOA activity. Rather, those children who were both maltreated and had low MAOA activity were more likely to develop conduct disorder than either children who were maltreated but had high MAO activity or children who were not maltreated but had low MAOA activity. Thus, both environment and genes mattered. A study of over 2,000 twins found the same thing: that being maltreated was linked to later antisocial behavior only via genetics (Jaffee et al., 2004).

Neurobiological Factors   Neuropsychological deficits, as suggested above, have been implicated in the childhood profiles of children with conduct disorder (Lynam & Henry, 2001; Moffitt, Lynam, & Sylva, 1994). These deficits include poor verbal skills, difficulty with executive functioning (the ability to anticipate, plan, use self-control, and solve problems), and problems with memory. In addition, children who develop conduct disorder at an earlier age (i.e., life-course-persistent type) have an IQ score of one standard deviation below age-matched peers without conduct disorder, and this IQ deficit is apparently not attributable to lower socioeconomic status, race, or school failure (Lynam, Moffitt, & Stouthamer-Loeber, 1993; Moffitt & Silva, 1988).

Psychological Factors   An important part of typical child development is the growth of moral awareness—the acquisition of a sense of what is right and wrong and the ability, even desire, to abide by rules and norms. Most people refrain from hurting others not only because it is illegal but because it would make them feel guilty to do otherwise. Children with conduct disorder, like psychopathic adults (see Chapter 12), seem to be deficient in this moral awareness, lacking remorse for their wrongdoing (Cimbora & McIntosh, 2003).

Behavioral theories that look to both modeling and operant conditioning provide useful explanations of the development and maintenance of conduct problems. For example, children who are physically abused by parents are likely to be aggressive when they grow up (Coie & Dodge, 1998). Children may also imitate aggressive acts seen elsewhere, such as on television (Huesmann & Miller, 1994). Since aggression is often an effective, albeit unpleasant, means of achieving a goal, it is likely to be reinforced. Thus, aggressive behavior is likely to be maintained.

This kind of social mimicry may at least partially explain the dramatic surge in delinquent behavior in adolescents who had not previously shown conduct problems. Perhaps these adolescents imitate the behavior of persistently antisocial peers who are seen as enjoying high-status possessions and sexual opportunities (Moffitt, 1993).

In addition, parenting characteristics such as harsh and inconsistent discipline and lack of monitoring are consistently associated with antisocial behavior in children. Perhaps children who do not experience negative consequences for early misbehavior later develop more serious conduct problems (Coie & Dodge, 1998).

A social-cognitive perspective on aggressive behavior (and, by extension, conduct disorder) comes from the work of Kenneth Dodge and associates. In one of his early studies (Dodge & Frame, 1982), Dodge found that the cognitive processes of aggressive children had a particular bias; these children interpreted ambiguous acts, such as being bumped in line, as evidence of hostile intent. Such perceptions may lead these children to retaliate aggressively for actions that may not have been intended as provocative. This can create a vicious cycle: their peers, remembering these aggressive behaviors, may tend to be aggressive more often against them, further angering the already aggressive children (see Figure 14.3). Dodge has constructed a social-information processing theory of child behavior that focuses on how children process information about their world and how these cognitions markedly affect their behavior (Crick & Dodge, 1994).

Peer Influences Investigations of how peers influence aggressive and antisocial behavior in children have focused on two broad areas: (1) acceptance or rejection by peers and (2) affiliation with deviant peers. Studies have shown that being rejected by peers is causally related to aggressive behavior, particularly in combination with ADHD (Hinshaw & Melnick, 1995). Other studies have shown that being rejected by peers can predict later aggressive behavior, even after controlling for prior levels of aggressive behavior (Coie & Dodge, 1998). Associating with other deviant peers also increases the likelihood of delinquent behavior (Capaldi & Patterson, 1994). One question that remains to be answered is whether children with conduct disorder choose to associate with like-minded peers, thus continuing on their path of antisocial behavior, or if simply being around deviant peers can help initiate antisocial behavior.

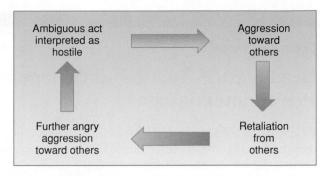

Figure 14.3 Dodge's cognitive theory of aggression. The interpretation of ambiguous acts as hostile is part of a vicious cycle that includes aggression toward and from others.

Sociocultural Factors Poverty and urban living are associated with higher levels of delinquency. Unemployment, poor educational facilities, disrupted family life, and a subculture that deems delinquency acceptable are all contributing factors (Lahey et al., 1999; Loeber & Farrington, 1998). The combination of early antisocial behavior in the child and socioeconomic disadvantage in the family predicts early criminal arrests (Patterson, Crosby, & Vuchinich, 1992).

A study of African American and white youths drawn from the Pittsburgh Youth Study indicates that the commonly found greater severity of delinquent acts among African Americans appears to be linked to their living in poorer neighborhoods, not to their race (Peeples & Loeber, 1994). The researchers designated neighborhoods as "underclass" or "non-underclass" based on factors such as family poverty, families with no one employed, male joblessness, and nonmarital births. In the total sample—ignoring differences in socioeconomic status—African American youths were more likely than white youths to have committed serious delinquent acts (e.g., car theft, breaking and entering, aggravated assault). But African American youths who were not living in underclass neighborhoods did not differ from white youths in serious delinquent behavior. Social factors matter. The strongest correlates of delinquency other than neighborhood were hyperactivity and lack of parental supervision; once these factors were controlled, residence in underclass neighborhoods was significantly related to delinquent behavior, whereas ethnicity was not.

Treatment of Conduct Disorder

The treatment of conduct disorder poses a formidable challenge to contemporary society. Sociologists and politicians, as well as community psychologists, working on the assumption that poor economic conditions create most of the problem, argue for a fairer distribution of income and for job programs and other large-scale efforts to alleviate the material deprivation of people with low socioeconomic status. In contrast, we emphasize psychological methods aimed at particular individuals and their families, rather than considering broader sociocultural factors. However, as we will see, addressing the multiple systems involved in the life of a child (family, peers, school, neighborhood) may be critical to the success of treatment efforts.

Family Interventions Some of the most promising approaches to treating conduct disorder involve intervening with the parents and families of the child. Gerald Patterson and colleagues have worked for over four decades developing and testing a behavioral program called **parental management training (PMT)**, in which parents are taught to modify their responses to their children so that prosocial rather than antisocial behavior is consistently rewarded. Parents are taught to use techniques such as positive reinforcement when the child

Focus on Discovery 14.3

Head Start: A Successful Community-Based Prevention Program

Head Start is a federally funded program whose goal is to prepare children from low-income families to succeed in the regular school setting. The impetus for the program came during the 1960s, when national attention in the United States was directed to the problems of hunger and civil rights.

The core of the Head Start program is community-based preschool education, focusing on the early development of cognitive and social skills. Head Start contracts with professionals in the community to provide children with health and dental services, including vaccinations, hearing and vision testing, medical treatment, parent training, and nutrition information (Head Start Bureau: http://www.acf.hhs.gov/programs/hsb/). Mental health services are another important component of the Head Start program. Psychologists may identify children with psychological problems and consult with teachers and staff to help make the preschool environment sensitive to psychological issues; for example, they may share knowledge of child development, consult on an individual case, or help staff address parents' concerns. Head Start programs are designed to be sensitive to cultural and ethnic factors affecting children and their families. Social workers can serve as advocates for a child's family, linking families with needed social services and encouraging parents to get involved with their children's education.

A comparison of Head Start children with other disadvantaged children who attended either a different preschool or no preschool showed that Head Start children improved significantly more than both groups on social-cognitive ability and motor impulsivity; the relative improvement was strongest for African American children, particularly those whose initial ability was below average. Although the Head Start program succeeded in enhancing the functioning of the neediest children, they were still behind their peers in terms of absolute cognitive levels after one year in the program (Lee, Brooks-Gunn, & Schnur, 1988). Other reports confirm the value of Head Start in helping poor children improve their intellectual functioning (e.g., Cronan et al., 1996; Perkins, 1995; Schleifer, 1995). The National Head Start Impact study, mandated by Congress in 1998, is a randomized, controlled clinical trial of Head Start that is studying close to 6,000 children in Head Start programs across the country. The study began in 2002, and results should be available in December 2006. This comprehensive study will help to answer questions about the efficacy of Head Start programs across domains (cognitive, social, communication, health) as well as about how Head Start impacts families. More detailed analyses will allow for the examination of what particular types of interventions work best in particular locations and with particular types of children.

Family therapy can be effective in treating conduct disorder. (David Young-Wolff/PhotoEdit.)

exhibits positive behaviors and time-out and loss of privileges for aggressive or antisocial behaviors.

Both parents' and teachers' reports of children's behavior and direct observation of behavior at home and at school support the program's effectiveness (Patterson, 1982). PMT has been shown to alter parent–child interactions, which in turn is associated with a decrease in antisocial and aggressive behavior (Dishion & Andrews, 1995; Dishion, Patterson, & Kavanagh, 1992). PMT has also been shown to improve the behavior of siblings and reduce depression in mothers involved in the program (Kazdin, 1985).

A study of chronic adolescent offenders found that both parent training and court-provided family treatment reduced rates of criminal offense (Bank et al., 1991). However, the parent-training approach, which included teaching parents to monitor their adolescents more closely and use age-appropriate rewards and consequences, led to more rapid improvement. Longer-term follow-ups suggest that the beneficial effects of PMT persist one to three years later (Brestan & Eyberg, 1998; Long et al., 1994). Recently, parent and teacher training approaches have been incorporated into larger community-based programs such as Head Start and have been shown to reduce childhood conduct problems and increase positive parenting behaviors (Webster-Stratton, 1998; Webster-Stratton, Reid & Hammond, 2001). (See Focus on Discovery 14.3 for more on Head Start.)

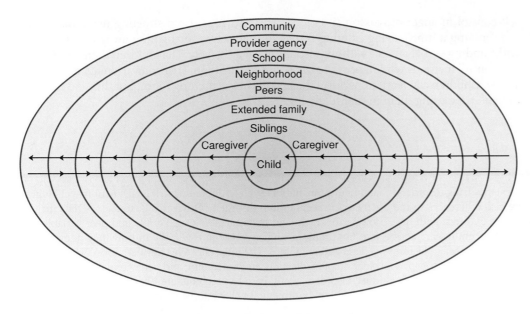

Community
Provider agency
School
Neighborhood
Peers
Extended family
Siblings
Caregiver   Caregiver
Child

Figure 14.4 Multisystemic treatment (MST) includes consideration of many different factors when developing a child's treatment, including family, school, community, and peers.

Multisystemic Treatment   A promising treatment for serious juvenile offenders is Scott Henggeler's **multisystemic treatment (MST)**, which has demonstrated reductions in arrests 4 years following treatment (Borduin et al., 1995). MST involves delivering intensive and comprehensive therapy services in the community, targeting the adolescent, the family, the school, and, in some cases, the peer group (Figure 14.4). The treatment is based on the view that conduct problems are influenced by multiple factors within the family and between the family and other social systems.

The strategies used by MST therapists are varied, incorporating behavioral, cognitive, family-systems, and case-management techniques. The therapy's uniqueness (and, apparently, its effectiveness; see Henggeler et al., 1998) lies in emphasizing individual and family strengths, identifying the context for the conduct problems, using present-focused and action-oriented interventions, and using interventions that require daily or weekly efforts by family members. Treatment is provided in "ecologically valid" settings, such as the home, school, or local recreational center, to maximize the chance that improvement will carry through into the regular daily lives of children and their families.

In comparison with adolescents who received an equivalent number of sessions (about 25) of traditional individual therapy in an office setting, adolescents who received MST showed fewer behavior problems and far fewer arrests over the following four years. For example, whereas more than 70 percent of the adolescents receiving traditional therapy were arrested in the four years following treatment, only 22 percent of those completing MST were arrested. In addition, assessment of other family members indicated that parents involved in MST had fewer psychiatric symptoms, and families were more supportive and showed less conflict and hostility in videotaped interactions. In contrast, the quality of interactions in the families of the adolescents receiving traditional individual therapy deteriorated following treatment. Even the adolescents receiving MST who dropped out of treatment after about four sessions were arrested significantly less than adolescents who completed the full course of traditional individual therapy.

Cognitive Therapy   The research on PMT and MST that we have just discussed suggests that intervention with parents and families is a critical component of success; however, such treatment is expensive and time-consuming (though clearly less so than incarceration), and some families may not be able or willing to become involved in it. Other research indicates that individual cognitive therapy with conduct-disordered children can improve their behavior, but family treatments remain the most effective.

Teaching children cognitive skills to control their anger shows promise in helping them reduce their aggressive behavior. In anger-control training, aggressive children are taught self-control in anger-provoking situations. They learn to use distracting techniques such as humming a tune, saying calming things to themselves, or turning away as a means of withstanding verbal attacks without responding aggressively. The children then apply these self-control methods while a peer provokes and insults them (Hinshaw, Henker, & Whalen, 1984). Children can learn to perform these skills in the therapy room, but they have a more difficult time using them in their daily lives.

Quick Summary

ADHD and conduct disorder are referred to as externalizing disorders. They appear across cultures, although there are also differences in the manifestation of externalizing symptoms in different cultures. Both disorders are more common in boys than girls, though recent research has begun to examine externalizing problems in girls. A number of factors work together to cause ADHD and conduct disorder. Genetic factors play a particularly important role in ADHD, but are also implicated in conduct disorder. Neurobiological research has implicated areas of the brain and neurotransmitters such as dopamine in ADHD; neuropsychological deficits are seen in both disorders. Other risk factors for ADHD include low birth weight and maternal smoking. Family and peer variables are also important factors to consider, especially in how they interact with genetic vulnerabilities. The most effective treatment for ADHD is a combination of medication, such as Ritalin, and behavioral therapy. For conduct disorder, family-based treatments are effective, as are treatments that include multiple points for intervention, as in MST.

Check Your Knowledge 14.2

Fill in the blank.
1. Moffitt and colleagues have provided a good deal of evidence for two types of conduct disorder. The _____ type is associated with an early age of onset and continued problems into adolescence and adulthood. The _____ type begins in the teenage years and is hypothesized to remit by adulthood, though a recent follow-up study has not supported the idea that this type remits.

2. Comorbidity is common in conduct disorder. Other problems that co-occur with conduct disorder include: _____, _____, _____, and _____.
3. A successful treatment for conduct disorder that involves the family is called _____ _____ _____. Another successful community-focused treatment that works with the child, parents, peers, and schools is _____ _____.

Depression and Anxiety in Children and Adolescents

Internalizing disorders such as depression and various anxiety disorders commonly co-occur with externalizing disorders as we have noted with respect to ADHD and conduct disorder. Furthermore, depression and anxiety disorders commonly co-occur with each other among children as they do among adults. Also, recent research indicates that depression and anxiety can be distinguished in children and adolescents in much the same way as among adults—that is, children with depression show low levels of positive affect and high levels of negative affect, and children with anxiety show high levels of negative affect but do not show low levels of positive affect (Lonigan, Phillips, & Hooe, 2003). Next, we consider in more detail some of the etiological factors and treatment considerations for childhood depression and anxiety.

Depression

There are both similarities and differences in the symptomatology of children and adults with major depressive disorder (Garber & Flynn, 2001). Children and adolescents ages 7 to 17 and adults both tend to show the following symptoms: depressed mood, inability to experience pleasure, fatigue, concentration problems, and suicidal ideation. Children and adolescents differ from adults in showing higher rates of suicide attempts and guilt, and lower rates of early-morning wakefulness, early-morning depression, loss of appetite, and weight loss.

As in adults, depression in children is recurrent. Longitudinal studies have demonstrated that both children and adolescents with major depression are likely to continue to exhibit significant depressive symptoms when assessed even four to eight years later (Garber, Kelly, & Martin, 2002; Lewinsohn et al., 2000).

In general, depression occurs in less than 1 percent of preschoolers (Kashani & Carlson, 1987; Kashani, Holcomb, & Orvaschel, 1986) and in 2 to 3 percent of school-age children (Cohen et al., 1993; Costello et al., 1988). In adolescents, rates of depression are comparable to those of adults, with particularly high rates (7 to 13 percent) for girls (Angold & Rutter, 1992; Kashani et al., 1987).

This prevalence among adolescent girls is almost twice that among adolescent boys and is the same as that found among women. (In adults, depression is also twice as common among women as among men.) Although adolescent girls experience depression more often than adolescent boys, there are no differences in the types of symptoms they experience (Lewinsohn et al., 2003). Interestingly, the gender difference does not occur before age 12; in fact, depression is found more often among boys during the early years (Anderson et al., 1987), and the full gender difference does not emerge consistently until adolescence (Hankin et al., 1998). Understanding the cause and timing of this gender difference may yield some further clues to the etiology of depression.

Etiology of Depression in Childhood and Adolescence   What causes a young person to become depressed? As with adults, evidence suggests that genetic factors play a role (Klein et al., 2001). Indeed, the results of genetic studies with adults (see Chapter 8) apply to children and adolescents also, since genetic influences are present from birth, though they may not be expressed right away.

Studies of depression in children have focused also on family and other relationships as sources of stress that might interact with a biological diathesis. Having a mother or father who is depressed increases the chances of being depressed as a child or adolescent; less is known about the reasons for these linkages (Garber et al., 2002; Kane & Garber, 2004; Lewinsohn et al., 2000). We know that depression in either or both spouses is often associated with marital conflict; we should expect, therefore, that depression will have negative effects on the children in a household, and it does (Hammen, 1997).

Depressed children and their parents have been shown to interact with each other in negative ways; for example, they show less warmth and more hostility toward each other than is the case with nondepressed children and their parents (Chiariello & Orvaschel, 1995). Children and adolescents experiencing major depression also have poor social skills and impaired relationships with siblings and friends (Lewinsohn et al., 1994). These patterns are likely to be both a cause and a consequence of depression. Depressed children have fewer and less satisfying contacts with their peers, who often reject them because they are not enjoyable to be around (Kennedy, Spence, & Hensley, 1989). These negative interactions in turn may aggravate the negative self-image and sense of worth that the depressed child already has (Coyne, 1976). Frequent criticism from parents may be especially harmful to the child's sense of competency and self-worth (Cole & Turner, 1993; Stark, Schmidt, et al., 1996).

Consistent with both Beck's theory (1967) and the learned helplessness theory of depression (Abramson et al., 1989) (see Chapter 8), cognitive distortions and negative attributional styles are associated with depression in children and adolescents in ways similar to what has been found with adults (Garber et al., 2002; Lewinsohn et al., 2000). For example, cognitive research with depressed children indicates that their outlooks are more negative than are those of nondepressed children and resemble those of depressed adults (Prieto, Cole, & Tageson, 1992). However, some research indicates that cognitive distortions in children may be a reflection of depression rather than a cause (Cole et al., 1998). Additional research that incorporates knowledge about children's normal cognitive development will help clarify the role of cognitive factors in childhood depression (Cole, Jacquez, & Manschman, 2001).

Treatment of Childhood and Adolescent Depression   Therapy with depressed children and adolescents has been studied far less than therapy with adults (Hammen, 1997).

This relative neglect may stem from the fact that depressed young people don't attract as much adult attention as those who act out, such as children with conduct disorder (Kaslow & Thompson, 1998).

Research on the safety and efficacy of medications for childhood and adolescent depression has lagged behind research with adults (Emslie & Mayes, 2001). In general, evidence suggests that selective serotonin reuptake inhibitors (SSRIs) are superior to tricyclic antidepressants (Emslie et al., 2000; Lynch, Glod, & Fitzgerald, 2001; Wagner & Ambrosini, 2001). However, some studies have shown that antidepressant drugs are no better than placebos in children and adolescents (Geller et al., 1992; Keller et al., 2001). A recent randomized clinical trial comparing Prozac, cognitive behavioral therapy (CBT), and both combined for adolescents with depression found that the combined treatment was the most effective (March et al., 2004). Concerns over the safety of antidepressant medications with children, particularly with respect to suicidality, have prompted a series of recent hearings in the United States and Britain. For example, in the study cited above (March et al., 2004), 7 out of 439 adolescents attempted suicide, of whom 6 were in the Prozac group, and 1 was in the CBT group. (See Focus on Discovery 14.2 for more on this complex issue.)

Most psychosocial interventions are modeled after clinical research with adults. For example, interpersonal therapy has been modified for use with depressed adolescents, by focusing on issues of concern to adolescents, such as peer pressure, the stress inherent in the transition from childhood to adulthood, and the conflict between dependency on parents (and parental figures, like teachers) and the drive to be independent (Moreau et al., 1992). Cognitive behavioral treatments in school settings appear to be effective and are associated with more rapid reduction of symptoms than family or supportive therapy (Curry, 2001). About 63 percent of depressed adolescents treated with CBT show significant improvement at the end of treatment (Lewinsohn & Clarke, 1999). A case report illustrating CBT with a depressed adolescent is presented. However, a recent study indicated that this favorable outcome does not hold up during posttreatment follow-up (Birmaher et al., 2000). In addition, the randomized clinical trial discussed above (March et al., 2004) found that Prozac alone was more effective than CBT alone in treating adolescents with depression.

Treatment of depressed children and adolescents may be best accomplished with a broad-spectrum approach that involves not only the child or adolescent but also the family and the school (Hammen, 1997; Stark, Napolitano, et al., 1996; Stark et al., 1998). Often therapy will focus on a depressed parent in addition to the depressed child; depressed parents probably communicate to their children their own pessimistic views of themselves and the world, and children are influenced strongly by their parents' ideas.

Clinical Case: Sharon

When initially seen, Sharon was extremely dysphoric, experienced recurrent suicidal ideation, and displayed a number of vegetative signs of depression ... [After being] placed on antidepressant medication ... she was introduced to a cognitive behavioral approach to depression ... She was able to understand how her mood was affected by her thoughts and behavior and was able to engage in behavioral planning to increase the occurrence of pleasurable and mastery-oriented events. Sharon manifested extremely high standards for evaluating her performance in a number of areas, and it became clear that her parents also ascribed to these standards, so that family therapy sessions were held to encourage Sharon and her parents to reevaluate their standards.

Sharon had difficulty with the notion of changing her standards and noted that when she was not depressed she actually valued her perfectionism. At that point she resisted the therapy because she perceived it as trying to change something she valued in herself. With this in mind, we began to explore and identify those situations or domains in which her perfectionism worked for her and when and how it might work against her. She became increasingly comfortable with this perspective and decided she wanted to continue to set high standards regarding her performance in mathematical course work (which was a clear area of strength), but she did not need to be so demanding of herself regarding art or physical education. Adapted from Braswell and Kendall (1988, p. 194).

Anxiety

Just about every child experience fears and worries as part of the normal course of development. Common fears, most of which are outgrown, include fear of the dark and of imaginary creatures (in children under 5) and fear of being separated from parents (in children under 10). In general, as with adults, fears are reported more often for girls than for boys (Lichtenstein & Annas, 2000), though this sex difference may be due at least in part to social pressures on boys that make them reluctant to admit that they are afraid of things. For fears and other worries to be classified as disorders according to DSM-IV-TR criteria, children's functioning must be impaired; unlike adults, however, children need not regard their fear as excessive or unreasonable, because children sometimes are unable to make such judgments. Based on these criteria, about 12 to 20 percent of children and adolescents would be diagnosed as having an anxiety disorder, making these the most common disorders of childhood (Achenbach et al., 1995; Shaffer et al., 1996). Although most unrealistic childhood fears dissipate over time, it is also the case that most anxious adults can trace their problems back to childhood.

The seriousness of some childhood anxiety problems should therefore not be underestimated. Not only do children suffer, as do adults, from the aversiveness of being anxious—simply put, anxiety doesn't feel good—but their anxiety may also work against their acquisition of skills appropriate to various stages of their development. For example, a child who is painfully shy and finds interacting with peers virtually intolerable is unlikely to learn important social skills. This deficit will persist as the child grows into adolescence and will form the foundation of still further social difficulties. Then whether in the workplace or at college, the adolescent's worst fear—"people will dislike and reject me"—is likely to be realized as his or her awkward, even off-putting behavior toward others produces rejecting and avoiding responses.

School Phobia   One childhood fear, **school phobia**, sometimes called *school refusal*, has serious academic and social consequences for the child and can be extremely disabling. Two types of school phobia have been identified. The more common type is associated with *separation anxiety*—children worry constantly that some harm will befall their parents or themselves when they are away from their parents. When at home, such children shadow one or both of their parents and often try to join them in bed. Since the beginning of school is often the first circumstance that requires lengthy and frequent separations of children from their parents, separation anxiety is often a principal cause of school phobia.

A second type of school phobia is associated with a true fear of school—either a fear specifically related to school or a more general fear (social phobia). Children with this type of school phobia generally begin refusing to go to school later in life and have more severe and pervasive avoidance of school. Their fear is more likely to be related to specific aspects of the school environment, such as worries about academic failure or discomfort with peers.

Experts agree that if school phobia is untreated (or if it doesn't dissipate without professional intervention) in childhood, it can have long-term negative consequences in both adolescence and adulthood.

Social Phobia   Most classrooms have in attendance at least one or two children who are extremely quiet and shy. Often these children will play only with family members or familiar peers, avoiding strangers both young and old. Their shyness may prevent them from acquiring skills and participating in a variety of activities enjoyed by most of their age-mates, for they avoid playgrounds and stay out of games played by neighborhood children. Although some children who are shy may simply be slow to warm up, truly withdrawn children never do, even after prolonged exposure to new people. Extremely shy children may refuse to speak at all in unfamiliar social circumstances, a condition called *selective mutism*. In crowded rooms they cling and whisper to their parents, hide behind the furniture, cower in corners, and may even have tantrums. At home they ask their parents endless questions about situations that worry them. Withdrawn children usually have warm and satisfying

School phobia is most commonly associated with separation anxiety disorder, an intense fear of being away from parents or other attachment figures. (David Young-Wolff/PhotoEdit.)

relationships with family members and family friends, and they show a desire for affection and acceptance.

The point at which this kind of behavior becomes a problem severe enough to be diagnosed as social phobia varies; few reliable statistics have been compiled on the frequency of this disorder. One estimate is that 1 percent of children and adolescents have social phobia (Kashani & Orvaschel, 1990); it is more of a problem with adolescents, who have a more acute concern about the opinions of others than younger children do.

Some children exhibit intense anxiety in specific social situations, showing social phobia similar to that of adults (see p. 124). When such children were asked to keep daily diaries of anxiety-producing events, they reported experiencing anxiety three times more frequently than did other children, with concerns about such activities as reading aloud before a group, writing on the board, and performing in front of others. They reported crying, avoidance, and somatic complaints such as shakiness and nausea when faced with these tasks (Beidel, 1991).

Theories of the etiology of social phobia in children are generally similar to theories of social phobia in adults. For example, research has shown that children with anxiety disorders overestimate the danger in many situations and underestimate their ability to cope with them (Boegels & Zigterman, 2000). The anxiety created by these cognitions then interferes with social interaction, causing the child to avoid social situations and thus not to get much practice at social skills. Another suggestion is that withdrawn children may simply not have the social know-how that facilitates interaction with their age-mates. The finding that isolated children make fewer attempts to make friends and are less imaginative in their play may indicate a deficiency in social skills. Finally, isolated children may have become so because they have in the past spent most of their time with adults; these children interact more freely with adults than with other children (Scarlett, 1980).

PTSD   Only recently have professionals addressed the development of posttraumatic stress disorder (PTSD) in children and adolescents. Children who are exposed to traumas such as chronic abuse, community violence, and natural disasters may experience symptoms similar to those experienced by traumatized adults. As with adults, these symptoms fall into three broad categories: (1) reexperiencing the traumatic event, as in nightmares, flashbacks, or intrusive thoughts; (2) avoiding trauma-related situations or information and experiencing a general numbing of responses, as in feelings of detachment or anhedonia; and (3) hyper-arousal, which can include irritability, sleep problems, and hypervigilance (Davis & Siegal, 2000). Some symptoms in children differ from those in adults; for example, children may exhibit signs of agitation instead of extreme fear or hopelessness.

Theories about the causes of PTSD in children are similar to the theories for adults. There must be exposure to a trauma, either experienced or witnessed. Like adults, children who have a propensity to experience anxiety may be at more risk for developing PTSD following exposure to trauma. Specific risk factors for children may include level of family stress, coping styles of the family, and past experiences with trauma (Martini et al., 1990). Some theorists suggest that parental reactions to trauma can help to lessen children's distress; specifically, if parents appear in control and calm in the face of stress, a child's reaction may be less severe (Davis & Siegal, 2000).

Very few studies have evaluated the efficacy of treatment of PTSD among children and adolescents, but the limited research suggests that cognitive behavioral treatments, along with family involvement, are beneficial (Yule & Canterbury, 1996).

Treatment of Anxiety in Childhood and Adolescence   How are childhood fears overcome? Many simply dissipate with time and maturation. For the most part, treatment of such fears is similar to that employed with adults, with suitable modifications to accommodate the different abilities and circumstances of childhood.

Perhaps the most widespread means of helping children overcome fears, employed by millions of parents, is to expose them gradually to the feared object, often while acting simultaneously to inhibit their anxiety. If a little girl fears strangers, a parent takes her by the hand and walks her slowly toward the new person. Offering rewards for moving closer to a feared object or situation can also be encouraging to a fearful child. Treatments based on modeling and on operant conditioning involve exposure to what is feared.

The only treatment approach that has empirical support for the treatment of anxiety in children and adolescents is cognitive behavioral therapy (Compton et al., 2004). Evidence indicates that such therapy can be helpful to many fearful and socially avoidant children (Kendall et al., 2004). This type of treatment typically involves working with both children and parents and includes psychoeducation, cognitive restructuring, exposure, modeling, skills training, and relapse prevention (Kendall, Aschenbrand, & Hudson, 2003; Velting, Setzer, & Albano, 2004). One of the more widely used treatments developed by Philip Kendall is called the Coping Cat (Kendall et al., 2003). This treatment is used with children between the ages of 7 and 13; it focuses on confronting fears, developing new ways to think about fears, exposure to feared situations, practice, and relapse prevention. Parents are also included in a couple of sessions. At least two randomized controlled clinical trials have shown this treatment to be effective (Kendall, 1994; Kendall et al., 1997). A follow-up study of children who received this treatment found that after 7 years, the majority of children treated were still anxiety free. Furthermore, the children who remained anxiety free after 7 years were less likely to have used drugs such as alcohol or marijuana than children for whom the treatment was less effective (Kendall, Safford, Flannery-Schroeder, & Webb, 2004).

Quick Summary

Anxiety disorders and depression in children are referred to as internalizing disorders. Depression in childhood and adolescence looks similar to depression in adulthood, although there are notable differences. In childhood, depression affects boys and girls equally, but in adolescence girls are affected twice as often as boys. Research on cognitive factors in childhood depression supports the notion that maladaptive cognitions and schemas play a role; however, this work must consider the developmental stage of the child. Treatment for depression among children is facing a good deal of controversy, at least with medication. A recent randomized clinical trial found that a combination of medication and CBT was the most effective treatment. Concerns about suicide risk and medications need to be addressed.

Anxiety and fear are typical in childhood. When fears interfere with functioning, such as keeping a child from school, intervention is warranted. Theories about the causes of anxiety disorder in children are similar to theories in adulthood, though less research has been done with children on, for example, cognitive factors. Cognitive behavioral therapy is an effective intervention for a number of different anxiety disorders in childhood. Other problems, such as PTSD in childhood, require additional study.

Learning Disabilities

Clinical Case: Tim

Several years ago Tim was a student in one of our undergraduate courses who showed an unusual pattern of strengths and weaknesses. His comments in class were exemplary, but his handwriting was sometimes indecipherable, and his spelling was very poor. After the instructor had noted these problems on his midterm examination, Tim came to see him and explained that he was dyslexic and that it took him a long time to complete the weekly reading assignments and to write papers and exams. The instructor decided to give Tim extra time for written work because he was obviously of superior intelligence and highly motivated to excel. Excel he did, earning an A in the course and on graduation admittance to a leading law school.

A **learning disability** is a condition in which a person shows inadequate development in a specific area of academic, language, speech, or motor skills that is not due to mental retardation, autism, a demonstrable physical disorder, or deficient educational opportunities. Children with a learning disability are usually of average or above average intelligence but have difficulty learning some specific skill in the affected area (e.g., arithmetic or reading), and thus their progress in school is impeded.

Clinical Descriptions

The term "learning disabilities" is not used by DSM-IV-TR but is used by most health professionals to group together three disorders that do appear in DSM-IV-TR: learning disorders, communication disorders, and motor skills disorder. Any of these disorders may apply to a child who fails to develop to the degree appropriate to his or her intellectual level in a specific academic, language, or motor skill area. Learning disabilities are often identified and treated within the school system rather than through mental health clinics. An older study suggested that the disorders are only slightly more common in boys (Shaywitz et al., 1990), but a recent study of four large epidemiological samples indicates that reading disorders, at least, are far more common in boys than in girls (Rutter et al., 2004). Though individuals with learning disabilities usually find ways to cope with their problems, their academic and social development is nonetheless affected, sometimes quite seriously.

Learning Disorders   DSM-IV-TR divides **learning disorders** into three categories: reading disorder (dyslexia), disorder of written expression, and mathematics disorder. None of these diagnoses are appropriate if the disability can be accounted for by a sensory deficit, such as a vision or hearing problem.

Tom Cruise, a highly successful actor, suffers from dyslexia. (AP/Wide World Photos.)

- Children with **reading disorder**, better known as **dyslexia**, have significant difficulty with word recognition, reading comprehension, and typically written spelling as well. When reading out loud they omit, add, or distort the pronunciation of words to an extent unusual for their age. In adulthood, problems with reading, comprehension, and written spelling can persist. This disorder, present in 5 to 10 percent of school-age children, does not preclude success. For example, Tom Cruise, a well-known and accomplished actor, has dyslexia.
- **Disorder of written expression** is an impairment in the ability to write (including spelling errors, errors in grammar and punctuation, and very poor handwriting) that is serious enough to interfere significantly with academic achievement or daily activities that require writing skills. Few systematic studies have yet been conducted on the prevalence of this disorder, which the college student Tim in the Clinical Case had in addition to his dyslexia.
- Children with **mathematics disorder** may have difficulty rapidly and accurately recalling arithmetic facts, counting objects correctly and quickly, and aligning numbers in columns.

Communication Disorders   Several categories of **communication disorders** have been distinguished:

- In **expressive language disorder**, the child has difficulty expressing himself or herself in speech. The child may seem eager to communicate but have inordinate difficulty finding the right words; for example, he or she may be unable to come up with the word *car* when pointing to a car passing by on the street. By age 4, the child speaks only in short phrases. Old words are forgotten when new ones are learned, and the use of grammatical structures is considerably below age level.
- Unlike children who have trouble finding words, youngsters with **phonological disorder** comprehend and are able to use a substantial vocabulary, but their speech is not

clear; *blue* comes out *bu*, and *rabbit* sounds like *wabbit*, for example. They have not learned articulation of the later-acquired speech sounds, such as *r, sh, th, f, z, l,* and *ch*. With speech therapy, complete recovery occurs in almost all cases, and milder cases may recover spontaneously by age 8.

- **Stuttering** is a disturbance in verbal fluency that is characterized by one or more of the following speech patterns: frequent repetitions or prolongations of sounds, long pauses between words, substituting easy words for those that are difficult to articulate (e.g., words beginning with certain consonants), and repeating whole words (e.g., saying "go-go-go-go" instead of just a single "go"). Sometimes bodily twitching and eye blinking accompany the verbal problems. Stuttering can interfere with academic, social, and occupational functioning and can prevent otherwise capable people from fulfilling their potential. It is frequently worse when the person is nervous and often improves or even disappears when the person sings. About three times as many males as females have the problem, which usually shows up at around age 5 and almost always before age 10. DSM-IV-TR estimates that up to 80 percent of individuals with stuttering recover, most of them without professional intervention, before the age of 16.

A speech therapist works with a child with phonological disorder by having him practice the sounds he finds difficult. (Hattie Young/Photo Researchers.)

Motor Skills Disorder   In **motor skills disorder**, also referred to as *developmental coordination disorder*, children show marked impairment in the development of motor coordination that is not explainable by mental retardation or a disorder such as cerebral palsy. The young child may have difficulty tying shoelaces and buttoning shirts and, when older, with building models, playing ball, and printing or handwriting. The diagnosis is made only if the impairment interferes significantly with academic achievement or with the activities of daily living.

Etiology of Learning Disabilities

Most research on learning disabilities concerns dyslexia, perhaps because it is the most prevalent of this group of disorders. Although studies on mathematics disorder are beginning to emerge, research has advanced more slowly in this area.

Etiology of Dyslexia   In the past, psychological theories focused on perceptual deficits as the basis for dyslexia. One popular hypothesis suggested that children with reading problems perceive letters in reverse order or mirror image, mistaking, for example, a d for a b. However, more recent findings have not supported this hypothesis (Wolff & Melngailis, 1996); most children make letter reversals when first learning to read, but even dyslexic individuals very rarely make letter reversals after age 9 or 10.

Family and twin studies confirm that there is a heritable component to dyslexia (Pennington, 1995; Raskind, 2001). Furthermore, there is fairly good consensus among investigators today that the core deficits in dyslexia include problems in language processing. Evidence from psychological, neuropsychological, and neuroimaging studies supports this contention. Research points to one or more problems in language processing that might underlie dyslexia, including perception of speech and analysis of the sounds of spoken language and their relation to printed words (Mann & Brady, 1988), difficulty recognizing rhyme and alliteration (Bradley & Bryant, 1985), problems with rapidly naming familiar objects (Scarborough, 1990; Wolf, Bally, & Morris, 1986), and delays in learning syntactic rules (Scarborough, 1990). Many of these processes fall under what is called *phonological awareness*, which is believed to be critical to the development of reading skills (Anthony & Lonigan, 2004).

Studies using various brain-imaging techniques support the idea that children with dyslexia have a problem in phonological awareness. These studies show that the left temporo-parietal-occipital regions of the brain appear to be centrally involved in dyslexia, and these areas of the brain are important for phonological awareness. For example, a study using fMRI found that, compared with nondyslexic children, dyslexic children failed to

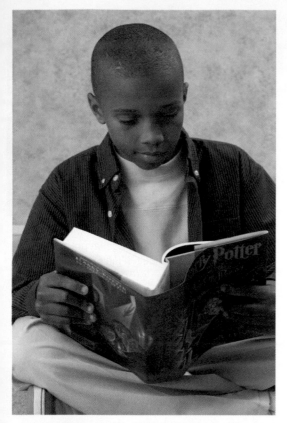

Recent interventions for dyslexia have improved children's reading. (Scholastic Studio 10/Index Stock.)

activate the temporoparietal area during a phonological processing task (Temple et al., 2001). A larger study using fMRI found that compared to children without dyslexia, children with dyslexia showed less activation in the left temporoparietal and occipitotemporal areas while doing a number of reading relevant tasks, such as identifying letters and sounding out words (Shaywitz et al., 2002). A recent treatment study showed that after a year of intensive treatment for reading problems, children with dyslexia were better readers and also showed greater activation in the left temporoparietal and occipitotemporal areas while completing a reading task, compared to a group of children who received a less intensive treatment (Shaywitz et al., 2004).

Similar findings using fMRI have been found with adults with dyslexia (Horwitz, Rumsey, & Donahue, 1998; Klingberg et al., 2000). A newer fMRI study with adults examined three different types of readers (Shaywitz et al., 2003). The first group was called persistently poor readers (PPR)—they had trouble reading early in school (second grade) and later in school (ninth or tenth grade). The second group was called accuracy improved or compensated readers (AI)—they had trouble reading early in school but not later in school. The third group was called nonimpaired readers (NI)—they had no trouble with reading either early or late in school. On behavioral reading tasks completed outside the scanner, the PPR group performed more poorly than the AI and NI groups. On many tests, the AI group performed as well as the NI group, suggesting they had in fact compensated for their early reading problems. However, the brain-imaging results told a different story. Specifically, the NI group activated the traditional areas of the brain linked to reading: the left temporo-parietal-occipital regions. However, the AI group did not show as much activation in these areas but did show activation in areas on the right side of the brain, suggesting that their compensation for early reading problems relied on areas of the brain not traditionally involved in reading. Paradoxically, the PPR group also activated the left side of the brain linked with reading. However, this group of poor readers also activated other areas of the brain associated with memory, suggesting that they were trying to rely on memorization of words to read rather than on language areas more efficiently used in reading.

Other brain abnormalities, possibly heritable, may also contribute to dyslexia. For example, autopsies of the brains of right-handed individuals with childhood dyslexia have revealed microscopic abnormalities in the location, number, and organization of neurons in what is called the posterior language area of the cortex (Galaburda, 1989, 1993).

It should be noted that the fMRI studies discussed above were done with children and adults in the United States who spoke English. A study examining Chinese children with dyslexia failed to find a problem with the temporoparietal area of the brain during reading tasks; instead, the left middle frontal gyrus showed less activation (Siok et al., 2004). The investigators speculate that the differences between the languages of English and Chinese may account for the different brain regions involved. Reading English requires putting together letters that represent sounds. Reading Chinese, in contrast, requires putting together symbols that represent meanings. Indeed, reading Chinese requires mastery of nearly 6,000 different symbols. Thus, Chinese relies more on visual processing, while English relies more on sound processing.

Etiology of Mathematics Disorder   Three subtypes of mathematics disorder have been proposed (Geary, 1993). The first involves a deficit in semantic verbal memory (memory for the meaning of words) and leads to problems with memorizing and retrieving arithmetic facts, even after extensive drilling. This type of math disorder appears to be associated with some dysfunction in the left hemisphere of the brain and often occurs together with a reading disorder.

The second subtype of math disorder involves the use of developmentally immature strategies for solving arithmetic problems and frequent errors in solving simple problems. For example, when first-grade children with this subtype are asked to add 3 and 4, they first count to three on their fingers, then count four more. In contrast, children this age with more typical math abilities start by putting out four fingers (without counting them) and then count three more (Geary & Brown, 1991; Geary, Brown, & Samaranayake, 1991). No evidence is yet available on the etiology of this type of disability, which appears to involve a developmental lag and generally improves with age.

A third and less common subtype of math disorder apparently involves impaired visuo-spatial skills, resulting in misaligning numbers in columns or making place-value errors (putting decimal points in wrong places). This type of disorder is much less likely to be associated with reading disorders than is the semantic-memory subtype.

No studies have been done on the heritability of mathematics disorders, but there is evidence of some genetic influence on individual variations in math skills. In particular, the type of math disability that involves poor semantic memory is most likely to be heritable. A study of over 250 twin pairs conducted through the Colorado Learning Disabilities Research Center suggested that common genetic factors underlie both reading and math deficits in children with both disorders (Gillis & DeFries, 1991).

Treatment of Learning Disabilities

The anxiety of parents whose otherwise typical child lags behind in reading or cannot speak effectively for his or her age cannot be underestimated. Several strategies are currently being used to treat learning disabilities, both in school programs and in private tutoring. Traditional linguistic approaches, used primarily in cases of reading and writing difficulties, focus on instruction in listening, speaking, reading, and writing skills in a logical, sequential, and multisensory manner, such as reading out loud under close supervision. In young children, readiness skills, such as letter discrimination, phonetic analysis, and learning letter–sound correspondences, may need to be taught before explicit instruction in reading is attempted. Findings from the National Reading Panel, a comprehensive review of the research on teaching children to read, indicate that phonics instruction is beneficial for children with reading difficulties. Phonics instruction involves helping children master the task of converting sounds to words (National Institute of Child Health and Human Development, 2000). Like the case of Tim described above, individuals with dyslexia often can succeed in college with the aid of instructional supports, such as tape-recorded lectures, Web-cast lectures that can be re-reviewed, tutors, and untimed tests. Colleges are required by law to provide special services to help such students, and public schools are now required to provide transitional vocational and career planning for older adolescents with learning disabilities.

In recent years, there has been an exciting development in treating communication disorders (Merzenich et al., 1996; Tallal et al., 1996). Based on previous findings that children with such disorders have difficulty discriminating certain sounds, the researchers developed special computer games and audiotapes that slow speech sounds. After intensive training with these modified speech stimuli for 1 month, children with severe language disorders were able to improve their language skills by approximately 2 years, to the point at which they were functioning as typically developing children do. Similar training using unmodified speech stimuli resulted in very little progress.

Based on their promising initial findings, these investigators expanded the treatment, now called Fast ForWord, and conducted a larger study including 500 children from the United States and Canada. Children received daily training for 6 to 8 weeks, and results again indicated that the intervention was effective. Children improved in speech, language, and auditory processing skills by about 1 1/2 years of ability (Tallal et al., 1998). The researchers speculate that this training method may even help prevent dyslexia, since many reading-disordered children had difficulties understanding language as young children.

Most children with learning disabilities have probably experienced a great deal of frustration and failure, eroding their motivation and confidence. Whatever their design, treatment programs should provide opportunities for children to experience feelings of mastery and self-efficacy. Rewarding small steps can be useful in increasing the child's motivation, helping the child focus attention on the learning task, and reducing behavioral problems caused by frustration. In addition to targeting academic skills, treatment for children with learning disabilities should include strategies to address the secondary social and emotional adjustment problems they experience. For example, educating children and parents about the disability, addressing their emotional reactions to the disability, and teaching them strategies to adapt are all helpful in improving overall adjustment (Culbertson, 1998).

Mental Retardation

 DSM-IV-TR Criteria for Mental Retardation

- Significantly below average intellectual functioning, IQ less than 70
- Deficits in adaptive social functioning in at least two of the following areas: communication, self-care, home living, interpersonal skills, use of community resources, ability to make own decisions, functional academic skills, leisure, work, health, and safety
- Onset before age 18

In this section, we first examine the DSM-IV-TR perspective on **mental retardation** and then discuss the approach of the American Association of Mental Retardation, the principal professional organization devoted to research, education, and application in the field of mental retardation.

Diagnosis and Assessment of Mental Retardation

Mental Retardation in DSM-IV-TR   The DSM-IV-TR diagnostic criteria for mental retardation, an Axis II disorder, include (1) significantly below average intellectual functioning, (2) deficits in adaptive behavior, and (3) an onset prior to age 18.

Intelligence-Test Scores   The first component of the DSM-IV-TR criteria requires a judgment of intelligence. Approximately two-thirds of the population achieves IQ (intelligent quotient) test scores between 85 and 115. Those with a score below 70 to 75, two standard deviations below the mean of the population, meet the criterion of "significant subaverage general intellectual functioning." Approximately 3 percent of the population falls into this category.

Adaptive Functioning   Adaptive functioning refers to mastering childhood skills such as toileting and dressing; understanding the concepts of time and money; being able to use tools, to shop, and to travel by public transportation; and becoming socially responsive. An adolescent, for example, is expected to be able to apply academic skills, reasoning, and judgment to daily living and to participate in group activities. An adult is expected to be self-supporting and to assume social responsibilities.

Several tests have been constructed to assess adaptive behavior. Best known are the Adaptive Behavior Scale, or ABS (Nihira et al., 1975), and the Vineland Adaptive Behavior Scales (Sparrow, Ballo, & Cicchetti, 1984; see Table 14.3). Although impairments in adaptive functioning have long been included in the definition of mental retardation, only recently have the tests been adequately standardized with firmly established norms. One problem with many assessments of adaptive behavior is that they fail to consider the environment to which the person must adapt. A person who lives in a small rural community where everyone is acquainted may not need skills as complex as those needed by someone who lives in New York City. Children who are competent working at farm chores, walking to school, and shopping at the local store may, when transported to a city, be considered deficient in adaptive behavior if they are not able to ride the subway to school or buy groceries at a store where a foreign language is spoken. By the same token, city children might find themselves at a loss with some of the activities expected of children living on a farm. An effective and valid assessment of adaptive behavior should therefore consider the interaction between the child and the surroundings in which he or she must function.

Table 14.3 Sample Items from the Vineland Adaptive Behavior Scales

Age (Years)	Adaptive Ability
2	Says at least 50 recognizable words. Removes front-opening coat, sweater, or shirt without assistance.
5	Tells popular story, fairy tale, lengthy joke, or plot of television program. Ties shoelaces into a bow without assistance.
8	Keeps secrets or confidences for more than 1 day. Orders own meal in a restaurant.
11	Uses the telephone for all kinds of calls without assistance. Watches television or listens to radio for information about a particular area of interest.
16	Looks after own health. Responds to hints or indirect cues in conversation.

Source: From Sparrow et al., 1984.

Age of Onset   The third DSM-IV-TR criterion is that mental retardation must be manifested before age 18, to rule out classifying as mental retardation any deficits in intelligence and

When assessing adaptive behavior, the environment must be considered. A person living in a rural community may not need the same skills as those needed by someone living in New York City, and vice versa. [(Left) Gene Peach/Liaison Agency, Inc./Getty Images. (Right) Joseph Rodriguez/Black Star.)]

adaptive behavior that result from injury or illnesses occurring later in life. Children with severe impairments are often diagnosed during infancy. Most children considered mentally retarded, however, are not identified as such until they enter school. These children have no obvious physiological, neurological, or physical manifestations, and their problems become apparent only when they are unable to keep up with their peers in school.

Levels of Mental Retardation   Table 14.4 shows the four levels of mental retardation recognized in DSM-IV-TR, each corresponding to a specific range of IQ scores. However, because IQ is not the sole basis of diagnosis, some persons falling in the mildly retarded range based on IQ but having no deficits in adaptive behavior would not be considered mentally retarded. In practice, the IQ criterion is usually applied only after deficits in adaptive behavior have been identified.

The Approach of the American Association of Mental Retardation   The American Association of Mental Retardation (AAMR) is an organization whose mission is to "promote progressive policies, sound research, effective practices, and universal human rights for people with intellectual disabilities" (AAMR Web site, www.aamr.org). AAMR has been in

Table 14.4 DSM-IV-TR Categories of Mental Retardation

Mild Mental Retardation (50–55 to 70 IQ). About 85 percent of all those with IQs of less than 70 are classified as having mild mental retardation.

Moderate Mental Retardation (35–40 to 50–55 IQ). About 10 percent of those with IQs of less than 55 are classified as having moderate mental retardation.

Severe Mental Retardation (20–25 to 35–40 IQ). About 3 to 4 percent of those with IQs less than 40 are classified as having severe mental retardation.

Profound Mental Retardation (below 20–25 IQ). About 1 to 2 percent of people with IQs less than 25 are classified as having profound mental retardation.

Source: DSM-IV-TR, 2000.

Table 14.5 The AAMR Definition of Mental Retardation

Mental retardation is a disability characterized by significant limitations both in intellectual functioning and in adaptive behavior as expressed in conceptual, social, and practical adaptive skills.

This disability originates before age 18.

Five Assumptions Essential to the Application of the Definition

1. Limitations in present functioning must be considered within the context of community environments typical of the individual's age, peers and culture.
2. Valid assessment considers cultural and linguistic diversity as well as differences in communication, sensory, motor, and behavioral factors.
3. Within an individual, limitations often coexist with strengths.
4. An important purpose of describing limitations is to develop a profile of needed supports.
5. With appropriate personalized supports over a sustained period, the life functioning of the person with mental retardation generally will improve.

Source: © 2002 American Association on Mental Retardation. Reproduced with permission of the American Association on Mental Retardation in the format Textbook via Copyright Clearance Center.

---

existence since 1876 and has routinely published guidelines for classifying and defining mental retardation that are less focused on identifying severity of disability and more on determining what steps are necessary to facilitate higher functioning. The 10th edition of the AAMR guidelines for defining mental retardation was published in 2002; the guidelines are presented in Table 14.5. These guidelines are followed by professionals more than are the DSM-IV-TR criteria.

Professionals are encouraged to identify an individual's strengths and weaknesses on psychological, physical, and environmental dimensions with a view toward determining the kinds and degrees of support needed to enhance the person's functioning in different domains. The approach focuses more on what people can do than on what they cannot do and directs professional attention to how best to make positive changes in the people's lives.

The AAMR approach encourages a more individualized assessment of a person's skills and needs than does the DSM-IV-TR. For example, a survey of over 200 people with severe mental retardation (IQs between 20 and 40) found that these individuals varied greatly in their communication skills, with some communicating only through nonverbal signals that could seldom be interpreted by caregivers and others able to combine symbols (through spoken words, manual signs, or communication boards) to make their needs known (McLean, Brady, & McLean, 1996).

As an example of the AAMR approach to classification, consider Roger, a 24-year-old man with an IQ of 45 who has attended a special program for mentally retarded individuals since he was 6. According to DSM-IV-TR, he would be considered moderately mentally retarded. Based on this diagnosis he would not be expected to be able to live independently, get around on his own, or progress beyond second grade. The AAMR classification system, however, would emphasize what is needed to maximize Roger's functioning. Thus, a clinician might discover that Roger can use the bus system if he takes a route familiar to him, and thus he might be able to go to a movie by himself from time to time. And although he cannot prepare complicated meals, he might be able to learn to prepare frozen entrées in a microwave oven. The assumption is that by concentrating and building on what he can do, Roger will make more progress.

In the schools, an individualized placement is based on the person's strengths and weaknesses and on the amount of instruction needed. A student who needs considerable one-on-one instruction because of deficient intellectual functioning may be placed in the same classroom with a child who needs intensive instruction because of emotional problems or physical disabilities. Students are identified by the classroom environment they are judged to need. This approach can lessen the stigmatizing effects of being considered retarded and may also encourage a focus on what can be done to improve the student's learning rather than on how to label the child.

Etiology of Mental Retardation

At this time, the primary cause of mental retardation can be identified in only 25 percent of the people affected. The causes that can be identified are typically neurobiological.

Genetic or Chromosomal Abnormalities   Chromosomal abnormalities occur in just under 5 percent of all recognized pregnancies. The majority of these pregnancies end in miscarriage. In all, about one-half of 1 percent of newborns have a chromosomal abnormality (Smith, Bierman, & Robinson, 1978). A significant proportion of these infants die soon after birth. Of the babies who survive, the majority have **Down syndrome**, or *trisomy 21*. Down syndrome is found in approximately 1 in 800 to 1,200 live births.

Down syndrome is named after the British physician Langdon Down, who first described its clinical signs in 1866. In 1959 the French geneticist Jerome Lejeune and colleagues identified its genetic basis. Human beings normally possess 46 chromosomes, inheriting 23 from each parent. Individuals with Down syndrome almost always have 47 chromosomes instead of 46. During maturation of the egg, the two chromosomes of pair 21, the smallest ones, fail to separate. If the egg unites with a sperm, there will be three of chromosome 21—thus the technical term trisomy 21.

People with Down syndrome have mental retardation as well as some distinctive physical signs, such as short and stocky stature; oval, upward-slanting eyes; a prolongation of the fold of the upper eyelid over the inner corner of the eye; sparse, fine, straight hair; a wide and flat nasal bridge; square-shaped ears; a large, furrowed tongue, which protrudes because the mouth is small and its roof low; and short, broad hands with stubby fingers.

About 40 percent of children with Down syndrome have heart problems; a small minority may have blockages of the upper intestinal tract; and about one in six dies during the first year. Mortality after age 40 is high. At autopsy, brain tissue generally shows deterioration similar to that in Alzheimer's disease (p. 503).

Another chromosomal abnormality that can cause mental retardation is **fragile X syndrome**, which involves a mutation in the fMR1 gene on the X chromosome (National Fragile X Foundation, www.fragilex.org). Physical symptoms associated with fragile X include facial features such as large, underdeveloped ears, a long, thin face, and a broad nasal root. In males, the testicles may be enlarged. Many such individuals exhibit mental retardation and behavior problems. Others have normal IQ but show problems such as learning disabilities, difficulties with frontal-lobe and right-hemisphere tasks, and mood lability. There is evidence that some cases of autistic disorder are caused by a form of fragile X (Baily et al., 2001; Brown et al., 1986). Some individuals with fragile X have very few problems but have been found to have social difficulties, such as shyness or poor eye contact (Dykens et al., 1988).

(Top) The normal complement of chromosomes is 23 pairs; (Bottom) In Down syndrome there are three copies (a trisomy) of chromosome 21. (Kunkel/Phototake.)

Recessive-Gene Diseases   Several hundred recessive-gene diseases have been identified, and many of them cause mental retardation. Genetic counseling can help prospective parents determine whether their backgrounds suggest that they are at risk for carrying certain of these recessive genes. Here we discuss one recessive-gene disease, phenylketonuria.

In **phenylketonuria (PKU)** the infant, born without obvious signs of difficulty, soon begins to suffer from a deficiency of a liver enzyme, phenylalanine hydroxylase. This enzyme is needed to convert phenylalanine, an amino acid contained in protein, to tyrosine, an amino acid that is essential for the production of certain hormones, such as epinephrine. Because of this enzyme deficiency, phenylalanine and its derivative phenylpyruvic acid are not broken down and instead build up in the body's fluids. This buildup eventually causes irreversible brain damage because the unmetabolized amino acid interferes with the process of myelination, the sheathing of neuron axons, which is essential for the rapid transmittal of impulses and thus of information. The neurons of the frontal lobes, the site of many

Child with Down syndrome. (Terry McKoy/Index Stock.)

important mental functions, such as rational decision making, are particularly affected, so mental retardation is profound.

States require that newborns be tested for PKU. If excess phenylalanine is found in the blood, a special diet is recommended for the baby. (Mary Kate Denny/PhotoEdit.)

Although PKU is rare, with an incidence of about 1 in 14,000 live births, it is estimated that 1 person in 70 is a carrier of the recessive gene. A blood test is available for prospective parents who have reason to suspect that they might be carriers. Pregnant women who carry the recessive gene must monitor their diet closely so that the fetus will not be exposed to toxic levels of phenylalanine (Baumeister & Baumeister, 1995). State laws require testing newborns for PKU. After the newborn with PKU has consumed milk for several days, an excess amount of unconverted phenylalanine can be detected in the blood. If the test is positive, the parents are urged to provide the infant a diet low in phenylalanine.

Parents are encouraged to introduce the special diet as early as possible and to maintain it indefinitely. Studies have indicated that children whose dietary restrictions stop at age five to seven begin to show subtle declines in functioning, particularly in IQ, reading, and spelling (Fishler et al., 1987; Legido et al., 1993). Even among children with PKU who maintain the diet, however, deficits in perceptual, memory, and attentional abilities have been observed (Banich et al., 2000; Huijbregts et al., 2002).

Infectious Diseases While in utero the fetus is at increased risk of mental retardation resulting from maternal infectious diseases such as rubella (German measles). The consequences of these diseases are most serious during the first trimester of pregnancy, when the fetus has no detectable immunological response, that is, its immune system is not developed enough to ward off infection. Cytomegalovirus, toxoplasmosis, rubella, herpes simplex, and syphilis are all maternal infections that can cause both physical deformities and mental retardation of the fetus. The mother may experience slight or no symptoms from the infection, but the effects on the developing fetus can be devastating. Women can have their blood tested to determine whether they are immune to rubella; nearly 85 percent of American women are. Women who are not immune are advised to be vaccinated at least six months before becoming pregnant. A fetus that contracts rubella from the mother is likely to be born with brain lesions that cause mental retardation.

HIV infection can also cause mental retardation. When not treated for HIV infection during pregnancy and delivery, an HIV-positive woman is more likely to pass on the virus to the developing fetus, and about half these infected infants develop mental retardation. Some develop typically at first but decline in cognitive and motor functioning as their HIV condition worsens; others remain HIV infected for many years without any impairment in intelligence.

Infectious diseases can also affect a child's developing brain after birth. Encephalitis and meningococcal meningitis may cause irreversible brain damage and even death if contracted in infancy or early childhood. In adulthood, these infections are usually far less serious. There are several forms of childhood meningitis, a disease in which the protective membranes of the brain are acutely inflamed and fever is very high.

Accidents In the United States, accidents are the leading cause of severe disability and death in children over one year of age. Falls, near drownings, and automobile accidents are among the most common mishaps in early childhood and may cause head injuries leading to varying degrees of mental retardation. Laws mandating that children sit in safety seats and wear seat belts in automobiles and that they wear protective helmets when bicycling could play a major role in reducing the incidence of mental retardation in children.

Environmental Hazards Several environmental pollutants can cause poisoning that results in mental retardation. One such pollutant is mercury, which may be ingested by eating affected fish. Another is lead, which is found in lead-based paints, smog, and the exhaust from automobiles that burn leaded gasoline. Lead poisoning can cause kidney and brain damage as well as anemia, mental retardation, seizures, and death. Lead-based paint is now prohibited in the United States, but it is still found in older homes, where children may pick and eat pieces that flake off.

Treatment of Mental Retardation

Residential Treatment   Since the 1960s, there have been serious and systematic attempts to educate children with mental retardation as fully as possible. Most people with mental retardation can acquire the competence needed to function effectively in the community. The trend has been to provide these individuals with educational and community services rather than institutionalizing them in hospitals where they receive mainly custodial care.

Since 1975, individuals with mental retardation have had a legal right to appropriate treatment in the least restrictive setting. Ideally, adults with mental retardation live in small- to medium-sized residences that are integrated into the community. Medical care is provided, and trained, live-in supervisors and aides attend to the residents' special needs around the clock. Residents are encouraged to participate in the household routines to the best of their abilities. Many adults with mental retardation have jobs and are able to live independently in their own apartments. Others live semi-independently in apartments housing three to four adults; generally, a counselor provides aid in the evening.

Behavioral Treatments   Early-intervention programs using behavioral techniques have been developed to improve the level of functioning of individuals with mental retardation. Several pilot projects are aimed at children with Down syndrome during infancy and early childhood to typically include systematic home- and treatment-center-based instruction in language skills, fine and gross motor skills, self-care, and social development. Specific behavioral objectives are defined, and children are taught skills in small, sequential steps (Reid, Wilson, & Faw, 1991).

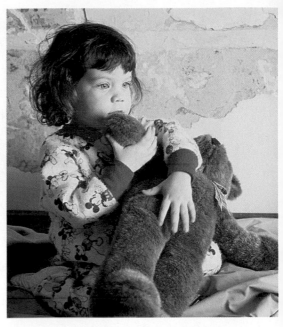

Although lead-based paint is now illegal, it can still be found in older homes. Eating these paint chips can cause lead poisoning, which can cause mental retardation. (James Keyser/Time Inc. Picture Collection.)

Children with severe mental retardation usually need intensive instruction to be able to feed, toilet, and groom themselves. To teach a child a particular routine, the therapist usually begins by dividing the targeted behavior, such as eating, into smaller components: pick up spoon, scoop food from plate onto spoon, bring spoon to mouth, remove food with lips, chew, and swallow food. Operant-conditioning principles are then applied to teach the child these components of eating. For example, the child may be reinforced for successive approximations to picking up the spoon until he or she is able to do so.

This operant approach, sometimes called *applied behavior analysis*, is also used to reduce inappropriate and self-injurious behavior. Children who live in institutions are especially prone to stereotyped behaviors performed in isolation—repetitive, rhythmic, self-stimulatory motions, such as rocking back and forth, swaying, and rolling the head—and to aggression against the self or toward other children and staff. These behaviors can often be reduced by reinforcing substitute behaviors.

Studies of these programs indicate consistent improvements in fine motor skills, acceptance by others, and self-help skills. However, the programs appear to have little effect on gross motor skills and linguistic abilities, and no long-term improvements in IQ or school performance have been demonstrated.

Cognitive Treatments   Many children with mental retardation fail to use strategies in solving problems, and when they do use strategies, they often do not use them effectively. Self-instructional training teaches these children to guide their problem-solving efforts through speech.

For example, one group of researchers taught high school students with IQs below 40 to make their own buttered toast and clean up after themselves (Hughes, Hugo, & Blatt, 1996). A teacher would demonstrate and verbalize the steps involved in solving a problem, such as the toaster's being upside down or unplugged. The young people learned to talk themselves through the steps using simple verbal or signed instructions. For example, when the toaster was presented upside down, the person would be taught to first state the problem ("Won't go in"), then to state the response ("Turn it"), self-evaluate ("Fixed it"), and self-reinforce ("Good"). They were rewarded with praise and high fives when they verbalized and solved the problem correctly. Several studies have demonstrated that even

Computer-assisted instruction is well suited for applications in the treatment of mental retardation. (Robin Nelson/PhotoEdit.)

individuals with severe mental retardation can learn self-instructional approaches to problem solving and then generalize the strategy to new tasks, including taking lunch orders at a cafeteria and performing janitorial duties (Hughes & Agran, 1993).

Computer-Assisted Instruction   Computer-assisted instruction is increasingly found in educational and treatment settings of all kinds; it may be especially well suited to the education of individuals with mental retardation. The visual and auditory components of computers maintain the attention of distractible students; the level of the material can be geared to the individual, ensuring successful experiences; and the computer can meet the need for numerous repetitions of material without becoming bored or impatient as a human teacher might. For example, computers have been used to help mentally retarded individuals learn to use an ATM (Davies, Stock, & Wehmeyer, 2003). Palm-top computers can be enormously helpful by serving as aids for reminders, directions, instructions, and daily tasks.

Quick Summary

Learning disorders, communication disorders, and motor skills disorders are all referred to by mental health professionals as learning disabilities. Most research has been conducted on learning disorders, particularly dyslexia. Children with dyslexia have significant difficulty with word recognition, reading comprehension, and typically written spelling as well. New research has uncovered how the brain is involved in dyslexia, particularly areas of the brain that support language, including the temporoparietal and occipitotemporal areas. However, important cultural differences have been noted, suggesting that there may not be one universal mechanism to account for dyslexia. The ways in which different languages are supported by the brain will be an important part of future research. Interventions for dyslexia involve intensive work on reading and language skills. Not only are these interventions successful, but they may also promote changes in the brain that could contribute to the longer term success of the treatment.

The DSM-IV-TR continues to include categories of mental retardation based on IQ scores (mild, moderate, severe, profound). However, most professionals agree that this approach is not particularly helpful for treatment. The approach of the AAMR stresses the importance of identifying an individual's strengths and weaknesses. There are a number of known causes of mental retardation, including chromosomal abnormalities, brain injury, infections, and toxins. Environmental influences such as poverty and nutrition are believed to play a part in milder forms of mental retardation.

Check Your Knowledge 14.3

Multiple choice.

1. Which of the following is not considered a learning disability?
   a. mathematics disorder
   b. dyslexia
   c. mental retardation
   d. expressive language disorder
2. A recent study examining children with dyslexia who spoke either Chinese or English found:
   a. the left middle frontal gyrus showed less activation during reading among Chinese-speaking children with dyslexia
   b. the left temporoparietal cortex showed less activation during reading among Chinese-speaking children with dyslexia

   c. the left middle frontal gyrus showed less activation during reading among English-speaking children with dyslexia
   d. the left temporoparietal cortex showed more activation during reading among English-speaking children with dyslexia
3. Which of the following has not been established as a cause for mental retardation?
   a. chromosomal abnormalities such as trisomy 21
   b. PKU
   c. lead poisoning
   d. all the above have been found to cause mental retardation

Autistic Disorder

Imagine that you are in a special-education classroom for children. You are taking a course on child disabilities, and one of the requirements is to volunteer some time in this class. One of the children in the room is standing in front of a fish tank. You notice his graceful, deft movements, his dreamy smile, and the remote look in his eyes. You start talking to him about the fish, but instead of acknowledging your comment, or even your presence, he begins rocking back and forth while continuing to smile, as if enjoying a private joke. Later, you ask the teacher about the boy, and she tells you that he has autistic disorder.

Clinical Descriptions

Autistic disorder was identified in 1943 by a psychiatrist at Harvard, Leo Kanner, who, in the course of his clinical work, noted 11 disturbed children who behaved in ways that were not common in children with mental retardation or schizophrenia. He named the syndrome *early infantile autism* because he observed that "there is from the start an extreme autistic aloneness that, whenever possible, disregards, ignores, shuts out anything that comes to the child from the outside" (Kanner, 1943).

Kanner considered autistic aloneness the most fundamental symptom. He also learned that these 11 children had been unable from the beginning of life to relate to people in the ordinary way. They were severely limited in language and had a strong, obsessive desire for everything about them to remain unchanged. Despite its early description by Kanner and others (Rimland, 1964), the disorder was not accepted into official diagnostic nomenclature until the publication of DSM-III in 1980.

Autistic disorder begins in early childhood and can be evident in the first months of life. It occurs fairly infrequently in the general population, affecting about one of every 750–1,000 children. Studies show that about four times more boys than girls have autism (Volkmar, Szatmari, & Sparrow, 1993). There has been a large increase in the number of autism diagnoses over the past 25 years—close to a 300 percent increase in California, for example (Maugh, 2002) (see Focus on Discovery 14.2 for more on this). Autism is found in all socioeconomic, ethnic, and racial groups.

Pervasive Developmental Disorders   DSM-III introduced the term **pervasive developmental disorders,** and DSM-III-R, DSM-IV, and DSM-IV-TR have retained it. In DSM-IV-TR, autistic disorder is but one of several pervasive developmental disorders; the others are Rett's disorder, childhood disintegrative disorder, and Asperger's disorder.

- **Rett's disorder** is very rare and is found only in girls. Development is entirely normal until the first or second year of life, when the growth of the child's head decelerates. She loses the ability to use her hands for purposeful movements, instead engaging in stereotyped movements such as hand wringing or hand washing; walks in an uncoordinated manner; learns only poorly to speak and to understand others; and is profoundly retarded. The child does not relate well to others, though this may improve later in life.

- **Childhood disintegrative disorder** occurs in children who have had normal development in the first 2 years of life followed by significant loss of social, play, language, and motor skills. Abnormalities in social interaction and communication and the presence of stereotyped behavior are very similar to those in autism. There has been considerable debate concerning the validity of childhood disintegrative disorder and whether it is distinct from autistic disorder (Hendry, 2000).

- **Asperger's disorder** is often regarded as a mild form of autism. Social relationships are poor and stereotyped behavior is intense and rigid, but language and intelligence are intact. It is not clear if Asperger's disorder differs qualitatively from autistic disorder or if it differs only in severity. More research has been conducted in the last 5 years on Asperger's disorder, perhaps due to the recognition of this condition among adults who for years wondered why they were different from others (*New York Times*, April 29, 2004).

DSM-IV-TR Criteria for Autistic Disorder

- A total of six or more items from A, B, and C below, with at least two from A and one each from B and C:

  A. Impairment in social interactions as manifested by at least two of the following:

  Marked impairment in use of nonverbal behaviors such as eye contact, facial expression, body language

  Deficit in development of peer relationships appropriate to developmental level

  Lack of spontaneous sharing of things or activities with others

  Lack of social or emotional reciprocity

  B. Impairment in communication as manifested by at least one of the following:

  Delay in or total lack of spoken language without attempts to compensate by nonverbal gestures

  In those who have some speech, marked impairment in ability to initiate or sustain a conversation with another

  Repetitious or idiosyncratic language

  Lack of developmentally appropriate play

  C. Repetitive or stereotyped behaviors or interests, manifested by at least one of the following:

  Abnormal preoccupation with objects or activities

  Rigid adherence to certain rituals

  Stereotyped mannerisms

  Abnormal preoccupation with parts of objects

- Delays or abnormal functioning in at least one of the following areas, beginning before age 3: social interactions, language for communication with others, or imaginative play

- Disturbance not better described as Rett's disorder or childhood disintegrative disorder

When applied to autism, the term "pervasive developmental disorder" implies that autism involves a serious abnormality in the developmental process itself and thus differs from the mental disorders that originate in adulthood. Because there is not much research on the other pervasive developmental disorders, we focus here on autism. The DSM-IV-TR criteria for autistic disorder are presented in the box in the margin.

Autism and Mental Retardation   Approximately 80 percent of children with autism score below 70 on standardized intelligence tests, which sometimes makes it difficult to distinguish between autistic disorder and mental retardation. There are important differences, however. Children with mental retardation usually score poorly on all parts of an intelligence test, but children with autism may score differently on different parts. Generally, children with autism do worse than children with mental retardation on tasks requiring abstract thought, symbolism, or sequential logic, all of which may be associated with their language deficits (Carpentieri & Morgan, 1994). They usually obtain better scores on items requiring visual-spatial skills, such as matching designs in block-design tests and putting together disassembled objects (Rutter, 1983). Sometimes they may have isolated skills that reflect great talent, such as the ability to multiply two four-digit numbers rapidly in their heads. They may also have exceptional long-term memory, being able to recall the exact words of a song heard years earlier. Sensorimotor development is the area of greatest relative strength among children with autism. These children, who may show severe and profound deficits in cognitive abilities, can be quite graceful and adept at swinging, climbing, or balancing, whereas children with mental retardation are much more delayed in areas of gross-motor development, such as learning to walk.

Autistic individuals with an IQ score greater than 70 or 80 are sometimes referred to as high-functioning. Studies comparing these high-functioning individuals with a control group matched on age, IQ, and education may still find differences between the groups. A recent study of language, for example, found that high-functioning individuals with autism performed faster but less accurately on a sentence comprehension test compared to a control group without autism but with equivalent IQ scores (Just et al., 2004). As part of this study, fMRI revealed that the patterns of brain activation also differed between the two groups. Specifically, compared to the control group, the high-functioning group showed greater activation in the areas of the brain linked to language comprehension and less activation in the areas linked to language production. In addition, the connectivity of the different areas of the brain linked with language was significantly lower among the high-functioning autism individuals than among the control group, suggesting that there is less coordination among the areas of the brain that support language processing among individuals with autism.

Social and Emotional Disturbances   We mentioned earlier that autistic aloneness is a central part of the disorder. In a sense, children with autism do not withdraw from society—they never fully joined it to begin with.

Typically, infants show signs of attachment, usually to their mothers, as early as 3 months of age. In children with autism this early attachment is less pronounced. Parents of autistic children must work harder to make contact and share affection with their babies. Children with autism rarely try to engage their parents in play, and they do not point to, show, or share objects of play with others.

Children with autism can have profound problems with the social world (Dawson et al., 2004). They rarely approach others and may look through or past people or turn their backs on them. For example, one study found that children with autism rarely offered a spontaneous greeting or farewell, either verbally or through smiling, making eye contact, or gesturing, when meeting or departing from an adult (Hobson & Lee, 1998). Another study found that 1-year-old autistic children attended to other people's faces far less often at their birthday parties than did children without autism (Osterling & Dawson, 1994). Few children with autism initiate play with other children, and they are usually unresponsive to any who may approach them. Children with autism do sometimes make eye contact, but their gaze has an unusual quality. Typically, developing children gaze to gain someone's attention or to direct the other person's attention to an object; children with autism generally do not (Dawson et al., 2004).

When someone else initiates play, children with autism may be compliant and engage in the activity for a period of time. Physical play, such as tickling and wrestling, may not be enjoyable to children with autism. Observations of their spontaneous play in an unstructured setting reveal that children with autism spend much less of their time engaged in symbolic play, such as making a doll drive to the store or pretending that a block is a car, than do either mentally retarded or normal children of comparable mental age (Sigman et al., 1987). Autistic children are more likely to twirl a favorite block continually for hours on end.

Consistent with the findings showing that autistic children do not pay attention to other people's faces or capture their gaze, recent fMRI studies have found that individuals with autism do not show activation in the fusiform gyrus, the area of the brain most often associated

Children with autism do not often play or socially interact with other children. (Ellen B. Senisi.)

with identifying faces, when completing face perception or identity tasks (Pierce et al., 2001, 2004). Instead, other areas of the brain show activation during these tasks, suggesting perhaps a less efficient system for identifying faces. A different fMRI study examined blood flow changes in the brain during processing of emotional facial expressions. In individuals with autism, the areas of the brain associated with the processing of faces (temporal-lobe region) and emotion (amygdala) were not activated during this task (Critchley et al., 2001).

Some children with autism appear not to recognize or distinguish one person from another, but some of these children can become preoccupied with and form strong attachments to simple inanimate objects (e.g., keys, rocks, a wire-mesh basket, light switches, a large blanket) and to more complex mechanical objects (e.g., refrigerators and vacuum cleaners). If the object is something they can carry, they may walk around with it in their hands, and this may prevent them from learning to do more useful things.

Recently some researchers have proposed that children with autism have a deficient "theory of mind" and that this is their core deficit leading to the kinds of social dysfunctions we have described here (Gopnik, Capps, & Meltzoff, 2000; Sigman, 1994). *Theory of mind* refers to a person's understanding that other people have desires, beliefs, intentions, and emotions that may be different from one's own. This ability is crucial for understanding and successfully engaging in social interactions. Theory of mind typically develops over the period between 2 1/2 and 5 years of age. Children with autism seem not to undergo this developmental milestone and thus seem unable to understand others' perspectives and emotional reactions. Some theorists suggest that autistic children lack empathy; therefore, for example, when a parent shows distress or pain, the child with autism withdraws rather than showing concern, and this withdrawal may indicate the child's inability to understand and empathize with another's feelings. Research has also shown that individuals with autism (and those with Asperger's disorder) have disturbances in areas of the brain linked to abilities needed for a theory of mind (Castelli et al., 2002).

Although high-functioning autistic children can learn to understand emotional experiences, they "answer questions about...emotional experiences like normal children answer difficult arithmetic questions" (Sigman, 1994, p. 15), with concentrated effort. Laboratory studies of children with high-functioning autism have found that they may recognize others' emotions without really understanding them (Capps, Yirmiya, & Sigman, 1992; Capps et al., 1999). For example, when asked to explain why someone was angry, a child with autism responded "because he was yelling" (Capps, Losh, & Thurber, 2000).

Communication Deficits   Even before they acquire language, children with autism show deficits in communication. Babbling, a term describing the utterances of infants before they begin to use words, is less frequent in infants with autism and conveys less information than it does in other infants (Ricks, 1972). By 2 years of age, most typically developing children use words to represent objects in their surroundings and construct one- and two-word sentences to express more complex thoughts, such as "Mommy go" or "Me juice." In contrast, children with autism lag well behind in these abilities and often show other language disturbances.

One such feature is **echolalia**, in which the child echoes, usually with remarkable fidelity, what he or she has heard another person say. The teacher may ask an autistic child, "Do you want a cookie?" The child's response may be, "Do you want a cookie?" This is immediate echolalia. In delayed echolalia the child may be in a room with the television on and appear to be completely uninterested. Several hours later or even the next day, the child may echo a word or phrase from the television program. Mute autistic children who later acquire some functional speech through training usually first pass through a stage of echolalia.

In the past, most educators and researchers believed that echolalia served no purpose. Now, however, some believe that echolalia may be an attempt to communicate (Prizant, 1983). For example, the child who was offered a cookie may decide later that he or she does want one, approach the teacher and say, "Do you want a cookie?" The child may not know what the words mean, but has understood that they are connected with getting a cookie.

Another language abnormality common in the speech of children with autism is **pronoun reversal** in which children refer to themselves as "he," "she," or "you" (or even by their own name). For example:

> Parent: What are you doing, Johnny?
> Child: He's here.
> Parent: Are you having a good time?
> Child: He knows it.

Pronoun reversal is closely linked to echolalia—when autistic children use echolalic speech, they refer to themselves as they have heard others speak of them and misapply pronouns. Children with autism are very literal in their use of words. If a father provided positive reinforcement by putting his daughter on his shoulders when she learned to say the word "yes," then the child might say "yes" to mean she wants to be lifted onto her father's shoulders. Or a child may say "do not drop the cat" to mean "no," because a parent had used these emphatic words when the child was about to drop the family feline.

Repetitive and Ritualistic Acts   Children with autism can become extremely upset over changes in their daily routines and surroundings. An offer of milk in a different drinking cup or a rearrangement of furniture may make them cry or precipitate a temper tantrum.

An obsessional quality pervades the behavior of autistic children in other ways as well. In their play they may continually line up toys or construct intricate patterns with household objects. As they grow older, they may become preoccupied with train schedules, subway routes, and number sequences. Children with autism are also likely to perform a more limited number of behaviors than nonautistic children and are less likely to explore new surroundings.

Children with autism are also given to stereotypical behavior, peculiar ritualistic hand movements, and other rhythmic movements, such as endless body rocking, hand flapping, and walking on tiptoe. They spin and twirl string, crayons, sticks, and plates, twiddle their fingers in front of their eyes, and stare at fans and other spinning things. Researchers often describe these as self-stimulatory activities. The children may become preoccupied with manipulating an object and may become very upset when interrupted.

Prognosis for Autistic Disorder   What happens to such severely disturbed children when they reach adulthood? Kanner (1973) reported on the adult status of 9 of the 11 children described in his original paper on autism. Two had developed epileptic seizures; one of these had died, and the other was in a state mental hospital. Four others had spent most of their lives in hospitals. Of the remaining three, one was still mute but was working on a farm and as an orderly in a nursing home. The other two had made satisfactory

Individuals with autism frequently engage in stereotyped behavior, such as ritualistic hand movements. (Nancy Pierce/Photo Researchers.)

recoveries; although both still lived with their parents and had little social life, they were gainfully employed and had developed some recreational interests.

Similar outcomes have been found in more recent population-based, follow-up studies (Gillberg, 1991; Nordin & Gillberg, 1998; Von Knorring & Hagglof, 1993). Generally, children with higher IQs who learn to speak before age six have the best outcomes, and a few of these function fairly well in adulthood. Follow-up studies focusing on high-functioning autistic individuals have indicated that most do not require residential care and some are able to attend college and support themselves through employment (Yirmiya & Sigman, 1991). Still, many independently functioning adults with autism continue to show impairment in social relationships (Howlin, Mawhood, & Rutter, 2000). Focus on Discovery 14.4 describes a woman with autism whose adult life is remarkable for its professional distinction blended with autistic social and emotional deficits.

Prior to the passage of the Developmentally Disabled Assistance and Bill of Rights Act in 1975, children with autism were often excluded from educational programs in the public schools. Thus most of the autistic children followed into adulthood had not had the benefit of intensive educational interventions or behavioral programs. Additional follow-up studies are needed to determine whether the prognosis for autism will remain as universally devastating as it was before the training and education of people with autism were taken seriously by society (Howlin & Goode, 1998).

Etiology of Autistic Disorder

The earliest theorizing about the etiology of autism was that psychological factors were responsible for its development. This narrow and faulty perspective has been replaced in recent years by theories based on evidence that genetic and neurological factors are important in the etiology of this puzzling syndrome.

Psychological Factors The best known psychoanalytic proposal on the cause of autism was formulated by Bruno Bettelheim (1967). His basic supposition was based on the observations that autism closely resembles the apathy and hopelessness found among inmates of German concentration camps during World War II and that therefore something extremely damaging must have taken place in early childhood. Bettelheim hypothesized the following scenario: a young infant has rejecting parents and is able to perceive their negative feelings; the infant finds that his or her own actions have little impact on the parents' unresponsiveness; and the child thus comes to believe that he or she can have no impact on the world and then builds the "empty fortress" of autism as protection against pain and disappointment. There is, however, no empirical support for this theory. More recent psychoanalytic theories on the causes of autistic disorder (Roser & Buchholz, 1996; Tustin, 1994) have been proposed, but these do not have empirical support either.

Like the psychoanalytically oriented theorists, some behavioral theorists postulated that certain childhood learning experiences cause autism. For example, one theorist suggested that parental inattention, especially by the mother, prevents establishment of the associations that make human beings social reinforcers (Ferster, 1961). Parents who have not become reinforcers cannot control the child's behavior, and the result is autistic disorder. There is also no support for this theory.

Despite the lack of empirical support for these psychological theories, they have gained enough recognition to place a tremendous emotional burden on parents who were told that they were at fault for their child's autism. Thus, these theories are not only unsupported, but pernicious as well.

Genetic Factors Evidence strongly suggests a genetic component for autistic disorder. For example, the risk of autism among siblings of people with the disorder is about 75 times greater than it is among siblings of people who do not have autistic disorder (McBride, Anderson, & Shapiro, 1996). Even stronger evidence for genetic transmission of autism comes from twin studies, which have found 60 to 91 percent concordance for autism between identical twins, compared with concordance rates of 0 to 20 percent between fraternal twins (Bailey et al., 1995; Le Couteur et al., 1996).

Focus on Discovery 14.4

The Story of a High-Functioning Autistic Woman

Temple Grandin is an autistic woman. She also has a Ph.D. in animal science, runs her own business designing machinery for use with farm animals, and is on the faculty at Colorado State University. Two autobiographical books (Grandin, 1986, 1995) and a profile by neurologist Oliver Sacks (1995) provide a moving and revealing portrait of the mysteries of autism. (Because of her high level of intellectual functioning, the diagnosis of Asperger's syndrome might be applicable. Controversy exists, however, as to whether this should be a separate diagnostic entity or viewed as a less severe form of autism.)

Temple Grandin, Ph.D., was diagnosed with autism in early childhood, but has had a successful academic career. (Rosalie Winard Photography.)

Lacking understanding of the complexities and subtleties of human social intercourse, deficient in the ability to empathize with others, Grandin sums up her relationship to the nonautistic world saying, "Much of the time I feel like an anthropologist on Mars" (Sacks, 1995, p. 259).

Grandin recalls from her childhood sudden impulsive behavior and violent rages, as well as hyperfocused attention, "a selectivity so intense that it could create a world of its own, a place of calm and order in the chaos and tumult" (Sacks, 1995, p. 254). She describes "sensations heightened, sometimes to an excruciating degree [and] she speaks of her ears, at the age of 2 or 3, as helpless microphones, transmitting everything, irrespective of relevance, at full, overwhelming volume" (Sacks, 1995, p. 254).

Grandin was diagnosed with autism in 1950 at age three. She had no speech at all, and doctors predicted that institutionalization would be her fate. However, with the help of a therapeutic nursery school and speech therapy and with the support of her family, she learned to speak by age six and began to make more contact with others. Still, as an adolescent observing other children interact, Grandin "sometimes wondered if they were all telepathic" (Sacks, 1995, p. 272), so mysterious

did she find the ability of normal children to understand each other's needs and wishes, to empathize, to communicate.

Visiting her one day at her university, Sacks made several observations that convey the autistic flavor of this uncommon person:

She sat me down [in her office] with little ceremony, no preliminaries, no social niceties, no small talk about my trip or how I liked Colorado. She plunged straight into talking of her work, speaking of her early interests in psychology and animal behavior, how they were connected with self-observation and a sense of her own needs as an autistic person, and how this had joined with the [highly developed] visualizing and engineering part of her mind to point her towards the special field she had made her own: the design of farms, feedlots, corrals, slaughterhouses— systems of many sorts for animal management.

She spoke well and clearly, but with a certain unstoppable impetus and fixity. A sentence, a paragraph, once started, had to be completed; nothing left implicit, hanging in the air. (Sacks, 1995, pp. 256–257)

Having traveled all day, missing lunch, feeling hungry and thirsty, Sacks hoped in vain for Grandin to notice his fatigued and needy state and offer him something to drink or suggest they go somewhere for a bite. After an hour, realizing that this was not going to happen, he asked for some coffee:

There was no "I'm sorry, I should have offered you some before," no intermediacy, no social junction. Instead she immediately took me to a coffeepot that was kept brewing in the secretaries' office upstairs. She introduced me to the secretaries in a somewhat brusque manner, giving me the feeling, once again, of someone who had learned, roughly, "how to behave" in such situations without having much personal perception of how other people felt—the nuances, the social subtleties involved. (Sacks, 1995, p. 257)

In her own writings Grandin points out that many autistic people are great fans of *Star Trek*, and especially the characters of Spock and Data, the former a member of the Vulcan race, purely intellectual, logical beings who eschew any consideration of the emotional side of life, and the latter an android, a highly sophisticated computer housed in a human body and, like Spock, lacking in emotion. (One of the dramatic themes involving both characters was, of course, their flirtation with the experience of human emotion, portrayed with particular poignancy by Data. This is a theme in Grandin's life as well.) As Grandin wrote at age 47:

All my life I have been an observer, and I have always felt like someone who watches from the outside. I could not participate in the social interactions of high school life.

Even today, personal relationships are something I don't really understand. I've remained celibate because doing so helps me avoid the many complicated situations that are too difficult for me to handle. [M]en who want to date often don't understand how to relate to a woman. They [and I myself] remind me of Data, the android on Star Trek. In one episode, Data's attempts at dating were a disaster. When he tried to be romantic [by effecting a change in a subroutine of his computer program], he complimented his date by using scientific terminology. Even very able adults with autism have such problems. (1995, pp. 132–133)

Some of the deficiencies of people with autism make them charmingly honest and trustworthy. "Lying," wrote Grandin, "is very anxiety-provoking because it requires rapid interpretations of subtle social cues [of which I am incapable] to determine whether the other person is really being deceived" (Grandin, 1995, p. 135).

Grandin's professional career is impressive. She uses her remarkable powers of visualization and her empathy for farm animals to design machines such as a chute leading cows to slaughter that takes them on a circular route, protecting them from awareness of their fate until the moment of death. She has also designed and built a "squeeze machine," a device that provides comforting hugs without the need for human contact. It has "two heavy, slanting wooden sides, perhaps four by three feet each, pleasantly upholstered with a thick, soft padding. They [are] joined by hinges to a long, narrow bottom board to create a V-shaped, body-sized trough. There [is] a complex control box at one end, with heavy-duty tubes leading off to another device, in a closet. [An] industrial compressor exerts a firm but comfortable pressure on the body, from the shoulders to the knees' " (Sacks, 1995, pp. 262–263). Her explanation of the rationale behind this contraption is that as a little girl she longed to be hugged but was also very fearful of physical contact with another person. When a favorite, large-bodied aunt hugged her, she felt both overwhelmed and comforted. Terror commingled with pleasure.

> She started to have daydreams—she was just five at the time—of a magic machine that could squeeze her powerfully but gently, in a huglike way, and in a way entirely commanded and controlled by her. Years later, as an adolescent, she had seen a picture of a squeeze chute designed to hold or restrain calves and realized that that was it: a little modification to make it suitable for human use, and it could be her magic machine. (Sacks, 1995, p. 263)

After watching her demonstrate the machine and trying it himself, Sacks observed:

> It is not just pleasure or relaxation that Temple gets from the machine but, she maintains, a feeling for others. As she lies in her machine, she says, her thoughts often turn to her mother, her favorite aunt, her teachers. She feels their love for her, and hers for them. She feels that the machine opens a door into an otherwise closed emotional world and allows her, almost teaches her, to feel empathy for others. (Sacks, 1995, p. 264)

Sacks has great admiration for Grandin's professional success and for the interesting and productive life she has made for herself, but when it comes to human interactions it is clear that she does not get it. "I was struck by the enormous difference, the gulf, between Temple's immediate, intuitive recognition of animal moods and signs and her extraordinary difficulties understanding human beings, their codes and signals, the way they conduct themselves" (p. 269).

Accounts such as those of Grandin and Sacks can provide insight into how people adapt to their own idiosyncrasies, using the sometimes peculiar gifts they have been given and working around the deficiencies with which they have been saddled. "Autism, while it may be pathologized as a syndrome, must also be seen as a whole mode of being, a deeply different mode or identity, one that needs to be conscious (and proud) of itself," wrote Sacks (p. 277). "At a recent lecture, Temple ended by saying, 'If I could snap my fingers and be nonautistic, I would not—because then I wouldn't be me. Autism is part of who I am'" (p. 291).

A series of studies following twins and families with an autistic member suggests that autism is linked genetically to a broader spectrum of deficits in communication and social interaction (Bailey et al., 1995; Bolton et al., 1994; Folstein & Rutter, 1977a, b). For example, almost all the nonautistic identical twins of autistic adults are unable to live independently or maintain a close and confiding relationship. In addition, most of the identical twins without autism evidenced communication deficits, such as delayed development of language abilities or reading impairments, as well as severe social deficits, including no social contacts outside the family, lack of responsiveness to social cues or conventions, and little or no spontaneous affection shown toward caregivers. In contrast, fraternal twins of children with autism are almost always normal in their social and language development and marry and live independently in adulthood (Le Couteur et al., 1996). Taken together, the evidence from family and twin studies strongly supports a genetic basis for autistic disorder.

Neurological Factors More and more research is linking the language, social, and emotional deficits in autism to the brain. A number of studies examining the brain in autism have been well replicated, allowing for a clearer picture of what may go wrong in the brain among individuals with autism. What remains to be figured out is why the brain goes awry early in development.

Studies using magnetic resonance imaging (MRI) found that, overall, the brains of autistic adults and children are larger than the brains of adults and children without autism (Courchesne, Carnes, & Davis, 2001; Piven et al., 1995, 1996). This same finding has been supported by studies using the measurement of head circumference as an indicator of brain size (Courchesne, Carper, & Akshoomoff, 2003). What makes these findings more interesting and puzzling is that most children with autism are born with brains of a relatively normal size; however, between the ages of 2 and 4, the brains of children with autism become significantly larger (Courchesne, 2004). Having a larger than normal brain is not necessarily a good thing, as it might indicate that neurons are not being pruned correctly. The pruning of neurons is an important part of brain maturation; older children have fewer connections between neurons than do babies. Adding further to this puzzle, brain growth in autism appears to slow abnormally in later childhood. It will be important for investigators to figure out how this pattern of brain growth is linked to the signs and symptoms of autism. It is worth noting that the areas of the brain that are "overgrown" in autism include the frontal, temporal, and cerebellar, which have been linked with language, social, and emotional functions.

Other areas of the brain are implicated in autism as well. Sixteen MRI and autopsy studies from nine independent research groups all found abnormalities in the cerebellum of autistic children (Haas et al., 1996), and more recent studies have confirmed this finding (e.g., Hardan et al., 2001). Another study found that the commonly observed tendency of autistic children to explore their surroundings less than other children do is correlated with a larger than normal cerebellum (Pierce & Courchesne, 2001). Neurological abnormalities in individuals with autism suggest that in the course of development, their brain cells fail to align properly and do not form the network of connections found in normal brains.

Treatment of Autistic Disorder

The earliest efforts at treatment of autistic disorder were psychological in nature, and some of them have shown promise. More recently, various treatments that combine psychological treatment and drugs have been studied as well, but with few positive results. Treatments for children with autism are usually aimed at reducing their unusual behavior and improving their communication and social skills.

It is important to note that even though genetic and neurological factors in the etiology of autism have much more empirical support than psychological factors, it is the psychological treatments that currently show the most promise, not medications. The lesson is that a neurological defect may well be treatable psychologically.

Ivar Lovaas, a behavior therapist, is noted for his operant-conditioning treatment of autistic children. (Courtesy of Susan Oliver Young.)

Behavioral Treatment Ivar Lovaas, a leading clinical researcher at the University of California at Los Angeles, conducted an intensive operant-conditioning-based program of behavioral treatment with young (under four years old) children with autism (Lovaas, 1987). Therapy encompassed all aspects of the children's lives for more than 40 hours a week over more than two years. Parents were trained extensively so that treatment could continue during almost all the children's waking hours. Nineteen children receiving this intensive treatment were compared with 40 children who received a similar treatment for less than 10 hours per week. Both groups of children were rewarded for being less aggressive, more compliant, and more socially appropriate—for example, talking and playing with other children. The goal of the program was to mainstream the children, the assumption being that autistic children, as they improve, benefit more from being with typically developing peers than from remaining by themselves or with other seriously disturbed children.

The results of this landmark study were dramatic and encouraging. The measured IQs for the intensive-therapy group averaged 83 in first grade (after about two years in the intensive therapy) compared with about 55 for the other group; 12 of the 19 reached the normal range, compared with only 2 (of 40) of the others. Furthermore, 9 of the 19 in the intensive-therapy group were promoted to second grade in a regular public school, whereas only 1 of the much larger group achieved this level of functioning. A follow-up of these children 4 years later indicated that the intensive-treatment group maintained their gains in IQ, adaptive behavior, and grade promotions in school (McEachin, Smith, & Lovaas, 1993). Although critics have pointed out weaknesses in the study's methodology and outcome measures (Schopler, Short, & Mesibov, 1989), this ambitious program confirms the benefits of intensive therapy with the heavy involvement of both professionals and parents in dealing with the challenges of autistic disorder.

One of the weaknesses of the study was that it was not a randomized, controlled clinical trial. To date, there has only been one randomized, controlled clinical trial to examine the efficacy of intensive behavioral treatment on a broader scale (although another is currently underway). This study compared an intensive behavioral treatment (about 25 hours a week, instead of 40) to a treatment that consisted of parent training only (Smith, Groen, & Wynn, 2000). Although the behavioral treatment was more effective than parent training alone, the children in this study did not show the same gains as in the study discussed above (Lovaas, 1987), perhaps due to the fact that the treatment was implemented for fewer hours.

Other research suggests that education provided by parents is more beneficial to the child than is clinic- or hospital-based treatment. Parents are present in many different situations and thus can help children generalize the gains they make. For example, one group of researchers demonstrated that 25 to 30 hours of parent training was as effective as 200 hours of direct clinic treatment in improving the behavior of children with autism (Koegel et al., 1982). This research group has also focused on comparing different strategies for behavioral parent training, with interesting discoveries. They found that parents could be more effective when taught to focus on increasing their children's general motivation and responsiveness rather than being taught to focus on changing individually targeted problem behaviors in a sequential manner (Koegel, Bimbela, & Schreibman, 1996). For example, allowing the child to choose the teaching materials, providing natural reinforcers (e.g., play and social praise) rather than edible reinforcers, and reinforcing attempts to respond as well as correct responses all led to improved family interactions and more positive communication between parents and their autistic children. This more focused approach to treatment is called *pivotal response treatment* (PRT), a term based on the notion that intervening in a key, or pivotal, area may lead to changes in other areas. At least 10 studies have found PRT to be effective (reviewed in Koegel, Koegel, & Brookman, 2003).

Drug Treatment   The most commonly used medication for treating problem behaviors in children with autism is haloperidol (trade name Haldol), an antipsychotic medication frequently used in the treatment of schizophrenia. Some controlled studies have shown that this drug reduces social withdrawal, stereotyped motor behavior, and such maladaptive behaviors as self-mutilation and aggression (Anderson et al., 1989; McBride et al., 1996; Perry et al., 1989). Many children do not respond positively to the drug, however, and it has not shown any positive effects on other aspects of autistic disorder, such as abnormal interpersonal relationships and language impairments (Holm & Varley, 1989). Haloperidol also has potentially serious side effects (Posey & McDougle, 2000). In a longitudinal study, over 30 percent of children with autism developed drug-related dyskinesias, or jerky muscle disturbances, although most went away after the drug was withdrawn (Campbell et al., 1997).

Evidence that children with autism may have elevated blood levels of serotonin (Anderson & Hoshino, 1987) encouraged research on medications that reduce the action of serotonin. In the early 1980s a large, multisite study was conducted in 20 medical centers to examine the effectiveness of fenfluramine, a drug known to lower serotonin levels in rats and monkeys. There was an initial flurry of enthusiastic claims that the drug effected dramatic improvement in the behavior and thought processes of children with autism (Ritvo et al., 1983), but later studies delivered much more modest findings. Although fenfluramine may work with some autistic children to slightly improve their social adjustment, attention span, activity level, and stereotyped behavior, no consistent effect has been shown on cognitive measures such as IQ or language functioning. Reviews concur that the effects of fenfluramine are at best subtle, and the drug certainly does not represent a cure for autism (Leventhal et al., 1993; Rapin, 1997).

Researchers have also studied naltrexone, an opioid receptor antagonist, and found that this drug reduces hyperactivity in children with autism and produces a moderate improvement in the initiation of social interactions (Aman & Langworthy, 2000; P. A. Williams et al., 2001; Willemsen-Swinkels, Buitelaar, & van Engeland, 1996). One controlled study suggested mild improvements in the initiation of communication as well (Kolmen et al., 1995), but others found no changes in communication or social behavior (Feldman, Kolmen, & Gonzaga, 1999; Willemsen-Swinkels et al., 1995, 1996). The drug does not appear to affect the core symptoms of autism, and some evidence suggests that at some doses it may increase self-injurious behavior (Anderson et al., 1997).

In sum, pharmacological treatment of autism is, at this point, less effective than behavioral treatments.

Check Your Knowledge 14.4

True or false?
1. All children with autism also have mental retardation.
2. Children with autism have difficulty recognizing emotions in others.

3. Family factors play a key role in the etiology of autistic disorder.
4. Medication is an effective treatment for autistic disorder.

Summary

Clinical Descriptions

● Childhood disorders are often organized into two domains: externalizing disorders and internalizing disorders. Externalizing disorders are characterized by such behaviors as aggressiveness, noncompliance, overactivity, and impulsiveness; they include attention-deficit/hyperactivity disorder, conduct disorder, and oppositional defiant disorder. Internalizing disorders are characterized by such behaviors as depression, social withdrawal, and anxiety and include childhood anxiety and mood disorders.

● Attention-deficit/hyperactivity disorder (ADHD) is a persistent pattern of inattention and/or hyperactivity and impulsivity that is more frequent and more severe than what is typically observed in children of a given age. Conduct disorder is sometimes a precursor to antisocial personality disorder in adulthood, though many children carrying the diagnosis do not progress to that extreme. It is characterized by high and widespread levels of aggression, lying, theft, vandalism, cruelty to other people and to animals, and other acts that violate laws and social norms.

● Mood and anxiety disorders in children share similarities with the adult forms of these disorders. However, differences that reflect different stages of development are also important.

● Learning disorders are diagnosed when a child fails to develop to the degree expected for his or her intellectual level in a specific academic, language, or motor-skill area. These disorders are often identified and treated within the school system rather than through mental health clinics.

● The DSM-IV-TR diagnostic criteria for mental retardation are subaverage intellectual functioning and deficits in adaptive behavior, with onset before the age of 18. Most professionals, however, focus more on the strengths of individuals with mental retardation than on their assignment to a particular level of severity. This shift in emphasis is associated with increased efforts to design psychological and educational interventions that make the most of individuals' abilities.

● Autistic disorder, one of the pervasive developmental disorders, begins before the age of 2 1/2. The major symptoms are a failure to relate to other people; communication problems, consisting of either a failure to learn any language or speech irregularities, such as echolalia and pronoun reversal; and theory of mind problems.

Etiology

● There is strong evidence for genetic and neurobiological factors in the etiology of ADHD. Low birth weight and maternal smoking are also risk factors. Family factors interact with these genetic vulnerabilities.

● Among the apparent etiological and risk factors for conduct disorder are a genetic predisposition, inadequate learning of moral awareness,

modeling and direct reinforcement of antisocial behavior, negative peer influences, and living in impoverished and crime-ridden areas.

● Etiological factors for mood and anxiety disorders in children are believed to be the same as in adulthood, though additional research is needed.

● There is mounting evidence that the most widely studied of the learning disorders, dyslexia, has genetic and other neurobiological components.

● The more severe forms of mental retardation have a neurological basis, such as the chromosomal trisomy that causes Down syndrome. Certain infectious diseases in the pregnant mother, such as HIV, rubella, and syphilis, as well as illnesses that affect the child directly, such as encephalitis, can stunt cognitive and social development, as can malnutrition, severe falls, and automobile accidents that injure the brain. Environmental factors are considered the principal causes of milder mental retardation.

● Family and twin studies give compelling evidence of a genetic predisposition. Abnormalities have been found in the brains of autistic children, including an overgrowth of the brain by age 2 and abnormalities in the cerebellum.

Treatment

● A combined treatment including stimulant drugs, such as Ritalin, and reinforcement for staying on task has shown effectiveness in reducing the symptoms of ADHD.

● The most promising approach to treating young people with conduct disorder involves intensive intervention in multiple systems, including the family, school, and peer systems.

● The most effective intervention for mood and anxiety disorders is cognitive behavioral therapy. Medication is effective for depression among adolescents, though its use is not without controversy.

● The most widespread interventions for dyslexia are educational.

● Many children with mental retardation who would formerly have been institutionalized are now being educated in the public schools under the provisions of Public Law 94-142. In addition, using applied behavioral analysis, self-instructional training, and modeling, behavior therapists have been able to treat successfully many of the behavioral problems of individuals with mental retardation and to improve their intellectual functioning.

● The most promising treatments for autism are psychological in nature, involving intensive behavioral interventions and work with parents. Various drug treatments have been used but have proved less effective than behavioral interventions.

Answers to Check Your Knowledge Questions

14.1 1. T; 2. T; 3. T; 4. F
14.2 1. life-course-persistent, adolescent-limited; 2. ADHD, substance abuse, depression, anxiety; 3. parent management training, multi-systemic treatment.

14.3 1. c; 2. a; 3. d
14.4 1. F; 2. T; 3. F; 4. F

Key Terms

Asperger's disorder
attention-deficit/hyperactivity disorder (ADHD)
autistic disorder
childhood disintegrative disorder
communication disorders
conduct disorder
developmental psychopathology
disorder of written expression

Down syndrome (trisomy 21)
echolalia
expressive language disorder
externalizing disorders
fragile X syndrome
internalizing disorders
learning disability
learning disorders
mathematics disorder

mental retardation
motor skills disorder
multisystemic treatment (MST)
oppositional defiant disorder
parental management training (PMT)
pervasive developmental disorders
phenylketonuria (PKU)

phonological disorder
pronoun reversal
reading disorder (dyslexia)
Rett's disorder
school phobia
stuttering

15 Late Life and Psychological Disorders

Learning Goals

1. Be able to describe common misconceptions about age-related changes, and to understand genuine age-related changes.
2. Be able to discuss issues involved in conducting research on aging.
3. Be able to explain the symptoms of dementia and delirium, and understand current approaches to etiology and treatment.
4. Be able to describe the prevalence, etiology, and treatment of psychological disorders in the elderly.
5. Be able to explain the issues involved with community living, assisted living, and nursing homes.

Clinical Case: Henry

Henry was a 56-year-old businessman who was hospitalized for cervical disk surgery. Because of his busy schedule and his anxiety about surgery, he had canceled two previous admissions. Although Henry drank heavily, his drinking never interfered with his business performance. There were no immediate complications of the surgery. The patient seemed to be making a normal recovery initially. During the third postoperative night, though, he became quite restless and could not sleep. The next day he was visibly fatigued. The following night his restlessness became more pronounced, and he became fearful. As the night progressed, he thought that he saw people hiding in his room, and shortly before dawn he told the nurse that he saw some strange little animals running over his bed and up the drapes. At the time of morning rounds, the patient was very frightened. He was lethargic, distractible, and incoherent when he tried to discuss the events of the night before. He knew who he was and where he was but did not know the date or when he had had his surgery. During that day his mental status fluctuated, but by nightfall he had become grossly disoriented and agitated. At this point, psychiatric consultation was obtained.

The consultant's diagnosis was delirium, probably due to several factors: withdrawal from alcohol, use of strong analgesics, and stress of the operation. The treatment consisted of a reduction in pain medications, partial illumination of the room at night, a family member present at all times, along with 50 mg of chlorpromazine (Thorazine) three times daily and 500 mg of chloral hydrate at bedtime. Treatment reversed his confusional state within 2 days, and he was able to return home in a week with no symptoms (Strub & Black, 1981, pp. 89–90).

As we age, physiological changes are inevitable, and there may be many emotional and mental changes as well. This chapter examines how issues like these influence mental health in late life. We begin by reviewing some general topics critical to the study of late life. We look next at dementia and delirium, two cognitive disorders. Then we examine a set of questions about mental illness in late life. Are older people at lower risk for mental disorders than young people? Do emotional problems develop in people who did not have them when younger? Are late life manifestations of mental illness caused by the same factors that trigger early onsets? Which treatments successfully address mental health problems among the elderly? Finally, we discuss general issues of living situations for older adults.

Aging: Issues and Methods

In contrast to the esteem in which they are held in most Asian countries, older adults are generally not treated well in the United States. The process of growing old is feared by many, even abhorred. Perhaps our lack of regard for older adults stems from our own deep-seated fear of growing old. The old person with serious infirmities is an unwelcome reminder that we all may one day walk with an unsteady gait, see less clearly, taste food less keenly, and experience more physical illness.

The social problems of aging may be especially severe for women. Even with the consciousness-raising of the past three decades, our society does not readily accept women with wrinkles and sagging bodies. Although men with gray hair at the temples and even baldness often are seen as distinguished, signs of aging in women are not valued in the U.S. and many other countries. The cosmetics and plastic-surgery industries make billions of dollars each year exploiting the fear inculcated in women about looking their age.[1] According to some experts, however, being female confers certain mental health benefits as people age, as explored in Focus on Discovery 15.1.

The old are usually defined as those over the age of 65, an arbitrary point set largely by social policies rather than any physiological process. To have some rough demarcation points, gerontologists usually divide people over age 65 into three groups: the young-old, those aged 65 to 74; the old-old, those aged 75 to 84; and the oldest-old, those over age 85.

At the time of the last census, people 65 and older comprised 12.4 percent (35 million) of the United States population (U.S. Bureau of the Census, 2001). Figure 15.1 shows the dramatic increase in the number of older Americans over time. As of 1999, there were 70,000 Americans at least 100 years old; by the year 2050, that number is expected to grow more than 10-fold to over 800,000 (U.S. Bureau of the Census, 1999).

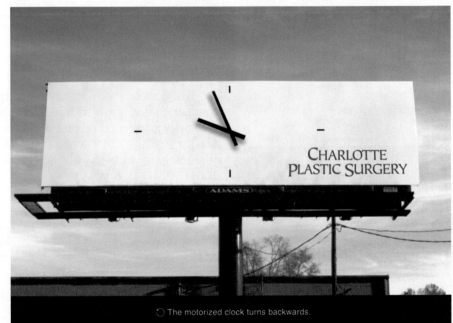

◯ The motorized clock turns backwards.

People spend billions of dollars per year on cosmetics and plastic surgery to reduce signs of aging. (Courtesy of BooneOakley.)

---

[1] We should point out, though, that increasing numbers of men are undergoing plastic surgery in an effort to look younger than their years.

Focus on Discovery 15.1

Gender and the Transition to Late Life

Older women in U.S. society face many threats to well-being. They are more likely than older men to be widowed or divorced (Moen, 1996); to live in poverty (Estes, Gerard, & Clarke, 1985); and to be the victims of crime, particularly domestic violence (Jones, 1987).

Despite these disadvantages, it has been observed that on some levels, women adapt more successfully to the aging process than do men. They enjoy a longer life expectancy than do men. More specific to mental health, the suicide rate for men rises steadily as they age, but the rate for women declines from their 50s across the rest of their life span (McIntosh, 1995).

Why are women resilient in late life? Women may come to late life with more experience navigating major role changes over the course of their lives (from, e.g., maternal and spousal roles to possible career-related roles to postparental roles). In contrast, men often remain in a more stable role of the provider until they reach late life and retirement. The ability to become involved in multiple social roles in late life is associated with fewer depressive symptoms, greater life satisfaction, and

higher perceived self-efficacy in both women and men (Turk-Charles, Rose, & Gatz, 1996).

One study examined the protectiveness of role flexibility and discrimination experience among a group of 65-year-old women (E. H. Davison, 1999). Women completed questionnaires to measure the amount of sexism and ageism they had experienced during their lives, their gender role flexibility (the degree to which they felt comfortable assuming the traditional roles of both sexes—e.g., being a mother of a small child 50 years ago and working outside the home), and subjective well-being. Consistent with theory, gender role flexibility predicted higher subjective well-being. Perceived discrimination predicted lower subjective well-being. These findings reinforce the notion that gender role flexibility is correlated with (and may contribute to) well-being in older women. Additionally, these data underscore the importance of considering the effects of discrimination on well-being in late life.

Given these statistics, it is not surprising that 69 percent of practicing psychologists conduct clinical work with older adults (Qualls et al., 2002). A major concern, though, is that fewer than 30 percent of psychologists report receiving any formal training about late life issues (Qualls et al., 2002). APA ethical principles state that it is important for psychologists working with the elderly to examine their stereotypes about late life (APA, 2004).

Ageism refers to discrimination against someone because of his or her age. In one form of ageism, countermyth, we especially applaud achievements of the elderly, as in former President Bush's parachute jump. (AP/Wide World Photos.)

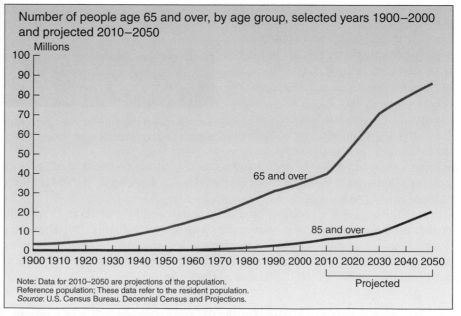

Number of people age 65 and over, by age group, selected years 1900–2000 and projected 2010–2050

65 and over

85 and over

Projected

Note: Data for 2010–2050 are projections of the population.
Reference population; These data refer to the resident population.
Source: U.S. Census Bureau. Decennial Census and Projections.

Figure 15.1   The number of old and old-old U.S. citizens is on the rise.

Myths about Late Life

Most people in the United States have certain assumptions about old age. Common myths include the idea that we will become doddering and befuddled. We worry that we will be unhappy, cope poorly with troubles, and become focused on our poor health. We worry that we will become lonely, and that our sex lives will become unsatisfying.

Each of these myths has been debunked. As we shall see, severe cognitive problems do not occur for most people in late life, though a mild decline in cognitive functioning is common (Park, O'Connell, & Thomson, 2003). Elderly people (age 60 and older) actually experience less negative emotion than do young people (age 18–30 years) (Lawton et al., 1992). Although some might suspect that these findings are artifacts of older individuals who may not want to describe negative feelings to researchers, laboratory studies also indicate that the elderly are skilled at regulating their emotions. For example, when older people are asked to think or talk about emotionally charged topics, they display less physiological reactivity than younger people do (Levenson, Carstensen, & Gottman, 1994). When viewing positive images, they show more robust brain activation in key emotion regions than younger people do (Mather et al., 2004). Older people are actually likely to underreport somatic symptoms, perhaps because of beliefs that aches and pains are an inevitable part of late life. People in late life are no more likely to meet criteria for somatization or hypochondriasis than are the young (Regier et al., 1988; Siegler & Costa, 1985).

Another myth, that older people are lonely, has received considerable attention. The truth is that the number of social activities is unrelated to psychological well-being among older people (Carstensen, 1996). As we age, our interests shift away from seeking new social interactions to cultivating those few social relationships that really matter to us, such as those with family and close friends. This phenomenon has been called **social selectivity**.

Contrary to stereotypes, many older people maintain an active interest in sex. Studies indicate that the frequency of sexual activity among those in their 70s is as high as it is among middle-aged people. (FPG International/Getty Images.)

When we have less time ahead of us, we tend to place a higher value on emotional intimacy than on learning more about the world. This preference applies not just to older people, but also to younger people who see themselves as having limited time, such as when they are preparing to move far away from their home (Frederickson & Carstensen, 1990) or if they have AIDS. When we can't see a future without end, we prefer to spend our limited time with our closest ties rather than with casual acquaintances, such as strangers in a recreation center for older adults. To those unfamiliar with these age-related changes, social selectivity could be misinterpreted as harmful social withdrawal.

Finally, contrary to popular belief, older people have considerable sexual interest and capacity (Deacon, Minichiello, & Plummer, 1995). For example, on average, sexual activity does not decrease between the ages of 46 and 71 (George & Weiler, 1981).

In sum, older adults have many positive life experiences, many coping mechanisms, and much wisdom on which to draw. Many stereotypes we hold about the elderly are false. Beyond questioning assumptions, it is important to recognize that the word diversity is well suited to the older population. Not only are older people different from one another, but they are more different from one another than are people in any other age group. People tend to become less alike as they grow older. That all old people are alike is a prejudice held by many people. A moment's honest reflection may reveal that certain traits come to mind when we hear that a person is age, say, 67. But to know that a person is 67 years old is actually to know very little about him or her. Each older person brings to late life a developmental history that makes his or her reactions to common problems unique.

The Problems Experienced in Late Life

We know that mental health is tied to the physical and social problems in a person's life. As a group, no other people have more of these problems than the aged. They have them all—physical decline and disabilities,

The quality of sleep diminishes as people age. (Corbis Digital Stock.)

As illustrated by John Glenn's space flight, advancing age need not lead to a curtailment of activities. (NASA/CNP/Archive Photos.)

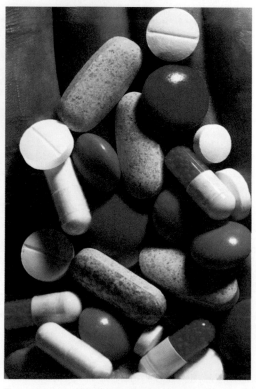

Polypharmacy is all too common in late life. (Tony Why/Phototake.)

sensory and neurological deficits, loss of loved ones, the cumulative effects of a lifetime of many unfortunate experiences, and social stresses such as ageism. (Ageism can be defined as discrimination against any person, young or old, based on chronological age, such as when a professor in his or her late 60s is considered too old to continue teaching at a university, or when a person older than 75 is ignored in a social gathering on the assumption that he or she has nothing to contribute to the conversation.) As many as 80 percent of elderly people have at least one major medical condition (National Academy on an Aging Society, 1999).

One particular facet of aging deserves particular attention. As people age, the quality and depth of sleep declines, so that by age 65, 25 percent of people report problems with insomnia (Mellinger, Balter, & Uhlenhuth, 1985). Rates of sleep apnea, a disorder in which a person stops breathing for seconds to minutes during the night, also increase with age (Prechter & Shepard, 1990). Insomnia is often caused by medication side effects (Rodin, McAvay, & Timko, 1988) or by pain from medical problems (Prinz & Raskin, 1978). Untreated and chronic sleep deficits can worsen both physical and psychological health problems and can even increase risk of mortality (Ancoli et al., 1996). Because older adults are often sensitive to side effects of medications, cognitive behavioral interventions may be superior to drug treatments for sleep problems (Morin et al., 1999).

Several problems are evident in the medical treatment available during late life. One of the main difficulties is that the chronic health problems of older people seldom diminish; physicians focused on identifying cures can become frustrated when none are available (Zarit, 1980). Another problem is due in part to the time pressure of the health care system: doctors may just write out a prescription in hopes of addressing the complaints rather than taking the time to find out what is really bothering an older patient. Doctors may not even check to see what other medications the patient is currently taking, or they may not know if the patient is seeing multiple doctors, a situation that is not unusual with older patients. *Polypharmacy*, the prescribing of multiple drugs to a patient, can result; this increases the risk of adverse drug reactions which may cause numerous side effects, toxicity, and allergic reactions. Often, physicians then prescribe more medications to combat the side effects, thus continuing the vicious cycle.

Further complicating the picture is the fact that most psychoactive drugs are tested on younger people; gauging the appropriate dose for the less efficient metabolism of the kidneys and liver of the older person represents a challenge for the medical practitioner—side effects and toxicity are much more common (Gallo & Lebowitz, 1999). The increased sensitivity to medication side effects is a particular problem with psychiatric medications—we will discuss some major problems in using antipsychotic medications, antidepressants, and benzodiazapines later in the chapter. One review of medical charts of more than 750,000 elderly patients found that more than one-fifth had filled a prescription for a medication deemed inappropriate for people over the age of 65 due to serious side effects (Curtis et al., 2004). Therefore, it is important that the primary care physician of the geriatric patient keep track of all prescribed medications taken, discontinue nonessential drugs, and prescribe only the necessary minimum dosages.

Research Methods in the Study of Aging

Research on aging requires an understanding of several special issues. Chronological age is not as simple a variable in psychological research as it might seem. Because other factors associated with age may be at work, we must be cautious when we attribute differences in age groups solely to the effects of aging. In the field of aging, as in studies of childhood development, a distinction is made among three kinds of effects (see Table 15.1):

- **Age effects** are the consequences of being a certain chronological age.
- **Cohort effects** are the consequences of growing up during a particular time period with its unique challenges and opportunities. For example, experiences like the Great

Table 15.1 Age, Cohort, and Time-of-Measurement Effects

Age Effects	Cohort Effects	Time-of-Measurement Effects
The effects of being a certain age; e.g., being old enough to receive Social Security	The consequences of having been born in a given year and having grown up during a particular time period; e.g., a sense of frugality may be increased among those who lived through the Great Depression of the 1930s	The effects of testing people at a particular time in history; e.g., people became more frank during the 1990s to surveys about their sexual behavior, as media discussion of sexuality increased

Depression, a world war, or 9/11 each shape experiences and attitudes. Similarly, the expectations for marriage have changed drastically in the past century, at least in Western societies, from a focus on stability to a focus on happiness and personal fulfillment.

- **Time-of-measurement effects** are confounds that arise because events at a particular point in time can have a specific effect on a variable that is being studied (Schaie & Hertzog, 1982). For example, people tested right after hurricane Katrina in New Orleans might demonstrate elevated levels of anxiety.

Two major research designs are used to assess developmental change: cross-sectional and longitudinal. In *cross-sectional studies*, the investigator compares different age groups at the same moment in time on the variable of interest. Suppose that in 1995 we took a poll in the U.S. and found that many interviewees over age 80 spoke with a European accent, whereas those in their 40s and 50s did not. Could we conclude that as people grow older, they develop European accents? Hardly! Cross-sectional studies do not examine the same people over time; consequently, they do not provide clear information about how people change as they age.

In *longitudinal studies*, the researcher periodically retests one group of people using the same measure over a number of years or decades. For example, the Baltimore Longitudinal Study of Aging is one of the longest-running studies of aging. Beginning in the 1950s, researchers have been following 1,400 men and women to see how their lifestyles, medical conditions, and psychological health change over time. In this study, a great deal has been learned about mental health and aging. For example, researchers were able to combat myths that people become more unhappy over time. Rather, people who were happy at age 30 tended to be happy as they moved into late life (Costa, Metter, & McCrae, 1994). In general, longitudinal designs allow us to trace individual patterns of consistency or change over time. Although longitudinal studies offer fundamental advantages, results can be biased by attrition, in which participants drop out of the study due to death, immobility, or lack of interest. When people are no longer available for follow-up because of death, this is called **selective mortality**. Selective mortality results in a particular form of bias, in that results obtained with the remaining sample are more relevant to drawing conclusions about relatively healthy people, and less relevant to drawing conclusions about unhealthy people. Beyond attrition due to death, people with the most problems are likely to drop out from a study, whereas the people who remain are usually healthier than the general population. This is a potentially important issue in

Cohort effects refer to the fact that people of the same chronological age may differ considerably depending on when they were born. (Marc Romanelli/Getty Images.)

studies of aging and mental health, as psychological disorders have been shown to predict disease and death (Kiecolt-Glaser & Glaser, 2002).

Quick Summary

As the number of older people in the United States burgeons, more and more mental health professionals are working with this population. Unfortunately, even mental health professionals tend to hold certain stereotypes about late life. It is important to recognize that as they age, most people tend to become more effective at regulating emotions, to remain invested in sexuality, to downplay medical symptoms, and to focus on core relationships over superficial social acquaintances and activities. The challenges of late life do include declining health and insomnia for many people. As increasing numbers of chronic health problems emerge,

polypharmacy becomes an issue for many. Compounding the hazards of polypharmacy, people become more sensitive to medication side effects and toxicity as they age.

In conducting research on aging, it is difficult to disentangle age effects, cohort effects, and time-of-measurement effects. Cross-sectional studies do not help distinguish age and cohort effects. Longitudinal studies provide more clarity about age and cohort effects, but the validity of findings can be challenged by attrition. One form of attrition, selective mortality, is particularly important to consider in studies of aging.

Check Your Knowledge 15.1

True or false?
1. Most elderly people have medical illnesses.
2. Most people develop major memory problems in late life.
3. Sexual interest typically declines as people age.
4. Side effects of medications are of less concern as people age, because most people adjust to them over time.
5. Most people become more unhappy as they age.
6. Cross-sectional studies follow the same group of people over time.

Cognitive Disorders in Late Life

Although most older people do not have cognitive disorders, these problems account for more admissions and hospital inpatient days than any other condition of geriatric adults (Zarit & Zarit, 1998). When mild cognitive impairment is considered, the most common mental health problem in late life is cognitive impairment, which is not a separate DSM category but is an important characteristic of more than one disorder (e.g., depression, dementia, delirium). We will examine two principal types of cognitive disorders, dementia, a deterioration of cognitive abilities, and delirium, a state of mental confusion. For each, we will consider the clinical description and types, as well as causal factors and treatment.

Dementia

Dementia is a general descriptive term for the deterioration of cognitive abilities to the point that social and occupational functions are impaired. Dementia comes on very slowly over a period of years; subtle cognitive and behavioral deficits can be detected well before the person shows any noticeable impairment (Small et al., 2000). In fact, the presence of these early problems, sometimes referred to as mild cognitive impairment, confers a greater risk (about 10 percent) of developing dementias, such as Alzheimer's disease, compared to adults without mild cognitive impairment (about 1 percent) (Bischkopf, Busse, & Angermeyer, 2002). Difficulty remembering things, especially recent events, is the most prominent symptom of dementia. People may leave tasks unfinished because they forget to return to them after an interruption. The person who had started to fill a teapot at the sink leaves the water running. As the dementia progresses, a parent is unable to remember the name of a daughter or son and later may not even recall that he or she has children or recognize them when they come to visit. Hygiene may be poor because the person forgets to bathe or dress adequately. Patients with dementia also get lost, even in familiar surroundings.

Judgment may become faulty, and the person may have difficulty comprehending situations and making plans or decisions. People with dementia lose control of their impulses; they may use coarse language, tell inappropriate jokes, shoplift, and make sexual advances to strangers. The ability to deal with abstract ideas deteriorates, and disturbances in emotions are common, including symptoms of depression, flatness of affect, and sporadic emotional outbursts. Delusions and hallucinations can occur (APA, 2000). Patients with dementia are likely to show language disturbances as well, such as vague patterns of speech. Despite intact sensory functioning, they may also have trouble recognizing familiar surroundings or naming common objects. Episodes of delirium, a state of great mental confusion (discussed in detail later), may also occur.

Clinical Case: Ellen

"I am so glad you came," Ellen says when I greet her. She is sitting at the dining room table sipping juice, a slender, almost frail woman. But Ellen has presence. She has the posture of a dancer: shoulders back, neck elongated, head up, and the gaunt face of a once beautiful woman, with large milky hazel eyes and high patrician cheekbones. She smiles and reaches for my hand. "It is so nice of you to visit," she says.

Ellen is gracious and polite, but the truth is, she doesn't remember me. She doesn't remember that we've visited a half dozen times before, that a few days ago we had tea together, that just yesterday I sat on her bed for a half hour massaging her hands with rosemary mint lotion. Ellen, like the 43 others living at this residential care facility, has Alzheimer's disease. Her short-term memory is shot, and her long-term memory is quirky and dreamlike, with images that are sometimes bright and lucid, and other times so out of focus that she can hardly make them out. Her life is like a puzzle someone took apart when she wasn't looking. She can see some of the pieces, but she can no longer see how they fit together (quoted from Kessler, 2004, p. 1).

The course of dementia may be progressive, static, or remitting, depending on the cause. Many people with progressive dementia eventually become withdrawn and apathetic. In the terminal phase of the illness, the person's personality loses its sparkle and integrity. Relatives and friends say that the person is just not himself or herself anymore. Social involvement with others keeps narrowing. Finally, the person is oblivious to his or her surroundings.

Worldwide prevalence estimates of dementia in the year 2000 were over 25 million, which represents about 0.4 percent of the world population (Wimo et al., 2003). The prevalence of dementia increases with advancing age. One study found a prevalence of 1 percent in people aged 65 to 74, 4 percent in those aged 75 to 84, and 10 percent in those over age 84 (George et al., 1991). The annual incidence, that is, the number of new cases developing in a year, in the United States has been estimated to be more than 5 percent for those over age 85 (Gao et al., 1998). Dementia is more common among women than men, perhaps because women live longer.

There are many different types of dementia. Here we discuss four: Alzheimer's disease is the most common; frontal-temporal is defined by the areas of the brain that are most affected; vascular dementia is the second most common type of dementia; and dementia with Lewy bodies is defined by the presence of Lewy bodies, abnormal deposits on neurons in different areas of the brain that are detected postmortem. Then, we briefly discuss dementia due to other causes.

Alzheimer's Disease   In **Alzheimer's disease**, initially described by the German neurologist Alois Alzheimer in 1906, the brain tissue irreversibly deteriorates, and death usually occurs within 12 years after the onset of symptoms. Over 50,000 Americans die each year from this disease, and in the year 2000, it was the seventh leading cause of death among men and women over the age of 65 (NCHS, 2004). The illness may begin with difficulties

In the photograph on the left of brain tissue from a patient with Alzheimer's disease, the waxy amyloid shows up as areas of dark pink. On the right are computer-generated images of a brain of a person with Alzheimer's disease and a normal brain. Note that the person's brain (left) has shrunk considerably owing to the loss of nerve cells. [(Left) Martin Rotker/Phototake; (right) Alfred Pasieka/Photo Researchers, Inc.]

in concentration and in memory for new material, and absentmindedness and irritability, shortcomings that may be overlooked for several years but that eventually interfere with daily living. Indeed, subtle deficits in learning and memory revealed by neuropsychological tests are found in people who will later develop the disease well before the onset of any clinical symptoms (Linn et al., 1995). As noted above, these deficits are sometimes referred to as mild cognitive impairment, but coming up with a clear and consistent definition of mild cognitive impairment remains a challenge for the field, as does disentangling the subtle cognitive decline that is typical among older adults from the decline that might predict the onset of Alzheimer's disease (Davis & Rockwood, 2004). As the disease develops, problems with language skills and word finding intensify. Visuospatial abilities decline, which can be expressed in **disorientation** (confusion with respect to time, place, or identity) and trouble copying figures. People with the disorder are typically unaware of their cognitive problems initially, and they may blame others for lost objects, even to the point of developing delusions of being persecuted. Memory continues to deteriorate, and the person becomes increasingly disoriented and agitated. Depression is common, occurring in up to 30 percent of people with Alzheimer's disease (Strauss & Ogrocki, 1996).

People with Alzheimer's disease have more **plaques** (small round β-amyloid protein deposits that are outside the neurons) and **neurofibrillary tangles** (twisted protein filaments composed largely of the protein, tau, in the cell bodies of neurons) than would be expected for a person's age. These plaques and tangles are present throughout the cerebral cortex and the hippocampus in acetylcholinergic (ACh) neurons.

These plaques and tangles appear related to a host of brain changes. At early stages, there seems to be a loss of neuronal synapses for ACh, as well as for glutamatergic synapses (Selkoe, 2002). Over time, neurons also begin to die. As neurons die, people with Alzheimer's develop atrophy (wasting away) of the cerebral cortex, the entorhinal cortex, and the hippocampus, and later the frontal, temporal, and parietal lobes. As neurons and synapses are lost, the fissures widen and the ridges become narrower and flatter. The ventricles also become enlarged. The cerebellum, spinal cord, and motor and sensory areas of the cortex are less affected, which is why Alzheimer's patients do not appear to have anything physically wrong with them until late in the disease process. For some time patients are able to walk around normally, and their overlearned habits, such as making small talk, remain intact, so that in short encounters strangers may not notice anything amiss. About 25 percent of patients with Alzheimer's disease eventually develop brain deterioration that leads to motor deficits.

Very strong evidence exists for a genetic basis for Alzheimer's in that concordance for MZ twins is greater than that for DZ twins (Bergem, Engedal, & Kringlen, 1997). Among early-onset (before age 60) cases, which account for fewer than 5 percent of all cases of Alzheimer's disease, the pattern of inheritance suggests the operation of a single, dominant gene.

The frequency of Alzheimer's disease increases with advanced age. (Will & Deni McIntyre/Science Source/Photo Researchers, Inc.)

Because people with Down's syndrome often develop Alzheimer's disease if they survive until middle age, interest focused initially on chromosome 21, which is aberrant in Down's syndrome (see p. 481). A gene controlling the formation of β-amyloid protein (which forms plaques) was found to be on the long arm of chromosome 21, and studies have demonstrated that this gene causes the development of about 5 percent of cases of early-onset Alzheimer's disease. Dominant genes causing a small percentage of early-onset cases of Alzheimer's disease have also been found on chromosomes 1 and 14.

The majority of late-onset cases of Alzheimer's disease exhibit a particular form of a gene on chromosome 19 called the apolipoprotein E 4 or APOE-4 allele. Having one E 4 allele increases the risk of Alzheimer's disease to 30 percent, and having two alleles brings the risk to above 90 percent (Cummings & Cole, 2002). People with two of the E 4 alleles show abnormal glucose metabolism in the cortex even before the onset of any symptoms, but this has not been shown among people of color (Reiman et al., 1996). The gene appears related to the production of β-amyloid proteins. Having a different form of this gene (the E 2 allele) lowers the risk of developing Alzheimer's disease. The E 4 allele is strongly related to Alzheimer's disease among Hispanics in the Caribbean (Romas et al., 2002).

Finally, the environment is likely to play a role in most cases of Alzheimer's, as demonstrated by reports of long-lived MZ twins who are discordant for the disorder. The reasoning is that if two people with the same genetic material (i.e., MZ twins) do not both develop a particular disorder, then environmental factors must play a role. Longitudinal studies suggest that head injuries (Gallo & Lebowitz, 1999) and depression increase the risk for Alzheimer's disease (Bassuk, Berkman, & Wypij, 1998).

Strong cognitive ability before disease onset may offer some protection from Alzheimer's. This possibility was demonstrated in a study of nuns. In the weeks before the nuns took their religious vows, they had written autobiographies. Years later, after the nuns died, researchers were able to code these autobiographies for their linguistic ability, general knowledge, vocabulary skills, and other cognitive abilities. Excerpts from two sisters illustrate the range of linguistic ability among the nuns.

- *Low linguistic ability: I was born in Eau Claire, Wis. on May 24, 1913 and was baptized in St. James church.*
- *High linguistic ability: The happiest day of my life so far was my First Communion Day which was in June nineteen hundred and twenty when I was but eight years of age, and four years later I was confirmed by Bishop D. D. (Snowden et al., 1996, p. 530).*

Low linguistic ability was found in 90 percent of those who developed Alzheimer's disease many years later and in only 13 percent of those who didn't (Snowden et al., 1996). Other studies have found that strong baseline mental ability reduces the risk for Alzheimer's and also that continuing to engage in cognitive activities (such as reading a newspaper regularly) reduces risk (Wilson et al., 2002). Unfortunately, plenty of people who are bright and read the newspaper daily still develop Alzheimer's disease. Researchers are focused on early identification of people at high risk for Alzheimer's, spurred in part by the hope that early intervention might mitigate or even prevent the later development of the disease.

Frontal-Temporal Dementia **Frontal-temporal dementia (FTD)** typically begins in the mid to late 50s, although many investigators believe that subtle changes in behavior, personality, and emotion can begin much earlier (e.g., Geschwind et al., 2001). The social and emotional changes in FTD are quite prominent, particularly to loved ones of the affected person. Unlike Alzheimer's disease, memory is not severely impaired in FTD. Instead, executive functions, which include things such as planning, problem solving, and goal-directed behavior, are more impaired in FTD compared to Alzheimer's (Kramer et al., 2003). Ability to recognize and comprehend emotion is also impaired in FTD (H. J. Rosen et al., 2002a,b).

The neuronal deterioration of FTD occurs predominantly in the amygdala, anterior temporal lobes, prefrontal cortex, and other regions involving serotonergic neurons (B. L. Miller et al., 1997). Pick's disease is one cause of frontal-temporal dementia. Like Alzheimer's disease, Pick's disease is a degenerative disorder in which neurons are lost. It is also

 DSM-IV-TR Criteria for Dementia

Of the Alzheimers type:

- Multiple cognitive deficits manifested by both A and B:
  A. Memory impairment
  B. One or more of the following: aphasia, apraxia (impairment in doing something even though motor components intact), agnosia, and disturbance in executive functioning
- Significant impairment and decline in social or occupational functioning
- Gradual onset and continuing cognitive decline
- Above cognitive deficits not due to any of the following:
  A. Other CNS conditions that cause such progressive declines, e.g., Parkinson's disease, brain tumor
  B. Systemic conditions known to cause dementia, e.g., hypothyroidism, niacin deficiency, syphilis, HIV infection
  C. Substance-induced conditions
- Cognitive deficits do not occur exclusively during an episode of delirium
- Cognitive deficits are not better accounted for by another Axis I disorder, for example, major depression or schizophrenia

Regions of the brain that are affected by frontal-temporal dementia. The image on the left is at the level of the caudate nuclei and the image on the right is at the level of the lateral ventricles. (Courtesy of David Knopman, Mayo Clinic.)

characterized by the presence of Pick bodies, spherical inclusions within neurons. Frontal-temporal dementia has a strong genetic component, although the specifics of the genetics are not as well understood as for Alzheimer's disease (Usman, 1997).

Vascular Dementia This type of frontal-subcortical dementia is the second most common dementia, next to Alzheimer's disease. It is diagnosed when a patient with dementia has neurological signs such as weakness in an arm or abnormal reflexes or when brain scans show evidence of cerebrovascular disease. Most commonly, the patient had a series of strokes in which a clot formed, impairing circulation and causing cell death. Genetic factors appear to be of no importance (Bergem et al., 1997), and risk for vascular dementia increases with the same risk factors described for cardiovascular disease in general—for example, a high level of "bad" (LDL) cholesterol, cigarette smoking, and elevated blood pressure (Moroney et al., 1999). Vascular dementias are more common among African Americans than whites, though the reasons for this difference are not well-understood (e.g., Froehlich, Bogardus, & Inouye, 2001).

Capillary with red blood cells

Nerve cells   Lewy body

Dementia with Lewy bodies is defined by the presence of abnormal deposits called Lewy bodies. In this form of dementia, the Lewy bodies are found on neurons throughout the brain. (Courtesy of James Lowe, University of Nottingham, Nottingham, United Kingdom)

Dementia with Lewy Bodies Although Lewy bodies, abnormal deposits on neurons in different areas of the brain, were first discovered by Frederick Lewy in the early 1900s, **dementia with Lewy bodies (DLB)** has only been considered a distinct type of dementia for 10 years, with the publication of recommended diagnostic criteria (McKeith et al., 1996). For years, mental health professionals and investigators believed Lewy bodies were a sure sign of Parkinson's disease. More recent research, however, has found that not all cases of Parkinson's have Lewy bodies, and that other dementias do have them. The symptoms associated with this type of dementia are often hard to distinguish from the symptoms of Parkinson's (such as the shuffling gait) and Alzheimer's disease (such as loss of memory). Other prominent symptoms include hallucinations and delusions, and there is hope that by uncovering the ways in which the brain dysfunction in DLB is linked to these symptoms, we may be able to better understand hallucinations and delusions in other disorders, such as schizophrenia. At this point, additional research is needed to determine whether DLB is a distinct type of dementia or whether the presence of Lewy bodies is a feature of a number of different dementias.

Dementias Caused by Disease and Injury A number of infectious diseases can produce dementia. Encephalitis, a generic term for any inflammation of brain tissue, is caused by viruses that enter the brain. Meningitis, an inflammation of the membranes covering the outer brain, is usually caused by a bacterial infection. The organism that produces the venereal disease syphilis (*Treponema pallidum*) can invade the brain and cause dementia.

HIV can also cause dementia. Although this kind of dementia is so far primarily a problem of younger people, older adults are one of the most rapidly growing HIV-infected groups in the United States, and they are becoming infected primarily through unprotected sex (Drummond, 1999). Rosenzweig and Fillit (1992) have cautioned that HIV- and AIDS-related symptoms in older adults may be misdiagnosed as Alzheimer's or as other forms of dementia. HIV-positive older adults are often misdiagnosed, because their doctors fail to consider the possibility that their patients are sexually active. Since the HIV virus proceeds to AIDS twice as fast in older as in younger adults, early detection is particularly important in this population. In an effort to educate older adults about safe sex, the American Association of Retired Persons (AARP) has produced and distributed the AIDS-prevention video *It Could Happen to Me*.

Finally, head traumas, brain tumors, nutritional deficiencies (especially of B-complex vitamins), kidney or liver failure, and endocrine-gland problems such as hyperthyroidism can result in dementia. Exposure to toxins (such as lead or mercury) and chronic substance use are both additional causes.

Treatment of Dementia   Despite numerous investigations, no treatment has been found that can reverse Alzheimer's disease. Some drugs, as described below, may provide some modest protection against decline in cognitive functions.

Medications and Prevention   Because Alzheimer's disease involves the death of brain cells that secrete acetylcholine, various medications are used to increase the levels of this neurotransmitter. Acetylcholinesterase inhibitors (drugs that interfere with the breakdown of acetylcholine), such as donepezil (Aricept) and galantamine (Reminyl), are the standard treatment for Alzheimer's disease (Cummings, 2000). Meta-analyses of dozens of trials indicate that both drugs are associated with less decrease in memory than is observed on placebo (Birks & Harvey, 2003; Loy & Schneider, 2004). At least one trial supports supplementing acetylcholinesterase inhibitors with Namenda (memantine), a drug that affects aspartate receptors believed to be involved in memory (Tariot et al., 2004). A vast amount of work is being conducted to identify new medical treatments for Alzheimer's. Some approaches that looked promising initially, however, have failed to gain support in ongoing research. For example, early enthusiasm for a possible amyloid vaccine was quelled by the emergence of serious side effects that led to the discontinuation of the human trial. No clinical trials have been conducted to examine the efficacy of medications to help manage the symptoms of FTD, although SSRIs have been prescribed with modest success (Pasquier et al., 2003).

Prevention strategies that focus on slowing the progression of dementia have received a great deal of attention in Alzheimer's research. Recall that β-amyloid plaques appear tied to the development of Alzheimer's disease. Based on this, research is focusing on ways of blocking the creation of amyloid from its precursor protein (Whyte, Bayreuther, & Masters, 1994). Early results suggest that nicotine delivered via patch might be helpful (White & Levin, 2004). The effects of nicotine await replication with a larger sample, and the benefits will need to be weighed against the possible health ramifications of nicotine. Statins, a class of drugs used to control cholesterol, also seem to be protective in early research (Rockwood et al., 2002). Unfortunately, statins have negative effects on the gastrointestinal system and the liver.

Management of other symptoms of Alzheimer's disease includes many of the drugs used to treat other disorders, for example, antidepressants for depression (Lyketsos et al., 2000). Atypical antipsychotic medication has become a common treatment supplement for acute relief of agitation and behavioral symptoms. Unfortunately, in a meta-analysis of 17 trials, elderly patients with dementia were 1.6 times more likely to die on atypical antipsychotic medications than they were on placebo (FDA, 2005).

Psychological Treatments   Supportive psychotherapy can help families and patients deal with the effects of the disease. Generally, the therapist allows opportunities for the person and the family to discuss the illness. The therapist also provides accurate information about the illness, helps family members care for the patient in the home, and encourages a realistic rather than a catastrophic attitude in dealing with the many specific challenges that this cognitive disorder presents (Knight, 1996). In contrast to what we have seen in dealing with virtually all other psychological problems, it may not be desirable to get patients to admit to their problems, for their denial may be the most effective coping mechanism available (Zarit, 1980). See Focus on Discovery 15.2 for more detail on treatments offered to support caregivers.

Once severe cognitive deficits are present, psychological treatment provides little long-term benefit. Before severe cognitive deficits emerge, though, psychological interventions employed with cognitively intact older adults can be useful for Alzheimer's patients (Kasl-Godley & Gatz, 2000).

Former President Ronald Reagan died from Alzheimer's disease. His daughter wrote the following about his disease, " . . . the past is like the rudder of a ship. It keeps you moving through the present, steers you into the future. Without it, without memory, you are unmoored, a wind-tossed boat with no anchor. You learn this by watching someone you love drift away" (Davis, 2002). (Reuter/Steve Grayson/Archive Photos.)

Focus on Discovery 15.2

Support for Caregivers

For every person with a severely disabling dementia living in an institution, there are at least two living in the community, usually supported by a family (especially wives and daughters). Caregiving for dementia requires much more time than caregiving for most other disorders (Ory et al., 1999), and has been shown to be extremely stressful across a number of cultures (Torti et al., 2004). Studies have documented unusually high levels of clinical depression and anxiety in adult family members caring for their parents or spouses with dementia as compared with noncaregiver controls (Dura, Stukenberg, & Kiecolt-Glaser, 1991). Other studies have found more physical illness (Potashnik & Pruchno, 1988) and decreased immune functioning (Kiecolt-Glaser et al., 1991) among caregivers. Further, for some caregivers, depression and loneliness persist long after their ill spouse has died (Robinson-Whelan et al., 2001). Even caregivers who had no history of psychological difficulties may develop anxiety and depressive disorders when faced with these challenges (Gatz, Bengtson, & Blum, 1990).

Despite the obvious toll of caretaking, some caregivers seem to adjust to these stresses without developing symptoms. A key question, then, is what predicts resiliency? Caregivers are less likely to develop depression and anxiety when the patient's problem behaviors are less severe, when social support is available, and when financial resources are adequate to handle medical expenses. African American caregivers typically report less stress and depression in their roles as caregivers than Caucasian Americans do (Connell & Gibson, 1997). Certain cognitive attitudes might be protective as well (e.g., Gatz et al., 1990). For example, it may be less stressful for a caregiver to adopt an accepting attitude toward the patient's behavior—"There's nothing I can do to change the situation, so let me just resign myself to it and make the necessary adjustments"—rather than take a more active approach—"How can I get mom to remember to put her coat on before leaving the house?" The latter attitude is more suitable to dealing with challenges that are amenable to modification (Folkman & Lazarus, 1985). In a study by Knight, Lutzky, and Olshevski (1992), efforts to help distressed caregivers solve problems and accept responsibility actually increased their stress as measured by cardiovascular reactivity. Knight and colleagues speculate that problem-solving training may reinforce the view that the caregiver is responsible for the patient's problem behaviors.

Families can be helped, however, to cope better with the stress of having a family member with Alzheimer's. For example, because people with Alzheimer's have great difficulty placing new information into

Caring for a relative with Alzheimer's disease is a source of severe stress. (David Young-Wolff/PhotoEdit.)

memory, they can engage in a reasonable conversation but forget a few minutes later what has been discussed. A caregiver may become impatient unless he or she understands that this impairment is to be expected because of the brain damage.

It is also useful for caregivers to understand that patients do not always recognize their limitations and may try to engage in activities beyond their abilities, sometimes dangerously so. It is important to set limits in light of their obliviousness to their own impairments. For example, caregivers often need to tell a relative with Alzheimer's disease that driving is off limits (and then remove car keys, as they can assume that the relative will forget the new rule).

Caregivers need support, encouragement, and opportunities to vent their feelings of guilt and resentment. Some may need permission and support to take time off (Olshevski, Katz, & Knight, 1999). Because the family caregivers are so powerfully affected, it is often recommended that they be given respites from their task. The patient may be hospitalized for a week, a health care worker may take over and give the family an opportunity for a holiday, or the patient may be enrolled at an adult day care center.

That said, recent reviews have suggested that it is hard to reduce caregiver burden: only programs that offer multiple components (e.g., psychoeducation about dementia, case management services, and cognitive behavioral strategies) consistently reduce caregiver's perceptions of distress and burden (Acton & Kang, 2001). A major study of 1,222 caregivers found that multicomponent programs were particularly helpful for female caregivers and for those with less education (Gitlin et al., 2003). When programs specifically focus on helping caregivers make behavioral changes in their own lives (e.g., increasing pleasant activities or exercise, social support), they do appear to help relieve depression among caregivers (Belle et al., 2003). Caregiver support programs have been found to be effective in improving the immune function of caregivers (Garand et al., 2002), decreasing medical costs of the person with dementia, as well as slowing the timing of institutionalization (Teri et al., 2003). Recently, researchers have shown that these programs can be offered effectively in HMO settings, in hopes of making them accessible for more people (Toseland et al., 2004). Unfortunately, these caregiver support programs remain inaccessible for many people; only half of physicians provide caregivers with such programs (C. S. Rosen et al., 2002).

It would seem that strategies aimed at dealing with declining memory ability would be helpful. Labels on drawers, appliances, and rooms may help orient some patients during the early stage of disease. Prominent calendars, clocks, and strategic notes, as well as an automatic dialer on a telephone, may help (Woods, 1994). Based on the empirical literature though, memory training effects are limited (Kasl-Godley & Gatz, 2000). On the other hand, family numbers can learn strategies to adapt to the memory loss. For example, families can ask questions that embed the answer. For example, it is much easier to respond to "Was the person you just spoke to on the phone Harry or Tom?" than to "Who just called?"

Behavioral approaches have been used to reduce disruptive behavior and depression in Alzheimer's patients. For example, self-care skills can be improved, verbal outbursts diminished, and depressed mood lifted (by encouraging pleasant activities) with the application of appropriate reinforcement contingencies (Kasl-Godley & Gatz, 2000).

Providing memory aids is one way of combating memory loss. (David Young-Wolff/PhotoEdit.)

The cognitive limitations of persons with dementia should always be treated with gentleness. Others should not talk about their disabilities in their presence, make fun of their occasional antics and forgetfulness, or discount their paranoid suspicions about others. Older people, even those with no biological disorder, are often infantilized or ignored by their juniors, a demeaning sign of disrespect.

Check Your Knowledge 15.2

1. A plaque is
   a. small round β-amyloid protein deposits
   b. protein filaments composed of the protein, tau
   c. a build-up of the myelin sheath surrounding neurons in the hippocampus
   d. a small white spot on a brain scan
2. A neurofibrillary tangle is
   a. small round β-amyloid protein deposits
   b. protein filaments composed of the protein, tau
   c. a build-up of the myelin sheath surrounding neurons in the hippocampus
   d. a small white spot on a brain scan
3. Which neurotransmitter is most involved in Alzheimer's disease?
   a. dopamine
   b. serotonin
   c. GABA
   d. acetylcholine
4. Which genes are most involved in Alzheimer's disease?
   a. the E 4 allele
   b. the C 5 allele
   c. the E 6 allele
   d. all of the above
5. How much do the medications for Alzheimer's disease help memory?
   a. a small amount
   b. a large amount, which is sustained for at least 2 years after medications are taken
   c. a large amount, but people relapse when they stop taking the medications
   d. There are no known treatments
6. Which of the following dementias is second in prevalence only to Alzheimer's?
   a. FTD
   b. Parkinson's disease
   c. dementia with Lewy bodies
   d. vascular dementia
7. FTD involves profound changes in:
   a. memory
   b. social and emotional behavior
   c. language
   d. attention

Delirium

The term **delirium** is derived from the Latin words *de*, meaning "out of," and *lira*, meaning "track." The term implies being off track or deviating from the usual state (Wells & Duncan,

**DSM-IV-TR Criteria
for Delirium**

- Disturbance of consciousness (reduced awareness of the environment and attentional difficulties)
- A change in cognition, such as language disturbance, memory deficit, or perceptual disturbance not better accounted for by a dementia
- Rapid onset (usually within hours or days), and fluctuation during the course of a day
- Evidence that symptoms are caused by a medical condition, such as malnutrition

1980). As illustrated in the clinical case of Henry at the beginning of this chapter, delirium is typically described as a clouded state of consciousness. The patient, sometimes rather suddenly, has great trouble focusing attention and cannot maintain a coherent stream of thought. The sleep–wake cycle becomes disturbed so that the person is drowsy during the day yet awake and agitated at night. Vivid dreams and nightmares are common. Delirious patients may be impossible to engage in conversation because of their wandering attention and fragmented thinking. In severe delirium, speech is rambling and incoherent. Bewildered and confused, some delirious individuals may become so disoriented that they are unclear about what day it is, where they are, and even who they are. Memory impairment, especially for recent events, is common.

In the course of a 24-hour period, people with delirium have lucid intervals and become alert and coherent. The person is generally worse during sleepless nights and in the dark. These daily fluctuations help distinguish delirium from other syndromes, especially Alzheimer's disease.

Perceptual disturbances are frequent in delirium. People mistake the unfamiliar for the familiar; for example, they may state that they are at home instead of in a hospital. Although illusions and hallucinations are common, particularly visual and mixed visual-auditory ones, they are not always present. Delusions—beliefs contrary to reality—have been noted in about 25 percent of older adults with delirium (Camus et al., 2000). These delusions tend to be poorly worked out, fleeting, and changeable.

Swings in activity and mood accompany these disordered thoughts and perceptions. Delirious people can be erratic, ripping their clothes one moment and sitting lethargically the next. Delirious patients are, however, usually in great emotional turmoil and may shift rapidly from one emotion to another—depression, anxiety, fright, anger, euphoria, and irritability. Fever, flushed face, dilated pupils, tremors, rapid heartbeat, elevated blood pressure, and incontinence of urine and feces are common. If delirium proceeds, the person may become stuporous and lethargic (Webster & Holroyd, 2000).

As noted in the diagnostic criteria, delirium is caused by medical conditions. The causes of delirium in older adults can be grouped into several general classes: drug intoxications and drug-withdrawal reactions, metabolic and nutritional imbalances (as in uncontrolled diabetes, thyroid dysfunction, kidney or liver failure, congestive heart failure, or malnutrition), infections or fevers (like pneumonia or urinary tract infections), neurological disorders (like head trauma or seizures), and the stress of major surgery, most commonly, hip surgery (Knight, 1996; Zarit & Zarit, 1998). As in the case of Henry at the start of this chapter, however, delirium usually has more than one cause.

People of any age are subject to delirium, but it is more common in children and older adults. Among older adults, it is particularly common in nursing homes and hospitals. For example, one study found that 6–12 percent of nursing home residents developed delirium in the course of 1 year (Katz, Parmelee, & Brubaker, 1991), and rates much higher than this have been found in elderly hospital patients (Meagher, 2001). For example, in one study, 46 percent of hip fracture patients experienced delirium (Marcantonio et al., 2001).

Why are older adults so vulnerable to delirium? Many explanations have been offered: the physical declines of late life, the increased susceptibility to chronic diseases, the many medications prescribed for older patients, and the greater sensitivity to drugs. One other factor, brain damage, increases the risk of delirium. Older individuals with dementia appear to be the most susceptible to delirium. A retrospective review of 100 hospital admissions of people of all ages who had a diagnosis of delirium revealed that 44 percent of them had delirium superimposed on another brain condition (Purdie, Honigman, & Rosen, 1981).

Unfortunately, delirium is often misdiagnosed (Knight, 1996). For example, when researchers systematically screened 133 hospitalized patients for delirium, they found that only one of the 15 identified cases had a note of delirium in the hospital chart (Cameron et al., 1987). Physicians are particularly unlikely to detect delirium when lethargy is present (Cole, 2004).

Table 15.2 Comparative Features of Dementia and Delirium

Dementia	Delirium
Gradual deterioration of abilities	Rapid onset
Deficits in memory for recent events	Trouble concentrating and staying with a train of thought
Not explained by another medical condition	Secondary to another medical condition
Usually progressive and nonreversible	Fluctuations over the course of a day
Treatment offers only minimal benefit	Usually reversible by treating underlying condition, but potentially fatal if cause, e.g., malnutrition, not treated
Prevalence increases with age	Prevalence is high in the very young as well as the old

Delirium is often misdiagnosed when a person has dementia. Table 15.2 compares the features of dementia and delirium. Knight (1996) offers a useful suggestion for distinguishing delirium from dementia:

The clinical "feel" of talking with a person with delirium is rather like talking to someone who is acutely intoxicated or in an acute psychotic episode. Whereas the demented patient may not remember the name of the place where she or he is, the delirious patient may believe it is a different sort of place altogether, perhaps mistaking a psychiatric ward for a used car lot . . . . (Knight, 1996, pp. 96–97)

Detecting and treating delirium is of fundamental importance. Untreated, the mortality rate for delirium is high; more than one-third of patients die within a year, either from exhaustion or from the condition causing the delirium, such as a drug overdose or malnutrition (McCusker et al., 2002). Beyond the risk of death, elderly adults who develop delirium in the hospital are at an increased risk for further cognitive decline (Jackson et al., 2004).

Treatment of Delirium   Complete recovery from delirium is possible if the syndrome is correctly identified and the underlying cause is treated promptly and effectively. The older adult who has a cognitive impairment must be examined thoroughly for all possible reversible causes of the disorder, such as drug intoxication, infections, fever, malnutrition, and head trauma, and then treated accordingly. Beyond treating the underlying medical conditions, the most common approach to treatment is to use atypical antipsychotic medications. It generally takes 1 to 4 weeks for the condition to clear; it takes longer in older patients than in younger patients.

Because of the high rates of delirium in hospitalized older adults, one study examined the efficacy of primary prevention strategies—in other words, the aim was to prevent delirium from starting. The researchers randomly assigned 852 inpatients who were 70 years of age or older to receive either standard medical care only or standard medical care along with an intervention designed to prevent onset of delirium. This intervention addressed risk factors for delirium such as sleep deprivation, immobility, dehydration, visual and hearing impairment, and cognitive impairment. The patients who received the intervention had significantly lower rates of delirium, and for those who did develop delirium, the durations of the episodes were significantly shorter (Inouye et al., 1999).

The high risk of delirium among people with dementia raises another set of prevention issues. Although these prevention goals are often neglected, the family of a person with dementia should learn the symptoms of delirium and know about its reversible nature. This is important because they may interpret the onset of delirium as a new stage of a progressive dementia. For example, a patient with Alzheimer's disease may run a high fever from an infection and begin to hallucinate and act bizarrely. These new symptoms, superimposed on the intellectual deterioration to which members of the family have become accustomed, may alarm them into concluding that the patient is losing ground irreversibly. They may rush into a premature decision to institutionalize the patient. With proper diagnosis and treatment, however, the person can usually return to the earlier state, and premature institutionalization can be avoided.

Quick Summary

Dementia is a broad term to capture cognitive decline, particularly a decrease in memory for recent events. As cognitive deficits become more widespread and profound, social and occupational functioning becomes more and more disturbed. Dementia affects approximately 1 percent of people between the ages of 65 and 74, but 10 percent of people over the age of 84. There are many types of dementia, including Alzheimer's, frontal-temporal, vascular, and dementia with Lewy bodies.

Alzheimer's disease is characterized by plaques and tangles in the brain. It has been related to the APOE-4 allele. The expression of genetic vulnerability, though, is influenced by environmental and psychological events, such as depression, head injury, and baseline cognitive ability and activity. The FDA has approved acetylcholinesterase inhibitors for the treatment of Alzheimer's disease, and a range of other medications are being tested. Currently available medications offer modest effects. Psychoeducation and memory training may be helpful for some patients during the early stages of Alzheimer's but are not helpful as the dementia symptoms become more profound. Caregivers of people with Alzheimer's are at high risk for depression and anxiety. Multimodal interventions that address a range of caregiver issues, including even periods of respite from caretaking, offer some protection against psychological symptoms. Frontal-temporal dementia (FTD) is characterized by neuronal deterioration in the amygdala, frontal, and temporal lobes. Picks disease is one form of FTD. The primary manifestation of FTD is marked changes in social and emotional behavior. Some research suggests FTD may be inherited, but additional research is needed. Vascular dementia affects subcortical areas of the brain and often occurs after a stroke. Genetic factors do not play a role in vascular dementia.

Diagnostic criteria for dementia with Lewy bodies were only recommended within the past 10 years. Because the symptoms overlap with those of other dementias, researchers are focused on whether this should be considered a distinct form of dementia.

Delirium is a cognitive disorder characterized by clouded consciousness, disorientation, and inability to follow conversation. Mood and symptoms tend to vary throughout the day. Delirium is most likely to affect children and older adults; among the elderly, it is particularly common in hospitals and nursing homes. By definition, delirium is secondary to an underlying medical condition. If delirium is diagnosed and the underlying medical condition is treated, full recovery can be expected. Delirium is often not detected, though, and the risk of further cognitive decline and even death is quite high when symptoms are not addressed.

Check Your Knowledge 15.3

1. Dementia is commonly characterized by _____.
   a. anxiety
   b. memory loss
   c. frank disorganization
   d. sad mood
2. Delirium is characterized by _____.
   a. anxiety
   b. memory loss
   c. frank disorganization
   d. sad mood
3. Mary, a 70-year-old woman, was hospitalized for hip surgery. Although there were no immediate complications of the surgery, her son became concerned when he visited her that night, because she was not making any sense. She thanked him for checking her into the Ritz Carlton and laughed giddily when he told her that she was in the hospital. Half an hour later, she began sobbing. Although she seemed fine the next morning, symptoms of acute confusion re-emerged by lunchtime. Which diagnosis is most likely for Mary?

   a. Alzheimer's disease
   b. frontal-temporal dementia
   c. mania
   d. delirium
4. Randy is a 75-year-old man in good health who is retired from a long and successful career as a CEO. Over the course of several months, he developed trouble remembering appointments, names, and items he had just read. His wife made a doctor's appointment for him after he burned two tea kettles in 1 week and got lost coming home from their favorite park. At the doctor's office, he denied any concerns, but testing revealed deficits in memory and language skills that seemed significant compared to the level of functioning he had enjoyed earlier in life. Which diagnosis is most likely for Randy?
   a. Alzheimer's disease
   b. frontal-temporal dementia
   c. mania
   d. delirium

Psychological Disorders in Late Life

Above, we described the cognitive disorders, which become more common as people age. Here, though, we turn to issues in understanding how aging relates to the other psychological disorders, such as depressive disorders, anxiety disorders, and substance abuse. We first look at the prevalence of mental disorders in late life. Then, we consider questions about whether there are unique aspects of etiology and treatment when these disorders occur among older adults compared to younger adults.

The DSM criteria for older adults are the same as those for younger adults. This is because the symptoms of mental disorders are assumed to be the same in adulthood and late life, even though little research supports this assumption (Gatz, Kasl-Godley, & Karel, 1996).

Prevalence: How Common Are Psychological Disorders in Late Life?

How likely are older people to have mental disorders? Current estimates indicate that persons over age 65 have the lowest overall prevalence of mental disorders of all age groups (see Table 15.3). Note that the rates of schizophrenia and bipolar disorder in late life are particularly low. [These rates are so low that we will not focus on schizophrenia and bipolar disorder within this chapter, other than to note that treatments for older and younger patients appear comparable (Jeste et al., 2003).] Prevalence rates for DSM-defined alcohol abuse or dependence are 3.1 percent for older men and 0.46 percent for older women (Helzer, Burnam, & McEvoy, 1991), averaging out to less than 2 percent. In one major NIMH survey (Regier et al., 1988), none of those aged 65 and older and only 0.1 percent of those between 45 and 64 years of age met criteria for a drug abuse or dependency disorder. These rates of substance abuse and dependence are much lower than the rates that have been determined for the general adult population (p. 296). Even rates of depression and anxiety appear lower than in younger populations. In sum, the majority of persons 65 years of age and older are free from serious psychopathology. Nonetheless, 10 to 20 percent do have psychological problems severe enough to warrant professional attention (Gatz et al., 1996).

Why are rates of psychopathology so low in late life? There are several completely different answers to these questions. Some have advised caution in interpreting such data, as a set of methodological issues must be considered. It also appears that there may be some processes related to aging that promote better mental health.

Methodologically, it must be considered that older adults may be more uncomfortable acknowledging and discussing mental health problems compared to younger people. Similarly, older people who grew up before experimentation with drugs became widespread might feel embarrassed about describing drug use. Beyond reporting bias, there are potential cohort effects. That is, the next generation of people to become old may manifest more depression, anxiety, and substance abuse than people who are already older (Zarit & Zarit, 1998).

Beyond these explanations, people with mental illness are at risk for dying earlier—before age 65—for several different reasons. Among heavy drinkers, the peak years for death from cirrhosis are between 55 and 64 years of age, and cardiovascular disease is also common (Shaper, 1990). Substance abuse, schizophrenia, and bipolar disorder are associated with increased mortality (Angst et al., 2002; Enger et al., 2004). Even milder psychological disorders compromise immune function, and as people age, they become particularly sensitive to these immune effects (Kiecolt-Glaser & Glaser, 2001). This may lead to worse outcomes for many medical conditions that are more common as people age. For example,

Table 15.3 One-Year Prevalence Rates of Mental Illness in Older and Younger Generations as Estimated in the Epidemiological Catchment Area Data

Disorder	One-Year Prevalence Rate (%)	
	Age 18–54	Age 55+
Any anxiety disorder	13.1	11.4
Simple phobia	8.3	7.3
Social phobia	2.0	1.0
Agoraphobia	4.9	4.1
Panic disorder	1.6	0.5
Obsessive-compulsive	2.4	1.5
Any mood disorder	7.1	4.4
Major depressive episode	6.5	3.8
Unipolar major depression	5.3	3.7
Dysthymia	1.6	1.6
Bipolar I	1.1	0.2
Bipolar II	0.6	0.1
Schizophrenia	1.3	0.6
Antisocial personality disorder	2.1	0.0
Anorexia nervosa	0.1	00

Source: U.S. Department of Health and Human Services, 1999.

Frojdh and colleagues (2003) conducted surveys with over 1,200 elderly people living in Sweden. Compared to those with low scores, those who obtained high scores on a self-report measure of depression were 2.5 times as likely to die within the next 6 years. Cardiovascular disease is also more common among people who are prone to worry (Kubanski et al., 1997). Because people with mental illness may die earlier, research studies on aging may suffer from the issue of selective mortality.

These three methodological issues—response biases, cohort effects, and selective mortality—could help explain the low prevalence of psychological disorders in late life. Most researchers, though, believe that aging is also genuinely related to better mental health. Above, we described research that suggests that the elderly are less unhappy and tend to cope better. This should translate into a decrease in psychological disorders. Some longitudinal studies suggest that many people who experience psychopathology early in life seem to age out of those symptoms. For example, longitudinal studies indicate that heavy drinkers tend to drink less as they enter late life (Fillmore, 1987). Indeed, even those with schizophrenia evidence a marked reduction, and sometimes a complete remission, of symptoms by the time they reach old age (Zarit & Zarit, 1998). Findings like these suggest that enhanced coping abilities developed across the life course may help protect people from mental illness during late life.

In sum, studies suggest lower rates of mental illness among the elderly. Although some methodological issues might explain part of this effect (low levels of disclosure, cohort effects, and selective mortality), it is also possible that some people become better adjusted as they age.

Beyond examining the prevalence rates of disorder, it is important to consider the incidence rates, or how many people are experiencing the onset of a new disorder. Generally, most people who have an episode of a psychological disorder late in life are experiencing a recurrence of a disorder that started earlier in life, rather than an initial onset. For example, most episodes of depression and anxiety are recurrences (Gallo & Lebowitz, 1999). In one study of older adults with GAD, 97 percent reported that their anxiety symptoms began before the age of 65 (Alwahhabi, 2003). Late onset is also extremely rare for schizophrenia (Karon & VandenBos, 1998). In contrast, late-onset alcoholism is more common (Liberto, Oslin, & Ruskin, 1996).

Medical Issues in Diagnosing Psychological Disorders

DSM criteria specify that a psychological disorder should not be diagnosed if the symptoms can be accounted for by a medical condition or medication side effects. Because medical conditions are more common in the elderly, it is particularly important to rule out such explanations. Medical problems such as thyroid problems, Addison's disease, Cushing's disease, Parkinson's disease, Alzheimer's disease, hypoglycemia, anemia, and vitamin deficiencies can produce symptoms that mimic schizophrenia, depression, or anxiety (Marengo & Westermeyer, 1996). Angina, congestive heart failure, and excessive caffeine consumption all may cause a faster heart rate which can be mistaken as a symptom of anxiety (Fisher & Noll, 1996). Age-related deterioration in the vestibular system (inner-ear control of one's sense of balance) can account for panic symptoms such as severe dizziness (Raj, Corvea, & Dagon, 1993). Antihypertensive medication, hormones, corticosteroids, and antiparkinsonism medications may contribute to depression or anxiety (Spar & LaRue, 1990).

Major Depressive Disorder

Despite the low prevalence, depressive disorders are estimated to account for nearly half the admissions of older adults to acute psychiatric care (Wattis, 1990). Women have more periods of depression than men for most of their lives, except possibly after age 85 (Gallo & Lebowitz, 1999). As with depression in younger people, depression in late life is highly comorbid with alcohol problems (Gallo & Lebowitz, 1999). Researchers initially believed that symptoms of depression differed in late life, but recent findings have identified only one consistent difference—cognitive symptoms (such as memory deficits and confusion) appear

Although depression is less common among older adults than younger ones, it accounts for a very large proportion of the psychiatric hospital admissions among the aged. (David Young-Wolff/ PhotoEdit.)

more pronounced when depression emerges in late life compared to earlier adulthood, discussed next.

Depression versus Dementia   Depression is likely to produce more cognitive impairment in the elderly than it does in younger people (Lockwood et al., 2000). Among elderly people with depression, those with later onset appear particularly at risk for cognitive impairment (Lockwood et al., 2000). The frequent presence of cognitive symptoms in late life depression can make it hard to differentiate whether memory problems are due to dementia or to depression. Indeed, cases of depression in older adults are often misdiagnosed as dementia because of the severe cognitive impairment. No single neuropsychological test can clearly differentiate people with depression from those with dementia, although researchers are working hard to develop a battery of specific memory tests that would help make this distinction (Swainson et al., 2001). When depressive symptoms are present, a good course of action is to treat them and hope that cognitive symptoms are improved in the process. A number of research studies have documented that cognitive symptoms of older individuals improve when their depression is treated (LaRue, 1992).

Of course, patients can have both dementia and depression. For example, an Alzheimer's patient can become depressed over his or her growing physical and cognitive limitations (Teri & Reifler, 1987). And the opposite direction of effects seems to occur as well: depression in middle-aged adults predicts increased risk for Alzheimer's disease as they age (Rosenblatt et al., 2003).

Etiology of Depression in Older Adults   As with younger adults, depression among older adults is related to a range of causes. Many of the causes of depression in older adults parallel those seen among younger adults. On the other hand, some new problems emerge during late life that can trigger depression.

A body of evidence has emerged about people who develop a first episode of depression after age 65. These late-onset first episodes seem particularly tied to vascular disease. For example, more than 20 percent of people develop a depressive episode in the 18 months after a myocardial infarction (Frasure-Smith et al., 1995). Moreover, when the brains of people with late onset depression are imaged, small white spots, called white matter hyperintensities (WMH), are often present (Camus et al., 2004). WMH are more common as people age, but they appear particularly common in people with cardiovascular risk factors. Taken together, these findings suggest that strokes and other vascular disease could explain the development of many late-onset depressions. The opposite direction of effects also has been shown; it is now well-established that depression also predicts a worse outcome for people with cardiovascular disease (Camus et al., 2004).

Beyond the specific ties to cardiovascular disease, poor physical health is a major risk factor for depression among older adults. A survey of 900 older adults living in the community found that 44 percent of people with depressive symptoms were medically ill (Blazer & Williams, 1980). Rates of depression appear particularly tied to physical disabilities, such as trouble walking (Gallo & Lebowitz, 1999).

As we grow older, we are more likely to experience a number of life events that would be expected to cause depression, such as the death of a spouse, social isolation, and retirement. For example, one might expect depression among people who are recently widowed, an experience more common among older adults. Although rates of depression do increase initially after people become widowed (Wilcox et al., 2003), most people, given time, recover well from bereavement. It may be helpful to counsel bereaved clients to examine their lives from a philosophical or a religious perspective. Similarly, social isolation is not as strongly linked to depression in late life as it is in middle age (Musetti et al., 1989), due perhaps to older people placing less emphasis on casual social contacts than younger people do (see earlier discussion of social selectivity in older adults). Furthermore, most people do not become depressed after retirement. Any ill effects of retirement may have more to do with the poor health and low incomes of some retirees and less with retirement per se (Pahkala, 1990). Successful adjustment to retirement is tied to positive marital relationships, high education, high job prestige before retirement, and high self-efficacy and self-esteem

(Kim & Moen, 2001). For many older adults, retirement ushers in a satisfying period of life (Wolfe, Morrow, & Frederickson, 1996). We would do well to assume that adaptation rather than depression is the common reaction to loss and stress in late life.

Treatment of Depression   Many physicians do not diagnose, and therefore do not treat, depression in primary care (Wolfe et al., 1996). In one study of 599 85-year-olds, only 25 percent of people who met criteria for major depressive disorder were diagnosed with such by their primary care doctor, and very few received appropriate treatment (Stek et al., 2004).

Although clinical lore holds that depressions in older patients are more resistant to treatment, we have known for a long time that these claims are not substantiated (Small & Jarvik, 1982). Rather, considerable evidence shows that depressed older adults can be helped by both psychological and pharmacological interventions. As with younger adults, research so far supports the use of cognitive, behavioral, and Interpersonal Psychotherapy (IPT) approaches (Gallagher-Thompson et al., 2000). Research also supports the use of short-term psychodynamic therapy for the treatment of late-life depression (Gallagher & Thompson, 1983). Similarly, antidepressant medications, particularly selective serotonin reuptake inhibitors (SSRIs) such as fluoxetine (Prozac), have been found to be more effective than placebos (Schneider et al., 2003). Either cognitive behavioral therapy or IPT provides additional relief when added to antidepressant medication (Reynolds et al., 1999; Thompson et al., 2001).

Despite the encouraging findings for antidepressant medications, either alone or in combination with psychological treatment, some caution is merited. Older adults are likely to be highly sensitive to the side effects of antidepressant drugs, such as postural hypotension (a fall in blood pressure when standing up), which causes some patients to become dizzy when they stand up and then to fall. (Falls in older adults are far more serious than they are for younger people. Broken bones take much longer to heal, and certain head injuries can be fatal.) These drugs also pose a danger to the cardiovascular system, increasing the risk of a heart attack. Moreover, older people generally are at high risk for toxic reactions to medications of all kinds. Worth noting also is a study examining the effects of antidepressants in older adults (Menting et al., 1996). This clinical trial found that about 76 percent of the SSRI patients experienced at least some side effects, 25 percent dropped out because of side effects, and about 41 percent dropped out overall. These results occurred even though most of the participants were relatively healthy elderly people. Although not all studies have found such high side effect rates, the lower tolerability of antidepressants among the elderly suggests that nonpharmacological approaches are particularly important (Scoggin & McElerath, 1994). Indeed, Landreville et al. (2001) found that elderly patients with depression reported that they would rather receive cognitive therapy than antidepressant medications.

Some psychiatrists recommend electroconvulsive therapy (p. 256) (Sackheim, 2004), particularly for geriatric patients who had an earlier favorable response to it (Janicak et al., 1993). ECT does, however, carry significant risks, and it should be considered only when other treatments have not been effective or are contraindicated, or when a rapid response (such as in the case of an acutely suicidal patient) is needed (Zarit & Zarit, 1998).

One innovative program addressed depression among elderly people with chronic medical illnesses. Although chronic medical illnesses increase risk for depression, problems with mobility can interfere with attending therapy sessions. Ciechanowski and colleagues (2004), then, looked at how therapy would work if it were offered in the home. The treatment they offered had a great deal in common with psychological treatments covered in Chapter 8; it included problem solving for improving life situations, increasing behavioral activation, and other standard techniques. If warranted, recommendations were made to primary care providers for antidepressant medications. In this way, the study was not designed to look at psychological treatment so much as to provide some form of depression treatment for this highly vulnerable population. People were randomly assigned to receive either depression treatment or treatment as usual (medical care). Findings of this study offer good news and bad news. On the good side, depression treatment was significantly more likely to produce remission (33 percent) than treatment as usual (12 percent). On the down side, even with treatment, two-thirds of people continued to experience depressive symptoms, and treatment also did not improve quality of life. The findings suggest that depression treatment helps, but also that it is hard to restore all aspects of life when older people face such severe medical conditions.

Another innovative treatment program has drawn on the finding that depression predicts poorer outcome among people with heart disease. That is, researchers investigated how well standard cognitive behavioral treatment (CBT) for depression worked for people who developed an episode of depression after a myocardial infarction. More than 2,400 patients were randomly assigned to receive CBT or standard medical care. Although CBT helped reduce depression, it did not seem to influence cardiovascular health (Berkman et al., 2003).

Suicide   The risk factors for suicide in the elderly are very parallel with those in younger people (see Chapter 8). For example, in older and younger people, depression is the major risk factor. Beyond depression, it is worth noting that physical illness, loss of loved ones, and dire financial circumstances, problems that are widespread among older adults, are important risk factors.

Butler, Lewis, and Sunderland (1998) argued that the suicide of older adults may be more of a rational or philosophical decision than it is among younger people. Consider, for example, the older person who faces the intractable pain and financial stress of a terminal illness. The debate over physician-assisted suicide (p. 264) is likely to focus increasing attention on suicide among elderly people.

Regardless of the reasons, the elevated suicide rates for people over age 65 are a concern: older adults are three times more likely to kill themselves than younger adults are (McIntosh, 1995). The suicide rate for men increases in a linear fashion with age from adolescence onward, whereas the rate for women peaks in their 50s and then slowly declines across the rest of the life span (McIntosh, 1995). Older white men are more likely to commit suicide than are members of any other group; the peak ages for committing suicide in this group are from 80 to 84 (Conwell, 2001). Marked increases have also been noted with age among African American men (Alston et al., 1995).

Older persons are less likely to communicate their intentions to commit suicide and more likely to use lethal methods than younger people are (Conwell, 2001). Once people are past age 65, their attempts rarely fail (Butler & Lewis, 1998). Furthermore, the statistics are probably underestimates; older adults have many opportunities to give up on themselves by neglecting their diet or medications, thus killing themselves in a more passive fashion.

One treatment program to reduce depression and suicidality in the elderly draws on the finding that elderly people are more likely to visit primary care doctors than to see specialty mental health providers. Bruce and colleagues (2004) screened patients over the age of 60 who were seeking medical care to see if they reported depressive symptoms. Patients with symptoms were offered an antidepressant medication, and if they did not want medication, they were offered a chance to receive psychological treatment. Interestingly, although the patients had not been seeking depression treatment, about 90 percent of patients accepted either medication or psychological treatment when they were offered. Compared to patients who received typical medical care, those who received either medication or psychological treatment obtained faster relief from their depression and from suicidal ideation, differences that lasted for a year.

Anxiety Disorders

In general, symptoms of anxiety disorders do not differ as people enter late life (Gretarsdortir et al., 2004). GAD is the most common anxiety disorder among the elderly (Alwahhabi, 2003). Post-traumatic stress disorder (PTSD) is seen in some older war veterans (Cook, 2001) and has been observed in older patients after such trauma as major health crises (Scogin, 1998). One study found that even after 50 years since the event, many veterans still

As with younger adults, anxiety disorders are more prevalent than depression. Worries about illnesses and becoming incapacitated may be a focus of concerns. (Zac Macaulay/The Image Bank/Getty Images.)

are affected by their war experiences (Hunt & Robbins, 2001). Despite their relevance, PTSD and acute stress disorder have received scant attention from researchers (Scogin, 1998).

Researchers know little about the causes of anxiety disorders in late life. Beyond ruling out medical explanations, causes of anxiety disorders are often related to the circumstances of getting older (Fisher & Noll, 1996)—threats of social isolation, poverty, and medical difficulties become more prominent as people age.

Anxiety problems in older adults seem to respond to the same types of psychological treatments found useful with younger adults (cf. Chapter 5), but less controlled research is available. For example, cognitive behavioral treatment has been found to be fairly helpful in reducing symptoms of anxiety (Wetherell, Gatz, & Craske, 2003). Researchers have developed accommodations, such as the use of more in-session summaries, to help compensate for memory loss that some older clients experience.

The short-acting benzodiazepines are the most widely used treatment for anxiety disorders in the elderly (Alwahhabi, 2003). Unfortunately, older adults are particularly sensitive to side effects from this class of medications—longitudinal research has shown that benzodiazepine use in older adults is predictive of increased morbidity, cognitive decline, and urinary incontinence, not to mention prolonged use after anxiety symptoms remit (Alwahhabi, 2003). Indeed, given the concerns about how dangerous these medications can be for older adults, the federal government has now instituted guidelines that long-term care facilities should limit the use of short-acting benzodiazepines to fewer than 10 continuous days, and fewer than 4 months for longer-acting benzodiazepines. Despite these guidelines, more than 20 percent of nursing home residents are prescribed benzodiazepines, and 8 percent use them for more than 4 months (Svarstad & Mount, 2001). A central goal, then, is to identify medications with fewer side effects. Busiperone (BusPar), which has fewer side effects, has been shown to be effective in one study of GAD. Surprisingly, researchers know little about antidepressant medications for treatment of anxiety in older adults, despite their efficacy in younger populations.

A concluding comment by Fisher and Noll (1996) in their review of anxiety disorders in elderly people could be applied to other psychological disorders as well.

> Although old age naturally presents the challenges of physical and emotional losses that may seem overwhelming to the young, the ability to competently cope with these losses [and challenges] is indeed probably the most remarkable aspect of the relationship between aging and anxiety. Perhaps through the study of the means by which the majority of older adults rise to the challenges associated with aging, researchers will better inform the treatment of anxiety across the lifespan. (Fisher & Noll, 1996, p. 323)

Delusional (Paranoid) Disorders

Symptoms of paranoia, such as Jeanine's fears that her husband and her neighbors were trying to hurt her (see Clinical Case), are found in many older psychiatric patients (Heston, 1987). For example, in a study of people age 85 and older, psychiatric interviews with family members and key informants suggested that 6.9 percent of people had experienced at least mild paranoid symptoms in the past year (Ostling & Skoog, 2002). In evaluating whether such symptoms merit diagnosis, though, clinicians must be sensitive to the fact that older people are often mistreated. Others may talk about them behind their backs, or even to their faces, and people may take advantage of older adults in many ways. That is, complaints from an older person concerning persecution may be justified.

Although paranoia in older patients may be the continuation of a disorder that began earlier in life, the most common cause of paranoia in late life is brain diseases such as delirium

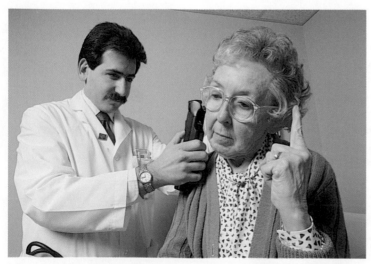

Loss of hearing is common in the elderly, and can create the sense that others are whispering behind their back. (J. Griffin/The Image Works.)

and dementia (Livingston et al., 2001). Paranoid ideation also has been linked to loss of hearing or sight (Ostling & Skoog, 2002). An older person who is having trouble hearing may believe that other people are whispering about him or her. Beyond cognitive and sensory declines, increases in social isolation can trigger paranoid symptoms (Gurland, 1991). This isolation limits the person's opportunities to check his or her suspicions about the world, making it easier for delusions to take hold. A good evaluation, then, will incorporate medical, cognitive, sensory, and social assessments.

If the symptoms are secondary to delirium or sensory impairment, treatment should address these issues. Otherwise, the treatment of paranoia is much the same for older adults as for younger adults. Although controlled data on the treatment of paranoia in older adults are lacking, supportive approaches to establish rapport, complemented by cognitive therapy, are recommended. Studies indicate that delusions in older patients can be treated with some success with antipsychotic medications (Schneider, 1996), although people who are experiencing paranoia are generally suspicious of the motives of those who give them drugs. Toxicity from medications must also be considered, given the particular sensitivity of older people to drugs.

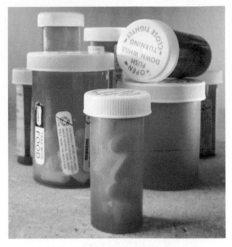

Medication misuse, whether deliberate or inadvertent, can be a serious problem among older patients and can cause delirium. (Eric Kamp/Phototake.)

Clinical Case: Jeanine

Jeanine was a 66-year-old married woman who reluctantly agreed to a clinical evaluation. She [had] a 6-week history of bizarre delusions and hallucinations of her husband spraying the house with a fluid that smelled like "burned food." She complained that he sprayed the substance everywhere around the house, including draperies and furniture, although she had never seen him do it. She could smell the substance almost constantly, and she said that it affected her head, chest, and rectum. She also complained that someone in the neighborhood

had been throwing bricks and rocks at her house. In addition, she suspected her husband of having affairs with other women, whose footprints she claimed to have seen near home.

During the interview, Jeanine was sullen toward the interviewer and extremely hostile toward her husband. She looked very sad at times and would occasionally wipe away a tear, but her predominant affect was extreme hostility about her husband's alleged behavior (Varner & Gaitz, 1982, p. 108).

Substance Abuse and Dependence

Although few people meet diagnostic criteria for alcohol or substance abuse, there are a fair number of people who drink heavily during late life (Molgaard et al., 1990). It is important, then, to consider that the physiological consequences of alcohol become more intense as people age. For example, tolerance for alcohol diminishes with age, in part because the ratio of body water to body mass decreases with time, resulting in higher blood-alcohol concentration per unit of alcohol imbibed (Morse, 1988). In addition, older people metabolize alcohol more slowly. Thus, the drug may cause greater changes in brain chemistry and may more readily bring on toxic effects, such as delirium, in older people. Several neuropsychological studies have shown that cognitive deficits associated with alcohol abuse, such as memory problems, are likely to be more pronounced in older than younger adults, even when the seriousness of drinking histories is comparable (Brandt et al., 1983). Although some intellectual functioning is recovered with abstinence, residual effects may remain long after the older person has stopped drinking.

Clinicians may be less likely to look for substance abuse in older people than in younger patients and instead may attribute symptoms such as poor motor coordination and impaired memory to a medical problem or to late-life depression. Indeed, substance problems often are comorbid with major depression (Liberto et al., 1996). Whether there is comorbidity or not, however, if substance abuse goes unrecognized, treatment will be severely compromised.

Medication Misuse The misuse of prescription and over-the-counter medicines is a much greater problem than alcohol or illegal drug abuse in the aged population (LaRue et al., 1985). Elderly people have a higher rate of legal drug intake than any other group; although they constitute only 13 percent of the population, they consume about one-third of all prescribed medications (Weber, 1996). When people now in middle age reach late life, the prevalence of prescription-drug abuse may be even greater, exacerbated by the "take a pill for your ills" mentality they have acquired. Older patients use more antianxiety medications than any other age group: rates of benzodiazepine use in community-dwelling older adults have been estimated at 14 to 37 percent (Wetherell, 1998).

The use of benzodiazapines and sleep aids can create physical as well as psychological dependency. Because older adults tend not to go to work regularly and may not even be seen in public for days or weeks at a time, consequences of drugs may continue for a long time without being noticed. The slurred speech and memory problems caused by drugs may be attributed by others to old age and dementia (LaRue et al., 1985), another example of how popular stereotypes can interfere with proper diagnosis and treatment. A former Valium addict and now a leader of Pills Anonymous groups in California stated the problem this way: "Closet junkies, that's what we call them here. They're at home. They're alone. They're afraid. They're just hiding. Their drug pusher is their doctor" (Weber, 1996, p. A36).

Since the current cohort of older adults is not as acculturated as are younger people to seeking help for psychological problems like drug abuse, many try without supervision to abstain from drugs, sometimes going cold turkey. Doing so can be very dangerous, even life-threatening, because withdrawal reactions place great demands on the cardiovascular system.

Check Your Knowledge 15.4

True or false?
1. Generally, mental illnesses occur more often as people age.
2. Most mental illnesses among older adults are continuations of illnesses that they had earlier in life.
3. The elderly are more likely to kill themselves than young people are.
4. Treatments for depression, anxiety, and schizophrenia in early life are not likely to work for someone who is in their late life.

Adjusting Treatment with Older Adults

Several barriers may prevent older people from receiving mental health care. First, older people may hold more negative beliefs about mental illness, and so may be less likely to seek treatment. Second, older people are less likely than younger adults to be assessed and referred for mental health care (Knight, 1996). Third, and perhaps most importantly, financial barriers may prevent access to care. Medicare, the major health care program for people age 65 and over, provides very little funding for mental health care. Only 2.5 percent of Medicare spending is for mental health care (Gottlieb, 1996). Medicare is also heavily biased toward inpatient care and nursing home care rather than outpatient care (Kiesler, 1992), even though outpatient management could save vast sums of money by preventing hospitalizations (Hughes et al., 1997).

Even when an elderly person can access treatment, clinicians tend to expect less success in treating older patients than in treating younger patients (Knight, 1996). Yet, as described above, research shows that psychological treatments can be successful for older patients. Indeed, with increasing years come increasing reflectiveness and a tendency to be philosophical about life (Neugarten, 1977), traits that augur well for psychotherapeutic interventions.

Although psychological treatment tends to be successful with this population, it may be important to adjust the process in several ways. Many of the emotional concerns of older adults may be realistic reactions to problems in aging, and pragmatic supports may be a better approach in those circumstances than attempts to help a person see the problem differently. For example, some clinicians focus on here-and-now practical problems in a more active and directive manner; they provide information, take the initiative in seeking out agencies for necessary services, and help the client through the maze of federal and local laws and offices that are in place to help them. Therapy also should foster a sense of control, self-efficacy, and hope. Some treatments focus on helping the older patient create a sense of meaning as he or she approaches the end of life.

It is also important to consider how cognitive characteristics of aging influence psychological treatment (Knight, 1996). For example, certain kinds of thinking simply take longer for many older people. Older people also tend to experience some diminution in the number of things that they can keep in mind at any one time. Explanations may have to be paced carefully. Therapists need to avoid the common tendency, when another person seems not to be following the thread of the conversation, to assume that impaired hearing is the cause of miscommunication.

Therapists, usually many years younger than these patients, can find that their interactions with patients touch on sensitive personal areas of their own, such as unresolved conflicts with their own parents, worries about their own aging process, and a reluctance to deal with issues of death and dying. As Knight, Kelly, and Gatz (1992) speculated, working with older adults "will challenge therapists intellectually and emotionally to reach a maturity beyond their years" (p. 546).

Beyond traditional psychotherapies, many people are developing innovative programs to help address problems associated with aging. For example, the growing specialization of behavioral gerontology (Nemeroff & Karoly, 1991) emphasizes helping older people to enhance their self-esteem and social contacts by focusing on specific, deceptively minor behaviors, such as controlling their hygiene better (Whitehead, Burgio, & Engel, 1985), increasing self-care and mobility (Burgio et al., 1986), and improving their telephone conversational skills (Praderas & MacDonald, 1986). Another recent development, though hardly a formal therapy, involves teaching older adults computer skills so that they can access the Internet and make the kinds of social contacts that were inconceivable only a few years ago (Cody et al., 1999).

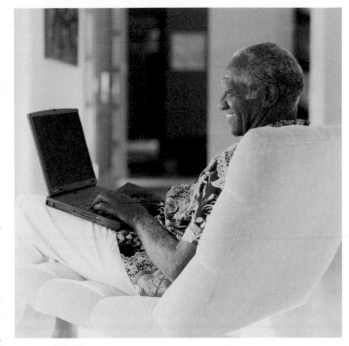

Being able to use a computer and access the Internet is one way older adults can increase their social contacts. (Digital Vision/Getty Images.)

Quick Summary

The prevalence of psychological disorders is lower among older adults than it is for any other age group. The psychological disorders that are present during late life usually represent a recurrence or continuation of symptoms that first emerged earlier in life. Some have argued that the low rates of mental illness could be an artifact of less disclosure among older people, could be a cohort effect, or could reflect selective mortality. Most researchers, though, believe that increased coping abilities might help explain the lower rates of disorder as people age. When psychological symptoms are present, it is particularly important to screen for medical causes among the elderly.

Certain issues should be considered in thinking about specific psychological disorders in late life. For example, cognitive symptoms may be a prominent symptom of depression during late life, so that differential diagnosis with dementia is important. Late-onset depression may also be related to cardiovascular conditions. Although the base rates of depression are low, suicide rates are high among the elderly, in part because suicide attempts made by older people are likely to be lethal.

Aside from cognitive disorders, anxiety disorders are the most common mental health problem faced in late life and may often be tied to the stresses involved in aging. Unfortunately, benzodiazepines are widely prescribed for the elderly despite clear evidence for dangerous side effects. Symptoms of paranoia become more common as people age, and may be triggered by sensory loss, dementia, or social isolation. Alcohol and substance abuse are rare, but inappropriate use of prescription or over-the-counter medications is a concern. Treatment for most conditions parallels the treatment used with younger adults, but some innovations have been made, such as offering treatment in the home, through primary care, or for people with heart disease.

Contrary to stereotypes, older people tend to benefit a great deal from psychological treatments. Therapists working with the elderly, though, may need to make adjustments, such as addressing genuine social and medical concerns in a pragmatic manner, and pacing explanations carefully. Therapists will often need to examine their own attitudes and feelings about aging.

Living Situations: Community Living, Nursing Homes, and Other Alternatives

At any given time 95 percent of older persons reside in the community. Many of these people are frail and have an urgent need for help with daily living arrangements. They tend to be poor, have three or more physical illnesses, and receive little assistance from the mental health system beyond medication (Meeks & Murrell, 1997). Some communities and for-profit agencies are organized to provide various services, such as:

- daily phone calls to older persons living alone to check that they are alright;
- home services, such as Meals on Wheels, which deliver hot meals;
- volunteers who cook meals, do household chores, and do minor repairs;
- home visits by health professionals, who provide assessments and treatment;
- adult day services, which provide health and social services in a group setting;
- senior centers, which serve hot lunches, help with state and federal forms, and also provide opportunities for socializing.

Available services can be matched with the needs of the older person (Evashwick, 2001).

Because mental health and physical health problems are so interwoven, interdisciplinary collaboration is critical with older clients. Focus on Discovery 15.3 describes the kind of interdisciplinary team effort that can serve the needs of older adults. A set of studies now clearly show that such community services as described above, coupled with careful coordination of services among health care providers, can enhance the quality of life as well as reduce hospitalization and institutionalization rates for older people (Johri, Beland, & Bergman, 2003).

Mere availability of services is not enough. Services must be coordinated, and in most localities they are not. All too often an older person and his or her family are shuffled from one agency to another, getting lost in Kafkaesque bureaucracies. Even professionals who have experience with the system often have difficulty working through it to get needed services for their clients. Frustrating rules can interfere with the very goals for which programs were instituted. In California, for example, Medicare does not always pay

Focus on Discovery 15.3

Interdisciplinary Teamwork in Geriatric Health Care

The health problems of older adults including psychological problems—are often more complex and chronic than are those of younger adults and of children (Birren & Schaie, 2001). Thus the guiding principle that organizes the thinking and the work of gerontological practitioners is interdisciplinary cooperation (Zeiss & Steffen, 1996). Professionals from several disciplines must work collaboratively to help older adults deal with psychological difficulties (Zeiss & Steffen, 1996). Figure 15.2 portrays how different professionals can work separately (the nonoverlapping areas) and collaboratively (the overlapping areas) to provide assessment and intervention. For example, although the medical doctor serves as the primary care physician, the cognitive screening (how well the patient remembers and thinks about things) can be done by the psychologist.

It is not easy to assemble or participate in such an interdisciplinary team, for the ethos in all these health-related disciplines is still discipline centered, even when the subject matter is not. Not all geriatric problems require such an approach, but as Zeiss and Steffen (1996) argue, even a seemingly straightforward health problem in an older adult can benefit from an interdisciplinary approach. They give an example of an 80-year-old woman with bronchitis. Can she be adequately treated by a physician alone? Maybe not. It may be essential to know that she is a caregiver for a husband with dementia, what other medications she is taking, what her immune status is, and other issues pertinent to her physical and emotional well-being. Social workers, psychologists, or other team members may be essential in planning not only acute treatment for her bronchitis but also backup care for her demented husband.

Coordination of care helps to prevent premature institutionalization among the elderly. Sadly, health care practices in the United States are behind other countries in developing "single point of entry" insurance systems, designed to facilitate coordinating health care needs across multiple agencies and providers (Johri et al., 2003).

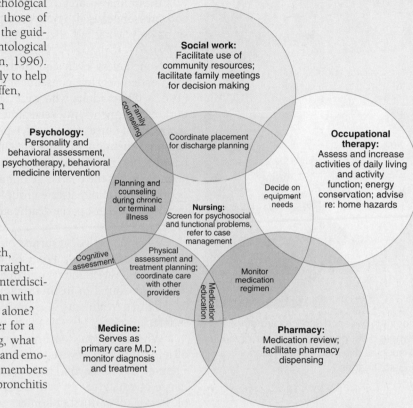

Figure 15.2 Geriatric interdisciplinary-team role map. Note both the separate and the overlapping areas of responsibility and expertise. From Zeiss, A. M., & Steffen, A. M. (1996). Interdisciplinary health care teams: The basic unit of geriatric care. In L. L. Carstensen, D. A. Edelstein, & L. Dornbrand (Eds.), *The practical handbook of clinical gerontology*. Thousand Oaks, CA: Sage.

for rehabilitation services, such as physical therapy after a broken hip has healed. As a consequence, many older people do not regain as much function as they might; thus, they may experience additional physical and emotional deterioration, exacerbations that require more expensive services.

A growing number of older persons live with family members who help manage tasks of daily living. Older people's relations with family members who must look after them can suffer, as the caretaker and the patient are likely to feel torn between anger and guilt over the new roles (Zarit, 1980). As changes in physical health or cognitive abilities become too daunting for community living, many people move to nursing homes, assisted living facilities, or retirement communities to receive more support.

Nursing Homes

The common myth about nursing homes is that families dump their older relatives into these institutions at the first sign of frailty. Rather, most families explore all their alternatives

Among community-based services are day care centers, where older people participate in various activities, such as exercise classes. (Lori Adamski/Getty Images.)

and exhaust their own resources before they institutionalize an older relative. Thus, the decision to institutionalize comes as a last resort.

Institutionalization can sometimes have a negative impact on family relations if heated disagreement arises about whether to place the parent in a nursing home. One study, however, found that for most families, moving the parent to a nursing home strengthened family ties and brought a renewed closeness between the parent and the child who was the primary caregiver. The care provided by the nursing home alleviated the strain and pressure caused by the multiple physical or mental problems of the parent. Relationships only worsened after the move for about 10 percent of families (Smith & Bengtson, 1979).

Nonetheless, even a good nursing home—and not all of them are run well—may have unintended negative consequences on some residents. Consider a classic study by Blenker (1967). Older adults who went to a family service center were randomly assigned to one of three treatments: intensive, intermediate, and minimal. Intensive treatment involved the services of a nurse and a social worker; intermediate treatment involved somewhat less professional attention; minimal treatment consisted of information and referral to community-based services. One might expect intensive treatment to have been the most effective, but after 6 months the death rate of members of the intensive-care group was four times that of people in the minimal-care group! The intermediate-care group was also better off than the intensive-care group; the death rate of its members was "only" twice that of the minimal-care group.

What happened? It turned out that the major factor was being placed in an institution such as a nursing home. A person was much more likely to be institutionalized if a nurse and social worker were intensively involved in planning his or her care, and the excessive death rates were found in institutionalized patients. Since people had been assigned randomly to the three treatments, it is unlikely that the death rates were related to any pretreatment differences.

What is it about some nursing homes that could contribute to decline? First, the stress of relocating to a new setting is believed to play a role in increased mortality (Schultz & Brenner, 1977). Beyond this, in the nursing home, the nature of care discourages maintenance of whatever self-care skills and autonomous activities the resident may be capable of. Residents of nursing homes, even if they are able to do so, are not permitted to cook, do their laundry, buy groceries, or tend the yard. Even more limiting, a resident able to feed himself or herself, but slowly and with occasional spills, will be assisted or even fed like a child at mealtimes to shorten the time devoted to serving meals and minimize messes. The resident then no longer thinks of himself or herself as able to eat without help, which is likely to lead to still more loss of function and lowered morale. See Focus on Discovery 15.4 for more discussion of the psychological consequences of nursing home care.

During the late 1980s a series of investigations into lax practices in nursing homes led to a number of governmental reforms. Despite resulting improvements in most nursing homes, serious problems remain with many of them (Senate Special Committee on Aging, March 2002). For example, nursing assistants are often inadequately trained, overworked, and underpaid—and it is the nursing assistants, not the professional nursing staff or physicians, who have by far the most contact with nursing home residents. Many nursing assistants do not speak the same language as the residents; some work two jobs for as many as 18 hours a day. Turnover in these positions is high. Despite the best intentions, nursing assistants are presented with an overwhelming set of challenges, owing in part to cutbacks in government funding to nursing homes and a resulting workload that is unreasonably heavy. Sometimes they lack even basic supplies, such as diapers, soap, and toilet paper. Nursing assistants along with many other health care professionals are often untrained in managing behaviorally disruptive residents. In one study, nursing assistants were found to have committed a set of harmful, even fatal errors, such as failure to wash hands, to note dehydration, and to attend to bedsores (Pyle, 1999). There is little doubt that nursing homes still need reform.

Focus on Discovery 15.4

Loss of Control in Nursing Homes

Is the loss of control over one's life that happens in nursing homes actually damaging to the person's physical and mental health? Ellen Langer and Judith Rodin believe that it is. Their research indicates that giving older nursing home residents control and responsibility can improve health. In one study, Langer and Rodin (1977) told one group of residents that they were given a variety of decisions to make themselves, instead of the staff's making decisions for them; they were also given plants to take care of. A control group was told how eager the staff was to take care of them; the plants they were given were looked after by the staff. Although initially matched on health and well-being, these two groups differed on measures of alertness, happiness, and general well-being at follow-up. Members of the group given enhanced responsibility—and presumably a sense of greater control—tested higher on these measures 3 weeks later, and even 18 months later. More importantly, 18 months later only

half as many members of the experimental group had died—7 of 47, compared with 13 of 44 for the control group.

Increased control is not positive under all circumstances and for all people, though (Rodin, 1986). With increased control comes more responsibility, and some people may convert this into unwarranted self-blame. For example, a caregiver may try to solve unsolvable memory problems for a dementia patient and blame themselves when they are unable to do so. And if the actual environment is not supportive of increased efforts to exert control, people are likely to feel worse. For example, if nursing home staff members discourage independence, a patient's efforts to be autonomous might provoke arguments. With this caveat in mind, Rodin concludes that health professionals as well as family members should look for ways to enhance control in older adults, particularly for those in institutional settings such as nursing homes.

National policy now mandates that people with primary mental illnesses should not be admitted to nursing homes. Despite that ruling, some people develop mental illnesses after admission, some people with mental illnesses were already living in nursing homes before the ruling, and others were admitted because diagnoses were not caught at admission. It has been estimated that 80 percent of people living in nursing homes have mental illness or dementia (Reichman et al., 1998), and 44 percent report significant symptoms of depression (Teresi et al., 2001).

Clearly then, there is a need for mental health services in these settings. Beyond evidence that psychological disorders can be effectively treated, interventions such as behavior therapy have been found to be quite effective in reducing unwanted behaviors and improving overall functioning in nursing home residents with dementia. In fact, medication can often be significantly reduced once behavior therapy has been implemented (Mansdorf et al., 1999).

Many nursing homes do provide mental health care. Indeed, one-third of mental health and substance-abuse treatment costs for the elderly are provided to nursing homes (Harwood et al., 2003). Nonetheless, nursing homes vary substantially in their ability to access quality mental health care. Almost half of nursing home administrators report that they do not have access to adequate mental health consultation (Reichman et al., 1998). Even when consultation is available, many nursing homes contact an off-site mental health provider who meets with a client and provides a written set of recommendations. One study of 523 nursing homes found that fewer than a third of written recommendations for mental health care were implemented by staff (Snowden & Roy-Byrne, 1998). These gaps in service are particularly sad, given that one study found that mental health interventions reduced deaths by 25 percent over a 2-year period for people with psychotic and anxiety disorders (Office of the Inspector General, 2001).

In an attempt to improve the quality of care, the federal government now mandates that the care provided to each client in a nursing home be evaluated using 24 quality control indices at admission, annually, and when a client experiences a significant change in status. Many of these indices are designed to

Nursing homes play a major role in the institutional care of the aged. They have often been criticized for the poor care they provide as well as the lack of stimulation in the environment. (Jose Luis Pelaez/Corbis Stock Market.)

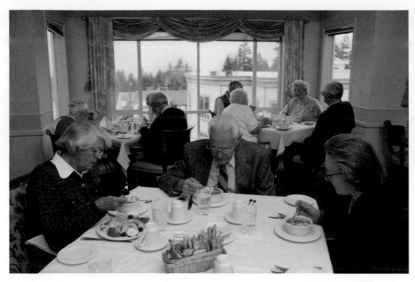

CCRCs often provide extensive opportunities for social contact. (Keith Brofsky/PhotoDisc, Inc./Getty Images.)

capture common problems with mental health care, including the inappropriate use of antipsychotic medications (to sedate patients when there is no psychotic disorder), ongoing use of benzodiazepines (which are dangerous for the elderly), use of sleeping pills more than twice per week, use of physical restraints on a daily basis, and untreated depression (Zimmerman, 2003). Average indices for each facility are included in a national database, to allow researchers, reviewers, and policy makers to make data-guided decisions.

Alternative Living Settings

Recently, the United States has seen a dramatic rise in assisted living, one alternative to nursing homes for many older adults who require assistance of one sort or another. The American Association of Retired Persons (AARP) reports that assisted living is the fastest growing category of housing for older adults in the United States (AARP, 1999). In contrast to nursing homes, assisted-living facilities resemble hotels, with separate rooms and suites for the residents as well as dining rooms and on-site amenities such as beauty and barber shops. The philosophy of assisted living stresses autonomy, independence, dignity, and privacy (AARP, 1999). Assisted living may sometimes go by other names, such as group homes or board-and-care. Many such residences are quite luxurious, with attentive staff, nursing and medical assistance readily available, daily activities, such as games and movies, and other services all designed to provide assisted care for older adults too infirm to live on their own but not so infirm as to require a nursing home. It is worth noting that nursing homes are usually much more expensive than even upscale assisted living facilities. Nonetheless, assisted living facilities can be quite costly, and as with nursing homes, there is a great deal of variability in quality of care.

In addition to assisted-living facilities and nursing homes, continuing care retirement communities (CCRCs) offer a continuum of care which enables residents to move from one housing option to another depending on their needs (AARP, 2001). These facilities combine independent living, assisted living, and nursing homes together on the same grounds. Residents may begin living in independent housing and move to other housing options as they require more assistance with their activities of daily living. The cost of living in these communities is quite high. Depending on the specific CCRC, residents may own or rent their apartment. The majority of CCRCs require their potential residents to pass a medical examination to assess their current health status.

Check Your Knowledge 15.5

1. The most common living situation for people in late life is
   a. in the community
   b. in a continuing care retirement community
   c. in a nursing home
   d. in a group home
2. National legislation focused on improving the quality of care in nursing homes has
   a. ignored mental health issues
   b. broadly described the need for mental health care
   c. provided specific guidelines about certain forms of mental health treatment
   d. There has been no national legislation.
3. National legislation mandates that older people with current psychological disorders
   a. should only be placed in nursing homes with good psychiatric coverage
   b. should not be placed in nursing homes
   c. does not address proper placement of this population

Summary

Aging: Issues and Methods

● Until recently, the psychological problems of older people were neglected by mental health professionals. As life expectancy continues to improve, it will become even more important to learn about the disorders suffered by some older people and the most effective means of treating them.

● Several stereotypes about aging are false. Generally, people in late life report low levels of negative emotion, are not inappropriately concerned with their health, and are not lonely. They report typically active sexual lives. On the other hand, poverty, stigma, and physical disease are common challenges for people as they age.

● In research studies, differences between a younger and an older group could reflect either cohort effects or effects of chronological age. Longitudinal studies are more helpful for making this distinction than cross-sectional studies are.

Cognitive Disorders in Late Life

● Serious cognitive disorders affect a small minority of older people. Two principal disorders have been distinguished: dementia and delirium.

● In dementia, the person's intellectual functioning declines and memory, abstract thinking, and judgment deteriorate. As the dementia progresses, the individual comes to seem like another person altogether and is, in the end, oblivious to his or her surroundings. A variety of diseases can cause this deterioration. The most common is Alzheimer's disease, a progressive, irreversible illness in which cortical cells waste away. Genes probably play some role in the etiology of Alzheimer's disease. A history of head injury and depression are also risk factors.

● Other forms of dementia include frontal-temporal dementia, vascular dementia, and dementia with Lewy bodies.

● Dementia usually responds only minimally to medication treatment, but the person and the family affected by the disease can be counseled on how to make the remaining time manageable and even rewarding. If adequate support is given to caregivers, many patients can be looked after at home.

● In delirium, there is sudden clouding of consciousness and other problems in thinking, feeling, and behaving: fragmented and undirected thought, incoherent speech, inability to sustain attention, hallucinations, illusions, disorientation, lethargy or hyperactivity, and mood swings. The condition is reversible, provided that the underlying cause is adequately treated. Causes include overmedication, infection of brain tissue, high fevers, malnutrition, dehydration, endocrine disorders, head trauma, cerebrovascular problems, and surgery.

Psychological Disorders in Late Life

● Data indicate that persons over age 65 have the lowest overall rates of mental disorders of all age groups. When older people experience psychological disorders, the symptoms are often a recurrence of a disorder that first emerged earlier in life.

● In older adults, depression tends to be accompanied by more cognitive impairment. When the onset of a first episode of depression occurs after age 65, cardiovascular disease is often a cause.

● Suicide attempts of older people are more likely to result in death than those of younger people, and the group with the highest rate of suicide is elderly Caucasian men.

● Anxiety disorders are more prevalent than depression among older adults.

● Delusional (paranoid) disorder may also be seen in older patients. Sometimes, onset occurs in the context of brain disorders, sensory losses, or increasing social isolation.

● Medication treatments for psychological disorders are similar in effectiveness during adulthood and late life, but must be used with caution because the elderly are more sensitive to side effects and toxicity.

Adjusting Treatment with Older Adults

● The treatments shown to help most psychological disorders in adulthood appear to be helpful for late life disorders. For example, cognitive, behavioral, and interpersonal psychotherapy are effective for depression, and cognitive behavioral treatment is effective for anxiety.

● Psychological treatments may need to be tailored to the needs of older people. Clinicians should sometimes be active and directive, providing information and seeking out the agencies that give the social services needed by their clients.

Living Situations: Community Living, Nursing Homes, and Other Alternatives

● Most older persons reside in the community.

● Nursing homes sometimes do little to encourage residents to maintain whatever capacities they have. Both physical and mental deterioration may occur. Serious neglect can be found in some nursing homes, and access to mental health care is limited. Several efforts have been made to correct these deficiencies.

● An increasingly popular alternative is assisted-living facilities.

Answers to Check Your Knowledge Questions

15.1. 1. T; 2. F; 3. F; 4. F; 5. F; 6. F
15.2. 1. a; 2. b; 3. d; 4. a; 5. a; 6. d; 7. b
15.3. 1. b; 2. c; 3. d; 4. a

15.4. 1. F; 2. T; 3. T; 4. F
15.5. 1. a; 2. c; 3. b

Key Terms

age effects	dementia	neurofibrillary tangles	time-of-measurement effects
Alzheimer's disease	dementia with Lewy bodies (DLB)	plaques	
cohort effects	disorientation	selective mortality	
delirium	frontal-temporal dementia (FTD)	social selectivity	

16 Psychological Treatment

Learning Goals

1. Be able to explain standards for psychotherapy research and issues in treatment outcome research.
2. Be able to discuss issues in adapting psychotherapies for people from diverse ethnic and cultural backgrounds.
3. Be able to identify the specific types of psychological treatments that have empirical support, and issues that clinicians must consider in applying these treatments.
4. Be able to describe different approaches to integrating psychotherapies and identifying common elements across treatments.
5. Be able to discuss the goals of community psychology and political trends in that field.

I n Chapters 1 and 2 we described the major approaches to psychological therapeutic intervention, and in Chapters 5 through 15 we reviewed how these approaches work for specific disorders. We now discuss some broader issues in psychological treatment. First, we consider overall standards and issues in evaluating psychotherapy research. Many authors have expressed concern about whether the results of psychotherapy research will generalize outside of the studies, and nowhere is this issue more profound than it is with respect to the generalizability of psychotherapy results for different cultural and ethnic groups. We highlight just a few of the issues involved in increasing cultural sensitivity within psychotherapy. Then, we review specific psychotherapies, such as psychoanalytic therapy and cognitive behavioral therapy, with an eye toward issues in implementing these treatments, but also specific data on how well each treatment works. As we discuss these treatments, we hope to enrich your understanding of them by offering small case studies to illustrate how some of these approaches work. We will also describe some treatments that have received less attention in previous chapters—existential therapies, couples therapies, and family therapies. The dizzying array of treatments that have been found to offer benefits, though, raises a fundamental question—how can we draw the best from each treatment approach? To provide some fuel for thought on that question, we discuss approaches to integration. Then, we close with a discussion of community psychology, a field that focuses on making interventions available on a broad social scale rather than with one person at a time.

Challenges in Evaluating Treatment Outcomes

Researchers have been studying treatment outcomes, or how well different therapies work, for decades. Outcome research is designed to address a simple question: does therapy work? The clear answer is yes. Hundreds of studies have examined whether people who

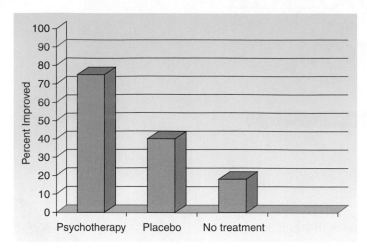

Figure 16.1 Summary of percent of people who achieve improvement across outcome for psychotherapy placebo and no treatment across studies. [Drawn from Lambert (2004). Psychotherapeutically-speaking—updates from the Division of Psychotherapy (29). With permission of the author and of APA.]

Troubled people may talk about their problems with friends or seek professional therapy. Treatment is typically sought by those for whom the advice and support of family or friends have not provided relief. [(Top) PhotoEdit; (bottom) Esbin-Anderson/The Image Works.]

receive psychotherapy fare better than those who do not. In meta-analyses of more than 300 studies, researchers have found that there is a moderately positive effect of treatment. About 75 percent of people who enter treatment achieve at least some improvement (Lambert & Ogles, 2004). As shown in Figure 16.1, these effects appear to be more powerful than the passage of time or support from friends and family. Eysenck (1952) had earlier questioned the effectiveness of most kinds of insight-oriented psychotherapy, finding that treated clients' rates of improvement were no better than the spontaneous remission rate. Eysenck's criticisms were compellingly rebutted by a number of scholars (e.g., Bergin, 1971) and continue to be rebutted by the accumulation of studies showing that therapy does work.

In the past 10 years, though, this research has begun to draw a great deal of attention from policy makers. In 1995, a task force for the American Psychological Association defined standards for research on psychotherapy and then published a report on the therapies that had received empirical support (see Table 16.1) (Task Force on Promotion and Dissemination of Psychological Treatments, 1995). The goal was to help clinicians draw more easily on this rapidly growing literature about **empirically supported treatments (ESTs)** to provide consumers with the best available treatments. These summaries might also help defend the role of psychotherapy with managed care agencies and insurance companies, who have increasingly demanded research evidence before they are willing to pay for treatments.

What are the standards for treatment **outcome research** to be seen as valid? Several different working groups have come up with slightly different answers to this question. At a minimum, most researchers agree that a treatment study should include the following criteria:

- a clear definition of the sample being studied, such as a description of diagnoses;
- a clear description of the treatment being offered, as in a treatment manual (described below);
- reliable and valid outcome measures;
- inclusion of a control or comparison treatment condition;
- random assignment of clients to treatment or comparison conditions; and
- a large enough sample for statistical tests.

Studies in which clients are randomly assigned to receive active treatment or a comparison (either no treatment, a placebo, or another treatment) are called **randomized controlled trials (RCTs)**. These studies can be considered an experiment, in which the independent variable is the treatment and the dependent variable is the clients' outcome.

Many different types of control groups can be included in psychotherapy research. Although some people argue that the inclusion of a control group may be unethical (Wolitzky, 1995), it is difficult to make a compelling case for any treatment when treatment outcome studies do not include a control group of some form. A no-treatment control group allows researchers to test whether the mere passage of time helps a person recover as much as treatment does. A stricter test compares the treatment group

Table 16.1   Examples of Empirically Supported Treatments for Adult Disorders

Depression
Cognitive therapy
Behavior therapy
Interpersonal psychotherapy

Generalized anxiety disorder
Cognitive therapy
Applied relaxation

Social phobia
Exposure alone
Exposure plus cognitive restructuring

Simple phobia
Systematic desensitization

Obsessive-compulsive disorder
Exposure and response prevention

Agoraphobia:
Exposure

Panic
Cognitive therapy for panic disorder
Exposure
Applied relaxation

PTSD
Exposure

Schizophrenia
Social skills training
Behavioral family therapy

Alcohol abuse and dependence
Community reinforcement approach
Behavioral marital therapy

Substance abuse and dependence
Relationship distress
Behavioral marital therapy
Emotion-focused therapy
Supportive-expressive therapy
Cognitive therapy
Relapse prevention
Behavior therapy

Sexual dysfunctions
Partner assisted sexual skills training

Bulimia
Cognitive behavior therapy
Interpersonal Psychotherapy

Source: Journal of Consulting and Clinical Psychology, 1998, 66(1). Updated from Chambless, D. L., Sanderson, W. C., Shoham, V., Johnson, S. B., Pope, K. S., Crits-Christoph, P., Baker, M., Johnson, B., Woody, S. R., Sue, S., Beutler, L., Williams, D. A., & McCurry, S. An update on empirically validated therapies. Available by Web at http://www.apa.org/divisions/div12/journals.html#Anchor-EMPIRICALLY-49575

to an attention-control group in which clients see a therapist regularly for support and encouragement (the "attention" component), but they do not receive what is considered to be the "active ingredient" in the kind of therapy being tested (e.g., gradual exposure to a feared situation in a behavioral treatment of a phobia). The strictest type of design includes an active-treatment control group, in which researchers compare the new treatment against a well-tested treatment. This type of design allows researchers to make comparative statements about two treatments.

The APA task force described above has focused on identifying treatments that are not just *efficacious* (those that produce improvements), but that are also *specific*, in that they perform better than an attention-control or placebo condition. It is important to note that many current research studies do not meet this condition.

As shown by the complexities that must be juggled in choosing a control group, designing treatment trials is difficult. Although many researchers agree with the APA task force's minimal standards for research studies, some aspects have been hotly debated. For example, failure for a treatment to appear on the APA task force list of empirically supported treatments (Table 16.1) could simply reflect a lack of careful studies. As you will see, most of the treatments listed are cognitive behavioral. Although we will discuss research supporting many other treatments in this chapter, cognitive behavioral treatments are featured in the APA list because the trials for these treatments have met the strict APA criteria. We turn toward three other issues that are a subject of debate: the use of treatment manuals, the nature of samples within treatment studies, and the generalizability of findings to the real world.

The Use of Treatment Manuals in Randomized Controlled Trials

Treatment manuals are detailed guides on how to conduct a particular psychological treatment—they provide specific procedures for the therapist to follow at each stage of treatment. The use of manuals has been a major advance in psychotherapy research (e.g., Nathan & Gorman, 2002) and is required to receive grant funding for treatment outcome research.

Manuals buy us greater internal validity (p. 112); we can more confidently attribute results to the action of the independent variable (in this case, the treatment offered). Without a manual, it is hard to know what therapists actually do, because a therapist's descriptions of a session or allegiance to an orientation might not capture what really happens (London, 1964). With manuals, someone reading a psychotherapy study can know what happened to clients in a given experimental condition. Even with a manual, though, maintaining precision in delivering the independent variable is a challenge—almost no other experiments in psychology attempt to control the independent variable for months (Westen, Novotny, & Thompson-Brenner, 2004).

Beyond challenges to internal validity, what about external validity? That is, do the results obtained from treatment manual–based studies generalize to psychotherapy practiced outside of a controlled study (Persons, 2001)? There is perhaps no more hotly debated topic in psychotherapy than this (Beutler, 1999; Goldfried & Davison, 1994).

The purpose of using treatment manuals is to clearly define the independent variable and to limit the amount that therapists vary in what they do. That is, the goal is to minimize differences across therapists. However, therapists vary even in randomized controlled trials (RCTs). For example, in the well-known NIMH Treatment of Depression Collaborative Research Program (p. 258), therapists differed in how well they implemented the manuals. Some therapists were more successful than others using the same manual (Blatt et al., 1996). Research suggests that sometimes these differences between therapists can be greater than the differences between treatments (Beutler, 1997).

Do we really want to force therapists to do the same things with each client? Some have argued that manuals might be too limiting for a good therapist. Outside of RCTs, therapists tend to tailor treatment to the client (Haaga & Stiles, 2000). That is, therapy in nonresearch settings can be more responsive to a client's needs because therapists are not constrained by the demands of a scientific study. In contrast, the very essence of treatment manuals is to minimize the tailoring of intervention to individual clients. The problem is that if a therapist adheres too rigidly to a treatment manual, the client can feel that his or her particular concerns are not being addressed (Henry et al., 1993).

Some of this debate about manuals could be resolved by research studies. Some reviews have suggested that manuals do not make a major difference in outcomes (Beutler et al., 2004). But the clear guidelines provided by manuals seem to help novice therapists more than experienced therapists (Multon, Kivlighan, & Gold, 1996). Further, in one meta-analysis of brief psychodynamic treatment studies, those that involved treatment manuals achieved greater gains than those with no treatment manuals (Anderson & Lambert, 1995). The challenge, then, might be to provide manuals that give therapists a clear road map but do not constrain experienced therapists to a point where their flexibility is diminished—a difficult balance, to be sure (Davison, 1998).

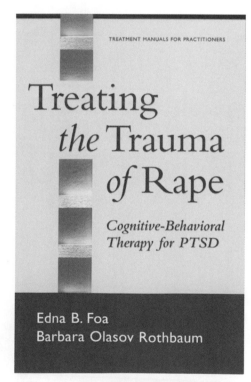

A treatment manual provides specific procedures for a therapist to use in working with a client. Although they are increasingly standard in research trials, many therapists still say they don't use them. From Edna B. Foa and Barbara Olasov Rothbaum, *Treating the Trauma of Rape: Cognitive-Behavioral Therapy for PTSD. Represented with permission of Guilford Publications.*

Defining a Sample

Randomized controlled trials (RCTs) typically focus on treating people who have a certain DSM diagnosis. For example, the large-scale NIMH RCT that we examined in Chapter 8 (p. 258) recruited people who met DSM criteria for major depressive disorder. But depressions are not all caused by the same factors (e.g., negative cognitive styles). Some have argued that we should be designing studies focused on people with similar psychological profiles (Persons, 1991). For example, clients with negative cognitive styles can be assigned to cognitive therapy, while those with significant family distress can be assigned to family therapy (Beevers & Miller, 2005). Beutler and colleagues (2003) have conducted a line of research to demonstrate the effectiveness of matching clients to treatment based on their coping styles. Hence, some have argued that it would be better to choose a treatment based on a person's level on different risk factors for psychopathology, rather than on their diagnosis.

Beyond concerns about the best basis for defining a sample, there are concerns about the number of people who are excluded in treatment research. In a typical RCT, researchers might include people who meet diagnostic criteria for a given disorder but exclude those who have more than one disorder, acute suicidality (for ethical reasons), or other characteristics. Some participants might not be willing to take part in a study in which they might be assigned to an ineffective treatment (the control condition). As it turns out, researchers exclude almost as many people as they recruit into these studies (Westen et al., 2004). For example, although most people who meet criteria for a single psychological disorder also meet criteria for at least one more disorder, most trials tend to focus on treating a single disorder at a time (Westen et al., 2004). This situation creates problems with generalizing from controlled studies to the actual practice of psychotherapy in the real world, a topic we consider next.

Treating Disorders in the Real World

Controlled RCTs, typically conducted in academic research settings, are designed to determine the **efficacy** of a treatment, that is, whether a treatment works under the purest of conditions. Because of the kinds of concerns just raised, academic research might not inform us about how these treatments work with broader samples in the hands of nonacademic therapists. We need to determine not just the efficacy of a treatment but also its **effectiveness**, that is, how well the treatment works in the real world. Studies of effectiveness might:

- include people with a broader range of problems (such as comorbid conditions);
- provide less intensive supervision of therapists;
- examine a broader range of outcomes, such as whether clients believe they were helped and feel satisfied with their lives at the end of treatment; and
- rely on briefer assessments.

As you might expect, when clients have more serious diagnostic complications and providers have less support, even medications tend to look less powerful than they do in careful efficacy studies. Effectiveness research can focus on how to foster better treatment in the community. For example, one recent study examined whether medication treatment of depression in the community was improved by providing psychiatrists with easily navigated hand-held computers programmed to provide quick feedback and assistance regarding treatment decisions (Trivedi et al., 2004). If it is hard to foster good medication treatment, one can imagine that interventions as complicated as a 16-session psychotherapy will be challenged by real-world hurdles too. Even though such studies may incorporate less experimental control, they are fundamentally important in evaluating how well these treatment approaches will work in the real world. Beyond some important surveys of how people see the therapy they have received (see *Consumer Reports*, 1995), effectiveness studies are beginning to appear in support of certain cognitive behavioral treatments of anxiety (e.g., Wade, Treat, & Stuart, 1998) and depression (e.g., Persons, Bostrom, & Bertagnolli, 1999).

Even with increasing evidence that these treatments work in the real world, there is a big gap between what happens in research centers and the real world (see Focus on Discovery 16.1 for a discussion of how business issues shape treatment in the real world). Even though more than 145 treatment manuals have been recognized as empirically supported

Focus on Discovery 16.1

Economic Systems Guiding Treatment Decisions in the Real World

No doubt you have heard of managed care. Insurance companies attempt to control costs (and maximize profits) by requiring prior pre-approval of treatments and by reducing the amount of payment for services. Managed care organizations aim to slow the rise of health care costs by applying business models to health care decisions. They have also demanded increased accountability from providers. Managed care organizations look to scientific evidence to decide which medical treatments to approve. More recently, these standards have been applied to psychological treatments (Chambless & Ollendick, 2001).

Who can object to trying to control costs? We all end up paying for one another's health care expenses one way or the other. But the picture is not that simple. Managed care is strongly opposed by some mental health professionals on the grounds that it intrudes on the privacy of clients as well as on the independent decision making of clinicians, who no longer have the freedom to choose the type of treatment or its duration for their clients.

Partly in response to managed care, a strategy from medicine called **stepped care** is becoming more widely used in psychology and psychiatry (Haaga, 2000). Briefly stated, stepped care refers to the practice of beginning treatment efforts with the least expensive intervention possible and moving on to more expensive interventions only if necessary (see Figure 16.2). For example, a client with mild depression might be offered a self-help book that has been shown to be effective in reducing symptoms (McKendree-Smith, Floyd, & Scogin, 2003). After a month, people who do not gain symptom relief would be offered psychotherapy or antidepressant medication.

Stepped care is consistent with the legal principle of "least restrictive alternative." As discussed in greater detail in the next chapter (p. 586), mental health professionals are supposed to provide that treatment which restricts the client's liberty to the least possible degree while remaining workable and effective [*In Re: Tarpley* 556 N.E. 2d, superseded by 581 N.E. 2d 1251 (1991)]. So, consistent with the principles of stepped care, psychological and psychiatric treatment should entail as little intrusion as possible.

There are risks associated with beginning with low-intensity treatments. If the initial intervention does not help, the client may lose heart and drop out of treatment altogether. Consider one example of stepped care. In a study of weight loss, researchers initially assigned 26 clients to receive basic education about how to lose weight. Only 4 of the 26 clients, though, were able to reach their desired weight (Black & Threlfall, 1986). Bibliotherapy was added, and the remaining 22 clients

reached their desired weight. In this type of circumstance, it would make sense to start with the more powerful intervention to avoid the demoralization that can arise when initial treatment efforts fail (Wilson, Vitonsek, & Loeb, 2000). Effective stepped care programs will depend on using minimal treatments that have strong research backing (Rosen, 2004). In some cases, such data are available. For example, brief written materials appear to be extremely helpful for many people who want to gain better control over drinking habits. Using well-tested written materials, then, makes sense as a starting ground for drinking-related treatment goals (Apodaca & Miller, 2003). Planning effective stepped care interventions requires a delicate juggling act to consider economics, illness severity, and the relative efficacy of different approaches.

Figure 16.2   Stepped care involves starting with the least expensive intervention and moving on to more expensive interventions only if needed. Sobell, M. B., & Sobell, L. C. (2000). Stepped Care as a Heuristic Approach to the Treatment of Alcohol Problems. *Journal of Consulting and Clinical Psychology*, 68, 573–579. Adapted with permission from *Addictive Behaviors across the Lifespan: Prevention, Treatment, and Policy Issues* (p. 150), by J. S. Baier, G. A. Marlatt, & R. J. McMahon (Eds.), 1993, Beverly Hills, CA: Sage.

(Chambless & Ollendick, 2001), therapists in the community seem relatively unaware of these manuals. For example, Addis and Krasnow (2000) reported that 23 percent of therapists surveyed said they had not heard of treatment manuals, and another 38 percent reported that they had heard of them but did not know what they were. Hopefully, more clinicians have heard about these treatment manuals since the survey was done, but clearly this demonstrates a need to work harder on getting research findings into the hands of therapists and consumers! One way to do this has been to recommend that graduate students in psychology be taught empirically supported treatments (Crits-Christoph et al., 1995).

Check Your Knowledge 16.1

Circle all that apply for the following questions.

1. Which of the following are the elements of an RCT by definition?
   a. randomization
   b. a comparison condition
   c. medications
   d. double-blind procedures
2. Which of these are common problems in treatment outcome studies?
   a. nonrepresentative samples
   b. no way to measure improvement

   c. variability across therapists
   d. treatment manuals constrain therapists
   e. lack of generalizability to the real world
   f. lack of clarity about treatment goals
3. The goal of effectiveness studies is to determine whether a treatment works
   a. under the best possible conditions
   b. under real-world conditions

The Importance of Culture and Ethnicity in Psychological Treatment

Above, we described concerns about who is recruited into treatment studies. As it turns out, one of the major gaps in treatment outcome studies has been the exclusion of people from diverse cultural and ethnic backgrounds. Most studies enroll predominantly white, non-Latino clients, so that samples often are not diverse enough to examine how treatment effects vary for differing groups of people. But there are many reasons to suspect that these treatments may not meet the needs of minority group members. For example, in studies of who seeks treatment in different settings, it appears that people from minority groups are much less likely to receive treatment for mental health conditions (USDHHS, 2002).

We believe it is important to consider some of the issues that may limit how well therapies work for people from different backgrounds. We do want to raise one caveat. Our discussion of ethnic and cultural factors in intervention runs the risk of stereotyping because we are going to review generalizations about the way a group of people react to psychological assistance. People from minority groups can differ as much from each other as their racial or ethnic group differs from another racial or ethnic group. It is important to consider the degree to which the person is *assimilated* into the majority culture and holds the same values as the majority culture (Sue & Sue, 2003). Nonetheless, a consideration of group characteristics is important and is part of a specialty called ethnic minority mental health.

It is usually assumed that clients do better with therapists who are similar to them in cultural and ethnic background. Indeed, many minority clients report that they would prefer to see someone from a similar background (Lopez, Lopez, & Fong, 1991). Such preferences may be particularly strong when a person maintains a strong identification with their ethnic group (Ponce & Atkinson, 1989). Therapists of similar background, perhaps even of the same gender, are expected to understand a person's life circumstances more quickly and may be more acceptable to the client. Despite this assumption, it has *not* been demonstrated that better outcomes are achieved when client and therapist are similar in race or ethnicity (Beutler, Machado, & Neufeldt, 1994), nor that clients are more likely to continue treatment when there is a match (Maramba & Nagayama-Hall, 2002). **Cultural competence** may matter more than ethnic matching. A therapist who is not a member of the same racial or

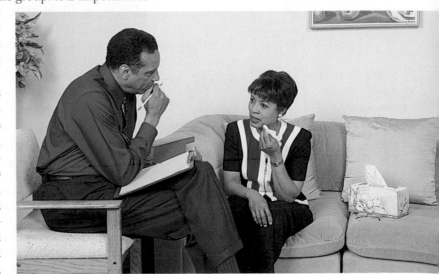

Although many minority clients report that they would like to see a minority therapist, cultural sensitivity appears to be more important to outcome than a match of ethnicity between the client and therapist. (Lew Merrim/Photo Researchers.)

ethnic group as the client might still understand the client and create a good therapeutic relationship if he or she is familiar with the client's culture (USDHHS, 2002). We provide a brief glimpse of the kinds of issues that a therapist should be knowledgeable about as one aspect of achieving cultural competence.

African Americans and Psychological Treatment

Racial stereotypes on the part of white therapists may be one barrier to African American clients receiving treatment. One experiment revealed that white therapists rated case study information about African American clients as reflecting more pathology than did African American therapists and also considered photographs of the clients less attractive (Atkinson et al., 1996).

Therapists need to accept that virtually all African Americans have encountered prejudice and racism, and many must wrestle with their rage at a majority culture that is sometimes insensitive to and unappreciative of the emotional consequences of growing up as a member of a feared, resented, and sometimes hated minority (USDHHS, 2002). And, like members of all the minority groups discussed in this section, many African Americans have been subjected to hate crimes, which obviously add to their sense of alienation from the mainstream culture. One survey of African American clients suggested that many felt that their therapists were insensitive to these issues (Thompson et al., 2004).

Latinos and Psychological Treatment

The life experiences of Latino Americans vary a great deal depending on the region they originally came from—Mexico, Cuba, Puerto Rico, or Central America. As is the case with other minority groups, generalizations are to be made with caution.

Therapy with most Latinos should appreciate their difficulty in expressing psychological concerns. Men in particular may have trouble expressing weakness and fear, which may be exacerbated by the growing independence of many Latina women as wage earners. In addition, religion plays a very strong role in most Latin cultures and therefore needs to be considered in any therapeutic approach with Latinos (USDHHS, 2002). Cognitive behavior therapy may be more acceptable than insight-oriented psychotherapy to some Latinos because it provides advice and problem solving around issues of immediate importance. The didactic style of cognitive behavior therapy may also serve to demystify the process and render it more educational than psychotherapeutic in nature, thus reducing the possible stigmatizing effects of "having one's head shrunk" (Organista & Munoz, 1996).

These considerations, however, apply generally to lower-income people, regardless of race or ethnicity. This means that socioeconomic class has to be considered. Consider Cuban-Americans. Because of the circumstances under which many Cubans came to the United States in the 1960s—being from the more privileged strata of Cuban society before Castro came into power in 1959—and given also their economic successes in many parts of the country, especially south Florida, there is no reason to assume that they and other higher income Latinos will find therapy less suitable than do Anglos.

Asian Americans, Pacific Islanders, and Psychological Treatment

Asian Americans and Pacific Islanders comprise more than three dozen distinct subgroups (e.g., Filipino, Chinese, Japanese, Vietnamese, Hawaiian, Samoan). They differ on dimensions such as how well they speak English, whether they came as refugees from war or terrorism in their homeland, and how much they identify with their native land (Sue & Sue, 2003). In general, these groups show a greater tendency than whites to be ashamed of emotional suffering and to be reluctant to seek out professional help.

The stereotype of Asian Americans as invariably being highly educated, earning good salaries, and being emotionally well-adjusted is belied by the facts. The discrimination suffered in the United States and in many other countries is as severe as that endured by other racial and ethnic minority groups (Sue & Sue, 2002). In the United States, for example, over 120,000 Japanese Americans—70,000 of them born in the United States (USDHHS, 2002)—were imprisoned in concentration camps and prisons for several years during World War II. More subtle discrimination is found in everyday occurrences in more recent times. Sue and Sue (2003) advise therapists to be sensitive to the personal losses that many Asian refugees have suffered and, especially in light of the great importance that family connections have for them, to the likelihood that they are very stressed from losses occurring to their families. Another way to put this is to appreciate the high rates of posttraumatic stress in Asian Americans who came to the United States as refugees.

Asian Americans in the United States are often caught between two cultures. One form of resolution is to identify vigorously with majority values and denigrate anything Asian, a kind of racial self-hate. Others, torn by conflicting loyalties, experience poorly expressed rage at a discriminatory Western culture. Acculturation, then, is important to consider.

Many cultural differences in values, particularly concerning relationships and emotional expression, have implications for how to conduct psychotherapy with Asian Americans and Pacific Islanders. Therapists should be aware that Asian Americans have a tendency to talk about stress in physical terms, such as headaches and fatigue, rather than to view their stress in psychological terms (Nguyen, 1985). Their values are also different from the majority culture in the United States. For example—and allowing for considerable individual variation—Asians respect structure and formality in interpersonal relationships, whereas a Western therapist is likely to favor informality and a less authoritarian attitude. (Quite the opposite holds for many Pacific Islanders such as Hawaiians, whose informality in relating to others is one of the things tourists like about vacationing on the Hawaiian Islands.) Respect for authority may take the form of agreeing readily to what the therapist proposes—and perhaps, rather than discussing differences openly, just not showing up for the next session. The acceptability of psychotherapy as a way to handle stress is likely to be much lower among Asian Americans, who tend to see emotional duress as something to be handled on one's own and through willpower (Kinzie, 1985). Asian Americans may also consider some areas off-limits for discussion with a therapist, for example, the nature of the marital relationship and especially sex. Finally, many Asian Americans prefer a structured approach to therapy over a reflective one (Iwamasa, 1993).

American Indians, Alaskan Natives, and Psychological Treatment

Like other minorities, American Indians and Alaskan Natives (sometimes referred to collectively as Native Americans or First Americans) are a highly heterogeneous group, with more than 500 tribes residing in the United States and many in Canada as well, speaking more than 200 languages, some of them as dissimilar to each other as English is to Chinese (Fleming, 1992).

American Indians and to a lesser but still significant extent Alaskan Natives have experienced severe institutional discrimination for over 300 years. They have been forbidden to speak their own language, driven from the land that their tribes had inhabited for hundreds of years, forbidden to engage in traditional native spiritual practices (in the case of American Indians), forced onto reservations in undesirable locations without regard for the special sanctity that land has for them, and subjected to other indignities. In recent years, however, their social and economic conditions have been improving, and tribes are achieving more control over their lives (USDHHS, 2002).

Because it is common for different family members to provide care for Native American children, the pattern of a child moving among different households is not necessarily a sign of trouble. A youngster's avoidance of eye contact is a traditional sign of respect but may be misconstrued by someone unfamiliar with the culture as quite the opposite and regarded as a problem to be remedied (Everett, Proctor, & Cartmell, 1989). As with members of other minority groups, conflicts about identification can be severe—young people can be torn between traditional values and those of the decidedly more privileged majority culture, which may underlie the high rates of truancy, substance abuse, and suicide among Native American young people (Red Horse, 1982). Drug abuse, especially alcoholism, is a widespread problem in some tribes and can lead to child abuse, particularly when there is family conflict. A value placed on cooperativeness rather than competitiveness can be misinterpreted by a culturally unaware therapist as lack of motivation. The importance of family may make it advisable to conduct treatment in the home and to engage family members in the process (Sue & Sue, 2003).

Psychotherapy Outcome Research in Ethnic Minority Populations

One review of the field reported that not a single study had shown that empirically supported treatments were valid for any specific minority group (Chambless & Ollendick, 2001). Although we have very little data on whether empirically supported treatments work with ethnic minority populations, here, we highlight work by a few researchers who have begun to provide data on whether currently available treatments work well when offered to people from different backgrounds.

For example, in one innovative study, Bolton and colleagues (2003) examined whether a group version of Interpersonal Psychotherapy for depression was efficacious for people living in Ugandan villages. Their findings suggested major improvements in depression among people who received Interpersonal Psychotherapy compared to those who were assigned to a control group.

Others have tested cognitive behavioral approaches in different populations within the United States. For example, Sanderson, Raue, and Wetzler (1998) examined cognitive behavior therapy for panic disorder in a small group of low-income clients, most of whom were Latino. The good news is that Sanderson found that cognitive behavioral treatment did lead to improvements. The bad news is that these improvements were not as large as had been found in other treatment studies.

This raises the need to consider adapting interventions to be more culturally sensitive. As outlined by Duran (2004), established treatments may need to be modified to change the role of the therapist, the types of intervention strategies used, the content of the intervention, and how to present certain content. For example, in refining an established treatment manual for stress management in an HIV-positive population, changes were made to the ways that assertiveness training was covered, new content was introduced on coping strategies and spirituality, and an array of other changes were made based on feedback from therapists and clients. Early results suggest that these efforts were a good idea; in a small group of HIV-positive Latino men, culturally sensitive treatment was found to produce significantly larger changes in depression, functioning, denial, and even HIV symptoms compared to a no-treatment control.

One approach to developing culturally sensitive interventions is to draw on strengths that might be promoted by a given culture. For example, Latino culture emphasizes family values and spirituality. Weisman (2005) modified traditional family therapy for schizophrenia to build on these values, with a more explicit focus on spirituality and family coping. It is hoped that tailoring interventions to these strengths can bolster their applicability.

Another example of innovative approaches is illustrated by the work of Ricardo Muñoz and colleagues, who have conducted research for years to examine how to treat depression among low-income, predominantly minority women in San Francisco. Their team first tailored cognitive behavioral therapy for depression so that it could be offered in a primary care group setting, such that it would be more widely accessible for people who might not seek out formal psychotherapy. Results of this intervention were successful (Muñoz et al., 1995). More recently, they modified the content of this intervention to be more specific to the concerns of African American women, including bolstering material to combat social isolation, to challenge myths of the superhuman African American woman, and to address family issues. Their initial findings suggest that African American women stated that they would rather receive the tailored intervention, and that it produced a significantly larger reduction in depressive symptoms than the traditional CBT intervention (Kohn et al., 2002).

Amy Weisman's research focuses on how to modify family treatment for schizophrenia to draw on strengths of Latino families. (Courtesy of Amy Weisman, University of Miami.)

Quick Summary

Over the past decade, a number of groups have attempted to provide clear standards for psychotherapy research and to summarize the current state of knowledge about the validity of psychotherapy. With some minor variations in criteria, these groups have tended to emphasize the importance of clearly defining the sample and treatment regimen, random assignment to either the active treatment or a control comparison, and reliable and valid measures of outcome. These efforts have gained increasing support, but have also provoked major debate. Treatment researchers and clinicians have raised concerns that control groups may not always be ethical, that treatment manuals can be constraining, that diagnosis might not be the best way to choose a treatment, and that the samples in treatment studies are not representative. One type of research focuses on the effectiveness of treatment, or the utility of a given treatment in the real world.

It is well established that minority groups are less likely to receive psychotherapy for psychological concerns. There is not support for the idea that matching therapist and client ethnicity is the answer to this question; rather, enhancing the cultural competence of therapists is the goal. Therapists need to be aware of cultural variability in stigma, emotional expression, attitudes toward mental illness, and disclosure. They also need to be aware of historical events and socioeconomic variables that influence clients. Despite a set of theories about what is important for good treatment outcome among minority populations, relatively little research has been done. Researchers who have tested treatment manuals developed for majority populations generally find such psychotherapies work with minority groups, but with less positive effect than seen in initial trials. A small set of dedicated researchers are working on ways to tailor treatment approaches to fit with culturally relevant values.

Specific Treatment Approaches: Issues and Treatment Outcome Research

With these general observations as background, we turn to an evaluation of several specific therapeutic approaches. For each therapy, we consider some issues in how to apply techniques and to refine the treatments, as well as the treatment outcome literature.

Psychoanalytic Treatment

One's paradigm affects one's criteria for evaluating how well therapy works. For example, in psychoanalysis, a principal criterion is the lifting of repressions, making the unconscious conscious. But how is that to be demonstrated? Attempts to assess outcome have sometimes relied on projective tests, such as the Rorschach, which in turn rely on the concept of the unconscious (Cook, Blatt, & Ford, 1995). For those who reject the very concept of an unconscious, data from projective tests will not be very convincing. Here, we will focus on research that has measured changes in symptoms, even though some would argue that the primary goal of psychoanalysis might be to increase insight.

As noted by several leading researchers in analytic therapy (Henry et al., 1994), it is difficult to distinguish between classical psychoanalysis and psychodynamic psychotherapy in practice. It is generally held that most classical psychoanalysts act in a fairly passive way, in contrast to those who practice psychodynamic psychotherapy, especially brief therapy. Freud, however, seems to have been much less remote and more directive than the classical analysts who followed him. In a report of a large psychoanalytic psychotherapy project, Wallerstein (1989) downplayed distinctions between classical psychoanalysis and psychodynamic treatment, noting that in actual practice, therapists tend to blend support, interpretation, and other elements. "All treatments (including even pure psychoanalyses) carry many more supportive components than they are usually credited with" (p. 205). With these cautions in mind, let us consider efforts to evaluate the efficacy of these therapies.

Outcome Research: Traditional Psychoanalytic Treatment   As Bachrach et al. (1991) pointed out, there are only four outcome studies of long-term psychoanalytic treatment. Major reviews of research on classical psychoanalysis suggest the following conclusions (Henry et al., 1994; Luborsky & Spence, 1978):

- Clients with severe psychopathology (e.g., schizophrenia) do not do as well as those with anxiety disorders. This is understandable in view of Freud's emphasis on less severe disorders rather than psychosis.
- People with more education tend to do better in analysis than those with less education.
- Poor outcomes are more likely when a therapist makes frequent interpretations of transference reactions—for example, indicating to a male client that his behavior toward the therapist seems to reflect unresolved conflicts with his mother.

Each of these studies of long-term psychoanalysis, though, has methodological problems, the most limiting of which is the lack of a control group. Because of this, we do not know whether psychoanalysis achieves more than the passage of time or the support of close others. This is not to say that psychoanalysis does no good, only that clear evidence is lacking as to its specific effectiveness.

Perhaps the most ambitious attempt to evaluate the effectiveness of psychoanalysis was the Menninger Foundation Psychotherapy Research Project, which began in the mid-1960s. In this study 42 clients—mostly Caucasian clients with anxiety, depression, or both—were seen in either psychoanalysis or short-term psychodynamic psychotherapy. In both groups about 60 percent of the clients improved. There were no significant differences between the two groups either immediately after treatment or at follow-up of 2 to 3 years (Wallerstein, 1986, 1989).

Outcome Research: Brief Psychodynamic Treatments   The picture emerging from outcome studies on brief psychodynamic treatment is inconsistent but generally positive. A meta-analysis of more than 25 studies suggested that brief psychodynamic therapy achieved moderately positive outcomes compared to no treatment (Anderson & Lambert, 1995). As reviewed by Goldfried, Greenberg, and Marmar (1990), brief psychodynamic therapy has been found to be helpful in treating bereavement (Marmar & Horowitz, 1988) and late-life depression (Thompson, Gallagher, & Breckenridge, 1987). Other literature reviews have found that brief psychodynamic therapy is useful with job-related distress and anxiety disorders (Koss & Shiang, 1994) including posttraumatic stress disorder (Horowitz, 1988) and psychopathy (Salekin, 2002). Overall, Anderson and Lambert (1995) suggested that brief psychodynamic therapies are likely to fare best when therapists use a manual and receive specific training in these approaches.

Several studies include comparisons with other active treatments. Rather than just asking if psychodynamic treatments are better than no treatment, these studies ask whether they work as well as cognitive behavioral treatment. In one review, the authors concluded that brief psychodynamic treatment achieved comparable results to other kinds of therapies (Anderson & Lambert, 1995). Similarly, one recent study found that brief psychodynamic therapy was as helpful as cognitive therapy for certain personality disorders (Svartberg, Stiles, & Seltzer, 2004). There is a fair amount of controversy about comparisons between treatments, though (see Lamberg & Ogles, 2004, for a discussion of how different reviewers find different patterns). Some of this debate may concern which studies and treatments should be included in a review. For example, Interpersonal Psychotherapy, a well-validated treatment for depression (see p. 252), builds on the psychodynamic emphasis on relationships, but it does not focus on the therapeutic relationship or a person's history. Should this be included in reviews of psychodynamic therapy? Reviewers differ on decisions such as this. As a result, some reviews find a small advantage for cognitive behavioral therapies, whereas others do not.

Experiential Therapies

Experiential therapies were developed in the mid-twentieth century. These therapies tend to include a major emphasis on the relationship with the therapist and on the process of activating emotions to help a person create new meaning (Elliot, Greenberg & Lietaer, 2004). To do so, the therapist uses **empathy**, the accurate awareness of the client's emotions. Experiential therapists emphasize the creative and expressive aspects of people, rather than the problematic and symptomatic features on which psychoanalysts often seem to concentrate. Because we have not reviewed these in much detail elsewhere in the book, we describe the key components of four of these approaches here: client-centered therapy, existential therapy, Gestalt therapy, and emotion-focused therapy.

Client-Centered Therapy   The American psychologist Carl Rogers (1902–1987) developed **client-centered therapy** based on a humanistic perspective. Humanism stresses the goodness of human nature. It holds that if unfettered by groundless fears and societal restrictions, human beings will develop normally, even exceptionally, much as a healthy plant will naturally develop from a seed if given enough light, air, and water without harmful or limiting conditions. Rogers (1951, 1961) developed a therapy that included the following assumptions:

1. People can be understood only from the vantage point of their own perceptions and feelings. That is, each person's unique ways of experiencing are the major determinants of behavior.
2. Healthy people are aware of the reasons for their behavior.
3. Healthy people are innately good and effective (e.g., able to achieve their goals); they become ineffective and disturbed only when faulty learning intervenes.
4. Healthy people are purposive and goal directed. They do not respond passively to the influence of their environment or to their inner drives, and they are self-directed.
5. Therapists should create conditions that will facilitate independent decision making by the client. Because of his positive view of people, Rogers assumed that their decisions would not only make them happy with themselves but also turn them into good, civilized people.
6. When people are not concerned with the evaluations, demands, and preferences of others, their lives are guided by an innate tendency for **self-actualization**, which refers to fulfilling one's potential as a human being.

Consistent with these views, Rogers avoided imposing goals on the client or manipulating events for them. According to Rogers, the client should take the lead and direct the course of the conversation and of the session. The therapist's job is to create conditions during the session that let the client return to his or her basic nature and make decisions leading to a more intrinsically gratifying life. Rogerians hold steadfastly to the rule that the person's innate capacity for growth and self-direction will assert itself provided that the therapeutic atmosphere is warm, attentive, and receptive.

The therapist promotes growth by totally accepting the person for who he or she is and providing what Rogers called **unconditional positive regard**. Other people set what Rogers called "conditions of worth"—"I will love you if." In contrast, the client-centered therapist values clients as they are—with unconditional positive regard—even if the therapist does not approve of their behavior. People have value merely for being people; the therapist must care deeply for and respect a client for the simple reason that he or she is another human being struggling to live and grow.

Existential Therapy   The existentialist point of view, like the humanistic one, emphasizes personal growth. Yet there are some important distinctions between the two. Existentialism is gloomier. Although it embraces free will and responsibility, existentialism stresses the anxiety that is inevitable in making important choices, the existential choices on which the quality of one's life depends, such as staying or not staying with a spouse, with a job, or even with this world. From the existentialist viewpoint, to be truly alive is to confront the anxiety that comes with existential choices. People must take responsibility for themselves, even when they are troubled.

Based on this view of humanity, the aim of **existential therapy** is to encourage clients to confront their anxieties concerning choices about how they will live, what they will value, and how they will relate to others. Therapists support their clients in examining

Carl Rogers, who developed client-centered therapy, proposed that the key ingredient in therapy is the attitude and style of the therapist rather than specific techniques. (Roger Ressmeyer/Corbis Images.)

what is really meaningful in life. According to this view, sometimes the most important and courageous choices will cause extreme discomfort. Life is not easy for those who are true to themselves.

Although existential therapy begins with a focus on internal feelings, changing behavior is an important goal—in particular, fostering open, honest, spontaneous, and loving relationships. At the same time, it emphasizes that each of us is ultimately alone; the paradox of life is that, despite the presence of others, we are inherently separate from them, that we came into the world alone and must create our own existence in the world alone. People must be encouraged to accept the responsibility for their own existence and to realize that within certain limits, they can redefine themselves at any moment and to behave and feel differently within their own social environment.

Gestalt Therapy   **Gestalt therapy**, derived from the work of Freidrich (Fritz) S. Perls (1893–1970), has both humanistic and existential elements. Like Rogers, Perls held that people have an innate goodness and that this basic nature should be allowed to express itself. Psychological problems originate in frustrations and denials of this inborn virtue.

A central goal of Gestalt therapy is to help clients understand and accept their needs, desires, and fears and to enhance their awareness of how they block themselves from satisfying their needs and reaching their goals. A basic assumption is that all of our perceptions are shaped by the needs and goals we bring to any situation. We engage with our social environment by projecting our needs, desires, and fears onto what is out there. Thus, if I am talking to a stranger, I do not merely react to the person as that person exists; I react to the stranger in the context of my needs. Sometimes unfinished business with a significant person from the past can affect how we deal with someone in the present.

Gestalt therapists focus on what a client is doing here and now in the session, without delving into the past. In Gestalt therapy the most important event in the client's life is what is happening at this moment—all that exists is the now. "Why" questions are discouraged because searching after causes in the past is considered an attempt to escape responsibility for making choices in the present, a familiar existential theme. (For more on specific Gestalt therapy techniques, see Focus on Discovery 16.2.)

Freidrich (Fritz) Perls, the colorful founder of Gestalt therapy. (Courtesy Harriet F. Schenker, Gestalt Institute of Cleveland.)

Emotion-Focused Therapy   Greenberg (2002) developed *emotion-focused therapy*, which incorporates elements of client-centered therapy and Gestalt process techniques. Within this approach, the therapist focuses on the idea that some emotions are adaptive, in that they are accurate responses to a given situation, whereas others are maladaptive—responses that are biased by previous experiences. Maladaptive emotions are based on an underlying loneliness, abandonment, worthlessness, anger, or inadequacy. When these feelings surface repetitively, they damage a person's relationships and lifestyle. The goal, then, is for a client to become more aware of these maladaptive emotions, to understand the source of these feelings, and to learn emotion regulation skills.

Outcome Research   More than 100 studies have been conducted on how well experiential approaches work (Elliot et al., 2004). Compared to wait-list and no-treatment controls, these treatments tend to have a positive effect. It does appear that experiential therapies, like most psychotherapies, are more likely to relieve symptoms of less severe problems, like anxiety and depression, than more severe problems, like schizophrenia. Of the different experiential treatments, emotion-focused therapy, developed by Greenberg and colleagues (1996), appears to have the strongest results.

Some of you may wonder whether these treatments fare better or worse than other types of therapy, such as cognitive behavioral therapy. There is more debate about this issue of how different treatments compare than we can cover well here. Although one review of studies suggested that CBT had an advantage (Grawe, Donati, & Bernauer, 1994 cited in Elliot et al., 2004), a more recent review suggests that if there is an advantage, it is probably fairly small (Elliot et al., 2004). CBT does appear to fare better than experiential treatments

Focus on Discovery 16.2

Gestalt Therapy Techniques

In Gestalt therapy, clients are cajoled into awareness of what is happening now. Gestalt therapy is noted for its emphasis on techniques, in contrast to the paucity of techniques in other humanistic and existential therapies. Here is a small sample of Gestalt techniques.

- *Language*. To help clients take responsibility for their lives, the therapist instructs them to change "it" language into "I" language.

  > *Therapist: What do you hear in your voice?*
  > *Patient: My voice sounds like it is crying.*
  > *Therapist: Can you take responsibility for that by saying, I am crying? (Levitsky & Perls, 1970, p. 142)*

  This simple change in language reduces the client's sense of being alienated from aspects of his or her very being. It helps the client see the self as active rather than passive.

- *The empty chair*. In the empty-chair technique, a client projects a feeling, person, object, or situation and then talks to the projection. For example, if a client is crying about childhood abuse, the Gestalt therapist might ask the client to pretend that the abuser is in an empty chair opposite the client and to speak to the abuser. This tactic often seems to help clients confront their feelings. In contrast, asking a client to talk *about* the abuse is assumed to encourage distance from feelings—which interferes with psychological well-being. A variation of the empty chair is the *two-chair technique*—the client moves to the chair that he or she has been talking to and responds as if he or she were the projected person or feeling.

- *Projection of feelings*. Gestalt therapists working with groups sometimes have people pair off, close their eyes, and imagine the face of someone that they are strongly attached to. They are encouraged to concentrate on their feelings about that person. Then all open their eyes and look at their partner. After a few moments, they are instructed to close their eyes again and think of something neutral, such as an arithmetic problem. They then open their eyes again and look a second time at their partner. Finally, they are asked whether there was an important difference in the way they felt about their partner in the two situations. This exercise is designed to exaggerate experience in all social interactions, namely, the continuous intrusion of our feelings into whatever is happening.

- *Attention to nonverbal and paralinguistic cues.* Therapists are trained to pay attention to nonverbal and paralinguistic cues given by the client. Nonverbal cues are body movements, facial expressions, gestures, and the like; paralinguistic cues are tone of voice, speech rate, and other such components of spoken language. Often without realizing it, people use nonverbal or paralinguistic cues to negate their words with their hands or their eyes. Perls placed emphasis

on observing these cues to determine what clients might really be feeling. "What we say is mostly lies or bullshit. But the voice is there, the gesture, the posture, the facial expression" (Perls, 1969, p. 54).

- *Metaphor*. Gestalt therapists often create unusual scenarios to make a problem more understandable. The following scene occurred in a session we observed:

  > *A husband and wife sat together on a sofa, bickering about the woman's mother. The husband seemed very angry with his mother-in-law, and the therapist surmised that she was getting in the way of his relationship with his wife. The therapist wanted to demonstrate to the couple how frustrating this must be for both of them, and he also wished to goad both of them into doing something about it. Without warning, he rose from his chair and wedged himself in between the couple. Not a word was said. The husband looked puzzled, then hurt, and gradually became angry at the therapist. He asked him to move so that he could sit next to his wife again. The therapist shook his head. When the husband repeated his request, the therapist removed his jacket and placed it over the wife's head so that the husband could not even see her. A long silence followed, during which the husband grew more and more agitated. The wife meanwhile was sitting quietly, covered by the therapist's coat. Suddenly the husband stood up, angrily removed the coat; then he pushed the therapist off the sofa. The therapist exploded in good-natured laughter. "I wondered how long it would take you to do something!" he roared.*

In the empty-chair technique, the client projects a person, object, or situation onto an empty chair and then talks to it. (Copyright John Wiley & Sons, Inc.)

The therapist's actions functioned as a metaphor that drove home several points in a way that mere words might not have. The husband reported tearfully that he had felt cut off from his wife by the therapist, in much the same way that he felt alienated from her by her mother. The mother was intruding, and he was not doing anything about it. He did not trust himself to assert his needs. The intervention made him wonder whether he might not be able to behave similarly toward his mother-in-law. As he spoke, his wife began to sob; she confided to her husband that all along she had wanted him to deal directly with her mother. So far so good. But then the therapist turned to the wife and asked her why she had not removed the coat herself! The husband grinned as the therapist gently chided the wife for being unduly passive about her marital problems. By the end of the session, the clients, although emotionally drained, felt more connected and expressed their resolve to alter their relationship with her mother.

Gestalt therapy forcefully conveys the message that a person can make the existential choice to be different at any time and that the therapist will not tolerate stagnation. No doubt this optimistic view helps many people change.

for anxiety disorders. Overall, however, the dominance of CBT approaches in Table 16.1 reflects that there are more carefully controlled trials available of CBT than of experiential therapies.

Exposure treatment is one of the most well-supported approaches for anxiety disorders. (Michael Newman/PhotoEdit.)

Behavioral Therapies

Exposure is one of the best-established behavioral approaches. Treatment outcome research supports the use of exposure to treat a wide variety of anxiety disorders, including simple phobias, posttraumatic stress disorder, obsessive-compulsive disorder, panic disorder, and agoraphobia (Chambless & Ollendick, 2001). Although most of the research has been done with adults, fearful children have also benefited from exposure treatment (Kazdin & Weisz, 1998). Exposure appears to consistently perform better than other treatment approaches for anxiety disorders (Emmelkamp, 2004).

Beyond exposure, operant techniques, which involve manipulating rewards and punishment, have been found to be successful with a wide range of behavioral problems in both adults and children. (See Focus on Discovery 16.3 for a discussion of some issues in therapeutic control of contingencies.) More recently, inroads on the problems of substance abuse have been made by reinforcing behavior that is incompatible with the use of a drug to deal with the stresses of everyday life (Higgins, Budney, & Sigmon, 2001). Linehan's dialectical behavior therapy (p. 409) also contains important operant elements for the management of suicidality. Another successful example of operant conditioning is **behavioral activation therapy** of depression (Jacobson, Martell, & Dimidjian, 2001), which involves helping a person engage in tasks that provide an opportunity for positive reinforcement. See Focus on Discovery 16.4 for a discussion of self-control and operant contingencies.

Operant techniques such as systematically rewarding desirable behavior and extinguishing undesirable behavior have been particularly successful in the treatment of many childhood problems (Kazdin & Weicz, 1998). One reason that operant-conditioning behavior therapy might be effective with children is that much of children's behavior is subject to the control of others. Children tend to be supervised fairly continually by teachers at school and by parents at home. The behavior therapist can work with parents and teachers to change rewards and punishments for a child. Before applying operant techniques, the therapist must determine that the problem behavior is, in fact, an operant—that it is under the control of a contingent reinforcer. A child who is crying because of physical pain, for example, should be attended to. A broad range of childhood problems are dealt with through operant conditioning, including bed-wetting, thumb-sucking, nail-biting, aggression, tantrums, hyperactivity, disruptive classroom behavior, poor school performance, language deficiency, extreme social withdrawal, mental retardation, autistic disorder, and asthmatic attacks (Kazdin & Weisz, 1998).

Maintaining Gains in Behavioral Therapy   A problem that is common to all treatments but perhaps especially to the behavioral therapies is that of maintaining gains after therapy ends. How can therapeutic changes last once clients return to their everyday situations, which might have helped create their problems in the first place?

For operant therapies, this challenge is particularly important, as the therapist has often been a source of reinforcement. This issue has been addressed in several ways. Because laboratory findings indicate that intermittent reinforcement—rewarding a response only a portion of the times it appears—makes new behavior more enduring, many operant programs move away from continuous schedules of reinforcement once desired behavior is occurring regularly. For example, if a teacher has succeeded in helping a disruptive child spend more time sitting by praising the child generously for each arithmetic problem finished while seated, the teacher will gradually reward the child for every other success, and ultimately only infrequently. Another strategy is to move from artificial reinforcers to those that occur naturally in the social environment. A token program might be maintained only long enough to encourage certain desired behavior, after which the person is weaned to naturally occurring reinforcers, such as praise from peers. If reinforcers are not likely to be available consistently in the natural environment, therapists sometimes manipulate surroundings to support behavioral changes. For example, in the treatment of autistic children, it is important for parents to learn how to provide reinforcement for good behavior (McEachin et al., 1993). Hence, parent training often becomes an integral part of behavior therapy for children. Similarly, treatment for many anxiety disorders now integrates work with partners and family members, so that new reinforcement contingencies can be set up in the home environment.

Cognitive Behavior Treatment

All cognitive approaches have one thing in common. They emphasize that how people construe themselves and the world is a major determinant of the kind of person they will be—and that people have choice in how they construe things. They assert that people can, sometimes with great effort, choose to think differently. By changing cognition, it is hoped that people can change their feelings, behaviors, and symptoms.

Clinical Case: An Example of Beck's Cognitive Therapy

The examples here illustrate ways of beginning to challenge a patient's negative perspective.

> *Therapist: You said that you feel like a failure since Bill left you. How would you define "failure"?*
> *Patient: Well, the marriage didn't work out.*
> *Therapist: So, you believe that the marriage didn't work out because you, as a person, are a failure?*
> *Patient: If I had been successful, then he would still be with me.*
> *Therapist: So, would we conclude that we can say, "People whose marriages don't work out are failures?"*
> *Patient: No, I guess I wouldn't go that far.*
> *Therapist: Why not? Should we have one definition of failure for you and another for everyone else?*

People who define "failure" as less than "extraordinarily successful" can see that their definitions are polarized in all-or-nothing terms—that is, "complete success" vs. "complete failure." A variation on this technique is to ask the patient how others would define "success" or "failure"...

> *Therapist: You can see that your definition of failure is quite different from the way other people might see it. Few people would say that a person who is divorced is*

a failure. Let's focus on the positive end right now. How would most people define "success" in a person?
> *Patient: Well, they might say that someone has success when they accomplish some of their goals.*
> *Therapist: OK. So, would we say that if someone accomplishes some goals they have success?*
> *Patient: Right.*
> *Therapist: Would we also say that people can have different degrees of success? Some people accomplish more goals than others?*
> *Patient: That sounds right.*
> *Therapist: So, if we applied this to you, would we say that you have accomplished some of your goals in life?*
> *Patient: Yes, I did graduate from college and I have been working for the past six years. I've been busy raising Ted—he had some medical problems a couple of years ago, but I got the right doctors for him.*
> *Therapist: So, would we call these some successful behaviors on your part?*
> *Patient: Right. I've had some successes.*
> *Therapist: Is there a contradiction, then, in your thinking—calling yourself a "failure" but saying that you have had several successes?*
> *Patient: Yes, that doesn't make sense, does it?*

Quoted from Leahy (2003).

Focus on Discovery 16.3

You're Changed If You Do and Changed If You Don't

Have you ever tried to persuade a friend to do something by asking him or her not to do it? Since Watzlawick and colleagues published *Pragmatics of Human Communication* in 1967, a small but committed number of psychotherapists have been drawn to **paradoxical interventions**. Therapists using these strategies typically suggest that the client continue or even increase the problem. If a person cannot go to sleep, he or she is asked to remain awake. If a client cannot stop thinking of a disturbing event, he or she is asked to think of it more often (Shoham & Rohrbaugh, 1999).

Randomized controlled trials (RCTs) indicate that such interventions are helpful in treating problems including agoraphobia, obsessions, behavior problems, and insomnia (Kim et al., 1991). Paradoxical instruction works best when embedded in what is called a "positive reframe," for example, praising an anxious client for his or her interpersonal sensitivity (Akillas Efran, 1995).

Shoham-Salomon and her co-workers postulate two mechanisms that could account for the results of paradoxical interventions: reactance and increases in self-efficacy. **Reactance** refers to the person's response to the perception that freedom is being limited—he or she makes efforts to restore freedom (Brehm & Brehm, 1981). A reactant person, when directed by the therapist to become more anxious, will see this directive as an infringement on his or her freedom and will protect against this perceived threat by becoming less anxious. Intuition tells us that paradoxical interventions might be effective when a person doesn't like to be controlled by others. Such a person might think: "So, he wants me to continue arriving late, huh? I'll show him—I'll start arriving early!"

When clients are not reactant, Shoham-Salomon proposes that the concept of self-efficacy could explain effects. As defined by Bandura (1977), **self-efficacy** is the belief that one is capable of performing a desired behavior. In this context, this entails the person's belief that he or she can control the symptom. Bandura's research suggests that self-efficacy is enhanced by successful experiences. Thus, when nonreactant clients are able to follow a paradoxical directive to increase anxiety, they may begin to believe that they can control the symptom. If they can make themselves worse, then maybe they can make themselves better.

Reactant and nonreactant people are expected to change in positive ways from paradoxical treatment, but for different reasons and at different times. The reactant person is expected to change quickly because he or she is defying the therapist's directive. The nonreactant client is not expected to change right away, but the groundwork is laid for later behavioral change via an increase in self-efficacy.

These predictions were confirmed in a study of procrastination in college students (a problem we are sure none of the readers of this book have!). We drew the title of this Focus on Discovery from an article with the same title (Shoham-Salomon, Avner, & Neeman, 1989). Participants were divided into reactant and nonreactant groups, based on ratings of spitefulness in tone of voice. The experimenters then assigned participants to receive one of two treatments, each conducted for two weekly sessions.

Paradoxical intervention The therapist explained that participants needed to understand their procrastination problem better. To this end they were to observe the problem carefully by trying to procrastinate deliberately. Students were instructed to gather all their study materials on their desks but to resist any impulse to study for half an hour while concentrating on procrastinating. Studying at these times was not permitted. If they succeeded in this unusual observation task for 6 days, on the seventh day they could either study or not study, as they wished and whenever they wished. At the second therapy session participants discussed this assignment. Those who were able to avoid studying were congratulated and reminded that not studying had allowed them to understand their problem and therefore to begin to deal with it. If a student reported having studied more, he or she was not praised; in fact, the therapist voiced skepticism and suggested that the change was probably only temporary. If students had not scheduled procrastination time, the therapist exhorted them to try it again in the coming week. Above all, participants were not encouraged to procrastinate less or study more.

In the study by Shoham-Salomon and colleagues, some students who had difficulty with procrastination were given the paradoxical directive not to study at certain times. (Penny Tweedie/Stone/Getty Images.)

Behavioral intervention. The contrasting intervention was behavioral; that is, a direct attempt was made to reduce procrastination and increase studying. Students were told that procrastination was a learned habit and that they needed to develop new behaviors incompatible with procrastination. They were directed to select a place in which they could study more effectively and to try to study as much as possible there, the idea being that these new stimulus conditions would become associated with improved study habits. Any reported successes were praised by the therapist.

Results showed that self-efficacy and time spent studying improved in both treatments, but the really interesting results concerned interactions between reactance and treatment modality. Higher reactance was correlated with less procrastination in the paradoxical but not in the behavioral group, as expected. That is, students who were motivated to restore freedom acted against the instructions of the therapist—told to study less, they studied more. This contrariness was not found among reactant students in the behavioral condition.

Increases in self-efficacy were correlated with more studying in the behavioral condition. But this link was not found in the paradoxical-treatment group, as predicted. The findings from this study were replicated in a second experiment.

Although this research has focused on less severe clinical issues, one current approach to therapy, called *motivational interviewing* (Miller & Rollnick, 1991), draws on principles of reactance and self-efficacy. This treatment, which was initially developed for substance abuse, attempts to bolster the person's belief that he or she can change (promoting self-efficacy). Therapists refrain from taking sides about whether a person should quit; rather, they steadfastly stay neutral in helping a person examine the pros and cons of quitting. The authors argue that if the therapist were to insist that a person should quit, it would promote reactance. A set of studies now provide evidence that a single session of motivational interviewing can enhance the odds that people with substance-abuse problems will engage in treatment and achieve success in reducing their substance use (Heather et al., 1996).

Although many would imagine that cognitive therapy might be dry and unemotional, many cognitions are affect-laden, sometimes referred to as "hot cognitions." Beck argued that "emotions are the royal road to cognition." That is, during highly distressed states, clients may have access to their most negative thoughts.

Over the past 30 years, though, many different variants of cognitive therapy have been developed. The earliest forms of cognitive behavior therapy (CBT) included Beck's cognitive therapy (p. 50) and Ellis' **rational-emotive behavior therapy (REBT)**. Although quite similar, these two therapies contrast in important ways. We review differences between these approaches. Then we discuss a cognitive therapy developed to prevent relapse in substance abuse, and a set of new treatments, referred to as the third wave of CBT. After discussing these various forms of CBT, we briefly review treatment outcome studies in CBT.

Beck's Cognitive Therapy Compared to Ellis' Rational Emotive Behavior Therapy

Beck hypothesizes that emotional distress is caused by underlying assumptions—such as believing that one is not a worthwhile or loveable person, or that the world is dangerous. Beck focuses on cognitive biases—such as selective abstraction and overgeneralization (cf. p. 247)—that filter experience in a way that maintains these negative beliefs about oneself and the world. A therapist and client work to identify a series of negative cognitions, to test the evidence for these cognitions, and to detect underlying patterns of negative thinking that point toward core maladaptive beliefs.

REBT is similar, but the basic premise is that demanding perfection from oneself and relationships is a principal cause of emotional distress. To a parent who became depressed after learning that his or her child had failed a test at school, Ellis would say something like, "So what if you are an inadequate parent? It is irrational to demand perfection and then to become depressed when you (or your child) fall short."

CBT and REBT also differ in style. Beck suggests that the therapist should avoid being overly didactic, but Ellis often uses minilectures. Beck proposes calling negative thoughts "unproductive ideas" to promote rapport. He does not favor adjectives such as irrational, which might be heard—with supportive humor, it must be pointed out—from Ellis. Ellis believes that forceful interventions are needed to disrupt well-learned thought patterns, so he will directly confront irrational beliefs, sometimes within minutes of meeting a client.

Marlatt's Relapse Prevention Therapy
One therapy that has received particular attention was developed by Marlatt and Gordon (1985) specifically to prevent relapse in substance abuse. His research on alcohol abuse sensitized them to the "abstinence violation effect"—the negative effects of a slip, as when a former drinker, after a successful period

Focus on Discovery 16.4

Self-Control—Outside a Behavioral Paradigm?

How do people change the way they think or behave? How do dieters resist a piece of chocolate cake, or alcoholics resist a drink, or angry people resist the urge to hurl a criticism at another person? Each of these indulgences requires people to control themselves, despite the conflicting possibility of reinforcement from taking another path. Self-control, then, involves consciously deciding to engage in a certain type of thought or behavior that requires some effort and is not explained by the immediate external contingencies. Most of us have decided to engage in some form of self-control.

Impulse control disorders, such as pathological gambling, may be related to poor self-control. (Doublas Kirkland/Corbis Images.)

Operant theory seems to assume that people passively respond to reinforcement and punishments in the environment. How can these models account for a person's ability to resist reinforcement in the hopes of improving life longer term?

Psychoanalytic writers posit that the ego controls the id's desire to indulge in immediate gratification. Behaviorists, especially Skinner (1953), have objected to this explanation, as there is no way to observe the ego. Skinner argued that people engage in self-control by arranging the environment so that only certain controlling stimuli are present. A person wishing to lose weight rids the house of fattening foods and avoids standing by the food table at a party. Behavior remains a function of the surroundings, but the surroundings are controlled by the person. One way to control the environment is to promise oneself reinforcement only after a certain goal is met (Bandura & Perloff, 1967). For example, one author of this book uses the strategy of promising herself a wonderful meal once she finishes a chapter. By setting up rewards for accomplishing a goal, self-control is promoted. Note that to account for self-control, behavior theorists incorporate cognition.

Muraven and Baumeister (2000) have described a model of self-control as an internal resource. They argue that we all have a certain amount of self-control, and that some people tend to have more than others. Like a muscle, self-control can be strengthened, but can also be exhausted. An interesting aspect of this model is the idea that there is probably a limit to how many self-control goals a person can pursue at one time. For example, people trying to control their emotions after a major breakup (self-control over emotional expression) may find it harder to stick with their diet (self-control over their eating patterns). This model would suggest that therapists should be careful not to assign their clients too many goals for self-improvement at once.

of abstinence, imbibes to a stupor after taking a single drink. Marlatt suggested that how a person thinks about a slip determines whether he or she will stay on the wagon or resume drinking to excess. The consequences of the slip are hypothesized to be worse if the person attributes it to internal, stable, and global factors believed to be uncontrollable—much as Abramson and colleagues (1978) theorized about helplessness and depression (see p. 248). An example would be a belief fostered by Alcoholics Anonymous (p. 332) that the lapse was caused by an uncontrollable disease process that overwhelms the person once a single drink is taken. Cognitive behavior therapists attempt to minimize the abstinence violation effect by encouraging the person to consider possible external, unstable, and specific factors that would drive a lapse, and by teaching strategies for coping with potential lapses.

The Third Wave of Cognitive Behavioral Therapy Over the past several years, clinical researchers have developed a new set of cognitive behavioral treatments, which have been labeled as the third wave of cognitive behavioral therapy. That is, one can consider strict behavioral approaches as the first wave, cognitive approaches as the second wave, and these approaches as a new step in the field. All three waves of treatments draw on models of conditioning and cognition, and they maintain a focus on observable changes in specific symptoms and behaviors. They also maintain a focus on building skills. But the third wave treatments differ by incorporating a focus on spirituality, values, emotion, and acceptance (Hayes et al., 2004). Some of the approaches that have been labeled as part of this third wave include dialectical behavior therapy (p. 409), acceptance and commitment therapy, integrative behavioral couples therapy (p. 552), and mindfulness-based cognitive therapy (p. 254). One theme that emerges across these manuals is acceptance (see Focus on Discovery 16.5). Another theme involves strategies to minimize emotional avoidance through the practice of mindfulness. That is, a person might be taught that much of the destructive power of emotions lies in the way we respond to them cognitively and behaviorally. A person might be taught to be more aware of emotions but to avoid immediate, impulsive reactions to that emotion. In the case of mindfulness-based cognitive therapy, this is facilitated through the use of meditation (Segal, Williams, & Teasdale, 2003).

Outcome Research   The effectiveness of Beck's cognitive therapy (CBT) has received more intensive study than other forms of CBT (Hollon, Haman, & Brown, 2002). A number of early experiments confirmed the favorable impact it has on depression (Rush et al., 1977; Shaw, 1977), and a meta-analysis of outcome studies of diverse therapies for depression concluded that Beck's therapy achieves greater short-term improvement than wait-list controls, medication treatment, noncognitive behavioral treatments, and a heterogeneous group of other psychotherapies (Dobson, 1989). Because older clients can be extremely sensitive to medications (p. 500), nonpharmacological interventions are especially appropriate for them. Beck's CBT also has proven effective in treating depression in children (Stark et al., 1998) as well as adolescents (Brent et al., 1997). The great interest in CBT led to the widely publicized comparative outcome study sponsored by the National Institute of Mental Health (Elkin et al., 1985), a study that, unlike other studies in the literature, did not find CBT superior to placebo for severe depression (recall our in-depth discussion on this milestone study, p. 258). More recently, a large collaborative study has found that CBT is as good as medications in treating severe depression and that its effects endure over a 1-year follow-up period (Hollon, Haman, & Brown, 2002). These findings are consistent with a recent meta-analysis that found CBT as effective as medications in treating even severe depression (DeRubeis et al., 1999). Beyond depression, a task force of the American Psychological Association concluded that Beck's cognitive therapy is an effective treatment for panic disorder, generalized anxiety disorder, social phobia, chronic pain, irritable bowel syndrome, and bulimia nervosa, and that it often fares better than medications alone (Chambless et al., 1996).

Because cognitive therapy involves clients in logical analysis of their life situation and empirical testing of their thoughts—challenging intellectual tasks—it has been assumed that more intelligent people are better suited to this approach (Whisman, 1993). This does not seem to be the case, however (Haaga et al., 1991). Perhaps intelligence is too general a concept, because it incorporates memory, reasoning, verbal skills, and quantitative skills. A more focused search for cognitive variables might prove more fruitful (Haaga, Rabois, & Brody, 1999).

One of the promising aspects of cognitive therapy is that people may learn skills that help them even after they stop seeing a therapist. For example, CBT appears to help prevent future episodes of depression (cf. Hollon, DeRubeis, & Evans, 1996). Given that as many as 50 percent of people with a first episode of depression will experience a second episode (APA, 2000), this is an important issue. In one study of CBT for drug abuse, researchers found that clients who received CBT actually improved further after treatment stopped (Carroll, Rounsaville, Nich, et al., 1994). The investigators speculated that CBT had taught clients coping skills that they were able to implement after therapy ended.

Beyond Beck's approach, other forms of CBT have received empirical support as well. A range of studies have shown positive effects of REBT for both adults and children (Chambless & Ollendick, 2001; Kendall et al., 1995). Marlatt's relapse prevention has been shown to work better than attention-control or no-treatment conditions in a series of randomized controlled trials for substance abuse and appears to have particular promise when researchers study clients over longer follow-up periods (Witkiewitz & Marlatt, 2004).

Although the number of treatment outcome studies available regarding third-wave approaches is small, the evidence so far is quite promising. These types of approaches have been found to be helpful for problems that are quite difficult to address, such as borderline personality disorder, recurrent major depression, severe marital distress, and opiate addiction (Hayes et al., 2004). It is also worth noting that these approaches have become extremely popular with therapists—so popular that some have cautioned that we need to hold back against adopting them until more data can be accrued (Corrigan, 2001). Indeed, Teasdale (2004), one of the developers of mindfulness-based cognitive therapy, has argued for the need to proceed cautiously, with a strong sense of theory, and a good knowledge of which conditions these third-wave treatments have been shown to help.

Couples Therapy

Although couples therapy has only been discussed briefly in earlier chapters, it is often used in the treatment of psychological disorders, particularly when marital distress appears to have either caused the psychological disorder or to have unfolded in response to the symptoms. Given this, we provide an overview of some of the basic goals in couples therapy, before we review treatment outcome data.

Conflict is inevitable in any long-term partner relationship, whether the two people are married or not, or of the opposite sex or not. Some couples adopt the strategy of avoiding disagreements and conflicts. For couples who believe in the fairy-tale ending, "And they lived happily ever after," signs of conflict are threatening and must be ignored. Such patterns may keep the peace for a short time, but dissatisfaction takes a toll over time. Because the partners do not quarrel, they may appear to be a perfect couple to observers, but the lack of open lines of communication produces emotional distance. Whereas disagreement among couples may be related to unhappiness in the short term, expression of differences predicts more satisfaction over time (Gottman & Krokoff, 1989).

When a problem involves a couple, treatment is most effective if the couple is seen together. (Michael Newman/PhotoEdit.)

One particularly destructive interaction pattern is known as the *demand–withdraw cycle*. In this pattern, one partner attempts to discuss a problem and the other withdraws from such efforts. This withdrawal generates more demands from the first spouse, who tries harder and harder to engage the other, only to be met with more avoidance. And so the cycle escalates. Christensen and Heavey (1990) suggest that there are sex differences in this pattern; women tend to assume the demanding role, whereas men usually withdraw. This process can reverse when the husband initiates discussion of his concerns (which men tend to do less often)—then, sometimes, the wife withdraws (Klinetob & Smith, 1996).

Couples therapies focus on reducing relationship distress and improving the functioning of the couple through treatment involving both partners. A principal focus is improving communication so that both partners' needs are met. Each partner is trained to listen empathically to the other and to state clearly to the partner what he or she understands is being said and what feelings underlie those remarks.

A common practice is to give couples specific homework assignments to practice new patterns of interaction that they have learned during sessions and to begin generalizing change from the consulting room to their everyday lives. Couples may be asked to practice paraphrasing each other's sentences for a specified time period, such as a half hour after dinner, as part of an active listening assignment. They may also be instructed to practice a new parenting skill with their children or to spend time doing a shared relaxing activity.

Most couples treatments focus on improving communication, satisfaction, trust, and positive feelings. Despite the common ground, there are also major differences across forms of couples therapy. Therapists choose techniques to match their theoretical orientation. A psychoanalytically oriented couples therapist will attend to possible unconscious factors

Table 16.2 Goals in Different Forms of Couples Therapy

Type of Couples Therapy	Chief Goal
Behavioral couples therapy	To increase the rate of pleasant interactions and decrease the rate of unpleasant interactions (Wood & Jacobson, 1985).
Cognitive behavioral couples therapy	To help the couple focus more on positive exchanges and less on negative exchanges, and to make less negative interpretations of each others' actions (Wheeler, Christenson, & Jacobson, 2001).
Integrative behavioral couples therapy	To supplement the behavioral approach with procedures designed to foster acceptance in couples (Christensen, Jacobson, & Babcock, 1995).
Emotionally focused therapy	To improve emotional engagement and responsiveness to each other's needs, to address "innate adaptive needs for protection, security, and connectedness with significant others" (Johnson & Greenberg, 1995, p. 124).
Psychodynamic insight-oriented couples therapy	To help clients understand the interpersonal dynamics and needs that each partner brings to the relationship, and how these influence their emotional reactions (Snyder, Wills, & Grady-Fletcher, 1991).

in each person's behavior toward the other, whereas a behavioral marital therapist will focus instead on maladaptive behavioral patterns that are being unwittingly reinforced in the relationship. Table 16.2 outlines the major emphases within different forms of couples therapies. See Focus on Discovery 16.5, for one example of a way that behavioral couples therapy has been expanded to include new ideas and procedures.

Treatment Outcome Studies of Couples Therapy So much outcome research has been done on couples therapy that there are now more than 47 reviews of couples therapy research! Luckily, many of these reviews arrive at similar conclusions. We focus on the conclusions from Baucom and colleagues (1998) and Sexton, Alexander, and Mease (2004):

- Behavioral couples therapy has been shown in more than two dozen studies in at least four countries to relieve relationship distress compared to no-treatment and placebo-controlled treatments.
- Many of the gains associated with behavioral couples therapy last when measured 1 year later.
- When the major concern is distress in the relationship, seeing the couple together is more successful than individual therapy is. When couples are seen in individual therapy to treat couples problems, about 10 percent get worse.
- Brief premarital training in communication skills can enhance future relationship satisfaction and even lower divorce rates compared with no-intervention controls (Markman et al., 1989).
- Adding a cognitive component to behavioral couples therapy does not appear to add to the positive outcomes (Montag & Wilson, 1992).

Hence, behavioral couples therapy has achieved support across a range of studies. Even so, the outcomes of behavioral couples therapy research are not as good as one might hope (Jacobson et al., 1984)—across all studies no more than half the treated couples are happily married at the end of treatment (even if they had improved during treatment). Interestingly, two therapies that include an emotionally relevant component have achieved positive results compared to behavioral couples therapy, including emotionally focused therapy (Johnson & Greenberg, 1995) and psychodynamic insight-oriented therapy (Snyder et al., 1991). Insight-oriented therapy was even found to be superior to behavioral couples therapy over a 4-year follow-up in terms of divorce rates and marital satisfaction (Snyder et al., 1991).

Focus on Discovery 16.5

Acceptance in Couples Therapy

The notion of acceptance has a time-honored history in clinical psychology and psychiatry, dating back at least to Sigmund Freud. As Christensen and Jacobson (2000) indicate, the use of interpretation in psychoanalytic couples therapy (e.g., Scharff, 1995) can lead to greater acceptance of displeasing behavior by attributing it to childhood wounds, thereby fostering sympathy for the partner who is behaving in negative ways. But the concept assumes greater meaning in the work of Carl Rogers, whose client-centered therapy rests on the belief that "conditions of worth" should not be set for others. Rather, we should try to accept clients as worthy people deserving of respect regardless of their behavior at any point in time. Albert Ellis's rational-emotive behavioral therapy also emphasizes acceptance by encouraging people to renounce many of the demands they impose on themselves and on others. As described on p. 409, Linehan's dialectical behavior therapy (1993) emphasizes the importance of the therapist developing a genuine attitude of caring and acceptance for the client with borderline personality disorder.

Drawing on earlier work, Neil Jacobson and Andrew Christensen (1996) developed an integrative behavioral couples therapy. The central goal of this therapy is to uncover the major variables driving marital distress, rather than to create superficial behavioral changes. For example, whereas traditional behavior therapists might focus on discrete observable behavior, such as lack of sex or frequent arguments, integrative therapists might focus on a partner's feeling that he or she is not loved or valued by the other partner. This shift in therapeutic attention provides one example of theoretical integration, in which cognitive behavioral therapies are enriched by attention to other schools of thought.

In integrative behavioral couples therapy, Jacobson and Christensen argue that behavioral couples therapists have overlooked the importance of the ability of people in a committed relationship to accept their partner while at the same time hoping for and encouraging change. They supplement traditional behavioral therapy techniques with a focus on acceptance. What is acceptance in Christensen's and Jacobson's terms? It refers to "a letting go of the struggle to change and in some cases even embracing those aspects of a partner which have . . . been precipitants of conflict . . . [it] implies that some conflicts cannot be resolved, and it attempts to turn areas of conflict into sources of intimacy and closeness" (Jacobson, 1992, p. 497). Acceptance does imply change—but the change is in the partner who is giving up efforts to change the other!

. . . What one partner sees as the other partner's 'uptightness' might be the 'stability' that first attracted him/her. Or alternatively, what one partner sees as the other's 'flakiness' or 'irresponsibility' might be the 'free-spiritedness' or 'rebelliousness' that so attracted him or her in the beginning of their relationship. The . . . therapist must help the partners notice the positive aspects of what they have come to see as purely negative behavior. And often this behavior is in some way related to a quality one partner once found attractive about the other (Wheeler et al., 2001, p. 617).

Jacobson's behavioral roots show, however, in his suggestions about how therapists can bring about change within the context of acceptance. He gives the example of a wife who found her husband's unavailability objectionable. [The assumption is that the man's unavailability was not due to such things as seeing other women. Jacobson was certainly attuned to the ethical and political dimensions of treatment (cf. Jacobson, 1989)]. In addition to the traditional goal of helping them improve their intimacy with each other, he encouraged the woman to develop some independent interests so that she would not rely so much on her husband on those occasions when he could not be present.

Is acceptance tantamount to resignation, to accepting a status quo that keeps one or both partners in a destructive relationship, one that perhaps demeans one partner in order to satisfy the selfish demands of the other? Jacobson and Christensen argue that acceptance is actually affirmative, holding out the promise of even greater intimacy. And as suggested here, some behavioral changes that were formerly—and unsuccessfully—worked toward in behavioral couples therapy with direct change attempts might actually be facilitated by embedding such efforts within a context of acceptance. Or, as they put it:

> . . . The purpose of "acceptance work" is not to promote resignation to the relationship as it is . . . . Rather, it is designed to help couples use their unsolvable problems as vehicles to establish greater closeness and intimacy. For couples who have difficulty changing their behavior, acceptance provides a viable alternative for building a closer relationship. For couples who do benefit from the traditional approach [that directly aims to change problematic behavior], [acceptance-based behavioral couples therapy] can facilitate further progress by providing an alternative way to establish a closer relationship, given that there are problems in every relationship that are impervious to change. Paradoxically, acceptance interventions are also predicted to produce change in addition to acceptance . . . because at times the pressure to change may be the very factor that prevents it from occurring" (Jacobson et al., 2000, pp. 351–352).

Some research has focused on couples therapy as a way to address symptoms in one of the partners. For example, couples therapy has been found to be helpful in the treatment of sexual disorders, and also appears to facilitate treatment entry among people with alcohol abuse (Sexton et al., 2004). Noting that depression can increase marital distress, but that marital distress also can create depression (Hooley & Teasdale, 1989), researchers have studied behavioral couples therapy as a treatment for depression (O'Leary & Beach, 1990). The findings indicate that couples therapy and Beck's individual cognitive therapy have similar effects on depression, and that couples therapy does more than cognitive therapy to increase marital satisfaction. Hence, psychological disorders that occur in the context of relationship problems may respond well to couples therapy.

Family Therapy

Family therapy is based on the idea that the problems of the family influence each member, and that the problems of each member influence the family. As such, family therapy has long been used to address specific symptoms of a given family member, particularly for the treatment of childhood problems. Over time, family therapy approaches have evolved to include a broader array of strategies, often carefully integrated into the school and community (Liddle, 1999).

Clinical Case: Clare

Clare, a 17-year-old female who lived with her parents and her 15-year-old brother was referred for family-focused treatment of bipolar disorder as an adjunct to medication treatment. She had received a diagnosis of bipolar I disorder in early adolescence and was treated with lithium carbonate and quetiapine, but had never fully responded to medications.

During an individual assessment session, Clare explained that she thought about suicide almost daily and had made two prior attempts, both by overdosing on her parents' medications. Clare had kept both attempts secret from her parents. Ethically, clinicians need to take steps to keep a client safe, and in this case, one measure would be to let Clare's parents know about her suicidality. The clinician explained this to Clare.

The first goal in family-focused treatment is to provide psychoeducation about bipolar disorder. As the symptoms of bipolar disorder were being reviewed, the clinician asked Clare to discuss her suicide attempts with her parents. When Clare did so, her parents were surprised. Although her mother and brother seemed less concerned, her father, who had experienced his own father's suicide, was quite concerned.

After psychoeducation, a goal in FFT is to choose one problem for the family to address and to help them learn new problem-solving skills in the process. In this family, the focus of problem solving was Clare's suicidality and how to keep her safe. To begin problem-solving, the therapist works with the family to define the problem and its context. The therapist asked the family to discuss situations that seemed to place Clare at most risk for suicide. The family was able to pinpoint that both previous attempts had followed interpersonal losses.

The next phase of problem solving is to generate potential solutions. To help with this process, the clinician posed questions to the family to address, including whether Clare could share her suicidal thoughts with her parents, how to establish whether she was safe, what responses would be helpful from them, and what other protective actions should be taken. Using this structure, the family was able to agree on the plan that Clare would notify her parents by phone or pager if need be when she was feeling self-destructive, and that her parents would respond in ways that would reduce the danger.

Clare and her parents generated a plan in which her parents would help Clare engage in positive and calming activities until her suicidal thoughts were less intrusive. Clare and her parents reported feeling closer and more optimistic.

The therapist then began to conduct the next phase of therapy, which consisted of training Clare to monitor her moods, to identify triggers for mood changes, and to help her cope with those triggers.

As is typical in FFT, the clinician introduced the communication enhancement module during session 8. A goal of this module is to roleplay new communication skills. Family members practice skills such as "active listening" by paraphrasing and labeling the others statements, and by asking clarifying questions. At first, Clare and her brother protested against the role play exercises.

Clare experienced another loss during this period, in that her one close long-term friend announced that she was going to be moving out of state. Clare made a suicide attempt with an overdose of Tylenol. Afterward, she became afraid, induced vomiting, and later told her parents about the attempt.

The next session focused on the suicide attempt. Her parents, and particularly her father, were hurt and angry. Clare reacted angrily and defensively. The therapist asked the family to practice "active listening" skills regarding Clare's suicidality. Clare explained that she had acted without even thinking about the family agreement, because she had been so distressed about the idea of losing her friend. Clare's parents were able to validate her feelings using active listening skills. The therapist reminded the parents that suicidal actions are common in bipolar disorder, and noted that Clare had been able to be honest about her suicide attempt, an indicator of better family connectedness. The therapist also recommended that Clare see her psychiatrist, who increased her dosage of lithium.

By the end of treatment after 9 months, Clare had not made any more suicide attempts, had become more willing to take her medications, and felt closer to her parents. Like many people with bipolar disorder, though, she remained mildly depressed. Clare and her family continued to see the therapist once every three months for ongoing support.

Adapted from Miklowitz and Taylor (2005).

Therapists are likely to use different forms of family therapy to treat different psychological disorders (Sexton et al., 2004). Family approaches for childhood conduct disorder may focus on improving parental monitoring and discipline. For adolescents with externalizing problems, the goal of family therapy may be to improve communication, to change roles, or to address a range of family problems. With severe psychopathologies like schizophrenia and bipolar disorder, family therapy is typically provided in addition to medication. For these disorders, family therapy focuses on reducing expressed emotion (criticism and hostility), improving understanding of the disorder, and helping families learn skills for managing symptom (Miklowitz et al., 2003; see the Clinical Case of Clare). For people with substance-abuse problems, family therapy has been used to help clients recognize the need for treatment. In sum, the goals and strategies of family therapy will be adjusted to meet the needs of different clients.

Family therapy has been found to be effective in reducing symptoms of a broad range of disorders, including agoraphobia, substance abuse, schizophrenia, and bipolar disorder (Lebow & Gurman, 1995). Family interventions for schizophrenia lead to substantially lower relapse rates, even 2 years after treatment (McFarlane et al., 2003).

Quick Summary

Humanistic and existential psychological approaches arose in the mid-twentieth century. Rogers's humanistic psychology put the client's needs first, emphasizing that self-actualization is the goal of treatment and that the therapist must display unconditional positive regard for the client. Existential and Gestalt approaches put more emphasis on recognizing the realities of life, which are often painful.

A large number of RCTs now support the efficacy of psychotherapy compared to wait-list controls or no treatment. More specifically, researchers have amassed evidence to support brief psychodynamic, experiential, cognitive behavioral, couples, and family therapies. Indeed, many therapies have garnered support, and the evidence that some therapies work better is a topic of debate. On the other hand, cognitive behavior therapy for anxiety disorders is particularly effective.

As evidence has accrued that therapy works well, clinical researchers have turned toward how to refine the concepts and techniques within these approaches. For example, behavior therapists have worked to address the maintenance of effects. Several new cognitive manuals focus on incorporating more broad-ranging concepts, such as spirituality, emotional avoidance, or acceptance. Marital therapists have added emotion or acceptance-based approaches.

Check Your Knowledge 16.2

1. Which treatment has **not** been shown to have efficacy compared to no-treatment control groups:
   a. traditional psychoanalysis
   b. short-term psychodynamic therapy
   c. experiential therapy
   d. behavior therapy
   e. cognitive therapy
2. In the few available studies, cognitive behavioral treatments appear to offer more relief than experiential treatments for which disorders?

   a. schizophrenia
   b. depression
   c. anxiety disorders
   d. all psychological disorders
3. A couple comes for treatment of incessant conflicts. They are likely to show the strongest marital improvements if you offer them:
   a. individual cognitive behavioral treatment for both partners
   b. couples therapy

Psychotherapy Integration

Research described above has established quite clearly that treatment works for most people. But nonetheless, a careful review of the data suggests there is room for improvement—some people with serious mental illness don't seek treatment, others leave treatment early, still others don't find treatment helps them change, and for a very few, problems actually worsen during treatment. A growing number of theorists have suggested that one way to address these issues would be to draw from the best ideas within different treatment approaches (Castonguay et al., 2003). These researchers build on a long tradition of integrative approaches to psychotherapy (e.g., Dollard & Miller, 1950; Marmor, 1971). Forty years ago Perry London (1964), in his critical analysis of insight and behavioral therapies, wrote,

> There is a quiet blending of techniques by artful therapists of either school, a blending that takes account of the fact that people are considerably simpler than the Insight schools give them credit for, but that they are also more complicated than the Action [behavior] therapists would like to believe (p. 39).

There are many ways to think about eclecticism. Eclecticism per se refers to a "pragmatic approach in which the therapist uses whatever techniques he or she believes are likely to be effective, with little or no underlying theory to guide these choices" (Arkowitz, 1992, p. 262). Many mental health professionals are skeptical about this approach because it lacks a rationale for choosing techniques. Without theoretical guidelines to help the therapist conceptualize the client's problem and related change strategies, eclecticism is equivalent to chaos. Here, we turn toward three approaches to integration that draw on careful theory (Westen, 2000): technical eclecticism, theoretical integration, and common factors approaches (see Table 16.3 for a summary).

Table 16.3 Different Approaches to Integration

Type of Integration	Definition
Technical eclecticism	Therapist works within one theoretical framework, but borrows techniques from other schools
Theoretical integration	Therapist integrates concepts from different schools
Common factors	Therapist draws on findings about variables that predict good outcomes across schools, such as a strong therapeutic relationship

Technical Eclecticism

Technical eclecticism is exemplified in Lazarus's multimodal approach (1997) and in Beutler's prescriptive psychotherapy (Beutler & Harwood, 1995). The therapist works within a particular theoretical framework, for example, cognitive behavior therapy, but sometimes imports techniques from other orientations without subscribing to the theories that spawned them. "Use whatever works" is the operating principle of the technical eclectic, but rationalize the use of a technique from one's own framework. For example, even though Lazarus conceptualizes treatment using behavioral principles, he might use techniques such as the Gestalt empty chair. In his approach, though, he uses this technique for behavioral rehearsal rather than as a way to help the client reclaim disowned parts of his or her personality, which is how the technique is conceptualized in Gestalt therapy.

Theoretical Integration

Theoretical integration aims to synthesize not only techniques but theories. Paul Wachtel (1997) provides one approach, *cyclical psychodynamics*, which integrates theory from both psychoanalysis and behavior therapy. Wachtel suggests that therapists should help the client change current behavior (the behavior therapist's credo), not only so that he or she can feel better in the here and now, but so that he or she can resolve repressed conflicts from the past (the goal of psychoanalytic approaches). He believes that people's current behavior maintains repressed problems via the feedback it brings from their present-day interactions with others. Wachtel holds to the psychodynamic notion that people's problems are set in motion by repressed past events, but he departs from most psychodynamic theorists by suggesting that therapy should target the current interpersonal cycles that maintain these conflicts.

For example, consider a young man who has repressed his extreme rage at his mother for having mistreated his father years ago, during his childhood. As a youngster, to control this rage, he developed defenses that took the form of overpoliteness and deference to women. Today this unassertiveness encourages some women to take advantage of him. Thus, he has come to resent women even more and to retreat still further. This man's submissiveness, originating in his buried childhood rage, is creating problems in the present and has revived his repressed rage. This confirmation of childhood beliefs keeps the early conflict alive. The cycle continues.

Wachtel would probably give the deferential young man some assertion training in hopes of breaking the vicious circle. After repeated disconfirmation of the belief that all women want to take advantage of him, the client could begin to let go of the repressed love–hate conflict with his mother.

Wachtel has some things to say to behavior therapists, too. He holds that behavior therapists can learn from their analytic colleagues about the kinds of problems people develop. For example, psychoanalytic theory tells us that children have strong and usually ambivalent feelings about their parents, some of which are so unpleasant that they are repressed, or at least are difficult to talk about openly. In a related vein, Wachtel argues that psychoanalysts are more likely than behavior therapists to consider the unusual concerns, wishes, and fears of their clients. Guided by the view that emotional problems derive from the repression of id impulses, they consider psychological difficulties to be reflections of darkly mysterious infantile wishes and fears. Behavior therapists tend to have a more straightforward, perhaps more prosaic, view of their clients' problems.

To a behavior therapist, the deferential young man might appear fearful of heterosexual relationships. Taking these fears at face value, the therapist would work to help the client reduce them, perhaps by a combination of desensitization, cognitive behavior therapy, and social skills training. But the behavior therapist would probably fail to explore the possibility, suggested by the psychoanalytic literature, that the young man is basically angry with women. Wachtel would advise the behavior therapist to be sensitive to the possibility of childhood conflicts. Such information could suggest a different behavioral intervention, aimed at the client's anger toward women, rather than apparent fear of them. In sum, Wachtel suggests ways that theories could be enriched in cognitive behavioral therapy, and that interventions could be enriched in psychoanalysis.

Arguments against Premature Theoretical Integration   We should note that some think that theoretical integration is not desirable. In other words, maybe at this point in the field, we still need different paradigms to fully study psychopathology and intervention.

> *A comprehensive conception of how the body works does not demand that every system or organ of the body operate according to the same principles. Thus, our view of how the circulatory system works is quite different from our view of the nervous system. The forces and actions of the human heart operate according to the principles of fluid mechanics, whereas the principles of electrochemistry apply to the transmission of nerve impulses through the neuron; yet these two quite different processes occur in the same human body and are coordinated harmoniously despite their apparently disparate functions.*
>
> *Similarly, human personality may operate in accordance with a complex interaction of seemingly disparate processes that act together, though each differently and in its own sphere. Thus, it is conceivable that the same individual may suffer at one time from a repressed conflict, a conditioned response, an incongruent self-image, and irrational cognitions; and that each of these dysfunctions may operate in semi-independent systems of psychic action that are amenable to rather different interventions, each of which is compatible with the "system" to which it is being applied. Diagnosis and therapy might then become concerned with the locus of the disorder or with which portion or portions of the multisystem psyche is involved (Garfield & Bergin, 1986, p. 10).*

Indeed, some have argued that theoretical integration is not possible. Even though Arnold Lazarus is a chief proponent for technical eclecticism (using techniques from different schools), he argues against theoretical integration. Lazarus argues that these schools of thought are so distinct that they do not even agree on what the definition of a fact or standards for evidence are.

Common Factors and Process Research

The goal of a **common factors** approach to psychotherapeutic integration is to understand the common ingredients that work across different forms of therapy (e.g., Goldfried, 2004).

Typical common factors include a strong rationale for how treatment will work (which might bolster hope), therapist expectations for change, and a strong therapeutic relationship (Wampold, 2001). One way people have approached common factors is to consider research about what predicts positive outcomes across different types of therapies. This type of approach often relies on **process research**.

While treatment outcome research often pits one treatment against another or a control treatment, process research is focused on what types of variables predict outcome within a given treatment. Many process researchers focus on observing what happens in session between a therapist and client. Carl Rogers (client-centered therapy) is rightfully credited with originating the field of psychotherapy process research. He and his students pioneered tape-recording of therapy sessions for research analysis of the therapeutic relationship.

Here, we focus on aspects of a topic that has been studied in more than 1,000 studies: the therapeutic relationship (Orlinsky, Ronnestad, & Willutzki, 2004). It is worth noting that this topic has been studied using different methods, including questionnaires as well as videotape coding of sessions. We focus on findings based on questionnaire measures.

The Therapeutic Alliance   Regardless of theoretical orientation, a good relationship between client and therapist is important. People are not likely to reveal deeply personal information if they do not trust their therapists. The heart of psychotherapy involves cooperation between a therapist and a client on making changes. In desensitization, for example, a client could readily sabotage the best efforts of the therapist by not imagining a particular scene or not practicing relaxation. And in virtually all therapies, clients are able to, and sometimes will, work against the therapist if relationship factors are neglected.

The term **therapeutic alliance** (also called the working alliance) describes the collaborative relationship between therapist and client, in which they share an affective bond and an ability to agree on treatment goals. In a meta-analysis across 79 studies, Martin, Garske, and Davis (2000) found that therapeutic alliance predicted a small but consistent amount of the variance in outcome across a broad range of psychological disorders, treatment approaches, and outcome measures. Overall, therapeutic alliance (measured with self-report scales given to the therapists or the client) accounted for at least 5 percent of the variability in outcome. This may seem like a really small piece of the pie! It is important to remember a few issues to put this in context. First, most therapists do establish good relationships with their clients—there may not be many terrible relationships being studied. Second, it is possible that other types of measures, like behaviorally based codes of actual interactions, would yield stronger effects. For example, across dozens of studies, clients' reports of empathy account for about 10 percent of the variance in outcome after treatment (Greenberg et al., 2001). Other variables that seem to be predictive include therapist friendliness and interpersonal flexibility (Beutler et al., 2004). Third, some data suggest that the quality of the therapeutic relationship influences variables that are not usually measured in these studies, such as whether a person leaves treatment (Horvath, 2001). Nonetheless, while it is clear that the therapeutic relationship is important, the research does not justify the assertion that the relationship alone produces change.

There are different views on how a good therapeutic alliance works (Henry et al., 1994). In client-centered therapy, a good relationship is assumed to be one of the critical ingredients for change (Elliott et al., 2004). In psychoanalysis, it might make interpretations more effective, thus having an indirect effect. Although the therapeutic relationship might not have received much attention in early cognitive approaches, it is central in some of the newer manuals, such as the manual for Linehan's dialectical behavior therapy. No matter how the alliance works, research suggests that a good relationship is an important factor for any therapeutic approach, not only for psychodynamic or client-centered approaches (Martin et al., 2000).

A great deal of research has been focused on how to promote a strong therapeutic relationship. Not surprisingly, these studies find that a therapist who can convey empathy and positive regard, to show their engagement in nonverbal behaviors (e.g., nodding their

A strong relationship between therapist and client is widely regarded as essential for implementing treatment procedures. A great deal of research has focused on the therapeutic alliance. (Esbin-Andersonage /Age Fotostock America, Inc.)

head, smiling, or leaning forward), and be flexible but set consistent goals for treatment will be able to promote stronger relationships (Ackerman & Hilsenroth, 2003). Beyond the therapists' behaviors, therapeutic relationships are also undoubtedly influenced by characteristics of the client, as well as of the therapy. It may be that when treatment begins to work, this will make a therapeutic relationship stronger. This seemed to be the case in one study on cognitive therapy of depression (Feeley, DeRubeis, & Gelfand, 1999). As with relationships in real life, the quality of a therapeutic relationship is probably guided by many different factors.

Process Research on Other Treatment Predictors　Beyond the therapeutic relationship, researchers have focused on determining whether treatments actually change underlying mechanisms as expected. That is, when cognitive therapy works, does it do so by changing negative cognitions? When emotion-focused therapy works, is it because a client has become more comfortable with expressing their emotions? To see how hard these questions are to answer, consider some of the findings on changes in cognition during therapy for depression.

If cognitive therapy works by changing cognition, certain patterns should appear over time: first, over the course of cognitive therapy, cognitions would become less negative; second, the improving negative cognitions would predict improvements in symptoms. Evidence for both of these patterns has emerged (Hollon et al., 1996; Simons, Garfield, & Murphy, 1984). You might expect this would answer the question of whether treatments actually change underlying mechanisms. But not quite yet. Some researchers have begun to examine cognitive changes that occur during other forms of treatment. In one study, Jacobson and his colleagues (1996) offered either traditional cognitive therapy or just one of the components of cognitive therapy—*behavioral activation*, which involves helping a person engage in more pleasant activities in the hopes they will gain more positive reinforcement. During behavioral activation, the therapist does not talk about cognition. As it turns out, behavioral activation achieved similar results to cognitive therapy in terms of changes in cognitive variables. These results suggest that you can change cognition without offering cognitive therapy.

Beck and others might argue that by changing behavior and social reinforcement, you will influence how a person thinks about their world. Bandura (1977) believes that behavioral procedures (e.g., getting a person to engage in a task and be successful) are actually a better way to change cognitive processes than verbal interventions. Bandura suggests that all therapeutic procedures, to the extent that they are effective, work their improvement by giving the person a sense of mastery or **self-efficacy**. He believes that the most effective way to gain a sense of self-efficacy (obviously a cognitive concept) is by changing overt behavior. All of this, of course, makes it very complicated to understand how much a given therapy changes a given mechanism—more than one mechanism may be involved, and changing one level may influence the other levels.

A set of researchers have called for more research focused on mechanisms of change in therapy. For example, Persons (2005) recommends conceptualizing the mechanisms that will be most important for a given person to obtain relief from symptoms, and gathering data on whether treatment is working to change those processes. Similarly, Rosen and Davison (2003) have argued that we should be defining empirically supported principles of change rather than empirically supported treatments. That is, they argue we should focus on the mechanisms that can successfully be changed in therapy, and cataloging the times when it would be most helpful to address those mechanisms. One example of this type of approach comes from work by David Clark (1994). Clark sees the driving force of panic disorder as cognitive misinterpretation of bodily sensations, such that a person believes that a small change in heart rate portends catastrophe. His treatment manual is designed to address this cognitive process. In support of his proposed mechanism, clients who took part in treatment and yet retained cognitive misinterpretations of bodily sensations at the end of treatment were likely to relapse within a year. Many researchers have argued that we should be more focused on testing our ability to change these sorts of mechanisms than on comparing entire treatment packages.

Quick Summary

Many researchers have voiced a call for integration of psychotherapies. Some argue for technical integration, or drawing techniques that work well into an already existing approach without changing the overarching theory, whereas others argue for more fundamental theoretical integration. Process research, including attempts to understand common factors, continues to receive a great deal of attention. Some feel that process research may help us avoid a proliferation of treatment manuals, by encouraging us to go back to the basic elements of which simpler strategies work for whom, at what time. Consistent with this goal, a number of researchers are trying to understand whether treatments actually change the mechanisms that they target, and which types of mechanisms are most important to change for symptom relief.

Check Your Knowledge 16.3

1. Treatment outcome studies test _____, and process studies test _____.
   a. which treatments work best
   b. which elements of treatments work best
2. Wachtel's integrative model incorporates (circle all that apply):
   a. psychodynamic conceptualizations of early childhood relationships influencing current relationships
   b. behavioral techniques to change current environmental features

   c. the psychoanalytic emphasis on the therapist as a blank slate
   d. a cognitive emphasis on maladaptive schemas
3. Arguments against theoretical integration include
   a. the lack of knowledge about common factors
   b. the poor evidence for behavioral techniques
   c. the absence of agreement on standards of evidence across fields
   d. none of the above

Community Psychology and Prevention Science

Community psychology aims to change large systems to help groups of people rather than individuals. Community psychologists are invested in reaching out to large populations to prevent the onset or recurrence of physical or mental disorders. This may involve mass-media campaigns, instructional programs in schools, or other techniques. The general strategy is twofold: (1) to reduce environmental risk factors and (2) to strengthen protective factors. This strategy has been called prevention science (Heller, Wyman, & Allen, 2000). As with individual psychotherapy, the theoretical rationales and the techniques used vary greatly.

We have previously described many community psychology programs. Examples include

- programs aimed at changing sexual practices to prevent HIV (p. 212);
- interventions to address depression when people seek primary care (p. 260);
- suicide prevention centers with telephone hotlines (p. 267);

Evaluation of Community Psychology

It has been suggested that the results of community psychology have been disappointing (Phares & Trull, 1997), but in recent years many projects have shown their worth (Heller et al., 2000). Indeed, we have featured the programs described above because of their positive results.

Evaluation of community psychology is particularly challenging because the interventions occur in the field, where it is difficult to set up experimental controls and thus harder to draw causal inferences (Linney, 1989). There can be many alternative explanations for the effect of a preventive intervention. For example, if a reduction in gang activity follows a school-based intervention aimed at that goal, it may be that a community center, such as the YMCA, or even a single, inspirational teacher had something to do with the observed change. Another concern in prevention science is the problem of attrition, or loss of participants (Mrazek & Haggerty, 1994). Unfortunately, those who drop out of an intervention could be at the highest risk and may constitute the group for which preventive efforts are most appropriate.

Political Factors in Community Psychology

The popularity of community psychology has risen and fallen over time. In the 1960s and 1970s, there was a shift to community activism in the prevention of mental disorders. In the past two decades, the number of community psychologists has declined. What causes these shifts? The answer is complex.

For many years, few people could afford psychotherapeutic services, which were usually in short supply and geared to intelligent and successful clients. The idea took hold among mental health professionals that psychotherapy aimed at changing the person might not be the best way to alleviate the psychological problems of most people. Focus began to shift from individual-level risk factors to large-scale social problems, such as poverty, over-crowding, poor education, segregation, the alienation felt in large cities, and the impersonal nature of many aspects of present-day living. Community psychology's emphasis on prevention became especially important in the United States, where a large gap had developed between the need for mental health care and the availability of services (Weissberg, Caplan, & Sivo, 1989).

The shift from intrapsychic to social factors probably also reflected the zeitgeist, or tenor of the times. The 1960s and early 1970s were a period of tremendous social upheaval and activism. Institutions of all kinds were being challenged. Cities and college campuses erupted in riots, and many ethnic minority groups demonstrated against racism and political repression. This social upheaval encouraged looking at social institutions for causes of individual suffering. At the same time, the Kennedy and Johnson administrations (1961–1969) lent the monetary clout of the federal government to a progressive liberalism. John Kennedy's New Frontier and Lyndon Johnson's Great Society programs poured tens of millions of dollars (equivalent to hundreds of millions today) into attempts to better the human condition.

After a growth spurt, the number of members of the APA Division on Community Psychology fell from a peak of 1,800 in 1983 to a current level of 1,000 in 2005 (Toro, 2005). A passing glance at the news would indicate that we still need community psychology. We have described the prevalence of rape, child abuse, violence, and homelessness in other chapters—ongoing problems of this magnitude call for interventions at a system level. Beyond evidence for social pressures on mental health, the high prevalence rates of depression, anxiety, and substance-abuse disorders demand approaches to identification and prevention that will reach a lot of people.

In the context of these ongoing social problems, the drop in the number of people entering community psychology is surprising. Speculatively, part of this may reflect shifts in values, to a more personal focus on individual and family issues rather than social issues. On the other hand, though, a number of the prevention goals initially championed by community psychologists have been adopted by clinical psychologists. For example, Jose Szapocznik has earned awards for his work on how community and school systems influence family and child mental health (APA, 2002), and the former president of the APA, Martin Seligman (1998), has conducted studies of how to prevent depression by teaching positive thinking skills to school children. Similarly, the activism of community psychologists (and others) helped psychologists in general become more aware of the need for cultural sensitivity. Some, then, would say that current clinical psychology incorporates some of the principles of community psychology. Nonetheless, we would argue that there is an ongoing need for people who specialize in understanding how broad social systems influence mental health, how to prevent mental health problems, and how to increase the accessibility and sensitivity of services for the needs of a diverse population.

Summary

Challenges in Evaluating Treatment Outcomes

● Research on the effectiveness of various forms of psychological treatments has been conducted for many decades. Overall, this research suggests that about 75 percent of people gain some improvement from therapy. Therapy also seems to be more helpful than a placebo or the passage of time.

● Efforts have been made to define standards for research on psychotherapy trials and to summarize current knowledge on which psychological treatments work. These standards typically include the need to randomly assign participants to treatment or a control, to use a treatment manual, to define the treated sample carefully, and to use reliable and valid outcome measures. It is hoped that these efforts will help disseminate the best available therapeutic practices to clinicians and their clients, as well as provide insurance companies with the data to support the use of psychotherapy.

● Controversy exists about the research standards: a large proportion of clients are excluded or will not take part in clinical trials, cultural diversity is lacking in most trials, many treatment approaches remain untested, and treatment manuals could constrain a talented therapist. A broader concern is that a huge gap exists between what happens in the research world and the real world. Efficacy research focuses on how well therapies work in carefully controlled experiments, whereas effectiveness research focuses on how well therapies work in the real world.

The Importance of Culture and Ethnicity in Psychological Treatment

● Clinicians offering treatment to minority individuals must be sensitive to the cultural values and events that shape the way people may approach relationships, therapy, and emotional expression. Little empirical research is available on how psychotherapies work for people from diverse backgrounds, but minority status is associated with less use of therapy. Researchers have developed modifications of some treatments to be more culturally sensitive.

Specific Treatment Approaches: Issues and Treatment Outcome Research

● Experiential psychotherapies, based on humanistic and existential psychology, emphasize freedom to choose, personal growth, and personal responsibility. Variants of these approaches include Rogers's client-centered therapy, existential therapy, Gestalt therapy, and emotion-focused therapy.

● Treatment outcome research supports the efficacy of psychodynamic, experiential, and cognitive behavioral approaches compared to no-treatment or treatment controls. Behavioral approaches offer a clear advantage for the treatment of anxiety and may be slightly more helpful than experiential approaches in other disorders. Generally, the literature on how these different active forms of psychotherapy compare to each other is quite small.

● Cognitive behavioral treatments have evolved over the past 10 years, and several manuals incorporate broader themes such as spirituality and meaning. Although there is less research available, the research findings about cognitive behavioral treatments are promising.

● Couples therapy helps distressed couples resolve the inevitable conflicts in any ongoing relationship of two adults living together. Behavioral therapies are clearly better than no treatment, but about half of couples report to significant distress after treatment. Promising evidence exists for integrative behavioral couples therapy and insight-oriented couples therapy as compared to standard behavioral marital therapy.

● Family therapy includes many different techniques. These therapies have been shown to be particularly successful in the treatment of externalizing disorders in children and adolescents, in helping people with substance abuse accept the need for treatment, and in reducing relapse in adults with schizophrenia and bipolar disorder.

Psychotherapy Integration

● There are three different approaches to therapy integration: technical eclecticism, theoretical integration, and common factorism. Technical eclectism refers to borrowing techniques from other approaches while maintaining a focused conceptual approach. Theoretical integration is exemplified by Wachtel's cyclical psychodynamics. Common factors research identifies variables that predict outcomes across a broad range of therapies, such as the quality of the therapeutic alliance or therapist empathy.

Community Psychology and Prevention Science

● Community psychology aims primarily at the prevention of disorder on a large scale. Political issues have shaped the popularity of this approach over time.

Answers to Check Your Knowledge Questions

16.1. 1. a, b; 2. a, c, d, e; 3. b
16.2. 1. a; 2. c; 3. b

16.3. 1. a, b; 2. a, b; 3. c

Key Terms

behavioral activation therapy	empirically supported treatments (ESTs)	randomized controlled trial (RCT)	technical eclecticism
client-centered therapy	existential therapy	rational-emotive behavior therapy (REBT)	theoretical integration
common factors	Gestalt therapy	reactance	therapeutic (working) alliance
cultural competence	outcome research	self-actualization	unconditional positive regard
effectiveness	paradoxical interventions	self-efficacy	
efficacy	process research	stepped care	
empathy			

17 Legal and Ethical Issues

Learning Goals

1. Be able to differentiate the legal concepts of insanity and the various standards for the insanity defense.
2. Be able to describe the issues surrounding competency to stand trial.
3. Be able to delineate the conditions under which a person can be committed to a hospital under civil law.
4. Be able to discuss the difficulties associated with predicting dangerousness, and the issues surrounding the rights to receive and refuse treatment.
5. Be able to describe the ethics surrounding psychological research and therapy.

A mendment I   *Congress shall make no law respecting an establishment of religion, or prohibiting the free exercise thereof; or abridging the freedom of speech, or of the press; or the right of the people peaceably to assemble, and to petition the Government for a redress of grievances.*

Amendment IV   The right of the people to be secure in their persons, houses, papers, and effects, against unreasonable searches and seizures, shall not be violated....

Amendment V   No person ... shall be compelled in any criminal case to be a witness against himself, nor be deprived of life, liberty, or property, without due process of law....

Amendment VI   In all criminal prosecutions, the accused shall enjoy the right to a speedy and public trial ... to be confronted with the witnesses against him; to have compulsory process for obtaining witnesses in his favor, and to have the Assistance of Counsel for his defense.

Amendment VIII   Excessive bail shall not be required, nor excessive fines imposed, nor cruel and unusual punishment inflicted.

Amendment XIII   ... Neither slavery nor involuntary servitude, except as a punishment for crime whereof the party shall have been duly convicted, shall exist within the United States, or any place subject to their jurisdiction....

Amendment XIV   ... No State shall ... deprive any person of life, liberty, or property, without due process of law; nor deny to any person within its jurisdiction the equal protection of the laws.

Amendment XV   ... The right of citizens of the United States to vote shall not be denied or abridged by the United States or by any State on account of race, color, or previous condition of servitude.

These eloquent statements describe and protect some of the rights of U.S. citizens and others residing in the United States. Against what are these rights being protected? Be mindful of the circumstances under which most of these statements were issued. After the Constitutional Convention had delineated the powers of government in 1787, the first Congress saw fit in 1789 to amend what had been framed and to set specific limits on the federal government. This was accomplished with what came to be called the Bill of Rights, which are the first 10 amendments to the Constitution. Amendments beyond the original 10 have been added since that time. The philosophical ideal of the U.S. government is to allow citizens the maximum degree of liberty consistent with preserving order in the community at large.

We open our final chapter in this way because the legal and mental health systems collaborate continually, although often subtly, to deny a substantial proportion of the U.S. population their basic civil rights. With the best of intentions, judges, governing boards of hospitals, bar associations, and professional mental health groups have worked over the years to protect society at large from the actions of people regarded as mentally ill or mentally defective and considered dangerous to themselves or to others. But in so doing they have denied many thousands of people their basic civil rights.

Mentally ill individuals who have broken the law or who are alleged to have done so are subject to **criminal commitment**, a procedure that confines a person in a mental hospital either for determination of competency to stand trial or after acquittal by reason of insanity. **Civil commitment** is a set of procedures by which a mentally ill and dangerous person who has not broken a law can be deprived of liberty and incarcerated in a mental hospital. Both commitments in effect remove individuals from the normal processes of the law. In this chapter we look at these legal procedures in depth. Then we turn to an examination of some important ethical issues as they relate to therapy and research.

Clinical Case: David

David had been hearing voices for several days. Unable to drown them out with music or talking, he became more and more troubled. The voices were telling him that he was the chosen one by God, chosen to rid the world of evil. David went to the emergency room of the local hospital seeking relief. Instead of being admitted, David was given a prescription for Haldol and sent on his way. Two days later, David took a loaded gun into the busy train station and began shooting. He killed 2 people and injured 14 others. When he was arrested, David told the police he was answering to God. His speaking was disorganized and hard to follow, and David expressed a number of paranoid beliefs.

David was found competent to stand trial because he understood that he was charged with murder and he was able to help his attorney with his defense. At trial, David entered a plea of "not guilty by reason of insanity" (NGRI). David's defense lawyer arranged for David to be evaluated by a psychologist. The psychologist concluded that David had schizophrenia, paranoid type, and that at the time of the crime he was unable to discern right from wrong (he thought his behavior was the right thing to do since God was directing him) and he was unable to conform his behavior to the requirements of the law. The prosecution did not dispute these findings, and

the case was settled before going to trial. David was committed to the local forensic hospital for an indeterminate period of time. He was to remain there until he was no longer dangerous and mentally ill. Periodic evaluations would be conducted to see if David could be transferred to a less secure hospital.

After seven years in the hospital, David had done very well. He took his prescribed medication (Zyprexa), was never in a physical altercation with other patients, participated in individual and group therapy, worked in the hospital machine shop, and served as a team leader for the unit he was living in. David felt horribly remorseful for the crimes he committed, and he recognized that he had schizophrenia that would require treatment for the rest of his life. The treatment team on the unit all agreed that David was no longer dangerous and that his schizophrenia was under control with the medications. They recommended that he be transferred to a less secure psychiatric hospital. David's attorney presented the case before a judge in the courtroom that was part of the hospital. The attorneys for the state objected to David's release, arguing that David could stop taking his medications and become violent again. The judge agreed that release was premature at this time and ordered that David remain in the forensic hospital for another year before being evaluated again.

Criminal Commitment

We examine first the role of psychiatry and psychology in the criminal justice system. Almost as early as the concept of mens rea, or "guilty mind," and the rule "No crime without an evil intent" had begun to be accepted in English common law, the concept of *insanity* was taken into consideration. Broadly speaking, insanity refers to a disordered mind, and a disordered mind may be regarded as unable to formulate and carry out a criminal purpose (Morse,

1992). In other words, a disordered mind cannot be a guilty mind; and only a guilty mind can engender culpable actions.

It is important to note at the beginning of our discussion that insanity is a legal concept, not a psychiatric or psychological concept. The legal definitions of insanity have changed across time as the result of many court proceedings. As we shall see, meeting the legal definition of insanity can be very different than meeting the diagnostic criteria for a particular mental disorder.

At first insanity was not a trial defense, but in England the Crown sometimes granted pardons to people who had been convicted of homicide if they were judged completely and totally mad (Morris, 1968). By the reign of Edward I (1272–1307) the concept of insanity had begun to be argued in court and could lessen punishment. During the course of the fourteenth century it became the rule of law that a person proved to be wholly and continually mad could be defended against a criminal charge.

In today's courts, judges and lawyers call on psychiatrists and clinical psychologists for assistance in dealing with criminal acts thought to result from the accused person's disordered mental state. Are such emotionally disturbed perpetrators less criminally responsible than those who are not distraught but commit the same crimes? Should such individuals even be brought to trial for transgressions against society's laws? Although efforts to excuse or protect an accused person by invoking the insanity defense or by judging him or her incompetent to stand trial are undoubtedly well-intentioned, invoking these doctrines can often subject those accused to a greater denial of liberties than they would otherwise experience.

The Insanity Defense

The **insanity defense** is the legal argument that a defendant should not be held responsible for an illegal act if it is attributable to mental illness that interferes with rationality or that results from some other excusing circumstance, such as not knowing right from wrong. A staggering amount of material has been written on the insanity defense, even though it is pleaded in less than 1 percent of all cases that reach trial and is rarely successful (Morse, 1982b; Steadman, 1979; Steadman et al., 1993).

In general, the insanity defense requires applying an abstract principle to specific life situations. As in all aspects of the law, terms can be defined in a number of ways—by defendants, defense lawyers, prosecutors, judges, and jurors—and testimony can be presented in diverse fashion, depending on the skill of the interrogators and the intelligence of the witnesses. Furthermore, because an insanity defense is based on the accused's mental condition at the time the crime was committed, retrospective, often speculative judgment on the part of attorneys, judges, jurors, and psychiatrists is required. And disagreement between defense and prosecution psychiatrists and psychologists is the rule.

There is an important difference between insanity and mental illness. A person can be diagnosed as mentally ill and yet be held responsible for a crime. Similarly, the most heinous or bizarre crime can be committed by someone who has no mental illness at all, despite our tendency to think someone must have been "crazy" to commit such a crime. Indeed, decades of social psychological research tell us that otherwise normal people can do horrendous, criminal acts under the right circumstances or contexts (Aronson, 2004).

The insanity pleas available in state and federal courts in the United States have been crafted from a series of legal definitions and precedents that we review below. Broadly, there are two different kinds of insanity pleas today. With the **not guilty by reason of insanity (NGRI)** plea, there is no dispute over whether the person actually committed the crime—both sides agree that the person did the crime. However, due to the person's insanity at the time of the crime, the defense attorney argues that the person should not be held responsible for the crime and should thus be acquitted of the crime. The successful NGRI plea indicates the person is not held responsible for the crime due to his or her mental illness. Individuals acquitted with the NGRI plea are committed indefinitely (i.e., they are not given a sentence or committed for predetermined period of time) to a forensic hospital. People are released from forensic hospitals if they are deemed no longer dangerous and no longer mentally ill (we discuss the difficulties in making these determinations below).

Table 17.1 Comparing NGRI and GBMI

	NGRI	GBMI
Responsibility for crime	Not responsible	Responsible
Where committed	Forensic hospital	Prison
Given sentence?	No	Yes
When released	When no longer dangerous and mentally ill	End of sentence, but could then be committed civilly if dangerous and mentally ill
Treatment given?	Yes	Possibly

A forensic hospital looks very much like a regular hospital except that the perimeter of the grounds is secured with gates, barbed wires, or electric fences. Inside the hospital, doors to the different units may be locked, and bars may be placed on windows on the lower floors. Patients do not stay in jail cells, however. They stay in either individual or shared rooms. Security staff are on hand to break up fights and keep patients safe. They typically do not carry weapons of any sort and they may be dressed in regular clothing rather than uniforms.

The second insanity plea available in some states is **guilty but mentally ill (GBMI)**. Initially adopted by Michigan in 1975, this plea allows an accused person to be found legally guilty of a crime—thus maximizing the chances of incarceration—but allows for psychiatric judgment on how to deal with the convicted person if he or she is considered to have been mentally ill when the act was committed. Thus, even a seriously ill person can be held morally and legally responsible for a crime, but can then, in theory, be committed to a prison hospital or other suitable facility for psychiatric treatment rather than to a regular prison for punishment. In reality, however, people judged GBMI are usually put in the general prison population where they may or may not receive treatment. As of 2000, 20 states had adopted some or all of the GBMI provisions; a few states have both NGRI and GBMI available. Table 17.1 compares these two insanity pleas. Three states—Idaho, Montana, and Utah—do not allow for any insanity defense.

We now turn to how these two pleas were developed by reviewing the legal precedents throughout history that set the stage for our current definitions of insanity.

Landmark Cases and Laws   In modern criminal law, several court rulings and established principles bear on the problems of legal responsibility and mental illness. Table 17.2 summarizes these rulings and principles.

Irresistible Impulse   The **irresistible impulse** concept was formulated in 1834 in a case in Ohio. According to this concept, if a pathological impulse or drive that the person could not control compelled that person to commit the criminal act, an insanity defense is legitimate. The irresistible-impulse test was confirmed in two subsequent court cases, *Parsons v. State* and *Davis v. United States*.[1]

The M'Naghten Rule   The **M'Naghten rule** was formulated in the aftermath of a murder trial in England in 1843. The defendant, Daniel M'Naghten, had set out to kill the British prime minister, Sir Robert Peel, but had mistaken Peel's secretary for Peel. M'Naghten claimed that he had been instructed to kill Lord Peel by the "voice of God." The judges ruled that

> *to establish a defense of insanity, it must be clearly proved that, at the time of the committing of the act, the party accused was labouring under such a defect of reason, from disease of the mind, as not to know the nature and quality of the act he was doing; or if he did know it, that he did not know he was doing what was wrong.*

---

[1] *Parsons v. State*, 2 So. 854, 866-67 (Ala. 1887); *Davis v. United States*, 165 U.S. 373, 378 (1897).

Table 17.2 Landmark Cases and Laws Regarding the Insanity Defense

Irresistible impulse (1834)	A pathological impulse or drive that the person could not control compelled that person to commit a criminal act.
M'Naghten rule (1843)	The person did not know the nature and quality of the criminal act in which he or she engaged, or, if the person did know it, the person did not know he or she was doing what was wrong.
Durham test (1954)	The person's criminal act is the product of mental disease or mental defect.
American Law Institute guidelines (1962)	1. The person's criminal act is a result of "mental disease or defect" that results in the person's not appreciating the wrongfulness of the act or in the person's inability to behave according to the law (combination of M'Naghten rule and irresistible impulse).
	2. "[T]he terms 'mental disease or defect' do not include an abnormality manifested only by repeated criminal or otherwise antisocial conduct" (American Law Institute, 1962).
Insanity Defense Reform Act	1. The person's criminal act is a result of severe mental illness or defect that prevents the person from understanding the nature of his or her crime.
	2. The burden of proof is shifted from the prosecution to the defense. The defense has to prove that the person is insane.
	3. If the person is judged to have recovered from mental illness, then instead of being released from the prison hospital, the person remains incarcerated for at least as long as he or she would have been imprisoned if he or she had been convicted.
Guilty but mentally ill (1975)	The person can be found legally guilty of a crime—thus maximizing the chances of incarceration—and the person's mental illness plays a role in how he or she is dealt with. Thus, even a seriously ill person can be held morally and legally responsible, but can then be committed to a prison hospital or other suitable facility for psychiatric treatment rather than to a regular prison for punishment.

By the beginning of the twentieth century this right–wrong test was being used in all the states except New Hampshire and in all federal courts. By the late 1980s it was the sole test in 18 states and in several others was applied in conjunction with irresistible impulse. However, a committee of the American Psychiatric Association expressed the view that understanding the difference between right and wrong was out of step with modern conceptions of insanity. It was in this context that a third important court decision was made.

The Durham Test   Judge David Bazelon ruled in 1954, in the case of *Durham v. United States*,[2] that the "accused is not criminally responsible if his unlawful act was the product of mental disease or mental defect." Bazelon believed that by referring simply to mental illness he would leave the profession of psychiatry free to apply its full knowledge. It would no longer be limited to considering impulses or knowledge of right and wrong.

Bazelon purposely did not incorporate in what would be called the **Durham test** any particular symptoms of mental disorder that might later become obsolete. The psychiatrist was accorded great liberty to convey to the court his or her own evaluation of the accused's mental condition. Forcing the jury to rely to this extent on expert testimony did not prove workable courtroom practice, however. Since 1972 the Durham test has not been used in any jurisdiction, and Bazelon eventually withdrew his support for it, feeling that it allowed too much leeway to expert witnesses.

American Law Institute Guidelines   In 1962 the American Law Institute (ALI) proposed its own guidelines, which were intended to be more specific and informative to lay jurors than were other tests. The **American Law Institute guidelines** state:

1. A person is not responsible for criminal conduct if at the time of such conduct as a result of mental disease or defect he lacks substantial capacity either to appreciate the criminality (wrongfulness) of his conduct or to conform his conduct to the requirements of law.

---

[2] *Durham v. United States*, 214 F.2d 862, 876 (D.C. Cir. 1954).

2. As used in the article, the terms "mental disease or defect" do not include an abnormality manifested only by repeated criminal or otherwise antisocial conduct (American Law Institute, 1962, p. 66).

The first ALI guideline combines the M'Naghten rule and the concept of irresistible impulse. The second concerns those who are repeatedly in trouble with the law; they are not to be deemed mentally ill only because they keep committing crimes. Indeed, the phrase "substantial capacity" in the first guideline is designed to limit an insanity defense to those with the most serious mental disorders. The second guideline excludes psychopathy as an excusing condition.

Until 1984 the ALI test was in use in more than half the states and in all federal courts. Some scholars, however, have argued that such words as substantial and appreciate introduce ambiguities that foster disagreements among expert witnesses as well as jurors as to whether a defendant's state of mind is sufficiently disturbed to justify a verdict of not guilty by reason of insanity (Simon & Aaronson, 1988).

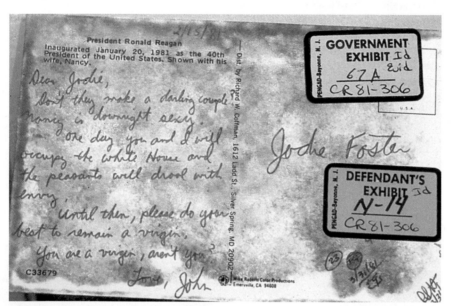

Insanity Defense Reform Act   In the 1980s a major effort began in the United States to clarify the legal defense of insanity. It sprang in large part from an NGRI verdict in the highly publicized trial of John Hinckley, Jr. for an assassination attempt against President Ronald Reagan in March 1981. After the NGRI verdict, the court received a flood of mail from citizens outraged that a would-be assassin of a U.S. president had not been held criminally responsible and had only been committed to an indefinite stay in a mental hospital until deemed mentally healthy enough for release. Their outrage reflects the public misperceptions about the insanity defense. The public often believes that a person is "getting away" with a crime when found NGRI and that they will be released from the hospital in short order. In reality, many people who are committed to a forensic hospital stay there longer than they would have stayed in prison had they been given a sentence (the case reviewed below of *Jones v. United States* vividly illustrates this). With respect to John Hinckley, he has been committed to St. Elizabeth's Hospital, a public mental hospital in Washington, D.C., for over 20 years. Although he can be released whenever his mental health is deemed adequate, this has not yet happened. In December 2003, a judge ruled that Hinckley could have six day-long unsupervised visits with his parents outside St. Elizabeth's hospital. These trips must be in the Washington, D.C. area and his parents must maintain daily contact with the hospital during the visits. The judge would not allow Hinckley to visit his parents at their home in Virginia, and the judge reaffirmed this decision in November 2004.

Because of the publicity surrounding the trial and the public outrage at the NGRI verdict, the insanity defense became a target of vigorous and sometimes vituperative criticism from many quarters. As Judge Parker, who presided at the trial, put it: "For many, the [Hinckley] defense was a clear manifestation of the failure of our criminal justice system to punish individuals who have clearly violated the law" (Simon & Aaronson, 1988, p. vii).

As a consequence of political pressures to "get tough" on criminals, Congress enacted in October 1984 the Insanity Defense Reform Act, addressing the insanity defense for the first time at the federal level. This new law, which has been adopted in all federal courts, contains several provisions designed to make it more difficult to plead NGRI.

John Hinckley, President Reagan's assailant, wrote this letter to actress Jodie Foster expressing his dream of marrying her and becoming president. (R. Mims/Corbis Sygma.)

• It eliminates the irresistible-impulse component of the ALI rules. This volitional and behavioral aspect of the ALI guidelines had been strongly criticized because one could regard any criminal act as arising from an inability to stay within the limits of the law. Such an interpretation would have the unacceptable consequence of excluding all criminals from the usual processes of the criminal justice system.

- It changes the ALI's "lacks substantial capacity ... to appreciate" to "unable to appreciate." This alteration in the cognitive component of the law is intended to tighten the grounds for an insanity defense by making more stringent the criterion for impaired judgment.

- The act also stipulates that the mental disease or defect must be "severe," the intent being to exclude insanity defenses on the bases of nonpsychotic disorders, such as antisocial personality disorder. (The ALI guidelines were developed to impose similar restrictions by the use of the word substantial to describe incapacity; this apparently was not considered strong enough in the immediate aftermath of the Hinckley acquittal.) Also abolished by the act were defenses relying on "diminished capacity" or "diminished responsibility," based on such mitigating circumstances as extreme passion or "temporary insanity." Again, the purpose was to make it harder to mount an insanity defense.

- It shifts the burden of proof from the prosecution to the defense. Instead of the prosecution's having to prove that the person was sane beyond a reasonable doubt at the time of the crime (the most stringent criterion, consistent with the constitutional requirement that people are considered innocent until proved guilty), the defense must prove that the defendant was not sane and must do so with "clear and convincing evidence" (a less stringent but still demanding standard of proof). Table 17.3 shows the different standards of proof used in U.S. courts. The importance of this shift can be appreciated by keeping in mind that if the prosecution bears the burden of proof beyond a reasonable doubt, then the defense need only introduce a reasonable doubt to defeat the prosecution's efforts to prove sanity. The heavier burden now placed on the defense is, like the other provisions, designed to make it more difficult to relieve a defendant of moral and legal responsibility.[3]

Table 17.3 Standards of Proof

Standard	Certainty Needed to Convict (%)
Beyond a reasonable doubt	95
Clear and convincing evidence	75
Beyond a preponderance of the evidence	51

- Finally, the new act responds to what many felt was the most troublesome feature of the existing laws—that the person could be released from commitment after a shorter period of time than would be allowed under an ordinary sentence. According to this act, if the person is judged to have recovered from mental illness, then instead of being released from the prison hospital, he or she can be incarcerated up to the maximum time allowable for the crime.

Guilty but Mentally Ill   Since 1975, over a dozen states have created what seems to be a compromise verdict—guilty but mentally ill (GBMI). This trend reflects the uneasiness of the legal and mental health professions in excusing a person who, in Thomas Szasz's terms, is **descriptively responsible** for a crime—that is, who indisputably committed the act—without being held **ascriptively responsible**—that is, without having to suffer some sort of negative societal consequence for breaking the law (see Focus on Discovery 17.1). A GBMI verdict, as mentioned, allows the usual sentence to be imposed but also allows for the person to be treated for mental illness during incarceration, a proposal Szasz made in the 1960s.

---

[3] According to Simon and Aaronson (1988), this provision arose in large measure from the inability of the prosecution to prove John Hinckley's sanity when he shot Reagan and three others. Several members of the jury testified after the trial to a subcommittee of the Senate Judiciary Committee that the judge's instructions on the burden of proof played a role in their verdict of NGRI. Even before the act, almost half the states required that the defendant must prove insanity, but only one, Arizona, had the "clear and convincing" standard. A majority of the states now place the burden of proof on the defense, albeit with the least exacting of legal standards of proof, "by a preponderance of the evidence."

Focus on Discovery 17.1

Thomas S. Szasz and the Case against Forensic Psychiatry and Psychology

Szasz's Polemic

> *By codifying acts of violence as expressions of mental illness, we neatly rid ourselves of the task of dealing with criminal offenses as more or less rational goal-directed acts, no different in principle from other forms of conduct. (Szasz, 1963, p. 141)*

This quotation from one of Thomas Szasz's most widely read books sets forth the basic theme of his argument against the weighty role that his own profession of psychiatry plays in the legal system. (Note that the quote is from 1963. Mental health specialists play an even greater role in the courts today.) We have already mentioned Szasz's distinction between descriptive and ascriptive responsibility: to hold a person criminally responsible is to ascribe legal responsibility for an act for which the person is descriptively responsible. A given social group makes the judgment whether a person who is descriptively responsible for a criminal act will receive criminal punishment. As Szasz points out, being criminally responsible is not an inherent trait that society uncovers. Rather, society at a given time and for a given criminal act decides whether it will hold the perpetrator legally responsible and punish him or her.

Szasz suggests that mental illness began to be used as an explanation for criminal behavior when people acted in a way that was threatening to society. According to Szasz, these exceptional cases all involved violence against people of high social rank. In the shooting of an English nobleman in 1724, a man named Arnold was believed to have as little understanding of his murderous act as "a wild beast." Another man, James Hadfield, was deemed deranged for attempting to assassinate King George III as he sat in a box at the Theatre Royal in 1800. And a third person, named Oxford, was regarded as insane for trying to kill Queen Victoria in 1840. The best-known case has already been mentioned, that of Daniel M'Naghten (1843), who killed Sir Robert Peel's private secretary after mistaking him for Peel. In all these cases from English law, which forms the basis for U.S. law, people of low social rank openly attacked their superiors. Szasz offers the provocative notion that "the issue of insanity may have been raised in these trials in order to obscure the social problems which the crimes intended to dramatize" (Szasz, 1963, p. 128).

Other cases in the United States and abroad, such as the assassinations of John and Robert Kennedy, South African Prime Minister Hendrik Verwoerd, Martin Luther King, Jr., and John Lennon, and the attempted assassination of Pope John Paul II, may to a degree reflect the social ills of the day. Moreover, events in the former Soviet Union provide examples of the role of politics in criminal and civil commitment. In *A Question of Madness*, the well-known Russian biochemist Zhores Medvedev (1972) told how Soviet psychiatrists collaborated with the state in attempting to muzzle his criticism of the government. They diagnosed him as suf-

fering from paranoid delusions, multiple personality, and other mental ailments that would make it dangerous for him to be at large in society.

Of course, Szasz does not claim that all insanity pleas involve an attempt to cover up social problems, for the vast majority of pleas of insanity are made in far more ordinary cases. Szasz sets forth a polemic much broader in scope. His basic concern is with individual freedom and responsibility for one's actions, which include the right to deviate from prevailing mores and the duty to assume responsibility for one's behavior.[a] Far from advocating that people be held less accountable for antisocial acts, he argues that legal responsibility should be extended to all, even to those whose actions are so far beyond the limits of convention that some explain their behavior in terms of mental illness. Szasz's overall lament is that the insanity plea discredits the person as a responsible human being and then subjects him or her to humiliating punishment defined and disguised as treatment (Szasz, 1963).

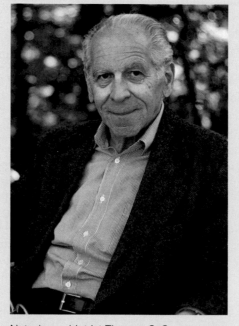

Noted psychiatrist Thomas S. Szasz argues strongly against the use of the insanity defense. (Courtesy Dr. Thomas Szasz.)

Evaluation of Szasz's Position

The Insanity Defense Reform Act of 1984, as well as changes in civil commitment to be described shortly, are consistent with the arguments that Szasz has put forward since the 1960s. These shifts toward holding mentally ill persons accountable for their actions and thereby more deserving of protection of their civil rights are perhaps due in part to Szasz's unrelenting attacks on the liaison between the law and the mental health professions.

However, Szasz has been criticized by those who believe that psychiatry and psychology should have an important role in deciding how to deal with people whose acts, whether criminal or not, seem attributable to mental illness. The abuses documented by Szasz should not blind us to the fact that—for whatever combination of neurobiological and psychological reasons—some people are at times a danger to others and to themselves and cannot judge and control their behavior in ways that are in line with societal laws and mores. Although Szasz and others object to mental illness as an explanation, it is difficult to deny that there is mental illness in the world. People do occasionally imagine persecutors, against whom they sometimes act with force. Some people do hallucinate and on this basis may behave in a dangerous fashion. Our concern for the liberties of one individual has always been tempered with our concern for the rights of others.

---

[a] In a provocative book, *The Abuse Excuse*, Alan Dershowitz, a well-known and high-profile law professor at Harvard University, argues that more and more lawbreakers are trying to avoid responsibility for their criminal acts by invoking one or another hardship in their past history as a reason for their unlawful actions (Dershowitz, 1994b).

Critics of the GBMI verdict argue that it does not benefit mentally ill criminal defendants and does not result in appropriate psychiatric treatment for those convicted (Woodmansee, 1996). A 1997 South Carolina Supreme Court case[4] found that South Carolina's GBMI statute did, to some degree, benefit defendants convicted under it. It mandated that convicted mentally ill people receive mental health evaluations before being placed in the general prison population. However, this particular benefit has not been shown to lead to better treatment in general.

One of the more famous cases involving the GBMI verdict was the February 15, 1992, conviction of Jeffrey Dahmer in Milwaukee, Wisconsin. He had been accused of and had admitted to butchering, cannibalizing, and having sex with the corpses of 15 boys and young men. Dahmer entered the insanity plea allowed in Wisconsin—guilty but mentally ill—and his sanity was the sole focus of an unusual trial that had jurors listening to conflicting testimony from mental health experts about the defendant's state of mind during the serial killings to which he had confessed. They had to decide whether he had had a mental disease that prevented him from knowing right from wrong or from being able to control his actions. Even though there was no disagreement that he was mentally ill, diagnosable as having some sort of paraphilia, Dahmer was deemed sane and therefore legally responsible for the grisly murders. The judge sentenced him to 15 consecutive life terms. Later, another inmate in prison killed him.

Jeffrey Dahmer, who admitted to butchering, cannibalizing, and having sex with the corpses of 15 boys and young men, was found guilty but mentally ill. (Reuters/Corbis Images.)

The Case of Jones v. United States   To illustrate the predicament that a person can get into by raising insanity as a condition for a criminal act, we consider a celebrated—some would call it infamous—Supreme Court case.[5]

Michael Jones was arrested, unarmed, on September 19, 1975, for attempting to steal a jacket from a department store in Washington, D.C. He was charged the following day with attempted petty larceny, a misdemeanor punishable by a maximum prison sentence of 1 year. The court ordered that he be committed to St. Elizabeth's Hospital for a determination of his competency to stand trial.

On March 2, 1976, almost six months after the alleged crime, a hospital psychologist reported to the court that Jones was competent to stand trial, although he had "schizophrenia, paranoid type." The psychologist also reported that the alleged crime resulted from Jones's condition, his paranoid schizophrenia. This comment is noteworthy because the psychologist was not asked to offer an opinion on Jones's state of mind during the crime, only on whether Jones was competent to stand trial. Jones then decided to plead not guilty by reason of insanity. Ten days later, on March 12, the court found him NGRI and formally committed him to St. Elizabeth's Hospital for treatment of his mental disorder.

On May 25, 1976, a customary 50-day hearing was held to determine whether Jones should remain in the hospital any longer. A psychologist from the hospital testified that Jones still suffered from paranoid schizophrenia and was a danger to himself and to others. A second hearing was held on February 22, 1977, 17 months after the commission of the crime and Jones's original commitment to St. Elizabeth's, for determination of competency. The defendant demanded release since he had already been hospitalized longer than the one-year maximum sentence he would have served had he been found guilty of the theft of the jacket. The court denied the request and returned him to St. Elizabeth's.

The District of Columbia Court of Appeals agreed with the original court. Ultimately, in November 1982, more than seven years after his hospitalization, Jones's appeal to the Supreme Court was heard. On June 29, 1983, by a five-to-four decision, the Court affirmed the earlier decision: Jones was to remain at St. Elizabeth's. His public defender reported to us several years ago that Jones has spent most of his committed years in St. Elizabeth's, living in the community for a period of time in the late 1980s, but always returning to the hospital (Fulton, personal communication, April 22, 1997).

The basic question Jones took to the Supreme Court was whether someone "who was committed to a mental hospital on being acquitted of a criminal offense by reason of insanity

---

[4] *South Carolina v. Hornsby*, 484 S.E.2d 869 (S.C. Sup. Ct. 1997).
[5] *Jones v. United States*, 463 U.S. 354 (1983).

must be released because he has been hospitalized for a period longer than he might have served in prison had he been convicted" (*Jones v. United States,* p. 700). Having already spent much more time in the prison hospital than he would have served in prison had he been convicted, Jones believed that he should be released. The Supreme Court, however, viewed matters differently (S Rep No. 1170, 84th Cong, 1st Sess 13 [1955], as cited in *Jones v. United States*):

> *An insanity acquittee is not entitled to his release merely because he has been hospitalized for a period longer than he could have been incarcerated if convicted. The length of a sentence for a particular criminal offense is based on a variety of considerations, including retribution, deterrence, and rehabilitation. However,* because an insanity acquittee was not convicted, he may not be punished. *The purpose of his commitment is to treat his mental illness and protect him and society from his potential dangerousness. There simply is no necessary correlation between the length of the acquittee's hypothetical criminal sentence and the length of time necessary for his recovery.* (p. 700, emphasis added)[6]
>
> *Where [the] accused has pleaded insanity as a defense to a crime, and the jury has found that the defendant was, in fact, insane at the time the crime was committed, it is just and reasonable . . . that the insanity, once established, should be presumed to continue and that the accused should automatically be confined for treatment until it can be shown that he has recovered.* (p. 705)
>
> *And because it is impossible to predict how long it will take for any given individual to recover—or indeed whether he ever will recover—Congress has chosen, as it has with respect to civil commitment, to leave the length of commitment indeterminate, subject to periodic review of the patient's suitability for release.* (p. 708)

What does this mean? Essentially, the Supreme Court ruled that since Jones was acquitted, he could not be punished for the crime. The constitutional justification for being punished is that the individual must be blameworthy. Jones's insanity left him legally blameless, for he could not possess mens rea, "a guilty mind." This is the logic of the insanity defense. Furthermore, according to the Court, since punishment cannot have any of its intended individual or societal effects on a mentally disturbed person—rehabilitation, deterrence, or retribution—it was irrelevant that Jones was being held longer than a normal prison sentence. Jones would have been released from prison sooner had he pleaded guilty.

In this case, the burden of proof was on Jones, the acquittee, to prove that he was no longer mentally ill or dangerous to society, whereas in the normal practice of justice in the United States, a person's accusers have the burden of proving him or her guilty. This situation differs as well from civil commitment (discussed later) in which the government, not the person, bears the burden of proof. Jones was denied this civil right.

The Court was concerned about Jones's illness-produced dangerousness. Jones argued in his petition to the Supreme Court that his theft of the jacket was not dangerous because it was not a violent crime. The Court stated, however, that for there to be violence in a criminal act, the act itself need not be dangerous. It cited a previous decision that a nonviolent theft of an article such as a watch may frequently result in violence through the efforts of the criminal to escape, or of the victim to protect his or her property, or of the police to apprehend the fleeing thief.[7]

The dissenting justices of the Court commented that the longer someone such as Jones had to remain in the hospital, the harder it would be for him to demonstrate that he was no longer a dangerous person or mentally ill. Extended institutionalization would likely make it more difficult for him to afford medical experts other than those associated with the hospital and to behave like someone who was not mentally ill.

> *The current [use of] psychotropic drugs . . . may render mental patients docile . . . but it does not "cure" them or allow them to demonstrate that they would remain non-violent if they were not drugged. . . . At petitioner's May 1976 hearing, the Government relied on testimony [from*

---

[6] At the time, this absence of correlation between the criminal act and the length of incarceration could also work the other way—specifically, "no matter how serious the act committed by the acquittee, he may be released within 50 days of his acquittal if he has recovered" (p. 708).

[7] *Overholser v. O'Beirne,* 302 F.2d 85, 861 (D.C. Cir. 1961).

hospital mental health experts] that petitioner was "not always responsive in a positive way to what goes on" and was "not a very active participant in the informal activities on the Ward" to support its contention that he had not recovered. (p. 716, n. 16)

Jones's case is unusual, even Kafkaesque. Most NGRI decisions are for crimes considerably more heinous than stealing a jacket. But the Jones case went all the way to the Supreme Court, and it illustrates some of the reasons that the insanity defense remains a controversial and emotionally charged issue for a society that values the rule of law and civil rights for its citizens.

Quick Summary

Insanity is a legal term, not a mental health term. Meeting the legal definition is not necessarily the same thing as having a diagnosable mental illness and vice versa. The insanity defense is the legal argument that a defendant should not be held responsible for an illegal act if it is attributable to mental illness that interferes with rationality or that results from some other excusing circumstance, such as not knowing right from wrong; the not guilty by reason of insanity (NGRI) plea signifies that an accused person should not be held responsible for the crime due to his or her mental illness. The guilty but mentally ill (GBMI) plea signifies that an accused person is legally guilty of a crime but can then, in theory, be committed to a prison hospital or other suitable facility for psychiatric treatment rather than to a regular prison for punishment.

The irresistible-impulse standard suggested that an impulse or drive that the person could not control compelled that person to commit the criminal act. The M'Naghten rule specified that a person could not distinguish right from wrong at the time of the crime because of the person's mental disease. The Durham test explicitly stated that the accused is not criminally responsible if his unlawful act was the product of mental disease or mental defect. The first part of the American Law Institute guidelines combines the M'Naghten rule and the concept of irresistible impulse. The second concerns those who are repeatedly in trouble with the law; they are not to be deemed mentally ill only because they keep committing crimes. The Insanity Defense Reform Act shifted the burden of proof from the prosecution to the defense, removed the irresistible-impulse component, changed wording of substantial capacity, and specified that mental illness must be severe. The Jones case illustrates a number of the complexities associated with the insanity defense.

Check Your Knowledge 17.1

Match the statement with the correct insanity standard
1. can't control behavior
2. found guilty
3. doesn't know right from wrong
4. due to mental disease or defect
5. affirmative defense

a. GBMI
b. Durham test
c. NGRI
d. irresistible impulse
e. M'Naghten rule

Competency to Stand Trial

The insanity defense concerns the accused person's mental state at the time of the crime. An important consideration before deciding what kind of defense to adopt is whether the accused person is competent to stand trial at all. In the U.S. criminal justice system, **competency to stand trial** must be decided before it can be determined whether they are responsible for the crime of which they are accused. It is possible for a person to be judged competent to stand trial and then be judged not guilty by reason of insanity.

The legal standard for being competent to stand trial has not changed since it was articulated by a 1960 U.S. Supreme Court decision:[8] "The test [is] whether [the defendant] has sufficient present ability to consult with his lawyer with a reasonable degree of rational understanding, and whether he has a rational as well as a factual understanding of the proceedings against him."

---
[8] *Dusky v. United States*, 362 U.S. 402 (1960).

Clinical Case: Yolanda

Yolanda, a 51-year-old African American woman, was arrested after taking a box of doughnuts from the local QuickMart. At the time of her arrest, she claimed she needed the doughnuts to feed the seven babies growing inside her. She said that Malcolm X was the father of her soon-to-be-born children and that she would soon assume the position of Queen of the New Cities. When asked what the New Cities were, she responded this was a new world order that would be in place following the alignment of the clouds with the planets Jupiter, Saturn, and Venus. Yolanda's public defender immediately realized that Yolanda was not ready for trial; she asked for a competency hearing and arranged for a psychologist to conduct an evaluation. Yolanda was diagnosed with schizophrenia, disorganized type, and her thinking disturbance was found to be so profound that she was not able to understand that she had been charged with theft. Furthermore, she was unable to help her attorney prepare a defense. Instead, Yolanda viewed her attorney as a threat to her unborn babies (she was not pregnant) and feared the attorney would keep her from assuming her rightful position as Queen. At her competency hearing, the judge declared that Yolanda was not competent to stand trial and that she be committed to the local forensic hospital for a period of three months, after which another competency evaluation would be held.

At the hospital, Yolanda was prescribed Olanzapine, and her thinking became more coherent and organized after two months. One of the unit's psychologists worked with Yolanda, teaching her about the criminal justice system. She worked to help Yolanda understand what the charge of theft meant and what a defense attorney, prosecuting attorney, judge, and jury were. At the end of three months, a different psychologist evaluated Yolanda and recommended that she was now competent to stand trial. Yolanda's public defender came to the hospital and met with her to discuss the case. Yolanda was able to help her attorney by telling her about her past hospitalizations and treatment history for schizophrenia. Yolanda realized she was not pregnant, but still held onto beliefs about the New Cities. Still, Yolanda understood that she had stolen the doughnuts and this was why she had to go to court. At her next competency hearing, Yolanda was deemed competent to stand trial. Two months later, she went to court again. This time, she entered a plea of NGRI. After a short trial, the judge accepted her NGRI plea and she returned to the forensic hospital. The treatment goals were now focused on helping Yolanda recover from schizophrenia and not on restoring her competency to stand trial.

Far greater numbers of people are committed to forensic or prison hospitals after being judged incompetent to stand trial—estimated at between 24,000 and 60,000 a year in the United States—than are tried and acquitted by reason of insanity.

With the 1966 Supreme Court case *Pate v. Robinson*[9] as precedent, the defense attorney, prosecutor, or judge may raise the question of mental illness whenever there is reason to believe that the accused person's mental condition might interfere with his or her upcoming trial. Another way to look at competency is that the courts do not want a person to be brought to trial **in absentia** ("not present")—which is a centuries-old principle of English common law—referring here to the person's mental state, not his or her physical presence. If after examination the person is deemed too mentally ill to participate meaningfully in a trial, the trial is routinely delayed, and the accused person is incarcerated with the hope that means of restoring adequate mental functioning can be found. This is what happened to Jones immediately after his arrest.

If a court fails to order a hearing when there is evidence that raises a reasonable doubt about competency to stand trial, or if it convicts a legally incompetent defendant, there is a violation of due process.[10] Once competency is questioned there must be a preponderance of evidence showing that the defendant is competent to stand trial.[11] As just indicated, the test to be applied is whether the defendant is able to consult adequately with his or her lawyer and whether he or she can understand the proceedings.[12] The court has to consider evidence such as irrational behavior as well as any medical or psychological data that might

[9] *Pate v. Robinson*, 383 U.S. 375 (1966).

[10] *United States v. White*, 887 F.2d 705 (6th Cir. 1989); *Wright v. Lockhart*, 914 F.2d 1093, cert. denied, 111 S.Ct. 1089 (1991).

[11] *United States v. Frank*, 956 F.2d 872, cert. denied, 113 S.Ct. 363 (1992); *United States v. Blohm*, 579 F.Supp. 495 (1983).

[12] *Frank*, 956 F.2d at 872; *Wright v. Lockhart*, 914 F.2d 1093 (8th Cir. 1990).

bear on the defendant's competency.[13] However, analogous to the insanity defense, being deemed mentally ill does not necessarily mean that the person is incompetent to stand trial; a person with schizophrenia, for example, may still understand legal proceedings and be able to assist in his or her defense (Winick, 1996). In Focus on Discovery 17.2, we consider the case of Andrea Yates, who was found competent to stand trial despite clear agreement that she was mentally ill.

Being judged incompetent to stand trial can have severe consequences for the individual. Bail is automatically denied, even if it would be routinely granted had the question of incompetency not been raised. The person is usually kept in a facility for the criminally insane for the pretrial examination. During this period the accused person is supposed to receive treatment to render him or her competent to stand trial.[14] In the meantime, he or she may lose employment and undergo the trauma of being separated from family and friends and from familiar surroundings for months or even years, perhaps making his or her emotional condition even worse and thus making it all the more difficult to show competency to stand trial. Until the 1970s, some people languished in prison hospitals for many years waiting to be found competent to stand trial.

A 1972 Supreme Court case, *Jackson v. Indiana*,[15] forced the states to a speedier determination of incompetency. The case concerned a mentally retarded deaf and mute man who was deemed not only incompetent to stand trial but unlikely ever to become competent. The Court ruled that the length of pretrial confinement must be limited to the time it takes to determine whether treatment during this detainment is likely to render the defendant competent to stand trial. If the defendant is unlikely ever to become competent, the state must, after this period, either institute civil commitment proceedings or release the defendant. Legislation in most states defines more precisely the minimal requirements for competency to stand trial, ending the latitude that has deprived thousands of people of their rights to due process (Fourteenth Amendment) and a speedy trial (Sixth Amendment). Defendants today cannot be committed for determination of competency for a period longer than the maximum possible sentence they face.[16]

Medicine has had an impact on the competency issue. The concept of "synthetic sanity" (Schwitzgebel & Schwitzgebel, 1980) has been used to argue that if a drug, such as Thorazine, temporarily produces a modicum of rationality in an otherwise deranged defendant, the trial may proceed. The likelihood that the defendant will again become incompetent to stand trial if the drug is withdrawn does not disqualify the person from going to court.[17] However, the individual rights of the defendant are to be protected against forced medication, because there is no guarantee that such treatment would render the person competent to stand trial and there is a chance that it might cause harm. A subsequent Supreme Court ruling[18] held that a criminal defendant generally cannot be forced to take psychotropic medication in an effort to render him or her competent to stand trial; one of the justices expressed strong reservations that a drugged defendant could ever get a fair trial. In general, the courts have responded to the existence of powerful psychoactive medications by requiring safeguards against their involuntary use to ensure that the defendant's civil rights are protected, even when a drug might restore legal competency to stand trial.[19]

In September 1999, the controversy appeared on the national scene. A judge ruled that the man who forced his way into the United States House of Representatives and shot two security officers could be made to take a psychoactive drug in an effort to make him competent to stand trial; his stated intention was to gain access to a secret machine that was exerting a malign control over people. However, in 2003 the Supreme Court ruled again that forced medication to restore competency could only be used in very limited

---

[13] *United States v. Hemsi*, 901 F.2d 293 (2d Cir. 1990); *Balfour v. Haws*, 892 F.2d 556 (7th Cir. 1989).

[14] *United States v. Sherman*, 912 F.2d 907 (7th Cir. 1990).

[15] *Jackson v. Indiana*, 406 U.S. 715 (1972).

[16] *United States v. DeBellis*, 649 F.2d 1 (1st Cir. 1981); *State v. Moore*, 467 N.W. 2d 201 (Wis. Ct. App. 1991).

[17] *State v. Hampton*, 218 So.2d 311 (La. 1969); *State v. Stacy*, no. 446 (Crim. App., Knoxville, Tenn., August 4, 1977); *United States v. Hayes*, 589 F.2d 811 (1979).

[18] *Riggins v. Nevada*, 504 U.S. 127 (1992).

[19] *United States v. Waddell*, 687 F. Supp. 208 (1988).

Focus on Discovery 17.2

Another Look at Insanity versus Mental Illness

On June 20, 2001, believing that her five children, ranging in age from six months to seven years, were condemned to eternal damnation, 37-year-old Andrea Yates, who lived with her husband and children in Houston, Texas, systematically drowned each child in a bathtub. As recounted on the CNN Web site:

> . . . when the police reached [the] modest brick home on Beachcomber Lane in suburban Houston, they found Andrea drenched with bathwater, her flowery blouse and brown leather sandals soaking wet. She had turned on the bathroom faucet to fill the porcelain tub and moved aside the shaggy mat to give herself traction for kneeling on the floor. It took a bit of work for her to chase down the last of the children; toward the end, she had a scuffle in the family room, sliding around on wet tile . . . . She dripped watery footprints from the tub to her bedroom, where she straightened the blankets around the kids in their pajamas once she was done with them. She called 911 and then her husband. 'It's time. I finally did it,' she said before telling him to come home and hanging up."

The nation was horrified by her actions, and in the months following the murders, information became known about Ms. Yates' frequent bouts of depression, especially after giving birth, as well as her several suicide attempts and hospitalizations for severe depression.

Eight months later her trial was held. The defense argued that she was mentally ill at the time of the murders—and for many periods of time preceding the events—and that she also could not distinguish right from wrong when she put her children to death. The prosecution argued that she did know right from wrong and should therefore be found guilty. On two things the defense and the prosecution agreed: (1) she had murdered her children; and (2) she was mentally ill at the time of the murder. Where they disagreed was on the crucial question as to whether her mental illness entailed not being able to distinguish right or wrong, the familiar M'Naghten principle of criminal responsibility. (Note: Despite her disturbed state of mind during the murders, she had been judged competent to stand trial.)

This trial shows the difficulty of making a successful insanity defense and is a vivid example of the critical difference between mental illness and insanity. No one disagreed that she was severely

depressed, probably psychotic, when she killed her five small children. But, as we have seen, mental illness is not the same as legal insanity. Employing the right–wrong principle, the jury deliberated for only 3 hours and 40 minutes on March 12, 2002, and delivered a verdict of guilty. They had rejected the defense's contention that Ms. Yates could not distinguish right from wrong at the time of the crime. On March 15, the jury decided to spare her life and recommended to the presiding judge that she get life in prison, not being eligible for parole for 40 years.

The trial and the guilty verdict occasioned impassioned discussion in the media and among millions of people in their everyday lives. How could the jury not have considered her insane? If such a person is not insane, who could be judged to be so? Should the right–wrong M'Naghten principle be dropped from the laws of half the states in the United States? Did not her phoning 911 to report what she had done prove that she knew she had done something very wrong? Did not the careful and systematic way she killed her children reflect a mind that, despite her deep depression and delusional thinking, could formulate a complex plan and execute it successfully? Had she received proper treatment from psychiatrists, especially from the one who had recently taken her off antidepressant medication that had been helping her and had sent her home without adequate follow-up?

These are but some of the questions that the Yates trial has raised

Andrea Yates, who drowned her five children, pled NGRI. Although she was suffering from mental illness, her plea was unsuccessful because she was judged capable of knowing right from wrong. (AP/Wide World Photos.)

and that will no doubt be debated in the years to come. They may even be debated in the Yates case. In January, 2005, an appeals court overturned Ms. Yates' murder conviction because the jury heard false testimony from one of the expert witnesses that may have unduly influenced their decision. One of the witnesses for the prosecution testified that Ms. Yates' behavior may have been influenced by an episode of the television show *Law and Order* that showed a woman with depression drowning her children. This testimony was used to bolster the prosecution's case that Ms. Yates knew right from wrong when she killed her children. However, there was no such episode on this television show, so Ms. Yates could not have been thus influenced. In November 2005, the Texas Court of Criminal appeals upheld the lower court's decision to overturn the conviction, thus leaving open the possibility of a retrial, a plea bargain, or a dismissal of charges.

circumstances.[20] In this case, St. Louis dentist Charles Sell was charged in 1997 with two different counts of fraud and with conspiring to kill a former employee and an FBI agent who arrested him. Mr. Sell was later diagnosed with delusional disorder and was found incompetent to stand trial. This was in essence a nonviolent crime, and the Supreme Court did not see that forced medication was justified in this case. The court ruled that forced medication could only be used if alternative treatments had failed, medication is likely to be effective, medication won't interfere with a person's right to defend him- or herself at trial, and there is an important government interest in trying the defendant for a serious crime.

If the defendant wishes, the effects of the medication must be explained to the jury, lest—if the defendant is pleading NGRI—the jury conclude from the defendant's relatively rational drug-produced demeanor that he or she could not have been insane at the time of the crime.[21] This requirement acknowledges that juries form their judgments of legal responsibility or insanity at least in part on how the defendant appears during the trial. If the defendant appears normal, the jury may be less likely to believe that the crime was an act of a disturbed mental state rather than of free will—even though an insanity defense has to do with the defendant's state of mind during the crime, not his or her psychological state during the trial.

Focus on Discovery 17.3 discusses the unusual challenge posed by dissociative identity disorder in criminal commitments.

Insanity, Mental Retardation, and Capital Punishment

As we have just seen, an accused person's mental state can be taken into consideration to determine whether he or she is competent to stand trial and/or should be held legally responsible for a criminal act. On very rare occasions the sanity or mental capacity of a person also becomes an issue after a conviction. The question is, should a person convicted of a capital offense and sentenced to be put to death by the state have to be legally sane at the time of the execution? Furthermore, what if the person is deemed so mentally retarded that he may not understand what is about to happen to him?

The question of insanity and capital punishment arose in April 1998 in California in the case of Horace Kelly, a 39-year-old man who had been found guilty of the brutal 1984 rapes and murders of two women and the slaying of an 11-year-old boy. Neither the issue of competency to stand trial nor an insanity defense to excuse him from criminal responsibility for the crimes had been raised at the time of his trial, but the man's lawyers argued—12 years later and just days before his scheduled execution by lethal injection—that Kelly's mental health had deteriorated during his imprisonment on death row to such an extent that one of his defense attorneys referred to him as a "walking vegetable." They made reference to a 1986 Supreme Court ruling stating that it is a violation of the Eighth Amendment (which prohibits cruel and unusual punishment) for an insane individual to be executed, even if the person was duly convicted and sentenced to death as a sane person.

We need to remember that insanity is a legal concept, and not everyone judged to be mentally ill is held to be legally insane. Evidence of mental illness (and possible insanity) during Kelly's imprisonment included psychiatrists' reports of delusions, hallucinations, and inappropriate affect. He was also described by fellow inmates and by guards as hoarding his feces and smearing them on the walls of his prison cell. By 1995, after 10 years on death row, one court-appointed psychiatrist concluded that Kelly was legally insane. On the other hand, another psychiatrist reported that when asked what being executed would mean for him, Kelly gave the rational reply that he would not be able to have a family; he was also able to name two of his victims and beat the psychiatrist in several games of tic-tac-toe.

In their effort to delay the execution, Kelly's lawyers argued that the stress on death row is so severe that some convicted felons inevitably go crazy there. Kelly was portrayed as particularly vulnerable, having endured a very troubled childhood, full of sexual and physical abuse from his parents, his siblings, and strangers. As a child, he was also subject

---

[20] *Sell v. United States*, 539 U.S. 02-5664 (2003).
[21] *State v. Jojola*, 553 F.2d 1296 (N.M. Ct. App. 1976).

Dissociative Identity Disorder and the Insanity Defense

Imagine that as you are having a cup of coffee one morning you hear pounding at the front door. You hurry to answer and find two police officers staring grimly at you. One of them asks, "Are you Jane Smith?" "Yes," you reply. "Well, ma'am, you are under arrest for grand theft and for the murder of John Doe." The officer then reads you your Miranda rights against self-incrimination, handcuffs you, and takes you to the police station, where you are allowed to call your lawyer.

This would be a scary situation for anybody. What is particularly frightening and puzzling to you and your lawyer is that you have absolutely no recollection of having committed the crime that a detective later describes to you. You are aghast that you cannot account for the time period when the murder was committed—in fact, your memory is startlingly blank for that entire time. And, as if this were not bizarre enough, the detective then shows you a videotape in which you are clearly firing a gun at a bank teller during a holdup. "Is that you in the videotape?" asks the detective. You confer with your lawyer, saying that it certainly looks like you, including the clothes, but you are advised not to admit anything one way or the other.

Let's move forward in time now to your trial some months later. Witnesses have come forward and identified you beyond a reasonable doubt. There is no one you know who can

Poster for the classic film about Jekyll and Hyde. (Jerry Ohlinger's Movie Material Store.)

testify that you were somewhere other than at the bank on the afternoon of the robbery and the murder. And it is clear that the jury is going to find you, in Szasz's terms, descriptively responsible for the crimes. But did you murder the teller in the bank? You are able to assert honestly to yourself and to the jury that you did not. And yet even you have been persuaded that the person in the videotape is you, and that that person committed the robbery and the murder.

Because of the strange nature of the case, your lawyer arranged prior to the trial to have you interviewed by a psychiatrist and a clinical psychologist, both of them well-known experts in forensics. Through extensive questioning they have decided that you have dissociative identity disorder (DID, formerly called multiple personality disorder) and that the crimes were committed not by you, Jane Smith, but by your rather violent alter, Laura. Indeed, during one of the interviews, Laura emerged and boasted about the crime, even chuckling over the fact that you, Jane, would be imprisoned for it.

This fictional account is not as far-fetched as you might think (recall the discussion of dissociative identity disorder in Chapter 6). Mental health lawyers have for some time been concerned with such scenarios as they have wrestled with various aspects of the insanity defense. But nearly all the people who successfully use

to what his mother called "trances," beginning at age two, with other signs of emotional and mental impairment throughout childhood and adolescence.

A federal judge decided in June 1998 and the U.S. Supreme Court concurred in April 1999 to stay (delay) Horace Kelly's execution and allow his lawyers to argue, among other things, that he should not be put to death because he was insane. After these arguments, Kelly's execution was permanently stayed. Among the many riveting questions that this case raises is the ethics of a mental health professional's working to improve a person's psychological condition to the extent that the person can be judged sane enough to be executed. And consider how the issue of synthetic sanity just described affects a death penalty situation: Does a person sentenced to death have the right to refuse psychotropic medication because he or she knows it would improve his or her mental condition enough so that he or she could be executed?

Increasing attention is being paid to this issue of synthetic sanity and the general question of whether it is constitutional to execute criminals who are deemed insane or mentally retarded at the time of their scheduled capital punishment. In February 2002, for example, the Georgia Board of Pardons and Paroles commuted the death sentence of a convicted rapist and murderer on the grounds that he was delusional (note that he had not been found NGRI and that he had been on death row for nearly 16 years). What makes this case significant is that the person had been forced to take psychoactive medication that improved his mental condition enough to meet the federal standard that only a person who is legally sane can be executed (Weinstein, 2002).

A man named Daryl Atkins was sentenced to death in Virginia for a kidnapping and murder he committed in 1996. His IQ was rated at 59, which placed him in the range of this defense are diagnosable as having schizophrenia (or more generally, as psychotic), and DID is regarded as a dissociative disorder (and used to be classified as one of the neuroses). Can DID be an excusing condition for a criminal act? Should Jane Smith be held ascriptively responsible for a crime committed by her alter, Laura? The quandary is clearly evident in the title of an article that addresses the DID issue: "Who's on Trial?" (Appelbaum & Greer, 1994).

Consider the widely accepted legal principle that people accused of crimes should be punished only if they are blameworthy. The several court decisions and laws we have reviewed in this chapter all rest on this principle. In reviews of the DID literature and of its forensic implications, Elyn Saks (1997) of the University of Southern California Law Center argues that DID should be regarded as a special case in mental health law, and that a new legal principle should be established. Her argument takes issue with legal practice that would hold a person with DID ascriptively responsible for a crime as long as the personality acting at the time of the crime intended to commit it.

What is intriguing about Saks's argument is that she devotes a major portion of it to defining personhood. What is a person? Is a person the body we inhabit? Well, most of the time our sense of who we are as persons does not conflict with the bodies we have come to know as our own, or rather, as us. But in DID there is a discrepancy. The body that committed the crimes at the bank was Jane Smith. But it was her alter, Laura, who committed the crimes. Saks argues that, peculiar as it may sound, the law should be interested in the body only as a container for the person. It is the person who may or may not be blameworthy, not the body. Nearly all the time they are one and the same, but in the case of DID they are not. In a sense, Laura committed the murder by using Jane's body.

Then is Jane blameworthy? The person Jane did not commit the crime; she did not even know about it. For the judge to sentence Jane, or more specifically, the body in the courtroom who usually goes by that name, would be unjust, argues Saks, for Jane is descriptively innocent. To be sure, sending Jane to prison would punish Laura, for whenever Laura would emerge, she would find herself imprisoned. But what of Jane? Saks concludes that it is unjust to imprison Jane because she is not blameworthy. Rather, we must find her not guilty by reason of dissociative identity disorder and remand her for treatment of the disorder.

Dissociative identity disorder would not, however, be a justification for a verdict of NGRI if the alter that did not commit the crime was aware of the other alter's criminal intent and did not do anything to prevent the criminal act. Under these circumstances, argues Saks, the first alter would be complicit in the crime and would therefore be somewhat blameworthy. A comparison Saks draws is to Robert Louis Stevenson's fictional character of Dr. Jekyll and Mr. Hyde. Jekyll made the potion that caused the emergence of Mr. Hyde, his alter, with the foreknowledge that Hyde would do evil. So even though Jekyll was not present when Hyde was in charge, he would nonetheless be blameworthy because of his prior knowledge of what Hyde would do—not to mention that he, Jekyll, has concocted the potion that created his alter, Hyde.

Saks is optimistic about the effectiveness of therapy for DID and believes that people like Jane/Laura can be integrated into one personality and then released to rejoin society. Saks goes so far as to argue that people with DID who are judged dangerous but who have not committed a crime should be subject to civil commitment, even though this would be tantamount to preventive detention. In this way, she suggests, future crimes might be avoided.[a]

---

[a] It should be recalled that a substantial number of mental health professionals dispute the existence of DID. For them Saks's arguments would not be persuasive.

the moderately retarded. His defense attorney argued that his intellectual limitations render capital punishment unconstitutional because he lacks understanding of the consequences of his actions and is therefore not as morally culpable for his acts as a person of normal intelligence. Eighteen of the 38 states that allow capital punishment already prohibit the execution of the mentally retarded on Eighth Amendment grounds against cruel and unusual punishment. In 2002, the United States Supreme Court ruled in a six-to-three decision in the case of *Atkins v. Virginia* that capital punishment of those with mental retardation constitutes cruel and unusual punishment, which is prohibited by the Eighth Amendment of the U.S. Constitution. The Supreme Court left open the question of what constitutes mental retardation, however, leaving it up to the states to decide how to remain within the requirements of the Eighth Amendment. The state of Virginia subsequently defined mental retardation as consisting of an IQ score of 70 or less along with difficulties in self-care and social interaction. In Virginia, a defendant must convince the jury of mental retardation using the standard "beyond a preponderance of the evidence" (see Table 17.3). Since 1998, Atkins was given an IQ test at least four times. He scored below 70 on two testing occasions (scores of 59 and 67), and above 70 on two other testing occasions (scores of 74 and 76). In August 2005, a Virginia jury decided that Daryl Atkins did not meet Virginia's definition of mental retardation. Thus, even though the Atkins case effectively abolished the practice of executing individuals with mental retardation, Daryl Atkins may well be put to death in Virginia because the jury's decision paved the way for the original death sentence to be carried out (as of this writing, attorneys for Atkins were preparing an appeal).

Check Your Knowledge 17.2

True or false?
1. The *Jackson* case established that individuals who will not be restored to competency should be found NGRI.
2. To be competent to stand trial, a person must be able to understand the charges and assist their attorney.

3. The Supreme Court ruled that executing mentally ill prisoners constitutes cruel and unusual punishment.

Civil Commitment

Historically, governments have had a duty to protect their citizens from harm. We take for granted the right and duty of government to set limits on our freedom for the sake of protecting us. Few drivers, for example, question the legitimacy of the state's imposing limits on them by providing traffic signals that often make them stop when they would rather go. Government has a long-established right as well as an obligation to protect us both from ourselves—the *parens patriae*, "power of the state"—and from others—the police power of the state. Civil commitment is one further exercise of these powers.

In virtually all states a person can be committed to a psychiatric hospital against his or her will if a judgment is made that he or she is (1) mentally ill and (2) a danger to self— that is, unable to provide for the basic physical needs of food, clothing, and shelter—or a danger to others (Perlin, 1994). (There is also something called "outpatient commitment," which we will describe later.) At present, dangerousness to others is more often the second criterion, and court rulings point to imminent dangerousness as the principal criterion (e.g., the person is right on the verge of committing a violent act).[22] In some states, a finding of imminent dangerousness must be evidenced by a recent overt act, attempt, or threat; however, there are some states that do not require an overt act [*In Re: Albright*, 836 P.2d 1 (Kan. App. 1992)]. Such commitment is supposed to last for only as long as the person remains dangerous.[23]

Specific commitment procedures generally fit into one of two categories, formal or informal. Formal or judicial commitment is by order of a court. It can be requested by any responsible citizen; usually the police, a relative, or a friend seeks the commitment. If the judge believes that there is a good reason to pursue the matter, he or she will order a mental health examination. The person has the right to object to these attempts to "certify" him or her, and a court hearing can be scheduled to allow the person to present evidence against commitment.

Informal, emergency commitment of mentally ill persons can be accomplished without initially involving the courts. For example, if a hospital administrative board believes that a voluntary patient requesting discharge is too disturbed and dangerous to be released, it is able to detain the patient with a temporary, informal commitment order.

Any person acting in an out-of-control, dangerous fashion may be taken immediately to a mental hospital by the police. Perhaps the most common informal commitment procedure is the 2PC, or two physicians' certificate. In most states, two physicians, not necessarily psychiatrists, can sign a certificate that allows a person to be incarcerated for some period of time, ranging from 24 hours to as long as 20 days. Detainment beyond this period requires formal judicial commitment.

Civil commitment affects far more people than criminal commitment. It is beyond the scope of this book to examine in detail the variety of state civil commitment laws and regulations; each state has its own, and they are in almost constant flux. Our aim is to present an overview that will provide a basic understanding of the issues and of current directions of change.

---

[22] *Suzuki v. Yuen*, 617 F.2d 173 (9th Cir. 1980).
[23] *United States v. DeBellis*, 649 F.2d 1 (1st Cir. 1981).

Preventive Detention and Problems in the Prediction of Dangerousness

The perception is widespread that mentally ill people account for a significant proportion of the violence that besets contemporary society, but this is not the case (Bonta, Law, & Hanson, 1998; Monahan, 1992). Only about 3 percent of the violence in the United States is clearly linked to mental illness (Swanson et al., 1990). Moreover, about 90 percent of people diagnosed as psychotic (primarily schizophrenia) are not violent (Swanson et al., 1990). Mentally ill persons—even allowing for their relatively small numbers—do not account for a large proportion of violent offenses, especially when compared with substance abusers and people who are in their teens and 20s, are male, and are poor (Mulvey, 1994). The MacArthur Violence Risk Assessment Study, a large prospective study of violent behavior among persons recently discharged from psychiatric hospitals, found that mentally ill patients who are not substance abusers are no more likely to engage in violence than are non-mentally ill individuals who are not substance abusers (Steadman et al., 1998). Thus, if substance abuse is not involved, mentally ill people are no more prone to violence than the average person. Also, when former patients do act aggressively, it is usually against family members or friends, and the incidents tend to occur at home (Steadman et al., 1998). In a later analysis from the MacArthur study, patients with delusions were not more violent than patients without

People with mental illness are not necessarily more likely to be violent than people without mental illness, contrary to the way movies often portray the mentally ill. (The Kobal Collection, Ltd.)

delusions, regardless of the content of their delusion (e.g., violent) or whether or not they had comorbid substance abuse (Appelbaum, Robbins, & Monahan, 2000). By and large, then, the general public is seldom affected by violence from the mentally ill.

Yet there is a strong connection in the public mind between violence and mental illness, and this belief is central to society's justification of civil commitment (Monahan & Shah, 1989; Steadman et al., 1998) as well as to the stigma attached to having been a patient in a psychiatric institution (Link et al., 1987; Steadman et al., 1998). We will examine the issues and the evidence.

The Prediction of Dangerousness   Civil commitment is necessarily a form of preventive detention; the prediction is made that a person judged mentally ill may in the future behave in a dangerous manner and should therefore be detained. But the entire U.S. legal and constitutional system is organized to protect people from preventive detention. Thus, unless mental illness comes into the picture, a person can generally be imprisoned only after having been found guilty of committing a crime (or, if accused and not yet convicted, denied bail if the crime was especially heinous and if the person poses a risk of leaving the jurisdiction to avoid trial). Furthermore, ordinary prisoners are routinely released from prison even though statistics show that most will commit additional crimes.

But what if a person openly threatens to inflict harm on others, such as an individual who for an hour each day stands in the street and shouts threats to people in a nearby apartment house? Does the state have to wait until the person acts on the threats? Usually not. In such a case the civil commitment process can be brought into play if the person is deemed not only an imminent danger to others but mentally ill as well (Perlin, 1994).

The likelihood of committing a dangerous act is central to civil commitment, but is dangerousness easily predicted? Early studies examining the accuracy of predictions that a person would commit a dangerous act found that mental health professionals were poor at making this judgment (e.g., Kozol, Boucher, & Garofalo, 1972; Monahan, 1973, 1976). Some researchers went on to argue that civil commitment for the purposes of preventive detention should be abolished. Monahan (1978), however, carefully scrutinized these studies and concluded that the ability to predict violence had not been adequately assessed. Most of the studies conformed to the following methodological pattern.

- People were hospitalized for mental illness and for being a danger to the community.
- While these people were in the hospital, it was again predicted that some of them would be violent if they were released into the community.
- After a period of time, these people were released, thus putting together the conditions for a natural experiment.
- Checks on the behavior of the released patients over the next several years did not reveal much dangerous behavior.

What is wrong with such research? Monahan pointed out that little if any consideration was given to changes that hospitalization itself might have effected. In the studies reviewed, the period of time spent in the hospital ranged from several months to 15 years. Prolonged periods of enforced hospitalization might very well make patients more docile, if for no other reason than that they become that much older.

Reconsideration of earlier research suggests that greater accuracy can be achieved than previously assumed in predicting dangerousness in the longer term (Monahan, 1984; Monahan & Steadman, 1994; Steadman et al., 1998). Violence prediction is most accurate under the following conditions (e.g., Campbell, Stefan, & Loder, 1994).

- If a person has been repeatedly violent in the recent past, it is reasonable to predict that he or she will be violent in the near future unless there have been major changes in the person's attitudes or environment. Thus, if a violent person is placed in a restrictive environment, such as a prison or high-security psychiatric hospital facility, he or she may well not be violent given the markedly changed environment.
- If violence is in the person's distant past, and if it was a single but very serious act, and if that person has been incarcerated for a period of time, then violence can be expected on release if there is reason to believe that the person's predetention personality and physical abilities have not changed and if the person is going to return to the same environment in which he or she was previously violent.
- Even with no history of violence, violence can be predicted if the person is judged to be on the brink of a violent act, for example, if the person is pointing a loaded gun at an occupied building.

In addition, as stated earlier, the presence of substance abuse significantly raises the rate of violence (Steadman et al., 1998). This finding supports including substance abuse as one of the factors to be considered when attempting to predict violence. [Substance abuse also predicts violence among non-mentally disordered individuals (Gendreau, Little, & Goggin, 1996).]

Violence among mentally ill individuals is often associated with medication noncompliance (Monahan, 1992). **Outpatient commitment** is one way of increasing medication compliance. It is an arrangement whereby a patient is allowed to leave the hospital but must live in a halfway house or other supervised setting and report to a mental health agency frequently and regularly. To the extent that outpatient commitment increases compliance with medication regimens and with maintaining regular contact with mental health professionals—and evidence indicates that it does (Munetz et al., 1996)—we can expect violence from formerly hospitalized patients to be reduced. Indeed, support services, such as halfway houses, can markedly reduce the chances that a person who might otherwise be prone to committing a violent act will actually commit one (Dvoskin & Steadman, 1994).

Preventive Detention and Sex Offenders   One example of preventive detention is provided by laws passed in seven states that enable some repeat and dangerous sex offenders to be deemed mentally ill when they are about to be released from prison and then to be civilly committed to a prison hospital for an indefinite period until treatment cures them of their presumed illness. Although this appears to some legal scholars to be unconstitutional—detaining a person for a crime that he or she may commit in the future—many argue that it makes sense to keep sexual predators out of society.

Proponents of these laws, usually called sexually violent predator acts, point to rapists and child molesters with long histories of recidivism. Based on past experience and sometimes on comments made by the prisoners themselves (e.g., one man said that the only way to keep him from victimizing children on his release would be to execute him), the probability may be high that such prisoners will harm people after their release. Should they not be prevented from doing so?

In 1997 the Supreme Court ruled that such preventive detention is in fact constitutional.[24] Even though we don't detain other kinds of criminals when they have served their time because of the likelihood that they will be recidivists, if a person is deemed mentally ill and dangerous, he or she can be civilly committed, as we have already discussed. This feature of civil commitment laws allows sexual predator laws to stand. (For a discussion of therapists' responsibilities to predict dangerousness, see Focus on Discovery 17.4.)

Toward Greater Protection of Patients' Rights

The United States Constitution is a remarkable document. It lays down the basic duties of elected federal officials and guarantees a set of civil rights. But there is often some distance between the abstract delineation of a civil right and its day-to-day implementation. Moreover, judges must interpret the Constitution as it bears on specific contemporary problems. Since nowhere in this cornerstone of U.S. democracy is there specific mention of mentally ill patients, lawyers and judges interpret various sections of the document to justify what they consider necessary in society's treatment of people whose mental health is in question.

In 1972, voluntary admissions to mental hospitals began to outnumber involuntary admissions. But a great number of people were still admitted and retained against their wishes, and it is impossible to know how many of those who admit themselves voluntarily do so under threat of civil commitment. One early survey (Gilboy & Schmidt, 1971) revealed that 40 percent of patients who had "voluntarily" admitted themselves to a psychiatric hospital in Chicago had actually been threatened with commitment by the police officers that had taken them there. Being hospitalized against one's wishes is less likely today, in large part due to changes in health care that emphasize outpatient care over inpatient care. In fact, it is increasingly difficult to hospitalize a patient today who is in real need of at least a short hospital stay—someone who is a danger to self or others.

Beginning in the 1970s, a number of court decisions were rendered to protect individuals from being involuntarily hospitalized unless absolutely necessary. For example, a 1976 federal court decision in Wisconsin, *Lessard v. Schmidt*,[25] gives a person threatened with civil commitment the right to timely written notice of the proceeding, opportunity for a hearing with counsel, the right to have the hearing decided by jury, Fifth Amendment protection against self-incrimination, and other similar procedural safeguards already accorded defendants in criminal actions, including being present at any hearing to decide the need for commitment.[26] Such protections are to be provided even under emergency commitment conditions.[27] A 1979 Supreme Court decision, *Addington v. Texas*,[28] further provides that the state must produce clear and convincing evidence that a person is mentally ill and dangerous before he or she can be involuntarily committed to a psychiatric hospital. In 1980, the Ninth Circuit Court of Appeals ruled that this danger must be imminent.[29] Clearly, the intent is to restrict the state's power to curtail individual freedoms because of mental illness. Although protection of the rights of mentally ill individuals adds tremendously to

[24] *Kansas v. Hendricks*, 117 S.Ct. 2072 (1997).

[25] *Lessard v. Schmidt*, 349 F.Supp. 1078 (E.D. Wisc. 1972), vacated and remanded on other grounds, 94 S.Ct. 713 (1974), reinstated in 413 F.Supp. 1318 (E.D. Wisc. 1976).

[26] *In Re: Lawaetz* 728 F.2d 225 (3d Cir. 1984).

[27] *Doremus v. Farrell*, 407 F.Supp. 509 (1975).

[28] *Addington v. Texas*, 441 U.S. 418 (1979).

[29] *Suzuki v. Yuen*, 617 F.2d at 173.

Focus on Discovery 17.4

The Tarasoff Case—The Duty to Warn and to Protect

The client's right to privileged communication—the legal right of a client to require that what goes on in therapy remain confidential—is an important protection, but it is not absolute. Society has long stipulated certain conditions in which confidentiality in a relationship should not be maintained because of the harm that can befall others. A famous California court ruling in 1974[a] described circumstances in which a therapist not only may but *must* breach the sanctity of a client's communication. First, what appear to be the facts in the case:

Clinical Case

In the fall of 1968, Prosenjit Poddar, a graduate student from India studying at the University of California at Berkeley, met Tatiana (Tanya) Tarasoff at a folk dancing class. They saw each other weekly during the fall, and on New Year's Eve she kissed him. Poddar interpreted this act as a sign of formal engagement (as it might have been in India, where he was a member of the Harijan or "untouchable caste"). [But] Tanya told him that she was involved with other men, and indicated that she did not wish to have an intimate relationship with him.

Poddar was depressed as a result of the rebuff, but he saw Tanya a few times during the spring (occasionally tape-recording their conversations in an effort to understand why she did not love him). Tanya left for Brazil in the summer, and Poddar, at the urging of a friend, went to the student health facility where a psychiatrist referred him to a psychologist for psychotherapy. When Tanya returned in October 1969, Poddar discontinued therapy. Based in part on Poddar's stated intention to purchase a gun, the psychologist notified the campus police, both orally and in writing, that Poddar was dangerous and should be taken to a community mental health center for psychiatric commitment.

The campus police interviewed Poddar, who seemed rational and promised to stay away from Tanya. They released him and notified the health service. No further efforts at commitment were made because the supervising psychiatrist apparently decided that such was not needed and, as a matter of confidentiality, requested that the letter to the police as well as certain therapy records be destroyed.

On October 27, Poddar went to Tanya's home armed with a pellet gun and a kitchen knife. She refused to speak to him. He shot her with the pellet gun. She ran from the house; he pursued, caught, and repeatedly and fatally stabbed her. Poddar was found guilty of voluntary

manslaughter rather than first- or second-degree murder. The defense established with the aid of the expert testimony of three psychiatrists that Poddar's diminished mental capacity, paranoid schizophrenia, precluded the malice necessary for first- or second-degree murder. After his prison term, he returned to India, where, according to his own report, he is happily married. (Schwitzgebel & Schwitzgebel, 1980, p. 205).

Under the privileged communication statute of California, the counseling center psychologist properly breached the confidentiality of the professional relationship and took steps to have Poddar civilly committed, for he judged Poddar to be an imminent danger. Poddar had stated that he intended to purchase a gun, and by his other words and actions he had convinced the therapist that he was desperate enough to harm Tarasoff. What the psychologist did not do, and what the court decided he should have done, was to warn the likely victim, Tanya Tarasoff, that her former friend had bought a gun and might use it against her. Such a warning would have been consistent with previous court decisions requiring physicians to warn the public when they are treating people with contagious diseases and requiring mental hospitals to warn others when a dangerous patient has left without being discharged (Knapp & Vandecreek, 1982). Or, as stated by the California Supreme Court in *Tarasoff*: "Once a therapist does in fact determine, or under applicable professional standards reasonably should have determined, that a patient poses a serious danger of violence to others, he bears a duty to exercise reasonable care to protect the foreseeable victims of that danger." The *Tarasoff* ruling, now being applied in other states as well,[b] requires clinicians, in deciding when to violate confidentiality, to use the very imperfect skill of predicting dangerousness.

Extending Protection to Foreseeable Victims

A subsequent California court ruling[c] held by a bare majority that foreseeable victims include those in close relationship to the identifiable victim. In this instance a mother was hurt by a shotgun fired by the dangerous patient, and her 7-year-old son was present when the shooting took place. The boy later sued the psychologists for damages brought on by emotional trauma. Since a young child is likely to be in the company of his or her mother, the court concluded in *Hedlund* that the *Tarasoff* ruling extended to the boy.[c]

Extending Protection Further to Potential Victims

A 1983 decision of a federal circuit court in California[d] extended *Tarasoff* still further. The court ruled that Veterans Administration psychiatrists should earlier have warned the murdered lover of an outpatient, Phillip

---

[a] *Tarasoff v. Regents of the University of California*, 529 P.2d 553 (Cal. 1974), vacated, reheard in bank, and affirmed, 131 Cal. Rptr. 14, 551 P.2d 334 (1976). The 1976 California Supreme Court ruling was by a four-to-three majority.

[b] *White v. United States*, 780 F.2d 97 (D.C. Cir. 1986); *Soutear v. United States*, 646 F.Supp. 524 (1986); *Dunkle v. Food Services East Inc.*, 582 A.2d. 1342 (1990); *People v. Clark*, 50 Cal. 3d 583, 789 P.2d 127 (1990).
[c] *Hedlund v. Superior Court*, 34 Cal.3d 695 (1983).
[d] *Jablonski by Pahls v. United States*, 712 F.2d 391 (1983).

Jablonski, that she was a foreseeable victim, even though the patient had never made an explicit threat against her to the therapists. The reasoning was that Jablonski, having previously raped and otherwise harmed his wife, would likely direct his continuing "violence . . . against women very close to him" (p. 392).

The court also found the hospital psychiatrists negligent in not obtaining Jablonski's earlier medical records. These records showed a history of harmful violent behavior, which, together with the threats his lover was complaining about, should have moved the hospital to institute emergency civil commitment. The court ruled that the failure to warn was a proximate or immediate cause of the woman's murder. Proper consideration of the medical records, said the judge, would have convinced the psychiatrists that Jablonski was a real danger to others and should be committed.

This broadening of the duty to warn and protect has placed mental health professionals in California in an even more difficult predicament, for the potentially violent patient need not even mention the specific person he or she may harm. It is up to the therapist to deduce who are possible victims, based on what he or she can learn of the patient's past and present circumstances. Ironically, Jablonski's lover realized that she was in danger; she had moved out of the apartment she was sharing with him and had complained to her priest and to the Veterans Administration psychiatrists themselves that she feared for her safety. One of the psychiatrists had even advised her to leave Jablonski, at least while he was being evaluated at the medical center. But "when [she] responded, 'I love him,' [the psychiatrist] did not warn her further because he believed she would not listen to him" (p. 393). The court found this warning "totally unspecific and inadequate under the circumstances" (p. 398).

Extending Protection to Property

Tarasoff was further extended by a Vermont State Supreme Court ruling, *Peck v. Counseling Service of Addison County*,[e] which held that a mental health practitioner has a duty to warn a third party if there is a danger of damage to property. The case involved a 29-year-old male patient who, after a heated argument with his father, told his therapist that he wanted to get back at his father and indicated that he might do so by burning down his father's barn. He proceeded to do just that. No people or animals were harmed in the fire; the barn housed no animals and was located 130 feet away from the parents' home. The court's conclusion that the therapist had a duty to warn was based on reasoning that arson is a violent act and therefore a lethal threat to people who may be in the vicinity of the fire. This ruling can be seen

Prosenjit Poddar was convicted of manslaughter in the death of Tatiana Tarasoff. The court ruled that his therapist, who had become convinced Poddar might harm Tarasoff, should have warned her of the impending danger. (AP/Wide World Photos.)

as an expansion of the *Hedlund* court decision as well; whereas *Hedlund* speaks of humans who may be at risk because of possible physical proximity to the endangered victim, *Peck* speaks of humans who could be harmed via threat to an inanimate object.

Extending Protection to Potential Victims as Yet Unknown

Many courts have augmented the duty to warn and protect to foreseeable victims of child abuse and even to possible victims as yet unknown. In one such case,[f] a medical student underwent a training analysis as one of the requirements to become a psychoanalyst. During the therapy he admitted that he was a pedophile. Later in his training he saw a male child as a patient as part of his psychiatric residency and sexually assaulted the boy. The court decided that the training analyst, who was not just the student's therapist but an instructor in the school, had reason to know that his patient-student "posed a specific threat to a specific group of persons, namely future minor patients, with whom [the student] would necessarily interact as part of his training" (p. 8). Even though, at the time the student revealed his pedophilia he did not have child patients (and thus there were no specific people whom the instructor could warn and take steps to protect), the supervisor—as his instructor, not just his therapist—was judged to have sufficient control over the student's professional training and activities (specifically, the power to keep the student from pursuing his interests in working with children) for the *Tarasoff* ruling to be relevant. The court decided that the supervisor could have and therefore should have "redirect[ed the student's] professional development without even compromising the confidentiality of [the student's] disclosures to him" (p. 8). Instead, the supervisor and, by virtue of his faculty status, the medical school in which he worked allowed the patient-student to pursue his interests in child psychiatry, which resulted in the sexual molestation of a child patient.

Extending Protection Based on Families' Reports

In 2004, a California appeals court ruled that therapists have a duty to warn a possible victim if the threat is reported by a member of the patient's family.[g] In this case, a therapist learned about a threat not from his patient, but from a family member of his patient. His patient

---

[e] *Peck v. Counseling Service of Addison County*, 499 A.2d 422 (Vt. 1985).

[f] *Almonte v. New York Medical College*, 851 F. Supp. 34, 40 (D. Conn. 1994) (denying motion for summary judgment).

[g] *Ewing v. Goldstein*, Cal. App.4th B163112.2d. (2004).

revealed to his parents that he had thoughts of killing his ex-girlfriend's new boyfriend. The parents contacted the therapist about this threat. The therapist did not contact the new boyfriend, who was later killed by his patient. Parents of the boyfriend sued for wrongful death, saying the therapist should have warned their son. The court agreed and ruled that a close family member is in essence a part of the patient, and thus a therapist does have a duty to warn potential victims if notified by a close family member of a patient. The court viewed the communication between a family member and the therapist about the threat as part of the patient's therapy and therefore "patient communication."

HIV and *Tarasoff*

Consider now the situation of a therapist who is treating an HIV-positive patient who has not disclosed his or her seropositive status to a partner and continues to engage in unsafe sex with that person. Where do the therapist's responsibilities lie? Emerging guidelines from professional associations such as the American Psychiatric Association support the therapist's breaking confidentiality as mandated by *Tarasoff* if the therapist is not successful in convincing the patient to disclose his or her status or engage in safer sexual behavior (American Psychiatric Association, 1992). This position is consistent with long-standing professional rules that require physicians to notify others of a patient's infectious disease so as to protect the public. The likelihood that the person is seropositive because of infidelity makes such actions fraught with difficulty for the patient's relationship with loved ones.

A relevant factor may be the mental competence of the patient. Some people who are HIV positive or have AIDS have impairments in their judgment and reasoning processes, which may prevent them from fully understanding the dangers their seropositive status poses to others through unsafe sex or needle sharing. Under such conditions especially, health professionals may have the legal and ethical duty to follow *Tarasoff* (Searight & Pound, 1994). Some states have enacted statutes that impose a duty to warn, whereas other states do not have a duty to warn but instead provide immunity (protection from prosecution or lawsuit) to health care providers if they decide to warn (Gostin & Hodge, 1998).

the burden of both civil courts and state and county mental-hospital staffs, it is a price a free society must pay.

We turn now to a discussion of several issues and trends that revolve around the greater protections being provided to those with mental disorders: the principle of the least restrictive alternative; the right to treatment; the right to refuse treatment; questions of free will in the law; and, finally, the way in which these several themes conflict in efforts to provide humane mental-health treatment while respecting individual rights. We shall see that competing interests operate to create a complex and continually changing picture.

Least Restrictive Alternative As noted earlier, civil commitment rests on presumed dangerousness, a condition that may vary depending on the circumstances. A person may be deemed dangerous if living in an apartment by himself or herself, but not dangerous if living in a residential treatment home and taking prescribed medications every day under medical supervision. The **least restrictive alternative** to freedom is to be provided when treating people with mental disorders and protecting them from harming themselves and others. A number of court rulings require that only those mentally ill patients who cannot be adequately looked after in less restrictive homes be confined in hospitals.[30] In general terms, mental health professionals have to provide the treatment that restricts the patient's liberty to the least possible degree while remaining workable.[31] It is unconstitutional to confine a nondangerous mentally ill patient who is capable of surviving on his or her own or with the help of willing and responsible family or friends.[32] Of course, this principle will have meaning only if society provides suitable residences and treatments, which rarely happens.

Least restrictive alternatives were supposed to be created when the deinstitutionalization movement took hold in the 1970s, but since the virtual cessation of federal funding for community mental health centers and other nonhospital placements in the 1980s, U.S. society has been faced with a growing number of people, usually formerly hospitalized patients, who are no longer dangerous and yet in need of more care than is available outside a hospital. Turkheimer and Parry (1992) argue that an awareness of the scarcity of less

---

[30] *Lake v. Cameron*, 267 F. Supp 155 (D.C. Cir. 1967); *Lessard*, 349 F. Supp. at 1078.
[31] *In Re: Tarpley*, 556 N.E.2d, superseded by 581 N.E.2d 1251 (1991).
[32] *Project Release v. Prevost*, 722 F.2d 960 (2d Cir. 1983).

restrictive alternatives has led to rather perfunctory protection of civil rights (e.g., attorneys may not argue vigorously against commitment) and to commitment of people even when they are not judged dangerous.

Right to Treatment   Another aspect of civil commitment that has come to the attention of the courts is the so-called right to treatment, a principle first articulated by Birnbaum (1960). If a person is deprived of liberty because he or she is mentally ill and is a danger to self or others, is the state not required to provide treatment to alleviate these problems? This important question has been the subject of several court cases since Birnbaum first articulated the issue.

The right to treatment has gained in legal status since the 1960s and was extended to all civilly committed patients in a landmark 1972 case, *Wyatt v. Stickney*.[33] In that case an Alabama federal court ruled that treatment is the only justification for the civil commitment of patients to a state mental hospital. As stated by Judge Frank Johnson, "to deprive any citizen of his or her liberty upon the altruistic theory that the confinement is for humane and therapeutic reasons and then fail to provide adequate treatment violates the very fundamentals of due process." Committed mental patients "have a constitutional right to receive such individual treatment as will give each of them a realistic opportunity to be cured or to improve his or her mental condition." This ruling, upheld on appeal, is frequently cited as ensuring protection of people confined by civil commitment, at least to the extent that the state cannot simply put them away without meeting minimal standards of care. In fact, when mentally retarded patients (as opposed to those judged to be mentally ill) are released from an institution, health officials are not relieved of their constitutional duty to provide reasonable care and safety as well as appropriate training.[34]

The *Wyatt* ruling was significant, for previously the courts had asserted that it was beyond their competence to pass judgment on the care given to mentally ill patients, and they had assumed that mental health professionals possessed special and exclusive knowledge about psychopathology and its treatment. Repeated reports of abuses, however, gradually prodded the U.S. judicial system to rule on what went on within the walls of mental hospitals. The *Wyatt* decision set forth very specific requirements—dayrooms of at least 40 square feet; curtains or screens for privacy in multipatient bedrooms; bedrooms limited to a maximum of five persons; a comfortable bed; one toilet per eight persons; the right of the patient to wear any clothing he or she wishes, provided it is not deemed dangerous; opportunities to interact with members of the opposite sex; and no physical restraints except in emergency situations. Further, to provide care 24 hours a day, 7 days a week, there should be, for every 250 patients, at least 2 psychiatrists, 3 additional physicians, 12 registered nurses, 90 attendants, 4 psychologists, and 7 social workers. When the *Wyatt* action was taken, Alabama state mental facilities averaged 1 physician per 2,000 patients, an extreme situation indeed.[35] Similar protections have been extended to people with mental retardation.[36]

The *Wyatt* ruling may have been weakened by a later Supreme Court decision, *Youngberg v. Romeo*,[37] regarding the treatment of a mentally retarded boy, Nicholas Romeo, who had been placed in physical restraints on occasion to keep him from hurting himself and others. While maintaining that patients have a right to reasonable care and safety, this 1982 decision deferred to the professional judgment of the mental health professionals responsible for the boy: "courts must show deference to the judgment exercised by a qualified professional . . . the decision, if made by a professional, is presumptively valid" (pp. 322,

Civil commitment supposedly requires that the person be dangerous. But in actual practice the decision to commit can be based on a judgment of severe disability, as in the case of some people who are homeless. (Corbis Images.)

---

[33] *Wyatt v. Stickney*, 325 F.Supp. 781 (M.D. Ala. 1971), enforced in 334 F.Supp. 1341 (M.D. Ala. 1971), 344 F.Supp. 373, 379 (M.D. Ala. 1972), aff'd sub nom *Wyatt v. Anderholt*, 503 F.2d 1305 (5th Cir. 1974).

[34] *Thomas S. v. Flaherty*, 902 F.2d 250, cert. denied, 111 S.Ct. 373 (1990).

[35] The underlying assumption is that patients civilly committed to public mental hospitals will receive adequate care, but the evidence for this level of care is weak. Even though the extremely negligent conditions that the *Wyatt* decision remedied in Alabama are seldom found today, it is questionable, argued Morse (1982c), whether forced hospitalization benefits patients. At the very least, however, public mental hospitals can provide shelter, food, protection, and custodial care, which many deinstitutionalized patients lack.

[36] *Feagley v. Waddill*, 868 F.2d 1437 (5th Cir. 1989).

[37] *Youngberg v. Romeo*, 102 S.Ct. 2452 (1982).

323). This decision gives more leeway to mental health professionals than the *Wyatt* ruling did. On the other hand, the 1990 *Thomas S. v. Flaherty* decision held that professional judgment is not the final word when it comes to constitutional protections of mentally retarded patients in public mental hospitals.

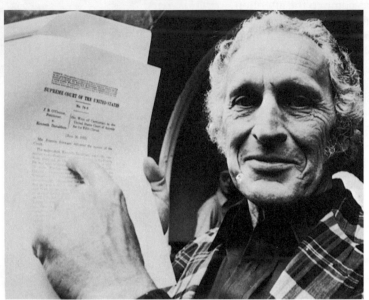

Kenneth Donaldson, displaying a copy of the Supreme Court opinion stating that nondangerous mental patients cannot be confined against their will under civil commitment. (AP/Wide World Photos.)

In a celebrated case, *O'Connor v. Donaldson*,[38] that eventually went to the Supreme Court in 1975, a civilly committed patient sued two state hospital doctors for his release and for monetary damages on the grounds that he had been incarcerated against his will for 14 years without being treated and without being dangerous to himself or to others. In January 1957, at the age of 49, Kenneth Donaldson was committed to the Florida state hospital at Chattahoochee on petition of his father, who felt that his son was delusional. At a brief court hearing a county judge found that Donaldson had paranoid schizophrenia and committed him for "care, maintenance, and treatment." The Florida statute then in effect allowed for such commitment on the usual grounds of mental illness and dangerousness, the latter defined as inability to manage property and to protect oneself from being taken advantage of by others.

In 1971, Donaldson sued Dr. O'Connor, the hospital superintendent, and Dr. Gumanis, a hospital psychiatrist, for release. Evidence presented at the trial in a U.S. District Court in Florida indicated that the hospital staff could have released Donaldson at any time following a determination that he was not a dangerous person. Testimony made it clear that at no time during his hospitalization had Donaldson's conduct posed any real danger to others or to himself. Furthermore, just before his commitment in 1957 he had been earning a living and taking adequate care of himself (and immediately on discharge he secured a job in hotel administration). Nonetheless, O'Connor had repeatedly refused the patient's requests for release, feeling it was his duty to determine whether a committed patient could adapt successfully outside the hospital. His judgment was that Donaldson could not. In deciding the question of dangerousness on the basis of how well the patient could live outside the institution, O'Connor was applying a more restrictive standard than that required by most state laws.

Several responsible people had attempted to obtain Donaldson's release by guaranteeing that they would look after him. In 1963, a halfway house formally requested that Donaldson be released to its care, and between 1964 and 1968 a former college classmate made four separate attempts to have the patient released to his custody. O'Connor refused, saying that the patient could be released only to his parents, who by this time were quite old.

The evidence indicated that Donaldson received only custodial care during his hospitalization. No treatment that could conceivably alleviate his assumed mental illness was undertaken. The milieu therapy that O'Connor claimed Donaldson was undergoing consisted of being kept in a large room with 60 other patients. Donaldson had been denied privileges to stroll around the hospital grounds or even to discuss his case with Dr. O'Connor. O'Connor also regarded as delusional Donaldson's expressed desire to write a book about his hospital experiences (which Donaldson did after his release; the book sold well).

The original trial and a subsequent appeal concluded that Donaldson was not dangerous and had been denied his constitutional right to treatment, based on the Fifth Amendment. Throughout this litigation Donaldson declared that he was neither dangerous nor mentally ill. But, went his claim, even if he were mentally ill, he should be released because he was not receiving treatment.

The Supreme Court ruled on June 26, 1975, that "a State cannot constitutionally confine . . . a nondangerous individual who is capable of surviving safely in freedom by

[38] *O'Connor v. Donaldson*, 95 S.Ct. 2486 (1975).

himself or with the help of willing and responsible family members or friends." In 1977, Donaldson settled for $20,000 from Dr. Gumanis and from the estate of Dr. O'Connor, who had died during the appeals process.

The Supreme Court decision on *O'Connor v. Donaldson* created a stir when it was issued and has since given mental health professionals pause in detaining patients. Although this decision is often cited as yet another affirmation of the right to treatment, the Supreme Court did not, in fact, rule on the constitutionality of this doctrine. Indeed, Chief Justice Warren E. Burger issued some warnings about the right to treatment.

> *Given the present state of medical knowledge regarding abnormal behavior and its treatment, few things would be more fraught with peril than [for] a State's power to protect the mentally ill [to depend on its ability to provide] such treatment as will give them a realistic opportunity to be cured. Nor can I accept the theory that a State may lawfully confine an individual thought to need treatment and justify that deprivation of liberty solely by providing such treatment. Our concepts of due process would not tolerate such a "trade off." (O'Connor v. Donaldson, pp. 588–589)*

The *Donaldson* decision did say that a committed patient's status must be periodically reviewed, for the grounds on which a patient was committed cannot be assumed to continue in effect forever. In other words, people can change while in a mental hospital and may no longer require confinement. This position seems straightforward enough, yet it may still be overlooked. For example, a 1986 court decision involved a woman with mental retardation who had spent her entire adult life in a state institution for the retarded after having been committed at age 15; during her 20 years of confinement she was never given a hearing to reconsider the grounds for the original commitment.[39]

Right to Refuse Treatment   If a committed patient has the right to expect appropriate treatment, since the need for help has resulted in loss of freedom, does he or she have the right to refuse treatment or a particular kind of treatment? The answer is yes, albeit with qualifications.

A state hospital may have adequate staff to provide up-to-date pharmacotherapy as well as group therapy but lack the professional resources to offer individual therapy. Suppose that a patient refuses the available treatments and insists on individual therapy. Would the patient later be able to sue the hospital for not offering the specific services requested? If the patient has the right to refuse certain forms of treatment, how far should the courts go in ensuring this right, remaining at the same time realistic about the state's ability to provide alternatives? When should the judgment of a professional override the wishes of a patient, especially one who is severely psychotic? Are the patient's best interests always served if he or she can veto the plans of those responsible for care (Winick, 1994), especially if refusing to take a therapeutic drug keeps a criminal defendant from being considered competent to stand trial (Winick, 1993) (recall the *Riggins v. Nevada* case discussed earlier)?

The right of committed patients to refuse psychoactive drugs is hotly debated. Significant legal and ethical issues surround the use of psychoactive medications (and such drugs are often the only kind of treatment a patient in a state hospital receives with any regularity). The side effects of most antipsychotic drugs are often aversive to the patient and are sometimes harmful and irreversible in the long run. Moreover, as many as one-third of the patients who take psychoactive drugs may not benefit from them.

Some court decisions illustrate the difficult issues that arise when the right to refuse treatment is debated. In a 1979 decision on some cases in which "unjustified polypharmacy" and "force or intimidation" had allegedly been applied without due consideration for the serious negative side effects of drugs, the judge in a New Jersey federal district court concluded that drugs can actually inhibit recovery and that therefore, except in emergencies, even an involuntarily committed patient can refuse to take them, based on the rights of privacy (First Amendment) and due process (Fourteenth Amendment).[40] The judge

---

[39] *Clark v. Cohen*, 794 F.2d 79, cert. denied, 479 U.S. 962 (1986).
[40] *Rennie v. Klein*, Civil Action No. 77-2624, Federal District Court of New Jersey, 14 September 1979.

ordered that advocates be available in each state mental hospital to help patients exercise the right to refuse treatment and that a listing of all the side effects of the drugs that might be given to the patients be posted in each hospital ward. In a reconsideration of this case, however, the judge stated that the opinion of the health professional must take precedence over the right to refuse treatment when patients are a danger to themselves or to others, in other words, in emergency situations.[41]

The question of the right to refuse medication continues to be the subject of lawsuits on behalf of both involuntary and voluntary mental hospital patients. Decisions on behalf of patients judged incompetent are frequently made by the hospital's professional staff. Although there is inconsistency across jurisdictions and the forensic picture is still developing, there is a trend toward granting even involuntarily committed patients certain rights to refuse psychoactive medication, based on the constitutional protections of freedom from physical invasion, freedom of thought, and the right to privacy.[42] In an extension of the least-restrictive-treatment principle, the court in *United States v. Charters* ruled that the government cannot force antipsychotic drugs on a person only on the supposition that at some future time he or she might become dangerous. Threat to the public safety has to be clear and imminent to justify the risks and restrictions that such medications pose, and it must be shown that less intrusive intervention will not likely reduce impending danger to others. In other words, forcible medication necessarily restricts liberty in addition to whatever physical risks it could bring; there has to be a very good reason to deprive even a committed patient of liberty and privacy via such intrusive measures.

The hands of mental health professionals are not tied, though. For example, it was ruled in a 1987 case that forcing a psychoactive drug on a former hospitalized patient did not violate his constitutional rights because he had been threatening to assassinate the president of the United States, he posed a threat to his own safety, and he could be shown by clear and convincing evidence to be seriously mentally impaired.[43] Decisions of health professionals are, however, subject to judicial review.[44]

Opponents of the right to refuse treatment are concerned that mental hospitals will revert to being warehouses of poorly treated patients. Psychiatrists fear that lawyers and judges will not accept that some people are too mentally ill to be able to make sound judgments about their treatment. In a book on what he calls America's mental health crisis, psychiatrist E. Fuller Torrey asserts that upwards of 90 percent of psychotic patients have no insight into their condition. Believing that they do not need any treatment, they subject themselves and their loved ones to sometimes desperate and frightening situations by refusing medication or other modes of therapy, most of which involve hospitalization (Torrey, 1996).

When someone already hospitalized is believed to be too psychotic to give informed consent about a treatment, mental health law sometimes invokes the doctrine of substituted judgment, the decision that the patient would have made if he or she had been able or competent to make a decision.[45] This principle creates as many problems as it solves. Deciding when a patient is competent to refuse treatment is one of the most controversial topics in the mental health law literature (e.g., Appelbaum & Grisso, 1995; Grisso & Appelbaum, 1995; Winick, 1997).

To complicate matters even further, research findings indicate that most committed patients, although showing impairment in their ability to think and make decisions, nonetheless demonstrate enough legally relevant abilities to be considered competent to participate in treatment decisions. Specifically, they show an ability to state a choice, to understand relevant information, to understand the nature of the situation they are in, and to think reasonably about the information pertaining to their treatment. This is especially so for depressed patients. Furthermore, patients diagnosed with schizophrenia that initially show major cognitive impairments that can interfere with their capacity to make treatment

[41] *Rennie v. Klein*, 720 F.2d 266 (3d Cir. 1983).

[42] *United States v. Charters*, 829 F.2d 479 (1987); *United States v. Watson*, 893 F.2d 970 (1990).

[43] *Dautremont v. Broadlawns Hospital*, 827 F.2d 291 (8th Cir. 1987).

[44] *United States v. Charters*, 863 F.2d 302, cert. denied, 494 U.S. 1016 (1990).

[45] *Guardianship of Weedon*, 565 N.E. 2d 432, 409 Mass. 196 (1991).

decisions for themselves usually improve enough after a few weeks of medication to be able to participate in decisions about their future therapy (Appelbaum & Grisso, 1995; Applebaum et al., 1999).

Law, Free Will, and Ethics   Mental health law experts and social scientists construe voluntariness somewhat differently. Social-science paradigms assign less importance to the concept of free will than does the law, which rests utterly on that idea (Morse, 1992). As psychologists familiar with actual practices in mental hospitals, we are sensitive to the subtle coercion that can operate on hospitalized patients, even those who entered voluntarily (Hoge et al., 1997). A hospital patient is subject to persuasion and pressure to accept the treatment recommendations of professional staff. Although one could argue that this is as it should be, the fact remains that even a "voluntary" and informed decision to take medication or to participate in any other therapy regimen is often (perhaps usually) less than free. The issue thus is more complicated and thorny than mental health law usually considers it to be—and the arguments of the legal profession do not lack for complexity and thorniness.

Rights to Treatment, to Refuse Treatment, and to Be Treated in the Least Restrictive Setting—Can They Be Reconciled?   We have reviewed several legal principles developed over the years that guide the courts and mental health professionals in meeting their constitutional obligations to civilly committed patients. Actions taken to implement one principle may conflict with another, however. The basic question is whether the right to be treated in the least restrictive fashion can be reconciled with both the right to treatment and the right to refuse treatment.

One approach to the conflict between right to treatment and right to refuse treatment is the so-called **advanced directive**, a legal document modeled after living wills. An advanced directive is composed by people who are legally competent and able to make decisions and specify how they want to be treated in the event that, sometime in the future, they need psychological or medical therapy but are mentally unfit to make decisions bearing on their therapy. The document may state what procedures the person consents to or refuses. Or the document may name another person to make such decisions. Many states now have laws that make such documents legally binding.

The use of advanced directives may enable people who are psychologically troubled but still competent to have more power over their future health care. But can such people really know what they will want or need if and when they become legally incompetent in the future? We can expect the debates on this issue of patient autonomy to continue.

Deinstitutionalization, Civil Liberties, and Mental Health

The cumulative impact of court rulings such as *Wyatt v. Stickney* and *O'Connor v. Donaldson* was to put mental health professionals on notice that they must be more careful about keeping people in mental hospitals against their will and that they must attend more to the specific treatment needs of committed patients. Pressure was placed on state governments to upgrade the quality of care in mental hospitals. In view of the abuses that have been documented in hospital care, these are surely encouraging changes. But the picture is not all that rosy. For judges to declare that patient care must meet certain minimal standards does not automatically translate into realization of that praiseworthy goal. Money is not in unlimited supply, and the care of mentally ill individuals has not been one of government's high priorities.

Beginning in the 1960s, many states embarked on a policy referred to as *deinstitutionalization*, discharging as many patients as possible from mental hospitals and discouraging admissions. Civil commitment is more difficult to achieve now than it was in the 1950s and 1960s, and committed patients are able, with the help of civil rights–minded lawyers, to refuse much of the treatment made available to them in the hospital. The population of state mental hospitals peaked in the 1950s at almost half a million patients; by the late 1990s the population had dropped to around 70,000. The maxim is now "Treat them in the community," the assumption being that virtually anything is preferable to institutionalization.

But what is this community that formerly hospitalized patients are supposed to find more helpful to them on discharge? Facilities outside hospitals are not prepared to cope with the influx of these patients. Some effective programs were described in Chapter 11, but these are very much the exception, not the rule. The state of affairs in many large urban areas is an unrelenting crisis for the hundreds of thousands of chronically ill patients who have been released since the 1960s without community services to help them. Many patients discharged from hospitals are eligible for benefits from the Veterans Administration and for Social Security Disability Insurance, but a large number are not receiving this assistance. Homeless persons do not have fixed addresses and need help in establishing eligibility and residency for the purpose of receiving benefits. The state of homelessness undoubtedly exacerbates the emotional suffering of formerly hospitalized patients. Mentally ill persons are an especially defenseless segment of the homeless population.

Deinstitutionalization may be a misnomer. *Transinstitutionalization* may be more apt, for declines in the census of mental hospitals have occasioned increases in the presence of mentally ill people in nursing homes, the mental health departments of nonpsychiatric hospitals, and prisons (Cloud, 1999; Kiesler, 1991), and these settings are by and large not equipped to handle the particular needs of mentally ill patients.

Indeed, jails and prisons have become the new "hospitals" for the mentally ill in the twenty-first century. A study by the Justice Department found that 16.2 percent of the population in prison or jails is seriously mentally ill (BJS, 1999). The Los Angeles County Jail may now be the largest mental "hospital" facility, with 1,500 inmates believed to have a serious mental illness (CAPT, 2000). Have we come that far from the days of deplorable institutions that we discussed in Chapter 1? Clearly, we need to do more.

> *"It is deplorable and outrageous that this state's prisons appear to have become a repository for a great number of its mentally ill citizens. Persons who, with psychiatric care, could fit well into society, are instead locked away, to become wards of the state's penal system. Then, in a tragically ironic twist, they may be confined in conditions that nurture, rather than abate, their psychoses."* Judge William Wayne Justice, Ruiz v. Johnson, 37 F. Supp.2d 855 (S.D. Texas, 1999).

Police officers are now called on to do the work of mental health professionals. They are often the first to come in contact with a mentally ill person and can make decisions as to whether a person should be taken to a hospital or jail. In several cities, mental health professionals have teamed up with police officers to form mobile crisis units (Lamb, Weinberger, & DeCuir, 2002). These units consist of trained mental health professionals who work in conjunction with local police to find the best option for a mentally ill person in the community. Because police officers are increasingly called on to work with mentally ill individuals, communities are recognizing the need for the police to receive the proper training. New laws passed in the past 5 years, including America's Law Enforcement and Mental Health Project Act (2000) and the later extension of this, called the Mentally Ill Offender Treatment and Crime Reduction Act (2004), provide funding for such training. These laws also provide funds to set up what are referred to as mental health courts in local communities. The idea is that mentally ill individuals who commit a crime may be better served by courts that can monitor treatment availability and adherence. Time will tell if these mental health courts do a better job of handling mentally ill persons who end up in the criminal justice system (Steadman, Davidson, & Brown, 2001).

The approach of building partnerships between mental health professionals and law enforcement led to the creation of the Consensus Project (www.consensusproject.org). The Council of State Governments coordinated a collaboration between criminal justice, mental health, and local and national lawmakers. A report entitled *Criminal Justice/Mental Health Consensus Project* was released in 2002, and it has been influential in increasing awareness of the large numbers of mentally ill people who are now housed in jails rather than in treatment facilities. The report outlines a number of policy ideas, all aimed at increasing cooperation between mental health and criminal justice and ultimately benefiting those with mental illness who are in the criminal justice system or who are at risk of becoming involved (e.g., sent to jail rather than treatment following a public outburst that reflects an exacerbation of illness).

Quick Summary

The legal standard for competency to stand trial requires that the accused understand the charges against him or her and can assist his or her attorney in the defense. If someone is judged incompetent to stand trial, the person receives treatment to restore competence and then returns to face the charges. The *Jackson* case specified that the pretrial period can be no longer than it takes to determine whether a person will ever become competent to stand trial. The use of medication to restore competency to stand trial can be used in limited circumstances.

The U.S. Supreme Court has ruled that it is unconstitutional (a violation of the Eighth Amendment, which prohibits cruel and unusual punishment) to execute people who are deemed legally insane or mentally retarded. Individual states can determine what constitutes mental retardation.

A person can be civilly committed to a hospital against his or her wishes if the person is mentally ill and a danger to self or others. Formal commitment requires a court order; informal commitment does not. Mentally ill patients who are not substance abusers are no more likely to engage in violence than are non-mentally ill individuals who are not substance abusers.

Early studies on the prediction of dangerousness had a number of flaws. Later research has shown that repeated acts of violence, a single serious violent act, being on the brink of violence, and medication noncompliance can maximize accuracy in predictions. Some states allow for sex offenders to be deemed mentally ill and civilly committed on release from prison.

Court cases have tried to balance individual's rights with the rights to protect society. The least restrictive alternative to freedom is to be provided when treating people with mental disorders and protecting them from harming themselves and others. A series of court cases have generally supported the notion that those individuals committed to a hospital have the right to receive treatment. Patients have the right to refuse treatment as well, except when doing so poses a danger to self or others.

The advanced directive is a legal document composed by people who are legally competent and able to make decisions and specify how they want to be treated in the event that, sometime in the future, they need psychological or medical therapy but are mentally unfit to make decisions bearing on their therapy.

Beginning in the 1960s, large numbers of patients were released from hospitals in what has been called deinstitutionalization. Unfortunately, there are not enough treatment options available in the community. Jails and prisons are now the new "hospitals" for mentally ill persons. Police officers are called on to do the work once reserved for mental health professionals. Partnerships between police, courts, and community mental health providers are promising for helping individuals with mental illness.

Check Your Knowledge 17.3

True or false?
1. Schizophrenia patients who have delusions are more likely to be violent than those patients without delusions.
2. Past violence is a predictor of future violence.
3. Court decisions have determined that hospitalized patients do not have a right to treatment unless they are dangerous.
4. Patients can refuse treatment if they are found incompetent to stand trial after being charged with a nonviolent offense.

Ethical Dilemmas in Therapy and Research

In this textbook we have examined a variety of theories and a multitude of data focusing on *what is* and *what is thought to be*. Ethics and values, often embodied in laws, are a different order of discussion. They concern *what ought to be*, having sometimes little to do with *what is*. It is extremely important to recognize the difference.

Within a given scientific paradigm we are able to examine what we believe is reality. As the study of philosophy and ethics reveals, however, the statements people have made for thousands of years about what *should be* are another matter. The Ten Commandments are such statements. They are prescriptions and proscriptions about human conduct. For example, the Eighth Commandment, Thou shalt not steal, in no way describes human conduct, for stealing is not uncommon. It is, instead, a pronouncement of an ideal to which people should aspire. The integrity of an ethical code that proscribes stealing does not depend on any evidence concerning the percentage of people who steal. Morals and data are two separate realms of discourse.

The legal trends reviewed thus far in this chapter place limits on the activities of mental health professionals. These legal constraints are important, for laws are one of society's strongest means of encouraging all of us to behave in certain ways. Mental health professionals also have professional and ethical constraints. All professional groups promulgate "shoulds" and "should nots," and by guidelines and mandates they limit to some degree what therapists and researchers should do with their patients, clients, and research participants. Courts as well have ruled on some of these questions. Most of the time what we believe is unethical is also illegal, but sometimes existing laws are in conflict with our moral sense of right and wrong. The American Psychological Association publishes a *Code of Ethics* that includes the ethical standards that constrain research and practice in psychology (APA, 2002). We examine now the ethics of making psychological inquiries and interventions into the lives of other human beings.

Ethical Restraints on Research

Basic to the nature of science is that what can be done will usually be attempted. The most reprehensible ethical insensitivity was evidenced in the brutal experiments conducted by German physicians on concentration camp prisoners during World War II. One experiment,

Defendants at the Nuremberg trials. (Corbis-Bettmann.)

for example, investigated how long people lived when their heads were bashed repeatedly with a heavy stick. Even if important information might be obtained from this kind of experiment, such actions violate our sense of decency and morality. The Nuremberg Trials, conducted by the Allies following the war, brought these and other barbarisms to light and meted out severe punishment to some of the soldiers, physicians, and Nazi officials who had engaged in or contributed to such actions, even when they claimed that they had merely been following orders.

It would be reassuring to be able to say that such gross violations of human decency take place only during incredible and cruel epochs such as the Third Reich, but unfortunately this is not the case. Spurred on by a blind enthusiasm for their work, researchers in the United States and other countries have sometimes dealt with human participants in reproachable ways.

Henry K. Beecher, a research professor at Harvard Medical School, surveyed medical research since 1945 and found that "many of the patients [used as participants in experiments] never had the risk satisfactorily explained to them, and ... further hundreds have not known that they were the participants of an experiment although grave consequences have been suffered as the direct result" (Beecher, 1966, p. 1354). One experiment compared penicillin with a placebo as a treatment to prevent rheumatic fever. Even though penicillin had already been acknowledged as the drug of choice for people with a streptococcal respiratory infection in order to protect them from later contracting rheumatic fever, placebos were administered to 109 service personnel without their knowledge or permission. More participants received penicillin than received the placebo, but three members of the control group contracted serious illnesses—two had rheumatic fever and one acute nephritis, a kidney disease. None of those who had received penicillin contracted such illnesses.

Half a century later, in January 1994, spurred on by Eileen Welsome, a journalist who won a Pulitzer Prize for her investigative reporting on the issue, the United States Energy Department began to publicize numerous experiments conducted in the 1950s through the 1970s that had exposed hundreds of people—usually without their informed consent or prior knowledge—to harmful doses of radiation. Particular concern was expressed because the overwhelming majority were people of low socioeconomic status, members of ethnic minorities, people with mental retardation, nursing home patients, or prisoners. The scientists, for the most part supported in their research with federal funds, understood that the risks were great even though relatively little was known about the harmful effects of radiation at the time. Some of these experiments involved giving women in the third trimester of pregnancy a radioactive tonic to determine safe levels of exposure and irradiating the testicles of prisoners to find out the degree of radiation that service personnel could endure without negative effects on sperm production. That these experiments took place many years after the Nuremberg Trials is particularly troubling.

The training of scientists equips them splendidly to pose interesting questions, sometimes even important ones, and to design research that is as free as possible of confounds. They have no special qualifications, however, for deciding whether a particular line of inquiry that involves humankind should be followed. Society needs knowledge, and a scientist has a right in a democracy to seek that knowledge. However, the ordinary citizens employed as participants in experiments must be protected from unnecessary harm, risk, humiliation, and invasion of privacy.

Several international codes of ethics pertain to the conduct of scientific research—the Nuremberg Code formulated in 1947 in the aftermath of the Nazi war-crime trials, the 1964 Declaration of Helsinki, and statements from the British Medical Research Council. In 1974, the U.S. Department of Health, Education, and Welfare began to issue guidelines and regulations governing scientific research that employs human and animal participants. In addition, a blue-ribbon panel, the National Commission for the Protection of Human Subjects of Biomedical and Behavioral Research, issued a report in 1978 that arose from hearings and inquiries into restrictions that the U.S. government might impose on research performed with patients in psychiatric institutions, prisoners, and children. These various codes and principles are continually being reevaluated and revised as new challenges are posed to the research community.

For the past 30 years the proposals of behavioral researchers, many of whom conduct experiments related to psychopathology and therapy, have been reviewed for safety and general ethical propriety by institutional review boards in hospitals, universities, and research institutes. Such committees—and this is significant—comprise not only behavioral scientists but also citizens from the community, lawyers, students, and specialists in a variety of disciplines, such as professors of English, history, and comparative religion. They are able to block any research proposal or require questionable aspects to be modified if in their collective judgment the research would put participants at too great a risk. Such committees also now pass judgment on the scientific merits of proposals, the rationale being that it is not ethical to recruit participants for studies that will not yield valid data (Capron, 1999; Rosenthal, 1995). In 2000, universities and other research institutions were required to begin certifying researchers on the basis of special coursework and examinations, to make it less likely that research participants will be put at risk. Researchers who receive funds from federal agencies, such as the National Institute of Mental Health, are also required to receive specialized training in research ethics.

Changes in the Declaration of Helsinki are being debated, spurred on by two recent developments in biomedical research. The first is an increase in research sponsored by for-profit organizations such as pharmaceutical companies. Faced with fierce competition and marketplace pressures to maximize profits, such companies may push for research that would not be approved by human subjects committees in nonprofit organizations such as universities. The globalization of research is a second factor in the possible attenuation of protection of human participants. Developing countries are particularly eager for partnerships in research and do not always have the same historical commitment to individual informed consent and safety that is prevalent in more industrialized and democratic countries. A potential danger is that utilitarian standards—will the research yield generally useful results?—are becoming more important than the focus of the past half century on the rights and safety of individual research participants.

In reaction to some ethical lapses in hospital-based research with mentally ill patients, the National Bioethics Advisory Commission recommends special precautions to ensure that research participants with mental illness fully understand the risks and benefits of any research they are asked to participate in and that particular care be taken to make certain that they can decline or withdraw from research without feeling coerced. Specifically, instead of simply allowing a guardian or family member to make the decision for the patient, the commission proposes that a health professional who has nothing to do with the particular study make a judgment on whether a given patient can give informed consent. The commission recommends also that if a guardian is allowed to give consent on behalf of a patient judged incompetent to do so, the guardian's own ability to give consent also be evaluated (Capron, 1999).

Informed Consent

The recent concern about conducting research with people with mental disorders underscores the all-important concept of **informed consent**. The investigator must provide enough information to enable people to judge whether they want to accept any risks inherent in being a participant in a research study. Prospective participants must be legally capable of giving consent, and there must be no deceit or coercion in obtaining it. For example, a psychologist might want to determine whether imagery helps college students associate one word with another. One group of students might be asked to associate pairs of words in their minds by generating a fanciful image connecting the two, such as a cat riding on a bicycle. Current standard operating procedure allows prospective participants to decide that the experiment is likely to be boring and to decline to participate. Furthermore, if people begin to participate as research participants, they are free to withdraw from the experiment at any time without fear of penalty.

Paired-associates research such as that just described is relatively innocuous, but what if the experiment poses real risks, such as ingesting a drug, or what if a patient with schizophrenia whose condition has improved by taking a drug is withdrawn from it so that the investigator can assess the effects of "drug washout"? Or what if the prospective participant is a child with mental retardation, unable to understand fully what is being asked? Such a person may not feel free or even be able to refuse participation.

As suggested earlier (Capron, 1999), problems with informed consent can be especially pronounced in clinical settings where there is a question of whether patients understand the nature of antipsychotic medication. Irwin et al. (1985) found that although most patients said they understood the benefits and side effects of their drugs, only a quarter of them could actually demonstrate such understanding when queried specifically. The authors concluded that simply reading information to hospitalized patients—especially the more severely ill ones—is no guarantee that they fully comprehend; therefore, informed consent cannot be said to have been obtained. The report of the National Bioethics Advisory Commission pointed to many published experiments involving mental patients in which no effort was made to determine whether the research participants had the decision-making capacity to give informed consent (Capron, 1999).

Still, as with the right to refuse treatment, there is recognition that being judged mentally ill—more specifically, being diagnosed with schizophrenia and being hospitalized—does not necessarily mean being incapable of giving informed consent (Appelbaum & Gutheil, 1991). An experiment by Grisso and Appelbaum (1991) found that, although patients with schizophrenia on average understood issues relating to treatment involving medication less well than did nonpsychiatric patients, there was a wide range of understanding among the patients; some showed as good understanding as did nonpsychiatric patients. In addition, although patients with schizophrenia may do more poorly than nonpatients on tests designed to assess decision-making skills, patients can give informed consent if a more detailed procedure describing a study is included—for example, one that describes what they will be asked to do and what they will see and explains that their participation is voluntary and that it in no way will impact their treatment (Carpenter et al., 2000; Wirshing et al., 1998).

The issue of informed consent is also of concern to researchers and clinicians who work with patients with Alzheimer's disease. Like the work with schizophrenia, having an Alzheimer's diagnosis does not necessarily mean a person cannot provide informed consent (Marson, Huthwaite, & Hupert, 2004). Measures have been developed to assess capacity for consent in this population, and this will continue to be an area of active research as the number of people over age 65 continues to increase (Marson, 2001).

These results point to the importance of examining each person individually for ability to give informed consent, rather than assuming that a person is unable to do so by virtue of being hospitalized for schizophrenia or Alzheimer's disease. Thus, although professional judgment is required, and may therefore be erroneous, being mentally ill will not necessarily mean that a patient cannot give informed consent.

Confidentiality and Privileged Communication

When individuals consult a psychiatrist or clinical psychologist, they are assured by professional ethics codes that what goes on in the session will remain confidential. **Confidentiality** means that nothing will be revealed to a third party, except only to other professionals and those intimately involved in the treatment, such as a nurse or medical secretary.

A **privileged communication** goes even further. It is communication between parties in a confidential relationship that is protected by law. The recipient of such a communication cannot legally be compelled to disclose it as a witness. The right of privileged communication is a major exception to the access courts have to evidence in judicial proceedings. Society believes that in the long term the interests of people are best served if communications to a spouse and to certain professionals remain off limits to the prying eyes and ears of the police, judges, and prosecutors. The privilege applies to such relationships as those between husband and wife, physician and patient, pastor and penitent, attorney and client, and psychologist and patient. The legal expression is that the patient or client "holds the privilege," which means that only he or she may release the other person to disclose confidential information in a legal proceeding.

There are important limits to a client's right of privileged communication, however. For example, according to the current California psychology licensing law (similar elements are present in other state laws), this right is eliminated for any of the following reasons.

- The client has accused the therapist of malpractice. In such a case, the therapist can divulge information about the therapy in order to defend himself or herself in any legal action initiated by the client.
- The client is less than 16 years old and the therapist has reason to believe that the child has been a victim of a crime such as child abuse. In fact, the psychologist is required to report to the police or to a child welfare agency within 36 hours any suspicion he or she has that the child client has been physically abused, including any suspicion of sexual molestation.
- The client initiated therapy in hopes of evading the law for having committed a crime or for planning to do so.
- The therapist judges that the client is a danger to self or to others and disclosure of information is necessary to ward off such danger (recall Focus on Discovery 17.4 on *Tarasoff*).

Who Is the Client or Patient?

Is it always clear to the clinician who the client is? In private therapy, when an adult pays a clinician a fee for help with a personal problem that has nothing to do with the legal system, the consulting individual is clearly the client. But an individual may be seen by a clinician for an evaluation of his or her competency to stand trial, or the clinician may be hired by an individual's family to assist in civil commitment proceedings. Perhaps the clinician is employed by a state mental hospital as a regular staff member and sees a particular patient about problems in controlling aggressive impulses.

It should be clear, although it sometimes is not, that in these instances the clinician is serving more than one client. In addition to the patient, he or she serves the family or the state, and it is incumbent on the mental health professional to inform the patient that this is so. This dual allegiance does not necessarily indicate that the patient's own interests will be sacrificed, but it does mean that discussions will not inevitably remain secret and that the clinician may in the future act in a way that displeases or even seriously compromises the interests of the individual.

Choice of Goals

Ideally the client sets the goals for therapy, but in practice it is naive to assume that some are not imposed by the therapist and may even go against the wishes of the client.

Setting goals may be particularly complex in family and couples therapy (Margolin, 1982). If several people are clients simultaneously—inevitable in family treatment—an intervention that benefits one or more individuals may well work to the disadvantage of one or more of the others in therapy. This can happen if one partner in couples therapy really wants to end the relationship, but the other sees the therapy as a way to save it. Because people often do not openly express their real concerns and wishes at the very beginning of therapy, the therapist can already be deeply enmeshed in their lives before learning that the two partners have conflicting goals. For this reason, among others, couples and family therapy is particularly challenging.

Sometimes the values held by therapists are subtle and difficult to discern. In an interesting examination of ethics in psychoanalysis and in behavior therapy, Paul Wachtel, whose ideas about psychotherapy integration we examined in the preceding chapter, writes of "the ethics of the lonely struggle" that, as a psychoanalyst himself, he sees as an unacknowledged characteristic of the insight therapies. He criticizes both psychoanalysis and the humanistic-existential approaches for an overemphasis on the need for people to change from within rather than being assisted, even directed, in their efforts to change in the manner customary in cognitive behavior therapy. By concentrating on people gaining their own insights and making behavioral changes pretty much on their own and by discouraging therapists from influencing their patients by directly teaching them new skills, insight-oriented therapists unwittingly teach an ethic of aloneness devoid of social support. He questions whether this is a proper message to convey to patients and to society-at-large. As he puts it,

> many [insight] therapists who criticize behavior therapy as an agent of cultural norms are themselves upholding one of the basic tenets of our capitalistic society, when they stress change based solely on autonomous action and deride the need for direct assistance from others. . . . It is, after all, just as human to be able to turn to others as it is to stand alone. (Wachtel, 1997, pp. 289–290)

The Ethical and Legal Dimensions of Recovered Memories

Perhaps one of the more difficult ethical and legal issues facing today's therapists involves the scientific controversies raised by so-called recovered memories (p. 176). The growing debate over the validity and reliability of reports of child abuse that surface when adults are in therapy has created considerable ethical and legal concern. One of the most important of the guidelines issued by the American Psychiatric Association (1993) stipulates that therapists should remain neutral when a patient reports abuse. Because a given symptom—for example, avoidance of sexual contact—may have many possible origins, it is not ethical according to the APA to attribute such symptoms to repressed memories of childhood sexual abuse without corroborating evidence.

A problem with this laudable stance is that some experts on sexual dysfunctions recommend that therapists inquire into possible sexual abuse whenever patients, especially women, report aversions to or disinterest in sex. The dilemma, then, is that some therapists who are predisposed by their theoretical leanings to believe that sexual abuse underlies a wide range of psychological disorders may be more likely to see it in a patient, perhaps even when none has occurred. By the same token, other therapists who do not believe that traumatic memories are often repressed may overlook childhood sexual abuse when it has taken place.

An incorrect diagnosis of recovered memories of sexual abuse can harm not only the patient but also the persons whom the patient accuses of having molested him or her years earlier. Courts in some jurisdictions have held that in addition to their duty to their patients, therapists may have a duty to those wrongly accused of abuse as a result of revelations during psychotherapy.[46]

The statute of limitations has been extended, allowing those who believe they were abused as children to file suit 20 or more years after the abuse purportedly occurred. However, there has been a backlash against these kinds of lawsuits as accused parents and others (e.g., clergy, youth leaders, and other professionals in positions of trust with children and adolescents) have begun to deny such charges vigorously, and some patients have recanted their allegations. This turn of events has resulted in lawsuits being filed against therapists both by the accused parties and by the patients (MacNamara, 1993).

One of the best-known legal incidents concerned Gary Romona, a man who claimed that an irresponsible therapist had implanted false memories into his adult daughter's mind. The daughter sued her father for allegedly having molested her when she was a child, but the father sued her therapist for having allegedly planted this erroneous idea into his daughter's mind. The father won a nearly half-million-dollar judgment (Kramer, 1995), at which point the daughter's suit against her father was dismissed. It is estimated that thousands of parents and other third parties have either already filed or plan to file lawsuits against therapists (Lazo, 1995). In addition to possible therapist bias, the concern in these lawsuits is with particular treatments that may increase susceptibility to suggestion, such as hypnosis and sodium amytal (truth serum).

It is not clear, however, whether such lawsuits will be allowed to go forward in the future. In a 1999 case in California, a parent falsely accused of molesting a child based on recovered memories elicited during therapy was not allowed to sue the therapist. The court ruled that a therapist must be free to act solely in the interests of the client and can be sued only by the client for negligent diagnosis or treatment. A therapist, the court said, is entitled to examine the possibility of past sexual abuse and should not be inhibited by the possibility of a suit by the alleged abuser.

With the scientific status of the validity of recovered memories very much in dispute, legal scholars as well as professional associations advise extreme caution in dealing with the issue. The danger of false positives—concluding that there was abuse when there wasn't—is as serious a matter as the danger of false negatives—concluding that there was no abuse when there was.

Quick Summary

Ethical restraints on research are necessary to avoid the abuses that have occurred in the past. Since the Nuremberg Codes of 1947, a number of ethical codes regarding psychological research have been developed. Research must be approved for safety and ethics by an institutional review board. Universities and other research institutions, as well as federal grant funding agencies, require that researchers receive specialized training and certification in research ethics, on the basis of special coursework and examinations, to make it less likely that research participants will be put at risk.

Special precautions must be taken to ensure that research participants with mental illness fully understand the risks and benefits of any research they are asked to participate in and that particular care be taken to make certain that they can decline or withdraw from research without feeling coerced. Informed consent procedures must include enough information about the research so that participants know about the risks and feel free to withdraw without penalty.

In therapy sessions, patients have the right to keep what is discussed confidential (can't be disclosed to a third party), and this discussion is considered a privileged communication (information in confidential relationship protected by law). However, confidentiality and the privileged communication can be broken if an individual is a danger to self or others, is suing a therapist for malpractice, is a child under 16 who has been the victim of a crime or abuse, or is trying to evade the law for a crime committed or planned.

The issue of recovered memories is filled with ethical dilemmas. The danger of concluding that there was abuse when there wasn't is as serious as concluding that there was no abuse when there was.

[46] See, for example, *Montoya v. Bebensee*, 761 P.2d 285 (Colo. Ct. App. 1988); *Peterson v. Walentiny*, No. 93-C-399-K (N.D. Okla., Jan. 6, 1995) (denying motion for summary judgment); but see *Bird v. W.C.W.*, 868 S.W. 2d 767 (Tex.1994). More recent cases include *Card v. Blakeslee*, 937 P.2d 846 (Colo. Ct. App. 1991) and *Althaus v. Cohen*, 710 A2d 1147 (Pa. Super. Ct. 1998).

Concluding Comment

An underlying theme of this book concerns the nature of knowledge. How do we decide that we understand a phenomenon? The rules of science that govern our definition of and search for knowledge require theories that can be tested, studies that can be replicated, and data that are public. This final chapter demonstrates again something emphasized at the very beginning of this book, namely, that the mental health professionals who conduct research and provide treatment are only human beings. They suffer from the same foibles that sometimes plague nonspecialists. They occasionally act with a certainty their evidence does not justify, and they sometimes fail to anticipate the moral and legal consequences of the ways in which they conduct research and apply the tentative findings of their young discipline. When society acts with great certainty on the basis of expert scientific opinion, particularly when that opinion denies to an individual the rights and respect accorded others, it may be well to let Szasz (1963) remind us that Sir Thomas Browne, a distinguished English physician, testified in an English court of law in 1664 that witches did indeed exist, "as everyone knew."

Despite these cautions, the field of abnormal psychology has made great strides. We know more about the causes and descriptions of mental illness than ever before. We are honing in on the development of effective treatments that last and do not have unpleasant side effects. To be sure, we have a long way to go, but this is an exciting time to be conducting research on psychopathology, and we hope that the students who have read this book will find their imaginations captured by the many issues and questions in this field and decide to make one of the mental health professions their career.

Summary

- Some civil liberties are rather routinely set aside when mental health professionals and the courts judge that mental illness has played a decisive role in determining an individual's behavior. This may occur through criminal or civil commitment.

- Criminal commitment sends a person to a hospital either before a trial for an alleged crime, because the person is deemed incompetent to stand trial, or after an acquittal by reason of insanity.

- Several landmark cases and principles in law address the conditions under which a person who has committed a crime might be excused from legal responsibility for it—that is, not guilty by reason of insanity. These involve the presence of an irresistible impulse, the notion that some people may not be able to distinguish between right and wrong (the M'Naghten rule), and the principle that a person should not be held criminally responsible if his or her unlawful act is the product of mental disease or mental defect (the Durham principle). The Insanity Defense Reform Act of 1984 made it harder for accused criminals to argue insanity as an excusing condition.

- Today, guilty but mentally ill, is in use in a number of states. This emergent legal doctrine reflects an uneasiness in legal and mental health circles about not holding people ascriptively responsible for crimes for which they are descriptively responsible.

- There is an important difference between mental illness and insanity. The latter is a legal concept. A person can be diagnosed as mentally ill and yet be deemed sane enough both to stand trial and to be found guilty of a crime.

- A person who is considered mentally ill and dangerous to self and to others, although he or she has not broken a law, can be civilly committed to an institution or be allowed to live outside of a hospital but only under supervision and with restrictions placed on his or her activities.

- Recent court rulings have provided greater protection to all committed mental patients, particularly those under civil commitment. They have the right to written notification, to counsel, to a jury decision concerning their commitment, and to Fifth Amendment protection against self-incrimination; the right to the least restrictive treatment setting; the right to be treated; and in most circumstances, the right to refuse treatment, particularly any procedure that entails considerable risk. However, there is a trend toward preventive detention when, for example, convicted sexual predators are about to be released from prison with every indication that they will harm others again.

- Ethical issues concerning research include restraints on what kinds of research are allowable and the duty of scientists to obtain informed consent from prospective human participants.

- In the area of therapy, ethical issues concern the right of clients to confidentiality, the question of who is the client (e.g., an individual or the state mental hospital that is paying the clinician), and the question of who sets the therapy goals.

- Diagnosis of sexual abuse in childhood based on so-called recovered memories has also presented ethical problems, as well as legal dilemmas, for therapists.

Answers to Check Your Knowledge Questions

17.1 1. d; 2. a; 3. e; 4. b; 5. c

17.2 1. F; 2. T; 3. T

17.3 1. F; 2. T; 3. F; 4. T

Key Terms

advanced directive
American Law institute guidelines
ascriptive responsibility
civil commitment
competency to stand trial

confidentiality
criminal commitment
descriptive responsibility
Durham test
guilty but mentally ill (GBMI)

in absentia
informed consent
insanity defense
irresistible impulse
least restrictive alternative

M'Naghten rule
not guilty by reason of insanity
    (NGRI)
outpatient commitment
privileged communication

Glossary

abnormal behavior. Patterns of emotion, thought, and action deemed pathological for one or more of the following reasons: infrequent occurrence, violation of norms, personal distress, disability or dysfunction, and unexpectedness.

acute stress disorder. A short-lived anxiety reaction to a traumatic event; if it lasts more than a month, it is diagnosed as posttraumatic stress disorder.

addiction. See *substance dependence.*

adoptees method. Research method that studies children who were adopted and reared completely apart from their abnormal parents, thereby eliminating the influence of being raised by disordered parents.

adrenal glands. Two small areas of tissue located just above the kidneys. The inner core of each gland, the medulla, secretes epinephrine and norepinephrine; the outer cortex secretes cortisol and other steroid hormones.

adrenaline. See *epinephrine.*

advanced directive. Legal document in which an individual—before becoming incapable of making such decisions—prescribes and proscribes certain courses of action to be taken to preserve his or her health or terminate life support.

affect. A subjective feeling or emotional tone often accompanied by bodily expressions noticeable to others.

age effects. The consequences of being a given chronological age. Compare *cohort effects.*

agonist. A drug that stimulates receptors normally specific to a particular neurotransmitter.

agoraphobia. Literally, fear of the marketplace. Fear of being in crowded or open places. Anxiety about situations in which it would be embarrassing or difficult to escape if panic symptoms occurred; most commonly diagnosed in some individuals with panic disorder.

AIDS (acquired immunodeficiency syndrome). A fatal disease transmitted by transfer of the human immunodeficiency virus, usually during sexual relations or by using needles previously infected by an HIV-positive person; it compromises the immune system to such a degree that the person ultimately dies from one of any number of infections.

allele. Any of the various forms in which a particular gene is found.

allostatic load. The physiological burden of high levels of stress hormones such as cortisol; may lead to disease susceptibility because of altered immune system functioning.

alogia. A negative symptom in schizophrenia, marked by poverty of speech and of speech content.

alternate-form reliability. See *reliability.*

altruistic suicide. As defined by Durkheim, self-annihilation that the person feels will serve a social purpose, such as the self-immolations practiced by Buddhist monks during the Vietnam War.

Alzheimer's disease. A dementia involving a progressive atrophy of cortical tissue and marked by memory impairment, intellectual deterioration, and, in more extreme cases, involuntary movements of limbs, occasional convulsions, and psychotic behavior. See also *plaques* and *neurofibrillary tangles.*

American Law Institute guidelines. Rules proposing that insanity is a legitimate defense plea if during criminal conduct, an individual could not judge right from wrong or control his or her behavior as required by law. Repetitive criminal acts are disavowed as a sole criterion. Compare *M'Naghten rule* and *irresistible impulse.*

amino acid. One of a large class of organic compounds important as the building blocks of proteins.

amnesia. Total or partial loss of memory that can be associated with a dissociative disorder, brain damage, or hypnosis.

amphetamines. A group of stimulating drugs that produce heightened levels of energy and, in large doses, nervousness, sleeplessness, and paranoid delusions.

amygdala. A subcortical structure of the temporal lobe involved in attention to emotionally salient stimuli and memory of emotionally relevant events.

anal stage. In psychoanalytic theory, the second psychosexual stage, which occurs during the second year of life when the anus is considered the principal erogenous zone.

analogue experiment. An experimental study of a phenomenon different from but related to the actual interests of the investigator; for example, animal research used to study human disorders, or research on mild symptoms used as a bridge to clinical disorders.

analytical psychology. A variation of Freud's psychoanalysis introduced by Carl Jung, focusing less on biological drives and more on factors such as self-fulfillment, collective unconscious, and religious symbolism.

anesthesia. An impairment or loss of sensation, usually of touch but sometimes of the other senses, that is often part of conversion disorder.

anger-in theory. The view that psychophysiological disorders, such as essential hypertension, arise from a person's not expressing anger or resentment.

angina pectoris. See *coronary heart disease.*

anhedonia. A negative symptom in schizophrenia or a symptom in depression in which the individual is unable to feel pleasure.

anomic suicide. As defined by Durkheim, self-annihilation triggered by a person's inability to cope with sudden and unfavorable change in a social situation.

anorexia nervosa. A disorder in which a person refuses to maintain normal weight, has an intense fear of becoming obese, and feels fat even when emaciated.

Antabuse (trade name for disulfiram). A drug that makes the drinking of alcohol produce nausea and other unpleasant effects.

antagonist. A drug that dampens the effect of a neurotransmitter on its receptors; for example, many dopamine antagonists block dopamine receptors.

anterior cingulate. In the subcortical region of the brain, the anterior portion of the cingulate gyrus, stretching about the corpus callosum.

antidepressant. Any drug that alleviates depression; also widely used to treat anxiety disorders.

antipsychotic drugs. Psychoactive drugs, such as Thorazine, that reduce psychotic symptoms but have long-term side effects resembling symptoms of neurological diseases.

antisocial personality disorder. Personality disorder defined by the absence of concern for others' feelings or social norms, a pervasive pattern of rule-breaking, and presence of conduct disorder by age 15.

anxiety. An unpleasant feeling of fear and apprehension accompanied by increased physiological arousal; in learning theory considered a drive that mediates between a threatening situation and avoidance behavior. Anxiety can be assessed by self-report, by measuring physiological arousal, and by observing overt behavior.

anxiety disorders. Disorders in which fear or tension is overriding and the primary disturbance; include phobic disorders, panic disorder, generalized anxiety disorder, obsessive-compulsive disorder, acute stress disorder, and posttraumatic stress disorder. These disorders form a major category in DSM-IV-TR.

Anxiety Sensitivity Index (ASI). A test that measures the extent to which people respond fearfully to their bodily sensations; predicts the degree to which unexplained physiological arousal leads to panic attacks.

anxiolytics. Minor tranquilizers or benzodiazepines used to treat anxiety disorders.

aphasia. The loss or impairment of the ability to use language because of lesions in the brain: executive, difficulties in speaking or writing the words intended; or receptive, difficulties in understanding written or spoken language.

appetitive phase. The first stage of the sexual response cycle, characterized by sexual interest or desire, often associated with sexually arousing fantasies.

aptitude test. A paper-and-pencil assessment of a person's intellectual functioning that is supposed to predict how the person will perform at a later time; well-known examples include the Scholastic Aptitude Test and the Graduate Record Examination.

ascriptive responsibility. The social judgment assigned to someone who has committed an illegal act and who is expected by society to be punished for it. Compare *descriptive responsibility.*

asociality. A negative symptom of schizophrenia marked by an inability to form close relationships and to feel intimacy.

Asperger's disorder. Pervasive developmental disorder believed to be a mild form of autism in which social relationships are poor and stereotyped behavior is intense and rigid, but language and intelligence are intact.

asthma. A psychophysiological disorder characterized by narrowing of the airways and increased secretion of mucus, often causing extremely labored and wheezy breathing.

asylums. Refuges established in western Europe in the fifteenth century to confine and provide for the mentally ill; forerunners of the mental hospital.

attention-deficit/hyperactivity disorder (ADHD). A disorder in children marked by difficulties in focusing adaptively on the task at hand, inappropriate fidgeting and antisocial behavior, and excessive non-goal-directed behavior.

attribution. The explanation a person has for why an event or behavior has occurred.

attributional style. A person's relatively consistent approach to attribution; for example, the consistent attribution of negative life events to internal, stable, and global causes is thought to dispose to depression.

atypical antipsychotic drugs. Any of several drugs, such as clozapine, used to treat schizophrenia that produce fewer motor side effects than traditional antipsychotics while reducing positive and disorganized symptoms at least as effectively; may, however, be associated with increased and serious side effects of other varieties.

autistic disorder. Pervasive developmental disorder in which the child's world is one of profound aloneness: speech is often absent, and the child has an obsessive need for everything to remain the same.

autonomic nervous system (ANS). The division of the nervous system that regulates involuntary functions; innervates endocrine glands, smooth muscle, and heart muscle; and initiates the physiological changes that are part of the expression of emotion. See *sympathetic* and *parasympathetic nervous systems*; compare *somatic nervous system.*

aversion therapy. A behavior therapy procedure that pairs a noxious stimulus, such as a shock, with situations that are undesirably attractive to make the situations less appealing.

aversive conditioning. Process believed to underlie the effectiveness of aversion therapy.

avoidance conditioning. Learning to move away from a stimulus that has previously been paired with an aversive stimulus such as electric shock.

avoidance learning. An experimental procedure in which a neutral stimulus is paired with a noxious one so that the organism learns to avoid the previously neutral stimulus.

avoidant personality disorder. Personality disorder defined by aloofness and extreme sensitivity to potential rejection, despite an intense desire for affiliation and affection.

avolition. A negative symptom in schizophrenia in which the individual lacks interest and drive.

barbiturates. A class of addictive synthetic sedatives; in large doses, can cause death by almost completely relaxing the diaphragm.

baseline. The state of a phenomenon before the independent variable is manipulated, providing a standard against which the effects of the variable can be measured.

behavior genetics. The study of individual differences in behavior that are attributable to differences in genetic makeup.

behavior therapy. A branch of psychotherapy conceived narrowly as the application of classical and operant conditioning to the alteration of clinical problems, but more broadly as applied experimental psychology in a clinical context.

behavioral activation (BA) therapy. Clinical approach to depression that seeks to increase participation in positively reinforcing activities.

behavioral assessment. A sampling of ongoing cognitions, feelings, and overt behavior in their situational context. Compare projective test and personality inventory.

behavioral inhibition. The tendency to exhibit anxiety or to freeze when facing threat. In infants, it is manifest as a tendency to become agitated and cry when faced with novel stimuli and may be an heritable predisposition for the development of anxiety disorders.

behavioral marital therapy. Clinical approach to depression in which a couple works to improve communication and satisfaction; more likely to relieve marital distress than individual cognitive therapy.

behavioral medicine. An interdisciplinary field concerned with integrating knowledge from medicine and behavioral science to understand health and illness, and to prevent as well as to treat psychophysiological disorders and other illnesses in which a person's psyche plays a role. See also *health psychology.*

behavioral observation. A form of behavioral assessment that entails careful observation of a person's overt behavior in a particular situation.

behaviorism. The school of psychology originally associated with John B. Watson, who proposed that observable behavior, not consciousness, is the proper subject matter of psychology. Contemporary behaviorists do use mediational concepts, provided they are firmly anchored to observables.

benzodiazepines. Any of several drugs commonly used to treat anxiety, such as Valium and Xanax.

beta blockers. Any of numerous beta-adrenergic antagonists, competitive inhibitors of a class of receptors for the hormone adrenaline; are approved as cardiovascular drugs but often used to treat social phobia, despite a lack of demonstrated efficacy.

binge eating disorder. Categorized in DSM-IV-TR as a diagnosis in need of further study; includes recurrent episodes of unrestrained eating.

biofeedback. Procedures that provide an individual immediate information on minute changes in muscle activity, skin temperature, heart rate, blood pressure, and other somatic functions, so that voluntary control over these bodily processes can be achieved, thereby ameliorating to some extent certain psychophysiological disorders.

bipolar I disorder. A diagnosis defined on the basis of at least one lifetime episode of mania. Most people with this disorder also experience episodes of major depression.

bipolar II disorder. A form of bipolar disorder, diagnosed in those who have experienced at least one major depressive episode and at least one episode of hypomania.

blindsight. Conversion disorder wherein patients have suffered lesions in the visual cortex and report themselves blind, but can perform well on some specific visual tests.

blocking. A disturbance associated with disorganized thinking in which a train of speech is interrupted by silence before an idea is fully expressed.

body dysmorphic disorder. A somatoform disorder marked by preoccupation with an imagined or exaggerated defect in appearance—for example, facial wrinkles or excess facial or body hair.

body mass index (BMI). Measure of body fat calculated by dividing weight in kilograms by height in meters squared; considered a more valid estimate of body fat than many others.

BOLD (blood oxygenation level dependent). The signal detected by functional MRI studies of the brain; measures blood flow and thus neural activity in particular regions.

borderline personality disorder. Personality disorder defined by impulsiveness and unpredictability, an uncertain self-image, intense and unstable social relationships, and extreme swings of mood.

brain stem. The part of the brain connecting the spinal cord with the cerebrum; contains the pons and medulla oblongata and functions as a neural relay station.

brief psychotic disorder. A disorder in which a person has a sudden onset of psychotic symptoms—incoherence, loose associations, delusions, hallucinations—immediately after a severely disturbing event; the symptoms last more than a few hours but no more than 2 weeks. Compare *schizophreniform disorder.*

brief therapy. Time-limited psychotherapy, usually ego-analytic in orientation and lasting no more than 25 sessions.

Briquet's syndrome. See *somatization disorder.*

bulimia nervosa. A disorder characterized by episodic uncontrollable eating binges followed by purging either by vomiting or by taking laxatives.

caffeine. Perhaps the world's most popular drug; a generalized stimulant of body systems, including the sympathetic nervous system. Though seldom viewed as a drug, caffeine is addictive, produces tolerance, and subjects habitual users to withdrawal.

Cannabis sativa. See *marijuana.*

cardiovascular disorders. Medical problems involving the heart and the blood circulation system, such as hypertension or coronary heart disease.

case study. The collection of historical or biographical information on a single individual, often including experiences in therapy.

catatonia. Constellation of schizophrenic symptoms including repetitive, peculiar, complex gestures, and in some cases, an almost manic increase in overall activity level.

catatonic features. Immobility or excessive and peculiar physical movements characterizing a subtype of episodes of MDD or mania.

catatonic immobility. A fixity of posture, sometimes grotesque, maintained for long periods, with accompanying muscular rigidity, trancelike state of consciousness, and waxy flexibility.

catatonic schizophrenia. A subtype of schizophrenia whose primary symptoms alternate between stuporous immobility and excited agitation.

catecholamines. Monoamine compounds, each having a catechol portion; include norepinephrine and dopamine, neurotransmitters in the central and autonomic nervous systems.

categorical classification. An approach to assessment in which a person is or is not a member of a discrete grouping. Compare *dimensional classification.*

cathartic method. A therapeutic procedure to relieve emotional suffering introduced by Breuer and developed further by Freud in the late nineteenth century, whereby a patient recalls and relives an earlier emotional catastrophe and reexperiences the tension and unhappiness.

central nervous system. The part of the nervous system that in vertebrates consists of the brain and spinal cord, to which all sensory impulses are transmitted and from which motor impulses pass out; supervises and coordinates the activities of the entire nervous system.

cerebellum. An area of the hindbrain concerned with balance, posture, and motor coordination.

cerebral cortex. The thin outer covering of each of the cerebral hemispheres; highly convoluted and composed of nerve cell bodies that constitute the gray matter of the brain.

cerebrum. The two-lobed structure extending from the brain stem and constituting the anterior (frontal) part of the brain; the largest and most recently developed portion of the brain, responsible for coordinating sensory and motor activities and performing higher cognitive processes.

childhood disintegrative disorder. Pervasive developmental disorder characterized by significant loss of social, play, language, and motor skills after the second year of life, with abnormalities in social interaction and communication similar to autism.

childhood sexual abuse (CSA). Sexual contact with a minor.

chlorpromazine. One of the phenothiazines, the generic term for one of the most widely prescribed antipsychotic drugs, sold under the name Thorazine.

chromosomes. The threadlike bodies within the nucleus of the cell, composed primarily of DNA and bearing the genetic information of the organism.

civil commitment. A procedure whereby a person can be legally certified as mentally ill and hospitalized, even against his or her will. Compare *criminal commitment*. Compare *outpatient commitment*.

classical conditioning. A basic form of learning, sometimes referred to as Pavlovian conditioning, in which a neutral stimulus is repeatedly paired with another stimulus (called the unconditioned stimulus, UCS) that naturally elicits a certain desired response (called the unconditioned response, UCR). After repeated trials the neutral stimulus becomes a conditioned stimulus (CS) and evokes the same or a similar response, now called the conditioned response (CR). Compare operant conditioning.

client-centered therapy. A humanistic-existential insight therapy, developed by Carl Rogers, that emphasizes the importance of the therapist understanding the client's subjective experiences and assisting the client to gain more awareness of current motivations for behavior: the goal is not only to reduce anxieties but also to foster actualization of the client's potential.

clinical interview. General term for conversation between a clinician and a patient that is aimed at determining diagnosis, history, causes for problems, and possible treatment options.

clinical psychologist. An individual who has earned a Ph.D. degree in psychology or a Psy.D. and whose training has included an internship in a mental hospital or clinic.

clinical significance. The degree to which effect size is large enough to be meaningful in predicting or treating a clinical disorder. Compare *statistical significance*.

cocaine. A pain-reducing, stimulating, and addictive alkaloid obtained from coca leaves that increases mental powers, produces euphoria, heightens sexual desire, and in large doses causes paranoia and hallucinations.

cognition. The process of knowing; the thinking, judging, reasoning, and planning activities of the human mind. Behavior is now often explained as depending on these processes.

cognitive behavior therapy (CBT). Behavior therapy which incorporates theory and research on cognitive processes such as thoughts, perceptions, judgments, self-statements, and tacit assumptions; a blend of both the cognitive and behavioral paradigms.

cognitive behavioral paradigm. General view that people can best be understood by studying how they perceive and structure their experiences and how this influences behavior.

cognitive biases. Tendencies to perceive events in a negative manner, for example, by attending to or remembering negative information more than positive information; hypothesized to be driven by underlying negative schemata.

cognitive enhancement therapy (CET). Also known as cognitive training, treatment that seeks to improve basic cognitive functions such as verbal learning ability in schizophrenic individuals, meanwhile reducing symptoms as well.

cognitive restructuring. Any behavior therapy procedure that attempts to alter the manner in which a client thinks about life so that he or she changes overt behavior and emotions.

cognitive therapy. See *cognitive restructuring*. See also *cognitive behavior therapy*.

cohort effects. The consequences of having been born in a given year and having grown up during a particular time period with its own unique pressures, problems, challenges, and opportunities. Compare *age effects*.

collective unconscious. Jung's concept that every human being carries within the wisdom, ideas, and strivings of those who have come before.

common factors. An approach to psychotherapeutic integration that aims to understand the common ingredients that work across different forms of therapy, such as rationale for how treatment will take place, therapist expectations for change, and a strong therapeutic relationship.

communication disorders. Learning disabilities in a child who fails to develop to the degree expected by his or her intellectual level in a specific language skill area; include expressive language disorder, phonological disorder, and stuttering.

community psychology. An approach to therapy that emphasizes prevention and seeking out potential difficulties in the natural surroundings rather than waiting for troubled individuals to initiate consultation. See also *prevention*.

comorbidity. The co-occurrence of two disorders, as when a person is both depressed and alcoholic.

competency to stand trial. A legal decision as to whether a person can participate meaningfully in his or her own defense.

compulsion. The irresistible impulse to repeat an irrational act over and over again. Compare *obsession*.

concordance. As applied in behavior genetics, the similarity in psychiatric diagnosis or in other traits within a pair of twins.

concurrent validity. See *validity*.

conditioned response (CR). See *classical conditioning*.

conditioned stimulus (CS). See *classical conditioning*.

conduct disorder. Pattern of extreme disobedience in youngsters, including theft, vandalism, lying, and early drug use; may be precursor of antisocial personality disorder.

confidentiality. A principle observed by lawyers, doctors, pastors, psychologists, and psychiatrists that dictates that the contents of a professional and private relationship are not divulged to anyone else. See also *privileged communication*.

construct validity. The extent to which scores or ratings on an assessment instrument relate to other variables or behaviors according to some theory or hypothesis.

content validity. See *validity*.

contingency. A close relationship, especially of a causal nature, between two events, one of which regularly follows the other.

control group. Those for whom the active condition of the independent variable is not administered, thus forming a baseline against which the effects of the active condition of the independent variable can be evaluated.

controlled drinking. A pattern of alcohol consumption that is moderate, avoiding the extremes of total abstinence and of inebriation.

conversion disorder. A somatoform disorder in which sensory or motor function are impaired, even though there is no detectable neurological explanation for the deficits.

coping. How people try to deal with problems, in particular the typically negative emotions elicited by stress; generally includes problem-focused, emotion-focused, and avoidance actions and efforts.

coronary heart disease (CHD). Angina pectoris, chest pains caused by insufficient supply of blood and thus oxygen to the heart; and myocardial infarction, or heart attack, in which the blood and oxygen supply is reduced so much that heart muscles are damaged.

corpus callosum. The large band of nerve fibers connecting the two cerebral hemispheres.

correlation. The tendency for two variables, such as height and weight, to covary.

correlation coefficient. A statistic ranging in value from -1.00 to $+1.00$ that measures the degree to which two variables are related. The sign indicates whether the relationship is positive or negative, and the magnitude indicates the strength of the relationship.

correlational method. The research strategy used to establish whether two or more variables are related without manipulating the independent variable. Relationships may be positive—as values for one variable increase, those for the other do also—or negative—as values for one variable increase, those for the other decrease. Compare *experiment*.

cortisol. A "stress hormone" secreted by the adrenal cortices; helps the body prepare to face threats.

co-twin. In behavior genetics research using the twin method, the member of the pair who is tested later to determine whether he or she has the same diagnosis or trait discovered earlier in the birth partner.

counseling psychologist. A doctoral level mental health professional whose training is similar to that of a clinical psychologist, though usually with less emphasis on research and serious psychopathology.

counterconditioning. Relearning achieved by eliciting a new response in the presence of a particular stimulus.

crack. A rock-crystal form of cocaine that is heated, melted, and smoked; more often used in poorer urban areas than conventional cocaine.

criminal commitment. A procedure whereby a person is confined in a mental hospital either for determination of competency to stand trial or after acquittal by reason of insanity. Compare *civil commitment*.

criterion validity. See *validity*.

critical incident stress debriefing (CISD). Crisis intervention therapy of a single long session, offered within 72 hours of the traumatic event, and administered regardless of whether the person has developed PTSD symptoms; controversial and possibly even harmful instead of efficacious.

cross-dependent. Acting on the same receptors, as methadone does with heroin.

cross-fostering. Research method that studies offspring who were adopted and reared completely apart from their biological parents, where the adoptive parent has a particular disorder but the biological parent does not, thereby introducing the influence of being raised by disordered parents.

cross-sectional design. Studies in which different age groups are compared at the same time. Compare *longitudinal studies*.

CT or CAT scan. Refers to computerized axial tomography, a method of diagnosis in which X-rays are taken from different angles and then analyzed by computer to produce a representation of the part of the body in cross section.

cultural competence. The capacity of a therapist to understand the patient's cultural framework and its implications for therapeutic work.

Cushing's syndrome. An endocrine disorder usually affecting young women, produced by oversecretion of cortisone and marked by mood swings, irritability, agitation, and physical disfigurement.

cyclothymic disorder. A form of bipolar disorder characterized by swings between elation and depression over at least a 2-year period, but with moods not so severe as manic or major depressive episodes.

cytokines. Immune system molecules, released by activated macrophages, which help initiate such bodily responses to infection as fatigue, fever, and activation of the HPA axis.

defense mechanisms. In psychoanalytic theory, reality-distorting strategies unconsciously adopted to protect the ego from anxiety.

delirium. A state of great mental confusion in which consciousness is clouded, attention cannot be sustained, and the stream of thought and speech is incoherent. The person is probably disoriented, emotionally erratic, restless or lethargic, and often has illusions, delusions, and hallucinations.

delirium tremens (DTs). One of the withdrawal symptoms that sometimes occurs when a period of heavy alcohol consumption is terminated; marked by fever, sweating, trembling, cognitive impairment, and hallucinations.

delusional (paranoid) disorder. A disorder in which the individual has persistent delusions and is very often contentious but has no disorganized thinking or hallucinations.

delusions. Beliefs contrary to reality, firmly held in spite of evidence to the contrary and common in paranoid disorders: of control, belief that one is being manipulated by some external force such as radar, television, or a creature from outer space; of grandeur, belief that one is an especially important or powerful person; of persecution, belief that one is being plotted against or oppressed by others.

dementia. Deterioration of mental faculties—memory, judgment, abstract thought, control of impulses, intellectual ability—that impairs social and occupational functioning and eventually changes the personality. See *Alzheimer's disease.*

dementia praecox. An older term for schizophrenia, believed then to be an incurable and progressive deterioration of mental functioning beginning in adolescence.

dementia with Lewy bodies (DLB). Form of dementia recently categorized as distinct from Parkinson's disease; characterized by shuffling gait, memory loss, and hallucinations and delusions.

demographic variable. A varying characteristic that is a vital or social statistic of an individual, sample group, or population; examples include age, sex, socioeconomic status, ethnic origin, and education.

demonology. The doctrine that a person's abnormal behavior is caused by an autonomous evil spirit.

denial. Defense mechanism in which a thought, feeling, or action is disavowed by the person.

dependent personality disorder. A disorder in which people are overly concerned about maintaining relationships. People with this disorder often allow others to make decisions for them and are reticent to make demands that could challenge relationships.

dependent variable. In a psychological experiment, the behavior that is measured and is expected to change with manipulation of the independent variable.

depersonalization. An alteration in perception of the self in which the individual loses a sense of reality and feels estranged from the self and perhaps separated from the body; may be a temporary reaction to stress and fatigue or part of panic disorder, depersonalization disorder, or schizophrenia.

depersonalization disorder. A dissociative disorder in which the individual feels unreal and estranged from the self and surroundings enough to disrupt functioning. People with this disorder may feel that their extremities have changed in size or that they are watching themselves from a distance.

derealization. Loss of the sense that the surroundings are real; present in several psychological disorders, such as panic disorder, depersonalization disorder, and schizophrenia.

descriptive responsibility. In legal proceedings, the judgment that the accused performed an illegal act. Compare *ascriptive responsibility.*

detoxification. The initial stage in weaning an addicted person from a drug; involves medical supervision of the sometimes painful withdrawal.

developmental psychopathology. The field that studies disorders of childhood within the context of normal life-span development.

diagnosis. The determination that the set of symptoms or problems of a patient indicates a particular disorder.

Diagnostic and Statistical Manual of Mental Disorders. See *DSM-IV-TR.*

dialectical behavior therapy. A therapeutic approach to borderline personality disorder that combines client-centered empathy and acceptance with behavioral problem solving, social skills training, and limit setting.

diathesis. Predisposition toward a disease or abnormality.

diathesis–stress. As applied in psychopathology, a view that assumes that individuals predisposed toward a particular mental disorder will be particularly affected by stress and will then manifest abnormal behavior.

dimensional classification. An approach to assessment in which a person is placed on a continuum. Compare *categorical classification.*

directionality problem. A difficulty that arises in the correlational method of research when it is known that two variables are related but it is unclear which is causing the other.

disorder of written expression. Difficulties writing without errors in spelling, grammar, or punctuation.

disorganized behavior. Symptom of schizophrenia that is marked by odd behaviors that do not appear organized, such as bouts of agitation, unusual dress, or childlike, silly behavior.

disorganized schizophrenia. In this subtype of schizophrenia (formerly called hebephrenia) the person has diffuse and regressive symptoms, is given to silliness, facial grimaces, and inconsequential rituals, and has constantly changeable moods and poor hygiene.

disorganized speech (thought disorder). Speech found in schizophrenia patients that is marked by poorly organized ideas and speech that is difficult for others to understand.

disorganized symptoms. Broad category of symptoms in schizophrenia that includes disorganized speech, disorganized thinking, and disorganized behavior.

disorientation. A state of mental confusion with respect to time, place, identity of self, other persons, and objects.

displacement. A defense mechanism whereby an emotional response is unconsciously redirected from an object or concept perceived as dangerous to a substitute less threatening to the ego.

dissociation. A process whereby a group of mental processes is split off from the main stream of consciousness, or behavior loses its relationship with the rest of the personality.

dissociative amnesia. A dissociative disorder in which the person suddenly becomes unable to recall important personal information to an extent that cannot be explained by ordinary forgetfulness.

dissociative disorders. Disorders in which the normal integration of consciousness, memory, or identity is suddenly and temporarily altered; include dissociative amnesia, dissociative fugue, dissociative identity disorder (multiple personality), and depersonalization disorder.

dissociative fugue. Disorder in which the person experiences total amnesia, moves, and establishes a new identity.

dissociative identity disorder (DID). A rare dissociative disorder (formerly called multiple personality disorder, or MPD) in which two or more fairly distinct and separate personalities are present within the same individual, each with his or her own memories, relationships, and behavior patterns, with only one of them dominant at any given time.

dizygotic (DZ) twins. Birth partners who developed from separate fertilized eggs and who are only 50 percent alike genetically, just as siblings born from different pregnancies involving the same father; also called fraternal twins. Compare *monozygotic twins.*

dopamine. Central nervous system neurotransmitter, a catecholamine that is also a precursor of norepinephrine and apparently figures in schizophrenia and Parkinson's disease.

dopamine theory. The view that schizophrenia arises from an increase in the number of dopamine receptors.

double-blind procedure. A method for reducing the biasing effects of the expectations of research participant and experimenter; neither is allowed to know whether the independent variable of the experiment is being applied to the participant.

Down syndrome (trisomy 21). A form of mental retardation caused by a third copy of a particular chromosome; involves an IQ usually less than 50 as well as distinctive physical characteristics.

DSM-IV-TR. The current Diagnostic and Statistical Manual of Mental Disorders of the American Psychiatric Association.

Durham test. A 1954 U.S. court ruling that an accused person is not ascriptively responsible if his or her crime is judged attributable to mental disease or defect.

dysfunction. An impairment or disturbance in the functioning of an organ, organ system, behavior, or cognition.

dyslexia (reading disorder). A learning disorder involving significant difficulty with word recognition, reading comprehension, and (typically) spelling.

dyspareunia. Persistent or recurrent pain during sexual intercourse not attributable to a medical problem.

dysthymic disorder. Depressive symptoms that last for at least 2 years but do not meet criteria for the diagnosis of major depressive disorder.

echolalia. The immediate or delayed repetition of the words of others, often found in autistic children.

ecological momentary assessment (EMA). Form of self-observation involving collection of data in real time (e.g., diaries) regarding thoughts, moods, and stressors.

Ecstasy. A relatively new hallucinogen, chemically similar to mescaline and the amphetamines.

effectiveness. How well a therapeutic treatment works in the real world, in the hands of broader samples of nonacademic, less supervised therapists. Compare *efficacy.*

efficacy. How well a therapeutic treatment works under rarified, academic research conditions. Compare *effectiveness.*

ego. In psychoanalytic theory, the predominantly conscious part of the personality, responsible for decision making and for dealing with reality.

ego analysis. An important set of modifications of classical psychoanalysis, based on a conception of the human being as having a stronger, more autonomous ego with gratifications independent of id satisfactions. Sometimes called ego psychology.

egoistic suicide. As defined by Durkheim, self-annihilation committed because the individual feels extreme alienation from others and from society.

Electra complex. In psychoanalytic theory, girls around age 4 have a sexual desire for the father which is repressed. Compare *Oedipus complex*.

electrocardiogram (EKG). A recording of the electrical activity of the heart, made with an electrocardiograph.

electroconvulsive therapy (ECT). A treatment that produces a convulsion by passing electric current through the brain; despite public concerns about this treatment, it can be useful in alleviating profound depression.

electrodermal responding. A recording of the minute electrical activity of the sweat glands on the skin, allowing inference of an emotional state.

electroencephalogram (FEG). A graphic recording of electrical activity of the brain, usually of the cerebral cortex, but sometimes of lower areas.

emotion. The expression, experience, and physiology that guide responses to problems and challenges in the environment.

empathy. Awareness and understanding of another's feelings and thoughts.

empirically supported treatments (ESTs). Approaches whose efficacy has been demonstrated and documented through research that meets the APA's standards for research on psychotherapy.

endocrine gland. Any of a number of ductless glands that release hormones directly into the blood or lymph. The secretions of some endocrine glands increase during emotional arousal.

endorphins. Opiates produced within the body; may have an important role in the processes by which the body builds up tolerance to drugs and is distressed by their withdrawal.

enzyme. A complex protein that acts as a catalyst in regulating metabolic activities.

epidemiology. The study of the frequency and distribution of illness in a population.

epinephrine. A hormone (a catecholamine) secreted by the medulla of the adrenal gland, with effects similar, but not identical, to those of stimulating the sympathetic nerves; causes an increase in blood pressure, inhibits peristaltic movements, and liberates glucose from the liver. Also called adrenaline.

episodic disorder. A condition, such as major depressive disorder, whose symptoms dissipate but that tends to recur.

essential hypertension. A psychophysiological disorder characterized by high blood pressure that cannot be traced to an organic cause; over time causes degeneration of small arteries, enlargement of the heart, and kidney damage.

etiology. All the factors that contribute to the development of an illness or disorder.

excitement phase. As applied by Masters and Johnson, the second stage of the sexual response cycle, characterized by pleasure associated with increased blood flow to the genitalia.

executive functioning. The cognitive capacity to plan how to do a task, how to devise strategies, and how to monitor one's performance.

exhibitionism. Marked preference for obtaining sexual gratification by exposing one's genitals to an unwilling observer.

existential therapy. An insight therapy that emphasizes choice and responsibility to define the meaning of one's life. In contrast with humanistic therapy, it tends to be less cheerful or sanguine in outlook, focusing more on the anxiety that is inherent in confronting one's ultimate aloneness in the world.

exorcism. The casting out of evil spirits by ritualistic chanting or torture.

experiment. The most powerful research technique for determining causal relationships; involves the manipulation of an independent variable, the measurement of a dependent variable, and the random assignment of participants to the several different conditions being investigated. Compare *correlational method*.

experimental effect. A statistically significant difference between two groups experiencing different manipulations of the independent variable.

explicit memory. Memory involving the conscious recall of experiences; the area of deficits typically seen in dissociative amnesia. Compare *implicit memory*.

exposure. Real-life (in vivo) or imaginal confrontation of a feared object or situation, especially as a component of systematic desensitization. See also *imaginal exposure*.

exposure and ritual prevention (ERP). The most widely used and accepted treatment of obsessive-compulsive disorder, in which the sufferer is prevented from engaging in compulsive ritual activity and instead faces the anxiety provoked by the stimulus, leading eventually to extinction of the conditioned response (anxiety).

expressed emotion (EE). Hostility, criticism, and emotional overinvolvement directed from other people toward the patient, usually within a family.

expressive language disorder. Communication disorder of childhood involving difficulties expressing thoughts and emotions in speech.

external validity. The extent to which the results of a study can be considered generalizable.

externalizing disorders. Domain of childhood disorders characterized by outward-directed behaviors, such as aggressiveness, noncompliance, overactivity, and impulsiveness; the category includes attention deficit hyperactivity disorder, conduct disorder, and oppositional defiant disorder. Compare *internalizing disorders*.

extinction. The elimination of a classically conditioned response by the omission of the unconditioned stimulus. In operant conditioning, the elimination of the conditioned response by the omission of reinforcement.

extraversion. Personality trait associated with frequent experiences of positive affect and social engagement.

eye movement desensitization and reprocessing (EMDR). Highly controversial therapeutic approach to trauma involving rapid oscillating eye movements along with classic imaginal exposure techniques; possibly efficacious, but no more so than cognitive or exposure therapies.

factitious disorder. Disorder in which the individual's physical or psychological symptoms appear under voluntary control and are adopted merely to assume the role of a sick person; called factitious disorder by proxy or Munchausen syndrome when a parent produces a physical illness in a child.

falsifiability. The extent to which a scientific assertion is amenable to systematic probes, any one of which could negate the scientist's expectations.

family method. A research strategy in behavior genetics in which the frequency of a trait or of abnormal behavior is determined in relatives who have varying percentages of shared genetic background.

family systems approach. A general approach to etiology and treatment that focuses on the complex interrelationships within families.

family-focused treatment (FET). With the goal of reducing the likelihood of relapse of bipolar disorder or schizophrenia, treatment that aims to educate the person's family about illness, enhance communication, and develop problem-solving skills.

fear. A reaction to real or perceived immediate danger in the present; can involve arousal, or sympathetic nervous system activity.

fear circuit. Set of brain structures, including the amygdala, that tend to be activated when the individual is feeling anxious or fearful; especially active among people with anxiety disorders.

fear-of-fear hypothesis. A cognitive model for the etiology of agoraphobia; suggests the condition is driven by negative thoughts about the consequences of having a panic attack in public.

female orgasmic disorder. A recurrent and persistent delay or absence of orgasm in a woman during sexual activity adequate in focus, intensity, and duration; in many instances the woman may experience considerable sexual excitement.

female sexual arousal disorder. Formerly called frigidity, the inability of a female to reach or maintain the lubrication–swelling stage of sexual excitement or to enjoy a subjective sense of pleasure or excitement during sexual activity.

fetal alcohol syndrome (FAS). Retarded growth of the developing fetus and infant; cranial, facial, and limb anomalies; and mental retardation caused by heavy consumption of alcohol by the mother during pregnancy.

fetishism. Reliance on an inanimate object for sexual arousal.

five-factor model. A personality theory that isolates five major dimensions of personality: neuroticism, extraversion, openness to experience, agreeableness, and conscientiousness.

fixation. In psychoanalytic theory, the arrest of psychosexual development at a particular stage through too much or too little gratification at that stage.

flashback. An unpredictable recurrence of experiences from an earlier drug trip.

flat affect. A lack of outward expression of emotion.

flight of ideas. A symptom of mania that involves a rapid shift in conversation from one subject to another with only superficial associative connections.

follow-up study. A research procedure whereby individuals observed in an earlier investigation are contacted at a later time for further study.

forced rape. The legal term for rape, forced sexual intercourse or other (especially) penetrative sexual activity with another person. Compare *statutory rape*.

forensic psychiatry or psychology. The branch of psychiatry or psychology that deals with the legal questions raised by disordered behavior.

fragile X syndrome. Malformation (or even breakage) of the X chromosome, associated with moderate mental retardation; symptoms include large, underdeveloped ears, a long, thin face, a broad nasal root, and enlarged testicles in males, as well as attention deficits and hyperactivity in many cases.

free association. A key psychoanalytic procedure in which the analysand is encouraged to give free rein to his or her thoughts and feelings, verbalizing whatever comes into the mind without monitoring its content. The assumption is that over time, repressed material will come forth for examination by both analysand and psychoanalyst.

frontal lobe. The anterior portion of each cerebral hemisphere, in front of the central sulcus; active in reasoning and other higher mental processes.

frontal-subcortical dementias. Dementias that involve impairment of both cognitive and motor functions; include Huntington's chorea, Parkinson's disease, normal pressure hydrocephalus, and vascular dementia.

frontal-temporal dementia (FTD). Dementia that begins typically in the mid to late 50s, characterized by deficits in executive functions such as planning, problem solving, and goal-directed behavior, as well as recognition and comprehension of emotions in others. Compare *Alzheimer's disease.*

frotteurism. The sexually oriented touching of an unsuspecting person, typically in public places that provide an easy means of escape.

fugue. See *dissociative fugue.*

functional magnetic resonance imaging (fMRI). Modification of magnetic resonance imaging (MRI) that allows researchers to take pictures of the brain so quickly that metabolic changes can be measured, resulting in a picture of the brain at work rather than of its structure alone.

functional social support. The quality of a person's relationships, for example, a good versus a distressed marriage. Compare *structural social support.*

G-proteins. Guanine nucleotide-binding proteins that serve to modulate activity within the postsynaptic cell, are implicated in mania and depression, and are possibly the intracellular target of lithium.

gamma-aminobutyric acid (GABA). Inhibitory neurotransmitter that may be involved in the anxiety disorders.

gender identity. The ingrained sense a person has of being either a man or a woman.

gender identity disorder. Adult disorder in which there is an incongruence between anatomic sex and self-identified gender.

gene. The smallest portion of DNA within a chromosome that functions as a piece of functional hereditary information.

gene expression. The switching on and off of the reading (transcription and translation) of genes into their products (usually proteins) and thus their associated phenotypes.

gene–environment interaction. The influence of genetics on an individual's sensitivity or reaction to an environmental event. Compare *reciprocal gene–environment interaction.*

general adaptation syndrome (GAS). Hans Selye's model to describe the biological reaction of an organism to sustained and unrelenting stress; the several stages culminate in death, in extreme circumstances.

general paresis. Infection of the central nervous system by the spirochete *Treponema pallidum,* which destroys brain tissue; marked by eye disturbances, tremors, and disordered speech as well as severe intellectual deterioration and psychotic symptoms.

generalized anxiety disorder (GAD). Disorder characterized by anxiety so chronic, persistent, and pervasive that it seems free-floating. The individual is jittery and strained, distractible, and worried that something bad is about to happen. A pounding heart, fast pulse and breathing, sweating, flushing, muscle aches, a lump in the throat, and an upset gastrointestinal tract are some of the bodily indications.

genetic marker. A DNA polymorphism linked to a gene critical to the inheritance of a particular form of psychopathology. See *linkage analysis.*

genetic paradigm. Since the early twentieth century, the approach to human behavior that focuses on both heritability of traits and complex interactions between genes and environment.

genital stage. In psychoanalytic theory, the final psychosexual stage, reached in adulthood, in which heterosexual interests predominate.

genotype. An individual's unobservable, genetic constitution, that is, the totality of genes present in the cells of an individual; often applied to the genes contributing to a single trait. Compare *phenotype.*

gerontology. The interdisciplinary study of aging and of the special problems of the elderly.

Gestalt therapy. A humanistic therapy, developed by Fritz Perls, that encourages clients to satisfy emerging needs so that their innate goodness can be expressed, to increase their awareness of unacknowledged feelings, and to reclaim parts of their personality that have been denied or disowned.

grandiose delusions. Found in paranoid schizophrenia, delusional disorder, and mania, an exaggerated sense of one's importance, power, knowledge, or identity. See also *delusions.*

Graves' disease. An endocrine disorder resulting from oversecretion of the hormone thyroxin, in which metabolic processes are sped up, producing apprehension, restlessness, and irritability.

gray matter. The neural tissue—made up largely of nerve cell bodies—that constitutes the cortex covering the cerebral hemisphere, the nuclei in lower brain areas, columns of the spinal cord, and the ganglia of the autonomic nervous system. Compare *white matter.*

group therapy. Method of treating psychological disorders whereby several persons are seen simultaneously by a single therapist.

guilty but mentally ill (GBMI). Insanity plea in which a mentally ill person can be held morally and legally responsible for a crime, but can then, in theory, be sent to a prison hospital or other suitable facility for psychiatric treatment rather than to a regular prison for punishment. In reality, however, people judged GBMI are usually put in the general prison population where they may or may not receive treatment. Compare *not guilty by reason of insanity.*

habituation. In physiology, a process whereby an organism's response to the same stimulus lessens with repeated presentations.

hallucinations. Perceptions in any sensory modality without relevant and adequate external stimuli.

hallucinogen. A drug or chemical, such as LSD, psilocybin, or mescaline, whose effects include hallucinations; often called psychedelic.

harmful dysfunction. Proposed definition of mental disorder that contains both a value judgment (harmful) and a putatively objective scientific component (dysfunction).

hashish. The dried resin of the cannabis plant, stronger in its effects than the dried leaves and stems that constitute marijuana.

health psychology. A branch of psychology dealing with the role of psychological factors in health and illness. See also *behavioral medicine.*

hebephrenia. Older term for disorganized schizophrenia.

heritability. The extent to which variability in a particular behavior/disorder within a population can be attributed to genetic factors.

heroin. An extremely addictive narcotic drug derived from morphine.

high-risk method. A research technique involving the intensive examination of people, such as the offspring of people with schizophrenia, who have a high probability of later becoming abnormal.

hippocampus. In the subcortical region of the brain, the long, tubelike structure that stretches from the septal area into the temporal lobe.

histrionic personality disorder. Personality disorder defined by overly dramatic behavior, emotional excess, and sexually provocative behavior.

homovanillic acid. A major metabolite of dopamine.

hopelessness theory. Cognitive theory of depression that began with learned helplessness theory, was modified to incorporate attributions, and has been modified again to emphasize hopelessness—an expectation that desirable outcomes will not occur, and that no available responses can change the situation.

hormone. A chemical substance produced by an endocrine gland and released into the blood or lymph that modulates a distant organ or organ system; affects functions such as metabolism, growth, and development of secondary sexual characteristics.

HPA axis. The neuroendocrine connections among hypothalamus, pituitary gland, and adrenal cortex, central to the body's response to stress.

humanistic therapy. An insight therapy that emphasizes freedom of choice, growth of human potential, the joys of being a human being, and the importance of the patient's phenomenology; sometimes called an experiential therapy. See also *existential therapy.*

Huntington's chorea. A fatal disease passed on by a single dominant allele; symptoms include spasmodic jerking of the limbs, psychotic behavior, and mental deterioration.

hydrocodone. An opiate combined with other drugs such as acetaminophen to produce prescription pain medications, including the commonly abused drug Vicodin. See also *oxycodone.*

5-hydroxyindoleacetic acid (5-HIAA). The major metabolite of serotonin.

hypertension. Abnormally high arterial blood pressure, with or without known organic causes. See *essential hypertension.*

hyperventilation. Very rapid and deep breathing associated with high levels of anxiety; causes the level of carbon dioxide in blood to be lowered with possible loss of consciousness.

hypnosis. A trancelike state or behavior resembling sleep, induced by suggestion, characterized primarily by increased suggestibility.

hypoactive sexual desire disorder. Absence of or deficiency in sexual fantasies and urges.

hypochondriasis. A somatoform disorder in which the person, misinterpreting rather ordinary physical sensations, is preoccupied with fears of having a serious disease. Compare *sexual aversion disorder.*

hypomania. An extremely happy or irritable mood accompanied by symptoms like increased energy and decreased need for sleep, but without the significant functional impairment associated with mania.

hypothalamus. In the subcortical region of the brain, the structure that regulates many visceral processes, including metabolism, temperature, perspiration, blood pressure, sleeping, and appetite.

hypotheses. Specific expectations or predictions about what should occur or be found if a theory is true or valid.

id. In psychoanalytic theory, that part of the personality present at birth, comprising all the energy of the psyche, and expressed as biological urges that strive continually for gratification.

ideas of reference. Delusional thinking that reads personal significance into seemingly trivial remarks or activities of others and completely unrelated events.

illusion. A misperception of a real external stimulus, such as hearing the slapping of waves as footsteps.

imaginal exposure. Treatment for anxiety disorders that involves visualizing feared scenes for extended periods of time. Frequently used in the treatment of posttraumatic stress disorder, when in vivo exposure to the initial trauma cannot be conducted.

imipramine. An antidepressant drug, one of the tricyclic group, trade name Tofranil.

implicit memory. Memory that underlies behavior but is based on experiences that cannot be consciously recalled;

typically not compromised in cases of dissociative amnesia. Compare *explicit memory.*

in absentia. Literally, "in one's absence." Courts are concerned that a person be able to participate personally and meaningfully in his or her own trial and not be tried in absentia because of a distracting mental disorder.

in vivo. As applied in psychology, taking place in a real-life situation.

inappropriate affect. Emotional responses that are out of context, such as laughter when hearing sad news.

incest. Sexual relations between close relatives, most often between daughter and father or between brother and sister.

incidence. In epidemiological studies of a particular disorder, the rate at which new cases occur in a given place at a given time. Compare *prevalence.*

incoherence. In schizophrenia, an aspect of disorganized thinking wherein verbal expression is marked by disconnectedness, fragmented thoughts, and jumbled phrases.

independent variable. In a psychological experiment, the factor, experience, or treatment that is under the control of the experimenter and that is expected to have an effect on participants as assessed by changes in the dependent variable.

index case (proband). The person who in a genetic investigation bears the diagnosis or trait in which the investigator is interested.

individual psychology. A variation of Freud's psychoanalysis introduced by Alfred Adler, focusing less on biological drives and more on such factors as people's conscious beliefs and goals for self-betterment.

informed consent. The agreement of a person to serve as a research participant or to enter therapy after being told the possible outcomes, both benefits and risks.

insanity defense. The legal argument that a defendant should not be held ascriptively responsible for an illegal act if the conduct is attributable to mental illness. See *not guilty by reason of insanity (NGRI)* and *guilty but mentally ill (GBMI).*

intelligence quotient (IQ). A standardized measure indicating how far an individual's raw score on an intelligence test is from the average raw score of his or her chronological age group.

intelligence test. A standardized means of assessing a person's current mental ability, for example, the Stanford–Binet test or the Wechsler Adult Intelligence Scale.

interleukin-6 (IL-6). A proinflammatory cytokine; elevated levels can result from stress as well as infection and have been linked to numerous diseases in older adults.

internal consistency reliability. See *reliability.*

internal validity. See *validity.*

internalizing disorders. Domain of childhood disorders characterized by inward-focused experiences and behaviors, such as depression, social withdrawal, and anxiety; the category includes childhood anxiety and mood disorders. Compare *externalizing disorders.*

interoceptive conditioning. Classical conditioning of panic attacks in response to internal bodily sensations of arousal (as opposed to the external situations that trigger anxiety).

interpersonal psychotherapy (IPT). A short-term, here-and-now focused psychological treatment initially developed for depression and influenced by the psychodynamic emphasis on relationships.

interpretation. In psychoanalysis, a key procedure in which the psychoanalyst points out to the analysand where resistance exists and what certain dreams and verbalizations reveal about impulses repressed in the unconscious; more generally, any statement by a therapist that construes the client's problem in a new way.

interrater reliability. See *reliability.*

irrational beliefs. Self-defeating assumptions that are assumed by rational-emotive therapists to underlie psychological distress.

irresistible impulse. The term used in an 1834 Ohio court ruling on criminal responsibility that determined that an insanity defense can be established by proving that the accused had an uncontrollable urge to perform the act.

la belle indifférence. The blasé attitude people with conversion disorder have toward their symptoms.

latency period. In psychoanalytic theory, the years between ages 6 and 12, during which id impulses play a minor role in motivation.

law of effect. A principle of learning that holds that behavior is acquired by virtue of its consequences.

learned helplessness theory. The theory of depression etiology that individuals acquire passivity and a sense of being unable to act and to control their lives, through unpleasant experiences and traumas against which their efforts were ineffective.

learning disabilities. General term for learning disorders, communication disorders, and motor skills disorder.

learning disorders. A set of developmental disorders encompassing dyslexia, mathematics disorder, and disorder of written expression; characterized by failure to develop in a specific academic area to the degree expected by the child's intellectual level.

least restrictive alternative. The legal principle according to which a hospitalized patient must be treated in a setting that imposes as few restrictions as possible on his or her freedom.

libido. Freudian term for the life-integrating instinct or force of the id; sometimes equated with sexual drive.

linkage analysis. A molecular genetic technique wherein occurrence of a disorder in a family is evaluated in parallel with inheritance of a known genetic (DNA) marker.

lithium. A drug useful in treating both mania and depression in bipolar disorder.

locus ceruleus. The brain region in the fear circuit that is especially important in panic disorder; the major source in the brain of norepinephrine, which helps trigger sympathetic nervous system activity.

longitudinal design. Investigation that collects information on the same individuals repeatedly over time, perhaps over many years, in an effort to determine how phenomena change. Compare *cross-sectional design.*

loose associations (derailment). In schizophrenia, an aspect of disorganized thinking wherein the patient has difficulty sticking to one topic and drifts off on a train of associations evoked by an idea from the past.

LSD. *d*-lysergic acid diethylamide, a drug synthesized in 1938 and discovered by accident to be a hallucinogen in 1943.

Luria–Nebraska test. A battery of neuropsychological tests that can detect impairment in different parts of the brain.

magnetic resonance imaging (MRI). A technique for measuring the structure (or, in the case of functional magnetic resonance imaging, the activity) of the living brain. The person is placed inside a large circular magnet that causes hydrogen atoms to move; the return of the atoms to their original positions when the current to the magnet is turned off is translated by a computer into pictures of brain tissue.

maintenance dose. An amount of a drug designed to enable a patient to continue to benefit from a therapeutically effective regimen of medication. It is often less than the dose required to initiate the positive change.

major depressive disorder (MDD). A disorder of individuals who have experienced episodes of depression but not

of mania. Depression episodes are marked by sadness or loss of pleasure, accompanied by symptoms such as feelings of worthlessness and guilt, withdrawal from others, loss of sleep, appetite, sexual desire, and either lethargy or agitation.

male erectile disorder. A recurrent and persistent inability to attain or maintain an erection until completion of sexual activity.

male orgasmic disorder. A recurrent and persistent delay or absence of ejaculation after an adequate phase of sexual excitement.

malingering. Faking a physical or psychological incapacity in order to avoid a responsibility or gain an end, where the goal is readily recognized from the individual's circumstances distinct from conversion disorder, in which the incapacity is assumed to be beyond voluntary control.

malleus maleficarum ("the witches' hammer"). A manual written by two Dominican monks in the fifteenth century to provide rules for identifying and trying witches.

mania. Intense elation or irritability, accompanied by symptoms such as excessive talkativeness, rapid thoughts, distractibility, grandiose plans, heightened activity, and insensitivity to the negative consequences of actions.

manic defense. Model in which mania is seen as a protection against a painful psychological state.

marijuana. A drug derived from the dried and ground leaves and stems of the female hemp plant, *Cannabis sativa.*

mathematics disorder. Learning disorder characterized by difficulty recalling arithmetic facts, counting objects, and aligning numbers in columns.

MDA (methylenedioxyamphetamine). A chemical component of Ecstasy, first synthesized in 1910 but not broadly known as a psychedelic until the 1960s.

MDMA (methylenedioxymethamphetamine). A chemical component of Ecstasy, initially used as an appetite suppressant for World War I soldiers and derived from precursors found in nutmeg, dill, saffron, and sassafras.

mediator. In psychology, an inferred state intervening between the observable stimulus and response, activated by the stimulus and in turn initiating the response; in more general terms, a thought, drive, emotion, or belief. See also *construct.*

melancholic. Subtype of major depressive disorder in which the individual is unable to feel better even momentarily when something good happens, regularly feels worse in the morning and awakens early, and suffers a deepening of other symptoms of depression.

meningitis. An inflammation of the meninges (layers of nonneural tissue surrounding the brain and spinal cord) through infection, usually by a bacterium, or through irritation.

mental age. The numerical index of an individual's cognitive development determined by standardized intelligence tests.

mental retardation. Subnormal intellectual functioning associated with impairment in adaptive behavior and identified at an early age.

mescaline. A hallucinogen and alkaloid that is the active ingredient of peyote.

mesmerize. The first term for hypnotize, after Franz Anton Mesmer, an Austrian physician who in the late eighteenth century treated and cured hysterical or conversion disorders with what he considered the animal magnetism emanating from his body and permeating the universe.

meta-analysis. A quantitative method of analyzing the results of a set of studies on a topic, by standardizing the results.

metabolic syndrome (of CHD). Combination of particular risk factors—abdominal obesity, insulin resistance, high blood pressure, low HDL cholesterol, and heightened inflammation—disposing to onset of coronary heart disease.

metabolism. The sum of the intracellular processes by which large molecules are broken down into smaller ones, releasing energy and wastes, and by which small molecules are built up into new living matter by consuming energy.

metabolite. A chemical breakdown product of an endogenous molecule, such as a neurotransmitter, or of an exogenous drug; used to gauge current or recent level of its precursor.

metacognition. The knowledge people have about the way they know and learn about their world, for example, recognizing the usefulness of a map in finding their way in a new city.

methadone. A synthetic addictive heroin substitute for treating those addicted to heroin that eliminates its effects and the cravings.

methamphetamine. An amphetamine derivative whose abuse skyrocketed in the 1990s.

mindfulness-based cognitive therapy (MBCT). Recent adaptation of cognitive therapy/restructuring that focuses on relapse prevention after successful treatment for recurrent episodes of major depression; aims to "decenter" the person's perspective in order to break the cycle between sadness and thinking patterns.

Minnesota Multiphasic Personality Inventory (MMPI). A lengthy personality inventory that identifies individuals with states such as anxiety, depression, masculinity–femininity, and paranoia, through their true–false replies to groups of statements.

mixed episodes. Bipolar episodes characterized by severe symptoms of both mania and depression within the same week.

M'Naghten rule. An 1843 British court decision stating that an insanity defense can be established by proving that the defendant did not know what he or she was doing or did not realize that it was wrong.

modeling. Learning by observing and imitating the behavior of others; or teaching by demonstrating and providing opportunities for imitation.

molecular genetics. Studies that seek to determine the components of a trait that are heritable by identifying relevant genes and their functions.

monoamine. An organic compound containing nitrogen in one amino group (NH). Some of the known neurotransmitters of the central nervous system, called collectively brain amines, are catecholamines and indoleamines, which are monoamines.

monoamine oxidase (MAO). An enzyme that breaks down monoamine neurotransmitters (such as dopamine, norepinephrine, and serotonin) in the synaptic cleft.

monoamine oxidase inhibitors (MAO inhibitors). A group of antidepressant drugs that prevent the enzyme monoamine oxidase from deactivating catecholamines and indolamines.

monozygotic (MZ) twins. Genetically identical twins who have developed from a single fertilized egg. Compare *dizygotic twins.*

mood disorders. Disorders, such as depressive disorders or mania, in which there are disabling disturbances in emotion.

moral treatment. A therapeutic regimen, introduced by Philippe Pinel during the French Revolution, whereby mentally ill patients were released from their restraints and were treated with compassion and dignity rather than with contempt and denigration.

morbidity risk. The probability that an individual will develop a particular disorder.

morphine. An addictive narcotic alkaloid extracted from opium, used primarily as an analgesic and as a sedative.

motor skills disorder. A learning disability characterized by marked impairment in the development of motor coordination that is not accounted for by a physical disorder such as cerebral palsy.

Mowrer's two-factor model. Mowrer's theory of avoidance learning according to which (1) fear is attached to a neutral stimulus by pairing it with a noxious unconditioned stimulus, and (2) a person learns to escape the fear elicited by the conditioned stimulus, thereby avoiding the unconditioned stimulus.

multiaxial classification system. Classification having several dimensions, all of which are employed in categorizing; DSM-IV-TR is an example.

multiple personality disorder (MPD). See *dissociative identity disorder (DID).*

multisystemic treatment (MST). Treatment for serious juvenile offenders that involves delivering intensive and comprehensive therapy services in the community, targeting the adolescent, the family, the school, and, in some cases, the peer group, in ecologically valid settings and using varied techniques.

myocardial infarction. Heart attack. See *coronary heart disease.*

narcissistic personality disorder. Personality disorder defined by extreme selfishness and self-centeredness, a grandiose view of one's uniqueness, achievements, and talents, an insatiable craving for admiration and approval from others, willingness to exploit to achieve goals, and expectation of much more from others than she or he is willing to give in return.

negative affect. Constellation of negative emotions that is elevated in both anxiety and depression.

negative reinforcement. The strengthening of a tendency to exhibit desired behavior by rewarding responses in that situation with the removal of an aversive stimulus.

negative symptoms. Behavioral deficits in schizophrenia, such as flat affect and apathy. Compare *positive symptoms.*

negative triad. In Beck's theory of depression, a person's negative views of the self, the world, and the future, in a reciprocal causal relationship with pessimistic assumptions (schemata) and cognitive biases such as selective abstraction.

neologism. A word made up by the speaker, usually meaningless to a listener.

nerve impulse. A wave of depolarization that propagates along the neuron and causes the release of neurotransmitter; action potential.

neurofibrillary tangles. Abnormal protein filaments present in the cell bodies of brain cells in patients with Alzheimer's disease.

neurologist. A physician who specializes in medical diseases that affect the nervous system, such as muscular dystrophy, cerebral palsy, or Alzheimer's disease.

neuron. A single nerve cell.

neuropsychological tests. Psychological tests, such as the Luria–Nebraska, that can detect impairment in different parts of the brain.

neuropsychologist. A psychologist who studies how brain dysfunction affects cognition, emotion, and behavior.

neuroscience paradigm. A broad theoretical view that holds that mental disorders are caused in part by some aberrant process directed by the brain.

neuroses. Old term for a large group of nonpsychotic disorders characterized by unrealistic anxiety, depression, and other associated problems; See *anxiety disorders.*

neuroticism. The tendency to react to events with greater than average negative affect; a strong predictor of onset of anxiety disorders and depression.

neurotransmitters. Chemical substances important in transferring a nerve impulse from one neuron to another; for example, serotonin and norepinephrine.

nicotine. The principal alkaloid of tobacco (an addicting agent).

nitrous oxide. A gas that, when inhaled, produces euphoria and sometimes giddiness.

nonshared environment. Factors distinct among family members, such as relationships with friends or specific experiences unique to a person. Compare *shared environment.*

nonverbal memories. Memories based on connections between sensory stimuli and external events.

norepinephrine. A catecholamine neurotransmitter of the central nervous system, disturbances in the tracts of which apparently figure in depression and mania. It is also a sympathetic nervous system neurotransmitter, a hormone released in addition to epinephrine and similar in action, and a strong vasoconstrictor.

not guilty by reason of insanity (NGRI). Insanity plea that specifies an individual is not to be held legally responsible for the crime because the person had a mental illness at the time of the crime. Different states and federal law have different standards for defining mental illness and what must be demonstrated by the defense. In most cases, the defense must show that because of the mental illness, the accused person could not conform his/her behavior to the law and did not know right from wrong when the crime was committed. Compare *guilty but mentally ill.*

nucleus. In anatomy, a mass of nerve cell bodies (gray matter) within the brain or spinal cord by which descending nerve fibers connect with ascending nerve fibers. Pl. nuclei.

obese. Currently defined as exhibiting a body mass index (BMI) of greater than 30.

object-relations theory. Variant of psychoanalytic theory that focuses on the way children internalize (*introject*) images of the people who are important to them (e.g., their parents), such that these internalized images (*object representations*) become part of the ego and influence how the person reacts to the world.

observer drift. The tendency of two raters of behavior to begin to agree with each other, achieving unusually high levels of reliability and differentiating their scores from those of other raters; regarded as a threat to reliable and valid behavioral assessment.

obsession. An intrusive and recurring thought that seems irrational and uncontrollable to the person experiencing it. Compare *compulsion.*

obsessive-compulsive disorder (OCD). An anxiety disorder in which the mind is flooded with persistent and uncontrollable thoughts or the individual is compelled to repeat certain acts again and again, causing significant distress and interference with everyday functioning.

obsessive-compulsive personality disorder. Personality disorder defined by inordinate difficulty making decisions, hyperconcern with details and efficiency, and poor relations with others due to demands that things be done just so, as well as their unduly conventional, serious, formal, and stingy emotions.

occipital lobe. The posterior portion of each cerebral hemisphere, situated behind the parietal lobe and above the temporal lobes; responsible for reception and analysis of visual information and for some visual memory.

Oedipus complex. In Freudian theory, the desire and conflict of the four-year-old male child who wants to possess his mother sexually and to eliminate the father rival. The threat of punishment from the father causes repression of these id impulses. Compare *Electra complex.*

operant conditioning. The acquisition or elimination of a response as a function of the environmental contingencies of reinforcement and punishment. Compare *classical conditioning.*

opiates. A group of addictive sedatives that in moderate doses relieve pain and induce sleep.

opium. One of the opiates, the dried, milky juice obtained from the immature fruit of the opium poppy; an addictive narcotic that produces euphoria and drowsiness while reducing pain.

oppositional defiant disorder. An externalizing disorder of children marked by high levels of disobedience to authority but lacking the extremes of conduct disorder.

oral stage. In psychoanalytic theory, the first psychosexual stage, which extends into the second year; during it the mouth is the principal erogenous zone.

orbitofrontal cortex. The portion of the frontal lobe located just above the eyes; one of three closely related brain regions that are unusually active in individuals with obsessive-compulsive disorder.

orgasm phase. The third stage of the sexual response cycle, characterized by a peak of sexual pleasure, generally including ejaculation in men and contraction of the outer vaginal walls in women.

outcome research. Research on the efficacy of psychotherapy. Compare *process research.*

outpatient commitment. A form of civil commitment consistent with the principle of least restrictive alternative, whereby the person is not hospitalized, but rather is allowed to remain free in the community under legal-medical constraints that ensure, for example, that prescribed medication is taken and other measures are observed.

oxycodone. An opiate combined with other drugs to produce prescription pain medications, including the commonly abused drug OxyContin. See also *hydrocodone.*

pain disorder. A somatoform disorder in which the person complains of severe and prolonged pain that is not fully explainable by organic pathology and is thus assumed to be caused or intensified by psychological factors.

panic attack. A sudden attack of intense apprehension, terror, and impending doom, accompanied by symptoms such as labored breathing, nausea, chest pain, feelings of choking and smothering, heart palpitations, dizziness, sweating, and trembling.

panic control therapy (PCT). A cognitive behavior treatment, based on the tendency of individuals with panic disorder to overreact to bodily stimuli, in which sensations are induced physically and coped with under safe conditions.

panic disorder. An anxiety disorder in which the individual has sudden, inexplicable, and frequent panic attacks; in DSM-IV-TR, diagnosed as with or without agoraphobia. See *panic attack.*

paradigm. A set of basic assumptions that outlines the universe of scientific inquiry, specifying both the concepts regarded as legitimate and the methods to be used in collecting and interpreting data.

paradoxical intervention. A therapeutic strategy that asks patients to increase or observe the frequency or intensity of a symptom, as in having anxious patients make themselves more anxious or note when and how severely they become anxious.

paranoia. The general term for delusions of persecution, of grandiosity, or both; found in several pathological conditions, delusional disorders, paranoid schizophrenia, and paranoid personality disorder, but can also be produced by large doses of certain drugs, such as cocaine or alcohol.

paranoid personality disorder. Personality disorder defined by expectation of mistreatment at the hands of others, suspicion, secretiveness, jealousy, argumentativeness, unwillingness to accept blame, and cold and unemotional affect.

paranoid schizophrenia. A type of schizophrenia in which the patient has numerous systematized delusions as well as hallucinations and ideas of reference. He or she may also be agitated, angry, and argumentative.

paraphilias. Sexual attraction to unusual objects and sexual activities unusual in nature.

parasympathetic nervous system. The division of the autonomic nervous system that is involved with maintenance; controls many of the internal organs and is active primarily when the organism is not aroused. Compare *sympathetic nervous system.*

parental management training (PMT). Behavioral program in which parents are taught to modify their responses to their children so that prosocial rather than antisocial behavior is consistently rewarded.

parietal lobe. The middle division of each cerebral hemisphere, situated behind the central sulcus and above the lateral sulcus; the receiving center for sensations of the skin and of bodily positions.

Parkinson's disease. A disease characterized by uncontrollable and severe muscle tremors, a stiff gait, a masklike, expressionless face, and withdrawal.

PCP. See *phencyclidine.*

pedophilia. A paraphilia defined by a marked preference for obtaining sexual gratification through contact with people defined legally as underage.

penile plethysmograph. A device for detecting blood flow and thus for recording changes in size of the penis.

personal therapy. A broad-spectrum cognitive behavioral approach to the problems faced by schizophrenia patients who have been discharged from the hospital; includes learning how to recognize inappropriate affect and how to notice small signs of relapse, cognitive restructuring to work at lowering stress levels, and muscle-relaxation techniques to detect and control anger and anxiety.

personality disorders. A group of disorders, listed separately on Axis II of the DSM-IV-TR, regarded as long-standing, inflexible, and maladaptive personality traits that impair social and occupational functioning.

personality inventory. A self-report questionnaire comprised of statements assessing habitual behavioral and affective tendencies.

pervasive developmental disorders. Severe childhood conditions, encompassing autistic disorder, Rett's disorder, childhood disintegrative disorder, and Asperger's disorder, marked by profound disturbances in social relations and oddities in behavior.

PET scan. Computer-generated picture of the living brain, created by analysis of emissions from radioactive isotopes injected into the bloodstream.

phallic stage. In psychoanalytic theory, the third psychosexual stage, extending from ages three to five or six, during which maximal gratification is obtained from genital stimulation.

phencyclidine (PCP). Also known by street names such as angel dust, PeaCE Pill, and zombie, this very powerful and hazardous drug causes profound disorientation, agitated and often violent behavior, and even seizures, coma, and death.

phenothiazine. The name for a group of drugs that relieve psychotic symptoms; their molecular structure, like that of the tricyclic drugs, consists of three fused rings. An example is chlorpromazine (Thorazine).

phenotype. The totality of physical characteristics and behavioral traits of an individual, or a particular trait exhibited by an individual; the product of interactions between genetics and the environment over the course of development. Compare *genotype.*

phenylketonuria (PKU). A genetic deficiency in a liver enzyme, phenylalanine hydroxylase, that causes severe mental retardation unless phenylalanine can be largely restricted from the diet.

phobia. An anxiety disorder in which there is intense fear and avoidance of specific objects and situations, recognized as irrational by the individual.

phonological disorder. Communication disorder in childhood in which some words sound like baby talk because the person is not able to make certain speech sounds.

placebo. Any inactive therapy or chemical agent, or any attribute or component of such a therapy or chemical, that affects a person's behavior for reasons related to his or her expectation of change.

placebo effect. The action of a drug or psychological treatment that is not attributable to any specific operations of the agent. For example, a tranquilizer can reduce anxiety both because of its special biochemical action and because the recipient expects relief. See *placebo.*

plaques. Small, round areas composed of remnants of lost neurons and beta-amyloid, a waxy protein deposit; present in the brains of patients with Alzheimer's disease.

plateau phase. According to Masters and Johnson, the second stage in sexual arousal, during which excitement and tension have reached a stable high level before orgasm.

pleasure principle. In psychoanalytic theory, the demanding manner by which the id operates, seeking immediate gratification of its needs.

polydrug abuse. The misuse of more than one drug at a time, such as drinking heavily and taking cocaine.

polygenic. As applied to psychopathology or any other trait, caused by multiple genes contributing their effects typically during multiple stages of development.

polymorphism. Any specific difference in DNA sequence that exists within a population.

pons. An area in the brain stem containing nerve-fiber tracts that connect the cerebellum with the spinal cord and with motor areas of the cerebrum.

positive affect. A constellation of particular positive emotions, such as excitement, that also reflect a general engagement with the environment; dampened in depression but not in anxiety.

positive reinforcement. The strengthening of a tendency to exhibit desired behavior by rewarding responses in that situation with a desired reward.

positive symptoms. Behavioral excesses in schizophrenia, such as hallucinations and bizarre behavior. Compare *negative symptoms.*

postpartum onset. Onset within 4 weeks postpartum, characterizing a subtype of episodes of MDD or mania.

posttraumatic model (of DID). Etiological model of dissociative identity disorder that assumes the condition begins in childhood as a result of severe physical or sexual abuse. Compare *sociocognitive model.*

posttraumatic stress disorder (PTSD). An anxiety disorder in which a particularly stressful event, such as military combat, rape, or a natural disaster, brings in its aftermath intrusive reexperiencings of the trauma, a numbing of responsiveness to the outside world, estrangement from others, and a tendency to be easily startled, as well as nightmares, recurrent dreams, and otherwise disturbed sleep.

poverty of content. Reduced informational content in speech, one of the negative symptoms of schizophrenia.

poverty of speech. Reduced amount of talking, one of the negative symptoms of schizophrenia.

predictive validity. See *validity*.

predisposition. An inclination or diathesis to respond in a certain way, either inborn or acquired; in abnormal psychology, a factor that lowers the ability to withstand stress and inclines the individual toward pathology.

prefrontal cortex. The region of the frontal lobe of the brain that helps maintain an image of threats and rewards faced, as well as maintain focus and plan relevant to those threats and rewards.

premature ejaculation. Inability of the male to inhibit his orgasm long enough for mutually satisfying sexual relations.

prepared learning. In classical conditioning theory, a biological predisposition to associate particular stimuli readily with the unconditioned stimulus.

prevalence. In epidemiological studies of a disorder, the percentage of a population that has the disorder at a given time. Compare *incidence*.

prevention. Primary prevention comprises efforts in community psychology to reduce the incidence of new cases of psychological disorder by such means as altering stressful living conditions and genetic counseling; secondary prevention seeks to detect disorders early, so that they will not develop into full-blown, perhaps chronic, disabilities; tertiary prevention attempts to reduce the long-term consequences of having a disorder, equivalent in most respects to therapy. See also *community psychology*.

primary prevention. See *prevention*.

privileged communication. The communication between parties in a confidential relationship that is protected by statute, which a spouse, doctor, lawyer, pastor, psychologist, or psychiatrist thus cannot be forced to disclose, except under unusual circumstances.

proband. See *index case*.

process research. Research on the mechanisms by which a therapy may bring improvement. Compare *outcome research*.

prognosis. A prediction of the likely course and outcome of an illness. Compare *diagnosis*.

projection. A defense mechanism whereby characteristics or desires unacceptable to the ego are attributed to someone else.

projective hypothesis. The notion that standard but highly unstructured stimuli, as found in the Rorschach assessment's series of inkblots, are necessary to bypass defenses in order to reveal unconscious motives and conflicts.

projective test. A psychological assessment device, such as the Rorschach series of inkblots, employing a set of standard but vague stimuli, on the assumption that unstructured material will allow unconscious motivations and fears to be uncovered.

pronoun reversal. A speech problem in which the child refers to himself or herself as "he," "she," or "you" and uses "I" or "me" in referring to others; often found in the speech of children with autistic disorder.

pruning. In neural development, the selective loss of synaptic connections, especially in the fine-tuning of brain regions devoted to sensory processing.

psilocybin. A psychedelic drug extracted from the mushroom *Psilocybe mexicana*.

psyche. In psychoanalytic theory, the totality of the id, ego, and superego, including both conscious and unconscious components.

psychiatrist. A physician (M.D.) who has taken specialized postdoctoral training, called a residency, in the diagnosis, treatment, and prevention of mental disorders.

psychoactive medications. Prescribed chemical compounds, for example Prozac, having a psychological effect that alters mood or thought process.

psychoanalysis. Primarily the therapy procedures pioneered by Freud, entailing free association, dream analysis, and working through the transference neurosis. More recently the term has come to encompass the numerous variations on basic Freudian therapy.

psychoanalyst (analyst). A therapist who has taken specialized postdoctoral training in psychoanalysis after earning an M.D. or a Ph.D. degree.

psychoanalytic (psychodynamic) paradigm. General view based on psychoanalytic theory.

psychoanalytic theory. Central Freudian assumption that psychopathology results from unconscious conflicts in the individual.

psychoeducational approaches. Especially with bipolar disorder and schizophrenia, the component of treatment that helps people learn about symptoms, expected time course, triggers for symptoms, and treatment strategies.

psychological factors affecting medical condition. A diagnosis in DSM-IV-TR that a physical illness is caused in part or exacerbated by psychological stress. See *psychophysiological disorders*.

psychological tests. Standardized procedures designed to measure performance on a particular task or to assess personality.

psychoneuroimmunology. Field that studies how psychological factors (especially stressors) impact the immune system (adversely).

psychopath. See *antisocial personality*.

psychopathologists. Mental health professionals who conduct research into the nature and development of mental disorders. Their academic backgrounds can differ; some are trained as experimental psychologists, others as psychiatrists, and still others as biochemists.

psychopathology. The field concerned with the nature and development of mental disorders.

psychopathy. A personality syndrome related to antisocial personality disorder, but defined by an absence of emotion, impulsivity, manipulativeness, and irresponsibility.

psychophysiological disorders. Disorders with physical symptoms that may involve actual tissue damage, usually in one organ system, which are produced in part by continued mobilization of the autonomic nervous system under stress; listed in DSM-IV-TR on Axis I as psychological factor affecting medical condition with the specific physical condition provided on Axis III.

psychophysiology. The discipline concerned with the bodily changes that accompany psychological events.

psychosis. A severe mental disorder in which thinking and emotion are so impaired that the individual is out of contact with reality.

psychotherapy. A primarily verbal means of helping troubled individuals change their thoughts, feelings, and behavior to reduce distress and to achieve greater life satisfaction.

psychotic features. A profound sadness and unjustified feelings of unworthiness, which also include delusions; can refer to delusions or hallucinations characterizing a subtype of episodes of MDD or mania.

punishment. In psychological experiments, any noxious stimulus imposed on an organism to reduce the probability that it will behave in an undesired way.

random assignment. A method of assigning people to groups by chance (e.g., using the flip of a coin). The procedure helps to ensure that groups are comparable before the experimental manipulation begins.

randomized controlled trials (RCTs). Studies in which clients are randomly assigned to receive either active treatment or a comparison (a placebo condition involving no treatment, or else an active-treatment control group that receives another treatment); experimental treatment studies, where the independent variable is the treatment type and the dependent variable is client outcome.

rape. See *forced rape* and see *statutory rape*.

rapid cycling. Term applied to bipolar disorders if the person has experienced at least four episodes within the past year.

rational-emotive behavior therapy (REBT). A cognitive-restructuring behavior therapy introduced by Albert Ellis and based on the assumption that much disordered behavior is rooted in absolutistic, unrealistic demands and goals, such as, "I must be universally loved."

rational-emotive therapy (RET). See *rational-emotive behavior therapy*.

rationalization. A defense mechanism in which a plausible reason is unconsciously invented by the ego to protect itself from confronting the real reason for an action, thought, or emotion.

reactance. Resistance to efforts by another to change the person.

reaction formation. A defense mechanism whereby an unconscious and unacceptable impulse or feeling that would cause anxiety is converted into its opposite so that it can become conscious and can be expressed.

reactivity. The phenomenon wherein behavior changes because it is being observed.

reading disorder. See *dyslexia*.

reality principle. In psychoanalytic theory, the manner in which the ego delays gratification and otherwise deals with the environment in a planned, rational fashion.

receptor. A protein embedded in a neural cell membrane that interacts with one or more neurotransmitters. Nonneural receptor proteins include hormone receptors.

reciprocal gene–environment interaction. The genetic predisposition for an individual to seek out certain environments that increase the risk of developing a particular disorder. Compare *gene–environment interaction*.

regression. A defense mechanism in which anxiety is avoided by retreating to the behavior patterns of an earlier psychosexual stage.

reinforcement. In operant conditioning, increasing the probability that a response will recur either by presenting a contingent positive event or by removing a negative one.

reliability. The extent to which a test, measurement, or classification system produces the same scientific observation each time it is applied. Reliability types include test-retest, the relationship between the scores that a person achieves when he or she takes the same test twice; interrater, the relationship between the judgments that at least two raters make independently about a phenomenon; split half, the relationship between two halves of an assessment instrument that have been determined to be equivalent; alternate-form, the relationship between scores achieved by people when they complete two versions of a test that are judged to be equivalent; and internal consistency, the degree to which different items of an assessment are related to one another.

repression. A defense mechanism whereby impulses and thoughts unacceptable to the ego are pushed into the unconscious.

residual schizophrenia. Diagnosis given to patients who have had an episode of schizophrenia but who presently show no psychotic symptoms, though signs of the disorder do exist.

resolution phase. The fourth and final stage of the sexual response cycle, characterized by an abatement of muscle tension, relaxation, and a sense of well-being.

response set. The tendency of an individual to respond in a particular way to questions or statements on a test—for example, with a False—regardless of the content of each query or statement.

retrospective reports. Recollections by an individual of past events.

Rett's disorder. A very rare pervasive developmental disorder found only in girls, with onset in the first or second year of life; symptoms include decelerated head growth, lost ability to use hands purposefully, uncoordinated walking, poor speech production and comprehension, and poor interpersonal relations. The child may improve later in life, but usually will remain severely or profoundly mentally retarded.

reuptake. Cellular process by which released neurotransmitters are taken back into the presynaptic cell, terminating their present postsynaptic effect but making them available for subsequent modulation of nerve impulse transmission.

reversal (ABAB) design. An experimental design in which behavior is measured during a baseline period (A), during a period when a treatment is introduced (B), during the reinstatement of the conditions that prevailed in the baseline period (A), and finally during a reintroduction of the treatment (B); commonly used in operant research to isolate cause–effect relationships.

reward system. System of brain structures whose modification may help explain why people are less motivated to pursue rewards during depression and overly focused on possible rewards during mania.

right to refuse treatment. A legal principle according to which a hospitalized patient may decline to participate in treatment.

right to treatment. A legal principle according to which a hospitalized patient must be provided some minimal amount and quality of professional intervention, enough to afford a realistic opportunity for meaningful improvement.

risk factor. A condition or variable that increases the likelihood of developing a disorder.

Rorschach Inkblot Test. A projective test in which the examinee is instructed to interpret a series of 10 inkblots reproduced on cards.

schema. A mental structure for organizing information about the world. Pl. schemata.

schizoaffective disorder. Diagnosis applied when a patient has symptoms of both mood disorder and either schizophreniform disorder or schizophrenia.

schizoid personality disorder. Personality disorder defined by emotional aloofness, indifference to the praise, criticism, and feelings of others, maintenance of few, if any, close friendships, and solitary interests.

schizophrenia. A group of psychotic disorders characterized by major disturbances in thought, emotion, and behavior; disordered thinking in which ideas are not logically related; faulty perception and attention; bizarre disturbances in motor activity; flat or inappropriate emotions; reduced tolerance for stress in interpersonal relations and withdrawal from people and reality, often into a fantasy life of delusions and hallucinations. See *schizoaffective disorder*, *schizophreniform disorder*, and *brief psychotic disorder*.

schizophreniform disorder. Diagnosis given to people who have all the symptoms of schizophrenia, for more than 2 weeks but less than 6 months. See *brief psychotic disorder*.

schizotypal personality disorder. Personality disorder defined by eccentricity, oddities of thought and perception (magical thinking, illusions, depersonalization, derealization), digressive speech involving overelaborations, and social isolation; under stress, behavior may appear psychotic.

school phobia. An acute, irrational dread of attending school, usually accompanied by somatic complaints; the most common phobia of childhood.

seasonal. Term applied by DSM-IV-TR to MDD or bipolar disorders if episodes happen regularly at a particular time of the year; therapy involves exposing patients to bright white light.

second messengers. Intracellular molecules whose levels are increased by sustained activity of neurotransmitter, for example, receptors, and which affect the resting states of ion channels or regulate gene expression of receptor molecules, thus modulating the cell's sensitivity to neurotransmitter.

secondary prevention. See *prevention*.

secondhand smoke. Also referred to as environmental tobacco smoke (ETS), the smoke from the burning end of a cigarette; contains higher concentrations of ammonia, carbon monoxide, nicotine, and tar than the smoke inhaled by the smoker.

secretory immunoglobulin A (sIgA). Antibody of the secretory immune system whose elevated level in the saliva correlates well with positive mood.

sedatives. Drugs that slow bodily activities, especially those of the central nervous system; used to reduce pain and tension and to induce relaxation and sleep.

selective abstraction. A cognitive bias in Beck's theory of depression wherein a person picks out from a complex situation only certain features and ignores aspects that could lead to a different conclusion.

selective mutism. A pattern of continuously refusing to speak in almost all social situations, including school, even though the child understands spoken language and is able to speak.

selective serotonin reuptake inhibitors (SSRIs). Any of various drugs that inhibit the presynaptic reuptake of the neurotransmitter serotonin, thereby prolonging its effects on postsynaptic neurons.

self-actualization. Fulfilling one's potential as an always growing human being; believed by client-centered therapists to be the master motive.

self-efficacy. In Bandura's theory, the person's belief that he or she can achieve particular goals.

self-monitoring. In behavioral assessment, a procedure whereby the individual observes and reports certain aspects of his or her own behavior, thoughts, or emotions.

sensate focus. A term applied to exercises prescribed at the beginning of the Masters and Johnson sex therapy program, in which partners are instructed to fondle each other to give pleasure but to refrain from intercourse, thus reducing anxiety about sexual performance.

separation anxiety disorder. A disorder in which the child feels intense fear and distress when away from someone on whom he or she is very dependent; said to be a significant cause of school phobia.

septal area. In the subcortical region of the brain, the area anterior to the thalamus.

serotonin. An indoleamine neurotransmitter of the central nervous system whose disturbances apparently figure in depression.

serotonin transporter gene. A particular gene critical to the gene–environment interactions that apparently contribute to the development of depression.

sex-reassignment surgery. An operation removing existing genitalia and constructing a substitute for the genitals of the opposite sex.

sexual aversion disorder. Avoidance of nearly all genital contact with other people.

sexual dysfunctions. Dysfunctions in which the appetitive or psychophysiological changes of the normal sexual response cycle are inhibited. Compare *hypoactive sexual desire disorder*.

sexual masochism. A marked preference for obtaining or increasing sexual gratification through subjection to pain or humiliation.

sexual orientation. An individual's self-identified preference for a sexual partner.

sexual response cycle. The general pattern of sexual physical processes and feelings, made up of five phases: appetitive interest, excitement, [plateau], orgasm, and resolution.

sexual sadism. A marked preference for obtaining or increasing sexual gratification by inflicting pain or humiliation on another person.

shaping. In operant conditioning, reinforcing responses that are successively closer approximations to the desired behavior.

shared environment. Factors that family members have in common, such as income level, child-rearing practices, and parental marital status and quality. Compare *nonshared environment*.

significant difference. See *statistical significance*.

single-subject experimental design. A design for an experiment conducted with a single subject. Typically, behavior is measured within a baseline condition, then during an experimental or treatment condition, and finally within the baseline condition again.

Skinner box. A laboratory apparatus in which an animal is placed for an operant-conditioning experiment; contains a lever or other device that the animal must manipulate to obtain a reward or avoid punishment.

social desirability. In completion of personality inventories, the tendency of the responder to give what he or she considers the socially acceptable answer, whether or not it is accurate.

social phobia. A collection of fears linked to the presence of other people.

social selection theory. An attempt to explain the correlation between social class and schizophrenia by arguing that people with schizophrenia tend to move downward in socioeconomic status. Compare *sociogenic hypothesis*.

social selectivity. The late-life shift in interest away from seeking new social interactions and toward cultivating those few social relationships that matter most, such as with family and close friends.

social worker. A mental health professional who holds a master of social work (M.S.W.) degree.

social-skills training. Behavior therapy procedures, such as modeling and behavior rehearsal, for teaching socially unknowledgeable individuals how to meet others, talk to them and maintain eye contact, give and receive criticism, offer and accept compliments, make requests and express feelings, and otherwise improve their relations with other people.

sociocognitive model (of DID). Etiological model of dissociative identity disorder that considers the condition to be the result of learning to enact social roles, though not through conscious deception, but in response to suggestion. Compare *posttraumatic model*.

sociogenic hypothesis. An idea that seeks causes in social conditions, for example, that being in a low social class can cause one to become schizophrenic. Compare *social selection theory*.

sociopath. See *antisocial personality*.

somatic arousal. Sweaty palms, fast heart rate, etc.; expected to increase in anxiety but not in depression.

somatic nervous system. The division of the nervous system that controls muscles under voluntary control. Compare *autonomic nervous system*.

somatization disorder (Briquet's syndrome). A somatoform disorder in which the person continually seeks medical help for recurrent and multiple physical symptoms that have no discoverable physical cause, despite a complicated medical history that is dramatically presented. Compare *hypochondriasis*.

somatoform disorders. Disorders in which symptoms suggest a physical problem but have no known physiological cause; believed to be linked to psychological conflicts and needs but not voluntarily assumed. See *somatization disorder (Briquet's syndrome), conversion disorder, pain disorder, and hypochondriasis*.

specific phobias. An unwarranted fear and avoidance of a specific object or circumstance, for example, fear of nonpoisonous snakes or fear of heights.

spectator role. As applied by Masters and Johnson, a pattern of behavior in which the individual's focus on and concern with sexual performance causes him or her to be an observer rather than a participant and thus impedes natural sexual responses.

standardization. The process of constructing a normed assessment procedure that meets the various psychometric criteria for reliability and validity.

state-dependent memory. The phenomenon wherein people are better able to remember an event if they are in the same state as when it occurred.

statistical significance. A result that has a low probability of having occurred by chance alone and is by convention regarded as important. Compare *clinical significance*.

statutory rape. Sexual intercourse between an adult and someone who is under the age of consent, as fixed by local statute. Compare *forced rape*.

stepped care. The practice of beginning treatment with the least intrusive intervention possible and moving on to more intensive efforts only if necessary.

stigma. The pernicious beliefs and attitudes held by a society, ascribed to groups considered deviant in some manner, such as the mentally ill.

stimulant. A drug, such as cocaine, that increases alertness and motor activity and at the same time reduces fatigue, allowing an individual to remain awake for an extended period of time.

stress. State of an organism subjected to a stressor; can take the form of increased autonomic activity and in the long term can cause breakdown of an organ or development of a mental disorder.

stress management. A range of psychological procedures that help people control and reduce their stress or anxiety.

stressor. An event that occasions stress in an organism, for example, loss of a loved one.

structural social support. A person's network of social relationships, for example, number of friends. Compare *functional social support*.

structured interview. An interview in which the questions are set out in a prescribed fashion for the interviewer; assists professionals in making diagnostic decisions based on standardized criteria.

stuttering. Communication disorder of childhood marked by frequent and pronounced verbal dysfluencies, such as repetitions of certain sounds.

sublimation. Defense mechanism entailing the conversion of sexual or aggressive impulses into socially valued behaviors, especially creative activity.

substance abuse. The use of a drug to such an extent that the person is often intoxicated throughout the day and fails in important obligations and in attempts to abstain, but there is no physiological dependence.

substance dependence. The abuse of a drug sometimes accompanied by a physiological dependence on it, made evident by tolerance and withdrawal symptoms; also called addiction.

substance-related disorders. Disorders in which drugs such as alcohol and cocaine are abused to such an extent that behavior becomes maladaptive; social and occupational functioning are impaired, and control or abstinence becomes impossible. Reliance on the drug may be either psychological, as in substance abuse, or physiological, as in substance dependence, or addiction.

subthreshold symptoms. Symptoms of a disorder that are clinically significant but do not meet full diagnostic criteria.

suicide. The intentional taking of one's own life.

suicide prevention centers. Staffed primarily by paraprofessionals who are trained to be empathic and to encourage suicidal callers—assumed to be ambivalent—to consider nondestructive ways of dealing with what is bothering them.

superego. In psychoanalytic theory, the part of the personality that acts as the conscience and reflects society's moral standards as learned from parents and teachers.

sympathetic nervous system. The division of the autonomic nervous system that acts on bodily systems—for example, contracting the blood vessels, reducing activity of the intestines, and increasing the heartbeat—to prepare the organism for exertion, emotional stress, or extreme cold. Compare parasympathetic nervous system.

symptom. An observable physiological or psychological manifestation of a disease.

synapse. Small gap between two neurons where the nerve signal passes electrically or chemically from the axon of the first to the dendrites, cell body, or axon of the second.

systematic desensitization. A major behavior therapy procedure that has a fearful person, while deeply relaxed, imagine a series of progressively more fearsome situations, such that fear is dispelled as a response incompatible with relaxation; useful for treating psychological problems in which anxiety is the principal difficulty.

tardive dyskinesia. A muscular disturbance of older patients who have taken phenothiazines for a very long time, marked by involuntary lip smacking and chin wagging.

technical eclecticism. An approach to psychotherapeutic integration in which the therapist works within a particular theoretical framework but occasionally imports techniques from other orientations—not subscribing to the theories that spawned them, but instead rationalizing the use of each technique from within one's framework.

temporal lobe. A large region of each cerebral hemisphere situated below the lateral sulcus and in front of the occipital lobe; contains primary auditory and general association areas.

tertiary prevention. See *prevention*.

test-retest reliability. See *reliability*.

tetrahydrocannabinol (THC). The major active chemical in marijuana and hashish.

thalamus. A major brain relay station consisting of two egg-shaped lobes; receives impulses from all sensory areas except the olfactory and transmits them to the cerebrum for higher processing.

Thematic Apperception Test (TAT). A projective test consisting of black-and-white pictures, each depicting a potentially emotion-laden situation, about each of which the examinee is instructed to make up a story. See also *projective hypothesis*.

theoretical integration. An approach to psychotherapeutic integration that aims to synthesize not only techniques, but theoretical perspectives and paradigms (e.g., psychoanalysis and behavior therapy).

theory. A formally stated and coherent set of propositions that explain and logically order a range of phenomena, generating testable predictions or hypotheses.

therapeutic (or working) alliance. The collaborative relationship between therapist and patient, in which they share an affective bond and an ability to agree on treatment goals.

third-variable problem. The difficulty in the correlational method of research whereby the relationship between two variables may be attributable to a third factor.

Thorazine. Trade name for chlorpromazine, one of the antipsychotic drugs and a member of the phenothiazine group.

thought suppression. Key feature of obsessive-compulsive disorder; has the paradoxical effect of inducing preoccupation with the object of thought.

thyroid gland. An endocrine structure whose two lobes are located on either side of the windpipe; secretes thyroxin.

time-of-measurement effects. A possible confound in longitudinal studies whereby conditions at a particular point in time can have a specific effect on a variable that is being studied over time.

time-out. An operant conditioning procedure in which, after bad behavior, the person is temporarily removed from a setting where reinforcers can be obtained and placed in a less desirable setting, for example, in a boring room.

token economy. A behavior therapy procedure, based on operant conditioning principles, in which hospitalized patients are given scrip rewards, such as poker chips, for socially constructive behavior. The tokens can be exchanged for desirable items and activities such as cigarettes and extra time away from the ward.

tolerance. A physiological process in which greater and greater amounts of an addictive drug are required to produce the same effect. See also *substance dependence*.

trait. A somatic characteristic; or an enduring psychological predisposition to respond in a particular way.

transference. The venting of the analysand's emotions, either positive or negative, by treating the psychoanalyst as the symbolic representative of someone important in the past.

transvestic fetishism. The practice of dressing in the clothing of the opposite sex, for the purpose of sexual arousal.

tricyclic antidepressants. A group of antidepressants with molecular structures characterized by three fused rings; interfere with the reuptake of norepinephrine and serotonin.

trisomy. See *Down syndrome*.

tryptophan. Amino acid that is the major precursor of serotonin; experimental depletion has found that a lowered serotonin level causes temporary depressive symptoms in people with a personal or family history of depression.

twin method. Research strategy in behavior genetics in which concordance rates of monozygotic and dizygotic twins are compared.

Type A behavior pattern. One of two contrasting psychological patterns revealed through studies seeking the cause of coronary heart disease. Type A people are competitive, rushed, hostile, and overcommitted to their work, and are believed to be at heightened risk for heart disease; Type B people are more relaxed and relatively free of pressure.

unconditional positive regard. According to Rogers, a crucial attitude for the client-centered therapist to adopt toward the client, who needs to feel complete acceptance as a person in order to evaluate the extent to which current behavior contributes to self-actualization.

unconditioned response (UCR). See *classical conditioning.*

unconditioned stimulus (UCS). See *classical conditioning.*

unconscious. A state of unawareness without sensation or thought; in psychoanalytic theory, the part of the personality, in particular the id impulses or energy, of which the ego is unaware.

undifferentiated schizophrenia. Diagnosis for patients whose symptoms either do not fit any listed category of schizophrenia or meet the criteria for more than one subtype.

vaginismus. Painful, spasmodic contractions of the outer third of the vagina, making penetration impossible or extremely difficult.

validity. In research, includes internal, the extent to which results can be confidently attributed to the manipulation of the independent variable, and external, the extent to which results may be generalized to other populations and settings. Validity as applied to psychiatric diagnoses includes concurrent, the extent to which previously undiscovered features are found among patients with the same diagnosis, and predictive, the extent to which predictions can be made about the future behavior of patients with the same diagnosis. Validity as applied to psychological and psychiatric measures includes content validity, the extent to which a measure adequately samples the domain of interest, and criterion, the extent to which a measure is associated in an expected way with some other measure (the criterion). See also *construct validity.*

ventricles. Cavities deep within the brain, filled with cerebrospinal fluid, that connect to the spinal cord.

voyeurism. Marked preference for obtaining sexual gratification by watching others in a state of undress or having sexual relations.

white matter. Neural tissue, particularly of the brain and spinal cord, consisting of tracts or bundles of myelinated (sheathed) nerve fibers. Compare *gray matter.*

withdrawal. Negative physiological and psychological reactions evidenced when a person suddenly stops taking an addictive drug; cramps, restlessness, and even death are examples. See *substance dependence.*

References

Abhey, S. E., & Stewart, D. E. (2000). Gender and psychosomatic aspects of ischemic disease. *Journal of Psychosomatic Research, 48,* 417–423.

Abikoff, H. B., & Hechtman, L. (1996). Multimodal therapy and stimulants in the treatment of children with attention-deficit hyperactivity disorder. In E. D. Hibbs & P. S. Jensen (Eds.), *Psychosocial treatments for child and adolescent disorders: Empirically based strategies for clinical practice* (pp. 341–369). Washington, DC: American Psychological Association.

Abou-Saleh, M. T., Younis, Y., & Karim, L. (1998). Anorexia nervosa in an Arab culture. *International Journal of Eating Disorders, 23,* 207–212.

Abramson, L. Y., Metalsky, G. I., & Alloy, L. B. (1989). Hopelessness depression: A theory-based subtype of depression. *Psychological Review, 96,* 358–372.

Abramson, L. Y., Seligman, M. E. P., & Teasdale, J. D. (1978). Learned helplessness in humans: Critique and reformulation. *Journal of Abnormal Psychology, 87,* 49–74.

Achenbach, T. M., Bird, H. R., Canino, G., Phares, V., Gould, M. S., & Rubio-Stipec, M. (1990). Epidemiological comparisons of Puerto Rican and U.S. mainland children: Parent, teacher and self-reports. *Journal of the American Academy of Child and Adolescent Psychiatry, 29,* 84–93.

Achenbach, T. M., Hensley, V. R., Phares, V., & Grayson, D. (1990). Problems and competencies reported by parents of Australian and American children. *Journal of Child Psychology and Psychiatry, 31,* 265–286.

Achenbach, T. M., Howell, C. T., McConaughy, S. H., & Stanger, C. (1995). Six-year predictors of problems in a national sample of children and youth: I. Cross-informant syndromes. *Journal of the American Academy of Child and Adolescent Psychiatry, 34,* 336–347.

Ackerman, S. J., & Hilsenroth, M. J. (2003). A review of therapist charcteristics and techniques positively impacting the therapeutic alliance. *Clinical Psychology Review, 23,* 1–33.

Acocella, J. (1999). *Creating hysteria: Women and multiple personality disorder.* San Francisco: Jossey-Bass.

Acton, G. J., & Kang, J. (2001). Interventions to reduce the burden of caregiving for an adult with dementia: A meta-analysis. *Research in Nursing and Health, 24,* 349–360.

Addis, M. E., & Krasnow, A. D. (2000). A national survey of practicing psychologists' attitudes toward psychotherapy treatment manuals. *Journal of Consulting and Clinical Psychology, 68,* 331–339.

Adler, A. (1930). *Guiding the child on the principles of individual psychology.* New York: Greenberg.

Adler, P. S., & Ditto, B. (1998). Psychophysiological effects of interviews about emotional events on offspring of hypertensives and normotensives. *International Journal of Psychophysiology, 28,* 263–271.

Adler, R. H., Zamboni, P., Hofer, T., & Hemmeler, W. (1997). How not to miss a somatic needle in a haystack of chronic pain. *Journal of Psychosomatic Research, 42,* 499–505.

Afflek, G., Apter, A., Tennen, H., Reisine, S., Barrows, E., Willard, A., et al. (2000). Mood states associated with transitory changes in asthma symptoms and peak expiratory flow. *Psychosomatic Medicine, 62,* 61–68.

Agras, W. S., Crow, S. J., Halmi, K. A., Mitchell, J. E., Wilson, G. T., & Kraemer, H. C. (2000). Outcome predictors for the cognitive-behavioral treatment of bulimia nervosa: Data from a multisite study. *American Journal of Psychiatry, 157,* 1302–1308.

Agras, W. S., Rossiter, E. M., Arnow, B., Schneider, J. A., Telch, C. F., Raeburn, S. D., Bruce, B., Perl, M., & Koran, L. M. (1992). Pharmacologic and cognitive-behavioral treatment for bulimia nervosa: A controlled comparison. *American Journal of Psychiatry, 149,* 82–87.

Agras, W. S., Rossiter, E. M., Arnow, B. et al. (1994). One-year follow-up of psychosocial and pharmacologic treatments for bulimia nervosa. *Journal of Clinical Psychiatry, 55,* 179–183.

Akillas, E., & Efran, J. S. (1995). Symptom prescription and reframing: Should they be combined? *Cognitive Therapy and Research, 19,* 263–279.

Akyuez, G., Dogan, O., Sar, V., Yargic, L. I., & Tutkun, H. (1999). Frequency of dissociative disorder in the general population in Turkey. *Comprehensive Psychiatry, 40,* 151–159.

Albee, G. W., Lane, E. A., & Reuter, J. M. (1964). Childhood intelligence of future schizophrenics and neighborhood peers. *Journal of Psychology, 58,* 141–144.

Albertini, R. S., & Phillips, K. A. (1999). Thirty-three cases of body dysmorphic disorder in children and adolescents. *Journal of the American Academy of Child and Adolescent Psychiatry, 38,* 453–459.

Alden, L. E. (1989). Short-term structured treatment for avoidant personality disorder. *Journal of Consulting and Clinical Psychology, 57,* 756–764.

Alden, L. E., Laposa, J. M., Taylor, C. T., & Ryder, A. G. (2002). Avoidant personality disorder: Current status and future directions. *Journal of Personality Disorders, 16,* 1–29.

Alexander, F. (1950). *Psychosomatic medicine.* New York: Norton.

Alexander, P. C., & Lupfer, S. L. (1987). Family characteristics and long-term consequences associated with sexual abuse. *Archives of Sexual Behavior, 16,* 235–245.

Alferi, S. M., Carver, C. S., Antoni, M. H., Weiss, S., & Duran, R. E. (2001). An exploratory study of social support, distress, and life disruption among low-income Hispanic women under treatment for early stage breast cancer. *Health Psychology, 20,* 41–46.

Allan, C., Smith, I., & Mellin, M. (2000). Detoxification from alcohol: A comparison of home detoxification and hospital-based day patient care. *Alcohol & Alcoholism, 35,* 66–69.

Allderidge, P. (1979). Hospitals, mad houses, and asylums: Cycles in the care of the insane. *British Journal of Psychiatry, 134,* 321–324.

Allen, Johns, L. C., Fu, C. H. Y., Broome, M. R., Vythelingum, G. N., & McGuire, P. K. (2004). Misattribution of external speech in patients with hallucinations and delusions. *Schizophrenia Research, 69,* 277–287.

Allnutt, S. H., Bradford, J. M., Greenberg, D. M., & Curry, S. (1996). Co-morbidity of alcoholism and the paraphilias. *Journal of Forensic Science, 41,* 234–239.

Alloy, L. B., Abramson, L. Y., Hogan, M. E., Whitehouse, W. G., Rose, D. T., Robinson, M. S., Kim, R. S., & Lapkin, J. B. (2000). The Temple-Wisconsin Cognitive Vulnerability to Depression Project: Lifetime history of Axis I psychopathology in individuals at high and low cognitive risk for depression. *Journal of Abnormal Psychology, 109,* 403–418.

Alloy, L. B., Abramson, L. Y., Whitehouse, W. G., Hogan, M. E., Tashman, N. A., Steinberg, D. L., Rose, D. T., & Donovan, P. (1999). Depressogenic cognitive styles: Predictive validity, information processing, personality characteristics, and developmental origins. *Behavior Research and Therapy, 37,* 503–531.

Almada, S. J. (1991). Neuroticism and cynicism and risk of death in middle aged men: The Western Electric study. *Psychosomatic Medicine, 53,* 165–175.

Alonso-Zaldivar, R. (1999, February 23). Alcohol-related road deaths analyzed. *Los Angeles Times,* pp. A12.

Alpert, J. E., Uebelacker, L. A., McLean, N. E., Nierenberg, A. A., et al. (1997). Social phobia, avoidant personality disorder and atypical depression: Co-occurrence and clinical implications. *Psychological Medicine, 27,* 627–633.

Altamura, C., Paluello, M. M., Mundo, E., Medda, S., & Mannu, P. (2001). Clinical and subclinical body dysmorphic disorder. *European Archives of Psychiatry and Clinical Neuroscience, 251,* 105–108.

Altman, D. G., Flora, J. A., & Farquhar, J. W. (1986, August). *Institutionalizing community-based health promotion programs.* Paper presented at the annual meeting of the American Psychological Association, Washington, DC.

Altshuler, L., Suppes, T., Black, D., Nolen, W. A., Keck, P. E., Jr., Frye, M. A., McElroy, S., Kupka, R., Grunze, H., Walden, J., Leverich, G., Denicoff, K., Luckenbaugh, D., & Post, R. (2003). Impact of antidepressant discontinuation after acute bipolar depression remission on rates of depressive relapse at 1-year follow-up. *American Journal of Psychiatry, 160,* 1252–1262.

Alwahhabi, F. (2003). Anxiety symptoms and generalized anxiety disorder in the elderly: A review. *Harvard Review of Psychiatry, 11,* 180–193.

Amador, X. F., Flaum, M., Andreasen, N. C., Strauss, D. H., Yale, S. A., et al. (1994). Awareness of illness in schizophrenia and schizoaffective and mood disorder. *Archives of General Psychiatry, 51,* 826–836.

Aman, M. G., & Langworthy, K. (2000). Pharmacotherapy for hyperactivity in children with autism and other pervasive developmental disorders. *Journal of Autism and Developmental Disorders, 30,* 451–459.

American Association of Retired Persons. (1999). *Assisted living in the United States.* Available at www.aarp.org. AARP Publication FS62R.

American Heart Association. (2002). *2002 Heart and stroke statistical update.* Dallas, Texas: American Heart Association.

American Heart Association. (2004). *Heart disease and stroke statistics-2004 update.* Dallas, Texas: American Heart Association.

American Law Institute. (1962). *Model penal code: Proposed official draft.* Philadelphia: Author.

American Psychiatric Association Board of Trustees. (1993). *Statement on memories of sexual abuse.* Washington, DC: American Psychiatric Association.

American Psychiatric Association. (1992). AIDS policy: Guidelines for outpatient psychiatric services. *American Journal of Psychiatry, 149,* 721.

American Psychiatric Association. (1993). Practice guidelines for major depressive disorder in adults. *American Journal of Psychiatry, 150,* All.

American Psychiatric Association. (1994). *Diagnostic and statistical manual of mental disorders (DSM-IV)* (4th ed.). Washington, DC: Author.

American Psychiatric Association. *Diagnostic and statistical manual of mental disorders (DSM-IV-TR).* First edition, 1952; second edition, 1968; third edition, 1980; revised, 1987; fourth edition, 1994; revised 2000. Washington, DC: Author.

American Psychological Association. (2002). Ethical principles of psychologists and code of conduct. *American Psychologist, 57,* 1060–1073. Available from the APA Web site: http://www.apa.org/ethics/code2002.html

American Psychological Association. (2004). Guidelines for psychological practice with older adults. *American Psychologist, 59,* 236–260.

Anand et al. (2000). Brain SPECT Imaging of Amphetamine-Induced Dopamine Release in Euthymic BPD Patients. *American Journal of Psychiatry, 157,* 1109–1114.

Anastopoulos, A. D., Shelton, T., DuPaul, G. J., & Guevremont, D. C. (1993). Parent training for attention deficit hyperactivity disorder: Its impact on parent functioning. *Journal of Abnormal Child Psychology, 20,* 503–520.

Ancoli Israel, S., Kripke, D. F., Klauber, M. R., Fell, R., Stepnowsky, C., & Estline, E., et al. (1996). Morbidity, mortality and sleep-disordered breathing in community dwelling elderly. *Sleep: Journal of Sleep Research and Sleep Medicine, 19,* 277–282.

Andersen, B. L., Cyranowski, J. M., & Aarestad, S. (2000). Beyond artificial, sex-linked distinctions to conceptualize female sexuality: Comment on Baumeister (2000). *Psychological Bulletin, 126*(3), 380–384.

Andersen, B. L., Cyranowski, J. M., & Espindle, D. (1999). Men's sexual self-schema. *Journal of Personality and Social Psychology, 76,* 645–661.

Anderson, B. L., Kiecolt-Glaser, J. K., & Glaser, R. (1994). A biobehavioral model of cancer stress and disease course. *American Psychologist, 49,* 389–404.

Anderson, C. A., Hinshaw, S. P., & Simmel, C. (1994). Mother-child interactions in ADHD and comparison boys: Relationships to overt and covert externalizing behavior. *Journal of Abnormal Child Psychology, 22,* 247–265.

Anderson, E. M., & Lambert, M. J. (1995). Short-term dynamically oriented psychotherapy: A review and meta-analysis. *Clinical Psychology Review, 15,* 503–514.

Anderson, G. M., & Hoshino, Y. (1987). Neurochemical studies of autism. In D. J. Cohen, A. M. Donnellan, & R. Paul (Eds.), *Handbook of autism and pervasive developmental disorders.* (pp. 166–191) New York: Wiley.

Anderson, J. C., (1996). Is childhood hyperactivity the product of western culture?. *Lancet 348,* 73–74.

Anderson, J. C., Williams, S., McGee, R., & Silva, A. (1987). DSM-III disorders in pre-adolescent children: Prevalence in a large sample from the general population. *Archives of General Psychiatry, 44,* 69–76.

Anderson, L. T., Campbell, M., Adams, P., Small, A. M., Perry, R., & Shell, J. (1989). The effects of haloperidol on discrimination learning and behavioral symptoms in autistic children. *Journal of Autism and Developmental Disorders, 19,* 227–239.

Anderson, M. C., & Green, C. (2001). Suppressing unwanted memories by executive control. *Nature, 410,* 366–369.

Anderson, S., Hanson, R., Malecha, M., Oftelie, A., Erickson, C., & Clark, J. M. (1997). The effectiveness of naltrexone in treating task attending, aggression, self-injury, and stereotypic mannerisms of six young males with autism or pervasive developmental disorders. *Journal of Developmental and Physical Disabilities, 9,* 211–221.

Andersson, T., Magnusson, D., & Wennberg, P. (1997). Early aggressiveness and hyperactivity as indicators of adult alcohol problems and criminality: A prospective longitudinal study of male subjects. *Studies on Crime and Crime Prevention, 6,* 7–20.

Andreasen, N. C. (1979). Thought, language, and communication disorders: 2. Diagnostic significance. *Archives of General Psychiatry, 36,* 1325–1330.

Andreasen, N. C., & Olsen, S. A. (1982). Negative versus positive schizophrenia. Definition and validation. *Archives of General Psychiatry, 39,* 789–794.

Andreasen, N. C., Olsen, S. A., Dennert, J. W., & Smith, M. R. (1982). Ventricular enlargement in schizophrenia: Relationship to positive and negative symptoms. *American Journal of Psychiatry, 139,* 297–302.

Anglin, M. D., Burke, C., Perrochet, B., Stamper, E., & Dawud-Noursi, S. (2000). History of the methamphetamine problem. *Journal of Psychoactive Drugs, 32,* 137–141.

Angold, A., Erkanli, A., Egger, H. L., & Costello, E. J. (2000). Stimulant treatment for children: A community perspective. *Journal of the American Academy of Child and Adolescent Psychiatry, 39,* 975–984.

Angold, A., & Rutter, M. (1992). Effects of age and pubertal status on depression in a large clinical sample. *Development and Psychopathology, 4,* 5–28.

Angrist, B., Lee, H. K., & Gershon, S. (1974). The antagonism of amphetamine-induced symptomatology by a neuroleptic. *American Journal of Psychiatry, 131,* 817–819.

Angst, F., Stassen, H. H., Clayton, P. J., & Angst, J. (2002). Mortality of patients with mood disorders: Follow-up over 34–38 years. *Journal of Affective Disorders, 68,* 167–181.

Angst, J. (1998). Sexual problems in healthy and depressed persons. *International Clinical Psychopharmacology, 13*(Suppl. 6), S1–S4.

Anthony, J. L., & Lonigan, C. L. (2004). The nature of phonological awareness: Converging evidence from four studies of preschool and early grade school children. *Journal of Educational Psychology, 96,* 43–55.

Antoni, M. H., Cruess, D. G., Cruess, S., et al. (2000). Cognitive-behavioral stress management intervention effects on anxiety, 24-Hr urinary norepinephrine output, and T-cytotoxic/suppressor cells over time among symptomatic HIV-infected gay men. *Journal of Consulting and Clinical Psychology, 68,* 31–45.

Antony, M. M., & Barlow, D. H. (2004). Specific phobias. In D. H. Barlow (Ed.), *Anxiety and its disorders: The nature and treatment of anxiety and panic* (pp. 380–417). New York: Guilford.

Apodaca, T. R., & Miller, W. R. (2003). A meta-analysis of the effectiveness of bibliotherapy for alcohol problems. *Journal of Clinical Psychology, 59,* 289–304.

Appel, L. J., Moore, T. J., Obarzanek, E., Vollmer, W. M., Svetkey, L. P., Sacks, F. M., Bray, G. A., Vogt, T. M., Cutler, J. A., Windhauser, M. M., Lin, P-H., & Karanja, N., for the DASH Collaborative Research Group. (1997). A clinical trial of the effects of dietary patterns on blood pressure. *New England Journal of Medicine, 336,* 1117–1124.

Appelbaum, P. S., & Greer, A. (1994). Who's on trial? Multiple personalities and the insanity defense. *Hospital and Community Psychiatry, 45,* 965–966.

Appelbaum, P. S., & Grisso, T. (1995). The MacArthur Treatment Competence Study: 1. Mental illness and competence to consent to treatment. *Law and Human Behavior, 19,* 105–126.

Appelbaum, P. S., Grisso, T., Frank, E., O'Donnel, S., & Kupfer, D. (1999). Capacities of depressed patients to consent to research. *American Journal of Psychiatry, 156,* 1380–1384.

Appelbaum, P. S., & Gutheil, T. (1991). *Clinical handbook of psychiatry and the law.* Baltimore: Williams & Wilkins.

Appelbaum, P. S., Robbins, P. C., & Monahan, J. (2000). Violence and delusions: Data from the MacArthur Violence Risk Assessment Study. *American Journal of Psychiatry, 157,* 566–557.

Apperloo, M. J. A., Van Der, Stege, Jolande, G., Hoek, A., & Weijmar Schultz, W. C. M. (2003). In the mood for sex: The value of androgens. *Journal of Sex and Marital Therapy, 29*(2), 87–102.

Appleby, P. R., Miller, L. C., & Rothspan, S. (1999). The paradox of trust for male couples: When risking is a part of loving. *Personal Relationships, 6,* 81–93.

Apt, C., & Hurlbert, D. H. (1994). The sexual attitudes, behavior, and relationships of women with histrionic personality disorder. *Journal of Sex and Marital Therapy, 20,* 125–133.

Apter, A. J., Affleck, G., Reisine, S. T., Tennen, H. A., Barrows, E., Wells, M., et al. (1997). Perception of airway obstruction in asthma: Sequential daily analyses of symptoms, peak expiratory flow rate, and mood. *Journal of Allergy and Clinical Immunology, 99,* 605–612.

Araujo, A. B., Durante, R., Feldman, H. A., Goldstein, I., & McKinley, J. B. (1998). The relationship between depressive symptoms and male erectile dysfunction: Cross-sectional results from the Massachusetts Male Aging Study. *Psychosomatic Medicine, 60,* 458–465.

Arbisi, P. A., Ben-Porath, Y. S., & McNulty, J. (2002). A comparison of MMPI-2 validity in African American and Caucasian psychiatric patients. *Psychological Assessment, 14,* 3–15.

Arentewicz, G., & Schmidt, G. (1983). *The treatment of sexual disorders: Concepts and techniques of couple therapy.* New York: Basic Books.

Arias, E., Anderson, R. N., Kung, H. C., Murphy, S. L., & Kochanek, K. D. (2003). *Deaths: Final Reports, 52.* Hyattsville, MD: National Center for Health Statistics. DHHS Publication No. 2003–1120.

Arkowitz, H. (1992). Integrative theories of therapy. In D. Freedheim (Ed.), *The history of psychotherapy: A century of change.* Washington, DC: American Psychological Association.

Arndt, I. O., Dorozynsky, L., Woody, G. E., McLellan, A. T., & O'Brien, C. P. (1992). Desipramine treatment of cocaine dependence in methadone-maintained patients. *Archives of General Psychiatry, 49,* 888–893.

Arnold, E. H., O'Leary, S. G., & Edwards, G. H. (1997). Father involvement and self-reported parenting of children with attention deficit hyperactivity disorder. *Journal of Consulting and Clinical Psychology, 65,* 337–342.

Arnold, E. M., Kirk, R. S., Roberts, A. C., Griffith, D. P., Meadows, K., & Julian, J., et al. (2003). Treatment of incarcerated, sexually-abused adolescent females: An outcome study. *Journal of Child Sexual Abuse, 12*(1), 123–139.

Arnold, L. E., Elliott, M., Sachs, L., et al. (2003). Effects of ethnicity on treatment attendance, stimulant response/dose, and 14-month outcome in ADHD. *Journal of Consulting and Clinical Psychology, 71,* 713–727.

Arnold, L. M., Keck, P. E., Jr., Collins J., Wilson, R., Fleck, D. E., Corey, K. B., Amicone, J., Adebimpe, V. R., & Strakowski, S. M. (2004). Ethnicity and first-rank symptoms in patients with psychosis. *Schizophrenia Research, 67,* 207–212.

Arnow, B., Kenardy, J., & Agras, W. S. (1992). Binge eating among the obese. *Journal of Behavioral Medicine, 15,* 155–170.

Aronson, E. (2004). *The social animal.* 9th edition. New York: Worth.

Artiles, A. J., & Trent, S. C. (1994). Overrepresentation of minority students in special education: A continuing debate. *Journal of Special Education, 27,* 410–437.

Ashton, H., & Young, A. H. (2003). GABA-ergic drugs: Exit stage left, enter stage right. *Journal of Psychopharmacology, 17,* 174–178.

Asmundson, G. J., Larsen, D. K., & Stein, M. B. (1998). Panic disorder and vestibular disturbance: An overview of empirical findings and clinical implications. *Journal of Psychosomatic Research, 44,* 107–120.

Aspinwall, L. G., Kemeny, M. E., Taylor, S. E., Schneider, S. G., & Dudley, J. P. (1991). Psychological predictors of gay mens' AIDS risk-reduction behavior. *Health Psychology, 10,* 432–444.

Associated Press. (1998). Bosnian Serb admits to raping four women. *Los Angeles Times,* pp. A6.

Atkinson, D. R., Brown, M. T., Parham, T. A., & Matthews, L. G. (1996). African American client skin tone and clinical judgments of African American and European American psychologists. *Professional Psychology: Research and Practice, 27,* 500–505.

Attia, E., Haiman, C., Walsh, B. T., & Flater, S. R. (1998). Does fluoxetine augment the inpatient treatment of anorexia nervosa? *American Journal of Psychiatry, 155,* 548–551.

Auerbach, J. D., Wypiijewska, C., Brodie, H., & Keith, H. (1994). *AIDS and behavior: An integrated approach.* Washington, DC, US: National Academy Press.

August, G. J., Realmuto, G. M., MacDonald, A. W., Nugent, S. M., & Crosby, R. (1996). Prevalence of ADHD and comorbid disorders among elementary school children screened for disruptive behavior. *Journal of Abnormal Child Psychology, 24,* 555–569.

Avissar, S., Nechamkin, Y., Barki-Harrington, L., Roitman, G., & Schreiber, G. (1997). Differential G protein measures in mononuclear leukocytes of patients with bipolar mood disorder are state dependent. *Journal of Affective Disorders, 43,* 85–93.

Avissar, S., Schreiber, G., Nechamkin, Y., Nehaus, I., Lam, G., et al. (1999). The effects of seasons and light therapy on G protein levels in mononuclear leukocytes in patients with seasonal, affective disorder. *Archives of General Psychiatry, 56,* 178–184.

Ayanian, J. Z., & Cleary, P. D. (1999). Perceived risks of heart disease and cancer among cigarete smokers. *JAMA, 281,* 1019–1021.

Azrin, N. H., Sisson, R. W., Meyers, R., & Godley, M. (1982). Alcoholism treatment by disulfiram and community reinforcement therapy. *Journal of Behaviour Therapy and Experimental Psychiatry, 13,* 105–112.

Bach, A. K., Wincze, J. P., & Barlow, D. H. (2001). Sexual dysfunction. In D. H. Barlow (Eds.), *Clinical handbook of psychological disorders* (pp. 562–608). New York: Guilford.

Bach, G. R. (1966). The marathon group: Intensive practice of intimate interactions. *Psychological Reports, 181,* 995–1002.

Bach, P. B., Cramer, L. D., Warren, J. L., & Begg, C. B. (1999). Racial differences in the treatment of early-stage lung cancer. *New England Journal of Medicine 341,* 1198–1205.

Bachrach, H., Galatzer-Levy, R., Skolnikoff, A., & Waldron, S. (1991). On the efficacy of psychoanalysis. *Journal of the American Psychoanalytic Association, 39,* 871–916.

Badner, J. A., & Gershon, E. S. (2002). Meta-analysis of whole-genome linkage scans of bipolar disorder and schizophrenia. *Molecular Psychiatry, 7,* 405–411.

Baer, J. S., & Lichtenstein, E. (1988). Cognitive assessment. In D. M. Donovan & G. A. Marlatt (Eds.), *Assessment of addictive behaviors* (pp. 189–213). New York: Guilford.

Baer, L., & Jenike, M. A. (1992). Personality disorders in obsessive-compulsive disorder. *Psychiatric Clinics of North America, 15,* 803–812.

Baer, R. A., & Sekirnjak, G. (1997). Detection of underreporting on the MMPI-II in a clinical population. Effects of information about validity scales. *Journal of Personality Assessment, 69,* 555–567.

Bagby, M. R., Nicholson, R. A., Bacchionchi, J. R., et al. (2002). The predictive capacity of the MMPI-2 and PAI validity scales and indexes to detect coached and uncoached feigning. *Journal of Personality Assessment, 78,* 69–86.

Bailey, A., LeCouteur, A., Gottesman, I., Bolton, P., Simonoff, E., Yuzda, E., & Rutter, M. (1995). Autism as a strongly genetic disorder: Evidence from a British twin study. *Psychological Medicine, 25,* 63–77.

Bailey, D. B., Jr., Hatton, D. D., et al. (2001). Autistic behavior, FMR1 protein, and developmental trajectories in young males with fragile X syndrome. *Journal of Autism and Developmental Disorders, 31,* 165–174.

Bailey, J. M. (2003). *The Man Who Would Be Queen.* Joseph Henry Press: Washington, DC.

Bailey, J. M., Dunne, M. P., & Martin, N. G. (2000). Genetic and environmental influences on sexual orientation and its correlates in an Australian twin sample. *Journal of Personality and Social Psychology, 78,* 524–536.

Baker, B., Paquette, M., Szalai, J., Driver, H., Perger, T., Helmers, K., et al. (2000). The influence of marital adjustment on 3-year left ventricular mass and ambulatory blood pressure in mild hypertension. *Archives of Internal Medicine, 160,* 3453–3458.

Baldessarini, R. J., & Hennen, J. (2004). Genetics of suicide: An overview. *Harvard Review of Psychiatry, 12,* 1–13.

Baldessarini, R. J., Tondo, L., Goodwin, F. K., Fireman, B., Simon, G. E., Hunkeler, E. M., et al. (2004). Suicide risk and treatments for patients with bipolar disorder; suicide risk in bipolar disorder during treatment with lithium and divalproex; reducing suicidal ideation and depressive symptoms in depressed older primary care patients: A randomized controlled trial. *JAMA: 290,* 1081–1519.

Ball, J., & Lehder Roberts, D. (2004). *Oxycodone, hydrocodone, and polydrug use 2002. The DAWN Report.* Office of Applied Statistics (OAS), Substance Abuse and Mental Health Services Administration (SAMHSA), U.S. Department of Health and Human Services.

Ball, J. C., & Ross, A. (1991). *The effectiveness of methadone maintenance treatment.* New York: Springer-Verlag.

Ball, S. A., Carroll, K. M., & Rounsaville, B. T. (1994). Sensation seeking, substance abuse, and psychopathology in treatment-seeking and community cocaine abusers. *Journal of Consulting and Clinical Psychology, 62,* 1053–1057.

Bancroft, J., Loftus, J., & Long, J. S. (2003). Distress about sex: A national survey of women in heterosexual relationships. *Archives of Sexual Behavior, 32,* 193–208.

Bandura, A. (1977). Self-efficacy: Toward a unifying theory of behavioral change. *Psychological Review, 84,* 191–215.

Bandura, A. (1986). *Social foundations of thought and action: A social cognitive theory.* Englewood Cliffs, NJ: Prentice Hall.

Bandura, A. (1997). *Self-efficacy: The exercise of control.* New York: Freeman.

Bandura, A., Blanchard, E. B., & Ritter, B. (1969). Relative efficacy of desensitization and modeling approaches for inducing behavioral, affective, and attitudinal changes. *Journal of Personality and Social Psychology, 13,* 173–199.

Bandura, A., & Menlove, F. L. (1968). Factors determining vicarious extinction of avoidance behavior through symbolic modeling. *Journal of Personality and Social Psychology, 8,* 99–108.

Bandura, A., & Perloff, B. (1967). Relative efficacy of self-monitored and externally imposed reinforcement systems. *Journal of Personality and Social Psychology, 7,* 111–116.

Banich, M. T., Passarotti, A. M., White, D. A., Nortz, M. J., & Steiner, R. D. (2000). Interhemispheric interaction during childhood: II. Children with early-treated phenylketonuria. *Developmental Neuropsychology, 18,* 53–71.

Bank, L., Marlowe, J. H., Reid, J. B., Patterson, G. R., & Weinrott, M. R. (1991). A comparative evaluation of parent-training interventions for families of chronic delinquents. *Journal of Abnormal Child Psychology, 19,* 15–33.

Bankier, B., Aigner, M., & Bach, M. (2001). Alexithymia in DSM-IV disorder: Comparative evaluation of somatoform disorder, panic disorder, obsessive-compulsive disorder, and depression. *Psychosomatics: Journal of Consultation Liaison Psychiatry, 42,* 235–240.

Banks, S. M., Salovey, P., Greener, S., Rothman, A. J., et al. (1995). The effects of message framing on mammography utilization. *Health Psychology, 14,* 178–184.

Barbarin, O. A., & Soler, R. E. (1993). Behavioral, emotional, and academic adjustment in a national probability sample of African-American children: Effects of age, gender, and family structure. *Journal of Black Psychology, 19,* 423–446.

Barch, D. M., Carter, C. S., Braver, T. S., et al. (2001). Selective deficits in prefrontal cortex function in medication-naïve patients with schizophrenia. *Archives of General Psychiatry, 58,* 280–288.

Barch, D. M., Carter, C. S., MacDonald, A. W., Braver, T. S., & Cohen, J. D. (2003). Context processing deficits in schizophrenia: Diagnostic specificity, four-week course, and relationship to clinical symptoms. *Journal of Abnormal Psychology, 112,* 132–143.

Barch, D. M., Csernansky, J. G., Conturo, T., & Snyder, A. Z. (2002). Working and long-term memory deficits in schizophrenia: Is there a common prefrontal mechanism? *Journal of Abnormal Psychology, 111,* 478–494.

Barefoot, J. C., Dahlstrom, G., & Williams, R. B. (1983). Hostility, CHD incidence, and total mortality: A 25-year follow-up study of 255 physicians. *Psychosomatic Medicine, 45,* 59–63.

Barkley, R. A. (1981). *Hyperactive children; A handbook for diagnosis and treatment.* New York: Guilford.

Barkley, R. A. (1990). *Attention-deficit hyperactivity disorder: A handbook for diagnosis and treatment.* New York: Guilford.

Barkley, R. A. (1997). Behavioral inhibition, sustained attention, and executive function: Constructing a unifying theory of ADHD. *Psychological Bulletin, 121,* 65–94.

Barkley, R. A. (1998). *Attention-deficit hyperactivity disorder: A handbook for diagnosis and treatment* (2nd ed.). New York: Guilford.

Barkley, R. A., DuPaul, G. J., & McMurray, M. B. (1990). A comprehensive evaluation of attention deficit disorder with and without hyperactivity defined by research criteria. *Journal of Consulting and Clinical Psychology, 58,* 775–789.

Barkley, R. A., Fischer, M., Edelbrock, C. S., & Smallish, L. (1990). The adolescent outcome of hyperactive children diagnosed by research criteria: 1. An 8 year prospective follow-up study. *Journal of the American Academy of Child and Adolescent Psychiatry, 29*, 546–557.

Barkley, R. A., Fischer, M., Smallish, L., & Fletcher, K. (2002). The persistence of Attention-Deficit Hyperactivity Disorder into young adulthood as a function of reporting source and definition of disorder. *Journal of Abnormal Psychology, 111*, 279–289.

Barkley, R. A., Fischer, M., Smallish, L., & Fletcher, K. (2003). Does the treatment of attention-deficit/hyperactivity disorder with stimulants contribute to drug use/abuse? A 13 year prospective study. *Pediatrics, 111*, 97–109.

Barkley, R. A., Grodzinsky, G., & DuPaul, G. J. (1992). Frontal lobe functions in attention deficit disorder with and without hyperactivity: A review and research report. *Journal of Abnormal Child Psychology, 20*, 163–188.

Barkley, R. A., Karlsson, J., & Pollard, S. (1985). Effects of age on the mother-child interactions of hyperactive children. *Journal of Abnormal Child Psychology, 13*, 631–638.

Barlow, D. H. (2004). *Anxiety and its disorders: The nature and treatment of anxiety and panic.* New York: Guilford.

Barlow, D. H., Abel, G. G., & Blanchard, E. B. (1979). Gender identity change in transsexuals. *Archives of General Psychiatry, 36*, 1001–1007.

Barlow, D. H., Blanchard, E. B., Vermilyea, J. A., Vermilyea, B. B., & DiNardo, P. A. (1986). Generalized anxiety and generalized anxiety disorder: Description and reconceptualization. *American Journal of Psychiatry, 143*, 40–44.

Barlow, D. H., Gorman, J. M., Shear, M. K., & Woods, S. W. (2000). Cognitive-behavioral therapy, imipramine, or their combination for panic disorder: A randomized controlled trial. *Journal of the American Medical Association, 283*, 2529–2536.

Barlow, D. H., Raffa, S. D., & Cohen, E. M. (2002). Psychosocial treatments for panic disorders, phobias, and generalized anxiety disorder. J. M. Gorman, P. E. Nathan (Eds.), *A guide to treatments that work* (2nd ed., pp. 301–335). London: Oxford University Press.

Barlow, D. H., Reynolds, E. J., & Agras, W. S. (1973). Gender identity change in a transsexual. *Archives of General Psychiatry, 29*, 569–576.

Barlow, D. H., Vermilyea, J., Blanchard, E., Vermilyea, B., DiNardo, P., & Cerny, J. (1985). The phenomenon of panic. *Journal of Abnormal Psychology, 94*, 320–328.

Barnett, P. A., & Gotlib, I. H. (1988). Psychosocial functioning and depression: Distinguishing among antecedents, concomitants, and consequences. *Psychological Bulletin, 104*, 97–126.

Barr, K. E. M., Farrell, M. P., Barnes, G. M., & Welte, J. W. (1993). Race, class, and gender differences in substance abuse: Evidence of middle class/underclass polarization among black males. *Social Problems, 40*, 314–327.

Barsky, A. J., Brener, J., Coeytaux, R. R., & Cleary, P. D. (1995). Accurate awareness of heartbeat in hypochondriacal and non-hypochondriacal patients. *Journal of Psychosomatic Research, 39*, 489–497.

Barsky, A. J., Fama, J. M., Bailey, E. D., & Ahern, D. K. (1998). A prospective 4- to 5-year study of DSM-III-R hypochondriasis. *Archives of General Psychiatry, 55*, 737–744.

Bartlik, B., & Goldberg, J. (2000). Female sexual arousal disorder. In S. R. Lieblum and R. C. Rosen (Eds.), *Principles and practice of sex therapy*, (3rd ed., pp. 85–117). New York: Guilford.

Basoglu, M., & Mineka, S. (1992). The role of uncontrollable and unpredictable stress in post-traumatic stress responses in torture survivors. In M., Basoglu (Ed.), *Tor-*

ture and its consequences: Current treatment approaches (pp. 182–225). New York: Cambridge University Press.

Bass, E., & Davis, L. (1994). *The courage to heal: A guide for women survivors of child sexual abuse.* New York: Harper Collins.

Bassuk, S. S., Berkman, L. F., & Wypij, D. (1998). Depressive symptomatology and incident cognitive decline in an elderly community sample. *Archives of General Psychiatry, 55*, 1073–1081.

Bateman, A. W., & Fonagy, P. (2004). Mentalization-based treatment of BPD. *Journal of Personality Disorders, 18*, 36–51.

Battaglia, M., Bernardeschi, L., Franchini, L., Bellodi, L., et al. (1995). A family study of schizotypal disorder. *Schizophrenia Bulletin, 21*, 33–45.

Baucom, D. H., Shoham, V., Mueser, K. T., Daiuto, A. D., & Stickle, T. R. (1998). Empirically supported couple and family interventions for marital distress and adult mental health problems. *Journal of Consulting and Clinical Psychology, 66*, 53–88.

Baumeister, A. A., & Baumeister, A. A. (1995). Mental retardation. In M. Hersen & R. T. Ammerman (Eds.), *Advanced abnormal child psychology* (pp. 283–303). Hillsdale, NJ: Lawrence Erlbaum.

Baumeister, R. F. (1990). Suicide as escape from self. *Psychological Review, 97*, 90–113.

Baumeister, R. F. (2000). Gender differences in erotic plasticity: The female sex drive as socially flexible and responsive. *Psychological Bulletin, 126*(3), 347–374.

Baumeister, R. F., & Butler, J. L. (1997). Sexual masochism: Deviance without pathology. In D. R., Laws & W., O'Donohue (Eds.), *Sexual deviance* (pp. 225–239). New York: Guilford.

Baumeister, R. F., Catanese, K. R., & Vohs, K. (2001). Is there a gender difference in strength of sex drive? Theoretical views, conceptual distinctions, and a review of relevant evidence. *Personality and Social Psychology Review, 5*(3), 242–273.

Baxter, L. R., Ackermann, R. F., Swerdlow, N. R., Brody, A., Saxena, S., Schwartz, J. M., Gregoritch, J. M., Stoessel, P., & Phelps, M. E. (2000). Specific brain system mediation of obsessive-compulsive disorder responsive to either medication or behavior therapy. In W. K. Goodman, M. V. Rudorfer, & J. D. Maser (Eds.), *Obsessive-compulsive disorder: Contemporary issues in treatment.* (pp. 573–610). Mahwah, NJ: Lawrence Erlbaum.

Bazanis, E., Rogers, R. D., Dowson, J. H., Taylor, P., Meux, C., Staley, C., et al. (2002). Neurocognitive deficits in decision-making and planning of patients with DSM-III-R borderline personality disorder. *Psychological Medicine, 32*, 1395–1405.

Beck, A. T. (1967). *Depression: Clinical, experimental and theoretical aspects.* New York: Harper & Row.

Beck, A. T. (1976). *Cognitive therapy and the emotional disorders.* New York: International Universities Press.

Beck, A. T., Butler, A. C., Brown, G. K., et al. (2001). Dysfunctional beliefs discriminate personality disorders. *Behaviour Research and Therapy, 39*, 1213–1225.

Beck, A. T., & Emery, R. (1987). *Anxiety disorders and phobias: A cognitive perspective.* NY: Basic Books.

Beck, A. T., & Freeman, A. (1990). *Cognitive therapy for personality disorders.* New York: Guilford Press.

Beck, A. T., Kovacs, M., & Weissman, A. (1975). Hopelessness and suicidal behavior: An overview. *Journal of the American Medical Association, 234*, 1146–1149.

Beck, A. T., & Rector, N. A. (2000). Cognitive therapy of schizophrenia: A new therapy for the new millennium. *American Journal of Psychotherapy, 54*, 291–300.

Beck, A. T., Rector, N., & Stolar, N. (2004, October). *The negative symptoms of schizophrenia: A cognitive perspective.*

Paper presented at the annual meeting of the Society for Research in Psychopathology, St. Louis, MO.

Beck, J. G. (1995). Hypoactive sexual desire disorder: An overview. *Journal of Consulting and Clinical Psychology, 63*, 919–927.

Beck, J. G., & Bozman, A. (1995). Gender differences in sexual desire: The effects of anger and anxiety. *Archives of Sexual Behavior, 24*, 595–612.

Becker, J. V., & Hunter, J. A. (1997). Understanding and treating child and adolescent sexual offenders. In T. H. Ollendick & R. J. Prinz (Eds.), *Advances in clinical child psychology* (pp. 177–196). New York: Plenum.

Becker, J. V., Kaplan, M. S., Cunningham-Rathner, J., & Kavoussi, R. J. (1986). Characteristics of adolescent incest sexual perpetrators: Preliminary findings. *Journal of Family Violence, 1*, 85–97.

Beecher, H. K. (1966). Ethics and clinical research. *New England Journal of Medicine, 274*, 1354–1360.

Beevers, C. G., & Miller, I. W. (2005). Unlinking negative cognition and symptoms of depression: Evidence of a specific treatment effect for cognitive therapy. *Journal of Consulting and Clinical Psychology, 73*, 68–77.

Beidel, D. C. (1991). Social phobia and overanxious disorder in school-age children. *Journal of the American Academy of Child and Adolescent Psychiatry, 30*, 545–552.

Bellack, A. S., & Hersen, M. (1998). *Behavioral assessment: A practical handbook* (4th ed.). Boston: Allyn & Bacon.

Bellack, A. S., Hersen, M., & Turner, S. M. (1976). Generalization effects of social skills training in chronic schizophrenics: An experimental analysis. *Behavior Research and Therapy, 14*, 391–398.

Belle, S. H., Czaja, S. J., Schulz, R., Zhang, S., Burgio, L. D., Gitlin, L. N., et al. (2003). Using a new taxonomy to combine the uncombinable: Integrating results across diverse interventions. *Psychology and Aging, 18*, 396–405.

Benkelfat, C., Ellenbogen, M. A., Dean, P., Palmour, R. M., & Young, S. N. (1994). Mood-lowering effect of tryptophan depletion: Enhanced susceptibility in young men at genetic risk for major affective disorders. *Archives of General Psychiatry, 51*, 687–700.

Benowitz, N. L., & Peng, M. W. (2000). Non-nicotine pharmacotherapy for smoking cessation. *CNS Drugs, 13*, 265–285.

Benowitz, N., Pérez-Stable, E., Herrera, B., & Jacob, P. (2002). Slower metabolism and reduced intake of nicotine from cigarette smoking in Chinese-Americans. *Journal of the National Cancer Institute, 94*, 108–115.

Ben-Porath, Y. S., & Butcher, J. N. (1989). The comparability of MMP-I and MMPI-2 scales and profiles. *Psychological Assessment, 1*, 345–347.

Berenbaum, H., & Oltmanns, T. F. (1992). Emotional experience and expression in schizophrenia and depression. *Journal of Abnormal Psychology, 101*, 37–44.

Berenbaum, S. A. (1999). Effects of early androgens on sex-typed activities and interests in adolescents with congenital adrenal hyperplasia. *Hormones and Behavior, 35*, 102–110.

Bergem, A. L., Engedal, K., & Kringlen, E. (1997). The role of heredity in late-onset Alzheimer's disease and vascular dementia: A twin study. *Archives of General Psychiatry, 54*, 264–270.

Bergin, A. E. (1971). The evaluation of therapeutic outcomes. In A. E. Bergin & S. L. Garfield (Eds.), *Handbook of psychotherapy and behavior change: An empirical analysis.* New York: Wiley.

Berkman, L. F., Blumenthal, J., Burg, M., Carney, R. M., et al. (2003). Effects of treating depression and low perceived social support on clinical events after myocardial infarction: The Enhancing Recovery in Coronary Heart

Disease Patients (ENRICHD) Randomized Trial. *JAMA,* *289,* 3106–3116.

Berman, L., Berman, J., Miles, M., Pollets, D., & Powell, J. A. (2003). Genital self-image as a component of sexual health: Relationship between genital self-image, female sexual function, and quality of life measures. *Journal of Sex and Marital Therapy, 29* (Suppl. 1), 11–21.

Bernstein, D. (1993). Paranoid personality disorder: A review of the literature and recommendations for DSM-IV. *Journal of Personality Disorders, 7,* 53–62.

Bernstein, D. P., Kasapis, C., Bergman, A., Weld, E., Mitropoulou, V., et al. (1997). Assessing Axis II disorders by informant interview. *Journal of Personality Disorders, 11,* 158–167.

Berrenberg, J. L., Dougherty, K. L., Erikson, M. S., Loew, J. L., Pacot, D. M., & Rousseau, C. N. S. (1993). *Saturation in AIDS education: Can we still make a difference?* Paper presented at the annual meeting of the Rocky Mountain and Western Psychological Associations, Phoenix, AZ.

Berry, J. C. (1967). *Antecedents of schizophrenia, impulsive character and alcoholism in males.* Paper presented at the 75th Annual Convention of the American Psychological Association, Washington, DC.

Bettelheim, B. (1967). *The empty fortress.* New York: Free Press.

Beutler, L. E. (1997). The psychotherapist as a neglected variable in psychotherapy: An illustration by reference to the role of therapist experience and training. *Clinical Psychology: Science and Practice, 4,* 44–52.

Beutler, L. E. (1999). Manualizing flexibility: The training of eclectic therapists. *Journal of Clinical Psychology, 55,* 399–404.

Beutler, L. E., & Harwood, T. M. (1995). Prescriptive psychotherapies. *Applied and Preventive Psychology, 4,* 89–100.

Beutler, L. E., Machado, P. P. P., & Neufeldt, S. A. (1994). Therapist variables. In S. L. Garfield, & A. E. Bergin (Eds.), *Handbook of psychotherapy and behavior change* (pp. 229–269). Oxford, England: John Wiley & Sons.

Beutler, L. E., Malik, M., Alimohamed, S., Harwood, T. M., Talebi, H., Noble, S., & Wong, E. (2004). Therapist variables. In M. J. Lambert (Ed.), *Bergin and Garfield's handbook of psychotherapy and behavior change* (5th ed., pp. 227–306). New York: John Wiley & Sons.

Beutler, L. E., Moleiro, C., Malik, M., Harwood, T. M., Romanelli, R., Gallagher-Thompson, D., & Thompson, L. (2003). A comparison of the dodo, EST, and ATI factors among comorbid stimulant-dependent, depressed patients. *Clinical Psychology and Psychotherapy, 10,* 69–85.

Bhatia, M. S., Nigam, V. R., Bohra, N., & Malik, S. C. (1991). Attention deficit disorder with hyperactivity among pediatric outpatients. *Journal of Child Psychology and Psychiatry, 32,* 297–306.

Bhave, S., Lindan, C. P., Hudes, E. S., Desai, S., Wagle, I., Tripathi, S. P., & Mandel, J. S. (1995). Impact of an intervention on HIV, sexually transmitted diseases, and condom use among sex workers in Bombay, India. *AIDS, 9,* S21–S30.

Biederman, J., & Faraone, S. (2004). The Massachusetts General Hospital studies of gender influences on attention-deficit/hyperactivity disorder in youth and relatives. *Psychiatric Clinics of North America, 27,* 215–224.

Biederman, J., Faraone, S., Mick, E., Spencer, T., Wilens, T., Kiely, K., Guite, J., Ablon, J. S., Reed, E., & Warbuton, R. (1995). High risk for attention deficit hyperactivity disorder among children of parents with childhood onset of the disorder: A pilot study. *American Journal of Psychiatry, 152,* 431–435.

Biederman, J., Faraone, S., Milberger, S., Curtis, S., Chen, L., Marrs, A., Ouellette, C., Moore, P., & Spencer, T. (1996). Predictors of persistence and remission of ADHD into adolescence: Results from a four-year prospective follow-up study. *Journal of the American Academy of Child and Adolescent Psychiatry, 35,* 343–351.

Biederman, J., Mick, E., Faraone, S. V., et al. (2000). Pediatric mania: A developmental subtype of bipolar disorder? *Biological Psychiatry, 48,* 458–466.

Bierut, L. J., Dinwiddie, S. H., Begleiter, H., Crowe, R. R., Hesselbrock, V., et al. (1998). Familial transmission of substance dependence: Alcohol, marijuana, cocaine, and habitual smoking: A report from the Collaborative Study on the Genetics of Alcoholism. *Archives of General Psychiatry, 55,* 982–994.

Biglan, A., Hops, H., & Sherman, L. (1988). Coercive family processes and maternal depression. In R. J. McMahon & R. DeV. Peter (Eds.), *Marriages and families: Behavioral treatments and processes* (pp. 72–103). New York: Brunner/Mazel.

Billings, A. G. (1979). Conflict resolution in distressed and nondistressed married couples. *Journal of Consulting and Clinical Psychology, 47,* 368–376.

Binzer, M., & Kullgren, G. (1996). Conversion symptoms: What can we learn from previous studies? *Nordic Journal of Psychiatry, 50,* 143–152.

Birks, J. S., & Harvey, R. (2003). Donepezil for dementia due to Alzheimer's disease. *The Cochrane Database of Systematic Reviews,* Issue 3. Art. No.: CD001190.

Birmaher, B., Brent, D. A., Kolko, D., Baugher, M., Bridge, J., Holder, D., Iyengar, S., & Ulloa, R. E. (2000). Clinical outcome after short-term psychotherapy for adolescents with major depressive disorder. *Archives of General Psychiatry, 57,* 29–36.

Birnbaum, M. (1960). The right to treatment. *American Bar Association Journal, 46,* 499–505.

Birren, J. E., & Schaie, K. W. (Eds.) (2001). *Handbook of the psychology of aging* (5th ed.). San Diego, CA: Academic Press.

Bischkopf, J., Busse, A., & Angermeyer, M. C. (2002). Mild cognitive impairment: A review of prevalence, incidence and outcome according to current approaches. *Acta Psychiatrica Scandinavia, 106,* 403–414.

BJS (1999). *Mental health and treatment of inmates and probationers.* Bureau of Justice Statistics Special Report. Department of Justice. NJC174463.

Black, D. R., & Threlfall, W. E. (1986). A stepped approach to weight control: A minimal intervention and a bibliotherapy problem-solving program. *Behavior Therapy, 17,* 144–157.

Black, D. W., Baumgard, C. H., & Bell, S. E. (1995). A 16- to 45-year follow-up of 71 men with antisocial personality disorder. *Comprehensive Psychiatry, 36,* 130–140.

Blair, R. J. D., Jones, L., Clark, F., & Smith, M. (1997). The psychopathic individual: A lack of responsiveness to distress cues? *Psychophysiology, 34,* 192–198.

Blair, R. J. R., Mitchell, D. G. V., Richell, R. A., Kelly, S., Leonard, A., Newman, C., et al. (2002). Turning a deaf ear to fear: Impaired recognition of vocal affect in psychopathic individuals. *Journal of Abnormal Psychology, 111,* 682–686.

Blanchard, J. J., & Brown, S. B. (1998). Structured diagnostic interviews. In C. R. Reynolds (Ed.), *Comprehensive clinical psychology, Volume 3, assessment* (pp. 97–130). New York: Elsevier.

Blanchard, J. J., Squires, D., Henry, T., Horan, W. P., Bogenschutz, M., et al. (1999). Examining an affect regulation model of substance abuse in schizophrenia: The role of traits and coping. *Journal of Nervous and Mental Disease, 187,* 72–79.

Blatt, S. J., Sanislow, C. A. III, Zuroff, D. C., & Pilkonis, P. A. (1996). Characteristics of effective therapists: Further analyses of data from the national institute of mental health treatment of depression collaborative research program. *Journal of Consulting and Clinical Psychology, 64,* 1276–1284.

Blazer, D. G., & Williams, C. D. (1980). Epidemiology of dysphoria and depression in the elderly population. *American Journal of Psychiatry, 137,* 439–444.

Blenker, M. (1967). Environmental change and the aging individual. *Gerontologist, 7,* 101–105.

Bliss, E. L. (1983). Multiple personalities, related disorders, and hypnosis. *American Journal of Clinical Hypnosis, 26,* 114–123.

Bloomfield, H. H. (1973). Assertive training in an outpatient group of chronic schizophrenics: A preliminary report. *Behavior Therapy, 4,* 277–281.

Blumenthal, J. A., Sherwood, A., Gullette, E. C. D., et al. (2002). Biobehavioral approaches to the treatment of essential hypertension. *Journal of Consulting and Clinical Psychology, 70,* 569–589.

Bockhoven, J. (1963). *Moral treatment in American psychiatry.* New York: Springer-Verlag.

Boegels, S. M., & Zigterman, D. (2000). Dysfunctional cognitions in children with social phobia, separation anxiety disorder, and generalized anxiety disorder. *Journal of Abnormal Child Psychology, 28,* 205–211.

Bogenschutz, M. P., & Nurnberg, H. (2004). Olanzapine versus placebo in the treatment of borderline personality disorder. *Journal of Clinical Psychiatry, 65,* 104–109.

Bohne, A., Keuthen, N. J., Wilhelm, S., Deckersback, T., & Jenike, M. A. (2002). Prevalence of symptoms of body dysmorphic disorder and its correlates: A cross-cultural comparison. *Psychosomatics, 43,* 486–490.

Bolger, N., Foster, M., Vinokur, A. D., & Ng, R. (1996). Close relationships and adjustment to a life crisis: The case of breast cancer. *Journal of Personality and Social Psychology, 70,* 283–294.

Bolton, P., Bass, J., Neugebauer, R., Verdeli, H., Clougherty, K. F., Wickramaratne, P., Speelman, L., Ndogoni, L., & Weissman, M. (2003). Group interpersonal psychotherapy for depression in rural Uganda: A randomized controlled trial. *JAMA, 289,* 3117–3124.

Bolton, P., MacDonald, H., Pickles, A., Rios, P., Goode, S., Crowson, M., Bailey, A., & Rutter, M. (1994). A case-control family history study of autism. *Journal of Child Psychology and Psychiatry, 35,* 877–900.

Bonanno, G. A., & Keltner, D. (1997). Facial expressions of emotion and the course of conjugal bereavement. *Journal of Abnormal Psychology, 106,* 126–137.

Bonanno, G. A., Wortman, C. B., Lehman, D. R., Tweed, R. G., Haring, M., Sonnega, J., et al. (2002). Resilience to loss and chronic grief: A prospective study from preloss to 18-months postloss. *Journal of Personality and Social Psychology, 83,* 1150–1164.

Bonta, J., Law, M., & Hanson, K. (1998). The prediction of criminal and violent recidivism among mentally disordered offenders. *Psychological Bulletin, 123,* 123–142.

Boon, S., & Draijer, N. (1993a). *Multiple personality disorder in the Netherlands.* Amsterdam: Swets & Zeitlinger.

Boon, S., & Draijer, N. (1993b). Multiple personality disorder in the Netherlands: A clinical investigation of 71 cases. *American Journal of Psychiatry, 150,* 489–494.

Borch-Jacobsen, M. (1997, April 24). Sybil: The Making of a Disease? An interview with Dr. Herbert Spiegel. *New York Review of Books.* NY, NY: New York Review of Books.

Borduin, C. M., Mann, B. J., Cone, L. T., Henggeler, S. W., Fucci, B. R., Blaske, D. M., & Williams, R. A. (1995). Multisystemic treatment of serious juvenile offenders:

Long-term prevention of criminality and violence. *Journal of Consulting and Clinical Psychology, 63*, 569–578.

Borkovec, T. D., Alcaine, O. M., & Behar, E. (2004). Clinical presentation and diagnostic features. In R. G. Heimberg, C. L. Turk, & D. S. Mennin (Eds.), *Generalized anxiety disorder* (pp. 77–108). New York: Guilford.

Borkovec, T. D., & Newman, M. G. (1998). Worry and generalized anxiety disorder. In P. Salkovskis (Ed.), *Comprehensive clinical psychology*. Oxford: Elsevier.

Bornstein, R. F. (1997). Dependent personality disorder in the DSM-IV and beyond. *Clinical Psychology: Science and Practice, 4*, 175–187.

Bornstein, R. F. (2003). Behaviorally referenced experimentation and symptom validation: A paradigm for 21st-century personality disorder research. *Journal of Personality Disorders, 17*, 1–18.

Bosanac, P., Burrows, G., & Norman, T. (2004). Olanzapine in anorexia nervosa. *Australian and New Zealand Journal of Psychiatry, 37*, 494.

Boscarino, J. A. (1997). Diseases among men 20 years after exposure to severe stress: Implications for clinical research and care. *Psychosomatic Medicine, 59*, 605–614.

Bosinski, H. A., Peter, M., Bonatz, G., Arndt, R., Heidenreich, M., et al. (1997). A higher rate of hyperadrenergic disorders in female-to-male transsexuals. *Psychoneuroendocrinology, 22*, 361–380.

Bouret, S. G., Draper, S. J., & Simerly, R. B. (2004). Trophic action of leptin on hypothalamic neurons that regulate feeding. *Science, 304*, 63–64.

Bouton, M. E., Mineka, S., & Barlow, D. H. (2001). A modern learning theory perspective on the etiology of panic disorder. *Psychological Review, 108*, 4–32.

Bowden, C. L., Calabrese, J. R., McElroy, S. L., et al. (2000). A randomized, placebo-controlled 12-month trial of divalproex and lithium in treatment of patients with bipolar I disorder. *Archives of General Psychiatry, 57*, 481–489.

Bowden, C. L., Lecrubier, Y., Bauer, M., Goodwin, G., Greil, W., Sachs, G., & von Knorring, L. (2000). Maintenance therapies for classic and other forms of bipolar disorder. *Journal of Affective Disorders, 59*, S57–S67.

Bower, G. H. (1981). Mood and memory. *American Psychologist, 36*, 129–141.

Bowers, M. B., Jr. (1974). Central dopamine turnover in schizophrenic syndromes. *Archives of General Psychiatry, 31*, 50–54.

Bowkett, S. (2003). Child abuse on the Internet: Ending the silence. *Clinical Child Psychology and Psychiatry, 8*, 556–557.

Boxall, B. (1995, September 3). Young gays stray from safer sex, new data shows. *Los Angeles Times*, pp. A1, A24.

Boyle, M. (1991). *Schizophrenia: A scientific delusion?* New York: Routledge.

Bradley, B. P., Mogg, K., Millar, N., & White, J. (1995). Selective processing of negative information: Effects of clinical anxiety, concurrent depression, and awareness. *Journal of Abnormal Psychology, 104*, 532–536.

Bradley, L., & Bryant, P. E. (1985). *Rhyme and reason in reading and spelling*. Ann Arbor: University of Michigan Press.

Bradley, S. J., & Zucker, K. J. (1997). Gender identity disorder: A review of the past 10 years. *Journal of the American Academy of Child and Adolescent Psychiatry, 36*, 872–880.

Brady, K., Pearlstein, T., Asnis, G., et al. (2000). Efficacy and safety of sertraline treatment of posttraumatic stress disorder. *JAMA, 283*, 1837–1844.

Brandon, T. H., Collins, B. N., Juliano, L. M., & Lazev, A. B. (2000). Preventing relapse among former smokers: A comparison of minimal interventions through telephone and mail. *Journal of Consulting & Clinical Psychology, 68*, 103–113.

Brandon, Y. H., Zelman, D. C., & Baker, T. B. (1987). Effects of maintenance sessions on smoking relapse: Delaying the inevitable? *Journal of Consulting and Clinical Psychology, 55*, 780–782.

Brandt, J., Buffers, N., Ryan, C., & Bayog, R. (1983). Cognitive loss and recovery in chronic alcohol abusers. *Archives of General Psychiatry, 40*, 435–442.

Bransford, J. D., & Johnson, M. K. (1973). Considerations of some problems of comprehension. In W. G. Chase (Ed.), *Visual information processing*. New York: Academic Press.

Braswell, L., & Kendall, P. C. (1988). Cognitive-behavioral methods with children. In K. S. Dobson (Ed.), *Handbook of cognitive-behavioral therapies*. New York: Guilford.

Bray, N. W., & Turner, L. A. (1987). Production anomalies (not strategic deficiencies) in mentally deficient individuals. *Intelligence, 11*, 49–60.

Brecher, E. M., & the Editors of Consumer Reports. (1972). *Licit and illicit drugs*. Mount Vernon, NY: Consumers Union.

Brehm, J. W. (1966). *A theory of psychological reactance*. New York: Academic Press.

Brehm, S. S., & Brehm, J. W. (1981). *Psychological reactance: A theory of freedom and control*. New York: Academic Press.

Bremner, J. D., Vythilingam, M., Vermetten, E., Southwick, S. M., McGlashan, T., Nazeer, A., et al. (2003). MRI and PET study of deficits in hippocampal structure and function in women with childhood sexual abuse and posttraumatic stress disorder. *American Journal of Psychiatry, 160*, 924–932.

Brennan, P. L., Schutte, K. K., & Moos, R. H. (1999). Reciprocal relations between stressors and drinking behavior: A three-wave panel study of late middle-aged and older women and men. *Addiction, 94*, 737–749.

Brent, D. A., Holder, D., Kolko, D., Birmaher, B., Baugher, M., et al. (1997). A clinical psychotherapy trial for adolescent depression comparing cognitive, family, and supportive therapy. *Archives of General Psychiatry, 54*, 877–885.

Breslau, N., Brown, G. G., DelDotto, J. E., Kumar, S., Ezhuthachan, S., Andreski, P., & Hufnagle, K. G. (1996). Psychiatric sequalae of low birth weight at 6 years of age. *Journal of Abnormal Child Psychology, 24*, 385–400.

Breslau, N., Chilcoat, H. D., Kessler, R. C., & Davis, G. C. (1999). Previous exposure to trauma and PTSD effects of subsequent trauma: Results from the Detroit Area Survey of Trauma. *American Journal of Psychiatry, 156*, 902–907.

Brestan, E. V., & Eyberg, S. M. (1998). Effective psychosocial treatment of conduct disordered children and adolscents: 29 years, 82 studies, and 5275 kids. *Journal of Clinical Child Psychology, 27*, 180–189.

Breuer, J., & Freud, S. (1982). *Studies in hysteria*. (J. Strachey, Trans. and Ed., with the collaboration of A. Freud). New York: Basic Books. (Original work published 1895.)

Brewerton, T. D., Lydiard, B. R., Laraia, M. T., Shook, J. E., & Ballenger, J. C. (1992). CSF Beta-endorphin and dynorphin in bulimia nervosa. *American Journal of Psychiatry, 149*, 1086–1090.

Brewin, C. R., Andrews, B., & Valentine, J. D. (2000). Meta-analysis of risk factors for posttraumatic stress disorder in trauma-exposed adults. *Journal of Consulting and Clinical Psychology, 68*, 748–766.

Brewin, C. R., & Holmes, E. A. (2003). Psychological theories of posttraumatic stress disorder. *Clinical Psychology Review, 23*, 339–376.

Brickman, A. S., McManus, M., Grapentine, W. L., & Alessi, N. (1984). Neuropsychological assessment of seriously delinquent adolescents. *Journal of the American Academy of Child Psychiatry, 23*, 453–457.

Brisson, C., Laflamme, N., Moisan, J., Miloît, A., Mâsse, B., & Vézina, M. (1999). Effect of family responsibilities and job strain on ambulatory blood pressure among white collar women. *Psychosomatic Medicine, 61*, 205–213.

Brody, A. L., Saxena, S., Stoessel, P., Gillies, L. A., Fairbanks, L. A., Alborzian, S., Phelps, M. E., Huang, S. C., Wu, H. M., Ho, M. L., Ho, M. K., Au, S. C., Maidment, K., & Baxter, L. R., Jr. (2001). Regional brain metabolic changes in patients with major depression treated with either paroxetine or interpersonal therapy: Preliminary findings. *Archives of General Psychiatry, 58*, 631–640.

Brookoff, D., Cook, C. S., Williams, C., & Mann, C. S. (1994). Testing reckless drivers for cocaine and marijuana. *The New England Journal of Medicine, 331*, 518–522.

Brown, A. S., Begg, M. D., Gravenstein, S., Schaefer, C. A., Wyatt, R. J., Bresnahan, M., Babulas, V. P., & Susser, E. S. (2004). Serologic evidence of prenatal influenza in the etiology of schizophrenia. *Archives of General Psychiatry, 61*, 774–780.

Brown, B. S., O'Grady, K. E., Farrell, E. V., Flechner, I. S., & Nurco, D. N. (2001). Factors associated with frequency of 12-Step attendance by drug abuse clients. *American Journal of Drug & Alcohol Abuse, 27*, 147–160.

Brown, D., Scheflin, A. W., & Whitfield, C. L. (1999). Recovered memories: The current weight of the evidence in science and in the courts. *The Journal of Psychiatry and Law, 27*, 5–156.

Brown, G. K., Beck, A. T., Steer, R. A., & Grisham, J. R. (2000). Risk factors for suicide in psychiatric outpatients: A 20-year prospective study. *Journal of Consulting and Clinical Psychology, 68*, 371–377.

Brown, G. L., & Goodwin, F. K. (1986). Cerebrospinal fluid correlates of suicide attempts and aggression. *Annals of the New York Academy of Science, 487*, 175–188.

Brown, G. P., Hammen, C. L., Craske, M. G., & Wickens, T. D. (1995). Dimensions of dysfunctional attitudes as vulnerabilities to depressive symptoms. *Journal of Abnormal Psychology, 104*, 431–435.

Brown, G. W., & Andrews, B. (1986). Social support and depression. In R. Trumbull & M. H. Appley (Eds.), *Dynamics of stress: Physiological, psychological, and social perspectives*. (pp. 257–282). New York: Plenum.

Brown, G. W., Bone, M., Dalison, B., & Wing, J. K. (1966). *Schizophrenia and social care*. London: Oxford University Press.

Brown, G. W., & Harris, T. O. (1978). *The Bedford College life-events and difficulty schedule: directory of contextual threat of events*. London: Bedford College, University of London.

Brown, G. W., & Harris, T. O., eds. (1989a). *Life events and illness*. New York: Guilford.

Brown, G. W., & Harris, T. O. (1989b). Depression. In Tirril O. Harris and George W. Brown (Eds.), *Life events and illness* (pp. 49–93). New York: Guilford.

Brown, S. A., Vik, P. W., McQuaid, J. R., Patterson, T. L., Irwin, M. R., et al. (1990). Severity of psychosocial stress and outcome of alcoholism treatment. *Journal of Abnormal Psychology, 99*, 344–348.

Brown, T. A., Campbell, L. A., Lehman, C. L., et al. (2001). Current and lifetime comorbidity of the DSM-IV anxiety and mood disorders in a large clinical sample. *Journal of Abnormal Psychology, 110*, 585–599.

Brown, W. T., Jenkins, E. C., et al. (1986). Fragile X and autism: a multicenter survey. *American Journal of Medical Genetics, 23*, 341–52.

Brownell, K. D., & Horgen, K. B. (2003). *Food fight: The inside story of the food industry, America's obesity crisis, and what we can do about it*. Chicago, IL: Contemporary Books.

Brownmiller, S. (1975). *Against our will: Men, women and rape*. New York: Simon & Schuster.

Bruce, M. L., Ten Have, T. R., Reynolds III, C. F., Katz, I. I., et al. (2004). Reducing suicidal ideation and depressive symptoms in depressed older primary care patients. *JAMA, 291,* 1081–1091.

Bruch, H. (1980). Preconditions for the development of anorexia nervosa. *American Journal of Psychoanalysis, 40,* 169–172.

Bryant, R. A., & McConkey, K. M. (1989). Visual conversion disorder: A case analysis of the influence of visual information. *Journal of Abnormal Psychology, 98,* 326–329.

Bryant, R. A., Sackville, T., Dang, S. T., Moulds, M., & Guthrie, R. (1999). Treating acute stress disorder: An evaluation of cognitive behavior therapy and supporting counseling techniques. *American Journal of Psychiatry, 156,* 1780–1786.

Buchanan, R. W., Breier, A., Kirkpatrick, B., Ball, P., & Carpenter, W. T. (1998). Positive and negative symptom response to clozapine in schizophrenic patients with and without the deficit syndrome. *American Journal of Psychiatry, 155,* 751–760.

Buchanan, R. W., Vladar, K., Barta, P. E., & Pearlson, G. D. (1998). Structural evaluation of the prefrontal cortex in schizophrenia. *American Journal of Psychiatry, 155,* 1049–1055.

Bucher, J. A., Houts, P. S., Nezu, C. M., & Nezu, A. M. (1999). Improving problem-solving skills of family caregivers through group education. *Journal of Psychosocial Oncology, 16,* 73–84.

Buchsbaum, M. S., Kessler, R., King, A., Johnson, J., & Cappelletti, J. (1984). Simultaneous cerebral glucography with positron emission tomography and topographic electroencephalography. In G. Pfurtscheller, E. J. Jonkman, & F. H. Lopes da Silva (Eds.), *Brain ischemia: Quantitative EEG and imaging techniques.* Amsterdam: Elsevier.

Bulik, C. M., Sullivan, P. F., & Joyce, P. R. (1999). Temperament, character and suicide attempts in anorexia nervosa, bulimia nervosa and major depression. *Acta Psychiatrica Scandinavica, 100,* 27–32.

Bulik, C. M., Sullivan, P. F., Wade, T. D., & Kendler, K. S. (2000). Twin studies of eating disorders: A review. *International Journal of Eating Disorders, 27,* 1–20.

Bulik, C. M., Wade, T. D., & Kendler, K. S. (2000). Characteristics of monozygotic twins discordant for bulimia nervosa. *International Journal of Eating Disorders, 29,* 1–10.

Bullers, S., Cooper, M. L., & Russell, M. (2001). Social network drinking and adult alcohol involvement: A longitudinal exploration of the direction of influence. *Addictive Behaviors, 26,* 181–199.

Burgio, L. D., Burgio, K. L., Engel, B. T., & Tice, L. M. (1986). Increasing distance and independence of ambulation in elderly nursing home residents. *Journal of Applied Behavior Analysis, 19,* 357–366.

Burke, B. L., Arkowitz, H., & Menchola, M. (2003). The efficacy of motivational interviewing: A meta-analysis of controlled clinical trials. *Journal of Consulting and Clinical Psychology, 71,* 843–861.

Burne, S. M., & McLean, N. J. (2002). The cognitive-behavioral model of bulimia nervosa: A direct evaluation. *International Journal of Eating Disorders, 31,* 17–31.

Burris, K. D., Molski T. F., Xu, C., Ryan, E., Tottori, K., Kikuchi, T., Yocca F. D., & Molinoff, P. B. (2002). Aripiprazole, a novel antipsychotic, is a high-affinity partial agonist at human dopamine D2 receptors. *Journal of Pharmacology and Experimental Therapies, 302,* 381–389.

Buss, A. H. (1966). *Psychopathology.* New York: Wiley.

Bustillo, J. R., Lauriello, J., Horan, W. P., & Keith, S. J. (2001). The psychosocial treatment of schizophrenia: An update. *American Journal of Psychiatry, 158,* 163–175.

Butcher, J. N., Dahlstrom, W. G., Graham, J. R., Tellegen, A., & Kraemer, B. (1989). *Minnesota Multiphasic Personality Inventory-2: Manual for administration and scoring.* Minneapolis: University of Minnesota Press.

Butler, L. D., Duran, R. E. F., Jasiukaitis, P., Koopman, C., & Spiegel, D. (1996). Hypnotizability and traumatic experience: A diathesis-stress model of dissociative symptomatology. *American Journal of Psychiatry, 153,* 42–63.

Butler, R. N., Lewis, M. I., & Sunderland, T. (1998). *Aging and mental health: Positive psychosocial and biomedical approaches* (5th ed.) Boston: Allyn & Bacon.

Butzlaff, R. L., & Hooley, J. M. (1998). Expressed emotion and psychiatric relapse: A meta-analysis. *Archives of General Psychiatry, 55,* 547–553.

Byne, W., Buchsbaum, M. S., Mattiace, L. A., et al. (2002). Postmortem assessment of thalamic nuclear volume in subjects with schizophrenia. *American Journal of Psychiatry, 159,* 59–65.

Caccioppo, J. T., Klein, D. J., Bernston, G. G., & Hatfield, E. (1998). The psychophysiology of emotion. In M. Lewis & E. Haviland (Eds.), *Handbook of emotions* (pp. 119–142). New York: Guilford.

Cadenhead, K. S., Light, G. A., Geyer, M. A., McDowell, J. E., & Braff, D. L. (2002). Neurobiological measures of schizotypal personality disorder: Defining an inhibitory endophenotype? *American Journal of Psychiatry, 159,* 869–871.

Cadoret, R. J., Yates, W. R., Troughton, E., Woodworth, G., & Stewart, M. A. (1995a). Adoption study demonstrating two genetic pathways to drug abuse. *Archives of General Psychiatry, 52,* 42–52.

Cadoret, R. J., Yates, W. R., Troughton, E., Woodworth, G., & Stewart, M. A. (1995b). Genetic-environment interaction in the genesis of aggressivity and conduct disorders. *Archives of General Psychiatry, 52,* 916–924.

Calabrese, J. R., Bowden, C. L., Sachs, G. S., Ascher, J. A., Monaghan, E., & Rudd, G. D. (1999). A double-blind placebo-controlled study of lamotrigine monotherapy in outpatients with bipolar I depression. *Journal of Clinical Psychiatry, 60,* 79–84.

Caldwell, M. B., Brownell, K. D., & Wilfley, D. (1997). Relationship of weight, body dissatisfaction, and self-esteem in African American and white female dieters. *International Journal of Eating Disorders, 22,* 127–130.

Calhoun, V. D., Pekar, J. J., & Pearlson, G. D. (2004). Alcohol intoxication effects on simulated driving: Exploring alcohol-dose effects on brain activation using functional MRI. *Neuropsychopharmacology, 29,* 2197–2107.

Calsyn, D. A., Saxon, A. J., Freeman, G., & Whitaker, S. (1992). Ineffectiveness of AIDS education and HIV antibody testing in reducing high-risk behaviors among injection drug users. *American Journal of Public Health, 82,* 573–575.

Cameron, D. J., Thomas, R. I., Mulvhill, M., & Bronheim, H. (1987). Delirium: A test of the Diagnostic and Statistical Manual III criteria on medical inpatients. *Journal of the American Geriatrics Society, 35,* 1007–1010.

Camí, J., & Farré, M. (2003). Drug addiction. *New England Journal of Medicine, 349,* 975–986.

Campbell, J., Stefan, S., & Loder, A. (1994). Putting violence in context. *Hospital and Community Psychiatry, 45,* 633.

Campbell, M., Armenteros, J. L., Malone, R. P., Adams, P. B., Eisenberg, Z. W., & Overall, J. E. (1997). Neuroleptic-related dyskinesias in autistic children: A prospective, longitudinal study. *Journal of the American Academy of Child and Adolescent Psychiatry, 36,* 835–843.

Campbell, S. B. (2002). *Behavioral problems in preschool children: Clinical and developmental issues* (2nd ed.). New York: Guilford.

Camus, V., Burtin, B., Simeone, I., et al. (2000). Factor analysis supports the evidence of existing hyperactive and hypoactive subtypes of delirium. *International Journal of Geriatric Psychiatry, 15,* 313–316.

Camus, V., KraehenbAhl, H., Preisig, M., Bala, C. J., & Waeber, G. (2004). Geriatric depression and vascular diseases: What are the links? *Journal of Affective Disorders, 81,* 1–16.

Canivez, G. L., & Watkins, M. W. (1998). Long-term stability of the Wechsler Intelligence Scale for Children (3rd ed.). *Psychological Assessment, 10,* 285–291.

Cannon, D. S., Baker, T. B., Gino, A., & Nathan, P. E. (1986). Alcohol-aversion therapy: Relation between strength of aversion and abstinence. *Journal of Consulting and Clinical Psychology, 54,* 825–830.

Cannon, T. D., Kaprio, J., Lonnqvist, J., Huttunen, M., & Koskenvuo, M. (1998). The genetic epidemiology of schizophrenia in a Finnish twin cohort: A population-based modeling study. *Archives of General Psychiatry, 55,* 67–74.

Cannon, T. D., & Mednick, S. A. (1993). The schizophrenia high-risk project in Copenhagen: Three decades of progress. *Acta Psychiatrica Scandanavica,* 33–47.

Cannon, T. D., Mednick, S. A., & Parnas, J. (1990). Antecedents of predominantly negative and predominantly positive-symptom schizophrenia in a high-risk population. *Archives of General Psychiatry, 47,* 622–632.

Cannon, T. D., van Erp, T. G., Rosso, I. M., et al. (2002). Fetal hypoxia and structural brain abnormalities in schizophrenic patients, their siblings, and controls. *Archives of General Psychiatry, 59,* 35–42.

Cannon, T. D., Zorilla, L. E., Shtasel, D., Gur, R. E., Gur, R. C., et al. (1994). Neuropsychological functioning in siblings discordant for schizophrenia and healthy volunteers. *Archives of General Psychiatry, 51,* 651–661.

Capaldi, D. M., & Patterson, G. R. (1994). Interrelated influences of contextual factors on antisocial behavior in childhood and adolescence for males. In D. C. Fowles, P. Sutker, & S. H. Goodman (Eds.), *Progress in experimental personality and psychopathology research* (pp. 165–198). New York: Springer-Verlag.

Capps, L., Losh, M., & Thurber, C. (2000). "The frog ate the bug and made his mouth sad": Narrative competence in children with autism. *Journal of Abnormal Child Psychology, 28,* 193–204.

Capps, L., Rasco, L., Losh, M., & Heerey, E. (1999, April). *Understanding of self-conscious emotions in high-functioning children with autism.* Paper presented at the Biennial Meeting of the Society for Research In Child Development. Albuquerque, NM.

Capps, L., Yirmiya, N., & Sigman, M. (1992). Understanding of simple and complex emotion in high-functioning children with autism. *Journal of Child Psychology and Psychiatry, 33,* 1169–1182.

Capron, A. M. (1999). Ethical and human rights issues in research on mental disorders that may affect decision-making capacity. *The New England Journal of Medicine, 340,* 1430–1434.

CAPT. (2000). Prisons: The nation's new mental institutions. *Outreach.* Online at http://www.psych-health.com/mental8. htm.

Cardno, A. G., Marshall, E. J., Coid, B., Macdonald, A. M., Ribchester, T. R., et al. (1999). Heritability estimates for psychotic disorders: The Maudsley Twin Psychosis Series. *Archives of General Psychiatry, 56,* 162–170.

Carlsson, A., Hanson, L. O., Waters, N., & Carlsson, M. L. (1999). A glutamatergic deficiency model of schizophrenia. *British Journal of Psychiatry, 174,* 2–6.

Carpeggiani, C., & Skinner, J. E. (1991). Coronary flow and mental stress: Experimental findings. *Circulation, 83,* 90–93.

Carpenter, W. T., Gold, J. M., Lahti, A. C., Queern, C. A., Conley, R. R., Bartko, J. J., Kovnick, J., & Appelbaum, P. S. (2000). Decisional capacity for informed consent in schizophrenia research. *Archives of General Psychiatry, 57,* 533–538.

Carpenter, W. T., Heinrichs, D. W., & Wagman, A. M. I. (1988). Deficit and nondeficit forms of schizophrenia: The concept. *American Journal of Psychiatry, 145,* 578–583.

Carpentieri, S. C., & Morgan, S. B. (1994). Brief report: A comparison of patterns of cognitive functioning of autistic and nonautistic retarded children on the Stanford-Binet (4th ed.). *Journal of Autism and Developmental Disorders, 24,* 215–223.

Carr, A. T. (1971). Compulsive neurosis: Two psychophysiological studies. *Bulletin of the British Psychological Society, 24,* 256–257.

Carr, E. G., Levin, L., McConnachie, G., Carlson, J. I., Kemp, D. C., & Smith, C. E. (1994). *Communication-based intervention for problem behavior.* Baltimore: Paul H. Brookes.

Carr, R. E. (1998). Panic disorder and asthma: Causes, effects, and research implications. *Journal of Psychosomatic Research, 44,* 43–52.

Carr, R. E. (1999). Panic disorder and asthma. *Journal of Asthma, 36,* 143–152.

Carrasco, J. L., Dyaz-Marsa, M., Hollander, E., Cesar, J., & Saiz-Ruiz, J. (2000). Decreased monoamine oxidase activity in female bulimia. *European Neuropsychopharmacology, 10,* 113–117.

Carroll, K. M., Ball, S. A., Nich, C., et al. (2001). Targeting behavioral therapies to enhance naltrexone treatment of opioid dependence: Efficacy of contingency management and significant other involvement. *Archives of General Psychiatry, 58,* 755–761.

Carroll, K. M., Rounsaville, B. J., Gordon, L. T., Nich, C., Jatlow, P., Bisighini, R. M., & Gawin, F. H. (1994). Psychotherapy and pharmacotherapy for ambulatory cocaine abusers. *Archives of General Psychiatry, 51,* 177–187.

Carroll, K. M., Rounsaville, B. J., Nich, C., Gordon, L. T., & Gawin, F. (1995). Integrating psychotherapy and pharmacotherapy for cocaine dependence: Results from a randomized clinical trial. In L. S. Onken, J. D. Blaine, & J. J. Boren (Eds.), *Integrating behavioral therapies with medications in the treatment of drug dependence* (pp. 19–36). Rockville, MD: National Institute on Drug Abuse.

Carroll, K. M., Rounsaville, B. J., Nich, C., Gordon, L. T., Wirtz, P. W., & Gawin, F. (1994). One-year follow-up of psychotherapy and pharmacotherapy for cocaine dependence. *Archives of General Psychiatry, 51,* 989–997.

Carroll, R. A. (2000). Assessment and treatment of gender dysphoria. In S. R. Lieblum & R. C. Rosen (Eds.), *Principles and practice of sex therapy* (pp. 368–397). New York: Guilford.

Carstensen, L. L. (1996). Evidence for a life-span theory of socioemotional selectivity. *Current Directions in Psychological Science, 4,* 151–156.

Carter, S., DeVries, A. C., Getz, L. L. (1995). Physiological substrates of mammalian monogamy: The prairie vole model. *Neuroscience & Biobehavioral Reviews, 19,* 303–314.

Carter, F. A., McIntosh, V. V. W., Joyce, P. R., Sullivan, P. F., & Bulik, C. M. (2003). Role of exposure with response prevention in cognitive-behavioral therapy for bulimia nervosa: Three-year follow-up results. *International Journal of Eating Disorders, 33,* 127–135.

Carver, C. S., Pozo, C., Harris, S. D., Noriega, V., Scheier, M., Robinson, D., Ketcham, A., Moffat, F. L., & Clark, K. (1993). How coping mediates the effect of optimism on distress: A study of women with early stage breast cancer. *Journal of Personality and Social Psychology, 65,* 375–390.

Carver, C. S., & Scheier, M. F. (1999). Stress, coping, and self-regulatory processes. In L. A. Pervin & O. P. John (Eds.), *Handbook of personality* (2nd ed., pp. 553–575). New York: Guilford Press.

Casey, J. E., Rourke, B. P., & Del Dotto, J. E. (1996). Learning disabilities in children with attention deficit disorder with and without hyperactivity. *Child Neuropsychology, 2,* 83–98.

Cashman, J. A. (1966). *The LSD story.* Greenwich, CT: Fawcett.

Casper, M. L., Barnett, E., Halverson, J. A., Elmes, G. A., Braham, V. E., Majeed, Z. A., Boom, A. S., & Stanley, S. (2000). *Women and heart disease: An atlas of racial and ethnic disparities in mortality* (2nd ed.). Office for Social and Environmental Health Research, West Virginia University, and the National Center for Chronic Disease Prevention and Health Promotion, Centers for Disease Control and Prevention, Atlanta, GA.

Caspi, A., McClay, J., Moffitt, T. E., Mill, J., Martin, J., Craig, I. W., Taylor, A., & Poulton, R. (2002). Role of genotype in the cycle of violence in maltreated children. *Science, 297,* 851–854.

Caspi, A., Sugden, K., Moffitt, T. E., Taylor, A., Craig, I. W., Harrington, H., et al. (2003). Influence of life stress on depression: Moderation by a polymorphism in the 5-HTT gene. *Science, 301,* 386–389.

Castellanos, F. X., Giedd, J. N., Marsh, W. L., Hamburger, S. D., Vaituzis, A. C., Dickstein, D. P., Sarfatti, S. E., Vauss, Y. C., Snell, J. W., Lange, N., Kaysen, D., Krain, A. L., Ritchie, G. F., Rajapaske, J. C., & Rapoport, J. L. (1996). Quantitative brain magnetic resonance imaging in attention-deficit/hyperactivity disorder. *Archives of General Psychiatry, 53,* 607–616.

Castellanos, F. X., Marvasti, F. F., Ducharme, J. L., Walter, J. M., Israel, M. E., Krain, A., Pavlovsky, C., & Hommer, D. W. (2000). Executive function oculomotor tasks in girls with ADHD. *Journal of the American Academy of Child and Adolescent Psychiatry, 39,* 644–650.

Castelli, F., Frith, C., Happe, F., & Frith, U. (2002). Autism, Asperger syndrome and brain mechanisms for the attribution of mental states to animated shapes. *Brain, 125,* 1839–1849.

Castle, D. J., & Murray, R. M. (1993). The epidemiology of late-onset schizophrenia. *Schizophrenia Bulletin, 19,* 691–700.

Castonguay, L. G., Reid, J. J., Jr., Halperin, G. S., & Goldfried, M. R. (2003). Psychotherapy integration. In T. A. Widiger and G. Stricker (Eds.), *Handbook of psychology: Clinical psychology* (Vol. 8, pp. 327–366). New York: John Wiley & Sons.

Cautela, J. R. (1966). Treatment of compulsive behavior by covert sensitization. *Psychological Record, 16,* 33–41.

Celebucki, C. C., Wayne, G. F., Connolly, G. N., Pankow, J. F., & Chang, E. I. (2005). Characterization of measured menthol in 48 U.S. cigarette sub-brands. *Nicotine & Tobacco Research, 7,* 523–531.

Centers for Disease Control and Prevention (2004). Cigarette use among American high school students 1991–2003, *MMWR, 53,* 499–502.

Cerny, J. A., Barlow, D. H., Craske, M. G., & Himadi, W. G. (1987). Couples treatment of agoraphobia: A two year follow-up. *Behavior Therapy, 18,* 401–415.

CEWG (2003). *Epidemiologic trends in drug abuse* (Volume I, June 2003). National Institute of Drug Abuse.

Chabrol, H., Peresson, G., Milberger, S., Biederman, J., & Faraone, S. V. (1997). ADHD and maternal smoking during pregnancy. *American Journal of Psychiatry, 154,* 1177–1178.

Chakravorty, B., Ahmed, A., & Buchanan, R. J. (2000). Midproject findings from a study of the National Collegiate Athletic Association's Policy on Smokeless Tobacco Use. *Substance Use and Misuse, 35,* 1431–1441.

Chambers, K. C., & Bernstein, I. L. (1995). Conditioned flavor aversions. In R. L. Doty (Ed.), *Handbook of olfaction and gustation* (pp. 745–773). New York: Marcel Dekker.

Chambers, R. A., Taylor, J. R., & Potenza, M. N. (2003). Developmental neurocircuitry of motivation in adolescence: A critical period of addiction vulnerability. *American Journal of Psychiatry, 160,* 1041–1052.

Chambless, D. L., & Ollendick, T. H. (2001). Empirically supported psychological interventions: Controversies and evidence. *Annual Review of Psychology, 52,* 685–716.

Chambless, D. L., Sanderson, W. C., Shoham, V., Johnson, S. B., Pope, K. S., Crits-Christoph, P., Baker, M., Johnson, B., Woody, S. R., Sue, S., Beutler, L. E., Williams, D. A., & McCurry, S. (1996). An update on empirically validated therapies. *The Clinical Psychologist, 49,* 5–18.

Chang, L., Cloak, C. C., & Ernst, T. (2003). Magnetic resonance spectroscopy studies of GABA in neuropsychiatric disorders. *Journal of Clinical Psychiatry, 64*(Suppl. 3), 7–14.

Charney, D. S., Nemeroff, C. B., Lewis, L., et al. (2002). National Depressive and Manic Depressive Association Consensus statement on the use of placebo in clinical trials of mood disorders. *Archives of General Psychiatry, 59,* 262–270.

Chase, A. (1980). *The legacy of malthus.* Urbana, IL: University of Illinois Press.

Chassin, L., Curran, P. J., Hussong, A. M., & Colder, C. R. (1996). The relation of parent alcoholism to adolescent substance abuse: A longitudinal follow-up. *Journal of Abnormal Psychology, 105,* 70–80.

Chassin, L., Pitts, S. C., DeLucia, C., & Todd, M. (1999). A longitudinal study of children of alcoholics: Predicting young adult substance use disorders, anxiety, and depression. *Journal of Abnormal Psychology, 108,* 106–119.

Chavira, D. A., Stein, M. B., & Malcarne, V. L. (2002). Scrutinizing the relationship between shyness and social phobia. *Journal of Anxiety Disorders, 16,* 585–598.

Chen, E., Bloomberg, G. R., Fisher, E. B., & Strunk, R. C. (2003). Predictors of repeat hospitalizations in children with asthma: The role of psychosocial and socioenvironmental factors. *Health Psychology, 22,* 12–18.

Chen, Y., Levy, D. L., Nakayama, K., Matthysse, S., et al. (1999). Dependence of impaired eye tracking on velocity discrimination in schizophrenia. *Archives of General Psychiatry, 56,* 155–161.

Chen, Y. P., Ehlers, A., Clark, D. M., & Mansell, W. (2002). Patients with generalized social phobia direct their attention away from faces. *Behaviour Research and Therapy, 40,* 677–687.

Chernoff, R. A. (1998). *The short- and long-term behavioral outcomes of HIV prevention interventions: A critical evaluation.* Unpublished manuscript. University of Southern California.

Chernoff, R. A., & Davison, G. C. (1997, August). *Values and their relationship to HIV/AIDS risk behavior.* Paper presented at the annual convention of the American Psychological Association, Chicago.

Chesney, M. A., Barrett, D. C., & Stall, R. (1998). Histories of substance use and risk behavior: Precursors to HIV seroconversion in homosexual men. *American Journal of Public Health, 88,* 113–116.

Chi, J. S., Poole, W. K., Kandefer, S. C., & Kloner, R. A. (2003). Cardiovascular mortality in New York City after September 11, 2001. *Amercian Journal of Cardiology, 92,* 857–861.

Chiariello, M. A., & Orvaschel, H. (1995). Patterns of parent–child communication: Relationship to depression. *Clinical Psychology Review, 15,* 395–407.

Chorpita, B. F., Brown, T. A., & Barlow, D. H. (1998). Perceived control as a mediator of family environment in etiological models of childhood anxiety. *Behavior Therapy, 29,* 457–476.

Chorpita, B. F., Vitali, A. E., & Barlow, D. H. (1997). Behavioral treatment of choking phobia in an adolescent: An experimental analysis. *Journal of Behavior Therapy and Experimental Psychiatry, 28,* 307–315.

Christenfeld, N., Gerin, W., Linden, W., Sanders, M., Mathur, J. D., et al. (1997). Social support effects on cardiovascular reactivity: Is a stranger as effective as a friend? *Psychosomatic Medicine, 59,* 388–398.

Christensen, A., & Heavey, C. L. (1990). Gender and social structure in the demand/withdraw pattern of marital conflict. *Journal of Personality and Social Psychology, 59,* 73–81.

Christensen, A., & Jacobson, N. S. (2000). *Reconcilable differences.* New York: Guilford.

Christensen, A., Jacobson, N. S., & Babcock, J. C. (1995). Integrative behavioral couple therapy. In A. S. Gurman, & N. S. Jacobson (Eds.), *Clinical handbook of couple therapy* (pp. 31–64). New York, NY: Guilford Press.

Christie, A. B. (1982). Changing patterns in mental illness in the elderly. *British Journal of Psychiatry, 140,* 154–159.

Chu, J. A., Frey, L. M., Ganzel, B. L., & Matthews, J. A. (2000). Memories of childhood abuse: Dissociation, amnesia, and corroboration. *American Journal of Psychiatry, 156,* 749–755.

Chua, S. T., & McKenna, P. T. (1995). Schizophrenia—a brain disease? *British Journal of Psychiatry, 166,* 563–582.

Ciechanowski, P., Wagner, E., Schmaling, K., Schwartz, S., Williams, B., Diehr, P., et al. (2004). Community-integrated home-based depression treatment in older adults: A randomized controlled trial. *JAMA, 291,* 1569–1577.

Cimbora, D. M., & McIntosh, D. N. (2003). Emotional responses to antisocial acts in adolescent males with conduct disorder: A link to affective morality. *Journal of Clinical Child and Adolescent Psychology, 32,* 296–301.

Cinciripini, P. M., Lapitsky, L. G., Wallfisch, A., Mace, R., Nezami, E., & Van Vunakis, H. (1994). An evaluation of a multicomponent treatment program involving scheduled smoking and relapse prevention procedures: Initial findings. *Addictive Behaviors, 19,* 13–22.

Clark, D. M. (1994). Cognitive therapy for panic disorder. In J. D. Maser, & B. E. Wolfe (Eds.), *Treatment of panic disorder: A consensus development conference* (pp. 121–132). Washington, DC, US: American Psychiatric Association.

Clark, D. M. (1996). Panic disorder: From theory to therapy. In P. M. Salkovskis (Ed.), *Frontiers of cognitive therapy* (pp. 318–344). New York: Guilford.

Clark, D. A. (1997). Twenty years of cognitive assessment: Current status and future directions. *Journal of Consulting and Clinical Psychology, 65,* 996–1000.

Clark, D. M. (1999). Anxiety disorders: Why they persist and how to treat them. *Behaviour Research and Therapy, 37,* S5–S27.

Clark, D. M., Ehlers, A., McManus, F., Hackmann, A., Fennell, M., Campbell, H., Flower, T., Davenport, C., & Louis, B. (2003). Cognitive therapy versus fluoxetine in generalized social phobia: A randomized control trial. *Journal of Consulting and Clinical Psychology, 71,* 1058–1067.

Clark, D. M., Salkovskis, P. M., Hackmann, A., Middleton, H., Anastasiades, P., & Gelder, M. (1994). A comparison of cognitive therapy, applied relaxation, and imipramine in the treatment of panic disorder. *British Journal of Psychiatry, 164,* 759–769.

Clark, D. M., Salkovskis, P. M., Hackmann, A., Wells, A., Ludgate, J., & Gelder, M. (1999). Brief cognitive therapy for panic disorder: A randomized controlled trial. *Journal of Consulting and Clinical Psychology, 67,* 583–589.

Clark, D. M., Salkovskis, P. M., Hackmann, A., Wells, A., Ludugate, J., & Gelder, M. G. (in press). Brief cognitive therapy for panic disorder: A controlled trial. *Journal of Consulting and Clinical Psychology.*

Clark, D. M., & Wells, A. (1995). A cognitive model of social phobia. In R. Heimberg, M. R. Liebowitz, D. A. Hope, & F. R. Schneier (Eds.), *Social phobia: Diagnosis, assessment and treatment.* (pp. 69–93). New York: Guilford.

Clark, L. A., & Livesley, W. J. (2002). Two approaches to identifying the dimensions of personality disorder: Convergence on the five-factor model. In T. A. Widiger, & P. T. J. Costa (Eds.), *Personality disorders and the five-factor model of personality* (pp. 161–176). Washington, DC, U.S.: American Psychological Association.

Clark, L. A., Watson, D., & Mineka, S. (1994). Temperament, personality, and the mood and anxiety disorders. *Journal of Abnormal Psychology, 103,* 103–116.

Classen, C., Koopman, C., Hales, R., & Spiegel, D. (1998). Acute stress disorder as a predictor of posttraumatic stress disorder. *American Journal of Psychiatry, 155,* 620–624.

Claude, D., & Firestone, P. (1995). The development of ADHD boys: A 12-year follow-up. *Canadian Journal of Behavioral Science, 27,* 226–249.

Clayton, R. R., Catterello, A., & Walden, K. P. (1991). Sensation seeking as a potential mediating variable for school-based prevention intervention: A two-year follow-up of DARE. *Health Communication, 3,* 229–239.

Cleckley, H. (1976). *The mask of sanity* (5th ed.). St. Louis: Mosby.

Climko, R. P., Roehrich, H., Sweeney, D. R., & Al-Razi, J. (1987). Ecstasy: A review of MDMA and MDA. *International Journal of Psychiatry in Medicine, 16,* 359–372.

Cloninger, R. C., Martin, R. L., Guze, S. B., & Clayton, P. L. (1986). A prospective follow-up and family study of somatization in men and women. *American Journal of Psychiatry, 143,* 713–714.

Cloud, J. (1999, June 7). Mental health reform: What it would really take. *Time Magazine,* 54–56.

Coccaro, E. F., & Kavoussi, R. J. (1995, May 20–25). *Fluoxetine in aggression in personality disorders* [New Research Abstracts]. Presented at the American Psychiatric Association 148th annual meeting, Miami.

Cody, M. J., Dunn, D., Hoppin, S., & Wendt, P. (1999). Silver surfers: Training and evaluating Internet use among older adult learners. *Communication Education, 48,* 269–286.

Cohen, D., Taieb, O., Flament, M., Benoit, N., Chevret, S., Corcos, M., Fossati, P., Jeammet, P., Allilaire, J. F., & Basquin, M. (2000). Absence of cognitive impairment at long-term follow-up in adolescents treated with ECT for severe mood disorder. *American Journal of Psychiatry, 157,* 460–462.

Cohen, R. M., Nordahl, T. E., Semple, W. E., Andreason, P., et al. (1997). The brain metabolic patterns of clozapine and fluphenazine-treated patients with schizophrenia during a continuous performance task. *Archives of General Psychiatry, 54,* 481–486.

Cohen, S., Doyle, W. J., Skoner, D. P., Rabin, B. S., & Gwaltney, J. M. (1997). Social ties and susceptibility to the common cold. *JAMA, 277,* 1940–1945.

Cohen, P., Cohen, J., Kasen, S., et al. (1993). An epidemiological study of disorders in late childhood and adolescence: I. Age- and gender-specific prevalence. *Journal of Child Psychology & Psychiatry, 34,* 851–867.

Cohen, S., Frank, E., Doyle, W. J., Rabin, B. S., et al. (1998). Types of stressors that increase susceptibility to the common cold in healthy adults. *Health Psychology, 17,* 214–223.

Cohen, S., Tyrell, D. A. J., & Smith, A. P. (1991). Psychological stress and susceptibility to the common cold. *New England Journal of Medicine, 325,* 606–612.

Cohen, S., & Wills, T. A. (1985). Stress, social support, and the buffering process. *Psychological Bulletin, 98,* 310–357.

Coie, J. D., & Dodge, K. A. (1998). Aggression and antisocial behavior. In W. Damon (Series Ed.) & N. Eisenberg (Vol. Ed.), *Handbook of child psychology: Volume 3: Social emotional and personality development* (pp. 779–862). New York: John Wiley & Sons.

Colapinto, J. (1997). The true story of Joan/John. *Rolling Stone,* 55-ff.

Cole, D., & Turner, J., Jr. (1993). Models of cognitive mediation and moderation in child depression. *Journal of Abnormal Psychology, 102,* 271–281.

Cole, D. A., Jacquez, F. M., & Manschman, T. L. (2001). Social origins of depressive cognitions: A longitudinal study of self-perceived competence in children. *Cognitive Therapy and Research, 25,* 377–395.

Cole, D. A., Martin, J. M., Peeke, L. G., Seroczynski, A. D., & Hoffman, K. (1998). Are cognitive errors of underestimation predictive or reflective of depressive symptoms in children: A longitudinal study. *Journal of Abnormal Psychology, 107,* 481–496.

Cole, D. A., Martin, J. M., Powers, B., & Truglio, R. (1990). Modeling causal relations between academic and social competence and depression: A multitrait-multimethod longitudinal study of children. *Journal of Abnormal Psychology, 105,* 258–270.

Cole, M. G. (2004). Delirium in elderly patients. *American Journal of Geriatric Psychiatry, 12,* 7–21.

Colfax, G., Vittinghoff, E., Husnik, M. J., et al. (2004). Substance use and sexual risk: A participant- and episode-level analysis among a cohort of men who have sex with men. *American Journal of Epidemiology, 159,* 1002–1012.

Colom, F., Vieta, E., Martinez-Aran, A., Reinares, M., Goikolea, J. M., Benabarre, A., Torrent, C., Comes, M., Corbella, B., Parramon, G., & Corominas, J. (2003). A randomized trial on the efficacy of group psychoeducation in the prophylaxis of recurrences in bipolar patients whose disease is in remission. *Archives of General Psychiatry, 60,* 402–407.

Comer, S. D., Hart, C. L., Ward, A. S., Haney, M., Foltin, R. W., & Fischman, M. W. (2001). Effects of repeated oral methamphetamine administration in humans. *Psychopharmacology, 155,* 397–404.

Compas, B. E., Haaga, D. A. F., Keefe, F. J., Leitenberg, H., & Williams, D. A. (1998). Sampling of empirically supported psychological treatments from health psychology: Smoking, chronic pain, cancer, and bulimia nervosa. *Journal of Consulting and Clinical Psychology, 66,* 89–112.

Compton, D. R., Dewey, W. L., & Martin, B. R. (1990). Cannabis dependence and tolerance production. *Advances in Alcohol and Substance Abuse, 9,* 129–147.

Compton, S. N., March, J. M., Brent, D., Albano, A. M., Weersing, R., & Curry, J. (2004). Cognitive-behavioral psychotherapy for anxiety and depressive disorders in children and adolescents: An evidence-based medicine review. *Journal of the American Academy of Child and Adolescent Psychiatry, 43,* 930–959.

Conceicao do Rosario-Campos, M., Leckman, J. F., Mercadante, M. T., et al. (2001). Adults with early-onset obsessive-compulsive disorder. *American Journal of Psychiatry, 158,* 1899–1903.

Condelli, W. S., Fairbank, J. A., Dennis, M. L., & Rachal, J. V. (1991). Cocaine use by clients in methadone programs: Significance, scope, and behavioral interventions. *Journal of Substance Abuse Treatment, 8,* 203–212.

Conger, J. J. (1951). The effects of alcohol on conflict behavior in the albino rat. *Quarterly Journal of Studies on Alcohol, 12,* 129.

Conley, R. R., Love, R. C., Kelly, D. L., & Bartko, J. J. (1999). Rehospitalization rates of patients recently discharged on a regimen of risperidone or clozapine. *American Journal of Psychiatry, 156,* 863–868.

Conley, R. R., & Mahmoud, R. (2001). A randomized double-blind study of risperidone and olanzapine in the treatment of schizophrenia or schizoaffective disorder. *American Journal of Psychiatry, 158,* 765–774.

Connell, C. M., & Gibson, G. D. (1997). Racial, ethnic, and cultural differences in dementia caregiving: Review and analysis. *Gerontologist, 37,* 355–364.

Connelly, M. (1992, March 7). 3 found dead after inhaling laughing gas. *Los Angeles Times,* pp. A1, A23.

Consumer Reports. (1995, November). Mental health: Does therapy help? *Consumer Reports,* pp. 734–739.

Conwell, Y. (2001). Suicide in later life: A review and recommendations for prevention. *Suicide and Life-Threatening Behavior, 31,* 32–47.

Cook, B., Blatt, S. J., & Ford, R. Q. (1995). The prediction of therapeutic response to long-term intensive treatment of seriously disturbed young adult inpatients. *Psychotherapy Research, 5,* 218–230.

Cook, J. M. (2001). Post-traumatic stress disorder in older adults. *PTSD Research Quarterly, 12(3),* 1–3.

Cook, M., & Mineka, S. (1989). Observational conditioning of fear to fear-relevant versus fear-irrelevant stimuli in rhesus monkeys. *Journal of Abnormal Psychology, 98,* 448–459.

Cooke, D. J., & Michie, C. (1999). Psychopathy across cultures: North America and Scotland compared. *Journal of Abnormal Psychology, 108,* 58–68.

Cookson, W. O. C. M., & Moffatt, M. F. (1997). Asthma: An epidemic in the absence of infection? *Science, 275,* 41–42.

Cookson, W. O. C. M., & Moffatt, M. F. (2000). Genetics of asthma and allergic disease. *Human Molecular Genetics, 9,* 2359–2364.

Coolidge, F. L., & Segal, D. L. (1998). Evolution of personality disorder diagnosis in the Diagnostic and Statistical Manual of Mental Disorders. *Clinical Psychology Review, 18,* 585–589.

Coolidge, F. L., Thede, L. L., & Young, S. E. (2002). The heritability of gender identity disorder in a child and adolescent twin sample. *Behavior Genetics, 32,* 251–257.

Coons, P. M., & Bowman, E. S. (2001). Ten-year follow-up study of patients with dissociative identity disorder. *Journal of Trauma and Dissociation, 2,* 73–89.

Coons, P. M., & Milstein, V. (1992). Psychogenic amnesia: A clinical investigation of 25 cases. *Dissociation: Progress in the Dissociative Disorders, 5,* 73–79.

Cooper, J. E., Kendell, R. E., Gurland, B. J., Sharpe, L., Copeland, J. R. M., & Simon, R. (1972). *Psychiatric diagnosis in New York and London.* London: Oxford University Press.

Cooper, M. L., Frone, M. R., Russell, M., & Mudar, P. (1995). Drinking to regulate positive and negative emotion: A motivational model of alcoholism. *Journal of Personality and Social Psychology, 69,* 961–974.

Cooper, P. J., Coker, S., & Fleming, C. (1994). Self-help for bulimia nervosa: A preliminary report. *International Journal of Eating Disorders, 16,* 401–404.

Copolov, D. L., Mackinnon, A., & Trauer, T. (2004). Correlates of the affective impact of auditory hallucinations in psychotic disorders. *Schizophrenia Bulletin, 30,* 163–171.

Corder, R., Douthwaite, J. A., Lees, D. M., Khan, N. Q., Viseu dos Santos, A. C., Wood, E. G., & Carrier, M. J.

(2001). Endothelin-1 synthesis is reduced by red wine. *Nature, 414,* 863–864.

Cornblatt, B., & Erlenmeyer-Kimling, L. E. (1985). Global attentional deviance in children at risk for schizophrenia: Specificity and predictive validity. *Journal of Abnormal Psychology, 94,* 470–486.

Cornelius, J. R., Salloum, I. M., Ehler, J. G., Jarrett, P. J., Cornelius, M. D., et al. (1997). Fluoxetine in depressed alcoholics: A double-blind, placebo-controlled trial. *Archives of General Psychiatry, 54,* 700–705.

Corrigan, P. W. (1991). Social skills training in adult psychiatric populations: A meta-analysis. *Journal of Behavior Therapy and Experimental Psychiatry, 22,* 203–210.

Corrigan, P. W. (2001). Getting ahead of the data: A threat to some behavior therapies. *The Behavior Therapist, 24,* 189–193.

Corwin, M. (1996). Heroin's new popularity claims unlikely victims. *Los Angeles Times,* pp. A1.

Coryell, W., & Schlesser, M. (2001). The dexamethasone suppression test and suicide prevention. *Archives of General Psychiatry, 158,* 748–753.

Costa, P. T., Jr., & McCrae, R. R. (1992). *NEO-PI-R.* Odessa, FL: Psychological Assessment Resources.

Costa, P. T., Metter, E. J., & McCrae, R. R. (1994). Personality stability and its contribution to successful aging. *Journal of Geriatric Psychiatry, 27,* 41–59.

Costello, E. J., Costello, A. J., Edelbrock, C., Burns, B. J., Dulcan, M. K., Brent, D., & Janiszewski, S. (1988). Psychiatric disorders in pediatric primary care. *Archives of General Psychiatry, 45,* 1107–1116.

Courchesne, E. (2004). Brain development in autism: Early overgrowth followed by premature arrests of growth. *Mental Retardation and Developmental Disabilities Research Reviews, 10,* 106–111.

Courchesne, E., Carnes, B. S., & Davis, H. R. (2001). Unusual brain growth patterns in early life in patients with autistic disorder: An MRI study. *Neurology, 57,* 245–254.

Courchesne, E., Carper, R., & Akshoomoff, N. (2003). Evidence of brain overgrowth in the first year of life in autism. *JAMA, 290,* 337–344.

Cox, B. J., Clara, I. P., & Enns, M. W. (2002). Posttraumatic stress disorder and the structure of common mental disorders. *Depression and Anxiety, 15,* 168–171.

Coyne, J. C. (1976). Depression and the response of others. *Journal of Abnormal Psychology, 85,* 186–193.

Coyne, J. C. (1994). Self-reported distress: Analog or ersatz depression? *Psychological Bulletin, 116,* 29–45.

Craske, M. G., & Barlow, D. H. (2001). Panic disorder and agoraphobia. In D. H. Barlow (Ed.), *Clinical handbook of psychological disorders* (pp. 1–59). New York: Guilford.

Craske, M. G., Maidenberg, E., & Bystritsky, A. (1995). Brief cognitive-behavioral versus nondirective therapy for panic disorder. *Journal of Behavior Therapy & Experimental Psychiatry, 26,* 113–120.

Creamer, M., Burgess, P., & McFarlane, A. C. (2001). Posttraumatic stress disorder: Findings from the Australian national survey of mental health and well-being. *Psychological Medicine, 31,* 1237–1247.

Creer, T. L. (1982). Asthma. *Journal of Consulting and Clinical Psychology, 50,* 912–921.

Creer, T. L., Renna, C. M., & Chai, H. (1982). The application of behavioral techniques to childhood asthma. In D. C. Russo & J. W. Varni (Eds.), *Behavioral pediatrics: Research and practice.* New York: Plenum.

Crick, N. R., & Dodge, K. A. (1994). A review and reformulation of social information-processing mechanisms in children's social adjustment. *Psychological Bulletin, 115,* 74–101.

Critchley, H. D., Daly, E. M., Bullmore, E. T., Williams, S. C. R., Van Amelsvoort, T., Robertson, D. M., Rowe,

A., Phillips, M., McAlonan, G., Howlin, P., & Murphy, D. G. M. (2001). The functional neuroanatomy of social behaviour: Changes in cerebral blood flow when people with autistic disorder process facial expressions. *Brain, 123,* 2203–2212.

Crits-Christoph, P., & Barber, J. P. (2002). Psychological treatments for personality disorders. In P. E. Nathan & J. M. Gorman (Eds.), *A guide to treatments that work.* New York: Oxford University Press.

Crits-Christoph, P., Chambless, D. L., Frank, E., Brody, C., et al. (1995). Training in empirically validated treatments: What are clinical psychology students learning? *Professional Psychology: Research and Practice, 26,* 514–522.

Critser, G. (2003). *Fatland: How Americans became the fattest people in the world.* Boston: Houghton Mifflin.

Croft, R. J., Mackay, A. J., Mills, A. T. D., & Gruzelier, J. G. H. (2001). The relative contributions of ecstasy and cannabis to cognitive impairment. *Psychopharmacology, 153,* 373–379.

Cronan, T. A., Cruz, S. G., Arriaga, R. I., & Sarkin, A. J. (1996). The effects of a community-based literacy program on young children's language and conceptual development. *American Journal of Community Psychology, 24,* 251–272.

Cronbach, L. J., & Meehl, P. E. (1955). Construct validity in psychological tests. *Psychological Bulletin, 52,* 281–302.

Crow, T. J. (1980). Molecular pathology of schizophrenia: More than one disease process? *British Medical Journal, 280,* 784–788.

Crowell, N. A., & Burgess, A. W. (1996). *Understanding violence against women.* National Research Council, Commission on Behavioral and Social Sciences and Education, Committee on Law and Justice, Panel on Research on Violence Against Women, Washington, DC: National Academy Press.

Csernansky, J. G., Mahmoud, R., & Brenner, R. (2002). A comparison of risperidone and haloperidol for the prevention of relapse in patients with schizophrenia. *The New England Journal of Medicine, 356,* 16–22.

Culbertson, J. L. (1998). Learning disabilities. In T. H. Ollendick, & M. Hersen, (Eds.), *Handbook of child psychopathology* (3rd ed.). New York: Plenum.

Cummings, J. L. (2000). Cholinesterase inhibitors: A new class of psychotropic compounds. *American Journal of Psychiatry, 157,* 4–15.

Cummings, J. L., & Cole, G. (2002). Alzheimer disease. *JAMA, 287,* 2335–2338.

Curry, J. F. (2001). Specific psychotherapies for childhood and adolescent depression. *Biological Psychiatry, 49,* 1091–1100.

Curtin, J. J., Lang, A. R., Patrick, C. J., & Strizke, W. G. K. (1998). Alcohol and fear-potentiated startle: The role of competing cognitive demands in the stress-reducing effects of intoxication. *Journal of Abnormal Psychology, 107,* 547–557.

Curtis, L. H., Ostbye, T., Sendersky, V., Hutchison, S., Dans, P. E., Wright, A., Woolsey, R. L., & Schulman, K. A. (2004). Inappropriate prescribing for elderly Americans in a large outpatient population. *Archives of Internal Medicine, 164,* 1621–1625.

D'Silva, K., Duggan, C., & McCarthy, L. (2004). Does treatment really make psychopaths worse? A review of the evidence. *Journal of Personality Disorders, 18,* 163–177.

Dallery, J., Silverman, K., Chutuape, M. A., Bigelow, G. E., & Stitzer, M. (2001). Voucher-based reinforcement of opiate plus cocaine abstinence in treatment-resistant methadone patients: Effects of reinforcer magnitude. *Experimental & Clinical Psychopharmacology, 9,* 317–325.

Dallman, M. F., Pecoraro, N., Akana, S. F., La Fleur, S. E., Gomez, F., Houshyar, H., Bell, M. E., Bhatnagar, S.,

Laugero, K. D., & Manalo, S. (2003). Chronic stress and obesity: A new view of comfort food. *Proceedings of the National Academy of Sciences, 100*, 11696–11701.

Dare, C., LeGrange, D., Eisler, I., & Rutherford, J. (1994). Redefining the psychosomatic family: Family process of 26 eating disordered families. *International Journal of Eating Disorders, 16*, 211–226.

Davidson, R. J., Pizzagalli, D., & Nitschke, J. B. (2002). The representation and regulation of emotion in depression: Perspectives from affective neuroscience. C. L. Hammen and I. H. Gotlib (Eds.), *Handbook of depression*. (pp. 219–244). New York: Guilford.

Davidson, R. J., Pizzagalli, D., Nitschke, J. B., & Putnam, K. (2002). Depression: Perspectives from affective neuroscience. *Annual Review of Psychology, 53*, 545–574.

Davies, D. K., Stock, S. E., & Wehmeyer, M. (2003). Application of computer simulation to teach ATM access to individuals with intellectual disabilities. *Education & Training in Developmental Disabilities, 38*, 451–456.

Davila, J., Hammen, C. L., Burge, D., Paley, B., & Daley, S. E. (1995). Poor interpersonal problem solving as a mechanism of stress generation in depression among adolescent women. *Journal of Abnormal Psychology, 104*, 592–600.

Davis, C. (1996). The interdependence of obsessive-compulsiveness, physical activity, and starvation: A model for anorexia nervosa. In W. F. Epling & W. D. Pierce (Eds.), *Activity nervosa: Theory, research, and treatment* (pp. 209–218). Mahwah, NJ: Lawrence Erlbaum.

Davis, C. (1997). Normal and neurotic perfectionism in eating disorders: An interactive model. *International Journal of Eating Disorders, 22*, 421–426.

Davis, H. S., & Rockwood, K. (2004). Conceptualization of mild cognitive impairment: A review. *International Journal of Geriatric Psychiatry, 19*, 313–319.

Davis, J. M. (1978). Dopamine theory of schizophrenia: A two-factor theory. In L. C. Wynne, R. L. Cromwell, & S. Matthysse (Eds.), *The nature of schizophrenia*. New York: Wiley.

Davis, K. L., Kahn, R. S., Ko, G., & Davidson, M. (1991). Dopamine and schizophrenia: A review and reconceptualization. *American Journal of Psychiatry, 148*, 1474–1486.

Davis, L., & Siegel, L. J. (2000). Posttraumatic stress disorder in children and adolescents: A review and analysis. *Clinical Child and Family Psychology Review, 3*, 135–153.

Davis, M. C., Matthews, K. A., & Twamley, E. W. (1999). Is life more difficult on Mars or Venus? A meta-analytic review of sex differences in major and minor life events. *Annals of Behavioral Medicine, 21*, 83–97.

Davison, E. H. (1999). *The interrelationships among subjective well-being, gender role flexibility, perceived sexism, and perceived ageism in older women*. Unpublished dissertation, University of California at Santa Barbara.

Davison, G. C., Haaga, D. A., Rosenbaum, J., Dolezal, S. L., & Weinstein, K. A. (1991). Assessment of self-efficacy in articulated thoughts: "States of Mind" analysis and association with speech anxious behavior. *Journal of Cognitive Psychotherapy: An International Quarterly, 5*, 83–92.

Davison, G. C., & Lazarus, A. A. (1994). Clinical innovation and evaluation: Integrating practice with inquiry. *Clinical Psychology: Science and Practice, 1*, 157–168.

Davison, G. C., Navarre, S. G., & Vogel, R. S. (1995). The articulated thoughts in simulated situations paradigm: A think-aloud approach to cognitive assessment. *Current Directions in Psychological Science, 4*, 29–33.

Davison, G. C., Robins, C., & Johnson, M. K. (1983). Articulated thoughts during simulated situations: A paradigm for studying cognition in emotion and behavior. *Cognitive Therapy and Research, 7*, 17–40.

Davison, G. C., & Thompson, R. F. (1988). Stress management. In D. Druckman & J. A. Swets (Eds.), *Enhancing human performance: Issues, theories, and techniques*. Washington, DC: National Academy Press.

Davison, G. C., Williams, M. E., Nezami, E., Bice, T. L., & DeQuattro, V. (1991). Relaxation, reduction in angry articulated thoughts, and improvements in borderline essential hypertension and heart rate. *Journal of Behavioral Medicine, 14*, 453–468.

Davison, G. C., & Zighelboim, V. (1987). Irrational beliefs in the articulated thoughts of college students with social anxiety. *Journal of Rational-Emotive Therapy, 5*, 238–254.

Dawson, G., Toth, K., Abbott, R., Osterling, J., Munson, J., Estes, A., & Liaw, J. (2004). Early social attention impairments in autism: Social orienting, joint attention, and attention to distress. *Developmental Psychology, 40*, 271–283.

Dawson, M. E., Schell, A. M., & Banis, H. T. (1986). Greater resistance to extinction of electrodermal responses conditioned to potentially phobic CSs: A noncognitive process? *Psychophysiology, 23*, 552–561.

Day, N. L., Leech, S. L., Richardson, G. A., Cornelius, M. D., Robles, N., & Larkby, C. (2004). Prenatal alcohol exposure predicts continued deficits in offspring size at 14 years of age. *Alcoholism: Clinical and Experimental Research, 26*, 1584–1591.

Day, N. L., & Richardson, G. A. (2004). An analysis of the effects of prenatal alcohol exposure on growth: A teratologic model. *American Journal of Medical Genetics Part C (Seminar in Medical Genetics), 127C*, 28–34.

Deacon, S., Minicchiello, V., & Plummer, D. (1995). Sexuality and older people: Revisiting the assumptions, *Educational Gerontology, 21*, 497–513.

Deep, A. L., Lilenfeld, L. R., Plotnicov, K. H., Pollice, C., & Kaye, W. H. (1999). Sexual abuse in eating disorder subtypes and control women: The role of cormorbid substance dependence in bulimia nervosa. *International Journal of Eating Disorders, 25*, 1–10.

DeFazio, A., & Cunningham, K. A. (1987). A paraphilia in a spinal-cord-injured patient: A case report. *Sexuality and Disability, 8*, 247–254.

de Graaf, R., Bijl, R. V., Ravelli, A., Smit, F., & Vollenbergh, W. A. M. (2002). Predictors of first incidence of DSM-III-R psychiatric disorders in the general population: Findings from the Netherlands mental health survey and incidence study. *Acta Psychiatrica Scandinavica, 106*, 303–313.

DeJong, W., & Kleck, R. E. (1986). The social psychological effects of overweight. In C. P. Herman, M. P. Zanna, & E. T. Higgins (Eds.), *Physical appearance, stigma, and social behavior*. Hillside, NJ: Lawrence Erlbaum.

DeKlyen, M., & Speltz, M. L. (2001). Attachment and conduct disorder. In J. Hill & B. Maughan (Eds.), *Conduct disorders in childhood and adolescence* (pp. 320–345). New York: Cambridge University Press.

Deldin, P. J., Deveney, C. M., Kim, A. S., Casas, B. R., & Best, J. L. (2001). A slow wave investigation of working memory biases in mood disorders. *Journal of Abnormal Psychology, 110*, 267–281.

De Leo, D., Buono, M. D., & Dwyer, J. (2002). Suicide among the elderly: The long-term impact of a telephone support and assessment intervention in northern Italy. *British Journal of Psychiatry, 181*, 226–229.

deLint, J. (1978). Alcohol consumption and alcohol problems from an epidemiological perspective. *British Journal of Alcohol and Alcoholism, 17*, 109–116.

DeLisi, L. E., Shaw, S. H., Crow, T. J., et al. (2002). A genome-wide scan for linkage to chromosomal regions in 382 sibling pairs with schizophrenia or schizoaffective disorder. *American Journal of Psychiatry, 159*, 803–812.

Depression Guidelines Panel. (1993). *Depression in primary care: Volume 2. Treatment of major depression. Clinical practice guideline No. 5*. (AHCPR publication No. 93-0551).

Rockville, MD: U.S. Department of Health and Human Services, Public Health Service, Agency for Health Care Policy and Research.

DePrince, A. P., & Freyd, J. J. (2004). Forgetting trauma stimuli. *Psychological Science, 15*, 488–492.

Depue, R. A., Collins, P. F., & Luciano, M. (1996). A model of neurobiology: Environment interaction in developmental psychopathology. In M. F. Lenzenweger & J. J. Haugaard (Eds.), *Frontiers of developmental psychopathology* (pp. 44–76). New York: Oxford University Press.

Depue, R. A., & Iacono, W. G. (1989). Neurobehavioral aspects of affective disorders. In L. W. Porter, & M. R. Rosenzweig (Eds.), *Annual review of psychology* (pp. 457–492). Palo Alto, CA: Annual Reviews, Inc.

DeRubeis, R. J., & Crits-Christoph, P. (1998). Empirically supported individual and group psychological treatments for adult mental disorders. *Journal of Consulting and Clinical Psychology, 66*, 37–52.

DeRubeis, R. J., Gelfand, L. A., Tang, T. Z., & Simons, A. D. (1999). Medications versus cognitive behavior therapy for severely depressed outpatients: Mega-analysis of four randomized comparisons. *American Journal of Psychiatry, 156*, 1007–1013.

Dershowitz, A. (1994a, May 15). "Abuse Excuse" du jour victimizes many. *Los Angeles Times*, pp. B5.

Dershowitz, A. (1994b). *The abuse excuse and other copouts, sob stories, and evasions of responsibility*. Boston: Little Brown.

De Souza, E. B., Battaglia, G., & Insel, T. L. (1990). Neurotoxic effect of MDMA on brain serotonin neurons: Evidence from neurochemical and radioligand binding studies. *Annual Proceedings of the New York Academy of Science, 600*, 682–697.

Detweiler, J. B., Bedell, B. T., Salovey, P., Pronin, E., & Rothman, A. J. (1999). Message framing and sunscreen use: Gain-framed messages motivate beach-goers. *Health Psychology, 18*, 9–196.

Deutsch, A. (1949). *The mentally ill in America*. New York: Columbia University Press.

Devine, V., Adelson, R., Goldstein, J., Valins, S., & Davison, G. C. (1974). Controlled test of the analgesic and relaxant properties of nitrous oxide. *Journal of Dental Research, 53*, 486–490.

Dew, M. A., Bromet, E. J., Brent, D., & Greenhouse, J. B. (1987). A quantitative literature review of the effectiveness of suicide prevention centers. *Journal of Consulting and Clinical Psychology, 55*, 239–244.

de Wit, H., & Zacny, J. (2000). Abuse potential of nicotine replacement therapies. In Palmer, K. J. (Ed) *Smoking cessation* (pp. 79–92). Kwai Chung, Hong Kong: Adis International Publications.

Dickerson, S. S., & Kemeny, M. E. (2004). Acute stressors and cortisol responses: A theoretical integration and synthesis of laboratory research. *Psychological Bulletin, 130*, 355–391.

Dickey, C. C., McCarley, R. W., & Shenton, M. E. (2002). The brain in schizotypal personality disorder: A review of structural MRI and CT findings. *Harvard Review of Psychiatry, 10*, 1–15.

DiClemente, R. J., Forrest, K. A., Mickler, S., & Principal Site Investigators. (1990). College students' knowledge and attitudes about AIDS and changes in HIV-preventive behaviors. *AIDS Education and Prevention, 2*, 201–212.

Dieserud, G., Roysamb, E., Braverman, M. T., Dalgard, O. S., & Ekeberg, O. (2003). Predicating repetition of suicide attempt: A prospective study of 50 suicide attempters. *Archives of Suicide Research, 7*, 1–15.

Dietz, P. E., Hazelwood, R. R., & Warren, J. (1990). The sexually sadistic criminal and his offenses. *Bulletin of the American Academy of Psychiatry and the Law, 18*, 163–178.

DiFranza, J. R., Richards, J. W., Paulman, P. M., Wolf-Gillespie, N., Fletcher, C., et al. (1991). RJR Nabisco's cartoon camel promotes Camel cigarettes to children. *Journal of the American Medical Association, 266,* 3149–3153.

DiMaggio, C., Martinez, M., & Menard, J.-F. (2001). Evidence of a cohort effect for age of onset of schizophrenia. *American Journal of Psychiatry, 158,* 489–492.

DiNardo, P. A., Guzy, L. T., Jenkins, J. A., Bak, R. M., Tomasi, S. F., & Copland, M. (1988). Etiology and maintenance of dog fears. *Behaviour Research and Therapy, 26,* 241–244.

DiNardo, P. A., O'Brien, G. T., Barlow, D. H., Waddell, M. T., & Blanchard, E. B. (1993). Reliability of the DSM-III-R anxiety disorders categories using the Anxiety Disorders Interview Schedule-Revised (ADIS-R). *Archives of General Psychiatry, 50,* 251–256.

Dinn, W. M., & Harris, C. L. (2000). Neurocognitive function in antisocial personality disorder. *Psychiatry Research, 97,* 173–190.

Dishion, T. J., & Andrews, D. W. (1995). Preventing escalation in problem behaviors with high-risk young adolescents: Immediate and 1-year outcomes. *Journal of Consulting and Clinical Psychology, 63,* 538–548.

Dishion, T. J., Patterson, G. R., & Kavanagh, K. A. (1992). An experimental test of the coercion model: Linking theory, measurement, and intervention. In J. McCord & R. E. Tremblay (Eds.), *Preventing antisocial behavior* (pp. 253–282). New York: Guilford.

Dixon, L., Scott, J., Lyles, A., Fahey, A., Skinner, A., & Shore, A. (1997). Adherence to schizophrenia PORT family treatment recommendations. *Schizophrenia Research, 24,* 221.

Dobson, K. S. (1989). A meta-analysis of the efficacy of cognitive therapy for depression. *Journal of Consulting and Clinical Psychology, 57,* 414–419.

Dodge, K. A., & Frame, C. L. (1982). Social cognitive biases and deficits in aggressive boys. *Child Development, 53,* 620–635.

Doerr, P., Fichter, M., Pirke, K. M., & Lund, R. (1980). Relationship between weight gain and hypothalamic-pituitary-adrenal function in patients with anorexia nervosa. *Journal of Steroid Biochemistry, 13,* 529–537.

Dohrenwend, B. P., Levav, P. E., Schwartz, S., Naveh, G., Link, B. G., Skodol, A. E., & Stueve, A. (1992). Socioeconomic status and psychiatric disorders: The causation-selection issue. *Science, 255,* 946–952.

Dolan, B. (1991). Cross-cultural aspects of anorexia and bulimia: A review. *International Journal of Eating Disorders, 10,* 67–78.

Dolder, C. R., Lacro, J. P., Dunn, L. B., & Jeste, D. V. (2002). Antipsychotic medication adherence: Is there a difference between typical and atypical agents? *American Journal of Psychiatry, 159,* 103–108.

Doll, H. A., & Fairburn, C. G. (1998). Heightened accuracy of self-reported weight in bulimia nervosa: A useful cognitive "distortion." *International Journal of Eating Disorders, 24,* 267–273.

Dollard, J., & Miller, N. E. (1950). *Personality and psychotherapy.* New York: McGraw-Hill.

Dougher, M. J. (1988). Clinical assessment of sex offenders. In B. K. Schwartz (Ed.), *A practitioner's guide to treating the incarcerated male sex offender* (pp. 77–84). Washington, DC: U.S. Department of Justice.

Draguns, J. G. (1989). Normal and abnormal behavior in cross-cultural perspective: Specifying the nature of their relationships. In J. J. Berman (Ed.), *Nebraska symposium on motivation.* Lincoln: University of Nebraska Press.

Dreznick, M. T. (2003). Heterosocial competence of rapists and child molesters: A meta-analysis. *Journal of Sex Research, 40,* 170–178.

Drug Enforcement Agency. (2000). *DEA Congressional Testimony.* May 16.

Drug Enforcement Administration. (2001). *Working to prevent the diversion and abuse of Oxycontin.* Drug Enforcement Administration, Office of Diversion Control, June 12.

Drummond, T. (1999, June 7). Never too old: Sexually active seniors are one of the fastest-growing HIV-infected populations in the U.S. *Time,* 84H.

Drury, V., Birchwood, M., Cochrane, R., & Macmillan, R. (1996). Cognitive therapy and recovery from acute psychosis: A controlled trial. *British Journal of Psychiatry, 169,* 593–601.

Duke, M. P. (1994). Chaos theory and psychology: Seven propositions. *Genetic, Social, & General Psychology Monographs, 120,* 267–286.

Duman, R. S., Malberg, J., & Nakagawa, S. (2001). Regulation of adult neurogenesis by psychotropic drugs and stress. *Journal of Pharmacology and Experimental Therapeutics, 299,* 401–407.

Dunham, H. W. (1965). *Community and schizophrenia: An epidemiological analysis.* Detroit: Wayne State University Press.

Duman, R. S., Heninger, G. R., & Nestler, E. J. (1997). A molecular and cellular theory of depression. *Archives of General Psychiatry, 54,* 597–606.

DuPaul, G. J. (1991). Parent and teacher ratings of ADHD symptoms: Psychometric properties in a community-based sample. *Journal of Clinical Child Psychology, 20,* 245–253.

DuPaul, G. J., & Henningson, P. N. (1993). Peer tutoring effects on the classroom performance of children with attention deficit hyperactivity disorder. *School Psychology Review, 22,* 134–143.

Dura, J. R., Stukenberg, K. W., & Kiecolt-Glaser, J. K. (1991). Anxiety and depressive disorders in adult children caring for demented parents. *Psychology and Aging, 6,* 467–473.

Duran, R. E. F., Bedoya, A., Stoelb, B., Antoni, M., & Schneiderman, N. (August, 2004). *Adapting a manualized group intervention for Spanish-speaking, HIV-positive men and women living with HIV: El Proyecto ARMESE.* Presentation at the Annual Conference of the American Psychological Association. Hawaii.

Durkheim, E. (1951). *Suicide.* (J. A. Spaulding & G. Simpson, Trans.). New York: Free Press. (Original work published 1897; 2nd ed., 1930.)

Durkin, K. L. (1997). Misuse of the internet by pedophiles: Implications for law enforcement and probation practice. *Federal Probation, 61,* 14–18.

Dusseldorp, E., van Elderen, T., Maes, S., Meulman, J., & Kraaij, V. (1999). A meta-analysis of psychoeducation programs for coronary heart disease patients. *Health Psychology, 18,* 506–519.

Dvoskin, J. A., & Steadman, H. J. (1994). Using intensive case management to reduce violence by mentally ill persons in the community. *Hospital and Community Psychiatry, 45,* 679–684.

Dworkin, R. H., & Lenzenwenger, M. F. (1984). Symptoms and the genetics of schizophrenia: Implications for diagnosis. *American Journal of Psychiatry, 141,* 1541–1546.

Dworkin, R. H., Lenzenwenger, M. F., & Moldin, S. O. (1987). Genetics and the phenomenology of schizophrenia. In P. D. Harvey and E. F. Walker (Eds.), *Positive and negative symptoms of psychosis.* Hillsdale, NJ: Lawrence Erlbaum.

Dykens, E., Leckman, J., Paul, R., & Watson, M. (1988). Cognitive, behavioral, and adaptive functioning in fragile X and non-fragile A retarded men. *Journal of Autism and Developmental Disorders, 18,* 41–52.

Eagles, J. M., Johnston, M. I., Hunter, D., Lobban, M., & Millar, H. R. (1995). Increasing incidence of anorexia nervosa in the female population of northeast Scotland. *American Journal of Psychiatry, 152,* 1266–1271.

Eaker, E. D., Pinsky, J., & Castelli, W. P. (1992). Myocardial infarction and coronary death among women: Psychosocial predictors from a 20 year follow-up of women in the Framingham study. *American Journal of Epidemiology, 135,* 854–864.

Eddy, K. T., Keel, P. K., Dorer, D. J., Delinksy, S. S., Franko, D. L., & Herzog, D. B. (2002). Longitudinal comparison of anorexia nervosa subtypes. *International Journal of Eating Disorders, 31,* 191–201.

Edelbrock, C., Rende, R., Plomin, T., & Thompson, L. A. (1995). A twin study of competence and problem behavior in childhood and early adolescence. *Journal of Child Psychology and Psychiatry and Allied Disciplines, 36,* 775–789.

Egan, T. (1990). As memory and music faded, Alzheimer patient met death. *The New York Times, 89,* A1, A16.

Egeland, J. A., Gerhard, D. S., Pauls, D. L., Sussex, J. N., Kidd, K. K., Allen, C. R., Hosterer, A. M., & Housman, D. E. (1987). Bipolar affective disorders linked to DNA markers on chromosome 11. *Nature, 325,* 783–787.

Ehlers, A., Clark, D. M., Hackmann, A., McManus, F., Fennell, M., Herbert, C., & Mayou, R. (2003). A randomized controlled trial of cognitive therapy, a self-help booklet, and repeated assessments as early interventions for posttraumatic stress disorder. *Archives of General Psychiatry, 60,* 1024–1032.

Ehlers, A., Mayou, R. A., & Bryant, B. (1998). Psychological predictors of chronic posttraumatic stress disorder after motor vehicle accidents. *Journal of Abnormal Psychology, 107,* 508–519.

Eich, E., Macaulay, D., Loewenstein, R. J., & Dihle, P. H. (1997). Memory, amnesia, and dissociative identity disorder. *Psychological Science, 8,* 417–422.

Eiser, C., Eiser, R. J., Town, C., & Tripp, J. (1991). Discipline strategies and parental perceptions of preschool children with asthma. *British Journal of Medical Psychology, 64,* 45–53.

Eisler, R. M., & Blalock, J. A. (1991). Masculine gender role stress: Implications for the assessment of men. *Clinical Psychology Review, 11,* 45–60.

Eissenberg, T., Bigelow, G. E., Strain, E. C., & Walsh, S. L. (1997). Dose-related efficacy of levomethadyl acetate for treatment of opioid dependence. *JAMA, 277,* 1945–1951.

Eley, T. C., Lichtenstein, P., & Moffitt, T. E. (2003). A longitudinal behavioral genetic analysis of the etiology of aggressive and nonaggressive antisocial behavior. *Development and Psychopathology, 15,* 383–402.

Elhwuegi, A. S. (2004). Central monoamines and their role in major depression. *Progress in Neuropsychopharmacology and Biological Psychiatry, 28,* 435–451.

Elkin, I., Gibbons, R. D., Shea, M. T., & Shaw, B. F. (1996). Science is not a trial (but it can sometimes be a tribulation). *Journal of Consulting and Clinical Psychology, 64,* 92–103.

Elkin, I., Parloff, M. B., Hadley, S. W., & Autry, J. H. (1985). NIMH Treatment of Depression Collaborative Research Program. *Archives of General Psychiatry, 42,* 305–316.

Elkin, I., Shea, M. T., Watkins, J. T., Imber, S. D., Sotsky, S. M., Collins, J. F., Glass, D. R., Pilkonis, P. A., Leber, W. R., Docherty, J. P., Fiester, S. J., & Parloff, M. B. (1989). NIMH Treatment of Depression Collaborative Research Program: 1. General effectiveness of treatments. *Archives of General Psychiatry, 46,* 971–983.

Elkis, H., Friedman, L., Wise, A., & Meltzer, H. T. (1995). Meta-analysis of studies of ventricular enlargement and cortical sulcal prominence in mood disorders. *Archives of General Psychiatry, 52,* 735–746.

Ellenberger, H. F. (1972). The story of "Anna O": A critical review with new data. *Journal of the History of the Behavioral Sciences, 8,* 267–279.

Elliott, R., Greenberg, L. S., & Lietaer, G. (2004). Research on experiential psychotherapies. In M. J. Lambert (Ed.), *Bergin and Garfield's handbook of psychotherapy and behavior change* (5th ed.). (pp. 493–539). New York: John Wiley & Sons

Ellis, A. (1962). *Reason and emotion in psychotherapy.* New York: Lyle Stuart.

Ellis, A. (1991). The revised ABC's of rational-emotive therapy (RET). *Journal of Rational-Emotive and Cognitive Behavior Therapy, 9,* 139–172.

Ellis, A. (1993). Changing rational-emotive therapy (RET) to rational emotive behavior therapy (REBT). *The Behavior Therapist, 16,* 257–258.

Ellis, A. (1995). Changing rational-emotive therapy (RET) to rational emotive behavior therapy (REBT). *Journal of Rational-Emotive and Cognitive Behavior Therapy, 13,* 85–89.

Elzinga, B. M., Phaf, R. H., Ardon, A. M., & van Dyck, R. (2003). Directed forgetting between, but not within, dissociative personality status. *Journal of Abnormal Psychology, 112,* 237–243.

Emmelkamp, P. M. G. (1986). Behavior therapy with adults. In S. L. Garfield & A. E. Bergin (Eds.), *Handbook of psychotherapy and behavior change* (3rd ed.). New York: Wiley.

Emmelkamp, P. M. G. (2004). Behavior therapy with adults. In M. J. Lambert (Ed.), *Bergin and Garfield's handbook of psychotherapy and behavior change* (5th ed., pp. 393–446). New York: John Wiley & Sons.

Emslie, G., & Mayes, T. N. (2001). Mood disorders in children and adolescents: Psychopharmacological treatment. *Biological Psychiatry, 49,* 1082–1090.

Emslie, G. J., Mayes, T. L., & Hughes, C. W. (2000). Updates in the pharmacologic treatment of childhood depression. *Psychiatric Clinics of North America, 23,* 813–835.

Engdahl, B., Dikel, T. N., Eberly, R., & Blank, A. (1997). Posttraumatic stress disorder in a community group of former prisoners of war: A normative response to severe trauma. *American Journal of Psychiatry, 154,* 1576–1581.

Enger, C., Weatherby, L., Reynolds, R. F., Glasser, D. B., & Walker, A. M. (2004). Serious cardiovascular events and mortality among patients with schizophrenia. *Journal of Nervous and Mental Disease, 192,* 19–27.

Enserink, M. (1999). Drug therapies for depression: From MAO inhibitors to substance. *Science, 284,* 239.

Epel, E. S., McEwen, B. S., & Ickovics, J. R. (1998). Embodying psychological thriving: Physical thriving in response to stress. *Journal of Social Issues, 54,* 301–322.

Epling, W. F., & Pierce, W. D. (1992). *Solving the anorexia puzzle.* Toronto, Canada: Hogrefe & Huber.

Epping-Jordan, J. E., Compas, B. E., & Howell, D. C. (1994). Predictors of cancer progression in young adult men and women: Avoidance, intrusive thoughts, and psychological symptoms. *Health Psychology, 13,* 539–547.

Epstein, J. A., Botvin, G. J., & Diaz, T. (2001). Linguistic acculturation associated with higher marijuana and polydrug use among Hispanic adolescents. *Substance Use & Misuse, 36,* 477–499.

Erdberg, P., & Exner, J. E., Jr. (1984). Rorschach assessment. In G. Goldstein & M. Hersen (Eds.), *Handbook of psychological assessment.* New York: Pergamon.

Erhardt, D., & Hinshaw, S. P. (1994). Initial sociometric impressions of attention-deficit hyperactivity disorder and comparison boys: Predictions from social behaviors and nonverbal behaviors. *Journal of Consulting and Clinical Psychology, 62,* 833–842.

Erikson, E. (1950). *Childhood and society.* New York: Norton.

Erlenmeyer-Kimling, L. E., & Cornblatt, B. (1987). The New York high-risk project: A follow-up report. *Schizophrenia Bulletin, 13,* 451–461.

Escobar, J. I., Burnam, M. A., Karno, M., Forsythe, A., Golding, J. M., et al. (1987). Somatization in the community. *Archives of General Psychiatry, 44,* 713–720.

Esser, G., Schmidt, M. H., & Woerner, W. (1990). Epidemiology and course of psychiatric disorders in school-age children: Results of a longitudinal study. *Journal of Child Psychology and Psychiatry, 31,* 243–263.

Estes, C. L., Gerard, L., & Clarke, A. (1985). Women and the economics of aging. In B. B. Hess & E. W. Markson (Eds.), *Growing old in America: New perspectives on old age* (3rd ed., pp. 546–562). New Brunswick: Transaction Books.

Evans, P. D., & Edgerton, N. (1990). Life events as predictors of the common cold. *British Journal of Medical Psychology, 64,* 35–44.

Evans, R. J. (2001). Social influences in etiology and prevention of smoking and other health threatening behaviors in children and adolescents. In A. Baum, T. A. Revenson, and J. E. Singer (Eds.), *Handbook of health psychology.* (pp. 459–468). Mahwah, NJ: Lawrence Erlbaum.

Evashwick, C. J. (2001). Definition of the continuum of care. In C. J. Evashwick (Ed.), *The continuum of long-term care* (pp. 3–13). Albany, NY: Delmar.

Everett, F., Proctor, N., & Cartmell, B. (1989). Providing psychological services to American Indian children and families. In D. R. Atkinson, G. Morten, & D. W. Sue (Eds.), *Counseling American minorities* (3rd ed.). Dubuque, IA: W.C. Brown.

Everill, J. T., & Waller, G. (1995). Reported sexual abuse and eating psychopathology: A review of the evidence for a causal link. *International Journal of Eating Disorders, 18,* 1–11.

Everson, S. A., Kaplan, G. A., Goldberg, D. A., & Salonen, J. T. (1996). Anticipatory blood pressure response to exercise predicts future high blood pressure in middle-aged men. *Hypertension, 27,* 1059–1064.

Everson, S. A., Kauhanen, J., Kaplan, G. A., Goldberg, D. E., Julkunen, J., et al. (1997). Hostility and increased risk of mortality and acute myocardial infarction: The mediating role of behavioral risk factors. *American Journal of Epidemiology, 146,* 142–152.

Exner, J. E. (1978). *The Rorschach: A comprehensive system: Volume 2. Current research and advanced interpretation.* New York: Wiley.

Exner, J. E., Jr. (1986). *The Rorschach: A comprehensive system: Volume 1. Basic foundations* (2nd ed.). New York: Wiley.

EXPLORE Study Team. (2004). Effects of a behavioural intervention to reduce acquisition of HIV infection among men who have sex with men: The EXPLORE randomised controlled study. *Lancet, 364,* 41–50.

Eysenck, H. J. (1952). The effects of psychotherapy: An evaluation. *Journal of Consulting Psychology, 16,* 319–324.

Faber, S. D., & Burns, J. W. (1996). Anger management style, degree of expressed anger, and gender influence cardiovascular recovery from interpersonal harassment. *Journal of Behavioral Medicine, 19,* 31–53.

Fabrega, H., Jr. (2002). Evolutionary theory, culture and psychiatric diagnosis. In M. Maj & W. Gaebel (Eds.), *Psychiatric diagnosis and classification* (pp. 107–135). New York: John Wiley & Sons.

Fairburn, C. G. (1985). Cognitive-behavioral treatment for bulimia. In D. M. Garner, & P. E. Garfinkel (Eds.), *Handbook of psychotherapy for anorexia nervosa and bulimia* (pp. 160–192). New York: Guilford.

Fairburn, C. G. (1997). Eating disorders. In D. M. Clark & C. G. Fairburn (Eds.), *Science and practice of cognitive behavior therapy* (pp. 209–243). New York: Oxford.

Fairburn, C. G., Agras, W. S., & Wilson, G. T. (1992). The research on the treatment of bulimia nervosa: Practical and theoretical implications. In G. H. Anderson & S. H. Kennedy (Eds.), *The biology of feast and famine: Relevance to eating disorders.* New York: Academic Press.

Fairburn, C. G., Cooper, Z., Doll, H. A., & Welch, S. L. (1999). Risk factors for anorexia nervosa: Three integrated case-control comparisons. *Archives of General Psychiatry, 56,* 468–478.

Fairburn, C. G., Jones, R., Peveler, R. C., Carr, S. J., Solomon, R. A., O'Connor, M. E., Burton, J., & Hope, R. A. (1991). Three psychological treatments for bulimia nervosa. *Archives of General Psychiatry, 48,* 463–469.

Fairburn, C. G., Jones, R., Peveler, R. C., Hope, R. A., & O'Connor, M. E. (1993). Psychotherapy and bulimia nervosa: The longer-term effects of interpersonal psychotherapy, behavior therapy, and cognitive therapy. *Archives of General Psychiatry, 50,* 419–428.

Fairburn, C. G., Marcus, M. D., & Wilson, G. T. (1993). Cognitive behaviour therapy for binge eating and bulimia nervosa: A comprehensive treatment manual. In C. G. Fairburn & G. T. Wilson (Eds.), *Binge eating: Nature, assessment, and treatment.* New York: Guilford.

Fairburn, C. G., Norman, P. A., Welch, S. L., O'Connor, M. E., Doll, H. A., & Peveler, R. C. (1995). A prospective study of outcome in bulimia nervosa and the long-term effects of three psychological treatments. *Archives of General Psychiatry, 52,* 304–312.

Fairburn, C. G., Shafran, R., & Cooper, Z. (1999). A cognitive behavioural theory of anorexia nervosa. *Behaviour Research and Therapy, 37,* 1–13.

Fairburn, C. G., Stice, E., Cooper, Z., Doll, H. A., Norman, P. A., & O'Connor, M. E. (2003). Understanding persistence in bulimia nervosa: A 5-year naturalistic study. *Journal of Consulting and Clinical Psychology, 71,* 103–109.

Fairburn, C. G., Welch, S. L., Doll, H. A., Davies, B. A., & O'Connor, M. E. (1997). Risk factors for bulimia nervosa: A community-based case-control study. *Archives of General Psychiatry, 54,* 509–517.

Fairburn, C. G., Welch, S. L., & Hay, P. J. (1993). The classification of recurrent overeating: The "binge eating disorder" proposal. *International Journal of Eating Disorders, 13,* 155–159.

Fairburn, C. G., Welch, S. L., Norman, P. A., O'Conner, M. E., & Doll, H. E. (1996). Bias and bulimia nervosa: How typical are clinic cases? *American Journal of Psychiatry, 153,* 386–391.

Fallon, B. (1995). Intracavernous injection therapy for male erectile dysfunction. *Urological Clinics of North America, 22,* 833–845.

Falloon, I. R. H., Boyd, J. L., McGill, C. W., Razani, J., Moss, H. B., & Gilderman, A. N. (1982). Family management in the prevention of exacerbation of schizophrenia: A controlled study. *New England Journal of Medicine, 306,* 1437–1440.

Falloon, I. R. H., Boyd, J. L., McGill, C. W., Williamson, M., Razani, J., Moss, H. B., Gilderman, A. M., & Simpson, G. M. (1985). Family management in the prevention of morbidity of schizophrenia. *Archives of General Psychiatry, 42,* 887–896.

Fals-Stewart, W., O'Farrell, T. J., Feehan, M., Birchler, G. R., Tiller, S., & McFarlin, S. K. (2000). Behavioral couples therapy versus individual-based treatment for male substance-abusing patients: An evaluation of significant individual change and comparison of improvement rates. *Journal of Substance Abuse Treatment, 18,* 249–254.

Fanous, A. H., Prescott, C. A., & Kendler, K. S. (2004). The prediction of thoughts of death or self-harm in a population-based sample of female twins. *Psychological Medicine, 34,* 301–312.

Faraone, S. V., Biederman, J., Jetton, J. G., & Tsuang, M. T. (1997). Attention deficit disorder and conduct disorder: Longitudinal evidence for a family subtype. *Psychological Medicine, 27,* 291–300.

Faraone, S. V., Biederman, J., Weber, W., & Russell, R. L. (1998). Psychiatric, neuropsychological, and psychosocial features of DSM-IV subtypes of attention-deficit/hyperactivity disorder: Results from a clinically referred sample. *Journal of the American Academy of Child and Adolescent Psychiatry, 37,* 185–193.

Faraone, S. V., Doyle, A. E., Mick, E., & Biederman, J. (2001). Meta-analysis of the association between the 7-repeat allele of the dopamine d(4) receptor gene and attention deficit hyperactivity disorder. *American Journal of Psychiatry, 158,* 1052–1057.

Faraone, S. V., Taylor, L., & Tsuang, M. (2002). The molecular genetics of schizophrenia: An emerging consensus. *Expert reviews in molecular medicine, 23.* http://www.expertreviews.org/02004751h.htm

Faravelli, C., Salvatori, S., Galassi, F., & Aiazzi, L. (1997). Epidemiology of somatoform disorders: A community survey in Florence. *Social Psychiatry and Psychiatric Epidemiology, 32,* 24–29.

Farina, A. (1976). *Abnormal psychology.* Englewood Cliffs, NJ: Prentice-Hall.

Farquhar, J. W. (1991). The Stanford cardiovascular disease prevention programs. *Annals of the New York Academy of Sciences, 623,* 327–331.

Farquhar, J. W., Fortmann, S. P., Flora, J. A., & Maccoby, N. (1990). Methods of communication to influence behaviour. In W. Holland, R. Detels, & G. Knox (Eds.), *Oxford textbook of public health* (2nd ed.). New York: Oxford University Press.

Farrell, A. D., & Danish, S. J. (1993). Peer drug associations and emotional restraint: Causes or consequences of adolescents' drug use? *Journal of Consulting and Clinical Psychology, 61,* 327–334.

Faustman, W. O., Bardgett, M., Faull, K. F., Pfefferman, A., & Cseransky, J. G. (1999). Cerebrospinal fluid glutamate inversely correlates with positive symptom severity in unmedicated male schizophrenic/schizoaffective patients. *Biological Psychiatry, 45,* 68–75.

Favaro, A., & Santonastaso, P. (1997). Suicidality in eating disorders: Clinical and psychological correlates. *Acta Psychiatrica Scandanavica, 95,* 508–514.

Febbraro, G. A. R., & Clum, G. A. (1998). Meta-analytic investigation of the effectiveness of self-regulatory components in the treatment of adult behavior problems. *Clinical Psychology Review, 18,* 143–161.

Feeley, M., DeRubeis, R. J., & Gelfand, L. A. (1999). The temporal relation of adherence and alliance to symptom change in cognitive therapy for depression. *Journal of Consulting and Clinical Psychology, 67,* 578–582.

Feingold, B. F. (1973). *Introduction to clinical allergy.* Springfield, IL: Charles C. Thomas.

Feldman, H. A., Goldstein, I., Hatzichristou, G., Krane, R. J., & McKinlay, J. B. (1994). Impotence and its medical and psychosocial correlates: Results of the Massachusetts male aging study. *Journal of Urology, 151,* 54–61.

Feldman, H. M., Kolmen, B. K., & Gonzaga, A. M. (1999). Naltrexone and communication skills in young children with autism. *Journal of the American Academy of Child & Adolescent Psychiatry, 38,* 587–593.

Feldman Barrett, L. (2003). So you want to be a social neuroscientist? *APS Observer, 16,* 5–7.

Ferguson, C. P., La Via, M. C., Crossan, P. J., & Kaye, W. H. (1999). Are SSRI's effective in underweight anorexia nervosa? *International Journal of Eating Disorders, 25,* 11–17.

Fergusson, D. M., & Horwood, L. J. (2000). Does cannabis use encourage other forms of illicit drug use? *Addiction, 95,* 505–520.

Fergusson, D. M., Horwood, L. J., & Lynskey, M. T. (1993). Prevalence and comorbidity of DSM-III-R diagnoses in a birth cohort of 15 year olds. *Journal of the American Academy of Child and Adolescent Psychiatry, 32,* 1127–1134.

Ferguson, K. J., & Spitzer, R. L. (1995). Binge eating disorder in a community-based sample of successful and unsuccessful dieters. *International Journal of Eating Disorders, 18,* 167–172.

Ferster, C. B. (1961). Positive reinforcement and behavioral deficits of autistic children. *Child Development, 32,* 437–456.

Fetkewicz, J., Sharma, V., & Merskey, H. (2000). A note on suicidal deterioration with recovered memory treatment. *Journal of Affective Disorders, 58,* 155–159.

Fiellin, D. A., O'Connor, P. G., Chawarski, M., Pakes, J. P., Pantalon, M. V., & Schottenfeld, R. S. (2001). Methadone maintenance in primary care: A randomized controlled trial. *JAMA, 286,* 1724–1731.

Filipek, P. A., Semrud-Clikeman, M., Steingard, R. J., Renshaw, P. F., Kennedy, D. N., & Biederman, J. (1997). Volumetric MRI analysis comparing subjects having attention-deficit hyperactivity disorder with normal controls. *Neurology, 48,* 589–601.

Fillmore, K. M. (1987). Prevalence, incidence and chronicity of drinking patterns and problems among men as a function of age: A longitudinal and cohort analysis. *British Journal of Addiction, 82,* 77–83.

Fillmore, K. M., & Caetano, R. (1980, May 22). *Epidemiology of occupational alcoholism.* Paper presented at the National Institute on Alcohol Abuse and Alcoholism's Workshop on Alcoholism in the Workplace, Reston, VA.

Finkelhor, D. (1983). Removing the child—Prosecuting the offender in cases of sexual abuse: Evidence from the national reporting system for child abuse and neglect. *Child Abuse and Neglect, 7,* 195–205.

Finlay-Jones, R. (1989). Anxiety. In G. W. Brown & T. O. Harris (Eds.), *Life events and illness* (pp. 95–112). New York: Guilford.

Finney, J. W., & Moos, R. H. (1998). Psychosocial treatments for alcohol use disorders. In P. E. Nathan & J. M. Gorman (Eds.), *A guide to treatments that work* (pp. 156–166). New York: Oxford University Press.

Fiorentine, R., & Hillhouse, M. P. (2000). Exploring the additive effects of drug misuse treatment and Twelve-Step involvement: Does Twelve-Step ideology matter? *Substance Use & Misuse, 35,* 367–397.

Fischer, M. (1971). Psychoses in the offspring of schizophrenic monozygotic twins and their normal co-twins. *British Journal of Psychiatry, 118,* 43–52.

Fishbain, D. A., Cutler, R., Rosomoff, H. L., & Rosomoff, R. S. (2000). Evidence-based data from animal and human experimental studies on pain relief with antidepressants: A structured review. *Pain Medicine, 1,* 310–316.

Fisher, B. S., Cullen, F. T., & Turner, M. G. (2000). *The sexual victimization of college women.* National Institute of Justice Bureau of Justice Statistics. Unpublished Manuscript. NCJ 182369. Available by Web at http://www.ojp.usdoj.gov

Fisher, J. E., & Noll, J. P. (1996). Anxiety disorders. In L. L. Carstensen, B. A. Edelstein, & L. Dornbrand (Eds.), *The practical handbook of clinical gerontology* (pp. 304–323). Thousand Oaks, CA: Sage.

Fishler, K., Azen, C. G., Henderson, R., Friedman, E. G., & Koch, R. (1987). Psychoeducational findings among children treated for phenylketonuria. *American Journal of Mental Deficiency, 92,* 65–73.

Fitzgibbons, M. L., Spring, B., Avellone, M. E., Blackman, L. R., Pingitore, R., & Stolley, M. R. (1998). Correlates of binge eating in Hispanic, black, and white women. *International Journal of Eating Disorders, 24,* 43–52.

Flaum, M., Amador, X., Gorman, J., Bracha, H. S., Edell, W., McGlashan, T., Pandurangi, A., Knedler, K. S., Robinson, D., Lieberman, J., Ontiveros, A., Tohen, M., McGorry, P. Tyrrell, G., Arndt, S., & Andreasen, N. C. (1998). DSM-IV Field trial for schizophrenia and other psychotic disorders. *DSM-IV sourcebook* (pp. 687–713). Washington, DC: American Psychological Association.

Fleming, C. M. (1992). American Indians and Alaska Natives: Changing societies past and present. In M. A. Orlandi, R. Weston, & L. G. Epstein (Eds.), *Cultural competence for evaluators: A guide for alcohol and other drug abuse prevention practitioners working with ethnic/racial communities* (OSAP cultural competence series 1, pp. 147–171). Rockville, MD: U.S. Department of Health & Human Services.

Flor, H., & Birbaumer, N. (1993). Comparison of the efficacy of electromyographic biofeedback, cognitive-behavioral therapy, and conservative medical interventions in the treatment of chronic musculoskeletal pain. *Journal of Consulting and Clinical Psychology, 61,* 653–658.

Foa, E. B. & Franklin, M. E. (2001). Obsessive-compulsive disorder. In D. H. Barlow (Ed.), *Clinical handbook of psychological disorders* (pp. 209–263). New York: Guilford.

Foa, E. B., & Meadows, E. A. (1997). Psychosocial treatments for posttraumatic stress disorder: A critical review. *Annual Review of Psychology, 48,* 449–480.

Foa, E. B., Riggs, D. S., Marsie, E. D., & Yarczower, M. (1995). The impact of fear activation and anger on the efficacy of exposure treatment for posttraumatic stress disorder. *Behavior Therapy, 26,* 487–499.

Folkman, S., & Lazarus, R. S. (1985). If it changes it must be a process: Study of emotions and coping during 3 stages of college examination. *Journal of Personality and Social Psychology, 48,* 150–170.

Folkman, S., & Moskowitz, J. T. (2000). Positive affect and the other side of coping. *American Psychologist, 55,* 647–654.

Folstein, S., & Rutter, M. (1977a). Genetic influences and infantile autism. *Nature, 265,* 726–728.

Folstein, S., & Rutter, M. (1977b). Infantile autism: A genetic study of 21 twin pairs. *Journal of Child Psychology and Psychiatry, 18,* 291–321.

Food and Drug Administration. (April 11, 2005). *Deaths with antipsychotics in elderly patients with behavioral disturbances.* Public Health Advisory available by Web at http://www.fda.gov/cder/drug/advisory/antipsychotics.htm

Ford, C. S., & Beach, F. A. (1951). *Patterns of sexual behavior.* New York: Harper.

Ford, C. V. (1995). Dimensions of somatization and hypochondriasis. Special Issue: Malingering and conversion reactions. *Neurological Clinics, 13,* 241–253.

Ford, C. V., & Folks, D. G. (1985). Conversion disorders: An overview. *Psychosomatics, 26,* 371–383.

Ford, J. M., Mathalon, D. H., Whitfield, S., Faustman, W. O., & Roth, W. T. (2002). Reduced communication between frontal and temporal lobes during talking in schizophrenia. *Biological Psychiatry, 51,* 485–492.

Forster, H. P., Emanuel, E., & Grady, C. (2001). The 2000 revision of the Declaration of Helsinki: A step forward or more confusion? *Lancet, 358,* 1449–1453.

Foucault, M. (1965). *Madness and civilization.* New York: Random House.

Fowler, I. L., Carr, V. J., Carter, N. T., & Lewin, T. J. (1998). Patterns of current and lifetime substance use in schizophrenia. *Schizophrenia Bulletin*, 24, 443–455.

Frackiewicz, E. J., Sramek, J. J., Herrera, J. M., Kurtz, N. M., & Cutler, N. R. (1997). Ethnicity and antipsychotic response. *Annals of Pharmacotherapy*, 31, 1360–1369.

Francis, D., Diorio, J., Liu, D., & Meaney, M. J. (1999). Nongenomic transmission across generations of maternal behavior and stress responses in the rat. *Science*, 286, 1155–1158.

Frank, E., Kupfer, D. J., Perel, J. M., Cornes, C., Jarrett, D. B., et al. (1990). Three-year outcomes for maintenance therapies in recurrent depression. *Archives of General Psychiatry*, 47, 1093–1099.

Frank, J. D. (1978). *Effective ingredients of successful psychotherapy.* Oxford, England: Brunner/Mazel.

Franklin, M. E., & Foa, E. B. (1998). Cognitive-behavioral treatments for obsessive-compulsive disorder. In P. E. Nathan & J. M. Gorman (Eds.), *A guide to treatments that work* (pp. 339–357). New York: Oxford University Press.

Franklin, T. R., Acton, P. D., Maldjian, J. A., Gray, J. D., Croft, J. R., Dackis, C. A., O'Brien, C. P., & Childress, A. R. (2002). Decreased gray matter concentration in the insular, orbitofrontal, cingulate, and temporal cortices of cocaine patients. *Biological Psychiatry*, 51, 131–142.

Frasure-Smith, N., Lesperance, F., & Talajic, M. (1995). Depresson and 18-month prognosis after myocardial infarction. *Circulation*, 91, 999–1005.

Frederickson, B. L., & Carstensen, L. L. (1990). Choosing social partners: How old age and anticipated endings make people more selective. *Psychology and Aging*, 5, 335–347.

Fredrickson, B. L., & Kahneman, D. (1993). Duration neglect in retrospective evaluations of affective episodes. *Journal of Personality and Social Psychology*, 65, 20–28.

Fredrickson, B. L., & Levenson, R. W. (1998). Positive emotions speed recovery from the cardiovascular sequelae of negative emotions. *Cognition and Emotion*, 12, 191–200.

Fredrickson, B. L., Maynard, K. E., Helms, M. J., Haney, T. L., Siegler, I. C., & Barefoot, J. C. (2000). Hostility predicts magnitude and duration of blood pressure response to anger. *Journal of Behavioral Medicine*, 23, 229–243.

Fredrickson, B. L., & Roberts, T. A. (1997). Objectification theory: Toward understanding women's lived experience and mental health risks. *Psychology of Women Quarterly*, 21, 173–206.

Fredrickson, B. L., Roberts, T. A., Noll, S. M., Quinn, D. M., & Twenge, J. M. (1998). That swimsuit becomes you: Sex differences in self-objectification, restrained eating, and math performance. *Journal of Personality and Social Psychology*, 78, 269–284.

Fredrikson, M., Annas, P., & Wik, G. (1997). Parental history, aversive exposure and the development of snake and spider phobia in women. *Behaviour Research and Therapy*, 35, 23–28.

Freeston, M. H., Dugas, M. J., & Ladoceur, R. (1996). Thoughts, images worry, and anxiety. *Cognitive Therapy and Research*, 20, 265–273.

French, S. A., Story, M., Neumark-Sztainer, D., Downes, B., Resnick, M., et al. (1997). Ethnic differences in psychosocial and health behavior correlates of dieting, purging, and binge eating in a population-based sample of adolescent females. *International Journal of Eating Disorders*, 22, 315–322.

Freud, A. (1946). *The ego and mechanisms of defense.* New York: International Universities Press.

Freud, A. (1966). *The ego and the mechanisms of defense.* New York: International Universities Press.

Freud, S. (1917). Mourning and melancholia. In *Collected*

papers (Vol. 4). London: Hogarth and the Institute of Psychoanalysis, 1950.

Freund, K. (1990). Courtship disorders. In W. L. Marshall, D. R. Laws, & H. E. Barbaree (Eds.), *Handbook of sexual assault: Issues, theories, and treatment* (pp. 195–207). New York: Plenum.

Frick, P. J., & Ellis, M. (1999). Callous-unemotional traits and subtypes of conduct disorder. *Clinical Child & Family Psychology Review*, 2, 149–168.

Fried, P., Watkinson, B., James, D., & Gray, R. (2002). Current and former marijuana use: Preliminary findings of a longitudinal study of effects on IQ in young adults. *CMAJ*, 166, 887–891.

Friedman, M. (1969). *Pathogenesis of coronary artery disease.* New York: McGraw-Hill.

Friedman, M., Thoresen, C. E., Gill, J. J., Powell, L. H., Ulmer, D., Thompson, L., Price, V. A., Rabin, D. D., Breall, W. S., Dixon, T., Levy, R., & Bourg, E. (1984). Alteration of type A behavior and reduction in cardiac recurrences in postmyocardial infarction patients. *American Heart Journal*, 108, 237–248.

Friedman, M., Thoresen, C. E., Gill, J. J., Ulmer, D., Thompson, L., Powell, L., Price, A., Elek, S. R., Rabin, D. D., Breall, W. S., Piaget, G., Dixon, T., Bourg, F., Levy, R., & Tasto, D. I. (1982). Feasibility of altering type A behavior pattern after myocardial infarction. *Circulation*, 66, 83–92.

Friedman, M., & Ulmer, D. (1984). *Treating type A behavior and your heart.* New York: Fawcett Crest.

Friedman, M. S., Powell, K. E., Hutwagner, L., Graham, L. M., & Teague, W. G. (2001). Impact of changes in transportation and commuting behaviors during the 1996 Summer Olympic Games in Atlanta on air quality and childhood asthma. *Journal of the American Medical Association*, 285, 897–905.

Friedmann, P. D., Lemon, S. C., & Stein, M. D. (2001). Transportation and retention in outpatient drug abuse treatment programs. *Journal of Substance Abuse Treatment*, 21, 97–103.

Friedrich, M. J. (2002). Epidemic of obesity expands its spread to developing countries. *JAMA*, 287, 1382–1386.

Froehlich, T. E., Bogardus, S. T., & Inouye, S. K. (2001). Dementia and race: Are there differences between African Americans and Caucasians? *Journal of the American Gerontological Society*, 49, 477–484.

Frojdh, K., Hakansson, A., Karlsson, I., Molarius, A., Frojdh, K., Hakansson, A., et al. (2003). Deceased, disabled or depressed—a population-based 6-year follow-up study of elderly people with depression. *Social Psychiatry and Psychiatric Epidemiology*, 38, 557–562.

Fromm-Reichmann, F. (1948). Notes on the development of treatment of schizophrenics by psychoanalytic psychotherapy. *Psychiatry*, 11, 263–273.

Frost, D. O., & Cadet, J.-L. (2000). Effects of methamphetamine-induced toxicity on the development of neural circuitry: A hypothesis. *Brain Research Reviews*, 34, 103–118.

Frost, H., Lamb, S. E., Moffett, J. A. K., Fairbank, J. C. T., & Moser, J. S. (1998). A fitness programme for patients with chronic low back pain: 2-year follow-up of a randomised controlled trial. *Pain*, 75, 273–279.

Fuller, R. K. (1988). Disulfiram treatment of alcoholism. In R. M. Rose & J. E. Barrett (Eds.), *Alcoholism: Treatment and outcome.* New York: Raven.

Fuller, R. K., & Allen, J. P. (2000). Patient-to-treatment matching. In G. Zernig & A. Saria et al. (Eds.), *Handbook of alcoholism* (pp. 363–368). Boca Raton, FL: CRC Press.

Fumeron, F., Betoulle, D., Nicaud, V., Evans, A., Kee, F., Ruidavets, J. B., Arveiler, D., Luc, G., & Cambien, F. (2002). Serotonin transporter gene polymorphism and

myocardial infarction: Étude Cas-TÄmoins de l'Infarctus du Myocarde (ECTIM). *Circulation*, 105, 2943–2945.

Fung, Y. K., & Lau, Y-S. (1989). Effects of prenatal nicotine exposure on rat striatal dopaminergic and nicotinic systems. *Pharmacology, Biochemistry & Behavior*, 33, 1–6.

Furnham, A., & Baguma, P. (1994). Cross-cultural differences in the evaluation of male and female body shapes. *International Journal of Eating Disorders*, 15, 81–89.

Galaburda, A. M. (1989). Ordinary and extraordinary brain development: Anatomical variation in developmental dyslexia. *Annals of Dyslexia*, 39, 67–80.

Galaburda, A. M. (1993). Neuroanatomical basis of developmental dyslexia. *Neurologic Clinics*, 11, 161–173.

Galea, S., Ahern, J., Resnick, H., Kilpatrick, D., Bucuvalas, M., Gold, J., Vlahov, D. (2002). Psychological sequelae of the September 11 terrorist attacks in New York City. *New England Journal of Medicine*, 346, 982–987.

Gallagher, D., & Thompson, L. W. (1983). Cognitive therapy for depression in the elderly. A promising model for treatment and research. In L. D. Breslau & M. R. Haug (Eds.), *Depression and aging: Causes, care and consequences.* New York: Springer-Verlag.

Gallagher-Thompson, D., McKibbin, C., Koonce-Volwiler, D., Menedez, A., Stewart, D., & Thompson, L. W. (2000). Psychotherapy for older adults. In C. R. Synder & R. E. Ingram (Eds.), *Handbook of psychological change* (pp. 614–636). New York: John Wiley & Sons.

Galli, V., McElroy, S. L., Soutullo, C. A., Kizer, D., Raute, N., et al. (1999). The psychiatric diagnoses of twenty-two adolescents who have sexually molested children. *Comprehensive Psychiatry*, 40, 85–88.

Gallo, C. L., & Pfeffer, C. R. (2003). Children and adolescents bereaved by a suicidal death: Implications for psychosocial outcomes and interventions. In A. Apter and R. A. King (Eds.), *Suicide in children and adolescents* (pp. 294–312). New York: Cambridge University Press.

Gallo, J. J., & Lebowitz, B. D. (1999). The epidemiology of common late-life mental disorders in the community: Themes for the new century. *Psychiatric Services*, 50, 1158–1166.

Gallo, L. C., & Matthews, K. A. (2003). Understanding the association between socioeconomic status and physical health: Do negative emotions play a role? *Psychological Bulletin*, 129, 10–51.

Ganellan, R. J. (1996). Comparing the diagnostic efficiency of the MMPI, MCMI-II, and Rorschach: A review. *Journal of Personality Assessment*, 67, 219–243.

Gann, M. K., & Davison, G. C. (1999). *Assessing psychological reactance: Defiant thoughts at the ATSS paradigm.* Unpublished manuscript. University of Southern California.

Gao, S., Hendrie, H. C., Hall, K. S., & Hui, S. (1998). Relationships between sex, age, and the incidence of dementia and Alzheimer's disease: A meta-analysis. *Archives of General Psychiatry*, 55, 809–816.

Garand, L., Buckwalter, K. C., Lubaroff, D., Tripp-Reimer, T., Frantz, R. A., & Ansley, T. N. (2002). A pilot study of immune and mood outcomes of a community-based intervention for dementia caregivers: The PLST intervention. *Archives of Psychiatric Nursing*, 16, 156–167.

Garb, H. N., & Schramke, C. J. (1996). Judgment research and neuropsychological assessment: A narrative review and meta-analyses. *Psychological Bulletin*, 120, 140–153.

Garb, I. I. N. (1997). Race bias, social class bias, and gender bias in clinical judgment. *Clinical Psychology: Science and Practice*, 4, 99–120.

Garber, J., & Flynn, C. (2001). Vulnerability to depression in childhood and adolescence. In R. M. Ingram and J. M. Price (Eds.), *Vulnerability to psychopathology: Risk across the lifespan* (pp. 175–225). New York: Guilford.

Garber, J., Kelly, M. K., & Martin, N. C. (2002). Developmental trajectories of adolescents' depressive symptoms: Predictors of change. *Journal of Consulting and Clinical Psychology, 70,* 79–95.

Garbutt, J. C., Mayo, J. P., Little, K. Y., Gillette, G. M., Mason, G. A., et al. (1994). Dose-response studies with protirelin. *Archives of General Psychiatry, 51,* 875–883.

Garcia-Andrade, C., Wall, T. L., & Ehlers, C. L. (1997). The firewater myth and response to alcohol in Mission Indians. *American Journal of Psychiatry, 154,* 983–988.

Garety, P. A., Fowler, D., & Kuipers, E. (2000). Cognitive-behavioral therapy for medication-resistant symptoms. *Schizophrenia Bulletin, 26,* 73–86.

Garfield, S. L. (1978). Research on client variables in psychotherapy. In S. L. Garfield & A. E. Bergin (Eds.), *Handbook of psychotherapy and behavior change* (2nd ed.). New York: Wiley.

Garfield, S. L., & Bergin, A. E. (1986). Introduction and historical overview. In S. L. Garfield & A. E. Bergin (Eds.), *Handbook of psychotherapy and behavior change* (3rd ed.). New York: Wiley.

Garfinkel, P. E., Goering, E. L., Goldbloom, S. D., Kennedy, S., Kaplan, A. S., & Woodside, D. B. (1996). Should amenorrhea be necessary for the diagnosis of anorexia nervosa? *British Journal of Psychiatry, 168,* 500–506.

Garfinkel, P. E., Kennedy, S. H., & Kaplan, A. S. (1995). Views on classification and diagnosis of eating disorders. *Canadian Journal of Psychiatry, 40,* 445–456.

Garland, R. J., & Dougher, M. J. (1991). Motivational interviewing in the treatment of sex offenders. In W. R. Miller & S. Rollnick (Eds.), *Motivating interviewing: Preparing people to change addictive behavior* (pp. 303–313). New York: Guilford.

Garner, D. M. (1997). Psychoeducational principles. In D. M. Garner & P. E. Garfinkel (Eds.), *Handbook of treatment for eating disorders* (pp. 145–177). New York: Guilford.

Garner, D. M., Garfinkel, P. E., Schwartz, D., & Thompson, M. (1980). Cultural expectation of thinness in women. *Psychological Reports, 47,* 483–491.

Garner, D. M., Olmsted, M. P., & Polivy, J. (1983). Development and validation of a multi-dimensional eating disorder inventory for anorexia nervosa and bulimia. *International Journal of Eating Disorders, 2,* 15–34.

Garner, D. M., Vitousek, K. M., & Pike, K. M. (1997). Cognitive-behavioral therapy for anorexia nervosa. In D. M. Garner & P. E. Garfinkel (Eds.), *Handbook of treatment for eating disorders* (pp. 94–144). New York: Guilford.

Gatchel, R. J., Baum, A., & Krantz, D. S. (1989). *An introduction to health psychology* (2nd ed.). New York: Random House.

Gatz, M., Bengtson, V. L., & Blum, M. J. (1990). Caregiving families. In J. E. Birren & K. W. Schaie (Eds.), *Handbook of the psychology of aging* (3rd ed., pp. 404–426). New York: Academic Press.

Gatz, M., Kasl-Godley, J. E., & Karel, M. J. (1996). Aging and mental disorders. In J. E. Birren & K. W. Schaie (Eds.), *Handbook of the psychology of aging.* San Diego, CA: Academic Press.

Gauthier, Y., Fortin, C., Drapeau, P., Breton, J., Gosselin, J., Quintal, L., Weisnagel, J., & Lamarre, A. (1978). Follow-up study of 35 asthmatic preschool children. *Journal of the American Academy of Child Psychiatry, 17,* 679–694.

Gauthier, Y., Fortin, C., Drapeau, P., Breton, J., Gosselin, J., Quintal, L., Weisnagel, J., Tetreault, L., & Pinard, G. (1977). The mother-child relationship and the development of autonomy and self-assertion in young (14–30 months) asthmatic children. *Journal of the American Academy of Child Psychiatry, 16,* 109–131.

Gaw, A. C. (2001). *Concise guide to cross-cultural psychiatry.* Washington, DC: American Psychiatric Association.

Ge, X., Conger, R. D., Cadoret, R. J., Neiderhiser, J. M., Yates, W., et al. (1996). The developmental interface between nature and nurture: A mutual influence model of child antisocial behavior and parent behaviors. *Developmental Psychology, 32,* 574–589.

Geary, D. C. (1993). Mathematical disabilities: Cognitive, neuropsychological, and genetic components. *Psychological Bulletin, 114,* 345–362.

Geary, D. C., & Brown, S. C. (1991). Cognitive addition: Strategy choice and speed-of-processing differences in gifted, normal, and mathematically disabled children. *Developmental Psychology, 27,* 398–406.

Geary, D. C., Brown, S. C., & Samaranayake, V. A. (1991). Cognitive addition: A short longitudinal study of strategy choice and speed-of-processing differences in normal and mathematically disabled children. *Developmental Psychology, 27,* 787–797.

Gebhard, P. H., Gagnon, J. H., Pomeroy, W. B., & Christenson, C. V. (1965). *Sex offenders.* New York: Harper & Row.

Geddes, J. R., Carney, S. M., Davies, C., Furukawa, T. A., Frank, E., Kupfer, D. J., & Goodwin, G. (2003). Relapse prevention with antidepressant drug treatment in depressive disorders: A systematic review. *Lancet, 361,* 653–661.

Geer, J. H., Davison, G. C., & Gatchel, R. I. (1970). Reduction of stress in humans through nonveridical perceived control of aversive stimulation. *Journal of Personality and Social Psychology, 16,* 731–738.

Geller, B., Cooper, T. B., Graham, D., Fetner, H., Marstellar, F., & Wells, J. (1992). Pharmacokinetically designed double-blind placebo-controlled study of nortriptyline in 6- to 12-year-olds with major depressive disorder. *Journal of the American Academy of Child and Adolescent Psychiatry, 31,* 34–44.

Gendall, K. A., Bulik, C. M., Joyce, P. R., McIntosh, V. V., & Carter, F. A. (2000). Menstrual cycle irregularity in bulimia nervosa: Associated factors and changes with treatment. *Journal of Psychosomatic Research, 49,* 409–415.

Gendreau, P., Little, T., & Goggin, C. (1996). A Meta-Analysis of the Predictors of Adult Offender Recidivism: What Works! *Criminology, 34,* 575–607.

General Register Office. (1968). *A glossary of mental disorders.* London.

George, L. K., Landoman, R., Blazer, D. G., & Anthony, J. C. (1991). Cognitive impairment. In L. N. Robins & D. A. Regier (Eds.), *Psychiatric disorders in America.* New York: Free Press.

George, L. K., & Weiler, S. J. (1981). Sexuality in middle and late life: The effects of age, cohort, and gender. *Archives of General Psychiatry, 38,* 919–923.

Geracioti, T. D., Baker, D. G., Ekhator, N. N., et al. (2001). CSF norepinephrine concentrations in posttraumatic stress disorder. *American Journal of Psychiatry, 158,* 1227–1230.

Gerlach, A. L., Wilhelm, F. H., Gruber, K., & Roth, W. T. (2001). Blushing and physiological arousability in social phobia. *Journal of Abnormal Psychology, 110,* 247–258.

Gernsbacher, M. A., Dawson, M., & Goldsmith, H. H. (2005). Three reasons not to believe in an autism epidemic. *Current Directions in Psychological Science, 14,* 55–58.

Gerra, G., Zaimovic, A., Ferri, M., Zambelli, U., Timpano, M., Neri, E., Marzocchi, G. F., Delsignore, R., & Brambilla, F. (2000). Long-lasting effects of (6)3,4-methylenedioxymethamphetamine (Ecstasy) on serotonin system function in humans. *Biological Psychiatry, 47,* 127–136.

Geschwind, D. H., Robidoux, J., Alarcon, M., et al. (2001). Dementia and neurodevelopmental predisposition: Cognitive dysfunction in presymptomatic subjects precedes dementia by decades in frontotemporal dementia. *Annals of Neurology, 50,* 741–746.

Ghaemi, S. N., Boiman, E. E., & Goodwin, F. K. (2000). Diagnosing bipolar disorder and the effect of antidepressants: A naturalistic study. *Journal of Clinical Psychiatry, 61,* 804–808.

Gibson, D. R. (2001). Effectiveness of syringe exchange programs in reducing HIV risk behavior and seroconversion among injecting drug users. *AIDS, 15,* 1329–1341.

Gidron, Y., Davidson, K., & Bata, I. (1999). The short-term effects of a hostility- reduction intervention in CHD patients. *Health Psychology, 18,* 416–420.

Gilbert, A. R., Rosenberg, D. R., Harenski, K., et al. (2001). Thalamic volumes in patients with first episode schizophrenia. *American Journal of Psychiatry, 158,* 618–624.

Gilbertson, M. W., Shenton, M. E., Ciszewski, A., Kasai, K., Lasko, N. B., Orr, S. P., et al. (2002). Smaller hippocampal volume predicts pathologic vulnerability to psychological trauma. *Nature Neuroscience, 5,* 1242–1247.

Gilbody, S., Whitty, P., Grimshaw, J., & Thomas, R. (2003). Educational and organizational interventions to improve the management of depression in primary care: A systematic review. *JAMA, 289,* 3145–3151.

Gilboy, J. A., & Schmidt, J. R. (1971). "Voluntary" hospitalization of the mentally ill. *Northwestern University Law Review, 66,* 429–439.

Gillberg, C. (1991). Outcome in autism and autistic-like conditions. *Journal of the American Academy of Child and Adolescent Psychiatry, 30,* 375–382.

Gillespie, K., Duffy, M., Hackmann, A., & Clark, D. M. (2002). Community based cognitive therapy in the treatment of post-traumatic stress disorder following the Omaha bomb. *Behaviour Research and Therapy, 40,* 345–357.

Gillis, J. J., & DeFries, J. C. (1991). Confirmatory factor analysis of reading and mathematics performance measures in the Colorado Reading Project. *Behavior Genetics, 21,* 572–573.

Ginzburg, H. M. (1986). Naltrexone: Its clinical utility. In B. Stimmel (Ed.), *Advances in alcohol and substance abuse* (pp. 83–101). New York: Haworth.

Gist, R., & Woodall, S. J. (2000). There are no simple solutions to complex problems. In Douglas Paton, John M. Violanti (Eds.), *Posttraumatic stress intervention: Challenges, issues, and perspectives.* (pp. 81–95). Springfield, IL: Charles C. Thomas Publisher.

Gitlin, L. N., Belle, S. H., Burgio, L. D., Czaja, S. J., Mahoney, D., Gallagher-Thompson, D., Burns, R., Hauck, W. W., Zhang, S., Schulz, R., & Ory, M. G. (2003). Effect of multicomponent interventions on caregiver burden and depression: The REACH Multisite Initiative at 6-month follow-up. *Psychology and Aging, 18,* 361–374.

Glass, C. R., & Arnkoff, D. B. (1997). Questionnaire methods of cognitive self-statement assessment. *Journal of Consulting and Clinical Psychology, 65,* 911–927.

Glassman, A. H., & Shapiro, P. A. (1998). Depression and the course of cardiovascular disease. *American Journal of Psychiatry, 155,* 4–11.

Glatt, S. J., Faraone, S. V., & Tsuang, M. (2003). Meta-analysis identifies an association between the dopamine D2 receptor gene and schizophrenia. *Molecular Psychiatry, 8,* 911–915.

Gleaves, D. H. (1996). The sociocognitive model of dissociative identity disorder: A reexamination of the evidence. *Psychological Bulletin, 120,* 42–59.

Gleaves, D. H., & Eberenz, K. P. (1994). Sexual abuse histories among treatment-resistant bulimia nervosa patients. *International Journal of Eating Disorders, 15,* 227–231.

Gleick, J. (1987). *Chaos: Making a new science.* New York: Penguin Books.

Glynn, L. M., Christenfeld, N., & Gerin, W. (1999). Gender, social support, and cardiovascular response to stress. *Psychosomatic Medicine, 61,* 234–242.

Godart, N. T., Flament, M. F., Lecrubier, Y., & Jeammet, P. (2000). Anxiety disorders in anorexia nervosa and bulimia nervosa: Co-morbidity and chronology of appearance. *European Psychiatry, 15,* 38–45.

Goldapple, K., Segal, Z., Garson, C., Lau, M., Bieling, P., Kennedy, S., & Mayberg, H. (2004). Modulation of cortical-limbic pathways in major depression. *Archives of General Psychiatry, 61,* 34–41.

Goldberg, T. E., & Weinberger, D. R. (2004). Genes and the parsing of cognitive processes. *Trends in Cognitive Sciences, 8,* 325–335.

Golden, C. J. (1981a). The Luria-Nebraska Children's Battery: Theory and formulation. In G. W. Hynd & J. E. Obrzut (Eds.), *Neuropsychological assessment and the school-age child: Issues and procedures.* New York: Grune & Stratton.

Golden, C. J. (1981b). A standardized version of Luria's neuropsychological tests: A quantitative and qualitative approach to neuropsychological evaluation. In S. B. Filskov & T. J. Boil (Eds.), *Handbook of clinical neuropsychology.* New York. Wiley.

Golden, C. J., Hammeke, T., & Purisch, A. (1978). Diagnostic validity of a standardized neuropsychological battery derived from Luria's neuropsychological tests. *Journal of Consulting and Clinical Psychology, 46,* 1258–1265.

Goldfried, M. R. (2004). Integrating integratively oriented brief psychotherapy. *Journal of Psychotherapy Integration, 14,* 93–105.

Goldfried, M. R., & Davison, G. C. (1994). *Clinical behavior therapy* (expanded edition). New York: John Wiley & Sons.

Goldfried, M. R., Greenberg, L. S., & Marmar, C. (1990). Individual psychotherapy: Process and outcome. *Annual Review of Psychology, 41,* 659–688.

Golding, J. M., Smith, G. R., & Kashner, T. M. (1991). Does somatization disorder occur in men? Clinical characteristics of women and men with unexplained somatic symptoms. *Archives of General Psychiatry, 48,* 231–235.

Goldman-Rakic, P. S., & Selemon, L. D. (1997). Functional and anatomical aspects of prefrontal pathology in schizophrenia. *Schizophrenia Bulletin, 23,* 437–458.

Goldstein, A. J., & Chambless, D. L. (1978). A reanalysis of agoraphobic behavior. *Behavior Therapy, 9,* 47–59.

Golier, J., & Yehuda, R. (1998). Neuroendocrine activity and memory-related impairments in posttraumatic stress disorder. *Development and Psychopathology, 10,* 857–869.

Gomez, F. C., Piedmont, R. L., & Fleming, M. Z. (1992). Factor analysis of the Spanish version of the WAIS: The Escala de Inteligencia Wechsler para Adultos (EIWA). *Psychological Assessment, 4,* 317–321.

Goodenow, C., Reisine, S. T., & Grady, K. E. (1990). Quality of social support and associated social and psychological functions in women with rheumatoid arthritis. *Health Psychology, 9,* 266–284.

Goodkin, K., Baldewicz, T. T., Blaney, N. T., et al. (2001). Physiological effects of bereavement and bereavement support group interventions. In M. Stroebe, R. O. Hansson, et al. (Eds.), *Handbook of bereavement research: Consequences, coping, and care* (pp. 671–703). Washington, DC, US: American Psychological Association.

Goodsitt, A. (1997). Eating disorders: A self-psychological perspective. In D. M. Garner & P. E. Garfinkel (Eds.), *Handbook of treatment for eating disorders* (pp. 205–228). New York: Guilford.

Goodwin, D. K. (February 17, 2003). The man in our memory. *New York Times Op-Ed section.*

Goodwin, F., & Jamison, K. (1990). *Manic-depressive illness.* New York: Oxford University Press.

Goodwin, F. K., Fireman, B., Simon, G. E., Hunkeler, E. M., Lee, J., & Revicki, D. (2003). Suicide risk in bipolar disorder during treatment with lithium and divalproex. *Journal of the American Medical Association, 290,* 1467–1473.

Gopnik, A., Capps, L., & Meltzoff, A. N. (2000). Early theories of mind: What the theory theory can tell us about autism. In S. Baren-Cohen, H. Tager-Flusberg, & D. Cohen (Eds.), *Understanding Other Minds* (2nd ed., pp. 50–72). Oxford, England: Oxford University Press.

Gordon, K. H., Perez, M., & Joiner, T. E. (2002). The impact of racial stereotypes on eating disorder recognition. *International Journal of Eating Disorders, 32,* 219–224.

Gorenstein, E. E., & Newman, J. P. (1980). Disinhibitory psychopathology: A new perspective and a model for research. *Psychological Review, 87,* 301–315.

Gorman, J. M., Kent, J., Martinez, J., Browne, S., Coplan, F., & Papp, L. A. (2001). Physiological changes during carbon dioxide inhalation in patients with panic disorder major depression, and premenstrual dysphoric disorder. *Archives of General Psychiatry, 58,* 125–131.

Gortner, E. T., Gollan, J. K., Dobson, K. S., & Jacobson, N. S. (1998). Cognitive-behavioral treatment for depression: Relapse prevention. *Journal of Consulting and Clinical Psychology, 66,* 377–384.

Gostin, L. O., & Hodge, J. G. (1998). Piercing the veil of secrecy in HIV/AIDs and other sexually transmitted diseases: Theories of privacy and disclosure in partner notification. *Duke Journal of Gender Law and Policy, 5,* 9–88.

Gotlib, I. H., & Krasnoperova, E. (1998). Biased information processing as a vulnerability factor for depression. *Behavior Therapy, 29,* 603–617.

Gotlib, I. H., Lewinsohn, P. R., & Seeley, J. R. (1995). Symptoms versus a diagnosis of depression: Differences in psychosocial functioning. *Journal of Consulting and Clinical Psychology, 63,* 90–100.

Gotlib, I. H., & Robinson, L. A. (1982). Responses to depressed individuals: Discrepancies between self-report and observer-rated behavior. *Journal of Abnormal Psychology, 91,* 231–240.

Gottesman, I., & Shields, J. (1972). *Schizophrenia and genetics: A twin study vantage point.* New York: Academic Press.

Gottesman, I. I., & Goldsmith, H. H. (1994). Developmental psychopathology of antisocial behavior: Inserting genes into its ontogenesis and epigenesis. In C. A. Nelson (Ed.), *Threats to optimal development.* Hillside, NJ: Lawrence Erlbaum.

Gottesman, I. I., McGuffin, P., & Farmer, A. E. (1987). Clinical genetics as clues to the "real" genetics of schizophrenia. *Schizophrenia Bulletin, 13,* 23–47.

Gottlieb, G. L. (1996). Financial issues. In J. Sadvoy, L. W. Lazarus, and L. F. Jarvik (Eds.), *Comprehensive review of geriatric psychiatry* (Vol II, 2nd ed., pp. 1065–1085). Washington, DC: American Psychiatric Press.

Gottman, J. M., & Krokoff, L. J. (1989). Marital interaction and satisfaction: A longitudinal view. *Journal of Consulting and Clinical Psychology, 57,* 47–52.

Gould, E., Otto, M. W., & Pollack, M. H. (1995). A meta-analysis of treatment outcome for panic disorder. *Clinical Psychology Review, 15,* 819–844.

Gould, R. A., Safren, S. A., Washington, D. O., & Otto, M. W. (2004). A meta-analytic review of cognitive-behavioral treatments. In R. G. Heimberg, C. L. Turk, & D. S. Mennin (Eds.), *Generalized anxiety disorder* (pp. 248–264). New York: Guilford.

Goyer, P., Andreason, P. J., Semple, W. E., Clayton, A. H., et al. (1994). Positron-emission tomography and personality disorders. *Neuropsychopharmacology, 10,* 21–28.

Goyette, C. H., & Conners, C. K. (1977). *Food additives and hyperkinesis.* Paper presented at the 85th Annual Convention of the American Psychological Association.

Graham, J. R. (1988). *Establishing validity of the revised form of the MMPI.* Symposium presentation at the 96th Annual Convention of the American Psychological Association, Atlanta.

Graham, J. R. (1990). *MMPI-2: Assessing personality and psychopathology.* New York: Oxford University Press.

Grandin, T. (1986). *Emergence: Labeled autistic.* Novato, CA: Arena Press.

Grandin, T. (1995). *Thinking in pictures.* New York: Doubleday.

Grant, B. F., & Dawson, D. A. (1997). Age of onset at alcohol use and its association with DSM-IV alcohol abuse and dependence: Results from the national longitudinal epidemiologic survey. *Journal of Substance Abuse, 9,* 103–110.

Gratzer, T., & Bradford, J. M. W. (1995). Offender and offense characteristics of sexual sadists: A comparative study. *Journal of Forensic Sciences, 40,* 450–455.

Green, M. F. (1996). What are the functional consequences of neurocognitive deficits in schizophrenia? *American Journal of Psychiatry, 153,* 321–330.

Green, M. F., Kern, R. S., Braff, D. L., & Mintz, J. (2000). Neurocognitive deficits and functional outcome in schizophrenia: Are we measuring the "right stuff"? *Schizophrenia Bulletin, 26,* 119–136.

Green, M. F., Marshall, B. D., Wirshing, W. C., Ames, D., Marder, S. R., McGurk, S., Kern, R. S., & Mintz, J. (1997). Does risperidone improve verbal working memory in treatment-resistant schizophrenia? *American Journal of Psychiatry, 154,* 799–804.

Green, M. F., Nuechterlein, K. H., Gold, J. M., et al. (2004). Approaching a consensus cognitive battery for clinical trials in schizophrenia: The NIMH-MATRICS conference to select cognitive domains and test criteria. *Biological Psychiatry, 56,* 301–307.

Green, R. (1976). One hundred ten feminine and masculine boys: Behavioral contrasts and demographic similarities. *Archives of Sexual Behavior, 5,* 425–446.

Green, R. (1987). Gender identity in childhood and later sexual orientation: Follow-up of 78 males. In A. Thomas & S. Chess (Eds.), *Annual progress in child psychiatry and child development, 1986* (pp. 214–220). Philadelphia, PA, US: Brunner/Mazel, Inc.

Green, R., & Blanchard, R. (1995). Gender identity disorders. In H. I. Kaplan & B. J. Sadock (Eds.), *Comprehensive textbook of psychiatry* (pp. 1347–1360). Baltimore, MD: Williams & Wilkins.

Green, R., & Fleming, D. T. (1990). Transsexual surgery follow-up: Status in the 1990s. In J. Bancroft, C. Davis, & D. Weinstein (Eds.), *Annual review of sex research* (pp. 163–174).

Greenberg, L. S. (2002). *Emotion-focused therapy: Coaching clients to work through their feelings* (pp. 171–191). Washington, DC, US: American Psychological Association.

Greenberg, L. S., Watson, J. C., Elliot, R., & Bohart, A. C. (2001). Empathy. *Psychotherapy: Theory, Research, Practice, Training, 38,* 380–384.

Greenblatt, J. C., Gfroerer, J. C., & Melnick, D. (1995). Increasing morbidity and mortality associated with abuse of methamphetamines—United States, 1991–1994. *Morbidity and Mortality Weekly Report, 44,* 882–886.

Greenfield, S. F., & O'Leary, G. (1999). Sex differences in marijuana use in the United States. *Harvard Review of Psychiatry, 6,* 297–303.

Gretarsdortir, E., Woodruff Borden, J., Meeks, S., Depp, C. A., Gretarsdottir, E., Woodruff Borden, J., et al. (2004). Social anxiety in older adults: Phenomenology, prevalence, and measurement. *Behaviour Research and Therapy*, 42, 459–475.

Grice, D. E., Halmi, K. A., Fichter, M. M., Strober, M., Woodside, D. B., Treasure, J. T., Kaplan, A. S., Magistretti, P. J., Goldman, D., Bulik, C. M., Kaye, W. H., & Berrettini, W. H. (2002). Evidence for a susceptibility gene for anorexia nervosa on chromosome 1. *American Journal of Human Genetics*, 70, 787–792.

Grifin, M. G., Resick, P. A., & Mechanic, M. B. (1997). Objective assessment of peritraumatic dissociation: Psychophysiological indicators. *American Journal of Psychiatry*, 154, 1081–1088.

Grillon, C. (2002). Startle reactivity and anxiety disorders: Aversive conditioning, context, and neurobiology. *Biological Psychiatry*, 52, 958–975.

Grilo, C. M., Shiffman, S., & Carter-Campbell, J. T. (1994). Binge eating antecedents in normal weight nonpurging females: Is there consistency? *International Journal of Eating Disorders*, 16, 239–249.

Grinker, R. R., & Spiegel, J. P. (1944). *Management of neuropsychiatric casualties in the zone of combat: Manual of military neuropsychiatry.* Philadelphia: W.B. Saunders.

Grinspoon, L., & Bakalar, J. B. (1995). Marijuana as medicine: A plea for reconsideration. *Journal of the American Medical Association*, 273, 1875–1876.

Grisso, T., & Appelbaum, P. S. (1991). Mentally ill and nonmentally ill patients' abilities to understand informed consent disclosures for medication: Preliminary data. *Law and Human Behavior*, 15, 377–388.

Groesz, L. M., Levine, M. P., & Murnen, S. K. (2002). The effect of experimental presentation of thin media images on body dissatisfaction: A meta-analytic review. *International Journal of Eating Disorders*, 31, 1–16.

Gross, C., Zhuang, X., Stark, K., Ramboz, S., Oosting, R., Kirby, L., Santarelli, L., Beck, S. & Hen, R. (2002). Serotonin1A receptor acts during development to establish normal anxiety-like behaviour in the adult. *Nature*, 416, 396–400.

Grossman, D. (1995). *On killing: The psychological cost of learning to kill in war and society.* Boston: Little, Brown.

Groth, N. A., Hobson, W. F., & Guy, T. S. (1982). The child molester: Clinical observations. In J. Conte & D. A. Shore (Eds.), *Social work and child sexual abuse.* New York: Haworth.

Gruber, K., Chutuape, M. A., & Stitzer, M. L. (2000). Reinforcement-based intensive outpatient treatment for inner city opiate abusers: A short-term evaluation. *Drug & Alcohol Dependence*, 57, 211–223.

Grundy, S. M., Brewer, B. Jr., Cleeman, J. I., et al. (2004). Definition of metabolic syndrome: report of the National Heart, Lung and Blood Institute/American Heart Association Conference on scientific issues related to definition. *Circulation*, 109, 433–438.

Gump, B. S., Matthews, K. A., & Räikkönen, K. (1999). Modeling relationships among socioeconomic status, hostility, cardiovascular reactivity, and left ventricular mass in African American and White children. *Health Psychology*, 18, 140–150.

Gunn, J. (1993). Castration is not the answer. *British Medical Journal*, 307, 790–791.

Gur, R. E., & Pearlson, G. D. (1993). Neuroimaging in schizophrenia research. *Schizophrenia Bulletin*, 19, 337–353.

Gur, R. E., Turetsky, B. I., Cowell, P. E., et al. (2000). Temporolimbic volume reductions in schizophrenia. *Archives of General Psychiatry*, 57, 769–776.

Gurland, B. (1991). Epidemiology of psychiatric disorders. In J. Sadavoy, L. W. Lazarus & L. F. Jarvik (Eds.), *Comprehensive review of geriatric psychiatry* (pp. 25–40). Washington, DC: American Psychiatric Press.

Gustad, J., & Phillips, K. A. (2003). Axis I comorbidity in body dysmorphic disorder. *Comprehensive Psychiatry*, 44, 270–276.

Gutman, D. A., & Nemeroff, C. B. (2003). Persistent central nervous system effects of an adverse early environment: Clinical and preclinical studies. *Physiology and Behavior*, 79, 471–478.

Guyll, M., & Contrada, R. J. (1998). Trait hostility and ambulatory cardiovascular activity: Responses to social interaction. *Health Psychology*, 17, 30–39.

Guyll, M., Matthews, K. A., & Bromberger, J. T. (2001). Discrimination and unfair treatment: Relationship to cardiovascular reactivity among African American and European American women. *Health Psychology*, 20, 315–325.

Gwynn, R. C. (2004). Risk factors for asthma in US adults: Results from the 2000 Behavioral Risk Factor Surveillance System. *Journal of Asthma*, 41, 91–98.

Haaga, D. A. (1987). Treatment of the type A behavior pattern. *Clinical Psychology Review*, 7, 557–574.

Haaga, D. A. F. (1989). Articulated thoughts and endorsement procedures for cognitive assessment in the prediction of smoking relapse. *Psychological Assessment: A Journal of Consulting and Clinical Psychology*, 1, 112–117.

Haaga, D. A. F. (1990). Issues in relating self-efficacy to smoking relapse: Importance of an "Achilles' Heel" situation and of prior quitting experience. *Journal of Substance Abuse*, 2, 191–200.

Haaga, D. A. F. (2000). Introduction to the special section on stepped care models in psychotherapy. *Journal of Consulting and Clinical Psychology*, 68, 547–548.

Haaga, D. A. F., DeRubeis, R. J., Stewart, B. L., & Beck, A. T. (1991). Relationship of intelligence with cognitive therapy outcome. *Behaviour Research and Therapy*, 29, 277–281.

Haaga, D. A. F., Dyck, M. J., & Ernst, D. (1991). Empirical status of cognitive theory of depression. *Psychological Bulletin*, 110, 215–236.

Haaga, D. A. F., Rabois, D., & Brody, C. (1999). Cognitive behavior therapy. In M. Hersen & A. S. Bellack (Eds.), *Handbook of comparative treatments for adult disorders* (2nd ed., pp. 8–61). New York: John Wiley & Sons.

Haaga, D. A. F., & Stiles, W. B. (2000). Randomized clinical trials in psychotherapy research: Methodology, design, and evaluation. In R. E. Ingram, & C. Snyder (Eds.), *Handbook of psychological change: Psychotherapy processes & practices for the 21st century* (pp. 14–39). New York, NY, John Wiley & Sons, Inc.

Haas, R. H., Townsend, J., Courchesne, E., Lincoln, A. J., Schreibman, L., & Yeung-Courchesne, R. (1996). Neurologic abnormalities in infantile autism. *Journal of Child Neurology*, 11, 84–92.

Hacking, I. (1998). *Mad travelers: Reflections on the reality of transient mental illness.* Charlottesville, VA: University Press of Virginia.

Haddock, G., Tarrier, N., Spaulding, W., Yusupoff, L. K., & McCarthy, E. (1998). Individual cognitive-behavior therapy in the treatment of hallucinations and delusions: A review. *Clinical Psychology Review*, 18, 821–838.

Halkitis, P. N., Parsons, J. T., & Stirratt, M. J. (2001). A double epidemic: Crystal methamphetamine drug use in relation to HIV transmission among gay men. *Journal of Homosexuality*, 41, 17–35.

Hall, G. C. (2001). Psychotherapy research with ethnic minorities: Empirical, ethical, and conceptual issues. *Journal of Consulting and Clinical Psychology*, 69(3), 502–510.

Hall, G. C., Hirschman, R., & Oliver, L. L. (1995). Sexual arousal and arousability to pedophilic stimuli in a community sample of normal men. *Behavior Therapy*, 26, 681–694.

Hall, S. M., Reuss, V. I., Munoz, R. F., Sees, K. L., Humfleet, G., et al. (1998). Nortriptyline and cognitive-behavioral therapy in the treatment of cigarette smoking. *Archives of General Psychiatry*, 55, 683–690.

Halmi, K. A., Sunday, S. R., Strober, M., Kaplan, A., Woodside, D. B., Fichter, N., Treasure, J., Berrettini, W. H., & Kaye, W. (2000). Perfectionism in anorexia nervosa: Variation by clinical subtype, obsessionality, and pathological eating behavior. *American Journal of Psychiatry*, 157, 1799–1805.

Hammen, C. (1997). Children of depressed parents: The stress context. In S. A. Wolchik, I. N. Sandler (Eds.), *Handbook of children's coping: Linking theory and intervention. Issues in clinical child psychology* (pp. 131–157). New York, NY. Plenum Press.

Hankin, B. J., Abramson, L. Y., Moffitt, T. E., Silva, P. A., McGee, R., et al. (1998). Development of depression from preadolescence to young adulthood: Emerging gender differences in a 10-year longitudinal study. *Journal of Abnormal Psychology*, 107, 128–140.

Hansen, W. B. (1992). School-based substance abuse prevention: A review of the state of the art in curriculum, 1980–1990. *Health Education Research: Theory and Practice*, 7, 403–430.

Hansen, W. B. (1993). School-based alcohol prevention programs. *Alcohol Health and Research World*, 18, 62–66.

Hansen, W. B., & Graham, J. W. (1991). Preventing alcohol, marijuana, and cigarette use among adolescents: Peer pressure resistance training versus establishing conservative norms. *Preventive Medicine*, 20, 414–430.

Hanson, R. K., & Bussiere, M. T. (1998). Predicting relapse: A meta-analysis of sexual offender recidivism studies. *Journal of Consulting and Clinical Psychology*, 66, 348–362.

Hanson, R. K., & Harris, A. J. R. (1997). Voyeurism: Assessment and treatment. In D. R. Laws & W. O'Donohue (Eds.), *Sexual deviance* (pp. 311–331). New York: Guilford.

Hanson, R. K., Hunsely, J., & Parker, K. C. H. (1988). The relationship between WAIS subtest reliability, "g" loadings, and meta-analytically derived validity estimates. *Journal of Clinical Psychology*, 44, 557–563.

Hardan, A. Y., Minshew, N. J., Harenski, K., & Keshavan, M. S. (2001). Posterior fossa magnetic resonance imaging in autism. *Journal of the American Academy of Child and Adolescent Psychiatry*, 40, 666–672.

Hardy, B. W., & Waller, D. A. (1988). Bulimia as substance abuse. In W. G. Johnson (Ed.), *Advances in eating disorders.* New York: JAI.

Hardy, J. (1993). Genetic mistakes point the way to Alzheimer's disease. *Journal of NIH Research*, 5, 46–49.

Hare, E. (1969). *Triennial statistical report of the Royal Maudsley and Bethlem Hospitals.* London: Bethlem and Maudsley Hospitals.

Hare, R. D., Harpur, T. J., Hakstian, R. A., Forth, A. E., Hart, S. D., et al. (1990). The revised Psychopathy Checklist: Reliability and factor structure. *Psychological Assessment*, 2, 338–341.

Hare, R. D., Hart, S. D., & Harpur, T. J. (1991). Psychopathy and the DSM-IV criteria for antisocial personality disorder. *Journal of Abnormal Psychology*, 100, 391–398.

Hariri, A. R., Drabant, E. M., Munoz, K. E., Kolachana, B. S., Mattay, V. S., Egan, M. F., Weinberger, D. R. (2005). A susceptibility gene for affective disorders and the response of the Human amygdala. *Archives of General Psychiatry*, 62, 146–152.

Harkin, A., Connor, T. J., Mulrooney, J., Kelly, J. P., & Leonard, B. E. (2001). Prior exposure to methylenedioxyamphetamine (MDA) induces serotonergic loss and changes in spontaneous exploratory and amphetamine-induced behaviors in rats. *Life Sciences, 68,* 1367–1382.

Harrison, J., Chin, J., & Ficarrotto, T. (1989). Warning: Masculinity may be dangerous to your health. In M. S. Kimmel & M. A. Messner (Eds.), *Men's lives* (pp. 296–309). New York: Macmillan.

Harrison, P. J., & Weinberger, D. R. (2004). Schizophrenia genes, gene expression, and neuropathology: On the matter of their convergence. *Molecular Psychiatry,* 1–29.

Harrow, M., Goldberg, J. F., Grossman, L. S., & Meltzer, H. Y. (1990). Outcome in manic disorders: A naturalistic follow-up study. *Archives of General Psychiatry, 47,* 665–671.

Harry Benjamin International Gender Dysphoria Association. (1998). *The standards of care of gender identity disorders* (5th version). Dusseldorf: Symposion.

Hart, E. L., Lahey, B. B., Loeber, R., Applegate, B., & Frick, P. J. (1995). Developmental changes in attention-deficit hyperactivity disorder in boys: A four-year longitudinal study. *Journal of Abnormal Child Psychology, 23,* 729–750.

Hart, S. D., & Hare, R. D. (1989). Discriminant validity of the Psychopathy Checklist in a forensic psychiatric population. *Psychological Assessment, 1,* 211–218.

Hartmann, H. (1958). *Ego psychology and the problem of adaptation.* New York: International Universities Press.

Hartung, C. M., & Widiger, T. A. (1998). Gender differences in the diagnosis of mental disorders: Conclusions and controversies of the DSM-IV. *Psychological-Bulletin, 123,* 260–278.

Hartz, D. T., Fredrick-Osborne, S. L., & Galloway, G. P. (2001). Craving predicts use during treatment for methamphetamine dependence: A prospective repeated-measures, within-subjects analysis. *Drug and Alcohol Dependence, 63,* 269–276.

Harvard Mental Health Letter. (1995, July). Schizophrenia update–Part II, *12,* 1–5.

Harvey, A. G., & Bryant, R. A. (2002). Acute stress disorder: A synthesis and critique. *Psychological Bulletin, 128,* 886–902.

Harvey, A. G., Watkins, E., Mansell, W., & Shafran, R. (2004). *Cognitive behavioural processes across psychological disorders: A transdiagnostic approach to research and treatment.* Oxford, England: Oxford University Press.

Harvey, P. D., Green, M. F., Keefe, R. S. I., & Velligan, D. (2004). Changes in cognitive functioning with risperidone and olanzapine treatment: A large-scale, double-blind, randomized study. *Journal of Clinical Psychiatry, 65,* 361–372.

Harvey, P. D., Green, M. F., McGurk, S., & Meltzer, H. Y. (2003). Changes in cognitive functioning with risperidone and olanzapine treatment: A large-scale, double-blind, randomized study. *Psychopharmacology, 169,* 404–411.

Harwood, H. J., Mark, T. L., McKusick, D. R., Coffey, R. M., King, E. C., & Genuardi, J. S. (2003). National spending on mental health and substance abuse treatment by age of clients, 1997. *Journal of Behavioral Health Services and Research, 30,* 433–443.

Hasin, D. F., van Rossem, R., McCloud, S., & Endicott, J. (1997). Differentiating DSM-IV alcohol dependence and abuse by course: Community heavy drinkers. *Journal of Substance Abuse, 9,* 127–135.

Haslam, C., Brown, S., Atkinson, S., & Haslam, R. (2004). Patients' experiences of medication for anxiety and depression: Effects on working life. *Family Practice, 21,* 204–212.

Haslam, N., & Kim, H. C. (2002). Categories and continua: A review of taxometric research. *Genetic, Social, and General Psychology Monographs, 128,* 271–320.

Hathaway, S. R., & McKinley, J. C. (1943). *MMPI manual.* New York: Psychological Corporation.

Hatzidimitriou, G., McCann, U. D., & Ricaurte, G. A. (1999). Altered serotonin innervation patterns in the forebrain of monkeys treated with (α)-3,4-methylenedioxymethamphetamine seven years previously: Factors influencing abnormal recovery. *Journal of Neuroscience 19,* 5096–5107.

Hawkins, J. D., Graham, J. W., Maguin, E., Abbott, R., et al. (1997). Exploring the effects of age of alcohol use initiation and psychosocial risk factors on subsequent alcohol misuse. *Journal of Studies on Alcohol, 58,* 280–290.

Hawton, K., Catalan, J., Martin, P., & Fagg, J. (1986). Long-term outcome of sex therapy. *Behaviour Research and Therapy, 24,* 665–675.

Hay, P., & Fairburn, C. G. (1998). The validity of the DSM-IV scheme for classifying eating disorders. *International Journal of Eating Disorders, 23,* 7–15.

Hayes, S. C., Masuda, A., Bissett, R., Luoma, J., & Guerrero, L. F. (2004). DBT, FAR and ACT: How empirically oriented are the new behavior therapy technologies? *Behavior Therapy, 35,* 35–54.

Haynes, S. N., & Horn, W. F. (1982). Reactivity in behavioral observation: A review. *Behavioral Assessment, 4,* 369–385.

Hazelrigg, M. D., Cooper, H. M., & Borduin, C. M. (1987). Evaluating the effectiveness of family therapies: An integrative review and analysis. *Psychological Bulletin, 101,* 428–442.

Heather, N., Rollnick, S., Bell, A., & Richmond, R. (1996). Effects of brief counselling among heavy drinkers identified on general hospital wards. *Drug and Alcohol Review, 15,* 29–38.

Heatherton, T. F., & Baumeister, R. F. (1991). Binge eating as escape from self-awareness. *Psychological Bulletin, 110,* 86–108.

Heatherton, T. F., Herman, C. P., & Polivy, J. (1991). Effects of physical threat and ego threat on eating behavior. *Journal of Personality and Social Psychology, 60,* 138–143.

Hechtman, L., Weiss, G., & Perlman, T. (1984). Hyperactives as young adults: Past and current substance abuse and antisocial behavior. *American Journal of Orthopsychiatry, 54,* 415–425.

Hecker, M. H. L., Chesney, M., Black, G. W., & Frautsch, N. (1988). Coronary-prone behavior in the Western Collaborative Group Study. *Psychosomatic Medicine, 50,* 153–164.

Heim, E., Valach, L., & Schaffner, L. (1997). Coping and psychosocial adaptation: Longitudinal effects over time and stages in breast cancer. *Psychosomatic Medicine, 59,* 408–418.

Heimberg, R. G., Dodge, C. S., Hope, D. A., Kennedy, C. R., Zollo, L. J., & Becker, R. E. (1990). Cognitive behavioral treatment for social phobia: Comparison with a credible placebo control. *Cognitive Therapy and Research, 14,* 1–23.

Heinrichs, R. W., & Zakzanis, K. K. (1998). Neurocognitive deficits in schizophrenia: A quantitative review of the evidence. *Neuropsychology, 12,* 426–445.

Heinssen, R. K., Liberman, R. P., & Kopelowicz, A. (2000). Psychosocial skills training for schizophrenia: Lessons from the laboratory. *Schizophrenia Bulletin, 26,* 21–46.

Heller, K., Wyman, M. F., & Allen, S. M. (2000). Future directions for prevention science: From research to adoption. In C. R. Snyder & R. E. Ingram (Eds.), *Handbook of psychological change: Psychotherapy processes & practices for the 21st century* (pp. 660–680). New York: John Wiley & Sons.

Heller, T. L., Baker, B. L., Henker, B., & Hinshaw, S. P. (1996). Externalizing behavior and cognitive functioning from preschool to first grade: Stability and predictors. *Journal of Clinical Child Psychology, 25,* 376–387.

Helmuth, L. (2003). In sickness or in health?. *Science, 302*(5646), 808–810.

Helweg-Larsen, M., & Collins, B. E. (1997). A social psychological perspective on the role of knowledge about AIDS in AIDS prevention. *Current Directions in Psychological Science, 6,* 23–26.

Helzer, J. E., Burnam, A., & McEvoy, L. T. (1991). Alcohol abuse and dependence. In L. Robins & D. Reiger (Eds.), *Psychiatric disorders in America: The Epidemiologic Catchment Area Study* (pp. 9–38). New York: Free Press.

Hendry, C. N. (2000). Childhood disintegrative disorder: Should it be considered a distinct diagnosis? *Clinical Psychology Review, 20,* 77–90.

Henggeler, S. W., Schoenwald, S. D., Borduin, C. M., Rowland, M. D., & Cunningham, P. B. (1998). *Multisystemic treatment of antisocial behavior in children and adolescents.* New York: Guilford.

Henningfield, J. E., Michaelides, T., & Sussman, S. (2000). Developing treatment for tobacco addicted youth—issues and challenges. *Journal of Child & Adolescent Substance Abuse, 9,* 5–26.

Henriksson, M. M., Aro, H. M., Marttunen, M. J., Heikkinen, M. E., Isometsa, E. T., Kuoppasalmi, K. I., & Lonnqvist, J. K. (1993). Mental disorders and comorbidity in suicide. *American Journal of Psychiatry, 150,* 935–940.

Henriques, J. B., & Davidson, R. J. (2000). Decreased responsiveness to reward in depression. *Cognition and Emotion, 14,* 711–724.

Henry, W. P., Schacht, T. E., Strupp, H. H., Butler, S. F., & Binder, J. L. (1993). Effects of training in time-limited dynamic psychotherapy: Mediators of therapists' responses to training. *Journal of Consulting and Clinical Psychology, 61,* 441–447.

Henry, W. P., Strupp, H. H., Schacht, T. E., & Gaston, L. (1994). Psychodynamic approaches. In S. L. Garfield & A. E. Bergin (Eds.), *Handbook of psychotherapy and behavior change* (pp. 467–508). Oxford, England: John Wiley & Sons.

Herbert, J. D. (1995). An overview of the current status of social phobia. *Applied and Preventive Psychology, 4,* 39–51.

Herman, C. P., Polivy, J., Lank, C., & Heatherton, T. F. (1987). Anxiety, hunger, and eating. *Journal of Abnormal Psychology, 96,* 264–269.

Herman, J. L., Perry, J. C., & van der Kolk, B. A. (1989). Childhood trauma in borderline personality disorder. *American Journal of Psychiatry, 146,* 490–495.

Herpetz, S. C., Dietrich, T. M., Wenning, B., et al. (2001a). Evidence of abnormal amygdala functioning in borderline personality disorder: A functional MRI study. *Biological Psychiatry, 50,* 292–298.

Herpetz, S. C., Werth, U., Lucas, G., et al. (2001b). Emotion in criminal offenders with psychopathy and borderline personality disorders. *Archives of General Psychiatry, 58,* 737–745.

Hersen, M., & Barlow, D. H. (1976). *Single case experimental designs: Strategies for studying behavior change.* New York: Pergamon.

Hersen, M., Bellack, A. S., Himmelhoch, J. M., & Thase, M. E. (1984). Effects of social skill training, amitriptyline, and psychotherapy in unipolar depressed women. *Behavior Therapy, 15,* 21–40.

Herz, M. I., Lamberti, J. S., & Mintz, J., et al. (2000). A program for relapse prevention in schizophrenia: A controlled study. *Archives of General Psychiatry, 57,* 277–284.

Herzog, D. B., Greenwood, D. N., Dorer, D. J., Flores, A. T., Ekeblad, E. R., Richards, A., Blais, M. A., & Keller, M. B. (2000). Mortality in eating disorders: A descriptive study. *International Journal of Eating Disorders, 28,* 20–26.

Heston, L. L. (1966). Psychiatric disorders in foster home reared children of schizophrenic mothers. *British Journal of Psychiatry, 112,* 819–825.

Heston, L. L. (1987). The paranoid syndrome after mid-life. In N. E. Miller & G. D. Cohen (Eds.), *Schizophrenia and aging* (pp. 249–257). New York: Guilford.

Hettema, J. M., Neale, M. C., & Kendler, K. S. (2001). A review and meta-analysis of the genetic epidemiology of the anxiety disorders. *American Journal of Psychiatry, 158,* 1568–1578.

Heuser, I., Yassouridis, A., & Holsboer, F. (1994). The combined dexamethasone CRH test: A refined laboratory test for psychiatric disorders. *Journal of Psychiatric Research, 28,* 341–346.

Hietala, J., Syvalahti, E., Vuorio, K., Nagren, K., Lehikoinen, P., et al. (1994). Striatal D2 dopamine receptor characteristics in drug-naive schizophrenic patients studied with positive emission tomography. *Archives of General Psychiatry, 51,* 116–123.

Higgins, S. T., Budney, A. J., & Sigmon, S. C. (2001). Cocaine dependence. In D. H. Barlow (Ed.), *Clinical handbook of psychological disorders: A step-by-step treatment manual* (pp. 434–469). New York, NY: Guilford Press.

Hill, A., Briken, P., Kraus, C., Strohm, K., & Berner, W. (2003). Differential pharmacological treatment of paraphilias and sex offenders. *International Journal of Offender Therapy and Comparative Criminology, 47*(4), 407–421.

Hill, H. A., Schoenbach, V. J., Kleinbaum, D. G., et al. (1994). A longitudinal analysis of predictors of quitting smoking among participants in a self-help intervention trial. *Addictive Behaviors, 19,* 159–173.

Hinrichsen, G. A. (1999). Treating older adults with interpersonal psychotherapy for depression. *Psychotherapy in Practice, 55*(8), 949–960.

Hinshaw, S. P. (1987). On the distinction between attentional deficits/hyperactivity and conduct problems/aggression in child psychopathology. *Psychological Bulletin, 101,* 443–463.

Hinshaw, S. P. (2002). Preadolescent girls with attention-deficit/hyperactivity disorder: I. Background characteristics, comorbidity, cognitive and social functioning, and parenting practices. *Journal of Consulting and Clinical Psychology, 70,* 1086–1098.

Hinshaw, S. P. Carte, E. T., Sami, N., Treuting, J. J., & Zupan, B. A. (2002). Preadolescent girls with attention-deficit/hyperactivity disorder: II. Neuropsychological performance in relation to subtypes and individual classification. *Journal of Consulting and Clinical Psychology, 70,* 1099–1111.

Hinshaw, S. P. (2006). *The mark of shame: The stigma of mental illness and an agenda for change.* New York: Oxford University Press.

Hinshaw, S. P., Henker, B., & Whalen, C. K. (1984). Self-control in hyperactive boys in anger-inducing situations: Effects of cognitive-behavioral training and of methylphenidate. *Journal of Abnormal Child Psychology, 12,* 55–77.

Hinshaw, S. P., Lahey, B. B., & Hart, E. L. (1993). Issues of taxonomy and comorbidity in the development of conduct disorder. *Development & Psychopathology, 5,* 31–49.

Hinshaw, S. P., & Lee, S. S. (2003). Oppositional defiant and conduct disorders. In E. J. Mash & R. A. Barkley (Eds.), *Child Psychopathology* (2nd ed., pp. 144–198). New York: Guilford.

Hinshaw, S. P., & Melnick, S. M. (1995). Peer relationships in boys with attention-deficit hyperactivity disorder with and without comorbid aggression. *Development and Psychopathology, 7,* 627–647.

Hinshaw, S. P., Owens, E. B., Wells, K. C., et al. (2000). Family processes and treatment outcome in the MTA: Negative/Ineffective parenting practices in relation to multimodal treatment. *Journal of Abnormal Child Psychology, 28,* 555–568.

Hinshaw, S. P., Zupan, B. A., Simmel, C., Nigg, J. T., & Melnick, S. (1997). Peer status in boys with and without Attention-Deficit Hyperactivity Disorder: Predictions from overt and covert antisocial behavior, social isolation, and authoritative parenting beliefs. *Child Development, 68,* 880–896.

Hinton, D., Ba, P., Peou, S., & Um, K. (2000). Panic disorder among Cambodian refugees attending a psychiatric clinic. *General Hospital Psychiatry, 22,* 437– 444.

Hinton, E., Um, K., & Ba, P. (2001). *Kyol Goeu* ('Wind Overload') Part II: Prevalence, characteristics, and mechanisms of *Kyol Goeu* and near *Kyol Goeu* episodes of Khmer patients attending a psychiatric clinic. *Transcultural Psychiatry, 38,* 433–460.

Hirsch, C. R., & Clark, D. M. (2004). Mental imagery and social phobia. In J. Yiend (Ed.), *Cognition, emotion and psychopathology: Theoretical, empirical and clinical directions* (pp. 232–250). Cambridge, England: Cambridge University Press.

Hjalmarson, A., Nilsson, F., Sjostrom, J., Wiklund, O. (1997). The nicotine inhaler in smoking cessation. *Archives of Internal Medicine, 157,* 1721–1728.

Ho, B.-C., Nopoulos, P., Flaum, M., Arndt, S., & Andreasen, N. C. (1998). Two-year outcome in first-episode schizophrenia: Predictive value of symptoms for quality of life. *American Journal of Psychiatry, 155,* 1196–1201.

Hobfoll, S. E., Jackson, A. P., Lavin, I. J., Britton, P. J., & Shepard, J. B. (1994). Reducing inner-city women's AIDS risk activities. *Health Psychology, 13,* 397– 403.

Hobfoll, S. E., Spielberger, C. D., Breznitz, S., Figley, C., Folkman, S., Lepper-Green, B., Meichenbaum, D., Milgram, N. A., Sandler, I., Sarason, I., & van der Kolk, B. (1991). War-related stress: Addressing the stress of war and other traumatic events. *American Psychologist, 46,* 848–855.

Hobson, R. P., & Lee, A. (1998). Hello and goodbye: A study of social engagement in autism. *Journal of Autism and Developmental Disorders, 28,* 117–127.

Hodges, E. L., Cochrane, C. E., & Brewerton, T. D. (1998). Family characteristics of binge-eating disorder patients. *International Journal of Eating Disorders, 23,* 145–151.

Hoebel, B. G., & Teitelbaum, P. (1966). Weight regulation in normal and hypothalamic hyperphagic rats. *Journal of Comparative and Physiological Psychology, 61,* 189–193.

Hoek, H. W., & van Hoeken, D. (2003). Review of the prevalence and incidence of eating disorders. *International Journal of Eating Disorders, 34,* 383–396.

Hoffman, G. W., Ellinwood, E. H., Jr., Rockwell, W. J., Herfkens, R. J., Nishita, J. K., & Guthrie, L. F. (1989). Cerebral atrophy in bulimia. *Biological Psychiatry, 25,* 894–902.

Hofmann, S. G., & Barlow, D. H. (2004). Social phobia (social anxiety disorder). In D. H. Barlow (Ed.). *Anxiety and its disorders: The nature and treatment of anxiety and panic.* (pp. 454–476). New York: Guilford.

Hofmann, S. G., Levitt, J. T., Hoffman, E. C., Greene, K., Litz, B. T., & Barlow, D. H. (2001). Potentially traumatizing events in panic disorder and other anxiety disorders. *Depression and Anxiety, 13,* 101–102.

Hogarty, G. E., Anderson, C. M., Reiss, D. J., Kornblith, S. J., Greenwald, D. P., et al. (1986). Family psychoeducation, social skills training, and maintenance chemotherapy in the aftercare treatment of schizophrenia: 1. One-year effects of a controlled study on relapse and expressed emotion. *Archives of General Psychiatry, 43,* 633–642.

Hogarty, G. E., Anderson, C. M., Reiss, D. J., Kornblith, S. J., Greenwald, D. P., Ulrich, R. F., Carter, M., & The Environmental-Personal Indicators in the Course of Schizophrenia (EPICS) Research Group. (1991). Family psychoeducation, social skills training, and maintenance chemotherapy in the aftercare treatment of schizophrenia. *Archives of General Psychiatry, 48,* 340–347.

Hogarty, G. E., Flesher, S., Ulrich, R., et al. (2004). Cognitive enhancement therapy for schizophrenia: Effects of a 2-year randomized trial on cognition and behavior. *Archives of General Psychiatry, 61,* 866–876.

Hogarty, G. E., Greenwald, D., Ulrich, R. F., Kornblith, S. J., DiBarry, A. L., Cooley, S., Carter, M., & Flesher, S. (1997a). Three-year trials of personal therapy among schizophrenic patients living with or independent of family, II: Effects on adjustment of patients. *Archives of General Psychiatry, 154,* 1514–1524.

Hogarty, G. E., Kornblith, S. J., Greenwald, D., DiBarry, A. L., Cooley, S., Flesher, S., Reiss, D., Carter, M., & Ulrich, R. (1995). Personal therapy: A disorder-relevant psychotherapy for schizophrenia. *Schizophrenia Bulletin, 21,* 379–393.

Hogarty, G. E., Kornblith, S. J., Greenwald, D., DiBarry, A. L., Cooley, S., Ulrich, R. F., Carter, M., & Flesher, S. (1997b). Three-year trials of personal therapy among schizophrenic patients living with or independent of family, I: Description of study and effects on relapse rates. *Archives of General Psychiatry, 154,* 1504–1513.

Hoge, S., Lidz, C., Eisenberg, M., Gardner, W., Monahan, J., Mulvey, E., Roth, L., & Bennet, N. (1997). Perceptions of coercion in the admission of voluntary and involuntary psychiatric patients. *International Journal of Law and Psychiatry, 20,* 167–181.

Holder, H. D., Longabaugh, R., Miller, W. R., & Rubonis, A. V. (1991). The cost effectiveness of treatment for alcoholism: A first approximation. *Journal of Studies on Alcohol, 52,* 517–540.

Hollingshead, A. B., & Redlich, F. C. (1958). *Social class and mental illness: A community study.* New York: Wiley.

Hollon, S., & DeRubeis, R. (2003). *Cognitive therapy for depression.* Presentation at the annual conference of the American Psychiatric Association, Philadelphia, PA.

Hollon, S. D., DeRubeis, R. J., & Evans, M. D. (1996). Cognitive therapy in the treatment and prevention of depression. In P. M. Salkovskis (Ed.), *Frontiers of cognitive therapy* (pp. 293–317). New York, NY: Guilford Press.

Hollon, S. D., Evans, M. D., & DeRubeis, R. J. (1990). Cognitive mediation of relapse prevention following treatment for depression: Implications of differential risk. In R. E. Ingram (Ed.), *Psychological aspects of depression* (pp. 117–136). New York: Plenum.

Hollon, S. D., Haman, K. L., & Brown, L. L. (2002). Cognitive-behavioral treatment of depression. In C. L. Hammen & I. H. Gotlib (Eds), *Handbook of depression* (pp. 383–403). New York: Guilford.

Hollon, S. D., Thase, M. E., & Markowitz, J. C. (2002). Treatment and prevention of depression. *Psychological Science in the Public Interest, 3,* 39–77.

Holm, V. A., & Varley, C. K. (1989). Pharmacological treatment of autistic children. In G. Dawson (Ed.), *Autism: Nature, diagnosis, and treatment* (pp. 386–404). New York: Guilford.

Holmes, T. H., & Rahe, R. H. (1967). The social readjustment rating scale. *Journal of Psychosomatic Research, 11,* 213–218.

Holzman, P. S. (1985). Eye movement dysfunctions and psychosis. *Review of Neurobiology, 27,* 179–205.

Hooley, J. M., & Teasdale, J. D. (1989). Predictors of relapse in unipolar depressives: Expressed emotion, marital distress, and perceived criticism. *Journal of Abnormal Psychology, 98,* 229–235.

Hope, D. A., Heimberg, R. G., & Bruch, M. A. (1995). Dismantling cognitive-behavioral group therapy for social phobia. *Behaviour Research and Therapy, 33,* 637–650.

Horney, K. (1942). *Self-analysis.* New York: Norton.

Horwitz, B., Rumsy, J. M., & Donahue, B. C. (1998). Functional connectivity of the angular gyrus in normal reading and dyslexia. *Proceedings of the National Academy of Science, 95,* 8939–8944.

Horowitz, M. J. (1988). *Introduction to psychodynamics: A new synthesis.* New York: Basic Books.

Horvath, A. O. (2001). The alliance. *Psychotherapy: Theory, Research, Practice Training, 38,* 365–372.

Houts, A. C. (2001). Harmful dysfunction and the search for value neutrality in the definition of mental disorder: Response to Wakefield, Part 2. *Behaviour Research and Therapy, 39,* 1099–1132.

Howe, M. L. (1998). Individual differences in factors that modulate storage and retrieval of traumatic memories. *Development and Psychopathology, 10,* 681–698.

Howes, R. J. (1998). Plethysmographic assessment of incarcerated sexual offenders: A comparison with rapists. *Sexual Abuse: A Journal of Research and Treatment, 10,* 183–194.

Howitt, D. (1995). Pornography and the paedophile: Is it criminogenic? *British Journal of Medical Psychology, 68,* 15–27.

Howlin, P., & Goode, S. (1998). Outcome in adult life for people with autism and Asperger's syndrome. In F. R. Volkmar, (Ed.), *Autism and pervasive developmental disorders* (pp. 209–241). New York: Cambridge University Press.

Howlin, P., Mawhood, L., & Rutter, M. (2000). Autism and developmental receptive language disorder—A follow-up comparison in early adult life. II. Social, behavioral, and psychiatric outcomes. *Journal of Child Psychiatry and Psychology, 41,* 561–578.

Hser, Y., Anglin, M. D., & Powers, K. (1993). A 24-year follow-up of California narcotics addicts. *Archives of General Psychiatry, 50,* 577–584.

Hsu, L. K. G. (1990). *Eating disorders.* New York: Guilford.

Huesmann, L. R., & Miller, L. S. (1994). Long-term effects of repeated exposure to media violence in childhood. In L. R. Huesmann (Ed.), *Aggressive behavior: Current perspectives* (pp. 153–186). New York: Plenum.

Huether, G., Zhou, D., & Ruther, E. (1997). Causes and consequences of the loss of serotonergic presynapses elicited by the consumption of 3,4-methylenedioxymethamphetamine (MDMA, "ecstasy") and its congeners. *Journal of Neural Transmission, 104,* 771–794.

Hughes, C., & Agran, M. (1993). Teaching persons with severe disabilities to use self-instruction in community settings: An analysis of applications. *The Journal of the Association for Persons with Severe Handicaps, 18,* 261–274.

Hughes, C., Hugo, K., & Blatt, J. (1996). Self-instructional intervention for teaching generalized problem-solving within a functional task sequence. *American Journal on Mental Retardation, 100,* 565–579.

Hughes, J. R. (2000). Reduced smoking: An introduction and review of the evidence. *Addiction, 95,* S3–S7.

Hughes, J. R., & Hatsukami, D. K. (1992). The nicotine withdrawal syndrome: A brief review and update. *International Journal of Smoking Cessation, 1,* 21–26.

Hughes, J. R., Higgins, S. T., Bickel, W. K., Hunt, W. K., & Fenwick, J. W. (1991). Caffeine self-administration, withdrawal, and adverse effects among coffee drinkers. *Archives of General Psychiatry, 48,* 611–617.

Hughes, J. R., Higgins, S. T., & Hatsukami, D. K. (1990). Effects of abstinence from tobacco: A critical review. In L. T. Kozlowski, H. Annis, H. D. Cappell, F. Glaser, M.

Goodstadt, Y. Israel, H. Kalant, E. M. Sellers, & J. Vingilis (Eds.), *Research advances in alcohol and drug problems.* New York: Plenum.

Hughes, S. L., Ulasevich, A., Weaver, F. M., et al. (1997). Impact of home care on hospital days: A meta-analysis. *Health Services Research, 32,* 415–432.

Huijbregts, S. C. J., de Sonneville, L. M. J., Licht, R., van Spronsen, F. J., Verkerk, P. H., & Sergeant, J. A. (2002). Sustained attention and inhibition of cognitive interference in treated phenylketonuria: Associations with concurrent and lifetime phenylalanine concentrations. *Neuropsychologia 40,* 7–15.

Hulley, S. Grady, D., Bush, T., Furberg, C., Herrington, D., Riggs, B., & Vittinghoff, E. (1998). Randomized trial of estrogen plus progestin for secondary prevention of coronary heart disease in postmenopausal women. Heart and Estrogen/progestin Replacement Study (HERS) Research Group. *Journal of the American Medical Association, 280,* 605–613.

Hunsley, J., & Bailey, J. M. (1999). The clinical utility of the Rorschach: Unfulfilled promises and an uncertain future. *Psychological Assessment, 11,* 266–277.

Huntjen, R. J. C., Postma, A., Peters, M. L., Woertman, L., & van der Hart, O. (2003). Interidentity amnesia for neutral, episodic information in dissociative identity disorder. *Journal of Abnormal Psychology, 112,* 290–297.

Hurlburt, R. T. (1979). Random sampling of cognitions and behavior. *Journal of Research on Personality, 13,* 103–111.

Hurlburt, R. T. (1997). Randomly sampling thinking in the natural environment. *Journal of Consulting and Clinical Psychology, 65,* 941–949.

Hurt, R. D., Sachs, D. P. L., & Glover, E. D. (1997). A comparison of sustained release buprioprion versus placebo for treatment of nicotine dependence. *New England Journal of Medicine, 337,* 1195–1202.

Hussong, A. M., Hicks, R. E., Levy, S. A., & Curran, P. J. (2001). Specifying the relations between affect and heavy alcohol use among young adults. *Journal of Abnormal Psychology, 110,* 449–461.

Hyland, M. E. (1990). The mood-peak flow relationship in adult asthmatics: A pilot study of individual differences and direction of causality. *British Journal of Medical Psychology, 63,* 379–384.

Hyman, S. E. (2002). Neuroscience, genetics, and the future of psychiatric diagnosis. *Psychopathology, 35,* 139–144.

Hynde, G. W., Hern, K. L., Novey, E. S., Eliopulos, D., Marshall, R., Gonzalez, J. J., & Voeller, K. K. (1993). Attention-deficit hyperactivity disorder and asymmetry of the caudate nucleus. *Journal of Child Neurology, 8,* 339–347.

Hypericum Depression Trial Study Group. (2002). Effect of *Hypericum perforatum* (St. John's wort) in major depressive disorder: A randomized controlled trial. *JAMA, 287,* 1807–1814.

Iacono, W. G., Morean, M., Beiser, M., Fleming, J. A., et al. (1992). Smooth pursuit eye-tracking in first episode psychotic patients and their relatives. *Journal of Abnormal Psychology, 101,* 104–116.

Ingram, C. (1996, September 26). Bill signed to let police tell of sex offenders' whereabouts. *Los Angeles Times,* pp. A3, A19.

Inouye, S. K., Bogardus, S. T., Jr., Charpentier, P. A., Leo-Summers, L., Acampora, D., Holford, T. R., & Cooney, L. M., Jr. (1999). A multicomponent intervention to prevent delirium in hospitalized older patients. *New England Journal of Medicine, 340,* 669–676.

Insel, T. R., Scanlan, J., Champoux, M., & Suomi, S. J. (1988). Rearing paradigm in a nonhuman primate affects response to B-CCE challenge. *Psychopharmacology, 96,* 81–86.

Institute of Medicine. (1990). *Treating drug problems.* Washington, DC: National Academy Press.

Institute of Medicine. (1999). *Marijuana and medicine: Assessing the science base.* Washington, DC: National Academy Press.

Institute of Medicine (2004). *Immunization safety review: Vaccines and autism.* Immunization Safety Review Board on Health Promotion and Disease Prevention. Washington, DC: National Academies Press.

Iribarren, C., Sidney, S., Bild, D. E., Liu, K., Markovitz, J. H., Roseman, J. M., & Matthews, K. A. (2000). Association of hostility with coronary artery calcification in young adults. *Journal of the American Medical Association, 283,* 2546–2551.

Irwin, M., Lovitz, A., Marder, S. R., Mintz, J., Winslade, W. J., van Putten, T., & Mills, M. J. (1985). Psychotic patients' understanding of informed consent. *American Journal of Psychiatry, 142,* 1351–1354.

Ishikawa, S. S., Raine, A., Lencz, T., Bihrle, S., & Lacasse, L. (2001). Autonomic stress reactivity and executive functions in successful and unsuccessful criminal psychopaths from the community. *Journal of Abnormal Psychology, 110,* 423–432.

Ivanoff, A., Jang, S. J., Smyth, N. J., & Linehan, M. M. (1994). Fewer reasons for staying alive when you are thinking of killing yourself: The Brief Reasons for Living Inventory. *Journal of Psychopathology and Behavioral Assessment, 16,* 1–13.

Ivarsson, T., Rästam, M., Weitz, E., Gilberg, I. C., & Gilberg, G. (2000). Depressive disorders in teenage-onset anorexia nervosa: A controlled longitudinal, partly community-based study. *Comprehensive Psychiatry, 41,* 398–403.

Iwamasa, G. Y. (1993). Asian Americans and cognitive behavioral therapy. *The Behavior Therapist, 16,* 233–235.

Jablonsky, A., Sartorius, N., Cooper, J. E., Anker, A., Korten, A., & Bertelson, A. (1994). Culture and schizophrenia. *British Journal of Psychiatry, 165,* 434–436.

Jackson, C. (1997). Testing a multi-stage model for the adoption of alcohol and tobacco behaviors by children. *Addictive Behaviors, 22,* 1–14.

Jackson, C., Winkleby, M. A., Flora, J. A., & Fortmann, S. P. (1991). Use of educational resources for cardiovascular risk reduction in the Stanford Five-City Project. *American Journal of Preventive Medicine, 7,* 82–88.

Jackson, J. C., Gordon, S. M., Hart, R. P., Hopkins, R. O., & Ely, E. W. (2004). The association between delirium and cognitive decline: A review of the empirical literature. *Neuropsychology Review, 14,* 87–98.

Jackson, K. M., Sher, K. J., & Wood, P. K. (2000). Trajectories of concurrent substance use disorders: A developmental, typological approach to comorbidity. *Alcoholism: Clinical & Experimental Research, 24,* 902–913.

Jackson, R. W., Treiber, F. A., Turner, J. R., Davis, H., & Strong, W. B. (1999). Effects of race, sex, and socioeconomic status upon cardiovascular stress responsivity and recovery in youth. *International Journal of Psychophysiology, 31,* 111–119.

Jacob, R. G., Thayer, J. F., Manuck, S. B., Muldoon, M. F., Tamres, L. K., et al. (1999). Ambulatory blood pressure responses and the circumplex model of mood: A 4-day study. *Psychosomatic Medicine, 61,* 319–333.

Jacobsen, L. K., Southwick, S. M., Kosten, T. R. (2001). Substance use disorders in patients with posttraumatic stress disorder: A review of the literature. *American Journal of Psychiatry, 158,* 1184–1190.

Jacobson, N. S. (1984). Variability in outcome and clinical significance of behavioral marital therapy: A reanalysis of outcome data. *Journal of Consulting and Clinical Psychology, 52,* 497–504.

Jacobson, N. S. (1989). The therapist-client relationship in cognitive behavior therapy: Implications for treating depression. *Journal of Cognitive Psychotherapy, 3*, 85–96.

Jacobson, N. S. (1992). Behavioral couple therapy: A new beginning. *Behavior Therapy, 23*, 493–506.

Jacobson, N. S., & Christensen, A. (1996). *Integrative couple therapy: Promoting acceptance and change.* New York: Norton.

Jacobson, N. S., Christensen, A., Prince, S. E., Cordova, J., & Eldridge, K. (2000). Integrative behavioral couple therapy: an acceptance-based, promising new treatment for couple discord. *Journal of Consulting and Clinical Psychology, 68*, 351–355.

Jacobson, N. S., Martell, C. R., & Dimidjian, S. (2001). Behavioral activation treatment for depression: Returning to contextual roots. *Clinical Psychology: Science and Practice, 8*, 255–270.

Jacobson, N. S., Dobson, K. S., Truax, P. A., Addis, M. E., Koerner, K., & Gollan, J. K., et al. (1996). A component analysis of cognitive-behavioral treatment for depression. *Journal of Consulting and Clinical Psychology, 64*, 295–304.

Jacobson, N. S., & Gortner, E. T. (2000). Can depression be de-medicalized in the 21st century?: Scientific revolutions, counter-revolutions and the magnetic field of normal science. *Behaviour Research & Therapy, 38*, 103–117.

Jacobson, N. S., & Hollon, S. D. (1996). Cognitive-behavior therapy versus pharmacotherapy: Now that the jury's returned its verdict, it's time to present the rest of the evidence. *Journal of Consulting and Clinical Psychology, 64*, 74–80.

Jacobson, N. S., Holzworth-Munroe, A., & Schmaling, K. B. (1989). Marital therapy and spouse involvement in the treatment of depression, agoraphobia, and alcoholism. *Journal of Consulting and Clinical Psychology, 57*, 5–10.

Jacobson, N. S., Dobson, K. S., Fruzzetti, A. E., & Schmaling, K. B. (1991). Marital therapy as a treatment for depression. *Journal of Consulting and Clinical Psychology, 59*, 547–557.

Jacobson, N. S., Roberts, L. J., Berns, S. B., & McGlinchey, J. B. (1999). Methods for defining and determining the clinical significance of treatment effects: Description, application, and alternatives. *Journal of Consulting and Clinical Psychology, 67*(3), 300–307.

Jaffe, J. H. (1985). Drug addiction and drug abuse. In Goodman & Gilman (Eds.), *The pharmacological basis of therapeutic behavior.* New York: Macmillan.

Jaffee, S. R., Caspi, A., Moffitt, T. E., Dodge, K. A., Rutter, M., Taylor, A., & Tully, L. A. (2005). Nature X nurture: Genetic vulnerabilities interact with child abuse to promote behavior problems. *Child Development, 76*, 356–370.

Jaffee, S. R., Moffitt, T. E., Caspi, A., Taylor, A., & Arseneault, L. (2002). Influence of adult domestic violence on children's internalizing and externalizing problems: An environmentally informative twin study. *Journal of the American Academy of Child and Adolescent Psychiatry, 41*, 1095–1103.

Jamison, K. R. (1992). *Touched with fire: Manic-depressive illness and the artistic temperament.* New York: Free Press.

Jampole, L., & Weber, M. K. (1987). An assessment of the behavior of sexually abused and nonsexually abused children with anatomically correct dolls. *Child Abuse and Neglect, 11*, 187–192.

Jandorf, L., Deblinger, E., Neale, J. M., & Stone, A. A. (1986). Daily vs. major life events as predictors of symptom frequency. *Journal of General Psychology, 113*, 205–218.

Jang, K. L., Livesley, W. J., Angleitner, A., Riemann, R., & Vernon, P. A. (2002). Genetic and environmental influences on the covariance of facets defining the domains of the five-factor model of personality. *Personality and Individual Differences, 33*, 83–101.

Janicak, P. G., Davis, J. M., Preskorn, S. H., & Ayd, F. J. (1993). *Principles and practice of psychopharmacological therapy.* Baltimore, MD: Williams & Wilkins.

Jansen, M. A., Glynn, T., & Howard, J. (1996). Prevention of alcohol, tobacco and other drug abuse. *American Behavioral Scientist, 39*, 790–807.

Jarrell, M. P., Johnson, W. G., & Williamson, D. A. (1986). *Insulin and glucose response in the binge purge episode of bulimic women.* Paper presented at the annual convention of the Association for Advancement of Behavior Therapy, Chicago.

Jarrett, R. B., Schaffer, M., McIntire, D., Witt-Browder, A., Kraft, D., & Risser, R. C. (1999). Treatment of atypical depression with cognitive therapy or phenelzine: A double blind, placebo controlled trial. *Archives of General Psychiatry, 56*, 431–437.

Jasnoski, M. L., & Kugler, J. (1987). Relaxation, imagery, and neuroimmunomodulation. *Annals of the New York Academy of Sciences, 496*, 722–730.

Jeans, R. F. I. (1976). An independently validated case of multiple personality. *Journal of Abnormal Psychology, 85*, 249–255.

Jelicic, M., Geraerts, E., Merckelbach, H., & Guerrieri, R. (2004). Acute stress enhances memory for emotional words, but impairs memory for neutral words. *International Journal of Neuroscience, 114*, 1343–1351.

Jellinek, E. M. (1952). Phases of alcohol addiction. *Quarterly Journal of Studies on Alcohol, 13*, 673–684.

Jenike, M. A., Baer, L., & Minichiello, W. E. (1986). *Obsessive-compulsive disorders: Theory and management.* Littleton, MA: PSG.

Jenike, M. A., & Rauch, S. L. (1994). Managing the patient with treatment-resistant obsessive-compulsive disorder: Current strategies. *Journal of Clinical Psychiatry, 55*, 11–17.

Jenkins, C. D. (1976). Recent evidence supporting psychologic and social risk factors for coronary disease. *New England Journal of Medicine, 294*, 1033–1038.

Jensen, P. S., Martin, D., & Cantwell, D. P. (1997b). Comorbidity in ADHD: Implications for research, practice, and DSM-V. *Journal of the American Academy of Child and Adolescent Psychiatry, 36*, 1065–1079.

Jernigan, D. H., Ostroff, J., Ross, C., & O'Hara III, J. A. (2004). Sex differences in adolescent exposure to alcohol advertising in magazines. *Archives of Pediatric and Adolescent Medicine, 158*, 702–704.

Jeste, D. V., Barak, Y., Madhusoodanan, S., Grossman, F., & Gharabawi, G. (2003). International multisite double-blind trial of the atypical antipsychotics risperidone and olanzapine in 175 elderly patients with chronic schizophrenia. *American Journal of Geriatric Psychiatry, 11*, 638–647.

Jezova, D., Jurankova, E., Mosnarova, A., Kriska, M., & Skultetyova, I. (1996). Neuroendocrine response during stress with relation to gender differences. *Acta Neurobiologae Experimentalis, 56*, 779–785.

Jiang, V., Babyak, M., Krantz, D. S., Waugh, R. A., Coleman, E., et al. (1996). Mental stress-induced myocardial ischemia and cardiac events. *JAMA, 275*, 1651–1656.

Jimerson, D. C., Lesem, M. D., Kate, W. H., & Brewerton, T. D. (1992). Low serotonin and dopamine metabolite concentrations in cerebrospinal fluid from bulimic patients with frequent binge episodes. *Archives of General Psychiatry, 49*, 132–138.

Jimerson, D. C., Wolfe, B. E., Metzger, E. D., Finkelstein, D. M., Cooper, T. B., et al. (1997). Decreased serotonin function in bulimia nervosa. *Archives of General Psychiatry, 54*, 529–536.

Johnson, B. A., & Ait-Daoud, N. (2000). Neuropharmacological treatments for alcoholism: Scientific basis and clinical findings. *Psychopharmacology, 149*, 327–344.

Johnson, D. R. (1987). The role of the creative arts therapist in the diagnosis and treatment of psychological trauma. *The Arts in Psychotherapy, 14*, 7–13.

Johnson, J., Weissman, M. M., & Klerman, G. L. (1990). Panic disorder, comorbidity, and suicide attempts. *Archives of General Psychiatry, 47*, 805–808.

Johnson, J. G., Cohen, P., Brown, J., Smailes, E. M., & Bernstein, D. P. (1999). Childhood maltreatment increases risk for personality disorders during early adulthood. *Archives of General Psychiatry, 56*, 600–606.

Johnson, N. J., Backlund, E., Sorlie, P. D., & Loveless, C. A. (2000). Marital status and mortality: The National Longitudinal Mortality Study. *Annals of Epidemiology, 10*, 224–238.

Johnson, S. L. (2005). Mania and dysregulation in goal pursuit: A review. *Clinical Psychology Review, 25*, 241–262.

Johnson, S. L., & Kizer, A. (2002). Bipolar and unipolar depression: A comparison of clinical phenomenology and psychosocial predictors. In C. L. Hammen & I. H. Gotlib (Eds.), *Handbook of depression* (pp. 141–165). New York, NY, US: Guilford Press.

Johnson, S. L., & Leahy, R. (Eds.). (2004). *Psychosocial approaches to bipolar disorder.* New York, NY: Guilford Press.

Johnson, S. L., & Miller, I. (1997). Negative life events and time to recovery from episodes of bipolar disorder. *Journal of Abnormal Psychology, 196*, 449–457.

Johnson, S. L., Sandrow, D., Meyer, B., Winters, R., Miller, I., Solomon, D., & Keitner, G. (2000). Increases in manic symptoms after life events involving goal attainment. *Journal of Abnormal Psychology, 109*, 721–727.

Johnson, S. L., Winett, C. A., Meyer, B., Greenhouse, W. J., & Miller, I. (1999). Social support and the course of bipolar disorder. *Journal of Abnormal Psychology, 108*, 558–566.

Johnson, S. M., & Greenberg, L. S. (1995). The emotionally focused approach to problems in adult attachment. In A. S. Gurman and N. S. Jacobson (Eds.), *Clinical handbook of couple therapy* (pp. 121–141). New York: Guilford.

Johnson, W. G., Tsoh, J. Y., & Varnado, P. J. (1996). Eating disorders: Efficacy of pharmacological and psychological interventions. *Clinical Psychology Review, 16*, 457–478.

Johnston, C., & Marsh, E. J. (2001). Families of children with attention-deficit/hyperactivity disorder: Review and recommendations for future research. *Clinical Child and Family Psychology Review, 4*, 183–207.

Johnston, L. D., O'Malley, P. M., & Bachman, J. G. (2001a). *Monitoring the future national results on adolescent drug use: Overview of key findings, 2000.* (NIH Publication No. 01-4923). Bethesda, MD: National Institute on Drug Abuse. (Also available on the Web at www.monitoringthefuture.org)

Johnston, L. D., O'Malley, P. M., & Bachman, J. G. (2001b). *Monitoring the future national results on adolescent drug use, 1975–2000. Volume I: Secondary school students* (NIH Publication No. 01-4924). Bethesda, MD: National Institute on Drug Abuse, c. 492 pp.

Johnston, L. D., O'Malley, P. M., & Bachman, J. G. (2001c). *Monitoring the future national results on adolescent drug use, 1975–2000. Volume II: College students and adults ages 19–40* (NIH Publication No. 01-4925). Bethesda, MD: National Institute on Drug Abuse, c. 238 pp.

Johri, M., Beland, F., & Bergman, H. (2003). International experiments in integrated care for the eldery: A synthesis of the evidence. *International Journal of Geriatric Psychiatry, 18*, 222–235.

Joiner, T. E. (1995). The price of soliciting and receiving negative feedback: Self-verification theory as a vulnerability to depression theory. *Journal of Abnormal Psychology, 104*, 364–372.

Joiner, T. E., Alfano, M. S., & Metalsky, G. I. (1992). When depression breeds contempt: Reassurance seeking, self-esteem, and rejection of depressed college students by their roommates. *Journal of Abnormal Psychology, 101*, 165–173.

Joiner, T. E., & Metalsky, G. I. (1995). A prospective test of an integrative interpersonal theory of depression: A naturalistic study of college roommates. *Journal of Personality and Social Psychiatry, 69*, 778–789.

Joiner, T. E., Vohs, K. D., & Heatherton, T. F. (2000). Three studies on the factorial distinctiveness of binge eating and bulimic symptoms among non-clinical men and women. *International Journal of Eating Disorders, 27*, 198–205.

Joiner, T. E. J., & Metalsky, G. I. (2001). Excessive reassurance seeking: Delineating a risk factor involved in the development of depressive symptoms. *Psychological Science, 12*, 371–378.

Joiner, T. E. J., Voelz, Z. R., & Rudd, M. D. (2001). For suicidal young adults with comorbid depressive and anxiety disorders, problem-solving treatment may be better than treatment as usual. *Professional Psychology: Research and Practice, 32*, 278–282.

Jones, G. M. (1987). Elderly people and domestic crime: Reflections on ageism, sexism, victimology *British Journal of Criminology, 27*, 191–201.

Jones, M. (1953). *The therapeutic community.* New York: Basic Books.

Jorenby, D. E., Leischow, S. J., Nides, M. A., Rennard, S. I., Johnston, J. A., et al. (1999). A controlled trial of sustained-release buprorion, a nicotine patch, or both for smoking cessation. *New England Journal of Medicine, 340*, 685–691.

Judd, L. J., Akiskal, H. S., Maser, J. D., Zeller, P. J., Endicott, J., et al. (1998). A prospective 12-year study of subsyndromal and syndromal depressive symptoms in unipolar major depressive disorders. *Archives of Gerneral Psychiatry, 55*, 694–701.

Judd, L. L. (1997). The clinical course of unipolar depressive disorders. *Archives of General Psychiatry, 54*, 989–992.

Jung, C. G. (1935). Fundamental psychological conceptions. In M. Barker & M. Game (Eds.), *A report of five lectures.* London: Institute of Medical Psychology.

Junginger, J., Barker, S., & Coe, D. (1992). Mood theme and bizarreness of delusions in schizophrenia and mood psychosis. *Journal of Abnormal Psychology, 101*, 287–292.

Junkert Tress, B., Schnierda, U., Hartkamp, N., Schmitz, N., Tress, W. (2001). Effects of short-term dynamic psychotherapy for neurotic, somatoform, and personality disorders: A prospective 1-year follow-up study. *Psychotherapy Research, 11*, 187–200.

Just, M. A., Cherkassky, V. L., Keller, T. A., & Minshew, N. J. (2004). Cortical activation and synchronization during sentence comprehension in high-functioning autism: Evidence of underconnectivity. *Brain, 127*, 1811–1821.

Kable, J. A., & Coles, C. D. (2004). The impact of prenatal alcohol exposure on neurophysiological encoding of environmental events at six months. *Alcoholism: Clinical and Experimental Research, 28*, 489–496.

Kafka, M. P. (1997). Hypersexual desire in males: An operational definition and clinical implications for males with paraphilias and paraphilia-related disorders. *Archives of Sexual Behavior, 26*(5), 505–526.

Kagan, J., & Snidman, N. (1999). Early childhood predictors of adult anxiety disorders. *Biological Psychiatry, 46*, 1536–1541.

Kalichman, S. C. (1995). *Understanding AIDS: A guide for mental health professionals.* Washington, DC: American Psychological Association.

Kalichman, S. C. (1996). *Answering your questions about AIDS.* Washington, DC: American Psychological Association.

Kamarck, T. M., Shiffman, S. M., Smithline, L., Goodie, J. L., Paty, J. A., et al. (1998). Effects of task strain, social conflict, and emotional activation on ambulatory cardiovascular activity: Daily life consequences of recurring stress in a multiethnic adult sample. *Health Psychology, 17*, 17–29.

Kamarck, T. W., Annunziato, B., & Amateau, L. M. (1995). Affiliations moderate the effects of social threat on stress-related cardiovascular responses: Boundary conditions for a laboratory model of social support. *Psychosomatic Medicine, 57*, 183–194.

Kamarck, T. W., Everson, S. A., Kaplan, G. A., Manuck, S. B., Jennings, J. R., et al. (1997). Exaggerated blood pressure responses during mental stress are associated with enhanced carotid atherosclerosis in middle-aged Finnish men. *Circulation, 96*, 3842–3848.

Kandel, D. B. (2002). *Stages and pathways of drug involvement: examining the gateway hypothesis.* New York: Cambridge University Press.

Kandel, D. B., Davies, M., Karus, D., & Yamaguchi, K. (1986). The consequences in young adulthood of adolescent drug involvement. *Archives of General Psychiatry, 43*, 746–754.

Kane, J. M., Marder, S. R., Schooler, N. R., et al. (2001). Clozapine and haloperidol in moderately refractory schizophrenia: A 6-month randomized and double-blind comparison. *Archives of General Psychiatry, 58*, 965–972.

Kane, J., Honigfeld, G., Singer, J., Meltzer, H., and the Clozapine Collaborative Study Group. (1988). Clozapine for treatment resistant schizophrenics. *Archives of General Psychiatry, 45*, 789–796.

Kane, P., & Garber, J. (2004). The relations among depression in fathers, children's psychopathology, and father-child conflict: A meta-analysis. *Clinical Psychology Review, 24*, 339–360.

Kanner, L. (1943). Autistic disturbances of affective contact. *Nervous Child, 2*, 217–250.

Kanner, L. (1973). *Childhood psychosis: Initial studies and new insights.* Washington, DC: V. H. Winston and Sons.

Kantorovich, N. V. (1930). An attempt at associative-reflex therapy in alcoholism. *Psychological Abstracts, 4*, 493.

Kaplan, H. I., & Sadock, B. J. (1991). *Synopsis of psychiatry: Behavioral sciences, clinical psychiatry.* Baltimore, MD: Williams & Williams.

Kaplan, H. S. (1974). *The new sex therapy.* New York: Brunner/Mazel.

Kaplan, H. S. (1997). Sexual desire disorders (hypoactive sexual desire and sexual aversion). In G. O. Gabbard & S. D. Atkinson (Eds.), *Synopsis of treatments of psychiatric disorders* (2nd ed., pp. 771–780). Washington, DC: American Psychiatric Press.

Kaplan, J. R., Manuck, S. B., Williams, J. K., & Strawn, W. (1994). Psychosocial influences on atherosclerosis: Evidence for effects and mechanisms in nonhuman primates. In J. Blascovich & E. S. Katkin (Eds.), *Cardiovascular reactivity* (pp. 3–26). Washington, DC: American Psychological Association.

Kaplan, M. (1983). A woman's view of DSM-III. *American Psychologist, 39*, 786–792.

Kaplan, M. S., & Kreuger, R. B. (1997). Voyeurism: Psychopathology and theory. In D. R. Laws & W. O'Donohue (Eds.), *Sexual deviance* (pp. 297–310). New York: Guilford.

Karasek, R. A. (1979). Job demands, job decision latitude, and mental strain: Implications for job redesign. *Administrative Science, 24*, 285–308.

Karon, B. P., & VandenBos, G. R. (1998). Schizophrenia and psychosis in elderly populations. In I. H. Nordhus, G. R. VandenBos, S. Berg, & P. Fromholt, (Eds.), *Clinical geropsychology* (pp. 219–227). Washington, DC: American Psychological Association.

Kashani, J. H., Beck, N. C., Hoeper, E. W., Fallahi, C., Corcoran, C. M., McAllister, J. A., Rosenberg, T. K., & Reid, J. C. (1987). Psychiatric disorders in a community sample of adolescents. *American Journal of Psychiatry, 144*, 584–589.

Kashani, J. H., & Carlson, G. A. (1987). Seriously depressed preschoolers. *American Journal of Psychiatry, 144*, 348–350.

Kashani, J. H., Holcomb, W. R., & Orvaschel, H. (1986). Depression and depressive symptoms in preschool children from the general population. *American Journal of Psychiatry, 143*, 1138–1143.

Kashani, J. H., & Orvaschel, H. (1990). A community study of anxiety in children and adolescents. *American Journal of Psychiatry, 147*, 313–318.

Kashden, J., & Franzen, M. D. (1996). An interrater reliability study of the Luria-Nebraska Neuropsychological Battery Form-II quantitative scoring system. *Archives of Clinical Neuropsychology, 11*, 155–163.

Kasl-Godley, J., & Gatz, M. (2000). Psychosocial intervention for individuals with dementia: An integration of theory, therapy, and a clinical understanding of dementia. *Clinical Psychology, 20*(6), 755–782.

Kaslow, N. J., & Thompson, M. P. (1998). Applying the criteria for empirically supported treatments to studies of psychosocial interventions for child and adolescent depression. *Journal of Clinical Child Psychology, 27*, 146–155.

Kassel, J. D., & Shiffman, S. (1997) Attentional mediation of cigarette smoking's effect on anxiety. *Health Psychology, 16*, 359–368.

Kassel, J. D., Stroud, L. R., & Paronis, C. A. (2003). Smoking, stress, and negative affect: Correlation, causation, and context across stages of smoking. *Psychological Bulletin, 129*, 270–304.

Kassel, J. D., & Unrod, M. (2000). Smoking, anxiety, and attention: Support for the role of nicotine in attentionally mediated anxiolysis. *Journal of Abnormal Psychology, 109*, 161–166.

Kassett, J. A., Gershon, E. S., Maxwell, M. E., et al. (1989). Psychiatric disorders in the first-degree relatives of probands with bulimia nervosa. *American Journal of Psychiatry, 146*, 1468–1471.

Kaszniak, A. W., Nussbaum, P. D., Berren, M. R., & Santiago, J. (1988). Amnesia as a consequence of male rape: A case report. *Journal of Abnormal Psychology, 97*, 100–104.

Katz, E. C., Gruber, K., Chutuape, M. A., & Stitzer, M. L. (2001). Reinforcement-based outpatient treatment for opiate and cocaine abusers. *Journal of Substance Abuse Treatment, 20*, 93–98.

Katz, H. M., & Gunderson, J. G. (1990). Individual psychodynamically oriented psychotherapy for schizophrenia patients. In M. I. Herz, S. J. Keith, & J. P. Docherty (Eds.), *Handbook of schizophrenia: Psychosocial treatment of schizophrenia* (pp. 69–90). Amsterdam: Elsevier.

Katz, I. R., Parmelee, P., & Brubaker, K. (1991). Toxic and metabolic encephalopathies in long-term care patients. *International Psychogeriatrics, 3*, 337–347.

Kawachi, I., Colditz, G. A., Ascherio, A., Rimm, E. B., Giovannucci, E., et al. (1994). Prospective study of phobic anxiety and risk of coronary heart disease in men. *Circulation, 89*, 1992–1997.

Kawachi, I., Sparrow, D., Spiro, A., Vokonas, P., & Weiss, S. T. (1996). A prospective study of anger and coronary heart disease: The normative aging study. *Circulation, 94,* 2090–2094.

Kawakami, N., Shimizu, H., Haratani, T., Iwata, N., & Kitamura, T. (2004). Lifetime and 6-month prevalence of DSM-III-R psychiatric disorders in an urban community in Japan. *Psychiatry Research, 121,* 293–301.

Kaye, W. H., Ebert, M. H., Raleigh, M., & Lake, R. (1984). Abnormalities in CNS monoamine metabolism in anorexia nervosa. *Archives of General Psychiatry 41,* 350–355.

Kaye, W. H., Greeno, C. G., Moss, H., Fernstrom, J., Lilenfeld, L. R., Wahlund, B., Weltzin, T. E., & Mann, J. J. L. (1998). Alterations in serotonin activity and platelet monoamine oxidase and psychiatric symptoms after recovery from bulimia nervosa. *Archives of General Psychiatry, 55,* 927–935.

Kaye, W. H., Gwirstman, H. E., George, D. T., et al. (1991). Altered serotonin activity in anorexia nervosa after long-term weight restoration. *Archives of General Psychiatry 48,* 556–562.

Kazdin, A. E. (1985). *Treatment of antisocial behavior in children and adolescents.* Homewood, IL: Dorsey.

Kazdin, A. E. (1994). Psychotherapy for children and adolescents. In A. E. Bergin & S. L. Garfield (Eds.), *Handbook of psychotherapy and behavior change* (4th ed., pp. 543–594). New York: John Wiley & Sons.

Kazdin, A. E., & Weisz, J. R. (1998). Identifying and developing empirically supported child and adolescent treatments. *Journal of Consulting and Clinical Psychology, 66,* 19–36.

Keane, T. M., & Barlow, D. H. (2004). Posttraumatic Stess Disorder. In D. H. Barlow (Ed.), *Anxiety and its disorders: The nature and treatment of anxiety and panic* (pp. 418–454). New York: Guilford.

Keane, T. M., Fairbank, J. A., Caddell, J. M., & Zimering, R. T. (1989). Implosive (flooding) therapy reduces symptoms of PTSD in Vietnam combat veterans. *Behavior Therapy, 20,* 245–260.

Keane, T. M., Gerardi, R. J., Quinn, S. J., & Litz, B. T. (1992). Behavioral treatment of post-traumatic stress disorder. In S. M. Turner, K. S. Calhoun, & H. E. Adams (Eds.), *Handbook of clinical behavior therapy* (2nd ed., pp. 87–97). New York: John Wiley & Sons.

Keane, T. M., Zimering, R. T., & Caddell, J. (1985). A behavioral formulation of posttraumatic stress disorder in Vietnam veterans. *The Behavior Therapist, 8,* 9–12.

Kearney, P. M., Whelton, M., Reynolds, K., Whelton, P. K., & He, J. (2004). Worldwide prevalence of hypertension: a systematic review. *Journal of Hypertension, 22,* 11–19.

Keel, P. K., & Klump, K. L. (2003). Are eating disorders culture-bound syndromes? Implications for conceptualizing their etiology. *Psychological Bulletin, 129,* 747–769.

Keel, P. K., & Mitchell, J. E. (1997). Outcome in bulimia nervosa. *American Journal of Psychiatry, 154,* 313–321.

Keel, P. K., Mitchell, J. E., Davis, T. L., & Crow, S. J. (2001). Relationship between depression and body dissatisfaction in women diagnosed with bulimia nervosa. *International Journal of Eating Disorders, 30,* 48–56.

Keel, P. K., Mitchell, J. E., Davis, T. L., & Crow, S. J. (2002). Long-term impact of treatment in women diagnosed with bulimia nervosa. *International Journal of Eating Disorders, 31,* 151–158.

Keel, P. K., Mitchell, J. E., Miller, K. B., Davis, T. L., & Crowe, S. J. (1999). Long-term outcome of bulimia nervosa. *Archives of General Psychiatry, 56,* 63–69.

Keilp, J. G., Sackeim, H. A., Brodsky, B. S., Oquendo, M. A., Malone, K. M., & Mann, J. J. (2001). Neuropsychological dysfunction in depressed suicide attempters. *Archives of General Psychiatry, 158,* 735–741.

Keller, M. B., Lavori, P. W., Kane, J. M., & Gelenberg, A. J. (1992). Subsyndromal symptoms in bipolar disorder: A comparison of standard and low serum levels of lithium. *Archives of General Psychiatry, 49,* 371–376.

Keller, M. B., Ryan, N. D., Strober, M., Klein, R. G., Kutcher, S. P., Birmaher, B., Hagino, O. R., Koplewicz, H., Carlson, G. A., Clarke, G. N., Emslie, G. J., Feinberg, D., Geller, B., Kusumakar, V., Papatheodorou, G., Sack, W. H., Sweeney, M., Wagner, K. D., Weller, E. B., Winters, N. C., Oakes, R., & McCafferty, J. P. (2001). Efficacy of paroxetine in the treatment of adolescent major depression: A randomized, controlled trial. *Journal of the American Academy of Child & Adolescent Psychiatry, 40,* 762–772.

Keller, M. B., Shapiro, R. W., Lavori, P. W., & Wolpe, N. (1982). Relapse in major depressive disorder: Analysis with the life table. *Archives of General Psychiatry, 39,* 911–915.

Keller, M. B., Yonkers, K. A., Warshaw, M. G., Pratt, L. A., Golan, J., Mathews, A. O., White, K., Swartz, A., Rich, J., & Lavori, P. (1994). Remission and relapse in subjects with panic disorder and agoraphobia: A prospective short interval naturalistic follow-up. *Journal of Nervous and Mental Disorders, 182,* 290–296.

Kellerman, J. (1989). *Silent partner.* New York: Bantam Books.

Kelley, M. L. (1990). *School-home notes: Promoting children's classroom success.* New York: Guilford.

Kelly, J. A. (1995). *Changing HIV risk behavior: Practical strategies.* New York: Guilford.

Kelly, J. A., Murphy, D. A., Washington, C. D., Wilson, T. S., Koob, J. J., Davis, D. R., Ledezma, G., & Davantes, B. (1994). The effects of HIV/AIDS intervention groups for high-risk women in urban clinics. *American Journal of Public Health, 84,* 1918–1922.

Kelly, J. A., & St. Lawrence, J. S. (1988a). *The AIDS health crisis: Psychological and social interventions.* New York: Plenum.

Kelly, J. A., St. Lawrence, J. S., Betts, R., Brasfield, T., & Hood, H. (1990). A skills training group intervention model to assist persons in reducing risk behaviors for HIV infection. *AIDS Education and Prevention, 2,* 24–35.

Kelly, J. A., St. Lawrence, J. S., Hood, H., & Brasfield, T. (1989). Behavioral intervention to reduce AIDS risk activities. *Journal of Consulting and Clinical Psychology, 57,* 60–67.

Kelsoe, J. R. (1997). The genetics of bipolar disorder. *Psychiatric Annals, 27,* 285–292.

Keltner, D., & Bonanno, G. A. (1997). A study of laughter and dissociation: Distinct correlates of laughter and smiling during bereavement. *Journal of Personality & Social Psychology, 73,* 687–702.

Keltner, D., & Kring, A. M. (1998). Emotion, social function, and psychopathology. *Review of General Psychology, 2,* 320–342.

Kemeny, M. E. (2003). The psychobiology of stress. *Current Directions in Psychological Science, 12,* 124–129.

Kempster, N. (1996, August 25). *Clinton orders tracking of sex offenders.* Los Angeles Times, pp. A20.

Kenardy, J., & Taylor, C. B. (1999). Expected versus unexpected panic attacks: A naturalistic prospective study. *Journal of Anxiety Disorders, 13,* 435–445.

Kendall, P. C. (1994). Treating anxiety disorders in youth: Results of a randomized clinical trial. *Journal of Consulting and Clinical Psychology, 62,* 100–110.

Kendall, P. C., Aschenbrand, S. G., & Hudson, J. L. (2003). Child-focused treatment of anxiety. In A. E. Kazdin & J. R. Weisz (Eds.), *Evidence-based psychotherapies for children and adolescents* (pp. 81–100). New York: Guilford.

Kendall, P. C., Flannery-Schroeder, E. C., Panichelli-Mindel, S., Southam-Gerow, M., Henin, A., & Warman, M. (1997). Therapy for youths with anxiety disorders: A second randomized clinical trial. *Journal of Consulting and Clinical Psychology, 65,* 366–380.

Kendall, P. C., & Ingram, R. E. (1989). Cognitive-behavioral perspectives: Theory and research on depression and anxiety. In D. Watson & P. C. Kendall (Eds.), *Personality, psychopathology, and psychotherapy* (pp. 27–53). San Diego, CA: Academic Press.

Kendall, P. C., Haaga, D. A. F., Ellis, A., Bernard, M., DiGiuseppe, R., & Kassinove, H. (1995). Rational-emotive therapy in the 1990s and beyond: Current status, recent revisions, and research questions. *Clinical Psychology Review, 15,* 169–185.

Kendall, P. C., Safford, S., Flannery-Schroeder, E., & Webb, A. (2004). Child anxiety treatment: Outcomes in adolescence and impact on substance use and depression at 7.4-year follow-up. *Journal of Consulting and Clinical Psychology, 72,* 276–287.

Kendell, R. E. (1975). *The role of diagnosis in psychiatry.* London: Blackwell.

Kendler, K. S. (1993). Twin studies of psychiatric illness: Current status and future directions. *Archives of General Psychiatry, 50,* 905–914.

Kendler, K. S. (1997). The diagnostic validity of melancholic major depression in a population-based sample of female twins. *Archives of General Psychiatry, 54,* 299–304.

Kendler, K. S., & Diehl, S. R. (1993). The genetics of schizophrenia: A current, genetic-epidemiologic perspective. *Schizophrenia Bulletin, 79,* 261–285.

Kendler, K. S., & Gardner, C. O. (1998). Boundaries of major depression: An evaluation of DSM-IV criteria. *American Journal of Psychiatry, 155,* 172–177.

Kendler, K. S., Hettema, J. M., Butera, F., Gardner, C. O., & Prescott, C. A. (2003). Life event dimensions of loss, humiliation, entrapment, and danger in the prediction of onsets of major depression and generalized anxiety. *Archives of General Psychiatry, 60,* 789–796.

Kendler, K. S., Karkowski, L. M., & Prescott, C. A. (1999). Causal relationship between stressful life events and the onset of major depression. *American Journal of Psychiatry, 156,* 837–841.

Kendler, K. S., & Karkowski-Shuman, L. (1997). Stressful life events and genetic liability to major depression: genetic control of exposure to the environment? *Psychological Medicine, 27,* 539–547.

Kendler, K. S., Karkowski-Shuman, L., & Walsh, D. (1996). Age of onset in schizophrenia and risk of illness in relatives. *British Journal of Psychiatry, 169,* 213–218.

Kendler, K. S., Myers, J., & Prescott, C. A. (2002). The etiology of phobias: An evaluation of the stress-diathesis model. *Archives of General Psychiatry, 59,* 242–249.

Kendler, K. S., Myers, J., Prescott, C. A., & Neale, M. C. (2001). The genetic epidemiology of irrational fears and phobias in men. *Archives of General Psychiatry, 58,* 257–267.

Kendler, K. S., Neale, M. C., Heath, A. C., Kessler, R. C., & Faves, L. J. (1994). A twin-family study of alcoholism in women. *American Journal of Psychiatry, 151,* 707–715.

Kendler, K. S., Neale, M. C., Kessler, R. C., Heath, A. C., et al. (1992). A population-based twin study of major depression in women: The impact of varying definitions of illness. *Archives of General Psychiatry, 49,* 257–266.

Kendler, K. S., Neale, M. C., & Walsh, D. (1995). Evaluating the spectrum concept of schizophrenia in the Roscommon Family Study. *American Journal of Psychiatry, 152,* 749–754.

Kendler, K. S., & Prescott, C. A. (1998). Cannabis use, abuse, and dependence in a population-based sample of female twins. *American Journal of Psychiatry, 155*, 1016–1022.

Kendler, K. S., & Prescott, C. A. (1999). Caffeine intake, tolerance, and withdrawal in women: A population-based twin study. *American Journal of Psychiatry, 156*, 223–228.

Kendler, K. S., Prescott, C. A., Myers, J., & Neale, M. C. (2003). The structure of genetic and environmental risk factors for common psychiatric and substance use disorders in men and women. *Archives of General Psychiatry, 60*, 929–937.

Kennedy, E., Spence, S. H., & Hensley, R. (1989). An examination of the relationship between childhood depression and social competence amongst primary school children. *Journal of Child Psychology and Psychiatry, 30*, 561–573.

Kernberg, O. F. (1985). *Borderline conditions and pathological narcissism*. Northvale, NJ: Jason Aronson.

Kerns, J. G., & Berenbaum, H. (2002). Cognitive impairments associated with formal thought disorder in people with schizophrenia. *Journal of Abnormal Psychology, 111*, 211–224.

Kerns, J. G., & Berenbaum, H. (2003). The relationship between formal thought disorder and executive functioning component processes. *Journal of Abnormal Psychology, 112*, 339–352.

Keshavan, M. S., Rosenberg, D., Sweeney, J. A., & Pettegrew, J. W. (1998). Decreased caudate volume in neuroleptic-naive psychotic patients. *American Journal of Psychiatry, 155*, 774–778.

Kessel, N., & Grossman, G. (1961). Suicide in alcoholics. *British Medical Journal, 2*, 1671–1672.

Kessler, L. (2004, August 22). Dancing with Rose: A strangely beautiful encounter with Alzheimer's patients provides insights that challenge the way we view the disease. *LA Times Magazine*.

Kessler, R. C., Crum, R. M., Warner, L. A., Nelson, C. B., et al. (1997). Lifetime co-occurrence of DSM-IIIR alcohol dependence with other psychiatric disorders in the National Comorbidity Study. *Archives of General Psychiatry, 54*, 313–321.

Kessler, R. C., McGonagle, K. A., Zhao, S., Nelson, C. B., et al. (1994). Lifetime and 12-month prevalence of DSM-III-R psychiatric disorders in the United States: Results from the National Comorbidity Study. *Archives of General Psychiatry, 51*, 8–19.

Kessler, R. C., Chiu, W. T., Demler, O., & Walters, E. E. (2005). Prevalence, Severity, and Comorbidity of 12-Month DSM-IV Disorders in the National Comorbidity Survey Replication. *Archives of General Psychiatry, 62*, 617–627.

Kessler, R. C., & McLeod, J. D. (1985). Social support and mental health in community samples. In S. Cohen & L. Syme (Eds.), *Social support and health* (pp. 219–240). Orlando, FL: Academic Press.

Kety, S. S., Rosenthal, D., Wender, P. H., & Schulsinger, F. (1968). The types and prevalence of mental illness in the biological and adoptive families of adopted schizophrenics. In D. Rosenthal & S. S. Kety (Eds.), *The transmission of schizophrenia*. Elmsford, NY: Pergamon.

Kety, S. S., Rosenthal, D., Wender, P. H., & Schulsinger, F. (1976). Mental illness in the adoptive and biological families of adopted individuals who have become schizophrenic. In R. R. Fieve, D. Rosenthal, & H. Brill (Eds.), *Genetic research in psychiatry*. Baltimore, MD: Johns Hopkins University Press.

Kety, S. S., Wender, P. H., Jacobsen, B., Ingraham, L. T., Jansson, L., et al. (1994). Mental illness in the biological and adoptive relatives of schizophrenic adoptees: Replication of the Copenhagen study in the rest of Denmark. *Archives of General Psychiatry, 51*, 442–468.

Keys, A., Brozek, J., Hsu, L. K. G., McConoha, C. E., & Bolton, B. (1950). *The biology of human starvation*. Minneapolis: University of Minnesota Press.

Keys, A., Taylor, H. L., et al. (1971). Mortality and coronary heart disease in men studied for 23 years. *Archives of Internal Medicine, 128*, 201–214.

Kidder, T. (1978). Soldiers of misfortune. *The Atlantic Monthly, 241*, 41–52.

Kiecolt-Glaser, J. K., Bane, C., Glaser, R., & Malarkey, W. B. (2003). Love, marriage, and divorce: newlyweds' stress hormones foreshadow relationship changes. *Journal of Consulting and Clinical Psychology, 71*, 176–188.

Kiecolt-Glaser, J., Dura, J. R., Speicher, C. E., & Trask, O. (1991). Spousal caregivers of dementia victims: Longitudinal changes in immunity and health. *Psychosomatic Medicine, 54*, 345–362.

Kiecolt-Glaser, J. K., Garner, W., Speicher, C. E., Penn, G. M., Holliday, J., & Glaser, R. (1984). Psychosocial modifiers of immunocompetence in medical students. *Psychosomatic Medicine, 46*, 7–14.

Kiecolt-Glaser, J. K., & Glaser, R. (2001). Stress and immunity: Age enhances the risks. *Current Directions in Psychological Science, 10*, 18–21.

Kiecolt-Glaser, J. K., & Glaser, R. (2002). Depression and immune function: Central pathways to morbidity and mortality. *Journal of Psychosomatic Research, 53*, 873–876.

Kiecolt-Glaser, J. K., Glaser, R., Williger, D., Stout, J., Messick, G., Sheppard, S., Ricker, D., Romischer, S. C., Briner, W., Bonnell, G., & Donnerberg, R. (1985). Psychosocial enhancement of immunocompetence in a geriatric population. *Health Psychology, 4*, 25–41.

Kiecolt-Glaser, J. K., McGuire, L., Robles, T. F., & Glaser, R. (2002). Psychoneuroimmunology and psychosomatic medicine: Back to the future. *Psychosomatic Medicine 64*, 15–28.

Kiesler, C. A. (1991). Changes in general hospital psychiatric care. *American Psychologist, 46*, 416–421.

Kiesler, C. A. (1992). U.S. mental health policy: Doomed to fail. *American Psychologist, 47*, 1077–1082.

Kihlstrom, J. F. (1994). Dissociative and conversion disorders. In D. J. Stein & J. E. Young (Eds.), *Cognitive science and clinical disorders*. San Diego, CA: Academic Press.

Kihlstrom, J. F., Tataryn, D. J., & Holt, I. P. (1993). Dissociative disorders. In P. B. Sutker & H. E. Adams (Eds.), *Comprehensive handbook of psychopathology* (pp. 203–234). New York: Plenum.

Killen, J. D., Fortmann, S. P., Newman, B., & Varady, A. (1990). Evaluation of a treatment approach combining nicotine gum with self-guided behavioral treatments for smoking relapse prevention. *Journal of Consulting and Clinical Psychology, 58*, 85–92.

Killen, J. D., Robinson, T. N., Haydel, K. F., Hayward, C., et al. (1997). Prospective study of risk factors for the initiation of cigarette smoking. *Journal of Consulting and Clinical Psychology, 65*, 1011–1016.

Killen, J. D., Taylor, C. B., Hayward, C., Haydel, K. F., Wilson, D. M., Hammer, L., Kraemer, H., Blair-Greiner, A., & Strachowski, D. (1996). Weight concerns influence the development of eating disorders: A 4-year prospective study. *Journal of Consulting and Clinical Psychology, 64*, 936–940.

Killen, J. D., Taylor, C. B., Hayward, C., Wilson, D. M., Haydel, K. F., et al. (1994). Pursuit of thinness and onset of eating disorders in a community sample of adolescent girls. *International Journal of Eating Disorders, 16*, 227–238.

Kim, E. (2005). The effect of the decreased safety behaviors on anxiety and negative thoughts in social phobics. *Journal of Anxiety Disorders, 19*, 69–86.

Kim, E. D., & Lipshultz, L. I. (1997). Advances in the evaluation and treatment of the infertile man. *World Journal of Urology, 15*, 378–393.

Kim, J. E., & Moen, P. (2001). Is retirement good or bad for subjective well-being? *Current Directions in Psychological Science Special Issue, 10*(3), 83–86.

Kim, R. S., Poling, J., & Ascher, L. M. (1991). An introduction to research on the clinical efficacy of paradoxical intention. In G. R. Weeks (Ed.), *Promoting change through paradoxical therapy* (rev. ed., pp. 216–250). Philadelphia, PA: Brunner/Mazel, Inc.

Kingree, J. B. (2001). Predictors of 12-step group preference among low-income treatment participants with alcohol problems. *Alcoholism Treatment Quarterly, 19*, 57–66.

Kinsey, A. C., Pomeroy, W. B., & Martin, C. E. (1948). *Sexual behavior in the human male*. Philadelphia: Saunders.

Kinzie, J. D. (1985). Overview of clinical issues in the treatment of Southeast Asian refugees. In T. C. Owan (Ed.), *Southeast Asian mental health treatment, prevention services, training, and research*. Washington, DC: National Institute of Mental Health.

Kinzl, J. F., Traweger, C., Trefalt, E., Mangweth, B., & Biebl, W. (1999). Binge eating disorder in females: A population based investigation. *International Journal of Eating Disorders, 25*, 287–292.

Kirmayer, L. J. (2001). Cultural variations in the clinical presentation of depression and anxiety: Implications for diagnosis and treatment. *Journal of Clinical Psychiatry, 62* (Suppl. 13), 22–28.

Kirmayer, L. J., Robbins, J. M., & Paris, J. (1994). Somatoform disorders: Personality and social matrix of somatic distress. *Journal of Abnormal Psychology, 103*, 125–136.

Kirmayer, L. J., & Young, A. (1998). Culture and somatization: Clinical, epidemiological, and ethnographic perspectives. *Psychosomatic Medicine, 60*, 420–430.

Kirsch, I. (2000). Are drug and placebo effects in depression additive? *Biological Psychiatry, 47*, 733–735.

Kirschbaum, C., Prussner, J. C., & Stone, A. A. (1995). Persistent high cortisol responses to repeated psychological stress in a subpopulation of healthy men. *Psychosomatic Medicine, 57*, 468–474.

Kisiel, C. L., & Lyons, J. S. (2001). Dissociation as a mediator of psychopathology among sexually abused children and adolescents. *American Journal of Psychiatry, 158*, 1034–1039.

Klaw, E., & Humphreys, K. (2000). Life stories of Moderation Management mutual help group members. *Contemporary Drug Problems, 27*, 779–803.

Klein, D. F., & Ross, D. C. (1993). Reanalysis of the National Institute of Mental Health Treatment of Depression Collaborative Research Program general effectiveness report. *Neuropsychopharmacology, 8*, 241–251.

Klein, D. N., Durbin, C. E., Shankman, S. A., & Santiago, N. J. (2002). Depression and personality. In C. L. Hammen & I. H. Gotlib (Eds.), *Handbook of depression* (pp. 115–140). New York, NY: Guilford Press.

Klein, D. N., Lewinsohn, P. M., Seeley, J. R., & Rohde, P. A. (2001). A family study of major depressive disorder in a community sample of adolescents. *Archives of General Psychiatry, 58*, 13–20.

Klein, D. N., Schwartz, J. E., Rose, S., & Leader, J. B. (2000). Five-year course and outcome of dysthymic disorder: A prospective, naturalistic follow-up study. *American Journal of Psychiatry, 157*, 931–939.

Kleinman, A. (1986). *Social origins of distress and disease: Depression, neurasthenia, and pain in modern China*. New Haven, CT: Yale University Press.

Klerman, G. L. (1988). Depression and related disorders of mood (affective disorders). In A. M. Nicholi, Jr. (Ed.), *The new Harvard guide to psychiatry.* Cambridge, MA: Harvard University Press.

Klerman, G. L., Weissman, M. M., Markowitz, J. C., Glick, I., Wilner, P. J., Mason, B., & Shear, M. K. (1994). Medication and psychotherapy. In A. E. Bergin & S. L. Garfield (Eds.), *Handbook of psychotherapy and behavior change* (4th ed., pp. 734–782). New York: John Wiley & Sons.

Klerman, G. L., Weissman, M. M., Rounsaville, B. J., & Chevron, E. S. (1984). *Interpersonal psychotherapy of depression.* New York: Basic Books.

Klinetob, N. A., & Smith, D. A. (1996). Demand-withdraw communication in marital interaction: Tests of interspousal contingency and gender role hypotheses. *Journal of Marriage and the Family, 58,* 945–957.

Klingberg, T., Hedehus, M., Temple, E., Salz, T., Gabrieli, J. D., Moseley, M. E., & Poldrack, R. A. (2000). Microstructure of temporo-parietal white matter as a basis for reading ability: Evidence from diffusion tensor magnetic resonance imaging. *Neuron, 25,* 493–500. *Interpersonal psychotherapy of depression.* New York: Basic Books.

Klinnert, M. D., Mrazek, P. J., & Mrazek, D. A. (1994). Early asthma onset: The interaction between family stressors and adaptive parenting. *Psychiatry, 57,* 51–61.

Klintsova, A. Y., Scamra, C., Hoffman, M., Napper, R. M. A., Goodlett, C. R., & Greenough, W. T. (2002). Therapeutic effects of complex motor training on motor performance deficits induced by neonatal binge-like alcohol exposure in rats: II. A quantitative stereological study of synaptic plasticity in female rat cerebellum. *Brain Research, 937,* 83–93.

Kluft, R. P. (1994). Treatment trajectories in multiple personality disorder. *Dissociation, 7,* 63–75.

Klump, K. L., McGue, M., & Iacono, W. G. (2000). Age differences in genetic and environmental influences on eating attitudes and behaviors in preadolescent and adolescent female twins. *Journal of Abnormal Psychology, 109,* 239–251.

Klump, K. L., McGue, M., & Iacono, W. G. (2002). Genetic relationships between personality and eating attitudes and behaviors. *Journal of Abnormal Psychology, 111,* 380–389.

Klump, K. L., Wonderlich, S., Lehoux, P., Lilenfeld, L. R. R., & Bulik, C. M. (2002). Does environment matter? A review of nonshared environment and eating disorders. *International Journal of Eating Disorders, 31,* 118–135.

Knapp, S., & Vandecreek, L. (1982). *Tarasoff:* Five years later. *Professional Psychology, 13,* 511–516.

Knight, B. G. (1996). *Psychotherapy with older adults* (2nd ed.). Thousand Oaks, CA: Sage.

Knight, B. G., Kelly, M., & Gatz, M. (1992). Psychotherapy and the older adult. In H. J. Freudenberger & D. K. Freedheim (Eds.), *History of psychotherapy: A century of change* (pp. 528–551). Washington, DC: American Psychological Association.

Knight, B. G., Lutzky, S. M., & Olshevski, J. L. (1992). *A randomized comparison of stress reduction training to problem solving training for dementia caregivers: Processes and outcomes.* Unpublished manuscript, University of Southern California, Los Angeles.

Knopp, E. H. (1984). *Retraining adult sex offenders.* New York: Safer Society Press.

Kochanek, K. D., Murphy, S. L., Anderson, R. N., & Scott, C. (2004). Deaths: Final data for 2002. *National vital statistics reports;* vol 53 no 5. Hyattsville, MD: National Center for Health Statistics.

Koegel, R. L., Bimbela, A., & Schreibman, L. (1996). Collateral effects of parent training on family interactions. *Journal of Autism and Developmental Disorders, 26,* 347–359.

Koegel, R. L., Koegel, L. K., & Brookman, L. I. (2003). Empirically supported pivotal response interventions with children with autism. In A. E. Kazdin & J. R. Weisz (Eds.), *Evidence-based psychotherapies for children and adolescents* (pp. 341–357). New York: Guilford.

Koegel, R. L., Schreibman, L., Britten, K. R., Burkey, J. C., & O'Neill, R. E. (1982). A comparison of parent training to direct child treatment. In R. L. Koegel, A. Rincover, & A. L. Egel (Eds.), *Educating and understanding autistic children.* San Diego, CA: College-Hill.

Koenigsberg, H. W., Reynolds, D., Goodman, M., New, A. S., Mitropoulou, V., & Trestman, R. L., et al. (2003). Risperidone in the treatment of schizotypal personality disorder. *Journal of Clinical Psychiatry, 64,* 628–634.

Koenigsberg, H. W., Woo-Ming, A. M., & Siever, L. J. (2002). Pharmacological treatments for personality disorders. In P. E. Nathan & J. M. Gorman (Eds.), *A guide to treatments that work.* New York: Oxford University Press.

Kohn, L. P., Oden, T., Munoz, R. F., Robinson, A., & Leavitt, D. (2002). Adapted cognitive behavioral group therapy for depressed low-income African American women. *Community Mental Health Journal, 38*(6), 497–504.

Kohn, M. L. (1968). Social class and schizophrenia: A critical review. In D. Rosenthal & S. S. Kety (Eds.), *The transmission of schizophrenia.* Elmsford, NY: Pergamon.

Kohut, H. (1971). *The analysis of the self.* New York: International Universities Press.

Kohut, H. (1977). *The restoration of the self.* New York: International Universities Press.

Koivuma-Honkanen, H., Honkanen, R., Viinamäki, H., Heikkilä, K., Kaprio, J., & Koskenvuo, M. (2001). Life satisfaction and suicide: A 20-year follow-up study. *American Journal of Psychiatry, 158,* 433–439.

Koller, E. A., Cross, J. T., Doraiswamy, P. M., & Malozowski, S. N. (2003). Pancreatitis associated with atypical antipsychotics: from the Food and Drug Administration's MedWatch surveillance system and published reports. *Pharmacotherapy, 23,* 1123–1130.

Kolmen, B. K., Feldman, H. E., Handen, B. L., & Janosky, J. E. (1995). Naltrexone in young autistic children: A double-blind, placebo-controlled crossover study. *Journal of the American Academy of Child and Adolescent Psychiatry, 34,* 223–231.

Konig, P., & Godfrey, S. (1973). Prevalence of exercise-induced bronchial liability in families of children with asthma. *Archives of Diseases of Childhood, 48,* 518.

Koob, G. F., Caine, B., Hyytia, P., Markou, A., Parsons, L. H., Roberts, A. J., Schulteis, G., & Weiss, F. (1999). Neurobiology of drug addiction. In M. D. Glantz & C. R. Hartel (Eds.), *Drug abuse: Origins and interventions* (pp. 161–190). Washington, DC: American Psychological Association.

Koons, C. R., Robins, C. J., Tweed, J. L., Lynch, T. R., Gonzalez, A. M., Morse, J. Q., et al. (2001). Efficacy of dialectical behavior therapy in women veterans with borderline personality disorder. *Behavior Therapy, 32,* 371–390.

Kopelowicz, A., & Liberman, R. P. (1998). Psychosocial treatments for schizophrenia. In P. E. Nathan & J. M. Gorman (Eds.), *A guide to treatments that work* (pp. 190–211). New York: Oxford University Press.

Kopelowicz, A., Liberman, R. P., & Zarate, R. (2002). Psychosocial treatments for schizophrenia. In P. E. Nathan & J. M. Gorman (Eds.), *A guide to treatments that work* (pp. 201–229). New York: Oxford University Press.

Koran, L. M., Hackett, E., Rubin, A., et al. (2002). Efficacy of sertraline in the long-term treatment of obsessive-compulsive disorder. *American Journal of Psychiatry, 158,* 88–95.

Koss, M. P., & Shiang, J. (1994). Research on brief psychotherapy. In A. E. Bergin & S. L. Garfield (Eds.), *Hand-*

book of psychotherapy and behavior change (4th ed., pp. 664–700). New York: John Wiley & Sons.

Kosten, T. R., Morgan, C. M., Falcione, J., & Schottenfeld, R. S. (1992). Pharmacotherapy for cocaine-abusing methadone-maintained patients using amantadine or desipramine. *Archives of General Psychiatry, 49,* 894–898.

Koston, T. R., & Ziedonis, D. M. (1997). Substance abuse and schizophrenia: Editors' introduction. *Schizophrenia Bulletin, 23,* 181–186.

Kotranski, L., Semaan, S., Collier, K., Lauby, J., Halbert, J., & Feighan, K. (1998). Effectiveness of an HIV risk reduction counseling intervention for out-of-treatment drug users. *AIDS Education and Prevention, 10,* 19–33.

Koutstaal, W., & Schacter, D. L. (1997). Inaccuracy and inaccessibility in memory retrieval: Contributions from cognitive psychology and neuropsychology. In L. A. Uyehara and P. S. Appelbaum (Eds.), *Trauma and memory: Clinical and legal controversies.* (pp. 93–137). London: Oxford University Press.

Kozak, M. J., Liebowitz, M., & Foa, E. B. (2000). Cognitive behavior therapy and pharmacotherapy for OCD: The NIMH-sponsored collaborative study. In W. K. Goodman, M. V. Rudorfer, and J. D. Maser (Eds.), *Obsessive-compulsive disorder: Contemporary issues in treatment.* Mahweh, NJ: Lawrence Erlbaum.

Kozel, N. J., & Adams, E. H. (1986). Epidemiology of drug abuse: An overview. *Science, 234,* 970–974.

Kozol, H., Boucher, R., & Garofalo, R. (1972). The diagnosis and treatment of dangerousness. *Crime and Delinquency, 18,* 37–92.

Kramer, E. F. (1995). Controversial litigation issue may be shifting our focus away from a more serious problem. *Res Gestae, 12,* 10–22.

Kramer, J. H., Jurik, J., Sha, S. J., Rankin, K. P., Rosen, H. J., Johnson, J. K., & Miller, B. L. (2003). Distinctive neuropsychological patterns in frontotemporal dementia, semantic dementia, and Alzheimer disease. *Cognitive and Behavioral Neurology, 16,* 211–218.

Krantz, S., & Hammen, C. L. (1979). Assessment of cognitive bias in depression. *Journal of Abnormal Psychology, 88,* 611–619.

Kranzler, H. R. (2000). Pharmacotherapy of alcoholism: Gaps in knowledge and opportunities for research. *Alcohol & Alcoholism, 35,* 537–547.

Kranzler, H. R., & van Kirk, J. (2001). Efficacy of naltrexone and acamprosate for alcoholism treatment: A meta-analysis. *Alcoholism: Clinical & Experimental Research, 25,* 1335–1341.

Krause, K.-H., Dresel, S. H., Krause, J., La Fougere, C., & Ackenheil, M. (2003). The dopamine transporter and neuroimaging in attention deficit hyperactivity disorder. *Neuroscience and Biobehavioral Reviews, 27,* 605–613.

Kreuger, R. B., & Kaplan, M. S. (2000). Evaluation and treatment of sexual disorders: Frottage. In L. Vandecreek and T. L. Jackson (Eds). *Innovations in clinical practice: A source book,* Volume 18(pp. 185–197). Sarasota, FL: Professional Resource Press/Professional Resource Exchange.

Kreyenbuhl, J., Zito, J. M., Buchanan, R. W., Soeken, K. L., & Lehman, A. F. (2003). Racial disparity in the pharmacological management of schizophrenia. *Schizophrenia Bulletin, 29,* 183–193.

Kring, A. M. (1999). Emotion in schizophrenia: Old mystery, new understanding. *Current Directions in Psychological Science, 8,* 160–163.

Kring, A. M. (2000). Gender and anger. In A. H. Fischer (Ed.), *Gender and Emotion,* (pp. 211–231). Cambridge: Cambridge University Press.

Kring, A. M., & Earnst, K. S. (1999). Stability of emotional responding in schizophrenia. *Behavior Therapy, 30,* 373–388.

Kring, A. M., & Neale, J. M. (1996). Do schizophrenics show a disjunctive relationship among expressive, experiential and physiological components of emotion? *Journal of Abnormal Psychology, 105,* 249–257.

Kruger, S., Seminowicz, D., Goldapple, K., Kennedy, S. H., & Mayberg, H. S. (2003). State and trait influences on mood regulation in bipolar disorder: Blood flow differences with an acute mood challenge. *Biological Psychiatry, 54,* 1274–1283.

Krystal, J. H., Cramer, J. A., Krol, W. F., et al. (2001). Naltrexone in the treatment of alcohol dependence. *The New England Journal of Medicine, 345,* 1734–1739.

Kubansky, L. D., & Kawachi, I. (2000). Going to the heart of the matter: Do negative emotions cause coronary heart disease? *Journal of Psychosomatic Research, 48,* 323–337.

Kubzansky, L. D., Kawachi, I., Spiro, A., Weiss, S. T., Vokonas, P. S., & Sparrow, D. (1997). Is worrying bad for your heart? A prospective study of worry and coronary heart disease in the Normative Aging Study. *Circulation, 95,* 818–824.

Kuehnle, K. (1998). Child sexual abuse evaluations: The scientist-practitioner model. *Behavioral Sciences & the Law, 16,* 5–20.

Kuhn, T. S. (1962). *The structure of scientific revolutions.* Chicago: University of Chicago Press.

Kuhn, T. S. (1970). *The structure of scientific revolutions.* Chicago: University of Chicago Press.

Kunst-Wilson, W. R., & Zajonc, R. B. (1980). Affective discrimination of stimuli that cannot be recognized. *Science, 207,* 557–558.

Kupfer, D. J. (2005). The increasing medical burden in bipolar disorder. *JAMA, 293,* 2528–2530.

Kupfer, D. J., First, M. B., & Regier, D. A. (2002). *A research agenda for DSM-V.* APPI: Arlington, VA.

Ladoceur, R., Dugas, M. J., Freeston, M. H., Leger, E., Gagnon, F., & Thibodeua, N. (2000). Efficacy of a new cognitive-behavioral treatment for generalized anxiety disorder: Evaluation in a controlled clinical trial. *Journal of Consulting and Clinical Psychology, 68,* 957–996.

Lahey, B. B., Loeber, R., Hart, E. L., Frick, P. J., Applegate, B., Zhang, Q., Green, S. M., & Russo, M. F. (1995). Four-year longitudinal study of conduct disorder in boys: Patterns and predictors of persistence. *Journal of Abnormal Psychology, 104,* 83–93.

Lahey, B. B., McBurnett, K., & Loeber, R. (2000). Are attention-deficit/hyperactivity disorder and oppositional defiant disorder developmental precursors to conduct disorder? In A. J. Sameroff & M. Lewis, et al. (Eds.), *Handbook of developmental psychopathology* (2nd ed., pp. 431–446). New York: Kluwer Academic/Plenum.

Lahey, B. B., Miller, T. L., Gordon, R. A., & Riley, A. W. (1999). Developmental epidemiology of the disruptive behavior disorders. In H. C. Quay & A. Hogan (Eds.), *Handbook of disruptive behavior disorders* (pp. 23–48). New York: Plenum.

Lalumiere, M. L., & Quinsey, V. L. (1994). The discriminability of rapists from nonsex offenders using phallometric measures. *Criminal Justice and Behavior, 21,* 150–175.

Lam, D. H., Bright, J., Jones, S., Hayward, P., Schuck, N., & Chisholm, D. et al. (2000). Cognitive therapy for bipolar illness—a pilot study of relapse prevention. *Cognitive Therapy and Research, 24,* 503–520.

Lamb, H. R., Weinberger, L. E., DeCuir, W. J. (2002). The police and mental health. *Psychiatry Services, 53,* 1266–1271.

Lambe, E. K., Katzman, D. K., Mikulis, D. J., Kennedy, S. H., & Zipursky, R. B. (1997). Cerebral gray matter volume deficits after weight recovery from anorexia nervosa. *Archives of General Psychiatry, 54,* 537–542.

Lambert, M. J., & Ogles, B. M. (2004). The efficacy and effectiveness of psychotherapy. In M. J. Lambert (Ed.), *Bergin and Garfield's handbook of psychotherapy and behavior change* (5th ed., pp. 139–193). Hoboken, NJ: John Wiley & Sons.

Lando, H. A. (1977). Successful treatment of smokers with a broad-spectrum behavioral approach. *Journal of Consulting and Clinical Psychology, 45,* 361–366.

Landreville, P., Landry, J., Baillargeon, L., Guerette, A., & Matteau, E. (2001). Older adults' acceptance of psychological and pharmacological treatments for depression. *Journal of Gerontology: Psychological Sciences, 56B(5),* P285–P291.

Lane, D., Carroll, D., Ring, C., Beevers, D. G., & Lip, G. H. Y. (2001). Mortality and quality of life 12 months after myocardial infarction: Effects of depression and anxiety. *Psychosomatic Medicine, 63,* 221–230.

Lane, E. A., & Albee, G. W. (1965). Childhood intellectual differences between schizophrenic adults and their siblings. *American Journal of Orthopsychiatry, 35,* 747–753.

Lang, A. R., Goeckner, D. J., Adessor, V. J., & Marlatt, G. A. (1975). Effects of alcohol on aggression in male social drinkers. *Journal of Abnormal Psychology, 84,* 508–518.

Langbehn, D. R., & Cadoret, R. J. (2001). The adult antisocial syndrome with and without antecedent conduct disorder: Comparisons from an adoption study. *Comprehensive Psychiatry, 42,* 272–282.

Langeluddeke, A. (1963). *Castration of sexual criminals.* Berlin: de Gruyter.

Langenbucher, J. W., & Chung, T. (1995). Onset and staging of DSM-IV alcohol dependence using mean age and survival hazard methods. *Journal of Abnormal Psychology, 104,* 346–354.

Langenbucher, J., Martin, C. S., Labouvie, E., Sanjuan, P. M., Bavly, L., & Pollock, N. K. (2000). Toward the DSM-V: The withdrawal-gate model versus the DSM-IV in the diagnosis of alcohol abuse and dependence. *Journal of Consulting & Clinical Psychology, 68,* 799–809.

Lannin, D. R., Mathews, H. F., Mitchell, J., Swanson, M. S., et al. (1998). Influence of socioeconomic and racial differences in late-stage presentation of breast cancer. *JAMA, 279,* 1801–1807.

Lantz, P. M., House, J. S., Lepkowski, J. M., Williams, D. R., et al. (1998). Socioeconomic factors, health behaviors, and mortality. *JAMA, 279,* 1703–1708.

Lanyon, R. I. (1986). Theory and treatment in child molestation. *Journal of Consulting and Clinical Psychology, 54,* 176–182.

LaRue, A. (1992). *Aging and neuropsychological assessment.* New York: Plenum.

LaRue, A., Dessonville, C., & Jarvik, L. F. (1985). Aging and mental disorders. In J. E. Birren & K. W. Schaie (Eds.), *Handbook of psychology of aging* (2nd ed.). New York: Van Nostrand-Reinhold.

Laumann, E. O., Gagnon, J. H., Michael, R. T., & Michaels, S. (1994). *The social organization of sexuality.* Chicago: University of Chicago Press.

Laumann, E. O., Paik, A., & Rosen, R. C. (1999). Sexual dysfunction in the United States: Prevalence and predictors. *JAMA, 281(6),* 537–544.

Lavoie, K. L., Miller, S. B., Conway, M., & Fleet, R. P. (2001). Anger, negative emotions, and cardiovascular reactivity during interpersonal conflict in women. *Journal of Psychosomatic Research, 15,* 503–512.

Law, M., & Tang, J. L. (1995). An analysis of the effectiveness of interventions intended to help people stop smoking. *Archives of Internal Medicine, 155,* 1933–1941.

Lawton, M., Kleban, M. H., Dean, J., & Rajagopal, D. (1992). The factorial generality of brief positive and negative affect measures. *Journals of Gerontology, 47,* P228–P237.

Lazarus, A. A. (1997). *Brief but comprehensive psychotherapy: The multimodal way.* New York: Springer-Verlag.

Lazarus, R. S. (1966). *Psychological stress and the coping process.* New York: McGraw-Hill.

Lazarus, R. S., & Folkman, S. (1984). *Stress, appraisal, and coping.* New York: Springer-Verlag.

Lazo, J. (1995). True or false: Expert testimony on repressed memory. *Loyola of Los Angeles Law Review, 28,* 1345–1413.

Leahy, R. L. (2003). *Cognitive Therapy Techniques: A Practitioner's Guide.* NY: Guilford Press.

Lebow, J. L., & Gurman, A. S. (1995). Research assessing couple and family therapy. *Annual Review of Psychology, 46,* 27–57.

Lechner, S. C., Antoni, M. H., Lydston, D., Laperrier, A., Ishii, M., Devieux, J., Stanley, H., Ironson, G., Schneiderman, N., Brondolo, E., Tobin, J., & Weiss, S. (2003). Cognitive–behavioral interventions improve quality of life in women with AIDS. *Journal of Psychosomatic Research, 54,* 253–261.

Le Couteur, A., Bailey, A., Goode, S., Pickles, A., Robertson, S., Gottesman, I., & Rutter, M. (1996). A broader phenotype of autism: The clinical spectrum in twins. *Journal of Child Psychology and Psychiatry and Allied Disciplines, 37,* 785–801.

Lee, S., Lee, A. M., Ngai, E., Lee, D. T. S., & Wing, Y. K. (2001). Rationale for food refusal in Chinese patients with anorexia nervosa. *International Journal of Eating Disorders, 29,* 224–229.

Lee, V. E., Brooks-Gunn, J., & Schnur, E. (1988). Does Head Start work? A 1-year follow-up comparison of disadvantaged children attending Head Start, no preschool, and other preschool programs. *Developmental Psychology, 24,* 210–222.

Leenaars, A. A., & Lester, D. (1995). Impact of suicide prevention centers on suicide in Canada. *Crisis, 16,* 39.

Legido, A., Tonyes, L., Carter, D., Schoemaker, A., DiGeorge, A., & Grover, W. D. (1993). Treatment variables and intellectual outcome in children with classic phenylketonuria: A single-center-based study. *Clinical Pediatrics, 32,* 417–425.

Lehman, A. F., Kreyenbuhl, J., Buchanan, R. W., et al. (2004). The schizophrenia patient outcomes research team (PORT): Updated treatment recommendations 2003. *Schizophrenia Bulletin, 30,* 193–217.

Lehman, A. F., Steinwachs, D. M., & the survey co-investigators from the Schizophrenia Patient Outcomes Research Team (PORT) client survey. (1998). Patterns of usual care for schizophrenia: Initial results from the Schizophrenia Patient Outcomes Research Team (PORT) client survey. *Schizophrenia Bulletin, 24,* 11–20.

Lehrer, P. M., Isenberg, S., & Hochron, S. M. (1993). Asthma and emotion: A review. *Journal of Asthma, 30,* 5–21.

Lehrer, P. M., & Woolfolk, R. L. (1993). *Principles and practice of stress management* (2nd ed.). New York: Guilford.

Leibenluft, E. (1996). Women with bipolar illness: Clinical and research issues. *American Journal of Psychiatry, 153,* 163–173.

Leiblum, S. R. (1997). Sexual pain disorders. In G. O. Gabbard & S. D. Atkinson (Eds.), *Synopsis of treatments of psychiatric disorders* (2nd ed., pp. 805–810). Washington, DC: American Psychiatric Press.

Leischow, S. J., Ranger-Moore, J., & Lawrence, D. (2000). Addressing social and cultural disparities in tobacco use. *Addictive Behaviors, 25,* 821–831.

Leit, R. A., Gray, J. J., & Pope, H. G. (2002). The media's presentation of the ideal male body: A cause for muscle dysmorphia? *International Journal of Eating Disorders, 31,* 334–338.

Leit, R. A., Pope, H. G., & Gray, J. J. (2001). Cultural expectations of muscularity in men: The evolution of playgirl centerfolds. *International Journal of Eating Disorders, 29,* 90–93.

Leitenberg, H., Gross, H., Peterson, H., & Rosen, J. C. (1984). Analysis of an anxiety model in the process of change during exposure plus response prevention treatment of bulimia nervosa. *Behavior Therapy, 15,* 3–20.

Lenzenweger, M. F. (2001). Reaction time slowing during high-load, sustained-attention task performance in relation to psychometrically identified schizotypy. *Journal of Abnormal Psychology, 110,* 290–296.

Lenzenweger, M. F., Dworkin, R. H., & Wethington, E. (1991). Examining the underlying structure of schizophrenic phenomenology: Evidence for a 3-process model. *Schizophrenia Bulletin, 17,* 515–524.

Leon, A. C., Portera, L., & Weissman, M. M. (1995). The social costs of anxiety disorders. *British Journal of Psychiatry, 166*(Suppl. 27), 19–22.

Leon, G. R., Fulkerson, J. A., Perry, C. L., & Early-Zald, M. B. (1995). Prospective analysis of personality and behavioral vulnerabilities and gender influences in the later development of disordered eating. *Journal of Abnormal Psychology, 104,* 140–149.

Leon, G. R., Fulkerson, J. A., Perry, C. L., Peel, P. K., & Klump, K. L. (1999). Three to four year prospective evaluation of personality and behavioral risk factors for later disordered eating in adolescent girls and boys. *Journal of Youth and Adolescence, 28,* 181–196.

Lerman, C., Caporaso, N. E., Audrain, J., Main, D., Bowman, E. D., et al. (1999). Evidence suggesting the role of specific genetic factors in cigarette smoking. *Health Psychology, 18,* 14–20.

Leslie, D. L., & Rosenheck, R. A. (2004). Incidence of newly diagnosed diabetes attributable to atypical antipsychotic medications. *American Journal of Psychiatry, 161,* 1709–1711.

Lester, D. (1991). Do suicide prevention centers prevent suicide? *Homeostasis in Health and Disease, 33,* 190–194.

Lester, D. (1995). Which nations establish suicide prevention centers? *Psycological Reports, 77,* 1298.

Leucht, S., Barnes, T. R. E., Kissling, W., Engel, R. R., Correll, C., & Kane, J. M. (2003). Relapse prevention in schizophrenia with new-generation antipsychotics: A systematic review and exploratory meta-analysis of randomized, controlled trials. *American Journal of Psychiatry, 160,* 1209–1222.

Leung, P. W., Luk, S. L., Ho, T. P., Taylor, E., Mak, F. L., & Bacon-Shone, J. (1996). The diagnosis and prevalence of hyperactivity in Chinese schoolboys. *British Journal of Psychiatry, 168,* 486–496.

Levav, I., Kohn, R., Golding, J. M., & Weissman, M. M. (1997). Vulnerability of Jews to major depression. *American Journal of Psychiatry, 154,* 941–947.

Levenson, R. W., Carstensen, L. L., & Gottman, J. M. (1994). Influence of age and gender on affect, physiology, and their interrelations: A study of long-term marriages. *Journal of Personality and Social Psychology, 67,* 56–68.

Levenston, G. K., Patrick, C. J., Bradley, M. M., & Lang, P. J. (2000). The psychopath as observer: Emotion and attention in picture processing. *Journal of Abnormal Psychology, 109,* 373–385.

Leventhal, B. L., Cook, E. H., Morford, M., Ravitz, A. J., Heller, W., & Freedman, D. X. (1993). Clinical and neurochemical effects of fenfluramine in children with autism. *The Journal of Neuropsychiatry and Clinical Neurosciences, 5,* 307–315.

Levitan, R. D., Kaplan, A. S., Joffe, R. T., Levitt, A. J., & Brown, G. M. (1997). Hormonal and subjective responses to intravenous meta-chlorophenylpiperazine in bulimia nervosa. *Archives of General Psychiatry, 54,* 521–528.

Levitsky, A., & Perls, F. S. (1970). The rules and games of Gestalt therapy. In J. Fagan & I. L. Shepherd (Eds.), *Gestalt therapy now: Theory, techniques, applications.* Palo Alto, CA: Science & Behavior Books.

Levy, F., Hay, D. A., McStephen, M., Wood, C., & Waldman, I. (1997). Attention-deficit hyperactivity disorder: A category or a continuum? Genetic analysis of a large-scale twin study. *Journal of the American Academy of Child and Adolescent Psychiatry, 36,* 737–744.

Lewinsohn, P. M., & Clarke, G. N. (1999). Psychosocial treatments for adolescent depression. *Clinical Psychology Review, 19,* 329–342.

Lewinsohn, P. M., & Gotlib, I. H. (1995). Behavioral and cognitive treatment of depression. In E. E. Becker & W. R. Leber (Eds.), *Handbook of depression* (pp. 352–375). New York: Guilford.

Lewinsohn, P. M., Joiner, T. E., & Rohde, P. (2001). Evaluation of cognitive diathesis-stress models in predicting major depressive disorder. *Journal of Abnormal Psychology, 110,* 203–215.

Lewinsohn, P. M., Petit, J. W., Joiner, T. E., & Seeley, J. R. (2003). The symptomatic expression of major depressive disorder in adolescents and young adults. *Journal of Abnormal Psychology, 112,* 244–252.

Lewinsohn, P. M., Roberts, R. E., Seeley, J. R., Rohde, P., Gotlib, I. H., & Hops, H. (1994). Adolescent psychopathology: 2. Psychosocial risk factors for depression. *Journal of Abnormal Psychology, 103,* 302–315.

Lewinsohn, P. M., Rohde, P., Seeley, J. R., Klein, D. N., & Gotlib, I. H. (2000). Natural course of adolescent major depressive disorder in a community sample: Predictors of recurrence in young adults. *American Journal of Psychiatry, 157,* 1584–1591.

Lewis, D. O., Yeager, C. A., Swica, Y., Pincus, J. H., & Lewis, M. (1997). Objective documentation of child abuse and dissociation on 12 murderers with dissociative identity disorder. *American Journal of Psychiatry, 154,* 1703–1710.

Li, F., Duncan, T. E., & Hops, H. (2001). Examining developmental trajectories in adolescent alcohol use using piecewise growth mixture modeling analysis. *Journal of Studies on Alcohol, 62,* 199–210.

Li, T.-K., Lumeng, L., McBride, W. J., & Waller, M. B. (1981). Indiana selection studies on alcohol related behaviors. In R. A. McClearn, R. A. Deitrich, & V. G. Erwin (Eds.), *Development of animal models as pharmacogenetic tools.* Washington, DC: U.S. Government Printing Office.

Liberman, R. P., Eckman, T. A., Kopelowicz, A., & Stolar, D. (2000). *Friendship and intimacy module.* Camarillo, CA: Psychiatric Rehabilitation Consultants, PO Box 2867, Camarillo, CA 93011.

Liberman, R. P., Wallace, C. J., Blackwell, G., Kopelowicz, J. V., et al. (1998). Skills training versus psychosocial occupational therapy for persons with persistent schizophrenia. *American Journal of Psychiatry, 155,* 1087–1091.

Liberto, J. G., Oslin, D. W., & Ruskin, P. E. (1996). Alcoholism in the older population. In L. L. Carstensen, B. A. Edelstein, & L. Dornbrand (Eds.), *The practical handbook of clinical gerontology* (pp. 324–348). Thousand Oaks, CA: Sage.

Lichenstein, P., & Annas, P. (2000). Heritability and prevalence of specific fears and phobias in childhood. *Journal of Child Psychology & Psychiatry & Allied Disciplines, 41,* 927–937.

Liddle, H. A. (1999). Theory development in a family-based therapy for adolescent drug abuse. *Journal of Clinical Child Psychology, 28,* 521–532.

Lieberman, J. A., Stroup, T. S., et al. (2005). Effectiveness of antipsychotic drugs in patients with chronic schizophrenia. *New England Journal of Medicine, 353,* 1209–1223.

Lieberman, M. A., Yalom, J. D., & Miles, M. B. (1973). *Encounter groups: First facts.* New York: Basic Books.

Liebowitz, M. R., Heimberg, R. G., Fresco, D. M., Travers, J., & Stein, M. B. (2000). Social phobia or social anxiety disorder: What's in a name? *Archives of General Psychiatry, 57,* 191–192.

Liechti, M. E., Baumann, C., Gamma, A., & Vollenweider, F. X. (2000). Acute psychological effects of 3,4-methylenedioxymethamphetamine (MDMA, 'Ecstasy') are attenuated by the serotonin uptake inhibitor citalopram. *Neuropsychopharmacology, 22,* 513–521.

Lief, H. I., & Hubschman, L. (1993). Orgasm in the postoperative transsexual. *Archives of Sexual Behavior, 22,* 145–155.

Light, K. C., Dolan, C. A., Davis, M. R., & Sherwood, A. (1992). Cardiovascular responses to an active coping challenge as predictors of blood pressure patterns 10 to 15 years later. *Psychosomatic Medicine, 54,* 217–230.

Lilenfeld, L. R., Kaye, W. H., Greeno, C. G., Merikangas, K. R., Plotnicov, K., et al. (1998). A controlled family study of anorexia nervosa and bulimia nervosa: Psychiatric disorders in first-degree relatives and effects of proband comorbidity. *Archives of General Psychiatry, 55,* 603–610.

Lilenfeld, L. R., Kaye, W. H., Greeno, C. G., Merikangas, K. R., Plotnicov, K., et al. (1999). Psychiatric disorders in women with bulimia nervosa and their first-degree relatives: Effects of comorbid substance dependence. *International Journal of Eating Disorders, 22,* 253–264.

Lilienfeld, S. O., Lynn, S. J., Kirsch, I., Chaves, J. F., et al. (1999). Dissociative identity disorder and the sociogenic model: Recalling lessons from the past. *Psychological Bulletin, 125,* 507–523.

Lilienfeld, S. O., & Marino, L. (1999). Essentialism revisited: Evolutionary theory and the concept of mental disorder. *Journal of Abnormal Psychology, 108,* 400–411.

Lilienfeld, S. O., Wood, J. M., & Garb, H. N. (2000). The scientific status of projective techniques. *Psychological Science in the Public Interest, 1,* 27–66.

Lilly, R., Quirk, A., Rhodes, T., & Stimson, G. V. (2000). Sociality in methadone treatment: Understanding methadone treatment and service delivery as a social process. *Drugs: Education, Prevention & Policy, 7,* 163–178.

Lim, K. O., Adalsteinssom, E., Spielman, D., Sullivan, E. V., Rosenbloom, M. J., & Pfefferman, A. (1998). Proton magnetic resonance spectroscopic imaging of cortical gray and white matter in schizophrenia. *Archives of General Psychiatry, 55,* 346–353.

Lim, S., & Kim, J. (2005). Cognitive processing of emotional information in depression, panic, and somatoform disorder. *Journal of Abnormal Psychology, 114,* 50–61.

Lindemann, E., & Finesinger, I. E. (1938). The effect of adrenalin and mecholyl in states of anxiety in psychoneurotic patients. *American Journal of Psychiatry, 95,* 353–370.

Linehan, M. M. (1987). Dialectical behavior therapy for borderline personality disorder. *Bulletin of the Menninger Clinic, 51,* 261–276.

Linehan, M. M. (1993). *Cognitive-behavioral treatment of borderline personality disorder.* New York, NY: Guilford Press.

Linehan, M. M. (1997). Behavioral treatments of suicidal behaviors: Definitional obfuscation and treatment outcomes. In D. M. Stoff & J. J. Mann (Eds.), *Neurobiology of suicide* (pp. 302–327). New York: Annals of the New York Academy of Sciences.

Linehan, M. M., Armstrong, H. E., Suarez, A., Allmon, D., & Heard, H. L. (1991). Cognitive-behavioral treatment of chronically parasuicidal borderline patients. *Archives of General Psychiatry, 48,* 1060–1064.

Linehan, M. M., Goodstein, J. L., Nielsen, S. L., & Chiles, J. A. (1983). Reasons for staying alive when you are thinking of killing yourself. *Journal of Consulting and Clinical Psychology, 51,* 276–286.

Linehan, M. M., & Heard, H. L. (1999). Borderline personality disorder: Costs, course, and treatment outcomes. In N. E. Miller, & K. M. Magruder (Eds.), *Cost-effectiveness of psychotherapy: A guide for practitioners, researchers, and policymakers* (pp. 291–305). London, Oxford University Press.

Linehan, M. M., Heard, H. L., & Armstrong, H. E. (1993). Naturalistic follow-up of a behavioral treatment for chronically parasuicidal borderline patients. *Archives of General Psychiatry, 50,* 971–974.

Linehan, M. M., Schmidt, H., Dimeff, L. A., Craft, J. C., Kanter, J., & Comtois, K. A. (1999). Dialectical behavior therapy for patients with borderline personality disorder and drug-dependence. *American Journal on Addictions, 8,* 279–292.

Linehan, M. M., & Shearin, E. N. (1988). Lethal stress: A social-behavioral model of suicidal behavior. In S. Fisher & J. Reason (Eds.), *Handbook of life stress, cognition, and health.* New York: Wiley.

Link, B., Cullen, F., Frank, J., & Wozniak, J. (1987). The social rejection of former mental patients: Understanding why labels matter. *American Journal of Sociology, 92,* 1401–1500.

Links, P., Steiner, M., Boiago, I., & Irwin, D. (1990). Lithium therapy for borderline patients: Preliminary findings. *Journal of Personality Disorders, 4,* 173–181.

Links, P. S., Heslegrave, R., & van Reekum, R. (1998). Prospective follow-up of borderline personality disorder: Prognosis, prediction outcome, and Axis II comorbidity. *Canadian Journal of Psychiatry, 43,* 265–270.

Linn, R. T., Wolf, P. A., Bachman, D. L., & Knoefel, J. E. (1995). The "preclinical phase" of probable Alzheimer's disease: A 13-year prospective study of the Framingham cohort. *Archives of Neurology, 52,* 485–490.

Linnet, K. M., Dalsgaard, S., Obel, C., et al. (2003). Maternal lifestyle factors in pregnancy risk of attention deficit hyperactivity disorder and associated behaviors: Review of the current evidence. *American Journal of Psychiatry, 160,* 1028–1040.

Linney, J. A. (1989). Optimizing research strategies in the schools. In L. A. Bond & B. E. Compas (Eds.), *Primary prevention and promotion in the schools* (pp. 50–76). Newbury Park, CA: Sage.

Liotti, M., Mayberg, H. S., McGinnis, S., Brannan, S. L., & Jerabek, P. (2002). Unmasking disease-specific cerebral blood flow abnormalities: Mood challenge in patients with remitted unipolar depression. *American Journal of Psychiatry, 159,* 1830–1840.

Lipsitz, J. D., Mannuzza, S., Klein, D. F., Ross, D. C., & Fyer, A. J. (1999). Specific phobia 10–16 years after treatment. *Depression and Anxiety, 10,* 105–111.

Litrownik, A. F., & Castillo-Cañez, I. (2000). Childhood maltreatment: Treatment of abuse and incest survivors. In C. R. Snyder & R. E. Ingram (Eds.), *Handbook of psychological change* (pp. 520–545). New York: John Wiley & Sons.

Litz, B. T., Gray, M. J., Bryant, R. A., & Adler, A. B. (2002). Early intervention for trauma: Current status and future directions. *Clinical Psychology: Science and Practice, 9,* 112–134.

Livesley, W. J., Jang, K. L., & Vernon, P. A. (1998). Phenotypic and genetic structure of traits in delineating personality disorder. *Archives of General Psychiatry, 55,* 941–948.

Livesley, W. J., Schroeder, M. L., Jackson, D. N., & Jung, K. L. (1994). Categorical distinctions in the study of personality disorder: Implications for classification. *Journal of Abnormal Psychology, 103,* 6–17.

Livingston, G., Kitchen, G., Manela, M., Katona, C., & Copeland, J. (2001). Persecutory symptoms and perceptual disturbance in a community sample of older people: The Islington study. *International Journal of Geriatric Psychiatry, 16,* 462–468.

Lobitz, W. C., & Post, R. D. (1979). Parameters of self-reinforcement and depression. *Journal of Abnormal Psychology, 88,* 33–41.

Lock, J., & LeGrange, D. (2001). Can family-based treatment of anorexia nervosa be manualized? *Journal of Psychotherapy Practice and Research, 10,* 253–261.

Lock, J., LeGrange, D., Agras, W. S., & Dare, C. (2001). *Treatment manual for anorexia nervosa: A family-based approach.* New York: Guilford.

Lockwood, K. A., Alexopoulos, G. S., Kakuma, T., & van Gorp, W. G. (2000). Subtypes of cognitive impairment in depressed older adults. *American Journal of Geriatric Psychiatry, 8,* 201–208.

Loeber, R., Burke, J. D., Lahey, B. B., Winters, A., & Zera, M. (2000). Oppositional defiant and conduct disorder: A review of the past 10 years, Part I. *Journal of the American Academy of Child & Adolescent Psychiatry, 39,* 1468–1484.

Loeber, R., & Farrington, D. P. (1998). *Serious and violent juvenile offenders: Risk factors and successful interventions.* Thousand Oaks, CA: Sage.

Loeber, R., & Hay, D. (1997). Key issues in the development of aggression and violence from childhood to early adulthood. *Annual Review of Psychology, 48,* 371–410.

Loeber, R., & Keenan, K. (1994). Interaction between conduct disorder and its comorbid conditions: Effects of age and gender. *Clinical Psychology Review, 14,* 497–523.

Loewenstein, R. J. (1991). Psychogenic amnesia and psychogenic fugue: A comprehensive review. In A. Tasman & S. M. Goldfinger (Eds.), *American psychiatric press review of psychiatry* (pp. 189–222). Washington, DC: American Psychiatric Press.

Loftus, E. F. (1993). The reality of repressed memories. *American Psychologist, 48,* 518–537.

Loftus, E. F. (1997). Memory for a past that never was. *Current Directions in Psychological Science, 6,* 60–62.

Logan, T. K., Cole, J., & Leukefeld, C. (2002). Women, sex, and HIV: Social and contextual factors, meta-analysis of published interventions, and implications for practice and research. *Psychological Bulletin, 128,* 851–885.

Lohmueller, K. E., Pearce, C. L., Pike, M., Lander, E. S., & Hirschhorn, J. N. (2003). Meta-analysis of genetic association studies supports a contribution of common variants to susceptibility to common disease. *Nature Genetics, 33,* 177–182.

Lollis, C. M., Strothers, H. S., Chitwood, D. D., & McGhee, M. (2000). Sex, drugs and HIV: Does methadone maintenance reduce drug use and risky sexual behavior? *Journal of Behavioral Medicine, 23,* 545–557.

London, P. (1964). *The modes and morals of psychotherapy.* New York: Holt, Rinehart & Winston.

Long, P., Forehand, R., Wierson, M., & Morgan, A. (1994). Does parent training with young noncompliant children have long-term effects? *Behaviour Research and Therapy, 32,* 101–107.

Long, W. R. (1995, November 24). A changing world proves deadly to Brazil Indians. *Los Angeles Times,* pp. A1, A47, A48.

Longshore, D., Urada, D., Evans, E., Hser, Y.-I., Prendergast, M., Hawken, A., Bunch, T., & Ettner, S. (2003). *Evaluation of the Substance Abuse and Crime Prevention Act, 2003 Report.* Online at http://www.uclaisap.org/prop36/reports.htm.

Lonigan, C. J., Phillips, B. M., & Hooe, E. S. (2003). Relations of positive and negative affectivity to anxiety and depression in children: Evidence from a latent variable longitudinal study. *Journal of Consulting and Clinical Psychology, 71,* 465–481.

Looman, J. (1995). Sexual fantasies of child molesters. *Canadian Journal of Behavioural Science, 27,* 321–332.

Looper, K. J., & Kirmayer, L. J. (2002). Behavioral medicine approaches to somatoform disorders. *Journal of Consulting and Clinical Psychology, 70,* 810–827.

Lopez, S. R. (1989). Patient variable biases in clinical judgment: Conceptual overview and methodological considerations. *Psychological Bulletin, 106,* 184–203.

Lopez, S. R. (1994). Latinos and the expression of psychopathology: A call for direct assessment of cultural influences. In C. Telles & M. Karno (Eds.), *Latino mental health: Current research and policy perspectives.* Los Angeles: UCLA.

Lopez, S. R. (1996). Testing ethnic minority children. In B. B. Wolman (Ed.), *The encyclopedia of psychology, psychiatry, and psychoanalysis.* New York: Holt.

Lopez, S. R. (2002). Teaching culturally informed psychological assessment: Conceptual issues and demonstrations. *Journal of Personality Assessment, 79,* 226–234.

Lopez, S. R., Lopez, A. A., & Fong, K. T. (1991). Mexican Americans' initial preferences for counselors: The role of ethnic factors. *Journal of Counseling Psychology, 38,* 487–496.

Lopez, S. R., Nelson, K. A., Snyder, K. S., & Mintz, J. (1999). Attributions and affective reactions of family members and course of schizophrenia. *Journal of Abnormal Psychology, 108,* 307–314.

Lopez-Ibor, J. J., Jr. (2003). Cultural adaptations of current psychiatric classifications: Are they the solution? *Psychopathology, 36,* 114–119.

LoPiccolo, J. (1992). Post-modern sex therapy for erectile failure. In R. C. Rosen & S. R. Leiblum (Eds.), *Erectile failure: Assessment and treatment.* New York: Guilford.

LoPiccolo, J., & Hogan, D. R. (1979). Multidimensional treatment of sexual dysfunction. In O. F. Pomerleau & J. P. Brady (Eds.), *Behavioral medicine: Theory and practice.* Baltimore, MD: Williams & Wilkins.

LoPiccolo, J., & Lobitz, W. C. (1972). The role of masturbation in the treatment of orgasmic dysfunction. *Archives of Sexual Behavior, 2,* 163–171.

Lovaas, O. I. (1987). Behavioral treatment and normal educational and intellectual functioning in young autistic children. *Journal of Consulting and Clinical Psychology, 55,* 3–9.

Lovallo, W. R., & Al'Absi, M. (1998). Hemodynamics during rest and behavioral stress in normotensive men at high risk for hypertension. *Psychophysiology, 35,* 47–53.

Loy, C., & Schneider, L. (2004). Galantamine for Alzheimer's disease. *The Cochrane Database of Systematic Reviews,* Issue 4. Art. No.: CD001747.pub2.

Lozano, B. L., & Johnson, S. L. (2001). Can personality traits predict increases in manic and depressive symptoms? *Journal of Affective Disorders, 63,* 103–111.

Luborsky, L., & Spence, D. P. (1978). Quantitative research on psychoanalytic therapy. In S. L. Garfield & A. E. Bergin (Eds.), *Handbook of psychotherapy and behavior change: An empirical analysis* (2nd ed.). New York: Wiley.

Lutgendorf, S., Antoni, M. H., Ironson, G., Klimas, N., Kumar, M., Starr, K., McCabe, P., Cleven, K., Fletcher, M. A., & Schneiderman, N. (1997). Cognitive-behavioral stress management decreases dysphoric mood and herpes simplex virus-type 2 antibody titers in symptomatic

HIV-seropositive gay men. *Journal of Consulting and Clinical Psychology, 65*, 31–43.

Lydiard, R. B., & Monnier, J. (2004). Pharmacological treatment. In R. G. Heimberg, C. L. Turk, & D. S. Mennin (Eds.), *Generalized anxiety disorder.* (pp. 351–381). New York: Guilford.

Lyketsos, C. G., Sheppard, J. M. E., Steele, C. D., Kopunek, S., Steinberg, M., & Baker, A. S., et al. (2000). Randomized, placebo-controlled, double-blind clinical trial of sertraline in the treatment of depression complicating alzheimer's disease: Initial results from the depression in alzheimer's disease study. *American Journal of Psychiatry, 157*, 1686–1689.

Lykken, D. T. (1957). A study of anxiety in the sociopathic personality. *Journal of Abnormal and Social Psychology, 55*, 6–10.

Lynam, D. R. (1998). Early identification of the fledgling psychopath: Locating the psychopathic child in the current nomenclature. *Journal of Abnormal Psychology, 107*, 566–575.

Lynam, D., & Henry, B. (2001). The role of neuropsychological deficits in conduct disorders. In J. Hill & B. Maughan (Eds.), *Conduct disorders in childhood and adolescence* (pp. 235–263). New York: Cambridge University Press.

Lynam, D., Moffitt, T. E., & Stouthamer-Loeber, M. (1993). Explaining the relation between IQ and delinquency: Race, class, test motivation, school failure, or self-control. *Journal of Abnormal Psychology, 102*, 187–196.

Lynam, D. R., & Widiger, T. A. (2001). Using the five-factor model to represent DSM-IV personality disorders: An expert consensus approach. *Journal of Abnormal Psychology, 110*, 401–412.

Lynch, A., Glod, C. A., & Fitzgerald, F. (2001). Psychopharmacologic treatment of adolescent depression. *Archives of Psychiatric Nursing, 15*, 41–47.

Lynch, J., Kaplan, G. A., Salonen, R., & Salonen, J. T. (1997). Workplace demands, economic reward, and the progression of atherosclerosis. *Circulation, 96*, 302–307.

Lynch, J., Krause, N., Kaplan, G. A., Tuomilehto, J., & Salonen, J. T. (1997). Workplace conditions, socioeconomic status, and the risk of mortality and acute myocardial infarction. *American Journal of Public Health, 87*, 617–622.

Lynch, J. W., Kaplan, G. A., Cohen, R. D., Tuomilehto, J., & Salonen, J. T. (1996). Do cardiovascular risk factors explain the relation between socioeconomic status, risk of all-cause mortality, cardiovascular mortality, and acute myocardial infarction? *American Journal of Epidemiology, 144*, 934–942.

Lynn, S. J., Lock, T., Loftus, E. F., Krackow, E., & Lilienfeld, S. O. (2003). The remembrance of things past: Problematic memory recovery techniques in psychotherapy. In S. J. Lynn and S. O. Lilienfeld (Eds.), *Science and pseudoscience in clinical psychology.* (pp. 205–239). New York: Guilford.

Lynskey, M. T., Heath, A. C., Bucholz, K. K., et al. (2003). Escalation of drug use in early-onset cannabis users vs co-twin controls. *JAMA, 289*, 427–433.

Lyon, H. M., Startup, M., & Bentall, R. P. (1999). Social cognition and the manic defense: Attribution, selective attention, and self-schema in bipolar affective disorder. *Journal of Abnormal Psychology, 108*, 273–282.

Lyons, M. J., True, W. R., Eisen, S. A., et al. (1995). Differential heritability of adult and juvenile antisocial traits. *Archives of General Psychiatry, 52*, 906–915.

Lystad, M. M. (1957). Social mobility among selected groups of schizophrenics. *American Sociological Review, 22*, 288–292.

Ma, G. X., & Shive, S. (2000). A comparative analysis of perceived risks and substance abuse among ethnic groups. *Addictive Behaviors, 25*, 361–371.

Ma, S. H., & Teasdale, J. D. (2004). Mindfulness-based cognitive therapy for depression: Replication and exploration of differential relapse prevention effects. *Journal of Consulting and Clinical Psychology, 72*, 31–40.

Maccoby, N., & Altman, D. G. (1988). Disease prevention in communities: The Stanford Heart Disease Prevention Program. In R. H. Price, E. L. Cowen, R. P. Lorion, & J. Ramos-McKay (Eds.), *14 ounces of prevention: A casebook for practitioners* (pp. 165–174). Washington, DC: American Psychological Association.

MacDonald, A. W., & Carter, C. S. (2003). Event-related fMRI study of context processing in dorsolateral prefrontal cortex of patients with schizophrenia. *Journal of Abnormal Psychology, 112*, 689–697.

MacDonald, V. M., Tsiantis, J., Achenbach, T. M., Motti-Stefanidi, F., & Richardson, C. (1995). Competencies and problems reported by parents of Greek and American children, ages 6–11. *European Child and Adolescent Psychiatry, 4*, 1–13.

MacGregor, M. W. (1996). Multiple personality disorder: Etiology, treatment, and techniques from a psychodynamic perspective. *Psychoanalytic Psychology, 13*, 389–402.

Macklin, M. L., Metzger, L. J., Litz, B. T., McNally, R. J., Lasko, N. B., et al. (1998). Lower precombat intelligence is a risk factor for posttraumatic stress disorder. *Journal of Consulting and Clinical Psychology, 66*, 323–326.

MacLeod, A. K., Haynes, C., & Sensky, T. (1998). Attributions about common bodily sensations: Their associations with hypochondriasis and anxiety. *Psychological Medicine, 28*, 225–228.

MacNamara, M. (1993). Fade away: The rise and fall of the repressed memory theory in the courtroom. *California Lawyer, 15*, 36–41.

Madonna, P. G., van Scoyk, S., & Jones, D. B. (1991). Family interactions within incest and nonincest families. *American Journal of Psychiatry, 148*, 46–49.

Maffei, C., Fossati, A., Agostini, I., Barraco, A., et al. (1997). Interrater reliability and internal consistency of the Structured Clinical Interview for Axis II Personality Disorders (SCID-II), Version 2.0. *Journal of Personality Disorders, 11*, 279–284.

Mahoney, L. J. (1977). Early diagnosis of breast cancer: The breast self-examination problem. *Progress in Clinical and Biological Research, 12*, 203–206.

Mahoney, M. J., & Moes, A. J. (1997). Complexity and psychotherapy: Promising dialogues and practical issues. In F. Masterpasque & A. Perna (Eds.), *The psychological meaning of chaos: Self-organization in human development and psychotherapy.* Washington, DC: American Psychological Association.

Maier, S. F., & Watkins, L. R. (1998). Cytokines for psychologists: Implications of bidirectional immune-to-brain communication for understanding behavior, mood, and cognition. *Psychological Review, 105*, 83–107.

Maj, M., Pirozzi, R., Magliono, L., & Bartoli, L. (1998). Long-term outcome of lithium prophylaxis in bipolar disorder: A 5-year prospective study of 402 patients at a lithium clinic. *American Journal of Psychiatry, 155*, 30–35.

Malamuth, N. M. (1998). An evolutionary-based model integrating research on the characteristics of sexually coercive men. In J. G. Adair and D. Belanger (Eds.), *Advances in psychological science, Volume 1: Social, personal, and cultural aspects.* (pp. 151–184). Hove, England: Psychology Press/Erlbaum.

Malamuth, N. M., & Brown, L. M. (1994). Sexually aggresive men's perceptions of women's communications: Testing three explanations. *Journal of Personality and Social Psychology, 67*, 699–712.

Malamuth, N. M., & Check, J. V. P. (1983). Sexual arousal to rape depictions: Individual differences. *Journal of Abnormal Psychology, 92*, 55–67.

Malaspina, D., Goetz, R. R., Yale, S., et al. (2000). Relation of familial schizophrenia to negative symptoms but not to the deficit syndrome. *American Journal of Psychiatry, 157*, 994–1003.

Malcolm, R., Herron, J. E., Anton, R. F., Roberts, J., & Moore, J. (2000). Recurrent detoxification may elevate alcohol craving as measured by the Obsessive Compulsive Drinking scale. *Alcohol, 20*, 181–185.

Maldonado, J. R., Butler, L. D., & Spiegel, D. (1998). Treatments for dissociative disorders. In P. E. Nathan & J. M. Gorman (Eds.), *A guide to treatments that work* (pp. 423–446). New York: Oxford University Press.

Maletzky, B. M. (1993). Factors associated with success and failure in the behavioral and cognitive treatment of sex offenders. *Annals of Sex Research, 6*, 241–258.

Maletzky, B. M. (1997). Exhibitionism: Assessment and treatment. In D. R. Laws & W. O'Donohue (Eds.), *Sexual deviance* (pp. 40–74). New York: Guilford.

Maletzky, B. M. (2000). Exhibitionism. In M. Hersen & M. Biaggio (Eds.), *Effective brief therapy: A clinician's guide* (pp. 235–257). New York: Plenum.

Maletzky, B. M. (2002). The paraphilias: research and treatment. In P. E. Nathan & J. M. Gorman (Eds.), *A guide to treatments that work* (pp. 525–558). New York: Oxford University Press.

Malik, S., Wong, N. D., Franklin, S. S., Kamath, T. V., L'Italien, G. J., Pio, J. R., & Williams, G. R. (2004). Impact of the metabolic syndrome on mortality from coronary heart disease, cardiovascular disease, and all causes in United States adults. *Circulation, 110*, 1245–1250.

Malina, A., Gaskill, J., McConaha, C., Frank, G. K., LaVia, M., Scholar, L., & Kaye, W. H. (2003). Olanzapine treatment of anorexia nervosa: A retrospective study. *International Journal of Eating Disorders, 33*, 234–237.

Malizia, A. L. (2003). Brain imaging and anxiety disorders. In D. Nutt and J. Ballenger (Eds.), *Anxiety disorders* (pp. 201–228). Malden, MA: Blackwell.

Malone, K. M., Oquendo, M. A., Haas, G. L., Ellis, S. P., Li, S., & Mann, J. J. (2000). Protective factors against suicidal acts in major depression: Reasons for living. *American Journal of Psychiatry, 157*, 1084–1088.

Manji, H. K., Chen, G., Shimon, H., Hsiao, J. K., Potter, W. Z., & Belmaker, R. H. (1995). Guanine nucleotide-binding proteins in bipolar affective disorder: Effects of long-term lithium treatment. *Archives of General Psychiatry, 52*, 135–144.

Mann, V. A., & Brady, S. (1988). Reading disability: The role of language deficiencies. *Journal of Consulting and Clinical Psychology, 56*, 811–816.

Mannuzza, S., Klein, R. G., Bonagura, N., Malloy, P., Giampino, T. L., & Addalli, K. A. (1991). Hyperactive boys almost grown up: 5. Replication of psychiatric status. *Archives of General Psychiatry, 48*, 77–83.

Mannuzza, S., Klein, R. G., & Moulton, J. L. (2003). Does stimulant medication place children at risk for adult substance abuse? A controlled, prospective follow-up study. *Journal of Child and Adolescent Psychopharmacology, 13*, 273–282.

Mansdorf, I. J., Calapai, P., Caselli, L., & Burstein, Y. (1999). Reducing psychotropic medication usage in nursing home residents: The effects of behaviorally oriented psychotherapy. *The Behavior Therapist, 22*, 21–39.

Mann, J. J., Huang, Y. Y., Underwood, M. D., Kassir, S. A., Oppenheim, S., & Kelly, T. M., et al. (2000). A serotonin transporter gene promoter polymorphism (5-HTTLPR) and prefrontal cortical binding in major depression and suicide. *Archives of General Psychiatry, 57*, 729–738.

Manuck, S. B., Kaplan, J. R., & Clarkson, T. B. (1983). Behaviorally induced heart rate reactivity and atherosclerosis in cynomolgus monkeys. *Psychosomatic Medicine, 49,* 95–108.

Maramba, G. G., & Nagayama-Hall, G. C. (2002). Meta-analyses of ethnic match as a predictor of dropout, utilization, and level of functioning. *Cultural Diversity and Ethnic Minority Psychology, 8,* 290–297.

Marcantonio, E. R., Flacker, J. M., Wright, R. J., & Resnick, N. M. (2001). Reducing delirium after hip fracture: A randomized trial. *Journal of the American Geriatrics Society, 49,* 516–522.

March, J., Silva, S., Petrycki, S., et al. (2004). Fluoxetine, cognitive-behavioral therapy, and their combination for adolescents with depression: Treatment for adolescents with depression study (TADS) randomized controlled trial. *JAMA, 292,* 807–820.

Marcus, J., Hans, S. L., Nagier, S., Auerbach, J. G., Mirsky, A. F., & Aubrey, A. (1987). Review of the NIMH Israeli Kibbutz-City and the Jerusalem infant development study. *Schizophrenia Bulletin, 13,* 425–438.

Marder, S. R., Wirshing, W. C., Glynn, S. M., Wirshing, D. A., Mintz, J., & Liberman, R. P. (1999). Risperidone and haloperidol in maintenance treatment: Interactions with psychosocial treatments. *Schizophrenia Research, 36,* 288.

Marengo, J., & Westermeyer, J. F. (1996). Schizophrenia and delusional disorder. In L. L. Carstensen, B. A. Edelstein, & L. Dornbrand (Eds.), *The practical handbook of clinical gerontology* (pp. 255–273). Thousand Oaks, CA: Sage.

Margolin, G. (1982). Ethical and legal considerations in marital and family therapy. *American Psychologist, 37,* 788–801.

Margraf, J., Ehlers, A., & Roth, W. T. (1986). Sodium lactate infusions and panic attacks: A review and critique. *Psychosomatic Medicine, 48,* 23–51.

Marijuana research findings. (1980). Washington, DC: U.S. Government Printing Office.

Markman, H. J., Floyd, F. J., Stanley, S. M., & Storaasli, R. D. (1988). Prevention of marital distress: A longitudinal investigation. *Journal of Consulting and Clinical Psychology, 56,* 210–217.

Markovitz, P. J., & Markovitz, P. J. (2004). Recent trends in the pharmacotherapy of personality disorders. *Journal of Personality Disorders, 18,* 99–101.

Markowitz, J. C. (1994). Psychotherapy of dysthymia. *American Journal of Psychiatry, 151,* 1114–1121.

Marks, I. M. (1995). Advances in behavioral-cognitive therapy of social phobia. *Journal of Clinical Psychiatry, 56,* 25–31.

Marlatt, G. A. (1983). The controlled drinking controversy: A commentary. *American Psychologist, 38,* 1097–1110.

Marlatt, G. A., & Gordon, J. R. (1985). (Eds.), *Relapse prevention: Maintenance strategies in the treatment of addictive behaviors.* New York: Guilford.

Marlowe, D. H. (2001). *Psychological and psychosocial consequences of combat and deployment: With special emphasis on the Gulf War.* Santa Monica, CA: RAND.

Marmar, C., & Horowitz, M. J. (1988). Diagnosis and phase-oriented treatment of post-traumatic stress disorders. In J. Wilson (Ed.), *Human adaptation to extreme stress: From the Holocaust to Vietnam.* New York: Brunner/Mazel.

Marmor, J. (1971). Dynamic psychotherapy and behavior therapy: Are they irreconcilable? *Archives of General Psychiatry, 24,* 22–28.

Marmot, M. G., Bosma, H., Hemingway, H., Brunner, E., & Stansfeld, S. (1997). Contribution of job control and other risk factors to social variations in coronary heart disease incidence. *The Lancet, 350,* 235–239.

Marques, J. K., Day, D. M., Nelson, C., & West, M. A. (1994). Effects of cognitive-behavioral treatment on sex offender recidivism: Preliminary results of a longitudinal study. *Criminal Justice and Behavior, 21*(1), 28–54.

Marrazzi, M. A., & Luby, E. D. (1986). An auto-addiction model of chronic anorexia nervosa. *International Journal of Eating Disorders, 5,* 191–208.

Marshall, L. A., & Cooke, D. J. (1999). The childhood experiences of psychopaths: A retrospective study of familial and societal factors. *Journal of Personality Disorders, 13,* 211–225.

Marshall, W. L. (1997). Pedophilia: Psychopathology and theory. In D. R. Laws & W. O'Donohue (Eds.), *Sexual deviance* (pp. 152–174). New York: Guilford.

Marshall, W. L., Barbaree, H. E., & Christophe, D. (1986). Sexual offenders against female children: Sexual preferences for age of victims and type of behaviour. *Canadian Journal of Behavioural Science, 18,* 424–439.

Marshall, W. L., Serran, G. A., & Cortoni, F. A. (2000). Childhood attachments, sexual abuse, and their relationship to adult coping in child molesters. *Sexual Abuse: A Journal of Research and Treatment, 12,* 17–26.

Marson, D. C. (2001). Loss of competency in Alzheimer's disease: Conceptual and psychometric approaches. *International Journal of Law and Psychiatry, 24,* 267–283.

Marson, D. C., Huthwaite, J. S., & Hebert, K. (2004). Testamentary capacity and undue influence in the elderly: A jurisprudent therapy perspective. *Law and Psychology Review, 28,* 71–96.

Martin, D. J., Garske, J. P., & Davis, M. K. (2000). Relation of the therapeutic alliance with outcome and other variables: A meta-analytic review. *Journal of Consulting and Clinical Psychology, 68,* 438–450.

Martin, J. E., Dubbert, P. M., & Cushman, W. C. (1991). Controlled trial of aerobic exercise in hypertension. *Circulation, 81,* 1560–1567.

Martini, D. R., Ryan, C., Nakayama, D., & Ramenofsky, M. (1990). Psychiatric sequelae after traumatic injury: The Pittsburgh regatta accident. *Journal of the American Academy of Child and Adolescent Psychiatry, 29,* 70–75.

Mason, B. J. (2001). Treatment of alcohol-dependent outpatients with acamprosate: A clinical review. *Journal of Clinical Psychiatry, 62,* 42–48.

Mason, F. L. (1997). Fetishism: Psychopathology and theory. In D. R. Laws & W. O'Donohue (Eds.), *Sexual deviance* (pp. 75–91). New York: Guilford.

Masse, L. C., & Tremblay, R. E. (1997). Behavior of boys in kindergarten and the course of substance use during adolescence. *Archives of General Psychiatry, 54,* 62–68.

Masson, J. M. (1984). *The assault on truth: Freud's suppression of the seduction theory.* New York: Farrar, Strauss, Giroux.

Masters, W. H., & Johnson, V. E. (1966). *Human sexual response.* Boston: Little, Brown and Company.

Masters, W. H., & Johnson, V. E. (1970). *Human sexual inadequacy.* Boston: Little, Brown and Company.

Mather, M., Canli, T., English, T., Whitfield, S., Wais, P., Ochsner, K., Gabrieli, J. D. E., & Carstensen, L. L. (2004). Amygdala responses to emotionally valenced stimuli in older and younger adults. *Psychological Science, 15,* 259–263.

Matsuda, L. A., Lolait, S. J., Brownstein, M. J., Young, A. C., & Bonner, T. I. (1990). Structure of a cannabinoid receptor and functional expression of the cloned cDNA. *Nature, 346,* 561–564.

Matt, G. E., Vazquez, C., & Campbell, W. K. (1992). Mood-congruent recall of affectively toned stimuli: A meta-analytic review. *Clinical Psychology Review, 12,* 227–255.

Matthews, K. A., Owens, J. F., Kuller, L. H., Sutton-Tyrrell, K., & Jansen-McWilliams, L. (1998). Are hostility and anxiety associated with carotid atherosclerosis in health postmenopausal women? *Psychosomatic Medicine, 60,* 633–638.

Matthews, K. A., Shumaker, S. A., Bowen, D. J., Langer, R. D., Hunt, J. R., et al. (1997). Women's healthy initiative: Why now? What is it? What's new? *American Psychologist, 52,* 101–116.

Mattson, M. E., Allen, J. P., Longabaugh, R., Nickless, C. J., Connors, G. J., & Kadden, R. M. (1994). A chronological review of empirical studies matching alcoholic clients to treatment. *Journal of Studies on Alcohol, 55,* 16–29.

Maugh II, T. H. (1998a, February 3). AIDS deaths down 44% in U.S.; new cases drop. *Los Angeles Times,* pp. A1–A11.

Maugh II, T. H. (1998b, July 5). Simpler therapy is new goal of AIDS research. *Los Angeles Times,* pp. A1, A18.

Maugh II, T. H. (2002, October 18). "Sobering" state report calls autism an epidemic. *Los Angeles Times,* pp. A1, A25.

Mayne, T. J. (2001). Emotions and health. In T. J. Mayne & G. A. Bonanno (Eds.), *Emotions: Current issues and future directions* (pp. 361–397). New York: Guilford.

McBride, P. A., Anderson, G. M., & Shapiro, T. (1996). Autism research: Bringing together approaches to pull apart the disorder. *Archives of General Psychiatry, 53,* 980–983.

McCabe, R. E., McFarlane, T., Polivy, J., & Olmsted, M. (2001). Eating disorders, dieting, and the accuracy of self-reported weight. *International Journal of Eating Disorders, 29,* 59–64.

McCarthy, B. W. (1986). A cognitive-behavioral approach to understanding and treating sexual trauma. *Journal of Sex and Marital Therapy, 12,* 322–329.

McCarty, D., Caspi, Y., Panas, L., Krakow, M., & Mulligan, D. H. (2000). Detoxification centers: Who's in the revolving door? *Journal of Behavioral Health Services & Research, 27,* 245–256.

McConaghy, N. (1993). *Sexual behavior: Problems and management.* New York: Plenum.

McConaghy, N. (1994). Paraphilias and gender identity disorders. In M. Hersen & R. T. Ammerman (Eds.), *Handbook of prescriptive treatments for adults* (pp. 317–346). New York: Plenum.

McCormick, N. B. (1999). When pleasure causes pain: Living with interstitial cystitis. *Sexuality and Disability, 17,* 7–18.

McCrady, B. S., & Epstein, E. E. (1998). Directions for research on alcoholic relationships: Marital- and individual-based models of heterogeneity. *Psychology of Addictive Behaviors, 9,* 157–166.

McCrae, R. R., & Costa, P. T., Jr. (1990). *Personality in adulthood.* New York: Guilford.

McCusker, J., Cole, M., & Abrahamowicz, M. (2002). Delirium predicts 12-month mortality. *Archives of Internal Medicine, 162,* 457–463.

McDonough, M., & Kennedy, N. (2002). Pharmacological management of obsessive-compulsive disorder: A review for clinicians. *Harvard Review of Psychiatry, 10,* 127–137.

McEachin, J. J., Smith, T., & Lovaas, O. I. (1993). Long-term outcome for children with autism who received early intensive behavioral treatment. *American Journal on Mental Retardation, 97,* 359–372.

McEwen, B. S., & Seeman, T. (1999). Protective and damaging effects of the mediators of stress: Elaborating the concepts of allostasis and allostatic load. In N. E. Adler, M. Marmot, B. E. McEwen, & J. Stewart (Eds.), *Socioeconomic status and health in industrial nations: social, psychological, and biological pathways* (pp. 30–47). *Annals of the New York Academy of Sciences, 896.* New York: New York Academy of Sciences.

McFall, R. M., & Hammen, C. L. (1971). Motivation, structure, and self-monitoring: Role of nonspecific factors in smoking reduction. *Journal of Consulting and Clinical Psychology, 37,* 80–86.

McFarlane, T., Polivy, J., & Herman, C. P. (1998). Effects of false weight feedback on mood, self-evaluation, and food intake in restrained and unrestrained eaters. *Journal of Abnormal Psychology, 107,* 312–318.

McFarlane, W. R., Dixon, L., Lukens, E., & Lucksted, A. (2003). Family psychoeducation and schizophrenia: A review of the literature. *Journal of Marital and Family Therapy, 29,* 223–245.

McFarlane, W. R., Lukens, E., Link, B., Dushay, R., Deakins, S., Newmark, M., Dunne, E. J., Horen, B., & Toran, J. (1995). Multiple-family groups and psychoeducation in the treatment of schizophrenia. *Archives of General Psychiatry, 52,* 679–687.

McGhie, A., & Chapman, J. S. (1961). Disorders of attention and perception in early schizophrenia. *British Journal of Medical Psychology, 34,* 103–116.

McGlashan, T. H., Grilo, C. M., Skodol, A. E., Gunderson, J. G., Shea, M. T., Morey, L. C., et al. (2000). The collaborative longitudinal personality disorders study: Baseline axis I/II and II/II diagnostic co-occurrence. *Acta Psychiatrica Scandinavica, 102,* 256–264.

McGlashan, T. H., & Hoffman, R. E. (2000). Schizophrenia as a disorder of developmentally reduced synaptic connectivity. *Archives of General Psychiatry, 57,* 637– 648.

McGue, M., Pickens, R. W., & Svikis, D. S. (1992). Sex and age effects on the inheritance of alcohol problems: A twin study. *Journal of Abnormal Psychology, 101,* 3–17.

McGuffin, P., Rijsdijk, F., Andrew, M., Sham, P., Katz, R., & Cardno, A. (2003). The heritability of bipolar affective disorder and the genetic relationship to unipolar depression. *Archives of General Psychiatry, 60,* 497–502.

McGuire, J., Nieri, D., Abbott, D., Sheridan, K., et al. (1995). Do *Tarasoff* principles apply in AIDS-related psychotherapy? Ethical decision making and the role of therapist homophobia and perceived client dangerousness. *Professional Psychology: Research and Practice, 26,* 608–611.

McGuire, P. K., Bench, C. J., Frith, C. D., & Marks, I. M. (1994). Functional anatomy of obsessive-compulsive phenomena. *British Journal of Psychiatry, 164,* 459–468.

McGuire, P. K., Shah, G. M. S., & Murray, R. M. (1993). Increased blood flow in Broca's area during auditory hallucinations in schizophrenia. *Lancet, 346,* 596–600.

McGuire, P. K., Silberswieg, D. A., & Frith, C. D. (1996). Functional neuroanatomy of verbal self-monitoring. *Brain 119,* 907–917.

McIntosh, J. L. (1995). Suicide prevention in the elderly (age 65–99). *Suicide and Life Threatening Behavior, 25,* 180–192.

McIntyre-Kingsolver, K., Lichtenstein, E., & Mermelstein, R. J. (1986). Spouse training in a multicomponent smoking-cessation program. *Behavior Therapy, 17,* 67–74.

McKeller, J., Stewart, E., & Humphreys, K. (2003). Alcoholics anonymous involvement and positive alcohol-related outcomes: Cause, consequence, or just a correlate? A prospective 2-year study of 2,319 alcohol dependent men. *Journal of Consulting and Clinical Psychology, 71,* 302–308.

McKendree-Smith, N. L., Floyd, M., & Scogin, F. R. (2003). Self-administered treatments for depression: A review. *Journal of Clinical Psychology, 59,* 275–288.

McKim, W. A. (1991). *Drugs and behavior: An introduction to behavioral pharmacology.* Englewood Cliffs, NJ: Prentice-Hall.

McKinley, N. M., & Hyde, J. S. (1996). The objectified body consciousness scale: Development and validation. *Psychology of Women Quarterly, 20,* 181–216.

McKown, C., & Weinstein, R. S. (2003). The development and consequences of stereotype consciousness in middle childhood. *Child Development, 74,* 498–515.

McLean, L. K., Brady, N. C., & McLean, J. E. (1996). Reported communication abilities of individuals with severe mental retardation. *American Journal on Mental Retardation, 100,* 580–591.

McMullen, S., & Rosen, R. C. (1979). Self-administered masturbation training in the treatment of primary orgasmic dysfunction. *Journal of Consulting and Clinical Psychology, 47,* 912–918.

McNally, R. J. (1997). Atypical phobias. In G. C. L. Davey (Ed.), *Phobias: A handbook of theory, research and treatment* (pp. 183–199). Chichester, England: John Wiley & Sons.

McNally, R. J. (2003a). Recovering memories of trauma: A view from the laboratory. *Current Directions in Psychological Science, 12,* 32–35.

McNally, R. J. (2003b). *Remembering trauma.* Cambridge, MA: Belknap Press of Harvard University Press.

McNally, R. J., Caspi, S. P., Riemann, B. C., & Zeitlin, S. B. (1990). Selective processing of threat cues in posttraumatic stress disorder. *Journal of Abnormal Psychology, 99,* 398–406.

McNally, R. J., Clancy, S. A., Barrett, H. M., & Parker, H. A. (2004). Inhibiting retrieval of trauma cues in adults reporting histories of childhood sexual abuse. *Cognition and Emotion, 18,* 479–493.

McNally, R. J., Lasko, N. B., Clancy, S. A., Macklin, M. L., Pitman, R. K., & Orr, S. P. (2004). Psychophysiological responding during script-driven imagery in people reporting abduction by space aliens. *Psychological Science, 15,* 493–497.

McNally, R. J., Ristuccia, C. S., & Perlman, C. A. (2005). Forgetting trauma cues in adults reporting continuous or recovered memories of childhood sexual abuse. *Psychological Science, 16,* 336–340.

McNeil, T. F., Cantor-Graae, E., & Weinberger, D. R. (2000). Relationship of obstetric complications and differences in size of brain structures in monozygotic twin pairs discordant for schizophrenia. *American Journal of Psychiatry, 157,* 203–212.

Meagher, D. J. (2001). Delirium: Optimizing management. *British Medical Journal, 322,* 144–149.

Meana, M., Binik, Y. M., Khalife, S., & Cohen, D. (1997). Dyspareunia: Sexual dysfunction or pain syndrome? *Journal of Nervous and Mental Disease, 185,* 561–569.

Meana, M., Binik, I., Khalife, S., & Cohen, D. (1998). Affect and marital adjustment in women's ratings of dyspareunic pain. *Canadian Journal of Psychiatry, 43,* 381– 385.

Meaney, M. J., Brake, W., & Gratton, A. (2002). Environmental regulation of the development of mesolimbic dopamine systems: A neurobiological mechanism for vulnerability to drug abuse? *Psychoneuroendocrinology, 27,* 127–148.

Mednick, S. A., & Schulsinger, F. (1968). Some premorbid characteristics related to breakdown in children with schizophrenic mothers. In D. Rosenthal & S. S. Kety (Eds.), *The transmission of schizophrenia.* Elmsford, NY: Pergamon.

Mednick, S. A., Huttonen, M. O., & Machon, R. A. (1994). Prenatal influenza infections and adult schizophrenia. *Schizophrenia Bulletin, 20,* 263–268.

Mednick, S. A., Machon, R., Hottunen, M. O., & Bonett, D. (1988). Fetal viral infection and adult schizophrenia. *Archives of General Psychiatry, 45,* 189–192.

Medvedev, Z. (1972). *A question of madness.* New York: Knopf.

Meeks, S., & Murrell, S. A. (1997). Mental illness in late life: Socioeconomic conditions, psychiatric symptoms, and adjustment of long term sufferers. *Psychology and Aging, 12,* 296–308.

Meier, B. (2003). *Pain killer: A "wonder" drug's trail of addiction and death.* Rodale Books.

Meier, D. E., Emmons, C. A., Wallenstein, S., Quill, T., Morrison, R. S., & Cassel, C. K. (1998). A national survey of physician-assisted suicide and euthanasia in the United States. *New England Journal of Medicine, 338,* 1193–1201.

Meilman, P., Leichliter, J. S., & Presley, C. A. (1999). Greeks and athletes: Who drinks more? *Journal of American College Health, 47,* 187–190.

Melamed, B. G., & Siegel, L. J. (1975). Reduction of anxiety in children facing hospitalization and surgery by use of filmed modeling. *Journal of Consulting and Clinical Psychology, 43,* 511–521.

Mellinger, G. D., Balter, M. B., & Uhlenhuth, E. H. (1985). Insomnia and its treatment. *Archives of General Psychiatry, 42,* 225–232.

Mellor, C. S. (1970). First rank symptoms of schizophrenia. *British Journal of Psychiatry, 117,* 15–23.

Melnick, S. M., & Hinshaw, S. P. (1996). What they want and what they get: The social goals of boys with ADHD and comparison boys. *Journal of Abnormal Child Psychology, 24,* 169–185.

Meltzer, H. Y. (2003). Suicide in schizophrenia. *Journal of Clinical Psychiatry, 64,* 1122–1125.

Meltzer, H. Y., Cola, P., & Way, L. E. (1993). Cost effectiveness of clozapine in neuroleptic-resistant schizophrenia. *American Journal of Psychiatry, 150,* 1630–1638.

Mennin, D. S., Heimberg, R. G., & Turk, C. L. (2004). Clinical presentation and diagnostic features. In R. G. Heimberg, C. L. Turk, & D. S. Mennin (Eds.), *Generalized anxiety disorder* (pp. 3–28). New York: Guilford.

Menting, J., Honig, A., Verhey, F., & Hartmans, M. (1996). Selective serotonin reuptake inhibitors (SSRIs) in the treatment of elderly depressed patients: A qualitative analysis of the literature on their efficacy and side-effects. *International Clinical Psychopharmacology, 11,* 165–175.

Menzies, R. G., & Clarke, J. C. (1995). The etiology of phobias: A nonassociative account. *Clinical Psychology Review, 15,* 23–48.

Merckelbach, H., Dekkers, T., Wessel, I., & Roefs, A. (2003). Dissociative symptoms and amnesia in Dutch concentration camp survivors. *Comprehensive Psychiatry, 44,* 65–69.

Merikangas, K. R., Stolar, M., Stevens, D. E., Goulet, J., Preisig, M. A., et al. (1998). Familial transmission of substance use disorders. *Archives of General Psychiatry, 55,* 973–981.

Merikangas, K. R., Zhang, H., Avenevoli, S., Acharyya, S., Neuenschwander, M., & Angst, J. (2003). Longitudinal trajectories of depression and anxiety in a prospective community study. *Archives of General Psychiatry, 60,* 993–1000.

Merzenich, M. M., Jenkins, W. M., Johnson, P., Schreiner, C., Miller, S. L., & Tallal, P. (1996). Temporal processing deficits of language-learning impaired children ameliorated by training. *Science, 271,* 77–81.

Meston, C. M., & Gorzalka, B. B. (1995). The effects of sympathetic activation on physiological and subjective sexual arousal in women. *Behaviour Research and Therapy, 33,* 651–664.

Meston, C. M., & Gorzalka, B. B. (1996). Differential effects of sympathetic activation on sexual arousal in sexually dysfunctional and functional women. *Journal of Abnormal Psychology, 105,* 582–591.

Metalsky, G. I., Joiner, T. E., Hardin, T. S., & Abramson, L. Y. (1993). Depressive reactions to failure in a natural setting: A test of the hopelessness and self-esteem theories of depression. *Journal of Abnormal Psychology*, *102*, 101–109.

Metz, M. E., Pryor, J. L., Nesvacil, L. J., Abuzzahab, F., et al. (1997). Premature ejaculation: A psychophysiological review. *Journal of Sex and Marital Therapy*, *23*, 3–23.

Meyer, B., Johnson, S. L., & Winters, R. (2001). Responsiveness to threat and incentive in bipolar disorder: Relations of the BIS/BAS scales with symptoms. *Journal of Psychopathology and Behavioral Assessment*, *23*, 133–143.

Meyer, G. J. (2002). Exploring possible differences and bias in the Rorschach Comprehensive System. *Journal of Personality Assessment*, *78*, 104–129.

Meyer, J. K. (1995). Paraphilias. In H. I. Kaplan & B. J. Sadock (Eds.), *Comprehensive textbook of psychiatry* (pp. 1334–1347). Baltimore, MD: Williams & Wilkins.

Meyer, V. (1966). Modification of expectations in cases with obsessional rituals. *Behaviour Research and Therapy*, *4*, 273–280.

Meyer, V., & Chesser, E. S. (1970). *Behavior therapy in clinical psychiatry.* Baltimore, MD: Penguin Books.

Meyerowitz, B. E., & Chaiken, S. (1987). The effect of message framing on breast self-examination attitudes, intentions, and behavior. *Journal of Personality and Social Psychology*, *52*, 500–510.

Meyerowitz, B. E., Richardson, J., Hudson, S., & Leedham, B. (1998). Ethnicity and cancer outcomes. Behavioral and psychosocial considerations. *Psychological Bulletin*, *123*, 47–70.

Micallef, J., & Blin, O. (2001). Neurobiology and clinical pharmacology of obsessive-compulsive disorder. *Clinical Neuropharmacology*, *24*, 191–207.

Miklowitz, D. J. (1985). *Family interaction and illness outcome in bipolar and schizophrenic patients.* Unpublished Ph.D. thesis, University of California at Los Angeles.

Miklowitz, D. J., George, E. L., Richards, J. A., Simoneau, T. L., & Suddath, R. L. (2003). A randomized study of family-focused psychoeducation and pharmacotherapy in the outpatient management of bipolar disorder. *Archives of General Psychiatry*, *60*, 904–912.

Miklowitz, D. J., & Goldstein, M. J. (1997). *Bipolar disorder: A family-focused treatment approach.* New York: Guidford.

Miklowitz, D. J., Simoneau, T. L., Sachs-Ericsson, N., Warner, R., & Suddath, R. (1996). Family risk indicators in the course of bipolar affective disorder. In E. Mundt et al. (Eds.), *Interpersonal factors in the origin and course of affective disorders* (pp. 204–217). London: Gaskell.

Miklowitz, D. J., & Taylor, D. O. (2005). Family-Focused Treatment of the Suicidal Bipolar Patient. Unpublished manuscript under review.

Milberger, S., Biederman, J., Faraone, S. V., & Chen, L. (1996). Is maternal smoking during pregnancy a risk factor for attention deficit hyperactivity disorder in children? *American Journal of Psychiatry*, *153*, 1138–1142.

Milich, R., Balentine, A., & Lynam, D. (2001). ADHD combined type and ADHD predominantly inattentive type are distinct and unrelated disorders. *Clinical Psychology: Science and Practice*, *8*, 463–488.

Miller, B. D., & Wood, B. L. (1994). Psychophysiologic reactivity in asthmatic children: A cholinergically mediated confluence of pathways. *Journal of the American Academy of Adolescent Psychiatry*, *33*, 1236–1245.

Miller, B. D., & Wood, B. L. (1997). Influence of specific emotional states on autonomic reactivity and pulmonary function in asthmatic children. *Journal of the American Academy of Child and Adolescent Psychiatry*, *36*, 669–677.

Miller, B. L., Ikonte, C., Ponton, M., & Levy, M. (1997). A study of the Lund Manchester research criteria for frontotemporal dementia: Clinical and single-photon emission CT correlations. *Neurology*, *48*, 937–942.

Miller, M. A., & Rahe, R. H. (1997). Life changes scaling for the 1990s. *Journal of Psychosomatic Research*, *13*, 279–292.

Miller, T. Q., & Volk, R. J. (1996). Weekly marijuana use as a risk factor for initial cocaine use: Results from a six wave national survey. *Journal of Child and Adolescent Substance Abuse*, *5*, 55–78.

Miller, W. R., & Rollnick, S. (Eds.). (1991). *Motivational interviewing: Preparing people to change addictive behavior.* New York: Guilford.

Miller, M. B. (2001). Paranoid, Schizoid, and Schizotypal personality disorders. In P. B. Sitker & H. E. Adams (Eds.), *Comprehensive Handbook of Psychopathology (3rd ed.),* (pp. 535–559). New York: Kluwer Academic/Plenum Publishers.

Miller, W. R., Zweben, A., DiClemente, C. C., & Rychtarik, R. G. (1992). Motivational Enhancement Therapy manual: A clinical research guide for therapists treating individuals with alcohol abuse and dependence. *NIAA Project MATCH Monograph*, Vol. 2, DHHS Publication No. (ADM) 92-1894.

Millon, T. (1996). *Disorders of personality: DSM-IV and beyond* (2nd ed.). New York: John Wiley & Sons.

Milos, G., Spindler, A., Schnyder, U., Martz, J., Hoek, H. W., & Willi, J. (2004). Incidence of severe anorexia in Switzerland: 40 years of development. *International Journal of Eating Disorders*, *35*, 250–258.

Mineka, S., & Öhman, A. (2002). Born to fear: Non-associative vs. associative factors in the etiology of phobias. *Behaviour Research and Therapy*, *40*, 173–184.

Mineka, S., Watson, D., & Clark, L. A. (1998). Comorbidity of anxiety and unipolar mood disorders. *Annual Review of Psychology*, *49*, 377–412.

Mineka, S., & Zinbarg, R. (1998). Experimental approaches to the anxiety and mood disorders. In J. G. Adair, D. Belanger, & K. L. Dion (Eds.), *Advances in psychological science, Volume. 1: Social, personal, and cultural aspects.* Hove, England: Psychology Press/Erlbaum, Taylor & Francis.

Minuchin, S., Baker, L., Rosman, B. L., Lieberman, R., Milman, L., & Todd, T. C. (1975). A conceptual model of psychosomatic illness in children. *Archives of General Psychiatry*, *32*, 1031–1038.

Mishkind, M. E., Rodin, J., Silberstein, L. R., & Striegel-Moore, R. H. (1986). The embodiment of masculinity: Cultural, psychological, and behavioral dimensions. *American Behavioral Scientist*, *29*, 545–562.

Mitchell, J. E. (1992). Subtyping of bulimia nervosa. *International Journal of Eating Disorders*, *11*, 327–332.

Mitchell, J. T., & Everly, G. S., Jr. (2000). Critical incident stress management and critical incident stress debriefings: Evolutions, effects and outcomes. John P. Wilson, Beverley Raphael (Ed.), *Psychological debriefing: Theory, practice and evidence.* (pp. 71–90). New York, NY: Cambridge University Press.

Mittleman, M. A., Maclure, M., Sherwood, J. B., Murly, R. P., Tofler, G. A., et al. (1997). Triggering of acute myocardial infarction onset by episodes of anger. *Circulation*, *92*, 1720–1725.

Moen, P. (1996). Gender, age, and the life course. In R. H. Binstock & L. K. George (Eds.), *Handbook of aging and the social sciences* (4th ed., pp. 171–187). San Diego, CA: Academic Press.

Moene, F. C., Landberg, E. H., Hoogduin, K. A., et al. (2000). Organic syndromes diagnosed as conversion disorder: Identification and frequency in a study of 85 patients. *Journal of Psychosomatic Research*, *49*, 7–12.

Moffitt, T. E. (1993). Adolescence-limited and life-course-persistent antisocial behavior: A developmental taxonomy. *Psychological Review*, *100*, 674–701.

Moffitt, T. E., & Caspi, A. (2001). Childhood predictors differentiate life-course persistent and adolescence-limited antisocial pathways among males and females. *Development and Psychopathology*, *13*, 355–375.

Moffitt, T. E., Caspi, A., Harrington, H., & Milne, B. J. (2002). Males on the life-course persistent and adolescence-limited antisocial pathways: Follow-up at age 26. *Development and Psychopathology 14*, 179–207.

Moffitt, T. E., Lynam, D., & Silva, P. A. (1994). Neuropsychological tests predict persistent male delinquency. *Criminology*, *32*, 101–124.

Moffitt, T. E., & Silva, P. A. (1988). IQ and delinquency: A direct test of the differential detection hypothesis. *Journal of Abnormal Psychology*, *97*, 330–333.

Mohr, D. C., & Beutler, L. E. (1990). Erectile dysfunction: A review of diagnostic and treatment procedures. *Clinical Psychology Review*, *10*, 123–150.

Molgaard, C. A., Nakamura, C. M., Stanford, E. P., Peddecord, K. M., & Morton, D. J. (1990). Prevalence of alcohol consumption among older persons. *Journal of Community Health*, *15*, 239–251.

Molnar, B. E., Buka, S. L., & Kessler, R. C. (2001). Child sexual abuse and subsequent psychopathology: Results from the National Comorbidity Survey. *American Journal of Public Health*, *91*(5), 753–760.

Monahan, J. (1973). The psychiatrization of criminal behavior. *Hospital and Community Psychiatry*, *24*, 105–107.

Monahan, J. (1976). The prevention of violence. In J. Monahan (Ed.), *Community mental health and the criminal justice system.* Elmsford, NY: Pergamon.

Monahan, J. (1978). Prediction research and the emergency commitment of dangerous mentally ill persons: A reconsideration. *American Journal of Psychiatry*, *135*, 198–201.

Monahan, J. (1984). The prediction of violent behavior: Toward a second generation of theory and policy. *American Journal of Psychiatry*, *141*, 10–15.

Monahan, J. (1992). Mental disorder and violent behavior: Perceptions and evidence. *American Psychologist*, *47*, 511–521.

Monahan, J., & Shah, S. (1989). Dangerousness and commitment of the mentally disordered in the United States. *Schizophrenia Bulletin*, *15*, 541–553.

Monahan, J., & Steadman, H. (1994). Toward a rejuvenation of risk assessment research. In J. Monahan & H. Steadman (Eds.), *Violence and mental disorder: Developments in risk assessment.* Chicago: University of Chicago Press.

Moniz, E. (1936). *Tentatives operatoires dans le traitement de ceretaines psychoses.* Paris: Mason.

Monroe, S. M., & Simons, A. D. (1991). Diathesis-stress theories in the context of life stress research: Implications for the depressive disorders. *Psychological Bulletin*, *110*, 406–425.

Monsen, K., & Monsen, J. T. (2000). Chronic pain and psychodynamic body therapy: A controlled outcome study. *Psychotherapy: Theory, Research, Practice, Training*, *37*, 257–269.

Monson, R., & Smith, C. R. (1983). Current concepts in psychiatry: Somatization disorder in primary care. *New England Journal of Medicine*, *308*, 1464–1465.

Montag, K. R., & Wilson, G. L. (1992). An empirical evaluation of behavioral and cognitive-behavioral group marital treatments with discordant couples. *Journal of Sex and Marital Therapy*, *18*, 255–272.

Moore, P., Landolt, H. P., Seifritz, E., Clark, C., Bhatti, T., & Kelsoe, J., et al. (2000). Clinical and physiological consequences of rapid tryptophan depletion. *Neuropsychopharmacology*, *23*, 601–622.

Moos, R. H., & Humphreys, K. (2004). Long-term influence of duration and frequency of participation in Alcoholics

Anonymous on individuals with alcohol use disorders. *Journal of Consulting and Clinical Psychology, 72*, 81–90.

Mora, S., Redberg, R. F., Cui, Y., Whiteman, M. K., Flaws, J. A., Sharrett, A. R., & Blumenthal, R. S. (2003). Ability of exercise testing to predict cardiovascular and all-cause death in asymptomatic women: a 20-year follow-up of the lipid research clinics prevalence study. *JAMA, 290*, 1600–1607.

Moran, M. (1991). Psychological factors affecting pulmonary and rheumatological diseases: A review. *Psychosomatics, 32*, 14–23.

Moreau, D., Mufson, L., Weissman, M. M., & Klerman, G. L. (1992). Interpersonal psychotherapy for adolescent depression: Description of modification and preliminary application. *Journal of the Academy of Child and Adolescent Psychiatry, 30*, 642–651.

Moreland, K., Wing, S., Diez Roux, A., & Poole, C. (2002). Neighborhood characteristics associated with the location of food stores and food services places. *American Journal of Preventive Medicine, 22*, 23–29.

Morenz, B., & Becker, J. V. (1995). The treatment of youthful sexual offenders. *Applied and Preventive Psychology, 4*, 247–256.

Morey, L. C., Gunderson, J., Quigley, B. D., & Lyons, M. (2000). Dimensions and categories: The "big five" factors and the DSM personality disorders. *Assessment, 7*, 203–216.

Morey, L. C. (1988). Personality disorders in DSM-III and DSM-IIIR: Convergence, coverage, and internal consistency. *American Journal of Psychiatry, 145*, 573–577.

Morf, C. C., & Rhodewalt, F. (2001). Unraveling the paradoxes of narcissism: A dynamic self-regulatory processing model. *Psychological Inquiry, 12*, 177–196.

Morgan, C. A. III, Hazlett, G., Wang, S., Richardson, E. G. Jr., Schnurr, P., Southwick, S. M. (2001). Symptoms of dissociation in humans experiencing acute, uncontrollable stress: A prospective investigation. *American Journal of Psychiatry, 158*, 1239–1247.

Morgan, M. J. (2000). Ecstasy (MDMA): A review of its possible persistent psychological effects. *Psychopharmacology, 152*, 230–248.

Morgenstern, J., Blanchard, K. A., Morgan, T. J., Labouvie, E., & Hayaki, J. (2001). Testing the effectiveness of cognitive-behavioral treatment for substance abuse in a community setting: Within treatment and posttreatment findings. *Journal of Consulting & Clinical Psychology, 69*, 1007–1017.

Morgenstern, J., Langenbucher, J., Labouvie, E., & Miller, K. J. (1997). The comorbidity of alcoholism and personality disorders in a clinical population; Prevalence rates and relation to alcohol typology variables. *Journal of Abnormal Psychology, 106*, 74–84.

Morin, C. M., Colecchi, C., Stone, J., Sood, R., & Brink, D. (1999). Behavioral and pharmacological therapies for late-life insomnia: A randomized controlled trial. *Journal of the American Medical Association, 281*, 991–999.

Morley, S. (1997). Pain management. In A. Baum, S. Newman, J. Weinman, R. West, & C. McManus (Eds.), *Cambridge handbook of psychology, health and medicine* (pp. 234–237). Cambridge, England: Cambridge University Press.

Morokoff, P. J., & Gilliland, R. (1993). Stress, sexual functioning, and marital satisfaction. *Journal of Sex Research, 30*, 43–53.

Moroney, J. T., Tang, M.-X., Berglund, L., Small, S., Merchant, C., et al. (1999). Low-density lipoprotein cholesterol and the risk of dementia with stroke. *JAMA, 282*, 254–260.

Morris, A. A. (1968). Criminal insanity. *Washington Review, 43*, 583–622.

Morris, N. (1966). Impediments to legal reform. *University of Chicago Law Review, 33*, 627–656.

Morse, R. M. (1988). Substance abuse among the elderly. *Bulletin of the Menninger Clinic, 52*, 259–268.

Morse, S. J. (1982a, June 23). In defense of the insanity defense. *Los Angeles Times.*

Morse, S. J. (1982b). Failed explanation and criminal responsibility: Experts and the unconscious. *Virginia Law Review, 678*, 971–1084.

Morse, S. J. (1982c). A preference for liberty: The case against involuntary commitment of the mentally disordered. *California Law Review, 70*, 54–106.

Morse, S. J. (1992). The "guilty mind": Mens rea. In D. K. Kagehiro & W. S. Laufer (Eds.), *Handbook of psychology and law* (pp. 207–229). New York: Springer-Verlag.

Moscicki, E. K. (1995). Epidemiology of suicidal behavior. In M. M. Silverman & R. W. Maris (Eds.), *Suicide prevention: Toward the year 2000* (pp. 22–35). New York: Guilford.

Moser, C., & Levitt, E. E. (1987). An exploratory-descriptive study of a sadomasochistically oriented sample. *The Journal of Sex Research, 23*, 322–337.

Moses, J. A., & Purisch, A. D. (1997). The evolution of the Luria-Nebraska Battery. In G. Goldstein & T. Incagnoli (Eds.), *Contemporary approaches to neuropsychological assessment* (pp. 131–170). New York: Plenum.

Moses, J. A., Schefft, B. A., Wong, J. L., & Berg, R. A. (1992). Interrater reliability analyses of the Luria-Nebraska neuropsychological battery, form II. *Archives of Clinical Neurology, 7*, 251–269.

Mowrer, O. H. (1947). On the dual nature of learning: A reinterpretation of "conditioning" and "problem-solving." *Harvard Educational Review, 17*, 102–148.

Mrazek, D. A., Schuman, W. B., & Klinnert, M. (1998). Early asthma onset: Risk of emotional and behavioral difficulties. *Journal of Child Psychology and Psychiatry and Allied Disciplines, 39*, 247–254.

Mrazek, P. J., & Haggerty, R. J. (1994). *Reducing risks for mental disorders: Frontiers for preventive intervention research.* Washington, DC: National Academy Press.

MTA Cooperative Group. (1999a). A 14-month randomized clinical trial of treatment strategies for attention-deficit/hyperactivity disorder. *Archives of General Psychiatry, 56*, 1073–1086.

MTA Cooperative Group. (1999b). Moderators and mediators of treatment response for children with attention-deficit/hyperactivity disorder. *Archives of General Psychiatry, 56*, 1088–1096.

Mueser, K., Bellack, A. S., & Blanchard, J. J. (1992). Comorbidity of schizophrenia and substance abuse: Implications for treatment. *Journal of Consulting and Clinical Psychology, 60*, 845–856.

Mueser, K. T., Bond, G. R., Drake, R. E., & Resnick, S. G. (1998). Models of community care for severe mental illness: A review of research on case management. *Schizophrenia Bulletin, 24*, 37–74.

Mueser, K. T., & Berenbaum, H. (1990). Psychodynamic treatment for schizophrenia: Is there a future? *Psychological Medicine, 20*, 253–262.

Mueser, K. T., & Liberman, R. P. (1995). Behavior therapy in practice. In B. Bongar & L. E. Beutler (Eds.), *Comprehensive textbook of psychotherapy: Theory and practice* (pp. 84–110). New York: Oxford University Press.

Mufson, L., Weissman, M. M., Moreau, D., & Garfinkel, R. (1999). Efficacy of interpersonal psychotherapy for depressed adolescents. *Archives of General Psychiatry, 56*, 573–579.

Multon, K. D., Kivlighan, D. M., & Gold, P. B. (1996). Changes in counselor adherence over the course of training. *Journal of Counseling Psychology, 43*, 356–363.

Mulvey, E. P. (1994). Assessing the evidence of a link between mental illness and violence. *Hospital and Community Psychiatry, 45*, 663–668.

Mundle, G., Bruegel, R., Urbaniak, H., Laengle, G., Buchkremer, G., & Mann, K. (2001). *Kurz- und mittelfristige Erfolgsraten ambulanter Entwoehnungsbehandlungen fuer alkoholabhaengige Patienten.* Eine 6-, 18-, und 36-Monats-Katamnese./Short- and medium-term outcome of outpatient treatment for alcohol dependent patients in Germany—A 6-, 18-, and 36-month follow-up. *Fortschritte der Neurologie Psychiatrie, 69*, 374–378.

Mundo, E., Maina, G., & Uslenghi, C. (2000). Multicentre, double-blind comparison of fluvoxamine and clomipramine in the treatment of obsessive-compulsive disorder. *International Clinical Psychopharmacology, 15*, 69–76.

Munetz, M. R., Grande, T., Kleist, J., & Peterson, G. A. (1996). The effectiveness of outpatient civil commitment. *Psychiatric Services, 47*, 1251–1253.

Muñoz, R. F., Ying, Y. W., Bernal, G., Perez-Stable, E. J., et al. (1995). Prevention of depression with primary care patients: A randomized controlled trial. *American Journal of Community Psychology, 23*, 199–222.

Munro, S., Thomas, K. L., & Abu-Shaar, M. (1993). Molecular characterization of a peripheral receptor for cannabinoids. *Nature, 365*, 61–65.

Muntner, P., He, J., Cutler, J. A., Wildman, R. P., & Whelton, P. K. (2004). Trends in blood pressure among adolescents and children. *JAMA, 291*, 2107–2113.

Muraven, M., & Baumeister, R. F. (2000). Self-regulation and depletion of limited resources: Does self-control resemble a muscle? *Psychological Bulletin, 126*, 247–259.

Murphy, J. (1976). Psychiatric labeling in cross-cultural perspective. *Science, 191*, 1019–1028.

Murphy, J. K., Stoney, C. M., Alpert, B. S., & Walker, S. S. (1995). Gender and ethnicity in children's cardiovascular reactivity: 7 years of study. *Health Psychology, 14*, 48–55.

Murray, C. J. L., & Lopez, A. D. (1996). *The global burden of disease: A comprehensive assessment of disease, injuries, and risk factors in 1990 and projected to 2020.* Cambridge, MA: Harvard University Press.

Musetti, L., Perugi, G., Soriani, A., & Rossi, V. M. (1989). Depression before and after age 65: A re-examination. *British Journal of Psychiatry, 155*, 330–336.

Musselman, D. L., Evans, D. L., & Nemeroff, C. B. (1998). The relationship of depression to cardiovascular disease: Epidemiology, biology, and treatment. *Archives of General Psychiatry, 55*, 580–592.

Mustonen, T. K., Spencer, S. M., Hoskinson, R. A., Sachs, D. P. L., & Garvey, A. J. (2005). The influence of gender, rance, and menthol content on tobacco exposure measures. *Nicotine & Tobacco Research, 7*, 581–590.

Myers, M. G., Stewart, D. G., & Brown, S. A. (1998). Progression from conduct disorder to antisocial personality disorder. *American Journal of Psychiatry, 155*, 479–485.

Myin-Germeys, I., van Os, J., Schwartz, J. E., et al. (2001). Emotional reactivity to daily life stress in schizophrenia. *Archives of General Psychiatry, 58*, 1137–1144.

Myrick, H. B., Kathleen, T., & Malcolm, R. (2001). New developments in the pharmacotherapy of alcohol dependence. *American Journal on Addictions, 10*, 3–15.

Nanke, A., & Rief, W. (2000). Biofeedback in the treatment of somatoform disorders. *Verhaltenstherapie, 10*, 238–248.

Nasser, M. (1986). Comparative study of the prevalence of abnormal eating attitudes among Arab female students of both London and Cairo Universities. *Psychological Medicine, 16*, 621–625.

Nasser, M. (1988). Eating disorders: The cultural dimension. *Social Psychiatry and Psychiatric Epidemiology, 23*, 184–187.

Nasser, M. (1997). *Culture and Weight Consciousness.* London: Routledge Press.

Nathan, P. E., & Gorman, J. M. (Eds.). (2002). *A guide to treatments that work (2nd ed.).* London: Oxford University Press.

National Academy on an Aging Society. (1999). *Challenges for the 21st century: Chronic and disabling conditions.* Retrieved from http://www.agingsociety.org/agingsociety/publications/chronic/index.html

National Center on Addiction and Substance Abuse at Columbia University (CASA; 2005). Under the Counter: The Diversion and Abuse of Controlled Prescription Drugs in the U.S.

National Center for Health Statistics. (2004). *Healthy People, 2004.* Online at: http://www.cdc.gov/nchs/hus.htm

National Center for Justice. (2003). *National Crime Victimization Survey.* Unpublished document, National Center for Justice, Document NCJ 206348.

National Center for Victims of Violent Crime. (2004). *Sexual violence.* Unpublished Document number 32291. Available by Web at http://www.ncvc.org/ncvc/main.aspx?dbID=DB Statistics584

National Drug Intelligence Center. (2001). *OxyContin diversion and abuse.* NDIC, Department of Justice, January 2001, Document ID: 2001-L0424-001. (Also available online at http://www.usdoj.gov/ndic/pubs/651/index.htm)

National Heart, Lung and Blood Institute. (1998). *Behavioral research in cardiovascular, lung, and blood health and disease.* Washington, DC: U.S. Department of Health and Human Services.

National Heart, Lung, and Blood Institute. (1998, June). *Clinical guidelines of the identification, evaluation, and treatment of overweight and obese adults.* NHLB accessed; July 25, 2001, www.nhlbi.nih.gov/guidelines/obesity/ob-home.htm

National Highway Transportation & Safety Administration. (2003). *Traffic safety facts 2003: Alcohol.* Washington, DC: National Center for Statistics and Analysis, U.S. Department of Transportation, DOT HS 809 761.

National Highway Transportation Safety Administration. (2005). 2004 Traffic Safety Annual Assessment—Early Results. National Center for Statistics and Analysis, US Department of Transportation, DOT HS 809 897.

National Institute on Alcohol Abuse and Alcoholism. (1997). Youth drinking: Risk factors and consequences. *Alcohol Alert,* 1–7.

National Institute on Alcohol Abuse and Alcoholism. (2001). *Alcohol Alert No. 51: Economic perspectives in alcoholism research.* Rockville, MD (Also available online at http://www.niaaa.nih.gov/publications/aa51-text.htm

National Institute on Alcohol Abuse and Alcoholism. (2002). *A call to action: Changing the culture of drinking at U.S. Colleges.* Task Force of the National Advisory Council on Alcohol Abuse and Alcoholism. National Institutes of Health, U.S. Department of Health and Human Service. (www.collegedrinkingprevention.gov). NIH Publication No. 02-5010.

National Institute of Child Health and Human Development. (2000). *Report of the National Reading Panel. Teaching children to read: An evidence-based assessment of the scientific research literature on reading and its implications for reading instruction* [online]. Available at http://www.nichd.nih.gov/publications/nrp/smallbook.htm

National Institute on Drug Abuse. (1982). *National survey on drug abuse.* Washington, DC: Author.

National Institute on Drug Abuse. (1983). *National survey on drug abuse: Main findings 1982* (DHHS Publication No. ADM 83-1263). Washington, DC: U.S. Government Printing Office.

National Institute on Drug Abuse. (1991). *National household survey on drug abuse: population estimates, 1991.* Washington, DC.

National Institute on Drug Abuse. (1998). *The economic costs of alcohol and drug abuse in the United States.* Rockville, MD: National Clearinghouse for Drug and Alcohol Information.

National Institute on Drug Abuse. (2000). Heroin abuse and addiction. *NIDA Research Report, NIH publication number 00-4165.* Rockville, MD (Also available online at http://165.112.78.61/ResearchReports/Heroin/Heroin.html

National Institute on Drug Abuse. (2004a). *NIDA InfoFacts: Crack and cocaine.* National Institute on Drug Abuse, National Institute of Health, U.S. Department of Health and Human Services (http://www.drugabuse.gov).

National Institute on Drug Abuse. (2004b). *NIDA InfoFacts: Inhalants.* National Institute on Drug Abuse, National Institute of Health, U.S. Department of Health and Human Services (http://www.drugabuse.gov).

National Institute on Drug Abuse. (2004c). *NIDA InfoFacts: Nationwide trends.* National Institute on Drug Abuse, National Institute of Health, U.S. Department of Health and Human Services (http://www.drugabuse.gov).

National Institute of Health Consensus Statement. (1998). *Diagnosis and treatment of attention deficit hyperactivity disorder (ADHD).* Rockville, MD: U.S. Government Printing Office.

National Institute of Mental Health (NIMH) Multisite HIV Prevention Trial Group. (1998). The NIMH multisite HIV prevention trial: Reducing HIV sexual risk behavior. *Science, 280,* 1889–1894.

NCHS. (2004). *NCHS data on Alzheimer's Disease.* National Center for Health Statistics, Centers for Disease Control (http://www.cdc.gov/nchs/data/factsheets/Alzheimers.pdf).

Neale, J. M., & Liebert, R. M. (1986). Science and behavior: An introduction to methods of research (3rd ed.). Englewood Cliffs, NJ: Prentice-Hall.

Neale, J. M., & Oltmanns, T. (1980). *Schizophrenia.* New York: Wiley.

Neisser, U. (1976). *Cognition and reality.* San Francisco: Freeman.

Neisser, U., & Harsch, N. (1991). Phantom flashbulbs: False recognitions of hearing the news about *Challenger.* In E. Winograd & U. Neisser (Eds.), *Affect and accuracy of recall: Studies of "flashbulb" memories.* New York: Cambridge University Press.

Nelson, E. C., Heath, A. C., Madden, P. A. F., Cooper, L., Dinwiddie, S. H., Bucholz, K. K., Glowinski, A., McLaughlin, T., Dunne, M. P., Statham, D. J., & Martin, N. G. (2002). Association between self-reported childhood sexual abuse and adverse psychosocial outcomes: A twin study. *Archives of General Psychiatry, 59,* 139–145.

Nelson, J. C., & Davis, J. M. (1997). DST studies in psychotic depression: A meta-analysis. *American Journal of Psychiatry, 154,* 1497–1503.

Nelson, M. D., Saykin, A. J., Flashman, L. A., & Riordin, H. J. (1998). Hippocampal volume reduction in schizophrenia as assessed by magnetic resonance imaging: A meta analytic study. *Archives of General Psychiatry, 55,* 433–440.

Nelson, R. O., Lipinski, D. P., & Black, J. L. (1976). The reactivity of adult retardates' self-monitoring: A comparison among behaviors of different valences, and a comparison with token reinforcement. *Psychological Record, 26,* 189–201.

Nelson, T. L., Palmer, R. F., & Pederson, N. L. (2004). The metabolic syndrome mediates the relationship between cynical hostility and cardiovascular disease. *Experimental Aging Research, 30,* 163–177.

Nemeroff, C. B., & Schatzberg, A. F. (1998). Pharmacological treatment of unipolar depression. In P. E. Nathan & J. M. Gorman (Eds.), *A guide to treatments that work* (pp. 212–225). New York: Oxford University Press.

Nemeroff, C. F., Stein, R. I., Diehl, N. S., & Smilack, K. M. (1994). From the Cleavers to the Clintons: Role choices and body orientation as reflected in magazine article content. *International Journal of Eating Disorders, 16,* 167–176.

Nemeroff, C. J., & Karoly, P. (1991). Operant methods. In F. H. Kanfer & A. P. Goldstein (Eds.), *Helping people change: A textbook of methods* (4th ed.). Elmsford, NY: Pergamon.

NESARC (2004). National Epidemiologic Survey on Alcohol and Related Conditions (NESARC), *Archives of General Psychiatry, 61,* 807–816.

Nestadt, G., Romanoski, A., Chahal, R., Merchant, A., et al. (1990). An epidemiological study of histrionic personality disorder. *Psychological Medicine, 20,* 413–422.

Nestle, M. (2002). *Food Politics: How the food industry influences nutrition and health.* Berkeley, CA: University of California Press.

Neugarten, B. L. (1977). Personality and aging. In J. E. Birren & K. W. Schaie (Eds.), *Handbook of the psychology of aging* (pp. 626–649). New York: Van Nostrand.

Neugebauer, R. (1979). Mediaeval and early modern theories of mental illness. *Archives of General Psychiatry, 36,* 477–484.

Neumeister, A., Konstantinidis, A., Praschak Rieder, N., Willeit, M., Hilger, E., & Stastny, J., et al. (2001). Monoaminergic function in the pathogenesis of seasonal affective disorder. *International Journal of Neuropsychopharmacology, 4,* 409–420.

Newlin, D. B., & Thomson, J. B. (1990). Alcohol challenge with sons of alcoholics: A critical review and analysis. *Psychological Bulletin, 108,* 383–402.

Newman, D. L., Moffitt, T. E., Caspi, A., & Silva, P. A. (1998). Comorbid mental disorders: Implications for treatment and sample selection. *Journal of Abnormal Psychology, 107,* 305–311.

Newman, J. P., Patterson, C. M., & Kosson, D. S. (1987). Response perseveration in psychopaths. *Journal of Abnormal Psychology, 96,* 145–149.

Newman, J. P., Schmitt, W. A., & Voss, W. D. (1997). The impact of motivationally neutral cues on psychopathic individuals: Assessing the generality of the response modulation hypothesis. *Journal of Abnormal Psychology, 196,* 563–575.

Nezu, A. A., Nezu, C. M., Friedman, S. H., Houts, P. S., & Faddis, S. (1997). The Project Genesis: Application of problem-solving therapy to individuals with cancer. *The Behavior Therapist, 20,* 155–158.

Nguyen, S. D. (1985). Mental health services for refugees and immigrants in Canada. In T. C. Owen (Ed.), *Southeast Asian mental health: Treatment, prevention, services, training, and research* (pp. 261–282). Washington, DC: National Institute of Mental Health.

Niederdeppe, J., Farrelly, M. C., & Haviland, M. L. (2004). Confirming "truth": More evidence of a successful tobacco countermarketing campaign in Florida. *American Journal of Public Health, 94,* 255–257.

Niedhammer, I., Goldberg, M., Leclerc, A., David, S., et al. (1998). Psychosocial work environment and cardiovascular risk factors in an occupational cohort in France. *Journal of Epidemiology and Community Health, 52,* 93–100.

Nietzel, M. T., & Harris, M. J. (1990). Relationship of dependency and achievement/ autonomy to depression. *Clinical Psychology Review, 10,* 279–297.

Nigg, J. T. (1999). The ADHD response inhibition deficit as measured by the stop task: Replication with DSM-IV combined type, extension, and qualification. *Journal of Abnormal Child Psychology, 27,* 393–402.

Nigg, J. T. (2001). Is ADHD a disinhibitory disorder? *Psychological Bulletin, 127,* 571–598.

Nigg, J. T., & Goldsmith, H. H. (1994). Genetics of personality disorders: Perspectives from personality and psychopathology research. *Psychological Bulletin, 115,* 346–380.

Nihira, K., Foster, R., Shenhaas, M., & Leland, H. (1975). *AAMD-Adaptive Behavior Scale.* Washington, DC: American Association on Mental Deficiency.

Nissen, M. J., Ross, J. L., Willingham, D. B., MacKenzie, T. B., & Schacter, D. L. (1988). Memory and awareness in a patient with multiple personality disorder. *Brain and Cognition, 8,* 117–134.

Noble, E. P. (2003). D2 dopamine receptor gene in psychiatric and neurologic disorders and its phenotypes. *American Journal of Medical Genetics, 116B,* 103–125.

Nobler, M. S., Oquendo, M. A., Kegeles, L. S., Malone, K. M., Campbell, C., Sackheim, H. A., et al. (2001). Decreased regional brain metabolism after ECT. *American Journal of Psychiatry, 158,* 305–308.

Nolen Hoeksema, S., Girgus, J. S., & Seligman, M. E. (1986). Learned helplessness in children: A longitudinal study of depression, achievement, and explanatory style. *Journal of Personality and Social Psychology, 51,* 435–442.

Noll, S. M., & Fredrickson, B. L. (1998). A mediational model linking self-objectification, body shame, and disordered eating. *Psychology of Women Quarterly, 22,* 623–636.

Nopoulos, P., Flaum, M., & Andreasen, N. C. (1997). Sex differences in brain morphology in schizophrenia. *American Journal of Psychiatry, 154,* 1648–1654.

Nordin, V., & Gillberg, C. (1998). The long-term course of autistic disorders: Update on follow-up studies. *Acta Psychiatrica Scandinavica, 97,* 99–108.

Norman, R. M., Malla, A. K., McLean, R. S., McIntosh, E. M., Neufeld, R. W., et al. (2002). An evaluation of a stress management program for individuals with schizophrenia. *Schizophrenia Research, 58,* 292–303.

Norton, G. R., Cox, B. J., & Malan, J. (1992). Non-clinical panickers: A critical review. *Clinical Psychology Review, 12,* 121–139.

Norton, J. P. (1982). *Expressed emotion, affective style, voice tone and communication deviance as predictors of offspring schizophrenia spectrum disorders.* Unpublished doctoral dissertation, University of California at Los Angeles.

Nourkova, V., Bernstein, D. M., & Loftus, E. F. (2004). Biography becomes autobiography: Distorting the subjective past. *American Journal of Psychology, 117,* 65–80.

Nowinski, J. (1999). Self-help groups for addictions. In B. S. McCrady & E. E. Epstein (Eds.). *Addictions: A comprehensive guidebook* (pp. 328–346). New York: Oxford University Press.

Noyes, R. (1999). The relationship of hypochondriasis to anxiety disorders. *General Hospital Psychiatry, 21,* 8–17.

Nunes, E. V., Quitkin, F. M., Donovan, S. J., Deliyannides, D., et al. (1998). Imipramine treatment of opiate-dependent patients with depressive disorders: A placebo-controlled trial. *Archives of General Psychiatry, 55,* 153–160.

O'Brien, W. H., & Haynes, S. N. (1995). Behavioral assessment. In L. A. Heiden & M. Hersen (Eds.), *Introduction to clinical psychology* (pp. 103–139). New York: Plenum.

O'Donnell, P., & Grace, A. A. (1998). Dysfunctions in multiple interrelated systems as the neurobiological bases of schizophrenic symptom clusters. *Schizophrenia Bulletin, 24,* 267–283.

O'Donohoe, W. (1993). The spell of Kuhn on psychology: An exegetical elixir. *Philosophical Psychology, 6,* 267–287.

O'Donohue, W., Dopke, C. A., & Swingen, D. N. (1997). Psychotherapy for female sexual dysfunction: A review. *Clinical Psychology Review, 17,* 537–566.

O'Donohue, W., & Plaud, J. J. (1994). The conditioning of human sexual arousal. *Archives of Sexual Behavior, 23,* 321–344.

O'Farrell, T. J. (1993). A behavioral marital therapy couples group program for alcoholics and their spouses. In T. J. O'Farrell (Ed.), *Treating alcohol problems: Marital and family interventions* (pp. 170–209). New York: Guilford Press.

O'Farrell, T. J., & Fals-Stewart, W. (2000). Behavioral couples therapy for alcoholism and drug abuse. *Journal of Substance Abuse Treatment, 18,* 51–54.

O'Farrell, T. J., Murphy, C. M., Neavins, T. M., & van Hutton, V. (2000). Verbal aggression among male alcoholic patients and their wives in the year before and two years after alcoholism treatment. *Journal of Family Violence, 15,* 295–310.

O'Leary, D. S., Block, R. I., Flaum, M., Schultz, S. K., Ponto, L. L., Boles, Watkins, G. L., Hurtig, R. R., Andreasen, N. C., & Hichwa, R. D. (2000). Acute marijuana effects on rCBF and cognition: A PET study. *Neuroreport: For Rapid Communication of Neuroscience Research, 11,* 3835–3841.

O'Leary, K. D., & Beach, S. R. (1990). Marital therapy: A viable treatment for depression and marital discord. *American Journal of Psychiatry, 147,* 183–186.

O'Leary, K. D., & Wilson, G. T. (1987). *Behavior therapy: Application and outcome.* Englewood Cliffs, NJ: Prentice-Hall.

O'Loughlin, J. O., Paradis, G., Kim, W., DiFranza, J., Meshefedjian, G., McMillan-Davey, E., Wong, S., Hanley, J., & Tyndale, R. F. (2005). Genetically decreased CYP2A6 and the risk of tobacco dependence: A prospective study of novice smokers. *Tobacco Control, 13,* 422–428.

O'Malley, S. S., Jaffe, A. J., Chang, G., Rode, S., Schottenfeld, R., et al. (1996). Six month follow-up of naltrexone and psychotherapy for alcohol dependence. *Archives of General Psychiatry, 53,* 217–224.

O'Neal, J. M. (1984). First person account: Finding myself and loving it. *Schizophrenia Bulletin, 10,* 109–110.

O'Neill, F. A., & Kendler, K. S. (1998). Longitudinal study of interpersonal dependency in female twins. *British Journal of Psychiatry, 172,* 154–158.

Obot, I. S., & Anthony, J. C. (1999). Association of school dropout with recent and past injecting drug use among African American adults. *Addictive Behaviors, 24,* 701–705.

Obot, I. S., & Anthony, J. C. (2000). School dropout and injecting drug use in a national sample of white non-hispanic american adults. *Journal of Drug Education, 30,* 145–155.

Obrist, P. A., Gaebelein, C. J., Teller, E. S., Langer, A. W., Grignolo, A., Light, K. C., & McCubbin, J. A. (1978). The relationship among heart rate, carotid dP/dt, and blood pressure in humans as a function of the type of stress. *Psychophysiology, 15,* 102–115.

Ockene, J. K., Mermelstein, R. J., Bonollo, D. S., Emmons, K. M., Perkins, K. A., Voorhees, C. C., & Hollis, J. F. (2000). Relapse and maintenance issues for smoking cessation. *Health Psychology, 19,* 17–31.

Oestling, S., & Skoog, I. (2002). Psychotic symptoms and paranoid ideation in a nondemented population-based sample of the very old. *Archives of General Psychiatry, 59,* 53–59.

Oetting, E. R., Deffenbacher, J. L., Taylor, M. J., Luther, N., Beauvais, F., & Edwards, R. W. (2000). Methamphetamine use by high school students: Recent trends, gender and ethnicity differences, and use of other drugs. *Journal of Child & Adolescent Substance Abuse, 10,* 33–50.

Office of Applied Studies. (2002). *Results from the 2001 National Household Survey on Drug Abuse: Volume I. Summary of national findings* (DHHS Publication No. SMA 02-3758, NHSDA Series H-17). Rockville, MD: Substance Abuse and Mental Health Services Administration.

Ogrodniczuk, J. S., & Piper, W. E. (2001). Day treatment for personality disorders: A review of research findings. *Harvard Review of Psychiatry, 9,* 105–117.

Öhman, A., Flykt, A., & Esteves, F. (2001). Emotion drives attention: Detecting the snake in the grass. *Journal of Experimental Psychology: General, 137,* 466–478.

Öhman, A., & Mineka, A. (2003). The malicious serpent: Snakes as a prototypical stimulus for an evolved module of fear. *Current Directions in Psychological Science, 12,* 5–9.

Öhman, A., & Soares, J. J. F. (1994). "Unconscious anxiety": Phobic responses to masked stimuli. *Journal of Abnormal Psychology, 103,* 231–240.

Olivardia, R., Pope, H. G., Mangweth, B., & Hudson, J. I. (1995). Eating disorders in college men. *American Journal of Psychiatry, 152,* 1279–1284.

Olshevski, J. L., Katz, A. D., & Knight, B. (1999). *Stress reduction for caregivers.* Philadelphia, PA: Brunner/Mazel.

Ono, Y., Yoshimura, K., Sueoka, R., Yaumachi, K., et al. (1996). Avoidant personality disorder and *taijin kyoufu:* Sociocultural implications of the WHO/ADAMHA International Study of Personality Disorders in Japan. *Acta Psychiatrica Scandinavica, 93,* 172–176.

Organista, K. C., & Munoz, R. F. (1996). Cognitive behavioral therapy with Latinos. *Cognitive and Behavioral Practice, 3,* 255–270.

Orlinsky, D. E., Ronnestad, M. H., & Willutzki, U. (2004). Fifty years of psychotherapy process-outcome research: Continuity and change. In M. J. Lambert (Ed.), *Bergin and Garfield's handbook of psychotherapy and behavior change* (5th ed.) (pp. 307–389). Hoboken, NJ: John Wiley & Sons.

Orr, S. P., Metzger, L. J., Lasko, N. B., Macklin, M. L., Hu, F. B., Shalev, A. Y., et al. (2003). Physiologic responses to sudden, loud tones in monozygotic twins discordant for combat exposure: Association with posttraumatic stress disorder. *Archives of General Psychiatry, 60,* 283–288.

Orth-Gomer, K., & Unden, A. L. (1990). Type A behavior, social support, and coronary risk: Interaction and significance for mortality in cardiac patients. *Psychosomatic Medicine, 52,* 59–72.

Öst, L.-G. (1992). Blood and injection phobia: Background and cognitive, physiological, and behavioral correlates. *Journal of Abnormal Psychology, 101,* 68–74.

Öst, L. G., Ferebee, I., & Furmark, T. (1997). One-session group therapy of spider phobia: Direct versus indirect treatments. *Behaviour Research and Therapy, 35,* 21–72.

Osterling, J., & Dawson, G. (1994). Early recognition of children with autism: A study of first birthday home videotapes. *Journal of Autism and Developmental Disorders, 24,* 247–257.

Ostling, S., & Skoog, I. (2002). Psychotic symptoms and paranoid ideation in a nondemented population-based sample of the very old. *Archives of General Psychiatry, 59,* 53–59.

Otto, M. W., Wilhelm, S., Cohen, L. S., & Harlow, B. L. (2001). Prevalence of body dysmorphic disorder in a community sample of women. *American Journal of Psychiatry, 158,* 2061–2063.

Ouimette, P. C., Finney, J. W., & Moos, R. H. (1997). Twelve-step and cognitive-behavioral treatment for substance abuse: A comparison of treatment effectiveness. *Journal of Consulting and Clinical Psychology, 65,* 230–240.

Owen, M. J., Williams, N. M., & O'Donovan, M. C. (2004). The molecular genetics of schizophrenia: new findings promise new insights. *Molecular Psychiatry, 9*, 14–27.

Owen, P. P., & Laurel-Seller, E. (2000). Weight and shape ideals: Thin is dangerously in. *Journal of Applied Social Psychology, 54*, 682–687.

Pahkala, K. (1990). Social and environmental factors and depression in old age. *International Journal of Geriatric Psychiatry, 5*, 99–113.

Pantelis, C., Velakoulis, D., McGorry, P. D., et al. (2003). Neuroanatomical abnormalities before and after onset of psychosis: A cross-sectional and longitudinal MRI comparison. *The Lancet, 361*, 281–288.

Paris, J. (1999). *Nature and nurture in psychiatry: A predisposition—stress model of mental disorders.* Washington, DC: American Psychiatric Association.

Paris, J. (2002). Implications of long-term outcome research for the management of patients with borderline personality disorder. *Harvard Review of Psychiatry, 10*, 315–323.

Paris, J. (2003). Personality disorders over time: Precursors, course and outcome. *Journal of Personality Disorders, 17*, 479–488.

Park, H. L., O'Connell, J. E., & Thomson, R. G. (2003). A systematic review of cognitive decline in the general elderly population. *International Journal of Geriatric Psychiatry, 18*, 1121–1134.

Paschall, M. J., Flewelling, R. L., & Faulkner, D. (2000). Alcohol misuse in young adulthood: Effects of race, educational attainment, and social context. *Substance Use and Misuse, 35*, 1485–1506.

Pasquier, F., Fukui, T., Sarazin, M., Pijnenburg, Y., Diehl, J., Grundman, M., & Miller, B. L. (2003). Laboratory investigations and treatment in frontotemporal dementia. *Annals of Neurology, 54* (Suppl 5), S32–S35.

Patrick, C. J. (1994). Emotion and psychopathy: Some startling new insights. *Psychophysiology, 31*, 319–330.

Patterson, C. M., & Newman, J. P. (1993). Reflectivity and learning from aversive events: Toward a psychological mechanism for the syndromes of disinhibition. *Psychological Review, 100*, 716–736.

Patterson, G. R. (1982). *Coercive family process.* Eugene, OR: Castilia.

Patterson, G. R. (1974). A basis for identifying stimuli which control behaviors in natural settings. *Child Development, 45*, 900–911.

Patterson, G. R., Crosby, L., & Vuchinich, S. (1992). Predicting risk for early police arrest. *Journal of Quantitative Criminology, 8*, 335–355.

Paul, G. L., & Lentz, R. J. (1977). *Psychosocial treatment of chronic mental patients: Milieu versus social learning programs.* Cambridge, MA: Harvard University Press.

Paul, G. L., & Menditto, A. A. (1992). Effectiveness of inpatient treatment programs for mentally ill adults in public psychiatric facilities. *Applied and Preventive Psychology: Current Scientific Perspectives, 1*, 41–63.

Paul, G. L., Stuve, P., & Cross, J. V. (1997). Real-world inpatient programs: Shedding some light. *Applied and Preventive Psychology.*

Paulhus, D. L. (1998). Interpersonal and intrapsychic adaptiveness of trait self-enhancement: A mixed blessing? *Journal of Personality and Social Psychology, 74*, 1197–1208.

Paxton, S. J., Schutz, H. K., Wertheim, E. H., & Muir, S. L. (1999). Friendship clique and peer influences on body image concerns, dietary restraint, extreme weight-loss behaviors, and binge eating in adolescent girls. *Journal of Abnormal Psychology, 108*, 255–264.

Payne, A., & Blanchard, E. B. (1995). A controlled comparison of cognitive therapy and self-help support groups in the treatment of irritable bowel syndrome. *Journal of Consulting and Clinical Psychology, 63*, 779–786.

Peeples, F., & Loeber, R. (1994). Do individual factors and neighborhood context explain ethnic differences in juvenile delinquency? *Journal of Quantitative Criminology, 10*, 141–157.

Pelham, W. E., Gnagy, E. M., Greiner, A. R., Hoza, B., Hinshaw, S. P., Swanson, J. M., Simpson, S., Shapiro, C., Bukstein, O., Baron-Myak, C., & McBurnett, K. (2000). Behavioral versus behavioral plus pharmacological treatment for ADHD children attending a summer treatment program. *Journal of Abnormal Child Psychology, 28*, 507–525.

Penn, D. L., Chamberlin, C., & Mueser, K. T. (2003). The effects of a documentary film about schizophrenia on psychiatric stigma. *Schizophrenia Bulletin, 29*, 383–391.

Penn, D. L., & Mueser, K. T. (1996). Research update on the psychosocial treatment of schizophrenia. *American Journal of Psychiatry, 153*, 607–617.

Pennebaker, J. W., Kiecolt-Glaser, J. K., & Glaser, R. (1988). Disclosure of traumas and immune function: Health implications for psychotherapy. *Journal of Consulting and Clinical Psychology, 56*, 239–245.

Pennington, B. F. (1995). Genetics of learning disabilities. *Journal of Child Neurology, 10*, S69–S77.

Perez, M., & Joiner, T. E. (2003). Body image dissatisfaction and disordered eating in black and white women. *International Journal of Eating Disorders, 33*, 342–350.

Perez, M., Voelz, Z. R., Pettit, J. W., & Joiner, T. E. (2002). The role of acculturative stress and body dissatisfaction in predicting bulimic symptomatology across ethnic groups. *International Journal of Eating Disorders, 31*, 442–454.

Perkins, D. D. (1995). Speaking truth to power: Empowerment ideology as social intervention and policy. *American Journal of Community Psychology, 23*, 765–794.

Perlin, M. L. (1994). *Law and mental disability.* Charlottesville, VA: The Michie Company.

Perls, F. S. (1969). *Gestalt therapy verbatim.* Moab, UT: Real People Press.

Perry, J. C., Banon, E., & Ianni, F. (1999). Effectiveness of psychotherapy for personality disorders. *American Journal of Psychiatry, 156*, 1312–1321.

Perry, R., Campbell, M., Adams, P., Lynch, N., Spencer, E. K., Curren, E. L., & Overall, J. E. (1989). Long-term efficacy of haloperidol in autistic children: Continuous versus discontinuous administration. *Journal of the American Academy of Child and Adolescent Psychiatry, 28*, 87–92.

Persing, J. S., Stuart, S. P., Noyes, R., & Happel, R. L. (2000). Hypochondrisis: The patient's perspective. *International Journal of Psychiatry in Medicine, 30*, 329–342.

Persons, J. B. (1991). Psychotherapy outcome studies do not accurately represent current models of psychotherapy: A proposed remedy. *American Psychologist, 46*, 99–106.

Persons, J. B. (2005). Empiricism, mechanism, and the practice of cognitive behavior therapy. *Behavior Therapy, 36*, 107–118.

Persons, J. B., Bostrom, A., & Bertagnolli, A. (1999). Results of randomized controlled trials of cognitive therapy for depression generalize to private practice. *Cognitive Therapy Research, 23*, 535–548.

Persons, J. B., Thase, M. E., & Crits-Christoph, P. (1996). The role of psychotherapy in the treatment of depression: Review of two practice guidelines. *Archives of General Psychiatry, 53*, 283–290.

Perugi, G., Akiskal, H. S., Giannotti, D., Frare, F., et al. (1997). Gender-related differences in body dysmorphic disorder. *Journal of Nervous and Mental Disease, 185*, 578–582.

Peters, M. (1977). Hypertension and the nature of stress. *Science, 198*, 80.

Peterson, C., Maier, S. F., & Seligman, M. E. P. (1993). *Learned helplessness: A theory for the age of personal control.* London: Oxford University Press.

Peterson, J. L., Coates, T. J., Catania, J., Hauck, W. W., Acree, M., Daigle, D., Hillard, B., Middleton, L., & Hearst, N. (1996). Evaluation of an HIV risk reduction intervention among African American homosexual and bisexual men. *AIDS, 10*, 319–325.

Peterson, C., Maier, S. F., & Seligman, M. E. P. (1993). *Learned Helplessness: A theory for the age of personal control.* London: Oxford University Press.

Petry, N. M., Martin, B., Cooney, J. L., & Kranzler, H. R. (2000). Give them prizes and they will come: Contingency management for treatment of alcohol dependence. *Journal of Consulting & Clinical Psychology, 68*, 250–257.

Pfefferbaum, A., Sullivan, E. V., Rosenbloom, M. J., Mathalon, D. H., & Lim, K. O. (1998). A controlled study of cortical grey matter and ventricular changes in alcoholic men over a 5-year interval. *Archives of General Psychiatry, 55*, 905–912.

Phares, E. J., & Trull, T. J. (1997). *Clinical psychology.* Pacific Grove, CA: Brooks/Cole.

Philips, K. A., Albertini, R. S., & Rasmussen, S. A. (2002). A randomized placebo-controlled trial of fluoxetine in body dysmorphic disorder. *Archives of General Psychiatry, 59*, 381–388.

Philips, K. A., McElroy, S. L., Dwight, M. M., et al. (2001). Delusionality and response to open-label fluvoxamine in body dysmorphic disorder. *Journal of Clinical Psychiatry, 62*, 87–91.

Philips, K. A., McFlroy, S. L., Keck, P. E., Pope, H. G., & Hudson, J. L. (1993). Body dysmorphic disorder: 30 cases of imagined ugliness. *American Journal of Psychiatry, 150*, 302–308.

Phillips, D. P. (1974). The influence of suggestion on suicide: Substantive and theoretical implications of the Werther effect. *American Sociological Review, 39*, 340–354.

Phillips, D. P. (1985). The found experiment: A new technique for assessing impact of mass media violence on real-world aggressive behavior. In G. Comstock (Ed.), *Public communication and behavior* (Vol. 1). New York: Academic Press.

Phillips, M. R., Li, X., & Zhang, Y. (2002). Suicide rates in China, 1995–99. *Lancet, 359*, 835–840.

Pierce, J. P., Choi, W. S., Gilpin, E. A., Farkas, A. J., & Berry, C. C. (1998). Tobacco ads, promotional items linked with teen smoking. *JAMA, 279*, 511–515.

Pierce, K., & Courchesne, E. (2001). Evidence for a cerebellar role in reduced exploration and stereotyped behavior in autism. *Biological Psychiatry, 49*, 655–664.

Pierce, K., Haist, F., Sedaghadt, F., & Corchesne, E. (2004). The brain response to personally familiar faces in autism: Findings of fusiform activity and beyond. *Brain, 127*, 1–14.

Pierce, K., Muller, R. A., Ambrose, J., Allen, G., & Courchesne, E. (2001). Face processing occurs outside the fusiform 'face area' in autism: Evidence from functional MRI. *Brain, 124*, 2059–2073.

Pike, K. M., Dohm, F., Striegel-Moore, R. H., Wilfley, D. E., & Fairburn, C. M. (2001). A comparison of black and white women with binge eating disorder. *American Journal of Psychiatry, 158*, 1455–1460.

Pilling, S., Bebbington, P., Kuipers, E., Garety, P., Geddes, L., Martindale, B., Orbach, G., & Morgan, C. (2002). Psychological treatments in schizophrenia: II. Meta-analyses of randomized controlled trials of social skills training and cognitive remediation. *Psychological Medicine, 32*, 783–791.

Piper, A., Jr., Pope, H. G., Jr., & Borowiecki III, J. J. (2000). Custer's last stand: Brown, Schefln, and Whitfiled's latest attempt to salvage "dissociative amnesia." *Journal of Psychiatry and the Law, 28,* 149–213.

Piven, J., Arndt, S., Bailey, J., & Andreasen, N. (1996). Regional brain enlargement in autism: A magnetic resonance imaging study. *Journal of the American Academy of Child and Adolescent Psychiatry, 35,* 530–536.

Piven, J., Arndt, S., Bailey, J., Havercamp, S., Andreasen, N. C., & Palmer, P. (1995). An MRI study of brain size in autism. *American Journal of Psychiatry, 152,* 1145–1149.

Placidi, G. P., Oquendo, M. A., Malone, K. M., Huang, Y. Y., Ellis, S. P., & Mann, J. J. (2001). Aggressivity, suicide attempts, and depression: Relationship to cerebrospinal fluid monoamine metabolite levels. *Biological Psychiatry, 50,* 783–791.

Plomin, R. (1999). Genetics and general cognitive ability. *Nature, 402,* C25–C29.

Plomin, R., DeFries, J. C., Craig, I. W., & McGuffin, P. (2003). *Behavioral Genetics in the Postgenomic Era.* Washington, DC: APA Books.

Plomin, R., & McGuffin, P. (2003). Psychopathology in the postgenomic era. *Annual Review of Psychology, 54,* 205–228.

Plotkin, D. A., Mintz, J., & Jarvik, L. F. (1985). Subjective memory complaints in geriatric depression. *American Journal of Psychiatry, 142,* 1103–1105.

Polich, J. M., Armor, D. J., & Braiker, H. B. (1980). Patterns of alcoholism over four years. *Journal of Studies on Alcohol, 41,* 397–415.

Polivy, J. (1976). Perception of calories and regulation of intake in restrained and unrestrained eaters. *Addictive Behaviors, 1,* 237–244.

Polivy, J., Heatherton, T. F., & Herman, C. P. (1988). Self-esteem, restraint and eating behavior. *Journal of Abnormal Psychology, 97,* 354–356.

Polivy, J., & Herman, C. P. (1985). Dieting and binging: A causal analysis. *American Psychologist, 40,* 193–201.

Polivy, J., Herman, C. P., & Howard, K. (1980). The Restraint Scale. In A. Stunkard (Ed.), *Obesity.* Philadelphia: Saunders.

Polivy, J., Herman, C. P., & McFarlane, T. (1994). Effects of anxiety on eating: Does palatability moderate distress-induced overeating in dieters? *Journal of Abnormal Psychology, 103,* 505–510.

Pollack, M. H., Zainelli, R., Goddard, A., et al. (2001). Paroxetine in the treatment of generalized anxiety disorder: Results of a placebo-controlled, flexible dosage trial. *Journal of Clinical Psychiatry, 62,* 350–357.

Polonsky, D. C. (2000). Premature ejaculation. In R. C. Rosen and S. R. Leiblum (Eds.), *Principles and practice of sex therapy* (3rd ed., pp. 305–332). New York: Guilford.

Pomerleau, O. F., Collins, A. C., Shiffman, S., & Pomerleau, C. S. (1993). Why some people smoke and others do not: New perspectives. *Journal of Consulting and Clinical Psychology 61,* 723–731.

Ponce, F., & Atkinson, D. (1989). Mexican-Americans and acculturation, counselor ethnicity, counseling style, and perceived counselor credibility. *Journal of Counseling Psychology, 36,* 203–208.

Poole, D. A., Lindsay, D. S., Memon, A., & Bull, R. (1995). Psychotherapy and the recovery of memories of childhood sexual abuse: U.S. and British practitioners' opinions, practices and experiences. *Journal of Consulting and Clinical Psychology, 63,* 426–437.

Pope, K. S. (1998). Pseudoscience, cross-examination, and scientific evidence in the recovered memory controversy. *Psychology, Public Policy, and Law, 4,* 1160–1181.

Porter, S., Yuille, J. C., & Lehman, D. R. (1999). The nature of real, implanted, and fabricated memories for emotional childhood events: Implications for the recovered memory debate. *Law and Human Behavior, 23,* 415–537.

Posey, M. J., & McDougle, C. M. (2000). The pharmacotherapy of target symptoms associated with autistic disorder and other pervasive developmental disorders. *Harvard Review of Psychiatry, 8,* 45–63.

Potashnik, S., & Pruchno, R. (1988, November). *Spouse caregivers: Physical and mental health in perspective.* Paper presented at the meeting of the Gerontological Society of America, San Francisco.

Potkin, S. G., Alva, G., Fleming, K., et al. (2002). A PET study of the pathophysiology of negative symptoms in schizophrenia. *American Journal of Psychiatry, 159,* 227–237.

Powell, L. H., Friedman, M., Thoresen, C. E., Gill, J. J., & Ulmer, D. K. (1984). Can the type A behavior pattern be altered after myocardial infarction? A second year report from the Recurrent Coronary Prevention Project. *Psychosomatic Medicine, 46,* 293–313.

Powell, R. A., & Gee, T. L. (2000). "The effects of hypnosis on dissociative identity disorder: A reexamination of the evidence": Reply. *Canadian Journal of Psychiatry, 45,* 848–849.

Power, K. G., Simpson, R. J., Swanson, V., Wallace, I. A., Feistner, A. T. C., & Sharp, D. (1990). A controlled comparison of cognitive-behaviour therapy, diazepam, and placebo, alone and in combination, for the treatment of generalized anxiety disorder. *Journal of Anxiety Disorders, 4,* 267–292.

Praderas, K., & MacDonald, M. L. (1986). Telephone conversational skills training with socially isolated impaired nursing home residents. *Journal of Applied Behavior Analysis, 19,* 337–348.

Prechter, G. C., & Shepard, J. W. J. (1990). Sleep and sleep disorders in the elderly. In R. J. Martin (Ed.), *Cardiorespiratory disorders during sleep* (pp. 365–386). Armonk, NY: Futura Publishing Co.

Prentky, R., & Burgess, A. W. (1990). Rehabilitation of child molesters: A cost-benefit analysis. *American Journal of Orthopsychiatry, 60*(1), 108–117.

Price, R. A., Cadoret, R. J., Stunkard, A. J., & Troughton, E. (1987). Genetic contributions to human fatness: An adoption study. *American Journal of Psychiatry, 144,* 1003–1008.

Prien, R. F., & Potter, W. Z. (1993). Maintenance treatment for mood disorders. In D. L. Dunner (Ed.), *Current psychiatric therapy.* Philadelphia: Saunders.

Prieto, S. L., Cole, D. A., & Tageson, C. W. (1992). Depressive self-schemas in clinic and nonclinic children. *Cognitive Therapy and Research, 16,* 521–534.

Prinz, P., & Raskind, M. (1978). Aging and sleep disorders. In R. Williams & R. Karacan (Eds.), *Sleep disorders: Diagnosis and treatment.* New York: Wiley.

Prizant, B. M. (1983). Language acquisition and communicative behavior in autism: Toward an understanding of the "whole" of it. *Journal of Speech and Hearing Disorders, 48,* 296–307.

Project MATCH Research Group. (1997). Matching alcoholism treatments to client heterogeneity: Project MATCH posttreatment drinking outcomes. *Journal of Studies on Alcohol, 58,* 7–29.

Pryor, T., Wiederman, M. W., & McGilley, B. (1996). Clinical correlates of anorexia subtypes. *International Journal of Eating Disorders, 19,* 371–379.

Pu, T., Mohamed, E., Imam, K., & El-Roey, A. M. (1986). One hundred cases of hysteria in eastern Libya. *British Journal of Psychiatry, 148,* 606–609.

Purdie, F. R., Honigman, T. B., & Rosen, P. (1981). Acute organic brain syndrome: A view of 100 cases. *Annals of Emergency Medicine, 10,* 455–461.

Putnam, F. W. (1993). Dissociative disorders in children: Behavioral profiles and problems. *Child Abuse and Neglect, 17,* 39–45.

Putnam, F. W. (1996). A brief history of multiple personality disorder. *Child and Adolescent Psychiatric Clinics of North America, 5,* 263–271.

Putnam, F. W., Guroff, J. J., Silberman, E. K., Barban, L., & Post, R. M. (1986). The clinical phenomenology of multiple personality disorder: Review of 100 recent cases. *Journal of Clinical Psychiatry, 47,* 285–293.

Pyle, A. (1999, May 28). Seeking a remedy for nursing homes' ills. *Los Angeles Times,* pp. A1–A30.

Qualls, S. H., Segal, D. L., Norman, S., Niederehe, G., & Gallagher-Thompson, D. (2002). Psychologists in practice with older adults: Current patterns, sources of training, and need for continuing education. *Professional Psychology: Research and Practice, 33,* 435–442.

Rachman, S. (1977). The conditioning theory of fear acquisition: A critical examination. *Behaviour Research and Therapy, 15,* 375–387.

Rachman, S. (1997). A cognitive theory of obsessions. *Behaviour Research and Therapy, 35,* 793–802.

Rachman, S., & DeSilva, P. (1978). Abnormal and normal obsessions. *Behaviour Research and Therapy, 16,* 233–248.

Rachman, S. J. (1966). Sexual fetishism: An experimental analogue. *Psychological Record, 16,* 293–296.

Rachman, S. J., & Wilson, G. T. (1980). *The effects of psychological therapy* (2nd ed.). Elmsford, NY: Pergamon.

Räikkönen, K., Matthews, K. A., Flory, J. D., & Owens, J. F. (1999). Effects of hostility on ambulatory blood pressure and mood during daily living. *Health Psychology, 18,* 44–53.

Räikkönen, K., Matthews, K. A., & Salomen, K. (2003). Hostility predicts metabolic syndrome risk factors in children and adolescents. *Health Psychology, 22,* 279–286.

Raine, A., Lencz, T., Bihrle, S., et al. (2000). Reduced prefrontal gray matter and reduced autonomic activity in antisocial personality disorder. *Archives of General Psychiatry, 57,* 119–127.

Raj, B. A., Corvea, M. H., & Dagon, E. M. (1993). The clinical characteristics of panic disorder in the elderly: A retrospective study. *Journal of Clinical Psychiatry, 54,* 150–155.

Rao, Y., Hoffmann, E., Zia, M., et al. (2000). Duplications and defects in the CYP2A6 gene: Identification, genotyping, and in vivo effects on smoking. *Molecular Pharmacology, 58,* 747–755.

Rapaport, D. (1951). *The organization and pathology of thought.* New York: Columbia University Press.

Rapee, R., Mattick, R., & Murrell, E. (1986). Cognitive mediation in the affective component of spontaneous panic attacks. *Journal of Behavior Therapy and Experimental Psychiatry, 17,* 245–253.

Rapin, I. (1997). Autism. *New England Journal of Medicine, 337,* 97–104.

Rapoport, J. L., Swedo, S. E., & Leonard, H. L. (1992). Childhood obsessive compulsive disorder. *Journal of Clinical Psychiatry, 53*(4, Suppl.), 11–16.

Rappaport, J., & Chinsky, J. M. (1974). Models for delivery of service from a historical and conceptual perspective. *Professional Psychology, 5,* 42–50.

Raskind, W. H. (2001). Current understanding of the genetic basis of reading and spelling disability. *Learning Disability Quarterly, 24,* 141–157.

Rassin, E., Merckelbach, H., Muris, P., & Schmidt, H. (2001). The thought-action fusion scale: Further evidence for its reliability and validity. *Behaviour Research and Therapy, 39,* 537–544.

Rassin, E., Muris, P., Schmidt, H., & Merckelbach, H. (2000). Relationships between thought-action fusion, thought suppression and obsessive-compulsive symptoms: A structural equation modeling approach. *Behaviour Research and Therapy, 38,* 889–897.

Rather, B. C., Goldman, M. S., Roehrich, L., & Brannick, M. (1992). Empirical modeling of an alcohol expectancy memory network using multidimensional scaling. *Journal of Abnormal Psychology, 101,* 174–183.

Rauch, S. L., & Jenike, M. A. (1998). Pharmacological treatment of obsessive compulsive disorder. In Jack M. Gorman and Peter E. Nathan (Eds.), *A guide to treatments that work* (pp. 358–376). London: Oxford University Press.

Rauch, S. L., Phillips, K. A., Segal, F., Makris, N., Shin, L. M., Whalen, P. J., et al. (2003). A preliminary morphometric magnetic resonance imaging study of regional brain volumes in body dysmorphic disorder. *Psychiatry Research: Neuroimaging, 122,* 13–19.

Rauch, S. L., Whalen, P. J., Shin, L. M., McInerney, S. C., Macklin, M. L., Lasko, N. B., Orr, S. P., & Pitman, R. K. (2000). Exaggerated amygdala response to masked facial stimuli in posttraumatic stress disorder: A functional MRI study. *Biological Psychiatry, 47,* 769–776.

Rawson, R. A., Martinelli-Casey, P., Anglin, M. D., et al. (2004). A multi-site comparison of psychosocial approaches for the treatment of methamphetamine dependence. *Addiction, 99,* 708–717.

Reas, D. L., Williamson, D. A., Martin, C. K., & Zucker, N. L. (2000). Duration of illness predicts outcome for bulimia nervosa: A long-term follow-up study. *International Journal of Eating Disorders, 27,* 428–434.

Rechlin, T., Loew, T. H., & Joraschky, P. (1997). Pseudoseizure "status." *Journal of Psychosomatic Research, 42,* 495–498.

Red Horse, Y. (1982). A cultural network model: Perspectives for adolescent services and paraprofessional training. In S. Manson (Ed.), *New directions in prevention among American Indians and Alaskan Native communities.* Portland: Oregon Health Sciences University.

Redmond, D. E. (1977). Alterations in the function of the nucleus locus coeruleus. In I. Hanin & E. Usdin (Eds.), *Animal models in psychiatry and neurology.* New York: Pergamon.

Reed, J. C., & Reed, H. B. C. (1997). The Halstead-Reitan Neuropsychological Battery. In G. Goldstein & T. Incagnoli (Eds.), *Contemporary approaches to neuropsychological assessment* (pp. 93–130). New York: Plenum.

Reed, S. D., Katkin, E. S., & Goldband, S. (1986). Biofeedback and behavioral medicine. In F. H. Kanfer & A. P. Goldstein (Eds.), *Helping people change: A textbook of methods* (3rd ed.). Elmsford, NY: Pergamon.

Reeder, G. D., Pryor, J. B., & Harsh, I. (1997). Activity and similarity in safer sex workshops led by peer educators. *AIDS Education and Prevention, 9,* 77–89.

Rees, L. (1964). The importance of psychological, allergic and infective factors in childhood asthma. *Journal of Psychosomatic Research, 7,* 253–262.

Regeer, E. J., ten Have, M., Rosso, M. L., van Roijen, L. H., Vollebergh, W., & Nolen, W. A. (2004). Prevalence of bipolar disorder in the general population: A reappraisal study of the netherlands mental health survey and incidence study. *Acta Psychiatrica Scandinavica, 110,* 374–382.

Regier, D. A., Boyd, J. H., Burke, J. D., Jr., Rae, D. S., Myers, J. K., Kramer, M., Robins, L. N., George, L. K., Karno, M., & Locke, B. Z. (1988). One-month prevalence of mental disorders in the United States. *Archives of General Psychiatry, 45,* 977–986.

Regier, D. A., Boyd, J. H., Burke, J. D., & Rae, D. S. (1988). One-month prevalence of mental disorders in the united states: Based on five epidemiologic catchment area sites. *Archives of General Psychiatry, 45,* 977–986.

Regier, D. A., Narrow, W. E., Rae, D. S., & Manderscheid, R. W. (1993). The de facto US mental and addictive disorders service system: Epidemiologic catchment area prospective 1-year prevalence rates of disorders and services. *Archives of General Psychiatry, 50,* 85–94.

Reich, D., & Zanarini, M. C. (2001). Developmental aspects of borderline personality disorder. *Harvard Review of Psychiatry, 9,* 294–301.

Reichman, W. E., Coyne, A. C., Borson, S., et al. (1998). Psychiatric consultation in the nursing home: A survey of six states. *American Journal of Geriatric Psychiatry, 6,* 320–327.

Reid, D. H., Wilson, P. G., & Faw, G. D. (1991). Teaching self-help skills. In J. L. Matson & J. A. Mulick (Eds.), *Handbook of mental retardation.* New York: Pergamon Press.

Reilly-Harrington, N. A., Alloy, L. B., Fresco, D. M., & Whitehouse, W. G. (1999). Cognitive styles and life events interact to predict bipolar and unipolar symptomatology. *Journal of Abnormal Psychology, 108,* 567–578.

Reiman, E. M., Caselli, R. J., Yun, L., Chen, K., Bandy, D., et al. (1996). Preclinical evidence of Alzheimer's disease in persons homozygous for the e4 allele for apolipoprotein E. *New England Journal of Medicine, 334,* 752–756.

Reimherr, F. W., Strong, R. E., Marchant, B. K., Hedges, D. W., & Wender, P. H. (2001). Factors affecting return of symptoms 1 year after treatment in a 62-week controlled study of fluoxetine in major depression. *Journal of Clinical Psychiatry, 62,* 16–23.

Reiner, W. G., & Gearhart, J. P. (2004). Discordant sexual identity in some genetic males with cloacal exstrophy assigned to female sex at birth. *New England Journal of Medicine, 350,* 333–341.

Reiser, M. F., Brust, A. A., Shapiro, A. P., Baker, H. M., Ranschoff, W., & Ferris, E. B. (1950). Life situations, emotions and the course of patients with arterial hypertension. *Research Publications of the Association for Research in Nervous & Mental Disease, 29,* 870–880.

Reiss, D., Heatherington, E. M., Plomin, R., Howe, G. W., Simmens, S. J., et al. (1995). Genetic questions for environmental studies: Differential parenting and psychopathology in adolescence. *Archives of General Psychiatry, 52,* 925–936.

Reissing, E. D., Binik, Y. M., & Khalife, S. (1999). Does vaginismus exist? A critical review of the literature. *Journal of Nervous and Mental Disease, 187,* 261–274.

Renemeno, L., Booij, J., Schmand, B., van den Brink, W., & Gunning, B. (2000). Memory disturbances in "Ecstasy" users are correlated with an altered brain serotonin neurotransmission. *Psychopharmacology, 148,* 322–324.

Renneberg, B., Goldstein, A. J., Phillips, D., & Chambless, D. L. (1990). Intensive behavioral group treatment of avoidant personality disorder. *Behavior Therapy, 21,* 363–377.

Renvoize, E. B., & Beveridge, A. W. (1989). Mental illness and the late Victorians: A study of patients admitted to three asylums in York, 1880-1884. *Psychological Medicine, 19,* 19–28.

Rescorla, R. A. (1988). Pavlovian conditioning: It's not what you think it is. *American Psychologist, 43,* 151–160.

Resick, P. A., Nishith, P., Weaver, T. L., Astin, M. C., & Feuer, C. A. (2002). A comparison of cognitive-processing therapy with prolonged exposure and a waiting condition for the treatment of chronic posttraumatic stress disorder in female rape victims. *Journal of Consulting and Clinical Psychology, 70,* 867–879.

Ressler, K. J., & Nemeroff, C. B. (1999). Role of norepinephrine in the pathophysiology and treatment of mood disorders. *Biological Psychiatry, 46,* 1219–1233.

Rey, J. M., Martin, A., & Krabman, P. (2004). Is the party over? Cannabis and juvenile psychiatric disorder: The past 10 years. *Journal of the American Academy of Child and Adolescent Psychiatry, 43,* 1194–1205.

Reynolds, C. F. I., Miller, M. D., Pasternak, R. E., Frank, E., Perel, J. M., Cornes, C., et al. (1999). Treatment of bereavement-related major depressive episodes in later life: A controlled study of acute and continuation treatment with nortriptyline and interpersonal psychotherapy. *American Journal of Psychiatry, 156,* 202–208.

Reynolds, C. R., Chastain, R. L., Kaufman, A. S., & McLean, J. E. (1997). Demographic characteristics and IQ among adults: Analysis of the WAIS-R standardization sample as a function of the stratification variables. *Journal of School Psychology, 25,* 323–342.

Richards, P. S., Baldwin, B. M., Frost, H. A., Clark-Sly, J. B., Berrett, M. E., & Hardman, R. K. (2000). What works for treating eating disorders? Conclusions of 28 outcome reviews. *Eating Disorders, 8,* 189–206.

Richards, R. L., Kinney, D. K., Lunde, I., Benet, M., & Merzel, A. (1988). Creativity in manic-depressives, cyclothymes, their normal relatives, and control subjects. *Journal of Abnormal Psychology, 97,* 281–288.

Richardson, J. D., Kilo, Hargreaves, K. M. (1998). Cannabinoids reduce hyperalgesia and inflammation via interaction with peripheral CBI receptors. *Pain, 75,* 111–119.

Ricks, D. M. (1972). *The beginning of vocal communication in infants and autistic children.* Unpublished doctoral dissertation, University of London.

Ridenour, T. A., Miller, A. R., Joy, K. L., & Dean, R. S. (1997). "Profile" analysis of the personality characteristics of child molesters using the MMPI-2. *Journal of Clinical Psychology, 53,* 575–586.

Ridker, P. M., Cook, N. R., Lee, I.-M., Gordon, D., Gaziano, J. M., Manson, J. E., Hennekens, C. H., & Buring, J. E. (2005). A Randomized trial of low-dose aspirin in the primary prevention of cardiovascular disease in women. *JAMA, 352,* 1293–1304.

Ridley, M. (2003). *Nature via Nurture: Genes, Experience, and what makes us human.* Great Britain: Harpers Collins..

Rieder, R. O., Mann, L. S., Weinberger, D. R., van Kammen, D. P., & Post, R. M. (1983). Computer tomographic scans in patients with schizophrenia, schizoaffective, and bipolar affective disorder. *Archives of General Psychiatry, 40,* 735–739.

Rief, W., & Auer, C. (2001). Is somatization a habituation disorder? Physiological reactivity in somatization syndrome. *Psychiatry Research, 101,* 63–74.

Riley, A. J., & Riley, E. J. (1978). A controlled study to evaluate directed masturbation in the management of primary orgasmic failure in women. *British Journal of Psychiatry, 133,* 404–409.

Rimland, B. (1964). *Infantile autism.* New York: Appleton-Century-Crofts.

Rind, B., Tromovitch, P., & Bauserman, R. (1998). A meta-analytic examination of assumed properties of child sexual abuse using college students. *Psychological Bulletin, 124,* 22–53.

Ringwalt, C., Ennett, S. T., & Holt, K. D. (1991). An outcome evaluation of Project DARE (Drug Abuse Resistance Education). *Health Education Research, 6,* 327–337.

Rinne, T., van den Brink, W., Wouters, L., & van Dyck, R. (2002). SSRI treatment of borderline personality disorder: A randomized, placebo-controlled clinical trial for female patients with borderline personality disorder. *American Journal of Psychiatry, 159,* 2048–2054.

Ritsher, J. B., Struening, E. L., Hellman, F., & Guardino, M. (2002). Internal validity of an anxiety disorder screening instrument across five ethnic groups. *Psychiatry Research, 111,* 199–213.

Ritvo, E. R., Freeman, B. J., Geller, E., & Yuwiler, A. (1983). Effects of fenfluramine on 14 outpatients with the syndrome of autism. *Journal of the American Academy of Child Psychiatry, 22,* 549–558.

Ritz, T., Dahme, B., & Roth, W. T. (2004). Behavioral interventions in asthma: Biofeedback techniques. *Journal of Psychosomatic Research, 56,* 711–720.

Ritz, T., & Roth, W. T. (2003). Behavioral interventions in asthma: Breathing training. *Behavior Modification, 27,* 710–730.

Roan, S. (1992, October 15). Giving up coffee tied to withdrawal symptoms. *Los Angeles Times,* pp. A26.

Robbins, S. J., Ehrman, R. N., Childress, A. R., Cornish, J. W., & O'Brien, C. P. (2000). Mood state and recent cocaine use are not associated with levels of cocaine cue reactivity. *Drug and Alcohol Dependence, 59,* 33–42.

Robins, C. J., & Chapman, A. L. (2004). Dialectical behavior therapy: Current status, recent developments, and future directions. *Journal of Personality Disorders, 18,* 73–89.

Robins, L. N., & Price, R. K. (1991). Adult disorders predicted by childhood conduct problems: Results from the NIMH epidemiologic catchment area project. *Psychiatry: Journal for the Study of Interpersonal Processes, 54,* 116–132.

Robinson, D., Woerner, M. G., Alvir, J., Bilder, R., Goldman, R., et al. (1999). Predictors of relapse following response from a first episode of schizophrenia or schizaffective disorder. *Archives of General Psychiatry, 56,* 241–247.

Robinson, L. A., Klesges, R. C., Zbikowski, S. M., & Glaser, R. (1997). Predictors of risk for different stages of adolescent smoking in a biracial sample. *Journal of Consulting and Clinical Psychology, 65,* 653–662.

Robinson, N. S., Garber, J., & Hillsman, R. (1995). Cognitions and stress: Direct and moderating effects on depression versus externalizing symptoms during the junior high school transition. *Journal of Abnormal Psychology, 104,* 453–463.

Robinson, T. E., & Berridge, K. C. (1993). The neural basis of drug craving: An incentive sensitization theory of addiction. *Brain Research Reviews, 18,* 247–191.

Robinson, T. E., & Berridge, K. C. (2003). Addiction. *Annual Review of Psychology, 54,* 25–53.

Robinson-Whelan, S., Tada, Y., McCallum, R. C., McGuire, L., & Kiecolt-Glaser, J. K. (2001). Long-term caregiving: What happens when it ends? *Journal of Abnormal Psychology, 110,* 573–584.

Robles, T. F., & Kiecolt-Glaser, J. K. (2004). The physiology of marriage: Pathways to health. *Physiology and Behavior, 79,* 409–416.

Rockwood, K., Kirkland, S., Hogan, D. B., et al. (2002). Use of lipid-lowering agents, indication bias, and the risk of dementia in community-dwelling elderly people. *Archives of Neurology, 59,* 223–227.

Rodin, J. (1986). Aging and health: Effects of the sense of control. *Science, 233,* 1271–1276.

Rodin, J., & Ickovics, J. R. (1990). Women's health: Review and research agenda as we approach the 21st century. *American Psychologist, 45,* 1018–1034.

Rodin, J., & Langer, E. J. (1977). Long-term effects of a control-relevant intervention with the institutionalized aged. *Journal of Personality and Social Psychology, 35,* 897–902.

Rodin, J., McAvay, G., & Timko, C. (1988). A longitudinal study of depressed mood and sleep disturbances in elderly adults. *Journal of Gerontology: Psychological Sciences, 43,* 45–53.

Roelofs, K., Hoogduin, K. A. L., Keijsers, G. P. J., et al. (2002). Hypnotic susceptibility in patients with conversion disorder. *Journal of Abnormal Psychology, 111,* 390–395.

Roemer, L., Molina, S., & Borkovec, T. D. (1997). An investigation of worry content among generally anxious individuals. *Journal of Nervous and Mental Disease, 185,* 314–319.

Roemer, L., Orsillo, S. M., & Barlow, D. H. (2004). Generalized anxiety disorder. In D. H. Barlow (Ed.), *Anxiety and its disorders: The nature and treatment of anxiety and panic* (pp. 477–515). New York: Guilford.

Roesch, S. C., & Weiner, B. (2001). A meta-analytic review of coping with illness: Do causal attributions matter? *Journal of Psychosomatic Research, 50,* 205–219.

Roffman, R. A., Stephens, R. S., Curtin, L., Gordon, J. R., Craver, J. N., Stern, M., Beadnell, B., & Downey, L. (1998). Relapse prevention as an intervention model for HIV risk reduction in gay and bisexual men. *AIDS Education and Prevention, 10,* 1–18.

Rogers, C. R. (1951). *Client-centered therapy.* Boston: Houghton Mifflin.

Rogers, C. R. (1961). *On becoming a person: A therapist's view of psychotherapy.* Boston: Houghton Mifflin.

Rogers, R. D. (2003). Neuropsychological investigations of the impulsive personality disorders. *Psychological Medicine, 33,* 1335–1340.

Rogler, L. H., & Hollingshead, A. B. (1985). *Trapped: Families and schizophrenia* (3rd ed.). Maplewood, NJ: Waterfront Press.

Romans, S. E., Gendall, K. A., Martin, J. L., & Mullen, P. E. (2001). Child sexual abuse and later disordered eating: A New Zealand epidemiological study. *International Journal of Eating Disorders, 29,* 380–392.

Romas, S. N., Santyana, V., Williamson, J., et al. (2002). Familial Alzheimer disease among Caribbean Hispanics. *Archives of Neurology, 59,* 87–91.

Romero, D. (1992, March 7). Two drugs crash the party scene. *Los Angeles Times,* pp. A1, A22–23.

Rose, J, E., Brauer, L. H., Behm, F. M., Cramblett, M. Calkins, K., & Lawhon, D. (2004). Psychopharmacological interactions between nicotine and ethanol. *Nicotine and Tobacco Research, 6,* 133–144.

Rosen, C. S., Chow, H. C., Greenbaum, M. A., Finney, J. F., Moos, R. H., Sheikh, J. I., et al. (2002). How well are clinicians following dementia practice guidelines? *Alzheimer Disease and Associated Disorders, 16,* 15–23.

Rosen, G. M. (2004). Remembering the 1978 and 1990 Task Forces on Self-Help Therapies. *Journal of Clinical Psychology, 60,* 111–113.

Rosen, G. M., & Davison, G. C. (2003). Psychology should list empirically supported principles of change (ESPs) and not credential trademarked therapies or other treatment packages. *Behavior Modification, 27,* 300–312.

Rosen, H. J., Pace-Savitsky, K., Perry, R. J., Kramer, J. H., Miller, B. L., & Levenson, R. L. (2002b). Recognition of emotion in the frontal and temporal variants of frontotemporal dementia. *Neurology, 58,* 1608–1615.

Rosen, H. J., Perry, R. J., Murphy, J., Kramer, J. H., Mychack, P., Schuff, N., Weiner, M., Levenson, R. L., & Miller, B. L. (2002a). Emotion comprehension in the temporal variant of frontotemporal dementia. *Brain, 125,* 2286–2295.

Rosen, R. C. (2000). Medical and psychological interventions for erectile dysfunction: Toward a combined treatment approach. In S. R. Lieblum & R. C. Rosen (Eds.), *Principles and practice of sex therapy* (pp. 276–304). New York: Guilford.

Rosen, R. C., & Leiblum, S. R. (1995). Treatment of sexual disorders in the 1990s: An integrated approach. *Journal of Consulting and Clinical Psychology, 63,* 877–890.

Rosen, R. C., Leiblum, S. R., & Spector, I. (1994). Psychologically based treatment for male erectile disorder: A cognitive-interpersonal model. *Journal of Sex and Marital Therapy, 20,* 67–85.

Rosen, R. C., & Rosen, L. (1981). *Human sexuality.* New York: Knopf.

Rosenblatt, A., Mehta, K. M., Romanoski, A., Eaton, W., & Lyketsos, C. (2003). Major depression and cognitive decline after 11.5years: Findings from the ECA study. *Journal of Nervous and Mental Disease, 191,* 827–830.

Rosenfarb, I. S., Goldstein, M. J., Mintz, J., & Neuchterlein, K. H. (1994). Expressed emotion and subclinical psychopathology observable within transactions between schizophrenics and their family members. *Journal of Abnormal Psychology, 104,* 259–267.

Rosenheck, R., Cramer, J., Allan, E., Erdos, J., Frisman, J., et al. (1999). Cost-effectivness of clozapine in patients with high and low levels of hospital use. *Archives of General Psychiatry, 56,* 565–572.

Rosenkranz, M. A., Jackson, D. C., Dalton, K. M., Dolski, I., Ryff, C. D., Singer, B. H., Muller, D., Kalin, N. H., & Davidson, R. J. (2003). Affective style and *in vivo* immune response: Neurobehavioral mechanisms. *PNAS, 100,* 11148–11152.

Rosenman, R. H., Brand, R. J., Jenkins, C. D., Friedman, M., Straus, R., & Wurm, M. (1975). Coronary heart disease in the Western Collaborative Group Study: Final followup experience of 8 years. *Journal of the American Medical Association, 233,* 872–877.

Rosenthal, N. E., Carpenter, C. J., James, S. P., Parry, B. L., Rogers, S. L. B., & Wehr, T. A. (1986). Seasonal affective disorder in children and adolescents. *American Journal of Psychiatry, 143,* 356–358.

Rosenzweig, R., & Fillit, H. (1992). Probable heterosexual transmission of AIDS in an aged woman. *Journal of the American Geriatric Society, 40,* 1261–1264.

Roser, K., & Buchholz, E. S. (1996). Autism from an intersubjective perspective. *Psychoanalytic Review, 83,* 305–323.

Rosman, B. L., Minuchin, S., & Liebman, R. (1975). Family lunch session: An introduction to family therapy in anorexia nervosa. *American Journal of Orthopsychiatry, 45,* 846–852.

Rosman, B. L., Minuchin, S., & Liebman, R. (1976). Input and outcome of family therapy of anorexia nervosa. In J. L. Claghorn (Ed.), *Successful psychotherapy.* New York: Brunner/Mazel.

Ross, C. A. (1989). *Multiple personality disorder: Diagnosis, clinical features, and treatment.* New York: Wiley.

Ross, C. A. (1991). Epidemiology of multiple personality disorder and dissociation. *Psychiatric Clinics of North America, 14,* 503–517.

Ross Gower, J., Waller, G., Tyson, M., & Elliott, P. (1998). Reported sexual abuse and subsequent psychopathology among women attending psychology clinics: The mediating role of dissociation. *British Journal of Clinical Psychology, 37,* 313–326.

Rossiter, E. M., & Agras, W. S. (1990). An empirical test of the DSM-IIIR definition of binge. *International Journal of Eating Disorders, 9,* 513–518.

Rost, K., Kashner, T. M., & Smith, G. R. (1994). Effectiveness of psychiatric intervention with somatization disorder patients: Improved outcomes at reduced costs. *General Hospital Psychiatry, 16,* 381–387.

Rothbaum, B. O., & Foa, E. B. (1993). Subtypes of posttraumatic stress disorder and duration of symptoms. In J. R. T. Davidson & E. B. Foa (Eds.), *Post-traumatic stress disorder: DSM-IV and beyond* (pp. 23–35). Washington, DC: American Psychiatric Press.

Rothbaum, B. O., Foa, E. B., Murdock, T., Riggs, D. S., & Walsh, W. (1992). A prospective examination of post-traumatic stress disorder in rape victims. *Journal of Traumatic Stress, 5,* 455–475.

Rothbaum, B. O., Hodges, L., Alarcon, R., Ready, D., Shahar, F., Graap, K., Pair, J., Hebert, P., Gotz, D., Will, B., & Baltzell, D. (1999). Virtual reality exposure therapy for PTSD Vietnam veterans: A case study. *Journal of Traumatic Stress, 12*(2), 263–271.

Rothman, A. J., & Salovey, P. (1997). Shaping perceptions to motivate healthy behavior: The role of message framing. *Psychological Bulletin, 121,* 3–19.

Roughgarden, J. (2004). *Evolution's rainbow: Diversity, gender, and sexuality in nature and people.* Berkeley, CA: University of California Press.

Rowland, D. L., Cooper, S. E., & Slob, A. K. (1996). Genital and psychoaffective responses to erotic stimulation in sexually functional and dysfunctional men. *Journal of Abnormal Psychology, 105,* 194–203.

Roy, A. (1982). Suicide in chronic schizophrenia. *British Journal of Psychiatry, 141,* 171–180.

Roy, A. (1994). Recent biologic studies on suicide. *Suicide and Life Threatening Behaviors, 24,* 10–24.

Roy, A. (1995). Suicide. In H. I. Kaplan & B. J. Sadock (Eds.), *Comprehensive textbook of psychiatry* (pp. 1739–1752). Baltimore, MD: Williams & Wilkins.

Roy-Byrne, P. P., & Cowley, D. S. (1998). Pharmacological treatment of panic, generalized anxiety, and phobic disorders. In P. E. Nathan & J. M. Gorman (Eds.), *A guide to treatments that work* (pp. 319–338). New York: Oxford University Press.

Roy-Byrne, P. P., Katon, W., Cowley, D. S., & Russo, J. (2001). A randomized effectiveness trial of collaborative care for patients with panic disorder in primary care. *Archives of General Psychiatry, 58,* 869–876.

Ruberman, W., Weinblatt, E., Goldberg, J. D., & Chaudhary, B. S. (1984). Psychosocial influences on mortality after myocardial infarction. *New England Journal of Medicine, 311,* 552–559.

Rubia, K., Overmeyer, S., Taylor, E., Brammer, M., Williams, S. C. R., et al. (1999). Hypofrontality in attention deficit hyperactivity disorder during higher-order motor control: A study with functional MRI. *American Journal of Psychiatry, 156,* 891–896.

Rubin, A. J. (1998a, August 15). Court rules FDA cannot regulate tobacco as a drug. *Los Angeles Times,* pp. A1–A10.

Rubin, A. J. (1998b, September 15). Fight ensues to block undoing of doctor-assisted suicide law. *Los Angeles Times,* pp. A5.

Rude, S. S., Valdez, C. R., Odom, S., & Ebrahimi, A. (2003). Negative cognitive biases predict subsequent depression. *Cognitive Therapy and Research, 27,* 415–429.

Rumbak, M. J., Kelso, T. M., Arheart, K. L., & Self, T. H. (1993). Perception of anxiety as a contributing factor in asthma: Indigent versus non-indigent. *Journal of Asthma, 30,* 165–169.

Rush, A. J., Beck, A. T., Kovacs, M., & Hollon, S. D. (1977). Comparative efficacy of cognitive therapy and pharmacotherapy in the treatment of depressed outpatients. *Cognitive Therapy and Research, 1,* 17–39

Rutherford, J., & Noegel, R. (1993). Genetic influences on eating attitudes in a normal female twin population. *Psychological Medicine, 23,* 425–436.

Rutherford, M. J., Cacciola, J. S., & Alterman, A. I. (1999). Antisocial personality disorder and psychopathy in cocaine-dependent women. *American Journal of Psychiatry, 156,* 849–856.

Rutledge, T., Reis, S. E., Olson, M., Owens, J., Kelsey, S. F., Pepine, C. J., Reichek, N., Rogers, W. J., Merz, N. B., Sopko, G., Cornell, C. E., & Matthews, K. A. (2001).

Psychosocial variables are associated with atherosclerosis risk factors among women with chest pain: The WISE study. *Psychosomatic Medicine, 63,* 282–288.

Rutter, M. (1983). Cognitive deficits in the pathogenesis of autism. *Journal of Child Psychology and Psychiatry, 2,* 513–531.

Rutter, M., Caspi, A., Fergusson, D., Horwood, L. J., Goodman, R., Maughan, B., Moffitt, T. E., Meltzer, H., & Carroll, J. (2004). Sex differences in developmental reading disability: New findings from 4 epidemiological studies. *JAMA, 291,* 2007–2012.

Rutter, M., & Silberg, J. (2002). Gene-environment interplay in relation to emotional and behavioral disturbance. *Annual Review of Psychology, 53,* 463–490.

Sabo, S. Z., Nelson, M. L., Fisher, C., Gunzerath, L., Brody, C. L., et al. (1999). A genetic association for cigarette smoking behavior. *Health Psychology, 18,* 7–13.

Sacco, R. L., Elkind, M., Boden-Albala, B., Lin, I., Kargman, D. E., et al. (1999). The protective effect of moderate alcohol consumption on ischemic stroke. *JAMA, 281,* 53–60.

Sachs, G. S., & Thase, M. E. (2000). Bipolar disorder therapeutics: Maintenance treatment. *Biological Psychiatry, 48,* 573–581.

Sackeim, H, A. (2001). Electroconvulsive therapy in late-life depression. In H. A. Sackeim & S. P. Roose (Eds.), *Late-life depression* (pp. 241–278). New York, NY: Oxford University Press.

Sackeim, H. A., & Lisanby, S. H. (2001). Physical treatments in psychiatry: Advances in electroconvulsive therapy, transcranial magnetic stimulation, and vagus nerve stimulation. In M. M. Weissman (Ed.), *Treatment of depression: Bridging the 21st century* (pp. 151–174). Washington, DC: American Psychiatric Publishing.

Sackeim, H. A., Nordlie, J. W., & Gur, R. C. (1979). A model of hysterical and hypnotic blindness: Cognition, motivation and awareness. *Journal of Abnormal Psychology, 88,* 474–489.

Sackeim, H. A., Prudic, J., Devenand, D. P., et al. (2000). A prospective, randomized, double-blind comparison of bilateral and right unilateral electroconvulsive shock therapy at different stimulus intensities. *Archives of General Psychiatry, 57,* 425–434.

Sacks, O. (1995). *An anthropologist on Mars.* New York: Knopf.

Saffer, H. (1991). Alcohol advertising bans and alcohol abuse: An international perspective. *Journal of Health Economics, 10,* 65–79.

Sakel, M. (1938). The pharmacological shock treatment of schizophrenia. *Nervous and Mental Disease Monograph, 62.*

Saks, E. R. (1997). *Jekyll on trial: Multiple personality disorder and criminal law.* New York: New York University Press.

Salamone, J. D. (2000). A critique of recent studies on placebo effects of antidepressants: Importance of research on active placebos. *Psychopharmacology, 152,* 1–6.

Salan, S. E., Zinberg, N E., & Frei, E. (1975). Antiemetic effect of delta-9-THC in patients receiving cancer chemotherapy. *New England Journal of Medicine, 293,* 795–797.

Salekin, R. T. (2002). Psychopathy and therapeutic pessimism: Clinical lore or clinical reality? *Clinical Psychology Review, 22,* 79–112.

Salekin, R. T., Rogers, R., & Sewell, K. W. (1997). Construct validity of psychopathy in a female offender sample: A multitrait-multimethod evaluation. *Journal of Abnormal Psychology, 106,* 576–585.

Salem, J. E., & Kring, A. M. (1998). The role of gender differences in the reduction of etiologic heterogeneity in schizophrenia. *Clinical Psychology Review, 18,* 795–819.

Salkovskis, P. M. (1996). Cognitive-behavioral approaches to understanding obsessional problems. In R. M. Rapee

(Ed.), *Current controversies in anxiety disorders.* New York: Guilford.

Salzman, C., Goldenberg, I., Bruce, S. E., & Keller, M. B. (2001). Pharmacologic treatment of anxiety disorders in 1989 versus 1996: Results from the Harvard/Brown anxiety disorders research program. *Journal of Clinical Psychiatry, 62,* 149–152.

Sanday, P. R. (1981). The socio-cultural context of rape: A cross-cultural study. *The Journal of Social Issues, 37,* 5–27.

Sandberg, S., Järvenpää, S., Paton, J. Y., & McCann, D. C. (2004). Asthma exacerbations in children immediately following stressful life events: A Cox's hierarchical regression. *Thorax, 49,* 1046–1051.

Sanderson, W. C., Rapee, R. M., & Barlow, D. H. (1989). The influence of an illusion of control on panic attacks induced via inhalation of 5.5% carbon dioxide-enriched air. *Archives of General Psychiatry, 46,* 157–162.

Sanderson, W. C., Raue, P. J., & Wetzler, S. (1998). The generalizability of cognitive behavior therapy for panic disorder. *Journal of Cognitive Psychotherapy, 12,* 323–330.

Sanger, T. M., Lieberman, J. A., Tohen, M., Grundy, S., et al. (1999). Olanzapine versus haloperidol in first-episode psychosis. *American Journal of Psychiatry, 156,* 79–87.

Santarelli, L. Saxe, M., Gross, C., Surget, A., Battaglia, F., Dulawa, S., Weisstaub, N., Lee, J., Duman, R., Arancio, O., Belzung, C., & Hen, R. (2003). Requirement of hippocampal neurogenesis for the behavioral effects of antidepressants. *Science, 301,* 805–809.

Sartorius, N., Jablensky, A., Korten, A., Ernberg, G., et al. (1986). Early manifestations and first-contact incidence of schizophrenia in different cultures: A preliminary report on the initial evaluation phase of the WHO Collaborative Study on Determinants of Outcome of Severe Mental Disorders. *Psychological Medicine, 16,* 909–928.

Sartorius, N., Shapiro, R., & Jablonsky, A. (1974). The international pilot study of schizophrenia. *Schizophrenia Bulletin, 2,* 21–35.

Saulsman, L. M., & Page, A. C. (2004). The five-factor model and personality disorder empirical literature: A meta-analytic review. *Clinical Psychology Review, 23,* 1055–1085.

Savage, D. G. (1996, December 11). High court debates sexual predator law. *Los Angeles Times,* pp. A26.

Sawyer, N. G., Spurrier, N., Whaites, L., Kennedy, Martin, A. J., & Baghurst, P. (2001). The relationship between asthma severity, family functioning, and the health-related quality of life of children with asthma. *Quality of Life Research, 9,* 1105–1115.

Sayette, M. A., & Wilson, G. T. (1991). Intoxication and exposure to stress: Effects of temporal patterning. *Journal of Abnormal Psychology, 100,* 56–62.

Sbrocco, T., Weisberg, R. B., Barlow, D. H., & Carter, M. M. (1997). The conceptual relationship between panic disorder and male erectile dysfunction. *Journal of Sex and Marital Therapy, 23,* 212–220.

Scarborough, H. S. (1990). Very early language deficits in dyslexic children. *Child Development, 61,* 128–174.

Scarlett, W. (1980). Social isolation from age-mates among nursery school children. *Journal of Child Psychology and Psychiatry, 21,* 231–240.

Schaefer, L. C., Wheeler, C. C., & Futterweit, W. (1997). Gender identity disorders (transsexualism). In G. O. Gabbard & S. D. Atkinson (Eds.), *Synopsis of treatments of psychiatric disorders* (2nd ed., pp. 843–858). Washington, DC: American Psychiatric Press.

Schaie, K. W., & Hertzog, C. (1982). Longitudinal methods. In B. B. Wolman (Ed.), *Handbook of developmental psychology.* Englewood Cliffs, NJ: Prentice-Hall.

Scharff, J. S. (1995). Psychoanalytic marital therapy. In N. S. Jacobson & A. S. Gurman (Eds.), *Clinical handbook of couple therapy*. New York: Guilford.

Scheff, T. J. (1966). *Being mentally ill: A sociological theory*. Chicago: Aldine.

Scheier, M. F., & Carver, C. S. (1987). Dispositional optimism and physical well-being: The influence of generalized outcome expectancies on health. *Journal of Personality and Social Psychology, 55*, 169–210.

Schiavi, R. C. (1997). Male erectile disorder. In G. O. Gabbard & S. D. Atkinson (Eds.), *Synopsis of treatments of psychiatric disorders* (2nd ed., pp. 781–788). Washington, DC: American Psychiatric Press.

Schleifer, M. (1995). Should we change our views about early childhood education? *Alberta Journal of Educational Research, 41*, 355–359.

Schlundt, D. G., & Johnson, W. G. (1990). *Eating disorders: Assessment and treatment*. Needham Heights, MA: Allyn & Bacon.

Schmidt, E., Carns, A., & Chandler, C. (2001). Assessing the efficacy of rational recovery in the treatment of alcohol/drug dependency. *Alcoholism Treatment Quarterly, 19*, 97–106.

Schmidt, N. B., Lerew, D. R., & Jackson, R. J. (1999). Prospective evaluation of anxiety sensitivity in the pathogenesis of panic: Prospective evaluation of spontaneous panic attacks during acute stress. *Journal of Abnormal Psychology, 106*, 355–364.

Schmidt, N. B., Woolaway-Bickel, K., & Bates, M. (2000). Suicide and panic disorder: Integration of the literature and new findings. In M. D. Rudd and T. E. Joiner (Eds.), *Suicide science: Expanding the boundaries* (pp. 117–136). New York: Kluwer Academic/Plenum.

Schmitt, D. P., et al. (2003). Universal sex differences in the desire for sexual variety: Tests from 52 nations, 6 continents and 13 islands. *Journal of Personality and Social Psychology, 85*, 85–104.

Schneider, J. (1996). Geriatric psychopharmacology. In L. L. Carstensen, B. A. Edelstein, & L. Dornbrand (Eds.), *The practical handbook of clinical gerontology* (pp. 481–542). Thousand Oaks, CA: Sage.

Schneider, K. (1959). *Clinical psychopathology*. New York: Grune & Stratton.

Schneider, L. S., Nelson, J. C., Clary, C. M., Newhouse, P., Krishnan, K. R. R., & Shiovitz, T., et al. (2003). An 8-week multicenter, parallel-group, double-blind, placebo-controlled study of sertraline in elderly outpatients with major depression. *American Journal of Psychiatry, 160*, 1277–1285.

Schoeneman, T. J. (1977). The role of mental illness in the European witch-hunts of the sixteenth and seventeenth centuries: An assessment. *Journal of the History of the Behavioral Sciences, 13*, 337–351.

Schooler, C., Flora, J. A., & Farquhar, J. W. (1993). Moving toward synergy: Media supplementation in the Stanford Five-City Project. *Communication Research, 26*, 587–610.

Schopler, E., Short, A., & Mesibov, G. (1989). Relation of behavioral treatment to "normal functioning": Comment on Lovaas. *Journal of Consulting and Clinical Psychology, 57*, 162–164.

Schottenfeld, R. S., Pakes, J., O'Conner, P., et al. (2000). Thrice-weekly versus daily buprenorphine maintenance. *Biological Psychiatry, 47*, 1072–1079.

Schreiber, F. L. (1973). *Sybil*. Chicago: Regnery.

Schuckit, M. A. (1983). The genetics of alcoholism. In B. Tabakoff, P. B. Sulker, & C. L. Randall (Eds.), *Medical and social aspects of alcohol use*. New York: Plenum.

Schuckit, M. A. (1994). Low level of response to alcohol as a predictor of future alcoholism. *American Journal of Psychiatry, 151*, 184–189.

Schuckit, M. A., Daeppen, J.-B., Danko, G. P., Tripp, M. L., Smith, T. L., et al. (1999). Clinical implications for four drugs of the DSM-IV distinction between substance with and without a physiological component. *American Journal of Psychiatry, 156*, 41–49.

Schuckit, M. A., Daeppen, J.-B., Tipp, J. E., Hesselbrock, M., & Bucholz, K. K. (1998). The clinical course of alcohol-related problems in alcohol dependent and non-alcohol dependent drinking women and men. *Journal of Studies on Alcohol, 59*, 581–590.

Schuckit, M. A., & Smith, T. L. (1996). An 8-year follow-up of 450 sons of alcoholic and control subjects. *Archives of General Psychiatry, 53*, 202–210.

Schuckit, M. A., Smith, T. L., Danko, G. P., Bucholz, K. K., Reich, T., & Bierut, L. (2001). Five-year clinical course associated with DSM-IV alcohol abuse or dependence in a large group of men and women. *American Journal of Psychiatry, 158*, 1084–1090.

Schuckit, M. A., Smith, T. L., Kalmijn, J., Hsuang, J., Hesselbrock, V., & Bucholz, K. (2000). Response to alcohol in daughters of alcoholics: A pilot study and comparison with sons of alcoholics. *Alcohol and Alcoholism, 35*, 242–248.

Schuckit, M. A., Tipp, J. E., & Smith, T. L. (1997). Periods of abstinence following the onset of alcohol dependence in 1,853 men and women. *Journal of Studies on Alcohol, 58*, 581–589.

Schuepbach, W. M. M., Adler, R. H., & Sabbioni, M. E. E. (2002). Accuracy of clinical diagnosis of 'psychogenic disorders' in the presence of physical symptoms suggesting a general medical condition: A 5-year follow-up in 162 patients. *Psychotherapy and Psychosomatics, 71*, 11–17.

Schultz, R., & Brenner, G. (1977). Relocation of the aged: A review and theoretical analysis. *Journal of Gerontology, 32*, 323–333.

Schwartz, G. E. (1973). Biofeedback as therapy: Some theoretical and practical issues. *American Psychologist, 28*, 666–673.

Schwartz, M. B., Chambliss, O. H., Brownell, K. D., Blair, S., & Billington, C. (2003). Weight bias among health professionals specializing in obesity. *Obesity Research, 11*, 1033–1039.

Schwartz, J. E., Warren, K., & Pickering, T. G. (1994). Mood, location and physical position as predictors of ambulatory blood pressure and heart rate: Application of a multilevel random effects model. *Annals of Behavioral Medicine, 16*, 210–220.

Schwartz, S. H., & Inbar-Saban, N. (1988). Value self-confrontation as a method to aid in weight loss. *Journal of Personality and Social Psychology, 54*, 396–404.

Schweizer, E., Rickels, K., Case, G., & Greenblatt, D. J. (1990). Long-term therapeutic use of benzodiazapines: Effects of gradual taper. *Archives of General Psychiatry, 47*, 908–915.

Schwitzgebel, R. L., & Schwitzgebel, R. K. (1980). *Law and psychological practice*. New York: Wiley.

Scientific perspectives on cocaine abuse. (1987). *Pharmacologist, 29*, 20–27.

Scoggin, F., & McElreath, L. (1994). Efficacy of psychosocial treatments for geriatric depression: A quantitative review. *Journal of Consulting and Clinical Psychology, 62*, 69–74.

Scogin, F. (1998). Anxiety in old age. In I. H. Nordhus, G. R. VandenBos, S. Berg, & P. Fromholt (Eds.), *Clinical geropsychology* (pp. 205–209). Washington, DC: American Psychological Association.

Scroppo, J. C., Drob, S. L., Weinberger, J. L., & Eagle, P. (1998). Identifying dissociative identity disorder: A self-report and projective study. *Journal of Abnormal Psychology, 107*, 272–284.

Scully, J. A., Tosi, H., & Banning, K. (2000). Life event checklists: Revisiting the Social Readjustment Rating Scale after 30 years. *Educational and Psychological Measurement, 60*, 864–876.

Searight, H. R., & Pound, P. (1994). The HIV-positive psychiatric patient and the duty to protect: Ethical and legal issues. *International Journal of Psychiatry in Medicine, 24*, 259–270.

Seeman, T. E., Singer, B. H., Rowe, J. W., Horwitz, R. I., & McEwen, B. S. (1997). Price of adaption—allostatic load and its health consequences: MacArthur studies of successful aging. *Archives of Internal Medicine, 157*, 2259–2268.

Seeman, T. E., & Syme, S. L. (1987). Social networks and coronary artery disease: A comparison of the structure and function of social relations as predictors of disease. *Psychosomatic Medicine, 49*, 381–406.

Sees, K. L., Delucchi, K. L., Masson, C., et al. (2000). Methadone maintenance vs 180-day psychosocially enriched detoxification for treatment of opioid dependence. *JAMA, 283*, 578–589.

Segal, Z. V., Gemar, M., & Williams, S. (1999). Differential cognitive response to a mood challenge following successful cognitive therapy or pharmacotherapy for unipolar depression. *Journal of Abnormal Psychology, 108*, 3–10.

Segal, Z. V., Williams, J. M., & Teasdale, J. D. (2001). *Mindfulness-based cognitive therapy for depression*. New York: Guilford.

Segal, Z. V., Williams, J. M. G., & Teasdale, J. D. (2003). Mindfulness-based cognitive therapy for depression: A new approach to preventing relapse. *Psychotherapy Research, 13*, 123–125.

Segerstrom, S. C., & Miller, G. E. (2004). Psychological stress and the immune system: A meta-analytic study of 30 years of inquiry. *Psychological Bulletin, 130*, 601–630.

Segerstrom, S. C., Taylor, S. E., Kemeny, M. E., & Fahey, J. L. (1998). Optimism is associated with mood, coping, and immune change in response to stress. *Journal of Personality and Social Psychology, 74*, 1646–1655.

Segraves, K. B., & Segraves, R. T. (1991). Hypoactive sexual desire disorder: Prevalence and comorbidity in 906 subjects. *Journal of Sex and Marital Therapy, 17*, 55–58.

Segraves, R. T. (2003). Recognizing and reversing sexual side effects of medications. In S. B. Levine, C. B. Candace, et al. (Eds.). *Handbook of clinical sexuality for mental health professionals* (pp. 377–391). New York: Brunner-Routledge.

Segraves, R. T., & Althof, S. (1998). Psychotherapy and pharmacotherapy of sexual dysfunctions. In P. E. Nathan & J. M. Gorman (Eds.), *A guide to treatments that work*. NY: Oxford.

Segrin, C. (2000). Social skills deficits associated with depression. *Clinical Psychology Review, 20*, 379–403.

Seligman, M. E. P. (1971). Phobias and preparedness. *Behavior Therapy, 2*, 307–320.

Seligman, M. E. P. (1974). Depression and learned helplessness. In R. J. Friedman & M. M. Katz (Eds.), *The psychology of depression: Contemporary theory and research*. Washington, DC: Winston-Wiley.

Seligman, M. E. P. (1998). President's column: Positive social science. *APA Monitor, 29*, 2–5.

Seligman, M. E., Maier, S. F., & Geer, J. H. (1968). Alleviation of learned helplessness in the dog. *Journal of Abnormal Psychology, 73*, 256–262.

Selkoe, D. J. (2002). Alzheimer's disease is a synaptic failure. *Science, 298*, 789–791.

Selling, L. S. (1940). *Men against madness*. New York: Greenberg.

Selye, H. (1950). *The physiology and pathology of exposure to stress*. Montreal: Acta.

Sensky, T., Turkington, D., Kingdon, D., et al. (2000). A randomized controlled trial of cognitive-behavioural therapy for persistent symptoms in schizophrenia resistant to medication. *Archives of General Psychiatry Psychiatry*, 57, 165–172.

Serdula, M. K., Mokdad, A. H., Williamson, D. F., Galuska, D. A., et al. (1999). Prevalence of attempting weight loss and strategies for controlling weight. *JAMA*, 282, 1353–1358.

Sexton, T. L., Alexander, J. F., & Mease, A. L. (2004). Levels of evidence for the models and mechanisms of therapeutic change in family and couple therapy. In M. J. Lambert (Ed.), *Bergin and Garfield's handbook of psychotherapy and behavior change* (5th ed., pp. 590–646). Hoboken, NJ: John Wiley & Sons.

Shachnow, J., Clarkin, J., DiPalma, C.-S., Thurston, F., et al. (1997). Biparental psychopathology and borderline personality disorder. *Psychiatry—Interpersonal and Biological Processes*, 60, 171–181.

Shaffer, D., Fisher, P., Dulcan, M., Davis, D., Piacentini, J., Schwab-Stone, M., et al. (1996). The NIMH Diagnostic Interview Schedule for Children, Version 2.3 (DISC 2.3): Description, acceptability, prevalence rates, and performance in the MECA study. *Journal of the American Academy of Child and Adolescent Psychiatry*, 49, 865–877.

Shaffer, D., Fisher, P., Lucas, C. P., et al. (2000). NIMH Diagnostic Interview for Children Version IV (NIMH DISC-IV): Description, differences from previous versions, and reliability of some common diagnoses. *Journal of the American Academy of Child & Adolescent Psychiatry*, 39, 28–38.

Shaper, A. G. (1990). Alcohol and mortality: A review of prospective studies. *British Journal of Addiction*, 85, 837–847.

Shapiro, D., Goldstein, I. B., & Jamner, L. D. (1995). Effects of anger and hostility, defensiveness, gender and family history of hypertension on cardiovascular reactivity. *Psychophysiology*, 32, 425–435.

Shapiro, D., Jamner, L. D., & Goldstein, I. B. (1993). Ambulatory stress psychophysiology: The study of "compensatory and defensive counterforces" and conflict in a natural setting. *Psychosomatic Medicine*, 55, 309–323.

Shapiro, D., Tursky, B., & Schwartz, G. E. (1970). Control of blood pressure in man by operant conditioning. *Circulation Research*, 26, 127–132.

Sharkansky, E. J., King, D. W., King, L. A., et al. (2000). Coping with Gulf War combat stress: Mediating and moderating effects. *Journal of Abnormal Psychology*, 109, 188–197.

Shaw, B. F. (1977). Comparison of cognitive therapy and behavior therapy in the treatment of depression. *Journal of Consulting and Clinical Psychology*, 45, 543–551.

Shaw, D. S., Bell, R. Q., & Gilliom, M. (2000). A truly early starter model of antisocial behavior revisited. *Clinical Child and Family Psychology Review*, 3, 158–172.

Shaw, D. S., Owens, E. B., Giovannelli, J., & Winslow, E. B. (2001). Infant and toddler pathways leading to early externalizing disorders. *Journal of the American Academy of Child and Adolescent Psychiatry*, 40, 36–43.

Shaywitz, B. A., Shaywitz, S. E., Blachman, B. A., et al. (2004). Development of left occipitotemporal systems for skilled reading in children after a phonologically-based intervention. *Biological Psychiatry*, 55, 926–933.

Shaywitz, S. E., Shaywitz, B. A., Fletcher, J. M., & Escobar, M. D. (1990). Prevalence of reading disability in boys and girls. *Journal of the American Medical Association*, 264, 998–1002.

Shaywitz, S. E., Shaywitz, B. A., Fulbright, R. K., et al. (2003). Neural systems for compensation and persistence: Young adult outcome of childhood reading disability. *Biological Psychiatry*, 54, 25–33.

Shaywitz, B. A., Shaywitz, S. E., Pugh, K. R., et al. (2002). Disruption of posterior brain systems for reading in children with developmental dyslexia. *Biological Psychiatry*, 52, 101–110.

Shea, M. T., Elkin, I., Imber, S. D., Sotsky, S. M., Watkins, J. T., Collins, J. F., Beckham, E., Glass, D. R., Dolan, R. T., & Parloff, M. B. (1992). Course of depressive symptoms over follow-up: Findings from the National Institute of Mental Health Treatment of Depression Collaborative Research Program. *Archives of General Psychiatry*, 49, 782–787.

Shea, M. T., Stout, R., Gunderson, J., Morey, L. C., Grilo, C. M., & McGlashan, T., et al. (2002). Short-term diagnostic stability of schizotypal, borderline, avoidant, and obsessive-compulsive personality disorders. *American Journal of Psychiatry*, 159, 2036–2041.

Sheler, J. L. (2003). A stubborn scandal: A year later, the church falls short on many reforms. US News and World Report. Available online at USNews.com

Sheline, Y. I. (2000). 3D MRI studies of neuroanatomic changes in unipolar major depression: The role of stress and medical comorbidity. *Biological Psychiatry*, 48, 791–800.

Sheline, Y., Barch, D., Donnelly, J. M., Ollinger, J. M., Snyder, A. Z., & Mintun, M. A. (2001). Increased amygdala response to masked emotional faces in depressed subjects resolves with antidepressant treatment: An fMRI study. *Biological Psychiatry*, 50, 651–658.

Shelton, R. C., Mainer, D. H., & Sulser, F. (1996). cAMP-dependent protein kinase activity in major depression. *American Journal of Psychiatry*, 153, 1037–1042.

Sher, K. J., Bartholow, B. D., & Nanda, S. (2001). Short- and long-term effects of fraternity and sorority membership on heavy drinking: A social norms perspective. *Psychology of Addictive Behaviors*, 15, 42–51.

Sher, K. J., & Levenson, R. W. (1982). Risk for alcoholism and individual differences in the stress-response-dampening effects of alcohol. *Journal of Abnormal Psychology*, 91, 350–367.

Sher, K. J., Martin, E. D., Wood, P. K., & Rutledge, P. C. (1997). Alcohol use disorders and neuropsychological functioning in first year undergraduates. *Experimental and Clinical Psychopharmacology*, 5, 304–315.

Sher, K. J., Walitzer, K. S., Wood, P. K., & Brent, E. F. (1991). Characteristics of children of alcoholics: Putative risk factors, substance use and abuse, and psychopathology. *Journal of Abnormal Psychology*, 100, 427–448.

Sher, K. J., Wood, M. D., Wood, P. K., & Raskin, G. (1996). Alcohol outcome expectancies and alcohol use: A latent variable cross-lagged panel study. *Journal of Abnormal Psychology*, 105, 561–574.

Shergill, S. S., Brammer, M. J., Williams, S. C., Murray, R. M., & McGuire, P. K. (2000). Mapping auditory hallucinations in schizophrenia using functional magnetic resonance imaging. *Archives of General Psychiatry*, 57, 1033–1038.

Sherman, D. K., Iacono, W. G., & McGue, M. K. (1997). Attention-deficit hyperactivity disorder dimensions: A twin study of inattention and impulsivity-hyperactivity. *Journal of the American Academy of Child and Adolescent Psychiatry*, 36, 745–753.

Shiffman, S., Fischer, L. A., Paty, J. A., Gnys, M., et al. (1994). Drinking and smoking: A field study of their association. *Annals of Behavioral Medicine*, 16, 203–209.

Shiffman, S., Gwaltney, C. J., Balabanis, M. H., Liu, K. S., Paty, J. A., Kassel, J. D., Hickcox, M., & Gnys, M. (2002). Immediate antecedents of cigarette smoking: An analysis from ecological momentary assessment. *Journal of Abnormal Psychology*, 111 531–545.

Shiffman, S., Paty, J. A., Gwaltney, C. J., & Dang, Q. (2004). Immediate antecedents of cigarette smoking: An analysis of unrestricted smoking patterns. *Journal of Abnormal Psychology*, 113, 166–171.

Shiffman, S., & Waters, A. J. (2004). Negative affect and smoking lapses: A prospective analysis. *Journal of Consulting and Clinical Psychology*, 72, 192–201.

Shneidman, E. S. (1973). Suicide. In *Encyclopedia Britannica*. Chicago: Encyclopedia Britannica.

Shneidman, E. S. (1987). A psychological approach to suicide. In G. R. VandenBos & B. K. Bryant (Eds.), *Cataclysms, crises, and catastrophes: Psychology in action*. Washington, DC: American Psychological Association.

Shneidman, E. S., Farberow, N. L., & Litman, R. E. (Eds.). (1970). *The psychology of suicide*. New York: Jason Aronson.

Shobe, K. K., & Kihlstrom, J. F. (1997). Is traumatic memory special? *Current Directions in Psychological Science*, 6, 70–74.

Shoham, V., & Rohrbaugh, M. J. (1999). Paradoxical interventions. In W. E. Craighead & C. Nemeroff (Eds.), *Encyclopedia of psychology and neuroscience*. New York: John Wiley & Sons.

Shoham-Salomon, V., Avner, R., & Neeman, R. (1989). You're changed if you do and changed if you don't: Mechanisms underlying paradoxical interventions. *Journal of Consulting and Clinical Psychology*, 57, 590–598.

Shontz, F. C., & Green, P. (1992). Trends in research on the Rorschach: Review and recommendations. *Applied and Preventive Psychology*, 1, 149–156.

Shumaker, S. A., Legault, C., Kuller, L., et al. (2004). Conjugated equine estrogens and incidence of probable dementia and mild cognitive impairment in postmenopausal women: Women's health initiative memory study. *JAMA*, 291, 2947–2958.

Shumaker, S. A., Legault, C., Rapp, S. R., et al. (2003). Estrogen plus progestin and the incidence of dementia and mild cognitive impairment in postmenopausal women. *JAMA*, 289, 2651–2662.

Sieg, K. G., Gaffney, G. R., Preston, D. F., & Hellings, J. A. (1995). SPECT brain imaging abnormalities in attention deficit hyperactivity disorder. *Clinical Nuclear Medicine*, 20, 55–60.

Siegel, D., DiClemente, R., Durbin, M., Krasnovsky, F., & Saliba, P. (1995). Change in junior high school students' AIDS-related knowledge, misconceptions, attitudes, and HIV-preventive behaviors: Effects of a school-based intervention. *AIDS Education and Prevention*, 7, 534–543.

Siegle, G. J., Steinhauer, S. R., Thase, M. E., Stenger, V. A., & Carter, C. S. (2002). Can't shake that feeling: Event-related fMRI assessment of sustained amygdala activity in response to emotional information in depressed individuals. *Biological Psychiatry*, 51, 693–707.

Siegler, I. C., & Costa, P. T., Jr. (1985). Health behavior relationships. In J. E. Birren & K. W. Schaie (Eds.), *Handbook of the psychology of aging* (2nd ed.). New York: Van Nostrand-Reinhold.

Siegman, A. W., Townsend, S. T., Civelek, A. C., & Blumenthal, R. S. (2000). Antagonistic behavior, dominance, hostility, and coronary heart disease. *Psychosomatic Medicine*, 62, 248–257.

Siever, L. J., Torgersen, S., Gunderson, J. G., Livesley, W. J., & Kendler, K. S. (2002). The borderline diagnosis III: Identifying endophenotypes for genetic studies. *Biological Psychiatry*, 51, 964–968.

Sigman, M. (1994). What are the core deficits in autism? In S. H. Broman & J. Grafman (Eds.), *Atypical cognitive deficits in developmental disorders: Implications for brain function* (pp. 139–157). Hillsdale, NJ: Lawrence Erlbaum.

Sigman, M., Ungerer, J. A., Mundy, P., & Sherman, T. (1987). Cognition in autistic children. In D. J. Cohen, A. M. Donnellan, & R. Paul (Eds.), *Handbook of autism and pervasive developmental disorders* (pp. 103–120). New York: Wiley.

Silberg J., Pickles A, Rutter M., Hewitt J., Simonoff E., et al. (1999). The influence of genetic factors and life stress on depression among adolescent girls. *Archives of General Psychiatry, 56*, 225–32.

Silberg, J., Rutter, M., Meyer, J., Maes, H., Hewitt, J., Simonoff, E., Pickles, A., Loeber, R., & Eaves, L. (1996). Genetic and environmental influences on the covariation between hyperactivity and conduct disturbance in juvenile twins. *Journal of Child Psychology and Psychiatry, 37*, 803–816.

Silverman, K., Evans, S. M., Strain, E. C., & Griffiths, R. R. (1992). Withdrawal syndrome after the double-blind cessation of caffeine consumption. *New England Journal of Medicine, 327*, 1109–1114.

Silverman, K., Higgins, S. T., Brooner, R. K., Montoya, I. D., Cone, E. J., Schuster, C. R., & Preston, K. I. (1996). Sustained cocaine abstinence in methadone maintenance patients through voucher-based reinforcement therapy. *Archives of General Psychiatry, 53*, 409–413.

Simeon, D., Gross, S., Guralnik, O., Stein, D. J., Schmeidler, J., & Hollander, E. (1997). Feeling unreal: 30 cases of DSM-III-R depersonalization disorder. *American Journal of Psychiatry, 154*, 1107–1112.

Simmel, C., Brooks, D., Barth, R. P., & Hinshaw, S. P. (2001). Prevalence of externalizing symptomatology in an adoptive sample: Pre-adoption risk factors and post-adoption functioning. *Journal of Abnormal Child Psychology, 29*, 53–69.

Simon, G., Ormel, J., VonKorff, M., & Barlow, W. (1995). Health care costs associated with depressive and anxiety disorders in primary care. *American Journal of Psychiatry, 152*, 352–357.

Simon, G. E. (1998). Management of somatoform and factitious disorders. In P. E. Nathan & J. M. Gorman (Eds.), *A guide to treatments that work* (pp. 408–422). New York: Oxford University Press.

Simon, G. E., & Gureje, O. (1999). Stability of somatization disorder and somatization symptoms among primary care patients. *Archives of General Psychiatry, 56*, 90–95.

Simon, G. E., VonKorff, M., Piccinelli, M., Fullerton, C., & Ormel, J. (1999). An international study of the relation between somatic symptoms and depression. *New England Journal of Medicine, 341*, 1329–1335.

Simon, G. E., Von Korff, M., Rutter, C. M., & Peterson, D. A. (2001). Treatment process and outcomes for managed care patients receiving new antidepressant prescriptions from psychiatrists and primary care physicians. *Archives of General Psychiatry, 58*, 395–401.

Simon, R. J., & Aaronson, D. E. (1988). *The insanity defense: A critical assessment of law and policy in the post-Hinckley era.* New York: Praeger.

Simon, S. L., Domier, C., Carnell, J., Brethen, P., Rawson, R., & Ling, W. (2000). Cognitive impairment in individuals currently using methamphetamine. *American Journal on Addictions, 9*, 222–231.

Simonoff, E. (2001). Genetic influences on conduct disorder. In J. Hill and B. Maughan (Eds.), *Conduct disorders in childhood and adolescence* (pp. 202–234). Cambridge, England: Cambridge University Press.

Simons, A. D., Garfield, S. L., & Murphy, G. E. (1984). The process of change in cognitive therapy and pharmacotherapy for depression: Changes in mood and cognition. *Archives of General Psychiatry, 41*, 45–51.

Singer, R., & Ryff, C. D. (1999). Hierarchies of life histories and associated health risks. In N. E. Alder, M. Marmot, B. E. McEwen, & J. Stewart (Eds.), *Socioeconomic status and health in industrial nations: social, psychological, ad biological pathways* (pp. 96–115). New York: New York Academy of Sciences.

Sinha, S. S., Mohlman, J., & Gorman, J. M. (2004). Neurobiology. In R. G. Heimberg, C. L. Turk, & D. S. Mennin (Eds.), *Generalized anxiety disorder* (pp. 187–218). New York: Guilford.

Sintchak, G. H., & Geer, J. H. (1975). A vaginal plethysmograph system. *Psychophysiology, 12*, 113–115.

Siok, W. T., Perfetti, C. A., Lin, Z., & Tan, L. H. (2004). Biological abnormality of impaired reading is constrained by culture. *Nature, 431*, 71–76.

Sisson, R. W., & Azrin, N. H. (1989). The community-reinforcement approach. In R. K. Hester & W. R. Miller (Eds.), *Handbook of alcoholism treatment approaches: Effective alternatives* (pp. 242–258). New York: Pergamon.

Sizemore, C. C., & Pittillo, E. S. (1977). *I'm Eve.* Garden City, NY: Doubleday.

Sizemore, J. P. (1995). Alabama's confidentiality quagmire: Psychotherapists, AIDS, mandatory reporting, and Tarasoff. *Law and Psychology Review, 19*, 241–257.

Skinner, B. F. (1953). *Science and human behavior.* New York: Macmillan.

Skinstad, A. H., & Swain, A. (2001). Comorbidity in a clinical sample of substance abusers. *American Journal of Drug and Alcohol Abuse, 27*, 45–64.

Sklar, L. A., & Anisman, H. (1979). Stress and coping factors influence tumor growth. *Science, 205*, 513–515.

Skolnick, A. S. (1998). Guidelines for treating erectile dysfunction issued. *JAMA, 277*, 24–26.

Skoog, G., & Skoog, I. (1999). A 40-year follow-up of patients with obsessive-compulsive disorder. *Archives of General Psychiatry, 56*, 121–130.

Slater, E. (1961). The thirty-fifth Maudsley lecture: Hysteria 311. *Journal of Mental Science, 107*, 358–381.

Slater, E., & Glithero, E. (1965). A follow-up of patients diagnosed as suffering from hysteria. *Journal of Psychosomatic Research, 9*, 9–13.

Sloan, D. M., Strauss, M. E., & Wisner, K. L. (2001). Diminished response to positive stimuli by depressed women. *Journal of Abnormal Psychology, 110*, 488–493.

Slutske, W. S., Heath, A. C., Dinwiddie, S. H., Madden, P. A. F., Bucholz, K. K., Dunne, M. P., Statham, D. J., & Martin, N. G. (1997). Modeling genetic and environmental influences in the etiology of conduct disorder: A study of 2,682 adult twin pairs. *Journal of Abnormal Psychology, 106*, 266–279.

Small, B. J., Fratiglioni, L., Viitanen, M., et al. (2000). The course of cognitive impairment in preclinical Alzheimer disease. *Archives of Neurology, 57*, 839– 844.

Small, G. W., & Jarvik, L. F. (1982). The dementia syndrome. *Lancet*, 1443–1446.

Smart, R. G., & Ogburne, A. C. (2000). Drug use and drinking among students in 36 countries. *Addictive Behaviors, 25*, 455–460.

Smith, D. W., Bierman, E. L., & Robinson, N. M. (1978). *The biologic ages of man: From conception through old age.* Philadelphia: Saunders.

Smith, G. (1992). The epidemiology and treatment of depression when it coincides with somatoform disorders, somatization, or panic. *General Hospital Psychiatry, 14*, 265–272.

Smith, G. T., Goldman, M. S., Greenbaum, P. E., & Christiansen, B. A. (1995). Expectancy for social facilitation from drinking: The divergent paths of high expectancy and low expectancy adolescents. *Journal of Abnormal Psychology, 104*, 32–40.

Smith, J., Frawley, P. J., & Polissar, L. (1991). Six- and twelve-month abstinence rates in inpatient alcoholics treated with aversion therapy compared with matched inpatients from a treatment registry. *Alcoholism: Clinical and Experimental Research, 15*, 862–870.

Smith, J. E., & Meyers, R. J. (2000). CRA: The Community Reinforcement Approach for treating alcohol problems. In M. J. Dougher (Ed.). *Clinical behavior analysis* (pp. 207–230). Reno, NV: Context Press.

Smith, J. E., Meyers, R. J., & Miller, W. R. (2001). The community reinforcement approach to the treatment of substance use disorders. *American Journal on Addictions, 10*, 51–59.

Smith, K. A., Fairburn, C. G., & Cowen, P. J. (1999). Symptomatic relapse in bulimia nervosa following acute tryptophan depletion. *Archives of General Psychiatry, 56*, 171–176.

Smith, K. F., & Bengston, V. L. (1979). Positive consequences of institutionalization: Solidarity between elderly parents and their middle aged children. *The Gerontologist, 5*, 438–447.

Smith, M. L., Glass, G. V., & Miller, T. I. (1980). *The benefits of psychotherapy.* Baltimore, MD: Johns Hopkins University Press.

Smith, M. U., & Katner, H. P. (1995). Quasi-experimental evaluations of three AIDS prevention activities for maintaining knowledge, improving attitudes, and changing risk behaviors of high school seniors. *AIDS Education and Prevention, 7*, 391–402.

Smith, S. S., Jorenby, D. E., Fiore, M. C., Anderson, J. E., Mielke, M. M., Beach, K. E., Piasecki, T. M., & Baker, T. B. (2001). Strike while the iron is hot: Can stepped-care treatments resurrect relapsing smokers? *Journal of Consulting & Clinical Psychology, 69*, 429–439.

Smith, T., Groen, A., & Wynn, J. W. (2000). Randomized trial of intensive early intervention for children with pervasive developmental disorder. *Research in Developmental Disabilities, 21*, 297–309.

Smith, Y. L. S., van Goozen, S. H. M., & Cohen Kettenis, P. T. (2001). Adolescents with gender identity disorder who were accepted or rejected for sex reassignment surgery: A prospective follow-up study. *Journal of the American Academy of Child and Adolescent Psychiatry, 40*, 472–481.

Snowdon, D. A., Kemper, S. J., Mortimer, J. A., Greiner, L. H., et al. (1996). Linguistic ability in early life and cognitive function and Alzheimer's disease in late life: Findings from the nun study. *JAMA, 275*, 528–534.

Snowden, M., & Roy-Byrne, P. (1998). Mental illness and nursing home reform: OBRA-87 ten years later. *Psychiatric Services, 49*, 220–233.

Snyder, D. K., Wills, R. M., & Grady-Fletcher, A. (1991). Long-term effectiveness of behavioral versus insight-oriented marital therapy: A 4-year follow-up study. *Journal of Consulting and Clinical Psychology, 59*, 138–141.

Snyder, S. H. (1974). *Madness and the brain.* New York: McGraw-Hill.

Sobell, L. C., Toneatto, A., & Sobell, M. B. (1990). Behavior therapy. In A. S. Bellack & M. Hersen (Eds.), *Handbook of comparative treatments for adult disorders* (pp. 479–505). New York: John Wiley & Sons.

Sobell, M. B., & Sobell, L. C. (1976). Second-year treatment outcome of alcoholics treated by individualized behavior therapy: Results. *Behaviour Research and Therapy, 14*, 195–215.

Sobell, M. B., & Sobell, L. C. (1993). *Problem drinkers: Guided self-change treatment.* New York: Guilford.

Sobell, M. B., & Sobell, L. C. (2000). Stepped care as a heuristic approach to the treatment of alcohol problems. *Journal of Consulting and Clinical Psychology, 68*, 573–579.

Soloff, P. H., Meltzer, C. C., Greer, P. J., et al. (2000). A fenfluramine-activated FDG-PET study of borderline personality disorder. *Biological Psychiatry, 47*, 540–547.

Solomon, D. A., Keller, M. B., Leon, A. C., Mueller, T. I., Lavori, P. W., Shea, M. T., Coryell, W., Warshaw, M., Turvey, C., Maser, J. D., & Endicott, J. (2000). Multiple recurrences of major depressive disorder. *American Journal of Psychiatry, 157,* 229–233.

Sorensen, J. L., & Copeland, A. L. (2000). Drug abuse treatment as an HIV prevention strategy: A review. *Drug & Alcohol Dependence, 59,* 17–31.

Soyka, M., Horak, M., Morhart, V., & Moeller, H. J. (2001). *Modellprojekt "Qualifizierte ambulante Entgiftung."* /Qualified outpatient detoxification. *Nervenarzt, 72,* 565–569

Spanos, N. P. (1994). Multiple identity enactments and multiple personality disorder: A sociocognitive perspective. *Psychological Bulletin, 116,* 143–165.

Spanos, N. P., Weekes, J. R., & Bertrand, L. D. (1985). Multiple personality: A social psychological perspective. *Journal of Abnormal Psychology, 94,* 362–376.

Spar, J. E., & LaRue, A. (1990). *Geriatric psychiatry.* Washington, DC: American Psychiatric Press.

Sparrow, S. S., Ballo, D. A., & Cicchetti, D. V. (1984). *Vineland Adaptive Behavior Scales.* Circle Pines, MI: American Guidance Service.

Spencer, S. J., Steele, C. M., & Quinn, D. M. (1999). Stereotype threat and women's math performance. *Journal of Experimental Social Psychology, 35,* 4–28.

Spencer, T., Biederman, J., Wilens, T., Harding, M., O'Donnell, D., & Griffin, S. (1996). Pharmacotherapy of attention-deficit hyperactivity disorder across the life cycle. *Journal of the American Academy of Child and Adolescent Psychiatry, 35,* 409–432.

Spengler, A. (1977). Manifest sadomasochism of males: Results of an empirical study. *Archives of Sexual Behavior, 6,* 441–456.

Spiess, W. F. J., Geer, J. H., & O'Donohue, W. T. (1984). Premature ejaculation: Investigation of factors in ejaculatory latency. *Journal of Abnormal Psychology, 93,* 242–245.

Spitzer, R. L., Gibbon, M., Skodol, A. E., Williams, J. B. W., & First, M. B. (Eds.). 1994. *DSM-IV casebook: A learning companion to the Diagnostic and Statistical Manual of Mental Disorders* (4th ed.). Washington, DC: American Psychiatric Press.

Spitzer, R. L., Gibbon, M., & Williams, J. B. W. (1996). *Structured clinical interview of DSM-IV Axis I disorders.* New York: N. Y. State Psychiatric Institute, Biometrics Research Department.

Spitzer, R. M., Stunkard, A., Yanovski, S., Marcus, M. D., Wadden, T., et al. (1993). Binge eating disorders should be included in DSM-IV. *International Journal of Eating Disorders, 13,* 161–169.

Spoth, R. A., Guyll, M., & Day, S. X. (2002). Universal family-focused interventions in alcohol-use prevention: Cost-benefit analyses of two interventions. *Journal of Studies on Alcohol, 63,* 219–228.

Spoth, R. A., Redmond, C., Shin, C., & Azevedo, K. (2004). Brief family intervention effects on adolescent substance initiation: School-level growth curve analyses 6 years following baseline. *Journal of Consulting and Clinical Psychology, 72,* 535–542.

Sprich, S., Biederman, J., Crawford, M. H., Mundy, E., & Faraone, S. V. (2000). Adoptive and biological families of children and adolescents with ADHD. *Journal of the American Academy of Child and Adolescent Psychiatry, 39,* 1432–1437.

Staats, A. W., & Staats, C. K. (1963). *Complex human behavior.* New York: Holt, Rinehart & Winston.

Stack, S. (2000). Media impacts on suicide: A quantitative review of 293 findings. *Social Science Quarterly, 81,* 957–971.

Stack, S. (2001). Occupation and suicide. *Social Science Quarterly, 82,* 384–396.

Stacy, A. W., Newcomb, M. D., & Bentler, P. M. (1991). Cognitive motivation and drug use: A 9-year longitudinal study. *Journal of Abnormal Psychology, 100,* 502–515.

Stanford, J. L., & Greenberg, R. S. (1989). Breast cancer incidence in young women by estrogen receptor status and race. *American Journal of Public Health, 79,* 71–73.

Stanley, M. A., & Turner, S. M. (1995). Current status of pharmacological and behavioral treatment of obsessive-compulsive disorder. *Behavior Therapy, 26,* 163–186.

Stanton, A. H., Gunderson, J. G., Knapp, P. H., Frank, A. E., Vanicelli, M. L., Schnitzer, R., & Rosenthal, R. (1984). Effects of psychotherapy in schizophrenia. *Schizophrenia Bulletin, 10,* 520–563.

Stanton, M. D., & Bardoni, A. (1972). Drug flashbacks: Reported frequency in a military population. *American Journal of Psychiatry, 129,* 751–755.

Stark, K. D., Napolitano, S., Swearer, S., Schmidt, K., Jaramillo, D., & Hoyle, J. (1996). Issues in the treatment of depressed children. *Applied and Preventive Psychology, 5,* 59–83

Stark, K. D., Schmidt, K., Joiner, T. E., & Lux, M. G. (1996). Cognitive triad: Relationship to depressive symptoms, parents' cognitive triad, and perceived parental messages. *Journal of Abnormal Child Psychology, 24,* 615–631.

Stark, K. D., Swearer, S., Sommer, D., Hickey, B. B., Napolitano, S., Kurowski, C., & Dempsey, M. (1998). School-based group treatment for depressive disorders in children. In T. R. Kratochwill & K. C. Stoiber (Eds.), *Handbook of group intervention for children and families* (pp. 68–99). Boston: Allyn & Bacon.

Steadman, H. J. (1979). *Beating a rap: Defendants found incompetent to stand trial.* Chicago: University of Chicago Press.

Steadman, H. J., Davidson, S., & Brown, C. (2001). Mental health courts: Their promise and unanswered questions. *Law and Psychiatry, 52,* 457–458.

Steadman, H. J., McGreevy, M. A., Morrissey, J. P., Callahan, L. A., Robbins, P. C., & Cirincione, C. (1993). *Before and after Hinckley: Evaluating insanity defense reform.* New York: Guilford.

Steadman, H. J., Mulvey, E. P., Monahan, J., Robbins, P. C., Appelbaum, P. S., Grisso, T., Roth, L. H., & Silver, E. (1998). Violence by people discharged from acute psychiatric inpatient facilities and by others in the same neighborhoods. *Archives of General Psychiatry, 55,* 393–401.

Steele, C. M., & Josephs, R. A. (1988). Drinking your troubles away: 2. An attention-allocation model of alcohol's effects on psychological stress. *Journal of Abnormal Psychology, 97,* 196–205.

Steiger, H., Gauvin, L., Jabalpurwala, S., & Séguin, J. R. 1999. Hypersenstivity to social interactions in bulimic syndromes: Relationship to binge eating. *Journal of Consulting and Clinical Psychology, 67,* 765–775.

Stein, E. A., Pankiewicz, J., Harsch, H. H., Cho, J.-K., Fuller, S. A., et al. (1998). Nicotine-induced limbic cortical activation in the human brain: A functional MRI study. *American Journal of Psychiatry, 155,* 1009–1015.

Stein, L. I., & Test, M. A. (1980). Alternative to mental hospital treatment: I. Conceptual model, treatment program, and clinical evaluation. *Archives of General Psychiatry, 37,* 392–397.

Stein, M. B. (1998). Neurobiological perspectives on social phobia: From affiliation to zoology. *Biological Psychiatry, 44,* 1277–1285.

Stein, M. B., Liebowitz, M. R., Lydiard, R. B., Pitts, C. D., Bushnell, W., & Gergel, I. (1998). Paroxetine treatment of generalized social phobia (social anxiety disorder): A randomized clinical trial. *Journal of the American Medical Association, 280,* 708–713.

Steinberg, J. S., Arshad, A., Kowalski, M., et al. (2004). Increased incidence of life-threatening ventricular arrhythmias in implantable defibrillator patients after the world trade center attack. *Journal of the American College of Cardiology, 44,* 1261–1264.

Steinhausen, H. C., & Metzke, C. W. (1998). Youth self-report of behavioral and emotional problems in a Swiss epidemiological study. *Journal of Youth and Adolescence, 27,* 429–441.

Stek, M. L., Gussekloon, J., Beekman, A. T. F., van Tilburg, W., & Westendorp, R. G. J. (2004). Prevalence, correlates and recognition of depression in the oldest old: The Leiden 85-plus study. *Journal of Affective Disorders, 78,* 193–200.

Steketee, G., & Frost, R. O. (1998). Obsessive-compulsive disorder. In A. S. Bellack & M. Herse (Eds.), *Comprehensive clinical psychology: Volume 6. Adults: Clinical formulation and treatment.* Oxford: Pergamon.

Steketee, G., & Barlow, D. H. (2004). Obsessive-compulsive disorder. In D. H. Barlow (Ed.). *Anxiety and its disorders: The nature and treatment of anxiety and panic.* (pp. 516–550). New York: Guilford.

Stephens, R. S., Roffman, R. A., & Simpson, E. E. (1993). Adult marijuana users seeking treatment. *Journal of Consulting and Clinical Psychology, 61,* 1100–1104.

Steptoe, A. (1997). Stress management. In A. Baum, S. Newman, J. Weinman, R. West, & C. McManus (Eds.), *Cambridge encyclopedia of psychology, health and medicine* (pp. 262–264). Cambridge, England: Cambridge University Press.

Stern, G. S., & Berrenberg, J. L. (1979). Skill-set, success outcome, and mania as determinants of the illusion of control. *Journal of Research in Personality, 13,* 206–222.

Stern, R. S., & Cobb, J. P. (1978). Phenomenology of obsessive-compulsive neurosis. *British Journal of Psychiatry, 132,* 233–234.

Stevenson, J., & Jones, I. H. (1972). Behavior therapy technique for exhibitionism: A preliminary report. *Archives of General Psychiatry, 27,* 839–841.

Stewart, W. F., Ricci, J. A., Chee, E., Hahn, S. R., & Morganstein, D. (2003). Cost of lost productive work time among US workers with depression. *Journal of the American Medical Association, 289,* 3135–3144.

Stice, E. (2001). A prospective test of the dual-pathway model of bulimic pathology: Mediating effects of dieting and negative affect. *Journal of Abnormal Psychology, 110,* 124–135.

Stice, E., & Agras, W. S. (1999). Subtyping bulimics along dietary restraint and negative affect dimensions. *Journal of Consulting and Clinical Psychology, 67,* 460–469.

Stice, E., Barrera, M., & Chasin, L. (1998). Prospective differential prediction of adolescent alcohol use and problem use: Examining the mechanisms of effect. *Journal of Abnormal Psychology, 107,* 616–628.

Stice, E., Burton, E. M., & Shaw, H. (2004). Prospective relations between bulimic pathology, depression, and substance abuse: Unpacking comorbidity in adolescent girls. *Journal of Consulting and Clinical Psychology, 72,* 62–71.

Stice, E., & Fairburn, C. G. (2003). Dietary and dietary-depressive subtypes of bulimia nervosa show differential symptom presentation, social impairment, comorbidity, and course of illness. *Journal of Consulting and Clinical Psychology, 71,* 1090–1094.

Stice, E., & Shaw, H. (2004). Eating disorder prevention programs: A meta-analytic review. *Psychological Bulletin, 130,* 206–227.

Stockmeier, C. A. (2003). Involvement of serotonin in depression: Evidence from postmortem and imaging studies of serotonin receptors and the serotonin transporter. *Journal of Psychiatric Research, 37,* 357–373.

Stone, A. A., Bovbjerg, D. H., Neale, J. M., Napoli, A., Valdimarsdottir, H., et al. (1992). Development of common cold symptoms following experimental rhinovirus infection is related to prior stressful life events. *Behavioral Medicine, 18,* 115–120.

Stone, A. A., Cox, D. S., Valdimarsdottir, H., Jandorf, L., & Neale, J. M. (1987). Evidence that secretory IgA antibody is associated with daily mood. *Journal of Personality and Social Psychology, 52,* 988–993.

Stone, A. A., & Neale, J. M. (1982). Development of a methodology for assessing daily experiences. In A. Baum and J. Singer (Eds.), *Environment and health.* Hillsdale, NJ: Lawrence Erlbaum.

Stone, A. A., & Neale, J. M. (1984). The effects of "severe" daily events on mood. *Journal of Personality and Social Psychology, 46,* 137–144.

Stone, A. A., Neale, J. M., Cox, D. S., Napoli, A., Valdimarsdottir, H., & Kennedy-Moore, E. (1994). Daily events are associated with a secretory immune response to an oral antigen in men. *Health Psychology, 13,* 440–446.

Stone, A. A., Reed, B. R., & Neale, J. M. (1987). Changes in daily event frequency precede episodes of physical symptoms. *Journal of Human Stress, 13,* 70–74.

Stone, A. A., Schwartz, J., Neale, J. M., Shiffman, S., Marco, C. A., et al. (1998). A comparison of coping assessed by Ecological Momentary Assessment and retrospective recall. *Journal of Personality and Social Psychology, 74,* 1670–1680.

Stone, A. A., & Shiffman, S. (1994). Ecological momentary assessment (EMA) in behavioral medicine. *Annals of Behavioral Medicine, 16,* 199–202.

Stone, G. (1982). Health Psychology, a new journal for a new field. *Health Psychology, 1,* 1–6.

Stone, M. H. (1986). Exploratory psychotherapy in schizophrenia-spectrum patients: A reevaluation in the light of long-term follow-up of schizophrenic and borderline patients. *Bulletin of the Menninger Clinic, 50,* 287–306.

Stone, M. H. (1987). Psychotherapy of borderline patients in light of long-term follow-up. *Bulletin of the Menninger Clinic, 51,* 231–247.

Stone, M. H. (1993). *Abnormalities of personality. Within and beyond the realm of treatment.* New York: Norton.

Stone, S. V., & Costa, P. T. (1990). Disease-prone personality or distress-prone personality? The role of neuroticism in coronary heart disease. In H. S. Friedman (Ed.), *Personality and disease.* New York: John Wiley & Sons.

Stopa, L., & Clark, D. M. (2000). Social phobia and interpretation of social events. *Behaviour Research and Therapy, 38,* 273–283.

Stormer, S. M., & Thompson, J. K. (1996). Explanations of body image disturbance: A test of maturational status, negative verbal commentary, and sociological hypotheses. *International Journal of Eating Disorders, 19,* 193–202.

Story, M., French, S. A., Resnick, M. D., & Blum, R. W. (1995). Ethnic/racial and socioeconomic differences in dieting behaviors and body image perceptions in adolescents. *International Journal of Eating Disorders, 18,* 173–179.

Stoving, R. K., Hangaard, J., Hansen-Nord, M., & Hagen, C. (1999). A review of endocrine changes in anorexia nervosa. *Journal of Psychiatric Research, 33,* 139–152.

Strain, E. C., Bigelow, G. E., Liebson, I. A., & Stitzer, M. L. (1999). Moderate- vs low-dose methadone in the treatment of opioid dependence. *JAMA, 281,* 1000–1005.

Strassberg, D. S., de Gouveia Brazao, C. A., Rowland, D. L., Tan, P., & Slob, A. K. (1999). Clomipramine in the treatment of rapid (premature) ejaculation. *Journal of Sex and Marital Therapy, 25,* 89–101.

Strassberg, D. S., Kelly, M. P., Carroll, C., & Kircher, J. C. (1987). The psychophysiological nature of premature ejaculation. *Archives of Sexual Behavior, 16*(4), 327–336.

Strauss, J. S., Carpenter, W. T., & Bartko, J. J. (1974). The diagnosis and understanding of schizophrenia: Part 3. Speculations on the processes that underlie schizophrenic signs and symptoms. *Schizophrenia Bulletin, 1,* 61–69.

Strauss, M. E., & Ogrocki, P. K. (1996). Confirmation of an association between family history of affective disorder and the depressive syndrome in Alzheimer's disease. *American Journal of Psychiatry, 153,* 1340–1342.

Streeton, C., & Whelan, G. (2001). Naltrexone, a relapse prevention maintenance treatment of alcohol dependence: A meta-analysis of randomized controlled trials. *Alcohol & Alcoholism, 36,* 544–552.

Striegel-Moore, R. H., Cachelin, F. M., Dohm, F.-A., Pike, K. M., Wilfely, D. E., & Fairburn, C. G. (2001). Comparison of binge eating disorder and bulimia nervosa in a community sample. *International Journal of Eating Disorders, 29,* 157–165.

Striegel-Moore, R. H., & Franco, D. L. (2003). Epidemiology of binge eating disorder. *International Journal of Eating Disorders, 34,* S19–S29.

Striegel-Moore, R. H., Garvin, V., Dohm, F.-A., & Rosenheck, R. (1999a). Eating disorders in a national sample of hospitalized male and female veterans: Prevalence and psychiatric comorbidity. *International Journal of Eating Disorders, 25,* 405–414.

Striegel-Moore, R. H., Garvin, V., Dohm, F. A., & Rosenheck, R. (1999b). Psychiatric comorbidity of eating disorders in men: A national study of hospitalized veterans. *International Journal of Eating Disorders, 25,* 399–404.

Striegel-Moore, R. H., Schreiber, G. B., Lo, A., Crawford, P., Obarzanek, E., & Rodin, J. (2000). Eating disorder symptoms in a cohort of 11 to 16-year-old black and white girls: The NHLBI growth and health study. *International Journal of Eating Disorders, 27,* 49–66.

Striegel-Moore, R. H., Wilson, G. T., Wilfley, D. E., Elder, K. A., & Brownell, K. D. (1998). Binge eating in an obese community sample. *International Journal of Eating Disorders, 23,* 27–36.

Stritzke, W. G. K., Patrick, C. J., & Lang, P. J. (1995). Alcohol and emotion: A multidimensional approach incorporating startle probe methodology. *Journal of Abnormal Psychology, 104,* 114–122.

Strober, M., Freeman, R., Lampert, C., Diamond, J., & Kaye, W. (2000). Controlled family study of anorexia nervosa and bulimia nervosa: Evidence of shared liability and transmission of partial syndromes. *American Journal of Psychiatry, 157,* 393–401.

Strober, M., Freeman, R., Lampert, C., Diamond, J., & Kaye, W. (2001). Males with anorexia nervosa: A controlled study of eating disorders in first-degree relatives. *International Journal of Eating Disorders, 29,* 264–269.

Strober, M., Freeman, R., & Morrell, W. (1997). The long-term course of severe anorexia nervosa in adolescents: Survival analysis of recovery, relapse, and outcome predictors over 10–15 years in a prospective study. *International Journal of Eating Disorders, 22,* 339–360.

Strober, M., Lampert, C., Morrell, W., Burroughs, J., & Jacobs, C. (1990). A controlled family study of anorexia nervosa: Evidence of family aggregation and lack of shared transmission with affective disorders. *International Journal of Eating Disorders, 9,* 239–253.

Strub, R. L., & Black, F. W. (1981). *Organic brain syndromes: An introduction to neurobehavioral disorders.* Philadelphia: F.A. Davis.

Stuart, F. M., Hammond, D. C., & Pett, M. A. (1987). Inhibited sexual desire in women. *Archives of Sexual Behavior, 16,* 91–106.

Styron, W. (1992). *Darkness visible: A memoir of madness.* New York: Vintage.

Substance Abuse and Mental Health Services Administration. (1997b). Preliminary results from the 1996 National Household Survey on Drug Abuse (DHHS Pub. No. SMA 97-3149). Rockville, MD: Office of Applied Studies: Substance Abuse and Mental Health Services Administration.

Substance Abuse and Mental Health Services Administration. (1998). *Substance abuse among older adults.* Treatment Improvement Protocol (TIP) Series #26. Rockville, MD: U.S. Department of Health and Human Services.

Substance Abuse and Mental Health Services Administration. 2004. *Overview of Findings from the 2003 National Survey on Drug Use and Health* (Office of Applied Studies, NSDUH Series H-24, DHHS Publication No. SMA 04-3963). Rockville, MD.

Suddath, R. L., Christison, G. W., Torrey, E. F., Cassonova, M. F., Weinberger, D. R., et al. (1990). Anatomical abnormalities in the brains of monozygotic twins discordant for schizophrenia. *New England Journal of Medicine, 322,* 789–793.

Sue, S. (1999). Science, ethnicity, and bias: Where have we gone wrong? *American Psychologist, 54,* 1070–1077.

Sue, D. W., & Sue, D. (1990). *Counseling the culturally different: Theory and practice.* (2nd ed.). Oxford, England: John Wiley & Sons.

Sugarman, P., Dumughn, C., Saad, K., Hinder, S., & Bluglass, S. (1994). Dangerousness in exhibitionists. *Journal of Forensic Psychiatry, 5,* 287–296.

Sullivan, J. M. (2000). Cellular and molecular mechanisms underlying learning and memory impairments produced by cannabinoids. *Learning and Memory, 7,* 132–139.

Sullivan, P. F. (1995). Mortality in anorexia nervosa. *American Journal of Psychiatry, 152,* 1073–1075.

Sullivan, P. F., Neale, M. C., & Kendler, K. S. (2000). Genetic epidemiology of major depression: Review and meta-analysis. *American Journal of Psychiatry, 157,* 1552–1562.

Suls, J., & Bende, J. (2005). Anger, anxiety, and depression as risk factors for cardiovascular disease, The problems and implications of overlapping affective dispositions. *Psychological Bulletin, 131,* 260–300.

Suomi, S. J. (1999). Behavioral inhibition and impulsive aggressiveness: Insights from studies with rhesus monkeys. In L. Balter & C. S. Tamis-LeMonda (Eds.) *Child psychology: A handbook of contemporary issues* (pp. 510–525). New York: Psychology Press.

Suomi, S. J. (2000). A biobehavioral perspective on developmental psychopathology: Excessive aggression and serotonergic dysfunction in monkeys. In A. J. Sameroff, M. Lewis, et. al. (Eds.) *Handbook of developmental psychopathology* (2nd ed., pp. 237–256). Dordrecht, Netherlands: Kluwer Academic Publishers.

Surles, R. C., Blanch, A. K., Shern, D. L., & Donahue, S. A. (1992). Case management as a strategy for systems change. *Health Affairs, 11,* 151–163.

Susser, E., & Wanderling, J. (1994). Epidemiology of nonaffective acute remitting psychosis versus schizophrenia: Sex and sociocultural setting. *Archives of General Psychiatry, 51,* 294–301.

Susser, E., Neugebauer, R., Hoek, H. W., Brown, A. S., Lin, S., et al. (1996). Schizophrenia after prenatal famine: Further evidence. *Archives of General Psychiatry, 53,* 25–31.

Susser, E., Valencia, E., Berkman, A., Sohler, N., Conover, S., Torres, J., Betne, P., Felix, A., & Miller, S. (1998). Human immunodeficiency virus sexual risk reduction in homeless men with mental illness. *Archives of General Psychiatry, 55,* 266–272.

Sussman, S. (1996). Development of a school-based drug abuse prevention curriculum for high-risk youth. *Journal of Psychoactive Drugs, 28,* 169–182.

Sussman, T., Dent, C. W., & Lichtman, K. L. (2001). Project EX: Outcomes of a teen smoking cessation program. *Addictive Behaviors, 26,* 425–438.

Sussman, S., Dent, C. W., McAdams, L., Stacy, A. W., Burton, D., & Flay, B. R. (1994). Group self-identification and adolescent cigarette smoking: A 1-year prospective study. *Journal of Abnormal Psychology, 103,* 576–580.

Sussman, S., Dent, C. W., Simon, T. R., Stacy, A. W., Galaif, F. R., Moss, M. A., Craig, S., & Johnson, C. A. (1995). Immediate impact of social influence-oriented substance abuse prevention curricula in traditional and continuation high schools. *Drugs and Society, 8,* 65–81.

Sussman, S., Stacy, A. W., Dent, C. W., Simon, T. R., & Johnson, C. A. (1996). Marijuana use: Current issues and new research directions. *The Journal of Drug Issues, 26,* 695–733.

Sutcliffe, J. P., & Jones, J. (1962). Personal identity, multiple personality, and hypnosis. *International Journal of Clinical and Experimental Hypnosis, 10,* 231–269.

Sutker, P. B., & Adams, H. E. (2001). *Comprehensive handbook of psychopathology* (3rd ed.). New York: Kluwer Academic/Plenum.

Sutker, P. B., Uddo, M., Brailey, K., Vasterling, J. J., & Errera, P. (1994). Psychopathology in war-zone deployed and nondeployed Operation Desert Storm troops assigned grave registration duties. *Journal of Abnormal Psychology, 103,* 383–390.

Suzuki, K., Takei, N., Kawai, M., Minabe, Y., & Mori, N. (2003). Is *Taijin Kyofusho* a culture-bound syndrome? *American Journal of Psychiatry, 160,* 1358.

Svarstad, B. L., & Mount, J. K. (2001). Chronic benzodiazepine use in nursing homes: Effects of federal guidelines, resident mix, and nurse staffing. *Journal of the American Geriatrics Society, 49,* 1673–1678.

Svartberg, M., Stiles, T. C., & Seltzer, M. H. (2004). Randomized, controlled trial of the effectiveness of short-term dynamic psychotherapy and cognitive therapy for cluster C personality disorders. *American Journal of Psychiatry, 161,* 810–817.

Swain, J., Koszycki, D., Shlik, J., & Bradwein, J. (2003). In D. Nutt and J. Ballenger (Eds.), *Anxiety disorders* (pp. 269–295). Malden, MA: Blackwell.

Swainson, R., Hodges, J. R., Galton, C. J., Semple, J., Michael, A., Dunn, B. D., Iddon, J. L., Robbins, T. W., & Sahakian, B. J. (2001). Early detection and differential diagnosis of Alzheimer's disease and depression with neuropsychological tasks. *Dementia and Geriatric Cognition Disorders, 12,* 265–280.

Swanson, J., McBurnett, K., Christian, D. L., & Wigal, T. (1995). Stimulant medications and the treatment of children with ADHD. In T. H. Ollendick & R. J. Prinz (Eds.), *Advances in clinical child psychology* (Vol. 17, pp. 265–322). New York: Plenum.

Swanson, J. M., Kraemer, H. C., Hinshaw, S. P., et al. (2001). Clinical relevance of the primary findings of the MTA: Success rates based on severity of ADHD and ODD symptoms at the end of treatment. *Journal of the American Academy of Child and Adolescent Psychiatry, 40,* 168–179.

Swanson, J. W., Holzer, C. E., Ganju, V. K., & Jono, R. T. (1990). Violence and psychiatric disorder in the community: Evidence from the Epidemiological Catchment Area surveys. *Hospital and Community Psychiatry, 41,* 761–770.

Sweet, J. J., Carr, M. A., Rossini, E., & Kasper, C. (1986). Relationship between the Luria-Nebraska Neuropsychological Battery and the WISC-R: Further examination using Kaufman's factors. *International Journal of Clinical Neuropsychology, 8,* 177–180.

Sweet, R. A., Mulsant, B. H., Gupta, B., Rifai, A. H., Pasternak, R. E., et al. (1995). Duration of neuroleptic treatment and prevalence of tardive dyskinesia in late life. *Archives of General Psychiatry, 52,* 478–486.

Szasz, T. S. (1963). *Law, liberty, and psychiatry.* New York: Macmillan.

Szasz, T. S. (1999). *Fatal freedom: The ethics and politics of suicide.* Westport, CT: Praeger.

Szczypka, M. S., Kwok, K., Brot, M. D., Marck, B. T., Matsumoto, A. M., Donahue, B. A., & Palmiter, R. D. (2001). Dopamine production in the caudate putamen restores feeding in dopamine-deficient mice. *Neuron, 30,* 819–828.

Tallal, P., Merzenich, M., Miller, S., & Jenkins, W. (1998). Language learning impairment: Integrating research and remediation. *Scandinavian Journal of Psychology, 39,* 197–199.

Tallal, P., Miller, S. L., Bedi, G., Byma, G., Wang, X., Nagarajan, S. S., Schreiner, C., Jenkins, W. M., & Merzenich, M. M. (1996). Language comprehension in language-learning impaired children improved with acoustically modified speech. *Science, 271,* 81–84.

Tallmadge, J., & Barkley, R. A. (1983). The interactions of hyperactive and normal boys with their mothers and fathers. *Journal of Abnormal Child Psychology, 11,* 565–579.

Tannock, R. (1998). Attention deficit hyperactivity disorder: Advances in cognitive, neurobiological, and genetic research. *Journal of Child Psychology and Psychiatry, 39,* 65–100.

Tariot, P. N., Farlow, M. R., Grossberg, G. T., Graham, S. M., McDonald, S., & Gergel, I. (2004). Memantine treatment in patients with moderate to severe Alzheimer disease already receiving Donepezil: A randomized controlled trial. *JAMA, 291,* 317–324.

Task Force on Promotion and Dissemination of Psychological Procedures. (1995). Training in and dissemination of empirically-validated psychological treatments: Report and recommendations. *The Clinical Psychologist, 48,* 3–23.

Taylor, C. B., Hayward, C., King, R., et al. (1990). Cardiovascular and symptomatic reduction effects of alprazolam and imipramine in patients with panic disorder: Results of a double-blind, placebo-controlled trial. *Journal of Clinical Psychopharmacology, 10,* 112–118.

Taylor, J., Iacono, W. G., & McGue, M. (2000). Evidence for a genetic etiology of early-onset delinquency. *Journal of Abnormal Psychology, 109,* 634–643.

Taylor, J., Loney, B. R., Bobadilla, L., Iacono, W. G., & McGue, M. (2003). Genetic and environmental influences on psychopathy trait dimensions in a community sample of male twins. *Journal of Abnormal Child Psychology, 31,* 633–645.

Taylor, S. E., Kemeny, M. E., Aspinwall, L. G., Schneider, S. G., Rodriguez, R., & Herbert, M. (1992). Optimism, coping, psychological distress, and high-risk sexual behavior among men at risk for acquired immunodeficiency syndrome (AIDS). *Journal of Personality and Social Psychology, 63,* 460–473.

Teasdale, J. D. (1988). Cognitive vulnerability to persistent depression. *Cognition and Emotion, 2,* 247–274.

Teasdale, J. D. (2004, September). Mindfulness and the third wave of cognitive-behavioural therapies. Keynote Address at the 34th Annual Conference of the European Association for Behavioural and Cognitive Therapies. Manchester, England.

Teasdale, J. D., Segal, Z. V., Williams, J. M. G., Ridgeway, V. A., Soulsby, J. M., & Lau, M. A. (2000). Prevention of relapse/recurrence in major depression by mindfulness-based cognitive therapy. *Journal of Consulting & Clinical Psychology, 68,* 615–623.

Telch, M. J. & Harrington, P. J. (unpublished manuscript). Anxiety sensitivity and unexpectedness of arousal in mediating affective response to 35% carbon dioxide inhalation.

Telch, M. J., Lucas, J. A., Schmidt, N. B., & Hanna, H. H. (1993). Group cognitive-behavioral treatment of panic disorder. *Behaviour Research and Therapy, 31,* 279–287.

Telch, M. J., Shermis, M. D., & Lucas, J. A. (1989). Anxiety sensitivity: Unitary personality trait or domain-specific appraisals? *Journal of Anxiety Disorders, 3,* 25–32.

Temple, E., Poldrack, R. A., Salidas, J., Deutsch, G. K., Tallal, P., Merzenich, M. M., & Gabrieli, J. D. E. (2001). Disrupted neural responses to phonological and orthographic processing in dyslexic children: An fMRI study. *Neuroreport, 12,* 299–307.

Teresi, J., Abrams, R., Holmes, D., Ramirez, M., & Eimicke, J. (2001). Prevalence of depression and depression recognition in nursing homes. *Social Psychiatry and Psychiatric Epidemiology, 36,* 613–620.

Teri, L., Gibbons, L. E., McCurry, S. M., Logsdon, R. G., Buchner, D. M., Barlow, W. E., et al. (2003). Exercise plus behavioral management in patients with Alzheimer disease: A randomized controlled trial. *JAMA, 290,* 2015–2022.

Teri, L., & Reifler, B. V. (1987). Depression and dementia. In L. L. Carstensen & B. A. Edelstein (Eds.), *Handbook of clinical gerontology.* New York: Pergamon.

Terry, D. J., & Hynes, G. J. (1998). Adjustment to a low-control situation: Reexamining the role of coping responses. *Journal of Personality and Social Psychology, 74,* 1078–1092.

Thapar, A., Fowler, T., Rice, F., et al. (2003). Maternal smoking during pregnancy and attention deficit hyperactivity disorder symptoms in offspring. *American Journal of Psychiatry, 160,* 1985–1989.

Thase, M. E. (2000). Psychopharmacology in conjunction with psychotherapy. In C. R. Snyder & R. E. Ingram (Eds.), (2000) *Handbook of psychological change.* New York: Wiley, pp. 474–497.

Thase, M. E., Jindal, R., & Howland, R. H. (2002). Biological aspects of depression. In C. L. Hammen and I. H. Gotlib (Eds.), *Handbook of depression.* (pp. 192–218). New York: Guilford.

Thase, M. E., & Rush, A. J. (1997). When at first you don't succeed: Sequential strategies for antidepressant nonresponders. *Journal of Clinical Psychiatry, 58*(Suppl. 13), 23–29.

Theobald, H., Bygren, L. O., Carstensen, J., & Engfeldt, P. A. (2000). Moderate intake of wine is associated with reduced total mortality and reduced mortality from cardiovascular disease. *Journal of Studies on Alcohol, 61,* 652–656.

Thigpen, C. H., & Cleckley, H. (1954). *The three faces of Eve.* Kingsport, TN: Kingsport Press.

Thoits, P. A. (1985). Self-labeling processes in mental illness: The role of emotional deviance. *American Journal of Sociology, 92,* 221–249.

Thomas, G., Reifman, A., Barnes, G. M., Farrell, & M. P. (2000). Delayed onset of drunkenness as a protective factor for adolescent alcohol misuse and sexual risk taking: A longitudinal study. *Deviant Behavior, 21,* 181–200.

Thomas, K. M., Drevets, W. C., Dahl, R. E., Ryan, N. D., Birmaher, B., & Eccard, C. H., et al. (2001). Amygdala response to fearful faces in anxious and depressed children. *Archives of General Psychiatry, 58,* 1057–1063.

Thomas, C., Turkheimer, E., & Oltmanns, T. F. (2003). Factorial structure of pathological personality as evaluated by peers. *Journal of Abnormal Psychology, 112,* 81–91.

Thompson, G. O. B., Raab, G. M., Hepburn, W. S., Hunter, R., Fulton, M., & Laxen, D. P. H. (1989). Blood-lead levels and children's behaviour: Results from the Edinburgh lead study. *Journal of Child Psychology and Psychiatry, 30,* 515–528.

Thompson, L. W., Coon, D. W., Gallagher-Thompson, D., Sommer, B. R., & Koin, D. (2001). Comparison of desipramine and cognitive/behavioral therapy in the treatment of elderly outpatients with mild-to-moderate depression. *American Journal of Geriatric Psychiatry, 9,* 225–240.

Thompson, L. W., Gallagher, D., & Breckenridge, J. S. (1987). Comparative effectiveness of psychotherapies for depressed elders. *Journal of Consulting and Clinical Psychology, 55,* 385–390.

Thompson, P. M., Hayashi, H. M., Simon, S. L. et al. (2004). Structural Abnormalities in the Brains of Human Subjects Who Use Methamphetamine. *Journal of Neuroscience, 24,* 6028–6036.

Thompson, V. L., Bazile, A., & Akbar, M. (2004). African Americans' perceptions of psychotherapy and psychotherapists. *Professional Psychology: Research and Practice, 35,* 19–26.

Thoresen, C. E., Friedman, M., Powell, L. H., Gill, J. J., & Ulmer, D. K. (1985). Altering the type A behavior pattern in postinfarction patients. *Journal of Cardiopulmonary Rehabilitation, 5,* 258–266.

Thyer, B. A., & Curtis, G. C. (1984). The effects of ethanol on phobic anxiety. *Behaviour Research and Therapy, 22,* 599–610.

Tiefer, L. (2001). A new view of women's sexual problems: Why new? Why now? *Journal of Sex Research, 38,* 89–96.

Tiefer, L. (2003). Female sexual dysfunction (FSD): Witnessing social construction in action. *Sexualities, Evolution and Gender, 5,* 33–36.

Tiefer, L., Hall, M., and Tavris, C. (2002). Beyond dysfunction: A new view of women's sexual problems. *Journal of Sex & Marital Therapy, 28,* 225–232.

Tiefer, L., Pedersen, B., & Melman, A. (1988). Psychosocial follow-up of penile prosthesis implant with patients and partners. *Journal of Sex and Marital Therapy, 14,* 184–201.

Tienari, P., Wynne, L. C., Moring, J., et al. (1994). The Finnish adoptive family study of schizophrenia: Implications for family research. *British Journal of Psychiatry, 164,* 20–26.

Tienari, P., Wynne, L. C., Laksy, K., Moring, J., Nieminen, P., & Sorri, A., et al. (2003). Genetic boundaries of the schizophrenia spectrum: Evidence from the Finnish adoptive family study of schizophrenia. *American Journal of Psychiatry, 160,* 1587–1594.

Tienari, P., Wynne, L. C., Moring, J. et al. (2000). Finnish adoptive family study: Sample selection and adoptee DSM-III diagnoses. *Acta Psychiatrica Scandinavica, 101,* 433–443.

Tihonen, J., Kuikka, J., Rasanen, P., Lepola, U., Kopenen, H., Liuska, A., Lehmusvaara, A., Vainio, P., Kononen, M. et al. (1997). Cerebral benzodiazepine receptor binding and distribution in generalized anxiety disorder: A fractal analysis. *Molecular Psychiatry, 2,* 463–471.

Tillfors, M., Furmark, T., Ekselius, L., & Fredrikson, M. (2001). Social phobia and avoidant personality disorder as related to parental history of social anxiety: A general population study. *Behaviour Research and Therapy, 39,* 289–298.

Timko, C., Moos, R. H., Finney, J. W., & Lesar, M. D. (2001). Long-term outcomes of alcohol use disorders: Comparing untreated individuals with those in Alcoholics Anonymous and formal treatment. *Journal of Studies on Alcohol, 61,* 529–540.

Tobin, D. L., Griffing, A., & Griffing, S. (1997). An examination of subtype criteria for bulimia nervosa. *International Journal of Eating Disorders, 22,* 179–186.

Tobler, N. S., Roona, M. A., Ochshorn, P., Marshall, D. G., Streke, A. V., & Stackpole, K. M. (2000). School-based adolescent drug prevention programs: 1998 meta-analysis. *Journal of Primary Prevention, 20,* 275–336.

Tomasson, K., Kent, D., & Coryell, W. (1991). Somatization and conversion disorders: Comorbidity and demographics at presentation. *Acta Psychiatrica Scandinavica, 84,* 288–293.

Tonigan, J. S., Miller, W. R., & Connors, G. J. (2000). Project MATCH client impressions about Alcoholics Anonymous: Measurement issues and relationship to treatment outcome. *Alcoholism Treatment Quarterly, 18,* 25–41.

Torgersen, S. (1986). Genetics of somatoform disorder. *Archives of General Psychiatry, 43,* 502–505.

Torgersen, S., Kringlen, E., & Cramer, V. (2001). The prevalence of personality disorders in a community sample. *Archives of General Psychiatry, 58,* 590–596.

Toro, P. A. (2005). Community psychology: Where do we go from here? (2004 Division 27 Presidential Address). *American Journal of Community Psychology, 35,* 9–16.

Torrey, E. F. (1996). *Out of the shadows: Confronting America's mental health crisis.* New York: John Wiley & Sons.

Torrey, E. F., Taylor, E., Bowler, A., & Gottesman, I. (1994). Schizophrenia and manic depressive disorder. In *The biological roots of mental illness as revealed by the landmark study of identical twins.* New York: Basic Books.

Torti, F. M., Gwyther, L. P., Reed, S. D., Friedman, J. Y., & Schulman, K. A. (2004). A multinational review of recent trends and reports in dementia caregiver burden. *Alzheimers Disease and Associated Disorders, 18,* 99–109.

Toseland, R. W., McCallion, P., Smith, T., & Banks, S. (2004). Supporting caregivers of frail older adults in an HMO setting. *American Journal of Orthopsychiatry, 74,* 349–364.

Tran, G. Q., Haaga, D. A. F., & Chambless, D. L. (1997). Expecting that alcohol will reduce social anxiety moderates the relation between social anxiety and alcohol consumption. *Cognitive Therapy and Research, 21,* 535–553.

Tremont, G., & Stern, R. A. (2000). Minimizing the cognitive effects of lithium therapy and electroconvulsive therapy using thyroid hormone. *International Journal of Neuropsychopharmacology, 3,* 175–186.

Trierweiler, S. J., Neighbors, H. W., Munday, C., Thompson, E. E., Binion, V. J., Gomez, J. P. (2000). Clinician attributions associated with the diagnosis of schizophrenia in African American and non-African American patients. *Journal of Consulting and Clinical Psychology, 68,* 171–175.

Trimpey, J., Velten, E., & Dain, R. (19993). Rational recovery from addictions. In W. Dryden & L. K. Hill (Eds). *Innovations in rational-emotive therapy* (pp. 253–271). Thousand Oaks, CA: Sage.

Trinder, H., & Salkovskis, P. M. (1994). Personally relevant instrusions outside the laboratory: Long-term suppression increases intrusion. *Behaviour Research and Therapy, 32,* 833–842.

Trivedi, M. H., Kern, J. K., Grannemann, B. D., Altshuler, K. Z., & Sunderajan, P. (2004). A computerized clinical decision support system as a means of implementing depression guidelines. *Psychiatric Services, 55,* 879–885.

True, W. R., Rice, J., Eisen, S. A., Heath, A. C., Godlberg, J., Lyons, M. J., & Nowak, J. (1993). A twin study of genetic and environmental contributions to liability for posttraumatic stress symptoms. *Archives of General Psychiatry, 50,* 257–264.

True, W. R., Xiam, H., Scherrer, J. F., Madden, P., Bucholz, K. K., et al. (1999). Common genetic vulnerability for nicotine and alcohol dependence in men. *Archives of General Psychiatry, 56,* 655–662.

Trull, T., Stepp, S. D., & Durrett, C. A. (2003). Research on borderline personality disorder: An update. *Current Opinion in Psychiatry, 16,* 77–82.

Trull, T. J., Widiger, T. A., & Frances, A. (1987). Covariation of criteria for avoidant, schizoid, and dependent personality disorders. *American Journal of Psychiatry, 144,* 767–771.

Tsai, D. C., & Pike, P. L. (2000). Effects of acculturation on the MMPI-2 scores of Asian American students. *Journal of Personality Assessment, 74,* 216–230.

Tsai, J. L., et al. (2001). Culture, ethnicity, and psychopathology. In H. E. Adams & P. B. Sutker (Eds). *Comprehensive Handbook of Psychopathology,* (3rd., Ed. pp. 105–127). NY: Kluwer Academic/Plenum Publishers.

Tsai, G., Parssani, L. A., Slusher, B. S., Carter, R., Baer, L., et al. (1995). Abnormal excitatory neurotransmitter metabolism in schizophrenic brains. *Archives of General Psychiatry, 52,* 829–836.

Tseng, W. S. (2001). *Handbook of cultural psychiatry.* San Diego, CA: Academic Press.

Tsuang, M. T., Lyons, M. J., Meyer, J. M., Doyle, T., Eisen, S. A., et al. (1998). Co-occurrence of abuse of different drugs in men: The role of drug-specific and shared vulnerabilities. *Archives of General Psychiatry, 55,* 967–972.

Tully, L. A., Arseneault, L., Caspi, A., Moffitt, T. E., & Morgan, J. (2004). Does maternal warmth moderate the effects of birth weight on twins' attention-deficit/hyperactivity disorder (ADHD) symptoms and low IQ? *Journal of Consulting and Clinical Psychology, 72,* 218–226.

Tune, L. E., Wong, D. F., Pearlson, G. D., Strauss, M. E., Young, T., et al. (1993). Dopamine D2 receptor density estimates in schizophrenia: A positron-emission tomography study with "C-methylspiperone." *Psychiatry Research, 49,* 219–237.

Tuomilehto, J., Geboers, J., Salonen, J. T., Nissinen, A., Kuulasman, K., & Puska, P. (1986). Decline in cardiovascular mortality in North Karelia and other parts of Finland. *British Medical Journal, 293,* 1068–1071.

Tuomisto, M. T. (1997). Intra-arterial blood pressure and heart rate reactivity to behavioral stress in normotensive, borderline, and mild hypertensive men. *Health Psychology, 16,* 554–565.

Turk, C. L., Heimberg, R. G., & Hope, D. A. (2001). Social anxiety disorder. In D. H. Barlow (Ed.), *Clinical handbook of psychological disorders* (pp. 114–153). New York: Guilford.

Turk, D. C. (2001). Treatment of chronic pain: Clinical outcomes, cost-effectiveness, and cost benefits. *Drug Benefit Trends, 13,* 36–38.

Turk, D. C., Wack, J. T., & Kerns, R. D. (1985). An empirical examination of the "pain behavior" construct. *Journal of Behavioral Medicine, 8,* 119–130.

Turk-Charles, S., Rose, T., & Gatz, M. (1996). The significance of gender in the treatment of older adults. In L. L. Carstensen, B. A. Edelstein, & L. Dornbrand (Eds.), *The practical handbook of clinical gerontology* (pp. 107–128). Thousand Oaks, CA: Sage.

Turkheimer, E. (1998). Heritability and biological explanation. *Psychological Review, 105,* 782–791.

Turkheimer, E. (2000). Three laws of behavior genetics and what they mean. *Current Directions in Psychological Science, 9,* 160–164.

Turkheimer, E., Haley, A., Waldron, M., D'Onofrio, B., & Gottesman, I. I. (2003). Socioeconomic status modifies the heritability of IQ in young children. *Psychological Science, 6,* 623–628.

Turkheimer, E., & Parry, C. D. (1992). Why the gap? Practice and policy in civil commitment hearings. *American Psychologist, 47,* 646–655.

Turkheimer, E., & Waldron, M. C. (2000). Nonshared environment: A theoretical, methodological, and quantitative review. *Psychological Bulletin, 126,* 78–108.

Turkington, D., Kingdom, D., & Turner, T. (2002). Effectiveness of a brief cognitive-behavioural intervention in the treatment of schizophrenia. *British Journal of Psychiatry, 180,* 523–527.

Turner, C. F., Ku, S. M., Rogers, L. D., Lindberg, J. H., & Pleck, F. L. (1998). Adolescent sexual behavior, drug use, and violence: Increased reporting with computer survey technology. *Science, 280,* 867–873.

Turner, R. J., & Wagonfeld, M. O. (1967). Occupational mobility and schizophrenia. *American Sociological Review, 32,* 104–113.

Turner, S. M., Beidel, D. C., & Townsley, R. M. (1990). Social phobia: Relationship to shyness. *Behaviour Research and Therapy, 28,* 297–305.

Tustin, F. (1994). Autistic children who are assessed as not brain-damaged. *Association of Child Psychotherapists, 20,* 103–131.

Twamley, E. W., Jeste, D. V., & Bellack, A. S. (2003). A review of cognitive training in schizophrenia. *Schizophrenia Bulletin, 29,* 359–382.

Tyrer, P., Thompson, S., Schmidt, U., Jones, V., Knapp, M., Davidson, K., Catalan, J., Airlie, J., Baxter, S., Byford, S., Byrne, G., Cameron, S., Caplan, R., Cooper, S., Ferguson, B., Freeman, C., Frost, S., Godley, J., Greenshields, J., Henderson, J., Holden, N., Keech, P., Kim, L., Logan, K., Manley, C., MacLeod, A., Murphy, R., Patience, L., Ramsay, L., De Munroz, S., Scott, J., Seivewright, H., Sivakumar, K., Tata, P., Thornton, S., Ukoumunne, O. C., & Wessely, S. (2003). Randomized controlled trial of brief cognitive behaviour therapy versus treatment as usual in recurrent deliberate self-harm: the POPMACT study. *Psychological Medicine, 33,* 969–976.

Tyrka, A. R., Waldron, I., Graber, J. A. & Brooks-Gunn, J. (2002) Prospective predictors of the onset of anorexic and bulimic syndromes. *International Journal of Eating Disorders, 32,* 282–290.

U.S. Bureau of the Census. 1999. *Current population reports, special studies.* Washington, DC: U.S. Government Printing Office.

U.S. Bureau of the Census. 2001. *The 65-years and older population: 2000.* By L. Hertzel and A. Smith. Washington, DC: Census Bureau Report number C2KBR01-10.

U.S. Department of Health and Human Services. 1989. *Reducing the health consequences of smoking: 25 years of progress. A report of the surgeon general, Executive summary* (DHHS Publication No. CDC 89-8411). Washington, DC: U.S. Government Printing Office.

U.S. Department of Health and Human Services, National Center for Health Statistics. (1990, August 30). Monthly vital statistics.

U.S. Department of Health & Human Services. (1998a). *Healthy People 2000: Mid course review and 1995 revisions.* Washington, DC: U.S. Government Printing Office.

U.S. Department of Health and Human Services. (1998b). *NHLBI report of the task force on Behavioral Research in Cardiovascular, Lung, and Blood Health and Disease.* Washington, DC: U.S. Government Printing Office.

U.S. Department of Health and Human Services. 1999. *Mental Health: A report of the Surgeon General*—Executive summary, Rockville, MD: U.S. Department of Health and Human Services, Substance Abuse and Mental Health Services Administration, Center for Mental Health Services, National Institutes of Health, National Institute of Mental Health, 1999.

U.S. Department of Health and Human Services. (2001a). *Mental Health: Culture, Race, and Ethnicity—A supplement to mental health: A report of the Surgeon General.* Rockville, MD: U.S. Department of Health and Human Services, Substance Abuse and Mental Health Services Administration, Center for Mental Health Services.

U.S. Department of Health and Human Services. (2001b). *The Surgeon General's call to action to prevent and decrease overweight and obesity.* [Rockville, MD]: U.S. Department of Health and Human Services, Public Health Service, Office of the Surgeon General. Available from: U.S. GPO, Washington.

U.S. Department of Health and Human Services. 2002. *Supplement to Mental Health: A Report of the Surgeon General* (SMA-01-3613). Retrieved July 2, 2002, from http://www.mentalhealth.org/Publications/allpubs/SMA-01-3613/sma-01-3613.pdf

U.S. Department of Health and Human Services. (2004). *The health consequences of smoking: A report of the Surgeon General.* [Atlanta, Ga.]: Department of Health and Human Services, Centers for Disease Control and Prevention, National Center for Chronic Disease Prevention and Health Promotion, Office on Smoking and Health; Washington, DC.

Uchino, B. N., Cacioppo, J. T., & Kiecolt-Glaser, K. G. (1996). The relationship between social support and physiological processes: A review with emphasis on underlying mechanisms and implications for health. *Psychological Bulletin, 119,* 488–531.

Uchinuma, Y., & Sekine, Y. (2000). Dissociative identity disorder (DID) in Japan: A forensic case report and the recent increase in reports of DID. *International Journal of Psychiatry in Clinical Practice, 4,* 155–160.

Unger, J. B., Boley Cruz, T., Schuster, D., Flora, J. A., & Anderson Johnson, C. (2001). Measuring exposure to pro- and anti-tobacco marketing among adolescents: Intercorrelations among measures and associations with smoking status. *Journal of Health Communication, 6,* 11–29.

Upper, D., & Ross, S. M. (Eds.). 1980. *Behavioral group therapy 1980: An annual review.* Champaign, IL: Research Press.

Usman, M. A. (1997). Frontotemporal dementias. In P. D. Nussbaum (Ed.), *Handbook of neuropsychology and aging* (pp. 159–176). New York: Plenum.

Uvnas-Moberg, K. (1997). Physiological and endocrine effects of social contact. In S. C. Carter, I.I. Lederhendler, et al. (Eds.). *The integrative neurobiology of affiliation. Annals of The New York Academy of Sciences,* Vol. 807 (pp. 146–163), New York, NY, U.S.: New York Academy of Sciences.

Uvnas-Moberg, K. (1999). Physiological and endocrine effects of social contact. In C. S. Carter, I. I., Lederhendler, & Kirkpatrick, B., (Eds.), *The integrative neurobiology of affiliation* (pp. 245–262). Cambridge, MA: MIT Press.

Vacha-Haase, T., Kogan, L. R., Tani, C. R., & Woodall, R. A. (2001). Reliability generalization: Exploring variation of reliability coefficients of MMPI clinical scale scores. *Educational and Psychological Measurement, 61,* 45–49.

Vaglenova, J., Birru, S., Pandiella, N. M., & Breese, C. R. (2004). An assessment of the long-term developmental and behavioral teratogenicity of prenatal nicotine exposure. *Behavioural Brain Research, 150,* 159–170.

Vaillant, G. E. (1996). A long-term follow-up of male alcohol abuse. *Archives of General Psychiatry, 53,* 243–250.

Valenti, A. M., Narendran, R., & Pristach, C. A. (2003). Who are patients on conventional antipsychotics? *Schizophrenia Bulletin, 29,* 195–200.

Van Ameringen, M. A., Lane, R. M., Walker, J. R., et al. (2001). Sertraline treatment of generalized social phobia: A 20-week, double-blind, placebo-controlled study. *American Journal of Psychiatry, 158,* 275–281.

van den Broucke, S., Vandereycken, W., & Vertommen, H. (1995). Marital communication in eating disorders: A controlled observational study. *International Journal of Eating Disorders, 17,* 1–23.

van der Sande, R., Buskens, E., Allart, E., van der Graaf, Y., & van Engeland, H. (1997). Psychosocial intervention following suicide attempt: A systematic review of treatment interventions. *Acta Psychiatrica Scandinavica, 96,* 43–50.

van Egeren, L. F., & Madarasmi, S. (1987). A computerized diary for ambulatory blood pressure monitoring. In N. Schneiderman (Ed.), *Handbook on methods and measurements in cardiovascular behavioral medicine.* New York: Plenum.

van Elst, L. T., Thiel, T., & Hesslinger, B., et al. (2001). Subtle prefrontal neuropathology in pilot magnetic resonance spectroscopy study in patients with borderline personality disorder. *Journal of Neuropsychiatry and Clinical Neuroscience, 13,* 511–514.

van Erp, T. G. M., Saleh, P. A., Huttunen, M., et al. (2004). Hippocampal volumes in schizophrenic twins. *Archives of General Psychiatry, 61,* 346–353.

Van Oppen, P., de Haan, E., Van Balkom, A. J. L. M., Spinhoven, P., et al. (1995). Cognitive therapy and exposure in vivo in the treatment of obsessive compulsive disorder. *Behaviour Research and Therapy, 33,* 379–390.

van Kammen, W. B., Loeber, R., & Stouthamer-Loeber, M. (1991). Substance use and its relationship to conduct problems and delinquency in young boys. *Journal of Youth and Adolescence, 20,* 399–413.

van Praag, H., Plutchik, R., & Apter, A. (Eds.), 1990. *Violence and suicidality.* New York: Brunner/Mazel.

Varner, R. V., & Gaitz, C. M. (1982). Schizophrenic and paranoid disorders in the aged. In L. F. Jarvik & G. W. Small (Eds.), *Psychiatric clinics of North America.* Philadelphia: Saunders.

Veale, D. (2000). Outcome of cosmetic surgery and "DIY" surgery in patients with body dysmorphic disorder. *Psychiatric Bulletin, 24,* 218–221.

Veale, D., Boocock, A., Gournay, K., et al. (1996). Body dysmorphic disorder: A cognitive-behavioral model and pilot randomized controlled trial. *Behaviour Research and Therapy, 34,* 717–729.

Vega, W. A., Kolody, B., Aguilar-Gaxiola, S., Alderete, E., Catalana, R., & Caraveo-Anduaga, J. (1998). Lifetime prevalence of DSM-III-R psychiatric disorders among urban and rural Mexican Americans in California. *Archives of General Psychiatry, 55,* 771–778.

Velakoulis, D., Pantelis, C., McGorry, P. D., Dudgeon, P., Brewer, W., et al. (1999). Hippocampal volume in first-episode psychoses and chronic schizophrenia: A high-resolution magnetic resonance imaging study. *Archives of General Psychiatry, 56,* 133–141.

Velting, O. N., Setzer, N. J., & Albano, A. M. (2004). Update on and advances in assessment and cognitive–behavioral treatment of anxiety disorders in children and adolescents. *Professional Psychology: Research and Practice, 35,* 42–54.

Ventura, J., Neuchterlein, K. H., Lukoff, D., & Hardesty, J. D. (1989). A prospective study of stressful life events and schizophrenic relapse. *Journal of Abnormal Psychology, 98,* 407–411.

Verkes, J. R., Gijsman, H. J., Pieters, M. S. M., Schoemaker, R. C., de Visser, S., Kuijpers, M., Pennings, E. J. M., de Bruin, D., van de Wijngaart, G., van Gerven, J. M.A., & Cohen, J. (2001). Cognitive performance and serotonergic function in users of ecstasy. *Psychopharmacology, 153,* 196–202.

Vitousek, K., & Manke, F. (1994). Personality variables and disorders in anorexia nervosa and bulimia nervosa. *Journal of Abnormal Psychology, 103,* 137–147.

Vogel, V. G., Graves, D. S., Vernon, S. W., Lord, J. A., Winn, R. J., & Peters, G. N. (1990). Mammographic screening of women with increased risk of breast cancer. *Cancer*, 66, 1613–1620.

Volk, D. W., Austin, M. C., Pierri, J. N., et al. (2000). Decreased glutamic acid decarboxylase67 messenger RNA expression in a subset of prefrontal cortical γ-aminobutyric acid neurons in subjects with schizophrenia. *Archives of General Psychiatry*, 57, 237–248.

Volkmar, F. R., Szatmari, P., & Sparrow, S. S. (1993). Sex differences in pervasive developmental disorders. *Journal of Autism and Developmental Disorders*, 23, 579–591.

Volkow, N. D., Wang, G. J., Fischman, M. W., & Foltin, R. W. (1997). Relationship between subjective effects of cocaine and dopamine transporter occupancy. *Nature*, 386, 827–830.

Volkow, N. D., Wang, G.-J., Fowler, J. S., Logan, J., Jayne, M., Franceschi, D., Wong, C., Gatley, S. J., Gifford, A. N., Ding, Y. S., & Pappas, N. (2002). "Nonhedonic" food motivation in humans involves dopamine in the dorsal striatum and methylphenidate amplifies this effect. *Synapse*, 44, 175–180.

Volpicelli, J. R., Rhines, K. C., Rhines, J. S., Volpicelli, L. A., et al. (1997). Naltrexone and alcohol dependence: Role of subject compliance. *Archives of General Psychiatry*, 54, 737–743.

Volpicelli, J. R., Watson, N. T., King, A. C., Shermen, C. E., & O'Brien, C. P. (1995). Effects of naltrexone on alcohol "high" in alcoholics. *American Journal of Psychiatry*, 152, 613–617.

von Krafft-Ebing, R. (1902). *Psychopathia sexualis*. Brooklyn, NY: Physicians and Surgeons Books.

Wachtel, P. L. (1997). *Psychoanalysis, behavior therapy and the relational world*. Washington, DC: American Psychological Association.

Wade, T. D., Bulik, C. M., Neale, M., & Kendler, K. S. (2000). Anorexia nervosa and major depression: Shared genetic and environmental risk factors. *American Journal of Psychiatry*, 157, 469–471.

Wade, W. A., Treat, T. A., & Stuart, G. A. (1998). Transporting an empirically supported treatment for panic disorder to a service clinic setting: A benchmarking strategy. *Journal of Consulting and Clinical Psychology*, 66, 231–239.

Wagner, K. D., & Ambrosini, P. J. (2001). Childhood depression: Pharmacological therapy/treatment (pharmacotherapy of childhood depression). *Journal of Clinical Child Psychology*, 30, 88–97.

Wahl, O. F. (1999). Mental health consumers' experience of stigma. *Schizophrenia Bulletin*, 25, 467–478.

Wahlbeck, K., Cheine, M., Essali, A., & Adams, C. (1999). Evidence of clozapine's effectiveness in schizophrenia: A systemic review and meta-analysis of randomized trials. *American Journal of Psychiatry*, 156, 990–999.

Wakefield, J. (1992). Disorder as dysfunction: A conceptual critique of DSM-III-R's definition of mental disorder. *Psychological Review*, 99, 232–247.

Wakefield, J. C. (1999. Philosophy of science and the progressiveness of DSM's theory—neutral nosology: Response to Follette and Houts, Part 1. *Behaviour Research and Therapy*, 37, 963–969.

Wakefield, M., & Chaloupka, R. (2000). Effectiveness of comprehensive tobacco control programmes in reducing teenage smoking in the USA. *Tobacco Control*, 9, 177–186.

Waldenger, R. J., & Frank, A. E. (1989). Clinicians' experiences in combining medication and psychotherapy in the treatment of borderline patients. *Hospital and Community Psychiatry*, 40, 712–718.

Waldman, I. D., Rowe, D. C., Abramowitz, A., Kozel, S. T., Mohr, J. H., Sherman, S. L., Cleveland, H. H., Sanders, M. L., Gard, J. M., & Stever, C. (1998). Association and linkage of the dopamine transporter gene and attention-deficit hyperactivity disorder in children: Heterogeneity

owing to diagnostic subtype and severity. *American Journal of Human Genetics* 63, 1767–1776.

Waldron, I. (1976). Why do women live longer than men? *Journal of Human Stress*, 2, 1–13.

Walker, E. F., Davis, D. M., & Savoie, T. D. (1994). Neuromotor precursors of schizophrenia. *Schizophrenia Bulletin*, 20, 441–451.

Walker, E. F., & DiForio, D. (1997). Schizophrenia: A neural diathesis-stress model. *Psychological Review*, 104, 667–685.

Walker, E. F., Grimes, K. E., Davis, D. M., & Adina, J. (1993). Childhood precursors of schizophrenia: Facial expressions of emotion. *American Journal of Psychiatry*, 150, 1654–1660.

Waller, D. A., Kiser, S., Hardy, B. W., Fuchs, I., & Feigenbaum, L. P. (1986). Eating behavior and plasma beta-endorphin in bulimia. *American Journal of Clinical Nutrition*, 4, 20–23.

Wallerstein, R. S. (1986). *Forty-two lives in treatment: A study of psychoanalysis and psychotherapy*. New York: Guilford.

Wallerstein, R. S. (1989). The Psychotherapy Research Project of the Menninger Foundation: An overview. *Journal of Consulting and Clinical Psychology*, 57, 195– 205.

Walsh, B. T., Agras, S. W., Devlin, M. J., et al. (2000). Fluoxetine for bulimia nervosa following poor response to psychotherapy. *American Journal of Psychiatry*, 157, 1332–1334.

Walsh, B. T., Seidman, S. N., Sysko, R., & Gould, M. (2002). Placebo response in studies of major depression: Variable, substantial, and growing. *JAMA*, 287, 1840–1847.

Walsh, B. T., Wilson, G. T., Loeb, K. L., Devin, M. J., et al. (1997). Medication and psychotherapy in the treatment of bulimia nervosa. *American Journal of Psychiatry*, 154, 523–531.

Walters, G. L., & Clopton, J. R. (2000). Effect of symptom information and validity scale information on the malingering of depression on the MMPI-2. *Journal of Personality Assessment*, 75, 183–199.

Wampold, B. E. (2001). *The great psychotherapy debate: Models, methods, and findings*. Mahwah, NJ; Lawrence Erlbaum.

Wang, M. Q., Fitzhugh, E. C., Eddy, J. M., Fu, Q., et al. (1997). Social influences on adolescents' smoking progress: A longitudinal analysis. *American Journal of Health Behavior*, 21, 111–117.

Wang, P. S., Demler, O., & Kessler, R. C. (2002). Adequacy of treatment for serious mental illness in the United States. *American Journal of Public Health*, 92, 92–98.

Wannamethee, S. G., Shaper, A. G., & Walker, M. (1998). Changes in physical activity, mortality, and incidence of coronary heart disease in older men. *The Lancet*, 351, 1603–1608.

Warwick, H. M. C., Clark, D. M., Cobb, A. M., & Salkovskis, P. M. (1996). A controlled trial of cognitive-behavioral treatment of hypochondriasis. *British Journal of Psychiatry*, 169, 189–195.

Warwick, H. M. C., & Salkovskis, P. M. (2001). Cognitive-behavioral treatment of hypochondriasis. In Don R. Lipsitt and Vladan Starcevic (Eds.), *Hypochondriasis: Modern perspectives on an ancient malady*. (pp. 314–328). London: Oxford University Press.

Waters, A., Hill, A., & Waller, G. (2001). Internal and external antecedents of binge eating episodes in a group of women with bulimia nervosa. *International Journal of Eating Disorders*, 29, 17–22.

Watson, D., & Pennebaker, J. W. (1989). Health complaints, stress, and distress: Exploring the central role of negative affectivity. *Psychological Review*, 96, 234–254.

Watson, J. B., & Rayner, R. (1920). Conditioned emotional reactions. *Journal of Experimental Psychology*, 3, 1–14.

Watt, N. F. (1974). Childhood and adolescent roots of schizophrenia. In D. Ricks, A. Thomas, & M. Roll (Eds.), *Life history research in psychopathology* (Vol. 3). Minneapolis: University of Minnesota Press.

Watt, N. F., Stolorow, R. D., Lubensky, A. W., & McClelland, D. C. (1970). School adjustment and behavior of children hospitalized for schizophrenia as adults. *American Journal of Orthopsychiatry*, 40, 637–657.

Wattis, J. P. (1990). Diagnostic issues in depression in old age. *International Clinical Psychopharmacology*, 5, 1–6.

Waxman, J. G., Cohen, E. N., Patchias, E., & Greenberger, M. D. (2004). *Making the Grade: A national and state-by-state report card*. Online at http://www.nwlc.org

Weaver, I. C. G., Cervoni, N., Champagne, F. A., D'Allesio, A. C., Shakti, S., Seck, J. R., Dymov, S., Szyf, M., & Meaney, J. J. (2004). Epigenetic programming by maternal behavior. *Nature Neuroscience*, 7, 847–854.

Weber, T. (1996. Tarnishing the golden years with addiction. *Los Angeles Times, December 2*, pp. A1, A37.

Webster, J. J., & Palmer, R. L. (2000). The childhood and family background of women with clinical eating disorders: A comparison with women with major depression and women without psychiatric disorder. *Psychological Medicine*, 30, 53–60.

Webster, R., & Holroyd, S. (2000). Prevalence of psychotic symptoms in delirium. *Psychosomatics*, 41, 519–522.

Webster-Stratton, C. (1998). Preventing conduct problems in Head Start children: Strengthening parenting competencies. *Journal of Consulting and Clinical Psychology*, 66, 715–730.

Webster-Stratton, C., Reid, M. J., & Hammond, M. (2001). Preventing conduct problems, promoting social competence: A parent and teacher training partnership in Head Start. *Journal of Clinical Child Psychology*, 30, 283–302.

Wechsler, D. (1968). *Escala de Inteligencia Wechsler para Adultos*. New York: Psychological Corporation.

Wechsler Intelligence Scale for Children (3rd ed.). 1991. San Antonio: The Psychological Corporation.

Wegner, D. M., Schneider, D. J., Carter, S. R., & White, T. L. (1987). Paradoxical effects of thought suppression. *Journal of Personality and Social Psychology*, 53, 5–13.

Weickert, C. S., Straub, R. E., McClintock, B. W., et al. (2004). Human dysbindin (DTNBP1) gene expression in normal brain and in schizophrenic prefrontal cortex and mid brain. *Archives of General Psychiatry*, 61, 544–555.

Weidner, G., & Collins, R. L. (1993). Gender, coping, and health. In H. W. Krohne (Ed.), *Attention and avoidance*. New York: Springer-Verlag.

Weidner, G., Friend, R., Ficarroto, T. J., & Mendell, N. R. (1989). Hostility and cardiovascular reactivity to stress in women and men. *Psychosomatic Medicine*, 51, 36–45.

Weinberger, D. R. (1987). Implications of normal brain development for the pathogenesis of schizophrenia. *Archives of General Psychiatry*, 44, 660–669.

Weinberger, D. R., Berman, K. F., & Illowsky, B. P. (1988). Physiological dysfunction of dorsolateral prefrontal cortex in schizophrenia: 3. A new cohort and evidence for a monoaminergic mechanism. *Archives of General Psychiatry*, 45, 609–615.

Weinberger, D. R., Cannon-Spoor, H. E., Potkin, S. G., & Wyatt, R. J. (1980). Poor premorbid adjustment and CT scan abnormalities in chronic schizophrenia. *American Journal of Psychiatry*, 137, 1410–1413.

Weiner, B., Frieze, L., Kukla, A., Reed, L., Rest, S., & Rosenbaum, R. M. (1971). *Perceiving the causes of success and failure*. New York: General Learning Press.

Weiner, D. B. (1994). *Le geste de Pinel*: The history of psychiatric myth. In M. S. Micale & R. Porter (Eds.), *Discovering the history of psychiatry*. New York: Oxford.

Weinstein, H. (2002, February 19). Killer's sentence of death debated. Los Angeles Times, pp. A1, A14.

Weintraub, S., Prinz, R., & Neale, J. M. (1978). Peer evaluations of the competence of children vulnerable to psychopathology. Journal of Abnormal Child Psychology, 6, 461–473.

Weisberg, R. B., Brown, T. A., Wincze, J. P., & Barlow, D. H. (2001). Causal attributions and male sexual arousal: The impact of attributions for a bogus erectile difficulty on sexual arousal, cognitions, and affect. Journal of Abnormal Psychology, 110, 324–334.

Weisberg, R. W. (1994). Genius and madness? A quasi-experimental test of the hypothesis that manic-depression increases creativity. Psychological Science, 5, 361–367.

Weisman, A. (2005). Integrating culturally-based approaches with existing interventions for Hispanic/Latino families coping with schizophrenia. Psychotherapy, 42, 178–197.

Weisman, A. G., Nuechterlein, K. H., Goldstein, M. J., & Snyder, K. S. (1998). Expressed emotion, attributions, and schizophrenia symptom dimensions. Journal of Abnormal Psychology, 107, 355–359.

Weisman, C. S., & Teitelbaum, M. A. (1985). Physician gender and the physician–patient relationship: Recent evidence and relevant questions. Social Science and Medicine, 20, 1119–1127.

Weisner, T. S. (1984). Serious drinking, White man's drinking and teetotaling: Drinking levels and styles in an urban Indian population. Journal of Studies on Alcohol, 45, 237–249.

Weiss, G., & Hechtman, L. (1993). Hyperactive children grown up (2nd ed.). New York: Guilford.

Weissberg, R. P., Caplan, M. Z., & Sivo, P. J. (1989). A new conceptual framework for establishing school-based social competence promotion programs. In L. A. Bond, & B. E. Compas (Eds.), Primary prevention and promotion in the schools (Vol. 12, pp. 255–296). Newbury Park, CA: Sage.

Weissman, A. N., & Beck, A. T. (1978). Development and validation of the Dysfunctional Attitude Scale: A preliminary investigation. Paper presented at the annual meeting of the American Educational Research Association, Toronto.

Weissman, M. M., Bland, R. C., Canino, G. J., Faravelli, C., Grenwald, S., et al. (1997). The cross-national epidemiology of panic disorder. Archives of General Psychiatry, 54, 305–312.

Weissman, M. M., Bland, R. C., Canino, G. J., Faravelli, C., Greenwald, S., et al. (1996). Cross-national epidemiology of major depression and bipolar disorder. JAMA, 276, 293–299.

Weissman, M. M., Bland, R. C., Canino, G. J., Greenwald, S., Hwu, H. G., & Joyce, P. R., et al. (1999). Prevalence of suicide ideation and suicide attempts in nine countries. Psychological Medicine, 29, 9–17.

Weisz, J. R., Sigman, M., Weiss, B., & Mosk, J. (1993). Parent reports of behavioral and emotional problems among children in Kenya, Thailand and the United States. Child Development, 64, 98–109.

Weisz, J. R., Suwanlert, S. C., Wanchai, W., & Bernadette, R. (1987). Over- and undercontrolled referral problems among children and adolescents from Thailand and the United States: The wat and wai of cultural differences. Journal of Consulting and Clinical Psychology, 55, 719–726.

Weisz, J. R., Weiss, B., Suwanlert, S., & Wanchai, C. (2003). Syndromal structure of psychopathology in children of Thailand and the United States. Journal of Consulting and Clinical Psychology, 71, 375–385.

Wells, A. (1998). Cognitive therapy of social phobia. In N. Tarrier, A. Wells, & G. Haddock (Eds.), Treating com-

plex cases: The cognitive-behavioural approach (pp. 1–26). Chicester: John Wiley & Sons.

Wells, C. E., & Duncan, G. W. (1980). Neurology for psychiatrists. Philadelphia: F. A. Davis.

Wells, K. C., Epstein, J. N., Hinshaw, S. P., et al. (2000). Parenting and family stress treatment outcomes in attention deficit hyperactivity disorder (ADHD): An empirical analysis in the MTA study. Journal of Abnormal Child Psychology, 28, 543–553.

Welsh, R., Burcham, B., DeMoss, K., Martin, C., & Milich, R. (1997). Attention deficit hyperactivity disorder diagnosis and management: A training program for teachers. Frankfurt: Kentucky Department of Education.

Wender, P. H., Kety, S. S., Rosenthal, D., Schulsinger, F., Ortmann, J., & Lunde, I. (1986). Psychiatric disorders in the biological and adoptive families of adopted individuals with affective disorders. Archives of General Psychiatry, 43, 923–929.

West, R. (2001). Glucose for smoking cessation: Does it have a role? CNS Drugs, 15, 261–265.

Westen, D. (1998). The scientific legacy of Sigmund Freud: Toward a psychodynamically informed psychological science. Psychological Bulletin, 124, 333–371.

Westen, D. (2000). Integrative psychotherapy: Integrating psychodynamic and cognitive-behavioral therapy and technique. In C. R. Snyder & R. E. Ingram (Eds.), Handbook of psychological change: Psychotherapy processes & practices for the 21st century (pp. 217–242). New York: John Wiley & Sons.

Westen, D., Novotny, C. M ., & Thompson-Brenner, H. (2004). The empirical status of empirically supported psychotherapies: Assumptions, findings, and reporting in controlled clinical trials. Psychological Bulletin, 130, 631–663.

Westergaard, T., Mortensen, P. B., Pedersen, C. B., Wohlfahrt, J., & Melhye, M. (1999). Exposure to prenatal and childhood infections and the risk of schizophrenia: Suggestions from a study of sibship characteristics and influenza prevalence. Archives of General Psychiatry, 56, 993–998.

Wetherell, J. L. (1998). Treatment of anxiety in older adults. Psychotherapy, 35, 444–458.

Wetherell, J. L., Gatz, M., & Craske, M. G. (2003). Treatment of generalized anxiety disorder in older adults. Journal of Consulting and Clinical Psychology, 71, 31–40.

Whalen, C. K. (1983). Hyperactivity, learning problems, and the attention deficit disorders. In T. H. Ollendick & M. Hersen (Eds.), Handbook of child psychopathology. New York: Plenum.

Whalen, C. K., & Henker, B. (1985). The social worlds of hyperactive (ADDH) children. Clinical Psychology Review, 5, 447–478.

Whalen, C. K., & Henker, B. (1991). Therapies for hyperactive children: Comparisons, combinations, and compromises. Journal of Consulting and Clinical Psychology, 59, 126–137.

Whalen, P. J, (1998) Fear, vigilance, and ambiguity. Initial neuroimaging studies of the human amygdala. Current Directions in Psychological Science, 7, 177–188.

Wheeler, J. G., Christensen, A., & Jacobson, N. S. (2001). Couple distress. In D. H. Barlow (Ed.), Clinical handbook of psychological disorders: A step-by-step treatment manual (pp. 609–630). New York, NY, Guilford Press.

Whelton, P. K., Appel, L. J., Espeland, M. A., Applegate, W. B., Ettinger, W. H., Kostis, J. B., Kumanyika, S., Lacy, C. R., Johnson, K. C., Folmar, S., & Cutler, J. A. for the TONE Collaborative Research Group. 1998. Sodium reduction and weight loss in the treatment of hypertension in older persons: A randomized controlled trial of nonpharmacologic interventions in the elderly

(TONE). Journal of the American Medical Association, 279, 839–846.

Whelton, P. K., He, J., Appel, L. J., et al. (2002). Primary prevention of hypertension. Clinical and public health advisory from the national high blood pressure education program. JAMA, 288, 1882–1888.

Whisman, M. A. (1993). Mediators and moderators of change in cognitive therapy of depression. Psychological Bulletin, 114, 248–265.

Whisman, M. A., & Bruce, M. L. (1999). Marital dissatisfaction and incidence of major depressive episode in a community sample. Journal of Abnormal Psychology, 108, 674–678.

Whitaker, A. H., van Rossen, R., Feldman, J. F., Schonfeld, I. S., Pinto-Martin, J. A., Torre, C., Shaffer, D., & Paneth, N. (1997). Psychiatric outcomes in low birth weight children at age 6 years: Relation to neonatal cranial ultrasound abnormalities. Archives of General Psychiatry, 54, 847–856.

Whitaker, R. (2002). Mad in America. Cambridge, MA: Perseus.

White, H., & Levin, E. (2004). Chronic transdermal nicotine patch treatment effects on cognitive performance in age-associated memory impairment. Psychopharmacology, 171, 465–471.

White, K. S., & Barlow, D. H. (2004). Panic disorder and agoraphobia. In D. H. Barlow (Ed.), Anxiety and its disorders: The nature and treatment of anxiety and panic (pp. 328–379). New York: Guilford.

Whitehead, W. E., Burgio, K. L., & Engel, B. T. (1985). Biofeedback treatment of fecal incontinence in geriatric patients. Journal of the American Geriatrics Society, 33, 320–324.

Whitmore, E. A., Mikulich, S. K., Thompson, L. L., Riggs, P. D., Aarons, G. A., & Crowley, T. J. (1997), Influences on adolescent substance dependence: Conduct disorder, depression, attention deficit hyperactivity disorder, and gender. Drug and Alcohol Dependence 47, 87–97.

Whittal, M. L., Agras, S. W., & Gould, R. A. (1999). Bulimia nervosa: A meta-analysis of psychosocial and pharmacological treatments. Behavior Therapy, 30, 117–135.

Whittemore, A., Wu-Williams, A., Lee, M., Zheng, S., Gallagher, R., Jiao, D. A., Zhou, L., Wang, X., Chen, K., Jung, D., Teh, C. Z., Ling, C., Xu, J. Y., Paffenberger, R., & Henderson, B. E. (1990). Diet, physical activity and colorectal cancer among Chinese in North America and the People's Republic of China. Journal of the National Cancer Institute, 82, 915–926.

Whyte, S., Bayreuther, K., & Masters, C. L. (1994). Rational therapeutic strategies for Alzheimer's disease. In D. B. Calne (Ed.), Neurodegenerative diseases. Philadelphia: Saunders.

Widiger, T. A., & Costa, P. T., Jr. (1994). Personality and personality disorders. Journal of Abnormal Psychology, 95, 43–51.

Widiger, T. A., Frances, A., & Trull, T. J. (1987). A psychometric analysis of the social-interpersonal and cognitive-perceptual items for schizotypal personality disorder. Archives of General Psychiatry, 44, 741–745.

Wiederman, M. W., & Pryor, T. L. (2000). Body dissatisfaction, bulimia, and depression among women: The mediating role of drive for thinness. International Journal of Eating Disorders, 27, 90–95.

Wilcox, S., Evenson, K. R., Aragaki, A., Wassertheil Smoller, S., Mouton, C. P., & Loevinger, B. L. (2003). The effects of widowhood on physical and mental health, health behaviors, and health outcomes: The women's health initiative. Health Psychology, 22, 513–522.

Wildes, J. E., Emery, R. E., & Simons, A. D. 2001. The roles of ethnicity and culture in the development of eating disturbance and body dissatisfaction: A meta-analytic review. *Clinical Psychology Review, 21*, 521–551.

Willemsen-Swinkels, S. H. N., Buitelaar, J. K., & van Engeland, H. (1996). The effects of chronic naltrexone treatment in young autistic children: A double-blind placebo-controlled crossover study. *Biological Psychiatry, 39*, 1023– 1031.

Willemsen-Swinkels, S. H. N., Buitelaar, J. K., Weijnen, F. G., & van Engeland, H. (1995). Placebo-controlled acute dosage naltrexone study in young autistic children. *Psychiatry Research, 58*, 203–215.

Willford, J. A., Richardson, G. A., Leech, S. L., & Day, N. L. (2004). Verbal and visuospatial learning and memory function in children with moderate prenatal alcohol exposure. *Alcoholism: Clinical and Experimental Research, 28*, 497–507.

Willi, J., & Grossman, S. (1983). Epidemiology of anorexia nervosa in a defined region of Switzerland. *American Journal of Psychiatry, 140*, 564–567.

Williams, C. J. (1999, May 27). In Kosovo, rape seen as awful as death. *Los Angeles Times*, pp. A1, A18.

Williams, J., McGuffin, P., Nothen, M., Owen, M. J., & Group, E. C. (1997). A meta analysis of association between the 5-HT2a receptor T102C polymorphism and schizophrenia. *Lancet, 349*, 1221–1226.

Williams, J. B. W., Gibbon, M., First, M. B., Spitzer, R. L., Davies, M., et al. (1992). The Structured Clinical Interview for DSM-III-R (SCID): 2. Multisite test-retest reliability. *Archives of General Psychiatry, 49*, 630–636.

Williams, J. (2003). Dementia and genetics. In R. Plomin & J. D. DeFries, et al. (Eds.), *Behavioral genetics in the postgenomic era* (pp. 503–527). Washington, DC: American Psychological Association.

Williams, J. M. G., Watts, F. N., MacLeod, C., & Mathews, A. (1997). *Cognitive psychology and emotional disorders.* (2nd Ed.). New York: John Wiley & Sons.

Williams, K., Goodman, M., & Green, 1985. Parent-child factors in gender role socialization in girls. *Journal of the American Academy of Child Psychiatry, 24*, 720–731.

Williams, L. M. (1995). Recall of childhood trauma: A prospective study of women's memories of child sexual abuse. *Journal of Consulting and Clinical Psychology, 62*, 1167–1176.

Williams, P. A., Allard, A., Spears, L., Dalrymple, N., & Bloom, A. S. (2001). Brief report: Case reports on naltrexone use in children with autism: Controlled observations regarding benefits and practical issues in medication management. *Journal of Autism and Developmental Disorders, 31*, 103–108.

Williams, R. B., Marchuk, D. A., Gadde, K. M., Barefoot, J. C., Grichnik, K., Helms, M. J., Kuhn, C. M., Lewis, J. G., Schanberg, S. M., Stafford-Smith, M., Suarez, E. C., Clary, G. L., Svenson, I. K., & Siegler, I. C. (2001). Central nervous system serotonin function and cardiovascular responses to stress. *Psychosomatic Medicine, 63*, 300–305.

Williams, S. L., & Falbo, J. (1996). Cognitive and performance-based treatments for panic attacks in people with varying degrees of agoraphobic disability. *Behaviour Research and Therapy, 34*, 253–264.

Williamson, D. A., Goreczny, A. J., Davis, C. J., Ruggiero, L., & MacKenzie, S. L. (1988). Psychophysiological analysis of the anxiety model of bulimia nervosa. *Behavior Therapy, 19*, 1–9.

Willner, P., D'Aquila, P. S., Coventry, T., & Brain, P. (1995). Loss of social status: Preliminary evaluation of a novel animal model of depression. *Journal of Psychopharmacology, 9*, 207–213.

Wills, T. A., & Cleary, S. D. (1999). Peer and adolescent substance use among 6th–9th graders: Latent growth analysis of influence versus selection mechanisms. *Health Psychology, 18*, 453–463.

Wills, T. A., DuHamel, K., & Vaccaro, D. (1995). Activity and mood temperament as predictors of adolescent substance use: Test of a self-regulation model. *Journal of Personality and Social Psychology, 68*, 901–916.

Wills, T. A., Sandy, J. M., Shinar, O., & Yaeger, A. (1999). Contributions of positive and negative affect to adolescent substance use: Test of a bidimensional model in a longitudinal study. *Psychology of Addictive Behaviors, 13*, 327–338.

Wills, T. A, Sandy, J. M., & Yaeger, A. M. (2002). Stress and smoking in adolescence: A test of directional hypotheses. *Health Psychology, 21*, p. 122–130.

Wilsnack, R. W., Vogeltanz, N. D., & Wilsnack, S. C., et al. (2000). Gender differences in alcohol consumption and adverse drinking consequences: Cross-cultural patterns. *Addiction, 95*, 251–265.

Wilsnack, S., & Wilsnack, R. (1995). Drinking and problem drinking in US women: Patterns and research trends. In M. Galanter (Ed.), *Recent developments in alcoholism* (Vol. 12, pp. 29–60). New York: Plenum.

Wilson, G. T. (1995). Psychological treatment of binge eating and bulimia nervosa. *Journal of Mental Health (UK), 4*, 451–457.

Wilson, G. T. (1991). Chemical aversion conditioning in the treatment of alcoholism: Further comments. *Behaviour Research and Therapy, 29*, 405–420.

Wilson, G. T., Loeb, K. L., Walsh, B. T., Labouvie, E., Petkova, E., Liu, X., & Waternaux, C. (1999). Psychological and pharmacological treatment of bulimia nervosa: Predictors and processes of change. *Journal of Consulting and Clinical Psychology, 67*, 451–459.

Wilson, G.T., & Lawson, D.M. (1976). The effects of alcohol on sexual arousal in women. *Journal of Abnormal Psychology, 85*, 489–497.

Wilson, G. T., & Fairburn, C. G. (1998). Treatments for eating disorders. In P. Nathan & J. M. Gorman (Eds.), *A guide to treatments that work* (pp. 501–530). London, Oxford University Press.

Wilson, G. T., & Pike, K. M. (1993). Eating disorders. In D. H. Barlow (Ed.), *Clinical handbook of psychological disorders* (pp. 278–317). New York: Guilford.

Wilson, G. T., & Pike, K. M. (2001). Eating disorders. In D. H. Barlow (Ed.), *Clinical handbook of psychological disorders.* (3rd ed., pp. 332–375). New York: Guilford.

Wilson, G. T., Vitousek, K. M., Loeb, K. L. (2000). Stepped care treatment for eating disorders. *Journal of Consulting and Clinical Psychology, 68*, 564–572.

Wilson, M. (1993). DSM-III and the transformation of American Psychiatry: A history. *American Journal of Psychiatry, 150*, 399–410.

Wilson, R. S., Mendes de Leon, C., Barnes, L., et al. (2002). Participation in cognitively stimulation activities and risk of incident Alzheimer's disease. *JAMA, 287*, 742–748.

Wimo, A., Winblad, B., Aguero-Torres, A., & von Strauss, E. (2003). The magnitude of dementia occurrence in the world. *Alzheimer Disease and Associated Disorders, 17*, 63–67.

Winchel, R. M., Stanley, B., & Stanley, M. (1990). Biochemical aspects of suicide. In S. J. Blumenthal & D. J. Kupfer (Eds.), *Suicide over the life cycle: Risk factors, assessment and treatment of suicidal patterns* (pp. 97–126). Washington, DC: American Psychiatric Press.

Winick, B. J. (1993). Psychotropic medication in the criminal trial process: The constitutional and therapeutic implications of *Riggins v. Nevada. New York Law School Journal of Human Rights, 10*, 637–709.

Winick, B. J. (1994). The right to refuse mental health treatment: A therapeutic jurisprudence analysis. *International Journal of Law and Psychiatry, 17*, 99–117.

Winick, B. J. (1997). *The right to refuse mental health treatment.* Washington, DC: American Psychological Association.

Winkleby, M. A., Cubbin, C., Ahn, D. K., & Kraemer, H. C. (1999). Pathways by which SES and ethnicity influence cardiovascular risk factors. In N. E. Adler & M. Marmot (Eds.), *Socioeconomic status and health in industrialized nations: Social, psychological, and biological pathways. Annals of the New York Academy of Sciences*, (Vol. 896). New York: New York Academy of Sciences.

Winkleby, M. A., Kraemer, H. C., Ahn, D. K., & Varady, A. N. (1998). Ethnic and socioeconomic differences in cardiovascular disease risk factors. *JAMA, 280*, 356–362.

Winston, A., Laikin, M., Pollack, J., Samstag, L. W., McCullough, L., & Muran, J. C. (1994). Short-term psychotherapy of personality disorders. *American Journal of Psychiatry, 151*, 190–194.

Winters, K. C., & Neale, J. M. (1985). Mania and low self-esteem. *Journal of Abnormal Psychology, 94*, 282–290.

Wirshing, D. W., Wirshing, W. C., Marder, S. R., Liberman, R. P., & Mintz, J. (1998). Informed consent: Assessment of comprehension. *American Journal of Psychiatry, 155*, 1508–1511.

Wirz-Justice, A., Graw, P., Kraeuchi, K., Gisin, B., et al. (1993). Light therapy in seasonal affective disorder is independent of time of day or circadian phase. *Archives of General Psychiatry, 50*, 929–937.

Witkiewitz, K., & Marlatt, G. A. (2004). Relapse prevention for alcohol and drug problems: that was zen, this is tao. *American Psychologist, 59*, 224–235.

Wittchen, H.-U., Stein, M. B., & Kessler, R. C. (1999). Social fears and social phobia in a community sample of adolescents and young adults: Prevalence, risk factors, and comorbidity. *Psychological Medicine, 29*, 309–323.

Wolf, M., Bally, H., & Morris, R. (1986). Automaticity, retrieval processes, and reading: A longitudinal study in average and impaired readers. *Child Development, 57*, 988–1000.

Wolfe, R., Morrow, J., & Frederickson, B. L. (1996). Mood disorders in older adults. In L. L. Carstensen, B. A. Edelstein, & L. Dornbrand (Eds.), *The practical handbook of clinical gerontology* (pp. 274–303). Thousand Oaks, CA: Sage.

Wolfe, V. V. (1990). Sexual abuse of children. In A. S. Bellack, M. Hersen, & A. E. Kazdin (Eds.), *International handbook of behavior modification and therapy* (2nd ed., pp. 707–729). New York: Plenum.

Wolff, P. H., & Melngailis, I. (1996). Reversing letters and reading transformed text in dyslexia: A reassessment. *Reading and Writing, 8*, 341–355.

Wolff, S., Narayan, S., & Moyes, B. (1988). Personality characteristics of parents of autistic children: A controlled study. *Journal of Child Psychology and Psychiatry and Allied Disciplines, 29*, 143–153.

Wolitzky, D. (1995). Traditional psychoanalytic psychotherapy. In A. S. Gurman & S. B. Messer (Eds.), *Essential psychotherapies: Theory and practice.* New York: Guilford.

Wolpe, J. (1958). *Psychotherapy by reciprocal inhibition.* Stanford, CA: Stanford University Press.

Wolraich, M. L., Wilson, D. B., & White, J. W. (1995). The effect of sugar on behavior or cognition in children: A meta-analysis. *Journal of the American Medical Association, 274*, 1617–1621.

Women's Health Initiative Screening Committee. (2004). Effects of conjugated equine estrogen in postmenopausal women with hysterectomy: The women's health initiative randomized controlled trial. *JAMA, 291,* 1701–1712.

Women's Health Initiative study group. (1998). Design of the Women's Health Initiative observational study and clinical trial. *Controlled Clinical Trials, 19,* 61–109.

Wonderlich, S. A., Crosby, R. D., Mitchell, J. E., Thompson, K. M., Redlin, J., Demuth, G., Smyth, J., & Haseltine, B. (2001). Eating disturbance and sexual trauma in childhood and adulthood. *International Journal of Eating Disorders, 30,* 401–412.

Wonderlich, S. A., & Swift, W. J. (1990). Perceptions of parental relationships in the eating disorders: The relevance of depressed mood. *Journal of Abnormal Psychology 99,* 353–360.

Wonderlich, S. A., Wilsnack, R. W., Wilsnack, S. C., & Harris, T. R. (1996). Childhood sexual abuse and bulimic behavior in a nationally representative sample. *American Journal of Public Health, 86,* 1082–1086.

Wong, D. F., Wagner, H. N., Tune, L. F., Dannals, R. F., Pearlson, G. D., Links, J. M., et al. (1986). Positron emission tomography reveals elevated D2 dopamine receptors in drug-naive schizophrenics. *Science, 234,* 1558–1562.

Woodman, C. L., Noyes, R., Black, D. W., Schlosser, S., & Yagla, S. J. (1999). A 5-year follow-up study of generalized anxiety disorder and panic disorder. *Journal of Nervous and Mental Disease, 187,* 3–9.

Woodmansee, M. A. (1996). The guilty but mentally ill verdict: Political expediency at the expense of moral principle. *Notre Dame Journal of Law, Ethics and Public Policy, 10,* 341–387.

Wood, L. F., & Jacobson, N. S. (1985). Marital distress. In D. H. Barlow (Ed.), *Clinical handbook of psychological disorders: A step-by-step treatment manual* (pp. 344–416). New York, NY: Guilford Press.

Woods, B. (1994). Management of memory impairment in older people with dementia. *International Review of Psychiatry, 6,* 153–161.

Woods, C. M., Vevea, J. L., Chambless, D. L., & Bayen, U. J. (2002). Are compulsive checkers impaired in memory? A meta-analytic review. *Clinical Psychology: Science and Practice, 9,* 353–366.

Woodside, D. B., Shekter-Wolfson, L. F., Garfinkel, P. E., & Olmsted, M. P. (1995). Family interactions in bulimia nervosa: Study design, comparisons to established population norms and changes over the course of an intensive day hospital treatment program. *International Journal of Eating Disorders, 17,* 105–115.

Woody, S. R., & Rodriguez, B. F. (2000). Self-focused attention and social anxiety in social phobics and normal controls. *Cognitive Therapy and Research, 24,* 473–88.

World Health Organization. (2001). *World health report: New understanding, new hope.* Geneva: Author.

Worling, J. R. (1995). Sexual abuse histories of adolescent male sex offenders: Differences on the basis of the age and gender of their victims. *Journal of Abnormal Psychology, 104,* 610–613.

Woodside, D.B., Bulik, C. M., Halmi, K. A., et al. (2002). Personality, perfectionism, and attitudes towards eating in parents of individuals with eating disorders. *International Journal of Eating Disorders, 13,* 290–299.

Wouda, J. C., Hartman, P. M., Bakker, R. M., Bakker, J. O., et al. (1998). Vaginal plethysmography in women with dyspareunia. *Journal of Sex Research, 35,* 141–147.

Wright, M. J. (1991). Identifying child sexual abuse using the Personality Inventory for Children. *Dissertation Abstracts International, 52,* 1744.

Writing Committee for the ENRICHD Investigators. (2003). Effects of treating depression and low perceived social support on clinical events after myocardial infarction. *JAMA, 289,* 3106–3116.

Writing Group for the Women's Health Initiative Investigators. (2002). Risks and benefits of estrogen plus estrogen plus progestin in healthy postmenopausal women. Principle results from the Women's Health Initiative randomized controlled trial. *JAMA, 288,* 321–333.

Wu, L.-T., Pilowsky, D. J., & Schlenger, W. E. (2004). Inhalant abuse and dependence among adolescents in the United State. *Journal of the American Academy of Child and Adolescent Psychiatry, 43,* 1206–1214.

Wulsin, L., Bachop, M., & Hoffman, D. (1988). Group therapy in manic-depressive illness. *American Journal of Psychotherapy, 2,* 263–271.

Wurtele, S. K., & Miller-Perrin, C. L. (1987). An evaluation of side-effects associated with participation in a child sexual abuse prevention program. *Journal of School Health, 57,* 228–231.

Wylie, K. R. (1997). Treatment outcome of brief couple therapy in psychogenic male erectile disorder. *Archives of Sexual Behavior, 26,* 527–545.

Yalom, I. D., Green, R., & Fisk, N. (1973). Prenatal exposure to female hormones: Effect on psychosexual development in boys. *Archives of General Psychiatry, 28,* 554–561.

Yan, L. L., Liu, K., Matthews, K. A., Daviglus, M. L., Ferguson, T. F., & Kiefe, C. I. (2003). Psychosocial factors and risk of hypertension: The Coronary Artery Risk Development in Young Adults (CARDIA) Study. *JAMA, 290,* 2138–2148.

Yanovski, S. Z. (2003). Binge eating disorder and obesity in 2003: Could treating an eating disorder have a positive effect on the obesity epidemic? *International Journal of Eating Disorders, 34*(Suppl), S117–S120.

Yates, A. (1989). Current perspectives on the eating disorders. *Journal of the American Academy of Child and Adolescent Psychiatry, 28,* 813–828.

Yen, S., Shea, T., Pagano, M., Sanislow, C. A., Grilo, C. M., McGlashan, T. H., et al. (2003). Axis I and axis II disorders as predictors of prospective suicide attempts: Findings from the collaborative longitudinal personality disorders study. *Journal of Abnormal Psychology, 112,* 375–381.

Yerkes, R. M., & Dodson, J. D. (1908). The relation of strength of stimulus to rapidity of habit formation. *Journal of Comparative and Neurological Psychology, 18,* 459–482.

Yetman, N. R. (1994). Race and ethnic inequality. In C. Calhoun & G. Ritzer (Eds.), *Social problems.* New York: McGraw-Hill.

Yoast, R., Williams, M. A., Deitchman, S. D., & Champion, H. C. (2001). Report of the Council on Scientific Affairs: Methadone maintenance and needle-exchange programs to reduce the medical and public health consequences of drug abuse. *Journal of Addictive Diseases, 20,* 15–40.

Yonkers, K. A., Dyck, I. R., Warshaw, M., & Keller, M. B. (2000). Factors predicting the clinical course of generalised anxiety disorder. *British Journal of Psychiatry, 176,* 544–549.

Young, A. S., Klap, R., Sherbourne, C. D., & Wells, K. B. (2001). The quality of care for depressive and anxiety disorders in the United States. *Archives of General Psychiatry, 58,* 55–61.

Younglove, J. A., & Vitello, C. J. (2003). Community notification provisions of "Megan's Law" from a therapeutic jurisprudence perspective: A case study. *American Journal of Forensic Psychology, 21,* 25–38.

Yule, W., & Canterbury, R. (1996). The treatment of post-traumatic stress disorder in children and adolescents. *International Review of Psychiatry, 6,* 141–151.

Yung, A. R., McGorry, P. D., McFarlane, C. A., & Patton, G. (1995). The PACE Clinic: Development of a clinical service for young people at high risk of psychosis. *Australia Psychiatry 3,* 345–349.

Yung, A. R., Phillips, L. J., Hok, P. Y., & McGorry, P. D. (2004). Risk factors for psychosis in an ultra high-risk group: psychopathology and clinical features. *Schizophrenia Research, 67,* 131 142.

Zanarini, M. C., Skodol, A. E., Bender, D., Dolan, R., Sanislow, C., Schaefer, E., Morey, L. C., Grilo, C. M., Shea, M. T., McGlashan, T. H., & Gunderson, J. G. (2000). The Collaborative Longitudinal Personality Disorders Study: Reliability of axis I and II diagnoses. *Journal of Personality Disorders, 14,* 291–299.

Zane, M. D. (1984). Psychoanalysis and contextual analysis of phobias. *Journal of the American Academy of Psychoanalysis, 12,* 553–568.

Zarit, S. H. (1980). *Aging and mental disorders: Psychological approaches to assessment and treatment.* New York: Free Press.

Zarit, S. H., & Zarit, J. M. (1998). *Mental disorders in older adults. Fundamentals of assessment and treatment.* New York: Guilford.

Zatzick, D. F., Marmer, C. R., Weiss, D. S., Browner, W. S., Metzler, T. J., et al. (1997). Posttraumatic stress disorder and functioning and quality of life in a nationally representative sample of male Vietnam veterans. *American Journal of Psychiatry, 154,* 1690–1695.

Zeiss, A. M., & Steffen, A. M. (1996). Interdisciplinary health care teams: The basic unit of geriatric care. In L. L. Carstensen, B. A. Edelstein, & L. Dornbrand (Eds.), *The practical handbook of clinical gerontology* (pp. 423–450). Thousand Oaks, CA: Sage.

Zellner, D. A., Harner, D. E., & Adler, R. L. (1989). Effects of eating abnormalities and gender on perceptions of desirable body shape. *Journal of Abnormal Psychology, 98,* 93–96.

Zheng, H., Sussman, S., Chen, X., Wang, Y. Xia, J., Gong, J., Liu, C., Shan, J., Unger, J., & Johnson, C. A. (2004). Project EX—A teen smoking cessation initial study in Wuhan, China. *Addictive Behaviors, 29,* 1725–1733.

Ziegler, F. J., Imboden, J. B., & Meyer, E. (1960). Contemporary conversion reactions: A clinical study. *American Journal of Psychiatry, 116,* 901–910.

Zilboorg, G., & Henry, G. W. (1941). *A history of medical psychology.* New York: Norton.

Zimmer, D. (1987). Does marital therapy enhance the effectiveness of treatment for sexual dysfunction? *Journal of Sex and Marital Therapy, 13,* 193–209.

Zimmer, L., & Morgan, J. P. (1995). *Exposing marijuana myths: A review of the scientific evidence.* New York: The Lindemith Center.

Zimmerman, M. A., Ramirez-Valles, J., Suarez, E., De la Rosa, G., & Castro, M. A. (1997). An HIV/AIDS Prevention Project for Mexican Homosexual Men: An Empowerment Approach. *Health Education & Behavior 24,* 177–190.

Zimmerman, D. R. (2003). Improving nursing home quality of care through outcomes data: The MDS quality indicators. *International Journal of Geriatric Psychiatry, 18,* 250–257.

Zinbarg, R. E., Brown, T. A., Barlow, D. H., & Rapee, R. M. (2001). Anxiety sensitivity, panic, and depressed mood: A reanalysis teasing apart the contributions of the two levels in the hierarchical structure of the Anxiety Sensitivity Index. *Journal of Abnormal Psychology, 110,* 372–377.

Zlotnick, C., Johnson, S. L., Miller, I. W., Pearlstein, T., &

Howard, M. (2001). Postpartum depression in women receiving public assistance: Pilot study of an interpersonal-therapy-oriented group intervention. *American Journal of Psychiatry, 158,* 638–640.

Zubin, J., & Spring, B. (1977). Vulnerability: A new view of schizophrenia. *Journal of Abnormal Psychology, 86,* 103–126.

Zucker, K. J., & Blanchard, R. (1997). Transvestic fetishism: Psychopathology and theory. In D. R. Laws & W. O'Donohue (Eds.), *Sexual deviance* (pp. 280–296). New York: Guilford.

Zucker, K. J., & Bradley, S. J. (1995). *Gender identity disorder and psychosexual problems in children and adolescents.* New York: Guilford.

Zucker, K. J., Bradley, S. J., & Sanikhani, M. (1997). Sex difference in referral rates of children with gender identity disorder: Some hypotheses. *Journal of Abnormal Child Psychology, 25,* 217–227.

Zucker, K. J., Wild, J., Bradley, S. J., & Stern, A. (1993). Physical attractiveness of boys with gender identity disorder. *Archives of Sexual Behavior, 22,* 23–36.

Quotation and Illustration Credits

Permission was obtained from the following material.

Page 112, Figure 4.3. Pennebaker, J., Kiecolt-Glaser, J. K., & Glaser, R. (1988). *Journal of Consulting and Clinical Psychology, 56,* 243. Copyright © 1988 by the American Psychological Association. Reprinted with permission.

Page 117, Figure 4.4. Journal of Behavioral Therapy and Experimental Psyciatry, 38. Chorpita et al. "Behavioral treatment of choking phobia in an adolescent: An experimental analysis," 307–315, copyright © 1997, with permission from Elsevier.

Page 125, Figure 5.1. Adapted from Chavira, D.A., Stein, M.B., Malcarne, V.L. (2002). Scrutinizing the relationship between shyness and social phobia. *Journal of Anxiety Disorders,* 16, 585–598.

Page 143, Figure 5.4. Martin, J.H. (1996). Neuroanatomy Text and Atlas, second edition. NY- McGraw-Hill Professions Division. With permission, McGraw-Hill Companies.

Page 146. Figure 5.6. Clark, D.M. (1997). Panic disorder and social phobia. [In D.M. Clark and C.G. Fairburn (Eds.), Science and Practice of Cognitive Behaviour Therapy (pp. 121–153)]. With permission, Oxford University Press.

Page 166, Figure 6.1. Netter, F.H. Adapted. Anesthesias in conversion disorder can be distinguished from true neurological dysfunctions. The CIBA Collection of Medical Illustrations, plates 5 and 6. Copyright © CIBA Pharmaceutical Company, Division of CIBA-GEIGY Corporation. Reprinted by permission.

Page 169, Figure 6.2. Looper, K.J., & Kirmayer, L.J. (2002). Behavioral medicine approaches to somatoform disorders. *Journal of Consulting and Clinical Psychology,* 70, 810–827.

Page 185, Figure 6.3. Lewis et al. 1997. Reprinted with permission from the American Journal of Psychiatry. Copyright ©1997. American Psychiatric Association.

Page 192, Figures 7.2 and 7.3. Stone, A.A., Reed, B.R. & Neale, J. M. (1987). Number of undesirable events for the ten days preceding an episode of respiratory infection. *Journal of Human Stress, 13,* 70–74. Copyright © 1987. Reprinted with permission of the Helen Dwight Reid Educational Foundation. Published by Heldref Publications, 1319 Eighteenth Street, NW, Washington, DC 20036-1802.

Page 232, Figure 8.1. Kessler et al. (2003). Journal of the American Medical Association, 289, 3095–3105.

Page 239, Figure 8.4. Snyder (1986) p. 106

Page 241, Figure 8.5. Reprinted with permission from the *Annual Review of Review of Psychology,* Vol. 53, copyright © 2002 by Annual Reviews, www.annualreviews.org

Page 262, Figure 8.9. Arias, E., Andress R.N., Kung, H.C., Murphy, S.L., Kochanek, K. (2003) *Deaths: Final Data for 2001.* Hyattsville, Maryland: National Center for deals Statistics, 52.

Page 273, Figure 9.1 Stunkard, A.J., Sorensen, T., & Schulsinger, F. (1983). Use of the Danish Adoption Register for the study of obesity and thinness. In S.S. Kety, L.P. Rowland, R.L. Sidman, S.W. Matthysse (Eds.), *The genetics of neurological and psychiatric disorders.* New York: Raven Press, 1983. p. 119.

Page 352, quotation: McGhie, A. & Chapman, J.S. (1961). Disorders of attention and perception in early schizophrenia. *British Journal of Medical Psychology, 34,* 103–116. Reprinted by permission of British Psychological Society.

Page 389, Figure 12.1. Shea, M.T., Stout, R., Gunderson, J., Morey, L.C., Grilo, C.M. & McGlashan, T. et al. (2002). Short-term diagnostic stability of schizotypal, borderline, avoidant, and obsessive-compulsive personality disorders. *American Journal of Psychiatry,* 159, 2036–2041

Page 402, Figure 12.3. Blair, R.J.D., Jones, L., Clarks, F., & Smith, M. (1997). The psychopathic individual: A lack of responsiveness to distress cues? *Psychophysiology,* 34, 192–198.

Page 422, Figure 13.4. Masters, W.H. & Johnson, V.E. (1970). *Human sexual inadequacy.* Reprinted by permission of Masters & Johnson Institute.

Page 422, Figure 13.5. Enhancing Sexuality: A Problem-Solving Approach, 1997, Graywind Publications

Page 445, Figure 13.7. National Center for Justice (2003). Unpublished document, National Center for Justice, Document NCJ, 2063–48.

Page 462, Figure 14.1. From Blumstein, A., Cohen, J., & Farrington, D.P. *Criminology, 26,* 11. Copyright © 1988. The American Society of Criminology.

Page 480. Table 14.5. American Association on Mental Retardation. Reproduced with permission of the American Association on Mental Retardation in the format Textbook via Copyright Clearance Center.

Page 490–91, Focus on Discovery 14.4, quotation: Grandin, T. (1995). Excerpts from *Thinking in pictures,* 132–135. Copyright © 1995. Used by permission of Doubleday, a division of Bantam Doubleday Dell Publishing Group, Inc.

Page 498, Figure 15.1. U.S. Census Bureau, Decennial Census and Projections.

Page 523, Figure 15.2. Zeiss, A.M. & Steffan, A.M. (1996). Interdisciplinary health care terms: The basic unit of geriatric care. In Carstensen, L.L., Edelstein, D.A., & Dornbrand, L. (Eds.), *The practical handbook of clinical gerontology.* Thousand Oaks, CA: Sage.

Page 530, Figure 16.1. Drawn from Lambert, M.J. (2004). Psychotherapeutically speaking-updates from the Division of Psychotherapy (29). Available by we at http://www.divisionofpsychotherapy.org/updates.php

Page 534, Figure 16.2. Adapted with permission from *Addictive Behaviors across the Lifespan:* Prevention, Treatment, and Policy Issues (p. 150), by J.S. Baier, G.A. Marlatt, & R.J. McMahon (Eds.), 1993, Beverly Hills, CA: Sage.

Name Index

Subject Index

DSM-IV-TR Multiaxial Classification System

Axis I

Clinical syndromes:

Disorders Usually First Diagnosed in Infancy, Childhood, or
   Adolescence
Delirium, Dementia, Amnestic and other Cognitive Disorders
Substance-related Disorders
Schizophrenia and Other Psychotic Disorders
Mood Disorders
Anxiety Disorders
Somatoform Disorders
Factitious Disorder
Dissociative Disorders
Sexual and Gender Identity Disorders
Eating Disorders
Sleep Disorders
Impulse Control Disorders Not Elsewhere Classified
Adjustment Disorders

Axis II

Mental Retardation
Personality Disorders

Axis III

General Medical Conditions

Axis IV
Psychosocial and Environmental Problems

Check:

_____ Problems with primary support group.
     Specify:

_____ Problems related to the social environment.
     Specify:

_____ Educational problem.
     Specify:

_____ Occupational problem.
     Specify:

_____ Housing problem.
     Specify:

_____ Economic problem.
     Specify:

_____ Problems with access to health care services.
     Specify:

_____ Problems related to interaction with the legal system/crime.
     Specify:

_____ Other psychosocial and environmental problems.
     Specify: